Fundamental Perspectives on International Law

Fifth Edition

WILLIAM R. SLOMANSON

Thomas Jefferson School of Law

San Diego, California

THOMSON

WADSWORTH

Australia • Brazil • Canada • Mexico • Singapore • Spain
United Kingdom • United States

DEDICATION

Por la quinta vez para
LAMPC
Las luces de mi vida

THOMSON
WADSWORTH

Fundamental Perspectives on International Law, **Fifth Edition**
William R. Slomanson

Executive Editor: David Tatom
Associate Development Editor: Rebecca Green
Editorial Assistant: Eva Dickerson
Technology Project Manager: Michelle Vardeman
Senior Marketing Manager: Janise Fry
Marketing Assistant: Teresa Jessen
Marketing Communications Manager:
   Nathaniel Michelson
Project Manager, Editorial Production: Paul Wells
Creative Director: Rob Hugel

Art Director: Maria Epes
Print Buyer: Barbara Britton
Permissions Editor: Roberta Broyer
Production Service: International Typesetting
   and Composition
Copy Editor: Joan O'Brien
Cover Designer: Garry Harman
Compositor: International Typesetting
   and Composition
Printer: Transcontinental Printing/Louiseville

Printed in Canada
  2 3 4 5 6 7 10 09 08 07

Library of Congress Control Number: 2006920349

ISBN 13: 978-0-495-00745-6
ISBN 10: 0-495-00745-5

Thomson Higher Education
10 Davis Drive
Belmont, CA 94002-3098
USA

For more information about our products, contact us at:
Thomson Learning Academic Resource Center
1-800-423-0563

For permission to use material from this text or product, submit a request online at
http://www.thomsonrights.com.
Any additional questions about permissions can be submitted by e-mail to **thomsonrights@thomson.com.**

Summary of Contents

Contents

Table of Cases

*Principal case names are in **bold**. Cases cited within principal cases, other quoted material, and in endnotes are not included here.*

Table of Treaties, Resolutions, and Miscellaneous Instruments

This index contains titled accords, agreements, conventions, declarations, pacts, protocols, and treaties.

Abbreviations

CIS: Commonwealth of Independent States
NATO: North Atlantic Treaty Organization
UN: United Nations
NK: North Korea
EC: European Community
IAC: Inter-American Convention
CISG: Convention for the International Sale of Goods
UNCLOS: United Nations Convention on the Law of Sea

OECD: Organization for Economic Cooperation and Development
EHR: European Human Rights, *also known as* Human Rights and Fundamental Freedoms
GA: General Assembly
ICCPR: International Covenant on Civil and Political Rights
FCN: Friendship, Commerce, and Navigation

Preface

Reports about the demise of International Law have been greatly exaggerated. The fourth edition questioned whether 9-11 turned International Law on its head—or merely poured fresh wine into a vintage bottle. The fifth edition continues this critical analysis in the aftermath of the Iraq War. It assesses claims that US hegemony has trumped the collective security regime associated with the UN dream of beating swords into plowshares.

Many of our students think they know all the answers. We try to teach them, instead, to ask the right questions. This edition thus presents a number of fundamental inquiries: Why would the firing of a transgendered British police officer fall within the province of International Law? Does the presence of 180,000 foreign military troops negate Iraqi sovereignty? Is the United Nations defunct? Do all cross-border kidnappings necessarily violate International Law? How does the Internet challenge basic principles of sovereignty established in the seventeenth century treaty leading to the modern nation-State? Does the Middle East's new "Berlin Wall" deter or encourage terrorism? Is the preemptive use of force wrong, or necessary, for global security? Should the person who can prevent another "9-11" be tortured if he refuses to talk? Can a multinational corporation be liable for human rights violations under International Law? Should a Pakistani governing council's "honor" edict, that a woman be gang-raped for her brother's conduct, fall within the province of International Law? Can Canada's native Inuit tribes obtain relief from a human rights tribunal, based on the US decision not to ratify a global warming treaty? Will globalization help or hinder World Trade Organization objectives?

This book provides *worldwide* perspectives on International law. No one country can change International Law, although it may have a notable impact. The author's case selection thus includes 45 principal case studies from foreign and international tribunals, and 17 from the United States. Numerous foreign resources are embedded in this text, to provide global access to the content of International Law. Some attempts to cover this subject are doggedly focused on the views of the author. All writers of course pick and choose their sources. As you will learn in the first chapter on the sources of International Law, my restatement of this subject does not necessarily make it so. But this 5th edition should present worthy evidence of the actual content of International Law. The textual mention of author affiliations is designed to more clearly expose my resources, and to ameliorate textbook bias.

I have included numerous textual examples to illustrate classical and contemporary applications, while plugging historical gaps for the well-rounded student. Endnote and end-of-chapter bibliographic material typically refer the reader to *book*-length analyses of the issues. Where useful for further research, I have also included website and newspaper citations. Most of the latter refer to *New York Times on the Web*. That resource facilitates access to succinct accounts of the many newsworthy issues at hand. It does not equate to this author's adoption of all views therein expressed.

Rather than present a huge collage of arguably related bits and pieces, this is a smaller, tightly integrated volume. It is designed with two purposes in mind. First, to present the fundamental corpus of International Law via a painstaking attempt to clarify rather than mystify. Second, to provide a teaching tool that is suitable for the varied learning styles that each professor encounters. One may thus tilt the course format to suit institutional needs via the most desirable combination of the lecture, case, and problem/role-playing methods.

The general organization of the prior edition has been retained, consisting of an evolving pattern with distinct units. Learning how these virtual chessboard pieces interact will prepare International Law's disciples and detractors for life in the twenty-first century. After an opening chapter on the general scope of International Law, the next three chapters cast the State, organizational, and individual/corporate actors in their relative roles. Chapters 5 through 10 portray much of the practical substance of International Law. The remaining chapters focus on cross-cutting human rights, environmental, and economic themes. These are present, to some extent, in all chapters. They are the grist for more detailed analysis in the advanced courses on those subjects offered at many universities.

◆ FIFTH EDITION COMPONENTS

COURSE WEB PAGE

<http://home.att.net/~slomansonb/txtcsesite.html> One need not be confined by the all-too-familiar adage: "A book is obsolete on the day it is published." This edition builds upon the 4th edition's introduction of the electronic component of this book. There has been a cosmic improvement in the amount, reliability, and sustainability of digitalized material. This technical upgrade enhances access to treaties, resolutions, and other key international instruments in ways not possible with only a print text. Professors may thereby assign the referenced international materials most suitable for their particular courses. Students may access more of the unedited, full-version cases and materials for their particular research needs. They may thereby obtain more analytical and informational detail than possible in the snapshot version of International Law necessarily presented in a single print volume. From the course Web page, one may link to the following resources:

◆ International Law Updates Web Page—containing online information about key developments occurring after publication of the print portion of the 5th edition
◆ Miscellaneous Web Resources—including online dictionaries, graduate education opportunities, historical resources, maps, and travel requirements
◆ International Web site Appendix—containing useful links to global Internet portals
◆ Research Guide on International Resources
◆ Career Opportunities in International Law
◆ Glossary of Terms, which has been moved from the book to the Internet

◆ Case Reading and Analysis Suggestions for the non-law student

NEW MATERIALS AND SECTIONS

The Fifth Edition contains the following fresh materials:

◆ Updated and expanded analyses of matters presented in the prior edition
◆ More original documents, both in the printed text and on the course Web page—including the 2002 US National Security Strategy and its related exercise
◆ A *substantially* revised chapter on the Use of Force, which includes fresh influences such as the US Supreme Court cases on US military detentions
◆ New sections on the traditional Laws of War (§10.6) and post-9-11 applications (§10.7)
◆ New decisions from international tribunals including the International Court of Justice, the United Nations Compensation Commission, the European Court of Human Rights, and the International Commission for the Settlement of Investment Disputes
◆ New or revised role playing problems, to probe student comprehension, and course review
◆ A "Change" Web page at <http://home.att.net/~slomansonb/5th_ed_Change.html>, to facilitate the prior adopter's transition from the 4th to the 5th edition

INTERNET NOTES

The number of endnotes containing Web links has been increased, to provide more access to original materials. This feature is especially useful for research papers and presentations. Professors and students may thereby mine the rich vein of informational resources extractable from the Internet. Each end-of-chapter bibliography also provides "Additional Internet Resources."

CROSS-REFERENCES

A number of section cross-references appear as "(§_._)." This device promotes access to more detailed content about related materials in other sections of the book. Readers may thus collate like materials for class preparation and further research.

INSTRUCTOR'S MANUAL

This separate on-line resource analyzes the end-of-chapter problems to assist the professor with helping students review and synthesize the materials. It also contains a password-protected test bank of International Law examinations. The various examination categories (essay, etc.) are accessible via the above course Web page.

◆ ACKNOWLEDGMENTS

The author thanks the following individuals for their support during his preparation of this edition: Dean Rudolph Hasl, and past Dean Kenneth Vandevelde, of the Thomas Jefferson School of Law—for their generous support of this project via a sabbatical and research grant; Charu Dutt (New Delhi), and Rebecca Green (Fort Worth)—for their much appreciated attention to detail during the production process for this book; Michel Richter of the Academic Training Association (Amsterdam), Vjosa Osmani (Mitrovica), and Viola Trebicka (Tirana)—for their respective roles in funding and translating this book into Albanian; and Erica Saltzman (TJSL '07)—for her consistently valuable research assistance and editorial input from the student's perspective.

The author would also like to thank the following reviewers for their invaluable feedback on this project:

Robert Bledsoe, University of Central Florida
Isebill V. Gruhn, University of California, Santa Cruz
Wei-chin Lee, Wake Forest University
Mark D. Welton, U.S. Military Academy

William R. Slomanson
San Diego, California
January 1, 2006

CHAPTER ONE

What Is International Law?

CHAPTER OUTLINE

INTRODUCTION

COURSE NEED

The American Council on Education recently published a study concluding that: (1) universities are failing to meet the need and student demand for classes with international content; and (2) too many existing classes are historical and academic—failing to adequately reflect upon current affairs. While this latest in a series of such studies presented some strengths, the overall findings revealed the following weaknesses:

◆ Most institutions exhibited a low level of commitment to internationalization, as evidenced by the low percentage of institutions that included internationalization in their mission statement or as a priority in their strategic plan.
◆ The majority of students and faculty expressed support for international activities, but failed to participate in these activities.

. . .

[P]rofound changes in international relations have taken place. . . . All countries, large or small, strong or weak, rich or poor, are equal members of the international community. No country should seek hegemony, engage in power politics or monopolize international affairs.

. . .

Mankind is on the threshold of a new era. The peoples of all countries are faced with the increasingly urgent question of the kind of international order they will live under in the next century. The Parties call upon all countries to engage in an active dialogue on the establishment of a peaceful, stable, just and rational new international order, and they are prepared to take part in a joint discussion of any constructive proposals to this end.

—Russian-Chinese Joint Declaration on a Multipolar World and the Establishment of a New International Order (May 20, 1997). <http://www.fas.org/news/russia/1997/a52–153en.htm>.

◆ While the number of participants had increased, only a small portion of undergraduates participated in academic programs abroad and many of those that did had short-term experiences.
◆ Internationally oriented extracurricular activities attracted a very small minority of students.[1]

Your professor and your university are obviously serving these needs with this course.

Nigerian Professor Chris Okeke provides a succinct glimpse of the rationale for taking a course in International Law:

(i) To expose the students to a clear understanding of the fact of inter-dependence that . . . states and other subjects of International Law, do not live in isolation, but rather must necessarily be interdependent; (ii) To teach the students to appreciate the universal principles and rules designed to ensure normal relations . . . irrespective of the differences in their economic, political and social systems; (iii) To educate the students in the spirit of humanism, democracy and respect for the sovereignty of all nations and peoples; (iv) To make the students to be constantly aware of the need to fight for the extermination of the remnants (traces) of colonialism and all forms of racial and national oppression.[2]

One should not mistakenly perceive International Law as falling within the exclusive domain of academicians. Many career opportunities will be unveiled by the study of this subject.[3] One need only peruse the titles of the numerous specialized legal journals to appreciate the contemporary pervasiveness of International Law, in a diverse array of employment contexts.[4]

ENTRY POINT

There are a variety of potential entry points for a course in International Law. One would be historical.[5] The demise of the medieval feudal systems demonstrated the need for a State system that could function as a community of nations, linked by commonly accepted norms of conduct. For the last several hundred years, world leaders have thus referred to this system of rules as "International Law." More than 150 years ago, when the community of nations was far less integrated than today, the prominent commentator, James Kent, addressed the importance of studying this branch of the law:

A comprehensive and scientific knowledge of international law is highly necessary, not only to lawyers practicing in our commercial ports, but to every [person] who is animated by liberal views, and a generous ambition to assume stations of high public trust. It would be exceedingly to the discredit of any person

who should be called to take a share in the councils of the nation, if [he/she] should be found deficient in the great leading principles of this law; and . . . the elementary learning of the law of nations, as not only an essential part of the education of an American Lawyer, but as proper to be academically taught.[6]

One could also begin this course by studying the various schools of thought.[7] They had a profound impact on the evolution of this branch of law, although this book is not designed for a primarily theoretical approach.

One might begin, instead, by contemplating a world where "International Law" were marginalized, or ceased to exist. This is not mere hyperbole. After the Russian Revolution of 1917, Marxist advocates such as Lenin and Stalin, who would later rescind the Soviet marginalization of the international legal system, asserted that the radical nature of a communist State required a split with the community of nations as it had evolved since the 1648 state-centric Treaty of Westphalia.[8] The University of Amsterdam's Peter Malanczuk succinctly articulates this historical point-counterpoint in the following terms: "The Soviet Union originally denied that there could be one system of international law that applied equally to capitalist and socialist states and rejected the validity of older customary law and treaties concluded by the Tsarist government. The attitude changed later, but the Soviet Union remained on the fringe of international affairs until it attained the status of a great power after the Second World War."[9]

Assume for a moment that world leaders suddenly decided to totally disregard International Law. This hypothetical would be reminiscent of the Dark Ages, between the Pax Romana and the medieval Renaissance, which sparked the desire for creating modern nation States. Such a void actually materialized during the 1966–1976 Cultural Revolution in the People's Republic of China (PRC). All courses on International Law were canceled. The teachers were summarily dismissed and sent elsewhere for reeducation. The Chinese government made no apologies about its distrust of International Law.[10] As one Chinese writer characterized the need for this drastic program, "in the Western capitalist world, suppression of the weak by the strong and the eating of small fish by big fish are not only tacitly condoned by bourgeois international law but also are cloaked with a mantle of legality."[11]

When the PRC's Cultural Revolution ended in 1976, its leaders chose to participate in the quest for world peace, notwithstanding competitive ideologies within the community of nations. In a 1982 review of this phenomenon, the President of the Chinese Society of International Law recounted how the PRC had abandoned its parochial disregard of International Law. China's prior decision to sequester itself from the society of nations was counterproductive to its best national interests. Under a renewed commitment to facilitating international relations:

> China's international lawyers must begin to work diligently to rebuild her science of international law which serves to promote world peace and truly represents the interests of the people the world over. . . .
>
> We need to make an intensive study of not only the theory of international law, but the different realms and branches of international law as well to facilitate China's international activities and her legislative work. While doing scientific research in this field, we also have the responsibility to train a new generation of specialists and scholars in international law.[12]

◆ 1.1 DEFINITION AND SCOPE

This introductory text uses the terms *Law of Nations*, *International Law*, and *Public International Law* interchangeably unless otherwise distinguished.

Your study of this subject begins with a comparison of the internal laws of a nation and the international legal norms applied *between* nations. As classically articulated by Columbia University's Professor Louis Henkin:

> First, law is politics. . . . [T]he distinction between law and politics is only a half-truth. . . . Law is made by political actors (not by lawyers), through political procedures, for political ends. . . .
>
> Second . . . law is the normative expression of a political system. To appreciate the character of international law and its relation to the international political system, it is helpful to invoke (though with caution) domestic law as an analogue. Domestic (national law) . . . is an expression of a domestic political system in a domestic (national) society. . . .
>
> Similarly . . . , international law is the product of its particular "society," its political system. International law, too, is a construct of norms, standards, principles, institutions and procedures. . . . But the constituency

of the international society is different. The "persons" constituting international society are not individual human beings but political entities, "States," and the society is an inter-State system, a system [for centuries composed only] of States.[13]

HISTORICAL STATE-DRIVEN DEFINITION

International Law is the body of rules which nations consider binding in their mutual relations. One may resort to several traditional sources for a more detailed explanation. International jurists, for example, sometimes employ useful definitions in their legal opinions. As articulated in a decision of the Permanent Court of International Justice (PCIJ), predecessor of the current world court:

> International law governs relations between independent States. The rules of law binding upon States therefore emanate from their own free will as expressed in conventions [treaties] or by usages [customary state practice] generally accepted as expressing principles of law and established in order to regulate the relations between these co-existing independent communities or with a view to the achievement of common aims.[14]

Historically, individuals were not directly subjected to these rules. One might draw an analogy from the law within most countries. If your animal is harmed by another person, you would sue the responsible person. Your animal would not have the legal capacity to be the plaintiff in a court of law. Save for the exceptions noted in the chapter on individuals and corporate "persons," the individual does not have the legal status to seek redress from another country. A panel of US jurists, referring to Nazi Germany's wrongful confiscation of a Swiss citizen's property in 1938, classically characterized International Law as "the relationship among nations rather than among individuals. It is termed the Law of Nations, or International Law, because it is relative to States or Political Societies and not necessarily to individuals, although citizens or subjects of the earth are greatly affected by it."[15]

Opinio Juris State practice, in specific situations involving inter-State relations, is the primary source for determining the content of International Law. Professor Luigi Condorelli of the University of Geneva aptly characterizes this source of determining an applicable norm. A number of States may employ a common practice ultimately becomes the norm for international relations between all States. This feature of International Law is typically referred to in the academic literature as *opinio juris*. One may thus derive what States believe to be legally binding by reference to this repeated State practice. Note that International Law does not necessarily consist of what a number of States might actually do. Rather, it is a blend of their respective expectations and their actual practice.[16]

The ICJ, the United Nations' judicial branch, provided the caveat that "[n]ot only must the acts concerned amount to a settled practice, but they must also be such, or carried out in such a way, as to be evidence of a belief that this practice is rendered obligatory by the existence of a rule of law requiring it. . . . The States concerned must therefore feel that they are conforming to what amounts to a legal obligation. The frequency or even habitual character of the acts is not in itself enough [to constitute *opinio juris*]."[17] The Court cited the potential derivation of *opinio juris* from UN resolutions. In a subsequent analysis involving the alleged mining of Nicaraguan harbors by agents of the United States, the ICJ considered the General Assembly's 1970 Declaration on Principles of International Law Concerning Friendly Relations and Cooperation Among States in Accordance with the Charter of the United Nations. The Court explained that "the adoption by States of this text affords an indication of their 'opinio juris' as to [the applicable] customary international law on the question."[18]

Consent-Based Governance   This introductory definition of International Law would be incomplete without a reference to the linkage between national and International Law (§1.4). Algeria's Mohammed Bedjaoui, a judge of the ICJ, describes this unique interrelationship in the following terms:

The fundamental characteristic of this international law is thus that its function is to regulate the relations between States, in other words, between entities known to be sovereign and which, in principle, assert their full independence of [from] any legal order. This at once raises the problem . . . of how these States which affirm their sovereignty can be [simultaneously] subject to international law. If one postulates at the outset that there is no higher authority than the State, how can the norm[s] of international law be produced for and applied by such a sovereign State? As might be expected, there is only [one] possible answer to this question, namely that, historically, it

has not been possible for international law to be anything other than a law resting largely on consent, whether express or tacit, of States. . . . It is more a law of co-ordination (between the sovereign jurisdictions of individual States) than a law of subordination.[19]

International Law also serves the needs of its constituents. In the lucid description by Princeton's School of Public and International Affairs Dean Anne-Marie Slaughter:

each of its specialized regimes is based in the consent of states to a specific set of roles that allow them to reap gains from cooperation and thereby serve their collective interests.

. . .

International law provides the indispensable framework for the conduct of stable and orderly international relations. It does not transcend from on high. Rather, it's created by states to serve their collective interests. Consider, for instance, the concept of sovereignty itself, which is routinely described as the cornerstone of the international legal system. . . . It is a deliberate construct, invented and perpetuated by states seeking to reduce war and violence in a particular set of circumstances.[20]

A State may be expressly bound by International Law, but its obligations are premised upon its consent to be bound. As acknowledged by the PCIJ: "any convention creating an obligation . . . places a restriction upon the exercise of the sovereign rights of the state . . . [and] the right of entering into international engagements is an attribute of State sovereignty."[21]

"Civilized" Only?   There are wrinkles in the definitional fabric of International Law. Some commentators qualify the above consensus-based definition as requiring "democratic" and "civilized" components. Long before the demise of the Soviet Union, Moscow State University Professor Grigori Tunkin embraced this element of International Law, which supposedly consists of democratic norms. He described it in his prominent 1974 treatise as the "aggregate of norms which are created by agreement between states of different social systems, [which] reflect the concordant wills of states and have a generally *democratic* character. . . ."[22]

Other commentators add the qualification that International Law contains only those norms accepted by "civilized" nations. This limitation finds support in the

Statute of the ICJ. Article 38.1.c provides that the Court may rely on "the general principles of law recognized by civilized nations." Of course, what constitutes *civilized* conduct often dwells in the eye of the beholder.[23]

MODERN PARTICIPATION BY NON-STATE ACTORS

International Law historically governed only the conduct of States (Chapter 2). It is now applicable to international organizations (Chapter 3). In specified circumstances, it applies to individuals and corporations (Chapter 4).

The proliferation of international organizations since World War II expanded the scope of International Law.

Unlike an undirected cast of *prima donna*–like State actors, all seeking to play a leading role, many organizations have projected a noticeable vitality on to the international stage. State members have thus delegated certain sovereign powers to certain international organizations. The latter, in turn, have required State members to act as directed.

Non-governmental organizations (NGOs), made up of individuals who do not possess sovereign powers, sometimes steal the show. Their emerging role as international lobbyists actors is described in the following analysis:

◆

New Players on the International Stage

Peter Spiro

International Legal Personality

2 *Hofstra Law & Policy Symposium* 25–32 (1997)

III THE NEW ACTORS.

. . . What follows is a brief introduction to the most important non-state actors (NGOs, corporations, and subnational governments) and a concise description of the nature of their international presence and the legal status that is now accorded them.

1. Non-governmental organizations (NGOs).

NGOs are hardly new to the international scene. The Catholic Church is perhaps the original NGO, and the labor movement provides the other significant example of transnational non-governmental organizing from earlier eras. While both remain quintessential models today, they are now joined by a throng. An almost infinite variety of groupings has spawned institutional vehicles in the from of NGOs (defined as organizations of non-national definition and not-for-profit orientation). Among the more prominent NGO groupings are environmentalists, human rights advocates, women, children, gays, the elderly, consumers, and indigenous peoples, each of which has mobilized at the international level.

Many NGOs at least purport to represent memberships, and many act as advocates in and out of international institutional settings. Greenpeace and Amnesty International are perhaps the most prominent examples

of the modern advocacy NGO. These advocacy NGOs are noteworthy in at least two important respects. First, they now act directly to influence international decision-making institutions and not only through the channel of home states. Thus, a Greenpeace or Amnesty International [organization] will not stop at having members or national sections lobby their own governments. . . . Rather, they will move into the international stream as transnational entities seeking leverage wherever available. For example, Greenpeace (with a largely North Atlantic membership) has had its positions voiced and advanced by delegations from small island states and lesser developed countries. In that fashion, advocacy NGOs become players outside the control of the states from which they nominally hale.

These NGOs have also been afforded a limited formal status in some international decisionmaking contexts. . . . [such as] participation at UN-sponsored world conferences in recent years, including at Rio (on the environment), Cairo (population), and Beijing (women). Conferences on multilateral pacts on climate change and endangered species have afforded NGOs a place as observers to treaty monitoring proceedings. But . . . NGOs [have not] been formally extended a status even approaching parity with that of states. Nor have NGOs been afforded standing in international judicial forums,

---

Reprinted with permission of the Hofstra Law & Policy Symposium. Footnotes omitted.

with prominent exceptions at the level of regional organizations.

In practice, NGO influence has far exceeded that indicated by their tentative formal standing in international institutions. NGOs have prompted states to undertake significant international legal initiatives, especially with respect to human rights and environmental protection. They have also been able to pursue global political agendas outside of institutions, either by shaming states (or other relevant actors, most notably corporations) through exposure and/or by mobilizing sympathetic consumer constituencies within the integrated global economy. The former is by now a well-honed tactic of the human rights movement through which objectives are secured by public relations mechanisms. The recent controversy surrounding Royal Dutch Shell's proposed scuttling of an oil rig [the Brent Spar] in the North Sea presents one recent example of the latter. Shell had received all appropriate domestic and international approvals to leave the Brent Spar rig on the ocean floor. Greenpeace objected and launched a campaign to boycott Shell gasoline. Within weeks, Shell's sales in Germany were down 30%, at which point the oil giant relented. Shell has since sought out Greenpeace for consultations in planning the decommission of other rigs. Similar tactics were deployed against France to protect its recent nuclear testing program in the South Pacific. Although the tests were completed as planned, the success of Greenpeace's consumer action campaign may have contributed to France's decision not to undertake more tests in the future.

Brent Spar-type tactics are effective in proportion to a corporation's or state's dependence on consumer trade. . . . There will also be episodes in which the possible costs of boycott efforts will not outweigh the benefits of the activity that the NGO seeks to halt. This may help to explain Shell's continued presence in Nigeria notwithstanding objections to the human rights practices of the current regime there [*e.g.,* §11.4 *Unocal* case]. While NGO power is not absolute, it is significant and growing.

2. Corporations.

As with the case of NGOs, corporations have long enjoyed a presence at the international level. The Hudson's Bay and British East India Companies were effectively sovereign over their far-flung trading realms, engaging in such characteristically governmental activity as coining currency, concluding treaties, and making war. During the 1960s and 1970s, the activities of multinational corporations were subjected to international scrutiny in the face of lesser developed countries' claims of capitalist exploitation.

In the interwar era of the 1920s and 1930s, the International Chamber of Commerce [ICC] participated in a variety of League of Nations proceedings and even signed some League instruments as a party. Corporate alliances such as the ICC now participate in international contexts as NGOs, subject to the same requirements and enjoying the same rights as others under the consultative status system. Corporate interests have also organized themselves for the issues of the day, for example, by forming a highly effective Business Council on Sustainable Development to participate in multilateral forums relating to the international environment.

Corporations so grouped thus enjoy some formal status in international institutions. But, as with NGOs, the status is decidedly second class even as real-world corporate power grows. Except at the ILO [International Labor Organization], the corporate community does not enjoy a seat at the table, at least not in its own name. Corporations generally have no standing in public international judicial and dispute resolution bodies, even where they effectively may be the only real parties in interest. This may have been the case with the first decision handed down by the new World Trade Organization dispute resolution panel, which, though styled as a dispute between Brazil and the United States, was in fact more a dispute between two oil companies.

Excluding corporate actors from formal decision-making processes, as well as absolving them from ultimate accountability under international law, may have made sense in a world in which corporations had a clear national identity and could be adequately represented by and through particular states. Until recent years, this had held more and less true. Even during their vilification during the sixties and seventies, the so-called "multinationals" qualified as such by virtue of a mere presence in more than one country. The moniker "multinational" has not, as least until recently, implied true multinationality in the sense of being under the ultimate control of more than one nation, and thus in a sense being in the control of none. . . .

Today such national identity and control is no longer so apparent. Some large corporations are becoming truly multinational in the sense that it is now almost meaningless to describe them as, say, American or British or Dutch. Even a corporation so intertwined with US foreign relations as Coca-Cola is now moving to shed its national roots. The increasingly cosmopolitan nature of international corporate giants is reflected in corporate structures that make them difficult to regulate from any single state.

Indeed, it is becoming increasingly difficult for states to regulate even those corporations that maintain a strong national identification. As global capital becomes more mobile and the global economy more competitive, state efforts to constrain corporations may be doomed to fail in some contexts. The United States, for example, would find it very difficult, at best, to impose its domestic minimum wage laws on a US corporation's operations in Malaysia, for to do so would place the US corporation at a disadvantage against competitors from other nations not subject to the same regulation. In turn, a developing state like Malaysia could not itself impose a minimum wage so long as other countries did not do the same, for to do so would likely force the US corporation to relocate outside Malaysia. To the extent this description now reflects real-world conditions, the corporate community itself could become an ultimate repository of power.

No wonder that NGOs have moved on some issues to influence corporate behavior directly, rather than indirectly by winning state regulation to the same effect. Such has been the case with the Brent Spar incident and other boycott efforts. It has also characterized the shareholder responsibility movement, in which progressive interests enjoying large shareholding interests (most notably, US state and local pension funds as well as churches) pressure corporations through shareholder resolutions to adhere to environmental and human rights practices beyond those required by domestic or international law.

3. Subnational governments.

Subnational governments [like Catalonia, Quebec, or Tijuana] are assuming an unprecedented role in global affairs. Subnational governments active at the international level include provinces, localities, and perhaps most notably the constitutive units of federative nation-states. The international profile of subnational governments has been most enhanced in recent years in the economic cultural spheres. Sister-city arrangements [in different countries] blossomed in the 1980s, and it is now routine for subnational officials to undertake international promotional campaigns (through trade delegations or permanent trade offices) to attract foreign investment into their jurisdictions. These activities have been facilitated by advances in global travel and communications, as well as by the global economic integration that makes transnational investment possible (and indeed necessary) to economic growth.

. . .

◆ *Notes*

1. Prior to the post–World War II Nuremberg judgment, scholars paid inadequate attention to the role of *private* actors. The international legal system was described as falling within the exclusive realm of State actors. But certain forms of conduct violate the law of nations, whether undertaken on behalf of a State or by private individuals. University of Houston Professor Jordan Paust conveniently collates their "international" crimes as follows:

   Today, the number of specific international crimes that can be committed by private individuals has increased from earlier categories to include, among others, the following: genocide; other crimes against humanity; apartheid; race discrimination; hostage-taking; torture; forced disappearance of persons; terrorism; terrorist bombings; financing of terrorism; aircraft hijacking; aircraft sabotage and certain other acts against civil aviation; certain acts against the safety of maritime navigation, including boatjacking; murder, kidnapping, or other attacks on the person or liberty of internationally protected persons; trafficking in certain drugs; slavery; and mercenarism.[24]

2. The Swiss banking industry reached a settlement with lawyers representing Holocaust survivors in August 1998 after three years of negotiations. The Nazi regime had sent gold and other assets to Switzerland during World War II, a fact kept secret by the banks until a Swiss guard refused to shred some documentary proof in 1995. The World Jewish Congress (WJC), with offices in more than eighty countries, pressured the Swiss banking industry and Swiss authorities to

return these assets to their rightful owners. The Swiss banks thereby averted economic sanctions—not by US federal authorities, but by entities other than nations—including the cities of New York and Los Angeles. The latter entities, while governmental, are not "persons" under International Law (as opposed to the national government). Nor is the WJC an international person, seized with the capacity to officially function in the international legal arena. However, these actors forcefully influenced the Swiss government and the very powerful Swiss banking industry, to act on a major international relations issue, with extremely sensitive political overtones. For further details, see <www.lib.uchicago.edu/~llou/nazigold.html>.

SCOPE OF INTERNATIONAL LAW

As this course unfolds, you will appreciate that International Law is not entrenched in the governmental structure employed by most nations. The UN Secretary-General is not a chief executive officer, and does not command any armed force. The UN General Assembly is not a legislative body, which can require nations to act in accordance with its resolutions. The ICJ does not have the power to hear contentious cases, absent the express consent of the defendant nation. This is a comparatively primitive state of affairs. It is an international legal system in which the governed govern, in order to preserve their respective sovereignties. This coordinated system depends upon a blend of legal norms and politics to function properly. Thus, a State member of the community of nations is not bound to act in a certain way, unless it has expressly consented to a particular course of conduct. In the international legal system, where States essentially govern themselves, critics understandably assert that the "distinction between law and politics is artificial, even preposterous."[25]

Evolution The content of International Law evolves gradually, sometimes, and in other instances, briskly. Such changes can adversely impact the degree of stability needed for a smoothly functioning legal system. A leading commentator, writing on behalf of the US Department of State, thus lamented that "International law is, more or less, in a continual state of change and development. In certain of its aspects the evolution is gradual; in others it is avulsive. [W]hereas certain customs are recognized as obligatory, others are in retrogression and are recognized as nonobligatory, depending upon the subject matter and its status at a particular time."[26]

Universality? The definitional nature of this introductory section requires brief mention of two corollaries: (1) Is *universal* acceptance required for a rule to become part of the content of International Law? (2) Can a powerful country like the United States *unilaterally* change International Law?

First, universal acceptance is not required for a norm to be incorporated into the body of International Law. If enough nations acknowledge a particular norm, by consistently using it in their international relations, their consensus will cause the norm to become a part of International Law.[27] However, a State's sovereign nature authorizes it to expressly reject what others might characterize as "universal" or "customary." But the requisite acquiescence may ultimately bind that nation, should it choose not to tender an objection through diplomatic processes or treaty reservations to situations.

Second, no single nation, regardless of its political or military strength, has the power to create or modify International Law. For example, one nation's statute cannot create global obligations. This branch of law is not created, developed, or abolished by the demand of one country, or a small group of countries. Its contours are determined by the common consent of many nations. The United States enjoys a unique and powerful post-Cold War posture. But it can neither dominate nor withdraw from the community of nations.

Unipolarity? As you will study in other chapters, the United States helped launch some major human rights treaties, starting in the 1980s. It later withdrew its support of those initiatives, as well as the ICJ. In the 1990s, the United States refused to ratify the Kyoto Protocol on greenhouse gas emissions. In 2001, it withdrew from the Anti-Ballistic Missile Treaty. In 2002, the United States initiated a number of treaties, which have undermined the new International Criminal Court. The United States launched preemptive wars against Afghanistan and Iraq, without the support of the United Nations and many long-term allies.

The March 2005 supplement to the 2002 US National Defense Strategy (§10.7) contended that "[o]ur strength as a nation state will continue to be challenged by those who employ a strategy of the weak by using international fora, judicial process, and terrorism." This motley grouping appeared to sculpt the following into one mold: *international fora*—presumably the United Nations; *judicial process*—presumably recent US Supreme Court decisions limiting governmental authority in the war on terrorism; and *terrorists*—exemplified by the September 11th hijackers. This Department of Defense strategy bullet assumes that these actors uniformly employ impotent strategies to achieve their respective objectives. The Bush Administration, by contrast, offers its Pre-emptive Strike Doctrine as the most powerful strategy for ensuring national defense in the *War on Terror*.

Why? Powerful nations, not just the United States, view the egalitarian notion of "sovereign equality" as a perennial source of irritation. It occupies an awkward point on the continuum between reality and utopia. As articulated by Nico Krisch of Germany's Max Planck Society for the Advancement of Science:

> Large nations have always had problems with transforming their factual power into legal superiority, which leaves them discontented with international law as a tool of foreign policy. . . . As a result, the United States has chosen to retreat from international law: it has made extensive use of reservations and frequently refused to sign or ratify important new treaties. Instead, it has increasingly relied on institutions in which it enjoys superior status . . . and it has turned to unilateral means, and notably to its domestic law, as a tool of foreign policy.
>
> . . .
>
> In international law . . . sovereign equality is a far-reaching promise with a largely indeterminate content, while on a concrete level it embodies few, very formal rules that ensure only minimal protection against factual inequalities.[28]

One could surmise that the United States was surprised by the dynamics spawned by its own hand, which it could not control. There was overwhelming support for the first Persian Gulf War in Kuwait, but little for the second in Iraq. US frustration with the comparative lack of support for round two with Iraq did not necessarily mean a complete rejection of multilateralism. One of the best examples is jointly articulated by the President of New York's International Peace Academy and the Director of Singapore's Institute of Defense and Strategic Studies:

> September 11 confirmed the argument . . . that "the U.S. foreign policy agenda is being transformed by transnational challenges that no single country . . . can resolve on its own." The nature of the terrorist threat is such that the United States will need the cooperation of many state and non-state actors. . . . This requires the United States to embark on a multilateral venture of unprecedented complexity. It calls for a strategy of eliciting the cooperation and sacrifices of numerous states of different political and cultural complexions, as well as those of international institutions and nongovernmental organizations.[29]

Less powerful nations, including the Third World, present a moderate but undeniable form of checks and balances on US dominance. The Russian-Chinese Joint Declaration on a Multipolar World, in the opening textbox in this chapter, urgently articulates the theme that "[n]o country should seek hegemony . . . or monopolize international affairs." As the United States continues to engage in conduct, such as preemptive wars not authorized by the UN Security Council, what kind of order will the international community in fact tolerate? Evidence of this concern is aptly assessed in the Chinese Journal of International Law:

Revolt Against or From Within the West? TWAIL, the Developing World, and the Future Direction of International Law

DAVID P. FIDLER
2 Chinese Journal of International Law 29 (2003)

The literature developing under the moniker "Third World Approaches to International Law" (TWAIL) critically analyzes international law in order to promote a more just and equitable approach to the countries and peoples of the developing world. Mutha described TWAIL as a "broad dialectic of opposition to international law" that resists the illegitimate, predatory, oppressive, and unjust [European-based] regime of international law.

Gathii similarly argued that "Third World positions exists in opposition to, and as a limit on, the triumphal universalism of the . . . [current] consensus in international law.

. . .

TWAIL scholars have resurrected Third World opposition to international law because they perceive [that] it creates a hierarchy of cultures that privileges the West, underpins Western political and economic hegemony, and enshrines as global gospel the values, beliefs, and practices of Western liberal civilization. TWAIL seeks to (1) deconstruct the use of international law for creating and perpetuating Western hegemony; and (2) construct the bases for a post-hegemony global order.

. . .

The essential dilemma of the TWAIL quest has been identified many times in international relations theory—finding ground for reform between the extremes of utopianism and *realpolitik*. Structurally, the TWAIL quest would be ill-advised to attempt to destabilize the international system by challenging the military, economic, and political hegemony of the West. The current "War on Terrorism" has been sparked by a desire by radical Islamic groups to revolt against the West through violence and terror. I cannot see anything but suffering for the Third World in that strategy. The events of September 11, 2001 have already reshaped global politics in ways that make the United States and its anti-terrorism allies less tolerant of views that challenge Western political and philosophical hegemony.

◆ 1.2 SOURCES OF INTERNATIONAL LAW

INTRODUCTION

Nations, international organizations, domestic or international courts, and arbitrators routinely examine the established "sources" of International Law to see whether the particular rule—which some participant is advocating—is actually a part of the corpus of International Law. Absent general State consent, the proposed rule is not binding.

The word *sources* is a chameleon-like term in the jargon of International Law.[30] One should distinguish between a source, *where* the law may be found, and a source which is the substantive *content* of applicable law. In this section of the book, the term "source" refers to the forensic process involving *where* a decision maker or researcher looks, to ascertain the substantive legal rule which governs a dispute or academic discourse. In this context, the term "source" does not refer to the actual language of the relevant legal text. Instead, it is a category, or type of source where the applicable substantive rule is located.

The international community has routinely applied the following list of sources for ascertaining the content of International Law. Under Article 38.1 of the Statute of the ICJ:

The Court, whose function is to decide in accordance with international law such disputes as are submitted to it, shall apply:

 a. international conventions, whether general or particular, establishing rules expressly recognized by the contesting states;

 b. international custom, as evidence of a general practice accepted as law;

 c. the general principles of law recognized by civilized nations;

 d. . . . judicial decisions and the teachings of the most highly qualified publicists of the various nations, as subsidiary means for the determination of rules of law.

This portfolio of sources was extracted from Article 38 of the original world court Statute, unanimously adopted by the First Assembly of the League of Nations in 1920. This PCIJ source list evolved from the common practice of local or regional tribunals, which had used these same sources for finding evidence of the substantive content of International Law. The so-called "Permanent" court employed these sources for seeking the details about the actual content of International Law, until its judges fled from Holland during World War II. While scholars have debated the completeness of this list of sources,[31] it is the definitive list for international arbitral and judicial tribunals.

Article 38's Critics The 1944 Report of the Informal Inter-Allied Committee on the Future of the PCIJ stated that "although the wording of this provision is open to certain criticisms, it has worked well in practice and its retention is recommended."[32]

Some critics question whether this aging articulation of the sources of International Law has continuing vitality. Some Western, Russian, and Chinese scholars have articulated forceful counterarguments:

◆ Former University of Chicago Professor Morton Kaplan and former US Attorney General Nicholas Katzenbach argued that this list of sources became "stereotyped." It fails to acknowledge the ever-changing nature of the content of International Law, and thus even the shopping list of sources from which it is derived.

◆ Moscow State University Professor Grigori Tunkin poses doubts about the "imperfect formulation" of this Statute of the International Court of Justice Article 38 listing of sources. He comments that a "practice" might not be a *general* practice within the meaning of this Article, although it is recognized as a legally binding rule between two nations or within a particular region of the world.

◆ Chinese scholars perceive Article 38 as being a list of Western-derived sources reflecting the external policy of the ruling classes, because these "sources of bourgeois international law are the external policy of the bourgeoisie which is also the will of the ruling class of those big capitalist powers." Third World scholars embrace this latter perception, because of the Eurocentric roots of modern International Law. Many of their homelands were colonized by the dominant States that cultivated these rules, long before the global independence movement of the 1960s.

◆ That *opinio juris* (what States profess to believe) and State practice (what States actually do) are not sufficiently distinguished by Article 38's reference to "custom." There is much subjectivity associated with the word "custom." The bias or experience of the particular decision maker complicates the daunting task of assessing the degree to which perceived changes in Customary International Law (CIL) are merely in the eye of the beholder.[33]

Hierarchy Among Sources? The sequential arrangement of the sources within Article 38 of the ICJ Statute (as discussed earlier) suggests an implicit hierarchy. The first layer of this ordering is that treaties, customs, and general principles are the primary sources for finding the content of International Law. Judicial decisions and scholarly writings are expressly designated as the "subsidiary" sources for determining the content of International Law.

The possibility of an express hierarchy of sources was almost incorporated into the *predecessor* of Article 38 (when the "Committee of Jurists" drafted it for the PCIJ in 1920). The initial draft version provided that any listed sources were to be considered *en ordre successif*—in successive order. This phrase was deleted, however, at the First Assembly of the League of Nations. The League's records do not indicate whether the deletion was meant to avoid a hierarchy; or, alternatively, was so unnecessary as to render the words (*en ordre successif*) surplusage. A treaty is the usually best evidence of what is International Law; a custom is more readily articulated than a general principle; and so on.[34]

Contemporary commentators rank the comparative importance of this statutory list of sources. Many consider custom to be not only at the top, but also the essential basis for the other sources. University of Rome Professor Benedetto Conforti thereby insists that:

Customary rules properly are placed at the top of the hierarchy of international norms. Included as a special category of customary rules, are general principles of law common to all domestic systems. Custom is both the highest source of international norms, and the only source of general rules. Treaties are second in ranking. Their obligatory character [itself] rests on a customary rule, *pacta sunt servanda* [good faith performance], and their entire existence is regulated by a series of customary rules known as the law of treaties. Third in the hierarchy are sources provided by agreements, including, most importantly, acts of international organizations.[35]

Other commentators characterize treaties as the most fundamental source. Frankfurt University's Professor Rudolf Bernhardt asserts that custom is often superseded by treaties. His informative perspective is that "normal customary law . . . can as such be superseded by regional as well as universal treaties. States are in general free to conclude treaties, which depart from customary law. This happens every day. Treaties on economic relations between certain States, double taxation agreements, defence alliances and human rights treaties all change the legal relations between the participating States, impose additional and different obligations, limit the existing freedom and sovereign rights of the States concerned, and [thereby] change the applicable norms. In this context, treaties have a 'higher' rank than customary law."[36]

The quest to fill the ICJ Statute's Article 38.1 gap, to assist decision makers having to choose among conflicting sources, now features a third paradigm. One might address any relative Article 38.1 hierarchy in terms of "sliding variables" impacting the relative authority and pedigree within the Article 38.1 source list. International human rights law, for example, has spawned the most extensive array of treaties and case law. Saskatchewan College of Law's Professor Franciso Martin thus explains that "we can discern a pedigree based on the relative authority of the international body from which the pronouncement of international policy emanates. For example, decisions and resolutions from the Council of Europe, Organization of American States (OAS), and the Organization of African Unity have less authority than those of the United Nations because these regional intergovernmental organizations have fewer members, and because Article 103 of the UN Charter demands that the UN Charter supercede other international agreements."[37] A UN human rights resolution, or an ICJ court opinion, would be accorded more weight than a resolution of the Council of Europe or a case decided by its European Court of Human Rights.

This section of the textbook now explores the practical meaning of the sources of International Law as follows: Custom, Treaties, General Principles, Judicial Decisions, Scholarly Writings, and a write in candidate, not on the Article 38 list: UN Resolutions.

(1) CUSTOM

Decision makers often examine the customary practice of various nations, as a primary source for determining the content of the rule applicable to the legal issue at hand. An established State practice, accepted by many nations, qualifies as a binding custom. This source has a rich and diverse history dating back to the Roman Empire.[38] It has a persistent vitality because many international obligations were, and are, not expressed in treaties.

When is a custom "binding"? Moscow State University Professor Grigori Tunkin describes this question as one of the most important, and most complex, theoretical problems for diplomats, jurists, and researchers. It is therefore "natural that the question of customary norms of international law has been the object of constant attention of specialists for a century."[39] This complexity has evolved from the dual process of having to determine both where to find evidence of the custom's existence and what customs are obligatory components of International Law.

There is often a continuum, whereby a customary practice among a few nations ultimately ripens into a custom applicable to all nations—on a regional or global basis. The problem is how to determine whether a particular practice by *some* States has matured as a CIL that binds all nations. Oxford University Professor Ian Brownlie conveniently assembles the four elements for resolving whether a claimed practice in fact falls within the domain of CIL: (1) duration or passage of time; (2) substantial uniformity or consistency of usage by the affected nations; (3) generality of the practice, or degree of abstention; and (4) *opinio juris et necessitatis*—international consensus about, and recognition of, the particular custom as binding.[40]

The fourth element is arguably the most important, yet the most difficult to authenticate. The ICJ opinion in the 1969 North Sea Continental Shelf case authoritatively evaluated the requisite degree of international consensus. The issue in such cases was whether the United Nation's 1958 Convention on the Continental Shelf, containing an equidistance principle for allocating limited resources within the shelf, codified a customary rule that would be binding on nations that were *not* parties to that Convention. The Court explained that:

> Not only must the acts concerned amount to a settled practice, but they must also be such . . . as to be evidence of a belief that this practice is rendered obligatory by the existence of a rule of law requiring it. . . . The States concerned must therefore feel that they are conforming to what amounts to a legal obligation. . . . There are [otherwise] many international acts, e.g., in the field of ceremonial [behavior] and protocol, which are performed almost invariably, but which are motivated only by considerations of courtesy, convenience, or tradition, and not by any sense of legal duty.[41]

Regional Custom   A regional custom applied by a few nations is not necessarily tantamount to a custom practiced by all other members of the community of nations. Both categories of custom may be binding.

For example, Colombia claimed, in a 1950 ICJ case, that "American International Law" required Peru to recognize Colombia's grant of asylum in the Latin American region. Peru responded that the Colombian embassy improperly granted asylum to a Peruvian national seeking to overthrow Peru's government. Peru was unwilling to permit its Peruvian national to depart the Columbian Embassy, and then leave Peru without being prosecuted for treason. The Court rejected the existence of either a regional or universal custom requiring Peru's recognition of Colombia's grant of diplomatic asylum—a decision for which this distant Court in Europe was harshly criticized, especially among African nations.

Yet the ICJ tacitly approved the potential application of regional custom, where they could be proven to exist (§7.3 *Columbia v. Peru* case). The following key passage illustrates what Colombia needed to prove, in order to establish that this custom had become a part of CIL:"The Party which relies on custom . . . must prove that this [supposed] custom is established in such a manner that it has become binding on the other Party . . . [and] that the [claimed right of asylum] . . . is in accordance with a constant and uniform usage, practised by the States in question, and that this usage is the expression of a right appertaining to the State granting asylum [Colombia] and a duty incumbent on the territorial State [Peru]."[42]

Some commentators, however, contend that a practice must be universal before a custom can become binding under International Law.[43] This "requirement" has been advocated in socialist nations when International Law is not considered part of a legal hierarchy of laws that can bind a sovereign State. The practical problem with this contention is that universality is rarely achieved, in an international system composed of many diverse nations. International custom gradually evolves through compromise and consistency of application. New York University Professor James Hsiung, writing on Chinese recognition practice, provides a useful insight. It is impossible to measure precisely how strong the dissent must be, before an existing norm is changed—or precisely when a rejected norm ceases to exist. Dissent, or a change of consensus, if supported by a growing number of States, may thus bring about a new norm or at least indicate a revision in customary practice.[44]

Custom Applied   National courts have various methods for ascertaining the scope of an advocate's claim that a customary rule of International Law exists, and should thus be applied to the case at hand. For example, the London Court of Appeal articulated how such rules may be proven, in its pronouncement that "[r]ules of international law, whether they be part of our law or a source of our law, must be in some sense 'proved,' and they are *not* proved in English courts by expert evidence like [hearing testimony about] foreign law: they are 'proved' by [the trial judge] taking judicial notice of international treaties and conventions, authoritative textbooks, practice and judicial decisions of other courts in other countries which show that they have attained the position of general acceptance by civilized nations."[45]

The following case classically illustrates how a group of decision makers—in this instance, US federal judges analyzing international human rights and environmental issues—examined the Article 38.1 sources of International Law, in their quest to resolve whether or not there was an applicable customary practice regarding corporate responsibility for environmental pollution:

Flores v. Southern Peru Copper Corporation
UNITED STATES COURT OF APPEALS SECOND CIRCUIT
343 F.3d 140 (2003)

AUTHOR'S NOTE: This case interprets the federal Alien Tort Claims Act or ATCA. (This moniker *should* have been "ATS," because whether this statute actually authorized individuals to bring "Claims" under the ATS was not authoritatively resolved until the following year in the US Supreme Court's *Sosa* opinion [§11.5].

Most of the *Flores* court's substantive analysis of the ATS has been deleted. This opinion therefore focuses on the court's *method* for ascertaining whether the sources in the International Court of Justice Statute reveal a viable customary rule to apply in this case. *Flores* is one of the rare instances where a *United States* court has applied

Art. 38.1 of the ICJ Statute to determine the content of International Law.

The *Flores* court applied Article 38.1 of the ICJ Statute to the facts of this case. Its judges thereby found that the plaintiffs had failed to establish a viable claim arising under Customary International Law.

COURT'S OPINION:

. . .

Plaintiffs in this case are residents of Ilo, Peru, and the representatives of deceased Ilo residents. They brought personal injury claims under the ATCA against Southern Peru Copper Corporation ("SPCC"), a United States company, alleging that pollution from SPCC's copper mining, refining, and smelting operations in and around Ilo caused plaintiffs' or their decedents' severe lung disease. The ATCA states that "[t]he district courts shall have original jurisdiction of any civil action by an alien for a tort only, committed in violation of the law of nations or a treaty of the United States." Plaintiffs claimed that defendant's conduct violates the "law of nations," commonly referred to as "international law" or, when limited to non-treaty law, as "customary international law." In particular, they asserted that defendant infringed upon their customary international law "right to life," "right to health," and right to "sustainable development."

. . .

BACKGROUND
I. Statement of the Case

. . .

SPCC's operations emit large quantities of sulfur dioxide and very fine particles of heavy metals into the local air and water. Plaintiffs claim that these emissions have caused their respiratory illnesses and that this "egregious and deadly" local pollution constitutes a customary international law offense because it violates the "right to life," "right to health," and right to "sustainable development."[3]

. . .

DISCUSSION

. . .

Questions regarding the purpose and scope of the ATCA [enacted in 1789] did not attract substantial judicial

attention until . . . first recognized by a federal appellate court as a viable basis for relief in *Filartega v. Pena-Irala*, 630 F.2d 876 (2d Cir. 1980). . . .

In determining whether the plaintiffs had alleged a violation of the law of nations, the *Filartiga* Court first identified the appropriate sources of customary international law . . . . [I]t determined that, in considering whether a plaintiff has alleged a violation of customary international law, a . . . principle to have "ripened . . . into 'a settled rule of international law,'" . . . must command "'the general assent of civilized nations.'"

. . .

B. The "Law of Nations"

1. Definition of "Law of Nations" or "Customary International Law" for Purposes of the ATCA

. . . The determination of what offenses violate customary international law, however, is no simple task. Customary international law is discerned from myriad decisions made in numerous and varied international and domestic arenas. Furthermore, the relevant evidence of customary international law is widely dispersed and generally unfamiliar to lawyers and judges. These difficulties are compounded by the fact that customary international law—as the term itself implies—is created by the general customs and practices of nations and therefore does not stem from any single, definitive, readily-identifiable source.[22] All of these characteristics give the body of customary international law a "soft, indeterminate character," Louis Henkin, *International Law: Politics and Values* 29 (1995), that is subject to creative interpretation. Accordingly, in determining what offenses violate customary international law, courts must proceed with extraordinary care and restraint.

. . .

First, in order for a principle to become part of customary international law, . . . the principle must be more than merely professed or aspirational.

. . .

---

[3] On appeal, plaintiffs only pursue their claims that defendant's conduct violates customary international law rights to life and health; they no longer base their argument on a right to "sustainable development." [The latter "right" is addressed in §12.2 of this text.]

---

[22] "Custom is the oldest and the original source of international law as well as of law in general," the substance of which "is to be found in the practice of states." 1 *Oppenheim's International Law 25-26* (Sir Robert Jennings & Sir Arthur Watts, eds., 9th ed. 1996). The practice of states, in turn, "embraces not only their external conduct with each other, but is also evidenced by such internal matters as their domestic legislation, judicial decisions, diplomatic d[i]spatches, internal government memoranda, and ministerial statements in Parliaments and elsewhere."

2. Sources and Evidence of Customary International Law

In determining whether a particular rule is a part of customary international law—*i.e.,* whether States universally abide by, or accede to, that rule out of a sense of legal obligation and mutual concern—courts must look to concrete evidence of the customs and practices of States. As we have recently stated, "we look primarily to the formal lawmaking and official actions of States and only secondarily to the works of scholars as evidence of the established practice of States."

In *United States v. Yousef,* we explained why the usage and practice of States—as opposed to judicial decisions or the works of scholars—constitute the primary sources of customary international law. 327 F.3d at 99–103. In that case, we looked to the Statute of the International Court of Justice ("ICJ Statute")—to which the United States and all members of the United Nations are parties—as a guide for determining the proper sources of international law.

. . .

Moreover, as noted above, customs or practices based on social and moral norms, rather than international legal obligation, are not appropriate sources of customary international law because they do not evidence any intention on the part of States, much less the community of States, to be legally bound.

. . .

III. Plaintiffs Have Failed to Allege a Violation of Customary International Law

. . .

A. The Rights to Life and Health Are Insufficiently Definite to Constitute Rules of Customary International Law

As an initial matter, we hold that the asserted "right to life" and "right to health" are insufficiently definite to constitute rules of customary international law. As noted above, . . . we have required that a plaintiff allege a violation of a "clear and unambiguous" rule of customary international law. . . .

Far from being "clear and unambiguous," the statements relied on by plaintiffs to define the rights to life and heath are vague and amorphous. For example, the statements that plaintiffs rely on to define the rights to life and health include the following:

Everyone has the right to a standard of living adequate for the health and well- being of himself and of his family . . . .

– Universal Declaration of Human Rights, Art. 25.

The States Parties to the present Covenant recognize the right of everyone to the enjoyment of the highest attainable standard of physical and mental health.

– International Covenant on Economic, Social, and Cultural Rights, Art. 12. Human beings are . . . entitled to a healthy and productive life in harmony with nature.

– Rio Declaration on Environment and Development ("Rio Declaration"), United Nations Conference on Environment and Development, Principle 1.

These principles are boundless and indeterminate. They express virtuous goals understandably expressed at a level of abstraction needed to secure the adherence of States that disagree on many of the particulars regarding how actually to achieve them. . . . The precept that "[h]uman beings are . . . entitled to a healthy and productive life in harmony with nature," for example, utterly fails to specify what conduct would fall within or outside of the law. Similarly, the exhortation that all people are entitled to the "highest attainable standard of physical and mental health," proclaims only nebulous notions that are infinitely malleable.

. . .

For the foregoing reasons, plaintiffs have failed to establish the existence of a customary international law "right to life" or "right to health."

B. Plaintiffs Have Not Submitted Evidence Sufficient to Establish that Customary International Law Prohibits *Intra*national Pollution

Although customary international law does not protect a right to life or right to health, plaintiffs' complaint may be construed to assert a claim under a more narrowly—defined customary international law rule [claiming that a State cannot pollute, or allow those under its control to pollute, even if the effect is felt only *within* its borders] . . . .

In support of their claims, plaintiffs have submitted the following types of evidence: (i) treaties, conventions, and covenants; (ii) non-binding declarations of the United Nations General Assembly, (iii) other non-binding multinational declarations of principle; (iv) decisions of multinational tribunals, and (v) affidavits of international law scholars. We analyze each type of evidence submitted by the plaintiffs in turn.

1. Treaties, Conventions, and Covenants

Plaintiffs rely on numerous treaties, conventions, and covenants in support of their claims. Although these instruments are proper evidence of customary international law to the extent that they create legal obligations among the States parties to them, plaintiffs have not demonstrated that the particular instruments on which they rely establish a legal rule prohibiting intranational pollution.

. . .

All treaties that have been ratified by at least two States provide *some* evidence of the custom and practice of nations. However, a treaty will only constitute *sufficient proof* of a norm of customary international law if an overwhelming majority of States have ratified the treaty, *and* those States uniformly and consistently act in accordance with its principles.

. . .

2. Non-Binding General Assembly Declarations

Plaintiffs rely on several resolutions of the United Nations General Assembly in support of their assertion that defendant's conduct violated a rule of customary international law. These documents are not proper sources of customary international law because they are merely aspirational and were never intended to be binding on member States of the United Nations.

. . .

Our position is consistent with the recognition in *Filartiga* that the right to be free from torture embodied in the Universal Declaration of Human Rights, G.A. Res. 217A(III), U.N. GAOR, 3d Sess., U.N. Doc. A/810, at 71 (1948), has attained the status of customary international law. . . .

In considering the Universal Declaration's prohibition against torture, the *Filartiga* Court cited extensive evidence that States, in their domestic and international practices, repudiate official torture. In particular, it recognized that torture is prohibited under law by, *inter alia,* the constitutions of fifty-five States, and noted the conclusion expressed by the Executive Branch of our government—the political branch with principal responsibility for conducting the international relations of the United States—that "[t]here now exists an international consensus" against official torture that "virtually all governments acknowledge," . . . . Accordingly, although *Filartiga* did indeed cite the Universal Declaration, this non-binding General Assembly declaration was only relevant to *Filartiga*'s [1980, pre-U.N. Torture Convention] analysis insofar as it accurately described the actual customs and practices of States on the question of torture.

In the instant case, the General Assembly documents relied on by plaintiffs do not describe the actual customs and practices of States. Accordingly, they cannot support plaintiffs' claims.

3. Other Multinational Declarations of Principle

. . .

Plaintiffs also rely on Principle 1 of the [1992] Rio Declaration, 31 I.L.M. 874, which sets forth broad, aspirational principles regarding environmental protection and sustainable development. The Rio Declaration includes no language indicating that the States joining in the Declaration intended to be legally bound by it.

. . .

4. Decisions of Multinational Tribunals

Plaintiffs also rely on judicial decisions of international tribunals in support of their claims. . . .

With respect to the European Court of Human Rights, the Court is only empowered to "interpret[ ]" and "appl[y]" the rules set forth in the European Convention for the Protection of Human Rights and Fundamental Freedoms—an instrument applicable only to its regional States parties—not to create new [global] rules of customary international law. *See* . . . *also* ICJ Statute art. 38 (listing judicial decisions as "subsidiary," rather than primary, sources of customary international law). . . .

5. Expert Affidavits Submitted by Plaintiffs

Plaintiffs submitted to the District Court several affidavits by international law scholars in support of their argument that strictly *intra* national pollution violates customary international law. After careful consideration, the District Court declined to afford evidentiary weight to these affidavits. It determined that the affidavits "are even less probative [than plaintiffs' documentary evidence] of the existence of universal norms, especially considering the vigorous academic debate over the content of international law."

. . .

In its seminal decision in *Paquete Habana,* the Supreme Court designated "the works of jurists [*i.e.,* scholars] and commentators" as a possible source of customary international law. *Paquete Habana,* 175 U.S. at 700, 20 S.Ct. 290. However, the Court expressly stated that such works "are resorted to by judicial tribunals, *not for the speculations of their authors concerning what the law ought to be,* but for trustworthy evidence of what the law *really is." Id.* (emphasis added).

. . .

We have reviewed the [legal experts'] affidavits submitted by plaintiffs and agree with the District Court's conclusion that they are not competent evidence of customary international law.

. . .

CONCLUSION

For the reasons stated above, we affirm the judgment of the District Court dismissing plaintiffs' complaint for . . . failure to state a claim under the ATCA.

◆ *Notes & Questions*

1. The custom alleged in *Paquete Habana* was that State practice precluded coastal fishing boats—not involved in the Spanish-American war efforts—from being captured during a nineteenth-century US naval blockade of Cuba. The Supreme Court therein examined five centuries of State practice in various wars between other nations. It determined that such coastal fishers were routinely exempted from capture. Unlike the inland waterways of the Vietnam War era, where Mekong Delta coastal fishers often had guns stashed beneath their fishing cargo, these Cuban fishers were not aiding the enemy. The *Paquete Habana* dissent disagreed that the US conduct of the Spanish-American War proved that such practice was obligatory. The President had ordered that the US naval blockade be conducted in accordance with International Law. This exercise of his discretion could be rescinded at any time. An edited version of the *Paquete Habana* case appears as indicated below.

2. Like *Flores,* the custom alleged in *Filartega* was an Alien Tort Statute (ATS) claim. In Paraguay, a policeman tortured and killed the brother/son of the plaintiff citizens of Paraguay. They successfully claimed that there was a clear customary practice among nations, which prohibited such torture. In *Flores,* however, the same federal Court of Appeals in New York ruled against the Peruvian plaintiffs on their environmental ATS claim. Why was there was a different result in *Paquete Habana/Filartega* than in *Flores,* as to whether CIL was proven by the respective plaintiffs?

3. Long after *Paquete Habana,* the US Government confirmed its application that "customary international law is federal law, to be enunciated authoritatively by the federal courts." *Filiartega, Amicus Curiae* brief for the United States at 1. For the argument that, absent a clear rule from a federal statute or treaty, state courts and legislatures in the United States are free to treat as they wish, or ignore, CIL, see C. Bradley & J. Goldsmith, Customary International Law as Federal Common Law: A Critique of The Modern Position, 110 Harv. Law Rev. 815 (1997). This "revisionist scholars" position was rebuked by Professor Harold Koh, then Assistant Secretary of State for Democracy, Human Rights and Labor, in Is International Law Really State Law?, 111 HARV. LAW REV. 1824 (1998).

4. The March 2005 *Agent Orange* case applied ICJ Statute Article 38.1 to another environmental case. Relying on *Flores,* the court restated the proposition that: "A guide for determining proper sources of international law is the Statute of the International Court of Justice. . . to which the United States is a party." In re "Agent Orange" Product Liability Litigation, 373 F.Supp.2d 7 (E.D.N.Y. 2005). The court observed that: "Customary international law is binding on all states, even in the absence of a particular state's consent, but may be modified within a state by subsequent legislation or a treaty, provided that the customary international law was not a peremptory norm (*jus cogens)." Id.,* at 131. This latter term embraces norms such as the prohibition on genocide, from which no state may vary (§11.2).

5. Regarding the *Flores* substantive law claim, what occurred in Peru, is by no means unique. In April 2005, for example, 50,000–60,000 elderly residents protested over pollution from nearby factories in a rural village in China. Some 3,000 police officers halted this protest. In 2003, tens of thousands of Chinese

villagers protested pollution in another province—a symptom of social unrest related to industrializing economies. See Rural Chinese Riot as Police Try to Halt Pollution Protest, NY Times on the Web, Apr. 14, 2005. Chapter 12 addresses international environmental pollution law.

The Paquete Habana and the Lola

SUPREME COURT OF THE UNITED STATES
175 U.S. 677, 20 S.Ct. 290, 44 L.Ed. 320
(1900)
Go to course Web page at
<http://home.att.net/~slomansonb/txtcsesite.html>.
Under Chapter One, click Paquete Habana.

(2) TREATIES

An applicable international convention, commonly referred to as treaty, is the first of the ICJ Statute's list of sources for finding the content of International Law. A multilateral treaty is usually the most convenient way of securing reliable evidence of a consensus on the issue before an international decision maker. When ratified by many nations, a multilateral treaty is direct proof of rights and obligations accepted by multiple parties to that treaty. It is the primary source for ascertaining the nature of what the international participants have agreed to do or not do. As you will observe in Chapter 8 on Treaties, there is often an inverse correlation between the number of treaty parties and specificity. The more parties to the treaty, the less is the detail, thus achieving a greater degree of consensus on the underlying principles. Because of the enormous range of issues that are not addressed by express treaty terms, CIL is the quintessential gap filler.

A regional treaty is not intended to have universal applicability. It is nevertheless a useful source for ascertaining the rules which bind its local participants. The Charter of the Organization of American States, for example, provides that all international disputes between American states shall be submitted to the procedures set forth in the OAS Charter—"*before* being referred to the Security Council of the United Nations."[46] State parties thereby agree to first resort to regional OAS agencies, rather than proceeding directly to the UN Security Council. While the

UN Charter *encourages* such regionalism, this particular treaty *requires* its members to seek an OAS solution first, before pursuing a remedy in a more global forum. Conversely, non-OAS nations are free to lodge their claims in the United Nations, or any other appropriate forum.

Global multilateral treaties usually provide the best evidence of international consensus, even when they are not universally adopted. One example is the UN Law of the Sea Treaty, which entered into force in November 1994. It is the best evidence of the respective rights and obligations of the parties who have accepted it. When enough nations have ratified such a treaty, its entry into force is the best source for resolving maritime issues between the ratifying states. Such a treaty may also bind non-parties, as a matter of CIL, if it codifies the general practice of many nations. This process was confirmed by the ICJ in its statement that a treaty may have "generated a rule which, while only conventional or contractual in its origin [between ratifying states], has since passed into the general *corpus* of international law, and is now accepted as such by the *opinio juris*, so as to have become binding even for countries which have never, and do not, become parties to the Convention. There is no doubt that this process . . . constitutes indeed one of the recognized methods by which new rules of customary international law may be formed."[47]

(3) GENERAL PRINCIPLES

The prescribed list of sources includes "general principles of law recognized by civilized nations." Why is this source necessary? Treaties do not, and usually cannot, provide answers to every future dispute. International decision makers sometimes borrow gap-filling concepts from the internal law of various nations, such as "equity" and "good faith."[48]

One who is not a lawyer should not assume that common words have a fixed definition, even in a matured national legal system. "Pornography " is mentioned in many legal and social discourses. The US Supreme Court cannot define it, but knows it when it sees it.[49] The same is especially true for the international legal system. As pithily articulated by New York University Professor Thomas Franck on the state of International Law: "Even if 'everyone' were to agree, at least in theory, that fairness is a necessary condition . . . , this unfortunately would not assure that everyone shared the same sense of fairness or agreed on a fixed meaning. Fairness is not 'out there' waiting to be discovered, it is a product of social context and history. Plato did not consider slavery to be unfair. . . . It has been suggested that while we may not be able to define justice, we can probably recognize injustice. . . . What is considered allocationally fair has varied across time, and still varies across cultures."[50]

The incorporation of *general principles* into the ICJ source list for determining the content of International Law thereby "enabled the Court to replenish, without subterfuge, the rules of international law by principles of law tested within the shelter of more mature and closely integrated [national] legal systems."[51] Although there is scholarly disagreement about the proper scope of this source,[52] it is limited to the principles of national law, generally applied by many nations.

The international legal system has not enjoyed the same long-term evolution experienced by national legal systems and their predecessors. International tribunals decide far fewer cases than judges in national legal courts. Analytical problems may surface for the international decision maker who is confronted with insufficient resources for independently resolving a dispute. *General principles* therefore serves as a stopgap, because the international judge can deduce an apropos rule that has evolved in a national legal system.

Both world courts affirmed the pragmatic value of the "general principles" source. In an often-quoted statement from a 1937 PCIJ case, Judge Anzilotti drew upon the commonly applied equitable principle that a nonperforming nation cannot take advantage of another nation's nonperformance. He was convinced that this general principle was "so just, so equitable, so universally recognized, that it must be applied in international relations" as one of those general principles of law recognized by civilized nations under Article 38 of the Court's Statute. The propriety of using national legal principles in international adjudication was reconfirmed in a 1970 ICJ case, dealing with the general principle of judicial independence from other branches of government. Notwithstanding differences in degree among the various national legal systems, judicial independence from the other branches of government "may be considered as a universally recognized principle in most of the municipal [national] and international legal systems of the world."[53]

On the other hand, the ubiquitous availability of a general legal principle—although staunchly ingrained in many national legal systems—might not be shoe horned into international jurisprudence. The US Supreme Court has exercised the power of judicial review, for example, over actions by the political branches of government since 1803.[54] The ICJ, however, cannot directly review the legality of UN Security Council action (or inaction). As exemplified by the University of Amsterdam's Professor Erika de Wet:

> Since the political organs of the United Nations cannot be a party to contentious proceedings, the question of legality of Security Council resolutions will have to arise [if at all] in proceedings between states. . . . If a survey of municipal orders were to indicate that judicial review of the decisions of political organs within states was (or was not) emerging as a general principle of law, this could tip the scale of the debate one way or the other. For example if the rationale for accepting such [judicial] control would seem to have become generally accepted, the ICJ could transpose it to the international order through Article 38(1)(c) of its Statute. This presupposes that a comparison with judicial review in municipal law is justified in light of the difference in structure between municipal orders and the international legal order.[55]

Yet there are many "general principles that do "fit," as classically illustrated in the following case:

The AM&S Case
Australian Mining & Smelting Europe Ltd. v. *E.C. Commission*
EUROPEAN COMMUNITY COMMISSION
2 *Common market law reports* 264 (1982)

AUTHOR'S NOTE: A commission of the European Community (EC) initiated a proceeding questioning whether AM&S business activities violated regional competition laws. The EC sought documents prepared by the company's lawyers. AM&S did not want to comply, on the basis of a claimed attorney-client privilege from disclosure in legal proceedings. There was no provision in the various EC treaties and regulations regarding the viability of such a privilege from discovery in Community legal proceedings.

In 1979, AM&S (based in the United Kingdom) instituted proceedings to have Commission Decision 79/760/EEC of 6 July 1979 declared void. That provision required AM&S to produce a number of documents which the company claimed were insulated from discovery in these proceedings—on the basis of a supposed attorney-client privilege, which was not set forth in any Community law.

The following excerpt is the Second Opinion of the Advocate General (Sir Gordon Slynn). Under Community procedure, this EC official filed his opinion, analyzing the availability of the claimed privilege from discovery in proceedings pending before the EC's administrative and judicial tribunals. The Advocate General thus presented the analysis of whether there was a general principle (attorney-client privilege) in the laws of the various EC member States, and, whether it should apply in Community proceedings. The textbook author has supplied italics in certain passages.

COMMISSION'S OPINION: In February 1979, officials of the Commission required the applicants to make available documents which they wished to see in connection with an investigation . . . of competitive conditions concerning the production and distribution of zinc metal and its alloys and zinc concentrates in order to verify that there is no infringement of Articles 85 and 86 of the EEC Treaty [the European Community's basic competition provisions]. The applicants produced copies of most of the documents. Some, however, were not produced . . . on the basis that they were covered by legal confidentiality, which entitled the applicants to withhold them.

The parties were invited to state at the re-opened oral hearing their views on the law as to, and legal opinions relating to, the existence and extent of the protection granted in investigative proceedings instituted by public authorities . . . to correspondence passing between . . . [the lawyer and his client AM&S].

The Commission's investigative powers . . . [authorize it to] 'undertake all necessary investigations . . .' and, to that end, its authorised officials are empowered to examine books and business records, to take copies of them, and to ask for oral explanations. *There is no reference to any exemption or protection which may be claimed on the basis of legal confidence* [between lawyer and client].

Is that silence conclusive that no such protection is capable of applying in any form and in any situation? In my view it is not. The essential enquiry is, first, whether there is a principle of Community law existing independently of the regulation, and, secondly, whether the regulation does on a proper construction restrict the application of that principle. . . .

That general principles which have not been expressly stated in the Treaty or in subordinate legislation may exist as part of Community law, the observance of which the Court is required to ensure, needs no emphasis. . . . The Commission argue[s] that there has to be a consensus among the laws of all the member-States, and that the Court cannot establish a principle which goes beyond that accepted by any one of the member-States.

It cited no specific authority for that proposition, nor indicated what is the necessary level or degree of consensus required to establish the existence of a general principle.

That *national law may be looked at* on a comparative basis as an aid to consideration of what is Community law is shown in many cases. . . . Such a course is followed not to import national laws as such into Community law, but to use it *as a means of discovering an unwritten principle* of Community law. . . .

The Court has been provided with extracts from legislation, case decisions and the opinions of academic authors and a welter of case references. Rather than set those out *in extenso*, I propose to summarise what seems to me to be the relevant features for present purposes, fully conscious of the risks that a summary may oversimplify and is incomplete. I deal first with the general position as to the protection of legal confidence and then consider the position in relation to competition law.

In Belgium, it seems that confidential communications between lawyer and client are protected and cannot be seized or used as evidence. . . .

In Denmark, the rules of the professional secret prevents lawyers from giving evidence of confidential information confided to them in their professional capacity, and a lawyer can refuse to produce documents covered by professional secrecy. Communications between an accused person and his lawyer are protected in the hands of the accused under section 786 of the Code of Procedure. This rule seems to apply also in civil proceedings [like this one].

In Germany, confidential communications to a lawyer are protected in his hands, and breach of the professional confidentiality by a lawyer is a criminal offence.

WHAT IS INTERNATIONAL LAW? **21**

Thus such documents in the hands of the lawyer cannot be seized (section 97 of the Code of Criminal Procedure). . . .

In France, breach of the rule of professional secrecy is a criminal offence. . . .

In Greece, it seems that confidential communications in the hands of lawyers are protected in investigative proceedings instituted by judicial or administrative authorities. Documents in the hands of the client are covered by the general principle of privacy defined in Article 9 of the [Greek] Constitution. . . .

In Ireland and the United Kingdom, although there may be differences in detail, broadly the law of the two member-States is the same. . . . It should be repeated, however that it covers both (a) communications between a person and his lawyer for the purpose of obtaining or giving legal advice whether or not in connection with pending or contemplated legal proceedings and (b) communications between a person and his lawyer and other persons for the dominant purpose of preparing for pending or contemplated legal proceedings.

In Italy, as in most of the member-States, the law forbids lawyers from giving evidence of the information confided in them by their clients and entitles them to withhold documents covered by the doctrine of professional secrecy. . . . It seems that . . . professional secrecy is a reflection of the right to a fair trial guaranteed by Article 24 of the [Italian] Constitution.

In Luxembourg, rules of professional secrecy and *les droits de la dèfense* [rights of the defense], it would seem, protect legal confidences in the hands of the lawyer, and of the client after proceedings have begun, but little case law has been produced showing the application of these rules in practice.

Dutch law forbids the revelation of confidences by persons exercising a profession, such as lawyers. Coupled with this there is a right to refuse to give evidence on matters covered by professional secrecy. These matters include not only the information revealed by the client but also, in the case of lawyers, the legal advice they have given. . . .

This summary is substantially, if not entirely, accepted by the Commission, the applicants and the body representing the Bars of all the member-States as being a fair and acceptable statement of the laws of member-States.

It seems to me significant that they were able to reach agreement as to the existence of the principles which are set out in the document which they prepared to read to the Court.

From this it is plain, as indeed seems inevitable, that the position in all the member-States is not identical. It is to my mind equally plain that *there exists in all the member-States* a recognition that the public interest and the proper administration of justice demand as *a general rule* that a client should be able to speak freely, frankly and fully to his lawyer. . . . It springs essentially from the basic need of a man in a civilised society to be able to turn to his lawyer for advice and help, and if proceedings begin, for representation; it springs no less from the advantages to a society which involves complex law reaching into all the business affairs of persons, real and legal, that they should be able to know what they can do under the law, what is forbidden, where they must tread circumspectly, where they run risks. . . .

Judgment

. . .

The application [by AM&S] is based on the submission that in all the member-States written communications between lawyer and client are protected by virtue of a principle common to all those States, although the scope of that protection and the means of securing it vary from one country to another. According to the applicant, it follows from that principle . . . that the protection is properly claimed on the ground that the documents in question are in fact covered by legal privilege. . . .

(a) *The interpretation of Article 14 of Regulation 17* [conferring investigatory powers on the EC] . . .

(b) *Applicability of the protection of confidentiality in Community Law* . . .

However, the above rules do not exclude the possibility of recognising, subject to certain conditions, that certain business records are of a confidential nature. Community law, which derives from not only the economic but also the legal interpenetration of the member-States, must take into account the principles and concepts common to the laws of those States concerning the observance of confidentiality, in particular, as regards certain communications between lawyer and client. That confidentiality serves the requirement, the importance of which is recognised in all of the member-States, that any person must be able, without constraint, to consult a lawyer whose profession entails the giving of independent legal advice to all those in need of it.

. . .

(d) *The confidential nature of the documents at issue* . . .

In view of that relationship and in the light of the foregoing considerations, the written communications at issue must accordingly be considered, in so far as they emanate from an independent lawyer entitled to practice his profession in a member-State, as confidential and on that ground beyond the Commission's power of investigation under Article 14 of Regulation 17.

◆ *Notes & Questions*

1. Why did this opinion elaborate upon the laws of the various European Community (EC) member States, as opposed to the laws of the EC?

2. For an international restatement of the lawyer's general role, and related governmental responsibilities to ensure that it is not infringed by State action, see United Nations High Commissioner for Human Rights, Basic Principles on the Role of Lawyers (1990) at <http://www.unhchr.ch/html/menu3/b/h_comp44.htm>.

(4) JUDICIAL DECISIONS

Article 38.1 of the ICJ Statute includes "judicial decisions" as a source for determining the content of International Law. For a variety of reasons, international decision makers have drawn mostly upon national court decisions, as opposed to the jurisprudence of international tribunals. One limitation is the requirement for State consent to resolve cases in international tribunals. There is a comparatively large body of jurisprudence available in the form of national case law on issues arising under International Law.

When a particular issue is similarly resolved by the courts of various nations, an international tribunal may thus consider the routine resolution of that issue as evidence of a State consensus. British Professor Hersch Lauterpacht commented that the "decisions within any particular State, when endowed with sufficient uniformity and authority, may be regarded as expressing the *opinio juris*," meaning an expression of what that nation considers accepted practice.[56]

This Article 38 source is a "subsidiary" source for International Law-finding. A judge's decision does not *make* law. A judge normally *interprets* the law and applies it to a pending case in both national and international tribunals.

This is particularly true in civil law countries, where jurisprudence is based on the 1804 Napoleonic Code. There, judges have less discretion than that of their common law counterparts when interpreting the law created by the legislature—especially in totalitarian societies, where the chief executive either directly, or effectively, makes the laws.

The judges of the ICJ come from various legal systems. The court cannot be a binding "decision maker," in the same way that the US Supreme Court can overrule both legislative and executive action within its own national legal system. The judicial pronouncements of the court of one or many nations do not directly create or modify International Law. Such judicial decisions provide evidence, however, of how the judicial branch of one member of the community of nations has resolved the pending issue—but not the political (executive and legislative) branches of government, which determine national positions on international matters.

The judicial decisions' source for determining International Law has evolved to the point where some commentators have characterized it as the most important factor in the progressive development of International Law—referring, in this instance, to the jurisprudence of *international* tribunals. Some writers characterize such judicial decisions as being entitled to greater significance than the "subsidiary" status accorded them by Article 38.1 of the ICJ Statute. As stated by a prior President of the ICJ, decisions of international tribunals, "exercise considerable influence as an impartial and well-considered statement of the law by jurists of authority, made in light of actual problems which arise before them."[57]

But such decisions are coming under attack (at least in the United States). In 1815, the US Supreme Court made an ambitious statement, about the utility of resort to such decisions. The justices were resolving a commercial dispute over a government seizure of sugar belonging to a citizen of another country in time of war. The Court therein opined that:

> The law of nations is the great source from which we derive those rules [regarding ownership of seized enemy property] which are recognized by all civilized and commercial states throughout Europe and America. This law is in part unwritten, and in part conventional [meaning the subject of a treaty]. To ascertain that which is unwritten, we resort to the . . . decisions of the Courts of every country, so far as they are founded upon a law common to every country, [which] will be received not as [binding] authority, but with respect. The decisions of the Courts of every country show how the law of nations, in the given case, is understood in that country, and

will be considered in adopting the rule which is to prevail in this [case]. . . .

Such reliance came under attack in 2002. As then stated by Supreme Court Justice, Antonio Scalia: "Equally irrelevant are the practices of the 'world community,' whose notions of justice are (thankfully) not always those of our people. 'We must never forget that it is a Constitution for the United States of America that we are expounding. . . . [W]here there is not first a settled consensus among our own people, the views of other nations, however enlightened the Justices of this Court may think them to be, cannot be imposed upon Americans through the Constitution.'"[58]

In 2004, members of the US legislative branch joined in, expressing stern opposition to judicial reliance on such sources, per the following resolution:

Reaffirmation of American Independence Resolution

Congress of the United States, House of Representatives, Washington, DC 20515
May 13, 2004
<http://www.house.gov/feeney/reaffirmation.htm>

The Subcommittee on the Constitution today passed House Res. 568, the "Reaffirmation of American Independence Resolution," introduced by U.S. Rep. Feeney (R-FL) and U.S. Rep. Goodlatte (R-VA). [The text of this resolution by fifty-nine members of the House, was introduced as:]

"Today's approval is a salute to the framers of the Constitution and a victory for those dedicated to the protection of American sovereignty," stated Rep. Feeney. "This resolution reminds the Supreme Court that their role is interpreting U.S. law, not importing foreign law."

Article VI of the U.S. Constitution clearly states that the Constitution and the laws of the United States are the supreme law of the land. Yet, with growing frequency, Justices of the U.S. Supreme Court have relied upon decisions of foreign judicial courts. Five Supreme Court justices have written or joined opinions that cited foreign authorities—including courts in Jamaica, India, Zimbabwe, and the European Union—to justify their decisions. In a recent speech, Justice

Sandra Day O'Connor stated, "I suspect that over time [the U.S. Supreme Court] will rely increasingly . . . on international and foreign courts in examining domestic issues."

- ◆ Judges in the United States are charged to interpret both the intent of Congress and other American legislative bodies and whether the legislative intent of such bodies can be implemented within the bounds of the Constitution. The views of foreign bodies are not relevant to either of those charges unless they can aid in determining either the original meaning of the Constitution or the legislative intent of state or federal statutes.
- ◆ This Legislation affirms the sense of the House that U.S. judicial decisions should not be based on any foreign laws, court decisions, or pronouncements of foreign governments unless they are relevant to determining the meaning of American constitutional and statutory law. House Res. 568 has 59 House cosponsors.

This resolution, by certain members of the legislative branch of government, cannot bind the judicial branch because of US constitutional separation of powers principles. Nevertheless, the House Majority Leader added: "We've got Justice Kennedy writing decisions based upon international law, not the Constitution of the United States? That's just outrageous."[59] He was specifically referring to the following US Supreme Court decision (among others), as evidence of the evolving discontent about judicial reliance on foreign national and international decisions. The colloquy in this 2005 case vividly illustrates the judicial layer of this debate:

Roper v. Simmons

UNITED STATES SUPREME COURT
543 U.S. 551, 125 S.Ct. 1183, 161 L.Ed.2d 1 (2005)

J. Kennedy delivered the [majority] opinion of the court.

. . .

Our determination that the death penalty is disproportionate punishment for offenders under 18 finds confirmation in the stark reality that the United States is the only country in the world that continues to give official sanction to the juvenile death penalty. . . .

Article 37 of the United Nations Convention on the Rights of the Child, which every country in the world has ratified save for the United States and Somalia, contains an express prohibition on capital punishment for crimes committed by juveniles under 18. . . .

[O]nly seven countries other than the United States have executed juvenile offenders since 1990: Iran, Pakistan, Saudi Arabia, Yemen, Nigeria, the Democratic Republic of Congo, and China. Since then each of these countries has either abolished capital punishment for juveniles or made public disavowal of the practice. In sum, it is fair to say that the United States now stands alone in a world that has turned its face against the juvenile death penalty.

. . .

It is proper that we acknowledge the overwhelming weight of international opinion against the juvenile death penalty, resting in large part on the understanding that the instability and emotional imbalance of young people may often be a factor in the crime. The opinion of the world community, while not controlling our outcome, does provide respected and significant confirmation for our own conclusions.

. . .

The Eighth and Fourteenth Amendments forbid imposition of the death penalty on offenders who were under the age of 18 when their crimes were committed. The judgment of the Missouri Supreme Court setting aside the sentence of death imposed upon Christopher Simmons is affirmed.

. . .

Justice O'Connor, dissenting.

. . .

I turn, finally, to the Court's discussion of foreign and international law. Without question, there has been a global trend in recent years towards abolishing capital punishment for under-18 offenders. . . . I disagree with Justice Scalia's contention [joined by Justices Rhenquist and Thomas], that foreign and international law have no place in our Eighth Amendment [cruel and unusual punishment] jurisprudence. Over the course of nearly half a century, the Court has consistently referred to foreign and international law as relevant to its assessment of evolving standards of decency. [Cited authorities omitted.] . . . But this Nation's evolving understanding of human dignity certainly is neither wholly isolated from, nor inherently at odds with, the values prevailing in other countries. On the contrary, we should not be surprised to find congruence between domestic and international values, especially where the international community has reached clear agreement—expressed in international law or in the domestic laws of individual countries—that a particular form of punishment is inconsistent with fundamental human rights. At least, the existence of an international consensus of this nature can serve to confirm the reasonableness of a consonant and genuine American consensus.

. . .

Justice Scalia, with whom The Chief Justice and Justice Thomas join, dissenting.

. . .

Though the views of our own citizens are essentially irrelevant to the Court's decision today, the views of other countries and the so-called international community take center stage.

. . .

Unless the Court has added to its arsenal the power to join and ratify treaties on behalf of the United States, I cannot see how this evidence favors, rather than refutes, its position. That the Senate and the President——those actors our Constitution empowers to enter into treaties, see Art. II, § 2—have declined to join and ratify treaties prohibiting execution of under-18 offenders can only suggest that *our country* has either not reached a national consensus on the question, or has reached a consensus contrary to what the Court announces.

. . .

More fundamentally, however, the basic premise of the Court's argument—that American law should conform to the laws of the rest of the world—ought to be rejected out of hand. In fact the Court itself does not believe it. In many significant respects the laws of most other countries differ from our law—including not only such explicit provisions of our Constitution as the right to jury trial and grand jury indictment, but even many interpretations of the Constitution prescribed by this Court itself.

. . .

The Court has been oblivious to the views of other countries when deciding how to interpret our Constitution's requirement that "Congress shall make no law respecting an establishment of religion. . . ." Amdt. 1. Most other countries—including those committed to religious neutrality—do not insist on the degree of separation between church and state that this Court requires.

. . .

And let us not forget the Court's abortion jurisprudence, which makes us one of only six countries that allow abortion on demand until the point of viability.

. . .

The Court's special reliance on the laws of the United Kingdom is perhaps the most indefensible part of its opinion. . . . It is beyond comprehension why we should look, for that purpose, to a country that has developed, in the centuries since the Revolutionary War—and with increasing speed since the United Kingdom's recent submission to the jurisprudence of European courts [§9.6 of this textbook] dominated by continental jurists—a legal, political, and social culture quite different from our own. . . . The Court should either profess its willingness to reconsider all these matters in light of the views of foreigners, or else it should cease putting forth foreigners' views as part of the *reasoned basis* of its decisions. To invoke alien law when it agrees with one's own thinking, and ignore it otherwise, is not reasoned decisionmaking, but sophistry.

◆ *Notes & Questions*

1. This case deals with whether or not one nation's court should consider judicial opinions from other nations, specifically, for assistance in determining whether a juvenile should be exempt from the death penalty for a crime committed before the age of eighteen. Does the majority opinion, or dissent, make the more convincing argument about whether US courts should resort to foreign law?

   In yet another clash of Titans, Reagan appointee Justice Kennedy, later rejected Republican Party proposals to punish federal judges for such rulings. Speaking to a conference of federal judges, he claimed: "It's really quite wrong to say that the Supreme Court ignores international law and doesn't understand it." Referring to the title of a book by New York Times columnist Thomas Friedman on globalization, Kennedy said "the world is now flat, and the US is beginning to be involved in international law." At a postspeech panel, Yale University law school Dean Harold Koh called the Republican legislation (discussed earlier), which would prohibit judges from citing foreign law in their decisions, "outrageously ridiculous." Harris Meyer, Justice Kennedy Wades Into International Waters Again, Daily Business Review (May 17, 2005).

2. The US Supreme Court's *Paquete Habana* decision has been cited numerous times for its famous passage: "International law is a part of our law, and must be ascertained and administered by the courts . . . as often as questions of right depending upon it are duly presented for their determination." The Paquete Habana, 175 U.S. 677, 700, 20 S.Ct. 290, 299, 44 L.Ed. 320 (1900) (see edited version on course Web page). As you proceed through this course, keep both this articulation and Justice Scalia's dissent in the preceding Supreme Court's 2005 *Roper* decision, close at hand.

You should assess whether one statement ultimately proves more accurate than the other; whether the truth lies somewhere in between; or how a judge in your country should choose.

3. Other national supreme courts, in countries with jurisprudential systems similar to the United States, clearly embrace decisions from foreign sources. The High Court of Australia's unanimous position in a 1991 case, was as follows:

> To determine whether, in these circumstances, there exists a customary law obligation to try alleged war criminals in respect of extraterritorial war crimes, it is necessary to refer to the sources of international law. Article 38(1) of the Statute of the International Court of Justice is generally regarded as a complete statement of the sources of international law.
>
> . . .
>
> The present argument thus raises for consideration two questions: 1. what system of law does the community of nations recognize as applicable to the creation and definition of war crimes and crimes against humanity? and 2. what courts are recognized to possess universal jurisdiction to apply the relevant system of law?
>
> . . .
>
> Therefore, the question is whether the statutory offence created by s.9 of the [Australian War Crimes] Act corresponds with the international law definition of international crimes existing at the relevant time.

Polyukhovich v. The Commonwealth of Australia and Another (1991), 172 Clr 501 F.c. 91/026, opinion of Judge Brennan, paragraphs 27, 35, and 49, available at <http://www.austlii.edu.au/au/cases/cth/high_ct/172clr501.html>.

4. For further research resources on the US debate, see H. Harris, "We are The World"– Or Are We?: The United States' Conflicting Views on the Use of International Law and Foreign [c5]Decisions, 12 HUMAN RIGHTS BRIEF 5 (Washington, DC: Amer. Univ., 2005); Justice Antonin Scalia, Keynote Address: Foreign Legal Authority in the Federal Courts, in PROCEEDINGS OF THE 98TH ANNUAL MEETING 305 (Washington, DC: Amer. Soc. Int'l Law: 2004); S. Murphy, Interpretation of US Constitution by Reference to International Law, in Contemporary Practice of the United States, 97 AMER. J. INT'L L. 683 (2003); and C. Gerety, *Roper v. Simmons* and the Role of International Laws, Practices and Opinions in United States Capital Punishment Jurisprudence, 4 Chin. J. Int'l L. 565 (2005).

Impact of ICJ Opinions   The ICJ is fettered with a significant limitation not found in the national law of many UN members (particularly the common law countries such as Canada, the United Kingdom, and the United States). Under Article 38.1(d), judicial decisions are sources of the law, but "[s]ubject to the provisions of Article 59." That Article of the ICJ Statute provides that the "decision of the Court has no binding force except as between the parties and in respect of that particular case."

As stated by the PCIJ in 1926, the reason for this statutory limitation "is simply to prevent legal principles accepted by the Court in a particular case from being binding on other States or in other disputes."[60] Put another way, national sovereignty was intended to limit the role of ICJ opinions in a manner not applicable in national courts. The drafters of this provision acknowledged that such a limit would attract more States to submit their disputes to this distant tribunal in Holland. A bad result in one case would not haunt the losing State in a later dispute.

In practice, however, the ICJ has reapplied many principles from its earlier cases. As its case precedent has expanded, a number of its prior opinions have been the basis for resolving the same issues resurfacing in subsequent cases. Perusing current ICJ opinions reveals that the current world court is not satisfied with the limitation in Article 59, whereby deciding today might theoretically mean disregarding the Court's reasoning tomorrow. Otherwise, there would be little consistency in its decision-making process and less respect for its ability to participate in the progressive development of International Law.

(5) SCHOLARLY WRITINGS

Article 38.1 further authorizes the use of "the teachings of the most highly qualified publicists of the various nations, as subsidiary means for the determination of rules of law." Analyses by influential "publicists," meaning prominent commentators on International Law, is the remaining statutory method for ascertaining evidence of the content of International Law.

As a practical matter, one who is deciding a question of International Law typically *begins* with academic writings. Where there is a treaty provision, or a widely recognized customary practice directly on point, there would be no need to resort to any other source to answer the issue at hand. Publicists write about established or evolving norms, and their interstitial gaps, which may thus influence the rule-making process. But they can never *make* rules, customs, and treaties.

Scholarly writers serve a related purpose. Their commentaries also memorialize historical and contemporary developments in State practice. Professor Karol Wolfke of Poland characterizes scholarly writing as an essential instrument for analyzing a disputed issue, gathering information about prior resolutions of the same issue, and finding the latest trends in the ebb and flow of international legal norms. In addition to "attracting attention to international practice and appraising it, the writers indirectly influence its further evolution, that is, the development of custom."[61]

On the other hand, the need for such publicists has dwindled. As articulated during an American Society of International Law panel discussion, and applied by the judges in the foregoing *Flores* case:

> The ICJ Statute's emphasis on the works of "publicists," more commonly known as scholars or jurists, as a subsidiary or secondary source of customary international law suffers from an anachronism, as the work of international law scholars during the nineteenth and early twentieth century differed considerably from that of contemporary scholars. In "the nineteenth century . . . ," international law scholars "did the hard work of collecting international practices." The practice of relying on international law scholars for summaries and evidence of customary international law—that is, as secondary or "subsidiary" sources of international law—makes less sense today. . . .
>
> Without taking any view on the merits of different forms of scholarship, and recognizing the potential of theoretical work to advance scholarship, we note that [the earlier raw] compilations and digests are of greater value in providing "trustworthy evidence of what the law *really is*," whereas [today's] expressly theoretical or normative works make their contribution by setting forth the "speculations of . . .

authors concerning what the law *ought to be*." *The Paquete Habana,* 175 U.S. 677, 700, 20 S.Ct. 290, 44 L.Ed. 320 (1900) (emphases added).[62]

UN RESOLUTIONS

Article 38.1 of the ICJ Statute is not necessarily a closed list of sources. Resolutions of international organizations also assist international decision makers in search of the substantive content of International Law. There has been a vast proliferation of international organizations in the eighty years since the initial version of Article 38.1 was drafted for use by the current world court's predecessor.

The United Nations is "the" global organization of States. It does not have a specialized agenda like other large organizations, such as the World Trade Organization. Courts and writers, seeking evidence of State practice and State expectations in a given circumstance, have employed its resolutions as a compass for determining the general content of International Law. But first, one must distinguish between resolutions of the General Assembly, and those of the Security Council.

Security Council Resolutions   UN Security Council resolutions typically respond to aggressive uses of force in violation of the UN Charter. They are not normative or rule making. They are, instead, case-by-case reactions to violations of existing International Law principles, which may threaten world or regional peace [§3.3].

General Assembly Resolutions   The UN General Assembly is not an international legislature. Its State Members never furnished it with the sovereign-like power to enact laws to bind the community of nations (§3.3). The strongest argument against characterizing General Assembly resolutions as being either normative or rule making, may be drawn from the language of the UN Charter. It provides that the General Assembly's role is to make *recommendations*. Under Article 10, the Assembly "may discuss any questions or any matters within the scope of the present Charter, and . . . may make recommendations to the Members of the United Nations or to the Security Council. . . ." Under Article 11, the Assembly "may consider the general principles of cooperation in the maintenance of international peace and security . . . and may make recommendations with regard to such principles to the [other GA] Members or the Security Council or both. . . ." Otherwise, General Assembly resolutions would be characterized as "laws," greatly reducing the need for an Article 38.1 source listing for ascertaining the substance of International Law.

A former Legal Counsel of the United Nations characterized General Assembly resolutions as nonbinding, even when *universally* adopted. Pursuant to this view, the "General Assembly's authority is limited to the adoption of resolutions. These are mere recommendations having no legally binding force for member states. Solemn declarations adopted either unanimously or by consensus have no different status, although their moral and political impact will be an important factor in guiding national policies. . . . The General Assembly, through its solemn declarations, can therefore give an important impetus to the emergence of new rules, despite the fact that the adoption of declarations per se does not give them the quality of binding norms."[63]

To fully appreciate the importance of what follows, in the ensuing chapters of this course in International Law, one should now digest the distinction between *hard* and *soft* International Law. Recognizing the rationale for why UN resolutions do not appear on the Article 38 shopping list of International Law's sources, aids in making the valuable connection between hard law (e.g., treaty obligations) and soft law (e.g., UN General Assembly resolutions or aspirational treaties). Paul Szasz, the late Legal Advisor of the International Conference on the Former Yugoslavia, uses this distinction to explain how soft law, such as UN resolutions, often leads to hard law, like UN-sponsored treaties, in the following terms:

> Hard international law is, by definition, binding, at least on some international entities [states or IGOs (inter-governmental organizations)], although not necessarily on all. By contrast, soft international law is not binding, though perhaps superficially it may appear to be so; nevertheless, international entities habitually comply with it, and it is this feature that makes possible reference to it as "law." . . .
>
> Soft law is usually generated as a compromise between those who wish a certain matter to be regulated definitely and those who, while not denying the merits of the substantive issue, do not wish (at least for a time) to be bound by rigid and obligatory rules—perhaps because they fear they cannot obtain whatever domestic legislative approval is necessary.

There are several reasons why soft law deserves to be included in a study of international law, especially one concerning the international legislative process. In the first place, soft law has much of the predictive value of hard law in regard to how states are expected to act. Indeed, in an international community where even hard and fast obligations are not always observed, there is at best a continuum . . . between the predictive value of hard and soft law. Second, soft law does not often remain "soft." Frequently it becomes the precursor of hard law, either because states in complying with it eventually create customary law or because soft law may be part of the raw material taken into account when codifying or developing norms into treaty law; indeed, soft law in the form of solemn declarations is used often by the UN General Assembly as a stepping stone to treaty law.[64]

Some commentators take the next step. They avow that certain UN General Assembly resolutions are sources of International Law that can bind member nations, because of their normative distillation of emerging State practice. Such declarations are evidence of the customary practice of many States. Professor Krzysztof Skubiszewski, of the Polish Academy Institute of State and Law, notes that "[o]n various occasions, the developing States read into some recommendations the legal duty to conform to them. There is a whole gamut of arguments to justify this attitude. Some writers treat the nonbinding resolutions as a modern source (e.g., [ICJ] Judge [Mohammed] Bedjaoui). Others give an extensive interpretation of the powers of the resolution-making body ([ICJ] Judge T. O. Elias), so extensive that it obviously contravenes its constitutional position [as a body which only makes recommendations]."[65] Northwestern University Professor Anthony D'Amato adds the practical plea that, although books have been written on the subject *sources of International Law*, "there is no clear consensus. International law surely would be a much easier subject to study and master if U.N. resolutions could be treated as definitive statements of rules of international law. But . . . the U.N. is not a world legislature, and its resolutions are not the functional equivalent statutes."[66]

Several ICJ opinions lend credence to the argument that some General Assembly resolutions may be binding as a matter of CIL:

- In the *Certain Expenses Case*, involving the obligation of member nations to contribute to United Nations expenses, the Court commented that "Article 18 deals with the '*decisions*' of the General Assembly 'on important questions.' These 'decisions' . . . have dispositive force and effect . . . includ[ing] suspension of rights and privileges of membership, expulsion of Members and 'budgetary questions.'"
- In the *Namibia* case, dealing with South Africa's failure to comply with its trust obligations regarding the former South-West Africa, the ICJ stated that it would not be correct to assume that, because the General Assembly is in principle vested with only the power to recommend, "it is debarred from adopting . . . resolutions which make determinations or have operative design." In the separate opinion of the prominent British ICJ judge, Sir Hersch Lauterpacht, in the South-West Africa Voting Procedure case: "[a] Resolution recommending . . . a specific course of action creates some legal obligation which . . . is nevertheless a legal obligation and constitutes a measure of supervision."[67]
- In the 1986 *Nicaragua* case, for example, the Court considered the Declaration on Principles of International Law concerning Friendly Relations and Cooperation Among States in Accordance with the Charter of the United Nations to be binding. The Court's view was that this Declaration illustrated the *opinio juris* of all UN members—although it was not the product of any debate. In this limited sense, then, the ICJ employed the General Assembly's Declaration as a viable source of International Law.[68]

The position of a prominent group of US practitioners and academicians illustrates the evolving perception about the somewhat hybrid nature of General Assembly resolutions (and those of other, special purpose, global international organizations). The American Law Institute's Restatement of the Foreign Relations Law of the United States provides that, unlike States, international organizations historically "have no authority to make law, and their determinations of [what is] law ordinarily have no special weight. But their declaratory pronouncements provide some evidence of what the states voting for it regard the law to be. . . . Resolutions of universal international organizations, if not controversial and if adopted by consensus or virtual unanimity, are given substantial weight."[69]

The late Columbia University Professor Oscar Schachter questioned this assumption that such resolutions may be entitled to some degree of legal validity. A vote for a resolution may not be intended to signify agreement on the legal validity of the asserted norm. Governments do not always have that intent when they either vote for a resolution, or fail to object to it. They may fairly assume that, since Assembly resolutions are only recommendations, "their vote should mean no more than that. They may cast their vote solely on political grounds in the belief that a resolution of the General Assembly is entirely a political matter without legal effect."[70]

Regardless of the varied positions on General Assembly resolutions as an extra-statutory source, they are a useful resource for seeking evidence of international norms. Examples include the Assembly's unanimous affirmation of the principles contained in the Charter of the Nuremberg Tribunal punishing Nazi war criminals, and its unanimous resolution producing the ensuing Genocide Convention. These particular General Assembly resolutions expressed the opinions of all UN members that they would henceforth recognize global prohibitions against such State conduct.[71]

◆ 1.3 RELATED DISCIPLINES

This section of the text briefly summarizes some of the other disciplines that have influenced the development of International Law and vice versa. Like history, they are often ignored in law school studies. Each provides a fitting lens, however, for visualizing a number of norms in this course.

PRIVATE INTERNATIONAL LAW

Public International Law refers to the rules which States consider binding in their mutual relations. *Private* International Law encompasses a body of substantive law which each nation applies to private transactions. As succinctly defined by Oxford University's P. M. North: "The *raison d'être* of private international law is the existence in the world of a number of separate municipal systems of law—a number of separate legal units—that differ greatly from each other in the rules by which they regulate the various legal relations arising in daily life. Courts in one country must frequently take account of some rule of law that exists in another. . . . Consequently, nations have long found that they cannot, by sheltering behind the principle of territorial sovereignty, afford to disregard foreign rules of law merely because they happen to be at variance with their own internal system of law."[72]

Public and Private International Law have always been closely enmeshed. Since the seventeenth century, the term *jus gentium*, or law of nations, has been used to refer to the public sector of International Law. The Romans used this term, however, to describe the body of law that governed disputes between individual Roman citizens and foreigners. French and Italian scholars of the twelfth century developed principles, now referred to as "Conflict of Laws," for resolving such private transnational disputes.[73]

A number of model international treaties have been drafted for disputes involving individuals from two nations, where the result would depend on the different laws of the country where relief would be sought. Some examples are the 1971 Hague Convention on the Law Applicable to Road Traffic Accidents; the 1975 Inter-American Convention on Letters Rogatory—which addresses service of process and the discovery of documents in participating nations (§5.5); the 1980 UN Convention on Contracts for the International Sale of Goods (§13.1 CISG); the 1988 Hague Convention on the Law Applicable to Succession to the Estates of Deceased Persons; and the 2005 Draft Convention on the International Recovery of Child Support and Other Forms of Family Maintenance.

Illustration   The following example demonstrates the problem presented when individuals or corporations are subject to different legal results, depending on *where* a breach of contract suit is filed:

Assume that two individuals, respectively from Nations X and Y, enter into an oral contract in the amount of $100,000. It is legally enforceable under the laws of Nation X, but not the laws of Nation Y. Under X law, an oral contract involving any sale is enforceable in the courts of State X. No writing is required to prove its terms. Under Y law, however, a contract for any amount over $500 cannot be enforced unless it was a written contract. Y's legislature intends to discourage fraud, by requiring a written contract as evidence, should a party wish to sue to enforce any business deal over $500. Thus, if a suit to enforce this *oral* contract for $100,000 is brought in the courts of State X, the plaintiff has a chance of winning. If that same suit is brought in the

courts of State Y, however, it will be immediately dismissed—because there was no writing to memorialize the parties' agreement.

Assume that Nations X and Y decide to ratify the already-mentioned UN Convention on the Sale of Goods (CISG). Article 11 of the CISG states that a "contract of sale need not be concluded in or evidenced by writing. . . . It may be proved by any means, including witnesses." This treaty therefore authorizes international contracts, for any amount, to be enforced between individuals living in States X and Y, when there is no written evidence of their oral agreement. Article 11 supercedes the internal law result of State Y, so that oral contracts entered into by Y residents are enforceable, regardless of which nation is the forum for a breach of contract lawsuit. While the parties are free to expressly disavow the treaty's application to their particular transaction, it facilitates contract performance and trumps Y's law, which would otherwise bar an action based on an oral contract.

INTERNATIONAL RELATIONS

Disciplines of International Law and International Relations share the common feature of examining how States behave. The study of International Relations assesses the political variables affecting how nations behave.

International Relations emerged as a distinct field of study early in the twentieth century. Post-World War I teachers, scholars, and diplomats recognized the need for the study of International Relations, premised on the platitude that history should not repeat itself. This academic discipline soon underwent a great transformation because of the harsh reality of the events leading to World War II. Political science "realists" characterized International Law as being too abstract and inflexible to adjust to life in the trenches. As summarized by Princeton University's Anne-Marie Slaughter: "the discipline of international relations was . . . quickly dimmed by World War II. The fledgling discipline was thus weaned on Political Realism . . . [by] seasoned observers of the interwar period [who] reacted against Wilsonian liberal internationalism, which [had] presumed that the combination of democracy and international organization [the League of Nations] could vanquish war and power politics. They believed instead . . . [that] states in the international realm were champions only of their own national interest. . . . The only relevant laws were the 'laws of politics,' and politics was a 'struggle for power.'"[74]

Commencing in the late 1970s, International Relations theory resurfaced. Its analysts then began to acknowledge the contributions made by International Law and international organizations. These institutions were perceived as promoting positive State behavior in collaborative ways. International legal norms were recognized as actually assisting governments in their pursuit of desirable political interests. International Law was no longer a mere doctrinal paradigm to be dredged up only when convenient for some governmental objective.[75]

The Cold War, and its demise, had a decisive impact on International Relations theory. International communism was an artificial interlude in the complex geopolitics that froze the normal growth of nationalist aspirations during the Cold War era. For example, Marshal Tito's long reign over Yugoslavia prevented ethnic conflict. It did not prepare the way, however, for the national dissolution after his passing (1980), not to mention the demise of the Soviet Union (1989). The negative features of nationalism, based on ethnicity, surfaced with an unexpected fury. The 1990s could succinctly be described in terms of new republics that would define themselves via "ethnic and religious minorities who see no reason why they should be prevented from pursuing their own national destinies . . . at the expense of their neighbors." Their leaders seized upon nationalism as an effective strategy to justify their power grabs after the collapse of communist ideology.[76]

RELIGION

Historical Influence Before the Roman Empire, religion was the source of what is now referred to as the law of nations.[77] As you will study in Chapter 2, the seventeenth-century Treaty of Westphalia is credited with establishing the entity that evolved into the modern nation or "State." It ended the (in)famous Thirty Years' War in Europe, fought between Catholics and Protestants. In one graphic depiction, "the Continent burned for three decades, and its people bled in a series of battles among the Holy Roman Empire, France, Sweden, Denmark, Bohemia, and a host of smaller principalities. The Treaty of Westphalia restored the principle . . . that . . . the prince of a particular region determines the religion of his people. In today's language, that means that one sovereign cannot intervene in the internal affairs of another."[78]

The sometimes symbiotic relationship between law and religion has spawned both positive and negative consequences. Willamette University Professor James Nafziger presents a succinct analysis of the intriguing parallels between religion and International Law in the following excerpt. It provides a succinct insight into other materials which you will study in this course:

The Functions of Religion in the International Legal System

BY JAMES A. R. NAFZIGER

in Mark W. Janis & Carolyn Evans (ed.), RELIGION AND INTERNATIONAL LAW (1999)
at 159–165 (footnotes omitted)

Religion and international law often appear to be congruent. They share elements of ritual, tradition, authority and universality that "connect the legal order of any given legal society with that society's beliefs in an ultimate transcendent reality." There is, too, a certain sanctity to any body of law, just as there is an authoritative and often constitutive structure in religion. Judaism is based on a covenant. In Martin Buber's terminology of I and Thou, both religion and international law are essentially dialogue; both seek to prove orientation of knowledge and a greater realization of the meaning of life. In a sense, the whole concept and practice of global order presupposes a moral and teleological viewpoint that is essentially religious. United Nations Secretary General Javier Perez de Cuellar has referred to the UN Charter as "my religion." . . . As ethical systems, both law and religion address the global order in a profound manner; both are concerned with the manner in which we accept and organize the world and universe around us.

Sometimes, however, religion and positive international law are anything but congruent. They may even be in conflict. For example, prohibitions on whaling by national and international agencies, for the best of environmental reasons may conflict with indigenous religious practices. Prescriptions to protect the rights of women, such as those that were developed and codified in the Convention Against the Elimination of All Forms of Discrimination Against Women, have been rejected by some Islamic traditions.

. . .

Integration of law and religion can, of course, result by definition whenever religious institutions or ideas are deliberately made the subject of international prescription. Examples include the Lateran Treaty between Italy and the Vatican . . . and the recognition of the Vatican as a state. 'Right to life' provisions in human rights instruments that are intended or interpreted to prohibit abortion have religious foundations. An extraordinarily inflammatory issue was the [1975] 'Zionism is racism' resolution of the United Nations General Assembly. . . .

Several global instruments articulate a fundamental freedom of thought, conscience and religion . . . [including] the Universal Declaration of Human Rights, and the International Covenant on Civil and Political Rights, and the Declaration on the Elimination of All Forms of Intolerance and Discrimination Based on Religion or Belief. Regional conventions and accords contain similar provisions. Other human rights agreements protecting religious freedoms include the Convention on the Prevention and Punishment of the Crime of Genocide and the Convention Relating to the Status of Refugees. These provisions highlight the topic of religion's role in the international legal system.

. . .

Religious institutions and doctrine have helped shape and develop modern international law. Certain denominations—for example, the Society of Friends (Quakers), the Brethren in Christ (Mennonites), the Church of the Brethren, the United Society of Believers in Christ's Second Appearing (Shakers), and the Bahá'í Faith—have accorded a central role to peace and the development of global order. . . . Many other denominations and such ecumenical institutions as the World Council of Churches (WCC), influenced by Third World churches, actively pursue programs for the progressive development and implementation of international law. . . .

Religious groups may sometimes be inhibited from active participation in the development of global order because of their disassociation from any politically related institutions, as international law and legal institutions may be viewed. Conversely, some groups may be motivated to create and help implement international law precisely because the latter *does* have political implication that symbolize a constraint on secular, fractious sovereignty and a cosmopolitan expression of the limits of sovereign authority. . . . On the one hand, Shiite belief deliberately merges religion and the state, and Latin American liberation theology joins forces with Marxist and other political movements in exercising a 'preferential option for the poor.' On the other hand, some (but not all) Western versions of evangelism tend to be distinctly Separationist in order to protect their cherished civil liberties.

. . .

So far in attempts to understand the historic role of religion in shaping modern international law, the message seems to be that international law did not replace the old time religion, as conventional learning implies, but entered into a continuous dialectical interdependence with religion.

. . . Rules and principles of international extradition appear to have originated in sanctified delivery of criminals, "bound up in solemn religious formulas," practiced by ancient Chaldeans, Egyptians and Chinese. The doctrine and practice of asylum—a "right of sanctuary" blessed by the medieval church—is rooted in ancient Greece. Gandhi's Hindu strategy of *satyagraha* (passive resistance) helped define principles of self-determination and peaceful resolution of conflict in the modern world, and Confucian ideology has encouraged the growth of non-litigory methods for resolving international commercial disputes.

. . .

Even after fragmentation of medieval Christendom and the emergence of the nation-state system after the [Protestant] Reformation, the medieval concept of a universal law continued to encourage cosmopolitanism among Roma Catholic sovereigns. Legal thinking in the Protestant states that emerged from the Reformation concurred in formulating and applying legal rules that would transcend the State and conform with religious thinking. The Protestant perspective of Grotius and his contemporaries and his contemporaries and disciples included the idea of brotherhood and universal love based on natural law that was stoic-Christian in origin but secular in expression. Within the essentially Roman law framework of the new states, accepting a secular definition of natural law with Christian roots inspired greater respect for codifying extant community practices.

. . .

Several examples of specific doctrinal contributions . . . may help confirm the creative function of religious doctrine in the formulation of modern international law. At a very deep level of significance, there seem to be certain universal, religious doctrine in the formulation of modern international law. . . . For example . . . all of the major religions propound a Golden Rule—treat others as you would like to be treated—that is the basis of reciprocity . . . that has shaped humanitarian legal doctrine. Personal redemption by acceptance . . . may help explain "positivism's preoccupation with consent" [e.g., a treaty-based agreement or that a State cannot be forced to appear before the International Court of Justice without its consent]; and the rules and principles of state succession may be rooted in the historic need of a religiously defined polity to attribute an implied choice of permanent exclusion to an untolerated ethnic order or other excluded group. International environmental law is rooted in the basic Judeo-Christian values, as is the concept of a 'common heritage of mankind,' which has at times influenced international environmental law, the law of the sea, cultural property law, the law of outer space and the legal status of Antarctica.

. . .

One of the most important contributions of religious thinking to international law is the doctrine of a just war. It has proven to be endlessly controversial . . . but endlessly durable as well.

. . .

In the nuclear era, the [just war] doctrine has proven to be particularly uncertain. Some would argue that it has been superceded by Article 2(4) of the United Nations Charter [prohibiting the aggressive use of force] and more recent, cognate formulations of customary . . . law. These publicists recognize that although some use of military force is acceptable, the exception to non-use must be premised on not the requirement of justice but rather on the defense of peace and opposition to aggression. It is now said the Charter "clearly favors peace over justice."

. . .

◆ *Notes*

1. A comprehensive collection of resources on religious documents designed to protect people, property, and land from the consequences of war—dating from 1500 B.C. to the present—is available in the federal case reported as *In re "Agent Orange" Product Liability Litigation*, 373 F.Supp.2d 7 (E.D.N.Y. 2005). Another succinct overview of the relationship between law and religion is available in M. Janis, ASIL INSIGHT 93, Religion and International Law (Nov. 27, 2002), at <http://www.asil.org/insights/insigh93.htm>.

2. Regarding Islam (addressed later) and war, see Islam and the ethics of war, <http://www.bbc.co.uk/religion/ethics/war/islam.shtml>. See generally J. Esposito, THE OXFORD DICTIONARY OF ISLAM (New York: Oxford Univ. Press, 2003).

3. Among the best narrative overviews of Islamic law are: S. Jackson, Plenary: Basics of Islamic Law, Association of American Law Schools (AALS) Workshop on Islamic Law (Jan. 2004), available at: <http://www. aals.org/ am2004/islamiclaw/basics.htm> & A. An-Na'im, 1. Islamic Law and International Law, available at: <http://www.aals.org/am2004/islamiclaw/international.htm>.

The Vatican and "fundamentalism" are two serviceable case studies about the historical and current associations between law and religion.

The Vatican City-State   Vatican City is the site of the Apostolic (or Holy) See. This is the central government of the Roman Catholic Church. The Pope, as head of State, exercises a unique spiritual reign over the world's Catholics. The geographical premises of this tiny State are located within Rome, based on a 1929 treaty with Italy.

The Vatican City-State is the only religious entity that has achieved governmental recognition with a status resembling a sovereign State. It has also proposed diplomatic initiatives longer than any sovereign. Since the time of the Emperor Constantine in the fourth century AD, the Pope has officially received numerous foreign emissaries. The Vatican currently maintains diplomatic relations with more than 120 nations.

Some of the prominent developments in Vatican history include the following: its role in encouraging the medieval crusades; claiming to divide the Atlantic between Spain and Portugal in 1493; the 1867 US congressional withdrawal of funding for a US delegation to the "Papal States;" President Franklin Roosevelt's sending a personal representative to the Pope on the eve of the outbreak of World War II; criticism for effectively acquiescing in the Nazi takeover of Europe, including complicity in war crimes;[79] US President Reagan's rekindling of the Vatican-US relationship in 1984, resulting in the opening of the Vatican embassy in Washington, DC; and occasional US Department of State briefings for the Pope during visits to Washington, DC.

The Vatican's contemporary international role includes the mediation of international crises. In 1965, for example, the Vatican embassy negotiated a cease-fire in the Dominican Republic conflict, whereby US troops departed from the Republic. In 1990, Panama's leader, Manuel Noriega, sought refuge in Panama's Vatican embassy. The Vatican's role prompted Noriega's surrender to US troops who had surrounded the embassy, shortly after the US invasion of Panama. The Holy See (Vatican) achieved worldwide attention in 1994, during the UN Conference on Population in Cairo, Egypt. The Pope consolidated forces with Iran and Libya, to deflect a potential multilateral approach, which had planned to approve abortion as a means for limiting the world's population. In 1997, the Pope made a much-heralded visit to Fidel Castro in Cuba.

In a June 2004 meeting with President Bush at the Vatican regarding the Iraq War, the Pope urged as follows: "It is the evident desire of everyone that this situation now be normalized as quickly as possible with the active participation of the international community and, in particular, the United Nations organization, in order to ensure a speedy return of Iraq's sovereignty, in conditions of security for all its people." When later commenting on torture and terrorist attacks, the Pope added: "Torture is a humiliation of the human person, whoever he is . . . [and] there are other means to make people talk."[80]

Fundamentalist Movement The collapse of the Soviet Union unleashed vintage religious rivalries that the Cold War repressed for the four decades after the World War II. Postwar political order had been maintained by the North Atlantic Treaty Organization (NATO)-Warsaw Pact paradigm. Then came the subsequent breakdown in statehood, when larger States split into smaller sovereign powers.

A number of Western commentators replaced the former Evil Empire (US President Ronald Reagan's term for the Soviet Union) with a new demon. It is often characterized, or mischaracterized, as "Islamic" fundamentalism. The US post-Gulf War policy of respecting Iraq's borders, for example, is perceived by fundamentalists like Usama bin Laden as ignoring ethnic Kurdish and religious Shiite claims to autonomy in and around Iraq. Freezing Iraq's borders after the 1991 Persian Gulf War, for example, via no-fly zones aligned with ethnic divisions, arguably maintained the existing world order, rather than allowing a new one to evolve. As stated in a comprehensive study of what Western writers describe as the fundamentalist post-Cold War insurgence:

> [f]undamentalists are boundary-setters: they excel in marking themselves off from others by distinctive dress, customs, and conduct. But they are also, in most cases, eager to expand their borders by attracting outsiders who will honor fundamentalist norms, or by requiring that nonfundamentalists observe fundamentalist codes. The state is the final arbiter of disputes within its borders. In cases in which the state is "fundamentalist" (e.g., Iran, Sudan) or has been influenced by fundamentalist socio-political agendas (Pakistan, India, Egypt, Israel), the fundamentalism of the enclave is encouraged or even empowered to spill over its natural boundaries and permeate the larger society.[81]

A novel feature of the contemporary "fundamentalist struggle" involves what some Western observers would describe as terrorist reactions to modern threats to fundamentalist doctrine. In March 1994, for example, Muslim fundamentalists murdered two young schoolgirls in Algiers because they were unveiled. This action marked the bloody enforcement of a February 1994 vow, undertaken in the name of religion. Muslim women who do not cover their heads in public joined a growing list of targets, including the Algerian army, police, secularist intellectuals, artists, journalists, and certain unsympathetic foreigners. In 1996, the Taliban government in

Afghanistan began to enforce its perception of an ordered society, wherein women were virtually under house arrest. They could not leave their homes unless accompanied by a related male, attend school, work, or travel without a full-body garment (burqa).[82]

September 11th posed new opportunities for positive US interaction with fundamentalism. The United States then enjoyed a fresh opportunity to improve relations with countries in the crucial Middle East region. There were still anti-American rallies, for example, outside the gates of what used to be the US Embassy in Tehran—stormed in 1979 by Iranians as part of the country's Islamic revolution (§7.4 *Iran Hostage* case). During the months after 9-11, assembled protesters would again chant "Death to America," to mark twenty-two years since the pro-US regime fell. But the crowds were not of the size or intensity that they once were. As a sign of the attitude then blooming among many Iranians, flowers appeared outside of the gates of the US embassy.[83] These were a symbol, quickly removed by Iranian police, of a warming toward America. The United States then decided to pursue the Taliban in Afghanistan in 2002, and launch a preemptive war against Iraq in 2003. The latter action especially damaged US relations with the Muslim world, fueling the contemporary renewal of regional fundamentalism, culminating in many extremists crossing into Iraq to aid the anti-US insurgency.

Religious leaders have participated in cross-border power struggles, since the time of the medieval Crusades. A number of Muslim nations supported the Afghan Mujahedeen in its fourteen-year struggle to disengage occupying Soviet troops. Rival factions within Afghanistan subsequently tore it apart, however, with political power struggles waged in the name of Islam. Religious violence approximated that, done by the Inquisition and the crusades of the Roman Catholic Church. Mosques were special targets of violence because people use them as safe havens from battles fought by rival factions of the Mujahedeen. The famous Blue Mosque in Kabul was filled with women and children when it was bombed in March 1994. The traditional acquiescence in the use of mosques as sanctuaries was apparently forsaken by rival religious groups. Even the Soviet regime never dared to break that tradition during its occupation of Afghanistan (1979–1989).

The constancy and stability of classical Islamic law during the last 1200 years cannot be adequately explained in a one-volume introductory book on Public International Law; however, several key themes necessarily permeate any more detailed analysis. First, western legal thought focuses on the nation-State as the body wielding the ultimate authority in virtually all contexts. This is not the case with the Muslim counterparts. The legal system of most contemporary Muslim countries likewise assumes that the State produces legal authority. But there exists a dislocation between two perceptions of legal authority. One emanates from the nation-State, while the other is found elsewhere. This second source of authority has been the dominant Muslim conception. The western-derived perception of authority, lodged in the nation-State (with its origins in the Treaty of Westphalia in 1648), was introduced in these nations only during the last two centuries. As succinctly articulated by a prominent scholar from McGill University's Institute of Islamic Studies:

Juristic Authority vs. State Power: The Legal Crises of Modern Islam

WAEL B. HALLAQ

19 Journal of Law and Religion 243, 258 (2004)

. . .

[T]he transposition of the command of the law from the hands of the faqihs (the traditional legal professionals) to those of the state represents the most important phenomenon of modern legal reform, one that signified simultaneously the eternal loss of epistemic authority and the dawning of the much-abhorred authority of the state. The emergence of the state as carrier of legal authority (or, strictly speaking, legal power) is seen as doubly repugnant in Islamic countries not only because the state appropriated law from the community-rooted groups of the religious jurists, but also because it had shown itself, for over a millennium, to be an entity severely lacking in religiosity, piety and rectitude.

If Islamic law had represented to Muslims the best of "din" (religion) then the state stood for the worst of "dunya" (worldly existence). With the appropriation of law in the wake of the reforms, the state has sunk into even lower levels of repugnancy. It committed a third felony: it substituted God's law with a foreign law; and to make things much worse, a fourth felony, it chose none other than the law of the colonizers to do so.

If modern Muslims are demanding a return to the Shari'a, it is because of their perception that all these violations have wreaked havoc with their lives. The modern "Muslim" nation-state (however many contradictions may lie in this phraseology) has not commanded, nor is it likely to command, the conformity of the Muslim masses to its will, much less their respect.

Put differently, the modern "Muslim" nation state failed to gain authority over its subjects, for authority, unlike power, does not necessarily depend on coercion. When the traditional legal schools acquired authority, they did so by virtue of the erudition of their jurists who proved themselves not only devoted to the best interests of the umma ([masses] whom they served very well) but also the most competent human agency to discover God's law. Their erudition was their authority, and erudition implied, indeed entailed, a hermeneutical engagement with the divine texts without which no law could be conceived. The state, on the other hand, abandoned God and His jurists' law, and could find no other tools to replace it than the instruments of worldly coercion and imperial power.

COMPARATIVE LAW

Just as well-rounded students should consider the impact of religion and culture on International Law, they should also acknowledge the influence of Comparative Law. There are many diverse legal traditions throughout the globe. National representatives in any international context—such as diplomats at the United Nations or multilateral conferences, or judges and arbitrators deciding international disputes—are far more likely to reach a workable result if they acknowledge one another's respective legal cultures. Indigenous norms provide a lens through which one may more competently perceive the international legal process.

Differing legal traditions often impact international problem-solving strategy. For example, two of the more prominent legal cultures are civil law (based on French law) and common law (based on British law). The former is derived from Napoleon's Civil Code of 1804. The latter has its roots in earlier medieval judicial practice.[84] One of the most challenging phases in the contemporary development of the United Nations' Yugoslavian war crimes tribunal was determining the extent to which both the Common Law and Civil Law traditions would be utilized for conducting its proceedings.[85]

Comparative Law affects private transactions as well. Assume that a Civil Law lawyer and a Common Law lawyer are negotiating on behalf of their respective clients. Each should come to the conference table, prepared to address the question of how any disputes will be resolved, and under what terms. If the Civil Law tradition were applied, there would be no jury to resolve disputes. Nor would there be a discovery phase between pleadings and trial. Under the Common Law tradition, the trial judge does not routinely ask questions of trial witnesses. The Civil Law judge would not have the inherent powers exercised by Common Law judges.

◆ 1.4 NATIONAL-INTERNATIONAL LAW NEXUS

Publishing a one-volume textbook on International Law mandates some difficult choices. One of them is culling the application of International Law from governmental actors in nearly 200 countries, while paying due attention to the "International" portion of the term "International Law." The internal law of each nation governs the relations among individuals, corporate entities, institutions, and the government within that nation's borders. Illustrating how a nation incorporates International Law into its legal system is the specific objective of this section of the book.

GOVERNMENTAL ACTORS

The quest for illustrations can be complicated. Within each country, one could focus on the actions of: (a) the executive branch of the chosen government; (b) its constitutive and legislative enactments; or (c) the pervasiveness of court structures and local judicial opinions, which tend to compile interbranch conduct in their case analyses. The following examples expose the respective flavors associated with the situs of power within various national legal systems.

Constitutions   Article 15(4) of the Russian Constitution offers a glimpse of the relation between Federation Law and international treaties: "The commonly recognized principles and norms of the international law and the international treaties of the Russian Federation shall be a component part of its legal system. If an international treaty of the Russian Federation stipulates other rules than those stipulated by the [Federation] law, the rules of the international treaty shall apply." This effectively allows the executive's treaty power to trump inconsistent legislation.

It is no surprise that Section II, paragraphs (2) and (8) of the Bosnia-Herzegovina Constitution make internationally recognized human rights that country's first priority: "The rights and freedoms set forth in the European Convention for the Protection of Human Rights and Fundamental Freedoms and its Protocols shall apply directly in Bosnia and Herzegovina. These shall have priority over all other law. All competent authorities in Bosnia and Herzegovina shall cooperate with and provide unrestricted access to: any international human rights monitoring mechanisms established for Bosnia and Herzegovina; the supervisory bodies established by any of the international agreements listed in Annex I to this Constitution; the International Tribunal for the Former Yugoslavia . . . ; and any other organization authorized by the United Nations Security Council with a mandate concerning human rights or humanitarian law."

The 1998 Irish Constitution exudes a sense of long-term regional conflict: "Ireland affirms its devotion to the ideal of peace and friendly co-operation amongst nations founded on international justice and morality . . . [and] affirms its adherence to the principle of the pacific settlement of international disputes by international arbitration or judicial determination. . . . [while accepting] the generally recognised principles of international law as its rule of conduct in its relations with other States."[86]

Article VI(2) of the US Constitution provides that "This Constitution, and the Laws of the United States which shall be made in Pursuance thereof; and all Treaties made, or which shall be made, under the Authority of the United States, shall be the supreme Law of the Land." This approach suggests equality among these documents. In practice, the US Constitution always trumps inconsistent treaties (§8.3).

Executive Branch Communications   One can also look to communications within or between national executive branches for evidence of the role of International Law. The famous classic exchange of diplomatic correspondence between Mexico and the United States in 1938 provides a classic example. The United States claimed that international custom prohibited Mexico's expropriation of farm land owned by US citizens without compensation. Both nations professed their own convenient applications of the general principle of "reason, equity, and justice."

The US government wanted Mexico to compensate the US owners for the seized land. US Secretary of State Cordell Hull sent a communiqué to the Mexican Ambassador to the United States. Hull thereby generated an exchange of letters that would be a useful source for determining what these two countries considered to be the general principle governing expropriations—there being no applicable treaty. Hull wrote that "we cannot admit that a foreign government may take the property of American nationals in disregard of the rule of compensation under international law. Nor can we admit that any government unilaterally and through its municipal legislation can, as in this instant case, nullify this universally accepted principle of international law, based as it is on reason, equity and justice."

The Mexican ambassador disavowed the existence of a general principle of law requiring compensation under the circumstances. Under Mexico's view, "there is in international law no rule universally accepted in theory nor carried out in practice, which makes obligatory the payment of immediate compensation nor even of deferred compensation, for expropriations of a general and impersonal character like those which Mexico has carried out for the purpose of redistribution of the land. . . . As has been stated above, there does not exist in international law any principle universally accepted by countries, nor by the writers of treatises on this subject, that would render obligatory the giving of adequate compensation for expropriations of a general and impersonal [non-discriminatory] character."

US Secretary Hull responded that "[t]he Government of the United States merely adverts to a self-evident fact when it notes that the applicable precedents and recognized authorities on international law support its declaration that, under every rule of law and equity, no government is entitled to expropriate private property, for whatever purpose, without provision for prompt, adequate, and effective payment therefor. In addition, clauses appearing in the constitutions of almost all nations today, and in particular in the constitutions of the American republics, embody the principle of just compensation."

Not wishing this statement to remain undeflected, Mexico responded that "[n]umerous nations, in reorganizing their economy, have been under the necessity of modifying their legislation in such manner that the expropriation of individual interests nevertheless does not call for immediate compensation and, in many cases, not even subsequent compensation; because such acts are inspired by legitimate causes and the aspirations of social justice, they have not been considered unusual or contrary to international law."[87]

Mexico and the United States ultimately negotiated a settlement of this compensation dispute. The quoted diplomatic correspondence demonstrates the reliance of both governmental representatives on general principles of International Law as a source for resolving their dispute (discussed further in §4.4 on State responsibility for injury to aliens).

Judicial Institutions   There is limited space available to cover all potential applications of International Law on an intra-state level. The nature of internal judicial institutions, and the method for displaying their work product, conveniently illustrates the linkage between International Law on national law. Fortunately, cases dealing with International Law issues, from all over the world, are conveniently collated into one globally recognized source.[88]

Most court decisions involving issues arising under International Law are those of *national* courts. As explained by George Slyz, New York University Fellow for the Center for International Studies: "International Law has a long history of influencing and forming the basis for decisions of national courts. In the seventeenth century, for example, British and French courts regularly applied international prize law in cases concerning the lawfulness of seizures of a belligerent's commercial vessels during military conflict. Today, national courts increasingly confront issues of international law as a result of the unprecedented increase in activity on the part of international organizations' and states' "newfound willingness to submit their disputes to international tribunals."[89]

The remainder of this section focuses on the following questions:

◆ What is the relationship between a nation's internal law and International Law?
◆ How is International Law actually applied in its internal court system?
◆ When does national law take precedence over International Law?
◆ In what courts can suits involving International Law be brought?
◆ Can those courts avoid the resolution of such issues?

Scholars have traditionally used the term "municipal" law to distinguish the internal law of a nation from International Law. But the term "municipal" is ambiguous. Under US law, for example, a number of states of the United States have Municipal Courts. The term "national law" will therefore be used in this section as a synonym for commonly applied terms such as domestic, internal, local, and municipal law. Before launching into some useful case law examples, one should begin with an appreciation of the following historical debate.

MONIST-DUALIST DEBATE

Medieval scholars did not distinguish municipal law from International Law. The law of nations was considered to be a universal law that bound all of humanity.[90] Contemporary scholars have debated over the theoretical relationship between national and International Law for many decades. This controversy is typically described in terms of the "monist" *versus* "dualist" paradigm.

Monist Approach   The monist perspective is that the Law of Nations and the law of each nation form an integrated, universal legal order. International Law is inherently woven into the legal fabric of every nation. Under this theory, no nation can reject International Law in principle. It may have reservations about certain components. Because so many national leaders have acknowledged the existence of International Law, it may be characterized as a part of human existence that is unrestrained by national borders. International Law is thus an integral part of all national legal systems.

The position of the United Nations' ICJ is unmistakably clear: national law can never prevail should it conflict with International Law. As stated by the Court, in the 1988 case involving US attempts to close the

PLO Mission at the UN—under national antiterrorist legislation in conflict with its treaty obligation not to do so. The ICJ responded that it "would be sufficient to recall the fundamental principle of international law that international law prevails over domestic law. This principle was endorsed by judicial decision[s] as long ago as . . . 1872 in the *Alabama case* [§2.3] between Great Britain and the United States, and has frequently been recalled since, for example in the case . . . in which the Permanent Court of International Justice laid it down that it is a generally accepted principle of international law that in the relations between Powers who are contracting Parties to a treaty, the provisions of municipal law cannot prevail over those of the treaty."[91]

Some contemporary examples of circumstances, where a nation has incorporated some feature of International Law into its national law, lend support to the Monist principle, which espouses one integrated legal system:

◆ Article 39.1 of the South African Constitution emerged after the fall of the long-term Apartheid regime. It now mandates that, when judges are interpreting the Bill of Rights, they "must consider international law."
◆ The French Constitution provides that treaties are "laws" that must always prevail within the French legal system.
◆ Article 25 of the former West German Constitution provided that the "generally accepted rules of international law are binding upon the state power [to act] and upon every citizen." International Law thereby governed all controversies, because there could be no conflict with internal law.

The foremost proponent of the Monist approach was Austrian Professor Hans Kelsen. His articulation was that national law and International Law have always been a part of the same legal system of universal norms. In an earlier era, these norms provided the basis for a system that came to be known as International Law. The same behavioral norms also propelled national legal order. States, through individuals who served as their agents, were expected to behave as would individuals. International Law did not need to establish its primacy in relation to national law, given the interdependent, rather than hierarchical, relationship between these integrated legal systems.[92]

Dualist Approach Dualists reject the monist perception of International Law as articulating an unrealistic assessment of two autonomous legal regimes. Under this theory, International Law and national law are distinct legal orders. Each nation retains the sovereign power to integrate, or isolate, the norms of International Law. National and International Law are *not* parts of a unified whole.

The Dualist theory flows from the quintessential feature of State sovereignty: consent. The State model, created by the 1648 Peace of Westphalia, evangelized an immutable dogma–State may be bound without giving its approval. Were it otherwise, how could a State be sovereign? When a nation actively decides to incorporate International Law into its national law, only then is International Law the law of that land. As discussed in the "Sources" section of this chapter, a State's decision makers typically examine international customs and treaties to ascertain whether the requisite expression of consent exists. Just as general principles of national law may be incorporated into International Law, International Law may be similarly integrated into a State's national law. Without express incorporation, International Law is more of a common goal, or standard of achievement for each State member of the global legal community.

A judge must therefore apply his or her national law, such as executive and legislative directives, even if to do so would violate International Law. As illustrated in an opinion of the British Court of Appeals, International Law has no validity except insofar as its principles are accepted and adopted by the United Kingdom's internal law. British decision makers thus "seek to ascertain what the relevant rule is, and having found it they will treat it as incorporated into the domestic law, so far as it is not inconsistent with rules enacted by statutes or finally declared by their tribunals."[93]

The quintessential restatement of the contemporary dualist doctrine in the United States appeared just twenty-five years after the Supreme Court's 1900 statement that "International law is part of our law, and must be ascertained and administered by the courts of justice of appropriate jurisdiction as often as questions of right depending upon it are duly presented for their determination." In a significant departure from this Supreme Court articulation of Monist doctrine, an often-cited federal trial court opinion declared as follows:

a misconception exists here as to the status . . . of *so-called* international law when that law encounters a municipal enactment. If we assume for the present that the national legislation has, by its terms, made the acts complained of a crime against the United States even when committed on the high seas by foreign nationals upon a ship of foreign registry, then there is no discretion vested in the federal court, once it obtains jurisdiction, to decline enforcement. *International practice is law only in so far as we adopt it*, and like all common or statute law it bends to the will of the Congress. It is not the function of courts to annul legislation; it is their duty to interpret and by their judicial decrees to enforce it—and even when an act of Congress is declared invalid, it is only because the basic law is being enforced in that declaration. . . . The act may contravene recognized principles of international comity, but that affords no more basis for judicial disregard of it than it does for executive disregard of it.[94]

In the new millennium, one can anticipate a growing connectedness between international and domestic law. But the more powerful nations have prevailed in the Monist-Dualist context. One example is found in the 1988 *Bangalore Principles*, forged by prominent lawyers from Commonwealth countries (e.g., Australia, India, New Zealand, the United Kingdom), and judicial participants including Ruth Bader Ginsburg (then a judge of the US Federal Court of Appeals; now on the US Supreme Court). These privately-generated norms, although not the product of an international convention of States or a UN General Assembly resolution, are one of the more accurate articulations of the contemporary relationship between national and International Law:

(1) International law . . . is not, as such, part of the domestic law in most common law countries;

(2) Such law does not become part of domestic law until [a] Parliament so enacts or the judges . . . declare the norms thereby established to be a part of domestic law;

(3) The judges will not do so automatically, simply because the norm is part of international law or is mentioned in a treaty—even one ratified by their own country;

(4) But if an issue of uncertainty arises . . . obscurity in its meaning or ambiguity in a relevant statute), a judge may seek guidance in the general principles of international law, as accepted by the community of nations; and

(5) From this source material, the judge may ascertain and declare what the relevant rule of domestic law is. It is the action of the judge, incorporating the rule into domestic law, which makes it part of domestic law.[95]

Internal Law is No Defense   Monists and Dualists agree on one matter: no nation may assert its internal law in defense of a breach of International Law. As aptly articulated by the PCIJ in 1931: "a State cannot adduce as against another State its own Constitution with a view to evading obligations incumbent upon it under international law or treaties in force."

This principle was reaffirmed in the UN International Law Commission's 1949 Draft Declaration on the Rights and Duties of States. Every nation must carry out its obligations arising from treaties and other sources of International Law in good faith. A nation "may not invoke provisions in its constitution or its [other internal] laws as an excuse for failure to perform this duty." This unassailable principle was reaffirmed in the Commission's 2001 final draft which was adopted by the UN General Assembly.[96]

INTERNATIONAL LAW APPLIED

Who actually applies International Law? Diplomats, presidents, and other public servants determine the what, how, and when of International Law applications. Although each branch of most governments have occasion to apply International Law, a course such as this one will naturally focus on the judicial branch. While numerous legislative and executive materials are presented in this course, it is the judges who most noticeably apply International Law on an almost day-to-day basis.

In matters of International Law, one naturally thinks of a robed group of judges, ceremoniously sitting in the Peace Palace of the ICJ in the Netherlands. But that Court's annual docket, finally in double figures in recent years, illustrates that the bulk of judicial decision making about international legal issues is done elsewhere. The judges and arbitrators of the world's national legal systems decide issues arising under International Law on a routine basis. The University of Rome's Professor Benedetto Conforti thus describes them in the following terms:

Only through what we could term "domestic legal operators" can we describe the binding character of international law or, better still, its ability to be implemented in a concrete and stable fashion. "Domestic legal operators" are those charged by the State community to apply and enforce law and [thus] include judges, first and foremost. In every State system we find more or less similar provisions holding that actions must comply with international law as well as [with] municipal law. This being so, compliance with international law relies not so much on enforcement mechanisms available at the international level, but rather on the resolve of domestic legal operators such as public servants and judges to use to their limits the mechanisms provided by municipal law to ensure compliance with international norms. . . .[97]

The 2005 Vietnamese *Agent Orange* litigation provides a classic illustration of a functioning "domestic legal operator." One of the most respected US judges, drawing upon several resources, therein reproduced the general approach of US courts when they resolve claims arising under International Law: "In judging international human rights claims against domestic corporations or others, courts in the United States with jurisdiction act as quasi-international tribunals. The international law of human rights parallels and supplements national law, superceding and supplying the deficiencies of national constitutions and laws. International law allows states to exercise universal jurisdiction over certain acts which threaten the international community as a whole ands which are criminal in all countries, such as war crimes."[98]

SELECTED CASE STUDIES

The following materials provide a snapshot of the application of International Law by both new and established judicial structures within selected nations. The two case studies, near the end of this subsection, illustrate how local judges can avoid deciding issues arising under International Law (*Kadic v. Karadzic*); and how creative judges can mold national law to comply with international treaty obligations (*A v. Chief Constable of West Yorkshire Police*).

Belgium A 1993 Belgian law (§5.2) authorized Belgian courts to try anyone convicted of universal crimes, such as war crimes and genocide, to be tried there— even if the defendant had no ties with Belgium. The current law still authorizes such prosecutions, if the

defendant lives in Belgium. The trial of two Rwandan businessmen began in May 2005, after their arrest while living in Brussels. They are accused of providing trucks for machete-wielding militias to kill some 50,000 people in Rwanda, then rewarding them with beer.

Bosnia-Herzegovina Bosnia's war crimes court began to function in March 2005. It will ease the burden of the International Criminal Tribunal for the Former Yugoslavia (ICTY §9.5) by assuming a portion of the ICTY caseload. It will apply the Bosnian criminal code. The ICTY will end its work in 2010. This domestic court will then take over the ICTY's remaining cases.

This new Bosnian court is staffed primarily by international judges and prosecutors. It will review about 1,000 cases now pending in lower level Bosnian courts, taking over the ones considered particularly sensitive. Prior to the establishment of this national court, Bosnian courts were able to try only low-profile war crimes cases, after receiving approval by the ICTY.

Cambodia The United Nations' influence on Cambodia resulted in the latter's decision to establish a tribunal applying internationally-recognized legal principles, including the Laws of War (§10.6), in a special court established by the Cambodian National Assembly.

In 2003, Cambodia and the United Nations finally agreed on an internationally supported, but Cambodian-controlled, tribunal to prosecute the former members of the Khmer Rouge for their genocide and crimes against humanity, occurring from 1975–1979. Cambodia had been accused of foot-dragging, because current members of the government are former Khmer Rouge members. The General Assembly ratified this agreement, however, followed by Cambodian legislative ratification.

This hybrid national court differs from the UN Security Council's two ad hoc tribunals—for Rwanda and the former Yugoslavia. The latter are international tribunals established under the Council's UN Charter powers (§9.5). In April 2005, the United Nations certified that this court met international justice standards. There will be some international judges and prosecutors working with this essentially Cambodian-staffed court.[99]

Canada Canada consists of ten provinces (and two territories). Its federal government has the exclusive international legal personality to represent Canada in international legal matters.[100]

Following the British tradition, treaties must be enacted into law by the Parliament. Canadian courts apply CIL, depending on whether they perceive the relevant issue as involving an "incorporation" (also "adoption") or a "transformation" context. Incorporation refers to the instance whereby rules of International Law may be automatically incorporated/adopted into Canadian law via judicial examination. An act of the Parliament would be the exception. If the act conflicts with international custom, the act prevails. Transformation, on the other hand, does not authorize judicial adoption of a rule of CIL under any circumstance.[101] As stated in the nationally leading case: "Nor . . . would the clearest proof of unanimous assent on the part of other nations be sufficient to authorize the tribunals of this country to apply, without an Act of Parliament, what would practically amount to a new law . . . [because] we should be unjustifiably usurping the province of the legislature."[102]

The incorporation/transformation distinction, as to when a Canadian court may thus incorporate customary international legal norms directly into Canadian law, remains unclear.

Iraq The Iraqi Governing Council and the US government developed a special process for trying war crimes in Iraq. The Coalition Provisional Authority established this court, created its statute, and trained Iraqi lawyers and judges to staff it.

Unlike the four international war crimes tribunals run or overseen by the United Nations in Kosovo, Rwanda, Sierra Leone, and the former Yugoslavia, this tribunal will be administered by Iraqis and effectively supervised by the United States. It is an unusual tribunal for other reasons. The names of the tribunal's thirty-five judges and 400 staff members have been shielded for security reasons. This necessity may also fuel claims that Iraq is in fact still occupied (§6.2).

One of the interesting features of this tribunal's work product could be the impact of the US supply of landmines provided to Iraq for its war against Iran; as well as US corporations selling the chemical agents used against Iranian troops and Iraq's Kurdish population during the 1980–1990 Iran-Iraq War.[103]

Mexico Mexican law is clearer than Canadian law regarding the role of International Law in the domestic legal fabric. Certain international legal principles are expressly incorporated into the Mexican Constitution. These principles are thus expected to guide the President's conduct of foreign affairs. They include the self-determination of peoples, nonintervention, peaceful settlement of disputes, and a prohibition on the use or threat of force in international relations.[104]

Like the United States, the Mexican Constitution contains a supremacy clause: "This Constitution, the laws of the Congress . . . and all treaties made . . . by the President of the Republic, with the approval of the Senate, shall be the Supreme Law throughout the Union." Federal law thus governs, in the event of a conflict with one of Mexico's thirty-one states.[105]

Mexico's Treaty Law provides that there are two categories of treaties: a "treaty" and an "inter-institutional agreement" made by an entity within Mexico's public administration.[106] Treaties must be approved by the national Senate. An inter-institutional agreement may be "entered into between an entity of Mexico's public administration at the *federal*, *state*, or *municipal* level, and one or more foreign governmental entities or international organizations, regardless of its name, and whether it derives from a valid treaty or not."[107]

Rwanda In March 2005, traditional community courts in Rwanda began to try people accused of involvement in the 1994 genocide. The "gacaca" courts should relieve the overwhelmed conventional courts. Approximately 12,000 such courts have been so established, in over 100 locations in Rwanda. Under gacaca tradition, the suspects have to represent themselves. They are tried where they allegedly committed the crimes. The highest sentence the gacaca courts can hand down is life imprisonment. Whether this process will satisfy minimum international judicial standards is unclear.

Sierra Leone In 2002, the United Nations approved the Special Court for Sierra Leone (SCSL). It was established to try those responsible for the crimes committed there during its ten-year civil war. It is now trying cases under Article 1.1 of the court's Statute, providing that the "Special Court shall . . . have the power to prosecute persons who bear the greatest responsibility for serious violations of international humanitarian law [§10.6] and Sierra Leonean law committed in the territory of Sierra Leone since 30 November 1996, including those leaders who, in committing such crimes, have threatened the establishment of and implementation of the peace process in Sierra Leone."

This model supposedly delivers justice faster, and at a lower cost, than the UN courts for Rwanda and Yugoslavia. Its most intriguing work product is the *Child Recruitment* case, which chronicles the enslavement of the children of Sierra Leone for paramilitary purposes.[108]

The SCSL's jurisprudence presents an interesting discrepancy between it and other national courts in Sierra Leone. The latter may impose the death penalty. The SCSL may not impose the death penalty, pursuant to the international trend regarding the abolition of the death penalty—the subject of the First Protocol to the International Covenant on Civil and Political Rights (§11.2).

South Africa   The 1996 Constitution's presumption—not to interpret South African law contrary to the result dictated by International Law—enjoys constitutional status. Article 232 provides that "[c]ustomary international law is law in the Republic unless it is inconsistent with the Constitution or an Act of Parliament." Article 233 provides that, when interpreting any legislation,

every court "must prefer any reasonable interpretation of the legislation that is consistent with international law over any alternative interpretation that is inconsistent with international law."

This formula is found in the law of many of the more powerful nations. But the presumption favoring International Law is found only in judicial opinions.[109] This elevation to *constitutional* status, however, is a departure from the attitude of developing countries emerging from colonial domination. They have been generally unwilling to remain subjugated to an international regime whose essence is derived from "principles by which the Western Powers agreed to live and to conduct their business."[110]

United Kingdom   The two case studies in this section of the book begin with the following illustration of a UK application of International Law—to what one might have previously considered a comparatively mundane decision for the local police:

A (Respondent) v. Chief Constable of West Yorkshire Police (Appellant)
HOUSE OF LORDS: OPINIONS OF THE LORDS OF APPEAL
2004 UKHL 21, E.W.C.A. Civ 1584 (6 May 2004)

AUTHOR'S NOTE: The House of Lords is the last resort for judicial opinions in the United Kingdom. This appeal considers the well-known 1971 *Corbett* decision. As you read this 2004 case, think about why local law was slow to react to the intervening and more liberal European Community law. The analysis in the following pages suggests the tension between local and International Law.

Prior materials in this chapter address the current US debate about the degree to which domestic courts should rely upon international resources for resolving sensitive issues [§1.2]. This theme resurfaces here, and will reappear on a number of occasions in the remainder of this book.

COURT'S OPINION:
Lord Bingham of Cornhill
My Lords,

1. On 9 March 1998 the Chief Constable of West Yorkshire rejected Ms A's application to become a constable in the West Yorkshire Police on the ground that,

as a male-to-female transsexual, she could not perform the full searching duties required of a police constable. The issue in this appeal is whether he thereby discriminated against her unlawfully in breach of the Sex Discrimination Act 1975. . . .

2. The chief constable rejected Ms A's application in March 1998 on grounds which were in substance the following: (1) He was advised that in English domestic law Ms A remained a man, despite the change of gender she had effected and the gender reassignment surgery she had undergone, because her biological sex at birth was male and nothing that happened thereafter could change it. (2) He concluded that as (legally) a man Ms A could not lawfully search women pursuant to section 54 of the Police and Criminal Evidence Act 1984. (3) He concluded that as an apparent woman Ms A could not in practice search men pursuant to section 54. (4) He regarded it as necessary that a constable should be capable of searching either men or women pursuant to

section 54. In the course of these proceedings, but not . . . as early as March 1998, he inferred that he could not excuse Ms A from all section 54 searching duty without alerting her colleagues to her transsexual history, which he believed would be deeply unacceptable to her.

3. The advice given to the chief constable on English domestic law, summarised in (1) above, was correct. Such was the effect of *Corbett v Corbett* [1971] P 83. That case, it is true, concerned the capacity of a male-to-female transsexual to marry. . . . But there was nothing in English domestic law to suggest that a person could be male for one purpose and female for another, and there was no rule other than that laid down in *Corbett* and *R v Tan*.

4. Since section 54(9) of the 1984 Act required a constable carrying out a search under the section to be of the same sex as the person searched, it necessarily followed that if Ms A was (legally) a man she could not lawfully search a woman under the section.

5. Since it is a requirement laid down in paragraph A 3.1 of the Codes prescribed under section 66 of the 1984 [Police] Act that "Every reasonable effort must be made to reduce to the minimum the embarrassment that a person being searched may experience", it was plain that Ms A, who appeared in every respect to be a woman, could not, even if legally a man, be permitted to search a man.

. . .

8. . . . [I]t was a genuine occupational qualification of a constable to be capable of searching men or women under section 54, and Ms A could search neither. If the problem were purely one of domestic law, I very much doubt if this defence could be defeated.

9. To outflank it, Ms A relied on the law of the European Community. Her starting point was the duty imposed on British courts by section 2(1) of the European Communities Act 1972 to give legal effect to all rights, liabilities, obligations and restrictions from time to time arising by or under the Treaty of Rome. It is of course well-established that the law of the Community prevails over any provision of domestic law inconsistent with it. Ms A relied on the prohibition . . . of any "discrimination whatsoever on grounds of sex either directly or indirectly." This prohibition was qualified by reserving to member states the right to exclude from the field to which the Directive applied "those occupational activities . . . for which, by reason of their nature or the context in which they are carried out, the sex of the worker constitutes a determining factor." . . .

10. The sheet-anchor of Ms A's case was the important judgment of the European Court of Justice in *P v S and Cornwall County Council* (Case C-13/94) [1996] ICR 795, which concerned the dismissal of a male-to-female transsexual at a time when she had embarked on but not completed a course of gender reassignment surgery. . . . For present purposes the significance of the decision is twofold. First, it held in very clear and simple terms that the Directive prohibited unfavourable treatment on grounds of gender reassignment. Secondly, that prohibition was based not on a semantic analysis of the provisions of the Directive but on "the principle of equality, which is one of the fundamental principles of Community law" . . . and on the Court's duty to safeguard the dignity and freedom to which an individual is entitled. . . .

11. The question then arises whether the decisions of the European Court of Justice . . ., and the philosophical principles on which they rest, can cohabit with a rule of domestic law which either precludes the employment of a post-operative male-to-female transsexual as a constable of whom routine section 54 searching duties are required, or requires such a person to be willing to disclose her transsexual identity to working colleagues and, perhaps, members of the public. . . . In my opinion, effect can be given to the clear thrust of Community law only by reading "the same sex" in section 54(9) of the 1984 Act, and "woman", "man" and "men" in sections 1, 2, 6 and 7 of the 1975 Act, as referring to the acquired gender of a post-operative transsexual who is visually and for all practical purposes indistinguishable from non-transsexual members of that gender. No one of that gender searched by such a person could reasonably object to the search.

. . .

Lord Rodger of Earlsferry

16. Ms A is a post-operative male-female transsexual. Unhappily, in the past, when her situation became known in her local community, she suffered hostility, personal abuse, taunts and damage to her home and property; happily, she now lives in another community where she has always been known as a woman and where she experiences no such problems. In January 1997, she applied to become a police officer in the West Yorkshire Police Force, some distance from her home. In March 1998, the Chief Constable refused her application.

. . .

18. Because of what had happened in the past, Ms A was at pains to secure that she could conduct these proceedings without the facts being published in the media and her situation becoming known to the public. . . . In other words, the question is whether, in March 1998, the Chief Constable discriminated against Ms A unlawfully on the ground of her sex by refusing her application to become a police officer, at a time when he reasonably understood that she was unwilling to reveal, or to allow others to reveal, to her colleagues and to members of the public that she was a transsexual. It is particularly important to be clear on this point since, throughout, the Chief Constable has acted honourably and in good faith.

19. In March 1998 the Chief Constable had been advised that, even though she had successfully undergone all the usual treatment, including surgery, in law Ms A's sex was still male. In my view that advice on the domestic law of the United Kingdom was, and remains, correct. Section 54(9) of the Police and Criminal Evidence Act 1984 ("PACE") provides: "The constable carrying out a search shall be of the same sex as the person searched." Parliament's laudable aim is to afford protection to the dignity and privacy of those being searched in a situation where they may well be peculiarly vulnerable. While her application to join the force was pending, Ms A herself very properly drew attention to the possible problem posed by this provision. On the basis of the legal advice given to him, the Chief Constable considered that, because of section 54(9), Ms A could not lawfully search female suspects. And, in practice, she could not search male suspects. Nor could the Chief Constable arrange for Ms A not to have to carry out searches without it becoming known why he was doing so. Since he understood that she was not willing for this to happen, the Chief Constable decided that he could not accept her application to join the force.

. . .

21. My Lords, examination of the terms of section 7 soon shows that they were not drafted with the present kind of case in mind. In the first place, standing back, I find it impossible to say that being a man, as opposed to a woman, or vice versa, is a genuine occupational qualification for the office of police constable. Both men and women hold that office. More particularly, section 7(2)(b) provides that being a man, or being a woman, is a genuine occupational qualification "*only* where" the job needs to be held by a man, or a woman, to preserve decency or privacy. But, again, the office of police constable does not require to be held by a man, as opposed to a woman, or by a woman, as opposed to a man, in order to preserve decency or privacy. Here too, the fact that there are many officers of both sexes disproves any such suggestion. Indeed, section 54(9) of PACE presupposes that there will be officers of both sexes. Male officers search male suspects and female officers search female suspects, but otherwise they are employed on the same terms and have the same duties—just as, in practice, in many department stores selling clothes for both men and women, male assistants may be asked to measure male customers and female assistants female customers, but otherwise the assistants are employed on the same terms to carry out the same duties.

22. In reality, what the Chief Constable is arguing in the present case is not that being a man, as opposed to a woman, or a woman as opposed to a man, is a genuine occupational qualification for being a police officer, but rather that, in terms of section 7(2)(b), the job of police officer needs to be held by a man *who can decently search men* or a woman *who can decently search women.*

. . .

The Baroness Hale of Richmond
My Lords,

. . .

Domestic law

30. In the well-known case of *Corbett v Corbett (orse Ashley)* [1971] P 83, Ormrod J held that, for the purpose of the law of capacity to marry, the sex of a person was fixed at birth. . . . Since then, it has been assumed that a person's gender is fixed at birth for the purpose of all legal provisions which make a distinction between men and women.

. . .

European Community law

34. The Sex Discrimination Act 1975 anticipated the EEC Council Directive 76/207/EEC, on the implementation of the principle of equal treatment for men and women as regards access to employment, vocational training and promotion and working conditions (the 'Equal Treatment Directive'). By Article 1(1) of the Directive:

The purpose of the Directive is to put into effect in the Member States the principle of equal treatment for men and women as regards access to employment, including promotion and to vocational training and as regards working conditions and, on the conditions referred to in paragraph 2, social security. This principle is hereinafter referred to as the principle of equal treatment.

By Article 2:

(1) . . . the principle of equal treatment shall mean that there shall be no discrimination whatsoever on grounds of sex either directly or indirectly by reference in particular to marital or family status.(2) This Directive shall be without prejudice to the rights of member states to exclude from its field of application those occupational activities and, where appropriate, the training leading thereto, for which, by reason of their nature or the context in which they are carried out, the sex of the worker constitutes a determining factor.

. . .

Jurisprudence of the European Court of Human Rights

37. It is remarkable that, in each of the cases brought by trans people under the European Convention on Human Rights, the European Commission on Human Rights found a breach of a relevant article, whereas the [British] Court has been slower and more selective in taking that view. As long ago as 1979, . . . the Commission found that the refusal of Belgium to enable the registers of civil status to reflect lawful sex-changes violated the right to respect for private life in article 8. In *Rees v United Kingdom* (1986) 9 EHRR 56, the European Court of Human Rights, by a majority of 12 to 3, held that the refusal of the United Kingdom to issue a new birth certificate to a post operative trans person was not in breach of its positive obligations under Article 8. The Court was strongly influenced by the fact that in this country birth registration is regarded as a matter of historical record but that thereafter a trans person can be issued with a driving licence and passport in the new name and title and thus present himself in the new gender for many practical purposes. The Court took the same view in *Cossey v United Kingdom* (1990) 13 EHRR 622, but this time by the slender majority of 10 to 8. There was a powerful dissent by Judge Martens, pointing to the increasing legislative and judicial recognition of trans people in European states and elsewhere and to the fundamental human rights involved which in his view should not be defeated by technicalities:

The principle which is basic in human rights and which underlies the various specific rights spelled out in the Convention is respect for human dignity and human freedom. Human dignity and human freedom imply that a man should be free to shape himself and his fate in the way that he deems best fits his personality. A transsexual does use those very fundamental rights. He is prepared to shape himself and his fate. In doing so he goes through long, dangerous and painful medical treatment to have his sexual organs, as far as is humanly feasible, adapted to the sex he is convinced he belongs to. After these ordeals, as a post-operative transsexual, he turns to the law and asks it to recognise the *fait accompli* he has created . . . . This is a request which the law should refuse to grant only if it truly has compelling reasons, for . . . such a refusal can only be qualified as cruel. But there are no such reasons.

. . .

This appeal

. . .

56. It might be possible to regard this as simply a decision that discrimination on grounds of transsexuality is discrimination "on grounds of sex" for the purpose of the Directive. But there are many reasons to think that it is not so simple. The purpose of the Directive, set out in Article 1(1), is to "put into effect in the Member States the principle of equal treatment for men and women . . ." The opinion of Advocate General Tesauro was emphatic that "transsexuals certainly do not constitute a third sex, so it should be considered as a matter of principle that they are covered by the directive, having regard also to the above-mentioned recognition of their right to a sexual identity." The "right to a sexual identity" referred to is clearly the right to the identity of a man or a woman rather than of some "third sex". Equally clearly it is a right to the identity of the sex into which the trans person has changed or is changing. In sex discrimination cases it is necessary to compare the applicant's treatment with that afforded to a member of the opposite sex. In gender reassignment cases it must be necessary to compare the applicant's treatment with that afforded to a member of the sex to which he or she used to belong. Hence the Court of Justice observed that the transsexual "is treated unfavourably by comparison with persons of the sex to which he or she was deemed to belong before undergoing gender

reassignment." Thus, for the purposes of discrimination between men and women in the fields covered by the directive, a trans person is to be regarded as having the sexual identity of the gender to which he or she has been reassigned.

. . .

62. She meets entirely the plea of Advocate General Ruiz-Jarabo Colomer in *KB*, at para 79:

> Transsexuals suffer the anguish of being convinced that they are victims of an error on the part of nature. Many have chosen suicide. At the end of a long and painful process, in which hormone

treatment is followed by delicate surgery, medical science can offer them partial relief by making their external physical features correspond so far as possible to those of the sex to which they feel they belong. To my mind it is wrong that the law should take refuge in purely technical expedients in order to deny full recognition of an assimilation which has been so painfully won.

63. In my view community law required in 1998 that such a person be recognised in her reassigned gender for the purposes covered by the Equal Treatment Directive.

. . .

◆ *Notes & Questions*

1. In paragraph 21, Lord Rogers says that it is "impossible to say that being a man, as opposed to a woman, or vice versa, is a genuine occupational qualification for the office of police constable." Do you agree?
2. What did the 1971 *Corbett* decision decide? If the House of Lords had applied local law, rather than EC law, how would the result have differed? What was the ultimate result in *West Yorkshire*?

United States: Legal Hierarchy   The question of how US courts are to apply International Law is not explicitly answered by the US Constitution. Its legislative article proclaims that Congress has the power to "define and punish . . . Offenses against the Law of Nations." Another article provides that treaties "shall be the supreme Law of the Land." Yet neither of these constitutional provisions expressly incorporates International Law into the "laws" of the United States. The US Supreme Court professed to do so in its *Paquete Habana* case (§1.2). In 1900, the Court therein announced its famous articulation that "International law is part of our law, and must be ascertained and administered by the courts . . . as often as questions of right depending upon it are duly presented for their determination."[111]

The Constitution's drafters hoped that US law would develop in a way that would respond to the necessities of the era. Characterizing treaties with other nations as the "Law of the Land" would give the least offense to the established European powers in a position to

threaten the existence of the new republic. That is one reason why the Constitution's drafters did not address the possibility of an express conflict between national and International Law in this 1787 document.

The Supreme Court pronouncement in *Paquete Habana*—and the Constitutional language that treaties are "supreme"—would become subject to a number of qualifications. A hierarchy among the Constitution and treaties emerged. The US Constitution now trumps treaties. Further detail is provided in §8.3 on US Treaty Practice.

There are other layers within this hierarchy. The internal laws of the United States may be incompatible with CIL. The practice of States is a major source of this category of International Law (§1.2). However, US courts do not necessarily apply CIL.[112] US courts must adhere to the will of the Congress as expressed in federal legislation. If Congress intended that a US statute violate the customary practice of States, then a US judge must abide by the expressed will of Congress.

US courts do not blindly apply internal law, when to do so would unnecessarily conflict with International Law. Judges presume, where the legislation they are interpreting is not unrelenting, that Congress did not intend to violate International Law. This presumption is often used to interpret US legislation in a way that avoids violations of CIL. (*See, e.g., Larsen* case, §6.3, where Congress implicitly intended the application of US drug laws on the high seas.) This presumption cannot be invoked, however, if Congress unmistakably intended to disregard some principle of CIL. The applicability of this presumption was capably articulated in a 1925 Prohibition-era rum-running case—probably the leading description on point:

> If we assume for the present that the national legislation has, by its terms, made the acts complained of a crime against the United States . . . then there is no discretion vested in the federal court, once it obtains jurisdiction, to decline enforcement [on the basis of a violation of International Law]. International practice is law only in so far as we adopt it, and like all common or statute law it bends to the will of the Congress . . . [because] it . . . follow[s] that in construing the terms and provisions of a statute it [a court] may . . . assume that such principles were on the national conscience and that the congressional act did not deliberately intend to infringe them. In other words, unless it unmistakably appears that a congressional act was intended to be in disregard of a principle of international comity, the presumption is that it was intended to be in conformity with it.[113]

Likewise, legislation by the individual political subdivisions within the federated system of states may not override the will of Congress. In a US Supreme Court case directly on point, the state of Missouri could not properly pass legislation that effectively controlled matters within the federal government's constitutional Treaty Power. Missouri could not purport to control the hunting laws regarding migratory birds while they were en route from Canada, through the United States, to Mexico. This is a matter which fell squarely within the national Treaty Power, and it thus prevailed over Missouri's right of control the people and things (migratory animals) temporarily within its boundaries.[114]

United States: Who Can be Sued and Where? In US federal courts, each lawsuit must be based on a specific Constitutional grant of power to hear and determine the particular type of case. Article III of the Constitution furnishes the federal courts with the power to decide cases involving ambassadors, consular officers, and diplomats.[115]

Congress may restrict the application of this Constitutional power to certain courts. The federal Judicial Code thus limits the resolution of cases against ambassadors and consuls to only the federal courts. This restriction gives *exclusive* jurisdiction to the federal (but not state) courts. It promotes uniformity of decision in

judicial applications of International Law when foreign diplomats and consular officers are sued within the United States. The federal system resolves such cases, as opposed to fifty-one state and federal court systems resolving such matters in a potentially conflicting manner.

Federal courts share certain concurrent powers with the states of the United States. The respective court systems routinely resolve controversies between a state or its citizens and foreign countries or their subjects (§2.6 Sovereign Immunity). Disputes involving issues of International Law, other than cases that fall within the exclusive province of the federal courts, may be adjudicated in the courts of all fifty states and in the ninety-four federal districts.

Federal courts have interpreted the Supremacy Clause of the Constitution to require states of the United States to apply federal law when dealing with issues of International Law (§2.1). Decisions by federal courts take precedence over any conflicting decisions by state courts, when a question of International Law is presented in either system (state or federal). In other words, judges of the fifty states cannot decide an issue concerning International Law in a manner that conflicts with a federal decision on that point of law. The historical rationale is that the individual colonies no longer exercised any international powers, once the United States was formed. The 1787 US Constitution established the United States as a federal entity for this purpose, so that it would be distinguishable from the respective states.

The US Supreme Court confirmed this federal-state hierarchy, when it reasoned that "as a member of the family of nations, the right and power of the United States in that field [international law] are equal to the right and power of the other members of the international family. Otherwise, the United States is not completely sovereign." When the federal government decides *not* to recognize a foreign government, for example, state court judges cannot allow that government to appear in their courts as either a plaintiff or a defendant.[116] This approach is echoed by the EU, regarding matters over which the EU has the competence to resolve (§3.4).[117]

United States: Avoiding International Law Issues US courts have devised a number of jurisprudential doctrines for avoiding the resolution of issues arising under International Law. One can appreciate that the judicial branch should not leap into sensitive international relations, without due consideration of the relationship between the judicial and political branches of the government. One of the classic restatements of the rationale for judicial temperance is found in a 2005 US federal court dissenting opinion, wherein the majority of the judges reversed the trial court's dismissal of a lawsuit against the Vatican Bank:

> . . . [T]he ineffable fact remains that this functionally is a lawsuit against (1) the Vatican itself, (2) the Vatican Bank, which is an instrumentality of the sovereign state of the Vatican, and (3) untold others—including probably the Pope—seeking relief for World War II wrongs against foreigners committed by the Nazis and their allies in Europe almost sixty years ago.
>
> . . .
>
> This set of facts and circumstances involving a foreign sovereign strikes me as demanding a "single-voiced statement" of our government's views, not a series of judgments by our courts. . . . I conclude, therefore, that the foreign policy quintessence of this case renders it as a subject matter beyond the power of the judiciary to intrude or to inquire.
>
> . . .
>
> What the majority has unintentionally accomplished in embracing this case is nothing less than the wholesale creation of a World Court, an international tribunal with breathtaking and limitless jurisdiction to entertain the World's failures, no matter where they happen, when they happen, to whom they happen, the identity of the wrongdoer, and the sovereignty of one of the parties.
>
> . . .
>
> Our unauthorized transformation of our district courts into an open-door international tribunal far overreaches the authority of "the . . . [judicial] branch" of our government. This opinion, albeit well-intentioned, extends the concept of judicial authority into unknown territory and mistakenly exercises power and competence that plainly belongs to the President and to Congress. Today, it is the Vatican and the Holocaust. Tomorrow, will it be horrors from Haiti, Cuba, Rwanda, South Africa, the Soviet Union, Bosnia, Sudan, Somalia, North Korea, Iraq, and who knows where? The majority opinion sends our district judges on a crusade from which they are not equipped and which is doomed to flounder. . . . Similarly, one can only wonder why the beleaguered

[US] State Department would stand silently by and allow this case to continue. . . .[118]

The most prominent devices for avoiding the resolution of issues arising under International Law are the: Political Question Doctrine; Act of State Doctrine; and Lack of Standing to Sue Doctrine.

The *Political Question Doctrine* acknowledges that the judicial branch of government was not designed to exercise political functions. Judges do not wish to resolve controversies actually falling within the province of the political branches of government: the executive and the legislative branches. The conduct of foreign affairs is constitutionally committed to the president, who is the chief of the executive branch of government. When it is claimed that the United States has violated International Law, a "political question" is presented, often falling within the province of the President's foreign relations powers.

A number of these political questions were presented in various state and federal courts during the Vietnam War. President Nixon's decisions to mine North Vietnamese harbors and bomb Cambodia were legally challenged by individuals in the US Army and in the House of Representatives. Their lawsuits claimed that these US military actions violated the UN prohibition against the aggressive use of force in international relations. The courts dismissed such cases, however, on the grounds that they involved military decisions, which were insulated from judicial review. Thus, these actions presented *political* rather than judicially cognizable issues. The judiciary did not wish to second-guess the President's military strategy in foreign conflicts.[119]

In a more recent application, survivors and estate representatives brought a negligence suit against the United States on behalf of members of the crew of a Turkish destroyer. They sought money damages for the injuries and deaths which occurred in 1992—when a Turkish destroyer was struck by live missiles fired from an American warship during a NATO training exercise. The trial and appellate courts did not consider this case on its merits, because this action presented a nonjusticiable political question. As stated by the appellate court:

> Restrictions derived from the separation of powers doctrine prevent the judicial branch from deciding "political questions," controversies that revolve around policy choices and value determinations

constitutionally committed for resolution to the legislative or executive branches. . . .

Foreign policy and military affairs figure prominently among the areas in which the political question doctrine has been implicated. The Supreme Court has declared that "[m]atters intimately related to foreign policy and national security are rarely proper subjects for judicial intervention." The Constitution commits the conduct of foreign affairs to the executive and legislative branches of government. . . .

In a related manner, the political branches of government are accorded a particularly high degree of deference in the area of military affairs. The Constitution emphatically confers authority over the military upon the executive and legislative branches of government. . . . The Supreme Court has generally declined to reach the merits of cases requiring review of military decisions, particularly when those cases challenged the institutional functioning of the military in areas such as personnel, discipline, and training. . . .

As with many cases that directly implicate foreign relations and military affairs, the instant controversy raises a nonjusticiable political question.[120]

The *Act of State Doctrine* (AOS) avoids the judicial resolution of challenges to the conduct of *foreign* leaders or governments performed within their own territories, as opposed to political decisions of the US president.

The major Cold War application arose when the new Cuban government nationalized property belonging to US citizens in 1959. The United States did not approve of Fidel Castro's coming to power. It thus imposed a quota on Cuban sugar imports, resulting in Cuba's nationalizations of US business interests. In the ensuing suits in various US courts, individuals and businesses alleged violations of International Law, spawned by Cuba's inadequate compensation for these nationalizations. The US courts dismissed these claims because Cuba's conduct, emanating from Cuba, could not be challenged in US courts.

For the purpose of applying the AOS doctrine to dismiss a lawsuit, one may assume that Cuba violated International Law by its nationalization of alien property without the requisite compensation (§4.4 Injury to Aliens). In the famous *Sabbatino* case, the US Supreme Court authoritatively echoed the traditional position that every national government is "bound to respect the independence of every other sovereign State, and [that] the courts of one country will not sit in judgment on the acts of the government of another [country] done within its own territory. Redress of grievances by reason of such acts must be obtained through the means open to be availed of by sovereign powers as between themselves [i.e., diplomatic negotiations or litigation in international tribunals]."[121]

The dismissal of such suits under the AOS doctrine does not mean that there is no redress for the underlying grievances. It does mean that aggrieved individuals should pursue legislative or executive remedies with the responsible foreign government. An example of the latter would be for the affected US corporations to exert individual pressure on the US Department of State to negotiate for monetary compensation from Cuba on their behalf (*e.g.*, §13.1 Helms-Burton Act).

The courts are reluctant to resolve issues that touch upon the constitutional powers of the executive branch of government. The President conducts foreign affairs, not the courts. Judges do not want to hinder the international diplomacy by making pronouncements on sensitive points of International Law. The State Department, acting on behalf of the President, may be engaged in negotiations with another government on behalf of all US citizens harmed by that foreign government's actions. A US court judgment, for one US citizen in a particular case, heralding the foreign State's violation of International Law, could easily jeopardize some sensitive negotiations.

The Congress disliked the US Supreme Court's well-intentioned AOS pronouncement in *Sabbatino*. Judges in the US were effectively encouraged to dismiss suits, involving the adverse conduct of foreign governments against US citizens, which violated International Law. Congress therefore responded to the *Sabbatino* case by amending a federal statute to encourage courts to resolve such issues, unless the President deems it appropriate to apply the AOS doctrine (by requesting that the court dismiss such a case). The Hickenlooper Amendment provides as follows:

> no court in the United States shall decline on the ground of the federal act of state doctrine to make a determination of the merits giving effect to the principles of international law in a case in which . . . [a] right to property is asserted by any party . . . based on the confiscation . . . by an act of that state in violation of the principles of international law including the principles of compensation . . . : *Provided*, That this subparagraph shall not be applicable . . . in any case . . . [where] the President determines that application of the act of state doctrine [*i.e.*, dismissal] is required

in that particular case by the foreign policy interests of the United States and a suggestion to this effect is filed on his behalf in that case with the court.[122]

If the President (through the Department of State) does not file a suggestion with the court requesting an AOS dismissal, then the judge normally proceeds to decide the case—although the court may effectively pass judgment on the question of whether a foreign government or its agency has violated International Law. In a nutshell, Congress reversed the impact of the US Supreme Court's AOS decision. *Sabbatino* had directed trial courts to automatically decline to hear and determine such issues. The ensuing congressional directive dovetails the interests of the executive branch with those of the judicial

branch, in a way that accomplishes the same result. The courts normally proceed with such cases. They need not be concerned about embarrassing the President in the conduct of foreign relations. The State Department receives notice from the courts, anytime such an issue is pending. The President has an opportunity to effectively intervene for the purpose of seeking a dismissal.[123]

Both the Act of State and Political Question doctrines were addressed in a fascinating case involving a self-styled head of State, "President" Radovan Karadzic. He was served with process in New York City, while attending UN negotiations regarding Bosnia prior to the 1995 Dayton Peace Accords. There were numerous International Law issues in this case, including whether his "Republika Srpska" (within Bosnia) insulated him from suit:

Kadic v. Karadzic

UNITED STATES COURT OF APPEALS, SECOND CIRCUIT (1995)
70 Fed.3d 232, *rehearing den'd*, 74 Fed.3d 377, *cert. den'd* 518 US 1005

AUTHOR'S NOTE: Two groups of victims from Bosnia-Herzegovina brought actions against the self-proclaimed president of the unrecognized Bosnian-Serb entity, called Republika Srpska. They sued under the Alien Tort Statute (ATS) for violations of international law [textbook §11.5]. The United States District Court for the Southern District of New York dismissed these actions for lack of subject matter jurisdiction.

The Court of Appeals reversed, holding that the plaintiffs sufficiently alleged violations of Customary International Law, and the Laws of War, for purposes of applying the ATS; that plaintiffs had sufficiently alleged that the unrecognized Bosnian Serb entity of "Srpska" was a "State," whereby the defendant was effectively acting under "color of law" for purposes of the alleged violations of International Law; that the defendant was not immune from personal service of process, while he an invitee of the United Nations; and that these suits were not precluded by either the Political Question Doctrine or the Act of State Doctrine.

Most case citations have been omitted from this edited version of the case.

COURT'S OPINION:
III. Justiciability
We recognize that cases of this nature might pose special questions concerning the judiciary's proper role

when adjudication might have implications in the conduct of this nation's foreign relations. We do not read *Filartiga* [textbook §11.5, holding that foreign citizens may sue foreign citizens in the US for certain violations of the Law of Nations] to mean that the federal judiciary must always act in ways that risk significant interference with United States foreign relations. To the contrary, we recognize that suits of this nature can present difficulties that implicate sensitive matters of diplomacy historically reserved to the jurisdiction of the political branches. *See First National Bank v. Banco National de Cuba,* 406 US 759, 767, 92 S.Ct. 1808, 1813, 32 L. Ed.2d 466 (1972). We therefore proceed to consider whether, even though the jurisdictional threshold is satisfied in the pending cases, other considerations relevant to Justiciability weigh against permitting the suits to proceed.

Two nonjurisdictional, prudential doctrines reflect the judiciary's concerns regarding separation of powers: the political question doctrine and the act of state doctrine.... Although we too recognize the potentially detrimental effects of judicial action in cases of this nature, we do not embrace the rather categorical views as to the inappropriateness of judicial action urged by [certain judges] .... Not every case "touching foreign relations" is nonjusticiable, and judges should not reflexively invoke these doctrines to avoid difficult and somewhat sensitive decisions in the context of human rights. We believe a preferable approach is to weigh carefully the relevant considerations on a case-by-case basis. This will permit the judiciary to act where appropriate in light of the express legislative mandate of the Congress in section 1350 [Alien Tort Statute], without compromising the primacy of the political branches in foreign affairs. Karadzic maintains that these suits were properly dismissed because they present nonjusticiable political questions. We disagree. Although these cases present issues that arise in a politically charged context, that does not transform them into cases involving nonjusticiable political questions. . . .

A nonjusticiable political question would ordinarily involve one or more of the following factors: [1] a textually demonstrable constitutional commitment of the issue to a coordinate political department; or [2] a lack of judicially discoverable and manageable standards for resolving it; or [3] the impossibility of deciding without an initial policy determination of a kind clearly for nonjudicial discretion; or [4] the impossibility of a court's undertaking independent resolution without expressing lack of the respect due coordinate branches of government; or [5] an unusual need for unquestioning adherence to a political decision already made; or [6] the potentiality of embarrassment from multifarious pronouncements by various departments on one question.

With respect to the first three factors, we have noted in a similar context involving a tort suit against the PLO that "[t]he department to whom this issue has been 'constitutionally committed' is none other than our own 'the Judiciary.'" *Klinghoffer*, 937 F.2d at 49 [suit against the PLO for terrorist attack and death of a US citizen]. Although the present actions are not based on the common law of torts, as was Klinghoffer, our decision in *Filartiga* established that universally recognized norms of international law provide judicially discoverable and manageable standards for adjudicating suits brought under the Alien Tort Act, which obviates any need to make initial policy decisions of the kind normally reserved for nonjudicial discretion. Moreover, the existence of judicially discoverable and manageable standards further undermines the claim that such suits relate to matters that are constitutionally committed to another branch.

The fourth through sixth . . . factors appear to be relevant only if judicial resolution of a question would contradict prior decisions taken by a political branch in those limited contexts where such contradiction would seriously interfere with important governmental interests. Disputes implicating foreign policy concerns have the potential to raise political question issues, although, as the Supreme Court has wisely cautioned, "it is 'error to suppose that every case or controversy which touches foreign relations lies beyond judicial cognizance.'"

The act of state doctrine, under which courts generally refrain from judging the acts of a foreign state within its territory, might be implicated in some cases arising under section 1350 [Alien Tort Statute]. However, as in *Filartiga,* we doubt that the acts of even a state official, taken in violation of a nation's fundamental law and wholly unratified by that nation's government, could properly be characterized as an act of state.

In the pending appeal, we need have no concern that interference with important governmental interests warrants rejection of appellants' claims. After commencing their action against Karadzic, attorneys for the plaintiffs in Doe [trial court plaintiff] wrote to the Secretary of State to oppose reported attempts by Karadzic to be granted immunity from suit in the United States; a copy of plaintiffs' complaint was attached to the letter. Far from intervening in the case to urge rejection of the suit on the ground that it presented political questions, the Department responded with a letter indicating that Karadzic was not immune from suit as an invitee of the United Nations. After oral argument in the pending appeals, this Court wrote to the Attorney General to inquire whether the United States wished to offer any further views concerning any of the issues raised. In a "Statement of Interest," signed by the Solicitor General and the State Department's Legal Adviser, the United States has expressly disclaimed any concern that the political question doctrine should be invoked to prevent the litigation of these lawsuits: "Although there might be instances in which federal courts are asked to issue rulings under the Alien Tort Statute or the Torture Victim Protection Act that might raise a political question, this is not one of them." Though even an assertion of the political question doctrine by the Executive Branch, entitled to respectful consideration, would not necessarily preclude adjudication, the Government's reply to our inquiry reinforces our view that adjudication may properly proceed.

As to the act of state doctrine, the doctrine was not asserted in the District Court and is not before us on this appeal. Moreover, the appellee has not had the temerity to assert in this Court that the acts he allegedly committed are the officially approved policy of a state. Finally, as noted, we think it would be a rare case in which the act of state doctrine precluded suit under section 1350. Banco National was careful to recognize the doctrine "in the absence of . . . unambiguous agreement regarding controlling legal principles," such as exist in the pending litigation, and applied the doctrine only in a context—expropriation of an alien's property—in which world opinion was sharply divided. Finally, we note that at this stage of the litigation no party has identified a more suitable forum, and we are aware of none. Though the Statement of the United States suggests the general importance of considering

the doctrine of forum non convenience [which might otherwise require a dismissal because of where the events took place], it seems evident that the courts of the former Yugoslavia, either in Serbia or war-torn Bosnia, are not now available to entertain plaintiffs' claims, even if circumstances concerning the location of witnesses and documents were presented that were sufficient to overcome the plaintiffs? preference for a United States forum.

CONCLUSION

The judgment of the District Court dismissing appellants' complaints for lack of subject-matter jurisdiction is reversed, and the cases are remanded for further proceedings in accordance with this opinion.

◆ *Notes & Questions*

1. What was the nature of defendant Karadzic's political question defense?
2. A head of State of a foreign country can usually claim that he or she undertook acts of State, which should not be second-guessed by courts of another country as authoritatively announced in the *Sabbatino* case (and mentioned in *Karadzic*). In Credit Suisse v. Dist. Court, 130 Fed.3d 1342 (9th Cir. 1997), victims of human rights violations in the Philippines under the Marcos regime were barred from prosecuting their suit under the AOS doctrine. Did the US court in *Karadzic* violate the AOS principle?
3. In August 2001, the trial jury returned a $4.5 billion judgment against this fugitive. Karadzic was thus held accountable for acts of genocide, rape, and torture. He directed forces under his control to engage in a campaign of terror and ethnic cleansing, in the self-proclaimed Bosnian-Serb "State"of Republika Srpska—allegedly responsible for the mass murder of 7,800 Muslim men and boys in a UN enclave in Bosnia.
4. In June 2004, NATO peacekeeping forces in Bosnia literally erected a billboard campaign, offering Karadzic a free one-way ticket to The Hague's International Criminal Tribunal for Yugoslavia. NATO withdrew its forces by the end of 2004 (replaced by an EU force), and had hoped to capture Karadzic. He was also seen in Montenegro and Belgrade, when his

mother died in May 2005. By that time, he was in his tenth year of eluding capture for extradition to the ICTY.

In July 2004, sixty Bosnian Serb politicians and officials were dismissed for their failure to capture and arrest Karadzic. The International High Representative for Bosnia also froze the bank accounts of the main Bosnian Serb party, and several Serbian companies. This money was to be diverted to institutions seeking Karadzic's arrest.

The *Lack of Standing to Sue Doctrine* precludes a criminal defendant from asserting the rights of a third party (nation) who is not present in the litigation. The former general and dictator, Manuel Noriega, presented such a claim after the 1989 US invasion of Panama. He was taken to the United States by its military forces for prosecution under US drug-trafficking laws. The ensuing US trial-court decision (affirmed on appeal), avoided the issue of whether the US invasion violated International Law. The court relied on the principle that Panama, not Noriega, had the right (standing) to complain about any US violation of Panamanian sovereignty:

Initially, it is important to note that individuals lack standing to assert violations of international treaties in the absence of a protest from the offended government. Moreover, . . . violations of international law alone do not deprive a court of jurisdiction over a defendant in the absence of specific treaty language to that effect. To defeat the Court's personal jurisdiction, Noriega must therefore establish that the treaty in question is self-executing [textbook §8.1] in the sense that it confers individual rights upon citizens of the signatory nations. . . .

As a general principle of international law, individuals have no standing to challenge violations of international treaties in the absence of a protest by the sovereign involved. "[R]ights under international common law must belong to the sovereigns, not to individuals." "Under international law, it is the contracting foreign government that has the right to complain about a violation." The rationale behind this rule is that treaties are "designed to protect the sovereign interests of nations, and it is up to the offended nations to determine whether a violation of sovereign interests occurred and requires redress."

. . .

Thus, under the applicable international law, Noriega lacks standing to challenge violations of these treaties in the absence of a protest by the Panamanian government that the invasion of Panama and subsequent arrest of Noriega violated that country's territorial sovereignty.[124]

◆ 1.5 IS INTERNATIONAL LAW REALLY LAW?

Skeptics often assume that States act only in their own best interests, without any earnest regard for the legal expectations imposed by International Law. Critics thus seize upon the excesses of certain members of the League of Nations, and now the United Nations, as prominent examples of an ineffective legal system. This criticism is usually prefaced with the claimed lack of the same executive, legislative, and judicial branches of government which most national legal systems exhibit.

Consider this succinct counterpoint by Columbia University Professor Louis Henkin: "[A]lmost all nations observe almost all principles of international law and almost all of their obligations almost all of the time." Like other laws, International Law is rarely enforced, because it is usually obeyed. Hans Morgenthau, the major post-World War II critic of International Law, conceded that "to deny that international law exists as a system of binding legal rules flies in the face of all the evidence."

The underlying rationale for this tendency to honor international expectations was timelessly expressed by former US Secretary of State Elihu Root: "There is an indefinite and almost mysterious influence exercised by the general opinion of the world regarding the nation's character and conduct. The greatest and strongest governments recognize this influence and act with reference to it. They dread the moral isolation created by general adverse opinion and the unfriendly feeling that accompanies it, and they desire general approval and the kindly feeling that goes with it."[125]

The following hypothetical conversation has likely occurred on occasions after the news of a serious breach of International Law saturates front-page headlines. The following words may have been uttered during either of the twentieth century's World Wars; after the facts of the Holocaust were exposed to world view; while Iran was holding American and Canadian diplomats hostage for 444 days; or when Saddam Hussein's forces torched more than 600 oil wells upon Iraq's flight from Kuwait in 1991:

> Of course, International Law isn't really law. Those who purport to be international lawyers, and the ivory-tower professors who teach and write on the subject, have a vested interest in trying to convince their clients and students that International Law is something more than a myopic fantasy. The evidence is all around us: if International Law were really law, Hitler, Karadzic, and Hussein would have been stopped in their tracks! International Law, if it is "law" at all, is quite primitive. Unlike a national government, based on the Rule of Law, it lacks the essential powers of enforcement. Like God, one may refer to International Law with great reverence—while harboring doubts about its very existence!

A 1990 editorial appearing in a major US magazine echoed these sentiments by describing the term International Law as "self-canceling." In a prominent reporter's words, the term International Law "is virtually an oxymoron. Law without a sword is mere words: lacking an enforcement mechanism . . . [it is] merely admonition or aspiration . . . [and to be effective it] must be backed by coercion legitimized by a political process. The 'international community' has no such process."[126]

Whether such arguments merit only superficial appeal must be considered at the outset, before one can seriously proceed to study the field of International Law. There would be little sense in taking this course, or specializing in International Law or a related discipline, if the tangibility of this branch of law cannot be effectively illustrated.

International Law *is* primitive in comparison to national legal systems. It lacks the same legislative, executive, and judicial enforcement mechanisms. Under the terms of the UN Charter, for example, the General Assembly makes recommendations. It does not legislate. The customary practice of States, and norm-creating treaties, are the essential lawmakers in the international legal system (§1.2 Sources of International Law). As will be seen later in this text, the UN Secretary-General does *not* have the power to directly intervene in any conflict, beyond that which is expressly provided by the disputing parties or the veto-ridden Security Council. Thus, he or she cannot launch a military strike, has no standing forces, and can only refer matters affecting international peace to the Security Council.

On the other hand, the evolution of entities like the European Union (§3.4)—now twenty-five members strong, the globalization wrought by the World Trade Organization (§13.2), the International Corporation for Assigned Names and Numbers that governs Internet Protocols, suggest that the traditional label "primitive" is becoming an unwarranted moniker. As characterized by Vienna University Professor Markus Burgstaller:

> international law has to some extent "matured" into a legal system covering all aspects of relations not only among states but also aspects of relations between states and their federated units, between states and persons, between persons and several states, between states and international corporations, and between international organizations and their members. . . .
>
> This increasing demand for international regulation contrasts with widespread skepticism of the relevance of international law. Ever since Hugo Grotius wrote [in the eighteenth century] . . . in order to refute the views of those who held international law as nonexistent or irrelevant it has been common for writers to comment on the comparison of municipal and international law and to discuss the specific nature (primitiveness and/or weakness) of the latter [by] . . . critics who believe that international law is irrelevant because it lacks centralized legislative, judicial, or enforcement procedures.[127]

It is given that international dispute resolution mechanisms cannot be thrust upon any State without its consent. Unlike individuals who break the laws of their countries, States are coequal sovereigns in an international legal system that has not been designed to force them to appear in a courtroom to defend a claimed breach of International Law. As Chapter 9 will illustrate, the ICJ cannot exercise jurisdiction in a case absent a defendant State's express consent to the proceedings. States have historically refused to cede the requisite degree of sovereignty to enable an international organization to control them in the absence of their express consent.

Critics of the international legal system therefore claim that International Law is not a "law." This routine salvo is premised on the assumption that anything less than full and immediate enforcement power renders a legal system inherently impotent. Political "Realists" chastise the international legal system as being rather crude, in relation to the available enforcement powers in national legal systems. In the judgment of these critics, the limitations of the international legal system, although intrinsically imposed by State sovereignty, render it comparatively weak.

Yale law professor Jed Rubenfeld classically articulates this skepticism about the public's perceived role of International Law in the modern legal order:

> Some American international law specialists . . . are often perceived by the rest of the U.S. legal world to be speaking a foreign language, or not so much a language as a kind of gibberish lacking the basic grammar—the grammar of enforceability—that alone gives legal language a claim to meaning. Kosovo [which like Iraq, lacked an authorizing UN Security Council resolution for the 1999 bombing] symbolizes not merely an exceptional, exigent circumstance in which . . . the United States was justified in going outside the UN framework, but rather an entire attitude about that framework, according to which the UN system, while pretending to be a legal system, isn't really a legal system.
>
> . . .
>
> A deeper reason for the [US] skepticism lies in the indications that international law may be used as a vehicle for anti-American resentments. A case in point is the position taken by the "international community" with respect to the continuing use of capital

punishment in some American jurisdictions. Most Americans . . . can respect the moral arguments that condemn the death penalty. But what many Americans have trouble respecting or understanding is the concerted effort to condemn the United States as a human-rights violator because of the death penalty and to expel the United States from international organizations on that ground. When the international community throws down the gauntlet over the death penalty in America while merely clearing its throat about the slaughter in Yugoslavia, Americans can hardly be blamed if they see a sign that an anti-American agenda can be expected to find expression in international law.[128]

There are two responses to this critique. One is that these systemic limitations were instituted by the State members of the international legal community. They are simultaneously both the governors, and the governed. They function within a system designed to temper the efficacy of enforcement measures with what critics perceive as International Law's "self-canceling" respect for national sovereignty. As articulated by one of the most prominent US Supreme Court chief justices, in a statement which has been quoted and requoted for almost 200 years: "The jurisdiction of the nation within its own territory is necessarily exclusive and absolute. It is susceptible of no limitation not imposed by itself. Any restriction upon it, deriving vitality from an external source, would imply a diminution in sovereignty. . . ."[129]

To appreciate this debate, one should distinguish between law and its enforcement mechanisms. While six months elapsed after Iraq's invasion of Kuwait, a thirty-four-nation coalition pitted Arab against Arab in the ensuing Persian Gulf War. Prior to the Iranian hostage crisis of 1979–1980, States had observed the institution of diplomatic immunity for two millennia. It made little sense, even for nations at war, to "shoot the messenger." Iran admittedly ignored UN Security Council resolutions and a judgment of the ICJ, each calling for the release of the hostages. Yet it would be a mistake to conclude that, lacking an *immediate* enforcement mechanism in that instance, International Law does not exist. Iran became totally isolated by the terms of the international response to its egregious breach of diplomatic immunity. No nation adversely reacted when the United States froze billions of dollars of Iranian assets in the United States, as a means of pressuring Iran to comply

with International Law. In the previous generation, a number of Hitler's henchmen paid with their lives for their roles in waging Germany's aggressive war as a result of the work of the Allied Nuremberg War Crimes Tribunal.

The other response, to the critics who argue that International Law is not a "law," is that this deceptively simple monosyllabic word possesses a chameleon-like nature. Several of the most prominent professors have drawn upon a variety of resources, to illustrate its subtle nature in the following terms:

The task of defining "law" itself, let alone "international law," is not easy. The point is made clearly in Sir Fredrick Pollack, A First Book of Jurisprudence for Students of the Common Law [that] . . . those ideas which seem to be the most simple are really the most difficult to grasp with certainty and express with accuracy [because] . . . the greater has been a lawyer's opportunities of knowledge, and the more time he has given to the study of legal principles, the greater will be his hesitation in face of the apparently simple question: What is law?

No less difficult is the task of defining "international law"—or, more precisely, of reaching agreement on what we mean by "international law." Indeed, the very reality of international law is sometimes open to challenge, on the grounds that there can be no [hierarchy of] governing sovereign states or that it is not 'real law' because states obey it only when it is in their interest to do so. . . . Clearly some definitions of law would exclude international law.[130]

The following scenario presents some refreshing perspectives on International Law as a "law," straddled with its intrinsic problems of enforcement and national leaders who believe that might makes right.

TRAFFIC LIGHTS AND INTERNATIONAL LAW
A "law" represents the behavior that a particular community deems acceptable. The scofflaw may be indifferent to that law. Imagine you are driving through a busy intersection with the usual array of traffic signals. Most motorists conform to the law. They proceed only when the light is green and stop when the light is red. This routine observance of community expectations prompts the following question: Why do most motorists observe the commands emitted from the directional commands,

even when there is no policeman present to enforce the applicable rules?[131]

Conforming behavior does not necessarily result from fear of punishment. The motorists at the intersection observe the law due to their common desire to proceed safely. Otherwise, there would be chaos, were each driver to attempt to reach his or her respective destination via that intersection. If most drivers did not observe the traffic laws at the various intersections of human behavior, there would be numerous collisions. These incidents would defeat the common goal of safely proceeding. While compliance may delay the immediate progress of some hurried drivers, conformity with justifiable expectations would enable everyone to arrive at their destinations— even if they do not arrive on time. The few scofflaws are unlikely to ignore the traffic lights without at least minor (and in some cases major) consequences.

The international system similarly spawns an astonishing level of order between nations (motorists), because of the common interest they share in observing the fundamental expectations of global harmony (collision avoidance). While some States may occasionally ignore the norms of accepted behavior, the international community has nevertheless imposed a legal framework for establishing mutual expectations. Most State "drivers" within the international legal system engage in consistent and predictable behavior that does not offend the shared sense of global order.

The national decision to voluntarily observe International Law is premised on self-interest and the survival instinct emerging at various international intersections. Self-interested States recognize that it is in their best interest to comply with the mutual expectations of International Law. Like most motorists, who observe almost all traffic laws almost all of the time, national interests are served best by a prevailing international order.

While the above traffic light analogy is not flawless, it does exemplify the analogous operation of International Law as an important cog in the wheel of international relations. One may avoid the all-too-common misperception that the legitimacy of governance depends, for its very existence, on coercive enforcement rather than commonly shared values. Hence, observance of the law does not depend exclusively on military or economic enforcement measures. States have observed International Law, in most instances, without a UN standing army, and other comparable governmental institutions that are the benchmarks of national law.

◆ PROBLEMS

Problem 1.A (end of §1.1) A member of the class will serve as the blackboard recorder. Another class member will begin this exercise by defining "International Law." Others may then suggest modifications that would more fully, or more accurately, complete the definition.

Problem 1.B (end of §1.2) In 2002, a remote village council in Pakistan ordered the gang rape of Mukhtar Mai, as a punishment for her brother's alleged sexual relations with a woman from a rival tribe. Gang rape is not uncommon in such "matters of honor." This one received worldwide attention, however, because it was approved by a village council. Such councils do not have express governmental legal authority. They render such decisions, however, because of the limited reach of the central government's authority over these centuries-old feudal norms.

Four of the six men who carried out the village council's decree were later convicted and sentenced to death by an Islamic tribunal. A similar tribunal overturned these convictions in March 2005. Defense lawyers therein successfully claimed that the convictions had been improperly "influenced by media hype and government pressure." The Federal Shariah Court, the nation's highest Islamic tribunal, later reinstated the death sentences. Pakistan's secular Supreme Court then deemed this Shariah court's ruling unconstitutional. Human rights activists have been urging the government of Pakistan to strip all local councils of their power to mete out such punishment. Details are available in N. Kristof, *When Rapists Walk Free*, New York Times on the Web (Mar. 5, 2005), or Section A, Page 13, Column 1.

Unlike Pakistan, more developed countries typically have police, courts, and prosecutors at various levels in all regions. Two students will now debate, pro and con, whether International Law applies to this incident. What factors from §1.1 and §1.2 of this book could be applied? What is the reason(s) for your response?

Problem 1.C (end of §1.4) A US citizen was traveling in the Middle East. In October 1994, she was riding on a crowded public bus that was the target of a terrorist "suicide bomb" attack. She was killed when the bomb carrier left it on board the bus, killing twenty-one people and injuring many others during rush hour in Tel Aviv.

"Hamas" claimed responsibility. That group consists of people who employ such tactics as political bargaining chips to influence the Middle East peace process, being negotiated by the Palestinian Authority and various governments in the region. Hamas is seeking a greater Palestine than agreed to during the 1993 peace accords in Washington, DC.

Assume that the US Department of State is considering an Israeli plan that the United States and Israel jointly undertake a secret mission to go into whatever State necessary to find the Hamas perpetrators, and to extract them. Any captured Hamas members will be tried in Israel for their participation in this bombing.

You are the judge in a trial court in your state of the United States, where the deceased US citizen lived. The spouse of the murdered citizen has filed a suit against Hamas in your court. Needless to say, Hamas does not respond to this suit. The US Department of State, acting on behalf of the US President, files papers in this suit asking you to dismiss this case because of sensitive Department of State negotiations with Israel and the Palestinian Authority. The essential US Department of State positions are as follows:

(a) The Political Question Doctrine requires dismissal of this case.

(b) The Act of State Doctrine is applicable, thus requiring dismissal of this case.

(c) The Department of State lawyer says that if you deny the US Government's request to dismiss this case, and the Hamas bomber is captured and returned to the US for trial, the perpetrator will have the legal standing to claim that your court cannot prosecute him. In other words, the US government's lawyer argues that you will have to dismiss this case anyway.

How will you rule on each of these claims?

Problem 1.D (end of §1.5) The Serbian post-Cold War advances in Bosnia-Herzegovina triggered a great deal of international frustration. Various rules of International Law, particularly the prohibition against violating territorial sovereignty, were ignored, primarily, but not exclusively, by the Serbs. The United Nations, NATO, and the United States appeared to be powerless to act. The United States and other NATO members wanted to carefully weigh the timing and degree of responsive action, during a period when democracy and capitalism had not been staunchly incorporated into the various Yugoslavian territories involved in the Bosnian

conflict. (The United Kingdom similarly appeased Hitler at the outset of World War II, by its cautious response to German territorial advances taken in violation of the territorial sovereignty of various European States.) With the possible exception of Moscow, there was no international outcry when an embargo was launched against the former Yugoslavia by the international community, nor when NATO aircraft proceeded to bomb some Serbian positions in Bosnia.

Skeptics claimed that this level of inaction proved that International Law is not a "law." They viewed the international response to the clear Serbian aggression as being strangled by political concerns. One of these was the potential Russian reaction to any US-European measures against Serbia, Russia's traditional ally.

Two students (or groups) will debate the following issues in the preceding factual context: (a) whether International Law is really law; (b) whether swift and effective enforcement measures against scofflaws in the former Yugoslavia would have been the only genuine benchmark of an effective international legal system; and (c) whether the Bosnian crisis exposed the political reality that expressions of caution by the international community are no more than a disguise for the fact that there is no applicable law which can effectively govern the relations between States.

◆ BIBLIOGRAPHY

Careers

M. Janis & S. Swartz (ed.), CAREERS IN INTERNATIONAL LAW (2d ed. Chicago: Amer. Bar Ass'n, 2001)

L. Louis-Jacques, Researching Careers in International Law: Resources in Print and Electronic Format <http://www.lib.uchicago.edu/~llou/careers.html>

W. Slomanson, Career Opportunities in International Law <http://home.att.net/~slomansonb/career.html>

§1.1 Definition and Scope

B. Boczek, INTERNATIONAL LAW: A DICTIONARY (Oxford: Scarecrow, 2005)

C. Blakesley, et al., Application of the Law of the International System, ch. 1, in THE INTERNATIONAL LEGAL SYSTEM: CASES AND MATERIALS (5th ed. New York: Foundation Press, 2001)

B. Carter & P. Trimble, What is International Law?, ch.1, in INTERNATIONAL LAW (2d ed. Boston: Little, Brown—now Aspen, 1995)

L. Damrosch, et al., The Nature of International Law, ch.1, in INTERNATIONAL LAW, CASES AND MATERIALS 1 (4th ed. St. Paul: West, 2001)

M. Janis & J. Noyes, The Nature of International Law, ch.1, in INTERNATIONAL LAW: CASES AND COMMENTARY 1 (3d ed. St. Paul, MN: WestGroup, 2006)

M. Kaplan & N. Katzenbach, The Theoretical Framework of International Law, ch. 3 in THE POLITICAL FOUNDATIONS OF INTERNATIONAL LAW 56 (New York: John Wiley & Sons, 1961)

C. Parry & J. Grant, ENCYCLOPAEDIC DICTIONARY OF INTERNATIONAL LAW (2d ed. Oceana: 2003)

S. Scott, The Logical Structure of International Law, ch. 5, in INTERNATIONAL LAW IN WORLD POLITICS: AN INTRODUCTION 87 (Boulder, CO: Rienner, 2004)

§1.2 Sources of International Law

M. Akehurst, The Hierarchy of Sources of International Law, 47 BRITISH YEARBOOK INTERNATIONAL LAW 273 (1975)

D. Harris, The Sources of International Law, ch. 2 in CASES AND MATERIALS ON INTERNATIONAL LAW 21 (6th ed. London: Street & Maxwell, 2004)

M. Koskenniemi, THE LIBRARY OF ESSAYS IN INTERNATIONAL LAW: SOURCES OF INTERNATIONAL LAW (Aldershot, Eng.: Ashgate, 2000) (collection of prominent articles)

E. McWhinney, UNITED NATIONS LAW MAKING: CULTURAL AND IDEOLOGICAL RELATIVISM AND INTERNATIONAL LAW MAKING FOR AN ERA OF TRANSITION (New York: Holmes & Meier, 1984)

S. Rosenne, Where to Find the Law, ch. 2, in THE PERPLEXITIES OF MODERN INTERNATIONAL LAW 25 (Martinus Nijhoff: 2004)

Sources of International Law, 19 THESAURUS ACROASIUM: SUMMER 1991 (Thessaloniki, Greece: INST. INT'L PUB. L., 1992)

M. Villiger, CUSTOMARY INTERNATIONAL LAW AND TREATIES: A MANUAL ON THE THEORY AND PRACTICE OF THE INTERRELATION OF SOURCES (rev. 2d ed. The Hague, Neth.: Kluwer, 1997)

§1.3 Related Disciplines

PRIVATE INTERNATIONAL LAW

H. Chatsworth, Feminist Methods in International Law, in Symposium on Method in International Law, 93 AMER. J. INT'L LAW 291, at 379 (1999)

S. Symeonides, W. Perdue & A. von Mehren, CONFLICT OF LAWS: AMERICAN, COMPARATIVE, AND INTERNATIONAL (St. Paul, MN: WestGroup, 1998)

INTERNATIONAL RELATIONS

B. Arts, M Noortman & B. Reinalda (ed.), NON-STATE ACTORS IN INTERNATIONAL RELATIONS (Aldershot, Eng.: Ashgate, 2001)

D. Lieberman & M. Gurtov, REVEALING THE WORLD: AN INTERDISCIPLINARY READER FOR INTERNATIONAL STUDIES (Dubuque, IA: Kendal/Hunt, 1992)

W. McWilliams & H. Piotrowski, THE WORLD SINCE 1945: A HISTORY OF INTERNATIONAL RELATIONS (3d ed. Boulder, CO: Lynne Rienner, 1993)

R. Powell, Absolute and Relative Gains in International Relations Theory, 85 AMER. POL. SCIENCE REV. 1303 (1991)

C. Sjolander & W. Cox, BEYOND POSITIVISM: CRITICAL REFLECTIONS ON INTERNATIONAL RELATIONS (Boulder, CO: Lynne Rienner, 1994)

RELIGION

F. Halliday, NATION AND RELIGION IN THE MIDDLE EAST (Boulder, CO: Rienner, 2000) Religious Legal Systems, ch.14-15, in K. Zweigert & H. Kotz, AN INTRODUCTION TO COMPARATIVE LAW 303 (3d ed. Oxford, Eng.: Oxford Univ. Press, 1998) (Weir translation)

S. Rudolph & J. Piscatore (ed.), TRANSNATIONAL RELIGION AND FADING STATES (Boulder, CO: Westview Press, 1997)

COMPARATIVE LAW

M. Glendon, M. Gordon, & C. Osakwe, COMPARATIVE LEGAL TRADITIONS: TEXT, MATERIALS AND CASES ON THE CIVIL AND COMMON LAW TRADITIONS (2d ed. St. Paul: West, 1994)

Symposium: New Directions in Comparative Law, 46 AMER. J. COMP. LAW 597–783 (1999)

The Concept of Comparative Law, ch. 1 in K. Zweigert & H. Kotz, AN INTRODUCTION TO COMPARATIVE LAW 1 (3d rev. ed. Oxford, Eng.: Clarendon Press, 1998)

§1.4 National-International Law Nexus

C. Bradley & J. Goldsmith, States and Foreign Relations, ch. 2, in FOREIGN RELATIONS LAW: CASES AND MATERIALS (New York: Aspen, 2003)

K. Clarke, Testing Nontested Models of International Relations: Reevaluating Realism, 45 AMER. J. POL. SCI. 3 (2001)

B. Conforti, INTERNATIONAL LAW AND THE ROLE OF DOMESTIC LEGAL SYSTEMS (Dordrecht, Neth.: Martinus Nijhoff, 1993)

L. Erades, INTERACTIONS BETWEEN INTERNATIONAL AND MUNICIPAL LAW: A COMPARATIVE CASE LAW STUDY (The Hague, Neth.: T.M.C. Asser Inst., 1993)

J. Goldsmith & E. Posner, THE LIMITS OF INTERNATIONAL LAW (Oxford, Eng.: Oxford Univ. Press, 2005)

A. Oppenheimer (ed.), THE RELATIONSHIP BETWEEN EUROPEAN COMMUNITY LAW AND NATIONAL LAW: THE CASES (Grotius: Cambridge Univ. Press, 1994)

J. Paust, INTERNATIONAL LAW AS LAW OF THE UNITED STATES (2d ed. Durham, NC: Carolina Acad. Press, 2003)

K. Sik, International Law in the Municipal Legal Order of Asian States: Virgin Land, in R. MacDonald (ed.), ESSAYS IN HONOUR OF WANG TIEYA 737 (Dordrecht, Neth.: Martinus Nijhoff, 1994)

§1.5 Is International Law Really Law?

R. Bierzanek, Some Remarks on 'Soft' International Law, 17 POLISH YEARBOOK INT'L LAW 21 (1988)

P. Brewer, et al., International Trust and Public Opinion About World Affairs, 48 AMER. J. POL. SCI. 1 (2004)

D. Caron, Does International Law Really Matter?, in PROCEEDINGS OF THE 98TH ANNUAL MEETING 305 (AMER. SOC. INT'L LAW: Wash., D.C. 2004)

D. Georgiev, Politics or Rule of Law: Deconstruction and Legitimacy in International Law, 4 EUROPEAN J. INT'L LAW 1 (1993)

H. Kissinger, DOES AMERICA NEED A FOREIGN POLICY? (New York: Simon & Schuster, 2001)

H. Koh, Review Essay: Why Do Nations Obey International Law?, 106 YALE L. J. 2599 (1997)

G. Niemeyer, LAW WITHOUT FORCE: THE FUNCTION OF POLITICS IN INTERNATIONAL LAW (New Brunswick, NJ: Transaction, 2001) (unrevised version originally published in 1941)

E. Niou & P. Ordeshook, Stability in Anarchic International Systems, 84 AMER. POL. SCIENCE REV. 1207 (1990)

Additional Internet Resources

Academic Journals (international topics): <http://stu.findlaw.com/journals/international.html>

Careers in International Law: <http://home.att.net/~slomansonb/career.html>

GlobaLex (international and foreign law research): <http://www.nyulawglobal.org/globalex>

International Law Research Guides: <http://www.llrx.com/international_law.html>

Internet Research: <http://www.lib.uchicago.edu/~llou/forintlaw.html>

Library of Congress's Global Legal Information Network: <www.glin.gov>

◆ ENDNOTES

1. L. Siaya & F. Hayward, American Council on Education Center for Institutional and International Initiatives, Mapping Internationalization on U.S. Campuses: Final Report (ACE: Wash., DC, 2003). Web Executive Summary: <http://www.acenet.edu>, click Programs, click Center for Institutional and International Initiatives, click Mapping: Report, scroll to Additional Information, click Mapping.

2. C. Okeke, THE THEORY AND PRACTICE OF INTERNATIONAL LAW IN NIGERIA 277–278 (Enugu, Nigeria: Fourth Dimension Pub., 1986).

3. For job opportunity resources, see Career Opportunities in International Law at <http://home.att.net/~slomansonb/career.html>.

4. For a complete listing of university law reviews, see M. Hoffheimer, 2005 DIRECTORY OF LAW REVIEWS (Cincinnati, OH: LexisNexis, 2005), available at: <www.lexisnexis.com/lawreview>.

5. *Brief intros*: Historical Introduction, L. Damrosch, et al., in INTERNATIONAL LAW, CASES AND MATERIALS xxvii (4th ed. St. Paul: West, 2001) & A Brief History of Public International Law, ch. 15, in E. Paras, INTERNATIONAL LAW AND WORLD ORGANIZATIONS 389 (4th rev. ed. Manila: Rex Book Store, 1985) (*Greek* city-state legal hierarchy). *China*: L. Chen, The Confucian View of World Order, ch. 2, in *Religion and International Law* 36 (divinity basis for Chinese reprisals). *Epochs*: W. Grewe, THE EPOCHS OF INTERNATIONAL LAW 7 (Berlin: Walter de Gruyter Pub., 2000) (Beyers translation from German). *Europe*: A. Cassese, ch. 2, at 34 (European ascendancy) & ch. 3, at 55, Historical Evolution of the International Community: The New Setting

(1918-present), in INTERNATIONAL LAW IN A DIVIDED WORLD (Oxford, Eng.: Clarendon Press, 1986). *Greek-Roman Influence*: & The Historical Background of International Law, ch. 1 in C. Fenwick, INTERNATIONAL LAW 9 (4th ed. New York: Appleton-Century-Crofts, 1965) (Grecian influence on Roman law). *Grotius:* Baskin & Feldman, The Role of Hugo Grotius in the Formation and Development of the International Law Science, 1982 SOVIET YEARBOOK. INT'L L. 275 (1983) (English trans.) ("father of International Law") & H. Lauterpacht, The Grotian Tradition in International Law, 23 BRIT. YEARBOOK. INT'L LAW 1 (1946) (derivation of term "International Law"). *India*: V. Nanda, International Law in Ancient Hindu India, ch. 3, in M. Janis & C. Evans (ed.), RELIGION AND INTERNATIONAL LAW 51 (The Hague: Kluwer, 1999) (Hindu disapproval of war) [hereinafter *Religion and International Law*]; *Islam*: W. Hallaq, A HISTORY OF ISLAMIC LEGAL THEORIES: AN INTRODUCTION TO SUNNI USUL AL~FIQH (Cambridge, Eng.: Cambridge Univ. Press, 1997).

6. J. Kent, 1 COMMENTARIES ON AMERICAN LAW 20 (2d ed. New York: O. Halsted, 1832).

7. *See, e.g.*, Kunz, Natural-Law Thinking in the Modern Science of International Law, 55 AMER. J. INT'L L. 951 (1961); Natural Law vs. Positivism, in G. Danilenko, LAW-MAKING IN THE INTERNATIONAL COMMUNITY 214–219 (Dordrecht, Neth.: Martinus Nijhoff, 1992); G. Schwarzenberger, The Grotius Factor in International Law and Relations: A Functional Approach, ch. 12, in H. Bull, B. Kingsbury, & A. Roberts (eds.), HUGO GROTIUS AND INTERNATIONAL RELATIONS 301 (Oxford, Eng.: Oxford Univ. Press, 1992).

8. This treaty is considered to be the ancestor of the modern nation State. The entire treaty text is provided by Yale Law School at <www.yale.edu/lawweb/avalon/westphal.htm>.

9. M. Akehurst, A MODERN INTRODUCTION TO INTERNATIONAL LAW 23 (7th rev. ed. London: Allen & Unwin, 1997).

10. *See* Wang T., Teaching and Research of International Law in Present Day China, 22 COLUM. J. TRANSNAT'L L. 77 (1983).

11. H. Chiu, Communist China's Attitude toward International Law, 60 AMER. J. INT'L L. 245, 250 (1966) (quoting Chinese-language source).

12. Huan, Foreword to first edition, CHINESE YEARBOOK OF INTERNATIONAL LAW 4 (Taipei: Inst. Int'l Relations, 1983).

13. Louis Henkin, International Law: Politics, Values and Functions, 216 RECUEIL DES COURS (Hague Academy of Int'l Law) 22 (1989).

14. The SS Lotus (France v. Turkey), 1927 PCIJ, Series A, No. 10, 18. Web: <http://www.worldcourts.com/pcij/eng/decisions/1gateway/1927.09.07_lotus.htm>.

15. Dreyfus v. Von Finck, 534 F.2d 24, 30 (2d Cir. 1976), cert. den'd, 429 US 825 (1976), disavowed on other grounds, Filartiga v. Pena-Irala, 630 F.2d 876 (2d Cir. 1980).

16. This concept, its development, and State usage is analyzed by Professor Condorelli in "Custom," ch. 7 in M. Bedjaoui (ed.), INTERNATIONAL LAW: ACHIEVEMENTS AND PROSPECTS 179, 187–192 (Paris: UNESCO, 1991) [hereinafter *Bedjaoui*].

17. North Sea Continental Shelf Cases (Fed. Rep. Germany v. Denmark/Netherlands), 1969 ICJ Rep. 4, 44. Web:

<http://www.icj-cij.org/icjwww/idecisions/isummaries/icssummary690220.htm>.

18. Case Concerning Military and Paramilitary Activities (Nicaragua v. US), 1986 ICJ Rep. 101 [hereinafter *Nicaragua case*].

19. General Introduction, in *Bedjaoui,* (cited in note 16 earlier), at 2.

20. Anne Marie Slaughter, What Good is International Law?: Leading Through Law, 27 WILSON QUARTERLY 37 (2003) [hereinafter *Leading Through Law*].

21. S.S. Wimbledon (U.K. et al v. Germany), 1923 P.C.I.J., Ser. A, No. 1, at 25. Web: <http://www.worldcourts.com/pcij/eng/decisions/1gateway/1923.08.17_wimbledon.htm>.

22. G. Tunkin, THEORY OF INTERNATIONAL LAW 251 (Cambridge, MA: Harv. Univ. Press, 1974) (italics added) [hereinafter *Tunkin*].

23. *See* resources collected in W. Duong, Partnerships with Monarchs—Two Case Studies, 25 UNIV. PENN. J. INT'L L. 1171, 1190 n.36 (2004) (danger of legal favoritism toward Anglo-American jurisprudence which has caused divergence in North-South dialogue).

24. J. Paust, The Reality of Private Rights, Duties, and Participation in the International Legal Process, 25 MICH. J. INT'L L. 1229, 1239–1240 (2004) (crime-by-crime footnote authorities omitted).

25. *See, e.g.*, M. McDougal & W. Reisman, International Law as a Process of Authoritative Decision, ch. 1, §1 in INTERNATIONAL LAW IN CONTEMPORARY PERSPECTIVE 4 (Mineola, NY: Foundation Press, 1981).

26. M. Whiteman, DIGEST OF INTERNATIONAL LAW 1 (Wash., DC: US Dep't State, 1963).

27. J. Charney, Universal International Law, 87 AMER. J. INT'L L. 529 (1993).

28. N. Kirsch, More Equal than the Rest? Hierarchy, Equality and US Predominance in International Law, ch. 5, in M. Byers & G. Nolte (ed.), UNITED STATES HEGEMONY AND THE FOUNDATIONS OF INTERNATIONAL LAW 135, at 136–137 (Cambridge: 2003).

29. D. Malone & Yuen Foong Khong, Resisting the Unilateral Impulse: Multilateral Engagement and the Future of U.S. Leadership 421, at 426, in UNILATERALISM AND U.S. FOREIGN POLICY: INTERNATIONAL PERSPECTIVES (Lynne Rienner: 2003).

30. *See* Different Meanings of the Term 'Sources of Law,' in V. D. Degan, SOURCES OF INTERNATIONAL LAW 1 (The Hague, Neth.: Martinus Nijhoff, 1995).

31. *See, e.g.*, I. Brownlie, PRINCIPLES OF PUBLIC INTERNATIONAL LAW 5 (6th ed. Oxford, Eng.: Oxford Univ. Press, 2003) [hereinafter *Brownlie*]; J. Brierly, THE LAW OF NATIONS 56 (Waldock 6th ed. Oxford, Eng.: Clarendon Press, 1976). *But see* G. Maris, INTERNATIONAL LAW: AN INTRODUCTION 44 (New York: Univ. Press of Amer., 1984) ("Amidst the chaos . . . is a lack of a set rule of sources").

32. ALLIED REPORT: CMD. DOC. 6531 (1944, at 36).

33. *Western criticism*: M. Kaplan & N. Katzenbach, THE POLITICAL FOUNDATIONS OF INTERNATIONAL LAW 231–236 (New York: John Wiley & Sons, 1961); *Soviet criticism*: Tunkin [cited in note 22 above], at 118; *Chinese criticism:* H. Chiu, Communist China's Attitude Toward International Law, 60 AMER. J. INT'L L. 245, 257 (1966), quoting Ying T'ao, Recognize the True Face of Bourgeois International Law from a Few Basic Concepts, in STUDIES IN INTERNATIONAL PROBLEMS 46–47 (1960) (Chinese-language periodical criticism). *Eye of the beholder:* Legitimacy Deficit in Article 38(1)(b)'s Jurisprudence, ch. 3 in B. Chigara, LEGITIMACY DEFICIT IN CUSTOM: A DECONSTRUCTIONIST CRITIQUE 102 (Aldershot, Eng.: Ashgate, 2001).

34. *See* M. Akehurst, The Hierarchy of the Sources of International Law, 47 BRITISH YEARBOOK INT'L L. 273, 274 (1974).

35. The Hierarchy of International Norms, in B. Conforti, INTERNATIONAL LAW AND THE ROLE OF DOMESTIC LEGAL SYSTEMS 115–116 (Dordrecht, Neth.: Martinus Nijhoff, 1993) (Provost translation) [hereinafter *Conforti*].

36. R. Bernhardt, Hierarchy Among the Sources of International Law?, in D. Constantopoulos (ed.), SOURCES OF INTERNATIONAL LAW, XIX THESAURUS ACROASIUM 209 (Thessaloniki, Greece: Inst. Pub. Int'l Law, 1992).

37. F. Martin, Delineating a Hierarchical Outline of International Law Sources and Norms, 65 SASKATCHEWAN L.R. 333, 359 (2002).

38. *See* The Elements of International Custom, ch. 1 in K. Wolfke, CUSTOM IN PRESENT INTERNATIONAL LAW 1 (2d rev. ed. Dordrecht, Neth.: Martinus Nijhoff, 1993).

39. *Tunkin* (cited in note 22 earlier), at 113–114.

40. *Brownlie* (cited in note 31 earlier), at 7–10.

41. 1969 ICJ Rep. 3, 44 [hereinafter *Continental Shelf Case*].

42. Asylum Case (Colombia v. Peru), 1950 ICJ REP. 266, 276.

43. *See, e.g.*, G. Danilenko, Customary Rule Formation in Contemporary International Law, 1982, SOVIET YEARBK. INT'L L. 169, 170 (1983) (English translation).

44. J. Hsiung, China? Recognition Practice and International Law, in J. Cohen (ed.), CHINA'S PRACTICE OF INTERNATIONAL LAW: SOME CASE STUDIES 14, 17 (Cambridge, MA: Harv. Univ. Press, 1972).

45. Trendtex Trading Corp. v. Central Bank of Nigeria, 1 ALL ENGLISH REP. 881, No. 902B03 (1977) (italics added). Web: <http://www.uniset.ca/other/css/19772WLR356.html>.

46. Article 20, 2 US TREATIES 2394, 119 U.N.T.S. 3 (italics added).

47. Continental Shelf Case (cited in note 41 earlier), at 41–42.

48. *Equity*: C. Rossi, EQUITY AND INTERNATIONAL LAW: A LEGAL REALIST APPROACH TO INTERNATIONAL DECISION-MAKING 87 (Irvington, NY: Transnatl, 1993). *Good faith*: J. F. O'Connor, GOOD FAITH IN INTERNATIONAL LAW 17 (Aldershot, Eng.: Dartmouth, 1991).

49. In the often-quoted, and classic, words of US Supreme Court Justice Stevens in one of the major pornography cases: "I shall not today attempt further to define the kinds of material I understand to be embraced within that shorthand description; and perhaps I could never succeed in intelligibly doing so. But I know it when I see it. . . . Jacobellis v. State of Ohio, 378 U.S. 184, 197, 84 S.Ct. 1676, 1683 (1964) (concurring opinion).

50. Thomas Frank, Fairness in International Law and Institutions 14 (Oxford, Eng.: Clarendon Press, 1995).

51. Bin Cheng, Foreword to General Principles of Law as Applied by International Courts and Tribunals at xi (Cambridge, Eng.: Grotius Publications, 1987).

52. *See, e.g.,* General Principles of Law, in R. Jennings & A. Watts, I Oppenheim's International Law (Part 1) 12, at 37n.2 (9th ed. Essex, Eng.: Longman, 1992) [hereinafter *Jennings*].

53. *PCIJ case*: Diversion of Water from the Meuse, PCIJ Series A/B, No. 70, at 25 (1937). Web: <http://www.worldcourts. com/pcij/eng/decisions/1gateway/1937.06.28_meuse.htm>. *ICJ case:* Barcelona Traction Case, 1970 ICJ Rep. 3, 33. Web (ICJ summary): <http://www.icj-cij.org/icjwww/idecisions/isummaries/ibtsummary700205.htm>.

54. *Marbury v. Madison*, 1 Cranch 137, 177, 2 L.Ed. 60 (1803).

55. E. de Wet, Judicial Review as an Emerging General Principle of Law and its Implications for Proceedings before the ICJ, ch. 3 in The Chapter VII Powers of the United Nations Security Council 70–71 (Hart: 2004).

56. H. Lauterpacht, The Development of International Law by the International Court 20 (rev. ed. London: Stevens & Sons, 1958).

57. *Jennings* (cited in note 52 earlier), at 41.

58. *1815 Supreme Court:* Thirty Hogsheds of Sugar v. Boyle, 13 US (9 Cranch) 191, 3 L.Ed. 701, 703 (1815). *2002 Supreme Court*: Atkins v. Virginia, 536 U.S. 304, 347–348, 122 S.Ct. 2242, 2264, 153 L.Ed.2d 335 (2002) (J. Scalia, dissenting, joined by Justices Rhenquist and Thomas).

59. Associated Press, DeLay Continues Attacks on Federal Courts, New York Times on the Web, Apr. 20, 2005.

60. Case Concerning the Factory at Chorzow (Germany v. Poland), 1926B1929 PCIJ, ser. A, No. 7, 19 (Judgment of May 25, 1926). Web: <http://www.worldcourts.com/pcij/eng/decisions/1gateway/1927.07.26_chorzow.htm>.

61. K. Wolfke, Custom in Present International Law 77 (2d rev. ed. Dordrecht, Neth.: Martinus Nijhoff, 1993).

62. Flores v. Southern Peru Copper Corp., 343 F.3d 140, 157 n.26 (2d Cir. 2003).

63. E. Suy, Innovations in International Law-Making Processes, in R. McDonald et al. (eds.), The International Law and Policy of Human Welfare 187, 190 (Alphen aan den Rijn, Neth.: Sitjhoff & Noordhoff, 1978).

64. P. Szasz, General Law-Making Processes (from Part I: The UN System as a Source of Law), in O. Schachter & C. Joyner (eds.), 1 United Nations Legal Order, at 45B46 (Cambridge, Eng.: Cambridge Univ. Press, 1995).

65. K. Skubiszewski, Law-Making by International Organizations, in XIX Thesaurus Acroasium: Sources of International Law 364 (Thessaloniki, Greece: Inst. Public Int'l Law, 1992).

66. A. D'Amato, International Law: Process and Prospect 75B76 (2d ed. Dobbs Ferry, NY: Transnat'l, 1995).

67. The three quoted cases are: Certain Expenses of the United Nations: 1962, ICJ Rep. 151, at 163; Legal Consequences for States of the Continued Presence of South Africa in Namibia (South-West Africa) Notwithstanding Security Council Resolution 276 (1970): 1971 ICJ Rep. 16, at 50; South–West Africa Voting Procedure: 1955 ICJ Rep. 67, at 118.

68. *Nicaragua case* (cited in note 18 earlier), at 99–100 & 188.

69. *Restatement* (cited in note 25 earlier), Comment *c*. to §103.

70. O. Schachter, Resolutions and Political Texts, ch. VI in International Law in Theory and Practice 88 (Dordrecht, Neth.: Martinus Nijhoff, 1991).

71. *See* M. Bergman, The Norm-Creating Effect of a General Assembly Resolution on Transnational Corporations, in F. Snyder & S. Sathirathai (eds.), Third World Attitudes toward International Law: An Introduction 231 (Dordrecht, Neth.: Martinus Nijhoff, 1987) (some resolutions are Anorm-creating@sources) & O. Asamoah, The Legal Significance of the Declarations of the General Assembly of the United Nations (The Hague: Martinus Nijhoff, 1966) (resolutions as sources when restating customary practice).

72. P. M. North & J. J. Fawcett, Private International Law 3–4 (13th ed. London: Butterworths, 1999).

73. M. McDougal, "Private" International Law: Jus Gentium Versus Choice of Law Rules or Approaches, 38 Amer. J. Comp. L. 521 (1990).

74. A. M. Burley, International Law and International Relations Theory: A Dual Agenda, 87 Amer. J. Int'l L. 205, 207 (1993).

75. *See, e.g.*, R. Keohane, After Hegemony: Cooperation and Discord in the World Political Economy 246 (Princeton: Princeton Univ. Press, 1984) *and* Arthur Stein, Why Nations Cooperate: Circumstance and Choice in International Relations 113 (Ithaca, NY: Cornell Univ. Press, 1990).

76. *Minorities:* M. Slann, Introduction: Ethnonationalism and the New World Order of International Relations, ch. 1 in B. Schechterman & M. Slann (eds.), The Ethnic Dimension in International Relations 3 (Westport, CT: Praeger, 1993). *Leaders*: Principles, Leaders, and the Use of Force: The Case of Yugoslavia, ch. 5 in James Goodby, Europe Undivided: The New Logic of Peace in U.S.-Russian Relations 112 (Wash., DC: U.S. Inst. of Peace, 1998). *See generally* N. Petersen (ed.), The Baltic States in International Law (Copenhagen: Danish Inst. Int'l Studies, 1993).

77. *See* D. Bederman, Religion and the Sources of International Law in Antiquity, in *Religion and International Law* (cited in note 5 earlier), at 2–3.

78. *Leading Through Law* (cited in note 20 earlier), at 37.

79. *Nazi takeover:* J. Cornwell, Hitler's Pope: The Secret History of Pius XII (New York, NY: Viking Press, 1999). *War crimes:* "Defendants participated in the activities of the [WWII Croatian] Ustasha Regime in furtherance of the commission of war crimes, crimes against humanity, crimes against peace, torture, rape, starvation, physical and mental abuse, summary execution and genocide." Alperin v. Vatican Bank, 410 F.3d 532, 543 (9th Cir., 2005), cert. denizd, 2006 Westlaw 88991 (2006) (as alleged in this class action Complaint) [hereinafter *Alperin*].

80. For an historical account of the Holy See's foreign relations, see R. Araujo, The International Personality and Sovereignty of the Holy See, 50 Cath. U.L.Rev. 291 (2001).

Pope quotation: R. Stevenson, Bush Meets with Pope at Vatican, New York Times on the Web (June 4, 2004) and Pope Says War No Excuse for Human Rights Abuses, New York Times on the Web (Dec. 13, 2005).

81. M. Marty & R. Appleby (eds.), INTRODUCTION TO FUNDA-MENTALISMS AND THE State 4 (Chicago: Univ. of Chicago Press, 1993).

82. This regime is premised in part on biblical interpretation. For example: "Men are a degree above women. The *Qur'an,* verse 2:228. Other verses . . . include Verse 4:34, highlighting . . . that men are in charge of women; Verse 2:282, that the evidentiary value of a woman's testimony is half that of a man's; Verse 24:30 that women remain inside their houses in seclusion, and to veil in case they had to venture out of their houses; Verses . . . where despite a number of safeguards for women inequality of men and women remains as the husband can repudiate his wife, whereas she cannot do the same." S. Ali, GENDER AND HUMAN RIGHTS IN ISLAM AND INTERNATIONAL LAW: EQUAL BEFORE ALLAH, BUT UNEQUAL BEFORE MAN? 44–45 (The Hague: Kluwer, 2000).

83. *See* H. LaFranchi, War, Surprisingly, Opens Diplomatic Doors, Christian Science Monitor (Nov. 9, 2001), available at: <http://www.csmonitor.com/2001/1109/p2s1-uspo.html>.

84. *See generally* Common Law and Civil Law–Comparison of Methods and Sources, in R. Schlesinger et al., COMPARA-TIVE LAW: CASES–TEXT–MATERIALS 229 (5th ed. Mineola, NY: Foundation Press, 1988).

85. *See* International Tribunal for the Prosecution of Persons Responsible for Serious Violations of International Humanitarian Law Committed in the Territory of the Former Yugoslavia Since 1991: Rules of Procedure and Evidence, 33 INT'L LEGAL MAT'LS 484 (1994).

86. Article 29 of the Irish Constitution, adopted Dec., 1999, in conformity with the Apr., 1998 "Good Friday Agreement," designed to eliminate the long-term hostilities with the United Kingdom over Northern Ireland.

87. G. Hackworth, DIGEST OF INTERNATIONAL LAW 655B661 (Wash., DC: US Gov't Print. Off., 1942).

88. The most comprehensive compilation is contained in INTERNATIONAL LAW REPORTS, by Grotius Publications. Access is facilitated by J. Barker, CONSOLIDATED TABLES OF CASES AND TREATIES: VOLUMES 1–80 (Cambridge, Eng.: 1991). One may therein select a particular treaty, and quickly ascertain the identity and citation for national cases, which have interpreted that treaty.

89. G. Slyz, International Law in National Courts, ch. 5, in T. Franck & G. Fox (eds.), INTERNATIONAL LAW DECISIONS IN NATIONAL COURTS 71 (Irvington-on-Hudson, NY: Transnational, 1996).

90. *See* E. Dickson, The Law of Nations as Part of the National Law of the United States, 101 UNIV. PENN. L. REV. 26, 26–27 (1952).

91. Applicability of the Obligation to Arbitrate Under Section 21 of the United Nations Headquarters Agreement of 26 June 1947, 1988 ICJ REP. 12, para. 57.

92. H. Kelsen, General Theory of Law and the State 363B380 (Cambridge, MA: Harv. Univ. Press, 1945).

93. Chung Chi Cheung v. Regina, 1939 Court of Appeals 160 (1939). *See generally*, J. Becker, THE AMERICAN LAW OF NATIONS: PUBLIC INTERNATIONAL LAW IN AMERICAN COURTS (Huntington, NY: Juris, 2001).

94. *Supreme Court:* The Paquete Habana and The Lola, set forth on Course Web Page, Chap. 1. *Trial court:* The Over the Top, 5 F.2d 838, 842 (D.C. Conn. 1925) (italics added).

95. M. Kirby, The Growing *Rapproachment* Between International Law and National Law, at 333, in A. Anghie & G. Sturgess (ed.), LEGAL VISIONS OF THE 21ST CENTURY: ESSAYS IN HONOUR OF JUDGE CHRISTOPHER WEERAMANTRY (The Hague: Kluwer, 1998).

96. *PCIJ quote*: Polish Nationals in Danzig, 1931 PCIJ REP., SER. A/B, NO. 44, at 24. *ILC quote*: 1949 YEARBK OF THE INT'L LAW COMMISSION 286, 289 (1949). *2001 final draft:* see §2.5 on State Responsibility.

97. Conforti, (cited in note 35 earlier), at 8–9.

98. Amended Memorandum, Order and Judgment, In re "Agent Orange" Product Liability Litigation, 373 F.Supp.2d 7 (E.D.N.Y. 2005) (authorities and quotation marks omitted).

99. Further details, and updates, are available at the American Society of International Law's Special Tribunal for Cambodia, at <http://www.globalpolicy.org/intljustice/camindx.htm.> Regarding the US refusal to financially support this tribunal, scroll to Articles 2005, then click A Cold War Hangover in US on Cambodia, reprinted from Roger Cohen, International Herald Tribune (April 9, 2005).

100. *See* G. LaForest, May the Provinces Legislate in Violation of International Law?, 39 CAN. BAR REV. 78 (1961).

101. H. Kindred et al., INTERNATIONAL LAW: CHIEFLY AS INTER-PRETED AND APPLIED IN CANADA 166–168 (6th ed. Toronto: Edmond Montgomery, 2000).

102. Regina v. Keyn, 2 Ex. D. 63, at 203 (1876) (Decided Nine Years after Canadian Independence from the UK). *See generally*, R. St. J. Macdonald, in R. Macdonald, G. Morris, & D. Johnston (Ed.), CANADIAN PERSPECTIVES ON INTERNA-TIONAL LAW AND ORGANIZATION 88 (1974).

103. Further details, and updates, are available at the American Society of International Law's The Iraq Tribunal: Toward a Trial for Saddam Husscin and Other Top Baath Leaders, at <http://www.globalpolicy.org/intljustice/iraqindex.htm>. For further detail on the past US role in Iraq, scroll to Articles 2005, then click Judgment at Baghdad, reprinted from The Nation (Mar. 12, 2005).

104. Mexican Const., Art. 89, para. X, available at: <http://www.ilstu.edu/class/hist263/docs/1917const.html>.

105. Mexican Const., Art. 133.

106. Ley de Tratados, Secretaría de Relaciones Exteriores, México. D.F., at 11 (1992).

107. J. Vargas, Vol. 2 MEXICAN LAW: A TREATISE FOR LEGAL PRACTITIONERS AND INTERNATIONAL INVESTORS, §1.37, 23–24 (St. Paul, MN: WestGroup, 1998) (translation from 1992 Treaty Law) (italics added). *See generally* M. Vazquez, DERECHO INTERNACTIONAL PUBLICO (10th ed. Mexico City: Editorial Purrua, 1991) (Spanish language text).

108. *Court* comparison: Further details, and updates, are available at the American Society of International Law's Special

Court for Sierra Leone, at <http://www.globalpolicy.org/intljustice/sierraindx.htm>. A succinct history of this country is available at <http://www.globalpolicy.org/security/issues/slindex.htm>. The basic documents of this court are available at <http://www.sc-sl.org/documents.html>. *Child Recruitment* case: Appeals Chamber's Decision on Preliminary Motion Based on Lack of Jurisdiction (Child Recruitment), Prosecutor v. Sam Hinga Norman, SCLC-2004-14-AR72 (E) (May 31, 2004). *SC-SL Statute*: <http://www.sc-sl.org/scsl-statute.html>. For the gripping detail about the related truth commissions, working in harmony with this court, see William Schabas, Truth Commissions and Courts Working in Parallel: The Sierra Leone Experience, in PROCEEDINGS OF THE 98TH ANNUAL MEETING 189 (Amer. Soc. Int'l Law: Wash., DC, 2004).

109. Further detail is available in Andre Stemmet, The Influence of Recent Constitutional Developments in South Africa on The Relationship Between International Law and Municipal Law, 33 INT'L LAWYER 47 (1999).

110. S. Prakash Sinha, New Nations and the Law of Nations 23 (A.W. Sijthoff: 1967).

111. *Punish Offenses*: Art. I, Section 8, Clause 10. *Law of the Land*: Article VI, clause 2. *Supreme Court*: 175 US 677 (1900).

112. *See generally*, J. Rogers, Treaties and Statutes Against the Background of Customary International Law, ch. 9, in INTERNATIONAL LAW AND UNITED STATES LAW 170 (Aldershot, Eng.: Ashgate, 1999)

113. Schroeder v. Bissell, 5 Fed.2d 838 (D.C. Conn., 1925). Such cases build upon the 1804 statement by the US Supreme Court that "an act of congress ought never to be construed to violate the law of nations, if any other possible construction remains." Murray v. Schooner Charming Betsy, 2 Cranch 64, 117–118 (1804).

114. Missouri v. Holland, 252 U.S. 416, 40 S.Ct. 382, 64 L. Ed. 641 (1920).

115. *See* 28 USCA §1351. The diplomatic immunity afforded by the 1961 Vienna Convention on Diplomatic Relations has effectively withdrawn the possibility of a §1351 suit against a diplomat (§7.4).

116. *See* Russian Socialist Federated Soviet Republic v. Cibrario, 235 N.Y. 255, 139 N.C. 259 (1923) (dismissing state court suit *against* Russia's unrecognized Bolshevik government) & Wulfsohn v. Russian Socialist Federated Soviet Republic, 234 N.Y. 372, 138 N.C. 24 (1923) (dismissing state court suit *by* that unrecognized government).

117. *US Federal supremacy*: United States v. Curtiss-Wright Export Corp., 299 US 304, 57 S.Ct. 216, 220, 81 L. Ed. 255 (1936). *European Union*: P. Dubinsky, The Essential Function of Federal Courts: The European Union and the United States Compared, XLII AMER. J. COMPARATIVE L. 295 (1994).

118. *Alperin* (cited in note 79 earlier), at 565–570.

119. *See, e.g.,* DaCosta v. Laird, 471 F.2d 1146 (2d Cir. 1973) (Vietnam harbor mining) & Holtzman v. Schlesinger, 484 F.2d 1307 (2d Cir. 1973) (Cambodian bombing). *See generally*, J. Charney, Judicial Deference in Foreign Relations, in L. Henkin, M. Glennon, & W. Rogers (eds.), FOREIGN AFFAIRS AND THE US CONSTITUTION 98 (Ardsley-on-Hudson, NY: Transnat'l Pub., 1990).

120. Aktepe v. USA, 105 F.3d 1400 (11th Cir., 1997), *cert. den'd*, 118 S.Ct. 685 (1998). *See generally*, M. Glennon, Foreign Affairs and the Political Question Doctrine, in L. Henkin, M. Glennon, & W. Rogers (eds.), FOREIGN AFFAIRS AND THE US CONSTITUTION 107 (Ardsley-on-Hudson, NY: Transnat'l Pub., 1990).

121. Banco Nacional de Cuba v. Sabbatino, 376 U.S. Rep. 398, 416, 84 S.Ct. 923, 934, 11 L. Ed. 2d 804 (1964).

122. 22 USC §2370(e)(2), as amended.

123. *See* Senate Foreign Relations Committee Report on [the second] Hickenlooper Amendment, S. REP. No. 1188, pt. I, 88th Cong., 2d Sess. 24 (1964).

124. United States of America v. Manuel Antonio Noriega, 746 Fed.Supp. 1506, at 1533–1534 (footnotes and case law authorities omitted), *aff'd*, 117 F.3d 1206 (11th Cir., 1997), *cert. den'd*, 118 S.Ct. 1389 (1998).

125. *Henkin* quote: L. Henkin, Preface, in HOW NATIONS BEHAVE: LAW AND FOREIGN POLICY (2d ed. New York: Columbia Univ. Press, 1979) at 47 (italics removed). *Morgenthau* quote: H. Morgenthau, Politics Among Nations: The Struggle for Power and Peace 251 (2d ed. 1954). *Root* quote: Address at Wash., DC, Apr. 24, 1908, reprinted in 2 PROCEEDINGS OF THE AMERICAN SOCIETY OF INTERNATIONAL LAW 14, 19 (1908).

126. G. Will, The Perils of 'Legality,' in Newsweek, at 66 (Sept. 10, 1990).

127. Markus Burgstaller, THEORIES OF COMPLIANCE WITH INTERNATIONAL LAW 21–22 (Martinus Nijhoff: 2005).

128. J. Rubenfeld, What Good is International Law?: The Two World Orders, 27 WILSON QUARTERLY 22, 32 (2003).

129. The Schooner Exchange v. McFadden, 136 US (7 Cranch) 116, 136 (1812) (Marshall, C. J.) (italics added).

130. B. Weston, R. Falk & H. Chatsworth, ch. 1, The Concept of International Law, in INTERNATIONAL LAW AND WORLD ORDER: A PROBLEM-ORIENTED COURSEBOOK 20 (3d ed. St. Paul, MN: WestGroup: 1997).

131. Saint Peter's College (New Jersey) political science Professor Richard Thurston inspired the development of this useful analogy.

CHAPTER TWO

States

INTRODUCTION

This chapter focuses on the *primary* actor under International Law—the State and its associated entities. As suggested by the adjacent text box description, the term "State" can be ambiguous. As aptly characterized by Jawarhal Nehru University's Professor Bhupinder Chimni, in his expose on the economic recolonization of the Third World: "The State is the principal subject of international law. But the relationship between State and international law continually evolves. Each era sees the material and ideological reconstitution of the relationship between state sovereignty and international law. The changes are primarily driven by dominant social forces and States of the time."[1]

After defining the contours of legal capacity, this chapter surveys the unprecedented alteration in the infrastructure of International Law caused by the vast increase

NEW YORK (August 24, 2000)—Afghanistan's ruling Taliban movement appealed to the world Thursday to give it official recognition and the seat at the United Nations that is still held by its opponents. "Afghanistan has completed all the criteria for official recognition," Afghan ambassador to Pakistan Maulvi Mohammad Saeed-ur-Rehman Haqqani told a news conference. . . .

The Taliban Islamic Emirate's appeal for world recognition preceded next month's U.N. General Assembly session where the question of the Afghan seat is likely to come up. "Law and order prevails in the country and there is a unified government ruling the country," Haqqani said. "There is peace and prosperity and people. . . . The people of Afghanistan are happy with the sovereignty of the Islamic Emirate of Afghanistan and, therefore, we expect the international community would help the people of Afghanistan."

—Reuters News Service, Afghan Taliban Demand World Recognition. Full story available at: <http://www.globalpolicy.org/security/issues/afghan/000825.htm>.

in the number of State actors after World War II. This phenomenon was caused by events that included the 1960s decolonization movement and the 1990s splintering of larger States into smaller ones.

When an entity is a "State," it possesses special rights, and incurs special obligations, including the following:

◆ *Recognition* by other States and organizations.
◆ *State responsibility* under International Law (substantive rules governing State conduct).
◆ Entitlement to *sovereign immunity* from suit by a foreign nation, and the historic immunity for its leader for acts undertaken while in office, no matter how heinous.

◆ 2.1 LEGAL PERSONALITY

A State's legal personality gives it the capacity to conduct relations on an international level. Individuals and corporate entities within that State do not have the same status under International Law. They lack the legal capacity to engage in international relations and cannot undertake State action within the community of nations.

If you were the CEO of a corporation, and I were to steal some of your corporate property, your corporation would have the legal capacity to sue me to recover the value of your stolen asset (or to initiate a criminal action). Assume, instead, that I am a government agent in another country. I nationalize the identical corporate asset. Your country would possess the legal capacity to sue my country in the International Court of Justice (ICJ). You or your corporation would not have the legal power to sue me or my State under general principles of International Law. Commentators often refer to your State's entitlement to take such action as illustrating its capacity to act on the "international plane" or the "international level."

Former UN Secretary-General Boutros-Ghali affirmed the primacy of the State in international affairs in his 1992 *Agenda for Peace Report* to the General Assembly. He therein stated that "[t]his wider mission [of making the United Nations stronger and more efficient] . . . will demand the concerted attention and effort of individual States, or regional and non-governmental organizations and of all of the United Nations system . . . [but the] foundation stone of this work is and must remain the State. Respect for its fundamental sovereignty and integrity are crucial to any common international progress." This principle was reaffirmed at the outset of his ensuing 1995 edition: "For almost three centuries, a set of principles of international cooperation has been in the making. . . . In

almost every area, . . . nations working together, through the United Nations, are setting the global agenda."[2]

This view of the State as the primary international actor is not new. More than four decades earlier, one of the most prominent International Law scholars described the continuing dominance of the State as the central feature of the international system. Professor Wolfgang Friedmann of Columbia University acknowledged this primacy because it "is by virtue of their lawmaking power and monopoly that states enter into bilateral and multilateral compacts, that wars can be started or terminated, that individuals can be punished or extradited . . . and [the very notion of 'State' would be] eventually superseded *only* if national entities were absorbed in[to] a world state. . . ."[3]

These are the preliminary questions for your study of the State in International Law: What does the term "State" mean? Under what conditions does an entity become a "State" (elements of statehood)? What is the relationship between a "State" (e.g., Germany's Bavaria) within a group of associated "States" (i.e., the German nation) under International Law?

"STATE"

Like many other legal terms, the word *State* means different things to different people. In the International Law context, a State is typically defined as a group of societies within a readily defined geographical area, united to ensure their mutual welfare and security. Commentators have long debated the appropriate nomenclature for describing this entity, advocating terms like "nation" or "State." The terms *State, nation, nation-State, community, country, people, government,* and *sovereign* are often used interchangeably. The following words in the Preamble to the UN Charter (italics added) provide a convenient example of such usages: "We the *peoples* of the United *Nations* . . . [h]ave resolved to combine our efforts . . . [through] our respective *Governments*. . . ."

There are some subtle differences among such terms, but heads of State, diplomats, speakers, and writers do not always offer such detail for their respective audiences. Reading the following short list of definitions will generate a healthy degree of caution when one is attempting to digest such discourses on International Law:

◆ *State:* "a person of international law [that] should possess the following qualifications: (a) a permanent population; (b) a defined territory; (c) government;

and (d) capacity to enter into relations with other States."

◆ *Nation:* "a practical association of human individuals who consider themselves to be a nation (on the basis of a shared religion, history, language or any other common feature)."

◆ *Nation-State:* the joinder of two terms, typically referring to a specific geographic area constituting a sovereign entity and possibly containing more than one group of nationals (individual citizens) based on shared religion, history, or language.

◆ *Community:* "a group of persons living in a given country or locality, having race, religion, language and traditions of their own, and united by the identity of such . . . in a sentiment of solidarity. . . ."

◆ *Country:* the territorial element of the term State, with attendant borders that define its land mass.

◆ *People:* "the permanently residing population of a territory with an internationally legal status (state, mandate territory, etc.)."

◆ *Government:* in International Law, the political group or entity responsible for engaging in foreign relations, which is the "true and lawful government of the state . . . which ought to exercise sovereignty, but which may be deprived of this right by a government *de facto*."

◆ *Sovereign:* occasional synonym for State or nation, although it actually describes "the evolving relationship between state and civil society, between political authority and the community . . . [being] as both an idea and an institution integral to the structure of Western thought . . . and to a geopolitical discourse in which territory is sharply demarcated and exclusively controlled."[4]

ELEMENTS OF STATEHOOD

When an entity achieves Statehood, it is entitled to the following—as classically restated in the Charter of the Organization of American States: "the State has the right to defend its integrity and independence, to provide for its preservation and prosperity, and consequently to organize itself as it sees fit, to legislate concerning its interests, to administer its services, and to determine the jurisdiction and competence of its courts. The exercise of these rights is limited only by the exercise of the rights of other States in accordance with international law."[5]

Not all State-like entities can properly lay claim to that status under International Law. So when is an entity entitled to Statehood in the international sense of the word? Are so-called "rogue States" nevertheless States under International Law?[6]

Four elements normally vest a State with "international legal personality." Under the 1933 Montevideo Inter-American Convention on the Rights and Duties of States, a "State as a person of international law should possess the following qualifications: (a) a permanent population; (b) a defined territory; (c) government; and (d) capacity to enter into relations with other States."[7] The simultaneous presence of these elements identifies a sovereign entity entitled to such international personality.

These treaty-based legal criteria for statehood have been widely adopted. Yet the level of acceptance has not been matched by simplicity of application. One reason is that the absence of one or more of these distinct elements, even over a period of time, does not necessarily deprive a State of its international personality. Analytical problems most often arise when larger States break up into smaller ones, as did the former Yugoslavia after the demise of the Soviet Union; or when one part of a nation attempts to secede, as in the American Civil War of the 1860s; and Quebec's potential secession from Canada;[8] or a foreign power's exercise of *de facto* control over another State—like Nazi Germany's expansion in Europe, or South Africa's long but unentitled dominion of the South-West Africa Trust Territory (now Namibia). Nevertheless, the above four *Montivideo* elements of Statehood are the essentials.

Population Component   The permanent population element is probably the least important of these elements of statehood. Neither a minimum population nor an express grant of nationality to the inhabitants is required for qualification as a State.[9] Nor does the absence of part of the population over a period of time necessarily vitiate State status. The nomadic tribes on the Kenya-Ethiopia border, for example, have been an ambulatory element of each nation's population for centuries. The transient nature of this significant component of each State's population has not diminished the permanence of either bordering State.

Deficiencies with the other elements of statehood—defined territory and a government engaging in foreign relations—have posed more serious problems.

Territorial Component   The territorial element of Statehood is blurred by mutually exclusive claims to the same territory. A classic example is the former Arab-Israeli territorial conflict, which had its roots in the United

Nations' plan to partition Palestine. This plan, devised in 1947 to divide Palestine into an Arab State and a Jewish State, was not implemented due to the Middle East War that erupted in 1948. Israel was able to expand its territory beyond that provided for by the UN plan, displacing millions of Arabs.

Columbia University's Professor Philip Jessup represented the United States in the UN Security Council in 1948 and later became a judge of the ICJ. He used the following illustration to demonstrate why Israel nevertheless satisfied the doctrinal elements of statehood as early as 1948:

On the Condition of Statehood

3 UN Security Council Official Records
383rd Meeting, at 9–12 (1948)

Over a year ago the United States gave its support to the principles of the majority plan proposed by the United Nations Special Committee on Palestine. That plan envisaged the creation of both a Jewish State and an Arab State in Palestine. We gave our support to the resolution of 29 November 1947 by which the General Assembly recommended a plan for the future government of Palestine involving, as one of its elements, the establishment of a Jewish State in part of Palestine. . . .

The Security Council now has before it the application of the Provisional Government of Israel for membership [in the United Nations]. The consideration of the application requires an examination of . . . the question of whether Israel is a State duly qualified for membership. Article 4 of the Charter of the United Nations specifies the following:

"Membership in the United Nations is open to peace-loving States which accept the obligations contained in the present Charter and, in the judgment of the Organization, are able and willing to carry out these obligations. . . ."

The first question which may be raised in analyzing Article 4 of the Charter and its applicability to the membership of the State of Israel, is the question of whether Israel is a State, as that term is used in Article 4 of the Charter. It is common knowledge that, while there are traditional definitions of a State in international law, the term has been used in many different ways. We are all aware that, under the traditional definition of a State in international law, all the great writers have pointed to four qualifications: first, there must be a people; second, there must be a territory; third, there must be a government; and, fourth, there must be capacity to enter into relations with other States of the world.

In so far as the question of capacity to enter into relations with other States of the world is concerned, learned academic arguments can be and have been made to the effect that we already have, among the Members of the United Nations, some political entities which do not possess full sovereign freedom to form their own international policy, which traditionally has been considered characteristic of a State. We know, however, that neither at San Francisco nor subsequently has the United Nations considered that complete freedom to frame and manage one's own foreign policy was an essential requisite of United Nations membership.

I do not dwell upon this point because . . . Israel is free and unhampered. On this point, I believe that there would be unanimity that Israel exercises complete independence of judgment and of will in forming and in executing its foreign policy. The reason for which I mention the qualification of this aspect of the traditional definition of a State is to underline the point that the term "State," as used and applied in Article 4 of the Charter of the United Nations, may not be wholly identical with the term "State" as it is used and defined in classic textbooks of international law.

When we look at the other classic attributes of a State, we find insistence that it must also have a Government. No one doubts that Israel has a Government. I think the world has been particularly impressed with the way in which the people of Israel have organized their government and have established a firm system of administration and of law-making under the most difficult conditions. Although, pending their scheduled elections, they still modestly and appropriately call themselves the Provisional Government of Israel, they have a legislative body which makes laws, they have a judiciary which interprets and applies those laws, and they have an executive which carries out the laws and which has at its disposal a considerable force responsive to its will.

According to the same classic definition, we are told that a State must have a people and a territory. Nobody questions the fact that the State of Israel has a people. It is an extremely homogeneous people, a people full of loyalty and of enthusiastic devotion to the State of Israel.

The argument seems chiefly to arise in connection with territory. One does not find in the general classic treatment of this subject any insistence that the territory of a State must be exactly fixed by definite frontiers. We all know that, historically, many States have begun their existence with their frontiers unsettled. Let me take as one example my own country, the United States of America. Like the State of Israel in its origin, it had certain territory along the seacoast. It had various indeterminate claims to an extended territory westward. But, in the case of the United States, that land had not even

been explored, and no one knew just where the American claims ended and where French and British and Spanish claims began. To the North, the exact delimitation of the frontier with the territories of Great Britain was not settled until many years later. And yet, I maintain that, in the light of history and in the light of the practice and acceptance by other States, the existence of the United States of America was not in question before its final boundaries were determined.

The formulae in the classic treatises somewhat vary, one from the other, but both reason and history demonstrate that the concept of territory does not necessarily include precise delimitation of the boundaries of that territory. The reason for the rule that one of the necessary attributes of a State is that it shall possess territory is that one cannot contemplate a State as a kind of disembodied spirit. Historically, the concept is one of insistence that there must be some portion of the earth's surface which its people inhabit and over which its Government exercises authority.

◆ *Notes*

1. For insights on the "Palestine" issue, *see* the Palestine Mandate, based on the 1917 Balfour Declaration "in favor of the establishment in Palestine of a national home for the Jewish people, it being clearly understood that nothing should be done which might prejudice the civil and religious rights of existing non-Jewish communities in Palestine." *See* Preambular wording at: <http://www.yale.edu/lawweb/avalon/mideast/palmanda.htm>. Article 8 of the League Mandate provided that: "The Administration of Palestine shall be responsible for enacting a nationality law . . . to facilitate the acquisition of Palestinian citizenship by Jews who take up their residence in Palestine." See <http://en.wikisource.org/wiki/Palestine_Mandate>. On the US position enunciated to the United Nations in 1947: "In the final analysis the problem of making any solution work rests with the people of Palestine." *Point 10*, at <http://www. yale.edu/lawweb/avalon/decade/decad164.htm>. On the occasion of the UN Partition of Palestine: "Independent Arab and Jewish States and the Special International Regime for the City of Jerusalem . . . shall come into existence in

Palestine two months after the evacuation of the armed forces of the mandatory Power [the U.K.] has been completed but in any case not later than 1 October 1948. The boundaries of the Arab State, the Jewish State, and the City of Jerusalem shall be as described . . . below." Part I, A (Termination of British Mandate & Partition of Palestine), available at <http://www.yale.edu/lawweb/avalon/un/res181.htm>. But as recently as October 2005, Iran's President, Mahmoud Ahmadinejad proclaimed that: "Israel must be wiped off the map." Further detail is provided in the §6.2 *Palestinian Wall Case*, and Problem 2.A at the end of this chapter.

2. Prior to the 1995 Dayton peace agreement establishing various geopolitical entities within Bosnia, the Serbs in Bosnia sought to maintain control of an area they referred to as "Republica Srpska." Their objective was to drive out Muslims and Croats, to establish a Serb enclave within Bosnia. In the §1.4 *Kadic v. Karadzic* case, the issue was whether Karadzic was "acting under color of state law," for purposes of establishing his responsibility for numerous atrocities occurring in the Srpska area of Bosnia. On the question of

whether this area within Bosnia was a "State," the court noted as follows:

> The definition of a state is well established in international law: Under international law, a state is an entity that has a defined territory and a permanent population, under the control of its own government, and that engages in, or has the capacity to engage in, formal relations with other such entities. "[A]ny government, however violent and wrongful in its origin, must be considered a *de facto* government if it was in the full and actual exercise of sovereignty over a territory and people large enough for a nation" . . .

Appellants' allegations entitle them to prove that Karadzic's regime satisfies the criteria for a state, for purposes of those international law violations requiring state action. Srpska is alleged to control defined territory, control populations within its power, and to have entered into agreements with other governments. It has a president, a legislature, and its own currency. These circumstances readily appear to satisfy the criteria for a state in all aspects of international law. Moreover, it is likely that the state action concept, where applicable for some violations like "official" torture, requires merely the semblance of official authority. The inquiry, after all, is whether a person purporting to wield official power has exceeded internationally recognized standards of civilized conduct, not whether statehood in all its formal aspects exists. *Kadic v. Karadzic,* 70 Fed.3d 232 (2nd Cir., 1995), *rehearing den'd,* 74 Fed.3d 377 (2nd Cir., 1996), *cert. den'd* 518 U.S. 1005 (1997).

Government Component The "government" element of statehood is problematic when separate entities, operating in different regions within a State, claim that each is the legitimate government of the entire territory. Modern examples include Nationalist and Communist China, North and South Korea, and the two Vietnamese governments of the 1960s and 1970s. In each instance, separate entities—possessing administrative and legislative authority—claimed the exclusive right to govern. External interference by other States contributed to the rigidity that caused each government to adopt and maintain inflexible postures regarding the potential for a shared power arrangement.

Another example of this overlapping governance arises in the awkward situation where an established government *should* be maintaining political order, but civil war or external threat have impacted its ability to actually "lead the way." The "Finland" of 1917 is a classic example. Shortly after achieving independence from what was destined to become a strong centralized Soviet Union, the Finnish government was engaged in a territorial dispute with Russia regarding some islands off Finland's coast. The League of Nations appointed jurists to analyze the issue, when Finland attained independence. They also explored the fundamental requirement of an effective government (for statehood). Under their succinct description of this element:

> the conditions required for the formation of a sovereign State did not exist. In the midst of revolution and anarchy, certain elements essential to the existence of a State . . . were lacking for a fairly considerable period. Political and social life was disorganized; the [civil] authorities were not strong enough to assert themselves; civil war was rife; further, . . . the Government had been chased from the capital and forcibly prevented from carrying out its duties; the armed camps and the police were divided into two opposing forces, and Russian troops, and after a time Germans also, took part in the civil war. . . . It is therefore difficult to say at what exact date the Finnish Republic, in the legal sense of the term, actually became a definitely constituted sovereign State. This certainly did not take place until a stable political organization had been created, and until the public authorities [of Finland] had become strong enough to assert themselves throughout the territories of the State without the assistance of foreign troops.

Somalia, depicted in the 2001 movie "Black Hawk Down," exemplifies the contemporary problem of an African nation that obtained its independence in the 1960s, but has since had perennial governance problems. In 1993, the UN Secretary-General fled for his life, during a visit designed to support the unsuccessful Somalian UN peacekeeping effort. The currently recognized, transitional Parliament and president in exile sit in Kenya's capitol city of Nairobi. It is unsafe for these elected leaders to return to Somalia. Clan-based militias have been responsible for the deaths of 500,000 people since the 1991 ouster of Somalia's former dictator. The nation's infrastructure has been devastated. There is no civil service, treasury, or buildings within which to meet. Thirteen peace efforts since 1991 formed two governments that have failed, because they never assumed effective control of Somalia.

After the 2003 US invasion of Iraq, the Coalition Provisional Authority was the recognized occupying power. When it dissolved on June 30, 2004, a fresh Iraqi interim government began to exercise sovereignty. But its control was not complete, in the traditional Westphalian sense. It did not have "effective control" of Iraq at the moment of its creation, nor later, as demonstrated by the raging insurgency. Elections of course provided a degree of legitimacy. But the presence of some 150,000 foreign coalition military troops, and a roughly equal number of police and various Iraqi security forces, failed to secure Iraq's borders. The onslaught of foreign "jihadists" determined to get the United States completely out of Iraq, and to topple any US-backed regime, militated against the characterization of Iraq's government as exhibiting effective control over Iraq.[10]

Foreign Relations Component The attribute requiring the "capacity to enter into relations with other States" is arguably the most decisive criterion for statehood. Under International Law, to be considered a "State," an entity must function independently of any authority, other than which might be imposed by International Law. Not all entities referred to as a "State" possess this capacity.

Some provincial entities engage in foreign relations, although another and more powerful governmental entity in the region disputes its legal right to do so. This typically occurs when there is a "breakaway" province, wherein the inhabitants seek to establish their right of self-determination (§2.3). Taiwan, for example, was a province of China for thousands of years. A number of countries recognize Taiwan as an independent nation. Chechnya yields another example. In January 2000, Afghanistan's Taliban government became the first State to recognize Chechnya. Chechnya opened an embassy in Kabul and commenced the process of appointing its first Ambassador (to Afghanistan).[11]

An entity may possess the characteristics of sovereignty, without actually being in control of its populace and territory. Foreign relations responsibilities may be entrusted to another State. Certain dependent States may be monitored by other more established States. The

governmental functions of such "mandated" (League of Nations) or "trust" territories (United Nations) will be addressed in Chapter 3 on the UN Trusteeship Council.

Under International Law, only the *national* government has the legal capacity to engage in foreign relations. Yet an increasing number of local state governments typically engage in international trade relations, crime control, and other governmental matters. The more that these nonfederal political entities operate in cross-border fashion, the more likely a conflict between the state and federal approach to a problem. One might question, for example, the appearance of nine US states— but not the federal government—at the December 2004 Buenos Aires annual conference on climate change. On the eve of the Kyoto Protocol on greenhouse emissions entering into force, the United States was not formally represented—and to no one's surprise, given their objections to this treaty on economic grounds (§12.2). But two dozen US states have taken steps to pursue emissions control programs.

A classic illustration of the potential State-state conflict within one nation was presented by the so-called Massachusetts Burma Law. The US Supreme Court stuck down a state law imposing sanctions on Massachusetts businesses that traded with Burma. The federal approach to dealing with Burma's human rights problem was more liberal. The national government desired more flexibility in dealing with the human rights record of Burma's military government (which renamed the country Myanmar). The Supreme Court characterized the Massachusetts law as "an obstacle to the accomplishment of Congress's full objectives under the federal Act. We find that the state law undermines the intended purpose . . . of at least three provisions of the federal Act, that is, its delegation of effective discretion to the President to control economic sanctions against Burma, its limitation of sanctions [applicable] solely to United States persons and new investment, and its directive to the President to proceed diplomatically in developing a comprehensive, multilateral strategy toward Burma."

The Court ruled similarly in its 2003 Holocaust Victim Insurance Relief Act case, wherein federal law preempted a California law requiring insurance companies to disclose certain information about policies they or their affiliates wrote in Europe, between 1920 and 1945. A strongly-worded four justice dissent agreed that the California Legislature should not speak on foreign policy issues. However, that was not the effect of this particular state law. Although "the federal approach differs from California's, no executive agreement or other formal expression of foreign policy disapproves state disclosure laws like the HVIRA. Absent a clear statement aimed at disclosure requirements by the 'one voice' to which courts properly defer in matters of foreign affairs, I would leave intact California's enactment."[12]

◆ 2.2 SHIFTING STATE INFRASTRUCTURE

Earlier sections of this book introduced the fundamentals regarding the development, definition, and general application of International Law. This section focuses on the dramatic change that has occurred in the makeup of the community of nations since World War II. The 1648 Treaty of Westphalia, which produced nation-States as we know them, evolved over the ensuing 300 years to yield approximately fifty nations by the close of World War II. In the last sixty years, however, the makeup of a number of those original countries has not only changed, but there are now nearly 200 diverse States (Exhibit 2.1).

Why such drastic change in so short a period? The contemporary rules of modern International Law, by comparison, evolved over a span of three centuries. The imprint on its development was marked by a comparatively homogenous group of nations, primarily in Europe. The European essence of International Law is captured by Holland's Professor J. H. Verzijl, who in 1955 noted emphatically that "there is one truth that is not open to denial or even to doubt, namely, that the actual body of international law, as it stands today, is not only the product of the conscious activity of the European mind, but has also drawn its vital essence from a common source of European beliefs, and in both of these aspects it is mainly of Western European origin."[13]

Predictably, this Western-derived basis for International Law has been criticized by scholars from both Western and non-Western nations. Queen's University (Ireland) Professor George Alexandrowicz characterized this European essence of International Law as being unacceptably ethnocentric. In his view, "Asian States, who for centuries had been considered members of the family of nations, found themselves in an *ad hoc* created legal vacuum which reduced them from the status of international personality [statehood] to the status of candidates competing for such personality."[14]

One can also criticize past indiscretions. The Berlin Congress of 1885, referred to more transparently as the West Africa Conference, resolved that the African continent was sufficiently uncivilized to warrant its colonization in the best interests of all nations. In a valiant, egalitarian gesture, this conference of European powers deemed slavery abolished. That institution was then conveniently characterized as violating the laws of nature. The real reason for this abolition, however, was prompted by the limited workforce[s] on the Western Coast of Africa, depopulated by the three-centuries-long export trade of slave labor to the Americas.

In 1945, fifty sovereign nations gathered at San Francisco to develop an agreement to set the basic parameters for future international relations (UN Charter). Since then, this community has quadrupled in size to nearly 200 States, most of whom are UN members. The "charter" members no longer exercise the degree of control they enjoyed at inception, when five of them were able to "call the shots" as the permanent, nonrotating members of the Security Council: China, the Soviet Union, Great Britain, France, and the United States. These were the most influential participants in the conduct of world affairs at the close of World War II. Many of them had colonies, countries, or some form of protectorates under their control at the time.

As you peruse Exhibit 2.1, observe the influx of new States in two notable eras. One was the 1960s, when colonialism was starting to give way to the self-determination of peoples, especially in Africa (§2.4). The other relevant era was the 1990s, after the collapse of the Soviet Union. The Cold War had effectively suppressed popular aspirations, both "good" and "bad," among the populations of Eastern Europe and other places. Suddenly, the Soviet Union splintered into a number of independent nations no longer tied to policies dictated from Moscow. Yugoslavia splintered into a group of independent States. Within those new countries, there would be even further attempts to adjust sovereign control by making small States out of larger predecessors—spawned in part by the "ethnic cleansing" designed to divvy up Bosnia, Serbia, and other Balkan theaters.

◆ 2.3 RECOGNITION

Recognition has a variety of meanings. It generally refers to one State's willingness to establish or maintain official relations with another State, its government, or some belligerent group within another State. The materials in this section focus on recognition of an individual State by another, with a brief comparison of *collective* recognition of a State by an international organization of States.

Writers and jurists have described recognition as one of the most chaotic and theoretically confusing topics in International Law. It is certainly one of the most sensitive and controversial.[15] Recognition of another State, or an entity within it, typically involves a mixture of political, military, and international considerations described later.

Prominent examples include: the 1903 US recognition of the nation of Cuba, in exchange for maintaining a US military base at Guantanamo Bay (§10.7 *Rasul* case); the continued US refusal to recognize the Castro government, since its 1959 coup d'état; and the twenty-two member Arab League refusal to recognize Iraq's US-appointed Governing Council in 2003. As an indicator of the political nature of recognition, the latter refusal was rooted in this postinvasion governing entity's being "dismissed by many in Iraq and across the Arab world as a puppet of Iraq's U.S. and British occupiers."[16] The Arab League recognized the US-installed Iraqi Governing Council as being suitable for filling Iraq's seat in the Arab League, left empty, during the US-initiated war in Iraq. As of two years later, only Australia, the United States, and the United Kingdom had recognized the Iraqi Governing Council as the *de jure* government of Iraq.

RECOGNITION BY A STATE

Recognition of States   The first of the three distinct State recognition scenarios is whether to recognize another "State" (as opposed to a new "government"). Argentina's former Judge of the ICJ aptly describes recognition of a new State as "a unilateral act whereby one or more States admit, whether expressly or tacitly, that they regard the . . . political entity as a State; consequently, they also admit that the . . . entity is an international legal personality, and as such is capable of acquiring international rights and contracting international obligations."[17] But the term "recognition of States" means different things to different people. As acknowledged by Senior Researcher Olivier Ribbelink, at the T.M.C. Asser Institute in The Netherlands:

A distinction must be made between recognition of States and recognition of governments. Recognition of a State only becomes an issue with the appearance of a "new" State. When there is no new State, [unlike a new government,] the issue does not arise. Recognition of a State means that, according to the recognising State, that specific State fulfils the criteria for statehood [§2.1]. . . .

However, sometimes individual States do add their own criteria or conditions. For example, Switzerland which stated that another . . . exclusively political and extremely important criterion is that Switzerland wishes to be able to control ("maitriser") the effects of an act of recognition, which is taken to mean that it is essential to recognize a State only when its security is by and large assured and guaranteed ("assurèe et garantie").[18]

Receiving recognition is one of the highest-ranking political goals for a new State. Its leaders desire equality of status with the other members of the international community. Statehood, and the distinct but related recognition decision by other States, enables new States to engage in international relations. Recognition is a minimum requirement that, much like needing "jacks or better to open" in a poker game, yields an enhanced stake in the game. Russia, for example, was keenly interested in the international recognition of its new republic, formed after a forty-year Cold War that stagnated its economy and embroiled it in adverse relations with democratic nations. The United States recognized Russia (and a number of other members of the former Soviet Union) almost immediately after creation of the Commonwealth of Independent States in 1991. The United States delayed recognition of Ukraine, on the other hand, until it was clear to the United States that Ukraine could function in harmony with the same Russia that had dominated Ukraine for nearly 600 years.

A new State may be recognized almost immediately, or in some cases, years after it is formed. The very existence of the German Democratic Republic (formerly East Germany) was considered a breach of the Soviet Union's duties under its post–World War II treaties with the Allied powers regarding the administration of German territory. It was obviously a "State," in terms of its *de facto* status (§2.1 elements). Many Western nations did not recognize East Germany's *de jure* existence, however, until 1973. A series of unilateral recognitions ultimately cured what many Western nations perceived as an illegal State regime.

There may also be delayed recognition of a State, although it is recognized by some or many other States. The Vatican did not recognize the State of Israel until

EXHIBIT 2.1   SOVEREIGN STATES: FROM UN INCEPTION TO THE PRESENT

UN MEMBERS	AMERICAS		EUROPE		ASIA & OCEANIA		AFRICA	
1945 ORIGINAL MEMBERS	Argentina	Guatemala	Belgium	Norway	Australia	Saudi Arabia	Egypt	South Africa
	Bolivia	Haiti	Belorussia	Poland	"China"	Syria	Ethiopia	
	Brazil	Honduras	◆ '91 name change to Belarus	Turkey	◆ Taiwan until '71		Liberia	
	Canada	Mexico		Ukraine	◆ now PRC seated			
	Chile	Nicaragua	Czecho-slovakia	USSR	India			
	Colombia	Panama	◆ split '93 into Czech Republic and Slovak Republic	◆ until '91	Iran			
	Costa Rica	Paraguay		◆ now Russian Federation	Iraq			
	Cuba	Peru		United Kingdom	Lebanon			
	Dominican Republic	United States		Yugoslavia	New Zealand			
	Ecuador	Uruguay	Denmark	◆ split '92	Philippines			
	El Sal-vador	Venezuela	France	◆ now Serbia and Monte-negro				
			Greece					
			Luxem-bourg					
			Nether-lands					
1945–1965	Jamaica	Trinidad and Tobago	Albania	Ireland	Afghanistan	Laos	Benin	Guinea
			Austria	Italy	Burma	Malaysia	Burundi	Madagascar
			Bulgaria	Malta	◆ now Myanmar	Maldives	Burkina Faso	Malawi
			Cyprus	Portugal	Cambodia	Mongolia	Cameroon	Mali
			Finland	Romania	◆ now Kampuchea	Nepal	Central African Republic	Mauritania
			Hungary	Spain	Indonesia	Pakistan		Niger
			Iceland	Sweden	Israel	Singapore	Chad	Nigeria
					Japan	Sri Lanka	Côte d'Ivoire (Ivory Coast)	Rwanda
					Jordan	Thailand		Senegal
					Kuwait	Yemen		Sierra Leone
							Congo	Somalia
							Democratic Republic of the Congo	Sudan
								Togo
								Tunisia
							Gabon	Uganda
							Ghana	Zambia
1965–1985	Antigua and Barbuda	Belize (was British Honduras)	Federal Republic of Germany ◆ until 1990 ◆ now Germany	German Democratic Republic ◆ until 1990 ◆ now Germany	Bahrain	Democratic Yemen Yemen and Democratic Yemen merged 1990	Algeria	Comoros
	The Bahamas	Dominica			Bangladesh		Angola	Equatorial Guinea
	Barbados	Grenada			Bhutan		Botswana	Gambia
		Guyana			Brunei		Brunei Darussalam	Guinea-Bissau
							Cape Verde	Guyana

EXHIBIT 2.1 SOVEREIGN STATES: FROM UN INCEPTION TO THE PRESENT (CONTINUED)

UN MEMBERS	AMERICAS		EUROPE		ASIA & OCEANIA		AFRICA	
1965–1985	Saint Kitts and Nevis Saint Lucia	Saint Vincent and the Grenadines Suriname			Fiji Oman Papua New Guinea Qatar Solomon Islands	United Arab Emirates Vanuatu Vietnam Western Samoa	Kenya Lesotho Libya Mauritius Morocco Mozambique Papua New Guinea São Tomé and Principe Seychelles Swaziland Tanganyika ♦ until 1961	Tanzania ♦ Tanganyika and Zanzibar merge 1964/ now United Republic of Tanzania United Arab Republic ♦ Egypt & Syria brief merger Zaire ♦ now Democratic Republic of Congo Zanzibar ♦ until 1963
1985–PRESENT			Andorra Armenia Azerbaijan Bosnia and Herzegovina Croatia Czech Republic Estonia Germany ♦ former East and West Germanies	Georgia Latvia Liechtenstein Lithuania Macedonia Moldova Monaco San Marino Slovakia Slovenia Switzerland	Kazakhstan Kiribati Kyrgyzstan Marshall Islands Micronesia Nauru North Korea	Palau South Korea Tajikistan Timor-Leste Tonga Turkmenistan Tuvalu Uzbekistan	Djibouti Eritrea	Namibia Zimbabwe

NON-UN MEMBERS

Aruba,[a] Cook Islands,[b] Holy See (Vatican City), Gaza/West Bank or Palestine (PLO),[c] Kosovo,[d] Niue,[e] Taiwan, Western Sahara (located in Southern Morocco-sovereignty unresolved). The Holy See has the status of "Non-Member State Maintaining Permanent Observer Missions at UN Headquarters."

[a] Seceded from the Netherlands Antilles in 1986; now separate, autonomous member of the Kingdom of the Netherlands; movement toward full independence halted at Aruba's request in 1990

[b] Free association with New Zealand

[c] UN Observer status, nonvoting GA seat

[d] Under UN administration (geographically within Serbia)

[e] Free association with New Zealand

Table does not include territorial possessions of the above-listed States. For further details, *see* CIA Country Studies on the World Wide Web: <http://www.cia.gov/cia/publications/factbook/docs/history.html> and UN Membership Web site: <www.un.org/Overview/unmember.html>.

1994, forty-five years after Israel was admitted to the United Nations as a member State. The Vatican's recognition, not given until after the Israel-Palestine Liberation Organization (PLO) accords of 1993, was premised on many centuries of distrust between Catholics and Jews. The week before this recognition occurred, Israel's largest-selling newspaper (*Yedioth Ahronoth*) stated: "The Catholic Church is one of the most conservative, oppressive, corrupt organizations in all human history. . . . The reconciliation can be done only if the Catholic Church and the one who heads it fall on their knees and ask forgiveness from the souls of the millions of tortured who went to heaven in black smoke, under the blessing of the Holy See." This news account was referring to the Catholic Church's Inquisition of the Middle Ages, and its passive stance during the World War II Holocaust. Many Israelis believe that the Catholic Church did nothing to halt, or may have clandestinely supported, Nazi Germany's appalling treatment of Europe's Jews.[19]

De jure recognition may be prematurely granted. The European Community [now European Union (EU)] recognized Slovenia and Croatia approximately six months after their vote of independence from the former Yugoslavia. This was an arguably premature decision, which many claim to be the spark that fueled the fires between ethnic rivals in the former Yugoslavia. Recognition of Bosnia-Herzegovina was arguably premature. The Russian newspaper *Pravda* reported in its February 27, 1993, issue that the "international carnage has been largely caused by the hasty recognition [by countries including Russia] of the independence of the unstable state of Bosnia and Herzegovina." This perspective is premised on Bosnia-Herzegovina not being in control of its territory during the flurry of international recognitions shortly after its secession from the former Yugoslavia.

Belgrade immediately protested that the EU's premature recognition of former territories of Yugoslavia violated International Law. Belgrade thus asserted that the virtually immediate international recognition by other countries violated Yugoslavia's territorial sovereignty over its secessionist regions. One can readily argue that there was no *de facto* basis for recognition by other countries (of Bosnia-Herzegovina), given the lack of control exercised over the territory and populace by the new Bosnian government. However, the political nature of recognition decisions suggests that Yugoslavia's claim of premature recognition did not trigger any State responsibility for harm to Yugoslavia.

Recognition decisions are granted or denied for a variety of reasons. Since the recognizing State is usually satisfied that the legal elements of statehood are present, the essential decision of whether to recognize another State has been traditionally quite political in nature. Examples include:

1. Whether the new State has been recognized by other members of the international community
2. Ethnocentric motives stemming from the perceived inferiority of certain nations, which effectively limited the recognition of new States from outside the European community for many decades
3. A need to appease certain regimes, as when Great Britain recognized the nineteenth-century Barbary Coast, whose pirates were stealing British ships and cargoes
4. Humanitarian motives, whereby many states refused to recognize Southern Rhodesia (now Zimbabwe) because of its internal racial policies
5. Commercial and military motives.[20]

There are two theories of recognition discourse: the *constitutive* theory and the *declaratory* theory. Under the constitutive perception, members of the community of nations must recognize a new State in order to constitute or establish its *de jure* international legal personality. The declaratory view, on the other hand, is that recognition is not required for the new State to be considered legitimate. Recognition merely declares or acknowledges the existing fact of statehood.

Although the constitutive theory is still advocated by some States and scholars,[21] recognition is not a necessary condition for statehood under International Law. Recognition is a matter of political decision making at the international level. States have no duty to recognize a new State, merely because it possesses all the legal attributes of statehood. Instead, recognition is a matter of discretion. It is a political act with legal consequences. The former Yugoslavia became the Federal Republic of Yugoslavia (FRY), and is now Serbia and Montenegro, which is as much a "State" as it is now independent, former political subdivisions. The latter entity is now recognized by many countries, who in the 1990s refused to recognize the Yugoslavian "rump" State (FRY).

The prevailing declaratory theory is manifested in regional treaties that specifically negate recognition as an element of the definition of statehood. Less powerful

States do not want external recognition decisions to influence their political objectives. They do not want the more powerful nations to use recognition as a ploy to exact political concessions. Under Article 12 of the Charter of the Organization of American States, for example, the "political existence of the State is independent of recognition by other States. Even before being recognized,

the State has the right to defend its integrity and independence, to provide for its prosperity, and consequently to organize itself as it sees fit. . . . The exercise of these rights is limited only by the exercise of rights of other States in accordance with international law."

The practical consequences of nonrecognition are addressed in the following case:

Cyprus v. Turkey

EUROPEAN COURT OF HUMAN RIGHTS GRAND CHAMBER
Application no. 25781/94 May 10, 2001
<http://www.echr.coe.int/Eng/Judgments.htm>

AUTHOR'S NOTE: In 1974, Turkey began its occupation of a portion of the island of Cyprus over the objection of Greece. This was done for the expressed purpose of protecting the Turkish minority just after Greek Cypriots staged an unsuccessful coup that would have unified Cyprus and Greece. This was nevertheless an illegal occupation, because of the UN Charter prohibition on the use or threat of force in international relations. In 1997, the UN Secretary-General vowed an end to this occupation—a predicament that remains unresolved.

This court (§9.6) sits in Strasbourg, France. Under International Law, individuals harmed by government action are normally expected first to pursue local remedies provided by the alleged defendant nation—usually their own country—before seeking assistance from an international tribunal. The central issue in this case is whether the courts established by the Turkish occupying forces in northern Cyprus were legally capable of providing such domestic remedies. A majority of the judges said that they could do so. A number of judges dissented, however. As you read this opinion, consider whether you would be a majority or dissenting judge:

COURT'S (MAJORITY) OPINION . . .
3. The applicant Government alleged with respect to the situation that has existed in Cyprus since the start of Turkey's military operations in northern Cyprus in July 1974 that the Government of Turkey ("the respondent Government") have [sic] continued to violate the [European] Convention [on Human Rights]. . . .

THE CIRCUMSTANCES OF THE CASE . . .
13. The complaints raised in this application arise out of the Turkish military operations in northern Cyprus in

July and August 1974 and the continuing division of the territory of Cyprus. . . .

14. A major development in the continuing division of Cyprus occurred in November 1983 with the proclamation of the "Turkish Republic of Northern Cyprus" (the "TRNC") and the subsequent enactment of the "TRNC Constitution" on 7 May 1985.

This development was condemned by the international community. On 18 November 1983, the United Nations Security Council adopted Resolution 541 (1983) declaring the proclamation of the establishment of the "TRNC" legally invalid and calling upon all States not to recognise any Cypriot State other than the Republic of Cyprus. A similar call was made by the Security Council on 11 May 1984 in its Resolution 550 (1984). In November 1983 the Committee of Ministers of the Council of Europe decided that it continued to regard the government of the Republic of Cyprus as the sole legitimate government of Cyprus and called for respect of the sovereignty, independence, territorial integrity and unity of the Republic of Cyprus.

15. According to the respondent Government, the "TRNC" is a democratic and constitutional State, which is politically independent of all other sovereign States including Turkey, and the administration in northern Cyprus has been set up by the Turkish-Cypriot people in the exercise of its right to self-determination and not by Turkey. Notwithstanding this view, it is only the Cypriot government, which is recognised internationally as the government of the Republic of Cyprus in the context of diplomatic and treaty relations and the working of international organisations.

16. United Nations peacekeeping forces ("UNFI-CYP") maintain a buffer-zone. A number of political initiatives have been taken at the level of the United Nations aimed at settling the Cyprus problem on the basis of institutional arrangements acceptable to both sides. . . .

18. The instant application is the first to have been referred to the Court. The applicant Government requested the Court in their memorial to "decide and declare that the respondent State [Turkey] is responsible for continuing violations . . . of the Convention . . . .

These allegations were invoked with reference to four broad categories of complaints: alleged violations of the rights of Greek-Cypriot missing persons and their relatives; alleged violations of the home and property rights of displaced persons; alleged violations of the rights of enclaved Greek Cypriots in northern Cyprus; alleged violations of the rights of Turkish Cypriots and the Gypsy community in northern Cyprus.

[Here, the court addresses the alleged violations of the rights of Greek-Cypriot missing persons and their property in the TRNC, which is governed by military courts.]

THE LAW . . .
3. As to the respondent State's responsibility under the Convention in respect of the alleged violations

69. The respondent Government disputed Turkey's liability under the Convention for the allegations set out in the application. In their submissions to the Commission, the respondent Government claimed that the acts and omissions complained of were imputable exclusively to the "Turkish Republic of Northern Cyprus" (the "TRNC"), an independent State established by the Turkish-Cypriot community in the exercise of its right to self-determination and possessing exclusive control and authority over the territory north of the United Nations buffer-zone. . . .

70. As in the proceedings before the Commission, the applicant Government contended before the Court that the "TRNC" was an illegal entity under international law since it owed its existence to the respondent State's unlawful act of invasion of the northern part of Cyprus in 1974 and to its continuing unlawful occupation of that part of Cyprus ever since. The respondent State's attempt to reinforce the division of Cyprus through the proclamation of the establishment of the "TRNC" in 1983 was vigorously condemned by the international community, as evidenced by the adoption

by the United Nations Security Council of Resolutions 541 (1983) and 550 (1984) and by the Council of Europe's Committee of Ministers of its resolution of 24 November 1983 (see paragraph 14 earlier).

71. The applicant Government stressed that even if Turkey had no legal title in international law to northern Cyprus, Turkey did have legal responsibility for that area in Convention terms, given that she exercised overall military and economic control over the area. This overall and, in addition, exclusive control of the occupied area was confirmed by irrefutable evidence of Turkey's power to dictate the course of events in the occupied area. In the applicant Government's submission, a Contracting State to the Convention could not, by way of delegation of powers to a subordinate and unlawful administration, avoid its responsibility for breaches of the Convention, indeed of international law in general. To hold otherwise would, in the present context of northern Cyprus, give rise to a grave lacuna in the system of human-rights protection and, indeed, render the Convention system there inoperative. . . .

FOR THESE REASONS, THE COURT . . .
4. *Holds* by sixteen votes to one that the facts complained of in the application fall within the "jurisdiction" of Turkey . . . and therefore entail the respondent State's responsibility under the Convention;

5. *Holds* by ten votes to seven that, for the purposes of former Article 26 (current Article 35 § 1) of the Convention, remedies available in the "TRNC" may be regarded as "domestic remedies" of the respondent State. . . .

PARTLY DISSENTING OPINION OF JUDGE PALM
[joined by five other judges]

While sharing most of the Court's conclusions in this complex case, I feel obliged to record my dissent in respect of one major issue: the significance attached by the Court to the existence of a system of remedies within the "TRNC." I consider the Court's approach to this question to be so misguided that it taints the judgment as a whole. . . .

In its *Loizidou v. Turkey* judgment of 18 December 1996 (*merits*) the Court found that Article 159 of the [TRNC] fundamental law was to be considered as invalid against the background of the refusal of the international community to regard the "TRNC" as a State under international law. It did not "consider it desirable, let alone necessary . . . to elaborate a general theory concerning the lawfulness of legislative and administrative acts of the "TRNC" (p. 2231, §§ 44–45). The Court was obviously concerned to limit its reasoning . . . to avoid straying into areas of particular complexity and delicacy concerning the "legality" of acts of an "outlaw" regime. It is my firm view that the Court should be equally careful in the present case to avoid elaborating a general theory concerning the validity and effectiveness of remedies in the "TRNC" . . .

Such a policy of judicial restraint in this area is supported by three main considerations. In the first place, any consideration of remedies gives rise to the obvious difficulty that the entire court system in the "TRNC" derives its legal authority from constitutional provisions whose validity the Court cannot recognise—for the same reasons that it could not recognise Article 159 in the *Loizidou* case—without conferring a degree of legitimacy on an entity from which the international community has withheld recognition. An international court should not consider itself free to disregard either the consistent practice of States in this respect or the repeated calls of the international community not to facilitate the entity's assertion of statehood. . . . The artificiality of this approach which reflects the reality that the "TRNC" has no standing in the international community or indeed before the Court and is recognised by Turkey alone is, in itself, a reason for the Court to exercise great caution before giving a broad ruling on the status of such "remedies" under the Convention.

Of course, I accept that even in a situation of illegality it is clearly in the interests of the inhabitants that some form of court system is set up to enable basic everyday disputes to be settled by a source of authority. Moreover, it is not to be excluded that the decisions of such courts, particularly in civil matters—divorce, custody arrangements, contracts and the like—could be recognised by the courts of other countries. Such recognition has indeed occurred from time to time, notably after the situation of illegality has ended. However, it is precisely because of the importance of such arrangements for the local population—if the situation permits that recourse be had to them—that an international court should be reluctant to venture into any examination of their legality unless it is strictly necessary to do so. Any other approach may ultimately be harmful to the *de facto* utility of such a system. For example, a finding of "illegality"

may discourage the use of such fora to settle disputes. Equally, a finding upholding the lawfulness of such arrangements in the present case could give rise to a call by the legitimate Cypriot government that such tribunals be shunned by the Greek-Cypriot community so as not to compromise the government's internationally asserted claim of illegality. The Court should not assume too readily that it is acting for the benefit of the local population in addressing the legality of such arrangements. . . .

In the present judgment the Court unwisely embarks on the elaboration of a general theory of remedies in the "TRNC." . . .

More importantly, such a general conclusion has, as a direct consequence, that the European Court of Human Rights may recognise as legally valid decisions of the "TRNC" courts and, implicitly, the provisions of the Constitution instituting the court system. Such an acknowledgment, notwithstanding the Court's constant assertions to the contrary, can only serve to undermine the firm position taken by the international community which through the United Nations Security Council has declared the proclamation of the "TRNC's" statehood "legally invalid" and which has stood firm in withholding recognition from the "TRNC." . . .

Partly Dissenting Opinion of Judge Marcus-Helmons

(Translation) . . .

Accordingly, . . . requiring the inhabitants of Cyprus to exhaust domestic remedies before the "TRNC" before applying to the European Court of Human Rights when, moreover, those remedies are known to be ineffective obviously constitutes an additional obstacle for the inhabitants to surmount in their legitimate desire to secure an end to the violation of a fundamental right by applying to Strasbourg. . . .

[T]he judgment the Court seems to jump to hasty and ill-advised conclusions which it considers to be a widely held opinion on this subject. As evidence of this, one need only examine, among other sources, the case law of the Supreme Court of the United States on the validity of the confederate acts of the South during the Civil War. It should be noted that the southern authorities were legal until they seceded (the position thus being totally different from one in which courts are illegally established after a military invasion by a neighbouring State). Shortly after the Civil War ended, the Supreme Court recognised in the cases [citations omitted] and within very strict limits that the administrative acts and judgments of the confederate courts had some validity to the extent that their aim and execution did not conflict with the authority of the national Government and did not infringe citizens' constitutional rights. . . .

◆ *Notes & Questions*

1. What was the majority's decision, and its reasoning for that decision?

2. Why did the dissenters disagree? Was their objective to deprive Greek Cypriots in Northern Cyprus from having any remedy in the TRNC military courts or the European Court of Human Rights?

3. Which opinion makes the most sense? Should the issue related to the TRNC's recognition status trump Northern Cypriot access to any available remedies?

4. UN plan to reunite the island failed. Turkish Cypriots in the north voted in favor of the reunification plan, while Greek Cypriots in the south rejected it. Each of the respective referenda had to pass for reunification to occur. With the defeat of the planned reunification, Cyprus (and nine other nations) joined the EU in 2004; however, all EU laws and benefits will apply only in the internationally recognized south. Turkey remains a candidate for EU membership. In September 2005, the EU advised Turkey that its negotiations will be paralyzed if it does not recognize "Cyprus"—as opposed to "Northern Cyprus."

5. Should the legality of a regime within State X (e.g., the TRNC) impact State Y's political recognition decision? As succinctly articulated by Dr. David Raic, of the Hague Institute for the Internationalisation:

> States are under a legal obligation not to recognize effective territorial entities which have come into existence as a result of a violation of one or more specific fundamental rules of international law. In this case "nonrecognition is said to 'bar the legality' of the act or situation in question, unless other wise legalised."
>
> . . .
>
> In addition, . . . there is a clear relationship between nonrecognition and the criteria for statehood. . . . Indeed, serious attention is called for when States withhold recognition of situations or acts where one would normally expect their recognition . . . where States are of the opinion that they are under an international *legal obligation* to withhold recognition of an otherwise effective territorial entity claiming statehood.

D. Raic, STATEHOOD AND THE LAW OF SELF-DETERMINATION 90–91 (Hague: Kluwer, 2002).

Recognition of Governments The second category of recognition decisions involves whether a State will continue relations with the new *government* of a previously recognized State. A change of government may trigger a host of political concerns for both the government desiring recognition, as well as the State considering whether to grant recognition.

As with recognition of a new State, recognition of a new government may be lawfully withheld or withdrawn. States often reconsider prior recognition decisions when the government of an existing State changes, especially when there has been an unconstitutional change in government, such as a coup d'état in a former republic. When comparing the recognition of a State versus its government, one might make the analogy with a "tree" and the "leaves" that it drops from time to time. The tree is the State. The leaves are various governments. While governments (or forms of government) may come and go, the tree remains. Sometimes, another State may choose not to recognize either the tree or the leaf it bears. That same State may decide to withdraw recognition of the particular government.[22] Two of the three countries that recognized Afghanistan's Taliban government, Saudi Arabia, and the United Arab Emirates, withdrew their recognition of the Taliban, when it refused to surrender Usama bin Laden in the aftermath of September 11, 2001 (§10.7).

Professor Stefan Talmon from Germany's University of Tubingen succinctly defines recognition, and the associated controversy, as follows:

The confusion which characterizes the subject of recognition of governments is due not so much to the unsettled state of the principles involved as to the nebulous nature of the term "recognition." The lack of any clear definition of the term has sometimes led even [one nation's] government departments to argue whether they have accorded recognition to a certain government. . . .

By the term "recognition" or "nonrecognition" may be meant an indication of willingness or unwillingness on the part of the recognizing government to establish or maintain official, but not necessarily intimate, relations with the government in question. Especially in cases of prolonged official nonrecognition of established governments States frequently speak of their willingness to "normalize" their relations with the Government in question. . . .

In the majority of cases, however, no defining formula is added to the term "recognition" and the recognizing government simply states that it recognizes or that it does not recognize a certain government or authority.[23]

Why would a nation withhold the recognition of another's government? Recognizing States are often concerned about whether the populace under a new government has actually acquiesced in the change. In addition, a sudden change in the form of government can present significant economic, political, and military concern to other States. Another reason is to support international isolation of a "rogue" nation (a term which of course means different things to different people).

For example, many states did not recognize the Hanoi-installed Kampuchea government (Cambodia, 1975) because it took power while Prince Sihanouk's UN-recognized government was in exile. The United States did not recognize the government imposed by the 1991 military coup in Haiti. After the democratic election of a Haitian leader who was acceptable to the United States, only the Vatican has recognized the new Haitian government. This particular decision was arguably premised on the Catholic Church's distaste for the ousted President Aristide, who was a former Catholic priest. North Korea has been essentially isolated from the community of nations since the Korean War. Its government is now recognized by only a handful of nations including Austria, Denmark, Finland, Italy, Portugal, and Sweden. Prior to Iraq, the United States had the largest

concentration of troops of any nation in the world stationed on the border between North and South Korea. If its so-called "rogue" status diminishes with the adoption of democratic reforms, there would likely be a flood of recognitions of its current government.

A number of new governments react adversely to renewed recognition inquiries, just because there is a new government. Their perception is that the large and economically dominant States may employ a fresh round of recognition decision making to exact new concessions from less powerful States. While the recognizing State may be merely seeking assurances that prior international obligations will continue to be performed, it might also exact other less desirable concessions. When the new government is openly hostile to the recognizing State, the latter might break diplomatic relations, impose economic sanctions, or build up its military presence in or near the territory of the unrecognized government's territory.

Under the "Tobar Doctrine" (1907), a number of Latin American states entered into treaties providing for the derecognition of states when there was an interruption of the constitutional order. It was named after Carlos Tobar, the Foreign Relations Minister of Ecuador. Its stated objective was to reduce the threat of revolution and civil war in the Inter-American system, by emphasizing the need for all governments to support the establishment of constitutionalism and democracy. Some nations thus entered into treaties embracing this apparently uncontroversial theme. But the Tobar Doctrine was widely viewed, not as shoring-up democratic principles, but as a way to stifle challenges to the regional status quo. The Tobar Doctrine was succeeded by the "Estrada Doctrine" (1930), and the Montevideo Convention on the Rights and Duties of States (1933). These initiatives reasserted the rights of States not to be subjected to what they perceived as another form of intervention in their internal affairs.

The "Estrada Doctrine" was named after Genaro Estrada, Mexico's Secretary of Foreign Relations. He complained that a revolutionary change in government should not provide other countries with a fresh opportunity to reconsider whether the new government should be recognized. By adopting the Estrada Doctrine, a number of Latin American nations addressed their concern that larger developed nations were misusing their power to undermine new governments. Latin American countries viewed any external renewal of recognition agenda as no more than a device for treading on a new government's sovereign right to conduct both internal and foreign affairs as it deemed appropriate. How the new government came into existence was not a matter for external recognition decisions by foreign powers.[24]

On the other hand, governments pondering a recognition decision tend to profess a rather principled question about a new government, when it has usurped democratic processes via a violent overthrow of a democratic regime. In Haiti, the democratically elected leader was overthrown by a military coup in 1991. The "Hutu" leaders in Rwanda massacred hundreds of thousands of people in 1994. There was a mass exodus of refugees fleeing for their lives, due to the indiscriminate machete attacks by rebel forces in Rwanda. States with more democratic and less violent traditions thus tend to avoid international relations with literally "cutthroat" regimes. In such instances, the failure to reconsider recognition presents a moral dilemma. To what degree should the community of nations thus avoid a renewed recognition dialogue? To do so means turning its head the other way, thereby acquiescing in the continued operation of a new government carrying out mass executions of innocent civilians.

If recognition is a matter for *political* decision makers, then what is the *legal* impact of recognition? A new government faces difficult legal barriers when it is not recognized by a particular country or the community of nations. An unrecognized government cannot effectively represent its interests abroad. For example, the unrecognized government and its citizens do not have access to the courts of nonrecognizing States. Such governments must endure the fiscal or political consequences of nonrecognition.[25]

A classic illustration materialized in a 1952 federal judicial opinion from California. The government-operated Bank of China at Shanghai deposited $800,000 into a US bank in San Francisco (Wells Fargo). Mao Tse-Tung subsequently overthrew the government of China in 1949. Wells Fargo then received conflicting demands to the ownership of the deposited money from, what were then, the two national "Banks of China." The mainland's new People's Republic of China (PRC) was the alleged successor to the government and property belonging to the Chinese people. The other claimant was the ousted Nationalist Chinese government, then seated in Taiwan (formerly Formosa).

Judge Goodman had to resolve which Bank of China

would receive the proceeds. He explored several grounds for resolving this matter, including (a) statehood; (b) which entity more clearly represented the Chinese people; (c) an equitable division of the deposit; and (d) whether Formosa's recognition by the US executive branch would legally foreclose the judicial ability to decide in favor of what was then the nonrecognized PRC government. Judge Goodman found that both "China's" were States. Both appeared to represent the People of China, the real owner. The Nationalist government was the original depositor. The mainland's communist authority now presided over the vast majority of Chinese people. President Truman announced that the United States recognized the Nationalist regime as the legitimate government for all of China. Judge Goodman thus felt bound to award the money to the Nationalist government.[26]

There are still remarkable recognition-related questions in US courts. Almost fifty years after Judge Goodman's decision, a US federal appellate court had to determine whether Taiwan would be entitled to the same benefits as a treaty ratified by the PRC. Beijing signed the Convention with the declaration that the Convention "shall of course apply to the entire Chinese territory including Taiwan." The underlying question was whether the US derecognition of Taiwan resulted in Taiwan being bound by China's international agreements.

In another instance, after Hong Kong reverted to PRC control (1997), litigants continued to ask US courts to identify the appropriate Chinese entity for seeking extradition from US law officials. The judicial response, like Judge Goodman's 1952 decision, was that the *executive* branch of the US government makes recognition decisions. The judicial branch thus lacks any independent power to decide whether the Hong Kong government is a legitimate "government," now that it is a subsovereign of the PRC.

The political recognition terrain has been continually arrant. Twenty-seven countries currently recognize Taiwan as an independent nation (which includes the recognition of its government). In 1979, the international community shifted from general recognition of Taiwan to the PRC. The US Congress reacted with the Taiwan Relations Act. It pledged to sell defensive arms to Taiwan, and assist, were mainland China to attack. The United States has since counseled restraint, via its long-term, but vague "One China, two solutions" policy. The United Nations then required Taiwan to yield the China seat to the PRC. In the 1990s, US President Clinton sent a naval battle group to the area, when China threatened to attack Taiwan. President Bush specified that the United States would defend Taiwan, if China were to attack. The March 2005 round of this debate flared when the National People's Congress enacted its Anti-Succession Act, authorizing the use of force—should Taiwan take further steps toward independence. China therein asserted that it "shall employ non-peaceful means and other necessary measures to protect China's sovereignty and territorial integrity." China also claims to have 700 missiles aimed at Taiwan, only 100 miles away, but has not specified the threshold for their deployment. In April 2005, the two political parties who fought the original war, ended sixty years of hostility. Each thereby pledged to thwart Taiwan's independence movement.[27]

Recognition of Belligerency   The third form of recognition decision materializes when a State decides to recognize a condition of belligerency within another State. Belligerents typically seek to overthrow the governments. Other nations may wish to officially recognize the belligerent force, or to covertly provide support to one side or the other in a civil war. The belligerent group, while not the recognized government, may nevertheless achieve a limited degree of legal personality under International Law. A revolutionary group attempting to seize power in its own country, or a portion of it, might thus be "recognized." The recognition may come initially from the existing government in the State of the belligerency, or externally from a foreign State.

The essential elements for achieving this status requires a group to:

1. Be the appropriate representative for a recognizable group
2. Exhibit some form of recognizable government
3. Field a military arm
4. Control some specific territory
5. Achieve external recognition, such as the Confederate States during the US Civil War.

Once recognized externally, such recognition then confers certain rights upon the belligerent entity—as well as on the government that opposes the belligerent entity. The US Supreme Court long ago provided a convenient listing, which includes the "rights of block-

ade, visitation, search and seizure of contraband articles on the high seas, and abandonment of claims for reparation on account of damages suffered by our citizens from the prevalence of warfare."[28]

When another country is not a party to a dispute between the belligerent forces and the forces of the regular government, it is expected to remain neutral until the belligerency is resolved. This duty of neutrality is at least as old as the historical State-centric system that has driven International Law from the time of the 1648 Treaty of Westphalia between the Holy Roman Emperor, the King of France, and their respective treaty allies. That focal treaty thus provided: "That nevertheless, neither the Emperor, nor any of the States of the Empire, shall meddle with the Wars which are now on foot between them. That if for the future any Dispute arises between these two Kingdoms, the above said reciprocal Obligation of not aiding each others Enemies, shall always continue firm."[29]

Upon such recognition, the duty to remain neutral means that an uninvolved State shall:

1. Not take sides to assist either the belligerent or the regular government
2. Not allow its territory to be used as a base for hostilities by the belligerent forces (British-Confederacy illustration earlier)
3. Acquiesce in restrictions imposed by the parties to the dispute if it wishes to remain entitled to respect of neutral State rights
4. Declare any change in status, as when it decides to side with the belligerency or the regular government
5. Must accept State responsibility under International Law for any violation of its duty of neutrality[30]

Switzerland breached this duty during World War II by providing banking assistance to Germany and sending war materials to Japan. Angola, Rwanda, Uganda, and Zambia failed to remain neutral when they provided military aid to rebels who took over some cities in the Congo in 1997. A handful of multilateral treaties on neutrality[31] generally supplement the Laws of War (which you will study in Chapter 10 on Use of Force).

Recognition of a belligerency effectively helps a group within a State to achieve its political quest for self-determination. In 1837, for example, a group of private American supporters were aiding a Canadian rebellion against British rule. They helped by running a ship, carrying men and supplies, back and forth, across the Niagra River into Canada. When the British learned of this, they sank the ship at its mooring on the US side of the border. While this famous incident is known more for its impact on the right to self-defense (§10.2), the United States would have been in violation of its third-party duty of neutrality, had Secretary of State Thomas Jefferson acquiesced in these incursions into Canadian waters.

Great Britain later recognized the Confederate States of the United States as "belligerents," when the Civil War with the Northern states of the United States began in 1861. Great Britain did not, however, observe its State duty to remain neutral as required under International Law. Ships for the Confederate South were built in British ports and prepared for war with the Union forces in the United States. As a result, the Treaty of Washington of 1871 inaugurated the *Alabama Claims* international arbitration proceedings. Two years later, Great Britain paid over $15 million to the United States as a consequence of the damages done by five vessels built for the belligerent Confederate forces. Ironically, Russian vessels paid port calls to New York and San Francisco in 1863, perceived by many observers as a tacit message that Russia then supported the Union in its quest to defeat the Confederacy. Czarist Russia observed its duty of neutrality because it took no active role in aiding the Union during the Civil War.

In 1981, France and Mexico officially recognized a leftist guerilla movement, which had fought for several years against the Colombian government. By recognizing this national liberation front as a "representative political force in Colombia," those nations acknowledged the rebels' right to participate in negotiations to end the Colombian civil war. Then in 1992, the Colombian rebels were invited to Mexico City, where they signed a cease-fire agreement with Colombian leaders. In May 2005, the Spanish parliament approved a resolution supporting the Prime Minister's proposal to engage in an open dialogue with the "ETA (Euskadi Ta Askatasuna)" Basque-area separatist movement— should it, in turn, renounce violence.

Al-Qaida would undoubtedly kill for the opportunity to be recognized as a "belligerent" entity. Its captured members have, instead, been characterized by the United States as "illegal combatants" not entitled to any rights under the Geneva Conventions (§10.7). If al-Qaida were recognized as a belligerent entity—as was the South in the US Civil War, the PLO in the Middle East, or the Basque-region ETA in Spain—it would also acquire obligations as a price tag in its global war on the United States, US allies, and moderate Arab governments.

Unlike traditional belligerent entities, however, al-Qaida has no territorial aspirations. It does not claim to be the legitimate government of a specific populated territory. Yet the US Bush Administration has made the novel claim to be "at war" with al-Qaida, arguably asserting that the latter is an international belligerency recognized by the US war on terrorism. Some key features of International Law may have changed since 9–11, but the ability of a State to be at war with a group of individuals, located in terrorist cells in various countries, is not one of them. Nor would most nations observe the right of neutrality, because of al-Qaida's methods in its quest for a new world order.

RECOGNITION BY AN INTERNATIONAL ORGANIZATION

An international organization consisting of a group of States may decide to extend (or withhold) its collective recognition. Article 1(2) of the League of Nations Covenant provided for a form of collective recognition. It permitted admission to this world body only if applicants expressed a commitment to observing international obligations. A State or other territory could attain League membership "if its admission is agreed to by two-thirds of the Assembly, provided it shall give effective guarantees of its sincere intention to observe international obligations, and shall accept . . . regulations . . . in regard to its military, naval, and air forces and armaments."

As noted by a prominent Finnish statesman in 1926, if the League of Nations did not succeed "in repelling an aggression or in preventing an occupation . . . of the territory of a Member, the other Members must not recognize that *de facto* change as final and valid *de jure*. If one of the direct consequences of that unlawful aggression has been the establishment of a new State, the Members of the League of Nations should . . . refuse to recognize that new State the existence of which is conflicting with the supreme values [of the League]. . . ."[32]

The United Nations does not collectively recognize States. The UN Charter contains prohibitions against force, as did the League Charter. Unlike the League, mere admission into the United Nations is not regarded as an act of collective recognition. The charter drafters thought it unwise to imply recognition from admission into this second-generation world body. In 1950, the Secretary-General expressly stated that the United Nations "does not possess any authority to recognize either a new State or a new government of an existing State. To establish the rule of collective recognition by the United Nations would require either an amendment to the Charter or a treaty to which all members would adhere."[33] This is one reason why the United Nations is more universal than was the League of Nations. The individual State members retain the discretion to deny recognition to a new State that has been admitted to UN membership by the organization.

The EU has taken the leading role in developing criteria for international recognition by an international organization. EU recognition requirements are comparatively objective, given that State articulations practice have not been very lucid about pinpointing the subjective criteria for recognizing other States. In 1991, the EU promulgated its Guidelines on the Recognition of New States in Eastern Europe and in the former Soviet Union. This announcement was expressly linked to its commitment to the law of self-determination of States. The EU and its member States adopted the following five criteria that States seeking recognition must satisfy:

1. respect for UN Charter provisions and its European counterpart (Conference on Security and Co-operation in Europe);
2. guarantees for ethnic and national minorities;
3. respect for the inviolability of all frontiers, which can be changed only by peaceful means and common agreement;
4. acceptance of international commitments regarding disarmament and nuclear nonproliferation; and
5. arbitration or like resolution of all disputes regarding succession and regional disputes.[34]

Similar to League of Nations practice, the EU will thereby withhold recognition from States, territories, or colonies, which are the product of international aggression. Recognition will not be given to States that violate territorial sovereignty, or fail to observe international human rights guarantees. A number of nations, including the United States heartily supported this new objective approach in the development of the International Law of recognition. It is now the only official listing of recognition factors.[35]

◆ 2.4 CHANGES IN STATE STATUS

Upon losing or achieving varying degrees of autonomy, an entity's international legal personality can change in a number of ways:

◆ Afghanistan was occupied by the Soviet Union from 1979–1989. During this period, it was unable to govern its people and territory. When attacked by the United States in 2002, it reverted to the status of an occupied territory. Although it later conducted elections, the remaining North Atlantic Treaty Organization (NATO) operation necessarily raised some question about the degree to which it is a completely independent sovereign.

◆ The fifteen former State members of the Soviet Union were governed by Moscow. This union began to disintegrate in 1989, with the collapse of the central government's ability to control so large an area and populace, under its form of economic and political management.

◆ Two States may join together—East and West Germany joined to become the reunited "Germany" in 1990, after the demise of the US/USSR Cold War.

◆ A State may cease to exist—Kuwait would have been absorbed into Iraq, absent the international response to Iraq's 1990 invasion of Kuwait.

◆ Groups within a State may secede to create their own State—Bosnia-Herzegovina, Croatia, Macedonia, and Slovenia seceded from the former Yugoslavia during a two-year period beginning in 1992.

◆ One State may peacefully separate into two States—in 1993, Czechoslovakia divided into the new States of the Czech Republic and Slovakia.

◆ A former colony may become a part of a State, and then achieve independence—Eritrea became a State in 1993, having previously been part of Ethiopia.

◆ States such as Afghanistan and Iraq may be invaded, followed by the imposition of a transitional government by an occupying power—which may or may not lead to a full transfer of sovereignty.

◆ A portion of a State may be placed under international administration, such as the UN's occupation of East Timor and Kosovo.[36]

This section addresses the changes in status that are especially important in current world affairs: succession, secession, and self-determination.

SUCCESSION

Succession means that one State takes over the territory of another State, which thereby ceases to exist. There are treaties that loosely define the term. Under Article 2 of both the 1978 Vienna Convention on Succession of States in Respect of Treaties, and the 1983 Vienna Convention on Succession of States in Respect of State Property, Archives, and Debts, the term succession of States "means the replacement of one State by another in the responsibility for the international relations of the territory."[37]

Succession occurs in a variety of circumstances including breakups and mergers. Contemporary examples include the 1993 split of Czechoslovakia into two States: the Czech Republic and Slovakia. These republics, in their respective territories, succeeded to the territory formerly occupied by the former State of Czechoslovakia. This split was referred to as the "velvet divorce" because of the bloodless nature of Czechoslovakia's separation into two distinct States. Atypically, this particular breakup was not bred by civil war or external pressure.

The converse situation is a merger, exemplified by the 1990 merger of the three territories of the Federal Republic of (West) Germany, the (East) German Democratic Republic, and the City of Berlin. The legal status of Berlin was never fully resolved, although the significant issues were laid to rest by a treaty, which effectively merged Berlin into the new integrated State of "Germany." This particular merger was fully agreed to by all the nations with any territorial interest: East Germany, West Germany, France, the (former) Soviet Union, the United Kingdom, and the United States.[38] These entities thereby succeeded to the territory that once consisted of two sovereign States and a special zone, whereby all three lost their formerly distinct international legal personalities in the process.

Succession may also occur in the more controversial scenario when a State, or a portion of it, is occupied and administered by another State. Nazi Germany's puppet State in France, referred to as the "Vichy State," ruled within the southern part of the country from 1940–1942. It subsequently maintained a shadowy existence for two more years, before dissolving in 1944. The 1974 Turkish invasion of the northern portion of Cyprus spawned a rather complicated succession scenario that has lasted over three decades.[39]

Succession can also result from independence and partition. Contemporary India is an example of both. In 1947, the territory of India achieved full independence. The new State of India replaced the former territory of the same name, which had long been under British control. The Indian territory was split into two distinct States: India and Pakistan. This partition of the former territory of India established two new international States, each with its own international legal personality.

There are numerous succession scenarios involving States, recognition, succession between international organizations, a succeeding State's responsibilities to an international organization, continuity of membership in the United Nations and in other organizations.[40] The most practical feature of this potpourri of subissues is the lingering three-part question about the effect that succession has on the following: (1) preexisting treaties made by the predecessor State; (2) successor State property rights and debt obligations; and (3) the resulting nationality of the inhabitants of the successor State.

Does the successor State take over the treaty obligations of the succeeded State? The historical view is that a new State commences its career with a clean slate. But global (and even intra-regional) perspectives are by no means uniform. When the original thirteen American colonies obtained their independence from Great Britain in 1776, the newly formed "United States" announced the emergent right of freedom from the obligations incurred by any prior treaties undertaken or affecting the territories occupied by these colonies. The former Spanish colonies of South America likewise began their statehood with a clean slate. Yet when Colombia separated from Spain in 1823, the US position was that Colombia remained bound by Spain's prior treaty commitments to the United States. In 1840, when the Texas territory gained independence from Mexico, the United States declared that all US treaty commitments with Mexico regarding Texas remained in effect.[41]

Today, there is no universal rule regarding State succession and prior *bilateral* treaty obligations, which are purely "political," as opposed to those, which are less political in nature. Political treaties such as international alliances and neutrality arrangements of the predecessor State. Generally, such treaties cease to exist when the State that concluded them ceases to exist. They specifically depend upon, and assume the existence of the contracting State, and no longer function when that State dissolves. Although there is some disagreement, nonpolitical treaties concluded by an extinct predecessor State, such as those involving commerce and extradition, generally fail to survive the extinction of the preceding State which adopted them. Yet the same treaties are likely to survive the succession, where two or more States agree to unify. When Nazi Germany absorbed Austria into Germany, the commerce treaties of the former State of Austria did not bind the successor German State. Yet the commercial treaties of the former East and West Germanies would bind today's successor State of unified Germany.

Multilateral treaties present a slightly clearer picture. They survive succession when they contain norms that have been adopted by many nations. The successor State cannot claim a "clean slate" to avoid humanitarian treatment of the citizens of the predecessor State, when such treatment is the subject of a multilateral treaty which the predecessor has ratified. This liability of the new or succeeding State is already rooted in norms of Customary International Law existing independently of the treaty, even where the succeeding State has not become a treaty party to that multilateral treaty.[42]

Does the successor State take over the property and debts of the succeeded State? The property and the debts of an extinct State normally become the property of the successor State. The public international debts of an extinct State are a common illustration of this theme. Why? Because the successor State is expected to absorb both the benefits and the burdens maintained by the former State.

An exception is often claimed when the debts of the succeeded State are contrary to the basic political interests of the successor State. International arbitrators have adopted the view that a successor State cannot be expected to succeed to such debts when they are repugnant to the fundamental interests or public policy of the succeeding State. When Yugoslavia reclaimed the territory of the "Independent Croatian State"—an unrecognized puppet regime established on Yugoslavian territory during World War II—the successor State of Yugoslavia did not have to assume the debts of the former unrecognized fascist administration.[43]

The 1983 Vienna Convention on Succession of States in Respect of State Property, Archives, and Debts addresses this question, although it has not yet received sufficient ratifications to enter into force. The successor State is entitled to the property of the former State. Succession does not extinguish obligations owed by the former State to either public or private creditors. The Succession treaty provides that succession "does not as such affect the rights . . . of creditors."[44]

Must the successor State provide its citizenship to the citizens of the succeeded State? When a State ceases to exist, so does the citizenship that it has previously conferred on its inhabitants. The former citizens of the extinct State must then look to the internal law of the successor State for their citizenship rights. This is generally a matter of internal law, rather than International Law. Yet international practice does suggest that new States confer their citizenship on those who were citizens of the succeeded State, based on habitual residence. On the other hand, the new State may not force its citizenship on individuals within what has become a subjugated State. This would preclude Israel, for example, from imposing its citizenship on people within the "occupied territories" (§6.2) it has acquired as a result of various wars.[45]

Succession of Governments   Unlike the possible avoidance of obligations when a new *State* comes into existence, a new *government* may not claim a "clean slate." Otherwise, the stability of international relations would be significantly undermined if questions of succession to obligations arose every time a new government assumed power. International Law theory provides further support for the view that new governments cannot avoid international obligations because, unlike a State, a government is not an international person.

SECESSION

While *succession* involves the takeover of another State's territory, *secession* is the breakup of a State, typically for the purpose of achieving independent statehood. Modern examples of secession arose in India and Yugoslavia. When Great Britain's rule over India ended in 1947 (during the British withdrawal from Asia), Pakistan was created by partitioning part of India's northeastern territory. In 1971, Bangladesh separated from Pakistan (mostly for religious reasons). In Yugoslavia, conflicts previously suppressed by the Cold War erupted in the 1990s. After the Soviet Union dissolved, ethnic conflict and resurgent nationalism spawned the breakup of the former Yugoslavia into five separate States. As noted in the ICJ case at the end of this section, East Timor effectively seceded from Indonesia, having previously a Portuguese colony for 500 years.[46]

Some observers have characterized the contemporary rash of secessionist movements as a rather dangerous phenomenon. The University of Arizona's Philosophy

Professor Allen Buchanan succinctly characterizes this development in these terms: "[if] each ethnic group, each 'people,' is entitled to its own state, then it [secession movements] is a recipe for virtually limitless upheaval, an exhortation to break apart the vast majority of existing states, given that most [States] if not all began as empires and include a plurality of ethnic groups or peoples within their present boundaries. . . . Secession can shatter old alliances . . . tip balances of power, create refugee populations, and disrupt international commerce. It can also result in a great loss of human life. And regardless of whether it acts or refrains from acting, each state takes a stand on each secessionist movement—if only by recognizing or not recognizing the independence of the seceding group."[47]

As with the prior succession (takeover) analysis, questions of what obligations continue may also arise after a secession. For example, had the Confederacy won the American Civil War of the 1860s, it is not clear whether the South would have retained the international obligations incurred by the United States for that portion of the United States. Prior to the end of World War II, international practice clearly supported the rule that a new State (seceding from another) could begin its existence without any restraints imposed by the treaty commitments of the State from which it seceded. After secession, the State from which another has seceded continued to be bound by its own existing treaty commitments, which do not depend on the continued existence of the State that has seceded.

Since World War II, the unequivocal rule that authorized a fresh start for seceding States, became somewhat equivocal. New States that have seceded from others still enjoy a "clean slate," but not as to treaties creating norms intended to bind all States. Humanitarian treaties are the prime example. These normally codify the existing customary practice of States. When Pakistan separated from India in 1947, it acknowledged a continuing obligation to remain a party to the 1921 Convention for the Suppression of Traffic in Women and Children. Pakistan's recognition of this obligation was specifically premised on India's acceptance of the 1921 treaty, when the Pakistani territory was still a part of India.[48]

SELF-DETERMINATION

Of the various modes of altering a territory's status, self-determination may be the least understood and most important. Self-determination is the inhabitants' right to choose how they will organize and be governed. They might not prefer self-governance, or, alternatively, they may opt for some form of autonomy that may or may not be statehood. Puerto Rico has been a part of the United States for 100 years. Its people have not chosen to become an independent sovereign, nor have they chosen to become a state within the federated system of states within the United States. If a majority of the people were to prefer complete independence from the United States, much like the evenly divided people of Canada's Quebec province, then they would *not* be enjoying their right of self-determination.

The UN Charter serves as a key rallying point for the modern law of self-determination. Article 1.2 of the Charter provides that one of the United Nation's essential purposes is "respect for the principle of equal rights and self-determination of peoples. . . ." The cornerstone is the Article 73 Declaration Regarding Non-Self-Governing Territories: "Members of the United Nations [that] have or [will] assume responsibilities for the administration of territories whose peoples have not yet attained a full measure of self-government recognize the principle that the interests of the inhabitants of these territories are paramount, and accept as a sacred trust the obligation to promote to the utmost . . . the well-being of the inhabitants of these territories. . . ."

A key UN development surfaced in 1960, in the midst of the movement to decolonize the many territories controlled by the original members. In Resolution 1514(XV), the General Assembly proclaimed—over objections by Western nations—that the "subjection of peoples to alien subjugation . . . constitutes a denial of fundamental human rights, is contrary to the Charter of the United Nations . . . [because all] peoples have the right to self-determination . . . [and any inadequacy] of political, economic, social or educational preparedness should never serve as a pretext for delaying independence." That resolution also provides that:

2. All peoples have the right to self-determination; by virtue of that right they freely determine their political status and freely pursue their economic, social and cultural development.

. . .

5. Immediate steps shall be taken, in Trust and Non-Self-Governing Territories or all other territories which have not yet attained independence, to transfer all powers to the peoples of those territories,

without any conditions or reservations, in accordance with their freely expressed will and desire, without any distinction as to race, creed or colour, in order to enable them to enjoy complete independence and freedom.

General Assembly Resolution 1541 further contemplates that non-self-governing territories might enjoy several possible outcomes in the quest for self-determination: (a) emergence as a sovereign independent State; or (b) free association with an independent State; or (c) integration with an independent State. Principle IX of that resolution declared that any "integration should be the result of the freely expressed wishes of the territory's peoples acting with full knowledge of the change in their status, their wishes having been expressed through informed and democratic processes, impartially conducted and based on universal adult suffrage. The United Nations could, when it deems it necessary, supervise these processes."

The subsequent Declaration on Principles of International Law Concerning Friendly Relations and Cooperation Among States in Accordance with the Charter of the United Nations (Resolution 2625 [XXV]) adds that:

> The establishment of a sovereign and independent State, the free association or integration with an independent State or the emergence into any other political status freely determined by a people constitute modes of implementing the right of self-determination by that people. . . . Every State has the duty to promote, through joint and separate action, realization of the principle of equal rights and self-determination of peoples in accordance with the provisions of the Charter, and to render assistance to the United Nations in carrying out the responsibilities entrusted to it by the Charter regarding the implementation of the principle.

One of the classic examples of self-determination *denied* was the situation in Namibia (formerly South-West Africa). It was controlled by South Africa, originating with a League of Nations mandate. South Africa refused to comply with various UN resolutions demanding that South Africa relinquish its control of South-West Africa. After seventy-four years of domination and a blistering decision from the ICJ,[49] South-West Africa finally achieved its own sovereign

identity and was admitted to the United Nations as the nation of Namibia in 1990. The regional achievement of self-determination, through the decolonization movement of the 1960s, is graphically illustrated in Exhibit 2.1. It features the huge number of African colonies, prior to the 1960s, which achieved statehood and thus surpassed the number of original UN members in 1945.

As the African decolonization movement shifted from rhetoric to reality, the rather general right of self-determination was further refined. Article 1.1 of both the 1966 International Covenant on Civil and Political Rights and the 1966 International Covenant on Economic, Social, and Cultural Rights provided the next building block. It provides that "[a]ll peoples have the right of self-determination. By virtue of that right they freely determine their political status and freely pursue their economic, social and cultural development." While the General Assembly approved these covenants with near unanimity, certain Western powers maintained their reservations about the so-called right of self-determination and its nuanced shift from "States" to the "peoples."[50]

Prominent contemporary self-determination scenarios include the:

◆ *Palestinians in the West Bank and Gaza (§6.2 Palestinian Wall Case).* The Palestinians living in several nations of the Middle East have claimed the right of self-determination over "Palestine" since the UN partition plan of 1947, which would have created a Palestinian State (in addition to Israel).

◆ *Baltics.* These were overtaken by the Soviet Union in the 1940s, unrecognized by many other States, in spite of *de facto* Soviet control. In February 1991, Estonians, Latvians, and Lithuanians voted for independence from the Soviet Union. Soviet President Gorbachev declared these votes "illegal" and then dispatched more Soviet troops to the area to maintain the "civil order." After twenty deaths, and the EU's withholding of $1 billion in food aid to the Soviet Union in protest, the Kremlin withdrew its special troops in an effort to diffuse the confrontation over the Baltic right of self-determination. The EU soon recognized the Baltics as independent States, noting that it "warmly welcome[d] the restoration of sovereignty and independence of the Baltic states which they lost in 1940."

◆ *Chechens.* The struggle for full autonomy of the inhabitants of Russia's predominantly Muslim region of Chechnya dates back to AD 965. During World War II, Stalin deported thousands of this area's inhabitants to Central Asia. In December 1994, a remarkable 40-mile human chain of 100,000 people protested Russia's continuing military assault on Chechnya.

◆ *Nunavuts.* In 1992, the Canadian government signed an accord with Eskimo leaders to create a native-run territory in Canada's Northwest Territories to be called Nunavut. The agreement called for the establishment of Nunavut, with the Nunavut government gradually assuming greater power in that portion of Canada. The Arctic Eskimos ratified a land claim agreement via a referendum, which in turn resulted in the Canadian government's passing legislation, establishing Nunavut in 1999.

◆ *Western Saharans.* Spain colonized this territory in 1884. A dispute arose between Mauritania and Morocco. This legal controversy lingered in the General Assembly from 1966 to 1974. The Assembly resolved that the inhabitants possessed a right to self-determination, strongly recommending that there should be a referendum so that they could vote to determine the status of Western Sahara. The ICJ avoided a clear answer via its conclusion that "the Court has not found legal ties of such a nature as might affect the application of resolution 1514 (XV) in the decolonization of Western Sahara and, in particular, of the principle of self-determination through the free and genuine expression of the will of the peoples of the Territory.[51] Western Sahara was thereafter partitioned between Mauritania and Morocco. The Spanish army departed in 1976, based on an agreement reached the year before. Morocco and Mauritania took over this territory. An indigenous liberation movement protested the 1975 partition agreement, however. In 1979, Mauritania ceded its portion of Western Sahara, and Moroccan troops took over. There has been no referendum of the inhabitants. Control over the territory remains politically unsettled, because of hostilities between the Moroccan government and the indigenous liberation front. A UN-administered cease-fire between independence-oriented guerrillas and territorial authorities has been in effect since September 1991. In summer 1998, a UN mediator secretly met with Indonesian authorities, separatist guerillas, and other members of the local population; however, a promised referendum has not yet occurred. UNSC Reso. 1598 (2005) called upon the the Polisario Front to release all remaining prisoners of war in compliance with international humanitarian law, and for Morocco to continue to cooperate with the Red Cross to resolve the fate of persons who are unaccounted for since the beginning of the latest round in this conflict. This unheeded nightmare continues to crave some humanitarian intervention. In October 2005, the Algerian-backed Polisario Front located and produced hundreds of African immigrants. Morocco had banished them to the Western Sahara.

◆ *Greek Cypriots.* The 2004 referenda, in both the Turkish Cypriot North and Greek Cypriot South, the failed UN reunification plan, and Cyprus's new EU membership applicable to just the southern portion of Cyprus have all combined to effectively deny Cypriots in both parts of the country to their respective claims to realize their desired self-determination (§2.3 *Cyprus v. Turkey* case).

◆ *Iraqi People.* The initial postwar government was US-installed. Each major ethnic group (Shiite, Sunni, and Kurd) vied for control within the US-backed elected government. There are still 150,000 US troops remaining in Iraq. No foreign military contingent is subject to the control of any entity within Iraq's elected government. Military Status of Forces agreements immunize foreign forces from Iraqi prosecution for civil or criminal violations of Iraq's

Case Concerning East Timor
(*Portugal* v. *Australia*)

INTERNATIONAL COURT OF JUSTICE

June 30, 1995

General List No. 84

1995 ICJ 90 (1995)

Go to course Web page at
<http://home.att.net/~slomansonb/
txtcsesite.html>.

Under Chapter Two, click <u>Case Concerning
East Timor.</u>

laws. As more and more bombings kill more and more Iraqis, one can only hope that this is the form of self-determination desired by the so-called silent majority.

The ICJ's subsequent self-determination case more clearly defined the contemporary contours:

◆ 2.5 STATE RESPONSIBILITY

INTRODUCTION

This section briefly addresses State responsibility under International Law. Once statehood is acquired, a State incurs obligations associated with its international status. It is required to make reparations for any international wrongdoing. A State could thus breach an obligation, which impacts just one State; or alternatively, the entire community of nations.[52]

Before delving into the specific content of International Law in this section and subsequent chapters, it will be useful to contemplate the general consequences of a State's wrongful conduct. First of all, a State can incur such liability for either intentional or negligent conduct. When a State commits a wrongful act against another State, its breach of International Law activates the requirement that it make reparations for that harm. Otherwise, States would not be coequal sovereigns under International Law.

Three fundamental elements trigger State responsibility: (1) the existence of a legal obligation recognized by International Law; (2) an act or omission that violates that obligation; and (3) some loss or articulable damage caused by the breach of the obligation.[53]

These elements are drawn from a variety of sources, including various judicial and arbitral awards. The Permanent Court of International Justice (PCIJ) tendered the quintessential articulation in 1928: "it is a principle of international law, and even a greater conception of [all] law, that any breach of an engagement [responsibility to another State] involves an obligation to make reparation."[54] Germany sued Poland, seeking reparations for Poland's breach of its treaty obligation *not* to expropriate a German factory once it was built in Poland.

Support for this principle can also be found in many arbitral decisions. In 1985, the crew of the Greenpeace vessel Rainbow Warrior protested French nuclear testing in the South Pacific. French agents then destroyed the vessel in a New Zealand harbor, thus killing one of the crew members. New Zealand was obviously upset because of this salient breach of its territorial sovereignty. France thus agreed to transfer the responsible French agents to its base in the Pacific, where they would remain for at least three years. They were clandestinely repatriated to France, however, without New Zealand's consent. In the ensuing 1986 arbitration, the UN Secretary-General ruled that France had thus incurred State responsibility for the acts of its agents and the related violation of its treaty commitment to incarcerate them in the geographical region, which was the scene of the crime. The *Rainbow Warrior Arbitration* affirmed that "the legal consequences of a breach of a treaty, including the determination of the circumstances that may exclude wrongfulness . . . and the appropriate remedies for breach, are subjects that belong to the customary law of state responsibility."[55]

There is a persistent question about whether a finding of fault or intent on the part of a State's agents required for State responsibility when one State harms another. The ICJ's 1949 *Corfu Channel* opinion suggests that some showing of fault is required for liability to arise. Great Britain sued Albania when British naval vessels hit mines that had been recently laid in an international strait off Albania's coast. Albania denied any knowledge of the presence of those mines—notwithstanding rather suspicious circumstances. The Court decided that "it cannot be concluded . . . that that state [Albania] necessarily knew, or ought to have known, of any unlawful act perpetrated therein, nor yet that it necessarily knew, or should have known, the authors [of the act of mine laying in the strait]."[56]

The UK's University of Leicester Professor Malcolm Shaw points out, however, that this lone passage from the Court is not tantamount to its general adoption of a "fault" requirement that would limit State responsibility. While judicial and academic opinions are divided on this matter, most tend to agree that there is a strict liability standard. Therefore, the State's fault, intent, or apparent knowledge are not necessary conditions for State responsibility. Albania, under this standard, would have been liable for the damages to the British warships—even if it did not *intend* to harm another State, citizens, or property. A State can thus be liable for a failure to act, as when there are floating mines in its territorial waters through which foreign vessels routinely navigate.[57]

DRAFT ARTICLES

The study of International Law would be far simpler if the rules were only contained in a multilateral treaty to which all nations could agree. Three international drafting commissions have attempted to codify the Law of State Responsibility under International Law. From 1924 to 1930, a Committee of Experts working with the League of Nations presented the first phase in this lengthy endeavor. Its draft articles were limited to the responsibility of States for injuries within their respective territories to foreign citizens or their property. The next phase, from 1949 to 1961, was undertaken by the UN's International Law Commission (ILC)—a group of prominent international legal scholars nominated by the governments of UN member States.[58] The length of this renewed endeavor is partially attributable to the remarkable increase in UN membership (Exhibit 2.1). From 1963 to date, the next wave of attempted codification of the law of State responsibility appeared to crest at the UN Charter. The drafters for this phase broadened their efforts to cover State responsibility for all topics within the Charter's reach.

A set of draft articles was finally adopted by the ILC's members in 1996. States were asked to provide responses by the beginning of 1998. Some did, which thus required more drafting.[59] The rules contained in the latest draft (2001) focus on *procedural* rules, as opposed to substantive rules that could have directly addressed what acts or omissions give rise to State responsibility for a breach of International Law. This model law of State responsibility is thus couched in only the most general of terms, despite more than seventy years of laborious efforts to produce an acceptable draft for an international conference. Article 1 almost bashfully provides that "[e]very internationally wrongful act of a State entails the international responsibility of that State." Article 2 adds that "[t]here is an internationally wrongful act of a State when conduct consisting of an action or omission: (a) is attributable to the State under international law; and (b) constitutes a breach of an international obligation of the State." One could thus readily predict that the ILC may never produce a comprehensive set of *substantive* rules.[60]

Former Article 19, deleted from the final 2001 adopted text, was the most controversial draft article. It defined specifically prohibited State conduct. If it had survived the final cut, it would have restated the law of State responsibility for "international crimes and delicts." Its deleted Subsection 3 included the following: aggression, failure to safeguard self-determination of peoples, slavery, genocide, apartheid, and massive pollution of the atmosphere or of the seas. These terms were not defined in any detail, which likely explains the decision to delete this article from the 2001 text adopted by the ILC—prior to submission to the UN General Assembly. The Assembly will decide if and when to adopt a resolution encouraging States to ratify this draft treaty on State Responsibility.[61]

◆ 2.6 SOVEREIGN IMMUNITY

This section of the chapter on States introduces an important adjunct to State status. Although a State may incur State responsibility for certain conduct, its status as a sovereign entity may shield it from having to respond to suits in the courts of another country. In this context, when sovereign immunity applies, one State's judge(s) cannot assert jurisdiction over another State in its courts. Reparations, if any, must be sought in some other forum, usually via diplomatic intervention (§7.1).

This attribute of sovereignty, immunity from suit in the courts of another country, is premised on one of the fundamental building blocks of International Law: all States are entitled to equality. State B, being a coequal sovereign entity in the community of nations, should not be subjected to a lawsuit in the courts in State A without B's consent. Although the State A plaintiff is entitled to a remedy from the government or an agency of State B, it may be preferable to resolve the dispute through diplomatic negotiations, rather than in the courts of State A.

This equality is often expressed in the constitutive documents of international organizations. Article 2.1 of the UN Charter provides that the "Organization is based on the principle of the sovereign equality of all its Members." Article 9 of the Charter of the Organization of American States provides that "States are juridically [legally] equal, enjoy equal rights and equal capacity to exercise these rights, and have equal duties. The rights of each State depend not upon its power to ensure the exercise thereof, but upon the mere fact of its existence as a person under international law."

One of the classic illustrations of the rationale for sovereign immunity is contained in the following excerpt from a 2001 US judicial opinion. The US Government successfully requested dismissal of an Auschwitz survivor's claim, thus supporting Germany's argument that it had sovereign immunity for its acts during World War II: "We think that something more nearly express . . . is wanted [in the US Foreign Sovereign Immunities Act] before we impute to the Congress an intention that the federal courts assume jurisdiction over the countless human rights cases that might well be brought by the victims of all the ruthless military juntas, presidents-for-life, and murderous dictators of the world, from Idi Amin to Mao Zedong."[62]

The historical lineage of sovereign immunity is somewhat sketchy. As stated by the Supreme Court of Canada: "The principle of sovereign immunity originated somewhat obscurely centuries ago in a period when the sovereign personified the state, and when sovereign interventions were generally limited to matters of public order, the conduct of international affairs and the defence of the state. . . . Sovereign immunity developed from the doctrine of the law of nations, which governs the international community of states based on the notions of sovereignty and equality of states. . . . These notions form the basis of an old Latin maxim: 'Par in parem imperium non habet,' which translates as 'An equal has no authority over an equal.'"[63]

In 1976, the United States enacted the first statute generally governing sovereign immunity. That legislation spawned a trend by nations wishing to make such determinations more objective. Congress wished to transfer more of the sovereign immunity decision making from the executive branch to the judicial branch of the government. As restated by the US Supreme Court's major policy opinion, the legislative history of the 1976 Act expressed the purpose to free the executive branch of the "Government from the case-by-case diplomatic pressures, to clarify the governing standards, and to 'assur[e] litigants that decisions are made on purely legal grounds under procedures that insure due process.'"[64]

You studied the Act of State (AOS) doctrine in §1.4 of this textbook. As an example, a State A corporation seeks retribution in a civil action for a harm allegedly done to the corporation by State B. The plaintiff corporation is essentially asking a State A court to decide the validity of some State B action that allegedly violates International Law, such as an uncompensated expropriation of A's subsidiary in State B. Defendant State B—or A's executive branch of the government—asks the State A court *not* to adjudicate State B's alleged substantive liability.[65] The AOS defense is similar, but distinct from a State B immunity defense. The comparison of these two potential defenses is ably articulated by the British Barrister and Oxford professor Hazel Fox:

> As regards the act of state doctrine some marked differences of scope and effect are observable between that defense and a plea of immunity . . . made . . . by reason of the . . . [legal] personality of the foreign State.
>
> First, the effect of the doctrine in the former [AOS] invokes the aid of the national court to go some way to endorsing the validity of the act of the foreign state, whereas in immunity the court remains neutral, merely deciding that it is not the appropriate forum. . . . Finally, . . . the act of state doctrine applies the political and moral values of the forum State. In contrast, immunity aims at a value-free assessment, an objective ascertainment as to which of the two States is the appropriate one to exercise jurisdiction [to provide some remedy for the alleged harm].[66]

The scope of *sovereign immunity* includes issues spawned by the alleged misconduct of States, Heads of State, State governmental agencies conducting State business, diplomats, and military forces operating in foreign theaters. State practice can thus be classified in terms of two general types of immunity: *absolute* and *restricted*.

ABSOLUTE IMMUNITY

State Nations have historically employed the *absolute* theory of sovereign immunity. The Kenya Court of Appeal provided a useful restatement of this theory. A resident of Kenya sued a British soldier for allegedly causing a motor accident in Kenya. The Claims Commission within Britain's Ministry of Defence—a government agency of Great Britain—was sued because it would normally be vicariously liable for the soldier's conduct undertaken in the course of his employment. The immunity upheld by Kenya's appellate decision illustrates the rationale for dismissing the governmental defendant:

> it is a matter of international law that our courts will not entertain an action against certain privileged persons and institutions unless the privilege is waived. The class . . . includes foreign sovereigns or heads of state and governments, foreign diplomats and their staff, consular officers and representatives of international organisations like UNO [UN] and OAU [Organization of African Unity]. Mr. Frazer for the

appellant [British governmental agency] cited the English case [citation omitted]. . . .

The general principle is undoubtedly that, except by consent, the courts of this country will not issue their process so as to entertain a claim against a foreign sovereign for debt or damages. The reason is that, if the courts here once entertained the claim, and in consequence [thereby] gave judgment against the foreign sovereign, they [the courts rendering the judgment] could be called on to enforce it by execution against its property here. Such execution might imperil our relations with that country and lead to [reciprocal] repercussions impossible to foresee. . . .

As was held in *Mighell v. Sultan of Johore* [1894] 1 QB 149, the courts in one country have no jurisdiction over an independent foreign sovereign of another country, unless he submits to the jurisdiction. There has been no [such] submission here.[67]

Just after World War II, absolute sovereign immunity applications began to focus on whether the defendant government's particular activity was closely associated with its political objectives within the host State. Thus, the *purpose* of that government's apparent commercial activity was controlling, rather than the fact that a private business could carry out the same project. The following case from Poland is a useful illustration. A woman named Aldona was a typist employed by the weekly magazine Voice of England. This magazine was published in Kraków, Poland, by the British Foreign Office of the government of the United Kingdom. Ms. Aldona was dismissed from her job. She was not paid the remainder of the salary due to her under the contract with the magazine. She sued Great Britain in a Polish court for the breach of her contract by the British agency publishing the magazine. The Polish courts dismissed her case because the defendant was a foreign sovereign. Aldona asserted that this dispute involved a mere contract of employment between a private person and a commercial magazine that was a profit-making enterprise. The magazine just happened to be published by an agency of the British government for diplomatic and other political purposes.

Aldona's unsuccessful argument was that publishing a magazine should be characterized as "economic" rather than a "diplomatic" or some other State-related activity. Her lawyer argued that if Great Britain's magazine could thereby avoid paying her, on the basis of a dismissal on grounds of sovereign immunity, the contractual obligations

of the British government in Poland would be meaningless. The Polish court first assessed the reciprocity concerns (suggested in the foregoing case from Kenya). Absent a dismissal in this case, the Polish government or its State-run entities would not fare well in British courts. Subsequent suits against a Polish governmental entity in Great Britain would likely invite a British judge to allow a suit to proceed against Polish government agencies operating in Great Britain. The Polish court noted that, while the British magazine was a commercial entity, because it was selling magazines for a profit, its underlying *purpose* was an inoffensive political activity on the part of the United Kingdom. The Polish Supreme Court also tied up an important loose end sometimes overlooked in sovereign immunity analyses: the plaintiff has a remedy, but it is not in the courts. Rather, the plaintiff's home State may enter into diplomatic negotiations on her behalf (§4.1). Under the Polish Supreme Court's analysis:

Polish Courts were unable, given the principle of reciprocity, to accept for deliberation the claim submitted by Aldona S., even if it concerned a commercial enterprise on behalf of the British authorities. However, such is really not the case, for the [lower Polish] Court of Appeal held that the publishing house of "Voice of England" is not a commercial enterprise. The objection of the plaintiff that this does not concern diplomatic but [rather] economic activity cannot be admitted as valid, for although the activity may not be diplomatic, it is political by its content, and economic only by its form. . . .

Finally, the last objection of the plaintiff, that refusal of legal protection would render the obligations of the British Foreign Office as a publisher of a magazine in the territory of our State incomplete and unreal, is also unfounded, for, if the plaintiff does not wish to seek justice before English courts, she may take advantage of general international usage in connection with immunity from jurisdiction, and approach the [Polish] Ministry of Foreign Affairs, which is obliged to take up the matter with the [British] Ministry of Foreign Affairs of a foreign country with a view to obtain satisfaction for a just claim. This approach frequently produces speedier results than court procedure.[68]

Head of State The scope of absolute sovereign immunity may also depend on what entities are embraced within the term "State." There is a distinction between heads of State and the State itself. For 2,000 years, absolute immunity has been universally recognized for heads of State regarding their public and private acts while they are in office. In the famous case cited in the earlier Kenya court decision, *Mighell v. Sultan of Johore,* Great Britain extended sovereign immunity to a foreign head of State who was sued there, for breach of his promise to marry. The case against the sultan was thus dismissed without considering the merits of the plaintiff's case.[69]

For this application of sovereign immunity, there was an iron-clad rule for nearly 2,000 years: a foreign head of State was not subject to *any* civil or criminal prosecution, during and after leaving office. This rule was sired by perceptions of necessity and reciprocity. The uniform customary international practice effectuated a form of *golden rule.*

In 1989, Manuel Noriega, Panama's former head of State, presented the first aberration in contemporary practice. The United States invaded Panama; waited for him outside of the Vatican embassy; seized him when he exited; then returned him to the United States for trial on drug-trafficking charges. This was perhaps the first time, since Roman leaders brought back captured foreign leaders in chains 2,000 years ago, that a foreign ruler was captured abroad and returned to the territory of the captors for trial. The United States relied on various legalities, including a state of war, which of course was commenced by the US invasion. The United States further asserted that this capture was an act of self-defense, premised on the danger that Noriega's dictatorship posed for US security interests in Panama. Noriega's capture and subsequent trial in the United States was labeled as a "gross violation" of International Law by the former president of the American Society of International Law. A US court nevertheless rejected Noriega's 1997 claim of head of State immunity in 1997.[70] In other US cases, however, the heads of State of the PRC and Zimbabwe have been accorded absolute immunity from prosecution in the United States.[71]

The Augusto Pinochet litigation made a significant contribution to toppling the centuries old immunity accorded to Heads of State, which had continued after they left office. *Pinochet* thus provided a significant spark to an evolving paradigm: one which questioned whether it still made sense to extend absolute immunity to an ex-ruler, who engages in such heinous

Judgment of the House of Lords
Regina v. Bartle and the Commissioner of Police for the Metropolis and Others Ex Parte Pinochet on 24 March 1999
On Appeal from a Divisional Court of the Queen's Bench Division
Go to course Web page at
<http://home.att.net/~slomansonb/ txtcsesite.html>.
Under Chapter Two,
click Ex Parte Pinochet.

conduct in office, that it could hardly be considered State policy.[72]

Slobodan Milosevic was the first head of State to be prosecuted by an *international* tribunal. His trial for genocide and various other crimes began in 2002, when the Serbian government turned him over to the International Criminal Tribunal for the Former Yugoslavia. The proceedings by this UN Security Council-initiated court in the Netherlands thus unsettled the millenniums-old rule of absolute immunity for sitting and former heads of State. Prosecution of other heads of State is now within the treaty-based jurisdiction of the International Criminal Court (ICC) in the Netherlands (§9.5). Under Article 27.1 of the Rome Statute of the ICC, the ICC's jurisdiction applies without regard to an individual's official capacity, and "[i]n particular . . . a Head of State or Government . . . ."

A tribunal like the ICC is specifically designed to try individuals without regard to their capacity as heads of State. States considering whether to prosecute such matters still tend to honor the historic immunity from arrest, prosecution, or extradition. While there have been some exceptions, such as in the textbook §1.4 *Karadzic* case, most States continued to honor tradition. During Chinese President Jiang Zemin's visit to the United States in 2002, he was served with a civil suit by the Falun Gong religious sect. The trial court authorized service, based on allegations that the PRC's President outlawed Falun Gong in 1999; but authorized ensuing torture, forced labor, reeducation, and murder of various members in the PRC. He was served in

Chicago. He failed to respond. Plaintiffs applied for a default judgment. The US government then intervened, to assert his head of State immunity. The trial court granted the requested dismissal. The federal appellate court's 2004 affirming opinion commented, in no uncertain terms, that:

"[I]t is a guiding principle . . . in such cases, that the courts should not so act as to embarrass the executive arm in its conduct of foreign affairs. . . ."

"Separation-of-powers principles impel a reluctance in the judiciary to interfere with or embarrass the executive in its constitutional role as the nation's primary organ of international policy." The determination to grant or not grant immunity can have significant implications for this country's relationship with other nations. A court is ill-prepared to assess these implications and resolve the competing concerns the Executive Branch is faced with in determining whether to immunize a head of state.

. . . Pursuant to their respective authorities, Congress or the Executive Branch can create exceptions to blanket immunity. In such cases the courts would be obliged to respect such exceptions. In the present case the Executive Branch has recognized the immunity of President Jiang from the appellants' suit. The district court was correct to accept this recognition as conclusive.[73]

Other Government Officials The leading treaty, on the degree to which government officials are entitled to their historical immunity from criminal prosecution, is the Statute of the ICC. In ICC proceedings, governmental capacity is irrelevant when an individual commits an international crime within the court's jurisdiction (§9.5).

As there have been no ICC trials yet, international legal analysts must draw upon the customary sources of International Law, to obtain information about its relevant content (§1.2). The leading contemporary case evidence is found in the following opinion:

Case Concerning the Arrest Warrant of 11 April 2000
(*Democratic Republic of the Congo* v. *Belgium*)
INTERNATIONAL COURT OF JUSTICE
General List No. 121 (Feb. 14, 2002)
<http://www.icj-cij.org/icjwww/idecisions.htm>

AUTHOR'S NOTE: A Belgian trial court judge issued an arrest warrant for the Democratic Republic of the Congo's Minister of Foreign Affairs. Belgium's arrest warrant was rooted in the Congolese defendant's alleged human rights atrocities, which were prohibited by the Geneva Conventions.

In the following key passages, the Court thus states the rationale for Belgium's violation of International Law—notwithstanding the heinous crimes allegedly committed by the Congo's Foreign Minister—and the recognized exceptions, which were inapplicable in this particular case:

COURT'S OPINION: . . .
58. The Court has carefully examined State practice, including national legislation and those few decisions of national higher courts, such as the House of Lords or the French Court of Cassation. It has been unable to deduce from this practice that there exists under customary international law any form of exception to the rule according immunity from criminal jurisdiction and inviolability to incumbent Ministers for Foreign Affairs, where they are suspected of having committed war crimes or crimes against humanity.

. . .

60. The Court emphasizes, however, that the *immunity* from jurisdiction enjoyed by incumbent Ministers for Foreign Affairs does not mean that they enjoy *impunity* in respect of any crimes they might have committed, irrespective of their gravity. Immunity from criminal jurisdiction and individual criminal responsibility are quite separate concepts. While jurisdictional immunity is procedural in nature, criminal responsibility is a question of substantive law. Jurisdictional immunity may well bar prosecution for a certain period or for certain offences; it cannot exonerate the person to whom it applies from all criminal responsibility.

61. Accordingly, the immunities enjoyed under international law by an incumbent or former Minister for Foreign Affairs do not represent a bar to criminal prosecution in certain circumstances.

First, such persons enjoy no criminal immunity under international law in their own countries, and may thus be tried by those countries' courts in accordance with the relevant rules of domestic law.

Secondly, they will cease to enjoy immunity from foreign jurisdiction if the State, which they represent or have represented decides to waive that immunity.

Thirdly, after a person ceases to hold the office of Minister for Foreign Affairs, he or she will no longer enjoy all of the immunities accorded by international law in other States. Provided that it has jurisdiction under international law, a court of one State may try a former Minister for Foreign Affairs of another State in respect of acts committed prior or subsequent to his or her period of office, as well as in respect of acts committed during that period of office in a private capacity.

Fourthly, an incumbent or former Minister for Foreign Affairs may be subject to criminal proceedings before certain international criminal courts, where they have jurisdiction. Examples include the International Criminal Tribunal for the former Yugoslavia, and the International Criminal Tribunal for Rwanda, established pursuant to Security Council resolutions under Chapter VII of the United Nations Charter, and the future International Criminal Court created by the 1998 Rome Convention. The latter's Statute expressly provides, in Article 27, paragraph 2, that "[i]mmunities or special procedural rules which may attach to the official capacity of a person, whether under national or international law, shall not bar the Court from exercising its jurisdiction over such a person." . . .

71. The Court also notes that Belgium admits that the purpose of the international *circulation* of the disputed arrest warrant was "to establish a legal basis for the arrest of Mr. Yerodia . . . abroad and his subsequent extradition to Belgium." The Respondent maintains, however, that the enforcement of the warrant in third States was "dependent on some further preliminary steps having been taken" and that, given the "inchoate" quality of the warrant as regards third States, there was no "infringe[ment of] the sovereignty of the [Congo]." It further points out that no Interpol Red Notice was requested until 12 September 2001, when Mr. Yerodia no longer held ministerial office.

The Court cannot subscribe to this view. As in the case of the warrant's issue, its international circulation from June 2000 by the Belgian authorities, given its nature and purpose, effectively infringed Mr. Yerodia's immunity as the Congo's incumbent Minister for Foreign Affairs and was furthermore liable to affect the Congo's conduct of its international relations. Since Mr. Yerodia was called upon in that capacity to undertake travel in the performance of his duties, the mere international circulation of the warrant, even in the absence of "further steps" by Belgium, could have resulted, in particular, in his arrest while abroad. The Court observes in this respect that Belgium itself cites information to the effect that Mr. Yerodia, "on applying for a visa to go to two countries, [apparently] learned that he ran the risk of being arrested as a result of the arrest warrant issued against him by Belgium," adding that "[t]his, moreover, is what the [Congo] . . . hints when it writes that the arrest warrant 'sometimes forced Minister Yerodia to travel by roundabout routes'." Accordingly, the Court concludes that the circulation of the warrant, whether or not it significantly interfered with Mr. Yerodia's diplomatic activity, constituted a violation of an obligation of Belgium towards the Congo, in that it failed to respect the immunity of the incumbent Minister for Foreign Affairs of the Congo and, more particularly, infringed the immunity from criminal jurisdiction and the inviolability then enjoyed by him under international law. . . .

SEPARATE OPINION OF PRESIDENT GUILLAUME . . .

15. . . . The adoption of the United Nations Charter proclaiming the sovereign equality of States, and the appearance on the international scene of new States, born of decolonization, have strengthened the territorial principle. International criminal law has itself undergone considerable development and constitutes today an impressive legal *corpus*. It recognizes in many situations the possibility, or indeed the obligation, for a State other than that on whose territory the offence was committed to confer jurisdiction on its courts to prosecute the authors of certain crimes where they are present on its territory. International criminal courts have been created. But at no time has it been envisaged that jurisdiction should be conferred upon the courts of every State in the world to prosecute such crimes, whoever their authors and victims and irrespective of the place where the offender is to be found. To do this would, moreover,

risk creating total judicial chaos. It would also be to encourage the arbitrary for the benefit of the powerful, purportedly acting as agent for an ill-defined "international community". Contrary to what is advocated by certain publicists, such a development would represent not an advance in the law but a step backward.

◆ Notes & Questions

1. The UN Charter provides—and in this case, the Court refers to—the principle that a State may not exercise its authority on the territory of another State, because of sovereign equality among all Members of the United Nations. No Belgian official went into the Congo to arrest the Congo's Foreign Minister. No other country arrested him. It was evident that he has committed the crimes charged. Was the ICJ thus overreacting to Belgium's attempt to enforce the provisions of the clearly applicable substantive rules of international human rights law?

2. *Should* International Law be altered to circumvent Justice Guillaume's rationale for concurring in the dismissal of this case? The whole court did not address the potential application of the Belgian law beyond its borders, as a potential violation of International Law. This feature of the case is presented in the French President's separate opinion, set forth in §5.2 of this book.

3. The important Paragraph 61, exception for trying a government official without violating International Law, was classically applied to a former government official in the new Special Court for Sierra Leone in May 2004. Former Head of State, Charles Taylor (yet to be extradited) is thus subject to its criminal proceedings. Prosecutor v. Charles Ghankay Taylor, summarized on the Court's Web site at <http://www.sc-sl.org/taylor.html>.

4. Further details and research resources are available in P. Bekker (US), World Court Orders Belgium to Cancel an Arrest Warrant Issued Against the Congolese Foreign Minister, ASIL INSIGHT (February 2002) & Myint Zan (Vanatu), Democratic Republic of Congo v. Belgium: Arrest Warrant of 11 April 2000; Crimes against Humanity: 'Immunity' versus 'Impunity,' Vol.7, J. SO. PACIFIC LAW, available at <http://law.vanuatu.usp.ac.fj/jspl/2003%20Volume7-Number1/Immunity_v_Impurity>.

5. The German courts considered a case filed in November 2004 against US Secretary of State, Donald Rumsfeld, regarding Iraq's Abu Grahib prison scandal. The New York-based Center for Constitutional Rights (CCR) and Berlin's Republican Lawyers' Association asserted that there was nowhere else to go. They relied on the German Code of Crimes Against International Law, introduced in 2002. It grants German courts universal jurisdiction in cases involving war crimes or crimes against humanity—when military and civilian commanders fail to prevent their subordinates from committing such acts. Before the case was dismissed, Rumsfeld canceled a planned visit to Germany. Details about this case and the German law are available at <http://www.dw-world.de/dw/article/0,1564,1413907,00.html>.

Diplomats   The immunity of State diplomats and consular officials is established by treaty. The relevant Vienna Conventions are addressed in §7.2.

Military Forces   An *occupying* foreign military force is not subject to prosecution in the tribunals of the occupied nation. This does not prevent responsibility under International Law, as discussed under the Laws of War in §10.6 of this book. In most cases, however, State A's military force is present in State B, via the invitation and consent of State B. Historically, only State A could prosecute a State A soldier or civilian dependent who committed a crime in State B—on or off base.

Post-World War II pressures arose which cast doubt on the practical utility of this feature of absolute immunity, especially for sensational crimes that sparked local attention. A classic illustration arose in Japan and Great Britain, when US military dependents (spouses) killed their US husbands who were on active military duty in those countries. In this situation, the degree of jurisdiction of any State A or State B tribunal depends on treaties known as Status of Forces Agreements (SOFA). Years before these homicides, the US-Japan-UK SOFAs provided that military dependents would be tried by a federal statute known as the Uniform Code of Military

Justice (UCMJ). This code does not provide for a civilian jury of one's peers, as required by the US Constitution for civilian defendants. These women were thus freed because, at the time, there was no law under which to try them. The US Supreme Court held that the SOFAs, which relied on UCMJ proceedings to try the wives, were applied in a manner that violated the wives' right to a civilian jury of their peers.[74]

For crimes arising under International Law, the ICC's Statute does not deprive the ICC of jurisdiction when the potential defendant is in the military (or a Head of State). However, Article 98 provides for complete immunity from an ICC prosecution when there is a treaty agreement that bars either local prosecution, or extradition of a defendant to the ICC from the detaining country.

National courts occasionally consider cases filed against military leaders. In May 2003, a Belgian trial court considered a case filed against US General Tommy Franks, who was commander of US forces during the Iraq War. Nineteen Iraqis claimed that they were victims of cluster bombs and US attacks on ambulances and civilians. Belgium's Foreign Minister deplored this lawsuit as an abuse of "universal jurisdiction" (textbook §5.2) then available to the Belgian courts.[75]

RESTRICTIVE IMMUNITY

The entry into force of the Statute for the ICC effectively restricted the absolute immunity historically enjoyed by heads of State. The foregoing ICJ Belgian Warrant case lists the various contemporary exceptions to the traditional immunity of other government officials. These limitations in criminal jurisdiction were actually predated, and influenced by, a parallel development in commercial matters after World War II. That is the revision of what *was* the historical rule of *absolute* sovereign immunity, when a State was engaged in "for-profit" business ventures.

In 1952, the US government led the way by shifting, from an across-the-board *absolute* immunity approach for its civil cases, to one of *restrictive* immunity. Foreign governments would thereafter be immune from suit in US courts *only* when the sovereign was acting like a sovereign and not a private merchant.

In 1976, signatories to the European Convention on State Immunity therein expressed their concern about this tendency to restrict the cases in which a State may claim immunity before foreign courts. Under Article 2

of this treaty, a State party cannot claim immunity from the jurisdiction of a court of another contracting State if it has undertaken to submit to the jurisdiction of that court either: (a) an international agreement; (b) an express term contained in a contract in writing; or (c) an express consent given after a dispute between the parties has arisen. The essential theme was to ensure that a State would have to give its express consent to being sued in the courts of another European State.[76]

Under the *contemporary* restrictive theory of sovereign immunity, most States no longer automatically extend absolute immunity to foreign government-owned or -operated entities. An entity operated by a State, in its capacity as a trader competing with other private merchants, is not *necessarily* given immunity from suit under the newer restrictive theory of sovereign immunity. As illustrated in the following materials in this section, *this* application of sovereign immunity analysis affects a State engaged in a commercial enterprise, as opposed to conduct that can be undertaken *only* by a sovereign nation (such as declaring war). For example, the US-based Boeing and Lockheed corporations are private corporations that build military aircraft. They may benefit, if the US government decides to engage in a military conflict with another nation. But only the US government has the legal competence to engage in military combat, as opposed to either of these private corporations, which could not require a flight unit to fly sorties into a combat theater.

Assume that a foreign government owns the company that builds its war planes (e.g., in a communist society where there is no *private* property). That government-owned company orders parts from Lockheed or Boeing. It fails to pay for those parts, as promised. Formerly, the US companies would not be able to sue that foreign government or its State-owned entities in a US court for breach of contract. A US court would not be permitted to hear the merits of such a claim because of the old rule, which provided for the absolute immunity of a foreign government to a suit in a US court. Modernly, the foreign government and/or its State-operated instrumentality will *not* be immune from a suit in a US court. That this government was contracting for the *public* purpose of defending itself is now virtually irrelevant. That foreign government effectively placed itself in the position of a private defense contractor who owes money to the US company for the delivered parts.

Certain States, such as the PRC, still adhere to the absolute immunity theory.[77] Most States currently apply some form of the restrictive standard for resolving sovereign immunity questions. Western nations typically restrict a foreign sovereign's immunity from suit, based on how the State is *acting,* rather than its disclosed *purpose.* Major distinctions are fabricated on distinctions like whether the State's conduct is: (1) sovereign versus private; (2) public versus private; (3) commercial versus noncommercial; or (4) political versus trade-related.

These enumerated distinctions are easily stated, but difficult to apply. In a commonly-cited US restatement of the circumstances required to grant immunity from suit, a federal court appeared to articulate an immunity test (for those situations where the executive branch has not spoken) in cases involving: (a) administrative acts within the United States, such as expulsion of an alien; (b) legislative acts such as nationalization; (c) acts concerning the armed forces; (d) acts concerning diplomatic activity; and (e) any public loan.

Now consider an Austrian Supreme Court case, to see if the Austrian court should have also found sovereign immunity if it had applied the standard discussed. In the relevant passage in the court's opinion:

The plaintiff was an Austrian citizen whose automobile was damaged in a collision with a car owned by the US government in Austria. The driver of the US car was delivering mail to the US embassy. The lawyer for the US claimed sovereign immunity from suit in the Austrian courts, premised on the underlying purpose of the trip. The lower court, and the Austrian Supreme Court, allowed the case to proceed, however. It was the act of driving itself, rather than its underlying purpose, that would shape the scope of sovereign immunity in Austrian foreign sovereign immunity analysis. Any qualified driver can drive a car on an Austrian highway. Negligence on the highway, not the underlying purpose of delivering US government mail, therefore vitiated sovereign immunity for the US in the Austrian courts. As stated by the Austrian Supreme Court: "We must always look at the act itself which is performed by State organs, and not at its motive or purpose. We must always investigate the act of the State from which the claim is derived. Whether an act is of a private or sovereign nature must always be deduced from the nature of the legal transaction . . . the action taken or the legal relationship arising [as from the collision on an Austrian highway]. . . ."

[T]he act from which the plaintiff derives his claim for damages against the defendant is not the collection of mail but the operation of a motor car . . . and action as a road user. By operating a motor car and using the public roads the defendant moves in spheres in which private individuals also move.[78]

◆ *Notes & Questions*

1. Does the Austrian court's emphasis on the nature of the act, resulting in the lawsuit, rather than its underlying purpose, refer to the collection and delivery of embassy mail, or does it refer to the driving of a car on an Austrian highway? Would the immediately prior US court's approach be useful to the facts of the Austrian case? The Austrian court referred to the distinction between private and sovereign acts. Was the delivery of mail to the US embassy in Austria a sovereign act of the US government, or was it merely an act, which the judge could characterize as private? *Should* the United States have been entitled to sovereign immunity in the Austrian Supreme Court case?

2. Does the Austrian court's emphasis on the "nature of the act," rather than its underlying purpose, refer to the collection and delivery of embassy mail, or does it refer to the driving of a car on an Austrian highway?

3. The UN's ILC presented its Draft Articles on Jurisdictional Immunities of States and Their Property to the General Assembly in 1991. Article 10.1 contains the following State immunity formulation: "If a State engages in a commercial transaction with a foreign natural or [corporate] juridical person and, by virtue of the applicable rules of private international law, differences relating to the commercial transaction fall within the jurisdiction of a court of another State, the State cannot invoke immunity from that jurisdiction in a proceeding arising out of that commercial transaction."

The General Assembly adopted a final draft, which was opened for signature from 17 January 2005 to 17 January 2007. This ILC draft is evidence that State practice has generally shifted from absolute to restrictive immunity in civil cases—undoubtedly for commercial transactions, and probably for negligent harm to individual and corporate plaintiffs. See <http:// www.un.org/law/jurisdictionalimmunities> & D. Stewart, Introductory Note, 44 INT'L LEGAL MAT'LS 801 (2004). The ILC's draft articles on State responsibility for *criminal* conduct are addressed in §2.5 of this book.

Judges typically apply a two-step process when analyzing the scope of sovereign immunity: (1) Is the entity claiming this defense a "State," for purposes of a sovereign immunity analysis? (2) Is the entity's conduct, which is the reason for the suit, really sovereign, or essentially commercial in nature? If the activity is "sovereign," then the case is normally dismissed. If "commercial," then the State is acting in a way that a private citizen trader may act, thus requiring the State to litigate the underlying claim on the merits. This analysis often presents a very close question, as illustrated in the following case from the Philippines Supreme Court:

The Holy See v. *Starbright Sales Enterprises, Inc.*
PHILIPPINES SUPREME COURT (1994)
102 Int'l Law Rep. 163 (1995)

AUTHOR'S NOTE: In 1990, Starbright brought this suit in the Philippine courts against The Holy See (HS, or The Vatican). The HS had sold the land in dispute to Starbright, who sought an annulment of the sale, and damages, because the seller had failed to evict some squatters.

The HS claimed that it was entitled to sovereign immunity from suit in the Philippine courts. The HS claimed that it had acquired the property as the site for its official mission in the Philippines, and then sold it. The reason for the sale was that the presence of the squatters—who may have had some right to be there—made development of this land for a diplomatic mission impossible.

The trial court determined that the HS had waived its sovereign immunity by entering into this commercial contract to sell the land. The Supreme Court reversed the trial court's finding, however, resulting in dismissal of this suit.

COURT'S OPINION:
The following is the text of the judgment of the Court, delivered by Quiason J [court's footnotes and citations omitted]: . . .

Petitioner is The Holy See who exercises sovereignty over the Vatican City in Rome, Italy, and is represented in the Philippines by the Papal Nuncio.

Private respondent, Starbright Sales Enterprises, Inc., is a domestic corporation engaged in the real estate business.

This petition arose from a controversy over a parcel of land . . . located in the Municipality of Paranaque, Metro Manila, and registered in the name of petitioner. . . .

In view of the refusal of the squatters to vacate the lots sold to private respondent, a dispute arose as to who of the parties has the responsibility of evicting and clearing the land of squatters. . . .

I

On 23 January 1990, private respondent filed a complaint . . . [in] Manila for annulment of the sale of the three parcels of land, and specific performance and damages against petitioner, represented by the Papal Nuncio, and three other defendants: namely Msgr Domingo A. Cirilos, Jr., the PRC and Tropicana (Civil Case No. 90–183).

The complaint alleged that: (1) On 17 April 1988, Msgr Cirilos, Jr., on behalf of petitioner and the PRC, agreed to sell to Ramon Licup Lots 5-A, 5-B and 5-D at the price of P1,240.00 per square meter; . . . (5) thereafter, private respondent demanded from Msgr Cirilos that the sellers fulfill their undertaking and clear the property of squatters; however, Msgr Cirilos informed private respondent of the squatters' refusal to vacate the lots, proposing instead either that the private respondent undertake the eviction or that the earnest money be returned to the latter; (6) private respondent counterproposed that if it would undertake the eviction of the squatters, the purchase price of the lots should be reduced . . . (11) private respondent is willing and able to comply with the terms of the contract to sell and has actually made plans to develop the lots into a townhouse project, but in view of the sellers' breach, it lost profits of not less than P30,000,000.00. . . .

On 8 June 1990, petitioner and Msgr Cirilos separately moved to dismiss the complaint . . . for lack of jurisdiction based on sovereign immunity from suit, and Msgr Cirilos for being an improper party. An opposition to the motion was filed by private respondent.

On 20 June 1991, the trial court issued an order denying, among others, petitioner's motion to dismiss after finding that petitioner "discarded [its] sovereign immunity by entering into the business contract in question. . . ."

Petitioner forthwith elevated [appealed] the matter to us. In its petition, petitioner invokes the privilege of sovereign immunity on its own behalf and on behalf of its official representative, the Papal Nuncio.

On 9 December 1991, a Motion for Intervention was filed before us by the Department of Foreign Affairs, claiming that it has a legal interest in the outcome of the case as regards the diplomatic immunity of petitioner [Holy See] and that it "adopts by reference, the allegations contained in the petition of the Holy See insofar as they refer to arguments relative to its claim of sovereign immunity from suit."

Private respondent [Starbright] opposed the intervention of the Department of Foreign Affairs. In compliance with the resolution of this Court, both parties and the Department of Foreign Affairs submitted their respective memoranda. . . .

II

The other procedural question raised by private respondent is the personality or legal interest of the Department of Foreign Affairs to intervene in the case on behalf of The Holy See.

In public international law, when a State or international agency wishes to plead sovereign or diplomatic immunity in a foreign court, it requests the Foreign Office of the State where it is sued to convey to the court that said defendant is entitled to immunity.

In the United States, the procedure followed is the process of "suggestion," where the foreign State or the international organization sued in an American court requests the Secretary of State to make a determination as to whether it is entitled to immunity. If the Secretary of State finds that the defendant is immune from suit, he, in turn, asks the Attorney General to submit to the court a "suggestion" that the defendant is entitled to

immunity. In England, a similar procedure is followed, only the Foreign Office issues a certification to that effect instead of submitting a "suggestion."

In the Philippines, the practice is for the foreign government or the international organization to first secure an executive endorsement of its claim of sovereign or diplomatic immunity. But how the Philippine Foreign Office conveys its endorsement to the courts varies. . . .

In the case of bench, the Department of Foreign Affairs, through the Office of Legal Affairs moved with this Court to be allowed to intervene on the side of petitioner. The Court allowed the said Department to file its memorandum in support of petitioner's claim of sovereign immunity.

In some cases, the defense of sovereign immunity was submitted directly to the local courts by the respondents through their private counsels. In cases where the foreign States bypass the Foreign Office, the courts can inquire into the facts and make their own determination as to the nature of the acts and transactions involved.

III

The burden of the petition is [to prove] that respondent trial court has no jurisdiction over petitioner, being a foreign State enjoying sovereign immunity. On the other hand, private respondent insists that the doctrine of non-suability is not anymore absolute and that petitioner had divested itself of such a cloak when, of its own free will, it entered into a commercial transaction for the sale of a parcel of land located in the Philippines.

A. The Holy See

Before we determine the issue of petitioner's non-suability, a brief look into its status as a sovereign State is in order.

Before the annexation of the Papal States by Italy in 1870, the Pope was the monarch and, as The Holy See, was considered a subject of international law. With the loss of the Papal States and the limitation of the territory under The Holy See to an area of 108.7 acres, the position of The Holy See in international law became controversial.

In 1929, Italy and The Holy See entered into the Lateran Treaty, where Italy recognized the exclusive dominion and sovereign jurisdiction of The Holy See over the Vatican City. It also recognized the right of The Holy See to receive foreign diplomats, to send its own diplomats to foreign countries, and to enter into treaties according to international law.

The Lateran Treaty established the statehood of the Vatican City "for the purpose of assuring to The Holy See absolute and visible independence and of guaranteeing to it indisputable sovereignty also in the field of international relations. . . ."

The Vatican City fits into none of the established categories of States, and the attribution to it of "sovereignty" must be made in a sense different from that in which it is applied to other States. In a community of national States, the Vatican City represents an entity organized not for political but for ecclesiastical purposes and international objects. Despite its size and object, the Vatican City has an independent government of its own, with the Pope, who is also head of the Roman Catholic Church, as The Holy See or Head of State, in conformity with its traditions and the demands of its mission in the world. Indeed, the world-wide interests and activities of the Vatican City are such as to make it in a sense an "International State."

One authority wrote that the recognition of the Vatican City as a State has significant implication–that it is possible for any entity pursuing objects essentially different from those pursued by States to be invested with international personality.

Inasmuch as the Pope prefers to conduct foreign relations and enter into transactions as The Holy See and not in the name of the Vatican City, one can conclude that in the Pope's own view, it is The Holy See that is the international person.

The Republic of the Philippines has accorded The Holy See the status of a foreign sovereign. The Holy See, through its Ambassador, the Papal Nuncio, has had diplomatic representations with the Philippine Government since 1957. This appears to be the universal practice in international relations.

B. Sovereign Immunity

As expressed in Section 2 of Article II of the 1987 [Philippine] Constitution, we have adopted the generally accepted principles of international law. Even without this affirmation, such principles of international law are deemed incorporated as part of the law of the land as a condition and consequence of our admission in the society of nations.

There are two conflicting concepts of sovereign immunity, each widely held and firmly established.

According to the classical or absolute theory, a sovereign cannot, without its consent, be made a respondent in the courts of another sovereign. According to the newer or restrictive theory, the immunity of the sovereign is recognized only with regard to public acts or acts *jure imperii* of a State, but not with regard to private acts or acts *jure gestionis*.

Some States passed legislation to serve as guidelines for the executive or judicial determination when an act may be considered as *jure gestionis*. The United States passed the Foreign Sovereign Immunities Act of 1976, which defines a commercial activity as "either a regular course of commercial conduct or a particular commercial transaction or act." Furthermore, the law declared that the "commercial character of the activity shall be determined by reference to the nature of the course of conduct or particular transaction or act, rather than by reference to its purpose." The Canadian Parliament enacted in 1982 an Act to Provide for State Immunity in Canadian courts. The Act defines a "commercial activity" as any particular transaction, act or conduct or any regular course of conduct that by reason of its nature is of a "commercial character."

The restrictive theory, which is intended to be a solution to the host of problems involving the issue of sovereign immunity, has created problems of its own. Legal treatises and the decisions in countries which follow the restrictive theory have difficulty in characterizing whether a contract of a sovereign State with a private party is an act *jure gestionis* or an act *jure imperii*.

The restrictive theory came about because of the entry of sovereign States into purely commercial activities only remotely connected with the discharge of governmental functions. This is particularly true with respect to the Communist States, which took control of nationalized business activities and international trading.

This Court has considered the following transactions by a foreign State with private parties as acts *jure imperii*: (1) the lease by a foreign government of apartment buildings for use of its military officers; (2) the conduct of public bidding for the repair of a wharf at a United States naval station; and (3) the change of employment status of base employees.

On the other hand, this Court has considered the following transactions by a foreign State with private parties as acts *jure gestionis*: (1) the hiring of a cook in the recreation center, consisting of three restaurants, a cafeteria, a bakery, a store, and a coffee and pastry shop at the

John Hay Air Station in Baguio City, to cater to United States servicemen and the general public; and (2) the bidding for the operation of barbers' shops in Clark Air Base in Angeles City. The operation of the restaurants and other facilities open to the general public is undoubtedly for profit as a commercial and not a governmental activity. By entering into the employment contract with the cook in the discharge of its proprietary function, the United States Government impliedly divested itself of its sovereign immunity from suit.

In the absence of legislation defining what activities and transactions shall be considered "commercial" and as constituting acts *jure gestionis,* we have to come out with our own guidelines, tentative [as] they may be.

Certainly, the mere entering into a contract by a foreign State with a private party cannot be the ultimate test. Such an act can only be the start of the inquiry. The logical question is whether the foreign State is engaged in the activity in the regular course of business. If the foreign State is not engaged regularly in a business or trade, the particular act or transaction must then be tested by its nature. If the act is in pursuit of a sovereign activity, or an incident thereof, then it is an act *jure imperii*, especially when it is not undertaken for gain or profit. . . .

In the case at bench, if petitioner [Holy See] has bought and sold lands in the ordinary course of a real estate business, surely the said transaction can be categorized as an act *jure gestionis*. However, petitioner has denied that the acquisition and subsequent disposal of Lot 5-A were made for profit but claimed that it acquired said property for the site of its mission or the Apostolic Nunciature in the Philippines. Private respondent failed to dispute said claim.

Lot 5-A was acquired by petitioner as a donation to the Archdiocese of Manila. The donation was made not for commercial purpose, but for the use of petitioner to construct thereon the official place of residence of the Papal Nuncio. The right of a foreign sovereign to acquire property, real or personal, in a receiving State, necessary for the creation and maintenance of its diplomatic mission, is recognized in the 1961 Vienna Convention on Diplomatic Relations (Articles 20–22). This treaty was concurred in by the Philippine Senate and entered into force in the Philippines on 15 November 1965.

In Article 31(a) of the Convention, a diplomatic envoy is granted immunity from the civil and administrative jurisdiction of the receiving State over any real action relating to private immovable property situated in the territory of the receiving State which the envoy holds on behalf of the sending State for the purposes of the mission. If this immunity is provided for a diplomatic envoy, with all the more reason should immunity be recognized as regards the sovereign itself, which in this case is The Holy See.

The decision to transfer the property and the subsequent disposal thereof are likewise clothed with a governmental character. Petitioner did not sell Lot 5-A for profit or gain. It merely wanted to dispose of the same because the squatters living thereon made it almost impossible for petitioner to use it for the purpose of the donation. The fact that squatters have occupied and are still occupying the lot, and that they stubbornly refuse to leave the premises, has been admitted by private respondent in its complaint.

The issue of petitioner's non-suability can be determined by the trial court without going to trial in the light of the pleadings, particularly the admission of private respondent. Besides, the privilege of sovereign immunity in this case was sufficiently established by the Memorandum and Certification of the Department of Foreign Affairs. As the department tasked with the conduct of the Philippines' foreign relations, the Department of Foreign Affairs has formally intervened in this case and officially certified that the Embassy of The Holy See is a duly accredited diplomatic mission to the Republic of the Philippines exempt from local jurisdiction and entitled to all the rights, privileges and immunities of a diplomatic mission or embassy in this country. The determination of the executive arm of government that a State or instrumentality is entitled to sovereign or diplomatic immunity is a potential question that is conclusive upon the courts. Where the plea of immunity is recognized and affirmed by the Executive branch, it is the duty of the courts to accept this claim so as not to embarrass the Executive arm of the government in conducting the country's foreign relations. . . .

IV

Private respondent [Starbright] is not left without any legal remedy for the redress of its grievances. Under both public international law and transnational law, a person who feels aggrieved by the acts of a foreign sovereign can ask his own government to espouse his case through diplomatic channels.

Private respondent can ask the Philippine Government, through the Foreign Office, to espouse its claims against The Holy See. Its first task is to persuade the Philippine Government to take up with The Holy See the validity of its claims. Of course, the Foreign Office shall first make a determination of the impact of its espousal on the relations between the Philippine Government and The Holy See. Once the Philippine Government decides to espouse the claim, the latter ceases to be a private cause.

According to the Permanent Court of International Justice, the forerunner of the International Court of Justice:

By taking up the case of one of its subjects and by resorting to diplomatic action or international judicial proceedings on his behalf, a State is in reality asserting its own rights—its right to ensure, in the person of its subjects, respect for the rules of international law.

Wherefore, the petition for *certiorari* is granted and the compliant in Civil Case No 90–183 against petitioner is dismissed.
SO ORDERED.

Most sovereign immunity questions involve acts of a recognized State, or one of its agencies, undertaking some activity abroad whose results leads to a suit against it in another nation's courts. An aggrieved individual has the power to immediately file a suit to recover the alleged losses. Resorting to one's home country for diplomatic representation may be far more time consuming—assuming that the home State is willing to undertake its citizen's plea for help.

Perhaps the most dramatic example in US history is presented below. When reading it, consider whether sovereign immunity should be discarded as a vintage anachronism, because it is a holdover from an era when States did not do business to the extent that they do today. On the other hand, sovereign immunity may serve a utilitarian purpose in international relations. When a judicial entity proceeds with such a suit, there is always the risk that the proceedings may offend the sensibilities of another nation. Some situations are best handled via executive branch diplomacy.

The contemporary law of sovereign immunity is not uniformly perceived by the various legal systems of the world, nor necessarily even by American judges. In this case alone, the trial, intermediate appellate, and Supreme Courts all differed on whether Saudi Arabia's sovereign immunity was waived by its recruiting and training employees in the United States. At the Supreme Court level, the justices were intensely divided on the question of whether the victim's claim, seeking money damages because of torture at the hands of Saudi government agents, should be dismissed on the technical basis that the relevant legislation protects even this egregious governmental conduct from being aired in an American courtroom.

Only five of the nine justices agreed with the "majority's" opinion written by Justice Souter. One of those nine justices agreed with most, but not all, of the opinion. Two of them concurred with the result, but disagreed with some of the reasoning. Four justices concurred in part and dissented in part. Needless to say, the sovereign immunity shield is not uniformly handled, even by judges on the same court (all of whom were well schooled in the same nation's legal system).

Saudi Arabia v. *Nelson*

SUPREME COURT OF THE
UNITED STATES
507 US 349, 113 S.Ct. 1471, 123 *L. Ed.* 47
(1993)
Go to course Web page at <http://home.att.net/
~slomansonb/txtcsesite.html>.
Under Chapter Two, click on
Saudi Arabia v. Nelson.

Claims regarding Saudi Arabia's violations of International Law still abound. In September 2005, a New York federal court considered claims filed by "9-11" survivors and insurance carriers against Saudi princes and a charitable organization previously labeled a Specially Designated Global Terrorist Entity by the US Treasury Department. The princes were dismissed on sovereign immunity grounds, but not the referenced organization known as the Rabita Trust. The case was continued as to this entity, in deference to the above executive branch designation. In Re Terrorist Attacks on September 11, 2001, 392 F.Supp.2d 539 (S.D.N.Y. 2005).

◆ PROBLEMS

Problem 2.A (§2.1, after excerpt *On Condition of Statehood*) The Jessup excerpt presents the argument in favor of Israel's condition of statehood. Problem 2.A builds upon that paradigm with the related question of Palestinian statehood. The PLO was created in 1964 to "liberate" Palestine from Israeli control. Its members include people who are citizens of various Arab States. Their ancestors inhabited that territory since ancient times, long before the Western nation-State model was incorporated into International Law in 1648. Materials about the PLO are available on the Palestinian National Authority Web site at <http://www.pna.net> (and in the §6.2 *Palestinian Wall* case).

In 1919, the Palestinian people were provisionally recognized as a State by the League of Nations, as indicated in the 1922 Mandate for Palestine addressed to Great Britain. The United Nation's 1947 partition plan [UN Gen. Ass. Res. 181(II)] would have created a Palestinian State, but for the outbreak of war between Arab States and the new State of Israel. The drive for a Palestinian State gained momentum in the 1970s. The creation of the State of Palestine has international support only insofar as it would occupy the additional territories conquered by Israel in various Middle East wars in the 1960s and 1970s, but not that portion of "Palestine" that became the independent State of Israel in 1948. The PLO historically denied Israel's right to exist, in what it considered as "Palestine," dating from biblical times. Palestinians have routinely characterized the UN partition plan of 1947 as a criminal act that denied them rights they believed were guaranteed by the 1919 recognition of Palestine and 1922 League Mandate to Great Britain.

Led by Yasir Arafat, the PLO initially insisted that a Palestinian State should *replace* Israel, because the Jewish state had no right to exist in its current location. The PLO later softened its position by recognizing Israel's right to exist in relation to the 1993 agreements brokered by President Clinton (although the more militant members of "Hamas" have disagreed). The Palestinian National Authority claims that it should thus be given territory taken by Israel, during various Middle East conflicts after the 1947 UN partition plan. The 1998

peace negotiations included Israel's demand that the PLO revoke the provision in the 1964 Covenant that calls for Israel's destruction. Israel's borders have not been fixed by international agreement with its neighbors. The PLO argues that Palestine's borders are not yet established.

In 1974, the PLO was invited to participate in the UN General Assembly's debate on the Palestine question, and in an effort to secure peace in the Middle East. (See G.A. Res. 3210, 29 UN GAOR Supp. [No. 108] at 3, UN Doc. A/RES/3210[XXIX] [1974], and G.A. Res. 3375, 30 UN GAOR Supp. [No. 27] at 3, UN Doc. A/RES/3375[XXX] [1975].) The PLO was then officially recognized by Austria, India, and the Soviet Union. In July 1998, the PLO was also accorded a unique, nonvoting "observer" status in the UN General Assembly. The PLO can now raise issues, cosponsor draft resolutions, and make speeches in the General Assembly. Participation in the United Nations was previously limited to traditional States and less controversial nongovernmental organizations (such as the International Red Cross).

In 1987, the US Congress enacted legislation entitled the Anti-Terrorism Act. It was designed to close the PLO's UN observer mission in New York City. The basis for the desired closure was that the PLO's alleged terrorist activities could flow into the United States through the PLO's observer mission at the United Nations. The US government subsequently filed a lawsuit in a US court, under the US antiterrorist law, seeking to close the mission. The PLO responded from Algiers by proclaiming the existence of the new and independent "State of Palestine." This 1988 declaration includes the assertions that "the people of Palestine fashioned its national identity" and "the Palestinian people have not ceased its valiant defence of its homeland . . . [of Palestine, which] was subjected to a new kind of foreign occupation" when Israel took over. *See* Palestine National Council Political Communiqué and Declaration of Independence, reprinted in 27 INT'L LEGAL MAT'LS 1660, 1668 (1988). It contains much of the history surrounding this conflict. This Palestinian declaration of statehood was immediately recognized by the Soviet Union. As of 1988, then, the PLO claimed that the State of Palestine finally achieved *de facto,* if not *de jure,* existence as a State.

In 1989, the ICJ ruled against the United States on its unilateral attempt to close the PLO mission at the UN headquarters in New York City. The Reagan administration unsuccessfully argued that the antiterrorist legislation required closure "irrespective of any international legal obligations that the United States may have. . . ." The United States noted that since the PLO was not a State, the space for its observer mission had been provided only as a mere courtesy, and that the United States could do so because it was the host government for the United Nation's New York facilities. One basis for countering the US position materialized in mid-1988. Jordan's King Hussein severed all forms of legal and administrative ties between Jordan and the West Bank, wherein Jewish settlers had been introduced by Israel, and which the PLO claims as to be its territory.

The UN General Assembly adopted Resolution 43/177 in December 1988, whereby it accorded observer-*State* status, thus augmenting the mere *observer* status the PLO achieved years before. As of 1990, 114 States had recognized the newly proclaimed State of Palestine, some twenty States more than the ninety-three that recognized Israel.

The 1993 accords established a program resulting in a partial turnover of autonomy over Gaza and the West Bank to the Palestinian National Authority—although this so-called "land for peace" process became subsequently bogged down. In 1998, PLO Chairman, Arafat, announced that he would thus proclaim the *de jure* statehood of Palestine within two years, regardless of Israel's negotiating posture. He died before doing so.

In March 1999, the EU began to consider its potential collective recognition of a "Palestinian State." The EU reaffirmed the Palestinians' right to self-determination, but did not actually recognize "Palestine" as a State. Since then, attacks and counterattacks in the Middle East have confirmed that when there's a peace agreement in the air, there are usually bodies on the ground. In 2002, UN Security Counsel Resolution 1397 became the first to refer to "a vision of a region where two States, Israel and Palestine, live side-by-side within secure and recognized borders. . . ."

In March 2005, a US federal court affirmed a default judgment against the PLO and the Palestinian Authority. Relatives of a husband, wife, and infant son filed this wrongful death claim after they were murdered at a wedding in Israel. The defendants claimed that political recognition was not a prerequisite for a finding of statehood. After applying the usual elements of statehood, the court found that the Palestinian Authority had not yet exercised sufficient government control over Palestine to satisfy the test for statehood. As concluded by the court: "We recognize that the status of the Palestinian territories is in many ways sui generis. Here, however, the defendants have not carried their burden of showing that Palestine satisfied the requirements for statehood under the applicable principles of international law at any point in time. In view of the unmistakable legislative command that sovereign immunity shall only be accorded to states . . . the defendants' sovereign immunity defense must fail."[79]

Assume that the PLO is now applying to the United Nations for full State membership in the General Assembly. Had the PLO already satisfied any or all of the four traditional elements of statehood *before* the 1993? Did the 1994 Palestinian autonomy agreements do that? Is there now a State of Palestine after the autonomy agreements here? What is its nature; for example, is it a State within the international community of nations? *See generally* Israel-Palestine Liberation Organization, Agreement on the Gaza Strip and the Jericho Area, 33 INT'L LEGAL MAT'LS 622 (1994) & H. Hillel, COUNTDOWN TO STATEHOOD: PALESTINIAN STATE FORMATION IN THE WEST BANK AND GAZA (Albany, NY: State Univ. of NY Press, 1998).

Problem 2.B (end of §2.3) Under UN Security Council Resolution 777, the former State of "Yugoslavia" ceased to exist at the United Nations. (See *Bosnia v. FRY*, on course Web page, Chapter Three.) In 1992, the former Yugoslavia split into what are currently five States: Bosnia-Herzegovina, Croatia, Macedonia, Slovenia, and the remaining "rump" State of Yugoslavia (consisting of Serbia and Montenegro).

The Macedonian province ultimately became a nation-State, was recognized by a number of countries, and is now a member of the United Nations. Selection of the name "Republic of Macedonia" was fraught with irony. Greece was furious about the name chosen for this new country (Macedonia). It already had a province named Macedonia. The name "Macedonia" deeply resonates among the Greek population. Alexander the Great resided in this particular Greek province during his famous conquests of the Roman era. Now, Greece's northern province of "Macedonia" and the new "Republic of Macedonia" share a common international border of approximately 300 kilometers. Greece feared that the Republic of Macedonia—by selecting that particular name—effectively demonstrated territorial aspirations for the future assimilation of the Greek province of Macedonia into the bordering country of Macedonia. Greece refers to this area in the new Republic as "Skopje" (also the name Macedonia's capital city). The UN Secretary-General suggested that Macedonia at least change its name to "New Macedonia," if the term *Macedonia* were going to remain a part of Macedonia's official country name.

The EU did not immediately recognize Macedonia, when it declared its independence from the former Yugoslavia. Macedonia was then a territory desperately seeking recognition from other States. The EU had recognized Slovenia and Croatia, approximately six months after their votes of independence from the former Yugoslavia. Regarding Macedonia, however, the EU leadership expressed that "there are still important matters to be addressed before a similar step by the Community and its member States will be taken." This was a smokescreen designed to temporarily delay the recognition of the new State of "Macedonia," due to Greece's continuing objections to the recognition of Macedonia by member States of the EU. The EU then promulgated its Recognition Guidelines (§2.4) as the device for structuring mutually agreed-upon succession, secession, and self-determination of the territories of the former Yugoslavia. All applicants for collective recognition by the EU were then required to comply with these requirements, as well as obtain approval of the UN Secretary-General, the Security Council, and the EU Conference on Yugoslavia for resolving such conflicts. This disputed region was admitted to the United Nations, under the name "Former Yugoslav Republic of Macedonia," to sidestep Greek objections. In November 2004, the United States decided to bear the wrath of its NATO ally Greece by recognizing Macedonia under its constitutional name "Republic of Macedonia." Macedonia has since sent troops in support of the US efforts in Afghanistan and Iraq.

The EU chose not to expressly recognize Macedonia. Instead, it determined that its member States could "recognize that State as a sovereign and independent State . . . and under a name that can be accepted by all parties concerned [*i.e.*, Greece] . . . [while] member States look forward to establishing with the authorities in Skopje [Macedonia's capital city] a fruitful cooperative relationship."

Questions: (1) Is Macedonia a "recognized" State? (2) What would Macedonia have done to satisfy EU Guidelines for Recognition? (3) Should Macedonia be recognized by other States outside of the EU? *See generally* Yung Wei, Recognition of Divided States: Implication and Application of Concepts of "Multi-System Nations," "Political Entities," and "Intra-National Commonwealth," 34 INT'L LAWYER 997 (2000).

Problem 2.C (end of §2.4) Palestinians inhabit various countries in the Middle East. Although Israel and the PLO began to implement an autonomy agreement as to Gaza and the City of Jericho in 1994, the UN partition plan of 1947 supposedly "created" a Palestinian State—much of which was lost as a result of the ensuing wars between various Arab States and Israel.

Are Palestinians within the States of Israel, Jordan, Lebanon, and Syria entitled to:

(1) Secession
(2) Succession
(3) Self-determination
(4) All of the above
(5) None of these alternatives.

Problem 2.D (after §2.4 *East Timor* Case) In July 1998, the United States began to give military aid to two Colombian Army units. The disclosed purpose was to protect human rights in Colombia. The US Department of State then commented that the aid includes night vision goggles, communications equipment, river boats, and aircraft for the ostensible purpose of counter-narcotics operations.

Critics warned, however, that the real purpose for this "aid" is to augment the US role in Colombia's antiguerilla war against indigenous forces desiring to overthrow the Colombian government. Colombian authorities noted that they have needed this material, in a huge area within southern and eastern Colombia containing strongholds of the Revolutionary Armed Forces (RAF) of Colombia. The RAF is one of Latin America's largest rebel forces.

Assume that the RAF has access to the UN general assembly or a media broadcast regarding this development in Colombia. The leader of the RAF claims that the US assistance to the Colombian Army has violated the indigenous population's right to self-determination. Three students (or groups) represent, respectively, the RAF, Colombia, and the United States. They will now deliberate whether the various UN resolutions and ICJ cases (e.g., East Timor and Western Sahara) support the

RAF's claim that the Colombian government and the United States are thereby violating the Colombian people's right to self-determination.

Problem 2.E (end of §2.4) Europe's gypsies apparently began their westward exodus from India in the tenth century. They have been a migratory people with no territory, political influence, or formal organization. Their itinerant wandering is both the hallmark of their culture and their greatest conflict with structured societies. It is difficult to educate, tax, and count them in any one nation's population census. The Nazis slaughtered many gypsies in a genocidal campaign to achieve "racial purity" during World War II. They were more recently been driven from their homes by Bosnian Serbs and Croat military forces. Thousands fled to Italy and Germany in the 1990s, only to face attack by neo-Nazis and expulsion under strict immigration laws.

In 1997, the Czech Republic's President Havel admonished Czechs to end their intolerance of gypsies after a wave of them departed for Canada in the pursuit of a safe harbor. In 1991, a Sub-Commission of the UN Commission on Human Rights invited States containing "Roma" (gypsy) communities to take all necessary steps to ensure equality and guarantee the protection and security of gypsies within their various host States. UN Doc. E/CN.4/1992/2, further details on this general dilemma for host States, and international humanitarian law, are provided in the Gypsy Law Symposium, XLV AMER. J. COMP. LAW 225–442 (1997). The Gypsy International Recognition and Compensation Action, filed in Switzerland in February 2002, seeks reparations against IBM for its role in helping the Nazis commit mass murder. IBM's punch-card machines allegedly enhanced the efficiency of the Nazi extermination campaign.

Perhaps 1 million Spanish gypsies now roam throughout Spain making camp in makeshift villages, living literally on the edge of civilization, and outside of towns and on the fringes of Spain's larger cities. Gypsies gathered in Seville, Spain, in May 1994 for the first Gypsy Congress. This Congress was conducted under the auspices of the European Commission, the executive agency of the EU. The Commission is trying to help gypsies help themselves in the current violence, surfacing with a fury in Europe's waves of ethnic violence that materialized after the Cold War.

Are Spain's gypsies entitled to self-determination? If so, *how* would that right be implemented? *See generally*,

G. Lewy, THE NAZI PROSECUTION OF THE GYPSIES (New York: Oxford Univ. Press, 2000); M. Tsekos, Minority Rights: The Failure of International Law to Protect the Roma, 9 HUM. RIGHTS BRIEF, Issue No. 3, at 26 (Wash., DC: Amer. Univ. Coll. Law, 2002); and T. Acton, A Three-cornered Choice: Structural Consequences of Value-Priorities in Gypsy Law as a Model for More General Understanding of Variations in the Administration of Justice, 51 AMER. J. COMPARATIVE L. 639 (2003).

Problem 2.F (§2.6, after *Nelson Case* on Course Web page) Assume that after the US Supreme Court's *Nelson* opinion, the US senator who went to the aid of the Nelsons—while the husband was confined in Saudi Arabia—decides to help future litigants in another way. Senator Hawk proposes the following legislation to Congress as an amendment to the 1976 Foreign Sovereign Immunities Act (FSIA):

> Be it hereby enacted that, from this day forward, all courts in the United States will, in doubtful cases involving the "commercial nature" of the act or conduct complained of, grant sovereign immunity to democratic sovereigns, but deny it for authoritarian States and their instrumentalities. In the latter instance, US courts shall proceed to hear the merits of the underlying tort or contract disputes.

Two students will debate the propriety of this proposed legislation. They will specifically address: (1) whether Congress should thereby give democratic regimes greater sovereign immunity than authoritarian regimes; and (2) what impact that the 1996 revision to the FSIA *has*, or *could* have, for the purpose of future sovereign immunity cases. (*See* post *Nelson* **Notes & Questions**.)

Problem 2.G (§2.6, after *Nelson Case* on Course Web page) Section 1.2 of this book (Sources of International Law) addressed the concept of "*jus cogens*." It includes State conduct that violates International Law in a manner that provides no defense such as Nazi Germany's official genocidal policy. Section 2.6 mentions the *Pinochet* litigation, whereby the British House of Lords determined that the conduct of this former head of State vitiated the derivative immunity he would otherwise have enjoyed, because of his violations of the international Torture Convention.

In 2001, a US federal appellate court considered, but rejected, an Auschwitz survivor's claim that Germany could not claim sovereign immunity from suit in the United States. While the events described in this case clearly fell within the "*jus cogens*" doctrine, the US court nevertheless dismissed this case in the following terms:

> Sampson's complaint alleges horrors which are beyond belief, and the evils he describes cannot be condemned in strong enough terms. In 1939, Sampson was imprisoned in the Lodz ghetto in Poland. He was subsequently transported by cattle car to the Auschwitz concentration camp, where he was forced to perform slave labor. At Auschwitz, the Gestapo killed all sixty members of his family. Sampson somehow survived, and he is now a United States citizen and resident of Chicago. . . .
>
> The United States government filed a brief as amicus curiae (the "United States") in support of Germany's argument that it had sovereign immunity for its acts during World War II. . . .
>
> We think that something more nearly express . . . is wanted before we impute to the [United States] Congress an intention that the federal courts assume jurisdiction over the countless human rights cases that might well be brought by the victims of all the ruthless military juntas, presidents-for-life, and murderous dictators of the world, from Idi Amin to Mao Zedong. Such an expansive reading of [the Foreign Sovereign Immunities Act] § 1605(a)(1) would likely place an enormous strain not only upon our courts but, more to the immediate point, upon our country's diplomatic relations with any number of foreign nations. In many if not most cases the outlaw regime would no longer even be in power and our Government could have normal relations with the government of the day—unless disrupted by our courts, that is, Sampson v. Fed. Rep. Germany, 250 F.3d 1145, 1146–47 & 1152 (7th Cir., 2001).

Three students, or teams, will respectively represent Mr. Sampson, Germany, and the United States. They will present their respective positions on whether this court should have ruled in favor of *retaining* jurisdiction over this suit (rather than dismissing it). Hearing this case on its merits would have provided plaintiff Sampson with the opportunity to prove his case against the Federal Republic of Germany.

All parties agree to the following points: (1) Under International Law doctrine, States are bound by the *jus cogens* limitation on their conduct, even if they do not consent to its application. (2) Germany publicly acknowledged that its actions violated *jus cogens* norms (Nazi genocide policy). (3) The contemporary application of *restrictive* sovereign immunity replaced the absolute approach, which prevailed before the end of World War II. (4) Under US law, exceptions to the 1976 Foreign Sovereign Immunities Act (FSIA) have been narrowly construed. (5) US courts have generally determined that, under the FSIA, a foreign sovereign's waiver of its immunity from litigation will normally be inferred only as a last resort—because of the potential impact on foreign relations.

◆ BIBLIOGRAPHY

§2.1 Legal Personality

J. Hickey, Jr. (ed.), International Legal Personality, 2 HOFSTRA LAW & POLICY SYMPOSIUM 1–170 (articles on various topics)

J. Jackson, Sovereignty Modern: A New Approach to an Outdated Concept, 97 AMER. J. INT'L L. 782 (2003)

R. Lapidoth, AUTONOMY: FLEXIBLE SOLUTIONS TO ETHNIC CONFLICTS (Wash., DC: US Inst. Peace, 1997)

O. Okafor, RE-DEFINING LEGITIMATE STATEHOOD: INTERNATIONAL LAW AND STATE FRAGMENTATION IN AFRICA (The Hague: Martinus Nijhoff, 2000)

A. Osiander, THE STATES SYSTEM OF EUROPE, 1640–1990: PEACEMAKING AND THE CONDITIONS OF INTERNATIONAL STABILITY (Oxford, Eng.: Oxford Univ. Press, 1994)

S. Pegg, INTERNATIONAL SOCIETY AND THE DE FACTO STATE (Aldershot, Eng.: Ashgate, 1998)

John T. Scott, The Sovereignless State and Locke's Language of Obligation, 94 AMER. POL. SCI. REV. 3 (2000)

N. Wallace-Bruce, CLAIMS TO STATEHOOD IN INTERNATIONAL LAW (New York: Carlton Press, 1994)

W. Zartman (ed.), COLLAPSED STATES: THE DISINTEGRATION AND RESTORATION OF LEGITIMATE AUTHORITY (Boulder, CO: Rienner, 1995)

§2.2 Shifting State Infrastructure

G. Abi-Saab, The Newly Independent States and the Rules of International Law, 8 HOWARD LAW J. 95 (1962)

R. Anand, CONFRONTATION OR COOPERATION: INTERNATIONAL LAW AND THE DEVELOPING COUNTRIES (New Delhi: Banyan, 1986)

W. Friedmann, THE CHANGING STRUCTURE OF INTERNATIONAL LAW (New York: Columbia Univ. Press, 1964)

K. Ginther & W. Benedek (eds.), NEW PERSPECTIVES AND CONCEPTIONS OF INTERNATIONAL LAW: AN AFRO-EUROPEAN DIALOGUE (Vienna: Springer-Verlag, 1983)

E. McWhinney, The "New" Countries and the "New" International Law: The United Nations' Special Conference on

Friendly Relations and Cooperation Among States, 60 AMER. J. INT'L LAW1 (1966)

S. Sinha, Treatment of Asian and African Peoples under International Law during the Past Four Centuries, ch. 1 in NEW NATIONS AND THE LAW OF NATIONS 11 (Leiden, Neth.: A.W. Sijthoff, 1967)

W. Zartman (ed.), COLLAPSED STATES: THE DISINTEGRATION AND RESTORATION OF LEGITIMATE AUTHORITY (Boulder, CO: Reinner, 1995)

§2.3 Recognition

C. Chinkin, The Law and Ethics of Recognition: Cambodia and Timor, ch. 10 in P. Keal (ed.), ETHICS AND FOREIGN POLICY 190 (St. Leonards, Australia: Allen & Unwin, 1992)

T. Grant, THE RECOGNITION OF STATES: LAW AND PRACTICE IN DEBATE AND EVOLUTION (Westport, CT: Praeger, 1999)

L. Kato, Recognition in International Law: Some Thoughts on Traditional Theory, Attitudes of and Practice by African States, 19 INDIAN J. INT'L LAW 299 (1970)

S. Talmon, RECOGNITION IN INTERNATIONAL LAW: A BIBLIOGRAPHY (The Hague: Martinus Nijhoff, 2000)

§2.4 Changes in State Status

SUCCESSION

S. Bernanzez, Succession of States, ch. 18 in M. Bedjaoui (ed.), INTERNATIONAL LAW: ACHIEVEMENTS AND PROSPECTS 381 (Dordrecht, Neth.: Martinus Nijhoff, 1991)

V. D. Degan, Equity in Matters of State Succession, ch. 14 in R. Macdonald, ESSAYS IN HONOUR OF WANG TIEYA 201 (Dordrecht, Neth.: Martinus Nijhoff, 1994)

R. Lapidoth & M. Hirsch (eds.), THE ARAB-ISRAELI CONFLICT AND ITS RESOLUTION: SELECTED DOCUMENTS (Dordrecht, Neth.: Martinus Nijhoff, 1992)

SECESSION

A. Eide, In Search of Constructive Alternatives to Secession, in C. Tomuschat (ed.), MODERN LAW OF SELF-DETERMINATION 139 (Dordrecht, Neth.: Martinus Nijhoff, 1993)

D. Murswiek, The Issue of a Right of Secession "Reconsidered," in C. Tomuschat (ed.), MODERN LAW OF SELF-DETERMINATION 21 (Dordrecht, Neth.: Martinus Nijhoff, 1993)

SELF-DETERMINATION

S. Anaya, INDIGENOUS PEOPLES IN INTERNATIONAL LAW (Oxford, Eng.: Oxford Univ. Press, 1996)

A. Cassese, SELF-DETERMINATION OF PEOPLES: A LEGAL REPRISAL (Cambridge, Eng.: Cambridge Univ. Press, 1995)

E. Hasani, SELF-DETERMINATION, TERRITORIAL INTEGRITY AND INTERNATIONAL STABILITY: THE CASE OF YUGOSLAVIA (Vienna: Nat'l Defense Academy, 2003)

E. Jensen, WESTERN SAHARA: ANATOMY OF A STALEMATE (Boulder, CO: Reinner, 2004)

R. Lapidoth & M. Hirsch (eds.), THE ARAB-ISRAELI CONFLICT AND ITS RESOLUTION: SELECTED DOCUMENTS (Dordrecht, Neth.: Martinus Nijhoff, 1992)

GENERAL

J. Duursma, FRAGMENTATION AND THE INTERNATIONAL RELATIONS OF MICRO-STATES (Cambridge, Eng.: Cambridge Univ. Press, 1996)

G. Ginsburgs, FROM SOVIET TO RUSSIAN INTERNATIONAL LAW: STUDIES IN CONTINUITY AND CHANGE (The Hague, Neth.: Martinus Nijhoff, 1998)

G. Lyons & M. Mastanduno, BEYOND WESTPHALIA: STATE SOVEREIGNTY AND INTERNATIONAL INTERVENTION (Baltimore: John Hopkins Univ. Press, 1995)

S. Murphy (ed.), Barring of FRY [former Yugoslavia] Representative at UN Security Council, in Contemporary Practice of the United States Relating to International Law, 94 AMER. J. INT'L L. 677 (2000)

M. Olcott, CENTRAL ASIA'S NEW STATES: INDEPENDENCE, FOREIGN POLICY, AND REGIONAL SECURITY (Wash., DC: US Inst. Peace, 1996)

M. Schoiswohl, STATUS AND (HUMAN RIGHTS) OBLIGATIONS OF NON-RECOGNIZED DE FACTO REGIMES IN INTERNATIONAL LAW: THE CASE OF 'SOMALILAND' (Leiden, Neth: Martinus Nijhoff, 2004)

J. Scott, The Sovereignless State and Locke's Language of Obligation, 94 AMER. POL. SCI. REV. 3 (2000)

§2.5 State Responsibility

W. Butler, CONTROL OVER COMPLIANCE WITH INTERNATIONAL LAW (Dordrecht, Neth.: Martinus Nijhoff, 1991)

State Responsibility, ch. 8 in R. Wallace, INTERNATIONAL LAW: A STUDENT INTRODUCTION 166 (2d ed. London: Street & Maxwell, 1992)

THESAURUS ACROASIUM: RESPONSIBILITY OF STATES (Thessaloniki, Greece: Inst. Int'l Public Law & Int'l Relations, 1993)

J. Weiler, A. Cassese, & M. Spinedi (eds.), INTERNATIONAL CRIMES OF STATE: A CRITICAL ANALYSIS OF THE ILC'S DRAFT ARTICLE 19 ON STATE RESPONSIBILITY (Berlin: De Gruyter, 1989)

§2.6 Sovereign Immunity

J. Dellapenna, SUING FOREIGN GOVERNMENTS AND THEIR CORPORATIONS (2d ed. Wash., DC: Transnational, 2003)

J. Donoghue, Taking the "Sovereign" Out of the Foreign Sovereign Immunities Act: A Functional Approach to the Commercial Activity Exception, 17 YALE J. INT'L LAW 489 (1992)

OAS Inter-American Draft Convention on Jurisdictional Immunity of States, 22 INT'L LEGAL MAT'LS 292 (1983)

A. Perez, The Perils of Pinochet: Problems for Transitional Justice and a Supranational Governance Solution, 28 DENVER J. INT'L LAW & POLICY 175 (2000)

Y. Simbeye, IMMUNITY AND INTERNATIONAL CRIMINAL LAW (Aldershot, Eng.: Ashgate, 2004)

S. Sucharitkul, Immunity of States, ch. 16 in M. Bedjaoui (ed.), INTERNATIONAL LAW: ACHIEVEMENTS AND PROSPECTS 327 (Dordrecht, Neth.: Martinus Nijhoff, 1991)

US Foreign Sovereign Immunities Act of 1976, 15 INT'L LEGAL MAT'LS 1388 (1976)

Additional Internet Resources

Country Facts: <http://www.theodora.com/wfb/abc_world_fact_book.html>

Country Studies: <http://lcweb2.loc.gov/frd/cs/cshome.html#toc>

Foreign Government Web sites: <http://www.library.northwestern.edu/govpub/resource/internat/foreign.html>

G. Gong, The 19th Century Standard of "Civilization," in Asian Financial Crisis: Culture and Strategy, University of Pennsylvania (Sept. 29, 1998): <http://www.icasinc.org/f1998/gwgf1998.html>

National Judicial Web sites: <http://www.ncsconline.org/D_KIS/CourtWebSites/International.html>

National Laws: <http://www.loc.gov/law/guide/nations.html#I>

US CIA World Fact Book: <http://www.odci.gov/cia/publications/factbook/index.html>

US Library of Congress Country Studies: <http://lcweb2.loc.gov/frd/cs/cshome.html#toc>

World Legal Systems <http://www.uottawa.ca/world-legal-systems/eng-generale.htm>

World Maps: <http://lcweb2.loc.gov/frd/cs/cshome.html#toc>

◆ ENDNOTES

1. B. Chimni, Third World Approaches to International Law: A Manifesto, ch. 4, in A. Anghie, et al. (ed.), THE THIRD WORLD AND INTERNATIONAL ORDER: LAW, POLITICS AND GLOBALIZATION 47, 51–52 (Leiden, Neth.: Brill, 2003).

2. *1992*: B. Boutros-Ghali, AN AGENDA FOR PEACE: PREVENTATIVE DIPLOMACY, PEACEMAKING AND PEACE-KEEPING 9 (New York: UN, 1992). *1995*: B. Boutros-Ghali, AN AGENDA FOR PEACE: SUPPLEMENT TO AN AGENDA FOR PEACE 1 (New York: UN, 1995).

3. W. Friedmann, THE CHANGING STRUCTURE OF INTERNATIONAL LAW 214 (New York: Columbia Univ. Press, 1964)

4. *See generally* W. Rice, Nation v. State-Judgment for Nation, 44 AMER. J. INT'L L. 162 (1950); M. Brandon, State v. Nation: Fresh Evidence Admitted, 44 AMER. J. INT'L L. 577 (1950). *State*: Article 1, 165 LON TREATY SERIES 19, 49 US STAT. 3097. *Nation*: B. Driessen, A CONCEPT OF NATION IN INTERNATIONAL LAW 13 (The Hague, Neth.: T.M.C. Asser Inst., 1992). *Community*: Greco-Bulgarian Communities Case, 1930 PCIJ REP., SER. B, No. 17, at 33. *People*: Driessen, at 17. *Government*: J. Fox, DICTIONARY OF INTERNATIONAL & COMPARATIVE LAW 75 (2d ed. New York: Oceana, 1997). *Sovereign*: J. Falk & J. Camilleri, THE END OF SOVEREIGNTY? THE POLITICS OF A SHRINKING AND FRAGMENTING WORLD 11 (Hants, Eng.: Edward Elgar Pub., 1992).

5. Charter of the Organization of American States, Art 9, available at: <http://www.yale.edu/lawweb/avalon/decade/decad062.htm#art9>

6. Ptera Minnerop, The Classification of States and the Creation of States within the International Community, in 7 MAX PLANK YEARBOOK OF UNITED NATIONS LAW 79 (Leiden: Martinus Nijhoff: 2004). For attacks *on* a "rogue State" absent an attack *from* one, see The New National Security Strategy, *id*., at 158.

7. 165 LON TREATY SERIES 19, 49 US Stat. 3097.

8. Although Quebec has received the most attention, Nunavut's flag flew for the first time (April, 1999) in the now self-governing territory in the northernmost portion of Canada. This culminates twenty years of negotiations between Canada and its indigenous, aboriginal Inuit people, who number about 25,000.

9. M. Gunter, What Happened to the United Nations Ministate Problem? 71 AMER. J. INT'L L. 110 (1977) (no minimum population); Case Concerning Acquisition of Polish Nationality (Germany v. Poland), 1923 PCIJ, Ser. B, No. 7, at 18 (Judgment of Sept. 15, 1923) (express grant not required).

10. *Finland*: League of Nations, Commission of Jurists on Aaland Islands Dispute, OFFICIAL JOURNAL, SPECIAL SUPP. 4, at 8–9 (1920). *Iraq*: C. Le Mon, Legality of a Request by the Interim Iraqi Government for the Continued Presence of United States Military Forces, ASIL Insight (June 2004), available at: <http://www.asil.org/insights/insigh135.htm>.

11. The Associated Press reported this development, based on a report by Radio Shariat on January 23, 2000.

12. *Burma case*: Crosby v. National Foreign Trade Council, 530 U.S. 363, 373–374, 120 S.Ct. 2288, 2294, 147 L.Ed.2d 352 (2000). *Holocaust case*: American Insurance Association v. Garamendi, 539 U.S. 396, 430, 123 S.Ct. 2374, 2395, 156 L.Ed.2d 376 (2003) (J. Ginzburg dissenting).

13. J. H. Verzijl, Western European Influence on the Foundations of International Law, 1 INT'L RELATIONS 137 (1955).

14. *Non-Western writer*: K. Sastri, International Law and Relations in Ancient India, 1 INDIAN YEARBK. INT'L AFFAIRS 97 (1952). *Western writer*: C. Alexandrowicz, Mogul Sovereignty and the Law of Nations, 4 INDIAN YEARBK. INT'L AFFAIRS 317, 318 (1955).

15. P. Chandra, INTERNATIONAL LAW 28 (New Delhi: Vikas, 1985) ("chaotic"); D. O'Connell, INTERNATIONAL LAW 127 (2d ed. New York: Oceana, 1970) ("confusing"; J. Dugard, RECOGNITION AND THE UNITED NATIONS 28 (Cambridge, Eng.: Grotius, 1987) ("controversial") [hereinafter *Recognition and the UN*].

16. Arab Nations Refuse to Recognize Iraq's Governing Council, USA Today (Aug. 5, 2003).

17. J. Ruda, Recognition of States and Governments, ch. 21 in M. Bedjaoui (ed.), INTERNATIONAL LAW: ACHIEVEMENTS AND PROSPECTS 450 (Dordrecht, Neth.: Martinus Nijhoff, 1991). On the historical evolution of recognition practice, see G. Abi-Saab, International Law and the International Community: The Long Road to Universality 36–39 (The Role of "Recognition"), ch. 1 in R. MacDonald (ed.), ESSAYS IN HONOUR OF WANG TIEYA (Dordrecht, Neth.: Martinus Nijhoff, 1994).

18. J. Klabbers et al. (ed.), STATE PRACTICE REGARDING STATE SUCCESSION AND ISSUES OF RECOGNITION 34 & 38 (The Hague: Kluwer, 1999) [hereinafter *Klabbers*].

19. *See, e.g.*: "The career of Eugenio Pacelli–Pope Pius XII—from the beginning of this century is the story of a bid for unprecedented papal power that by 1933 had drawn the Catholic Church into complicity with the darkest forces of the era." Preface, viii, J. Cornwall, HITLER'S POPE: THE SECRET HISTORY OF PIUS XII (New York: Viking Press, 1999).

20. E. McDowell, Contemporary Practice of the United States Relating to International Law, 71 AMER. J. INT'L L. 337 (1977) (recognition by other States); C. Fenwick, INTERNATIONAL LAW 157–159 (4th ed. New York: Appleton-Century-Crofts, 1965) (ethnocentric motives); see The Helena, 4 CH. ROB. 3 (1801) (British case on pirate treaties), reprinted in W. Bishop, INTERNATIONAL LAW, CASES AND MATERIALS 301 (3d ed. Boston: Little, Brown & Co., 1971); G. Von Glahn, LAW AMONG NATIONS 69 (7th ed. Boston: Allyn and Bacon, 1996) (commercial and military motives).

21. Two academic treatises sparked this post-World War II debate about the nature of recognition. They are still the classics. *Compare* H. Lauterpacht, RECOGNITION IN INTERNATIONAL LAW 63 (Cambridge, Eng.: Cambridge Univ. Press, 1947) (recognition is not primarily a manifestation of national policy, but the fulfillment of an international duty) *with* T. Chen, THE INTERNATIONAL LAW OF RECOGNITION 61 (Green ed. London: Stevens, 1951) (recognition is merely declarative of the existing fact of statehood).

22. The author thanks Mary Durfee (Associate Professor of the Social Sciences Department at Michigan Technological University) for this useful analogy.

23. S. Talmon, RECOGNITION OF GOVERNMENTS IN INTERNATIONAL LAW: WITH PARTICULAR REFERENCE TO GOVERNMENTS IN EXILE 21–27 (Oxford: Clarendon Press, 1998) (footnotes omitted).

24. *Tobar Doctrine*: see C. Stansifer, Application of the Tobar Doctrine to Central America, 23 The Americas (Jan. 1967), at 251–72. *Estrada Doctrine*: Genaro Estrada's doctrinal statement is reprinted in 25 AMER. J. INT'L L. SUPP. 203 (1931). A provocative response was published in P. Jessup, The Estrada Doctrine, 25 AMER. J. INT'L LAW 719 (1930).

25. *See* P. Brown, The Legal Effects of Recognition, 44 AMER. J. INT'L L. 617 (1950); Comment, Effects in Private Litigation of Failure to Recognize New Foreign Governments, 19 UNIV. CHICAGO L. REV. 73 (1951).

26. Bank of China v. Wells Fargo Bank & Union Trust Co., 104 Fed. Supp. 59 (1952), affirmed, 209 F.2d 467 (1953).

27. *Fifty years later*: Mingtai Fire & Marine Insurance Co. v. United Parcel Service, 177 F.3d 1142 Cir., 1999), cert. den'd 528 U.S. 951 (1999). *Hong Kong*: Cheung v. US, 213 F.3d 82, 88–89 (2d Cir., 2000). *PRC legislation*: See J. Kahn, *60 Years Later, China Enemies End Their War*, New York Times on the Web (Apr. 30, 2005).

28. *Elements for recognition*: J. Paust, War and Enemy Status After 9/11: Attacks on the Laws of War, 28 Yale Int'l L. J. 325 (2003). *Rights conferred*: The Three Friends, 166 U.S. 1, 63, 17 S.Ct. 495, 502, 41 L.Ed. 897 (1897).

29. See course Web site at <http://home.att.net/~slomansonb/txtcsesite.html>, click on Chap. One Treaty of Westphalia.

30. *See generally* E. Chadwick, TRADITIONAL NEUTRALITY REVISITED: LAW, THEORY, AND CASE STUDIES (Hague: Kluwer, 2002); S. Neff, THE RIGHTS AND DUTIES OF NEUTRALS: A GENERAL HISTORY (Manchester, Eng.: Manchester Univ. Press, 2000); and Unilateral and Third Party Claims: Neutrality, Section 13.4, in C. Chinkin, THIRD PARTIES IN INTERNATIONAL LAW 299 (Oxford, Eng.: Clarendon Press, 1993).

31. They are conveniently collated in Neutrality, ch. XIII, in D. Schindler & J. Toman (ed.), THE LAWS OF ARMED CONFLICTS: A COLLECTION OF CONVENTIONS, RESOLUTIONS AND OTHER DOCUMENTS, Nos. 112–115, at 1399 (Leiden: Martinus Nijhoff, 2004).

32. *See* English translation in Collective Recognition and Non-Recognition Under the League of Nations, ch. 3, at 28 & arguments for and against this practice, ch. 4, in *Recognition and the UN* 41 (cited in note 15 above].

33. Memorandum on the Legal Aspects of the Problem of Representation in the United Nations, UN DOC. S/1466, Mar. 9, 1950.

34. EU Recognition Guidelines are reprinted in 31 INT'L LEGAL MAT'LS 1485 (1992).

35. *See, e.g.*, 2 FOREIGN POL. BULLETIN 39, 42 (Nov./Dec. 1991) (testimony of US Deputy Ass't of Dep't of State).

36. *East Timor*: N. Azimi & Chang Li Lin, THE UNITED NATIONS TRANSITIONAL ADMINISTRATION IN EAST TIMOR (Leiden, Neth.: Martinus Nijhoff, 2003). *Kosovo*: United Nations Interim Administration Mission in Kosovo (UN Web page) at <http://www. unmikonline.org>.

37. *1978 "treaty" succession*: UN Doc. A/CONF. 80/31. *1983 "property" succession*: UN DOC. A/CONF. 117/14 (the former has entered into force, although only the minimum fifteen nations have ratified it; the latter draft treaty has not entered into force).

38. *See* Treaty on the Final Settlement with Respect to Germany, 29 INT'L LEGAL MAT'LS 1186, 1188 (1990) ("united Germany shall comprise the territory of the [FRG, GDR,] . . . and the whole of Berlin").

39. K. Chrysostomides, THE REPUBLIC OF CYPRUS: A STUDY IN INTERNATIONAL LAW (The Hague: Martinus Nijhoff, 2000) (especially Chapter 7: "Unilateral Declaration of Independence" Contrary to International Law, at 237).

40. On State succession generally, see R. Jennings & A. Watts, 1 OPPENHEIM'S INTERNATIONAL LAW (Part I) §§60–70 (9th ed. Essex, Eng.: Longman, 1993) [hereinafter *Oppenheim*]. Recognition issues are addressed in *Klabbers* [cited in note 18 above]. Regarding treaties, property and debt, see P. Menon, THE SUCCESSION OF STATES IN RESPECT TO TREATIES, STATE PROPERTY, ARCHIVES, AND DEBTS (Lampeter, Wales: E. Mellon, 1991). A new State's responsibilities to an organization, of which the prior State was a member, is addressed in K. Buhler, STATE SUCCESSION AND MEMBERSHIP IN INTERNATIONAL ORGANIZATIONS: LEGAL THEORIES VERSUS POLITICAL PRAGMATISM (The Hague: Kluwer, 2001). Succession between international organizations is covered in P. Meyers, SUCCESSION BETWEEN INTERNATIONAL ORGANIZATIONS (London: Kegan Paul Int'l, 1993). Regarding UN membership, see K. Buhler, ch.2, State Succession, Identity/Continuity and Membership in the United *Nations* 187–326, in P. Eisemann & M. Koskenniemi (ed.), STATE SUCCESSION: CODIFICATION TESTED AGAINST THE FACTS (The Hague: Martinus Nijhoff, 2000).

41. *Colombia*: J. Moore, 5 DIGEST OF INTERNATIONAL LAW 341 (Wash., DC: US Gov't Printing Off., 1906). *Texas*: J. Moore, 3 HISTORY AND DIGEST OF THE INTERNATIONAL ARBITRATIONS

TO WHICH THE UNITED STATES HAS BEEN A PARTY 3223 (Wash., DC: US Gov't Print. Off., 1898).

42. *Oppenheim* (Part I), §62, 211–213 [cited in note 40 above].

43. International Arbitration entitled Regarding Dues for Reply Coupons Issued in Croatia, 23 INT'L L. REP. 591 (1956).

44. *See 1983 treaty*, Article 9 on property & Article 36 on debts [cited in note 37 above].

45. *Oppenheim* (Part I), §62, 218–219 [cited in note 40 above].

46. For further details, see I. Martin, SELF-DETERMINATION IN EAST TIMOR: THE UNITED NATIONS, THE BALLOT, AND INTERNATIONAL INTERVENTION (Boulder, CO: Rienner, 2001).

47. A. Buchanan, SECESSION: THE MORALITY OF POLITICAL DIVORCE FROM FORT SUMTER TO LITHUANIA AND QUEBEC 2 (Boulder, CO: Westview Press, 1991)

48. O. Schachter, The Development of International Law Through the Legal Opinions of the United Nations Secretariat, XXV BRITISH YEARBOOK INT'L L. 91, 107 (1948).

49. Namibia (South-West Africa) Case, 1971 ICJ REP. 55.

50. *Res. 1514*: Declaration on the Granting of Independence to Colonial Countries and Peoples, UN GAOR 15TH SESS., SUPP. No. 16 (A/4884), at 66. *Res. 1541*: UN GAOR 15TH SESS., SUPP. No. 16 (A/4684), at 29. RES. 2625: UN GAOR 25TH SESS., SUPP. NO. 8 (A/8028), at 121. *CPR Covenant*: 999 U.N.T.S. 171. *ESC Covenant*: 999 U.N.T.S. 3. 1970 Declaration: UN GAOR 25TH SESS., SUPP. NO. 8, (A/8028) at 121. *Reservations*: See, e.g., United Kingdom, UN GAOR 21ST SESS., THIRD COMM., 1496th Mtg., 16 Dec. 1966, at 10–11.

51. Western Sahara (Advisory Opinion), 1975 ICJ REP. 12, para 162; reprinted in 14 INT'L LEGAL MAT'LS 1355 (1975).

52. To further explore those breaches, which supposedly impact *all* nations, as opposed to harming only one/several nations, see A. de Hoogh, OBLIGATIONS ERGA OMNES AND INTERNATIONAL CRIMES: A THEORETICAL INQUIRY INTO THE IMPLEMENTATION AND ENFORCEMENT OF THE INTERNATIONAL RESPONSIBILITY OF STATES (Hague: Kluwer, 1996).

53. Whether actually *damage* is required is the subject of an intense debate. *See* A. Tanzi, Is Damage a Distinct Condition for the Existence of an Internationally Wrongful Act? in M. Spinedi & B. Simma (eds.), UNITED NATIONS CODIFICATION OF STATE RESPONSIBILITY (New York: Oceana, 1987).

54. Case Concerning the Factory at Chorzow, PCIJ SER. A, No. 17, at 29 (1928).

55. Rainbow Warrior Arbitration, 82 INT'L L. REP. 499, 551 (1991). *See* UN Secretary-General's opinion contained in 81 AMER. J. INT'L L. 325 (1987). Further details are provided in Problem 12.C.

56. 1949 ICJ REP. 4, 18.

57. State Responsibility, ch. 14, in M. Shaw, INTERNATIONAL LAW 699–700 (5th ed. Cambridge, Eng.: Cambridge Univ. Press, 2003).

58. *See* UN, THE WORK OF THE INTERNATIONAL LAW COMMISSION 121 (New York: UN, 1996). On the various phases of the ILC's work, see I. Sinclair, THE INTERNATIONAL LAW COMMISSION, ch. II, at 45 (Cambridge, Eng.: Grotius, 1987). Various provisions, their genesis, and their development are discussed in S. Rosenne, THE INTERNATIONAL LAW COMMISSION'S DRAFT ARTICLES ON STATE RESPONSIBILITY (Dordrecht, Neth.: Martinus Nijhoff, 1991).

59. ILC draft reprinted in 37 INT'L LEGAL MAT'LS 440 (1998). For the State responses, see <www.law.cam.ac.uk/rcil/ILCSR/Statresp.htm>. That Web site also identifies the Articles adopted on "Second Reading" by the Drafting Committee (1998–2000), as well as the literature on State Responsibility from various regions of the world. The final draft is UN DOC. A/CN.4/L.602/REV.1 (July 26, 2001). is available at <http://www.un.org/law/ilc/texts/decfra.htm>.

60. *See* University of Law Study at Padova's (Italy) Professor Andrea Gattini, Smoking/No Smoking: Some Remarks on the Current Place of Fault in the ILC Draft Articles on State Responsibility, in Symposium: State Responsibility, 10 EUROPEAN J. INT'L L. 399 (1999).

61. *Articles and Commentary*: J. Crawford, THE INTERNATIONAL LAW COMMISSION'S ARTICLES ON STATE RESPONSIBILITY: INTRODUCTION, TEXT AND COMMENTARIES (Cambridge: Cambridge Univ. Press, 2002). *Symposium*: The ILC's State Responsibility Articles, 96 AMER. J. INT'L L. 773–890 (2002).

62. Sampson v. Fed. Rep. Germany, 250 F.3d 1145, 1146–1147 & 1152 (7th Cir., 2001).

63. Karlheinz Schreiber v. Federal Republic of Germany and the Attorney General of Canada, 2002 Can. Sup. Ct. 62 §13 (2002).

64. Verlinden B.V. v. Central Bank of Nigeria, 461 U.S. 480, 488, 103 S.Ct. 1962, 1969, 76 L.Ed.2d 81 (1983), quoting 1976 H.R. REPORT NO. 94–1487, at 7.

65. See, specifically, Hickenlooper quote in text accompanying Chapter 1 endnote 120 and the principale case application in *Kadic v. Karadzic*.

66. State Immunity as a Personal Plea, Distinguished from the Doctrines of Act of State and Non-justiciability, ch. 11, in H. Fox, THE LAW OF STATE IMMUNITY 477, at 481 (Oxford, Eng.: Oxford Univ. Press, 2002).

67. Ministry of Defence v. Ndegwa, 103 INT'L LAW REP. 235 (Kenya Court App., 1983).

68. Aldona S. v. United Kingdom, Supreme Court of Poland (1948), reported in 90 JOURNAL DU DROIT INTERNATIONAL 191 (1963).

69. 1 Queen's Bench 149 (1893), reported in ALL ENG. Rep. 1019 (1963).

70. *Violation of International Law*: L. Henkin, The Invasion of Panama Under International Law: A Gross Violation, 29 COLUMBIA J. TRANSNAT'L L. 293 (1991). *Rejection of Head of State immunity*: US v. Noriega, 117 F.3rd 1206 (11th Cir., 1997), *cert. den'd*, 118 US 1389 (1998).

71. *See* S. Andrews, U.S. Courts Rule on Absolute Immunity and Inviolability of Foreign Heads of State: The Cases against Robert Mugabe and Jiang Zemin, ASIL INSIGHT (Nov. 2004) at <http://www.asil.org/insights/2004/11/insight041122.html>.

72. N. Roht-Arriaza, THE PINOCHET EFFECT: TRANSNATIONAL JUSTICE IN THE AGE OF HUMAN RIGHTS (Philadelphia: Univ. Penn Press, 2004).

73. *Rome Statute*: see <www.un.org/icc/romestat.htm>. *Immunity case*: Wei Ye v. Jiang Zemin and Falun Gong Control Office, 383 F.3d 620, 626–627 (7th Cir. 2004) (parentheticals

removed). *See also*: Tachiona v. U.S., 386 F.3d 205 (2nd Cir., 2004) (US successfully appealed judgment against Zimbabwe's president, who was, while acting in different capacity, nevertheless immune from suit).

74. Reid v. Covert, 354 U.S. 1, 77 S.Ct 1222, 1 L.Ed.2d 1148 (1957).

75. See R. Bernstein, Belguim: War Crimes Complaint Against Franks, NYT on the Web (May 15, 2003).

76. European Convention on State Immunity, available at <http://wwwserver.law.wits.ac.za/humanrts/euro/ets74.html>.

77. D. Fienerman, Sovereign Immunity in the Chinese Case and Its Implications for the Future of International Law, in R. MacDonald (ed.), ESSAYS IN HONOUR OF WANG TIEYA 251 (Dordrecht, Neth.: Martinus Nijhoff, 1994).

78. *US case*: Victory Transport Inc. v. Comisaria General de Abastecimientos y Transportes, 336 F.2d 354, 360 (1964). *Austrian case*: Collision with Foreign Government Owned Motor Car, Supreme Court of Austria, reported in 40 Int'l L. Rep. 73 (1961).

79. Ungar v. PLO, 402 F.3d 274 (1st Cir. 2005).

CHAPTER THREE

Organizations

INTRODUCTION

Chapter 2 addressed the legal identity and characteristics of the State, the primary actor in international affairs. This chapter continues with a related building block: the attributes of the international organization—a supporting actor, with increasing influence in global affairs.

There are important contrasts between the legal capacity of States and international organizations. Each State is an independent sovereign entity, enjoying equal status with other States under International Law—regardless of size or power. Each State is endowed with this fundamental attribute: plenary power over persons and things within its borders. A public international organization, on the other hand, owes its existence to the discretion of the States that created it—unlike a nongovernmental organization, which is not beholden to any State or group of States for its existence.

THE PREOCCUPATION OF THE UNITED NATIONS founders was with State security . . .

The central challenge for the twenty-first century is to fashion a new and broader understanding . . . of what *collective* security means . . . [because] no State can stand wholly alone. Collective strategies, collective institutions and a sense of collective responsibility are indispensable.

The case for collective security today rests on three basic pillars. Today's threats recognize no national boundaries, are connected, and must be addressed at the global and regional as well as the national levels. No State, *no matter how powerful,* can by its own efforts alone make itself invulnerable to today's threats. . . . Stated baldly, without mutual recognition of threats there can be no collective security. Self-help will rule, mistrust will predominate and cooperation for long-term mutual gain will elude us.—Report of the UN High-level Panel on Threats, Challenges and Change, at 11–12 (Dec. 2, 2004) (italics added), at <http://www.un.org/secureworld>, click Document.

This chapter presents a preliminary description of the legal essence of international organizations, followed by some classification characteristics. It will initially focus on the key *global* organization—the United Nations—followed by the most comprehensive *regional* organization—the European Union (EU). The salient features of several selected regional organizations are depicted in this chapter. Economic international organizations are presented in Chapter 13.

◆ 3.1 LEGAL PERSONALITY

INTRODUCTION

What is an "international organization (IO)?"[1] It is a formal institution, established by agreement of the affiliated members who created it. The common feature of most IOs is that their members all benefit from an organization working toward their desired objectives.

IOs typically serve the needs of either States or individuals who join or work for some nongovernmental association operating in more than one country.[2] Another type of organization affiliates itself with various governments. According to the popular myth, the International Criminal Police Organization (Interpol) has the capacity to operate independently of national governments. Its agents supposedly track and arrest international fugitives across the globe. In fact, Interpol cannot act without the express consent of the national police of any State wherein it maintains a presence. Interpol does not possess any independent police power to apprehend criminals throughout the world.[3]

This course focuses on *public* international organizations (PIO) consisting of State members, as opposed to nongovernmental international organizations like Amnesty International (AI) and Doctors Without Borders (§11.4). Furthermore, a basic course in International Law normally devotes scant attention to PIOs other then those that routinely deal with major ethnic and military conflicts.[4]

To qualify as a PIO, an entity must be: (1) established by some form of international agreement among States;

(2) created as a new international legal entity that functions independently of State sovereign control; and (3) created under International Law.[5]

Most organizations—such as the United Nations or the EU—are established by treaty. Others may be the product of an agreement reached at a ministerial or summit meeting of State representatives or heads of State. The Organization of Oil Producing Countries (OPEC), for example, was founded at a 1960 meeting of governmental representatives in Baghdad. To have international legal personality, the organization also must be provided with the capacity to enjoy rights, and incur obligations, in its relations with member (or nonmember) States. The 1947 General Agreement on Tariffs and Trade (GATT) was essentially an international agreement about each State's published tariffs. There was no sovereign entity, capable of requiring State compliance with GATT's goals, until the World Trade Organization materialized in 1995 (§13.2). Agreements between two nations to provide for public transportation does not create an entity that is directly governed by International Law. The French-British Channel Tunnel created a biinternational governing entity, not unlike a corporation. The French-Swiss agreement on the Bâle-Mulhouse Airport specifically provides that French law shall apply to airport operations—not the customary State practice you studied in §1.2 on Sources of International Law.[6]

There is a striking parallel in the growth of States and IOs since the close of World War II. The number of States increased dramatically, from fifty-one to nearly two hundred (Exhibit 3.1). There has been an equally spectacular growth in the number of international organizations, from several hundred to nearly five thousand. Exhibit 3.1 illustrates the exponential growth in these organizations:

EXHIBIT 3.1 INTERNATIONAL ORGANIZATIONS BY YEAR AND TYPE (1909–1997)*

Year	Nongovernmental	Intergovernmental	Total All Types
1909	176	37	213
1951	832	123	955
1960	1,268	154	1,422

*Adapted from Union of International Associations, Vol. 3, *Yearbook of International Organizations 1997–1998,* Table 2, Appendix 3, at 1749 (34th ed. Munich: K.G. Saur Munchen Publishers, 1998).

EXHIBIT 3.1 INTERNATIONAL ORGANIZATIONS BY YEAR AND TYPE (1909–1997) (CONTINUED)

Year	Nongovernmental	Intergovernmental	Total All Types
1968	3,318	229	3,547
1976	6,222	252	6,474
1978	9,521	289	9,810
1983	17,030	2,549	19,579
1985	20,634	3,546	24,180
1987	23,248	3,897	27,145
1989	20,063	4,068	24,131
1991	23,635	4,565	28,200
1993	28,901	5,103	34,004
1995	36,054	5,668	41,722
1996	38,243	5,885	44,128
1997	40,306	6,115	46,421

The notion of an international organization pursuing the common objectives of its member States is not a twentieth-century development. Peace and religion were early motivators. The Egyptian Pharaoh Ikhnaton envisioned an international theological order some 3,400 years ago. The Amphictyon League of the ancient Greek city-states organized themselves with a view toward lessening the brutality of war. The medieval poet Dante proposed a global super-State, operating under control of a central court of justice. Yet these were not organizations in the contemporary sense described below, and there were no permanent organizational institutions.

The following excerpt traces the evolution of international organizations:

Principles of the Institutional Law of International Organizations

Dr. Chittharanjan Amerasinghe

Introduction, Chap. One (1996), pages 1–8

History of International Organizations

Bilateral and even multilateral relations between States have a long history, but the establishment of public international organizations functioning as institutions is essentially a development of the late nineteenth century. Consular relations designed to protect interests in commerce, and diplomatic relations concerned with representation of States, go far back in history: the former to the times of the ancient Greeks and Romans; the latter to a somewhat later period, taking its modern shape in the fifteenth century. It is in these institutions that the origins of the more complex institutions which started evolving in the early nineteenth century can be found.

When bilateral relationships based on the existence of diplomatic embassies or missions were found to be inadequate to meet more complex situations arising from problems concerning not just two but many States, a means had to be found for representation in the same forum of the interests of all the States concerned. This was the international conference. It was the ad hoc temporary conference convened for a specific purpose and terminating once agreement was reached on the subject matter and a treaty was adopted that evolved ultimately into permanent international organizations with organs that function on a permanent basis and meet periodically.

The Peace of Westphalia of 1648 was the result of such a conference, as was the settlement in 1815 through the Congress of Vienna and the Treaty of Versailles in 1919. There were other conferences such as the Congress of Berlin of 1871 and the Hague Conferences of 1899 and 1907 which concerned other matters than peace. Conferences were convened to solve problems on a multilateral basis. The result of the conference would generally be a formal treaty or convention or, where such an agreement was not desirable or obtainable, a memorandum or minutes of the conference.

...

These conferences proved inadequate for the solution of [specific, long-term] political problems. They were even more inadequate for the regulation of relations between the peoples of the different countries which were the result of their common interests. Thus, in the nineteenth century, there developed associations, international in character, among groups other than governments. There followed similar developments among governments which were, however, at that time rather in the administrative than in the political field.

In the western hemisphere, there were somewhat different but significant developments. The pan-American system resorted to conferences at a regional level, beginning in 1826, though they did not yield tangible results till the Washington Conference of 1885. These conferences had a periodic character after that and culminated in the formation of the OAS [Organization of American States]. They contributed to the techniques of international organizations in several ways: (i) the conferences were not convened at the initiative of any one State, but the time and place of each were decided by the previous one; (ii) the agenda of each conference was prepared by the governing body of the standing administrative organ, the Pan-American Union (established in 1912); (iii) a greater possibility existed to undertake preparatory work before each conference than in the case of ad hoc conferences; and (iv) the periodic character of the conferences made possible the development of more elaborate and formal procedural arrangements.

By contrast, the non-governmental unions or associations sprang from the realization by non-governmental bodies, consisting of both private individuals and corporate associations, that their interests had an international character which required that those interests be promoted in cooperation with similar bodies in other countries through permanent international associations. Perhaps the first conference of a private nature which led to the establishment of an association was the one which formulated the World Anti-Slavery Convention of 1840. Since then there have been a plethora of private associations or unions established, including the International Committee of the Red Cross (1863), the International Law Association (1873), the Inter-Parliamentary Union (1889) and the International Chamber of Commerce (1919), to mention only a few. Because of the proliferation of these private unions, in 1910 the Union of International Associations was formed to co-ordinate their activities, among other things. These private unions ... anticipated and antedated the development of the public unions. Their appearance suggests that the growth of the international organization was the result of a universal human need.

The public international union which appeared also in the nineteenth century, especially in its second half, is more important for the development of the modern international organization. The public unions which sprang up at that time were international administrative unions—agencies which had a certain permanency and dealt with non-political technical activities. These were also associations of governments or administrations as contrasted with private bodies. The Congress of Vienna had proclaimed the principle of freedom of navigation which led to the appearance of many river commissions. A good example of these was the Rhine Commission which was invested with considerable powers, including both legislative and political powers. There were commissions for other rivers, such as the Danube, Elbe and Po. Numerous other administrative unions in many fields appeared pursuant to needs as they arose. The Universal Telegraphic Union was established in 1865 with an administration as its central organ. The Universal Postal Union was established in 1874. There were other unions which sprang up such as the International Union of Railway Freight Transportation (1890), the International Bureau of Industrial Property (1883), the International Bureau of Literary Property

(1886) and the International Office of Public Health (1907).

Such unions generally had periodical conferences or meetings of the representatives of member States, decisions being taken usually by unanimous vote, and a permanent secretariat (bureau) which performed the administrative tasks. One of the principal contributions of the unions to the concept of the international organization was the institutional element which was secured through a standing organ, the bureau, and provided the stepping stone from the technique of the conference to that of the organization. In some cases there were permanent deliberative or legislative organs as well (e.g., the UPU and the International Telegraphic Union). The trend toward the permanence of association was very marked.

. . .

It was in 1919 after the Treaty of Versailles, when the League of Nations was created, that an attempt was made to create a political organization of an open and universal character. Since then the public inter-governmental or inter-State organization has become firmly established in international relations, a development which culminated in the establishment of the United Nations and its specialized agencies.

The nineteenth century has been described as 'the era of *preparation for* international organization,' this chronological period being between 1815 and 1914, while the years which have passed since the momentous event of 1914 must in a sense be regarded as 'the era of *establishment of* international organization, which, in these terms comes to be regarded as a phenomenon of the twentieth century.' The institutionalization today in inter-State relations has led to international organizations influencing far more than in the past the shaping of international relations and the development of the international law intended for their regulation. In an important sense great power diplomacy conducted at summit meetings has now given way increasingly to a new form of multilateralism achieved through international organizations like the UN as negotiating arenas available to all States.

Pervasiveness of International Organizations

Public international organizations have grown exceedingly numerous, especially since the Second World War. They are of diverse nature and of different sizes in terms of membership. They range from those that deal on a global basis with matters of general concern, such as peace (the UN) and Development . . . , to those that are concerned with the regimes of particular rivers (the river commissions) or control of whaling, on a much more limited scale. They have clearly had a significant impact on the lives of people in individual countries, while positively influencing relations between nations and creating an effective and friendly modality for the conduct of international intercourse. . . . At the same time, it is clear that international organizations . . . [are] a response to the needs of international intercourse rather than as a fulfillment of a philosophical or ideological desire to achieve world government. What has evolved is a large number of international organizations, basically unconnected with each other though such connections, especially in the UN system, may subsequently be established. . . .

Despite the fears and concerns of some governments that international organizations are increasing too fast and that they are a burden on their exchequers, they are still proliferating at a considerable rate. Generally, it is unusual for a new problem in international relations to be considered without at the same time some international organization being developed to deal with it. For instance, concern with the instability of commodities markets led to the establishment in the 1980s of the Common Fund for Commodities[,] and the competition for newly discovered wealth of the international seabed area resulted in the creation of the ISA [§6.3 International Seabed Authority] under the Law of the Sea Convention in 1982, based on the concept of 'the common heritage of mankind.' More recently in the 1990s the problems of international trade . . . led to the development of the WTO. International society has, in spite of the diversity of culture and political systems, been progressively drawn closer together and become more unified. People and their governments now look far beyond national frontiers and feel a common responsibility for the major problems of the world. . . . Many of those problems have overflowed national boundaries, or called for attention beyond national limits, become international and demanded regulation and treatment in a wide sphere, with the consequence that governments have sought increasingly to deal with them through international organizations.

. . .

LEGAL CAPACITY UNDER INTERNATIONAL LAW

The International Court of Justice (ICJ) provided an insightful analysis of an IO's legal capacity in the following case. In November 1947, UN General Assembly Resolution 181(II) partitioned the former British Mandate, referred to as "Palestine," to create new Jewish and Arab States. This resolution was accepted by the Jewish community, but rejected by Arab States in the Middle East. Shortly after Israel declared its statehood in May 1948, hostilities began in and around what is now the State of Israel. Two weeks later, UN Security Council Resolution 50 called for a cessation of hostilities.

A Swedish citizen, Count Bernadotte, was appointed the UN Mediator in Palestine for the purpose of negotiating a settlement. He was killed while pursuing this objective within the Palestinian territory. General Assembly Resolution 194(III) of December 1948 expressed a "deep appreciation of the progress achieved through the good offices of the late United Nations Mediator in promoting a peaceful adjustment of the future situation of Palestine, for which cause he sacrificed his life."[7] The issue for the ICJ was whether the UN Charter gave this IO the legal capacity to demand reparations from the responsible State or States whose agents kill UN employees:

Reparation for Injuries Suffered in the Service of the United Nations

ADVISORY OPINION, INTERNATIONAL COURT OF JUSTICE (1949)

1949 *International Court of Justice Reports* 174

AUTHOR'S NOTE: This is an International Court of Justice (ICJ) "advisory" opinion. There is no State defendant [§9.4]. The UN requested that the Court render its opinion on the issue of whether the UN had a legal right—distinct from a member State—to sue for damages to the UN, in its capacity as an organization employing international civil servants. In addition to the death of the UN's Mediator in Palestine, its agents from various countries were being injured or killed while performing duties on behalf of the organization. Prior to the Court's decision in this case, only the victim's State of citizenship had the exclusive right to seek reparations for harm to that State—because of the death of its citizen [§4.1].

In 1947, the UN claimed that there could be State responsibility, to an international organization, for injury to aliens (UN employees) allegedly caused by Israel, Jordan, and Egypt, where these individuals were working for the UN—in three separate incidents. The UN claimed that the responsible States failed to protect these individuals from private criminal acts. In the case of Israel, for example, two UN employees in Palestine were shot while driving through the Jewish portion of Jerusalem. The UN sought compensation from Israel for the loss of their lives. Its claim was brought for Israel's "failure to exercise due diligence and to take all reasonable measures for the prevention of the assassination; liability of the government for actions committed by irregular forces in territory under the control of the Israel[i] authorities; and failure to take

all measures required by international law and by the Security Council... to bring the culprits to justice." Israel refused to pay any compensation, claiming that only the State of the victim's nationality had the legal capacity to assert the State liability of Israel.[8]

The Court analyzed whether the alleged harm to the UN, in its legal capacity as an international organization, could be reconciled with—or supplant—the right to seek reparations by the State of the victim's nationality. Put another way, if a Swedish citizen is killed while abroad, only Sweden could seek reparations from the responsible State, prior to creation of the UN. Could the UN Charter be read as furnishing the UN with the legal personality to sue in an international court, for wrongs done to the UN in its capacity as the employer of the deceased?

COURT'S OPINION: The questions asked of the Court relate to the "capacity to bring an international claim;" accordingly, we must begin by defining what is meant by that capacity, and consider the characteristics of the Organization, so as to determine whether, in general, these characteristics do, or do not, include for the Organization a right to present an international claim [for injury to a UN agent].

Competence to bring an international claim is, for those possessing it, the capacity to resort to the customary methods recognized by international law for the establishment, the presentation and the settlement of claims.

Among these methods may be mentioned protest, request for an enquiry, negotiation, and request for submission to an arbitral tribunal or to the Court in so far as this may be authorized by the Statute [of the ICJ].

This capacity certainly belongs to the State; a State can bring an international claim against another State. Such a claim takes the form of a claim between two political entities [*i.e.*, States], equal in law, similar in form, and both the direct subjects of international law. It is dealt with by means of negotiation, and cannot, in the present state of the law as to international jurisdiction, be submitted to a tribunal, except with the consent of the States concerned. . . .

But, in the international sphere, has the Organization such a nature as involves the capacity to bring an international claim? In order to answer this question, the Court must first enquire whether the Charter has given the Organization such a position that it possesses, in regard to its Members, rights which it is entitled to ask them to respect. In other words, does the Organization possess international personality? . . .

The Charter has not been content to make the Organization created by it merely a centre "for harmonizing the actions of nations in the attainment of these common ends" (Article I, para. 4). It has equipped that centre with organs and has given it special tasks. It has defined the position of the Members in relation to the Organization by requiring them to give it every assistance in any action undertaken by it (Article 2, para. 5) and to accept and carry out the decisions of the Security Council; by authorizing the General Assembly to make recommendations to the Members; by giving the Organization legal capacity and privileges and immunities in the territory of each of its Members; and by providing for the conclusion of agreements between the Organization and its Members. Practice—in particular the conclusion of conventions to which the Organization is a party—has confirmed this character of the Organization, which occupies a position in certain respects in detachment from its Members, and which is under a duty to remind them, if need be, of certain obligations. . . . The "Convention on the Privileges and Immunities of the United Nations" of 1946 creates rights and duties between each of the signatories and the Organization (see, in particular, Section 35). It is difficult to see how such a convention could operate except upon the international plane and as between parties possessing international personality.

In the opinion of the Court, the Organization was intended to exercise and enjoy, and is in fact exercising and enjoying, functions and rights which can only be explained on the basis of the possession of a large measure of international personality and the capacity to operate upon an international plane. It is at present the supreme type of international organization, and it could not carry out the intentions of its founders if it was devoid of international personality. It must be acknowledged that its Members, by entrusting certain functions to it, with the attendant duties and responsibilities, have clothed it with the competence required to enable those functions to be effectively discharged.

Accordingly, the Court has come to the conclusion that the Organization is an international person. That is not the same thing as saying that it is a State, which it certainly is not, or that its legal personality and rights and duties are the same as those of a State. Still less is it the same thing as saying that it is a "super-State," whatever that expression may mean. It does not even imply that all its rights and duties must be upon the international plane, any more than all the rights and duties of a State must be upon that plane. What it does mean is that it is a subject of international law and capable of possessing international rights and duties, and that it has capacity to maintain its rights by bringing international claims.

The next question is whether the sum of the international rights of the Organization comprises the right to bring the kind of international claim described in the Request for this Opinion. That is a[n international organization's] claim against a State to obtain reparation in respect of the damage caused by the injury of an agent of the Organization in the course of the performance of his duties. Whereas a State possesses the totality of international rights and duties recognized by international law, the rights and duties of an entity such as the Organization must depend upon its purposes and functions as specified or implied in its constituent documents and developed in practice. The functions of the Organization are of such a character that they could not be effectively discharged if they involved the concurrent action, on the international plane, of fifty-eight or more Foreign Offices, and the Court concludes that the Members have endowed the Organization with capacity to bring international claims when necessitated by the discharge of its functions.

Having regard to its purposes and functions already referred to, the Organization may find it necessary, and has in fact found it necessary, to entrust its agents with important missions to be performed in disturbed parts of the world. Many missions, from their very nature, involve the agents in unusual dangers to which ordinary persons are not exposed. For the same reason, the injuries suffered by its agents in these circumstances will sometimes have occurred in such a manner that their national State would not be justified in bringing a claim for reparation on the ground of diplomatic protection, or, at any rate, would not feel disposed to do so. Both to ensure the efficient and independent performance of these missions and to afford effective support to its agents, the Organization must provide them with adequate protection.

The obligations entered into by States to enable the agents of the Organization to perform their duties are undertaken not in the interest of the agents, but in that of the Organization. When it claims redress for a breach of these obligations, the Organization is invoking its own right, the right that the obligations due to it should be respected. . . . In claiming reparation based on the injury suffered by its agent, the Organization does not represent the agent, but is asserting its own right, the right to secure respect for undertakings entered into towards the Organization. . . .

The question of reconciling action [this right to sue that is claimed] by the Organization with the rights of a national State may arise in another way; that is to say, when the agent bears the nationality of the defendant State. . . .

The action of the Organization is in fact based not upon the nationality of the victim but upon his status as agent of the Organization. Therefore it does not matter whether or not the State to which the claim is addressed regards him as its own national, because the question of nationality is not pertinent to the admissibility of the claim. . . .

◆ Notes & Questions

1. Article 104 of the UN Charter (<http://home.att.net/~slomansonb/txtcsesite.html>, under Chapter Three, click UN Charter) furnishes the "capacity as may be necessary" to exercise its functions and fulfill its purposes within the territory of each member State. What UN Charter gap was filled by the Reparations case?

2. Under Article 100 of the Charter, UN employees performing UN duties cannot "seek or receive instructions from any government or from any other authority external to the Organization." Assume that a UN agent—a citizen of Sweden—is carrying out a mission on behalf of the United Nations in Sweden. The Reparations case suggests reasons for conferring the protection of the United Nations on the injured individual, even though the UN employee is presumably still entitled to similar protection by his or her home State. Why?

3. There have been a number of incidents whereby the United Nations—or other international organizations such as the EU—might sue to establish State responsibility, under the theory spawned by the ICJ's *Reparations Case:*

   ◆ In December 1991, the body of UN Colonel John Higgins was returned to the United Nations from Lebanon. While on a UN peacekeeping operation in 1989, he was kidnaped and later brutally murdered.

   ◆ In January 1991, five European Community (now EU) truce observers were shot down in their helicopter by Serbian Yugoslavian military forces in Croatia. Of course, neither Lebanon nor what was then Yugoslavia claimed responsibility for the deaths of these agents while on peacekeeping missions for, respectively, the United Nations and the EU. It is precisely in this situation that these international organizations would hold the right, under the Reparations rationale, to seek redress from the responsible States.

   ◆ In December 1992, Cambodia's Khmer Rouge freed eleven UN peacekeepers who had been kidnaped and threatened with execution. As a belligerent entity (§2.3: Recognition of Belligerency), the Khmer Rouge would bear responsibility under International Law for any harm that might have come to these UN peacekeepers.

   ◆ In November 1997, gunmen stormed aboard a boat moored off Somalia to kidnap five aid workers from the United Nations and the EU.

   ◆ In February 1998, four UN observers from the Czech Republic, Sweden, and Uruguay (two of the UN employees) were kidnaped by a heavily armed gang in Tbilisi, Georgia. The gang then presented the government of Georgia with the following demand: If seven prisoners accused of plotting to kill the President of Georgia were not released, these UN employees would be killed. Georgian police surrounded the house where the kidnaped UN personnel were being held and eventually captured the surviving gang members.

◆ In July 1998, four UN employees from Poland, Uruguay, Japan, and Tajikistan were shot in the former Soviet republic of Tajikistan. UN Secretary-General Kofi Annan said that they had been "ambushed and ruthlessly executed."

◆ In 2003, a truck bomb explosion killed eight UN staff members at Baghdad's UN headquarters, including the UN's top representative—resulting in the UN's departure from Iraq.

4. In 1994, General Assembly Resolution 49/59 adopted the Convention on the Safety of United Nations and Associated Personnel. Article 7 provides that "United Nations and associated personnel, their equipment and premises shall not be made the object of attack. . . . "Article 9 requires each state party to enact national law making it a crime to either attack UN personnel or to attack the official premises of any UN personnel, which is likely to endanger his or her person. The need for such a treaty is apparent from a subsequent UN report on casualties between 1992 and 1998. 173 UN staffers were killed, and 80 were still missing, as of September 2000. The UN Blue Helmet was once comparable to a security blanket. It is now a target.

In 1997, the United Kingdom enacted legislation whereby crimes against UN personnel are crimes against the United Kingdom—just as if those acts had occurred in the United Kingdom. This statute is a contemporary example of the *Reparations* theme being implemented under both national and International Law. In 1995, a Serbian tank fired on UN personnel in Kosovo, severely injuring a British soldier. For the resulting case, which analyzes both the Convention and the statute, *see* Regina v. Ministry of Defence Ex Parte Walker, at: <http://www.parliament.the-stationery-office.co.uk/pa/ld199900/ldjudgmt/jd000406/walker-1.htm> (Judgment, House of Lords, 6 April 2000).

5. *Question:* 500 UN hostages were held in Sierra Leone beginning in May 2000. This was another blow to UN peacekeeping efforts in Africa. Four Keynan peacekeepers were killed. Another dozen from various African nations were wounded. The United States, England, and France declined an invitation to provide reinforcement troops. The West shied away from African peacekeeping, after the death of eighteen US marines in UN's Somalian mission in 1993. 100 Nigerians were detained, before being released without their weapons. You are the UN's lawyer: Under International Law, who would you be able to sue, and why?

6. The *Reparations Case* addressed the UN's capacity to be a plaintiff, seeking damages for harm to one of its international civil servants, in an *international* court. The following US legislation, enacted four years earlier, related to the UN's permission to operate on US soil (at its New York City headquarters). Congress thereby generally enabled designated international organizations to exercise the legal capacity to operate—within the United States, and under US national law:[9]

§288. . . . [T]he term "international organization" means a public international organization in which the United States participates pursuant to any treaty . . . and which shall have been designated by the President . . . as being entitled to enjoy the privileges, exemptions, and immunities provided in this subchapter. . . .

§288a. International organizations shall enjoy the status, immunities, exemptions, and privileges set forth in this section, as follows:

(a) International organizations shall, to the extent consistent with the instrument creating them, possess the capacity—
   (i) to contract;
   (ii) to acquire and dispose of real and personal property;
   (iii) to institute legal proceedings.

This legislation did not specifically say that any particular IO could be a plaintiff (or a defendant) in a US court, nor did it mention whether an IO could sue the United States. A case decided four years after the above legislation was enacted, and one year after the ICJ's *Reparations Case,* provided some answers. The United

Nations contracted with the United States, whereby the latter was to deliver emergency supplies (milk) for children in Europe. The shipper hired by the United States damaged the milk in some cases, and never delivered it in others. A US federal court was required to examine the related issues spawned by this alleged breach of contract: (1) Did the United Nations have the legal capacity to bring a lawsuit—other than in the ICJ? (2) If so, could the United Nations sue a member nation in *that* nation's domestic courts? The following critical passages provided an affirmative answer to both questions:

> The International Court of Justice has held [*see* above *Reparations Case*] that the United Nations is a legal entity separate and distinct from the member States. While it is not a state nor a super-State, it is an international person, clothed by its Members with the competence necessary to discharge its functions. Article 104 of the Charter of the United Nations provides that "the Organization shall enjoy in the territory of each of its Members such legal capacity as may be necessary for the exercise of its functions and the fulfillment of its purposes" . . . [and] the President has removed any possible doubt by designating the United Nations as one of the organizations entitled to enjoy the privileges conferred by the International Organizations Immunities Act.
>
> . . .
>
> Whether the United Nations may sue the United States is a more difficult question. . . .
>
> The broad purpose of the International Organizations Immunities Act was to vitalize the status of international organizations of which the United States is a member and to facilitate their activities. A liberal interpretation of the Act is in harmony with this purpose.
>
> The considerations which might prompt a restrictive interpretation are not persuasive. It is true that . . . international organizations on a grand scale are a modern phenomenon. The wide variety of activities in which they engage is likely to give rise to claims against their members that can most readily be disposed of in national courts. The present claim is such a claim. . . .
>
> International organizations, such as the United Nations and its agencies, of which the United States is a member, are not alien bodies. The interests of the

> United States are served when the United Nations' interests are protected. A prompt and equitable settlement of any claim it may have against the United States will be the settlement most advantageous to both parties. The courts of the United States afford a most appropriate forum for accomplishing such a settlement.[10]

This key 1950 US domestic court decision could have led the way in an identifiable international trend for resolving disputes between States and IOs. Today, however, there are limited fora within which to pursue such claims. The ICJ is not one of them, because "only States" can be parties to cases heard by the world court (§9.4). And as cautioned by Vienna University's Dr. August Reinisch, regarding State alternatives: "it is . . . generally accepted that international organizations may become legally liable according to domestic law. The enforcement aspect, however, is in many cases more controversial. The obvious reason for this legal insecurity as far as the availability of an adjudicative organ to determine and enforce legal accountability is concerned lies in the lack of explicit provisions for such organs or in the explicit exclusion of possible fora [regarding IO liability] . . . the predominant position on the domestic level where existing courts are frequently deprived of their adjudicative power as far as international organizations are concerned."[11]

CONTEMPORARY ROLES

The Ford Foundation, a US-based research and policy-making institution, has traditionally advocated for increased reliance on international organization as a practical vehicle for effecting positive changes in State-to-State relations. Its studies embrace the concept of international cooperation, in an era when the State is still the principal international player. In a 1990 study on international organizations and law, this Foundation articulated a shifting paradigm whereby international organizations and nongovernmental organizations could both assume a greater role in the progressive development of international order. As asserted in this foundation's serviceable position paper regarding the need for more effective international organizations:

> [I]t is abundantly clear that no single nation now dominates our age. The United States, the architect of the postwar order, is no longer able to control events

singlehandedly, if it ever could. Japan, the European Community, the newly industrializing countries . . . and the dominant nations in some regions have become influential international actors. . . . Partly as a consequence of this diffusion of power, international organizations face far different challenges now than they did forty years ago. The United Nations, Breton Woods institutions [establishing the International Monetary Fund], and the international trade system are all under strain. . . .

Linking the fields of international organizations and international law to multilateral cooperation . . . suggests an underlying conviction that institutionalized global cooperation is a necessity . . . [that] should be based in law and should include enforceable rights and obligations.[12]

The comprehensive December 2004 Report of the United Nation's High-Level Panel on Threats, Challenges and Change echoed this sentiment fourteen years later:

We must not underestimate the difficulty of reaching a new consensus about the meaning and responsibilities of *collective* security. Many will regard one or more of the threats we identify as not really being a threat to international peace and security. Some believe that HIV/AIDS is a horrible disease, but not a security threat. Or that terrorism is a threat to some States, but not all. Or that civil wars in Africa are a humanitarian tragedy, but surely not a problem for international security. Or that poverty is a problem of development, not security.

. . .

What is needed today is nothing less than a new consensus between alliances that are frayed, between wealthy nations and poor, and among peoples mired in mistrust across an apparently widening cultural abyss. The essence of that consensus is simple: we *all* share responsibility for each other's security. And the test of that consensus will be action.

. . .

The attacks of 11 September 2001 revealed that States, as well as collective security institutions, have failed to keep pace with changes in the nature of threats. The technological revolution that has radically changed the worlds of communication, information-processing, health and transportation has eroded borders, altered migration and allowed individuals the world over to share information at a speed inconceivable two decades ago. Such changes have brought many benefits but also great potential for harm. Smaller and smaller numbers of people are able to inflict greater and greater amounts of damage, without the support of any State. A new threat, transnational organized crime, undermines the rule of law within and across borders. Technologies designed to improve daily life can be transformed into instruments of aggression. We have yet to fully understand the impact of these changes, but they herald a fundamentally different security climate— one whose unique opportunities for cooperation are matched by an unprecedented scope for destruction.[13]

The UN's International Law Commission (ILC) is currently engaged in defining the contours of organizational responsibilities arising under International Law. You will recall that the ILC presented the Draft Articles on State Responsibility to the General Assembly (GA) in 2001 (§2.5). It is currently pursuing a like blueprint for defining the obligations of international organizational as well. In 2003, General Assembly Resolution 58/77 therefore "requested a number of international organizations to provide comments and materials 'especially on questions of attribution [of conduct to international organizations] and of responsibility of member States for conduct that is attributed to an international organization.'" In April 2004, the ILC then presented its report on responsibility of international organizations to the international legal community via the GA.

The classic example of potential organizational responsibility for an international delict arose from the 1999 bombing of the territory of the Federal Republic of Yugoslavia. That military action spawned extensive debate about whether the negative implications of the Kosovo conflict should be attributed to the North Atlantic Treaty Organization (NATO) qua international organization—as opposed to some or all of its members (§10.5 Humanitarian Intervention). A number of NATO nations were sued in the ICJ and the European Court of Human Rights.[14] In both venues, various respondent States argued that any conduct allegedly violating International Law should be attributed to NATO—rather than to the national participants in that war. Neither action resolved the merits of this response.

By comparison, there is undisputed State responsibility for violations of International Law, when a State organ acts on behalf of the State. This customary restatement of *State* responsibility could be applied to an international organization as well. The relevant ILC draft principle thus provides as follows: "the conduct of an organ of an international organization, of one of its officials or another person entrusted with part of the organization's functions shall be considered as an act of that organization under international law, whatever position the organ, official or person holds in the structure of the organization."[15]

The practical impact of this ILC project will materialize at various points in this book—including §9.5 on International Criminal Courts; §10.3 on Peacekeeping Operations; §10.6 on Laws of War; and §11.2 on the UN role in promoting human rights. Those sections will demonstrate the need for clarity of definition, to help solidify the customary and treaty-based protection of individuals in conflict zones managed by international organizations. In the case of Kosovo, for example, the results would apply to NATO, for its 1999 bombing—and the United Nations, for claims arising during its ensuing half-dozen year occupation. The resulting ILC restatement of principles should arguably apply with equal force, to the use of force, by *both* States and international organizations.

◆ 3.2 ORGANIZATIONAL CLASSIFICATION

International organizations can be sorted in many ways. This section focuses on what an organization is designed to do, based on who created it and why.

TRADITIONAL MODEL

The traditional paradigm of organizational classification employs a "functional" approach. International organizations are thereby: (1) public or private; (2) administrative or political; (3) global or regional; and (4) either possess, or do not possess, supranational power.[16] One could also initiate a discussion of IOs from a host of other perspectives. These include the "rationalist," "revolutionary," "realist," and "critical" theories for assessing IOs.[17]

The "functional" model is a convenient starting point for characterizing the power and purpose of the myriad of contemporary international organizations. Typically, a group of States agree to establish a "public" organization—

a process with the potential for derogations from State sovereignty. States often enter into written treaties to inaugurate international trade or communications associations. Those bodies then implement the joint decisions of the State representatives.

"Private" international organizations are typically established by non–State entities (individuals or corporations). Nongovernmental representatives then execute the mission of the particular organization—hence, the term "Non-Governmental Organization" (NGO). This latter type of international organization is not created by a treaty between sovereign States. Examples include the International Chamber of Commerce (headquartered in Paris) and AI (headquartered in London).

The *administrative v. political* distinction is somewhat blurred by modern practice. Administrative international organizations tend to have goals that are far more limited than those of their political analogues. The UN's International Telecommunications Union, for example, serves an administrative purpose that is not associated with maintaining or directing political order. Among other things, it allocates radio frequencies for communication in outer space. Many political IOs, on the other hand, are intergovernmental entities designed to maintain military or political order. The United Nations was conceived to implement a system of collective security to discourage the unilateral use of military force. The United Nations also serves as a forum for improving the economic and social conditions of its member States.

The *global v. regional* distinction is arguably less useful than the other traditional distinctions. The United Nations is the quintessential example of a global organization. Its impact, however, is not necessarily global. It is not a world government. It often serves as a forum for debating regional problems. Not all regional organizations are, in fact, regional. The press often refers to NATO as a Western European association. Yet the geographical position of certain long-term members such as the United States, Canada, and Iceland makes it difficult to characterize NATO's function as being limited to Western Europe—especially now that NATO is welcoming certain former Warsaw Pact members from the former Soviet Union (§3.5).

The final traditional distinction involves organizations possessing, or not possessing, *power over member States* requiring them to act or not act in particular ways. One definitional problem is that many international organizations are "supranational." They are associations of States with independent organs for implementing the goals of the participants. It would be incorrect, however, to characterize the United Nations as having supranational power. It cannot dispatch a peacekeeping force independently of the approval of the five permanent members of the Security Council (SC). Nor does the SC traditionally dispatch troops without the consent of the State or States where they are to be stationed. In the EU, on the other hand, members have ceded some of their sovereign powers to community organs, which may—and do—require member States to act in ways that would not occur unilaterally.

IGOS & INGOS

Another useful classification distinction is the international *governmental* organization (IGO) versus the international nongovernmental organization [INGO (IGO v. INGO)], as heralded by the University of Aberdeen (Scotland) Professor Clive Archer.[18] This distinction builds upon UN Economic and Social Council Resolution 288(x) of 1950. It provided that every "international organization that is not created by means of international governmental agreements [treaties] shall be considered as a nongovernmental international organization."

The United Nations is a global IGO. Its membership consists of States throughout the world. The EU is an IGO that operates on a primarily regional international level.

Examples of INGOs include AI (London), the International Olympic Committee (Lausanne, Switzerland), the American Society of International Law (Washington, DC), and the International Campaign to Ban Land Mines. AI's members are individuals, from all over the globe, who are concerned about State observance of international human rights norms. They thus promote AI's agenda through various Web sites.[19] AI was not founded by a conference of governmental leaders, but by a British lawyer. No State sends official representatives to its meetings. The Olympic Committee is another worldwide international organization, promoting sports competition to enhance State friendships (§4.2 *Perez v. IOC* case). In 1998, its work under UN auspices promoted an agreement by 179 nations that there would be no hostilities during the Winter Olympics in Japan. The International Campaign to Ban Land Mines consists of about 1,200 groups in ninety countries. This organization received the Nobel Peace Prize for its work, which influenced 122 nations to sign the global treaty banning land mines in 1996. The American Society of International Law (Washington, DC) is composed of lawyers, judges, and professors from all over the world. It conducts seminars in and outside of the United States. It is a professional association devoted to the study of International Law to promote State observance of International Law.

The relationship between States and NGOs designed to pique State consciousness is often strained. The 1995 Fourth World Conference on Women was sponsored by the United Nations in Beijing, with representatives from 189 countries in attendance. Some 30,000 individuals and NGOs also attended, but had to conduct a parallel event in a tent city that is 35 miles from Beijing. They were thus precluded from direct participation in this official State conference. As noted by the US representative, Secretary of State Madeline Albright: "Freedom to participate in the political process of our countries is the inalienable right of every woman and man. Deny that, and you deny everything." In December 2005, Russian legislation restricted NGO activities, especially those funded by western institutions such as Human Rights Watch and AI. In her critical response, US Secretary of State Condoleeza Rice responded that Russia should understand "the importance of nongovernmental organizations to a stable, democratic environment."

Some IOs consist of both IGOs and INGOs. Governments and private corporations have jointly formed an IO to improve telecommunications. The Communication Satellite Corporation (COMSAT) is a mix of both States, which do possess international legal capacity, and nongovernmental corporations, which do not possess such capacity under International Law. They have nevertheless combined to achieve the delivery of better worldwide communications.

The relationship between IGOs and INGOs may be somewhat symbiotic, whereby dissimilar organs unify to serve mutually beneficial interests. For example, certain nongovernmental organizations possess a special status at the United Nations. The Palestine Liberation Organization (PLO), the International Committee for the Red Cross, and the American Society of International Law have been accorded special "observer status" by different UN organs. When the GA meets at the UN headquarters in New York City, the PLO sends representatives to monitor the proceedings. As of July 1998, its representative may raise issues, cosponsor draft resolutions, and make speeches in the GA. Various INGOs thereby participate in the work of the United Nations. They are neither States nor governmental organizations, but they do enjoy some degree of legal personality on the international level via their special status within the GA.

The International Red Cross, a private international union, promoted the intergovernmental Geneva Conventions of 1864, 1906, 1929, and 1949 (§10.6). The Red Cross sometimes acts in ways that do not have the support of the parties in conflict. The North Vietnamese opposed the Red Cross position on the degree of protection afforded to the US and South Vietnamese prisoners in the North during the Vietnam War. The Geneva Convention was characterized by the North Vietnamese as being inapplicable to an undeclared war. The Red Cross pressed all States to reconvene another Geneva Convention in 1977, which established added protections for prisoners in undeclared wars.[20] On the other hand, the Bosnian Serbs applauded the Red Cross assistance with the 1994 evacuation of thousands of Muslims and Croatians from the town of Prijefor in Bosnia. Although the objective was to save them from the Bosnian Serbs, this atypical Red Cross evacuation indirectly helped the Serbs in promoting their goal of ethnic cleansing.

PURPOSE

One might compare the respective purposes of the United Nations and North American Free Trade Agreement (§13.3 NAFTA), to see that modern organizations cannot always be neatly pigeon-holed into one category or another. The UN Charter's mission statement is so broadly worded that it defies a succinct characterization, in terms of any singular purpose. Member States therein provided that:

The Purposes of the United Nations are:

1. To maintain international peace and security . . . ;
2. To develop friendly relations among nations based on respect for the principle of equal rights and self-determination of peoples . . . ;
3. To achieve international cooperation in solving international problems of an economic, social, cultural, or humanitarian character . . . ;
4. To be a centre for harmonizing the actions of nations in the attainment of these common ends.

NAFTA's purpose, on the other hand, is more limited, more specific, and more binding (as opposed to the UN Charter, which represents a common standard of achievement). While social improvements and cultural exchanges might also be facilitated by NAFTA, its essential objective is to reduce trade barriers for the economic benefit of its trading partners. NAFTA Article 102.1 illustrates this contrast in purpose vis-a-vis the comparatively broad and egalitarian UN Charter objectives:

The objectives of this Agreement . . . are to: (a) eliminate barriers to trade in, and facilitate the cross-border movement of, goods and services between the territories of the Parties; (b) promote conditions of fair competition in the free trade area; (c) increase substantially investment opportunities in the territories of the Parties; (d) provide adequate and effective protection and enforcement of intellectual property rights [copyright, trademark, and patent protection] in each Party's territory; (e) create effective procedures for the implementation and application of this Agreement, for its joint administration and for the resolution of disputes; and (f) establish a framework for further trilateral, regional and multilateral cooperation to expand and enhance the benefits of this Agreement.[21]

Al-Qaida, a relatively new INGO, is an amorphous group of individuals claiming allegiance to the Saudi-born multimillionaire Usama bin Laden (UBL). As defined in the US indictment of the September 11th "20th hijacker," Zacarias Moussaoui, this NGO and its leader: "issued a statement entitled 'The Nuclear Bomb of Islam,' under the banner of the 'International Islamic Front for Fighting the Jews and the Crusaders.' Al-Qaida therein stated that 'it is the duty of the Muslims to prepare as much force as possible to terrorize the enemies of God.'" In its mission statement, signed by five individuals including UBL in 1998, al-Qaida announced that "in compliance with God's order, we issue the following fatwa to all Muslims: The ruling to kill the Americans and their allies—both civilian and military—is an individual duty for every Muslim who can do it in any country in which it is possible to do it, in order to liberate the al-Aqsa Mosque [Jerusalem] and the holy mosque [Mecca] from their grip, and in order for their armies to move out of all the lands of Islam, defeated and unable to threaten any Muslim." Furthermore,

"Al-Qaida's goal . . . is to overthrow nearly all Muslim governments, which are viewed as corrupt, to drive Western influence from those countries, and eventually to abolish state boundaries."[22]

In prior sections of this book, you learned that States and certain international organizations are international persons. The prominent NGOs thirst for this status as well. However, even those which are international in scope, pursuing global objectives, must function under the domestic laws of the State wherein they choose to operate. They must deal with shifts in attitudes, depending on who holds political power at the moment—as classically illustrated in the following case:

Center for Reproductive Law and Policy v. George W. Bush

UNITED STATES SECOND DISTRICT COURT OF APPEALS

304 F.3d 183 (2002)

Sotomayor, Circuit Judge:
This suit was brought by a domestic organization that advocates reproductive rights and by attorneys employed by the organization. Plaintiffs challenge the so-called "Mexico City Policy," pursuant to which the United States government requires foreign organizations, as a condition of receiving government funds, to agree neither to perform abortions nor to promote abortion generally. . . . The district court dismissed the case . . . . The district court was following the general rule . . . that a federal court may not assume it has jurisdiction over a matter and proceed directly to the merits. The instant case is exceptional, however. . . .

BACKGROUND
. . . Plaintiff The Center for Reproductive Law & Policy ("CRLP") is a nonprofit advocacy organization devoted to the promotion of reproductive rights. Individual plaintiffs Janet Benshoof, Anika Rahman, Katherine Hall Martinez, Julia Ernst, Laura Katzive, Melissa Upreti and Christina Zampas are CRLP staff attorneys engaged in the organization's global mission of reproductive law reform. Defendant George W. Bush is the President of the United States. Defendant Colin Powell is the U.S. Secretary of State and is thus responsible for "ensuring program and policy coordination among agencies of the United States Government in carrying out the policies set forth in the Foreign Assistance Act. . . ." 22 U.S.C. §6593(b)(2). Defendant Andrew Natsios is the Administrator of the United States Agency for International Development ("USAID"). At issue in this case is the so-called "Mexico City Policy"[1] of the United States government, whereby foreign non-governmental organizations ("NGOs") receiving U.S. government funds must agree to a provision called the "Standard Clause," which prohibits the organizations from engaging in activities that promote abortion (also referred to as the "challenged restrictions").

The Foreign Assistance Act of 1961 ("FAA") authorizes the President "to furnish assistance, on such terms and conditions as he may determine, for voluntary population planning." 22 U.S.C. §2151b(b). . . .

The challenged restrictions originated in August 1984, when President Ronald Reagan announced the Mexico City Policy ("the Policy"). The Policy expressed the government's disapproval of abortion as an element of family planning programs and set forth various ways in which the government would prohibit its funds from being used to support abortion overseas. Among these, it was announced that "the United States will no longer contribute to separate nongovernmental organizations which perform or actively promote abortion as a method of family planning in other nations."

Pursuant to the Mexico City Policy, USAID incorporated the "Standard Clause" into its family planning assistance agreements and contracts. The Standard Clause provides that in order to be eligible for USAID funding, a foreign NGO must certify in writing that it "will not, while receiving assistance under the grant, perform or actively promote abortion as a method of family planning

---

[1] The term derives from a United Nations conference held in Mexico City in 1984, at which the United States delegation presented a policy statement outlining the type of abortion-related restrictions at issue in this case.

in AID-recipient countries or provide financial support to other foreign nongovernmental organizations that conduct such activities." The restrictions established in the Standard Clause extend to *all* activities of recipient NGOs, not merely to projects funded by USAID. Thus, in order to receive U.S. government funds, a foreign NGO may not engage in *any* activities that promote abortion. These restrictions do not apply to domestic NGOs such as plaintiff CRLP.

The Mexico City Policy was rescinded by President Bill Clinton in January 1993, but was reinstated by President George W. Bush in March 2001. President Bush issued an official memorandum that restored the abortion-related restrictions discussed above, including the Standard Clause. Accordingly, as a condition of receiving U.S. government funds, foreign NGOs again are required to agree not to perform or actively promote abortion as a method of family planning.[2]

Plaintiffs . . . primary claim . . . is that, as a result of the challenged restrictions, foreign NGOs are chilled from interacting and communicating with domestic abortion rights groups such as plaintiff CRLP, thus depriving plaintiffs of their rights to freedom of speech and association in carrying out the mission of the organization. . . . Finally, plaintiffs attempt to bring a claim under customary international law, the substance of which appears to be identical to their First Amendment claim.

The district court dismissed the action in its entirety on the ground that plaintiffs lack standing under Article III of the Constitution. The court first noted that because the challenged restrictions apply only to foreign NGOs, not to domestic organizations such as CRLP, the Mexico City Policy does not affect plaintiffs directly.

. . .

DISCUSSION
I. First Amendment Claim
A. *Plaintiffs' Allegations*
The crux of plaintiffs' First Amendment claim is their contention that the restrictions chill foreign NGOs from collaborating with domestic NGOs like CRLP because such collaboration may be viewed as promoting abortion and thus would jeopardize the foreign NGOs' receipt of U.S. government funds. Plaintiffs argue that such collaboration is essential to their ability

to carry out their mission as advocates of reproductive rights and that depriving them of this ability violates their freedom of speech and association.

Specifically, plaintiffs allege that they depend on collaboration with foreign NGOs in order to advocate abortion law reform in foreign countries; to gather reliable information regarding abortion laws; to disseminate publications and reports; to reach audiences worldwide in order to promote abortion law reform; to access victims and witnesses of human rights abuses; to lobby the United States government to rescind the Restoration Memorandum; to influence international conferences, international legal tribunals, and world public opinion; to increase protection for the right to abortion in the United States; and to engage in open and free discussion about abortion.

Plaintiffs list several countries in which they currently have projects involving these activities and where foreign NGOs have agreed to the Standard Clause, and they allege that all of these activities are significantly hindered in those countries. . . . Plaintiffs also invoke their right to receive information, claiming that the Standard Clause "interferes with Plaintiffs' ability to obtain information necessary to accomplish their abortion law reform efforts from USAID recipient [foreign NGOs]," and impedes plaintiffs' access to victims and witnesses of human rights abuses related to reproductive issues. Plaintiffs explain that foreign NGOs are often the only vehicle to provide access to both general information and first-hand accounts regarding conditions in foreign countries, and that obtaining such information is necessary for domestic NGOs to fulfill their mission of advocating reproductive rights—including their ability to lobby the United States government.

. . .

C. *The Standing Issue*
The district court dismissed the instant case, not on the merits . . . but for lack of constitutional standing [§1.4 Lack of Standing to Sue Doctrine]. A federal court has jurisdiction only if . . . (1) that the plaintiff has suffered an "injury in fact," i.e., an invasion of a judicially cognizable interest which is concrete and particularized as well as actual or imminent, rather than conjectural or hypothetical; (2) that there is a causal connection such that the

---

[2]"Abortion as a method of family planning" does not include "abortions performed if the life of the mother would be endangered if the fetus were carried to term or abortions performed following rape or incest (since abortion under these circumstances is not a family planning act)." Restoration Memorandum, 66 Fed.Reg. at 17,306.

injury is fairly traceable to the challenged conduct; and (3) that it is likely, as opposed to merely speculative, that the injury will be redressed by a favorable decision.

. . .

III. Equal Protection Claim
A. Plaintiffs Have "Competitive Advocate Standing"

. . .

Though plaintiffs do not employ the term, this argument is essentially a theory that this Court has dubbed "competitive advocate standing." We have acknowledged the possibility that a plaintiff may have standing to bring an equal protection claim where the government's allocation of a particular benefit "creates an uneven playing field" for organizations advocating their views in the public arena. In order to "satisfy the rule that he was personally disadvantaged," a plaintiff must "show that he personally competes in the same arena with the party to whom the government has bestowed the assertedly illegal benefit."

Plaintiffs have standing under this theory. CRLP is an advocacy organization that communicates its viewpoint regarding issues of abortion and reproductive rights, and it competes with anti-abortion groups engaged in advocacy around the very same issues. The Standard Clause has bestowed a benefit on plaintiffs' competitive adversaries by rewarding their suppliers of information, the foreign NGOs, with government grants, while withholding those grants from suppliers of information who would deal with CRLP. This is precisely the type of situation that the doctrine of competitive advocate standing contemplates. . . .

B. The Equal Protection Claim is Without Merit

. . . The Supreme Court has made clear that the government is free to favor the anti-abortion position over the pro-choice position, and can do so with public funds. Plaintiffs' equal protection challenge is thus without merit.

CONCLUSION

For the reasons stated, we affirm the district court's dismissal of this action, though on different grounds.

◆ *Notes & Questions*

1. The government action described in this case currently affects both foreign and domestic NGOs. Why is the US NGO at a competitive disadvantage? Did the court deny the relief sought by the Center for Reproductive Rights because it disagreed with the plaintiff on the merits of its case against the president (and other defendants)?

2. Should the ability of foreign and domestic NGOs to deal with each other, regarding conduct that is not illegal, depend on which president is in office?

3. A variety of NGOs, and their impacts on States and other organizations, is available in B. Arts, M. Noortmann & B. Reinalda, NON-STATE ACTORS IN INTERNATIONAL RELATIONS (Aldershot, Eng.: Ashgate, 2001). A symposium, the product of a conference on NGOs, is available in On the Possibilities and Limitations of NGO Participation in International Law and its Processes, in PROCEEDINGS OF THE NINETY-FIFTH ANNUAL MEETING OF THE AMERICAN SOCIETY OF INTERNATIONAL LAW: (Wash., DC: Amer. Soc. Int'l Law, 2001).

FUNCTIONAL SHIFT

Many global and regional alliances are shifting from political to economic orientations. The Warsaw Pact, a prominent figure in international affairs until 1991, is military history. Many of the former Soviet Union member States are being admitted into NATO by way of its Partnership for Peace Program.

The Arab League is splintered. Egypt was expelled due to President Sadat's decision to enter into friendly treaty relations with Israel. The League virtually fell apart during the Persian Gulf War (PGW). Members who formerly advocated Israel's demise fought their Arab League ally Iraq, which, among other things, protected Israel from Iraqi attack. The contemporary PLO autonomy further confirms the lack of unity about conquering Israel—the traditional military and political foe of League members (see, e.g., Arab Boycott §10.1).

The Organization of African Unity (OAU) is expanding upon its traditional political purpose. South Africa's rejection of apartheid, and the presidency of Nelson Mandela, inadvertently deprived the OAU of the one issue that united its otherwise fractious membership. The OAU is currently pursuing economic objectives, to a much greater degree than in the past, now that the racial vestiges of colonialism are no longer official state policy in South Africa (§3.5).

Numerous international common markets and free trade areas are working to advance the economic objectives of member States throughout the globe, especially now that the Cold War no longer drives international relations (§13.3).

◆ 3.3 UNITED NATIONS

At one point before launching the Iraq War in 2003, US President Bush expressed his frustration that the United Nations would be "irrelevant," if it failed to provide a SC resolution authorizing the use of force against Iraq (which it did not do). Just three years earlier, world leaders including President Bill Clinton acknowledged that:

> 1. We, Heads of State and Government, have gathered at United Nations Headquarters in New York from 6 to 8 September 2000, at the dawn of a new Millennium, to reaffirm our faith in the Organization and its Charter as indispensable foundations of a more peaceful, prosperous and just world.
>
> . . .
>
> 3. We reaffirm our commitment to the purposes and principles of the Charter of the United Nations, which have proved timeless and universal. Indeed, their relevance and capacity to inspire have increased, as nations and peoples have become increasingly interconnected and interdependent.
>
> . . .
>
> 32. We solemnly reaffirm, on this historic occasion, that the United Nations is the indispensable common house of the entire human family, through which we will seek to realize our universal aspirations for peace, cooperation and development. We, therefore, pledge our unstinting support for these common objectives, and our determination to achieve them.[23]

After digesting this section of the book, you will be in a better position to make a personal assessment about the true role of the United Nations, whether too much or too little has been expected of it, and whether the above Millennium Declaration by 152 world leaders provides an accurate vision of what the United Nations can actually accomplish in this twenty-first century.

This section of your text covers three central themes: events preceding creation of the United Nations (Historical Backdrop); the UN's major institutions (UN Organization); and its successes and failures (UN Assessment).

HISTORICAL BACKDROP

League of Nations   This was the first global international organization and the direct predecessor of the United Nations. The League of Peace, a private organization in the United States, proposed a League of Nations in a 1914 newspaper editorial at the outset of World War I. Great Britain's League of Nations Society began to promote this ideal in 1916. The South African statesman, who coauthored the Covenant of the League of Nations (and the UN Charter), proposed that the peoples in the territories formerly belonging to Russia, Austria-Hungary, and Turkey create an international organization to resolve their territorial disputes. All States would thereby abide by the fundamental principle that resolutions by "the league of nations should be substituted for any policy of national annexation."[24]

US President Woodrow Wilson was a key proponent of the League's creation. Drawing on the 1917 "Recommendations of Havana," prepared by the American Institute of International Law meeting in Cuba, Wilson's famous 1918 "Fourteen Points" speech to the US Congress advocated a "general association of nations [that] must be formed under specific covenants for the purpose of affording mutual guarantees of political independence and territorial integrity to great and small states alike." His essential purpose was to avoid a second world war, based on the popular notion of the day that this first global conflict be the "war to end all wars." World leaders reacted by expressing their hope that the League would be the ultimate mechanism for avoiding a repetition of the secret military alliances and mutual suspicions that permeated the international atmosphere. The fear of another war thus generated the creation of this organization to encourage open diplomacy and cooling-off periods whenever international tensions threatened peace.

Wilson witnessed the realization of his first point—the creation of an international organization dedicated to open "covenants of peace, openly arrived at, after which there shall be no private international understandings of any kind but diplomacy shall proceed always frankly and in public view." The 1919 League of Nations Covenant, part of the Treaty of Versailles, was ultimately signed by seventy-three States. Its twenty-six articles dealt with a variety of problems, although the central theme was how to control military aggression. It was a progressive development in international relations because it established a two-organ permanent diplomatic conference (a GA and a SC). The League was a central location for conference diplomacy. Unfortunately, it never achieved universality in terms of State participation.[25]

The dream that the League of Nations would maintain international peace and security failed the test of reality. The US Senate chose not to ratify the League of Nations Covenant. The senators feared a diminution of US sovereignty. They believed that membership would instead draw the United States into further wars.[26] The United States opted for isolationism, which was the death knell for the organization's potential effectiveness. League membership consisted essentially of only the war-torn European countries.

While the League enjoyed some successes during its twenty-year existence, its failures eroded global confidence in the ability of an organization to maintain harmonious international relations. The League was unable to control the offensive military objectives of its member States. By the time the Soviet Union (USSR) finally joined the League in 1934, Brazil, Germany, and Japan had already withdrawn. The USSR later invaded Finland, Japan expanded into Manchuria, Germany annexed Austria into the Third Reich, and Italy invaded Ethiopia. A few League members reacted by an almost submissive form of economic sanctions—a brief boycott of Italian-made shoes. The global economic depression of the 1930s, coupled with US isolationism, the expulsion of the USSR (after it invaded Finland), and a somewhat xenophobic atmosphere, all contributed to the demise of the League of Nations.

United Nations In 1942, a number of League members met to assess whether the League should continue. They decided that it should be replaced by another global international organization to pursue the ideal of collective security. The name "United Nations" was devised by US President Roosevelt.[27] It was first used in the "Declaration by United Nations" of January 1, 1942. Representatives of the twenty-six Allied nations therein pledged that their governments would continue their fight against the Axis powers.

The UN Charter was drawn up by the representatives of fifty allied countries during the UN Conference on International Organization, held in San Francisco from April through June 1945.[28] (Poland was not represented at the conference, although it later signed the Charter to become one of the original fifty-one member States.) Delegates deliberated the various proposals previously tendered by China, the USSR, the United Kingdom, and the United States during meetings held in 1944. The summer 1945 drafting conference in San Francisco barely preceded the atomic bombing of Japan in August, which effectively ended the war. The new "United Nations" was officially established on October 24, 1945. See Exhibit 3.2. That day is now celebrated globally as UN Day.

EXHIBIT 3.2 SELECTED CHRONOLOGY OF MAJOR UN EVENTS*

YEAR	EVENT	YEAR	EVENT
1945	UN Charter created and enters into force.	1949	GA establishes office of High Commissioner for Refugees (Chapter 12).
1946	First General Assembly (GA) London; reconvenes in New York.	1950	Soviet Union (SU) boycotts Security Council (SC) for failing to oust Nationalist (Formosa) government as representative for "China" seat. SC establishes Korean action under control of US (UN signed truce with North Korea in 1953).
1947	GA adopts plan to partition "Palestine" to create Arab and Jewish States.		
1948	GA adopts Universal Declaration on Human Rights (Chapter 11).		

*UN peacekeeping operations are addressed in §10.3.

EXHIBIT 3.2 SELECTED CHRONOLOGY OF MAJOR UN EVENTS (CONTINUED)

YEAR	EVENT	YEAR	EVENT
1952	Over South Africa's objections, GA begins study of apartheid (SC arms embargo against South Africa: voluntary 1963; mandatory 1977).	1974	GA bars South African delegation from participating in GA operations despite Western objections; GA calls for New International Economic Order.
1956	Hungary obtains SC resolution regarding SU invasion (unenforced). GA establishes first independent UN force to handle Suez Canal crisis.	1975	GA passes resolution, equating Zionism with racism (revoked in 1991).
1960	GA adopts Declaration on Granting Independence to colonies and peoples. GA: SU's Nikita Khrushchev accuses Secretary-General of abusing position.	1984	Office for Emergency Operations in Africa created for famine relief.
1962	SC attempts to negotiate solution to Cuban Missile Crisis.	1989	GA announces the UN Decade of International Law (Chapter 1).
1963	World Food Program established by UN Food and Agricultural Organization.	1990	Numerous SC and GA resolutions regarding Persian Gulf War (Chapter 10).
1967	SC adopts Resolution 242 calling for Israeli withdrawal from occupied territories after Six-Day War with Middle East Arab States.	1991	End of Cold War signals improved atmosphere for SC peace efforts.
1968	GA approves Treaty on Non-Proliferation of Nuclear Weapons, calling for ratification (1993: North Korea announces intent not to renew).	1992	UN concludes most expensive peace operation in history (Cambodia $2 billion).★ SC bans former Yugoslavia from SC seat; status unresolved until successful reapplication for membership in 2000.
1969	UN Convention on Elimination of All Forms of Discrimination becomes effective.	1993	US President's GA speech chides UN inability to fulfill agenda; promises US will pay past-due assessments if new funding formula developed. Secretary-General flees from attack by Somali residents. UN not key participant in Bosnia conflict. Russia's Yeltsin requests UN support for Russia to be guarantor of stability in former USSR. UN evacuates 700 refugees from Rwanda.
1971	GA expels Chinese Nationalist representative and seats PRC delegation.		
1972	Kurt Waldheim begins service as Secretary-General 1972–1986 (later accused of Nazi-era war crimes).	1994	GA establishes post of High Commissioner for Human Rights. US requests UN ban on worldwide arms sales

UN ORGANIZATION

The six principal organs of the United Nations are the: General Assembly (GA), Security Council (SC), Economic and Social Council (ESCO), Trusteeship Council (TC), Secretariat, and the International Court of Justice (ICJ). Numerous other UN organs and specialized agencies also exist within this system, as illustrated in Exhibit 3.3.

General Assembly The GA is composed of the UN's 191 member States. Various committees and commissions serve a variety of functions for the GA. They draft, receive, and consider reports on world events, supervise the UN's Trusteeship Council, participate in selection of the judges of the ICJ, approve budgets and applications for membership, and appoint the UN Secretary-General.

Six major committees drive the work of the General Assembly. They are designated the "First" through "Sixth" Committee. The following committee titles suggest the day-to-day work of the Assembly: First Committee—Disarmament and International Security; Second Committee—Economic and Financial; Third Committee—Social, Humanitarian, and Cultural; Fourth Committee—Special Political and Decolonization; Fifth Committee—Administrative and Budgetary; and Sixth Committee—Legal.[29]

The GA is primarily a global forum for resolving issues within the scope of the UN Charter. Articles 10–17 of the Charter enable the GA to "discuss," to "consider," to "initiate studies and make recommendations," and to "receive and consider annual and special reports." England's University of Leicester Professor Malcolm Shaw

EXHIBIT 3.2 SELECTED CHRONOLOGY OF MAJOR UN EVENTS (CONTINUED)

YEAR	EVENT	YEAR	EVENT
	to North Korea. SC authorizes French request for humanitarian intervention in Rwanda. UN establishes Rwanda peacekeeping operation. Bosnian Serbs isolate UN peacekeepers, making them virtual hostages.	2000	UN Millennium Summit draws 152 heads of State from all over the world to reaffirm UN's central position in world affairs.
1995	UN (Berlin) Greenhouse Conference negotiates new limits to control global warming.	2001	Slobodan Milosevic, Yugoslavia's former head of State extradited to UN's International Criminal Tribunal for trial of war crimes. UN resolutions regarding September 11, 2001 [§10.7]
1996	UN Conference on Human Settlements issues Habitat Agenda for urban living in 21st century; because of dues arrearage, US removed from panel regarding UN funding.	2002	UN Security Council Resolution 1442 referring to the threat that Iraq's "proliferation of weapons of mass destruction . . . poses to international peace and security," affords Iraq a final opportunity to comply with its disarmament obligations.
1997	In its first emergency session in 15 years, the GA demands that Israel stop building Jewish settlements in East Jerusalem. UN's International Criminal Tribunal for Former Yugoslavia conducts first international criminal trial since Nuremberg. New Secretary-General Kofi Annan installed to reform UN.	2003	*March*: UN Secretary General warns that if the US fails to win approval from the Security Council for an attack on Iraq, Washington's decision to act outside the Council would violate the United Nations charter. *October*: UNSC Resolution 1511 establishes Multinational UN Force led by US.
1998	Rome Conference establishes preliminary structure for first permanent International Criminal Court. Secretary-General advises US it must consult with UN before attacking Iraq.	2004	UN Security Council Resolution 1566 identifies acts of terrorism, specifying that there can be no political or other justification, calls upon all States to prevent and punish such acts and to become parties to all multilateral treaties on terrorism.
1999	UN takes over administration of Kosovo and East Timor. It is thus responsible for rebuilding the governmental functions, which has otherwise always been a matter of State competence. The Secretary-General announces the Observance by United Nations Forces of International Humanitarian Law, whereby UN forces are subject to Geneva Conventions.	2005	UN Security Council Resolution 1593 refers first case (Sudan) to the International Criminal Court.

thus characterizes the GA as "essentially a *debating chamber*, a forum for the exchange of ideas and the discussion of a wide-ranging category of problems."[30]

The GA became more than a mere debate chamber in 1950. Its members recognized that the SC's power to act in sensitive cases would be vitiated by the veto power of any of the five permanent members of the Council. The Assembly then adopted "Uniting for Peace Resolution" 377. Its purpose was to ensure a prompt UN response to threats to international peace—when the SC would not, or could not, take action. The effect of this resolution, permitting the GA to act in the absence of the express Charter authority to do so, augmented the SC's authority to maintain peace (§10.3).

In an attempt to avert the Iraq War, an NGO—New York City's Center for Constitutional Rights

(CCR)—brought public attention to Resolution 377. In its February 2003 Uniting for Peace campaign, CCR proposed that antiwar activists lobby their national representatives to the United Nations to lobby their national representatives to the United Nations, for the purpose of rescuing this matter from the SC's inability to act. This major human rights NGO launched this unsuccessful campaign on the following basis:

Long ago, the members of the United Nations recognized that such impasses would occur in the Security Council. They set up a procedure for insuring that such stalemates would not prevent the United Nations from carrying out its mission to "maintain international peace and security." In 1950, the United Nations by an almost unanimous vote adopted

EXHIBIT 3.3 UNITED NATIONS SYSTEM

The United Nations system

PRINCIPAL ORGANS

Trusteeship Council	Security Council	General Assembly	Economic and Social Council	International Court of Justice	Secretariat

Subsidiary Bodies
Military Staff Committee
Standing Committee and ad hoc bodies
International Criminal Tribunal for the Former Yugoslavia
International Criminal Tribunal for Rwanda
UN Monitoring, Verification and Inspection Commission (Iraq)
United Nations Compensation Commission
Peacekeeping Operations and Missions

Programmes and Funds
UNCTAD United Nations Conference on Trade and Development
  ITC International Trade Centre (UNCTAD/WTO)
UNDCP United Nations Drug Control Programme[1]
UNEP United Nations Environment Programme
UNICEF United Nations Children's Fund

UNDP United Nations Development Programme
  UNIFEM United Nations Development Fund for Women
  UNV United Nations Volunteers
UNCDF United Nations Capital Development Fund
UNFPA United Nations Population Fund

UNHCR Office of the United Nations High Commissioner for Refugees
WFP World Food Programme
UNRWA[2] United Nations Relief and Works Agency for Palestine Refugees in the Near East
UN-HABITAT United Nations Human Settlements Programme (UNHSP)

Research and Training Institutes
UNICRI United Nations Interregional Crime and Justice Research Institute
UNITAR United Nations Institute for Training and Research

UNRISD United Nations Research Institute for Social Development
UNIDIR[2] United Nations Institute for Disarmament Research

INSTRAW International Research and Training Institute for the Advancement of Women

Other UN Entities
OHCHR Office of the United Nations High Commissioner for Human Rights

UNOPS United Nations Office for Project Services
UNU United Nations University
UNSSC United Nations System Staff College

UNAIDS Joint United Nations Programme on HIV/AIDS

Subsidiary Bodies
Main committees
Other sessional committees
Standing committees and ad hoc bodies
Other subsidiary organs

Functional Commissions
Commissions on:
Human Rights
Narcotic Drugs
Crime Prevention and Criminal Justice
Science and Technology for Development
Sustainable Development
Status of Women
Population and Development
Commission for Social Development
Statistical Commission

Regional Commissions
Economic Commission for Africa (ECA)
Economic Commission for Europe (ECE)
Economic Commission for Latin America and the Caribbean (ECLAC)
Economic and Social Commission for Asia and the Pacific (ESCAP)
Economic and Social Commission for Western Asia (ESCWA)

Other Bodies
Permanent Forum on Indigenous Issues (PFII)
United Nations Forum on Forests
Sessional and standing committees
Expert, ad hoc and related bodies

Related Organizations
WTO[3] World Trade Organization
IAEA[4] International Atomic Energy Agency
CTBTO PREP.COM[5] PrepCom for the Nuclear-Test-Ban-Treaty Organization
OPCW[5] Organization for the Prohibition of Chemical Weapons

Specialized Agencies[6]
ILO International Labour Organization
FAO Food and Agriculture Organization of the United Nations
UNESCO United Nations Educational, Scientific and Cultural Organization
WHO World Health Organization
WORLD BANK GROUP
IBRD International Bank for Reconstruction and Development
IDA International Development Association
IFC International Finance Corporation
MIGA Multilateral Investment Guarantee Agency
ICSID International Centre for Settlement of Investment Disputes
IMF International Monetary Fund
ICAO International Civil Aviation Organization
IMO International Maritime Organization
ITU International Telecommunication Union
UPU Universal Postal Union
WMO World Meterological Organization
WIPO World Intellectual Property Organization
IFAD International Fund for Agricultural Development
UNIDO United Nations Industrial Development Organization
WTO[3] World Tourism Organization

Departments and Offices
OSG Office of the Secretary-General
OIOS Office of Internal Oversight Services
OLA Office of Legal Affairs
DPA Department of Political Affairs
DDA Department for Disarmament Affairs
DPKO Department of Peace-keeping Operations
OCHA Office for the Coordination of Humanitarian Affairs
DESA Department of Economic and Social Affairs
DGACM Department for General Assembly and Conference Management
DPI Department of Public Information
DM Department of Management
OHRLLS Office of the High Representative for the Least Developed Countries, Landlocked Developing Countries and Small Island Developing States
UNSECOORD Office of the United Nations Security Coordinator
UNODC United Nations Office on Drugs and Crime
UNOG UN Office at Geneva
UNOV UN Office at Vienna
UNON UN Office at Nairobi

Published by the UN Department of Public Information
DPI/2342—March 2004

NOTES: Solid lines from a Principal Organ indicate a direct reporting relationship; dashes indicate a non-subsidiary relationship. [1]The UN Drug Control Programme is part of the UN Office on Drugs and Crime. [2]UNRWA and UNIDIR report only to the GA. [3]The World Trade Organization and World Tourism Organization use the same acronym. [4]IAEA reports to the Security Council and the General Assembly (GA). [5]The CTBTO Prep.Com and OPCW report to the GA. [6]Specialized agencies are autonomous organizations working with the UN and each other through the coordinating machinery of the ECOSOC at the intergovernmental level, and through the Chief Executives Board for coordination (CEB) at the inter-secretariat level.

Resolution 377, the wonderfully named "Uniting for Peace." The United States played an important role in that resolutions adoption, concerned about the possibilities of vetoes by the Soviet Union during the Cold War.

Uniting for Peace provides that if, because of the lack of unanimity of the permanent members of the Security Council (France, China, Russia, Britain, United States), the Council cannot maintain international peace where there is a "threat to the peace, breach of the peace or act of aggression," the General Assembly "shall consider the matter immediately. . . ." The General Assembly can meet within 24 hours to consider such a matter, and can recommend collective measures to U.N. members including the use of armed forces to "maintain or restore international peace and security."

The Uniting for Peace resolution procedure has been used ten times since 1950. Its first use was by the United States.[31]

. . .

Since the end of World War II, world leaders have often addressed the GA on very sensitive problems in international relations. In 1960, Nikita Khrushchev spoke to the GA, accusing UN Secretary-General Dag Hammarskjold of abusing his position as head of this global organization. Yasir Arafat, the leader of the PLO, spoke to the GA in 1974. His objective was to seek UN assistance in consummating the statehood of the dormant State of Palestine. In 1993, US President Clinton spoke in an effort to convince this body to reduce what he characterized as its overextended commitment to worldwide peacekeeping engagements. President Bush addressed the Assembly in 2003, seeking authorization for a war against Iraq.

It is sometimes easier to define something by first acknowledging what it is not. The GA is *not* a world legislature. It may pass resolutions, some of which ultimately become treaties for State ratification. Other resolutions may indicate the degree of *opinio juris*—regarding a practice which States consider binding in their international relations (§1.3). The Assembly does not, however, have the power to enact legislation like a national legislature such as the US Congress, Mexican Parliament, or Japanese Diet. The majority of State members are unwilling to yield the requisite degree of sovereignty to authorize the GA to pass laws, which would bind all nations. As succinctly stated by the University of Pozman Professor Krzysztof Skubiszewski (Poland), "[w]e know both from the reading of the UN Charter and the history of its drafting (the defeat of the Philippine proposal on this right presented at the [1945] Conference in San Francisco) that no power to make law for states has been conferred on the General Assembly or any other organ of the United Nations. For such power, whether comprising legislation by virtue of unanimous vote, or by majority decision with the guarantees of the system of contracting out, or by majority decision binding for all, must always be based on an EXPLICIT AND UNEQUIVOCAL TREATY AUTHORIZATION."[32]

The GA's Charter prerogatives are thus limited to the initiation of studies and the recommendation of peaceful courses of action when confronted with pending hostilities. Its fundamental purpose is to promote international cooperation, in a political rather than military context. The Assembly's State members therefore collaborate regarding major economic, social, cultural, educational, human rights, and health issues. They sometimes recommend measures for the peaceful adjustment of any situation deemed likely to impair friendly relations among nations. Thus, there has been a proliferation of global conferences within the UN system. Issue-oriented *ad hoc* world conferences can focus worldwide attention on a particular social or economic problem, as well as spawning institutionalized follow-up activities.

Germany's University of Tubingen political science professor Volker Rittberger aptly acknowledges that such "[g]lobal conference diplomacy, which takes place in any of these institutional settings, represents a unique vehicle for facilitating and strengthening internationally-coordinated public policy-making . . . which is expected to cope with . . . resource shortages at the level of the individual decision-making unit, e.g., the central government of a nation state. . . . Moreover, . . . national decision-making units remain necessary, but are no longer exclusive participants in this decision-making system."[33]

The GA was effectively controlled by the United States throughout the 1950s. After a paradigm shift, associated with the induction of new independent States (former colonies), the "Third World" began to control the overall direction of the Assembly in the mid-1960s. One of the resulting agenda shifts was the seventy–seven nation announcement of a New International Economic Order (§13.4). This platform advocated an equitable redistribution of the world's wealth. The Assembly-driven Law of the Sea Treaty, for example, entered into force in 1994. Its contemporary applicability illustrates some of the ways in which this redistribution is intended to materialize. While economically powerful nations objected, the treaty text requires the powerful seagoing nations to deposit a portion of revenues they draw from mining and fishing into an agency which, in turn, is supposed to repatriate a portion of these revenues to the less powerful States (§6.3).

The UN GA provides an unparalleled form of recognition for the less powerful members of the international community. As aptly characterized by Political Science Professor M.J. Peterson of Amherst University, the "egalitarian nature of the Assembly . . . makes it the favorite political organ of weak states . . . because it gives them an influence over decisions that they lack elsewhere in the international system. . . . The Third World Coalition . . . uses the Assembly more intensely than did the US-led coalition, but its relative lack of power has exposed more clearly the limits on Assembly control over outcomes in world politics."[34]

Losing the seat in the GA would normally be a devastating blow to national prestige. No nation, especially the less powerful ones, would ever wish for the Assembly to exercise its UN Charter Article 6 power of expulsion. In 1979, Taiwan lost the "China" seat to the mainland People's Republic of China (PRC). This was not an Article 6 expulsion, but a matter of collective recognition of the government that more clearly represented the national population (§2.3). The most fascinating and debatable example involved the status of the United Nations' "Yugoslavia" seat, which remained empty between 1992 and 2000. The following case illustrates yet another curious intersection of law and politics, which in this instance, yielded a "phantom State." Some apparition had to be conjured, for the world court to have both: (a) original jurisdiction to proceed to its 1996 judgment; and (b) continuing jurisdiction in 2003, in order to deny the successor entity's ability to change that judgment:

> **Application for Revision of The Judgment of 11 July 1996 in the Case Concerning Application of The Convention on The Prevention and Punishment of The Crime of Genocide** (*Bosnia and Herzegovina v. Yugoslavia*)
>
> INTERNATIONAL COURT OF JUSTICE
> General List No. 122 (February 3, 2003)
> <http://www.icj-cij.org/icjwww/idecisions.htm>
> Go to course Web page at
> <http://home.att.net/~slomansonb/txtcsesite.html>.
> Under Chapter Three, click Bosnia v. FRY.

Security Council

(a) Purpose and Structure   The SC is the UN organ with the primary responsibility for maintaining peace. Under Article 39 of the Charter, the SC determines what constitutes a threat to peace and what security measures should be taken by the United Nations.

The SC is much smaller than the GA of all nations. The SC consists of fifteen countries. The Council's limited size was designed to facilitate prompt and effective action by the United Nations—in contrast to the debating atmosphere of the all-member GA. Nations can refer their disputes to the SC for resolution (as well as to the GA when it is in session). Unlike the Assembly, the Council functions continuously. A representative of each of the fifteen member States must be present at all times at UN Headquarters in New York City.

The SC includes five "permanent" members and ten "rotating" members, periodically elected by the GA. The five permanent members are China, France, Russia, the United Kingdom, and the United States. The "Russian" seat on the Council was formerly occupied by the Soviet Union until 1991 and now occupied by Russia. The "China" seat has been occupied by the PRC since the Republic of China (Nationalist Chinese government) was ousted by UN action in 1971.

The makeup of the SC has always generated debates about its failure to more democratically reflect the UN's overall composition. The GA is a comparatively diverse body, consisting of States from every corner of the world, innumerable cultures, all political systems, and every form of economic development. Under the original Charter, however, five of the (then only) eleven SC members occupied permanent seats on the Council. *Any one* of these five could block Council action by exercising its individual right to *veto* any proposed action. No rotating member possesses this extraordinary veto power. Action by the SC therefore requires a unanimous vote of the five permanent members and a majority vote of the fifteen total members.

There have been several significant movements seeking a change to the SC's composition. GA member States believed that the Council should not ignore the less powerful but more populated States within in Africa, Asia, and Latin America. In 1965, the United Nations altered its structure to magnify the presence of such nations—many of which were former colonies of the charter UN members. The number of Council seats was then increased from eleven to fifteen. The four fresh seats were designated as additional rotating seats as opposed to the five permanent seats. A number of commentators viewed this as a minor concession, however, in the struggle to ameliorate the powerful-nation dominance of the Council.

After the demise of the Soviet Union, and its attendant Cold War with the United States, Germany and Japan have consistently sought an upgrade of their status from occasional rotating members. They have sought their addition to the Council, which would thus result in seven permanent SC members. Unlike the US, the British and French governments are opposed to such a change, as evinced by British Foreign Secretary Douglas Hurd's widely reported 1993 application of the old adage: "If it ain't broke, don't fix it." US Secretary of State Warren Christopher responded that the SC may not be broke; however, "[i]t's time for some reorganizing." Ironically, the Japanese and German constitutions, each limit their ability to participate in SC military actions.[35]

The year 2004 spawned a number of high-level SC reform measures. A UN panel suggested two options: (1) adding six new permanent members; or (2) creating a new tier of semipermanent members—two each from Asia, Africa, Europe, and the Americas. Egypt independently launched its plea for a permanent seat. Its ambassador to the United Nations proclaimed, in words articulating like claims from other countries: "Egypt's regional and international contributions—in African, Arab, Islamic circles, in the Middle East and among developing countries and blooming economies . . . [thus] qualities her. . . ." Four other nations vowed to support each other's bids for an expanded SC: Brazil, Germany, India, and Japan. Their joint statement noted that the "Security Council must reflect the realities of the international community in the twenty-first century," drawing support in the four-fold increase of nations since the original fifty-one nations in 1945 (see §2.2 listing in Exhibit 2.1). Brazil's president added that Africa must be represented within the Council's permanent membership "to reflect today's realities—not perpetuate the post-World War II era." The French president also called for an increase from fifteen permanent and rotating nations to twenty or twenty-five. Chirac stated that: "You cannot simply take a snapshot of 1945 and apply it to 2004." Russian President Putin, speaking in support of India's permanent addition, expressed the view that any reform would be one-sided if new members did not have the veto power.[36]

Because of various limitations built into the UN Charter, by the nations that drafted it, there is a prominent distinction between promise and performance. Under Article 47 of the Charter, for example, the Council is responsible for submitting plans to UN members for establishing and maintaining a system to regulate armaments. Under Articles 41 and 42 of the Charter, the SC may decide what related measures are needed to implement its decisions. The Charter states that the Council may order the complete or partial interruption of economic relations with States that violate International Law. If the Council considers such sanctions inadequate, the Charter expressly authorizes its use of air, sea, or land forces as necessary to maintain or restore international peace and security. (Multinational operations under Security Council control are addressed in Chapter 10 of this book.)

For a variety of reasons, including that no Article 43 standing army ever materialized, the Council has had to resort to some rather ingenuous bases for taking action—or affirming action already taken by a UN member or coalition of States (such as NATO). Unlike the circumstances which prevail in each of the many liberal democracies within the UN's membership, there is no review process for assessing the legality of the Council's interventions—as will be addressed in relation to the ICJ, which lacks any judicial review power over the SC's executive acts.

The SC basked in comparatively provocative sunshine, in the aftermath of the dark Cold War period of the 1950s through the 1980s. In the 1990s, the Council established two special courts to deal with the atrocities in the former Yugoslavia and Rwanda (§9.5). The Yugoslavian tribunal tried the first former Head of State for genocide and war crimes (for which Slobodan Milosevic's claim of presidential immunity would be disregarded, when his trial began in 2002).

In another instance of a proactive approach not witnessed during the Cold War, the Council (slowly but) effectively responded to the 1998 bombings of the US embassies in Kenya and Tanzania—which had killed 224 people, and the 2001 commercial aircraft attacks on New York's World Trade Center and Washington's Pentagon—later killing nearly 3,000 people. Given the widespread belief that Usama Bin Laden planned the embassy bombings, the Council embarked upon a mission to secure his capture. The SC seized upon its Chapter VII powers to "delegate" them to member States. In Resolution 1189, the Council called upon all States to adopt "practical measures for security cooperation, for the prevention of such acts of terrorism. . . ." Resolution 1214 demanded "that the Taliban stop providing sanctuary and training for international terrorists and their organizations. . . . ." When Afghanistan did not comply, Resolution 1267 demanded that "the Taliban turn over Usama bin Laden without further delay. . . ." This resolution backed up the Councils's demand by authorizing an air embargo and the freezing of financial resources to which the country had access. It was followed by other resolutions that the United States would rely upon as a basis for its air strikes in Afghanistan.

During the Cold War between permanent Security Council members (United States and Soviet Union), the United Nations exercised only a minimal degree of control over several territories in conflict. The UN's peacekeeping role, not mentioned anywhere in the Charter, was dependent on the consent of parties engaged in the hostilities. Military forces, on loan to the UN by various

countries, occupied State territory as a buffer—designed to enforce postconflict peace agreements (§10.3). Peacekeeping was not necessarily peace*making*.

The Security Council's decision to rescue two areas of the world from ethnic tension—by assuming their administration, and operating as if it were a sovereign State—may be perhaps the most striking example of the Council's post-Cold War renaissance. The first of two such areas was East Timor (§2.4), where the UN rescued the residents from continuing violence resulting from the desire to break from Indonesian colonization. The second has been the administration of Kosovo (§3.5). There have been many problems with the UN's administration in each of these theaters.[37] No one can dispute, however, that this unique control of sovereign territory—by the only international organization ever to do so—was a marked departure from the UN's impotence to take proactive measures during the half-century Cold War.

In its major 2004 self-analysis, the UN High-Level Panel on Threats, Challenges and Change thus determined that:

224. Deploying peace enforcement and peacekeeping forces may be essential in terminating conflicts but are not sufficient for long-term recovery. Serious attention to the longer-term process of peacebuilding in all its multiple dimensions is critical; failure to invest adequately in peacebuilding increases the odds that a country will relapse into conflict.

. . .

227. . . . Given that many peace operations can expect resource shortfalls, the efficient use of resources is all the more important. . . . The Security Council should mandate and the General Assembly should authorize funding for disarmament and demobilization programmes from assessed budgets.

228. . . . A standing fund for peacebuilding should be established at the level of at least $250 million that can be used to finance the recurrent expenditures of a nascent Government, as well as critical agency programmes in the areas of rehabilitation and reintegration.[38]

The Council's October 2003 resolution on Afghanistan supported expansion of the NATO-led International Security Assistance Force beyond the capitol city of Kabul (Resolution 1510). Its June 2004 resolution endorsed US turnover of Iraq to the Interim Government of Iraq (Resolution 1546). While after the fact of the US invasion of these countries, the UN SC nevertheless opted to exercise its influence to monitor their occupation—sending a clear message about ending the respective occupations. One could of course argue that these measures were comparatively passive and arguably face-saving. But were they not preferable to total inaction by the United Nation?

(b) The Veto Dilemma   The League of Nations was plagued from the outset with its unanimity requirement for SC action. The UN strategy was initially perceived as an improvement. Nine of fifteen votes, rather than unanimity, is one of two conditions for SC action. The other condition has bedeviled the SC—almost from the outset: The United Nations cannot act if one of the five permanent members casts a veto, occasionally described as a dictatorship within a democracy.

Ironically, the word "veto" is not contained in the UN Charter. Article 48 merely states that action "shall be taken by all the Members of the United Nations or by some of them, as the Security Council may determine." Article 27.3 provides that the Council's substantive decisions "shall be made by an affirmative vote of nine members including the concurring vote of the permanent members. . . ." It is the Security Council's *Provisional Rules of Procedure* that contain the somewhat infamous veto provision adopted at the 1945 UN drafting conference in San Francisco. Mindful of the US decision not to join the League of Nations, and the Soviet Union's expulsion from the League for invading Finland, none of the five permanent Council members could be drawn into an armed conflict that it did not wish to enter.

National sovereignty was the real culprit in what would soon become apparent with the advent of the Cold War: powerful States did not want to cede sovereign powers to an external entity. The UNSC would otherwise be enabled to trump a State's unilateral decision about initiating, engaging in, or avoiding future hostilities. Giving this type of power to the SC would also tamper with a powerful State's ability to clandestinely support an "offending" State's action. Handing over such power to an international organization would limit a member's ability to remain indifferent to threats

to peace in distant corners of the globe. The State-oriented concern about the retention of sovereign discretion also thwarted materialization of the Article 43 standing army. Had such a force materialized, it would have functioned as an international police force able to react to threats to the peace in different ways than UN members might prefer.

The post-World War II veto dilemma pitted the two most powerful allies against one another, in a way that would severely limit the United Nations' overall ability to respond to threats to peace. The USSR temporarily boycotted SC meetings in 1950. The USSR had insisted that the PRC (communist mainland China) was the appropriate entity to occupy the "China" seat on the Council, rather than the then-seated Republic of China. The Nationalist government on Formosa—now Taiwan—had been unseated in Mao's successful communist uprising, but not at the United Nations. This historic absence of one of the permanent five SC member States allowed the Council to vote in favor of UN involvement in the Korean Conflict under the direction of a US military command. This would not have happened if the Soviet representative had been present for the vote, or possibly, if the "China" seat had been occupied by mainland China—which would soon be assisting North Korea during the 1950–1953 Korean conflict. This event led to the infamous Cold War "veto" which would ultimately paralyze the SC's pursuit of collective security.

Since its inception, this facet of superpower politics has been most evident when one of the five holders of the veto power have blocked an international response to their *own* threats to international peace. Recent examples by each Council member—armed with the knowledge that it could conveniently deflect SC action—arguably include the 1989 US invasion of Panama; France's involvement in the escape of the French agents responsible for the death of crew members on the Greenpeace vessel *Rainbow Warrior* in New Zealand in 1986; Great Britain's 1982 war with Argentina over the distant Falkland Islands just off Argentina's coast; the Soviet Union's occupation of Afghanistan in 1979; and any UN action which might have responded to the reported deaths of some 3,000 civilians in Beijing's Tiananmen Square during the 1989 democracy demonstration.

Effective UN Security Council control of international conflict is arguably unlikely without significant change in the SC's voting procedure. All members of the Permanent Five can thereby continue to "have their cake and eat it too." These SC members have all benefitted from the veto, which has been unfairly attributed to the obstructionism of just the former Soviet Union.

Although the frequency of the veto declined after the Cold War (1989), the circumstances giving rise to the many ensuing conflicts have not. There will be no effective international organizational control until there is a genuine interest by member States to integrate word and deed. In the words of UN Political Affairs Officer Anjali Patil, in her book on the SC veto: "It really doesn't matter who enjoys the veto power in the Security Council; international peace and security cannot be maintained until all States accept the need to identify with the whole of humanity. We have struggled over the centuries for absolute peace but have not yet achieved it. While creating the United Nations has enabled us to avoid a [third] world war, we have yet to create a genuine international society."[39]

Too many powerful UN members are obsessed with retaining their options via the historical application of virtually *complete* State sovereignty. This preoccupation allows too many States to say one thing and mean another. It demonstrates the continuing lack of an international commitment to reliance on the Security Council, as the tool for attaining the UN Charter ideal "to save succeeding generations from the scourge of war."

(c) Peacekeeping Operations UN Peacekeeping operations are addressed in §10.3 on the Use of Force by States and Organizations. There, the materials will address the UN's provocative role in the governance of post-conflict societies.

Economic and Social Council The League of Nations focused on military and political problems. The UN system is more inclusive, evinced by Charter recognition of the economic and social sparks for igniting conflict. UN priorities thus include the observance of human rights and the general welfare of the individual.

The UN Educational, Scientific, and Cultural Organization (UNESCO—headquartered in Paris) conducts studies and issues reports on international economic, social, cultural, educational, and health matters. The results of these studies are forwarded to the GA, to the

State members of the United Nations, and to other UN specialized agencies concerned with the promotion of human rights and fundamental freedoms for all people. ECOSOC also prepares draft conventions for submission to the GA. It thus arranges international conferences on matters within its competence. It is the lead international agency, for example, for addressing the impact of illegal drug trafficking. An index to its vast array of programs is available on the UN Web site.[40]

The rotating fifty-four member ECOSOC operates under the authority of the GA. Its job description is to promote: "(a) higher standards of living, full employment, and conditions of economic and social progress and development; (b) solutions of international economic, social, health, and related problems; and international cultural and educational cooperation; and (c) universal respect for, and observance of, human rights and fundamental freedoms for all without distinction as to race, sex, language, or religion."[41]

This institution unfortunately received more limelight than desired, when the US Reagan Administration began to shun participation in various UN agencies in the 1980s. It was the first UN agency from which the United States withdrew (1984). One disclosed reason was the US assertion that this vast UN bureaucracy had produced much paperwork, but without tangible benefits. In 1990, the United States reaffirmed its opposition to rejoining UNESCO. US Secretary of State James Baker's remarks provided telling insight into the US position as follows: "Bluntly stated, UNESCO needs the United States as a member far more than the United States needs UNESCO."

The United States returned to UNESCO in October 2003. (In the interim, this UN organ had lost the former 25 percent US contribution.) The US perspective changed about UNESCO having previously spread anti-American propaganda. The United States now pays 22 percent of this entity's budget.[42]

Trusteeship Council The TC has been a distinct UN organ consisting of selected UN members. It has been responsible for the administration of territories that are incapable of self-government. Under Article 77 of the Charter, certain member States have supervised territories detached from enemy States, typically as a result of war. Under Article 73 of the Charter, supervising States accepting a "trust" territory must observe the principle that the interests of the inhabitants of these territories are paramount to any interests of the supervising State. The supervising State must therefore accept the obligation to promote the well-being of the inhabitants.

This "big brother" plan was devised to promote the political, economic, social, and educational advancement of the supervised territories that were not yet capable of self-governance. This posture made sense when the Charter was drafted in 1945, long before the decolonization movement of the 1960s. Another trusteeship objective was to help these territories achieve self-government through the progressive development of independent political institutions (§2.4 Self-Determination). The United States, for example, administered the Trust Territory of the Pacific Islands beginning in 1947. Portions of the population later developed their own forms of government and constitutions. In 1986, the UN's TC determined that the United States had satisfied its obligation to administer most of this territory. The United States then declared its obligations to be discharged. The Micronesia and Marshall Islands portion of this US trust territory later joined the United Nations as independent States. Palau later became an independent nation. The speed of this internationally supervised development has depended on the particular circumstances of each territory, its people, and their stage of political advancement.

The TC's work has been completed, due to the success of the decolonization movement of the 1960s. It thus suspended operation in 1994, with the independence of Palau—the last remaining UN trust territory. It no longer conducts its annual TC meetings, although it may meet if its president, a majority of its members, or the GA/SC, so decide.

Although it successfully worked itself out of a job, the related performance of some UN members was not without its problems. The leading example of a breach of this trust relationship involved Namibia. This nation was originally a League of Nations "Mandate," analogous to the League-generated mandates like the British Mandate over Palestine. South Africa, the administrator for Nambia—when it was called South West Africa—refused to yield to decades of UN pressure to release its hold on this trust territory. South Africa finally agreed to permit Namibia to govern itself in 1990, whereafter Namibia joined the United Nations as an independent State member.

There have been other alleged breaches of trust. Nauru, a tiny republic in the central Pacific Ocean, sued

Australia in the ICJ in 1989. Nauru therein alleged neglect, because of Australia's exploitation and removal of phosphates earlier in the twentieth century. Natives claimed that they were barred from seeking outside legal help to avoid such depletions during the Australian administration. In 1967, the UN General Assembly terminated the Trusteeship. In 1992, the ICJ rejected Australia's contention that the UN's termination of the trusteeship barred the Court from hearing this breach of trust case. Eventually, the parties agreed to discontinue the case, which has been dismissed.[43]

One trust territory even sued its administrative host to terminate the trust relationship. The size of the Trust Territory of the Pacific Islands was reduced by the departure of Micronesia, the Marshall Islands, and the Commonwealth of the Northern Marianas—after the 1986 UN declaration that the US administration had been fulfilled as to these areas. The government of Palau then signed a Compact of Free Association with the United States. This agreement was initially rejected by the people of Palau, however, in a series of UN-observed plebiscites. In 1990, this remaining Trust Territory of the Pacific Islands sued the United States in a New York court in its bid for self-rule. The plaintiffs argued that continued UN trusteeship reneged on the lost promise of self-government. But any alteration of this trust relationship requires approval by the UN's SC under Charter Article 83. The US court dismissed this case, partially on the basis that US courts do not have the jurisdiction or power to hear cases to dissolve trust territory relationships—a power expressly reserved by the UN Charter to the SC in association with the TC.[44]

Although the TC appears to be a relic of another era, it may nevertheless have some contemporary utility. A number of States are "failing," in the sense that they are experiencing difficulties in continued self-government. Famine, civil war, and economic deprivation are some of the contemporary causes. Liberia dissolved into chaos in 1990 when rival factions began to assert tribal rivalries—slaughtering tens of thousands in the crossfire. Similar events occurred in Rwanda in 1994. "Older" States from other regions of the world such as Afghanistan, Mozambique, Somalia, and Zaire are bordering on the same fate. "Newer" States like Macedonia are just one step further away from such failed status. With contemporary limitations, especially financial problems, the United Nations is not in a good position to come to their rescue. As noted by the UN

Secretary-General in 1995: "Another feature of such [post-Cold War] conflicts is the collapse of State institutions, especially the police and judiciary, with resulting paralysis of governance, a breakdown of law and order, and general banditry and chaos. Not only are the functions of government suspended, its assets are destroyed or looted and experienced officials are killed or flee the country. . . . [Thus, the] United Nations is, for good reasons, reluctant to assume responsibility for maintaining law and order, nor can it impose a new political structure or State institutions. It can only help the hostile factions to help themselves and begin to live together again.[45]

The daunting question, of course, is under what circumstances should such States or other territories be declared temporary wards of the United Nations? One of many problems would be the predictable reprisals of various local warlords if—under the auspices of the United Nations—a State or group of States attempted to intervene, no matter how humanitarian the motive. Another practical limitation would be UN's financial instability, caused by an increasing number of States in arrears on their annual UN dues. In 1992, the UN Secretary-General stated that the United Nations was "considering" this option. Bosnia mediator, Britain's Lord Owen, and his US counterpart, Cyrus Vance, rejected this possibility for Bosnia. In nearby Kosovo, the United Nations operated this former Yugoslavian province in the aftermath of the 1999 NATO bombing of Kosovo (UNSC Resolution 1244). The other alternative, when a State's infrastructure has failed to function, is to idly observe such tragedies rather than intervening on humanitarian grounds. There is a price for such inaction: some have become breeding grounds for terrorism.

Secretariat The Secretariat administers all of the programs of the United Nations. At its zenith, a staff numbering over 26,000 persons (at Geneva, New York, Vienna, and Nairobi) is headed by the UN Secretary-General. Appointed by the GA on recommendation of the SC, this officer is the chief administrator of the United Nations.

Employees of the Secretariat, including the Secretary-General, are expected to execute their duties independently of any national allegiances. Article 100 of the UN Charter provides that in the "performance of their duties the Secretary-General and the staff shall not seek or receive instructions from any other authority external to the Organization. They shall refrain from any action which might reflect on their position as international officials responsible only to the Organization." State members of the United Nations must therefore respect the exclusively international character and responsibilities of their citizens while they are serving on the UN staff (§3.6).

An important, but somewhat obscure, function of the office of the Secretary-General (SG) is preventative diplomacy. While the public has traditionally perceived the role of this office as merely titular, the SG has often undertaken quite perilous negotiations to resolve international crises. Under Article 99 of the UN Charter, the SG "may bring to the attention of the Security Council any matter which in his opinion may threaten the maintenance of international peace and security." In Boutros Boutros-Ghali's *Agenda for Peace,* requested by the heads of State at the first meeting of the SC in 1992, he aptly notes the increasing importance of this role. In his words: "There is a long history of the utilization by the United Nations of distinguished statesmen to facilitate the processes of peace. . . . Frequently it is the Secretary-General himself who undertakes the task. While the mediator's effectiveness is enhanced by strong and evident support from the [Security] Council, the General Assembly and the relevant Member States acting in their national capacity, the good offices of the Secretary-General may at times be employed most effectively when conducted independently of the deliberative bodies."[46]

There is no clear theoretical framework, however, for linkage between the SG's Article 99 obligation to bring peace-threatening matters before the SC, and the SG's ability to directly gather the information needed to carry out his or her monumental task. This is a critical gap in need of reform. The problem is succinctly stated by Professor of Peace Studies Thomas Boudreau of St. John's University in Collegeville, Minnesota: "Without a theoretical framework that justifies and clarifies a specific reform, each effort to improve the Secretary-General's ability to prevent conflict threatens to become a piecemeal 'band-aid' solution. In short, there is a need to . . . define and develop a clear and consistent link between the Secretary-General's obligation under Article 99 and his ability to gather, ascertain, and evaluate information concerning conflict prevention.

There seems to be a bankruptcy of ideas in the realm of information gathering by the United Nations."[47]

To combat this concern, the Secretary-General's August 2005 report—In Larger Freedom: Towards Security, Development, and Human Rights for All—was designed to generate a dialogue for the September 2005 Millennium Summit (fifth year review of the achievement of the above-quoted Millennium Declaration). The Secretary therein promised that steps will be taken to create a cabinet-style decision-making mechanism. He sought the financial backing to arrange a one-time staff buyout to refresh and realign staff to meet current needs of the organization. A primary objective is to undertake a comprehensive review of the Office of Internal Oversight Services (OIOS), in the aftermath of the UN Oil-for-Food scandal, to strengthen the independence and authority of the OIOS.

International Court of Justice   The ICJ is the UN's judicial organ. Unlike its predecessor, the PCIJ (which was *not* an organ of the League of Nations), the drafters of the UN Charter presented the ICJ as a forum wherein international disputes could be resolved in the courtroom rather than on the battlefield.

The ICJ is headquartered at The Hague, in the Netherlands, and is generally viewed as not having fully lived up to the dream envisioned by drafters of the relevant UN Charter provisions (Articles 92–96), and the operational rules set forth in the companion Statute of the ICJ. Here, too, national sovereignty has been the culprit in tarnishing the 1945 vision of beating swords into plowshares.

Two prominent examples of the drafters' Charter-based limitations include the requirement of a State's consent to be sued in the ICJ and the Court's lack of judicial review regarding decisions by other UN organs (§9.4 of this text).

UN ASSESSMENT

This portion of the international organizations chapter summarizes the perspectives about how the United Nations has discharged its Charter functions. Some commentators claim that it is a merely a place to let off steam, operating as a conduit for the hegemony of its most powerful national members. The most accurate account is one that is drawn after a careful assessment of both sides of the UN balance sheet. Although there have

been pluses, many minuses can be attributed to the organization's prototypical limitations.

Inducing National Compliance   There is a widely perceived weakness, which ironically attests to the UN's resiliency under arduous circumstances. The criticism is that the United Nations has been historically powerless to effectively control the excesses of its member nations. While there has been no World War III, there have been numerous conflicts in its half-century existence. Critics have often wondered aloud why the United Nations exists if its purpose was to effectively manage conflict, rather than standing on the sidelines.

At the 1945 UN Charter drafting conference, the international community provided the SC with the ostensible power to handle future conflicts. They said one thing, but ultimately meant another. Article 43, for example, stated that the United Nations would have a military force at its disposal, to be staffed based upon future agreements. While troops *would* later become available, UN operations would always have to be carried out on an *ad hoc* voluntary basis. UN involvement would depend on the political consent of the affected States, as well as that of each of the five permanent SC members (because of their respective abilities to veto UN action). Unlike its member States, the United Nations would never have a standing army.[48]

The UN Charter was thus drafted to include broad standards of achievement, with which no State could openly disagree. But as is typical of most multinational treaty making, such treaties are not intended to be immediately binding (§8.2). One reason was that the Charter's blueprint for the post-World War II community of nations was the product of negotiations among State-centric representatives. Since the 1648 Treaty of Westphalia (§1.1), national sovereignty had been the cornerstone of national existence. Thus, the UN drafting was not inclined to cede clear-cut, sovereign-like powers to an international organization, which might later be controlled by potential competitors.

The following two analyses explore rationales for: (1) retaining the United Nations as the centerpiece for twenty-first century security needs—authored by Russian academics in the Chinese Journal of International Law, and (2) the UN's December 2004 broadly-based assessment of its own weaknesses—which must be addressed, if the international community hopes to attain "A More Secure World" (report title):

The Concept of the US National Security and International Law: A View from Moscow

Igor Lukashuk and Darya Boklan
2 *Chinese Journal of International Law* 587 (2003)

. . .

Increasing the level of international system governance is the key global issue, and the way it is resolved will determine the adjustment of other global problems. The focal nature of this issue has been many times underscored by statesmen and by the resolutions of intergovernmental organizations and NGOs. The UN Secretary General stated in the UN 2000 Progress Report that "more efficient world governance is required, under which I mean joint conduct of international affairs."

The concept of the foreign policy of Russia stresses the need "to increase the level of governance of the international system", which provides for "the strengthening of the role of international institutions and mechanisms in the world economy and politics." International law occupies an important place amongst such institutions and mechanisms. The level of international systems governance greatly depends upon the efficiency of international law.

Increasing the level of international system governance is directly connected with the increase of the role of law and ensuring legality at both the national and international levels. This focal principle has been stressed in the UN Millennium Declaration, adopted at the Millennium Summit in September 2000. The heads of states and governments declared their will "to strengthen respect for the rule of law in international and national affairs."

. . .

Preventive world policy is needed in this respect, aimed at the prevention of catastrophic scenarios. Such policy has to be implemented by the whole of the international community in compliance with the Purposes and Principles of the UN Charter. A contemporary world order may be successfully built up only on a multilateral basis with a wide circle of nations involved—that is, with the participation of the whole international community.

The UN has to play the key role in this process. It is within the UN framework that the foundations of the new world order, and correspondingly, those of the new legal order were formulated by the collective effort of nations at the turn of the 21st century. These basic principles have been stipulated by a number of resolutions adopted by the UN General Assembly in 2000 at its historic Millennium Session. Among these resolutions a special role belongs to the UN Millennium Declaration adopted at the Millennium Summit.

The Purposes and Principles of the UN Charter which "have proved timeless and universal" have been laid down in the foundation of the new world order. Moreover, "their relevance and capacity to inspire have increased, as nations and peoples have become increasingly interconnected and interdependent." Equitable and lasting peace all around the world has to be established on the basis of the mentioned purposes and principles.

The [UN] Millennium Declaration contains principal provisions for understanding the nature of new world order. Heads of states and governments have stated: "We recognize that, in addition to our separate responsibilities to our individual societies, we have a collective responsibility to uphold the principles of human dignity, equality and equity at the global level." This provision is of special importance for the USA. The USA, having power which exceeds many times the powers of other states, has to bear special responsibility for providing sustainable development to other nations. The concept of US national security must be based upon the above mentioned principle.

The Millennium Declaration has stipulated certain specific ways to obtain the above mentioned goals. A special emphasis should be put upon the fact that factors such as the increase of the general level of compliance with legislation and securing the rule of law in international and home affairs have been placed in the focus of attention. The role and capacities of the United Nations have to be substantially increased with the aim of making the UN a more efficient mechanism of securing peace in international stability.

. . .

The challenges of today provide for the basis of profound changes in the foreign policy of states. Foreign policy has to consider the new interrelationship of the national and common interests of all nations. It is impossible to secure the interests of one particular state without due regard to the common international interests. Increase in the importance of the interests of the international community does not mean infringement of the interests of any particular nation. The major goal is to attain the balance of interests of both sides. This goal is of primary importance, because without reaching it the proper functioning of the international community, as well as of the nations which constitute this community, would be impossible.

. . .

International law is an indispensable instrument for resolving these problems. Common security can be insured in the context of the international legal community, i.e. the community based upon the principles of the rule of law and its supremacy in politics. One of the main tasks of the United Nations is to create international community based upon the rule of law. Kofi Annan, the UN Secretary General, has underscored that the work aimed at creating the international community based upon the rule of law remains one of the main missions of the United Nations.

. . .

Having come to power in 2000, the new American Administration proclaimed that in its future endeavors, it would proceed from the national interests and not from those of some illusory international community. Many eminent experts underline the groundlessness of this approach. F. Cameron, former British diplomat and prominent political scientist, writes: "Contrary to what Condoleezza Rice stated in 2000, there is no contradiction between promoting national interests and a commitment to the interests of a far-from-illusionary international community."

The international community today is a kind of reality, the interests of which must be considered for the nations to make their foreign policy efficient. American scholars of authority recognize that the security of the USA is directly linked today to the global security and to the strengthening of the international community. "Americans have to make a conceptual breakthrough

and recognize the evident fact: they are part and parcel of the international community."

On 20 September 2001, after terrorist attacks on New York and Washington, President George Bush said: "Either you are with us, or you are with the terrorists." As it is known, most states declared their solidarity with the USA and its war against terrorism. However, this fact in no way means solidarity with the US Strategy of national security.

The above mentioned position of the US Administration cannot serve as the background for efficient policy. It is being subjected to criticism not only by authors of scientific literature but also by the mass media. Two prominent American experts write that meeting global challenges requires active partnership with allies as well as providing the United Nations and no other international organizations with instruments capable of preventing major conflicts, not least of all because the United States alone is not capable of meeting these challenges.

. . .

The US National Security Strategy, by ignoring the common interests of nations, inflicts a feasible blow upon the world legal order, which is based on the balance of the national and common interests of nations.

. . .

This strategy is incompatible with the main principles of contemporary international law and even with those of the past. American experts recognize that such a strategy presumes a refusal of the international order, which has been shaping international relations since the Treaty of Westphalia (1648). It is incompatible not only with the UN Charter, but also with NATO principles. R. Koen writes that the Bush Administration breaks international law and customs to pieces by stating that it can act in any way for the sake of self-defense. This is an impulse rather than a doctrine.

Many statesmen have criticized the US Administration's treatment of international law and of the United Nations. G. Schmidt writes that George Bush "has confirmed that his country is not going to consider either the UN, or other international institutions, or the commitments of the USA as far as the ratified agreements are concerned, or with documents signed by the American side."

. . .

The efficiency of international law is conditioned, first of all, by understanding the need of its existence, which maybe compared to traffic rules that are honored due to the understanding of their necessity [§1.6 Traffic Lights]. If someone should drive a tank in the opposite lane, it would inevitably cause a disaster.

Unfortunately, the political and legal thinking of leaders and the public at large is lagging behind the needs of the day. Building up the international law consciousness is therefore of paramount importance. It is only the building up of public awareness in the spirit of honoring human rights and the rights of other nations that can provide for democracy and legal order at the national and international levels. This argument was included in the UN Resolutions on the Decade of international law [1990–1999].

. . .

The opinion quoted above reveals the intention to get the protection of the mighty state, regardless of its "shameless egoism." However, history has testified to the fact that supremacy of one or of several states has never been able to secure either the national interests of other states, nor common international interests. Today a durable world order can be based only on the mutual consent of the international community, the UN being the most representative body of such consent. The democratic world order cannot be achieved without strengthening and expanding the authority of this universal organization.

. . .

The USA will be capable of retaining its leading role only by placing its might at the service of the international legal order, only by respecting interests of other states and those of the international community as a whole. In general, a lot will depend upon how the American Administration will bring the new strategy to life, upon how it will respect the realities of the global world. At the end of the day, the USA will understand that it is impossible to ignore traffic rules even if it is driving a tank.

♦

A More Secure World: Our Shared Responsibility
Report of the Secretary-General's
High-level Panel on Threats, Challenges and Change

(Part Four *Synopsis*: A More Effective United Nations
for the Twenty-first Century, at 64–65)

ANAND PANYARACHUN, CHAIRMAN
<http://www.un.org/secureworld>

The United Nations was never intended to be a utopian exercise. It was meant to be a collective security system that worked. The Charter of the United Nations provided the most powerful States with permanent membership on the Security Council and the veto. In exchange, they were expected to use their power for the common good and promote and obey international law. As Harry Truman, then President of the United States, noted in his speech to the final plenary session of the founding conference of the United Nations Organization, "we all have to recognize—no matter how great our strength—that we must deny ourselves the license to do always as we please."

In approaching the issue of United Nations reform, it is as important today as it was in 1945 to combine power with principle. Recommendations that ignore underlying power realities will be doomed to failure or irrelevance, but recommendations that simply reflect raw distributions of power and make no effort to bolster international principles are unlikely to gain the widespread adherence required to shift international behaviour.

Proposed changes should be driven by real-world need. Change for its own sake is likely to run the well-worn course of the endless reform debates of the past decade. The litmus test is this: does a proposed change help meet the challenge posed by a virulent threat?

Throughout the Panel's work, we have looked for institutional weaknesses in current responses to threats. The following stand as the most urgently in need of remedy:

◆ The General Assembly has lost vitality and often fails to focus effectively on the most compelling issues of the day.

◆ The Security Council will need to be more proactive in the future. For this to happen, those who contribute most to the Organization financially, militarily and diplomatically should participate more in Council decision-making, and those who participate in Council decision-making should contribute more to the Organization. The Security Council needs greater credibility, legitimacy and representation to do all that we demand of it.

◆ There is a major institutional gap in addressing countries under stress and countries emerging from conflict. Such countries often suffer from attention, policy guidance and resource deficits.

◆ The Security Council has not made the most of the potential advantages of working with regional and subregional organizations.

◆ There must be new institutional arrangements to address the economic and social threats to international security.

◆ The Commission on Human Rights suffers from a legitimacy deficit that casts doubts on the overall reputation of the United Nations.

◆ There is a need for a more professional and better organized Secretariat that is much more capable of concerted action.

The reforms we propose will not by themselves make the United Nations more effective. In the absence of Member States reaching agreement on the security consensus contained in the present report, the United Nations will underachieve. Its institutions will still only be as strong as the energy, resources and attention devoted to them by Member States and their leaders.

◆ Notes & Questions

1. The initial Moscow excerpt from the Chinese Journal of International Law states that the Bush Administration has operated, since 2002, solely from national rather than international interests. Could one counter that the United States is paying more attention to its national interests than in the past, as opposed to ignoring International Law? Russia appears to be more egalitarian than during the Cold War by its expressed concern with International Law compliance. Would this attitude be the joint influence of: (a) the demise of the comparatively powerful Soviet Union; and (b) the contemporary threat associated with there being only one remaining superpower (United States)? These and related matters will be addressed in more detail in future chapters covering international courts, Laws of War, and other perennial concerns within the ambit of "shared responsibility" expressed by these Russian authors.

2. The other excerpt (UN *Synopsis*)—and the entire self-assessment report—specifically avoid mentioning any particular conflict. As stated in the overall Report's transmittal letter, from this project's Chair to the Secretary-General: "Our mandate from you precluded any in-depth examination of individual conflicts and we have respected that guidance." If you were Kofi Annan, consider whether you would have thus excluded the following conflicts from consideration, in your quest to improve collective security: The US-led war in Iraq; the Palestinian conflict; Russia's conflict in Chechnya; the PRC's conflict with Taiwan; and Mexico's Zapatista conflict in Chiapas. Did such exclusions mean that the United Nations is no more than a polite international debate club? Alternatively, if you were the Secretary-General, would you be likely to accomplish more by *not* authorizing the discussion of any specific conflict in this otherwise comprehensive, ninety-nine page report? Why?

3. Does this United Nations Report mean that a remarkable change will be in fact undertaken at the United Nations? Will the UN organization now be able to overcome any military excesses of its sovereign members? Are there differences between the defunct League of Nations—which was unable to control conflicts

generated by its State members—and the United Nations that may shift this collective security *Synopsis* from dream to reality?

4. Not all reform necessarily requires changes in the UN Charter. See, e.g., L. Sohn, Important Improvements in the Functioning of the Principal Organs of the United Nations that Can Be Made Without Charter Revision, 91 AMER. J. INT'L L. 652 (1997).

During the Cold War, the United Nations was unable to beat swords into plowshares. A principal reason was political infighting among the permanent SC members. Even after after the demise of the Soviet Union, Russia and China entered into a treaty to restrain US emergence as the lone superpower, as expressed in the passage: "No country should seek hegemony, engage in power politics or monopolize international affairs." (Chapter One opening text box.)

In the 1990s, however, the SC began to exercise its authority in new ways, which would more directly deal with conflicts and more assertively address their consequences. These actions involved both internal and international hostilities, where an exercise of the SC's Chapter VII powers no longer depended solely upon State consent. In 1999, for example, the United Nations undertook an unusual role by assuming responsibility for the *governance* of Kosovo and East Timor, in a way that resembled the exercise of the sovereign power of States. This expanded UN role is addressed further in the Peacekeeping Operations portion of this text (§10.3).

In December 2005, the GA and SC established a novel UN Peacebuilding Commission. Its mandate will be coordinated by its UN Peacebuilding Support Office. The latter entity will explore integrated strategies, and pursue predictable financial investment, with the objective of developing the "best practices on issues that require extensive collaboration among political, military, humanitarian and [other] development actors." This new project will focus on country-specific meetings with the targeted nation, other nations within the same region, and the relevant financial institutions.

This regime could evaporate, however, if merely a matter of pouring fresh wine into an aging bottle. Regardless of configuration, neither the Peacebuilding Commission nor its Support Office can act against the wishes of any affected nation. Article 2.7 of the Charter prohibits meddling by any external institution other than the SC.

But the joint GA-SC resolutions have resolved to at least "[e]xtend the period of attention by the international community to post-conflict recovery." One thus hopes that those who have so resolved can match word and deed.[49]

Common Criticisms The United Nations has achieved the degree of success that one might expect from an international organization composed of totally autonomous States. They did not opt to yield the requisite degree of sovereignty to the United Nations, which otherwise would have empowered it to function against their wishes. This international organization was never intended to be a supreme legislative body. Nor did its State creators intend to endow it with executive powers. The United Nations could do little to force members to comply with the decisions of UN organs. This limitation was evidenced by the lack of Charter language vesting the Secretary-General with effective control over UN military operations.

There have been some successes in advancing human rights, resolving territorial disputes, promoting economic and social welfare programs, and developing draft treaties for State adoption. One is the UN Convention on the Law of the Sea (§6.3). The eight-year process, which produced this global constitution of the oceans, evinces a monumental undertaking that would not have materialized without an established global forum to promote it.

Critics tend to focus on the limitations of the SC and the GA. They often overlook the fact that the UN has commissioned numerous agencies (Exhibit 3.3) to pursue programs, which have improved living conditions for millions of people. UN economic and social welfare programs have eliminated certain diseases. They have generated hundreds of treaties dealing with a host of issues including narcotics, trade, slavery, atomic energy, road transportation, and famine-relief efforts in Africa.[50] The United Nations can similarly be credited with the global proliferation of human rights treaties in recent decades (§11.2).

Various UN agencies have also resolved a number of territorial disputes. The ICJ has decided many boundary disputes. The UN Committee on the Peaceful Uses of Outer Space undertook the foundational work necessary to conclude the 1967 Treaty on Principles Governing the Activities of States in the Exploration and Use of Outer Space Including the Moon and Other Celestial Bodies. The space treaties produced at the United Nations yielded a widely accepted paradigm for avoiding future territorial disputes and limiting the militarization of space (§6.4).[51]

One resulting perception is that the United Nations has lost none of its relevance, although the status quo is not necessarily satisfactory. Arpad Prandler of the Hungarian Branch of the International Law Association, has thus asserted as follows:

The Hungarian People's Republic . . . has taken a consistent stand . . . against concepts and suggestions which, though well-intentioned, have laid the blame on the Charter for both the failures of the World Organization and the negative tendencies for the international situation and which seek the cure for ills external to the Organization. . . . The aims and purposes of the Charter, namely the maintenance of international peace and security, the preservation and removal of threats to peace, the development of friendly relations among nations based on respect for the principle of equal rights and self-determination of peoples, and international cooperation in the economic, social and cultural fields are of unchanged significance and call for a fuller measure of implementation.

. . .

On the whole, the Organization . . . has stood the test of time. The United Nations Organization and its six principle organs . . . live up to their shared function stated by the Charter "to be a centre for harmonizing the actions of nations in the attainment of these common ends." . . .

It should also be emphasized that this position is neither in favour of conservatism nor in favour of the status quo, insofar as the Charter could not and cannot be regarded as the repertory of petrified dogmas. In our opinion the organic inner evolution of the world organization should still be supported which, subject to the substantive provisions of the Charter, leaves scope for undertaking an carrying out fresh and specific tasks. . . .

The Hungarian People's Republic has accordingly spared no effort—alongside other Member States—to explore the underutilized possibilities inherent in the Charter and to enhance the effectiveness and the and role of the Organization. . . . Like other socialist countries Hungary is nevertheless prepared to adopt a flexible attitude towards any proposal seeking to find a novel expedient that is politically justifiable,

practically feasible and legally adjustable to the system of the Charter.[52]

Another persistent view is that the United Nations has *not* accomplished its undoubtedly myopic goal of maintaining world peace. It is no stronger than the sum of its national parts.[53] Thus, one should acknowledge that only the resurrection of a deeply committed US interest can save this floundering organization. In the 1980s, for example, the Reagan Administration expressed that the United Nations needed the United States far more than the United States needed the United Nations. The United States began its withdrawal from various UN agencies. The ICJ determined that the United States had violated International Law by its activities in Nicaragua, although the United States had unsuccessfully attempted to withdraw from the ICJ's proceedings (§10.2). Then, "overnight," the *senior* Bush Administration could not embrace International Law enough—when the United States was soliciting Arab support to rescue Kuwait from Iraq's annexation in 1990.

One could thus pose the question: What would happen if the United Nations shut down today? Not unlike China's Cultural Revolution, where International Law was abandoned for a ten-year period (1966–1976), suppose the United Nations were discarded! In an iconoclastic passage, challenging UN-driven programs seeking the redistribution of the world's wealth and resources, the influential Heritage Foundation questions the continued vitality of the United Nations, as follows:

This obsession with the NIEO [§13.4 New International Economic Order] has converted the United Nations from an organization that might merely have been costly and annoying for Americans into a body which threatens those nations committed to democracy, liberty and economic development.

This raises the question, understandably, of whether the United Nations serves any positive purpose. If its influence is of no consequence or, indeed, negative, then the world may be better off without the U.N. . . . [T]he debate is not between competing theories, but is based on fact and history. The United Nations . . . no longer is simply a well-intentioned glimmer in an idealist's eye or an embryonic body whose missteps and failures understandably should be overlooked. It is a full-grown organization with a real record and history. A discussion of the U.N. and of whether the world would be better without it, therefore now moves beyond theories and good intentions to a record of comprised facts and data, successes and failures.

. . .

Only those situations improved by the U.N. argue for the continued existence of the organization. Even here, however, it is possible that other multinational organizations may be able to do as well or better than the UN.[54]

The comprehensive December 2004 Report of the Secretary-General's High-level Panel on Threats, Challenges and Change would predictably beg to differ. As pointed out in a key passage associated with the frustration of global politics during the Cold War: "Nonetheless, without the United Nations the post-1945 world would very probably have been a bloodier place. There were fewer inter-State wars in the last half of the twentieth century than in the first half. Given that during the same period the number of States grew almost fourfold, one might have expected to see a marked rise in inter-State wars. . . . The United Nations diminished the threat of inter-State war in several ways. Peace was furthered by the invention of peacekeeping; diplomacy was carried out by the Secretary-General; disputes were remedied under the International Court of Justice; and a strong norm was upheld against aggressive war."[55]

A third perspective is that the United Nations has enjoyed both successes and failures, but is now at a major crossroads for several reasons—not the least of which is its financial woes (described below.) This organization has more than its fair share of critics. Yet, an examination of the overall balance sheet reveals that is by no means politically bankrupt. As envisioned by Georgetown University Professor of Government Christopher Joyner: "From a more cynical perspective, the United Nations has been depicted in recent years as an ineffective international bureaucracy hobbled by waste, inefficiency, and mismanagement. While certain degrees of truth obviously reside in each of these impressions, none of them accurately reveals the whole picture, purposes, or activities of the United Nations or of its successes. Nor do they suggest the broad truth that the United Nations has emerged since World War II for nearly all states as the preeminent institutional source of international law." Professor Joyner then observes that "member states over the past five decades have persistently resorted to using

UN institutions and processes to create new international law to address problems accrued from changing circumstances and political developments."[56]

Critics have also attacked the United Nations as being no more than a "Turkish bath." This common perception is that the United Nations has failed because it serves only as a place to let off steam. Jeanne Kirkpatrick, formerly President Reagan's chief delegate to the UN Security Council, publicly analogized this body with a Turkish bath—unable to achieve the task of resolving international conflict. In 1986, UN General Assembly President Choudhury similarly proclaimed that the Assembly needs to be strengthened because it "has been reduced to a mere debating body."[57]

While not totally inaccurate, the Turkish bath analogy is misleading. Any UN inability to act, or to achieve uniform compliance with the unassailable Charter norms, could be—and often has been—characterized as a "complete failure." One desirable UN function is that it provides adversaries with an opportunity for global access to information about global, regional, and internal problems. UN members meet both regularly, and, when there is a crisis. Without this forum, there would be no comparable opportunity for discussions, which have brought the force of public opinion to bear on the conduct of certain nations. Distant events otherwise tend to receive little attention outside of the affected country or region, before they might erupt into war crimes, crimes against humanity, or other arenas within the ambit of Charter concerns. Immediate access to the UN's political organs, such as the GA or the SC, serves the national political agenda of establishing and maintaining dialogues on the issues that nations consider important to the preservation of international peace.

The major powers structured this organization in a way that would not compromise their respective national interests. The permanent SC members' assured that result via their respective national right to individually veto Council action. This provision, with its heyday during the Cold War, trumped the UN's potential for actually beating swords into plowshares. That all of these nations have immediate access to a public forum, in an electronic age with its instantaneous promulgation of all categories of information (§5.4), may be one reason why threats to peace have not resulted in nuclear winter. On the other hand, it is clear that the organization cannot achieve its Charter potential without significant reform.[58]

One of the most striking criticisms of the United Nations involves its inability to control genocide. The UN Charter's Preamble includes the following, as a cornerstone in the organization's foundation: that the United Nations was determined "to reaffirm faith in fundamental human rights, in the dignity and worth of the human person. . . ." To this end, the UN Preamble contains the further pledge that its members would "practice tolerance and live together in peace with one another as good neighbours. . . ." One should of course assign responsibility to the States where genocide has occurred, and third-party States for not intervening, in areas such as Rwanda (1994) (§9.5), Srebreniza (1995),[59] and Darfur (a Sudanese region receiving scant international attention until 2004) (§11.1).

There is further head-in-the-sand evidence in what the UN's widely heralded 2004 analysis of twenty-first century threats to the collective security of nations does *not* say. This epic report was designed to identify major threats to collective security. Yet there is no independent section on genocide in this otherwise comprehensive report.[60] The Secretary-General's direction—to avoid naming any country as being responsible—further reflects on the UN's inability to control this all-too-familiar feature of the contemporary international landscape. The Panel's response was to use the terms "mass atrocity" and "humanitarian disaster," rather than "genocide," and to once mention the Genocide Treaty almost in passing.

On a positive note, however, the Report at least lists the countries where acknowledging the existence of "genocide" is unavoidable; admits that the UN Security Council has been inconsistent and ineffective; and recognizes an "emerging" norm requiring the international community to react. Specifically:

> 199. The Charter of the United Nations is not as clear as it could be when it comes to saving lives within countries in situations of mass atrocity. . . .
> 200. . . . The principle of non-intervention in internal affairs cannot be used to protect genocidal acts or other atrocities, such as large-scale violations of international humanitarian law or large-scale ethnic cleansing, which can properly be considered a threat to international security and as such provoke action by the Security Council.
> 201. The successive humanitarian disasters in Somalia, Bosnia and Herzegovina, Rwanda, Kosovo and now Darfur, Sudan, have concentrated attention not on the immunities of sovereign Governments but their responsibilities, both to their own people and to the wider international community. . . .
> 202. The Security Council so far has been neither very consistent nor very effective in dealing with these cases, very often acting too late, too hesitantly or not at all. . . .
> 203. We endorse the emerging norm that there is a collective international responsibility to protect, exercisable by the Security Council authorizing military intervention as a last resort, in the event of genocide and other large-scale killing, ethnic cleansing or serious violations of international humanitarian law which sovereign Governments have proved powerless or unwilling to prevent.[61]

One who authors a textbook could provide chapter and verse on various views about the value of the United Nations, and what it should do to achieve effective reform. One fundamental perspective is crystal clear. Until the United Nations or the community of nations noticeably reduces the global level of hunger, poverty, infectious disease, and environmental degradation, there will be no effective security. Events like September 11, 2001, and the ensuing Iraq War will be the beginning of a very long—or possibly in the same sense, comparatively short—twenty-first century.

Financial Crises

(a) Member Dues Payable Yet another criticism leveled at the United Nations is the characterization that it is no more than a vast paper mill, existing to serve itself rather than its members. The United Nations is, of course, a very large business. At its zenith in the 1990s, it employed some 26,500 people throughout the world, while generating more than 1 billion pages of documents per year. Its six-official-language system of administration requires multiple translations and republication of the same information at virtually all levels. Under Article 111 of the Charter, the five original languages included those of the permanent members of the SC: Chinese, French, Russian, and English (United States and Great Britain). Spanish was initially included as an official language due to the large percentage of the world's population that spoke Spanish. Arabic was added for the same reason in 1977.

In the mid-1980s, certain countries began to withdraw from various organs of the United Nations and/or refused to pay their full annually assessed UN dues. The 1986 US assessment, for example, was approximately $200 million, or 25 percent of the UN's total $800 million annual budget. By 1993, the US dues assessment was $374 million in arrears, which the president promised to pay only if the United Nations would alter its funding formula to reflect growth in other national economies (such as Germany and Japan, which pay far less in annual dues). In addition, there is the distinct assessment for UN *peacekeeping* costs (31.7 percent of the total figure, often larger in absolute dollars than the *regular* annual budget assessments). Three days after September 11, 2001, both houses of Congress removed their objections to paying the entire amount that the United States owed the United Nations.

The United Nations finally established an independent Inspector General in 1994. The creation of this new watchdog post helped clear the way for the United States to repay the large amount of money it owed the United Nations. The US Congress was unwilling to pay the arrearage in UN-assessed dues until this position was created, resulting in the naming of a German diplomat to probe bureaucratic mismanagement and waste. The Inspector General is charged with the responsibility of strict financial oversight at the United Nations, as well as strengthening its accountability in ways that should generate greater confidence. There is the daunting question, however, of whether this measure has been the proverbial "too little, too late."

About 80 percent of the UN's budget is paid by only fifteen nations. Various UN agencies support a large number of staff in expensive cities such as Paris (UNESCO). It is understandable that traditional UN supporters, like the United States which pays 25 percent of the fixed annual budget, would demand more for its involvement—just as any private corporate structure would have to reorganize to meet the demands of its stockholders who perceive their stock as dwindling in value because of mismanagement.

Ironically, the US Department of State Legal Advisor concluded in 1978 that the United States, and all member States, must pay their assessed obligations. In his words, "the General Assembly's adoption and apportionment of the Organization's expenses create a binding legal obligation on the part of State members to pay their assessed shares." This analysis was based on Article 17 of the UN Charter and the 1962 ICJ case interpreting the Charter as requiring members to pay the organization's

expenses. Certain UN members had then objected to the UN peacekeeping commitments in the former Belgian Congo and the Middle East, unsuccessfully claiming that the related expenditures were not "expenses of the Organization" within the meaning of the Charter.[62]

By 1995, the US Congress was adamant about the perceived situation at the United Nations, where Republican Party leaders espoused the position that the United States was not getting a sufficient political return on its investment. In the UN Withdrawal Act of 1995, the House of Representatives proposed that the US Mission to the United Nations be closed by 1999 and that the UN Headquarters Agreement Act be repealed so that the United Nations would cease to function in New York City. Had this Act been adopted into law, the US Congress would not have authorized any annual dues or peacekeeping funds.[63]

The United Nations reacted by promulgating the 1996 Secretary-General Report on proposed administrative and budgetary reform. Its objective was to appease US complaints about UN waste.[64] In 1997, the Secretary-General notified the United States that it would lose voting rights if the arrearage remained unattended. The United States lost the first of two annual bids for a seat on the powerful Advisory Committee on Administrative and Budgetary Questions—a committee on which the United States served for fifty years, or since the inception of the United Nations. In 1998, the United States paid only $197 million of its regular 1998 dues, the minimum necessary to avoid losing its GA vote. A 1998 US Senate Bill would have paid the UN accrued arrearage, which was $819 million in annual dues, and the $107 million peacekeeping assessment. However, an otherwise supportive President Clinton was essentially forced to veto this legislation because it contained a distinct and abortion rider. UN Secretary-General Kofi Annan and the EU denounced the resulting dues rejection, partially because it came in the same week that the United States sought UN support for a military campaign against Iraq.

In 1999, the US Senate nearly unanimously approved a bill to pay $1 billion of its arrearage, conditioned on: (a) the annual UN assessment for the US portion of the *regular* budget be dropped from 25 to 20 percent; (b) the *peacekeeping* assessment be scaled back from 31 to 25 percent; and (c) a portion of the US dues payment be used for the US reimbursement of allies in their peacekeeping operations. President Clinton then signed legislation, which authorizes payment of $926 million to the United

Nations, subject to certain reforms, which must be certified by the US Secretary of State.[65] US citizen and media mogul Ted Turner donated $34 million to cover (just) the 2001 shortfall for the United States, having donated $1 billion to the United Nations in 1997. While the United Nations normally bars such contributions, these donations facilitated a reduction of the US administrative budget 25 to 22 percent—the first financial reform of the UN's regular budget in twenty-eight years. The US peacekeeping budget was also reduced from 31 to 27 percent, although US law requires a further reduction to 25 percent, as a condition for releasing congressionally allocated arrears now owed by the United States (over $1 billion). The budget of eighteen other nations will be increased to offset the US reduction.

In May 2000, a UN vote ousted the United States from the UN Human Rights Commission, in a matter which was apparently not related to the US dues arrearage. However, the US House of Representatives chose to respond by threatening to withhold some of the US dues owed to the United Nations.

There are many contemporary reform initiatives. In May 2005, a US congressional committee proposed the United Nations Reform Act of 2005.[66] It would condition the payment of the US dues payable to the United Nations to the latter's undertaking various reforms. If enacted into law, and there were no responsive reform, the United States would reduce its dues payments to fifty percent of its annual assessment by the United Nations. The United Nations would have until October 2007 to implement most of the thirty-nine reforms. If not, then the United States would hold back fifty percent of its dues payable—currently $330 million of the $1.5 billion total UN budget. The Secretary-General responded that the proposed legislation will interfere with the currently pending reforms—the most sweeping in the UN's sixty-year history. The US Congress also worked with the Washington, DC, US Institute of Peace to produce the June 2005 Task Force on the UN Report. Its major recommendations for reform include: (1) the creation of corporate style oversight bodies and personnel standards to improve UN employee performance; and (2) creation of a rapid reaction capability by its member States' armed forces—to prevent genocide, mass killing, and sustained major human rights violations. If implemented, this particular proposal would be the closest step toward actually implementing the latent UN Charter Article 43 standing army.[67]

(b) Oil-for-Food Scandal   This contemporary blemish continues to deface the UN's image. This $64,000,000,000 scandal allegedly involves half of the 4,500 contracting companies involved in contracting with the United Nations in the aftermath of the first PGW. The Secretary-General's son worked for a firm that allegedly profited from the illicit sales practices that diverted food and supplies from the Iraqi people. The senior Cypriot UN diplomat who managed this program was cited for his role in this scandal. Local employees of the UN mission in Baghdad kept this secret, until a UN whistle blower could no longer be ignored. This monitor claims that the United Nations fired him for reporting this corruption. In August 2005, a senior Russian UN diplomat was the first to be indicted. Cash stashed in red canvas diplomatic bags had been sent by diplomatic courier to the Iraqi Embassy in Moscow.

From 1997 until 2003 (just prior to the Iraq War), the SC had sanctioned Iraq, for its undisputed threats to international peace. An exception authorized the Iraqi government to sell enough oil to attend to the humanitarian needs of its people, spawned by the impact of the UN sanctions. During this period, Saddam Hussein personally profited by sales arrangements whereby the oil purchasers had to pay bribes. Supplies destined for the Iraqi people were instead diverted, in a way that helped the Iraqi military and the pockets of Hussein and his senior Baath Party associates—an estimated 20 to 25 percent of the overall $64,000,000,000 in the sale of Iraqi oil during the seven-year sanctions period.

The episode has fueled the continuing controversy about UN mismanagement, annual dues arrearage by UN member nations, and the need for reform—as noted earlier in this book's UN Assessment section. One response has been the Secretary-General's decision to waive the diplomatic immunity of any responsible UN official. It has also marred relations between the United States/United Kingdom and France/Russia—the latter having sought to continue the Oil-for-Food program after the fall of Baghdad. $11,000,000,000 of Iraq's oil sales were to French and Russian companies during the seven years in question.

The September 2005 UN Panel report concluded that this program was "corrupt and inefficient." It called for urgent reform, including creation of a new chief operating officer and an independent oversight board. The Secretary-General then accepted responsibility in his statement to the SC: "The report is critical of me personally, and I accept its criticism. . . . The inquiry committee has ripped away the curtain and shone a harsh light into the most unsightly corners of the organization."[68]

This continuing investigation has revealed that more than 2,000 companies in numerous nations (including the United States) were involved. A chief executive officer in the private sector would have been fired. So the United Nations must adopt the oversight reforms called for by the chief investigator—a former US Federal Reserve Board Chairman. Otherwise, the United Nations' already battered credibility will be damaged beyond repair.

◆ 3.4 EUROPEAN UNION

The UN Charter acknowledged the utility of other, autonomous international organizations. Article 52(1) recognizes the simultaneous "existence of regional arrangements or agencies for dealing with such matters relating to the maintenance of international peace and security as are appropriate for regional action provided that such arrangements or agencies and their activities are consistent with the Purposes and Principles of the United Nations." Under Article 52(3), the UN Security Council encourages the settlement of local disputes through regional organizations. These provisions complement Article 33(1), whereby the State parties to any dispute "shall, first of all, seek a solution by negotiation . . . [or] resort to regional agencies or arrangements, or other peaceful means of their own choice." States have developed a number of regional defense, economic, and political organizations. These entities sometimes operate in harmony with the United Nations at the global level, with individual States at the regional level, and sometimes without any regard for the United Nations.

Many prominent organizations cannot be covered in a course designed to provide fundamental perspectives. While some key military and political organizations will be profiled, this section of the book focuses exclusively on the EU. It is probably the best example of how a group of States has managed to integrate goals and results at the regional organizational level.

HISTORICAL BACKDROP

Long before the much-heralded European Union's Maestricht Treaty of 1992, the concept of an association of European States found political expression in both negative and positive ways. There were attempts to impose unity by Napoleon and Hitler. Napoleon sought to unite the Continent under French hegemony until his military demise at the beginning of the nineteenth century. Hitler sought the subjugation of Europe under the dictatorship of Germany's Third Reich.

Peaceful attempts to unite Europe followed World War I. In 1923, Austria led the Pan-European Movement. It beckoned creation of a United States of Europe modeled on the success of the Swiss struggle for regional unity after the 1648 Peace of Westphalia (§1.1), which led to the modern nation-State. In 1929, in speeches before the League of Nations Assembly in Geneva, French and German leaders proposed the creation of a European Community within the framework of the League of Nations.

These positive bids for peaceful unification were overcome by a dominant tide of nationalism and imperialism. The twentieth century's two "great wars" demonstrated the futility of the constant rivalry between European nations over many centuries. Europe's collapse, its political and economic exhaustion, and its outdated national structures signaled the need for a fresh start and a more radical approach to the post-World War II reordering of Europe.

This organization appears to have international legal personality, but actually draws upon that which its constituent entities that do possess the legal capacity to operate on the international level. As concisely illustrated by the University of Helsinki's Jan Klabbers:

> As many observers have noted, the Treaty establishing the European Union . . . does not explicitly confer international legal personality upon the European Union. . . . Some observers merely note the fact that [there is] no specific reference to the Union's international legal personality, but do not go beyond faintly hinting . . . that the European Union might not be able to act under international law. Others contend that, to the extent that the Union wishes to act internationally, it can do so only by means of borrowing powers and institutions from its composite elements that are endowed with international legal personality: the Communities.[69]

This lack of independent legal personality was one of the driving forces behind the 2005 referendums on the proposed EU Constitution. Article 1.7, entitled *Legal personality,* thus expressly, succinctly, and independently of any of the other 447 articles provides that: "The Union shall have legal personality." This would not have given the EU any powers not expressly delegated to it under this, or prior treaties establishing various Community organs. Had it been ratified by (all) member nations, however, the current entity—with all of its economic, political, social, and military designs—would now possess the required power to act independently of its supporting Community organs.

The contemporary EU is rooted in the creation of three proximate but distinct communities. The first was the European Coal and Steel Community formed by the 1951 Treaty of Paris. The 1957 Treaty of Rome established the European Economic Community and the European Atomic Energy Community. The initial goal was to create a common market (no internal tariff barriers) in coal and steel for the six member States of Belgium, France, West Germany, Italy, Luxembourg, and the Netherlands. This union would, it was hoped, secure peace by loosely integrating both the victorious and the vanquished European nations of prior world wars. Although France rejected the added aspiration of an international defense organization, the original members built an economic community premised on the free movement of workers, goods, and services. Mutually agreeable agricultural and commercial policies were adopted by the end of the 1970s. Further history is available on the EU's Web site and in the standard texts.[70] The current membership, and pending applications, are set forth in Exhibit 3.4.

COMMUNITY LAW

Maastricht Treaty The 1992 Treaty on EU was signed in Maastricht, the Netherlands.[71] It amended earlier treaties on various Community subjects, in a way that would bring all of them under one umbrella treaty and eliminate inconsistencies. The objectives stated in the Maastricht Treaty include some key features that define the anticipated future of this organization (Title I, Article B):

◆ "Creation of an area without internal frontiers" (much like states of other federated unions such as the US);
◆ Social cohesion through an economic and monetary union, which will ultimately create a single currency (historically printed by each individual country);
◆ The further assertion of "its identity on the international scene, in particular through the implementation of a common foreign and security policy including the eventual framing of a common defence policy, which might in time lead to a common defense" (leaning toward the League of Nations and OAS Charter provisions providing that an attack upon one member of the international organization is an attack against all—a provision not employed in the UN Charter); and
◆ Strengthening the "protection of the rights and interests of the nationals of its Member States through the introduction of a citizenship of the Union" (facilitating even smoother international travel than currently permitted within the EU).

The "Euro" is the currency of the European Monetary Union. The member nations have effectively yielded a degree of their sovereignty to a central bank located in Frankfurt. The French franc, for example, faded into obscurity in February 2002. The first franc

---

EXHIBIT 3.4 EUROPEAN UNION MEMBER STATES AND ASSOCIATED NATIONS

Current Members	Candidate Countries	Associated Nations[72]
Austria, Belgium, Czech Republic, Cyprus, Denmark, Estonia, Finland, France, Germany, Great Britain, Greece, Hungary, Ireland, Italy, Latvia, Lithuania, Luxembourg, Malta, Netherlands, Poland, Portugal, Slovak Republic, Slovenia, Spain, and Sweden (25)	Bulgaria, Croatia, Romania, and Turkey (4)	Loose form of association with southern Mediterranean, African, and Caribbean-Pacific States under the four "Lome Conventions" concluded during the 1970s and 1980s (69)

Source: <http://europa.eu.int/abc/governments/index_en.htm#candidate>

was a gold coin created in December 1360. It paid the ransom to the English to free King Jean le Bon, who was held captive for four years during the Hundred Years War. Members can qualify only if they achieve low inflation, low government budget deficits, and leaner social programs—at a time when unemployment in most member nations is relatively high (approximately 10 percent). Trading in the Euro began on the first day of 1999, with the use of hard currency to follow. The majority of nations within the EU have thus ceded control over their local interest rates to an international body. This has never been done before in any other treaty arrangement.

Amsterdam Treaty   This 1997 treaty contained new approaches regarding community social policies. It was a reaction to the criticism that the EU had focused exclusively on economic interests, to the detriment of: social security; employment rights in the event of layoffs possibly associated with controls mandated by Maastricht's economic guidelines; and social welfare. Thus, the Amsterdam Treaty is designed to reassure the public that basic social needs will not be sacrificed to market forces.

Nice Treaty   The potential addition of mostly eastern European nations (most of which became members in 2004) was one of the most contentious issues in EU history. The Nice Treaty required each of the then dozen members to approve of the accession of enough members to essentially double the size of the EU.[73] Ireland, the most economically challenged member of the EU (until 2004) initially rejected the addition of new EU members. Many Irish voters were concerned about the EU exercising too much control over domestic matters. They were concerned about existing members possibly having to subsidize the economies of the new lower-income nations. Many refugees had already come to Ireland looking for work. These voters feared that adoption of the Nice Treaty could turn this steady stream into a deluge. Nevertheless, ten new members were admitted to the EU in 2004, as listed in Exhibit 3.4 above.

EU Constitution   In 2003, Europe's leaders drafted what was supposed to become the EU's first constitution.[74] Europe's leaders backed this document, which was designed to move beyond a mere monetary and trade union. The proposed constitution generally provides,

for example, that member nations can act, only when the EU does not. But the people of all twenty-five EU nations were to agree to the proposed constitution, for it to become effective. Instead, several of the original, more powerful members conducted referendums in 2005, which resulted in "no" votes.

There are varied views about the cause. While some will argue they can be overcome,[75] the negatives have been spawned by an increasing mistrust of local government because of stagnant economies, high unemployment, immigration concerns, and the desire to maintain cultural differences. The popularity of French President Jacques Chirac declined, for example, in the face of a rising Muslim population. He had lobbied extensively for Turkish membership in the EU. A number of French citizens felt, however, that Turkey's comparative economic inferiority, its being one of the most populated countries in the region, and its potential for a larger share of representation in the various EU governmental organs, would yield a number of costly EU programs—especially the "right to housing assistance" under the proposed EU Constitution. Furthermore, Turkey has occupied the northern part of Cyprus since its 1974 invasion and establishment of a nonrecognized State-like entity (§2.3 *Cyprus v. Turkey* case).

A proposed constitutional reference to the Christian roots of Europe is yet another popular concern. Certain leaders add that religious references have no place in this document.

One might also attribute the popular reluctance to adopt this constitution as a product of the uncertainties associated with the 2004 EU expansion from fifteen to twenty-five countries. As aptly described by Professor Joseph Weiler of NYU's School of Law and the Brugge College of Europe:

There is something, indeed more than one thing, deceptive in the juxtaposition of enlargement and Constitution. First is the notion that these two concepts are different—as if the decision on enlargement was not a constitutional decision. The opposite is true. The enlargement decision was the single most important constitutional decision taken in the last decade, and arguably longer. For good or for bad, the change in number of Member States, in the size of Europe's [EU] population, its geography and topography, and in its cultural and political mix are all on a scale of magnitude which will make the new Europe a very, very different polity, independently of any constitutional structure adopted. [76]

In some instances, the national governments have opted to have their parliaments make this decision, rather than the people. People who did not trust their own governments were less likely to welcome even more unification via this governing document that would have been administered for all twenty-five EU members from Brussels and the other organizational power centers.

There are military concerns as well, now that the EU has an official defense policy. Established in December 2002, its purpose is: "to add to the range of instruments already at the European Union's disposal for crisis management and conflict prevention in support of the Common Foreign and Security Policy, the capacity to conduct EU-led crisis management operations, including military operations where NATO as a whole is not engaged." The EU has been flexing its military muscle in peacekeeping operations in Macedonia, the Democratic Republic of Congo, and now Bosnia. In November 2004, Bosnia's NATO peacekeeping was transferred to a 7,000-member EU force. Although 80 percent of the troops involved in this operation would merely be changing the insignia on their uniforms, many isolationists are concerned that this is a slippery slope which will lead to unwanted military engagements. There have been positive developments, such as the November 2004 EU negotiations with Iran to withdraw from its uranium enrichment program. But one might nevertheless conclude that many voters are effectively clinging to the Westphalian State-centric notion of national sovereignty, originally spawned by the Europe of 1648.

EU/UN COMPARISON

What makes the EU different from the United Nations? Both institutions have their critics.[77] Unlike the United Nations, however, the EU has a relatively homogeneous social, economic, and legal environment. The EU was initially designed to integrate the European nations economically. Europe was crushed by World War II; its nations had lost many of their colonies; and this region needed to unite to compete with large powers, including the United States to the west and the Soviet Union to the east.

The economic unification of Europe began with the reduction of trade barriers within the Community and the establishment of a common economic policy in relation to nonmember nations. The EU's strategy was thus designed for the creation of one central bank, followed by one European currency for all member States. By contrast, there is little likelihood of there ever being a central bank or a like economic program linking UN members.

Another essential objective of the EU's single market is the economic and political stability of Europe. Competitors within this Union will benefit because they will have larger markets, unimpeded by the usual customs inspections, tariffs, and other limitations on international business (Chapter 13). The comprehensiveness of the EU's rules govern minutiae such as the brands of ketchup to be used in US-owned fast-food restaurants in Paris, the angle of Ford headlights made in London, and the airing of "I Love Lucy" reruns in Amsterdam. Unlike the United Nations, the EU's institutions are generally endowed with the necessary sovereignty to require member States to treat their citizens in ways that they would not otherwise be required under national law.

EU'S EXPANDING ECONOMIC POWER

The national votes against the EU Constitution in 2005 may have failed to boost the EU's political clout. But its economic power is growing. The EU can pressure other nations to act, or refrain from acting in certain ways. In 1992, the EU imposed economic sanctions and an arms embargo on Libya—in a show of EU solidarity with the UN Security Council. Libya had refused to extradite its two indicted intelligence agents, who were later convicted of blowing up Pan Am 103 over Lockerbie, Scotland, in 1988. The EU expanded it sanctions regime by freezing Libyan bank accounts, and denying Libya the right to purchase oil-producing equipment from EU countries. Although the UN's sanctions against Libya ended in 1999, it was not until October 2004 that the EU lifted its twelve years of economic sanctions. This rewarded Libya for its agreement to scuttle plans to develop weapons of mass destruction.

In summer 2005, the EU—which had no political ties with Iraq during the twenty-four year reign of Saddam Hussein—opened a permanent mission in Baghdad. The EU spent $390 million on Iraq in 2003–2004, and $240 million in 2005. Europe was divided over the War in Iraq in the UN Security Council. The EU may thus be the vehicle for future fence-mending.

The European Commission, the EU's executive arm, can also require business entities in other countries to adhere to EU laws. This scenario arises when business entities in non-EU countries act in ways that threaten EU competition policy. The following 497,196,304 Euro (approximately $600,000,000) decision against the Microsoft Corporation is a dramatic illustration:

Commission of the European Communities v. Microsoft Corporation Commission Decision Relating to a Proceeding Under Article 82 of the EC Treaty

Case COMP/C-3/37.792 Microsoft (March 03, 2004)

<http://europa.eu.int/comm/competition/antitrust/cases/decisions/37792/en.pdf>

Go to course Web page at <http://home.att.net/~slomansonb/txtcsesite.html>.
Under Chapter Three, click European Commission v. Microsoft Corporation.

◆ 3.5 OTHER ORGANIZATIONS

While the EU has received much global attention in recent decades, a number of other international organizations are also influential actors in international affairs. Some major economic organizations, including the World Trade Organization, NAFTA, and the so-called "Group of 77" will be covered in Chapter 13 of this text (International Economic Relations). While a survey course in International Law cannot cover many international organizations, it can touch upon several of the principal military and political international organizations:

◆ North Atlantic Treaty Organization (NATO)
◆ Organization for Security and Cooperation in Europe
◆ Commonwealth of Independent States
◆ Organization of American States
◆ League of Arab States & Organization of the Islamic Conference
◆ African Union

NORTH ATLANTIC TREATY ORGANIZATION

NATO is the major military defense organization in the world. Its solidarity has occasionally waned, particularly when France withdrew in 1966.[78] France then expressed its concern about NATO being the subject of US domination, largely because of NATO's dependence on US military support. While the NATO Secretary-General has always been a European, its Supreme Commander has always been an American. France is now a member, although it has not committed to participating in NATO's military structure.

During the Cold War, NATO expanded three times: adding Greece and Turkey in 1952, West Germany in 1955, and Spain in 1982. At the height of the Soviet-US Cold War, NATO thus had more than 2 million military personnel deployed in Western Europe. The Soviet Union's parallel Warsaw Pact nations deployed about 4 million troops in Eastern Europe.

After the Soviet Union collapsed, NATO took a cautious approach to any potential eastward expansion, so that Moscow would not unnecessarily fear encirclement. In 1994, NATO developed its "Partnership for Peace Program." The Partnership for Peace Program involves joint military exercises, peacekeeping, and the exchange of military doctrine and weaponry.

One objective was to expand NATO's membership eastward, to incorporate the former members of the Soviet Union. The Heads of State Framework Agreement for this program provides that:

This Partnership is established as an expression of a joint conviction that stability and security in the Euro-Atlantic area can be achieved only through cooperation and common action. Protection and promotion of fundamental freedoms and human rights, and safeguarding of freedom, justice, and peace through democracy are shared values fundamental to the Partnership.

In joining the Partnership, the member States . . . subscribing to this Document recall that they are committed to the preservation of democratic societies, their freedom from coercion and intimidation, and the maintenance of the principles of international law.

They reaffirm their commitment to fulfil in good faith the obligations of the Charter of the United Nations and the principles of the Universal Declaration on Human Rights; specifically, to refrain from the threat or use of force against the territorial integrity or political independence of any State, to respect existing borders and to settle disputes by peaceful means. They also reaffirm their commitment to . . . the fulfillment of the commitments and obligations they have undertaken in the field of disarmament and arms control.[79]

Russia began to express concerns about the demise of its military Warsaw Pact, while NATO only expanded to embrace former Warsaw Pact members. One can appreciate this irony by reference to the NATO Secretary General's 1990 speech to the Supreme Soviet in Moscow, just before the Warsaw Pact was dissolved. Germany's Manfred Worner proposed an association as follows:

This visit in itself symbolizes the dramatic changes of the past year. The Cold War now belongs to the past. A new Europe is emerging . . . [yet] age-old fears and suspicions cannot be banished overnight; but they can be overcome. Never before has Europe had such a tangible opportunity to overcome the cycle of war and peace that has so bedeviled its history. . . .

I have come to Moscow today with a very simple message: we extend our hand of friendship to you. And I have come with a very direct offer: to cooperate with you. The time of confrontation is over. The hostility and mistrust of the past must be buried. We see your country, and all the other countries of the Warsaw Treaty Organization, no longer as adversaries but as partners in a common endeavor to build what you [might] call a Common European Home, erected on the values of democracy, human freedoms, and partnership. . . .

[The NATO Secretary General then proposed that] the Soviet Union gains partners that will help in its great domestic task of reform and renewal. Partners who will cooperate to ensure that the Soviet Union is an active and constructive part of the dynamic Europe of advanced industrial economies and technological interdependence of the 21st century. . . . Beyond confrontation we can address the immense global challenges of today and tomorrow: environmental degradation, drugs, terrorism, hunger, population, the

proliferation of immensely destructive military technologies in the Third World. . . . The Alliance I have the honour to represent wants partners in the building of a new Europe. . . . Let us look to a common future, and work for it with trust and imagination.[80]

In 2001—years after the Warsaw Pact folded, and the Partnership for Peace Program had resulted in NATO's expansion to include Poland, Hungary, and the Czech Republic—Russian President Vladimir Putin posed the rhetorical question of whether it was NATO's turn to either disperse or change. He proclaimed that:

NATO . . . has outlived its usefulness and should disband or be extended to include Russia.

If NATO does not reach out to embrace Russia, it should be scrapped and replaced by a new body that includes all of Europe and Russia.

. . .

The Warsaw Treaty does not exist, the Soviet Union does not exist, but NATO exists and . . . when we are told that it is a political organization, then, naturally, we may ask, why did you bomb Yugoslavia?[81]

Russia was invited to participate in NATO. It then signed the NATO Partnership agreement—one day after US troops finally withdrew from Berlin. The current NATO affiliates are as follows in Exhibit 3.5:

EXHIBIT 3.5 NATO MEMBERSHIP AND ASSOCIATED NATIONS

Member Nations	Partnership for Peace Program
Belgium, Bulgaria, Canada, Czech Republic, Denmark, Estonia, France, Germany, Greece, Hungary, Iceland, Italy, Latvia, Lithuania, Luxembourg, Netherlands, Norway, Poland, Portugal, Romania, Slovakia, Slovenia, Spain, Turkey, United Kingdom, United States (26)	Albania, Armenia, Austria, Azerbaijan, Belarus, Croatia, Finland, Georgia, Ireland, Kazakhstan, Kyrgyzstan, Republic, Moldova, Russia, Sweden, Switzerland, Macedonia, Tadjikistan, Turkmenistan, Ukraine, Uzbekistan (20)

One must of course distinguish between merely sign-ing a Partnership for Peace agreement and full NATO membership. The "Partnership" is only a step in what is a more complex process. Germany and the United States are split on the issue of whether Russia should ultimately become a full-fledged member of NATO. Germany's defense minister had warned that allowing Russia to become a member would "blow NATO apart." Vintage rivalries still spawn historical concerns about European security in a way that could arguably preclude the full integration of all "European" States into this regional military organization. Russia had recently proclaimed (in its 1997 joint declaration with China) the need for a *multipolar* world. This declaration envisioned a post–Cold War "new international order," wherein "[n]o country should seek hegemony, engage in power politics or monopolize international affairs."[82] In May 2005, Russia's Foreign Minister Sergei Lavrov declared—to the Russian Parliament's lower house—that Russia was not going to join NATO and the EU.

The West's position is that Russia is over reacting. A number of commentators have countered, however, that Russia is *not* being alarmist about US hegemony in Europe. NATO's Supreme Commander has always been a US military officer. That officer conducted NATO's Kosovo bombing campaign in 1999 (§10.5). There was no UN Security Council resolution authorizing this first of NATO's military campaigns. The NATO commander, just after the bombing stopped, also ordered the British theater commander to use force to secure the suddenly Russian-occupied airport in Kosovo (Problem 3.G). Some 20,000 NATO troops from thirty-four countries have been keeping the peace in Bosnia—with the powers to arrest war crimes suspects for trial in The Hague. The United States successfully provided financial incen-tives to entice the former Soviet ally, Yugoslavia, to turn over its former president for trial at the UN tribunal at The Hague.

Russia can make these points: (a) it is not a full-fledged member of NATO, and there has been open opposition to its becoming so; (b) NATO launched its first military campaign in 1999 in Kosovo, and took over military con-trol of Afghanistan in 2002; (c) most of the NATO nations have troops on the ground in Iraq, and NATO is setting up a military training center (for Iraqis); (d) the Bush Administration has announced its preemptive Strike Doctrine in the war on terrorism (§10.2); and (e) NATO

combat jets are within 3 minutes of St. Petersburg. One might therefore ask the following two questions: (1) What is the likely consequence of these two, long-term Cold War adversaries *not* enjoying like status in the world's strongest international military organization? (2) Will it matter, if the United States continues to be the only long-term superpower?

ORGANIZATION FOR SECURITY AND COOPERATION IN EUROPE

In terms of State memberships, the Organization for Security and Cooperation in Europe (OSCE) is the largest nonmilitary, regional security organization in the world. It has fifty-five participating States from Europe, Central Asia, and North America. Like NATO, the OCSE has a "Partnership" program, which facili-tates a dialogue between its members and other States in the region.[83] OSCE activities include early warn-ing, conflict prevention, crisis management, and post-conflict rehabilitation. Its members include Canada and the United States, while Japan enjoys official "observer" status. The former Yugoslavia's attempt to retain the "Yugoslavian" seat in the OSCE was rejected, until former President Slobodan Milosevic was no longer in power (as in the United Nations per the above §3.3 *Bosnia v. FRY* case).

The OSCE's roots date from the mid-1950s when the Soviet Union initiated "European Security Conferences" attended by representatives of Eastern European States. These meetings resulted in creation of the Warsaw Treaty Organization, which would become NATO's regional competitor. In the 1960s, the Warsaw Pact initiated addi-tional conferences seeking greater peace and security in Europe. Thanks to the artful diplomacy by the Federal Republic of Germany in the field of East-West relations, the CSCE (Conference on Security and Cooperation in Europe—the original name until 1995) was inaugurated in 1972, just after the conclusion of the first Strategic Arms Limitations Treaty between the United States and the Soviet Union. The OSCE's predecessor was thus established to deal with Cold War tension, and to provide for security from Vancouver to Vladivostok. The 1991 CSCE Madrid Conference produced the framework of the CSCE Parliament. The 1992 meeting of the Coun-cil of Ministers produced the Prague Document on the nonproliferation of nuclear weapons and limitations on arms transfers within Europe.[84]

There have been several defining moments in the CSCE/OSCE process. The first major achievement was the Helsinki Final Act of 1975. That instrument emphasizes concerns of regional security, economic matters, and humanitarian treatment. To ensure the equality of States—despite vast differences in economic, military, and political power—the organization's members resolved that its proceedings "shall take place outside military alliances." This has avoided a narrow NATO-versus-Warsaw Pact approach to regional problem solving. The OSCE functions somewhat like a remodeled United Nations, whereby diverse players on the European stage continually meet for purposes including the provision of "confidence-building" measures involving security and disarmament.

Other major achievements included the 1989 Concluding Document of Vienna. It contains a mandate for the Negotiation on Conventional Armed Forces in Europe talks. This was followed by the 1990 Conventional Forces in Europe (CFE) Treaty of Paris.[85] A number of participating States including France, which has not rejoined the military wing of NATO, perceive the OSCE process as the genuine European alternative to resolving regional problems. The OSCE has thus played a role in monitoring events in Bosnia, Chechnya, and Kosovo, with a view toward maintaining the commitments tendered by the respective parties in those conflicts. It was the OSCE that undertook responsibility for the conduct of national and municipal elections, arms control negotiations, and human rights monitoring in Bosnia under the 1995 Dayton Peace Accords. When Serbian authorities would not recognize the 1996 election results, the OSCE called upon them to abide by the results.

Yet another example of the lasting importance of this organization is its emphasis on human rights issues. The Conference on the Human Dimension meets annually to exchange information about questionable State practices and unresolved human rights problems. Prior to the destruction of the Berlin Wall, the United States tapped this organization as a vehicle for expressing concern that Eastern European members had failed to live up to professed objectives including the right to travel, freedom of religion, and freedom from psychiatric abuse while in detention. In March 1995, Russia's president, Boris Yeltsin, agreed to receive a permanent human rights mission from the CSCE to monitor events in Chechnya, the rebellious region consisting of mostly Muslims who seek independence.

Some limitations still hamper the OSCE process. Like the UN Charter, the 1975 Helsinki Final Act is a political, rather than a legally binding, document. It is not a treaty in the sense of creating immediate obligations, although some participants have argued that the 1975 Act resulted in some binding commitments by member States to at least continued participation in a Pan-European process.[86] This state of affairs should not be surprising, given the historical diversity of its member States. The OSCE historically exhibited a rather light institutional structure, until the creation of some permanent administrative and political organs in the early 1990s.

The OSCE's 1994 code of conduct on the political and military features of the region's security may be the most intriguing document within its voluminous work product. This code—the offspring of a prior French proposal—as noted in the introduction to the paragraph-by-paragraph code commentary: "is the most important normative document adopted by the OSCE participating states since the 1975 Helsinki Final Act. It . . . intrudes into an area of state power which has hitherto been normally considered taboo: armed forces . . . fill[ing] a normative gap . . . regulating the role and use of armed forces (at domestic as well as [the] external level) in the context of states wherein the rule of law prevails."[87] It is nevertheless a proposed code of conduct, not enforceable as a binding treaty, although arguably within the corpus of regional customary International Law (see this text's §1.2 on Sources of International Law).

Were this to occur, the fifty-five national members of the OSCE would have produced a document well ahead of its time, given the current UN and global preoccupation with collective security in the aftermath of 9-11 and the Iraq War.[88] For example, paragraph 3 of its first section provides that OSCE member nations "remain convinced that security is indivisible and that the security of each of them is inseparably linked to the security of all others. They will not strengthen their security at the expense of the security of other states. They will pursue their own security interests with the common efforts to strengthen security and stability within the OSCE area and beyond."[89]

One by-product of OSCE cooperation was the March 1995 Pact of Stability. It requires former East bloc States, wishing to join either the EU or NATO, to first settle any border disputes and ethnic conflicts.

The Pact requires that these former Soviet bloc countries agree to permit the OSCE to be the watchdog agency for ensuring compliance. If this bargain eventually performs as designed, new Yugoslavia-like conflicts will be resolved before they can erupt—also advancing the objectives of democracy and peaceful international relations on the European continent.

The OSCE is gradually assembling solid organizational infrastructure. In 1996, the OSCE heads of State announced the "Lisbon Summit Declaration." Its objective was to create a comprehensive security framework for Europe in the twenty-first century premised upon improved conflict-prevention measures, arms control, and meaningful assessment of security-related economic, social, and environmental problems. In 1997, the OSCE followed up by announcement of its Guidelines for a Charter on European Security.

The OSCE's 1999 Istanbul Conference determined the future direction for this organization by acknowledging that the OSCE would have to work in concert with other international organizations in Europe. The heads of State of the member nations restructured the OSCE's foundation in the following (abbreviated) Charter blueprint for the future:[90]

At the dawn of the twenty-first century we, the Heads of State or Government of the OSCE participating States, declare our firm commitment to a free, democratic and more integrated OSCE area where participating States are at peace with each other, and individuals and communities live in freedom, prosperity and security. To implement this commitment, we have decided to take a number of new steps. We have agreed to:

◆ Adopt the Platform for Co-operative Security, in order to strengthen co-operation between the OSCE and other international organizations and Institutions, thereby making better use of the resources of the international community;

◆ Develop the OSCE's role in peacekeeping, thereby better reflecting the Organization's comprehensive approach to security;

◆ Create Rapid Expert Assistance and Co-operation Teams (REACT), thereby enabling the OSCE to respond quickly to demands for assistance and for large civilian field operations;

◆ Expand our ability to carry out police-related activities in order to assist in maintaining the primacy of law;

◆ Establish an Operation Centre, in order to plan and deploy OSCE field operations;

◆ Strengthen the consultation process within the OSCE by establishing the Preparatory Committee under the OSCE Permanent Council.

We are committed to preventing the outbreak of violent conflicts wherever possible. The steps we have agreed to take in this Charter will strengthen the OSCE's ability in this respect as well as its capacity to settle conflicts and to rehabilitate societies ravaged by war and destruction. The Charter will contribute to the formation of a common and indivisible security space. It will advance the creation of an OSCE area free of dividing lines and zones with different levels of security.

This document is, of course, aspirational in nature. Like the UN Charter, it contains unassailable principles, with which no State member of this organization would openly disagree. One example of its hortatory nature is the phrase in paragraph 2, that "*We have put Europe's old divisions behind us*" (italics added). Since its promulgation, there have been continuous conflicts within the States covered by its call for cooperation.

COMMONWEALTH OF INDEPENDENT STATES

The Commonwealth of Independent States (CIS) is the partial successor to the former Soviet Union. In 1991, Belarus, Ukraine, and Russia established the Minsk Declaration, or Agreement Establishing the Commonwealth of Independent States. Two weeks after the establishment of the CIS, eight more former Soviet republics joined: Armenia, Azerbaijan, Kazakhstan, Kyrgyzstan, Moldova, Tajikastan, Turkmenistan, and Uzbekistan. Georgia and Moldova joined, respectively, in 1993 and 1994. The companion protocol, or Alma-Ata Declaration, facilitated former States of the Soviet Union becoming members of the CIS.[91] The Baltic members—Estonia, Latvia, and Lithuania—chose not to join. Each had finally gained long sought-after independence, and thus decided not to participate in what they considered to be a fresh version of the Soviet Union.

The CIS States inaugurated their international organization in the following document:

Agreement on the Establishment of the Commonwealth of Independent States

Signed on December 8, 1991 at the city of Minsk,
by the Republic of Belarus, the Russian Federation (RSFSR) and Ukraine
<http://www.therussiasite.org/legal/laws/CISagreement.html>

We . . . as the High Contracting Parties, do state that the Union of Soviet Socialist Republics, as a subject of international law and a geopolitical reality, hereby terminate its existence. Based on the historical community of our peoples and the relations that have formed between them, taking into account the bilateral agreements concluded between the High Contracting Parties, striving to build democratic law-based states, intending to develop our relations on the basis of mutual recognition and respect of state sovereignty, the inherent right to self-determination, the principles of equality and non-interference in internal affairs, a rejection of the use of force, economic or other methods of pressure, regulation of disputed issues though negotiations, and other generally recognized principles and norms of international law, believing that further development and strengthening of relations of friendship, good neighborhood and mutually beneficial cooperation between our states corresponds to the fundamental interests of their peoples and serves peace and security, confirming our adherence to the purposes and principles of the Charter of the United Nations, the Helsinki Final Act, and other documents of the Conference on Security and Co-operation in Europe, undertaking to observe generally recognized international norms on human and peoples' rights, have agreed upon the following:

. . .

Article 2

The High Contracting Parties hereby guarantee their citizens, irrespective of their nationality or other differences, equal rights and liberties. Each of the High Contracting Parties guarantees the citizen of the other Parties, as well as stateless person residing in its territory, irrespective of their nationality or other differences, civil, political, economic and cultural rights and liberties in accordance with generally recognized international norms on human rights.

. . .

Article 5

The High Contracting Parties shall recognize and respect the territorial integrity of one another and the inviolability of existing borders under the framework of the Commonwealth. They shall guarantee the openness of borders, freedom of movement for citizens and for the transfer of information.

. . .

Article 6

Member States of the Commonwealth will cooperate in ensuring international peace and security, implementing effective measures to reduce arms and military expenditures. They will strive to eliminate all nuclear weapons, general and full disarmament under strict international control. The Parties will respect one another's aspiration to achieve the status of a non-nuclear zone and neutral state.

Member States of the Commonwealth will preserve and support under a united command the common military and strategic space, including unified control over nuclear weapons, the procedure for the implementation of which shall be regulated by a special agreement. They shall also guarantee necessary conditions for the placement, functioning, material and social support for strategic military forces.

. . .

Article 12

The High Contracting Parties shall guarantee the performance of international obligations arising for them from the treaties and agreements of the former Union of Soviet Socialist Republics.

. . .

Article 14

The official location of the coordinating bodies of the Commonwealth shall be the city of Moscow. The activity of the bodies of the former Union of Soviet Socialist Republics in the territories of the member states of the Commonwealth shall be terminated.

. . .

The CIS treaty accomplished a number of objectives. First, in a manner akin to State succession (§2.4), the original founding States of the Soviet Union (1922) terminated the existence of this former international organization and announced the CIS succession which guaranteed the observance of the treaty obligations of the former Soviet Union (Article 12). The successor organization further recognizes current borders and each member republic's independence, sovereignty, and equality (Article 5). It also established a free-market ruble zone, embracing the republics' interdependent economies and a joint defense force for participating republics.

Regarding the materials, which will be studied in future chapters of this book, such as Chapter 4 on the status of the individual in International Law, this CIS instrument expressly provides for rights that are guaranteed to individuals regarding citizenship, statelessness, and human rights (Articles 2 and 5). The CIS States further expressed their aspiration for "implementing effective measures to reduce arms and military expenditures" as well as, one day, achieving a nuclear free zone (Article 6). While these expressions of intent are not necessarily a binding treaty commitment, they are nevertheless clear statements of intent to make this an organizational priority (§8.1).

In 2001, the Bush Administration announced its intent to rekindle the US missile defense shield program (dubbed "Star Wars"), in violation of the 1972 Anti-Ballistic Missile Treaty (§10.4). It would not be unreasonable for the CIS States to view this attempt to place "defensive" nuclear weapons in space as a threat of force. Ironically, the 1991 CIS Agreement's nuclear free zone goal was a rather significant departure from the Soviet Union's Cold War position on nuclear arms. The decade-later US policy announcement, regarding its so-called Star Wars Defense Shield, suggests one reason why the CIS States are concerned about a renewed arms race and the continuing eastward expansion of NATO.

ORGANIZATION OF AMERICAN STATES

The Organization of American States (OAS), headquartered in Washington, DC, is composed of all States of the Western Hemisphere, except Cuba (thirty-five member States). As a result of the 1962 Cuban Missile Crisis (§10.2), OAS members voted to suspend Cuba's participation because Cuba had "voluntarily placed itself outside of the inter-American system."[92] Of existing international organizations, the OAS is currently the world's oldest. In 1890, several nations created a bureau later known as the Pan American Union. It was subsequently incorporated into another entity called the Organization of American States in 1948. Its essential purposes are as follows:

◆

Charter of the OAS
Signed in Bogotá in 1948
As amended by the Protocol of Buenos Aires in 1967,
by the Protocol of Cartagena de Indias in 1985 and by the Protocol of Managua in 1993
<http://www.oas.org/EN/PINFO/CHARTER96/chart96e.htm>

IN THE NAME OF THEIR PEOPLES, THE STATES REPRESENTED AT THE NINTH INTERNATIONAL CONFERENCE OF AMERICAN STATES,

. . .

Resolved to persevere in the noble undertaking that humanity has conferred upon the United Nations, whose principles and purposes they solemnly reaffirm;

Convinced that juridical organization is a necessary condition for security and peace founded on moral order and on justice; and In accordance with Resolution IX of the Inter-American Conference on Problems of War and Peace, held in Mexico City,

HAVE AGREED upon the following

PART ONE
Chapter I   Nature and Purposes
Article l

The American States establish by this Charter the international organization that they have developed to achieve an order of peace and justice, to promote their solidarity, to strengthen their collaboration, and to defend their sovereignty, their territorial integrity, and their independence. Within the United Nations, the Organization of American States is a regional agency.

The Organization of American States has no powers other than those expressly conferred upon it by this Charter, none of whose provisions authorizes it to intervene in matters that are within the internal jurisdiction of the Member States.

Article 2
The Organization of American States, in order to put into practice the principles on which it is founded and to fulfill its regional obligations under the Charter of the United Nations, proclaims the following essential purposes:

a. To strengthen the peace and security of the continent;

b. To promote and consolidate representative democracy, with due respect for the principle of nonintervention;

c. To prevent possible causes of difficulties and to ensure the pacific settlement of disputes that may arise among the Member States;

d. To provide for common action on the part of those States in the event of aggression;

e. To seek the solution of political, juridical, and economic problems that may arise among them;

f. To promote, by cooperative action, their economic, social, and cultural development; and

g. To achieve an effective limitation of conventional weapons that will make it possible to devote the largest amount of resources to the economic and social development of the Member States.

Chapter II   Principles
. . .
Article 3
The American States reaffirm the following principles:

a. International law is the standard of conduct of States in their reciprocal relations;

b. International order consists essentially of respect for the personality, sovereignty, and independence of States, and the faithful fulfillment of obligations derived from treaties and other sources of international law;

c. Good faith shall govern the relations between States;

d. The solidarity of the American States and the high aims which are sought through it require the political organization of those States on the basis of the effective exercise of representative democracy;

e. Every State has the right to choose, without external interference, its political, economic, and social system and to organize itself in the way best suited to it, and has the duty to abstain from intervening in the affairs of another State. Subject to the foregoing, the American States shall cooperate fully among themselves, independently of the nature of their political, economic, and social systems;

f. The American States condemn war of aggression: victory does not give rights;

g. An act of aggression against one American State is an act of aggression against all the other American States;

h. Controversies of an international character arising between two or more American States shall be settled by peaceful procedures;

I. Social justice and social security are bases of lasting peace;

j. Economic cooperation is essential to the common welfare and prosperity of the peoples of the continent;

k. The American States proclaim the fundamental rights of the individual without distinction as to race, nationality, creed, or sex;

l. The spiritual unity of the continent is based on respect for the cultural values of the American countries and requires their close cooperation for the high purposes of civilization;

m. The education of peoples should be directed toward justice, freedom, and peace.

. . .

The OAS Charter broadly addresses nearly all facets of economic and political life in the Western Hemisphere, drawing on parallel provisions and organization found in the UN Charter. For example, it has both an organ of consultation, similar to the UN Security Council, and an international court, similar to the UN's ICJ (§9.6).

Under Article 1 of its Charter, the OAS is a "regional agency" of the United Nations. These two international organizations are distinct and do not share a hierarchical relationship. The OAS is neither controlled by, nor directly responsible to, the United Nations. The loose association between these organizations is an example of regionalism within a universal system. This was the preferred post-World War II apparatus for ensuring the coexistence of the new global organization and any regional groupings, which might wish to pursue local concerns. One example of this approach is suggested by the earlier League of Nations Covenant. It similarly provided that the League's creation would not affect the vitality of "regional undertakings like the Monroe Doctrine [US policy of excluding external powers from exerting any control in the Western Hemisphere] for securing the maintenance of peace."[93]

Article 4 of the OAS Charter establishes the organization's essential purposes: "(a) To strengthen the peace and security of the continent; (b) To prevent possible causes of difficulties and to ensure the pacific settlement of disputes that may arise among the Member States; (c) To provide for common action on the part of those States in the event of aggression; (d) To seek the solution of political, juridical and economic problems that may arise among them; and (e) To promote, by cooperative action, their economic, social and cultural development."

The OAS has changed its functional orientation several times. It was a commercial international organization when its predecessor was formed in 1890. After World War I, its members adopted a nonintervention theme to discourage unilateral action by any OAS member in hemispheric affairs.

To promote joint military responses to external threats, the twenty-one American States ratified the 1947 Rio Treaty. It proclaimed that "an armed attack by any State against an American State shall be considered as an attack against all the American States."[94] Each member thereby promised to assist the others in repelling such attacks. OAS members are still concerned with defense matters, as evinced by the 1948 OAS Charter's Article 3(g) provision that "An act of aggression against one American State is an act of aggression against all the other American States." The latter wording is not as clear an expression of collective self-defense (§10.2).

The organization's current emphasis is on the development of economic and political solidarity in the hemisphere. In 1987, for example, some member nations (other than the United States) began to pursue the possible economic reintegration of Cuba into the OAS.

The United Nations was not the only international organization seeking the restoration of Haiti's democratically elected president to power after the 1991 military coup. The OAS imposed an embargo on Haiti. In 1992, the United States thereby seized an oil tanker bound for Haiti in violation of the embargo. This was the first time that an OAS embargo actually resulted in such a seizure. In 1997, an earlier amendment to the Charter entered into force, authorizing suspension of any State whose democratic government is forcibly overthrown.

The OAS reached a milestone in its existence in 2000. It was able to mediate a border dispute with which the United Nations had struggled since 1980. Guatemala characterizes the resolution of this dispute as essential to the continuing validity of its acceptance of Belize's borders, after Belize declared independence from Great Britain in 1981. Then, the UN General Assembly urged Guatemala and Belize to find a peaceful solution to their territorial differences. In the interim, a territorial dispute between these two OAS members resulted in bloody confrontations between their military forces.

The OAS has also wrestled with its growing role as intermediary, between certain Latin American governments and their opponents. It has thus probed violence and democratic lapses in Bolivia and Venezuela. Guatemala's perception was that the General Assembly has failed to facilitate a satisfactory solution to the unresolved territorial claims involving several UN member States. Belize contended that its borders had been accepted by previous Guatemalan governments, the international community, the United Nations, and the OAS. In November 2000, pursuant to the OAS mediation efforts, delegations from Belize and Guatemala signed an agreement to adopt a comprehensive set of "confidence-building measures to avoid incidents between the two countries." Neither country thereby renounced sovereignty over the claimed territories. Yet this negotiation at least temporarily established a sufficient degree of trust to prevent further hostile incidents, as a prelude to resolving long-simmering territorial claims.[95]

ARAB LEAGUE *AND* ORGANIZATION OF THE ISLAMIC CONFERENCE

Arab League The League of Arab States is an international organization composed of twenty-two Middle Eastern states and the Palestine Liberation Organization (PLO). The League was established in 1945 to promote comprehensive cooperation among countries of Arabic language and culture.[96]

When Egypt first proposed the Arab League in 1943, Arab states wanted closer cooperation—but without the loss of complete self-rule which can result from a total union (like the EU). The original charter of the league thus created a regional organization of sovereign States, which was neither a union nor a federation. Among the goals the league set for itself were winning independence for all Arabs still under foreign rule in the Middle East, and to prevent the Jewish minority in Palestine (then governed by the British) from creating a Jewish state.

League members then established the Council of Arab Economic Unity in 1964 to promote an Arab Common Market and various other economic programs. The resulting institutions include the Arab Fund for Economic and Social Development for projects in Arab countries (1968), the Arab Bank for Economic Development in Africa (1973), and the Arab Monetary Fund (1976).

League objectives include political collaboration for preserving the independence and the State sovereignty of its members. The Council of the League deployed inter-League peacekeeping forces in Kuwait in 1961 and Lebanon in 1976. The latter effort eventually failed in 1989, however, when Syria refused League demands to withdraw its troops from Lebanon and Iraq (Syria's archenemy).

One of the League's long-term goals is to operate as a collective self-defense organization like NATO. Some

States within the League question why the United States unilaterally engaged in a missile strike against Iraq in 1993 (in response to a threat on the life of former President Bush), while it would not readily engage in such tactics against the Bosnian Serbs. In 1998, the Arab League protested the US bombing in the Sudan, when the United States thus responded to the bombing of its embassy in the Sudan (§7.2).

The political solidarity of the League was adversely affected by a number of events occurring in the latter part of the twentieth century. Under the Camp David Agreements of 1978, US President Jimmy Carter facilitated a series of meetings between Egypt and Israel, at Camp David near Washington, DC. This led Egypt's establishing independent ties with Israel. Since this was contrary to League policy, Egypt was suspended from the League in 1979 (and has since been reinstated). The 1991 Persian Gulf War further deteriorated Arab unity. Certain Arab members even went so far as to assist the United States in protecting Israel from League member Iraq's missile attacks.

In 1993, the Israeli deportation of Muslim fundamentalists to Lebanon also helped rekindle the League's anti-Israeli focus. The League sought worldwide support at the United Nations for the responsive SC resolution. Yet the evident lack of fervor in the private commentaries of Arab League representatives reflected a deep antipathy toward militant Arab fundamentalists. Many of them do not support the PLO's control of relations with Israel. Now that the PLO has negotiated an autonomy agreement with Israel, in the Gaza Strip and the City of Jericho, the League has less of an anti-Israeli flavor. (§10.1 addresses the Arab boycott of Israel.) Yet the League's political cohesion remains in a state of flux, because of worldwide claims that certain States within its membership have engaged in a systematic program of State terrorism to accomplish nationalistic goals.

This organization is one of the key players for nations waging the current war on terror, and concerned about their international reputation. It provides an external link to the international community—in a forum other than the UN Security Council, which cannot act without the imprimatur of permanent members such as the United States and United Kingdom. In 1998, for example, the Secretariat of the League "learned with resentment of the bombing by the United States [in Sudan on

August 20, 1998] . . . [and] consider[ed] this unjustified act a blatant violation of the sovereignty of a State member of the League of Arab States, and of its territorial integrity, as well as against all international laws and tradition, above all the Charter of the United Nations."[97]

In 2004, this organization rejected threatened UN sanctions against The Sudan, for the humanitarian crisis in Darfur. The League—during the interim period when Sudan's government was supposed to cooperate with the UN investigation—feared what it characterized as "forced foreign military intervention in the area."

Organization of the Islamic Conference   The Organization of the Islamic Conference (OIC) is the largest Muslim international organization in the world, established in Morocco in 1969. It is an intergovernmental organization of fifty-six States. They have therein pooled their resources, as stated on the organization's Web page, to "speak with one voice to safeguard the interest and ensure the progress and well-being of their peoples and those of other Muslims in the world over . . . in the wake of the criminal arson perpetrated on 21 August 1969 by Zionist elements against Al-Aqsa Mosque, in occupied Jerusalem. . . ."

The purposes expressed in its comparatively brief 1972 Charter are to: strengthen Islamic solidarity among Member States; coordinate action that will safeguard its holy places; support the struggle of the Palestinian people and assist them in recovering their rights and liberating their occupied territories; facilitate the right to self-determination and noninterference in the internal affairs of Member States.

The OIC's State members also "pledge[d] to refrain, in relations among Member States, from resorting to force or threatening to resort to the use of force against the unity and territorial integrity or the political independence of any one of them."[98]

In June 2004, this group expressed its support for the then new Iraqi Interim Government on the eve of its takeover from the US administrator. This support was characterized as a notable change for Arab nations in regard to the Iraq War. Yet one would *expect* the OIC to do so, as a means of actively assisting the new government in the aftermath of the prior US invasion and direct administration of Iraq. A year earlier, the OIC has authorized the then new US-installed Iraqi Governing Council to take Iraq's seat in the organization.

In June 2005, OIC Ambassador Atta El-Manan Bakhit urged the United States to "live up to its responsibility and not show leniency to perpetrators of qur'an desecration" reportedly occurring at the Guantanamo military base in Cuba.

AFRICAN UNION

The African Union (AU)—previously the Organization of African Unity—is rooted in the Western-derived institutions of colonial rule and the related treatment of nations on the African continent. This organization's traditional goal has been African political unity to promote self-determination. As succinctly described by the University of East Anglia (England) Professor Gino Naldi:

Pan-Africanism has its origins in nineteenth-century America where the American Colonization Society for the Establishment of Free Men of Color of the United States was formed in 1816 in response to the alienation and exploitation of the Negroes with the purpose of repatriating freed slaves. This led to the founding of Liberia in West Africa [by freed slaves from the US] as a free and sovereign State in 1847. Nevertheless, the Pan-African movement, which gathered momentum at the turn of the century, continued to struggle for the end of the colonial system in Africa and called for the dismantling of the colonial boundaries agreed upon at the Congress of Berlin in 1885 [premised upon Africa's supposed inability to govern itself without European influence]. . . . But it was the post–Second World War era that provided the impetus for self-determination in Africa. The demand for political, economic and cultural self-determination became a flood that the colonial powers could not dam. The independence of Ghana on 6 March 1957 marked the beginning of a new dawn in Africa.[99]

The OAU was established in 1963, and headquartered in Ethiopia. It consists of all of the independent nations in Africa. Morocco withdrew, and Zaire (now Democratic Republic of Congo) suspended its membership when the Western Sahara became an independent member in 1984—based on unresolved territorial claims (§2.4 Changes in State Status). Many of the organizational purposes, continued in the 2002 establishment of the African Union,[100] include:

African Union

<http://www.africa-union.org/home/Welcome.htm>,
click Constitutive Act.
(July 9, 2002)

We, Heads of State and Government of the Member States . . .

Inspired by the noble ideals which guided the founding fathers of our Continental Organization and generations of Pan-Africanists in their determination to promote unity, solidarity, cohesion and cooperation among the peoples of Africa and African States;

Considering the principles and objectives stated in the Charter of the Organization of African Unity and the Treaty establishing the African Economic Community;

Recalling the heroic struggles waged by our peoples and our countries for political independence, human dignity and economic emancipation;

Considering that since its inception, the Organization of African Unity has played a determining and invaluable role in the liberation of the continent, the affirmation of a common identity and the process of attainment of the unity of our continent and has provided a unique framework for our collective action in Africa and in our relations with the rest of the world.

Determined to take up the multifaceted challenges that confront our continent and peoples in the light of the social, economic and political changes taking place in the world; CONVINCED of the need to accelerate the process of implementing the Treaty establishing the African Economic Community in order to promote the socio-economic development of Africa and to face more effectively the challenges posed by globalization;

Guided by our common vision of a united and strong Africa and by the need to build a partnership between governments and all segments of civil society, in particular women, youth and the private sector, in order to strengthen solidarity and cohesion among our peoples;

Conscious of the fact that the scourge of conflicts in Africa constitutes a major impediment to the socio-economic development of the continent and of the need to promote peace, security and stability as a prerequisite for the implementation of our development and integration agenda;

Determined to promote and protect human and peoples' rights, consolidate democratic institutions and culture, and to ensure good governance and the rule of law;

Further Determined to take all necessary measures to strengthen our common institutions and provide them with the necessary powers and resources to enable them discharge their respective mandates effectively;

Recalling the Declaration which we adopted at the Fourth Extraordinary Session of our Assembly in Sirte, the Great Socialist People's Libyan Arab Jamahiriya, on 9.9. 99, in which we decided to establish an African Union, in conformity with the ultimate objectives of the Charter of our Continental Organization and the Treaty establishing the African Economic Community;

HAVE AGREED AS FOLLOWS:

. . .

Article 2 Establishment
The African Union is hereby established in accordance with the provisions of this Act.

Article 3 Objectives
The objectives of the Union shall be to:

(a) achieve greater unity and solidarity between the African countries and the peoples of Africa;

(b) defend the sovereignty, territorial integrity and independence of its Member States;

(c) accelerate the political and socio-economic integration of the continent;

(d) promote and defend African common positions on issues of interest to the continent and its peoples;

(e) encourage international cooperation, taking due account of the Charter of the United Nations and the Universal Declaration of Human Rights;

(f) promote peace, security, and stability on the continent;

(g) promote democratic principles and institutions, popular participation and good governance;

(h) promote and protect human and peoples' rights in accordance with the African Charter on Human and Peoples' Rights and other relevant human rights instruments;

(i) establish the necessary conditions which enable the continent to play its rightful role in the global economy and in international negotiations;

(j) promote sustainable development at the economic, social and cultural levels as well as the integration of African economies;

(k) promote co-operation in all fields of human activity to raise the living standards of African peoples;

(l) coordinate and harmonize the policies between the existing and future Regional Economic Communities for the gradual attainment of the objectives of the Union;

(m) advance the development of the continent by promoting research in all fields, in particular in science and technology;

(n) work with relevant international partners in the eradication of preventable diseases and the promotion of good health on the continent.

. . .

The AU's most distinctive (and successful) objectives were to resolve the political problems in South West Africa and South Africa. The Union thus supported the black nationalist movements in southern Africa. The six "Frontline Countries" constituted a bloc within the OAU, designed to assist the remaining colonial territories achieve independence. The primary goal of the Frontline Countries was to free South West Africa from South African rule—held in violation of numerous UN resolutions. This objective was accomplished with the independence, renaming, and entry into the United Nations of the new renamed State of Namibia in 1990. The other success was the plight of black South Africans, who were subject to white minority rule under that nation's former system of apartheid. These OAU internal institutions were dismantled just prior to Nelson Mandela's assumption of the presidency of South Africa in 1994. South Africa then joined the OAU.

The Charter tasks the organization to provide for the territorial integrity of its member States. In 1981–1982, the organization seized upon its implied powers in the predecessor OAU Charter to establish a peacekeeping force in Chad. However, that force's mandate was unclear and it lacked financing and organization. These circumstances thus led to failure—mostly because it was perceived by Chad's President as being an enforcement arm of the Chad government, rather than a neutral peacekeeping force.[101] When Liberia's 1990 civil war erupted, neither the OAU nor the United Nations attempted to mediate or keep the peace—although another African (economic) organization did send in forces.[102] The OAU played a minor role in the UN peacekeeping operations in the 1990s (*e.g.*, Somalia, Liberia, and Mozambique).

It has established a commission to mediate all disputes between African nations.[103] In 1998, an OAU delegation went to Ethiopia to mediate the territorial dispute involving invading Eritrean forces. The OAU's current orientation is essentially economic, however, premised on its 1991 treaty establishing the OAU's economic community.[104]

In both 2004 and 2005, the AU proposed a peace mission in the troubled Darfur region of The Sudan. International donors then pledged over $200,000,000 to fund the AU's peacekeeping operation (§10.3 Peacekeeping Operations).

The United Nations is not the only international organization suffering from membership delinquency in paying assessed shares of the annual budget. A number of African nations have fallen behind in their payments to the OAU. Given the concerns about the impact of this development on operational integrity, the OAU resolved that its member States must no longer threaten its continued operation in this manner. In 1990, the organization resolved to limit its annual budget ceiling to 10 percent above the amount expended in the previous year. Another remedial measure was to remind delinquent member States that they could not participate in organizational decision making or present candidates for OAU posts.[105]

◆ 3.6 ORGANIZATIONAL IMMUNITY

State responsibility under International Law was addressed in §2.5 of this book. State immunity from responsibility, in the form of insulation from suit in the courts of another State, was addressed in §2.6 of this book. After forty years of drafting, the UN's ILC recently presented draft articles to the UN General Assembly. The ILC has begun its work on the responsibility of international organizations.[106]

Compared to State immunity analysis, the immunity of an IO is more complex and less developed—especially for individuals harmed by employees or agents of an IO. As aptly articulated by the Catholic University of Nijmegen's Professor Karel Wellens: "the category of non-state claimants is still encountering the common procedural obstacle of jurisdictional immunity before the domestic courts, which is normally claimed by and frequently granted to international organizations. . . . The immature state of development of a remedial regime is, of course, embedded in the evolving process of elaboration and consolidation of the overall accountability regime for international organizations."[107]

One of the most under-reported examples is sexual abuse resulting in "U.N. Peacekeeping Babies." A March 2005 report, written by Jordan's Ambassador to the UN—and former peacekeeper—proposed remedies for the ongoing sexual exploitation of local women by UN peacekeepers. Given the problems with peacekeepers being drawn away from their UN mission, the proposal suggests that a trust fund be developed to assist the mothers of these babies—especially in the Democratic Republic of the Congo, where there have been numerous allegations of sexual misconduct. A permanent UN investigative team would include a local prosecutor. There would be special courts-martial at the scene of a crime for local prosecutions. At present, the United Nations has no tracking system for this flow of "peacekeeping babies." As reported by Refugees International: "A 'boys will be boys' attitude in peacekeeping missions breeds tolerance for exploiting and abusing local [Haitian and Liberian] women . . . [and such] behavior would not be accepted in the home country of these soldiers."[108]

This section focuses on the question of whether an international organization entitled to immunity from suit in the national courts of its member States. You will recall that State immunity analysis depends on whether the forum nation follows the "absolute" or the "restrictive" approach to sovereign immunity. The answer to the question of organizational immunity involves a similar rationale for shielding organizations from suits in their member States.

One reason for the dearth of available cases is that international organizations appear in national courts far less frequently than do States. When they do, decisions on the scope of immunity accorded to an international organization rest solely with the forum State's law. Traditionally, the executive branch of the government has been the decision maker on this issue. The courts then defer to such decisions, so that the respective branches of the government do not conflict. There is a modern trend, however, whereby many courts—rather than blindly adhering to such executive control—are engaging in "free evaluation of immunity issues by the courts themselves."[109]

UNITED NATIONS

The Convention on the Privileges and Immunities of the United Nations was adopted by the GA in 1946.[110] The key provisions provide as follows:

ART. IV, SECTION 11 Representatives of Members to the principal and subsidiary organs of the United Nations and to conferences convened by the United Nations, shall, while exercising their functions and during the journey to and from the place of meeting, enjoy the following privileges and immunities:

(a) Immunity from personal arrest or detention and from seizure of their personal baggage, and, in respect of words spoken or written and all acts done by them in their capacity as representatives, immunity from legal process of every kind;

(b) Inviolability for all papers and documents;

(c) The right to use codes and to receive papers or correspondence by courier or in sealed bags;

(d) Exemption in respect of themselves and their spouses from immigration restrictions, aliens registration or national service obligations in the State they are visiting or through which they are passing in the exercise of their functions;

(e) The same facilities in respect of currency or exchange restrictions as are accorded to representatives of foreign governments on temporary official missions;

(f) The immunities and facilities in respect of their personal baggage as are accorded to diplomatic envoys, and also;

(g) Such other privileges, immunities and facilities not inconsistent with the foregoing as diplomatic envoys enjoy, except that they shall have no right to claim exemption from customs duties on goods imported (otherwise than as part of their personal baggage) or from excise duties or sales taxes.

UN employees and their personal baggage are immune from arrest or the other interferences mentioned in the Convention. UN property and assets are immune from expropriation or detention. Under Article VI §22, the same general protection applies to *ad hoc* experts dispatched to gather information or perform other work for the United Nations, when they are not routine UN employees. This protection facilitates temporary assignments, while minimizing interruptions such as local arrests for espionage.

The degree of protection actually enjoyed by UN employees or special experts is not uniform. In 1989, the ICJ determined that Romania violated Section 22 of the Convention by detaining a special rapporteur of the Sub-Commission on Prevention of Discrimination and Protection of Minorities. In 2002, the United States expelled two Cuban diplomats posted to the United Nations, who were supposedly spying. This was a violation of the UN Convention, although the United Nations did not protest. In March 2004, British Intelligence officials monitored UN Secretary-General Kofi Annan's telephone calls during the period leading to the Iraq War. The 1946 immunities convention does not specifically refer to such monitoring—as does the Vienna Convention on Diplomatic and Consular Relations (§7.4). However, under UN Charter Article 100.2: "Each Member of the United Nations undertakes to respect the exclusive international character of the responsibilities of the Secretary-General and the staff." Article 2, Section 3 of the 1946 Convention provides that: "The premises of the United Nations shall be inviolable . . . [and] shall be immune from search . . . or any other form of interference. . . ."[111]

In 1998, the Court addressed immunity from national court judgments (Art. VIII, Section 30) against the UN's Special Rapporteur of the Commission on Human Rights on the Independence of Judges and Lawyers. He was named as a defendant in four civil defamation suits in Malaysia, resulting from statements he made in 1995 in an article in International Commercial Litigation, a magazine published in the United Kingdom and circulated in Malaysia. The UN Secretary-General issued notes confirming that, based on a determination by the UN Legal Counsel, his remarks were made in his official capacity as a Special Rapporteur—and that he should thus be immune from such litigation under the Convention. The Malaysian Ministry of Foreign Affairs asked the Malaysian courts to determine the immunity question. The High Court for Kuala Lumpur declined to find that he was protected by the claimed immunity. The Malaysian government considered the Secretary-General's notes merely to be "opinions," with no binding legal effect. After further attempts to stay the court proceedings or reach some settlement, the United Nations and Malaysia agreed to refer the matter to the ICJ. The President of the ICJ issued an order, based on the submission of written statements and responses from the parties. It called on the Government of Malaysia to stay all court proceedings in this matter and to accept the advisory opinion as decisive.[112]

The United Nations has mandated immunity for its employees—and supporting troops—in the administration of Kosovo. In 1999, the Security Council authorized Member States and relevant international organizations to establish the international security presence in Kosovo, known as KFOR (composed primarily of NATO military forces). One year later, the United Nations Interim Administration Mission in Kosovo (UNIMIK), announced a joint declaration on the status of KFOR and UNMIK. It outlines the privileges and immunities to which the organizational forces in Kosovo are entitled. While they must respect local law, to the extent that it does not conflict with the basic UN resolution (1244), the various components of KFOR enjoy wide latitude in the performance of their work in Kosovo. Should any KFOR employees breach the law, they cannot be (legally) detained. They can be prosecuted, but only by their home nation upon their return.

Can the United Nations *waive* the immunity of its employees? This occurred in two widely reported incidents in Kosovo. In 2002, an Egyptian working as a UN police officer killed his female translator in his apartment. The United Nations chose to waive its organizational immunity, thus resulting in his trial in the local judicial system, and a thirteen-year sentence. In 2004—the day after the King of Jordan publicly commented that the war in Iraq had created unprecedented animosity toward America across the Middle East—Jordanian (UN) police fired on vehicles carrying US (UN) police. Two Americans and one Jordanian were killed, leaving eleven others wounded. The Jordanians could not be interviewed until the United Nations waived their right to diplomatic immunity.[113]

The Article Two immunities thus include the provision that "[l]ocally recruited KFOR personnel shall be immune from legal process in respect of words spoken or written and acts performed by them in carrying out tasks exclusively related to their services to KFOR." Other personnel are:

a. immune from jurisdiction before courts in Kosovo in respect of any administrative, civil or criminal act committed by them in the territory of Kosovo. Such personnel shall be subject to the exclusive jurisdiction of their respective sending States; and

b. immune from any form of arrest or detention other than by persons acting on behalf of their respective sending States. If erroneously detained, they shall be immediately turned over to KFOR authorities.[114]

In the United States, the United Nations enjoys the same immunity that is enjoyed by foreign governments.[115] Because of local complaints about abuse of this immunity, however, the United Nations is bowing to pressure to waive its conventional immunity. In March 1999, the United Nations announced that it would authorize the wage garnishment of its staff members who fail to pay court ordered spouse and child support rather than permitting them to rely on institutional immunity to evade legal obligations under local state law. In December 2000, a United Nations official who, ironically, wrote and lectured on poverty in Africa, faces a lawsuit from a Zambian man who claims the official held him in indentured servitude for seventeen months. A lawsuit filed in New York accused the official of paying the plaintiff illegally low wages of $160 a month for working in their home nearly 70 hours per week.[116]

In the United Nations "Oil-for-Food" scandal (§3.3), the United Nations was monitoring Iraq's sale of oil for humanitarian purposes from 1997 to 2003. Secretary-General Kofi Annan resisted requests from the US Congress for interviews with UN staff, and for access to UN internal audits of this now defunct program. Annan ultimately waived diplomatic immunity in certain cases, resulting in the first indictment in August 2005.

OTHER ORGANIZATIONS

The scope of immunity for other international organizations is not as clear. In some nations, international organizational immunity is likened to diplomatic immunity (§7.4). Other nations draw upon the analogy to State immunity (§2.6).

In a 1990 arbitration, the Federal Republic of Germany (the "FRG" prior to German unification) sought to tax certain activities of the European Molecular Biology Laboratory (EMBL). This is an international organization, which had negotiated a Headquarters Agreement with the FRG, similar to the agreement between the United Nations and United States regarding the immunities of the organization's New York City facilities. The FRG imposed taxes and customs duties on income and goods related to this organization's canteen and guest house used by visiting staff and scientists, as well as maintenance of the residence of the Director-General of the EMBL. The organization believed that these taxes violated the Headquarters Agreement between Germany and the EMBL. When ruling in favor of the EMBL, the arbitrators noted the organization's special status, and immunity from taxes and duties, in the following terms:

Therefore it was inadmissible [for the FRG] to tend to limit the privileges and immunities of the EMBL, and to interpret them restrictively. For the privileges and immunities were not intended to provide international organizations with individual legal entitlements, but to contribute to an effective discharge of the responsibilities by the organization and make the latter independent from internal jurisdiction [of the FRG courts over EMBL]. . . .

Besides the general principle of the respect of the effective discharge of the responsibilities and of the independence of the organizations, the largely undisputed principle had to be respected that a host State must not draw financial advantages from the official activities of an international organization. Otherwise it would adversely affect the financial resources of the organization at the expense of the financial contribution of the other member States.[117]

In 2004, the new International Criminal Court began to execute privilege and immunities agreements with the countries wherein its employees would be working to gather prosecution evidence. This type of arrangement is necessary to ensure the safety, independence, and confidentiality required for such sensitive investigations.

Can IOs be sued in the courts of their member states? In Chapter 2 of this book, you studied the ability of an IO to pursue its own independent claim against a

State that harms a UN employee (ICJ *Reparations Case*). You also read about the United Nations being able to sue one of its member States (*Balfour* note case).

The following case classically illustrates a not-so-uncommon scenario, whereby employees sued an IO in courts of a member country:

Broadbent v. Organization of American States

UNITED STATES COURT OF APPEALS

District of Columbia Circuit

628 Fed.Rptr.2d 27 (1980)

AUTHOR'S NOTE: Plaintiff Broadbent and some co-workers lost their jobs at the General Secretariat of the Organization of American States (OAS). The plaintiffs included US citizens and foreign nationals residing in the US who were employed at the OAS's permanent headquarters in Washington, DC. They believed that they were wrongfully terminated.

They first filed a complaint with an OAS administrative tribunal set up to resolve personnel disputes. That OAS tribunal decided that these employees should be reinstated, awarding a small amount of money damages in the event that the OAS Secretary-General ultimately denied the reinstatement recommendation of the administrative panel. Plaintiffs then sued for $3 million in a federal court of the US—also located in Washington, D.C. They alleged that the OAS had improperly breached their employment contracts.

The defendant OAS responded by seeking dismissal of their suit. The federal trial court did just that, holding that the OAS was "absolutely" immune—under any circumstances—from such suits. The federal appellate court agreed that the OAS was entitled to organizational immunity. The appellate court's decision, however, was that "restrictive" immunity was the applicable standard to apply to an international organization, rather than the lower court's reliance on an absolute standard for gauging whether the organization was immune from suit.

Both the trial and appellate courts achieved the same result. They dismissed the case against the OAS. Their respective legal yardsticks differed in terms of which standard was applicable—absolute or restrictive immunity.

The restrictive standard would authorize prosecution of future suits against an international organization in US courts if, like State immunity, the organization's activities were sufficiently "commercial." The appellate court applied the Foreign Sovereign Immunities Act (FSIA) to the OAS, just as if it were a "State" within the meaning of the FSIA. If a foreign State would be entitled to immunity under the Act, so would an international organization like the OAS. The OAS was immune from suit if it was not conducting a "business" as if it were a private trader—when hiring and firing employees at the organization's Washington, DC headquarters.

COURT'S OPINION: Section 1605 of the FSIA provides that foreign states shall not be immune from the jurisdiction of American courts in any case based upon their commercial activity in the United States, with the commercial character of an activity determined by reference to its "nature" rather than to its "purpose." The conceptual difficulties involved in differentiating *jure gestionis* [acts by a private trader] from *jure imperli* [acts by a State] have led some commentators to declare the distinction unworkable. The restrictive immunity doctrine is designed to accommodate the legal interests of citizens doing business with foreign governments on the one hand, with the interests of foreign states in avoiding the embarrassment of defending the propriety of political acts before a foreign court.

In our view [the appellate court], the employment by a foreign state or international organization of internal administrative personnel—civil servants—is not properly characterized as "doing business." That view is supported by the legislative history of the FSIA, and the definition of "commercial activity" in §1603. The House [of Representatives] Report commented:

Commercial activity.—Paragraph (c) of section 1603 defines the term "commercial activity" as including a broad spectrum of endeavor, from an individual commercial transaction or act to a regular course of commercial conduct. A "regular course of commercial conduct" includes the carrying on of a commercial enterprise such as a mineral extraction company, an airline or a state trading corporation. Certainly, if an activity is customarily carried on for profit, its commercial nature could readily be assumed. At the other end of the spectrum, a single contract, if of the same character as a contract which might be made by a private person, could constitute a "particular transaction or act." . . . By contrast, . . . an activity whose essential nature is public or governmental . . . would not itself constitute a commercial activity. . . . Also public or governmental and not commercial in nature would be the employment of diplomatic, civil service, or military personnel, but not the employment of American citizens or third country nationals by the foreign state in the United States.

This report clearly marks employment of civil servants as noncommercial for purposes of restrictive immunity. The Committee Reports establish an exception from the general rule in the case of employment of American citizens or third country nationals by foreign states. The exception leaves foreign states free to conduct "governmental" matters through their own citizens. A comparable exception is not applicable to international organizations, because their civil servants are inevitably drawn from either American citizens or "third" country nations. In the case of international organizations, such an exception would swallow up the rule of immunity for civil service employment disputes.

The United States has accepted without qualification the principles that international organizations must be free to perform their functions and that no member state may take action to hinder the organization. The unique nature of the international civil service is relevant. International officials should be as free as possible, within the mandate granted by the member states, to perform their duties free from the peculiarities of national politics. The OAS charter, for example, imposes constraints on the organization's employment practices. Such constraints may not coincide with the employment policies pursued by its various member states. . . . An attempt by the courts of one nation to adjudicate the personnel claims

of international civil servants would entangle those courts in the internal administration of those organizations. Denial of immunity opens the door to divided decisions of the courts of different member states passing judgment on the rules, regulations, and decisions of the international bodies. Undercutting uniformity in the application of staff rules or regulations would undermine the ability of the organization to function effectively.

We hold that the relationship of an international organization with its internal administrative staff is noncommercial, and, absent waiver, activities defining or arising out of that relationship may not be the basis of an action against [the organization] regardless of whether international organizations enjoy absolute or restrictive immunity.

The appellants were staff members of the General Secretariat of the OAS. Their appointments, terms of employment, salaries and allowances, and the termination of employment were governed by detailed "Staff Rules of the General Secretariat" promulgated by the OAS. The Staff Rules further establish an elaborate grievance procedure within the OAS, with ultimate appeal to the Administrative Tribunal of the OAS.

The Tribunal is competent to determine the lawfulness of an employee's termination of employment. If an employee has been wrongfully discharged, the Tribunal may order reinstatement. If reinstatement is ordered, the Tribunal may also establish an indemnity to be paid to the employee in the event the Secretary General exercises his authority to indemnify the employee rather than effect the reinstatement.

The employment disputes between the appellants and OAS were disputes concerning the internal administrative staff of the Organization. The internal administration of the OAS is a non-commercial activity shielded by the doctrine of immunity. There was no waiver, and accordingly the appellants' action had to be dismissed.

◆ *Notes & Questions*

1. Section 2.6 of this book analyzes the distinction between the "absolute" and the "restrictive" immunity of States. How did the *Broadbent* trial and appellate courts apply that distinction, in very different ways, to an international organization?

2. There was no difference in the end result. Why?

3. Would it have made a difference if there had been no administrative tribunal at the OAS to handle such terminations?

4. In 1998, the same Court of Appeals stated that: (1) the scope of immunity accorded international organizations under the International Organizational Immunities Act (IOIA) of 1945 is probably broader than that of States under the Foreign Sovereign Immunities

Act (FSIA) of 1976. Atkinson v. Inter-American Development Bank, 156 Fed.3d 1335 (D.C. Cir., 1998). This court did not clearly resolve whether Congress generally intended that greater immunity be accorded international organizations than States. Aguado v. Inter-American Development Bank, 85 Fed.Appx. 776, 777 (D.C. Cir., 2004) (citing *Broadbent*).

◆ PROBLEMS

Problem 3.A (after §3.1 Reparations Case) In September 1991, in the aftermath of the PGW, a UN nuclear inspection team entered Iraq for the purpose of ensuring that it was not producing weapons of mass destruction. This inspection was to be conducted under a SC resolution requiring Iraq to divest itself of such weapons. Iraq responded by seizing forty-four UN team members, including citizens of several nations. Iraq claimed that some were spies. The SC then approved Iraqi demands. One was that the inspectors must make lists of Iraq's secret nuclear-weapons program papers that they intended to take with them for further analysis by the United Nations. This minor SC concession (allowing Iraq to make some demand of the United Nations) may have saved the lives of the UN's inspectors.

If they had been killed by Iraqi agents, to whom would Iraq have State responsibility for reparations under International Law? Should there be an exclusive remedy for this type of wrong, assertable by only one entity?

Problem 3.B (end of §3.2) In 1991, military leaders overthrew the democratically elected government of Haiti. The United States considered this coup to be quite adverse to the hemispheric interests of other democratic nations in and near the Caribbean.

Assume that sometime thereafter, the US president announces that the United States will undertake a "humanitarian intervention" in Haiti. The president announces that the purpose will be to "to help the people of Haiti restore democracy. Assume further that Haiti's military government responds to the US announcement with its own statement, as follows: "North American imperialism will never prevent the people of Haiti from achieving their rightful role in hemispheric affairs, which have been dominated by the US since establishment of international organizations including the Organization of American States (1890) and the UN (1945)."

The United Nations previously imposed an embargo on oil bound for Haiti. Assume that the United Nations either cannot or will not respond to this particular flare-up. The United States has just vetoed a proposed UN Security Council resolution that would prohibit the United States from acting unilaterally to invade Haiti. As covered in §3.3, the veto of one of the "permanent five" precludes Council action on such matters (e.g., from dispatching peacekeeping forces to Haiti). Further, Haiti's military leaders are unlikely to agree to a UN intervention which would threaten their continued control of Haiti's government.

Later, assume that there is a local response to the events in Haiti. The Organization of Central American States (OCAS) has asked its members—consisting of States in Central America—to participate in a peace process. The organs of this international organization cannot act without the unanimous consent of all members of the OCAS. The dual goal of this conference will be to establish regional containment of this hypothetical Haitian scenario and to avoid a further confrontation between the United States and Haiti. The OCAS is an independent international organization whose membership includes the United States and Haiti. UN administrators have referred to this international organization as one of the UN's regional agencies. Under Article 33 of the UN Charter, regional agencies are encouraged to resolve threats to international peace.

The Inter-American Economic and Social Council is part of the infrastructure of the Organization of Central American States. Its fundamental purpose is to promote the economic and social welfare of the member States of the OCAS through better utilization of all natural resources within the region. It has made many recommendations to OCAS member States dealing with economic and social matters. To accomplish its purpose, assume that Council members vote to conduct a research study of the effect of both the United States and the new Haitian regime on the economic and social well-being of this Caribbean nation. Council members believe that the economic scenario in Haiti will undoubtedly worsen as a result of social and military problems resulting from the US-Haitian confrontation. The Council study, not yet completed, will address these interrelated matters for the United States and other OCAS members. It will consider what collective action might be taken to avert the further escalation of hostilities in this region.

What is the nature of the OCAS—the international organization addressing this explosive situation?

Discuss the various ways in which one might classify this organization.

Problem 3.C (after Security Council Materials in §3.3) Membership on the Security Council has not been particularly democratic. It was not until May 2000 that Israel became aligned with any group of nations. While it is geographically part of the Asian Group, Israel was accepted into the Western European and Others Group. (Previously, Israel was the only UN member to be barred from *any* group, because of Arab-nation resistance.) Israel's admission was limited to four years, after which it was subject to reconfirmation. In two years, Israel was able to vie for participation in certain UN bodies for the first time. Another nondemocratic example is that only five States occupy *permanent* seats on the Council. As to the *rotating* seats, there are five groupings used for filling the rotating SC seats from among the UN's other 186 nonpermanent members.

The United States has backed the addition of Germany and Japan as future permanent members of the UN Security Council. Many other possible changes would arguably do a better job of making the Council "mirror" the Assembly, by more accurately reflecting the demographic composition of the community of nations. Consider the following options:

1. Should Great Britain and France each continue to occupy a permanent seat?
2. Alternatively, should either nation cede its seat to Germany, or should all three somehow rotate on this particular "permanent" slot on the Council—to be known as the "European Seat?"
3. Would Japan be entitled to a permanent seat, given its economic superiority in global affairs?
4. Should China share (rotate on) the permanent "Asian seat" with India, given the latter's immense population, which surpasses that of all Council members except China?
5. Should Germany, Japan, or any other nation be added as a permanent SC member—but without the right of veto, thus providing for *some* status on the Council? This would be permanent status, but without the attendant right of automatic veto which is currently exercisable by the original five permanent members.
6. Would any of these changes truly influence, in a positive way, the SC's ability to perform, without diminishing its power to act?
7. Should there be some *other* change?
8. Should there be *no* change at all?
9. Which of these would be the best option?

Class members will examine these various positions and resolve which alternative would best suit the following goals:

(a) Better representation of the community of nations on the SC
(b) More reliable conduct of Council business under its Article 39 (or other) mandate(s)

Problem 3.D (within §3.3, to further analyze "Subsequent Unilateral Action?") A major legal question arose, as of the US 1998 military buildup in the Persian Gulf: Could the United States unilaterally attack Iraq premised on aging 1991 UN resolutions—as opposed to soliciting a fresh UN Security Council resolution to authorize an attack on Iraq?

UN Charter Article 2.4 prohibits the use of force. The Charter-based exception being self-defense (Article 51) and SC authorization (Article 42). As will be seen in Chapter 10 on the use of force, State practice has arguably augmented the Article 51 requirement of an "armed attack" by relying on "anticipatory" self-defense—given advances in weapons technology since the Charter was drafted in 1945.

Resolution 678, passed before the PGW began, said that member States "can use all necessary force" to oust Iraq from Kuwait. However, seven years had passed by the time of the US saber rattling; Iraq had departed Kuwait; there had been a cease-fire; the United States did not have the benefit of the same worldwide resolve to go to war in 1998 (not that of permanent SC members China, France, and Russia, or any of the Arab nations that so staunchly supported the PGW in 1991); there was no provision in any SC resolution authorizing a UN member State to use force on its own initiative; and Article 2.4 of the UN Charter generally prohibits the use of force, which could be interpreted to require the express authorization of force by the SC rather than leaving a doubtful situation to the discretion of one member State.

The US support for its military buildup relied on several arguments: Resolution 678 could be still invoked, because peace and security had not been restored to the area; in 1994, Iraqi forces moved toward Kuwait, then pulled back when the United States dispatched a naval carrier group to the Gulf; in 1996, Iraq sent its forces into Northern Iraq to help a Kurdish group recapture a key city inside a safe haven protected by US-led forces; and Article 51 of the UN Charter accorded the right of collective self-defense because of the potential use of the biological and chemical weapons thought to be hidden in Saddam Hussein's large presidential palaces. Thus, the continuing threat of biological warfare would mean that the war had never really ended. Iraqi compliance with the cease-fire agreements would thereby be construed as a condition precedent to an effective cease-fire (Resolution 686).

Two students (or groups) will debate whether the United States possessed the authority to attack Iraq—as planned prior to the Secretary-General's successful intervention—*without* a fresh UN Security Council resolution. While some basic arguments have been provided, there are others. This exercise illustrates some of the problems with potential UN solutions to threats to peace.

Problem 3.E (after Trusteeship Council Materials in §3.3) The aftermath of the Cold War included the breakdown, if not splintering, of State sovereignty. For example, the Soviet Union collapsed into a number of smaller States. One State under its influence, Yugoslavia, further split into five additional States.

One consequence of the realization of statehood, especially by former colonies in Africa, has been the increasing frequency of what many have referred to as "failed States." These are States that have achieved independence but not sufficient economic and political stature to thrive. Warring tribes and ethnic groups are responsible for mass terror, executions, fleeing refugees, and economic hardship for the citizens of such countries.

Somalia is just one example of the negative facets of postcolonial statehood: a State that has "failed," or will fail, thus producing anarchy (as depicted in the movie Black Hawk Down). UN efforts to provide humanitarian relief have resulted in mass looting, anti-UN actions, and anti-UN sentiment expressed by various segments of the populace. The UN Secretary-General fled for his life during a 1993 visit to Somalia, during which he had hoped to bolster the spirit of the peacekeeping forces in Somalia. In 2004, UN Security Council Resolution 1558 deplored the massive flow of weapons and ammunition into and through Somalia in violation of the UN arms embargo. The government sits in exile in Nairobi, Kenya. When that government called for an African

Union peacekeeping force to help control Somalia's lawlessness, thousands of Somalians protested the potential infusion of foreign, non-Muslim troops.

Kosovo is geographically within Serbia. It has been occupied by NATO, and administered by the United Nations, since 1999. Background details are available at: <http://home.att.net/~slomansonb/txtcsesite.html>, click on <u>Thin Red Line</u> (Chapter 10). Kosovo may arguably be a candidate for trusteeship. Such a UN-sponsored administrative tool has previously been effectuated through supervision by a neighboring State.

Peruse Articles 75–85 of the UN Charter on the course Web site at: <http://home.att.net/~slomansonb/txtcsesite. html>, especially Articles 77 and 78. Then reconsider the definition of statehood in §2.1 of this textbook. Three students will now assume the roles of: (1) the UN's Trusteeship Council; and (2) Serbia (and Montenegro); and (3) a supervising nation, willing to take either Somalia or Kosovo under trusteeship. They will analyze/debate the following issues:

1. Should the United Nations bring such quasi-States "under its wings?" Should the United Nations attempt to reestablish the Trusteeship system in either place, because Somalia or Kosovo's arguable inability to control their own international affairs? Would the UN's current financial problems (§3.3) affect this debate?
2. Would that be best accomplished by reviving the trust system; or alternatively, by taking over Somalia's governmental functions, as the United Nations did in East Timor and Kosovo?
3. If the Trust device doable, *which* UN member State would administer these Trust Territories?
4. Would Kosovo—under UN administration from 1999 to the present—be a viable candidate for such a trusteeship? (The UN's comparatively brief administration of East Timor preceded its 2002 statehood and admission to the United Nations.)[118]
5. Should the UN Charter be amended to *delete* the entire concept of trusteeship?

Problem 3.F (within UN Assessment Materials, after "Financial Crisis," in §3.3) The UN Secretary-General originally threatened that the United States would lose its GA vote at the end of 1998 if it did not pay its arrearage of what was then more than $1.5 billion. (The US position in the SC would not be affected.) The US accounting system has generally created problems for the United Nations, because the United Nations expects dues to be paid at the beginning of the calendar year, but the United States has normally paid its dues around October 1.

As of the close of 1998, the year when the financial crisis began to receive an extraordinary degree of public attention, eighteen other nations had also fallen behind by failing to pay their dues for more than two years: Bosnia, Burundi, Cambodia, Comoros, Congo, Dominica, Equatorial Guinea, Georgia, Guinea-Bissau, Iraq, Liberia, Moldova, São Tomé, Somalia, Tajikistan, Togo, Vanuatu, and "Yugoslavia." The February 2002 list of countries actually barred the following countries from voting in the GA: Cape Verde, Central African Republic, Chad, Mauritania, Niger, and Seychelles. The materials in the text summarize some of the subsequent developments in this financial crisis.

Article 19 of the UN Charter provides as follows: "A member of the United Nations which is in arrears in the payment of its financial contributions to the Organization shall have no vote in the General Assembly if the amount of its arrears equals or exceeds the amount of the contributions due from it for the preceding two full years. The General Assembly may, nevertheless, permit such a Member to vote if it is satisfied that the failure to pay is due to conditions beyond the control of the Member." In May 2005, the US Congress first considered its United Nations Reform Act of 2005. The United States would thereby withhold one-half of its assessed dues, if certain reforms were not implemented by the annual payment date of October 1, 2007. *See* Course Web page, Chapter Three.

Three students, or groups, will analyze/debate whether the United States should thus lose its vote in the GA. They will represent: (1) the United States, (2) the United Nations, and (3) US allies which *have* timely paid their assessed dues. Japan and Germany, for example, shoulder (respectively) the greatest financial burdens, other than the United States.

Problem 3.G (after §3.6) Former US General Wesley Clark (and 2004 presidential contender) was the US Supreme Allied Commander in Europe during the 1999 Kosovo bombing campaign by NATO forces. A number of NATO countries actively participated in this military campaign—the first in NATO's history. There was no UN Security Council resolution to authorize this intervention in the former Yugoslavia. US and UK military

forces, acting under the authority of NATO, bombed various parts of Serbia, including Belgrade and Kosovo.

Just as the NATO bombing campaign ended, and before the UN Mission in Kosovo was operational, Russia—a traditional ally of Serbia—dispatched its military forces. They went on a two-day march, from where they were serving under the UN in Sarajevo, Bosnia. At that time, Russia was not associated with NATO's operations in Kosovo. The Russian troops were cheered as saviors by Pristina's Serbian population.

To avoid losing control of Kosovo's main airport to the Russians, General Clark—with the approval of NATO leader Javier Solana—ordered British troops to seize the airport from the small advance contingent of Russian forces who were occupying one end of the airport. Russian planes were in the air, outside of Kosovo, but were refused overflight permission from Hungary and Romania. The UK General, Sir Michael Jackson refused Clark's order, responding that—as General Jackson reportedly said to Clark—"I'm not going to start World War III for you."[119] The Russians later agreed to integrate their forces with NATO's forces in Kosovo.

Assume that, instead, General Jackson followed Clark's order. Many of the 200 Russian troops at the Pristina airfield are killed or wounded. After an intense diplomatic exchange, President Clinton appears to apologize. Russia wishes to use this incident, however, as a tool to focus global attention on this (hypothetical augmentation of the actual) event. Russia and the United States agree to an international arbitration. Russia pursues not only the United States and the United Kingdom as defendants, but also NATO.

Five students are the arbitrators, chosen as follows: one by Russia; one by the United States/United Kingdom; one by NATO; one from a nation that refused the Russian overflights to get to the Kosovo airport; and the UN's Legal Officer. Drawing upon the materials, especially in §3.1 and §3.6 of this chapter, the arbitrators will address the following questions in their debate: Is NATO *independently* responsible for the death/wounding of the Russian soldiers? Should liability, if any, instead be limited to the United States and United Kingdom? Should NATO, the United Kingdom, and the United States *all* be liable? What percentage of fault should be attributed to NATO, the United States, the United Kingdom, and/or Russia? Can NATO claim that it is immune from any liability for this incident? Would it be wise for NATO to *waive* any potential claim of immunity. One purpose might be to establish a leading role, whereby a major international organization would thereby accept the consequences of its members' actions—given the potential arbitral finding of organizational responsibility.

◆ BIBLIOGRAPHY

§3.1 Legal Personality

P. Bekker, THE LEGAL POSITION OF INTERGOVERNMENTAL ORGANIZATIONS: A FUNCTIONAL NECESSITY ANALYSIS OF THEIR LEGAL STATUS AND IMMUNITIES (Dordrecht, Neth.: Martinus Nijhoff, 1994)

W. Feld, R. Jordan, & L. Hurwitz, INTERNATIONAL ORGANIZATIONS: A COMPARATIVE APPROACH (3d ed. Westport, CT: Praeger, 1994)

R. Foot, S. MacFarlane & M. Mastanduno (ed.), US HEGEMONY AND INTERNATIONAL ORGANIZATIONS (Oxford, Eng.: Oxford Univ. Press, 2003)

F. Kirgis, INTERNATIONAL ORGANIZATIONS IN THEIR LEGAL SETTING (2d ed. St. Paul: West, 1993)

M. Martinez, NATIONAL SOVEREIGNTY AND INTERNATIONAL ORGANIZATIONS (The Hague: Kluwer, 1996)

M. Mendelson, The Definition of 'International Organization' in the International Law Commission's Current Project on the Responsibility of International Organizations, Ch. 32, in M. Ragazzi (ed.), INTERNATIONAL RESPONSIBILITY TODAY: ESSAYS IN MEMORY OF OSCAR SCHACHTER 371(Leiden, Neth.: Martinus Nijhoff, 2005)

D. Sarooshi, INTERNATIONAL ORGANIZATIONS AND THEIR EXERCISE OF SOVEREIGN POWERS (Oxford, Eng.: Oxford Univ. Press, 2005)

§3.2 Classification of Organizations

M. Bertrand & D. Warner (ed.), A NEW CHARTER FOR A WORLDWIDE ORGANIZATION? (The Hague: Kluwer Law Int'l, 1997)

V. Essien, International Organizations: A Selected Bibliography, 10 FORDHAM INT'L LAW J. 857 (1987 Supplement)

Persons Other than States as Subjects of International Law, in R. Jennings & A. Watts, 1 OPPENHEIM'S INTERNATIONAL LAW (Part I) §7, at 18–22 (9th ed. Essex, Eng.: Longman, 1993)

§3.3 United Nations

GENERALLY

A. Bennett, HISTORICAL DICTIONARY OF THE UNITED NATIONS (Lanham, MD: Scarecrow, 1995)

S. Bailey & S. Daws, THE PROCEDURE OF THE UN SECURITY COUNCIL (3d ed. Oxford, Eng.: Clarendon Press, 1998)

B. Conforti, THE LAW AND PRACTICE OF THE UNITED NATIONS (3d ed. The Hague, Neth.: Brill, 2005)

G. Dirks et al., STATE OF THE UNITED NATIONS, 1993: NORTH-SOUTH PERSPECTIVES (Providence, RI: Acad. Council on UN System, 1993)

R. Gregg, ABOUT FACE: THE UNITED STATES AND THE UNITED NATIONS (Boulder, CO: Lynne Reinner, 1993)

C. Joyner (ed.), THE UNITED NATIONS AND INTERNATIONAL LAW (Cambridge, Eng.: Cambridge Univ. Press, 1997)

R. Keohane, Governance in a Partially Globalized World, 95 AMER. POL. SCI. REV. 1 (2001)

M. Marin-Bosch, VOTES IN THE UN GENERAL ASSEMBLY (The Hague, Neth.: Kluwer, 1998)

K. Wellens (ed.), RESOLUTIONS AND STATEMENTS OF THE UNITED NATIONS SECURITY COUNCIL (1946–1992): A THEMATIC GUIDE (2d ed. Dordrecht, Neth.: Martinus Nijhoff, 1993)

R. Wells, PEACE BY PIECES—UNITED NATIONS AGENCIES AND THEIR ROLES: A READER AND BIBLIOGRAPHY (Metuchen, NJ: Scarecrow Press, 1991)

YEARBOOK OF THE UNITED NATIONS: (NY: UN) (annually published & cumulative CD version available)

REFORM

A. Abass, REGIONAL ORGANISATIONS AND THE DEVELOPMENT OF COLLECTIVE SECURITY: BEYOND CHAPTER VIII OF THE UN CHARTER (Oxford, Eng.: Hart, 2004)

B. Bourantonis & J. Weiner (ed.), THE UNITED NATIONS IN THE NEW WORLD ORDER: THE WORLD ORGANIZATION AT FIFTY (New York: St. Martin's Press, 1995)

B. Fassbender, UN SECURITY COUNCIL REFORM AND THE RIGHT OF VETO: A CONSTITUTIONAL PERSPECTIVE (The Hague, Neth: Kluwer, 1998)

H. Kelsen, THE LAW OF THE UNITED NATIONS: A CRITICAL ANALYSIS OF ITS FUNDAMENTAL PROBLEMS (New York: Praeger Press, 1950)

Report of the High-level Panel on Threats, Challenges and Change–A More Secured World: Our Shared Responsibility, 4 CHINESE J. INT'L L. 303 (2005)

D. Schweigman, THE AUTHORITY OF THE SECURITY COUNCIL UNDER CHAPTER VII OF THE UN CHARTER: LEGAL LIMITS AND THE ROLE OF THE INTERNATIONAL COURT OF JUSTICE (The Hague: Kluwer, 2001)

D. Sarooshi, THE UNITED NATIONS AND THE DEVELOPMENT OF COLLECTIVE SECURITY: THE DELEGATION BY THE UN SECURITY COUNCIL OF ITS CHAPTER VII POWERS (Oxford, Eng.: Oxford Univ. Press, 1999).

UN, UN MILLENNIUM DEVELOPMENT LIBRARY (14 Volume Set) (NY, UN: 2005) (focusing on overcoming poverty and achieving human development objectives)

§3.4 European Union

G. Berman et al., CASES AND MATERIALS ON EUROPEAN UNION LAW (2d ed. St. Paul, MN: WestGroup, 2002)

R. Creech, LAW AND LANGUAGE IN THE EUROPEAN UNION: THE PARADOX OF A BABEL "UNITED IN DIVERSITY" (Groningen, Neth: Europa Law Pub, 2005)

R. Frid, THE RELATIONS BETWEEN THE EC AND INTERNATIONAL ORGANIZATIONS: LEGAL THEORY AND PRACTICE (The Hague, Neth.: Kluwer, 1995)

R. Folsom, EUROPEAN UNION LAW IN A NUTSHELL (4th ed. St. Paul, MN: Thompson/West, 2004)

A. Kellerman, EU ENLARGEMENT: THE CONSTITUTIONAL IMPACT AT EU AND NATIONAL LEVEL (The Hague: TMC Asser Press, 2001)

W. Nicoll & T. Salmon, UNDERSTANDING THE NEW EUROPEAN COMMUNITY (New York: Harvester/Wheatsheaf, 1994)

A. Levasseur, R. Scott & A. Togoussidou-Meletis, THE LAW OF THE EUROPEAN UNION: A NEW CONSTITUTIONAL ORDER (Durham, NC: Carolina Acad. Press, 2005)

A. Toth, THE OXFORD ENCYCLOPAEDIA OF EUROPEAN COMMUNITY LAW (Oxford, Eng.: Clarendon Press, 1990)

§3.5 Other Organizations

S. Ali, THE INTERNATIONAL ORGANIZATIONS AND WORLD ORDER DICTIONARY (Santa Barbara, CA: ABC CLIO, 1992)

A. Bloed (ed.), THE CONFERENCE ON SECURITY AND COOPERATION IN EUROPE: BASIC DOCUMENTS, 1993–1995 (The Hague, Neth.: Martinus Nijhoff, 1997)

F. Kirgis, INTERNATIONAL ORGANIZATIONS IN THEIR LEGAL SETTING (2d ed. St. Paul: West, 1993)

G. Naldi (ed.), DOCUMENTS OF THE ORGANIZATION OF AFRICAN UNITY (London: Mainsail, 1992)

M. Pinto, Asian-African Legal Consultative Committee Annual Survey of Activities 1996–1997 in K. Sik, M. Pinto & S. Subedi, 7 ASIAN YEARBOOK OF INT'L LAW 345 (The Hague: Kluwer Law Int'l, 2001)

O. Stoetzer, The ORGANIZATION OF AMERICAN STATES (2d ed. Westport, CT: Praeger, 1993)

M. Schachter, HISTORICAL DICTIONARY OF INTERNATIONAL ORGANIZATIONS (Lanham, MD: Scarecrow, 1998)

§3.6 Organizational Immunity

C. Amerasinghe, Privileges and Immunities, ch. 10, in PRINCIPLES OF THE INSTITUTIONAL LAW OF INTERNATIONAL ORGANIZATIONS (2d ed Cambridge, Eng.: Cambridge Univ. Press, 2005)

M. Scharf, Privileges and Immunities, ch. IV (Inviolability) and V (Right of Entry), in THE LAW OF INTERNATIONAL ORGANIZATIONS: PROBLEMS AND MATERIALS 149 & 199 (Durham, NC: Carolina, 2001)

Additional Internet Resources

N. Blokker & R. Wessel, INTERNATIONAL ORGANIZATIONS LAW REVIEW: <http://www.brill.nl/m_catalogue_sub6_id21691.htm> (1st volume 2004, also in print)

European Research Papers Archive: <http://www.wu-wien.ac.at/erpa>

European Union Treaties: <http://europa.eu.int/eur-lex/en/treaties/dat/treaties_en.pdf>

Global Rights, Using the Inter-American System for Human Rights: A Practical Guide for NGOs:

Repertoire of the Practice of the Security Council: <http://www.un.org/Depts/dpa/repertoire/index.html#1946-1951>

UN Official Documents: <http://documents.un.org>, click Welcome, then Search

◆ ENDNOTES

1. A classic analysis of the terms "international" and "organization," as well as the distinctions between those terms, is provided in Definitions and History, ch. 1 in C. Archer, INTERNATIONAL ORGANIZATIONS (2d ed. London: Routledge, 1992) [hereinafter *Archer*].

2. *See,* e.g., M. Karns & K. Mingst, Nonstate Actors: NGOs, Networks, and Social Movements, ch. 6 in INTERNATIONAL ORGANIZATIONS: THE POLITICS OF GLOBAL GOVERNANCE, at 211 (Boulder, CO: Rienner, 2004).

3. *See* W. Slomanson, Civil Actions Against Interpol: A Field Compass, 57 TEMPLE LAW QUARTERLY 553 (1984).

4. *Ethnic* conflict: M. Esman & S. Telhami (ed.), INTERNATIONAL ORGANIZATIONS AND ETHNIC CONFLICT (Ithaca, NY: Cornell Univ. Press, 1995). *Military* conflict: H. McCoubrey & N. White, INTERNATIONAL ORGANIZATIONS AND CIVIL WARS (Aldershot, Eng.: Dartmouth Pub., 1995).

5. H. Schermers & N. Blokker, INTERNATIONAL INSTITUTIONAL LAW §33, at 26 (4th rev. ed. Leiden, Neth.: Brill, 2003).

6. Id., §§33-45, at 27–37.

7. Further details on the resolutions and related events are provided in R. Lapidoth & M. Hirsch (eds.), THE ARAB-ISRAELI CONFLICT AND ITS RESOLUTION: SELECTED DOCUMENTS 71 (Dordrecht, Neth.: Martinus Nijhoff, 1992).

8. Further details on these matters are available in 8 M. Whiteman, DIGEST OF INTERNATIONAL LAW 742 (Wash., DC: US Gov't Print. Off., 1967).

9. The US recognition legislation was the International Organizations Immunities Act, 59 STAT. 669, 22 USCA §§288(a)–(f).

10. Balfour, Guthrie & Co. v. United States, 90 Fed. Supp. 831, 832–833 (1950).

11. A. Reinisch, Do National Courts Provide an Appropriate Forum for Disputes Involving International Organizations? ch. 6 in INTERNATIONAL ORGANIZATIONS BEFORE NATIONAL COURTS, at 318–319 (Cambridge, Eng.: Cambridge Univ. Press, 2004).

12. Ford Foundation, INTERNATIONAL ORGANIZATIONS AND LAW 5 & 8 (New York: Ford Found., 1990).

13. A. Panyarachun (Chair), I Different Worlds 1945 and 2005, in A More Secure World: Our Shared Responsibility—Report of the United Nation's High-Level Panel on Threats, Challenges and Change, UN DOC. A/59/65 (italics added), available at <www.un.org/secureworld>, click Document [hereinafter High-Level Panel Report].

14. *ICJ:* Legality of the Use of Force (Yugoslavia v. Belgium), General List No. 105 (1999), proceedings available at <http://www.icj-cij.org/icjwww/idecisions.htm>. *ECHR:* Bankovic and Others v. Belgium and 16 other Contracting States, application no. 52207/99, §§ 14–27, ECHR 2001-XII, proceedings available at <http://www.echr.coe.int>.

15. G. Gaja, Special Rapporteur, General Rule on Attribution of Conduct to an International Organization, Art. 4, ILC Second Report on Responsibility of International

Organizations, ¶28.1, at 14, UN Doc. No. A/CN.4/541 (2004).

16. P. Sands & P. Klein, Bowett's Law of International Institutions, 16–19 (5th ed. London: Sweet & Maxwell, 2001).

17. N. White, Theories of International Organisation, ch. 1 in The Law of International Organisations 1–22 (Manchester, Eng.: Manchester Univ. Press, 1997).

18. Classification of International Organizations, ch. 2 in *Archer,* 38 (cited in note 1 above).

19. The host site for many of AI's constituencies is <http://www.amnesty.org>. This site links to numerous online reports, programs, and video presentations about AI's worldwide programs.

20. Protocols Additional to the Geneva Conventions of 12 August 1949 (Geneva: Int'l Comm. Red Cross, 1977).

21. NAFTA text: <http://www.nafta-sec-alena.org/english/index.htm> (click NAFTA).

22. *Indictment:* U.S. v. Moussaoui, 2003 Westlaw 1877700 (E.D.Va., 2003) (from original indictment). *Web page:* <http://www.fas.org/irp/world/para/docs/980223-fatwa.htm>. Originally published in the Arabic Newspaper al-Quds.al-Arabi (London), Feb. 23, 1998, at 3. Available at Cornell's Mid-East Web site: <http://www.library.cornell.edu/colldev/mideast/fatw2.htm>. *Further details:* Y. Alexander & M. Swetnam, Usama bin Laden's Al-Qaida: Profile of a Terrorist Network (Ardsley, NY: Transnat'l, 2001).

23. United Nations Millennium Declaration, UN Doc A/55/L.2 (Sept. 6, 2000) (Heads of State Summit at UN HQ in New York), available at: <http://www.unitednations.org.uk/info/millenniumdec.html>.

24. Succinct but authoritative histories are available in League of Nations, E. Osmanczyk, Encyclopedia of the United Nations and International Agreements 511–516 (2d ed. London: Taylor & Francis, 1990) [hereinafter *UN Encyclopedia*] and Y. Choue (ed.), World Encyclopedia of Peace 177 (2d ed. Seoul, Korea: Jin Wang Kim Pub., 1999) (Vol. 3). For the most scholarly studies, *see* F. Walters, A History of the League of Nations (London: Oxford Univ. Press, 1952); A. Zimmern, The League of Nations and the Rule of Law 1918–1935 (London: MacMillan, 1936). For illustrated histories, see G. Ostrower, The League of Nations from 1919–1929 & G. Gill, The League of Nations from 1929–1946 (Garden City Park, NY: Avery Pub. Group, 1996) (two volumes in same series).

25. *First Point: see* 2 Selected Literary and Political Papers and Addresses of Woodrow Wilson (New York: Grosset & Dunlap, 1952) for Wilson's "Fourteen Points" speech. *Text:* <http://www.unog.ch/library/archives/lon/lbryfset.html>, click "Library Documents," then click "The League of Nations Covenant."

26. For a contemporary expression of this concern, *see* H. Jacobson, W. Reisinger, & T. Mathers, National Entanglements in International Governmental Organizations, 80 Amer. Pol. Sci. Rev. 141 (1986).

27. *See generally,* T. Hoopes & D. Brinkley, FDR and the Creation of the U.N. (New Haven, CT: Yale Univ. Press, 1997) and A. Yoder, The Birth of the United Nations, Ch. 3,

in The Evolution of the United Nations System 27 (2d ed. Wash., D.C.: Taylor & Francis, 1993).

28. For a detailed analysis of the evolution of each article, see B. Simma (ed.), The Charter of the United Nations: A Commentary (2d ed. Oxford, Eng.: Oxford Univ. Press, 2002) [hereinafter *Simma*].

29. *Historical committee structure:* B. Finley, The Structure of the United Nations General Assembly: Its Committees, Commissions, and Other Organisms: 1974–1980s (White Plains, NY: Kraus Int'l, 1988). *1993 committee reorganization:* Schaff, More Organizational Changes at the UN, 22 Int'l J. Legal Info. 199 (1994). Further details about these committees are available on the GA Web site at <http://www.un.org/ga/55>.

30. M. Shaw, International Law 1090 (5th ed. Cambridge, Eng.: Grotius, 2003) (italics added).

31. CCR, A U.N. Alternative to War: "Uniting for Peace," available at: <http://ccr-ny.org/v2/whatsnew/report.asp?ObjID=OhZHHegENn&Content=186>, click Uniting for Peace Viewpoint. For draft letter to be sent by activists, to lobby their nation's UN representative to convene what would have been the eleventh such resolution to use this device, click Draft Letter to Secretary-General.

32. K. Skubiszewski, The United Nations General Assembly and Its Power to Influence National Action, in Proceedings and Committee Reports of the American Branch of the International Law Association 1964 Annual Meeting 153–154 (1964).

33. V. Rittberger, International Conference Diplomacy: A Conspectus, M. Boisard & E. Chossudovsky (ed.), Multilateral Diplomacy: The United Nations System at Geneva—A Working Guide 15, at 19 (2d rev. ed. The Hague: Kluwer, 1998).

34. M. J. Peterson, The General Assembly in World Politics 2–3 (Boston: Unwin Hyman, 1990).

35. Article 9 of the Japanese Constitution bars the maintenance of "war potential." *See* generally W. Slomanson, Judicial Review of War Renunciation in the Naganuma Nike Case: Juggling the Constitutional Crisis in Japan, 9 Cornell Int'l L.J. 24 (1975). Articles 26 and 87(a) of the former West German Constitution banned the use of military forces for other than defensive purposes. Germany sent peacekeeping troops to Somalia, and Japan has contributed financially to UN peacekeeping operations.

36. *2004 SC Panel: see* Farah Stockman, UN Panel to Recommend Security Council Expansion, Boston Globe (November 28, 2004 web version). *Decade of failure: see* B. Fassbender, All Illusions Shattered? Looking Back on a Decade of Failed Attempts to Reform the UN Security Council, in A. Bogdandy & R. Wolfrum (ed.), 7 Max Planck Yearbook of United Nations Law 183 (Leiden, Neth.: Martinus Nijhoff, 2004).

37. *East Timor: see* N. Azimi & Chang Li Lin, The United Nations Transitional Administration in East Timor (Leiden, Neth.: Martinus Nijhoff, 2003). *Kosovo: see* International Crisis Group (Brussels), Kosovo After Haradinaj: Europe Report N° 163 (May 2005), available at <http://www

.crisisgroup.org/home/index.cfm>, click <u>Kosovo After Haradinaj</u> for Executive Summary and Full Report.

38. *High-Level Panel* (cited in note 13), at 61–62.

39. Anjali Patil, THE UN VETO IN WORLD AFFAIRS 1946–1990: A COMPLETE RECORD AND CASE HISTORIES OF THE SECURITY COUNCIL'S VETO (Sarasota, FL: UNIFO Pub., 1992).

40. *See, e.g.*, ECOSOC, Commission on Narcotic Drugs Report of the Thirty-Sixth Session, UN DOC. E/CN.7/1993/12/ REV.1, SUPP. No. 9 (Vienna: UN, 1994). Basic details on the scope of this agency's work is available on the UN Web site at <www.un.org/esa>. Click Index to see all of the ECOSOC programs.

41. ECOSOC Home Page <http://www.un.org/esa/ coordination/ecosoc>, click <u>Overview</u>.

42. Further details are available in E. Sciolino, First Lady, in Paris, Oversees U.S. Return to UNESCO, NYT on the Web (Sept. 29, 2003).

43. *Termination not a bar to subsequent proceedings:* Certain Phosphate Lands in Nauru (Nauru v. Australia), ICJ Communiqué No. 92/18 (Judgment on Preliminary Objections of June 26, 1992). *Dismissal as a result of settlement:* ICJ Communiqué No. 93/29 (Sept. 13, 1993) (whereby issues will never be publicly adjudicated). A book-length treatment of this subject is available in C. Weeramantry, NAURU: ENVIRONMENTAL DAMAGE UNDER INTERNATIONAL TRUSTEESHIP (Melbourne: Oxford Univ. Press, 1992).

44. Morgan Guarantee Trust v. Republic of Palau, 924 Fed.Rptr.2d 1237 (2d Cir. 1991).

45. B. Boutros-Ghali, SUPPLEMENT TO AN AGENDA FOR PEACE: POSITION PAPER OF THE SECRETARY-GENERAL ON THE OCCASION OF THE FIFTIETH ANNIVERSARY OF THE UNITED NATIONS 9 (2d ed. New York: UN, 1995) [hereinafter *Agenda for Peace Supplement*].

46. B. Boutros-Ghali, AN AGENDA FOR PEACE: PREVENTATIVE DIPLOMACY, PEACEMAKING, AND PEACEKEEPING 21–22 (New York: UN, 1992) [hereinafter *Agenda for Peace*].

47. T. Boudreau, SHEATHING THE SWORD: THE U.N. SECRETARY-GENERAL AND THE PREVENTION OF INTERNATIONAL CONFLICT 105–106 (New York: Greenwood Press, 1991).

48. *See Simma*, 760–763 (cited in note 28 above).

49. *UN Governance:* R. Wedgewood & H. Jacobson (ed.), Symposium: State Reconstruction After Civil Conflict, 95 AMER. J. INT'L L. 1–119 (2001), especially, M. Matheson, United Nations Governance of Postconflict Societies, at 76. UN Peacebuilding: see details at: <http://www.un.org/peace/ *peacebuilding*>.

50. *See* Department of Public Information, YEARBOOK OF THE UNITED NATIONS 1999 [53rd annual volume of organizational activities] (New York: UN, 2002) & *UN Encyclopedia* (cited in note 24 above).

51. *See* N. Jasentuliyana, The Lawmaking Process in the United Nations, ch. 3, in N. Jasentuliyana (ed.), SPACE LAW: DEVELOPMENT AND SCOPE 33 (Westport, CT: Praeger, 1992); C. Christol, The Moon Treaty Enters into Force, 79 AMER. J. INT'L L. 163 (1985).

52. A. Prandler, The Unchanging Significance of the United Nations Charter and Some International Legal Aspects of Its Application, in H. Bokor-Szego (ed.), QUESTIONS OF INTERNATIONAL LAW, at 192–93 (Dordrecht, Neth.: Martinus Nijhoff, 1986) (italics deleted).

53. *See, e.g.,* E. Van Den Haag & J. Conrad, THE U.N. IN OR OUT: A DEBATE (New York: Plenum Press, 1988); T. Franck, NATION AGAINST NATION: WHAT HAPPENED TO THE U.N. DREAM AND WHAT THE US CAN DO ABOUT IT (New York: Oxford Univ. Press, 1985).

54. Heritage Foundation, Introduction to A World Without a United Nations: What Would Happen If the United Nations Were Shut Down, at III.11/8, in J. Muller (ed.), REFORMING THE UNITED NATIONS: NEW INITIATIVES AND PAST EFFORTS (Dordrecht, Neth.: Kluwer, 1997) (three volumes) [hereinafter *Reforming the UN*].

55. *High-Level Panel Report* (cited in note 13 above), para. 11, at 18 (bolding deleted).

56. C. Joyner, Conclusion: The United Nations as International Law-Giver 432–433, ch. 16, in C. Joyner (ed.), THE UNITED NATIONS AND INTERNATIONAL LAW (Cambridge, Eng.: Cambridge Univ. Press, 1997).

57. N.Y. Times, Sept. 17, 1986, at 3 (Choudhury's opening statement to Assembly's 41st session in New York).

58. Prominent contemporary studies are available in J. Miller (ed.), REFORMING THE UNITED NATIONS: THE QUIET REVOLUTION (Hague: Kluwer Law Int'l, 2001 (1996–2000); Secretary-General's 1992 and 1995 proposals in *Agenda for Peace* and *Supplement* (cited in notes 45 & 46 above]; *Reforming the UN* (cited in note 54 above]; B. Urquhart & E. Childers, RENEWING THE UNITED NATIONS SYSTEM (New York: Ford Found., 1994); S. Ogata et al., FINANCING AN EFFECTIVE UNITED NATIONS: A REPORT OF THE INDEPENDENT ADVISORY GROUP ON U.N. FINANCING (New York: Ford Found., 1993); and J. Leach et al., FINAL REPORT OF THE UNITED STATES COMMISSION ON IMPROVING THE EFFECTIVENESS OF THE UNITED NATIONS (Wash., DC: US Gov't Print. Off., 1993).

59. The defendant in the *Karadzic* case, in §1.4 of this book, is one of the individuals allegedly most responsible for this massacre of some 8,000 Muslim boys and men. A video depicting one of the events in this worst genocide since World War II was used in the Netherlands, May 2005 trial of former Yugoslavian President Milosevic—to provide further evidence of its existence. The Dutch government fell, as a result of its peacekeepers failing to stop this massacre. The comparative speed with which this massacre occurred (only several days) would normally militate against blaming the UN—but for the irony that it occurred in a UN safe haven, to which these Muslims flocked during the Bosnian war.

60. *High-Level Panel* (cited in note 13), at 8–10 (table of contents).

61. *Id.,* at 56–57 (bolding deleted).

62. *Legal Advisor:* H. Hansell, Memo. of Aug. 7, 1978, reprinted in 1979 DIGEST OF UNITED STATES PRACTICE IN INTERNATIONAL LAW 225, 226 (Wash., DC: US Gov't Print. Off., 1983). *Art. 17.2:* The expenses of the Organization shall be borne by the Members as apportioned by the General Assembly. *ICJ case:* Certain Expenses of the United Nations, 1962 ICJ REP. 168. An illustrative analysis of these points is

available in E. Zoller, The "Corporate Will" of the United Nations and the Rights of the Minority, 81 Amer. J. Int'l L. 610 (1987).

63. H.R. 2535, 104th Cong., Oct. 25, 1995, introduced by Rep. Scarborough. Web version at <http://thomas.loc.gov/cgi-bin/query/z?c104:H.R.2535:>.

64. *See, e.g.,* Report of the Secretary-General: Administrative and Budgetary Aspects of the Financing of the United Nations Peacekeeping Operations, U.N. Doc. A/51/389 (1996), reprinted in 37 Int'l Legal Mat'ls 700 (1998).

65. Sean D. Murphy, Contemporary Practice of the United States Relating to International Law, 94 Amer. J. Int'l L. 348 (2000).

66. For a related report by the President to the Congress, see 22 U.S. Code §287b(c)(3) (2002).

67. *Story:* See N. Wadhams, Bill Would Tie U.S. Dues to U.N. Reform, Associated Press (May 20, 2005) & U.N. Warms Against Linking Dies to U.N. Reform, Associated Press (May 21, 2005), available at: <http://cbn.com/cbnnews/Wire/050520d.asp>. *US UN Reform Act:* <http://www.govtrack.us/congress/billtext.xpd?bill=h109-2745>. *Scaled-back result:* see W. Hoge, Envoys Reach Compromise on Scaled-Back U.N. Reform Plans, NYT on the web (Sept. 13, 2005).

68. *UN Reform Act:* Perhaps the best reporting on this event is the two-part series by the Washington Times, The U.N. Oil for Food Scandal (Mar. 22–23, 2004), available at <www.washingtontimes.com>. See also CNN, Whistle-blower: 'Gaping Holes' in Oil-for Food (Mar. 17, 2005), available at <http://www.cnn.com>, search "Whistle-blower." TASK Force Report: see Task Force on the United Nations, available at <http://www.usip.org/un/index.html>. *UN Panel Report:* <http://www.iic-offp.org/Mgmt_Report.htm>.

69. J. Klabbers, Presumptive Personality: The European Union in International Law, ch. 14, in M. Koskenniemi (ed.), International Law Aspects of the European Union 231 (Hague: Martinus Nijhoff, 1998).

70. *EU website:* The History of the European Union: A chronology from 1946 to 2001, <http://europa.eu.int/abc/history/index_en.htm>. *Texts:* P. Craig & G. de Burca, The Development of European Integration, ch. 1 in EC Law: Text, Cases & Materials (Oxford, Eng.: Clarendon Press, 1995) & The History of the European Community, ch. 1 in G. Berrmann et al., Cases and Materials on European Union Law 3 (2d ed. St. Paul: West, 2002).

71. Available at: <http://europa.eu.int/en/record/mt/final.html>. The various EU treaties are available on the EU's Web site at <http://europa.eu.int/abc/treaties_en.htm>.

72. The 1975 "Lome I" Treaty and related documents are available in 14 INT'L LEGAL MAT'LS 595 (1975). The "Lome II" Treaties are available in 19 Int'l Legal Mat'ls 327 (1980). The 1984 modifications are available in 24 Int'l Legal Mat'ls 571 (1985) ("Lome III" Final Act). The 1989 Lome IV Agreement, joining sixty-nine States in an association with the Community, is reprinted in 29 Int'l Legal Mat'ls 783 (1990).

73. Treaty of Nice Amending the Treaty on European Union, The Treaties Establishing the European Communities And Certain Related Acts at: <http://www.nicetreatyonline.com/treatytext.htm>.

74. Treaty Establishing a Constitution For Europe, available on the European Union Web site at: <http://europa.eu.int/constitution/print_en.htm>.

75. *See, e.g.,* The generally positive essays contained in the two volumes of T. Tridimas & P. Nebbia, European Union Law for the Twenty-first Century (Oxford, Eng.: Hart, 2004).

76. J. Weiler, A Constitution for Europe?: Some Hard Choices, ch. 2, in G. Bermann & K. Pistor (ed.), Law and Governance in an Enlarged European Union 40 (Oxford, Eng.: Hart, 2004).

77. For an elaborate analysis of the negative aspects of European integration, *see* G. Harris, The Dark Side of Europe (2d ed. New York: Columbia Univ. Press, 1994) (written by a member of the European Parliament's Secretariat).

78. An analysis of the French position is available in E. Stein & D. Carreau, Law and Peaceful Change in a Subsystem: Withdrawal of France from NATO, 62 Amer. J. Int'l L. 577 (1968). Albania withdrew from the Warsaw Pact in 1968 after the Soviet invasion of Czechoslovakia.

79. 1994 Partnership for Peace Framework Document, para. 2, in NATO Online Library, at <http://www.nato.int/docu/comm/49-95/c940110b.htm>.

80. A Common Europe—Partners in Stability: Speeches by the Secretary General of NATO, reprinted in Change and Continuity in the North Atlantic Alliance 191–195 (Brussels: NATO, 1990).

81. Colin McMahon, Putin Calls for NATO to Change or Dissolve, Chicago Tribune, at A19, July 19, 2001.

82. *See* Russian-Chinese Joint Declaration on a Multipolar World and the Establishment of a New International Order, adopted in Moscow on 23 April 1997, available at <http://www.fas.org/news/russia/1997/a52—153en.htm>.

83. In addition to its six Mediterranean Partners for Co-operation, the OSCE maintains a special relationship with Japan, the Republic of Korea and Thailand. See program description at: <http://www.osce.org/ec/partners/cooperation/ partners/>.

84. *Parliament:* Final Resolution of the Madrid Conference Concerning the Establishment of the CSCE Parliamentary Assembly, 30 Int'l Legal Mat'ls 1344 (1991). *Arms:* Prague Document on Further Development of CSCE Institutions and Structures and Declaration on Non-Proliferation and Arms Transfers, 31 Int'l Legal Mat'ls 978 (1992).

85. *See* S. Croft (ed.), The Conventional Armed Forces in Europe Treaty: The Cold War Endgame (Aldershot, Eng.: Dartmouth Pub., 1994).

86. *See, e.g.,* P. van Djik, The Final Act of Helsinki: Basis for Pan-European System?, 1980 Netherlands Yearbook Int'l Law 110.

87. General Introduction, Victor-Yves Ghebali & A. Lambert, The OSCE Code of Conduct on Politico-Military Aspects of Security 1 (Leiden, Neth.: Brill, 2005)

[hereinafter *OSCE Code*]. This Code is also available on the OSCE Web site, at: <http://www.OSCE.org/item/4256.html>.

88. See generally *High-Level Panel Report* (cited in note 13 above].

89. *OSCE Code* (cited in note 87 above], at 28.

90. *1996:* Declaration on a Common and Comprehensive Security Model for Europe for the Twenty-First Century, 36 INT'L LEGAL MAT'LS 486 (1997). *1997:* Guidelines on an OSCE Document-Charter on European Security, 37 INT'L LEGAL MAT'LS 693 (1998). *1999:* OSCE Istanbul Charter For European Security. See generally OSCE 1975–2000 HANDBOOK (3d ed. Vienna: OSCE, 2000).

91. *Minsk Declaration: see* UN Doc. A/46/771 (1991), reprinted in 31 INT'L LEGAL MAT'LS 138 (1992). *Protocol:* 31 INT'L LEGAL MAT'LS 142 (1992). The various documents are reprinted in W. Butler, BASIC LEGAL DOCUMENTS OF THE RUSSIAN FEDERATION (New York: Oceana, 1992).

92. Meeting of Consultation of Ministers of Foreign Affairs of Jan. 31, 1962, reported in 46 US DEP'T STATE BULL. 281, No. 1182 (1962).

93. Article 21, League of Nations Covenant, available at: <http://history.acusd.edu/gen/text/versaillestreaty/ver001.html>.

94. Article 3.1, Inter-American Treaty of Reciprocal Assistance, 21 U.N.T.S. 243, 62 US STAT. 1681.

95. For further details, *see* M. Gorina-Ysern, OAS Mediates in Belize-Guatemala Border Dispute, ASIL Insight (December 2000), available at: <http://www.asil.org/insights.htm>.

96. The text of the constitutive agreement is reprinted in 39 AMER. J. INT'L L. 266 (1945). A commentary is available in Khadduri, The Arab League as a Regional Arrangement, 40 AMER. J. INTL L. 756 (1946).

97. Arab League Statement to UN Security Council Condemning US Bombing in Sudan, UN DOC. S/1998/789, dated August 21, 1998.

98. Available at: <http://www.oic-oci.org>.

99. G. Naldi, THE ORGANIZATION OF AFRICAN UNITY: AN ANALYSIS OF ITS ROLE 3 (London: Mainsail, 1989).

100. *See* Current Developments: The New African Union and its Constitutive Act, 96 AMER. J. INTL LAW 365 (2002); N. Udombana, The Institutional Structure of the African Union: A Legal Analysis, 33 CALIF. WEST. INT'L L.J. 69 (2002); and T. Maluwa, The OAU/African Union and International Law: Mapping New Boundaries or Revising Old Terrain?, in PROCEEDINGS OF THE 98th ANNUAL MEETING OF THE AMERICAN SOCIETY OF INTERNATIONAL LAW 232 (2004).

101. H. McCoubrey & N. White, PEACEKEEPING BY OTHER INTERNATIONAL ORGANIZATIONS, IN INTERNATIONAL ORGANIZATIONS AND CIVIL WARS 186–187 (Aldershot, Eng.: Dartmouth Pub., 1995).

102. This was the Economic Community of West African States (ECOWAS) force known as "ECOMOG". Regarding this economic community, *see generally* T. Shaw & J. Okolo, THE POLITICAL ECONOMY AND FOREIGN POLICY IN ECOWAS (New York: St. Martin's Press, 1994).

103. *See* T. Elias, The Commission of Mediation, Conciliation and Arbitration of the OAU, XL BRIT. YEARBOOK INT'L L. 336 (1964).

104. The treaty is reprinted in 30 INT'L LEGAL MAT'LS 1241 (1991).

105. Resolution on Arrears of Contribution, OAU Resolution 2 RADIO 660, reprinted in G. Knelt (ed.), DOCUMENTS OF THE ORGANIZATION OF AFRICAN UNITY 45 (London: Mainsail, 1992).

106. M. Ragazzi (ed.), INTERNATIONAL RESPONSIBILITY TODAY: ESSAYS IN MEMORY OF OSCAR SCHACHTER (Lieden, Neth.: Brill, 2005).

107. Karel Wellens, Conclusion, REMEDIES AGAINST INTERNATIONAL ORGANIZATIONS 263 & 265 (Cambridge, Eng.: Cambridge Univ. Press, 2002).

108. *Jordanian Report:* A Comprehensive Strategy to Eliminate Future Sexual Exploitation and Abuse in United Nations Peacekeeping Operations, available at: <http://daccess-ods.un.org/TMP/2285858.html>. *Story:* UN News Centre, UN Secretariat and Assembly Must Approve New Rules for UN Peacekeepers (June 9, 2005), available at: <http://www.un.org/apps/news/story.asp?NewsID=13761&Cr=peacekeep& Cr1=>. *Refugees International Report:* Must Boys Be Boys? Ending Sexual Exploitation & Abuse in UN Peacekeeping Missions, Oct. 18, 2005, available at: <http://www.refugeesinternational.org/content/publication/detail/6976>.

109. According Immunity to International Organizations, in A. Reinsch, INTERNATIONAL ORGANIZATIONS BEFORE NATIONAL COURTS at 129 (Cambridge, Eng.: Cambridge Univ. Press, 2000).

110. *Resolution:* Gen. Ass. Res. 22A, 1 Gen. Ass. Off. Records, Supp. at 25, UN Doc. A/64 (1946). *Convention:* 1 U.N.T.S. 15 (1946). Resolution: *Web version* (Univ. Minn.): <http://www1.umn.edu/humanrts/instree/p&i-convention.htm>.

111. *Jordanian incident:* T. Golden, U.S. Expels Two Cuban Diplomats for Spying, Moves to Evict Two More, NYT on the Web (Nov. 7, 2002). *British incident:* F. Kirgis, Alleged Monitoring of United Nations Telephone Calls, ASIL Insight (Mar. 2004), available at: <http://www.asil.org/insights/insigh127.htm>.

112. *Romanian case* (summary): Applicability of Article VI, Section 22, of the Convention on the Privileges and Immunities of the United Nations Advisory Opinion of 15 December 1989. *See* <http://www.icj-cij.org/icjwww/idecisions/isummaries/iecosocsummary891215.htm>. *Malaysian case:* (summary): Difference Relating to Immunity from Legal Process of a Special Rapporteur of the Commission on Human Rights, Advisory Opinion of 29 April 1999. *See* <http://www.icj-cij.org/icjwww/idecisions/isummaries/inumasummary19990429.htm>.

113. Jordanians Probed over Shooting, BBC News (Apr. 19, 2004), available at: <http://news.bbc.co.uk/1/hi/world/europe/3637033.stm>.

114. Art. 2.3 and 2.4, UNMIK/REG/2000/47 On the Status, Privileges and Immunities of KFOR and UNMIK and Their Personnel in Kosovo. See <http://www.unmikonline.org/regulations/2000/reg47-00.htm>.

115. US legislation: International Organizations Immunities Act Section 2(b), 22 USCA §288 (1945) (1979 ed., 59 STATS. 669).

116. C. Haughney, Suit Claims Indentured Servitude, Washington Post, Thursday, Jan. 4, 2001, at A10. *See* <http://washingtonpost.com/wp-dyn/articles/A15283-2001Jan3.html>.

117. European Molecular Biology Laboratory Arbitration, 29 June 1990, 105 INT'L LAW REP. 1, 19–20 (1990).

118. For further details, see *East Timor:* N. Azimi & Chang Li Lin, THE UNITED NATIONS TRANSITIONAL ADMINISTRATION IN EAST TIMOR (Leiden, Neth.: Martinus Nijhoff, 2003) & *Kosovo:* United Nations Interim Administration Mission in Kosovo (UN Web page) at <http://www.unmikonline.org>.

119. One of the few reports—other than on blogs—is available in the British Broadcasting Corporation news story: Wesley Clark's Credentials for Running Against President George Bush Rested Squarely on His Military Reputation, posted by the BBC two years later on Sept. 17, 2003. *See* <http://news.bbc.co.uk/1/hi/world/americas/3110020.stm>. A longer account is available in John Norris, COLLISION COURSE: NATO, RUSSIA AND KOSOVO (Westport, CT: Praeger, 2005).

CHAPTER FOUR

Individuals and Corporations

INTRODUCTION

Prior chapters defined International Law and analyzed the role of the various entities possessing legal capacity to act at the international level. This chapter analyzes the role of the other "player"—natural and corporate persons. Historically, individual citizens played no direct role in shaping the evolution of International Law—a system designed in 1648 to govern the conduct of States in their mutual relations. Although there are significant domestic legal distinctions between individuals and corporations, exploring that level of detail is beyond the scope of this survey course.[1] This chapter's use of the term "individual," generally refers to both people and corporations, unless otherwise indicated.

The first section of Chapter 4 explores the evolution of the individual's international legal personality. The enormous impact of the Nazi Third Reich spawned a robust postwar pressure to create more direct enforcement vehicles for prosecuting and protecting individuals under International Law.

[O]NE OF THE REVOLUTIONARY FEATURES OF the Community legal system is the fact that private parties, as well as the Member States, are subject to EC law. Thus, EC law has gone beyond the boundaries of International Law to produce a direct impact on the rights and obligations of Community Nationals. Accordingly, it was only fair that natural and legal [corporate] persons should be able to obtain a review not only of acts of the Member States, in contravention of EC law but also of acts of Community institutions that could be illegal or disproportionately harmful to their interests.

—A. Albors-Llorens, PRIVATE PARTIES IN EUROPEAN COMMUNITY LAW: CHALLENGING COMMUNITY MEASURES 7–8 (1996).

◆ 4.1 LEGAL PERSONALITY

INDIVIDUAL'S LEGAL CAPACITY

Historical Limitation The British philosopher Jeremy Bentham coined the term "International Law" in his famous treatise of 1789. It articulated the historical perspective that only the State could be governed by International Law because "[t]ransactions which may take place between individuals who are subjects of different states . . . are regulated by the internal laws, and decided upon by the internal tribunals, of the one or the other of these states. . . . There remain then the mutual transactions between sovereigns as such, for the subject of

Soldier Jones Hypothetical

Assume that States X and Y share a common border. State Y forces have been crossing into X from a small remote village in Y near the border. State Y villagers have been assisting State Y military forces by providing them with food and information about troop movements—just on the other side of the border in State X.

Jones is a soldier in the army of State X. His superior officer sends him into State Y on a secret mission designated *Operation Phoenix*. Its objective is to "neutralize" anyone who might help State Y forces cross into State X near the State Y village on this international border. Jones interprets "neutralize" to mean "kill." He kills most of the civilian men, women, and children in the State Y village and escapes back into State X.

The remaining relatives of the slaughtered villagers from State Y want Soldier Jones and State X to pay for this brutal massacre. *Operation Phoenix* undoubtedly violated International Law. This neutralization mission violated the territorial sovereignty of State Y. State X thereby conducted an extraterritorial military operation in State Y without Y's consent. Consider the following questions:

- ◆ Can the State Y relatives directly negotiate with State X? (If you were a Y relative, whose family had been slaughtered by State Y, does this option make sense—even if you could actually determine with whom to meet?)
- ◆ Can the State Y relatives pursue Soldier Jones in a State or international tribunal? Which one? (Would you have the financial resources to pursue this claim? What about the limitation imposed by §2.6 sovereign immunity?)
- ◆ State X has obviously violated International Law. Has Jones? (Who created the current system of International Law—and whose conduct is governed by those norms?)

Other limitations further preclude the villagers from a remedy against either Soldier Jones or State X, which will be analyzed in this section.

---

that branch of jurisprudence which may be properly and exclusively termed international."[2]

For the next two centuries, States would continue to be the essential "subjects" of International Law. They were the legal entities that created this body of rules to govern their relations with each other. Individuals and business entities have historically been the subjects of *national* law. The laws of Morocco, for example, govern the conduct of a person living in Morocco or a foreign corporation doing business in Morocco. If a private Moroccan corporation wants to purchase metal from Germany, it will have to consult the internal law of Morocco for any local import restrictions on German metal. Further, Moroccan law may prohibit that corporation from importing such metal for the purpose of making automatic machine guns. A violation of these laws, applicable to persons and corporations in Morocco, would subject this corporation and its owners to punishment under national law.

Under this historical approach, Soldier Jones would be incapable of violating International Law. He is an individual, not a State. Only State X could incur responsibility for directing him to slaughter the Y villagers. Under Bentham's classical view (and that of certain modern States), individuals lack the required "legal personality" or "legal capacity" to incur responsibility under International Law. Soldier Jones undoubtedly violated the national law of State Y, where he carried out his mission. It was his home State (X) that violated International Law by ordering its agent to carry out *Operation Phoenix*. Jones was acting as an agent of State X. Only X would possess the capacity to incur State responsibility as a legal "person" subject to the rules of International Law.

This perspective prevailed in most countries until World War II. The existence of a direct relationship between the individual and International Law was denied, especially by scholars in socialist countries. Chinese International Law texts published in the 1980s deny that individuals are necessarily the subjects of International Law.[3] One result is that the individual, who is not the subject of International Law, cannot accuse a State of breaching an obligation arising under

International Law. A 1983 study by the East Asian Legal Studies Department of the University of Maryland corroborates this perspective. Thus, the sovereign nature of the State would be effectively diminished by subjecting State power to the scrutiny by an individual. The "[r]ecognition of individual responsibility for personal acts under international law would . . . clash with Marxist principles regarding the class struggle in international relations. Moreover, the Chinese rejection of the concept of individuals as subject[s] of international law is an indisputable repudiation of the . . . conception of law which, by casting individuals in the role of international entities, attempted to circumvent the internal sovereign rule of the state. To the PRC, the only legitimate instrument to ensure the rights of individuals is the nation state."[4]

The Soviet approach presented an alternative. The status of the individual could be acknowledged by International Law, only to the extent that it was expressly recognized by the national law. Otherwise, the UN Charter principles of State sovereignty and freedom from external intervention would be meaningless. The Soviet perspective was that even international organizations, heralding the human rights of the individual, could not circumvent the primacy of the State. Doing so would be tantamount to international interference in the internal affairs of the Soviet Union.

Professor Lung-chu Chen of New York University argues that authoritarian regimes deny individual status in International Law to conveniently serve the totalitarian purposes of those States that govern without legitimate authority. They "will not tolerate their nationals complaining to other state elites or the larger community of mankind [*e.g.*, the UN] about the deprivations within their particular communities."[5]

The Vietnamese government chose not to espouse the claim of its citizens against the US companies that manufactured "Agent Orange." This product was a group of chemicals used by the United States during the Vietnam War to clear jungle foliage to limit enemy concealment and destroy crops, which they could use for food. Some 10,000 US war veterans have received US medical disability benefits, because of their exposure to this herbicide. The United States had no interest, or obligation, to hear the claims of these Vietnamese citizens. Their only recourse was to sue these chemical corporations in a US court. This suit was dismissed in March 2005, on the basis that "[t]here is no basis for any of the claims of plaintiffs under the domestic law of any nation or state or under any form of International Law."[6] In April 2005, the UN Security Council took action on behalf of the victims of the genocide in the Darfur region of the Sudan. Some half million people had been killed, driven away, or otherwise injured by the government-supported militia. These individuals had no recourse against their own government. The Council thus referred this matter to the International Criminal Court (§9.5), naming specific individuals who were to be prosecuted for their human rights violations. The Council also urged the African Union to provide forces to protect the Sudanese victims from further atrocities.

State Representation   What is the practical consequence of the individual's not being able to directly pursue such claims as a plaintiff under International Law? The State enjoys virtually exclusive discretion regarding whether or not to pursue a remedy on the international level. It can lodge a diplomatic claim or institute proceedings in an international tribunal on behalf of its citizens who are harmed by another country. In 1928, the Permanent Court of International Justice (PCIJ) explained that "[r]ights or interests of an individual the violation of which rights causes damage are always in a different plane to rights belonging to a State, which rights may also be infringed by the same act. The damage suffered by an individual is never, therefore, identical in kind with that which will be suffered by a State; it can only afford a convenient scale for the calculation of the reparation due the State [whose citizen has been harmed]."[7]

National law, of course, embraces the discretionary nature of the State to espouse the claims of its citizens. A US court in Florida dismissed such a case on the basis that the judicial branch of government does not have the power to hear such a claim, when it has already been denied by the executive branch. The plaintiff had alleged that her husband was the captain of a cargo ship, traveling from Miami to Montevideo, Uruguay. She claimed that a governor in Brazil arranged for the deceased husband's ship to be hijacked—whereupon agents of the governor tortured her husband. She contended that her husband died from the resulting injuries. She filed this action because she wanted the court to require the US Secretary of State to submit her claim to the Brazilian government. The federal court in Miami dismissed her Petition for *Mandamus* on the basis that it could not require the Department of State to act. In this situation, the US government had complete discretion *not* to pursue this claim against Brazil. In the words of the federal court:

> Mandamus is available only when a government agency has a duty to act on the part of an individual. It is not available to review the discretionary acts of government officials. . . .
>
> The action is, in effect, a demand that the State Department "espouse" Petitioner's claim. Espousal is the assertion of the private claim of United States nationals by the government against another sovereign. The Secretary of State has the discretion to determine whether to espouse a claim.
>
> The Court finds that espousal being a discretionary function, it does not have jurisdiction to provide the mandamus relief sought by Petitioner.[8]

Many international tragedies illustrate the application of this legal regime. Iran sued the United States in the International Court of Justice (ICJ) for the 1988 destruction of an Iranian commercial airliner, which was flying near a US naval vessel in the Persian Gulf. Its radar mistook that distant plane for an attacking fighter jet. Under International Law, Iran's State status provided it with the legal capacity to present a claim in an international tribunal against the United States for the acts of its military agents. The relatives of the Iranian citizens killed in the incident could not take such direct action against the United States. The Iranian relatives, of course, expected Iran to act on their behalf. Iran was harmed, under International Law, when its citizens were killed. This tragedy triggered Iran's discretionary decision to pursue a remedy against the offending nation. Iran claimed that the death of the Iranians on the ill-fated flight, and the destruction of the Iranian aircraft, constituted unprovoked violations of the right to fly over international waters. Further, any monetary compensation obtained by Iran for the destruction of the aircraft and the loss of life would belong to Iran. The victims' families would benefit, but only if Iran chose to give them any of the US compensation for its tragic mistake. Many States do turn over such recoveries to the individuals or relatives harmed in these circumstances. Because of poor international relations, however, the United States offered to provide compensation to the Iranian survivors conditioned on the special requirement that all payments would go directly to the victims' families, rather than pass through the hands of the Iranian government.[9]

EVOLVING "INTERNATIONAL" STATUS

As recounted by Antonio Cassese on the Faculty of Political Sciences at University of Florence, Italy, the scope of the individual's legal capacity evolved, particularly in the aftermath of World War II:

Individuals

BY ANTONIO CASSESE

in M. Bedjaoui (ed.), International Law:
Process and Prospects 114–120 (1991)

1. It is well known that States and insurgents [§2.3] are "traditional" subjects of the international community, in the sense that they have been the *dramatis personae* on the international scene from the beginning. Recently, especially after the Second World War, other poles of interest and activity have gained international status: international organizations; "peoples" finding themselves in certain conditions and being endowed with a representative structure (i.e., liberation movements; and individuals). The emergence of these "new" subjects is a distinct feature of modern international law.

. . .

4. Over a long period of time, during virtually the whole of the first stage of development of the international community (1648–1918), human beings have been under the exclusive sway of States. Individuals were only taken into consideration by international law *qua* individuals of a given State and in case of conflict, their interests were concretely safeguarded only if their national State decided to exercise diplomatic protection. . . . Thus, if individuals acquired some relevance in international affairs, it was as mere "objects" or, at best, "beneficiaries of international agreements."

. . .

8. After the Second World War international protection of human beings as such increased to a staggering extent. Individuals were no longer taken care of on the international level *qua* members of a group (minority or particular category); they began to be protected *qua individual human beings.*

9. Why did things change so drastically? The main reason was the conviction shared by all the victorious powers, that the Nazi aggression and the atrocities perpetrated had been the fruit of a victorious philosophy based on utter disregard for the dignity of man. One means of preventing a return to these horrors was the proclamation at all levels of some basic standards for respect for human rights.

. . .

18. . . . [O]ne should not underestimate the importance of individuals acting on the international scene.

First, one should bear in mind that it is not easy for States to deprive themselves of some of their sovereign prerogatives, in particular their traditional right to exercise full control over physical persons subject to their jurisdiction. Given the present structure of the world community and the fact that States are still the overlords, the limited status of individuals can be regarded as a remarkable progress. . . .

Second, whenever individuals are granted the right to petition international organs, they may act irrespectively of their nationality, whether they be citizens of the State complained of, or nationals of other States . . . or even stateless persons. The right of petition is therefore granted to physical persons *qua* human beings. No bond of nationality nor any other form of allegiance is taken into account. This represents a momentous innovation in its own right.

. . .

19. It is apparent from the foregoing remarks that individuals . . . [nevertheless] remain dependent on the will of their "creators." Like international organizations, individuals perform activities delegated to them by States . . . . On this score both organizations and individuals can be styled "*ancillary*" subjects of international law. . . .

20. It follows that, like international organizations, individuals are *derivative* subjects, in that they draw their existence from the formal decisions (normally a treaty) of other subjects [States]. . . . Consequently one may distinguish between *primary* and *secondary* subjects, the former embracing States, the latter encompassing individuals . . . .

◆ *Notes*

1. One entity Professor Cassese mentions, "*peoples,*" historically had no direct representation in international affairs. The UN Charter refers to this grouping in its Article 1.2 purpose "to develop friendly relations among nations based on respect for the principles of equal rights and self-determination of *peoples.*" In 1982, the United Nations thus created a Working Group on Indigenous Populations. In 1993, the General Assembly adopted a program of activities for the International Decade of the World's Indigenous People (1995–2004). It then identified the establishment of the Forum as one of the main objectives of the Decade. In July 2000, the UN's Economic and Social Council established a Permanent Forum on Indigenous Issues as a subsidiary organ of the Council. ECOSOC Res. 2000/22. This new forum formally integrates indigenous peoples and their representatives into the structure of the United Nations. It marks the first time that representatives of states and nonstate actors have been accorded *parity* in a permanent representative body within the United Nations Organization. As noted by UN High Commissioner for Human Rights, who is the coordinator of the Indigenous People Decade, this is an historic step forward: "The Permanent Forum promises to give indigenous peoples a unique voice within the UN system, commensurate with the unique problems which many indigenous people still face, but also with the unique contribution they make to the human rights dialogue, at the local, national and international levels."[10]

2. The early post-World War II movement toward European integration showed signs of relaxing one of the most rigid of the State-centric regime: an individual had no standing on the international level to lodge his or her claim, thus requiring the aid of a willing State. This limitation effectively meant that many wrongs went without a remedy. It was typically one's own State that caused the harm. But the 1950 European Convention for the Protection of Human

Rights and Fundamental Freedoms first spoke of lodging a claim against a State, in the European Court of Human Rights. Under Article 34: "The Court may receive applications from any person, nongovernmental organisation or group of individuals claiming to be the victim of a violation by one of the High Contracting Parties of the rights set forth in the Convention or the protocols thereto. The High Contracting Parties undertake not to hinder in any way the effective exercise of this right." Of course one could not do so, unless the offending State were a party to this treaty. However, this was the first major institution to at least offer the possibility of an individual, or nongovernmental organization, essentially functioning on the international level (i.e., individual v. State in an international forum). This treaty is available at: <http://conventions.coe.int/Treaty/EN/cadreprincipal.htm>.

3. Some *global* organizations accord the right of direct petition, by an individual to an international body. Individuals may thereby bring State breaches of the individual's treaty-based rights to the attention of the appropriate international enforcement body. This regime is dependent on the State ratification of treaties or protocols, which authorize such individual access to international proceedings.[11]

4. Under some contemporary regional treaties, *corporations* possess the power to pursue remedies when they are legally harmed by State conduct. They do not have to be represented by their home country (whom they may be suing). Under the North American Free Trade Agreement [NAFTA (§13.3)], for example, a NAFTA investor may sue for breach of certain NAFTA provisions by a NAFTA nation. The claim is heard by an international tribunal, normally composed of three members appointed by the investor and the NAFTA country being sued. Tribunals are formed under the investor's choice of commercial arbitration rules. (WTO disputes, on the other hand, can only be initiated by governments against other governments, as described in text §13.2)[12]

INDIVIDUAL/CORPORATE DEFENDANTS

Traditional doctrine espouses the following remedy for individual plaintiffs harmed by the action of a State: Their home State may choose to pursue a claim, in an

international context, for harm done to them by a foreign nation. The PCIJ characterized such claims in the following terms: "By taking up the case of one of its subjects and by resorting to diplomatic action or international judicial proceedings on his behalf, a state is in reality asserting its own rights—its right to ensure, in the person of its subjects, respect for the rules of international law."[13]

In the Soldier Jones Hypothetical, Jones, although an individual, could incur direct responsibility under International Law *if* his conduct amounted to an international crime such as genocide (but not murder). Jones would thereby directly violate International Law. If Jones had been assigned to kill all members of the hypothetical village for the purpose of eliminating a particular ethnic group—as opposed to merely securing a military target—he would then be directly punishable in an international tribunal, similar to Slobodan Milosevic who is being tried by a UN tribunal in the Netherlands, in part because his orders went beyond the "mere" ethnic cleansing of certain groups in the former Yugoslavia (§9.5). Whether murder or genocide, a relative of a deceased villager would not have the capacity to be a plaintiff in an international tribunal. Only States or international organizations have the general capacity to pursue claims in international proceedings.

In Chapter 2, you studied the contemporary diminution of immunity of Heads of State in the context of sovereign immunity. That immunity dates back to many centuries before the appearance of the State-centric system of International Law that evolved from the 1648 Treaty of Westphalia (§1.1). At about the same time, nations began to apply a customary practice whereby there was one type of individual who *was* able to operate on the "international" level: *the pirate*. Individual perpetrators of this crime were clearly subjects of International Law. They could be prosecuted in the courts of any nation, for violating the law of nations prohibiting piracy. Many jurists held that pirates were liable for their conduct directly under International Law, even when their conduct did not violate the law of the State where they could be found. Piracy was sufficiently heinous to be considered a crime against all nations. They were thus committing the original "international" crime against humanity (further addressed in §5.2 regarding universal jurisdiction, and Chapter 11 on human rights).[14]

The perspective that individuals could otherwise violate International Law—not just national law—surfaced with a fury, as a result of the horrors perpetrated by Germany's Nazi regime. Western scholars and jurists revived the theory that an individual could breach International Law. It was memorialized in the 1946 Judgment of the Nuremberg Tribunal, and the companion war crimes trials in Tokyo (§9.5). These major postwar tribunals tried individuals for conduct deemed to violate International Law, given that their actions did not violate either German or Japanese law. The resulting State denial of the dignity of the individual ultimately led France, England, the Soviet Union, and the United States to try the key Nazi and Japanese war criminals under the international agreements establishing the Nuremberg and Tokyo Military Tribunals.

The liability of the Nazi and Japanese defendants was based on the direct relationship between the individuals' conduct and International Law. The individual defendants claimed that they had no obligations under International Law. Their only duty was to their own nations, which in turn, would bear any resulting State responsibility for breaches of International Law. The International Military Tribunal at Nuremberg disagreed in the following terms: "Individuals have international duties which transcend the national obligations of obedience imposed by the individual State (to which they owe allegiance). He who violates the laws of war cannot obtain immunity while acting in pursuance of the authority of the State if the State in authorizing action moves outside its competence under international law." This trial generated an intense global interest in acknowledging the liability of the individual defendant—under International Law—premised largely on the unfathomable, genocidal conduct of these defendants. University of Denver Professor Ved Nanda thus comments that "[h]istory will perhaps recall that the single most significant international law development in the second half of the twentieth century was the dramatic shift in the individual's status from a mere object to a subject of international law. Indeed, the human being as an individual is becoming a full-fledged claimant with standing to seek redress in the international arena. The protection of internationally recognized human rights is by all accounts a revolutionary change."[15]

The potential for a corporation to violate International Law has also evolved. As noted in the above Vietnamese "Agent Orange" case, US corporations were being sued for the widespread use of this herbicide during the Vietnam War:

Defendants argue that corporations cannot be liable under international law. There is substantial support for this position.

. . .

Limiting civil liability to individuals while exonerating the corporation directing the individual's action [however,] . . . makes little sense in today's world. . . .

A corporation is not immune from civil legal action based on international law. The opinion on this point of [University of Houston] Professor Paust is compelling. "Companies and corporations have duties arising under international law, especially with respect to laws of war and human rights. Moreover, they have never been granted immunity under any known treaty or customary law with respect to violations of treaty-based or customary international law."[16]

◆ 4.2 NATIONALITY, STATELESSNESS, AND REFUGEES

An individual's nationality, often referred to as citizenship, is a bond between an individual and a State that establishes reciprocal rights and duties between them. This bond was once an automatic attribute of merely residence within the Roman Empire (except for certain "barbarians" who were not considered legal residents). In AD 212, the Edict of Caracalla conferred Roman citizenship on all individuals who lived within the area controlled by the Empire. There was no distinction between place of birth, parental citizenship, or whether one wished to become a Roman citizen or abandon that citizenship.[17]

This section analyzes contemporary citizenship rules, State competence in such matters, and the related consequences of citizenship. The four major components of this subject are nationality, dual nationality, statelessness, and refugees.

NATIONALITY

Scope Nationality is a legal, political, and social link between the individual and the State. In 1955, the ICJ defined nationality as "a legal bond having as its basis a social fact of attachment, a genuine connection of existence, interests and sentiments, together with the existence of reciprocal rights and duties. It may be said . . . that the individual upon whom it is conferred . . . is in fact more closely connected with the population of the State conferring nationality than with that of any other State. . . ."[18]

Nationality establishes mutual expectations for both the State that confers it and the individual who acquires it. The State has the right to require its citizens to serve in its military forces. The State may also tax an individual for earnings accrued anywhere in the world. The individual is correlatively entitled to certain expectations based on his or her nationality. One of the most important of these rights is the State protection of the individual. The home State normally assists its nationals, when they are mistreated by another State or its agents in another country. A Canadian citizen who is mistreated in Saudi Arabia may seek Canada's assistance. The protection is likely to materialize in some form of a Canadian diplomatic or consular official's inquiry/protest on behalf of the Canadian citizen who was harmed by Saudi conduct that violates international normative expectations.

Nations have not always protected their citizens abroad. The concept of nationality was not introduced in mainland China, for example, until the mid-nineteenth century. The Chinese government historically showed little interest in protecting its citizens when they were abroad. Choosing to live abroad was prima facie evidence of disloyalty. Residing among "barbarians" rendered Chinese citizens unworthy of the State's protection.[19]

Is nationality a matter of national law or International Law? If giving or withholding nationality were not subject to international legal norms, then a State would be free to deprive its citizens of citizenship against their wishes. In a 1915 case, the then new Turkish government, fearing that Turkish Armenians were a dangerous "foreign element with cousins in the Russian army," deported them to Syria and other Middle Eastern areas.

In 1923, the PCIJ proclaimed that States generally had unlimited discretion when making nationality decisions. Exceptions included those situations where there was a treaty obligation to confer, or the inability to confer, nationality under the particular circumstances. In one of the two prominent cases, France conferred French nationality on residents of Tunis and Morocco, notwithstanding a British protest on behalf of British citizens living in those territories. The Court was asked to decide whether this was a matter of national discretion, which fell exclusively within France's unbridled

power to decide. The Court responded that this matter involved an issue arising under International Law, although the conferring of nationality was normally a matter committed to the discretion of each State's national law. Thus, "nationality is not, in principle, regulated by international law, [however] the right of a State to use its discretion is nevertheless restricted only by obligations which it may have undertaken towards other States. In such a case, jurisdiction which, in principle, belongs solely to the State [*i.e.,* conferring nationality on residents of its territories] is limited by rules of international law." In the same year, the Court added an important limitation in the following Polish case: "One of the common problems which presented itself in connection with the protection of minorities, was that of preventing these States from refusing their nationality, on racial, religious or linguistic grounds, to certain categories of persons, in spite of the link which effectively attached them to the territory allocated to one or [the] other of these States."[20]

In 1939, Stalin and Hitler signed a nonaggression treaty containing a secret protocol placing various nations, including Estonia, under Soviet influence. Stalin ordered the deportation of 60,000 Estonian nationals to Siberia after taking away their Estonian citizenship. This was one of the war-related events, which would later stimulate international pressure to limit the wide latitude of discretion exercisable by States in nationality matters. The results of such pressures are addressed as follows, whereby postwar refugee and genocide treaties now pose further impediments.

Acquisition How is nationality acquired? Individual nationality, or citizenship, is acquired in three ways: (1) passively, by parentage; (2) passively, by being born in a State that considers a child born there its citizen; and (3) actively, by naturalization of an individual who voluntarily changes allegiance from one State to another.

Parentage Citizenship derived from parentage is a rule drawn from the ancient Roman law. The child's citizenship was that of the parents. This rule is referred to as *jus sanguinis,* or "blood rule" for establishing citizenship. A child born of Roman parents in any region of the world not under Roman control was nevertheless a Roman citizen. The *jus sanguinis* basis for acquiring nationality is applied in Europe, Latin America, and many English-speaking countries.

Birth Many countries apply a nationality-by-birth rule. This is the rule known as *jus soli,* or "soil rule" for determining citizenship. In the Middle Ages, birth within certain European territories automatically vested the newborn with that nation's citizenship. Under its contemporary application, a child born in England, whose parents are visiting Italian citizens, is an English citizen under the immigration and nationality laws of England. (This child would also be an Italian citizen because Italy follows the blood rule.)

Nationality determinations are often complicated by the simultaneous applicability of the laws of the country of the parents and the child's country of birth. Assume that a Japanese couple has a baby during a visit to the United States. Application of the parentage or *jus sanguinis* blood rule would make the baby a citizen of Japan. Application of the *jus soli* or soil rule would make the baby a citizen of the US. This child is a citizen of both countries and may have to choose one of two citizenships upon attaining adult status. To alleviate such problems in Europe, the Council of Europe's 1997 European Convention on Nationality—and the failed 2005 EU Constitution—provide that everyone has a right to nationality. A treaty party must automatically grant its nationality to persons having at least one parent who is a national of that State, which does not apply to persons born abroad. In that instance, the European Convention provides that there is an obligation to facilitate the acquisition of that State's nationality (although not automatically).[21] However, Ireland is now the only nation in the EU that automatically grants citizenship to anyone born within the nation.

There have been efforts to curtail the US application of the *jus soli* rule, which automatically confers US nationality upon those born on US soil. The US Constitution provides that "All persons born or naturalized in the United States . . . are citizens of the United States. . . ."[22] In 1993, California's Governor Pete Wilson made a proposal that, if adopted by Congress, would have amended the US Constitution. That change would have repealed this constitutional guarantee. Children of foreign nationals born on US soil, when undocumented, would no longer automatically be US citizens.

Naturalization Individuals may actively change their nationality through the process of naturalization. The national law of the country from which nationality is sought establishes its naturalization requirements. In a notable passage from a US Supreme Court opinion: "It is an accepted maxim of international law that every sovereign nation has the power, as inherent in sovereignty, and essential to self-preservation, to forbid the entrance of foreigners within its dominions, or to admit them only in such cases and upon such conditions as it may see fit to prescribe."[23]

Adjacent nations may have very different approaches. French and German leaders sought to, respectively, open and close the door to immigrants in the same month. In June 1993, France's National Assembly overwhelmingly approved a tougher immigration law that made it more difficult for foreign citizens to acquire French citizenship via marriage or residence with a family member in France. Immigration is one of France's most explosive social issues because of increasing crime, which the French press has attributed to "foreigners."

Germany's Chancellor Helmut Kohl contemporaneously urged the German Parliament to make it easier to become a German citizen. Responding to pressure after fatal attacks on Turks in Solingen, Germany, Kohl attempted to initiate a process that would change Germany's eighty-year-old nationality law, barring many lifelong residents (including some who were born in Germany) from applying for German citizenship, if they could not establish the legality of their presence in Germany. Later that year, however, Germany instead introduced a tough immigration policy, designed to halt the influx of immigrants spawned by the end of the Cold War. One year later (1994), illegal immigration had dropped by two-thirds, and the number of individuals seeking political asylum dropped by 72 percent.[24] On the other hand, German law did accommodate over 2 million ethnic Turks who lived in Germany for decades, without full citizenship rights. A 1913 citizenship law provided that citizenship was to be derived only from parentage. New legislation now provides that children born after January 1, 2000, whose parents have lived in Germany for at least eight years, are automatically German citizens.

One major problem in immigration law involves naturalization undertaken for reasons not related to habitual residence in the naturalizing country. Granting citizenship under these circumstances does not necessarily entitle an individual to claim that he or she is a national of the naturalizing State. The relatively lax nationality laws of one State may be in conflict with the more demanding laws of another. In 1955, the ICJ addressed this recurring problem in the following major case:

Nottebohm Case (*Liechtenstein v. Guatemala*)

INTERNATIONAL COURT OF JUSTICE (1955)

1955 *International Court of Justice Reports* 4

AUTHOR'S NOTE: Nottebohm was a German citizen residing in Guatemala. He operated a successful business in both Guatemala and Germany before World War II. Guatemala's laws discriminated against foreign citizens and business entities that were nationals of countries with which it was at war. German citizens could not do business in Guatemala.

Just before Guatemala declared war against Germany, Nottebohm went to Liechtenstein and applied for citizenship. His purpose was to avoid the discriminatory laws against foreign citizens so that he could continue his lucrative business in Guatemala. There was no state of war between Guatemala and Liechtenstein. Liechtenstein waived its usual three-year waiting period when it granted citizenship to Nottebohm. He immediately took an oath of allegiance, became a naturalized citizen of Liechtenstein, and was issued a passport prior to leaving for Guatemala.

When Nottebohm attempted to return to Guatemala as a citizen of Liechtenstein, however, he was unable to reenter. His property in Guatemala was seized by the government. Guatemala still considered Nottebohm a German national and would not recognize Liechtenstein's grant of nationality. In 1946, Liechtenstein first asserted its right to protect Nottebohm, whom it considered to be its naturalized citizen. In 1951, after unsuccessful negotiations with Guatemala, Liechtenstein instituted this suit in the International Court of Justice. Liechtenstein wanted to recover for damages to Nottebohm caused by Guatemala's treatment of a person that Liechtenstein considered its citizen.

The Court's opinion in this famous case addresses the requirements for the international recognition of citizenship conferred under national law. The legal question included whether Liechtenstein could present this claim on behalf of Nottebohm, and in turn, whether Guatemala had to recognize Nottebohm as a citizen of Liechtenstein.

COURT'S OPINION: [T]he Court must ascertain whether the nationality conferred on Nottebohm by Liechtenstein . . . bestows upon Liechtenstein a sufficient title to the exercise of protection in respect of

Nottebohm as against Guatemala. In this connection, Counsel for Liechtenstein said: "the essential question is whether Mr. Nottebohm, having acquired the nationality of Liechtenstein, that acquisition of nationality is one which must be recognized by other States."

Guatemala expressly stated that it could not recognise that Mr. Nottebohm, a German subject habitually resident in Guatemala, has acquired the nationality of Liechtenstein without changing his "habitual residence." There is here an express denial by Guatemala of Nottebohm's Liechtenstein nationality.

The naturalization of Nottebohm was an act performed by Liechtenstein in the exercise of its domestic jurisdiction. The question to be decided is whether that act has the international effect here under consideration.

International arbitrators have given their preference to the real and effective nationality, that which accorded with the facts, that based on stronger factual ties between the person concerned and one of the States whose nationality is involved. Different factors are taken into consideration, and their importance will vary from one case to the next: the habitual residence of the individual concerned is an important factor, but there are other factors such as the centre of his interests, his family ties, his participation in public life, attachment shown by him for a given country and inculcated in his children, etc. [I]nternational law leaves it to each State to lay down the rules governing the grant of its own nationality. On the other hand, a State cannot claim that the rules it has laid down are entitled to recognition by another State unless it has acted in conformity with this general aim of making the legal bond of nationality accord with the individual's genuine connection with the State which assumes the defence of its citizens by means of protection as against other States.

According to the practice of States, to arbitral and judicial decisions and to the opinion of writers, nationality is a legal bond having as its basis a social fact of attachment, a genuine connection of existence, interests and sentiments, together with the existence of reciprocal rights and duties. It may be said to constitute the juridical connection of the fact that the individual upon whom it is conferred either directly by the law or as the result of an act of the authorities, is in fact more closely connected with the population of the State conferring nationality than with that of any other State. Conferred by a State, it only entitles that State to exercise protection vis-à-vis another State, if it constitutes a translation into juridical terms of the individual's connection with the State, which has made him a national.

At the date when he applied for naturalization Nottebohm had been a German national from the time of his birth. His country had been at war for more than a month, and there is nothing to indicate that the application for naturalization then made by Nottebohm was motivated by any desire to dissociate himself from the Government of his country [Germany].

He had been settled in Guatemala for 34 years. He had carried on his activities there. It was the main seat of his interests. He returned there shortly after his naturalization, and it remained the centre of his interest and of his business activities. He stayed there until his removal as a result of war measures [passed by Guatemala] in 1943. He subsequently attempted to return there, and he now complains of Guatemala's refusal to admit him [now that he claims Liechtenstein rather than German nationality].

In contrast, his actual connections with Liechtenstein were extremely tenuous. No settled abode, no prolonged residence in the country at the time of his application for naturalization: the application indicates that he was paying a visit there and confirms the transient character of this visit by its request that the naturalization proceedings should be initiated and concluded without delay. If Nottebohm went to Liechtenstein in 1946, this was because of the refusal of Guatemala to admit him. No indication is given of the grounds warranting the waiver of the condition of residence. There is no allegation of any economic interests or of any activities exercised or to be exercised in Liechtenstein, and no manifestation of any intention whatsoever to transfer all or some of his interests and his business activities to Liechtenstein.

These facts clearly establish, on the one hand, the absence of any bond of attachment between Nottebohm and Liechtenstein and, on the other hand, the existence of a long-standing and close connection between him and Guatemala, a link which his naturalization in no way weakened. That naturalization was not based on any real prior connection with Liechtenstein, nor did it in any way alter the manner of life of the person upon whom it was conferred in exceptional circumstances of speed and accommodation. In both respects, it was lacking in the genuineness requisite to an act of such importance, if it is to be entitled to be respected by a State in the position of Guatemala. It was granted without regard to the concept of nationality adopted in international relations.

Naturalization was asked for not so much for the purpose of obtaining a legal recognition of Nottebohm's membership in fact in the population of Liechtenstein, as it was to enable him to substitute for his status as a national of a belligerent State [Germany] that of a national of a neutral State [Liechtenstein], with the sole aim of thus coming within the protection of Liechtenstein.

Guatemala is under no obligation to recognise a nationality granted in such circumstances. Liechtenstein consequently is not entitled to extend its protection to Nottebohm vis-à-vis Guatemala.

◆ *Notes & Questions*

1. The ICJ dismissed Liechtenstein's claim filed on behalf of Nottebohm. He was a citizen of Liechtenstein under its national law. Under International Law, however, Liechtenstein could not confer its citizenship on Nottebohm for the purpose of requiring other countries to treat him as if he were a citizen of Liechtenstein. As a result, Guatemala could appropriately characterize Nottebohm as a German citizen—remaining free to apply its discriminatory laws against the citizen of a country with which Guatemala was at war.

2. The court never decided the merits of this claim regarding Guatemala's alleged mistreatment of Nottebohm. He was not represented by a country with which he had the effective link of nationality. Liechtenstein therefore did not have the legal capacity to bring this claim. Only Germany possessed the right to question Guatemala's discriminatory treatment of Nottebohm, which it did not invoke during or after the war.

3. The *Nottebohm* case is often cited for its restatement of the factors for international recognition of naturalization by another State: residence, center of interests,

family ties, participation in public life, and attachment shown for a particular State.

4. The Caribbean island nation of Dominica provides its economic citizenship via its "passport to paradise" program. For the equivalent of US $50,000, the country can become a safe haven for fugitives, tax evaders, and corrupt foreign politicians—according to Emilia Puma, spokeswoman for the US Embassy in Barbados. A March 1999 US Department of State report cited Caribbean-based "economic citizenship" as an obstacle to fighting international crime. Belize, Grenada, and St. Kitts and Nevis also have economic citizenship for sale.

5. A US program authorizes people who invest US $1 million ($500,000 in depressed areas) and employ ten people to obtain a visa for two years. They may then apply for permanent residence.

New Forms of Citizenship   The next generation of citizenship options may involve citizenship that is provided by an international organization and citizenship in a borderless world.

Organizational Citizenship   As early as 1974, the Paris Summit of the Heads of State launched a study of "the conditions under which the citizens . . . of the Member States could be given social rights as members of the [European] community." Since then, the European Union (EU) has moved beyond a mere economic entity, including military structure (§3.4). The EU is addressing the full panoply of social and other needs that fall within the traditional competence of the State.

Article G of the 1992 Maastricht Treaty incorporates an earlier treaty creating the European Community. The "Citizenship of the Union" provision states as follows:

ARTICLE 8

1. Citizenship of the Union is hereby established. Every person holding the nationality of a Member State shall be a citizen of the Union.
2. Citizens of the Union shall enjoy the rights conferred by this Treaty and shall be subject to the duties imposed thereby.

The remaining provisions of Article 8 afford treaty-based protection for the following rights of citizens within the EU: the right to move and reside freely within the territory of the Member States; the right to

vote and be a candidate at municipal elections in the Member State in which he resides, although not a citizen of the Member State, under the same conditions as nationals of that State; protection by the diplomatic or consular authorities of any Member State, on the same conditions as the nationals of that State; and the right to petition the European Parliament about any matter which comes within the Community's fields of activity and which affects that citizen.[25]

Article I-10.1 of the failed 2005 EU Constitution contains a comparable article that carefully distinguishes between community citizenship and State nationality: "Every national of a Member State shall be a citizen of the Union. Citizenship of the Union shall be additional to national citizenship and shall not replace it." This essentially confers rights including: moving and residing freely within the territory of all member States; voting and standing as a candidate in elections to the European Parliament; and diplomatic representation in any member country in which another member State does not have consular representation available.

By analogy to the ICJ's *Nottebohm* case discussed earlier, if Germany, Guatemala, and Liechtenstein were all members of the same international organization, which provided citizenship rights as specified in Article 8 of the regional Maastricht Treaty, then the court would *not* have dismissed Liechtenstein's case. In 1955, there was of course no common citizenship provision, which accorded "community" rights to all citizens. If that were the case today, and all three countries involved were members of an international organization providing Article 8 rights, then the appropriate court would have an obligation to hear the merits of Nottebohm's claim—regardless of which of the three member nations were to present this claim. Further, Nottebohm, as an individual, would have the right of petition to the appropriate community (international) organ to present his own claim, without the necessary sponsorship of Liechtenstein (or Guatemala, or Germany).[26]

Citizenship in a Borderless World   As *Nottebohm* confirmed in 1955, citizenship or nationality, is the bond between the individual and the State. State Jurisdiction and the Internet (§5.4) presents the current impact of the Internet on the twenty-first century society. With the advent of the Information Age, or the electronic world of "cyberspace," citizenship may, one day, not be dependent on the relationship between the individual and the State, as has been the case, since the modern system of states dating from the 1648 Treaty of Westphalia.

"Globalization" (§13.1), a term meaning different things to different people, has profoundly affected contemporary notions of citizenship. The major corporations have annual budgets which dwarf that of many nations. Globalization will continue to revise the degree to which nation-States are sovereign, as borders become less relevant to our daily lives.[27] A representative comment on the impact of globalization illustrates the evolution:

This move to globalization has . . . conjured up thoughts of a new status of "world citizen;" a person with rights of travel anywhere. In a world without territorial borders that would be possible, and it would certainly herald a radical shift in the laws of migration. . . . International trade and development of a global economy represent a significant starting point . . . [whereby] the effect of these changes is a disjuncture between the formal authority of the state and the actual system of production, distribution and exchange. The global economy involves the internationalization of production and financial transactions. Moreover, the international corporation has been engaged in investment, production and exchange which has transcended nation-state borders.

So too we have regional economies and markets encouraged a borderless world by promoting free movement of goods and labour across nation-state borders.

. . .

In the twenty-first century, people will recognise themselves as members of a nation-state and members of a global community. Moreover, there is likely to be a continued growth of citizens of multiple nation-states as well as global citizens. The consequence can be articulated as people having more that [sic] one "legal status" and one "community" with which they identify.

. . .

How do these factors stand up in a borderless world? Habitual residence may not be a reality for those who are traveling often for the purpose of work, given the effect of the international economy on borders. Moreover if we concentrate on the "centre of a person's interests," this may no longer have a necessary connection to a nation-state. Family ties could very well be situated around the world, and participation in public life may be a public on a much greater scale through non-government international organizations.[28]

Given the contemporary pressure by international organizations to protect individual rights, one might also anticipate linkage between them and the forces of globalization, as State sovereignty contracts. The United Nations, for example, has now undertaken the governance of State territory (East Timor and Kosovo). Its membership is changing. Larger States are continuing to break up into smaller ones, as the fruits of self-determination ripen. The UN Secretary-General's October 1999 perspective supports this theme, in the sense that the individual and the State are effectively engaged in a role-reversal: "State sovereignty, in its most basic sense, is being redefined—not least by the forces of globalisation and international co-operation. States are now widely understood to be instruments at the service of their peoples, and not vice versa. At the same time individual sovereignty—by which I mean the fundamental freedom of each individual, enshrined in the charter of the UN and subsequent international treaties—has been enhanced by a renewed and spreading consciousness of individual rights. When we read the charter today, we are more than ever conscious that its aim is to protect individual human beings, not to protect those who abuse them."[29]

DUAL NATIONALITY

As noted by the former General Counsel of the US Immigration and Naturalization Service: "Dual or multiple citizenship has grown increasingly common, despite a global legal order nominally opposed to such a status Because that opposition is more and more at variance with the needs and realities of an interconnected globe, where travel is cheaper, swifter, and more frequent, it has been widely but unevenly eroded."[30]

A dual national possesses the citizenship of more than one nation. An individual may: (1) be born in a nation that applies the *jus soli* rule of automatic nationality by birth; and (2) simultaneously acquire the parents' citizenship, when their home nation applies the *jus sanguinis* rule of nationality of the parents.

Dual nationality is also spawned by those nations that allow their nationals to emigrate but not forfeit their original nationality status, should they decide to acquire a new citizenship. In 1998, Mexico joined the growing number of countries promoting dual nationality—in the sense that it no longer vitiates the original Mexican nationality, based solely on a Mexican becoming the citizen of another country. For example, although the individual becomes a citizen of the United States, he or she is also a dual national under Mexican law. This change in Mexican law ameliorated the concern of many Mexicans who migrate to the United States, who did not want to "betray" Mexico by opting for citizenship in the United States. Mexico's objectives include a desire to build a larger political base in the United States, whereby affected individuals will be able to vote and hold office in the United States, own property in Mexico, and influence issues of interest to both nations.

Members of an international community of nations do not always have the same approach to dual nationality. In the NAFTA region, for example, Canada approved dual citizenship in 1977. The United States, on the other hand, does not favor dual citizenship, partially because of diplomatic problems regarding which country should represent a dual national who has been harmed in a third nation.

An individual may encounter some unusual burdens as a result of dual nationality. One is being subject to the jurisdiction of two countries, each of which considers that person its national. Each nation might then command that individual to return, such as when his or her testimony is needed (§5.2). Both nations may wish to tax the income of such individuals or impress them into military service. Also, such individuals may not be able to predict which nation will protect them, if they are harmed in a third nation. For example, a famous international arbitration decision denied Italy the right to espouse a claim on behalf of an Italian citizen born of Italian parents. He was an Italian national under the law of Italy. He was Peruvian, however, by birth. The tribunal refused to recognize Italy's attempt to bring a claim on his behalf against Peru. The international arbitrator was unwilling to allow Italy to represent a Peruvian national in a suit against Peru. As described earlier, various attributes flow from the bond of nationality between a nation and its citizens who happen to be abroad. An individual's home nation may be expected to provide diplomatic protection in a dispute involving mistreatment of the individual by another nation that considers that person an alien. Here Peru was in the awkward position of purporting to protect a Peruvian national against action taken by Italy, for this dual national who was also an Italian citizen.[31]

Another disadvantage of dual nationality is the potential for expulsion during time of war. Ethiopia expelled a large number of Ethiopian nationals who obtained Eritrean citizenship, for example, after the Eritrean portion of Ethiopia became independent—followed by a war between these two countries. Ethiopia thus deprived them

of their Ethiopian nationality. International Law does not permit a nation to arbitrarily deprive its citizens of their nationality. Eritrea therefore sought relief from Ethiopia, in the Permanent Court of Arbitration in The Hague. The Eritrea Ethiopia Claims Commission therein rejected Eritrea's claim. International Humanitarian Law (§10.6) gives belligerents the power to expel nationals of the enemy State during times of conflict. Thus, "Ethiopia lawfully deprived a substantial number of dual nationals of their Ethiopian nationality following identification through Ethiopia's security committee process. Ethiopia could lawfully expel these persons as nationals of an enemy belligerent, although it was bound to ensure them the protections required by Geneva Convention IV and other applicable international humanitarian law. Eritrea's claim that this group was unlawfully expelled is rejected."[32]

Some multilateral treaties have attempted to ameliorate the adverse impact of dual citizenship, although they have accomplished little. The 1930 Hague Convention on Certain Questions Relating to the Conflict of Nationality Laws was the first multilateral treaty to address dual nationality. While it restates the basic nationality rules already discussed, none of its provisions resolves the dilemma posed for the individual dual national when two nations claim that person as their citizen. Under Article 3, for example, "a person having two or more nationalities may be regarded as its national by each of the States whose nationality he possesses." Under this early treaty on dual nationality, each nation may apply its own law to the same individual. Some relief was available via the wording of the 1930 Hague Protocol Relating to Military Obligations in Certain Cases of Double Nationality. This treaty provides a model for avoiding competing military service claims in the case of dual nationals. If it had been adopted by a sufficient number of countries, it would have eliminated double military service for individuals who were dual nationals. The 1964 Paris Convention Concerning the Exchange of Information with Respect to Acquisition of Nationality is another multilateral treaty designed to assist dual nationals. While useful for the purpose of acquiring information, none of its provisions addresses inconsistent obligations for dual nationals.[33]

The most effective devices for avoiding inconsistent burdens are the various bilateral treaties that specifically address dual nationality problems. The classic problem emerges when two States draft an individual into their respective armies. The Netherlands–Belgian Agreement of 1954, for example, concerning the Military Service of Young Men Possessing Both Belgian and Netherlands Nationality, is a good illustration of international cooperation. It avoids the potential unfairness of having to serve in two armies just because an individual is a dual national. Military service for one nation automatically precludes military service obligations in another nation.[34]

The 1997 European Convention on Nationality is the most recent attempt to alleviate burdens associated with dual nationality. In contrast to the 1930 Hague Convention, this instrument does not decide the issue of diplomatic protection. Article 17 merely refers to the existing rules of Customary International Law for resolving such issues—a reference that leaves much to the imagination. It does provide, at least in principle, that dual nationals are expected to fulfill any military obligation only once, although this standard does not apply in cases of an emergency mobilization of military forces.[35]

STATELESSNESS

Individuals are stateless when they lack the nationality of any State. Loss of one's original citizenship—typically conferred by birth or parentage, without obtaining a new citizenship—renders the individual stateless. Such individuals cannot claim the bond of citizenship with any State to protect them. There is no State to come to the aid of an individual in need of diplomatic representation.

During and after both world wars, numerous people became stateless. Many were refugees who lost their citizenship after fleeing from their native lands. They were not citizens of the State where they had found temporary refuge. Many fled certain Eastern European countries to avoid political persecution only to find that they had been deprived of their original citizenship for doing so. Under the 1948 Hungarian Nationality Act, for example, the government of Hungary could "deprive of his Hungarian nationality a person who . . . on going abroad contravenes or evades the statutory provisions relating to the departure from the country." The 1951 Polish Nationality Act provided that a Polish citizen who resided abroad would be deprived of Polish nationality if the government determined that such an individual "left the territory of the Polish State unlawfully" or "refused to return to Poland at the summons of the competent authority."

The 1948 Declaration of Human Rights thus articulated the United Nation's aspiration for comprehensive post–World War II nationality laws. Article 15.1 provides: "Everyone has the right to a nationality." Article 15.2 follows with its ambitious call for a world wherein "[n]o one shall be arbitrarily deprived of his nationality nor denied the right to change his nationality."

The phenomenon of statelessness is not limited to the two world wars. Many refugees fled Cuba in the 1960s, and Vietnam in the 1970s, because of political persecution. They lost their citizenship as a result of their decision to flee. They were stateless before they underwent any naturalization proceedings in the countries where they found temporary or permanent refuge.

The significance of statelessness is that affected individuals encounter great difficulty in traveling and obtaining work. The absence of identity documents, like a birth certificate or passport, typically precludes an alien from entering or working in most countries. It can materialize in very charged contexts, such as the sensitive Olympic dispute involving Cuba and the United States:

Perez v. International Olympic Committee

COURT OF ARBITRATION FOR SPORT
AD HOC DIVISION: SYDNEY OLYMPIC GAMES
(CAS Arbitration No. SYD 5) (19 Sept. 2000)
120 *International Law Reports* 1 (2002)

AUTHOR'S NOTE: The applicant represented Cuba in the 1992 Olympic Games. After he defected, the US granted him asylum. He competed in sports events for the US from 1997 to 1999, the year he became a naturalized US citizen. After being selected for the US kayak team for the 2000 Sydney Olympics, the International Olympic committee ("IOC") advised him that he was ineligible to compete, because he had not been a US citizen for three years prior to the 2000 Olympics. Cuba refused to waive this rule. The US Olympic Committee (USOC) challenged this IOC decision.

OLYMPIC COURT OF ARBITRATION OPINION:

1. Facts

1. The present proceedings have been commenced by Mr. Angel Perez (the Claimant) seeking a declaration that he may compete in the 2000 Sydney Olympic Games as a member of the US Olympic Team.

2. The Claimant was born in Havana in 1971 and competed for Cuba in the 1992 Olympic Games in Barcelona.

3. In May 1993, after a competition in Mexico, the Claimant did not return to Cuba. He entered the United States and immediately made an application for asylum under the US immigration laws. He has since been a resident of Miami, and has never returned to Cuba.

. . .

5. On 11 September 1995, the Claimant was awarded permanent residence status as a "Resident Alien" in the US ("Green Card").

6. The Claimant competed for the US in the kayak World championships in 1997, 1998, and 1999 in accordance with the Rules of the International Canoe Federation.

7. In September 1999, the Claimant obtained US citizenship.

8. On 21 August 2000, the United States Olympic Committee and USA Canoe/Kayak requested the IOC to grant Mr. Perez the right to participate in the Sydney 2000 Olympic Games. The IOC denied this request on 28 August 2000, for the following reasons:

The facts of this case clearly fall within paragraph 2 of the Bye-law [sic] to Rule 46 of the Olympic Charter. In particular, in view of:

(i) Mr. Perez having previously represented Cuba in an international competition as referred to in Paragraph 2 of the Bye-law to Rule 46 of the Olympic Charter.

(ii) Less than three years having passed since Mr. Perez has become a national of the United States; and

(iii) The NOC of Cuba not agreeing to reduce this three years period referred to in Paragraph 2 of the Bye-law to Rule 46 of the Olympic Charter, Mr. Perez is not eligible to represent the United States at the 2000 Sydney Olympic Games.

The IOC regrets that the parties concerned were not able to resolve this matter so as to allow Mr. Perez to compete for the United States, especially in view of the fact that it has been approximately eight years since Mr. Perez last represented Cuba.

9. On 12 September 2000, the USOC and USA Canoe/Kayak commenced proceedings before the Court of Arbitration for Sport Ad Hoc Division Sydney Olympic Games seeking a decision, which would allow Mr. Angel Perez to participate for the United States of America in the Kayak competition of the Sydney 2000 Olympic Games.

10. On 13 September 2000, the CAS Ad Hoc Division for the Sydney Olympic Games delivered an award dismissing the application.

2. Procedure

11. On 17 September 2000, the Claimant filed the application instituting the present proceedings. To the application was attached a letter dared 14 September 2000, signed by Edward W Gnehm, Ambassador of the United States of America, addressed "To Whom it May Concern" and affirming that the Claimant had been a national of the United States under US law "for a period considerably in excess of three years" before the beginning of the 2000 Olympic Games.

12. Hearings were conducted on 18 September 2000. . . .

13. The Cuban National Committee was provided a copy of the application and invited to attend the hearings as a third interested party entitled to be heard and to adduce evidence. It did not attend, but prior to the hearings filed a letter . . . reading in its entirety as follows (translation):

The Cuban Olympic Committee has restated on various occasions that Mr. Angel Perez, athlete in Canoe-Kayak, has not complied with the requirements of Rule 46 of the Olympic Charter.

In view of the above, the Cuban Olympic Committee confirms that Mr. Angel Perez is not eligible, and does not authorize him to represent the US Olympic Committee at the Sydney Olympic Games.

14. At the hearing, the Applicant produced an opinion on relevant Cuban law signed by Avelino J. Gonzales, Esq., a Cuban lawyer now practicing in Florida who is

a graduate and former Adjunct Professor of the University of Havana. The Respondent stated that it neither accepted nor rejected the opinion, but did not seek the opportunity to provide additional evidence.

3. The Parties' Arguments

3.1. The Claimant's Contentions

15. The Claimant argues that he became a US national more than three years before the opening of the Sydney Olympic Games, and that therefore he is entitled to participate, and to represent the United States, irrespective of the objection sought to be raised by Cuba under paragraph 2 of the Bye-law to Rule 46 of the Olympic Charter.

16. Secondly, the Claimant argues that even if it is found that he did not become a US national until 1999, he nevertheless should be treated as a stateless person as of 1993, with the consequence that he "changed his nationality" for the purposes of Rule 46 more than three years ago, and thus may participate as a US national irrespective of the Cuban objection.

3.2. The Respondent's Contentions

17. The Respondent considers that the Claimant has not proved that he acquired US nationality before 1999, and that on that basis Cuban approval was necessary for the Claimant to participate and represent the US in the Games.

18. As to the contention that the Claimant became stateless as of 1993, the Respondent takes the position that it does not wish to act adversarially [*sic*] in the context of what could be viewed as a debate between the Claimant and the Cuban National Committee, but that its only concern is the proper application of the Charter. Although invited to attend the hearing, the Cuban National Committee did not.

4. Legal Analysis

4.1. Legal Framework

19. These proceedings are governed by the CAS Arbitration Rules for the Games of the XXVII Olympiad in Sydney (the "ad hoc Rules") of CAS enacted by the International Council of Arbitration for Sport ("ICAS") on 29 November 1999. They are further subject to Chapter 12 of the Swiss Private International Law Act of 18 December 1987 as a result of the express choice of law contained in Article 17 ad hoc Rules and the choice of Lausanne, Switzerland, as the seat of the

Ad Hoc Division and of its panels of Arbitrators, pursuant to Article 7 of the ad hoc Rules.

. . .

4.3. Merits if the Application

A. The Claimants contention that he was a national of the United States for more than three years prior to the 2000 Sydney Games

25. The only evidence additional to that which was before us in CAS arbitration N° SYD 1 is the letter signed by the Ambassador of the United States in Australia (see Paragraph 11).

26. The award in that case held, at para. 11, that the Claimants there had not demonstrated that Mr. Perez had acquired US nationality before he was granted citizenship in September 1999. The Panel indicated (para. 10) that, if factors such as those invoked by the Claimants could suffice to confer nationality, there would be numerous examples of attempts—indeed successful attempts—to obtain it.

27. What is now contended is that the letter by the Ambassador is conclusive as to what it states, i.e. that the Claimant became a US national for a period considerably in excess of three years before the beginning of the 2000 Olympic Games.

28. The Panel accepts that the Ambassador's letter is a considered statement by an accredited representative of the United States. The Panel nevertheless does not regard it as conclusive. Although it appears to be the case that under US law a person may become a US national [i.e., acquire a "green card"] before being granted citizenship, the question remains whether this has occurred. If the Claimant became a US national at least three years prior to the 2000 Olympic Games as a result of the operation of US law, the Panel anticipates that this could be the subject of opinion evidence from United States lawyers competent in the field who could so opine and cite either judicial or administrative authority to support the conclusion. No such opinion evidence has been tendered.

29. The Panel therefore rejects the Claimant's submission that on the material in evidence before it, one should conclude that he acquired US nationality more than three years before the 2000 Olympic Games.

B. The Claimants alternative contention that Cuban consent is not required because he should be deemed to have become a stateless person in 1993

30. Paragraph 2 of the Bye-law to Rule 46 of the Olympic Charter provides that a competitor who has represented one country in the Olympic Games . . . , and who has changed his nationality or acquired a new nationality; shall not participate in the Olympic Games to represent his new country until three years after such change or acquisition.

31. The Claimant argues that as a result of the Cuban legal regime, he became a stateless person after his defection in 1993, and that even if he did not *acquire US nationality* until 1999, he should be deemed to have *changed his nationality* when he became stateless.

. . .

33. The conclusion of the Gonzales Opinion [para. 14 above] is that *"Mr. Perez became stateless when he defected from Cuba back in 1993."*

34. The substantive foundations of this conclusion are as follows:

— under Article 135.1 of the Cuban Penal Code, Law N° 62 of 29 December 1982, a defector in Mr. Perez's position could be sentenced to a minimum sentence of three years in prison, with a maximum of eight years;

— Mr. Perez would not be allowed to travel to Cuba without a visa granted by the Cuban Immigration Department; a Cuban living abroad could be sentenced to up to three years in prison for illegal entry under Article 214.1 of the Cuban Penal Code;

— Cubans residing abroad may not own a business or real property in Cuba;

— irrespective of past social security contributions when they lived in Cuba, Cubans who leave the country may not collect such benefits when they become eligible, if they live abroad;

— under Law 989 of 5 December 1961, individuals who have "abandoned definitively the country" are susceptible to the confiscation of all their property.

35. Mr Gonzales thus concludes that Mr. Perez was effectively deprived of his civic rights as a Cuban when he defected in 1993, and that he should therefore be treated as a stateless person from that date.

36. In the absence of any contrary evidence or explanation offered by the Cuban National Olympic Committee, which did not avail itself of the opportunity given

to it to appear, the Panel concludes that the Gonzales Opinion constitutes sufficient evidence to ground the conclusion that Mr. Perez was, as of 1993, deprived of what is generally recognized as fundamental civic rights. Issues of national law, when presented to an international tribunal such as this Panel, must be established by competent evidence adduced by the parties. The Panel is conscious of the fact that the propositions articulated by Mr. Gonzales may be susceptible to significant qualifications, or indeed rebuttal, but the Panel has no reason to question the evidence proffered in the absence of any challenge to it. This consideration is particularly relevant in circumstances where all interested parties, including the Cuban National Olympic Committee, know or should know that CAS is bound to operate with great speed in order to ensure that its decisions are not pointless given the exigencies of the Olympic schedule.

37. It remains to be examined whether there is an international notion of statelessness that may be applicable in Mr. Perez's situation, and if so what its consequence may be for the purposes of paragraph 2 of the Bye-law to Rule 46 of the Olympic Charter.

38. It is clear that "statelessness," as both a concept and status, is well known in international law.

39. The Panel was referred to several authorities, including Paul Weis, *Nationality and Statelessness* (2nd Edn 1979), and Guy S. Goodwin, *The Refugee in International law* (2nd Edn 1996).

40. Weis, a former Legal Adviser of the Office of the United Nations High Commissioner for Refugees, states that a person may become stateless by losing one nationality without acquiring another. There have been a number of international conventions dealing with statelessness which, generally speaking, have been directed to reducing instances of involuntary loss of nationality.

41. In its second session in 1947, the Commission on Human Rights of the United Nations adopted a Resolution on Stateless Persons in which it expressed the wish that early consideration be given by the United Nations to the legal status of persons who do not enjoy the protection of any government, "in particular pending the acquisition of nationality as regards their legal and social protection and their documentation."

42. The *UN* Secretariat (Social Department) has given the term "stateless persons" a meaning which includes persons who are not only *de jure* but also *de facto* stateless, i.e. "persons who without having been

deprived of their nationality no longer enjoy the protection and assistance of their national authorities."

43. Rule 46 of the Olympic Charter requires that "Any competitor in the Olympic Games must be a national of the country of the NOC which is entering him." The Bye-law to Rule 46 is directed to circumstances in which, broadly speaking, the right of an athlete to compete may be restricted notwithstanding he or she is at the time of the relevant Games a national of a particular country which has selected him or her as a competitor.

44. The purpose of nationality in international law is not to give governments any form of proprietary interest in individuals, as though they were chattels. Nor is it to enable those who govern a country to use individuals as the instruments of their policy. These considerations are reinforced in circumstances where, as here, the uncontradicted evidence is that in return for the dominion sought to be exercised over Mr. Perez seven years after his leaving the country, Cuba apparently withholds from him the benefits of fundamental civil rights, such as those of freedom of movement and respect for property (The present case is thus fundamentally different from that of *Miranda v. Cuban Olympic Committee,* CAS arbitration N° SYD 3, where the Claimant was not a defector and traveled annually to Cuba on a Cuban passport, thus reaffirming his Cuban nationality until the moment he acquired Canadian citizenship.) The notion that Cuba in these circumstances should be in a position to prevent Mr. Perez from competing is offensive to two core principles of the Olympic Charter, namely that the interests of athletes are fundamental (Rule 3 (1)), and that Olympic competition is among athletes and not countries (Rule 9 (1)).

45. Having regard to the principles of the Charter, particularly those expressed in Rules 2, 3, 9 and 31, the Panel considers that the word "nationality" in Rule 46 and its Bye-law should be construed broadly. In so far as it is relevant to consider whether a person has lost his or her nationality, the Panel is of the view that a person may be found to have lost it both in circumstances where he or she is *de jure* or *de facto* stateless.

46. As it is the only evidence of Cuban law before us and because the opinion is consistent at least with the Claimant having become *de facto* stateless, the Panel is of the view . . . that in 1993, the Claimant at least became *de facto* stateless. In other words, as a result of his defection, he was no longer effectively a national of Cuba for the purposes of Rule 46 notwithstanding that he may in a formal sense have remained a national of Cuba and been so regarded by the government of that country. Whatever may have happened between 1993 and 1999, he has clearly now become a national of the United States, and may, prima facie, be entered as a competitor in these Games by his new country.

47. The final question remains whether, under Bye-law 46.2, the Claimant "changed" his nationality more than three years prior to the 2000 Sydney Olympic Games.

48. By definition the word "change" means to "become or make different" or "alter" or "pass from one form to another" (Oxford Advanced Learners Dictionary).

49. If this word were construed literally, it could be argued that a person does not change nationality until he or she [fully] changes to another nationality.

50. It is the Panel's view that the word "change" should be given a broad meaning to include the situation where a person becomes stateless. If a text may be interpreted in two ways, the Panel has no hesitation in resolving the ambiguity in favour of an athlete who is guilty of neither wrong-doing nor even negligence in terms of the Olympic Charter. The word "change" is appropriate to describe the passing from one form to another, that is from "nationality" to "statelessness." Based on the evidence of Cuban law before the Panel which, in the absence of evidence of the contrary, it feels bound to accept, that is what happened here.

51. The Panel therefore concludes that the Claimant "changed his nationality" in 1993 for the purposes of paragraph 2 of the Bye-law to Rule 46 of the Olympic Charter, and that therefore consent under that Bye-law by the concerned NOCs, including the Cuban Olympic Committee, is not necessary for him to compete.

52. The Panel further concludes that the Claimant is eligible to participate in the 2000 Olympic Games on behalf of the United States.

5. Decision

1. The application is allowed.

2. The decision dated 28 August 2000 finding that the Claimant is not eligible to represent the United States at the 2000 Sydney Olympic Games is overturned.

3. The Claimant is eligible to participate and represent the United States in the 2000 Sydney Olympic Games.

◆ *Notes & Questions*

1. Why did Perez seek to establish that he was "state-less" for a period of time? When did he become a US "national" under the Court of Arbitration Opinion? Does the Perez opinion hold that he became a citizen of the United States earlier than when he was naturalized in 1999? What should be the purpose of "nationality" in International Law?

2. Why did Swiss law govern this dispute? See textbook §1.4 regarding Private International Law. Why did this case pose a question involving International Law? Is it because the Olympics are "international?"

3. Was this legal dispute between the United States and Cuba? The US Cuban-American community, especially in Miami, certainly thought so. See L. Robertson, Cuban Kayaker's Case Overturned—He'll Compete for U.S., Miami Herald (Sept. 18, 2000), available at: <http://www.latinamericanstudies.org/sports/kayaker.htm>.

4. In 1957, the Supreme Court of British Columbia reviewed a deportation order made by Canadian immigration authorities regarding an individual named Hanna. He had sought residence in Canada, and a waiver of compliance with its Immigration Act due to this classic illustration of statelessness. He was born at sea and had no known record of his birth. As a minor child, he crossed and recrossed the international boundaries of Ethiopia, French Somaliland, British Somaliland, and Eritrea—without encountering difficulty with the immigration officials of those countries. As he grew older, Hanna had difficulty with the immigration officers of these countries, because he could not possess any nationality. In Eritrea, Hanna stowed away on an Italian steamer, hoping to land at some country that would grant him asylum. But upon arriving at any port, he was immediately locked up and denied permission to land. After a year of aimless wandering and imprisonment, Hanna escaped from the Italian vessel and concealed himself in the hold of the Norwegian motor-ship Gudvieg. As a stowaway, he fared no better than before. He was effectively held prisoner aboard the Gudvieg for more than sixteen months, making several trips to Canada. Canadian immigration authorities, having initially refused his entry, ultimately granted him asylum—on the basis that otherwise, he would be effectively condemned to life imprisonment at sea. Re Immigration Act and Hanna (Supreme Court of British Columbia), 21 WESTERN WEEKLY REPORTER 400 (1957).

5. The 1989 Convention on the Rights of the Child (textbook §11.2) provides that a birth certificate is a child's primary right, because it is evidence of an official identity and nationality. Only Somalia and the United States have not ratified this Convention. In 1998, the United Nations International Children's Emergency Fund (UNICEF) presented its annual Progress of Nations Report. UNICEF therein reported that one-third of the world's children do not have a birth certificate, which is increasing by approximately 40 million children per year. This circumstance deprives the children of many developing countries from obtaining health care, vaccinations, and education, while subjecting many of them to premature military service. Many babies in China are not registered, so that families can avoid the People's Republic of China's (PRC) policy of one child per family.

6. In the aftermath of 9-11, and the wars in Afghanistan and Iraq, the United Staes was deporting aliens to countries that did not necessarily want them, or to places where the alien did not wish to go or return. In January 2005, the US Supreme Court determined that this could no longer be ordered without the consent of the transferee country. Jama v. Immigration and Customs Enforcement, 543 U.S. 335, 125 S.Ct. 694, 160 L. Ed. 2d 708 (2005).

International organizations have attempted to alleviate the problems caused by statelessness. In 1921, the League of Nations established the Office of the High Commissioner of Refugees in response primarily to people made stateless by the Russian Revolution of 1917. (Members of the United Nations would later establish the UN Relief and Rehabilitation Administration to deal with the statelessness resulting from World War II.) Several treaties therefore address, but have yet to resolve, this recurring problem. The goal of the 1930 Hague Protocol Concerning Statelessness was to provide nationality to those deprived of it because of political dissension or military conflict. This draft treaty never became effective, because too few nations ratified it. The ensuing Universal Declaration of Human Rights, although not a binding treaty, nevertheless established a moral obligation that discourages UN member States from intentionally creating stateless persons.

The UN Convention on the Reduction of Statelessness entered into force in 1975. It obliges its signatories to grant their citizenship to stateless people who are willing recipients and found within their borders. It also removes the State discretion to deprive inhabitants of citizenship except on grounds that are not associated with race, religion, and political beliefs. But there are only fifteen State members, hardly enough to signal a global commitment to the problem of statelessness. The UN High Commissioner for Refugees currently deals with such matters.

The 1997 European Convention on Nationality provides in its preambular wording that signatories should use their sovereign powers to avoid statelessness. Article 4 specifically provides that everyone has a right to nationality. Under this treaty, statelessness would be significantly reduced (presuming sufficient ratifications) in an area of the world that has produced millions of stateless persons because of two world wars. It would thus be the first legally binding multilateral treaty containing a comprehensive set of rules to govern nationality problems.[36]

The 1999 UN International Law Commission's Draft Articles on Nationality of Natural Persons in Relation to the Succession of States provide: "Every individual who, on the date of the succession of States, had the nationality of the predecessor State, irrespective of the mode of acquisition of that nationality, has the right to the nationality of at least one of the States concerned, in accordance with the present draft articles."[37]

REFUGEES

State treatment of international refugees is a problem, which overlaps with statelessness. The plight of refugees is a predicament, which has received much attention because of the twentieth century's two world wars. Shortly after World War II, it was immediately evident that refugee problems were not finally over. Rather than a series of spontaneous *ad hoc* agreements, UN members initiated a process leading to the 1951 Geneva Convention on the Status of Refugees—and its 1967 Protocol. The basic Convention applies to those who became refugees prior to 1951. The Protocol applies to refugees since then. A 2001 declaration of the 143 State members reaffirmed the central role of the Refugee Convention for the protection of the world's refugee problem.[38]

This objective of refugee law is to establish and maintain the fundamental rights of the individual. Former UN High Commissioner for Refugees Guy Goodwin-Hill captures the spirit of this objective in his articulation that "[a]s was the case with some of the inter-war arrangements, the objective of the 1951 Convention and the 1967 Protocol is to both establish certain fundamental rights . . . and to prescribe certain standards of treatment. The refugee may be stateless and therefore, as a matter of law, unable to secure the benefits accorded to nationals of his or her country of origin. Alternatively, even if nationality is retained, the refugee's unprotected status can make obtaining such benefits a practical impossibility. The Convention consequently proposes, as a minimum standard, that refugees should receive at least that treatment which is accorded to aliens generally."[39]

These agreements do three things: they define who are refugees, determine their legal status, and provide the administrative and diplomatic machinery for implementing protective treaty provisions.

Who are refugees under International Law? Article 1.A.(2) of the 1951 Refugee Convention defines a refugee as any person who "owing to [a] well-founded fear of being persecuted for reasons of race, religion, nationality, membership of a particular social group or political opinion, is outside the country of his nationality and is unable, or, owing to such fear, is unwilling to avail himself of the protection of that country; or who, not having a nationality and being outside the country of his former habitual residence as a result of such events, is unable, or . . . unwilling to return to it." The April 2004 Common European Asylum System implements the general terms of this Convention in the EU.[40]

What is the refugee's legal status under International Law? One of the most important treaty protections is described in Article 33.1 of the Convention. A State may not return an individual to his or her homeland if "his life or freedom would be threatened on account of his race, religion, nationality, membership of a particular social group or political opinion."

The largest refugee population is that of the Palestinians, estimated to be 4 million people. The UN General Assembly's 1948 Resolution 194 provided that "refugees wishing to return to their homes and live at peace with their neighbors should be permitted to do so. . . ." It would be reaffirmed many times since, including Resolution 3236, which confirms the "inalienable right of the Palestinians to return to their homes and property from which they have been displaced and uprooted." The 1967 war spawned numerous refugee camps scattered throughout the Middle East in the West Bank, Gaza,

Lebanon, Jordan, and Syria. The 2005 Israeli departure from Gaza satisfies a portion of Resolution 3236.

Israel has linked the repeated Palestinian calls for their "right of return" to events, which subsequently threatened its very existence. In 1948, the United Nations partitioned what was then known as "Palestine" into two parts one, which would be the State of Palestine and the other the State of Israel. Israel's new Arab neighbors rejected that partition by attacking Israel. The Arab League would soon decree its economic boycott of Israel, actually designed to extinguish the State of Israel (§10.1).

Refugee issues resurfaced with a renewed fury after the Cold War, in Bosnia, Rwanda, and Kosovo, to name just a few locations touched by this lamentable feature of the individual's traditionally passive role in International Law.

National Applications Nations have applied (or ignored) international refugee law in a variety of significant contexts. The Fifth Strafsenat of the Bundesgerichtshof of the Federal Republic of Germany affirmed the State Court of Berlin's manslaughter convictions of Egon Krenz, the former General Secretary of East Germany (GDR), and two others. The defendants had been found criminally liable for participating in resolutions passed by the GDR Politburo and National Security Counsel, leading to fatal shootings at the Berlin Wall between 1984 and 1989. The German court thus held that the actions of the accused were illegal and unjustified under both GDR border law and State Practice. While the shooting of refugees was legal, and even sanctioned under GDR law, such legal doctrines could serve as neither justification nor excuse for manslaughter. The Bundesgerichtshof found no mistake of law and affirmed the application of the German Reunification Agreement (addressed further in the §11.3 *Berlin Wall Border Guard* case).

The British House of Lords applied the Refugee Convention's "members of particular social group" language to two married Pakistani women. They sought refugee status in the United Kingdom, because they were at risk of being falsely accused of adultery in Pakistan. If returned, they would be subject to criminal proceedings for sexual immorality. If found guilty, the possible punishments included public flogging or stoning to death. The majority of the House panel held that evidence of state-sanctioned or state-tolerated discrimination—notwithstanding constitutional guarantees of equality—rendered women in Pakistan "members

of a particular social group" and thus entitled to protected status under Art 1A(2) of the 1951 Convention.

In 2004, the England and Wales Court of Appeal (EWCA) considered a refugee claim by a Russian army deserter. He refused to fight in the Chechen War, and then unsuccessfully sought asylum from the United Kingdom's Secretary of State and Immigration Appeal Tribunal. They determined that his application did not fit within the 1951 Refugee Convention. The EWCA returned this case to the Tribunal. The question was whether this war warranted "international condemnation." The EWCA thus determined that he might be entitled to refugee status, if his participation was premised upon a war that was contrary to the basic rules of human conduct as defined by International Law.[41] Australia extended like protection to a Chinese national born in 1996 to Chinese parents in an immigration detention center in Australia. An administrative tribunal found that the child was not a refugee, merely because the parents "feared" retaliation if they were returned home to China, notwithstanding its one child per family State policy. On appeal, the High Court of Australia determined that the parents' fear for their child was sufficient to meet the "fear" component of the Convention definition of refugee.[42]

The EU grew from fifteen to twenty-five countries in 2004. The newest members are largely former members of the Soviet Union (§3.4). The assessment might not be as promising as one would hope. Unlike the older member nations, they had to make notable concessions regarding the treatment of minorities and refugees. Now that they are EU members, they will—as one knowledgeable academic grouping notes—be "unwilling to remodel their domestic legislation again. . . . To be sure, the present Member States will lose much of their bargaining power vis-a-vis the candidate states once these have been admitted to the club. It is acknowledged by most working in the field . . . that the scope of subregional policies have yet to bring about a viable refugee protection framework that guarantees adequate protection to refugees in the applicant states."[43]

North Korea threatened to withdraw from regional nuclear weapons discussions, unless the United States repealed the October 2004 North Korean Human Rights Act. This US legislation removed barriers for North Koreans wishing to obtain asylum in the United States. It allocated $20,000,000 per year to help settle those North Koreans who apply for asylum.

In December 2005, Egyptian police killed a dozen Sudanese war refugees in Cairo. Hundreds had occupied a squatter's camp, established to protest: (a) the UN refusal to support their quest for refugee status; and (b) Egypt's refusal to resettle them in a third country. The UN Commissioner for Refugees merely responded: "There is no justification for such violence and loss of life."

US Interpretation   The most famous case decided by any national court of a State party to the 1951 Refugee Convention has also been the most widely criticized. The following US Supreme Court case applied the "return" provision to Haitian refugees who sought asylum in the United States. In 1991, a group of military leaders displaced the government of Jean-Bertrand Aristide, the first democratically elected president in Haitian history. All parties to the litigation agreed that since this military coup, "hundreds of Haitians have been killed, tortured, detained without a warrant, or subjected to violence and the destruction of their property because of their political beliefs. Thousands have been forced into hiding."

Following the coup, the US Coast Guard suspended repatriations for a period of several weeks, and the United States imposed economic sanctions on Haiti. In the meantime the Haitian exodus expanded dramatically. During the next six months, the Coast Guard interdicted more than 34,000 Haitians. Because so many of them could not be safely processed on Coast Guard cutters, the Department of Defense established temporary facilities at the US Naval Base in Guantanamo, Cuba, to accommodate them during the screening process. In May 1992, the US Navy determined that no additional migrants could safely be accommodated at Guantanamo. This background set the stage for the US action that allegedly violated its commitments under the treaty.

President Clinton directed the Coast Guard to intercept vessels illegally transporting passengers from Haiti to the United States and to return those passengers to Haiti without first determining whether they may qualify as "refugees" under the 1951 UN Convention Relating to the Status of Refugees. This reaction posed the question of whether such forced repatriation to Haiti violated the US Immigration and Nationality Act (INA) and Article 33 of the United Nations Protocol Relating to the Status of Refugees. The US Immigration Act was supposedly amended to codify the US treaty commitment under the 1951 Refugee Convention.

The treaty gap that triggered this litigation involved how to apply the term "return."[44] Did the French-language treaty term *refouler* broadly require a determination of refugee status for *all* returns—even on the high seas—or just those returns occurring after the asylum seeker has arrived within the territory (or territorial waters) of a State that is a party to the 1951 Refugee Convention?

The text and the history of the US legislation, like that of Article 33 of the UN Convention, are completely silent on the applicability of returns undertaken *outside* territorial borders or waters. The "Respondents" (Haitians) argued that the 1967 Protocol's broad remedial goals prohibit a nation from repatriating refugees to their potential oppressors—whether or not the refugees are the objects of the US return within or beyond US territory.

The drafters of the 1951 Convention, and the parties to the companion Protocol—like the drafters of the conforming 1980 US immigration law amendment—apparently did not contemplate that any nation would ever gather fleeing refugees and then return them to the very country from which they so desperately sought to escape:

◆

Sale v. Haitian Centers Council, Inc.

SUPREME COURT OF THE UNITED STATES, 1993
509 US 155, 113 S.Ct. 2549, 125 *L. Ed.* 2d 128

AUTHOR'S NOTE: The trial court decided against the Haitians, confirming the legality of President Clinton's directive requiring returns to Haiti without having an "Article 33 Refugee Convention" hearing.

The Court of Appeals disagreed. Its judges did not accept the US government's argument that the treaty did not bar returns made prior to the refugee's arrival in the US or its territorial waters. The 1980 amendment to the national immigration laws was apparently intended to conform US immigration law to the provisions of the Refugee Convention. This intermediate court's panel of judges read the Article 33.1 "return" provision as "plainly" covering all refugees, regardless of their location, and where they were found and immediately turned back by the US Coast Guard. The US was thus characterized as engaging in the act of "returning" these refugees on the high seas. This, said the intermediate court, thereby triggering the Article 33.1 requirement to require a determination of whether these "returns" would subject the Haitians to death or other heinous mistreatment on the basis of their political beliefs.

The US Supreme Court majority decided, however, that in spite of the moral weight of this argument, Article 33 was not intended to have such an extraterritorial effect. The treaty could not apply to a return ("refouler") occurring outside of US territorial waters, on the high seas between Haiti and the US. In the final paragraph, the majority of the Supreme Court's justices presented their final argument by quoting from the opinion of a lower court case with similar facts: "This case presents a painfully common situation in which desperate people, convinced that they can no longer remain in their homeland, take desperate measures to escape. Although the human crisis is compelling, there is no solution to be found in a judicial remedy" (implying the need for a diplomatic remedy or a treaty modification).

What follows is the dissent to the majority opinion. Justice Blackmun agreed with the intermediate appellate court which would have required a hearing before the Haitian refugees could be turned back by the US Coast Guard. According to Justice Blackmun, the lower court's judges correctly interpreted the "refouler" (return) provision of the Refugee Convention as prohibiting President Clinton's Executive Order to the Coast Guard in violation of the treaty.

JUSTICE BLACKMUN, DISSENTING: When, in 1968, the United States acceded to the United Nations Protocol Relating to the Status of Refugees, Jan. 31, 1967, it pledged not to "return (refouler) a refugee in any manner whatsoever" to a place where he would face political persecution. In 1980, Congress amended our immigration law to reflect the Protocol's directives. Today's majority nevertheless decides that the forced repatriation of the Haitian refugees is perfectly legal, because the word "return" does not mean return, because the opposite of "within the United States" is not outside the United States, and because the official charged with controlling immigration has no role in enforcing an order to control immigration. . . .

Article 33.1 of the Convention states categorically and without geographical limitation: "No Contracting State shall expel or return (*refouler*) a refugee in any manner whatsoever to the frontiers of territories where his life or freedom would be threatened on account of his race, religion, nationality, membership of a particular social group or political opinion."

The terms are unambiguous. Vulnerable refugees shall not be returned. The language is clear, and the command is straightforward; that should be the end of the inquiry. Indeed, until litigation ensued, the Government consistently acknowledged that the Convention applied on the high seas.

The majority, however, has difficulty with the Treaty's use of the term "return ('refouler')." "Return," it claims, does not mean return, but instead has a distinctive legal meaning. For this proposition the Court relies almost entirely on the fact that American law makes a general distinction between deportation and exclusion. Without explanation, the majority asserts that in light of this distinction the word "return" as used in the Treaty somehow must refer only to "the exclusion of aliens who are . . . 'on the threshold of initial entry'" [citation omitted].

. . . The text of the Convention does not ban the "exclusion" of aliens who have reached some indeterminate "threshold"; it bans their "return." It is well settled that a treaty must first be construed according to its "ordinary meaning." Article 31.1 of the Vienna Convention on the Law of Treaties. The ordinary meaning of "return" is "to bring, send, or put (a person or thing) back to or in a former position." Webster's Third New International Dictionary 1941 (1986). That describes precisely what petitioners [US government agencies] are doing to the Haitians. By dispensing with ordinary meaning at the outset, and by taking instead as its starting point the assumption that "return," as used in the Treaty, "has a legal meaning narrower than its common meaning," the majority leads itself astray.

The straightforward interpretation of the duty of nonreturn is strongly reinforced by the Convention's use of the French term refouler. The ordinary meaning of "refouler," as the majority concedes, is "[t]o repulse . . . ; to drive back, to repel." *Dictionnaire Larousse* 631 (1981). Thus construed, Article 33.1 of the Convention reads: "No contracting state shall expel or [repulse, drive back, or repel] a refugee in any manner whatsoever to the frontiers of territories where his life or freedom would be threatened. . . ." That, of course, is exactly what the Government is doing. It is no surprise that when the French press has described the very policy challenged here, the term it has used is *refouler*. See, e.g., Le bourbier haitien, *Le Monde*, May 31–June 1, 1992 ("[L]es Etats-Unis ont decide de refouler directement les refugies recueillis par la garde cotiere." (The United States has decided [de refouler] directly the refugees picked up by the Coast Guard). . . .

Article 33.1 is clear not only in what it says, but also in what it does not say: it does not include any geographical limitation. It limits only where a refugee may be sent "to," not where he may be sent from. This is not surprising, given that the aim of the provision is to protect refugees against persecution. . . .

The Convention that the [US] Refugee Act embodies was enacted largely in response to the experience of Jewish refugees in Europe during the period of World War II. The tragic consequences of the world's indifference at that time are well known. The resulting ban on refoulement, as broad as the humanitarian purpose that inspired it, is easily applicable here, the Court's protestations of impotence and regret notwithstanding.

The refugees attempting to escape from Haiti do not claim a right of admission to this country. They do not even argue that the Government has no right to intercept their boats. They demand only that the United States, land of refugees and guardian of freedom, cease forcibly driving them back to detention, abuse, and death. That is a modest plea, vindicated by the Treaty and the statute. We should not close our ears to it.

I dissent [from the majority's holding affirming President Clinton's Executive Order which authorizes returns to Haiti, without the required determination of refugee status under the Refugee Convention].

◆ Notes & Questions

1. The Supreme Court majority found that no treaty can impose uncontemplated extraterritorial obligations on those who ratify it, regardless of the general humanitarian intent of the treaty. Because the text of Article 33 did not *authorize* a signatory's "returns" outside of its territory, it could not be interpreted to *prohibit* such actions. Could one argue that the majority of the court effectively violated the "spirit" of the Article 33 "refouler" provision? Did the US Supreme Court majority's restrictive interpretation of the treaty's refoulement provision violate US obligations under the Refugee Convention? Alternatively, should such situations be left to the discretion of each State to apply either a broad or a narrow construction? Should the treaty be amended to clarify this point? If so, would there be a danger in reopening the treaty to national interpretations which could water down what rights are already expressed in the Convention and Protocol?

2. Justice Blackmun was not the only "dissenter." The majority's decision was chastised by the President of the American Society of International Law in the Society's Newsletter of Sept.–Oct. 1993. Society President Louis Henkin therein remarked that "the Supreme Court has adopted an eccentric, highly implausible interpretation of a treaty. It has interpreted those treaties . . . not as other state parties would interpret them, not as an international tribunal would interpret them, [and] not as the US Supreme Court would have interpreted them earlier in our history when the justices took the law of nations seriously, when they appeared to recognize that in such cases US courts were sitting in effect as international tribunals." Further analysis of Professor Henkin's point is available in M. Rogoff, Interpretation of International Agreements by Domestic Courts and the Politics of International Treaty Relations: Reflections on Some Recent Decisions of the United States Supreme Court, 11 AMER. UNIV. J. INT'L L. & POL'Y 559 (1996).

3. As the above 1993 Haitian case illustrates, no UN program or treaty has fully accomplished the goal of eradicating the problems identified in *Sale v. Haitian Centers Council, Inc.* The primary barrier is national distrust. Many countries share the concern about potential United Nations or treaty interference with nationality decisions that they would like to make on a case-by-case basis. Their view, effectively, is that the State's treatment of individuals remains a matter that should be exclusively within national jurisdiction. *Sale* arguably provided another illustration of the disdain shown by certain national courts for broad interpretations of their treaty commitments.

4. Consider this passage from perhaps the most authoritative statement about refugee law, penned by a former

UN High Commissioner for Refugees. He was referring to the principle of "non-refoulement" and contemporary applications of the 1951 Convention and its 1967 Protocol: "If each State remains absolutely free to determine the status of asylum seekers and either to abide by or ignore the principle of nonrefoulement, then the refugee's status in international law is denied and the standing, authority, and effectiveness of the principles and institutions of protection are seriously undermined. G. Goodwin-Hill, THE REFUGEE IN INTERNATIONAL LAW 169 (2d ed. Oxford, Eng.: Clarendon Press, 1996).

5. In a new challenge to Refugee Convention expectations, the US Border Patrol may—as of August 2004— return foreigners to their home country *without* a hearing before an immigration judge. A Department of Homeland Security notice authorizes an expedited removal process for aliens who cannot demonstrate to the border patrol agent, within 100 miles of any US border, that they have been in the United States for fourteen days before the encounter. T. Ridge, Designating Aliens for Expedited Removal, 69 FED. REGISTER No. 154 (Aug. 11, 2004). Amnesty International's response was that "Someone else, someone a few steps removed from the 'heat of battle,' needs to make the life-and-death judgment call whether those apprehended should be removed to their country of origin." B. Frelick, Playing by the Rules: Not Much Help for the Refugees, San Diego Union Tribune (Sept. 17, 2004).

◆ 4.3 CORPORATE NATIONALITY

INTRODUCTION

A corporation is considered a legal "person" under the national law of most nations. There are a variety of entities to which this section could apply. The most common form is that of the "corporation," a business entity created for the purpose of limiting liability beyond that which is available to a natural person. This section will use the term "corporation" to refer collectively to all such institutions.

This chapter previously addressed the legal bond of nationality linking the individual and his or her native State. There are instances where a corporation needs like protection on the international level. A corporation may be taxed by more than one country, each claiming that the corporation is its citizen. It may be nationalized by the host country, without adequate (or any) compensation to the shareholders (§4.4).

The genuineness of an individual's nationality link with a particular State is comparatively easy to establish (*Nottebohm*). The genuineness of a corporation's link with a particular country is a more complex question. Today's multinational enterprises are often owned by parent corporations and, in turn, by numerous shareholders residing in various countries. When the enterprise is harmed, it is the individual shareholders who are actually harmed. These investors sometimes seek the assistance of the States of their individual nationalities to help them obtain a remedy for the wrong done to the multinational enterprise. Other times they seek such help in the name of the corporation.

Studying corporations is also important, for reasons beyond determining with which State they are properly aligned—for purposes of diplomatic representation, arbitrations, or cases filed in regional or global tribunals. A number of these "multinationals" generate annual earnings eclipsing the gross national product of the nations wherein they operate. Some have thus wielded a heavy hand in terms of influencing State behavior. A 1909 US Supreme Court antitrust case provides a classic illustration. Costa Rica nationalized the plaintiff US corporation's assets. The apparent motive for this property taking was provided by another US corporation, which conspired with the government to monopolize the lucrative Central American banana trade.[45] UN codes of conduct have since evolved, in the contemporary effort to control the corporate potential for harming both nations and their inhabitants (§13.1).

Like a natural person, a business entity possesses nationality under International Law. It, too, can be harmed in and by foreign countries. Like individuals, corporations lack the international legal capacity to seek remedies for wrongs such as the corporation harmed by Costa Rica in the preceding paragraph. Historically, corporations have had to convince their home governments to present claims on their behalf, usually via diplomatic efforts on their behalf or the national pursuit of litigation in an international tribunal against the offending State. But States are not *obligated* to present such claims on an international level.

In an age when many corporations engage in business transactions throughout the globe, the issue of the corporation's legal situs—where it can claim citizenship—presents a judicial quagmire. A number of European nations treat a multinational corporation as a national of the country where its headquarters or home office is located. In the United States, a corporation is a US national if it is incorporated in one of the fifty US states.

HOME STATE?

Which country may legally espouse a claim on behalf of a corporation?

Hypothetical: Assume that Investco is a large multinational corporation located in Hong Kong. It is owned by shareholders from Brazil, France, Germany, South Africa, and the United States. Assume that the Chinese

government nationalizes Investco's assets after the 1997 takeover of Hong Kong. The PRC does so without any compensation. Under International Law, not all of the "shareholder" nations have the capacity to present a claim for compensation against China. By analogy, the ICJ determined that Mr. Nottebohm's receipt of a new nationality did not authorize Liechtenstein to present his property claim against Guatemala. A similar analysis is appropriate in the case of corporations, when they have ties with more than one nation. A tribunal would have to decide which of the various nations best represents Investco's corporate personality. Under International Law, the appropriate State is normally the State where Investco is incorporated. There are exceptions, however, which will be discussed in the following case.

Barcelona Traction, Light, and Power Co.

INTERNATIONAL COURT OF JUSTICE
1970 *International Court of Justice Reports* (Second Phase) 3 (1970)

AUTHOR'S NOTE: Barcelona Traction was incorporated in Canada. It operated a power company in Spain. It was declared bankrupt by a Spanish court, which ordered the seizure of its assets. Belgium, England, Canada, and the US all tried to assist Barcelona Traction in resisting the seizure.

Individual citizens in these countries owned the stock of the corporation. The shareholders believed that the Spanish authorities prematurely sought bankruptcy for some ulterior purpose. The corporation was a legal person, separate from its stockholders, and claiming that it was a corporate citizen of Canada. However, Canada exercised its State discretion, by choosing not to process this claim on behalf of the Canadian shareholders or the corporation.

Belgian nationals owned eighty-eight percent of the Barcelona Traction stock at the time the bankruptcy was declared. Belgium thus decided to prosecute this action in the ICJ against Spain, because the majority of the individual shareholders were Belgians.

The ICJ dismissed this suit. It ruled that Belgium could not represent Barcelona Traction. If the country of incorporation (Canada) was unwilling to pursue the claim, the State of the majority of the individual shareholders (Belgium) could not do so. Selected portions of the ICJ's opinion present the Court's rationale for vesting the country of incorporation with the exclusive right of representation on the international plane (in diplomatic

or international judicial proceedings). The paragraph numbers are those of the Court.

COURT'S OPINION:

. . .

70. In allocating corporate entities to States for purposes of diplomatic protection, international law is based, but only to a limited extent, on an analogy with the rules governing the nationality of individuals. The traditional rule attributes the right of diplomatic protection of a corporate entity to the State under the laws of which it is incorporated and in whose territory it has its registered office. . . . However, in the particular field of the diplomatic protection of corporate entities, no absolute test of the "genuine connection" has found general acceptance. . . .

71. In the present case, it is not disputed that the company was incorporated in Canada and has its registered office in that country. The incorporation of the company under the law of Canada was an act of free choice. Not only did the founders of the company seek its incorporation under Canadian law but it has remained under that law for a period of over 50 years. It has maintained in Canada its registered office, its accounts and its share registers. Board meetings were held there for many years; it has been listed in the records of the Canadian tax authorities. A close and permanent connection has been established, fortified by the passage of over half a century.

This connection is in no way weakened by the fact that the company engaged from the very outset in commercial activities outside Canada, for that was its declared object. Barcelona Traction's links with Canada are thus manifold.

72. Furthermore, the Canadian nationality of the company has received general recognition. Prior to the institution of proceedings before the Court, three other governments apart from that of Canada (those of the United Kingdom, the United States and Belgium) made representations concerning the treatment accorded to Barcelona Traction by the Spanish authorities. The United Kingdom Government intervened on behalf of bondholders and of shareholders. Several representations were also made by the United States Government, but not on behalf of the Barcelona Traction company as such.

. . .

75. The Canadian Government itself, which never appears to have doubted its right to intervene on the company's behalf, exercised the protection of Barcelona Traction by diplomatic representation for a number of years, in particular by its note of 27 March 1948, in which it alleged that a denial of justice had been committed in respect of the Barcelona Traction, Ebro and National Trust companies, and requested that the bankruptcy judgment be canceled. . . .

76. In sum, the record shows that from 1948 onwards the Canadian Government made to the Spanish Government numerous representations which cannot be viewed otherwise than as the exercise of diplomatic protection in respect of the Barcelona Traction company. Therefore this was not a case where diplomatic protection was [totally] refused or remained in the sphere of fiction. It is also clear that over the whole period of its diplomatic activity the Canadian Government proceeded in full knowledge of the Belgian attitude and activity.

. . .

78. The Court would here observe that, within the limits prescribed by international law, a State may exercise diplomatic protection by whatever means and to whatever extent it thinks fit, for it is its own right that the State is asserting. Should the natural [individuals] or legal [corporate] persons on whose behalf it is acting consider that their rights are not adequately protected, they have no remedy in international law. All they can do is to resort to municipal [internal] law, if means are available, with a view to furthering their cause or obtaining redress. . . . However, all these questions remain within the province of municipal law and do not affect the position internationally.

79. The State must be viewed as the sole judge to decide whether its protection will be granted, to what extent it is granted, and when it will cease. It retains in this respect a discretionary power the exercise of which may be determined by considerations of a political or other nature, unrelated to the particular case. Since the claim of the State is not identical with that of the individual or corporate person whose cause is espoused, the State enjoys complete freedom of action. Whatever the reasons for any change of attitude, the fact cannot in itself constitute a justification for the exercise of diplomatic protection by another government, unless there is some independent and otherwise valid ground for that.

. . .

88. It follows from what has already been stated above that, where it is a question of an unlawful act committed against a company representing foreign capital, the general rule of international law authorizes the national State of the company alone to make a claim.

. . .

96. The Court considers that the [unsuccessfully argued] adoption of the theory of diplomatic protection of shareholders as such, by opening the door to competing diplomatic claims, could create an atmosphere of confusion and insecurity in international economic relations. The danger would be all the greater inasmuch as the shares of companies whose activity is international are widely scattered and frequently change hands. It might perhaps be claimed that, if the right of protection belonging to the national States of the shareholders were considered as only secondary to that of the national State of the company, there would be less danger of difficulties of the kind contemplated. However, the Court must state that the essence of a secondary right is that it only comes into existence at the time when the original right ceases to exist [for example, the State of incorporation ceases to exist—as discussed in §2.4]. . . .

100. In the present case, it is clear from what has been said above that Barcelona Traction was never reduced to a position of impotence such that it could not have approached its national State, Canada, to ask for its diplomatic protection, and that, as far as appeared to the Court, there was nothing to prevent Canada from continuing to grant its diplomatic protection to Barcelona Traction if it had considered that it should do so.

. . .

◆ *Notes & Questions*

1. What general rule did the ICJ apply for determining which State could represent a multinational corporation in international (judicial or diplomatic) proceedings?
2. Are there any exceptions that would allow *another* State to present an international claim on behalf of a corporation?
3. The Court's language in this 1970 opinion solidly vests the appropriate State with the sole discretion to determine whether it will process a claim for a corporation. Should the shareholders be able to have their claims espoused by another country? In their own right, as individuals in a claim against a State?

Consider the following more recent case, decided under the International Convention on Settlement of Investment Disputes between States and Nationals of Other States. It presents the contemporary view of the relevant shareholder rights under International Law.

◆

CMS Gas Transmission Company (Claimant) v. The Republic of Argentina (Respondent)

INTERNATIONAL CENTRE FOR SETTLEMENT OF INVESTMENT DISPUTES (JULY 17, 2003)

Case No. ARB/01/8

42 *International Legal Materials* 788 (2003)

AUTHOR'S NOTE: CMS is a US corporation. It lodged this arbitration against Argentina in the International Centre for Settlement of Investment Disputes (ICSID), which is located in Washington, DC. Argentina had suspended a tariff adjustment formula, for gas transportation by an enterprise in which CMS had invested (by granting it licenses). Argentina enacted new privatization measures related to the gas sector of its national economy. Those measures applied to a company ("TGN") in which CMS had invested. Argentina's new regulations were allegedly applied in a way that therefore harmed CMS investments supposedly in violation of a bilateral investment treaty ("BIT") between the US and Argentina.

The following segment of this case addresses just the question of whether the CMS corporation had the legal standing ("*jus standi*") to seek relief from Argentina. The Republic essentially claimed that regardless of the *merits* of the CMS claim CMS was not the proper plaintiff to present this claim. Therefore, the CMS claim could not be heard by this tribunal ("admissibility").

TRIBUNAL'S OPINION:
Decision of the Tribunal on Objections to Jurisdiction

. . .

Objection to admissibility on the issue of the Claimant's jus standi

36. The Republic of Argentina has objected to the admissibility of the claim by CMS on the ground that the Claimant does not hold the rights upon which it bases its claim to wit, TGN being the licensee, and CMS only a minority shareholder in this company, only TGN could claim for any damage suffered. . . . It follows, in the Respondent's view, that CMS is claiming not for direct damages but for indirect damages which could result from its minority participation in TGN.

. . .

43. The parties have turned next to the discussion of the situation under international law, with particular reference to the meaning and extent of the Barcelona Traction decision. Counsel for the Republic of Argentina are right when arguing that that decision ruled out the protection of investors by the State of their nationality when that State is different from the State of incorporation of the corporate entity concerned. . . . However, Counsel for the Claimant [CMS] are also right . . . it did not rule out the possibility of extending protection to shareholders in a corporation in different contexts. Specifically, the International Court of Justice was well aware of the new trends in respect of the protection of foreign investors under the 1965

Convention and the bilateral investment treaties related thereto.

. . .

46. The Republic of Argentina has advanced the argument that, when shareholders have been protected separately from the affected corporation, this occurred in cases where the shareholders were majority or controlling, not *minority* shareholders as in the instant case. This fact may be true, but it is equally true, as argued by the Claimant . . . ; rather they were concerned with the possibility of protecting shareholders *independently* from the affected corporation, that is, solely with the issue of the corporate legal personality and its limits [italics added].

47. State practice further supports the meaning of this changing scenario. Besides accepting the protection of shareholders . . . , the concept of limiting it to majority or controlling participations has given way to a lower threshold in this respect. Minority and non-controlling participations have thus been included in the protection granted or have been admitted to [make a] claim in

their own right. Contemporary practice relating to . . . the decisions of the Iran-United States Tribunal and the rules and decisions of the United Nations Compensation Commission . . . evidence increasing flexibility in the handling of international claims.

48. The Tribunal therefore finds no bar in current international law to the concept of allowing claims by shareholders independently from those of the corporation concerned, not even if those shareholders are minority or non-controlling shareholders. Although it is true, as argued by the Republic of Argentina, that this is mostly the result of . . . specific treaty arrangements that have so allowed, . . . [and] is so prevalent that it can now be considered the general rule, certainly in respect of foreign investments and increasingly in respect of other matters. To the extent that customary international law or generally the traditional law of international claims might have followed a different approach—a proposition that is open to debate—then that [traditional] approach can [now] be considered the exception.

◆ *Notes & Questions*

1. Should the rule for a corporation (*Barcelona Traction*) or its shareholders (*CMS*)—regarding who can tender claims in an international forum—instead be the *Nottebohm* "genuine link" test applied to individuals?

2. Institutional background details about the International Centre for Settlement of Investment Disputes tribunal is available in R. Rayfuse (ed.), 1 ICSID REPORTS 3–280 (Cambridge, Eng.: Cambridge Univ. Press, 1993).

3. Assume that you represent the respondent Argentina. You would like your country to be able to predict when it can expect to be sued in its own local courts, as opposed to suits being filed against Argentina in international tribunals. You have now considered both the ICJ's *Barcelona Traction* and ICSID's *CMS* case. *CMS* is evidence that the brightline *Barcelona Traction* rule—only the State of incorporation can espouse claims on behalf of a corporation—is too rigid for contemporary cross-border investment. Your country wants to encourage more foreign investment. Should you therefore recommend that your nation continue to object to CMS-like claims being

heard in an international investment tribunal like ICSID?

◆ **4.4 INJURY TO ALIENS**

INTRODUCTION

Many forms of State responsibility are exhibited throughout this book. State responsibility is a vast component of International Law, which appears throughout the various chapters of any textbook on this subject. As discussed in §2.5, for example, there have been numerous attempts to achieve consensus on articulating this facet of International Law—mostly without success. This section of the book covers State responsibility for injury to aliens, a matter which dovetails with analyses of the individual and corporation under International Law. A State may be held accountable for the acts of its agents, harming aliens in a way that treats them differently from its own citizens.

Early commentators had practical reasons for focusing on this category of State responsibility. Many nationals of one State—who have lived, traveled, or worked in another State—have endured abuse and discrimination throughout recorded history. As noted by a leading study:

"Since ancient times foreigners have been regarded with suspicion, if not fear, either due to their non-conforming religious and social customs, their assumed inferiority, or because they were considered potential spies and agents of other nations. The Romans refused aliens the benefits of the *jus civile* [civil law], thirteenth-century England limited their recourse to the ordinary courts of justice [rather than all courts], and imperial Spain denied them trading rights in the New World." Word and deed often have yet to merge.

The December 2005 ultranationalist march through central Moscow suggests a modern analogy. The organized Movement Against Illegal Immigration then proclaimed that immigrants from the Caucus and Central Asia had "occupied Russian cities," and that Russians must oppose "the virus of tolerance."[46]

The development of the law of State responsibility for injury to aliens began approximately two centuries ago. One of the foremost commentators of the time, Emerich de Vattel, wrote in his influential book on the *Law of Nations:* "Whoever ill-treats a [foreign] citizen injures the State, which must protect the citizen."[47] His articulation was adopted by many international tribunals and commentators as the rationale for recognizing State responsibility for injury to aliens. Avoiding the escalation of this facet of discrimination became the linchpin in restatements of the law of State responsibility.

This branch of State responsibility relied on the internal tort law applied by many States. Tort law governs civil wrongs by an individual for unreasonable conduct that harms another individual. If someone takes the property of another without justification, that person is liable under the internal tort law of many nations. Writers and jurists believed that a State should be similarly liable when its unreasonable acts or omissions harmed aliens. Such protection was necessary because national law typically insulated the State from the claims of its own citizens. When State X nationalized the property of a foreign citizen without compensation, that citizen's home State Y could thus assert a case against State X because of X's responsibility for discriminating against an alien.

CODIFICATION ATTEMPTS

The law of State responsibility for injury to aliens is not codified in a comprehensive multilateral treaty. The International Law textbook used at Russia's Moscow State University urges that "codification is now an urgent task. Members of the League of Nations sought to codify

those norms of international law dealing with the responsibility of States for damage to the person or property of foreigners (which efforts served the interests of imperialist States)."[48]

Several attempts have been made to codify the law of State responsibility for injuries to foreign individuals and corporations. The first was the 1929 draft Convention on Responsibility of States for Damage Done on Their Territory to the Person or Property of Foreigners. It was compiled and produced under the auspices of the Harvard Law School Research in International Law Project during the period between the two world wars. Another campaign to codify this branch of State responsibility surfaced in 1953, when members of the UN General Assembly decided that "it is desirable for the maintenance of peaceful relations between States that the principles of international law governing State responsibility be codified." This UN resolution resulted in the drafting of several reports on various facets of State responsibility. Those reports did not, however, generate a written multilateral agreement.[49]

One of the most extensive presentations of the law of State responsibility toward aliens was published in 1961: the Draft Convention on the International Responsibility of States for Injury to Aliens. The authors were Harvard University Professors Louis Sohn and Marvin Baxter. Their work exemplifies the Western view that underdeveloped nations have a significant interest in importing foreign investment and technological assistance and can profit by the just treatment of foreign corporations and employees. The Sohn–Baxter perspective is that both developed and lesser-developed nations should encourage the fair and nondiscriminatory treatment of their citizens while abroad. This draft treaty does not incorporate the views of all commentators. It is an alternative, however, to the so-called Third World New International Economic Order (described below), whereby a State may treat aliens differently than its own citizens.[50]

Current UN efforts to codify State responsibility have not yet produced *final* draft articles on this particular feature of Sate responsibility. The recent 1998 draft is admittedly silent, because "one *should not* find in the state responsibility draft articles a discussion of the law governing, for example, expropriation of the property of foreign nationals."[51] This project, as it continues to develop, will hopefully contain draft treaty articles, which may serve as a generally acceptable basis for greater international cooperation on this premedieval problem.

CATEGORIES OF INJURY

What specific State conduct triggers responsibility for injury to aliens? While classification is no simple task, the customary violations may be listed as follows:

(1) Nonwealth injuries
(2) Denial of justice, including what some writers characterize as separate subcategories of wrongful arrest and detention, and lack of due diligence
(3) Confiscation of property
(4) Deprivation of livelihood

Nonwealth Injuries This form of State responsibility evolved from the unreasonable acts or omissions of State agents, which caused death or physical injury to foreign citizens. A 1983 report by the Panel on the Law of State Responsibility of the American Society of International Law defined nonwealth injury as "an injury inflicted by a State upon an alien either (1) directly through some act or omission causing physical or other personal injury to or the death of an alien, or (2) indirectly through some failure to act, including the failure under certain circumstances to prevent injury inflicted by another party, the failure to provide the injured alien with an effective remedy, or the failure to pursue, prosecute, and punish the responsible party."[52]

This category of harm is distinguished from the other types of State responsibility by its physical attributes. While a nonwealth injury can have economic consequences, the harm is not directed at the victim's pocket book. In October 1965, for example, Indonesian army forces conducted a campaign directed at Chinese nationals in Indonesia. Chinese citizens were beaten, arrested without cause, and murdered. Further, Indonesia's army issued permits allowing civilians to demonstrate for the purpose of persecuting Chinese nationals. The Chinese government sought and received assurances from Indonesia's central government that this violence would end. Had the Indonesian government refused the Chinese demands, it would have incurred further responsibility for physical nonwealth injuries to China's nationals.

Denial of Justice

Discrimination Against Aliens A State's discriminatory application of its domestic laws to an alien is described as a "denial of justice." This is a somewhat "procedural" form of injury, rather than a physical harm. The standard procedures, which apply to the benefit of a local citizen, are withheld from an alien.

There is no uniform definition of this form of injury. National and international tribunals have nevertheless found a denial of justice in countless cases. There are some limitations, however. In Latin American States, a "denial of justice" can occur only when the State has *completely* refused access to its courts—or, its courts will not take the necessary steps to render a decision. The regional perspective is that there can never be a denial of justice based on the quality or unsatisfactory nature of the procedures used by the tribunal when it is deciding an alien's claim. If there is some access to some tribunal, which will ultimately decide the particular matter, then a foreign citizen cannot complain about the quality of justice although different procedures apply in his or her own home state.[53]

Most nations adopt a broader interpretation of the term "denial of justice." A State can be responsible for injuring an alien when its tribunals do not provide adequate time or legal representation to prepare a defense. This must occur in a way that provides less protection than that afforded to the offending State's own citizens. If local citizens are allowed to seek legal assistance, it would be a denial of justice to withhold that right just because the prisoner is a foreign citizen.

International Minimum Standard Another subcategory of denial of justice is the unreasonable arrest and detention of an alien. Incarceration is thereby unlawful when it discriminates against aliens and unreasonably departs from generally accepted procedure. An arresting State would be liable if it failed to give a reason for the arrest or detention of an alien defendant, or if trial were delayed for an unreasonable time after arrest.

Can a State incur liability for a denial of justice when it treats foreign citizens in the same way that it treats its own citizens? A variation on the denial of justice theme arises when a State treats a foreign citizen in a substandard way, and then defends on the basis of equal treatment of all individuals in the same circumstances. This problem triggers the daunting question of whether there is an international minimum standard (IMS) below which no State may fall in its treatment of all individuals including its own citizens. The comparatively poor treatment of individuals is not discriminatory, as long as there is no discrimination against aliens. Both foreign and local citizens are subjected to the same type of treatment. If an IMS does exist, however, that State would not be able to use equality of treatment to justify its falling below the IMS regarding the treatment of both foreign and local citizens.

The historical maturation of such a standard has been retarded by economic and political differences between Western States and States in lesser-developed regions of the world. What is probably the most definitive (and equally broad) statement defining the IMS was made by US Secretary of State Elihu Root in 1910:

> Each country is bound to give to the nationals of another country in its territory the benefit of the same laws, the same administration, the same protection, and the same redress for injury which it gives to its own citizens, and neither more nor less: provided the protection which the country gives to its own citizens conforms to the established standard of civilization.
>
> There is [however] a standard of justice very simple, very fundamental, and of such general acceptance by all civilized countries as to form a part of the international law of the world. The . . . system of law and administration shall conform to this general standard. If any country's system of law and administration does not conform to that standard, although the people of the country may be content to live under it, no other country can be compelled to accept it as furnishing a satisfactory measure of treatment of its citizens.[54]

There have been some UN-driven codification attempts. They generally protect human rights in the prisoner's context. However, as is typical of broadly worded statements of principle with which no State could disagree, they prohibit torture and inhumane conditions without defining those terms. In 1955, the first UN Congress on the Prevention of Crime and the Treatment of Offenders sought to promote a general consensus about generally accepted treatment of prisoners and management of penal institutions. This Congress promulgated the Standard Minimum Rules for the Treatment of Prisoners, which was approved by the Economic and Social Council in its 1957 Resolution 663. While it expressly denied any intent to draft a model system of penal institutions, its work is still regarded as one of the seminal statements regarding international standards for the treatment of prisoners. Its *Basic Principle* is that "[t]here shall be no discrimination on grounds of race, colour, sex, language, religion, political or other opinion, national or social origin, property, birth or other status."

The 1988 UN General Assembly Resolution 43/173 then promulgated the Body of Principles for the Protection of All Persons Under and Form of Detention or Imprisonment. *Principle 1* provides that all persons "shall be treated in a humane manner and with respect for the inherent dignity of the human person." *Principle 6* adds that no one "shall be subjected to torture or cruel, inhuman or degrading treatment or punishment."[55]

An IMS has been uniformly asserted in the following circumstances: the complaining State asserts that the responsible State departed from generally accepted standards of justice for the latter's treatment of *all* individuals, both foreign and domestic. The responding State typically counters its actions by relying on the "national treatment" standard set forth in the 1933 Montevideo Convention on Rights and Duties of States (ratified mostly by Latin American nations). A foreign citizen is thereby entitled to no better treatment than the local citizens of the responding State. Equal treatment of local and foreign nationals precludes any international liability for injury to an alien.

There is no clear consensus about the existence or scope of the IMS, partially because of the comparative economic positions of the nations usually involved in these controversies. One of the few but enlightening cases applying the so-called IMS is the following 2003 North American Free Trade Agreement (NAFTA) panel case:

In The Proceeding Between
The Loewen Group, Inc. and Raymond L. Loewen (Claimants)
and United States of America (Respondent)

INTERNATIONAL CENTRE FOR SETTLEMENT OF INVESTMENT DISPUTES (June 26, 2003)

Case No. ARB(AF)/98/3

42 INTERNATIONAL LEGAL MATERIALS 811 (2003)

Go to course Web page at

<http://home.att.net/~slomansonb/txtcsesite.html>.

Under Chapter Four, click <u>Loewen v. US</u>.

Lack of Due Diligence   A State may incur responsibility under International Law, although the principal actor is *not* an agent of the State. A State's failure to exercise due diligence to protect a foreign citizen is wrongful if the unpunished act of a private individual is a crime under the laws of that State (or generally recognized as criminal conduct elsewhere in the principal legal systems of the world). Responsibility then arises under International Law if that State fails to apprehend or control the individual who has committed the crime against the foreign citizen.

Examples include the 1979 storming of the US embassy in Iran by Iranian citizens. Iran's leader denied that his government had arranged for them to storm the embassy and take US citizens hostage because they were foreign citizens from a disfavored nation. Iran nevertheless incurred State responsibility for failing to take any action to stop the crowds from stampeding the persons and property of these foreign citizens (§7.4). A more common example of such State responsibility is the indifference of lower-echelon officials, in circumstances where a local citizen would be given prompt assistance. States are expected to control such officials when they act, or fail to act, in a way that would protect a local citizen, and thus unreasonably discriminates against an alien who does not receive like treatment.

Confiscation of Property   There is a significant conflict between traditional Western expectations, and contemporary non-Western models, regarding whether either International Law *or* host State law should apply.

Right to Nationalize   The State generally possesses inherent power over persons and things within its borders. It may thus nationalize property belonging to foreigners (and local citizens). As succinctly stated by a contemporary Chinese scholar:

> Public international law regards nationalization as [a] lawful exercise of state power. This is because each state, being possessed of sovereignty, naturally has the right within its own territory to prescribe whatever economic and social system it chooses to establish. Speaking more concretely, each state has the exclusive right to regulate . . . conditions of acquisition, loss, and contents of ownership. Consequently, when one approaches this question from the standpoint of the principle of state sovereignty, one must recognize

that states enjoy the right to adopt nationalization measures. Nationalization belongs to matters of national jurisdiction and therefore . . . neither the United Nations nor other states have a right to intervene [when another country nationalizes the property of its citizens].[56]

"Confiscation" Limitation   Under the traditional Western view, a nationalization must be undertaken for a "public" purpose. It must also be accompanied by "prompt, adequate, and effective" repayment for the property taken by the government.[57]

There is no public purpose when the government takes property, which merely adds to the personal holdings of a dictator. Further, providing *some* compensation does not mean that the compensation is adequate. A nationalization violates the Western-derived formula if the terms of the compensation are less favorable than those provided to citizens of the host State, or the amount of compensation is below the fair market value of the property.

The standard for determining fair market value is subject to a great deal of controversy. Some States do not feel compelled to use any of them. Concepts like "fair market value," "replacement cost," and "book value" are rather indefinite terms when applied by experienced accountants, let alone officials or mediators from different legal or social systems.

In a case with major immense political undertones, Fidel Castro orchestrated the revolutionary takeover of Cuba in 1959. The United States subsequently imposed a quota on the amount of Cuban sugar importable into the United States. Castro characterized this singular US sugar quota as an act of "aggression, [done] for political purposes." The Cuban government then nationalized the sugar interests of US individuals and corporations, but not Cuban-owned sugar interests. Cuba was willing to pay for the nationalized sugar interests in its own government bonds—payable twenty years later, at a rate of interest well below that of similar bonds. This type of compensation was legal under the laws of Cuba. The US Department of State viewed it as inadequate, however, referring to it as "manifestly in violation of those principles of international law which have long been accepted by the free countries of the West. It is in its essence discriminatory, arbitrary and confiscatory." Payment in long-term bonds, at a comparatively low rate of interest, was neither prompt nor adequate. The State Department claimed that Cuba's purpose was discriminatory, because Cuba took the US property as a political response to the US import quota imposed on Cuban sugar.[58]

Non-Western Models A number of lesser-developed countries (LDCs) have adopted an alternative yardstick for measuring the appropriate degree of compensation in such cases. Their position is that the more-developed countries (MDCs), whose corporations operate within their borders, unfairly profit from long-term economic relationships. Foreign multinational corporations have thus been characterized as extracting enormous profits for distant shareholders, with little return for the local citizens. The LDCs do not perceive uncompensated nationalizations of foreign property as necessarily being confiscatory takings in violation of International Law.

One supporting argument is that the MDCs have effectively deprived the LDCs of their national sovereignty over natural resources, through unacceptable business arrangements that have historically taken unfair advantage of the LDCs. Huge profits, they argue, have been expatriated to the private shareholders of the MDC multinational corporations. Instead, more of these profits should be injected into the sagging economies of the world's LDCs. An uncompensated nationalization returns only a fraction of what has been improperly taken from the LDC, via one-sided business arrangements. This scenario has thus diluted national sovereignty over disappearing natural resources, with no tangible benefits for the LDCs.

Many LDCs decided to respond to the above Western-derived compensation requirements via their premise, as stated in the UN General Assembly Resolution of 1962 on Permanent Sovereignty over Natural Resources. Its objective was to machinate a paradigm in customary international practice, as it evolved while the LDCs were still colonial territories of the MDCs. A fresh standard for determining compensation for expropriations had to be determined under the national law of the host State where the taking occurs. This would be more representative than measuring compensation via the historical practice evolving from an era predating the existence of the vast majority of current members of the international community. The resulting Resolution therefore provides as follows: "[T]he owner shall be paid appropriate compensation, in accordance with the rules in force in the State taking such measures . . . [and] the national jurisdiction of the State taking such measures

shall be exhausted. However, upon agreement by sovereign States . . . settlement of the dispute shall be made through arbitration or international adjudication. . . ."[59]

There is tension between two competing policies in this East-West, or North-South, dialogue. One is the primacy of a State's territorial jurisdiction over persons and things within its borders. The opposing policy is the historical protection afforded to aliens by the external influence of International Law. The claimed applicability of both policies then spawns a dilemma which pits them against one another. The University of Minnesota's Professor Gerhard von Glahn describes what is clearly the Western perception of the proper balance between these twin goals:

> Each state is the sole judge of the extent to which aliens enjoy civil privileges within its jurisdiction. But beyond those permissive grants, each alien, as a human being, may be said to be endowed with certain rights, both as to person and to property, that are his by virtue of his being. It is primarily in connection with those basic rights that a responsibility by the host state arises. It is in this sphere that claims originate and . . . may be advanced against the host state by the government to which the alien owes allegiance.[60]

The essential feature of this counter to the Western formulation is that national law rather than International Law should govern theses MDC-LDC disputes. Foreign shareholders of the effected MDC corporation would be limited to the local remedies of the nationalizing State (if any). The LDC would neither be accused of violating International Law, nor would it have to engage in international adjudication—absent its express consent. This is one of the basic tenets of the New International Economic Order (NIEO) promulgated in 1974 by many nonaligned nations. It will be addressed later in this textbook (§13. 4), in the broader context of international economic relations. At present, with respect to this section's analysis of State responsibility for injury to aliens, Pace University (New York) Professor S. Prakash Sinha provides this summary:

> They challenge some of the rules of international law as not consistent with their view of the new order and they point to the need for international law to reflect a consensus of the entire world community,

including theirs, and promote the widest sharing of values. They criticize the system of international law as being a product of relations among imperialist States and of relations of an imperial character between imperialist States and colonial peoples. . . . Moved by the desire to cut inherited burdens, to free themselves from foreign control of their economies, and to obtain capital needed for their programmes of economic reconstruction, the newly independent States have resorted to expropriation of foreign interests. In their opinion, the validity of such expropriation is not a matter of international law.[61]

On the other hand, the widespread application of this approach could foster economic suicide. Adoption would frustrate the free flow of capital to a State whose leader suddenly nationalized foreign property without paying compensation. Other corporate structures would fear similar treatment by State X. The resulting lack of investment would retard its economic growth.

Neither the Western position (prompt, adequate, effective compensation) nor the Third World position (host State law determines compensation on case-by-case basis) has been adopted in any multilateral treaty. This tension has retarded universal applicability of some major treaties with components seeking to redistribute global wealth. The UN Law of the Sea Treaty, for example, became effective in 1994. However, it contains a number of equitable redistribution principles to which MDCs have objected (§6.3).

The Latin American variation to the LDC perception of Western economic hegemony is the "Calvo Doctrine." It evolved from the tenet that no government should have to accept financial responsibility for civil insurrection resulting in mistreatment of foreign citizens at the hands of insurgents rather than the defending government. The relevant adaptation of this concept is that a State may impose conditions on foreign individuals and corporations who wish to do business within that State's borders. It may thus require, as a condition of doing business there, that foreigners be treated on equal footing with local citizens. A foreign company doing business in a Calvo jurisdiction must thereby relinquish its right, arising under International Law, to seek the diplomatic assistance of its home State when there has been a nationalization. As exemplified by Article 27.1 of the Mexican Constitution, foreigners must agree to "consider themselves as [Mexican] nationals in respect to such

property, and bind themselves not to invoke the protection of their governments. . . ." This constitutional clause thereby waives the right to claim the assistance of a foreign government when the Mexican government has decided to nationalize foreign property.

Iran-US Claims Tribunal   One entity that could develop a wider degree of consensus on international expropriation norms is the Iran-US Claims Tribunal. The Iranian revolution that led to the International Court of Justice *Iranian Hostages Case* (§7.4), and the treaty which freed them in 1980, presented a rich opportunity for unifying the respective compensation rules.

In this instance, host-State takings were outspokenly anti-American. They were done with utter disregard for any international norms. The Iranian government nationalized, or otherwise controlled, virtually all foreign property in all conceivable industries. The governmental objective was to exorcize the "US Demon" in Iran. The United States responded by freezing Iranian assets in the United States. As part of the treaty agreement leading to release of the American hostages after 444 days in captivity, the United States made these Iranian assets available to this tribunal for the purpose of satisfying claims against Iran.

This tribunal is unlikely to break new ground, however (§9.6). Its mandate, agreed to by negotiators for the United States and Iran, is to decide all cases "on the basis of respect for law, applying such . . . rules and principles of commercial and international law as the Tribunal determines to be applicable. . . ."[62] The Tribunal has had the unenviable task of interpreting this "governing law" term, but only in the several of the nearly 500 cases it decided during its first ten years of existence. Most claimants avoided raising the issue of determining the precise international norms, perceiving the potential legal task as unproductively expensive due to the attendant ambiguity and complexity. As stated by a practicing lawyer who is one of the leading commentators on this issue: "In only a few cases has the issue been addressed, and in some of these, the awards suggest it was used more as a justification for achieving a result predetermined to be fair or equitable by the arbitrators than as a set of rules to be followed in reaching a reasoned decision based in law."[63]

Until a widely accepted treaty accomplishes a greater degree of international consensus, the debate about the appropriate compensation paradigm will continue to polarize the developed and developing States in this category of State responsibility for injury to aliens.

Deprivation of Livelihood Another category of State responsibility for injury to aliens is the unreasonable deprivation of a foreign citizen's ability to enjoy a livelihood. The withdrawal of his or her ability to continue practicing a certain occupation is an unacceptable deprivation if done for a discriminatory purpose.

The US Supreme Court case of *Asakura v. City of Seattle* is a useful illustration. Under a treaty between Japan and the United States, the citizens of both countries were entitled to enjoy equal employment rights with the citizens of each country. The city of Seattle subsequently passed a pawnbroker ordinance providing that "no such license shall be granted unless the applicant be a citizen of the United States." The Court determined that this ordinance "makes it impossible for aliens to carry on the business. It need not be considered whether the State, if it sees fit, may forbid and destroy business generally. Such a law would apply equally to aliens and citizens. . . ." The ordinance improperly discriminated against aliens in violation of the treaty specifically providing for equal treatment of Japanese citizens working in the United States. If the court had ruled against the plaintiff Japanese pawnbroker who challenged the ordinance, the United States would have incurred State responsibility for depriving foreign citizens of a livelihood during peacetime.[64]

◆ PROBLEMS

Problem 4.A (end of §4.1) Two Libyan military intelligence officers were responsible for blowing up Pan Am Flight 103 over Lockerbie, Scotland, in 1989. All 270 passengers, from various countries of the world including England and the United States, died violent deaths. UN Security Council Resolution 731 of 1992 demanded the trial of these two suspects in the West. The Arab League negotiated with Libya's leader to turn over the suspects for trial outside of Libya. England and the United States sought the extradition of these individuals from Libya for trial. Libya's leader (Colonel Gadhafi) refused all of these demands and requests.

A 1998 arrangement to try them in the Netherlands, as if the court there were sitting in Scotland—where the plane exploded—finally resolved this segment of a seemingly never-ending controversy. In May 2002, Libya

offered to pay the United States $2.7 billion to compensate the victims' families ($10 million each), in return for the United States and the United Nations terminating their respective sanctions against Libya.

Assuming that these two Libyan intelligence agents were not yet brought to trial from Libya, who could seek remedies for the deaths of the passengers on Pan Am Flight 103? Against whom? Where?

Problem 4.B (after Nottebohm Case §4.2) In June 1989, the best-known dissident in the PRC entered the US Embassy in Beijing to seek diplomatic asylum. Fang Lizhi, a prominent astrophysicist and human rights advocate, remained there until June 1990, refusing treatment for a heart ailment for fear of arrest. China's agreement to allow him to leave the US Embassy (without being arrested) for a new home in Great Britain signaled a thawing of Sino-US relations. The Chinese government acceded to US pressure to allow this dissident to leave China, possibly due to its desire to retain favorable trading status with the United States.

Assume, instead, that Fang Lizhi is *still* residing in the US Embassy in Beijing. His request for asylum has not yet been resolved. No diplomatic arrangements have been made regarding his safe passage out of the PRC. He therein declares his intent to "defect" to either the United States or Great Britain now that his immediate family is assembled with him in the US Embassy. They are ready to leave on short notice to any country that will take the family. The US ambassador initially says that "the granting of asylum at this critical time might jeopardize the US negotiations with China over human rights issues." After conferring with the US Secretary of State, and the British Foreign Minister, the parties decide that Fang Lizhi should apply for British citizenship. He has never been in Great Britain. The British government is apparently willing to waive all citizenship requirements, including a waiting period of three years (as in *Nottebohm*). After one week, Great Britain issues Fang Lizhi a British passport, which is delivered to him in the US Embassy in Beijing.

Assume further that (contrary to the actual facts in this case) the Chinese government protests, accusing the United States and Great Britain of meddling in Chinese affairs. The PRC is not willing to allow safe passage so that Fang Lizhi can leave China. The Chinese government's Minister of Foreign Affairs advises all concerned that this dissident, engaging in anti-State conduct, will be arrested the moment he leaves the embassy. In the eyes of the PRC, he remains a Chinese citizen and a traitor.

Students will represent China, Great Britain, and the United States. They will debate the following matters: What is Fang Lizhi's nationality? Must China recognize the British citizenship conferred on this dissident?

Problem 4.C (end of §4.2, after Sale v. Haitian Centers Council Case) As Justice Blackmun stated regarding Jewish refugees during the World War II era: "The tragic consequences of the world's indifference at that time are well known." One example might be the following incident. Even prior to US entry into World War II, the fate of the Jewish citizens and some other minorities of Nazi Germany was well known—see M. Gilbert, AUSCHWITZ AND THE ALLIES (New York: Holt, Rinehart & Winston, 1981). US families were willing and qualified to sponsor a number of Nazi Germany's Jewish children. In 1939, however, the US Congress defeated proposed legislation that would have rescued about 20,000 such children from Nazi Germany. The government's rationale was that this rescue would have exceeded the US immigration quota from Germany. *See* A Brief History of Immigration to the United States, in T. Aleinkoff & D. Martin, IMMIGRATION PROCESS AND POLICY 52 (St. Paul: West, 1985), which described this event as "what may be the cruelest single action in US immigration history."

In 1994, there were savage machete killings by the majority Hutus of the minority Tutsis in Rwanda. Some 1 million Rwandans fled into Zaire (renamed Democratic Republic of the Congo) and neighboring African nations. Assume that an organization like the *Sale* case's Haitian Council is trying to save several hundred Tutsi orphans. The successful rebel tribe leaders in Rwanda vow that such children will have no place in Rwanda's future if they remain. No other country is willing to take them.

Assume that the US Embassy's ambassador to Rwanda is approached by the Save the Rwanda Children Organization (SRCO). Its representative presents a plan whereby willing and qualified US citizens will accept Rwandan refugees in the United States. A part of this plan is an application to the United States for asylum for these children, who are being discriminated against on the basis of "membership in a particular social group" (the Tutsi minority) under Article 33.1 of the Refugee Convention.

The SRCO representative brings a small group of teenage Tutsi boys to this embassy meeting. They have been earmarked for slaughter, because of their family ties to the Tutsi rebels who are fighting to stop the Hutu-led massacre. After consultation with the US Department of State, the US Embassy officer declines to accept them, or any Tutsi children, on the basis that "the US does not have the capacity to become a haven for the world's refugees." The US refusal means that these children will probably be exterminated, possibly within a matter of hours.

Questions: (1) Would the 1951 Refugee Convention affect the ability of the United States to say "no" to this proposal, which will mean certain death for the children? What about the 1967 Protocol? (2) Blackmun's dissent in *Haitian Centers Council* scolds the Supreme Court majority for its refusal to apply the Refugee Convention on an "extraterritorial" basis; that is, in the international waters between Haiti and the United States which are heavily patrolled by the US Coast Guard. Could Blackmun's argument be extended to the above Rwandan children hypothetical, thereby requiring the United States to grant asylum to these Rwandan "refugees?"

Problem 4.D (§4.4 after "Denial of Justice" subsection) Harry Roberts was a US citizen, charged by Mexico with "assaulting a house." When he and several armed American companions gathered outside a house in Mexico, the owner summoned the Mexican police. After an exchange of small-weapons fire, the police arrested Roberts. The Mexican Constitution provided that prisoners had to be brought to trial within twelve months of their arrest. Roberts was in a Mexican jail for nineteen months without any hearing.[65]

The arbitration report further notes that "[w]ith respect to this point of unreasonably long detention without trial, the Mexican Agency contended that Roberts was undoubtedly guilty of the crime for which he was arrested; that therefore had he been tried he would have been sentenced to serve a term of imprisonment of more than nineteen months; and that, since, under Mexican law, the period of nineteen months would have been taken into account in fixing his sentence of imprisonment, it cannot properly be considered that he was illegally detained for an unreasonable period of time."

His conditions of incarceration were typical for Mexican prisons of that era, but less tolerable than prison conditions in other countries in the 1920s. The report of the international arbitration reveals that he was kept in a "room thirty-five feet long and twenty feet wide with stone walls, earthen floor, straw roof, a single window, a single door and no sanitary accommodations, all the prisoners depositing their excrement in a barrel kept in a corner of the room; that thirty or forty men were at times thrown together in this single room; that the prisoners were given no facilities to clean themselves; that the room contained no furniture . . . and that the food given them was scarce, unclean and of the coarsest kind."

After his release, Roberts obtained US assistance for presenting this case against Mexico. The US representative claimed that Mexico was responsible for a denial of justice to a US citizen. It had violated the IMS applicable to all prisoners. Mexico's representative countered that Roberts was treated the same as *all* prisoners, including Mexicans.

Jail conditions can be terrible, even in a comparatively strong economy like the United States. Its courts have occasionally enunciated a minimum constitutional standard for the treatment of prisoners. The following 1976 case from Alabama (fifty years after the *Roberts* international arbitration) is a classic example:

> There can be no question that the present conditions of confinement in the Alabama penal system violate any current judicial definition of cruel and unusual punishment, a situation evidenced by the defendants' [State of Alabama and its Board of Corrections] admission that serious Eighth Amendment [cruel and unusual punishment] violations exist. . . .
>
> Confinement itself within a given institution may amount to a cruel and unusual punishment prohibited by the [federal] Constitution where the confinement is characterized by conditions and practices so bad as to be shocking to the conscience of reasonably civilized people even though a particular inmate may never personally be subject to any disciplinary action.
>
> The conditions in which Alabama prisoners must live, as established by the evidence in these cases, bear no reasonable relationship to legitimate institutional goals. As a whole they create an atmosphere in which inmates are compelled to live in constant fear of violence, in imminent danger to their physical well-being, and without opportunity to seek a more promising future.

Pugh v. Locke, 406 F.Supp. 318, 329 (Dist. Ct. Ala, 1976), cert. granted in part, judgment reversed in part on other grounds, Alabama v. Pugh, 438 U.S. 781 (U.S. Ala. 1978).

Two students will represent Mexico and the United States. A third will represent a neutral country (not located in the western hemisphere). Assume that Mexico did not treat Roberts any differently than other prisoners. They will address the following questions associated with the US claim—that Mexico breached the IMS of treatment for aliens:

1. Should Roberts' guilt or innocence be considered?
2. In the absence of any relevant treaty in the 1920s, is there an applicable IMS?
3. Should your international tribunal announce an IMS? If so, what would it be?
4. Did Mexico's violation of its constitutionally required twelve-month period, from arrest to trial, automatically constitute a breach of the IMS?
5. Did the earlier-quoted Mexican prison conditions constitute a breach of the IMS?
6. What should be the result announced by the international arbitration between Mexico and the United States?

Problem 4.E (§4.4 after "Confiscation of Property" subsection)   Reynolds-Guyana (RG) was a foreign-owned mining corporation that mined bauxite in Guyana for a number of decades. The parent company was a US corporation. Guyana is a former British colony that achieved its independence and statehood in 1966. RG's profits were substantial, although there was an enormous start-up cost, including research and development.

In 1974, Guyana's government assessed an equally enormous "bauxite tax deficiency" against RG. The company immediately characterized this tax as being fabricated for confiscatory purposes. Guyana's Prime Minister responded that RG would be fully nationalized by the end of 1974. A US agency, the Overseas Private Investment Corporation, advised RG not to pay the bauxite tax deficiency. This agency then negotiated the sale of

RG's mining operations to a third party on terms acceptable to the government of Guyana.

Assume the following:

1. A 1973 Guyana law, passed on the eve of this 1974 controversy, provides that the Calvo Doctrine is incorporated into every contract involving any foreign business operation in Guyana.
2. This 1973 law contains a provision, similar to that contained in the Iran-US Claims Tribunal, stating that "any compensation dispute requires respect for the law, and the law to be applied to any nationalization is International Law."

The majority of RG shareholders are US citizens who have become quite wealthy as a result of their stock investment in RG. Negotiators are now deliberating about whether Guyana has incurred State responsibility to compensate RG's parent corporation (in the United States) for losses caused by the enormous bauxite deficiency tax. (In this hypothetical, there has been no sale to a third party, as occurred in the actual 1974 case.) Two students (or groups) represent Guyana and the US investors. They will now debate the effect of applying assumptions (1) and (2).

◆ BIBLIOGRAPHY

§4.1 Legal Personality

S. Anaya, INDIGENOUS PEOPLES IN INTERNATIONAL LAW (2d ed. Oxford, Eng.: Oxford Univ. Press, 2004)

C. Grossman & D. Bradlow, Conference on Changing Notions of Sovereignty and the Role of Private Actors in International Law: Are We Being Propelled Towards a People-Centered Transnational Legal Order? 9 AMER. UNIV. J. INT'L L. & POLICY 1 (1993)

R. Higgins, Conceptual Thinking about the Individual in International Law, in R. Falk et al., INTERNATIONAL LAW: A CONTEMPORARY PERSPECTIVE 476 (Boulder, CO: Westview Press, 1985)

M. Janis, Individuals and International Law, ch. 8, in AN INTRODUCTION TO INTERNATIONAL LAW 239 (4th ed. New York: Aspen, 2003)

A. Orakhelashvili, The Position of the Individual in International Law, 31 CAL. WEST. INT'L L. J. 241 (2001)

C. Warkentin, RESHAPING WORLD POLITICS: NGOS, THE INTERNET, AND GLOBAL CIVIL SOCIETY (Lanham, MD: Rowman & Littlefield, 2001)

§4.2 Nationality, Statelessness, and Refugees

G. Alfredsson & P. Macalister-Smith (eds.), THE LIVING LAW OF NATIONS: ESSAYS ON REFUGEES, MINORITIES, INDIGENOUS PEOPLES AND THE HUMAN RIGHTS OF OTHER VULNERABLE GROUPS (Kehl, Germany: N.P. Engel, 1996)

A. Bayefsky & J. Fitzpatrick (ed.), HUMAN RIGHTS AND FORCED DISPLACEMENT (Hague: Martinus Nijhoff, 2000)

J. Fitzpatrick (ed.), HUMAN RIGHTS PROTECTION FOR REFUGEES, ASYLUM-SEEKERS, AND INTERNALLY DISPLACED PERSONS: A GUIDE TO INTERNATIONAL MECHANISMS AND PROCEDURES (Ardsley, NY: Transnational Publishers, 2002)

E. Feller, V. Turk & F. Nicholson (ed.), REFUGEE PROTECTION IN INTERNATIONAL LAW: UNCHR'S GLOBAL CONSULTATIONS ON INTERNATIONAL PROTECTION (Cambridge, Eng.: Cambridge Univ. Press, 2003)

J. Hathaway, THE RIGHTS OF REFUGEES UNDER INTERNATIONAL LAW (Cambridge, Eng.: Cambridge Univ. Press, 2005)

H. Lambert, SEEKING ASYLUM: COMPARATIVE LAW AND PRACTICE IN SELECTED EUROPEAN COUNTRIES (Dordrecht, Neth.: Martinus Nijhoff, 1995)

D. Miller, ON NATIONALITY (Oxford, Eng.: Clarendon Press, 1995)

M. Saltzer, RIGHTS OF PASSAGE: THE PASSPORT IN INTERNATIONAL RELATIONS (Boulder, CO: Rienner, 2003)

P. Shah (ed.), THE CHALLENGE OF ASYLUM TO LEGAL SYSTEMS (London: Cavendish, 2005)

Y. Zilbershats, THE HUMAN RIGHT TO CITIZENSHIP (Ardsley, NY: Transnational, 2002)

§4.3 Corporate Nationality

F. Rigaux, Transnational Corporations, ch. 5, in M. Bedjaoui (ed.), INTERNATIONAL LAW: ACHIEVEMENTS AND PROSPECTS 121 (Dordrecht, Neth.; Boston: Martinus Nijhoff, 1991)

D. Saari, GLOBAL CORPORATIONS AND SOVEREIGN NATIONS: COLLISION OR COOPERATION? (Westport, CT: Quorum Books, 1999)

§4.4 Injury to Aliens

Injury to the Persons and Property of Aliens on State Territory, ch. 24, in I. Brownlie, PRINCIPLES OF PUBLIC INTERNATIONAL LAW 497 (6th ed. Oxford, Eng.: Clarendon Press, 2003)

R. Jennings & A. Watts, Property of Aliens: Expropriation, §407, in 1 OPPENHEIM'S INTERNATIONAL LAW (Part II) 911 (Essex, Eng.: Longman, 1992)

A. Mouri, THE INTERNATIONAL LAW OF EXPROPRIATION AS REFLECTED IN THE WORK OF THE IRAN/US CLAIMS TRIBUNAL (Dordrecht, Neth.: Martinus Nijhoff, 1994)

M. McDougal et al., The Protection of Aliens from Discrimination and World Public Order: Responsibility of States Conjoined with Human Rights, 70 AMER. J. INT'L LAW 432 (1976)

Jan Paulsson, DENIAL OF JUSTICE IN INTERNATIONAL LAW (Cambridge, Eng.: Cambridge Univ. Press, 2005)

Responsibility for Injuries to Aliens, in H. Kindred et al., INTERNATIONAL LAW: CHIEFLY AS INTERPRETED AND APPLIED IN CANADA 635 (6th ed. Toronto: Edmond Montgomery Pub., 2000)

Additional Internet Resources

Culture and Language: <http://globaledge.msu.edu/ibrd/>, click on <u>Culture and Language</u>

Population Law (Annual Review): <http://www.law.harvard.edu/programs/annual_review/>

◆ ENDNOTES

1. I. Seidl-Hohenveldern, CORPORATIONS IN AND UNDER INTERNATIONAL LAW (Cambridge, Eng.: Grotius, 1987).

2. J. Bentham, AN INTRODUCTION TO THE PRINCIPLES OF MORALS AND LEGISLATION 296 (Dover, NH: Longwood Press, 1970) (Burns & Hart edition).

3. *See* H. Chiu, Book Reviews and Notes, 82 AMER. J. INTL L. 892, 894–895 (1988).

4. D. Salem, THE PEOPLE'S REPUBLIC OF CHINA: INTERNATIONAL LAW AND ARMS CONTROL 13 (Baltimore: Univ. of Maryland, 1983).

5. L. Chen, The Individual, ch. 5 in AN INTRODUCTION TO CONTEMPORARY INTERNATIONAL LAW: A POLICY ORIENTED PERSPECTIVE 76, 77 (New Haven, CT: Yale Univ. Press, 1989).

6. In re "Agent Orange" Product Liability Litigation, 373 F.Supp.2d 7, 129 (E.D.N.Y. 2005) [hereinafter *Agent Orange*].

7. Case Concerning the Factory at Chorzow (Germany v. Poland), 1928 PCIJ, SER. A, NO. 17 (Judgment of Sept. 13, 1928).

8. Brown v. Warren Christopher, Secretary of State, No. 93–1375-CIV (S.D. Fla. Nov. 18, 1993) (unpublished opinion).

9. Iran and the United States ultimately settled this suit for $61.8 million, upon dismissal of the case from the ICJ's docket of cases. The order and surrounding facts are available in 35 INT'L LEGAL MAT'LS 550 (1996).

10. For background analysis, see John Carey and Siegfried Wiessner, ASIL Flash Insight: A New United Nations Subsidiary Organ: The Permanent Forum on Indigenous Issues, (April 2001), at: <http://www.asil.org/insights/insigh67.htm>.

11. *See generally,* P. Ghandi, THE HUMAN RIGHTS COMMITTEE AND THE RIGHT OF INDIVIDUAL PETITION: LAW AND PRACTICE (Aldershot, Eng.: Ashgate, 1998).

12. A comprehensive summary of laws, procedures, and NAFTA links is available at <http://www.naftaclaims.com>.

13. Mavrommatis Palestine Concessions case: PCIJ, SER. A, NO. 2 (1924), reported in 2 INT'L L. REP. 27. *See also* that "rules creating individual rights and obligations . . . [are] enforceable by the national courts." Danzig Railway Officials Case, PCIJ, SER. B, NO. 15 (1928), reported in 4 INT'L L. REP. 287.

14. See generally A. Rubin, THE LAW OF PIRACY (2d ed. Irvington-on-Hudson, NY: Transnational, 1998).

15. V. Nanda, International Law in the Twenty-First Century, ch. 5 in N. Jasentuliyana (ed.), PERSPECTIVES ON INTERNATIONAL LAW, at 83 (London: Kluwer, 1995).

16. *Agent Orange* (cited in note 6 above), at 54 & 58.

17. E. Paras, A Brief History of Conflict of Laws, ch. 15, in PHILIPPINE CONFLICT OF LAWS 438 (7th ed. Manila: Rex Book Store, 1990).

18. Nottebohm Case (Liechtenstein v. Guatemala), 1955 ICJ REP. 4.

19. Determination of Chinese Nationality, in 1 J. Cohen & H. Chiu, PEOPLE'S CHINA AND INTERNATIONAL LAW: A DOCUMENTARY STUDY 746 (Princeton, NJ: Princeton Univ. Press, 1974).

20. *France:* Nationality Decrees in Tunis and Morocco (Advisory Opinion), PCIJ, SER. B, NO. 4 (1923), reported in 1 World Court Rep. 145. *Poland:* Acquisition of Polish Nationality (Advisory Opinion), Permanent Court of International Justice, SER. B, NO.7, at 79 (1923 case interpreting nationality provision of WWI peace treaty between the Allied Powers and Poland).

21. European Convention on Nationality, Done at Strasbourg, Nov. 6, 1997, reprinted in 37 INT'L LEGAL MAT'LS 47 (1998) [hereinafter 1997 *Nationality Convention*].

22. US Const., Amend. XIV (1868). An analysis of this provision is available in J. Guendelsberger, Access to Citizenship for Children Born Within the State to Foreign Parents, 40 AMER. J. COMP. L. 379 (1992).

23. Nishimura Ekiu v. United States, 142 US 651, 659 (1892).

24. Details on the various national and international court decisions are available from the Finnish author Ruth Donner, The Principle of the "Link" in Nationality Law, ch. 2, in THE REGULATION OF NATIONALITY IN INTERNATIONAL LAW (2d ed. Irvington-on-Hudson, NY: Transnational, 1994).

25. Provisions Amending the Treaty Establishing the European Economic Community with a View to Establishing The European Community, Articles 8(a)-(d), available on the EU Web site at: <http://europa.eu.int/en/record/mt/title2.html>

26. Regarding the content and potential scope of organizational citizenship, *see* H. d'Oliveira, Union Citizenship: Pie in the Sky?, ch. 4 in A. Rosas & E. Antola (ed.), A CITIZENS' EUROPE: IN SEARCH OF A NEW ORDER 58 (London: Sage, 1995).

27. *See generally,* L. Green, Is World Citizenship a Legal Practicality?, 1987 CANADIAN YEARBOOK OF INTERNATIONAL LAW 151.

28. K. Rubenstein, Citizenship in a Borderless World, in A. Anghie & G. Sturgess (ed.), LEGAL VISIONS OF THE 21ST CENTURY: ESSAYS IN HONOUR OF JUDGE CHRISTOPHER WEERAMANTRY 183, at 184 & 200-202 (The Hague: Kluwer Law Int'l, 1998) (footnote omitted).

29. Kofi A. Annan, Two Concepts of Sovereignty, THE ECONOMIST (Sept. 18, 1999).

30. D. Martin, Introduction: The Trend Toward Dual Nationality, ch. 1, in D. Martin & K. Hailbronner (ed.), RIGHTS AND DUTIES OF DUAL NATIONALS: EVOLUTION AND PROSPECTS 3 (Hague: Kluwer, 2003).

31. Canevaro Case (Italy v. Peru), 2 REP. INT'L ARB. AWARDS 397 (1949).

32. Eritrea Ethiopia Claims Commission, Civilians Claims Eritrea's Claims 15, 16, 23 & 27-32, para. 82 (Dec. 17, 2004), available at : <http://www.pca-cpa.org/ENGLISH/RPC, click Eritrea-Ethiopia Claims Commission.

33. *Hague Convention:* Convention of 12 April 1930, 179 LEAGUE OF NATIONS TREATY SERIES 89 (1938). *Protocol:* Protocol of 12 April 1930, 178 LEAGUE OF NATIONS TREATY SERIES 227 (1937) (this series does not report all treaties in chronological order). *Paris Convention:* See K. Sik, The Netherlands and the Law Concerning Nationality, in 3 INTERNATIONAL LAW AND THE NETHERLANDS 3, 7 (Alphen aan den Rijn, Neth.: Sijtoff & Noordhoff, 1980).

34. Exchange of Notes at The Hague of 9 June 1954, 216 UN TREATY SERIES 121 (1955).

35. *See* European Convention on Nationality, Done at Strasbourg, Nov. 6, 1997, reprinted in 37 INT'L LEGAL MAT'LS 47 (1998), *Nationality Convention* (cited in note 21 above).

36. *See Nationality Convention* [cited in note 21 above] (three ratifications are required for this treaty to enter into force).

37. Article 1, Right to a Nationality, UN DOC. A/CN.4/L.573, 27 May 1999.

38. The work product of attending academicians is located in S. Kneebone (ed.), THE REFUGEES CONVENTION 50 YEARS ON: GLOBALISATION AND INTERNATIONAL LAW (Aldershot, Eng.: Ashgate, 2003).

39. G. Goodwin-Hill, THE REFUGEE IN INTERNATIONAL LAW 298 (2d ed. Oxford, Eng.: Clarendon Press, 1996).

40. See <http://ue.eu.int/ueDocs/cms_Data/docs/pressData/en/jha/80112.pdf>, search "status of refugees."

41. Krotov v. Secretary of State for the Home Dep't, EWCA Civ 69 (Feb. 11, 2004).

42. *German court:* Egon Krenz, Gunter Schabowski, and Gunter Kleiber, 5 STR 632/98 (November 8, 1999). British decision: Islam v. Secretary of State for the Home Office, Ex Parte Shah (Mar. 25, 1999). *Australian case:* Chen Shi Hai v. The Minister for Immigration and Multicultural Affairs, [2000] H.C.A. 19 (April 13, 2000), reprinted in 39 INT'L LEGAL MAT'LS 769 (2000).

43. R. Byrne, G. Noll & J. Vedsted-Hansen (ed.), Transformation of Asylum in Europe, ch. 9, in their NEW ASYLUM COUNTRIES?: MIGRATION CONTROL AND REFUGEE PROTECTION IN AN ENLARGED EUROPEAN UNION, at 429-430 (Hague: Kluwer, 2002).

44. *See generally,* H. Kahn, Legal Problems Relating to Refugees and Displaced Persons, in Hague Acad. Int'l Law, 149 RECUEIL DES COURS 287, 318 (1976).

45. American Banana v. United Fruit, 213 US 347, 29 S.Ct. 511, 53 L. Ed. 826 (1909).

46. *Early commentator:* F. Dawson & I. Head, National Tribunals and the Rights of Aliens, in 10 INTERNATIONAL LAW, at XI (Charlottesville, VA: Univ. Press of Va., 1971). *Modern analogy:* Kevin O'Flynn, Nationalists to Celebrate with Anti-Immigrant Rally, Moscow Times on the web, Nov. 3, 2005.

47. E. de Vattel, II THE LAW OF NATIONS 136 (New York: Oceana, 1964) (translation of original 1758 edition).

48. G. Tunkin, INTERNATIONAL LAW 224 (Moscow: Progress Publishers, 1982) (1986 trans.).

49. *1929 draft:* Responsibility of States, 23 AMER. J. INT'L L. SPECIAL SUPP. 131 (1929). *1953 attempt:* Gen. Ass. Res. 799 (VIII), Dec. 7, 1953, contained in G.A.O.R. (8th Session) Supp. (No. 17) at 52, UN DOC. A/2630.

50. The draft convention is reprinted in L. Sohn & M. Baxter, Responsibility of States for Injuries to the Economic Interests of Aliens, 55 AMER. J. INT'L L. 545, 548 (1961). These draft principles were approved by the American Society of International Law's Panel on the Law of State Responsibility in 1980.

51. Quote from D. Kaye, Introductory Note to 1998 draft, contained in 37 INT'L LEGAL MAT'LS 440 (1998) (italics added).

See S. Rosenne, THE INTERNATIONAL LAW COMMISSION'S DRAFT ARTICLES ON STATE RESPONSIBILITY: PART 1, Articles 1-35 (Dordrecht, Neth.: Martinus Nijhoff, 1991) (italics added); *and* M. Spinedi & B. Simma (eds.), UNITED NATIONS CODIFICATION OF STATE RESPONSIBILITY (New York: Oceana, 1987).

52. G. Yates, State Responsibility for Nonwealth Injuries to Aliens in the Postwar Era, in R. Lillich (Reporter), INTERNATIONAL LAW OF STATE RESPONSIBILITY FOR INJURIES TO ALIENS 213, 214 (Charlottesville, VA: Univ. Press of Va., 1983).

53. *Case examples:* The classic articulation is available in O. Lissitzyn, The Meaning of the Term "Denial of Justice" in International Law, 30 AMER. J. INT'L L. 632 (1936). *Latin American perspective:* I. Puente, The Concept of "Denial of Justice" in Latin America, 43 MICH. L. REV. 383 (1944).

54. E. Root, The Basis of Protection to Citizens Residing Abroad, 4 PROCEEDINGS OF THE AMERICAN SOCIETY OF INTERNATIONAL LAW 20-21 (Wash., DC: Amer. Soc. Int'l Law, 1910).

55. All details are conveniently provided in N. Rodley, THE TREATMENT OF PRISONERS UNDER INTERNATIONAL LAW, ANNEX 3 (1955 Minimum Rules), at 413 *and* ANNEX 4 (1988 Resolution), at 428 (2d ed. Oxford, Eng.: Oxford Univ. Press, 1999).

56. Li Hao-p'ei, Nationalization and International Law, in 1 PEOPLE'S CHINA AND INTERNATIONAL LAW: A DOCUMENTARY STUDY 719 (Princeton: Princeton Univ. Press, 1974).

57. This formulation appears in the diplomatic notes exchanged between Mexico and the United States in 1938. See §1.3 of this text (General Principles), and 2 RESTATEMENT (THIRD) OF THE LAW OF THE FOREIGN RELATIONS LAW OF THE UNITED STATES §712 (St. Paul: ALI Publishers, 1987) (containing extensive commentary and examples).

58. Facts and quotes appear in Banco Nacional de Cuba v. Sabbatino, 376 U.S. 398, 84 S.Ct. 923, 11 L. Ed. 2d 804 (1964).

59. UN Gen. Ass. Res. 1803(XVII), reproduced in 2 INT'L LEGAL MAT'LS 223 (1963).

60. G. von Glahn, LAW AMONG NATIONS: AN INTRODUCTION TO PUBLIC INTERNATIONAL LAW 190 (7th ed. Boston: Allyn & Bacon, 1996).

61. S. Sinha, Perspective of the Newly Independent States on the Binding Quality of International Law, in F. Snyder & S. Sathirathai, THIRD WORLD ATTITUDES TOWARD INTERNATIONAL LAW: AN INTRODUCTION 23, 29 (Dordrecht, Neth.: Martinus Nijhoff, 1987).

62. Undertakings of the Government of the United States of America and the Government of the Islamic Republic of Iran with Respect to the Declaration of the Government of the Democratic and Popular Republic of Algeria, Art. V, reproduced in 20 INT'L LEGAL MAT'LS 229, 232 (1981).

63. J. Westberg, International Transactions and Claims Involving Government Parties: Case Law of the Iran-United States Claims Tribunal 66 (Wash., DC: Int'l L. Inst., 1991).

64. 265 U.S. 332, 44 S.Ct. 515, 68 L.Ed. 1041 (1924).

65. Roberts v. Mexico (United States v. Mexico), General Claims Commission of 1926, 4 REP. INT'L ARB. AWARDS 77 (1974).

Extraterritorial Jurisdiction

INTRODUCTION

Prior chapters covered the preliminary essentials for defining International Law, and the actors who shape its contours. This chapter commences your course analysis of operational norms. Its focus is limitations on the frequent exercise of State power in an "extraterritorial" context.

This is the basic question: Under what circumstances can a State legally exercise its sovereign powers beyond its borders? This common feature of State practice often conflicts with the norm that sovereignty is not permeable.

◆ 5.1 DEFINITIONAL SETTING

State regulation of the activities of its inhabitants, and those whose conduct has an effect within its boundaries, is often described in terms of "jurisdiction" and "sovereignty." They are often used synonymously, but there are important distinctions.

YAHOO! IS AN INTERNET SERVICE PROVIDER WHICH has its principal place of business in Santa Clara, California. Its American website, www.yahoo.com, targets U.S. users and provides many services, including auction sites, message boards, and [former] chat rooms, for which Yahoo! users supply much of the content. Nazi discussions have occurred in Yahoo!'s [former] chat rooms and Nazi-related paraphernalia have appeared for sale on its auction website.

[T]he French Criminal Code bans exhibition of Nazi propaganda for sale and prohibits French citizens from purchasing or possessing such material.

On May 22, 2000, the French court . . . issued an order requiring Yahoo!—subject to a fine of 100,000 Francs (approximately $13,300) per day—to destroy all Nazi-related messages, images, and text stored on its server. . . .

—Yahoo! Inc. v. La Ligue Contre Le Racisme Et
    L'Antisemitisme, 379 F.3d 1120, 1121–1122 (9th Cir.,
    2004).

SOVEREIGNTY AND JURISDICTION

Sovereignty Sovereignty is the right of a State to govern exclusively the affairs of its inhabitants, and to be free from external control. A sovereign State has the international capacity to exchange diplomats with other States, to engage in treaty making, and to be immune from the jurisdiction of the courts of other States.

A State possesses sovereignty when it is able to act independently of the consent or control of any other State. International theorists describe State sovereignty in terms of a solid sphere, much like a billiard ball—whereby one nation cannot intrude into the internal affairs of another. When there is a clash between two or more such spheres of influence, the theoretical equality of every State rigidly repels the other "billiard ball" on the international playing surface.

The University of Belgrade Professor, Branimir Jankovic, traces these roots of sovereignty as follows:

> the idea of sovereignty originated when there appeared a growing opposition to feudal anarchy and to interference in the affairs of other states. The [emerging national] rulers of those times fought for their unlimited, sovereign authority, within their states as well as outside their borders. In this struggle to supersede the feudal retrogressive system and create a new social order, the idea of state sovereignty had a progressive significance. Although at first historically progressive, [sovereign] absolutism . . . was based upon an unlimited autocracy and brute force. It is in the ideology of absolutism that we find the roots of the theory of absolute sovereignty. . . . The sovereignty of a state means today its independence from external intervention. This is the supreme authority inherent in every independent state, limited only by the universally adopted and currently valid rules of international law. This supreme power extends within the borders of the national territory and is usually described as territorial sovereignty, or territorial jurisdiction of states.[1]

A classic example of the historic notion of European State-centric sovereignty is quite familiar to every first-year law student in the United States. The ubiquitous bedrock of modern jurisdictional analysis flows from the Supreme Court's 1877 definition of sovereignty,[2] borrowed directly from the then contemporary European State practice. The Court reversed the sale of land, pursuant to a judgment obtained without the knowledge of the owner. The seeds of European jurisdictional practice were replanted by the US Supreme Court as follows:

> every State possesses exclusive jurisdiction and sovereignty over persons and property within its territory. . . . The other principle of public law referred to follows from the one mentioned; that is, that no State can exercise direct jurisdiction and authority over persons or property without its territory. The several States are of equal dignity and authority, and the independence of one implies the exclusion of power from all others. And so it is laid down by jurists, as an elementary principle, that the laws of one State have no operation outside of its territory, except so far as is allowed by comity.

> . . .

> The . . . familiar rule that countries foreign to our own disregarded a judgment . . . where the defendant had not been served with process nor had a day in court; . . . 'The international law . . . as it existed among the States in 1790, was that a judgment rendered in one State, assuming to bind the person of a citizen of another, was void within the foreign State, when the defendant had not been served with process.' . . .[3]

The underlying seventeenth-century concept of sovereignty, to which the US Supreme Court refers, reigned unchallenged from its Westphalian roots until well into the twentieth century. It has since endured contemporary attacks. As aptly described by Professor John Jackson in his lecture series at Cambridge University in 2002:

> Although much criticized, the concept of "sovereignty" is still central to most thinking about international relations and particularly international law. The old "Westphalian" concept in the context of a nation-state's "right" to monopolize certain exercises of power with respect to its territory and citizens has been discredited in many ways . . . , but it is still prized and harbored by those who maintain certain "realist" views or who otherwise wish to prevent (sometimes with justification) foreign or international powers and authorities from interfering in a national government's decisions and activities. Furthermore, when one begins to analyze and dis-aggregate the concept of sovereignty, it quickly becomes apparent that it has many dimensions. Often, however, the term "sovereignty" is invoked in a context or manner designed to avoid and prevent analysis, sometimes with an advocate's intent to fend off criticism or justifications for international "infringements" on the activities of a nation-state or its internal stakeholders and power operators.[4]

Examples of the modern diminution of the traditional State-centric notion of "absolute" sovereignty include:

◆ Contemporary norms of Customary International Law, to the extent that they bind rogue States—

exemplified by Libya, when it sparred with the international community in the aftermath of its bombing a passenger jet over Lockerbie Scotland in 1988 (Problem 4.A)

◆ The post-World War II watering down of sovereign immunity, from the absolute to the "restrictive" approach, after (§2.6)

◆ European integration—spawned by the consent of the twenty-five EU States—yielding the requisite degree of State sovereignty for certain community institutions to require State members to act/refrain from acting on preadmission State preferences (§3.4)

◆ Evolving limitations on the rule of absolute immunity for heads of State, as also evinced in Chapter 2 of this book, *e.g.*, Article 27.1 of the 1998 Statute of the International Criminal Court (§9.5)

◆ National willingness of many countries to embrace the Kyoto environmental treaty, to plan against the dangers of global warming (§12.2)

◆ The majority of the community of nations participating in the World Trade Organization process, resulting in Geneva panel decisions restricting the conduct of even the most powerful nations (§13.2).

Jurisdiction The term "jurisdiction" has multiple meanings. The one now most relevant is the State's legal capacity to: (a) make, (b) enforce, and (c) adjudicate breaches of its substantive rules. A State's legislature has the power to enact laws governing conduct within, and often beyond, its borders. Yet the *un*authorized exercise of sovereign power in the territory of another State is typically protested as an exercise of "extraterritorial" jurisdiction, thus violating International Law. The offending State has the obligation not to interfere with another State's enjoyment of the right to control people and activities within its borders. The target State possesses the right, based on its status as a sovereign entity, to at least an apology, because it possesses equal rights and dignity, as do all members of the community of nations.

Applications One might commence by some exposure to early US history. The Piracies and Felonies Clause of the US Constitution specifically grants power for the punishment of offenses beyond the territorial limits of the United States (the only clause to do so). Early Supreme Court opinions addressed extraterritorial applications of US law, under the 1790 Act for the Punishment of Certain Crimes Against the United States. In a representative opinion, Chief Justice Marshall stated for the Court: "The question, whether this act extends farther than to American citizens, or to persons [not] on board American vessels, or to offences [not] committed against citzens [*sic*] of the United States, is not without its difficulties. The constitution having conferred on congress the power of defining and punishing piracy, there can be no doubt of the right of the legislature to enact laws punishing pirates, although they may be foreigners, and may have committed no particular offence against the United States."[5]

But most instances of an extraterritorial exercise of sovereign power do not involve piracy, which was the recurring "9-11" of an earlier era.[6] In a frequently quoted premise expressed over a century later by the Permanent Court of International Justice (PCIJ) (*S.S. Lotus* below): "the principal and foremost restriction imposed by international law upon a State is that—failing the existence of a permissive rule to the contrary—it may not exercise its power in the territory of another State." In 1804, the US Supreme Court likewise admonished—in circumstances *not* involving the historic, and widely accepted exercise of extraterritorial jurisdiction to punish pirates: "an act of Congress ought never to be construed to violate the law of nations if any other possible construction remains, and consequently can never be construed to violate . . . the law of nations as understood in this country."[7]

Many States have, at one time or another, engaged in both overt and covert activities within the territory of another State. What constitutes acceptable State practice is sometimes a matter of degree. Spying, for example, is a form of extraterritorial jurisdiction in the sense that Nation X clandestinely sends an X citizen into Nation Y to spy, or employs a Nation Y citizen to spy on his or her own country. Such activities are often executed in the name of counter-terrorism.[8] The United States, for example, constructed a secret tunnel under the former Soviet Union's new embassy in Washington, DC, jointly managed by the FBI and the National Security Agency. While diplomats and government agencies are not supposed to engage in this sort of activity, many spies/diplomats have been expelled for precisely this reason (§7.4). All nations profess to loathe spying, on the legal basis that the spying nation violates the territorial sovereignty of the nation spied upon. However, it is ironic that there is no international convention in which States could agree to prohibit spying.

One venue for such clandestine activity is the international organization. It may be used for the ulterior purpose of obtaining sensitive information about a targeted member nation. The United States has claimed that various UN representatives have thus been operatives for foreign nation information-gathering purposes. In January 1999, Iraq credibly established that US weapons inspectors, working for the UN's international weapons inspection team in Iraq, were undertaking simultaneous intelligence operations—apparently unknown to the chief weapons inspector, Britain's Richard Butler, who denied that the UN mission was being used for this purpose.

Some exercises of "extraterritorial" jurisdiction are far more acceptable than others. Many countries routinely apply their laws to conduct occurring beyond their national borders, in ways that do not adversely impact international relations. The 2000 Military Extraterritorial Jurisdiction Act was first applied to a woman who stabbed her husband to death on an Air Force base in Turkey, in May 2003. Under Title 18 of the US Code §3261, the US Justice Department may prosecute civilians who accompany military personnel on international assignments, if the host government chooses not to prosecute. But the 2002 US executive branch announcement—regarding the right to launch preemptive strikes in the name of self-defense (§10.2)—has been openly embraced by only one other national government (United Kingdom).

There are examples of extraterritorial jurisdiction that no State would condone. In July 2005, for example, Italy demanded that the United States show "full respect" for Italian sovereignty. The prime minister summoned the American ambassador to explain the US Central Intelligence Agency's abduction of a Muslim cleric from a street in Milan in 2003. An Italian judge had ordered the arrest of thirteen people linked to the Central Intelligence Agency, on charges of kidnaping Mr. Nasr and flying him to an Egyptian prison. The chief prosecutor also assessed the legal status of another six Americans who were allegedly involved in this abduction.[9]

The handful of recognized bases for an extraterritorial application of sovereign power are presented in the following section.

◆ 5.2 JURISDICTIONAL PRINCIPLES

States exercise both civil and criminal jurisdiction over events abroad. Both derive from principles firmly established by customary State practice in criminal matters.

Commentators use the term "International Criminal Law" (ICL) in two related but distinct contexts, referring to: (1) the penal features of International Law; and (2) the international application of a nation's criminal law. Courts and journalists are not always clear about where they diverge. The first usage involves crimes that are in essence "internationalized" by the community of nations. The classic illustration is genocide. In August, 2001, Bosnian Serb general Radislav Kristic was the first soldier to be convicted of genocide by the UN's International Criminal Tribunal for the former Yugoslavia. ICL, when used in *this* sense, refers to the general's conduct—related to the 1995 killing of 7,800 Muslim men and boys at an overrun UN safe haven. This was a very special kind of internationally based crime, which was distinct from 7,800 murder convictions under the law of the Bosnian nation.[10] The required genocidal element was specific intent, demonstrated with crystal clarity by Kristic's conduct, to eradicate Bosnian Muslims.

Otherwise, the term "ICL" is used (or misused) when referring to applications of national law to crimes, which involve two or more countries. As Sweden's Uppsala University Professor Iain Cameron succinctly explains:

a state can criminalize conduct which occurs outside its territory, and provide for prosecution of the actors should they come within its territory. A state's assertion of [its jurisdictional] competence in this way can be referred to as "extraterritorial criminal jurisdiction," although the actual prosecution and punishment of the offender is intraterritorial. All states apply their criminal law to events and conduct occurring outwith [without] their territories to a greater and lesser extent, and so all states apply rules which lay down the spatial scope of their criminal law and grant competence to their courts to try and punish people who have committed abroad [the] acts defined in their criminal codes as offences."[11]

The jurisdictional principles in this chapter authorize—and limit—a State's ability to proscribe and punish individuals who commit crimes beyond the borders of the prosecuting State. In 1935, a major study at the Harvard Law School confirmed the continuing need for expanding criminal jurisdiction in this international context. The Introductory Comment of the study explained it as follows: "From its beginning, the international community of States has had to deal in a pragmatic way with more or less troublesome problems of penal jurisdiction. In exercising such jurisdiction . . . States became increasingly aware of the overlappings and the gaps which produced conflicts [between two States wanting to prosecute the same criminal] and required cooperation. . . . In the [nineteenth] century, with the increasing facility of travel, transport and communication . . . the problems of conflict between the different national systems became progressively more acute."[12]

This relatively homogenous perspective about the nature of the national jurisdiction evolved. State practice no longer expects every application of national jurisdiction to smash into an impenetrable brick wall at the international border. As ably explained by Vanderbilt School of Law Professor Harold Maier: "Today, improvements in means of communications and transportation both facilitate international economic and social intercourse and support the proposition that the effects of governmental encroachments upon human liberty often transcend national boundaries . . . and the resulting need to regulate . . . can no longer be localised within national boundaries. These increasingly complex interrelationships between national, social, [environmental] and economic interests foster a recognition by the world community that there are occasions when both national and [international] community interests are served by permitting a nation to address, under its laws, activities carried on outside its national borders."[13]

International practice now acknowledges five customary bases for legitimate State regulation of individual or corporate conduct, occurring either partially or wholly beyond its borders. Exhibit 5.1 summarizes this significant intersection between national and International Law:

EXHIBIT 5.1 STATE "X" INTERNATIONAL JURISDICTIONAL GUIDE

Jurisdictional Principle		Conduct for Which State "X" May Prosecute
Territorial	(Subjective)	Defendant's conduct violates State X law
		Conduct starts *within* State X
		Completed within State X
	(Objective)	Defendant's conduct violates State X law
		Conduct starts *outside* State X
		Completed or has "effect" within State X
Nationality		Defendant's conduct violates State X law
		Defendant is a citizen (national) of X
		Conduct may start and end anywhere
Passive Personality		Defendant's conduct violates State X law
		Victim is a citizen (national) of X
		Conduct may start and end anywhere
Protective		Defendant's conduct violates State X law
		Conduct may start and end outside State X
		(Territorial must either start or end in X)
		(Protective need not have "effect" in X)
Universality		Defendant's conduct sufficiently heinous to violate the laws of all States
		Conduct started and completed anywhere
		All States may prosecute (not just X)

TERRITORIAL PRINCIPLE

Under this principle, the State's jurisdictional authority is derived from the location of the defendant's act. That conduct usually starts and ends within the State that is prosecuting the defendant. The State may thereby punish individuals who commit crimes within its borders. Of all jurisdictional principles, this application is the most widely accepted and the least disputed.

There are two applications of the territorial principle: "subjective" (internal) and "objective" (external). Assume that the defendant is a foreign citizen. A State may have the jurisdictional power to prosecute violators of its laws, without regard to that person's nationality. For example, Italy may wish to prosecute a Swiss citizen who plots the overthrow of the Italian government. That individual is captured by the Italian police in Rome, where he planned this *coup d'etat.* Italy possesses the subjective territorial jurisdiction to prosecute and punish this defendant, although he or she is a foreign citizen, because of this conduct taking place within Italy's borders. As stated by Italy's Court of Cassation, in response to a Swiss defendant's unsuccessful claim, that Italy would lack jurisdiction in such a case, there "is no rule of Italian public law or international law which exempts from punishment an alien who commits an act in Italy which constitutes a crime. . . . The crime of which the appellant [defendant] has been found guilty, is not less a crime because he is a Swiss national. . . ."[14]

Under International Law, Italy may also exercise its sovereign powers over those whose extraterritorial conduct violates its laws. The prior historical limitation—that a State could regulate only that conduct occurring within its geographical boundaries—no longer makes sense. Nineteenth-century national legislation began to reflect this internationalization of criminal activity, which was made possible by the evolution of technology and communication. Since then, geometric improvements in travel and communication have greatly enhanced the criminal's ability to commit a crime (or parts of a crime) in more than one country. Unlawful conduct of the earlier Swiss citizen may occur partially inside and partially outside of Italy—thus authorizing its objective application of the territorial principle although a segment of the punished conduct occurs in Switzerland (or elsewhere).

This facet of territorial jurisdiction is more easily abused. The prosecuted conduct may occur outside of the prosecuting nation. It may have the requisite effect within a nation to allow it to prosecute, based on accepted State practice. The leading international case on this "effects doctrine" was decided in 1927 by the PCIJ:

The S.S. Lotus (France v. Turkey)

PERMANENT COURT OF INTERNATIONAL JUSTICE

Permanent Court of International Justice Reports, Series A, No. 10 (1927)

AUTHOR'S NOTE: In 1923, the French mail steamer Lotus was in international waters, headed for Constantinople. The Lotus collided with an outbound Turkish coal ship, the Boz-Kourt. Eight Turkish seamen were killed in the collision. When the Lotus arrived in Turkey, Turkish authorities arrested and prosecuted the French ship's watch officer, Lieutenant Demons (as well as the Turkish vessel's captain) for involuntary manslaughter. Defendant Demons' negligence allegedly cost the lives of Turkish citizens as well as substantial property damage to the Turkish vessel.

France objected to Turkey's exercise of jurisdiction over its French citizen. The alleged criminal negligence did not occur on Turkish territory or in its territorial waters. After diplomatic protests, France and Turkey decided to submit France's objection to Turkey's exercise of its national jurisdiction to the PCIJ for a neutral resolution.

Some italics have been added. All footnotes were omitted.

COURT'S OPINION:

I

. . .

The violation, if any, of the principles of international law would have consisted in the taking of criminal proceedings against Lieutenant Demons. It is not therefore a question relating to any particular step in these proceedings [by Turkey] but of the very fact of the Turkish Courts exercising criminal jurisdiction. That is [because] the proceedings relate exclusively to the question whether Turkey has or has not, according to the principles of international law, jurisdiction to prosecute [France's citizen] in this case.

The Parties agree that the Court has not to consider whether the prosecution was in conformity with Turkish law. . . .

The prosecution was instituted [however] in pursuance of [the following] Turkish legislation.

. . .

[Art. 6 of the Turkish Penal Code provided that] Any foreigner who . . . commits an offence abroad to the prejudice of Turkey or of a Turkish subject . . . shall be punished in accordance with the Turkish Penal Code provided that he is arrested in Turkey.

. . .

[T]he question submitted to the Court is not whether that article is compatible with the principles of international law; it is more general. The Court is asked to state whether or not the principles of international law prevent Turkey from instituting criminal proceedings against Lieutenant Demons under Turkish law.

II

. . .

Now the first and foremost restriction imposed by international law upon a State is that . . . it may not exercise its power in any form in the territory of another State. In this sense, jurisdiction is certainly territorial; it cannot be exercised by a State outside its territory except by virtue of a permissive rule derived from international custom or from a convention.

It does not, however, follow that international law prohibits a State from exercising jurisdiction . . . [over] acts which have taken place abroad . . . . Far from laying down a general prohibition to the effect that States may not extend the application of their laws and the jurisdiction of their courts to persons, property and acts outside their territory, it leaves them in this respect a wide measure of discretion, which is only limited in certain cases by prohibitive rules; as regards other cases, every State remains free to adopt the principles which it regards as best and most suitable.

This discretion left to States by international law explains the great variety of rules which they have been able to adopt without objections or complaints on the part of other States. . . .

It follows from the foregoing that the contention of the French Government to the effect that Turkey must in each case be able to cite a rule of international law authorizing her to exercise jurisdiction, is opposed to the generally accepted international law.

. . .

III

. . .

Such a view would only be tenable if international law contained a general prohibition to States to extend the application of their laws and the jurisdiction of their courts to persons, property and acts outside their territory. . . . But this is certainly not the case under international law as it stands at present.

. . .

IV

. . .

[I]t is certain that the courts of many countries, even of countries which have given their criminal legislation a strictly territorial character, interpret criminal law in the sense that offences, the authors of which at the moment of commission are in the territory of another State, are nevertheless to be regarded as having been committed in the national territory [of the prosecuting State] if one of the constituent elements of the offence, *and more especially its effects,* have taken place there. . . . Again, the Court does not know of any cases in which governments have protested against the fact that the criminal law of some country contained a rule to this effect or that the courts of a country construed their criminal law in this sense. Consequently, once it is admitted that the effects of the offence were produced on the Turkish vessel, it becomes impossible to hold that there is a rule of international law which prohibits Turkey from prosecuting Lieutenant Demons because of the fact that the author of the offence was on board the French ship.

. . .

It follows that what occurs on board a vessel on the high seas must be regarded as if it occurred on the territory of the State whose flag the ship flies. If, therefore, a guilty act committed on the high seas produces its, effects on a vessel flying another flag or in foreign territory, the same principles must be applied as if the territories of two different States were concerned, and the conclusion must therefore be drawn that there is no rule of international law prohibiting the State to which the ship on which the effects of the offence have taken place belongs, from regarding the offence as having been committed in its territory.

. . .

This conclusion could only be overcome if it were shown that there was a rule of customary international law which, going further than the principle stated above, established the exclusive jurisdiction of the State whose flag was flown. The French Government has endeavoured to prove the existence of such a rule, having recourse for this purpose to the teachings of publicists, to decisions of municipal and international tribunals, and especially to conventions . . . creating exceptions to the principle of the freedom of the seas by permitting the war and police vessels of a State to exercise a more or less extensive control over the merchant vessels of another State. . . .

In the Court's opinion, the existence of such a rule has not been conclusively proved.

. . .

So far as the Court is aware there are no decisions of international tribunals in this matter; but some decisions of municipal courts have been cited. Without pausing to consider the value to be attributed to the judgments of municipal courts in connection with the establishment of the existence of a rule of international law, it will suffice to observe that the decisions quoted sometimes support one view and sometimes the other.

. . .

The offence for which Lieutenant Demons was prosecuted was an act—of negligence or imprudence—having its origin on board the [French ship] *Lotus,* whilst its effects made themselves felt on board the [Turkish ship] *Boz-Kourt.* . . . It is only natural that each should be able to exercise jurisdiction and to do so in respect of the incident as a whole. It is therefore a case of concurrent jurisdiction.

. . .

V

. . .

The Court, having heard both Parties, gives, by the President's casting vote—the votes being equally divided—judgment to the effect . . . that Turkey, by instituting criminal proceedings in pursuance of Turkish law against Lieutenant Demons, officer of the watch on board the *Lotus* at the time of the collision, has not acted in conflict with the principles of international law.

. . .

M. LODER, DISSENTING
Turkey, having arrested, tried and convicted a foreigner for an offence which he is alleged to have committed outside her territory, claims to have been authorized to do so by reason of the absence of a prohibitive rule of international law.

. . .

In other words, on the contention that, under international law, every door is open unless it is closed by treaty or by established Custom.

. . .

The fundamental consequence of their independence and sovereignty is that no municipal law, in the particular case under consideration no criminal law, can apply or have binding effect outside the national territory.

. . .

The criminal law of a State applies in the first place to all persons within its territory, whether nationals or foreigners, because the right of jurisdiction over its own territory is an attribute of its sovereignty.

. . .

The general rule that the criminal law of a State loses its compelling force and its applicability in relation to offences committed by a foreigner in foreign territory, a rule derived from the basic principle of the sovereignty and independence of States, has indeed undergone modifications and has been made subject to exceptions restricting its scope by the *mutual consent* of the different Powers in so far as territory properly so called is concerned.

But according to a generally accepted view, this is not the case as regards the high seas. There the law of the flag and national jurisdiction have retained their indisputable authority to the exclusion of all foreign law or jurisdiction.

◆ *Notes & Questions*

1. The PCIJ held that Turkey could exercise its national criminal jurisdiction over a "foreigner" who violated Turkish law, when the French officer committed an offense abroad. On these facts, "abroad" included international waters. Unlike State sovereign territory, such areas do not "belong" to anyone. The Court approved "wide discretion" for this application of Turkish law. As will be seen in the next chapter, this development is also referred to as the ability of a State to exercise its jurisdiction based on the "law of the flag." A Turkish vessel might thus be legally characterized as an extension of the Turkish territory. Which alternative form of the "territorial principle" did the Court approve in *Lotus*?

2. The Court also acknowledged the applicability of the "passive personality" principle in this case. The victims of the French officer's negligence were Turkish citizens, as was the vessel. This feature of extraterritorial jurisdiction is analyzed later.

3. State practice emerged, which conformed the PCIJ's articulation that Customary International Law was evolving in support of extraterritorial exercises of sovereignty. Ten years later, for example, Ireland expressly provided for this practice in Article 29.8 of its 1937 Constitution: "The State may exercise extra-territorial jurisdiction in accordance with the generally recognised principles of international law."

4. Note how the French Government referred the PCIJ to the various sources of International Law (textbook §1.2), in an endeavor to illustrate that none of them supported Turkey's "extraterritorial" exercise of its Penal Code to Lt. Demons.

5. The PCIJ's 1927 definition and application of territorial jurisdiction coincides with that applied by the §5.1 *Pennoyer v. Neff* US Supreme Court decision in 1887. Both incorporated the "international law" premised on European State practice when deciding these landmark cases.

NATIONALITY PRINCIPLE

A State may regulate the conduct of its own citizens, even when their acts occur entirely outside of that State. In 1992, US chess master Bobby Fischer defied a UN resolution imposing sanctions against the former Yugoslavia. No US citizen was permitted to travel to Yugoslavia because of US legislation, which required compliance with the UN resolution. When Fischer defied the travel ban, the US Treasury Department sent him a letter, warning him about the penalties for his refusal to comply. Although his conduct took place on foreign soil, the United States could rely upon the nationality principle of jurisdiction to legitimize any ensuing prosecution for his prohibited travel.

In the *Lotus* case discussed earlier, France could have prosecuted the French ship's officer for his negligence. Lieutenant Demons was a French citizen who damaged a French public vessel. This exercise of State jurisdiction would have been premised on the legal bond between a State and its citizens. That link generates reciprocal rights and obligations. As previously analyzed in the §4.2 *Nottebohm* case, a State is expected to protect its citizens when they are abroad—for as long as they owe it their allegiance. Conversely, a citizen's conduct may touch and concern the interests of his or her home State in a way that allows that State to request that the citizen return home. That State may also punish its citizen for certain conduct abroad, such as operating a public French vessel in a way that damaged it in a collision at sea, based on the nationality link between France and its citizen.

The nationality principle is invoked less frequently than the territorial principle. One practical reason is that the territorial and nationality principles often overlap. France would not *have* to invoke the nationality principle if it wanted to prosecute Lieutenant Demons. The territorial principle would be conspicuously available, because his negligence also harmed the French vessel in the Lotus collision—an extension of France's territory on the high seas. In *Lotus,* Turkey did not claim that its criminal jurisdiction was based in whole or in part on this principle, because the Lotus watch officer was not a Turkish citizen. Turkey might have done so, if the *Lotus* issues had included any wrongdoing by the captain of the Turkish vessel.

Under the nationality principle, States enjoy relatively unfettered legal control over their citizens. A State's treatment of its own citizens was historically not within the legal province of other states.[15] The following case explains why:

◆

Blackmer v. United States

SUPREME COURT OF THE UNITED STATES, 1932
284 US 421, 52 S.Ct. 252, 76 *L. Ed.* 375

AUTHOR'S NOTE: This was a tax case arising out of the famous Teapot Dome Scandal during the administration of President Warren Harding in the 1920s. In litigation related to this scandal, the Supreme Court found that some high-ranking politicians had obtained oil leases through corrupt means. Blackmer, a US citizen, had some information needed by the US authorities to investigate them. He had moved to France but had not relinquished his US citizenship.

A US consular officer in Paris served Blackmer with a notice to return to Washington to testify for the US government. His testimony would help to ascertain the facts during criminal and civil investigations of the scandal. After Blackmer ignored this court order to return to the United States, the trial judge found him in contempt of court for failing to appear. Blackmer then petitioned the US Supreme Court for relief from the lower court's contempt order and related fine. The following portion of the Supreme Court's opinion succinctly articulates the application of the nationality principle of jurisdiction requiring Blackmer's return.

COURT'S OPINION: Mr. Chief Justice Hughes delivered the opinion of the Court.

The petitioner, Harry M. Blackmer, a citizen of the United States resident in Paris, France, was adjudged guilty of contempt of the Supreme Court of the District of Columbia for failure to respond to subpoenas served upon him in France and requiring him to appear as a witness on behalf of the United States at a criminal trial in that court. Two subpoenas were issued, for appearances at different times, and there was a separate proceeding with respect to each. The two cases were heard together, and a fine of $30,000 with costs was imposed in each case, to be satisfied out of the property of the petitioner which had been seizer by order of the court. The decrees were affirmed by the Court of Appeals of the District, and this Court granted writs of certiorari.

The subpoenas were issued and served, and the proceedings to punish for contempt were taken, under the provisions of the Act of July 3, 1926. . . . [FN1] The statute provided that whenever the attendance at the trial of a criminal action of a witness abroad, who is "a citizen of the United States or domiciled therein," is desired by the Attorney General, or any assistant or district attorney acting under him, the judge of the court in which the action is pending may order a subpoena to issue, to be addressed to a consul of the United States and to be served by him personally upon the witness with a tender of traveling expenses. Upon proof of such service and of the failure of the witness to appear, the court may make an order requiring the witness to show cause why he should not be punished for contempt, and, upon the issue of such an order, the court may direct that property belonging to the witness and within the United States may be seized and held to satisfy any judgment which may be rendered against him in the proceeding. . . .

[FN1] The Act is as follows: "Be it enacted by the Senate and House of Representatives of the United States of America in Congress assembled, That whenever letters rogatory shall issue out of any court of the United States, either with or without interrogatories addressed to any court of any foreign country, to take the testimony of any witness, being a citizen of the United States or domiciled therein, and such witness, having been personally notified by it according to the practice of such court, to appear and testify pursuant to such letters rogatory and such witness shall neglect to appear . . . , the court out of which said letters issued may upon proper showing order that a subpoena issue addressed to any consul of the United States within any country in which such witness may be, commanding such witness to appear before the said court at a time and place therein designated.

Sec. 2. Whenever the attendance at the trial of any criminal action of a witness, being a citizen of the United States or domiciled therein, who is beyond the jurisdiction of the United States, is desired by the Attorney General or any assistant or district attorney acting under him, its judge of the court before which such action is pending, or who is to sit in the trial of the same, may, upon proper showing, order that a subpoena issue, addressed to any consul of the United States within any country in which such witness may be, commanding such witness to appear before the said court at a time and place therein designated."

. . .

While it appears that the petitioner removed his residence to France in the year 1924, it is undisputed that he was, and continued to be, a citizen of the United States. He continued to owe allegiance to the United States. By virtue of the obligations of citizenship, the United States retained its authority over him, and he was bound by its laws made applicable to him in a foreign country. Thus, although resident abroad, the petitioner remained subject to the taxing power of the United States. For disobedience to its laws through conduct abroad, he was subject to punishment in the courts of the United States. With respect to such an exercise of authority, there is no question of international law, but solely of the purport of the municipal law which establishes the duties of the citizen in relation to his own government. While the legislation of the Congress, unless the contrary intent appears, is construed to apply only within the territorial jurisdiction of the United States, the question of its application, so far as citizens of the United States in foreign countries are concerned, is one of construction, not of legislative power. Nor can it be doubted that the United States possesses the power inherent in sovereignty to require the return to this country of a citizen, resident elsewhere, whenever the public interest requires it, and to penalize him in case of refusal. Compare *Bartue* and the *Duchess of Suffolk's Case* [citations omitted].

What in England was the prerogative of the sovereign in this respect pertains under our constitutional system to the national authority which may be exercised by the Congress by virtue of the legislative power to prescribe the duties of the citizens of the United States. It is also beyond controversy that one of the duties which the citizen owes to his government is to support the administration of justice by attending its courts and giving his testimony whenever he is properly summoned. And the Congress may provide for the performance of this duty and prescribe penalties for disobedience. . . .

In the present instance, the . . . authority to require the absent citizen to return and testify necessarily implies the authority to give him notice of the requirement. As his attendance is needed in court, it is appropriate that the Congress should authorize the court to direct the notice to be given, and that it should be in the customary form of a subpoena. . . . The question of the validity of the provision for actual service of the subpoena in a foreign country is one that arises solely between the government of the United States and the citizen. The mere giving of such a notice to the citizen in the foreign country of the requirement of his government that he shall return is in no sence [sic] an invasion of any right of the foreign government and the citizen has no standing to invoke any such supposed right.

PASSIVE PERSONALITY PRINCIPLE

This form of jurisdiction is based on the nationality of the victim when the crime occurs outside of the prosecuting State's territory. It is probably the least used jurisdictional basis, given its potential for abuse.

An unlimited application of the passive personality principle would result in the potential prosecution of *anyone* in the world, *anywhere* in the world, who allegedly harm citizens of the prosecuting country. It is generally not used unless another principle is also applicable. In the above PCIJ *Lotus* case, Turkey relied on the passive personality principle to support its prosecution of the French ship's officer (in addition to its primary territoriality principle argument). His conduct harmed Turkish citizens and Turkish property interests. Because the conduct took place outside of Turkey, the Court cautiously acknowledged the theoretical applicability of this principle. Some of the judges expressed their belief that International Law does not permit assertions of jurisdiction exclusively on this basis. Judge Moore warned that jurisdiction based solely on the victim's citizenship would mean "that the citizen [victim] of one country, when he visits another country, takes with him for his 'protection' the law of his own country and subjects those with whom he comes into contact to the operation of that law. In this way an inhabitant of a great commercial city, in which foreigners congregate, may in the course of an hour unconsciously fall under the operation of a number of foreign criminal codes. . . ."[16]

Case Study: In 2002, a Mexican national was convicted of sexual contact with a minor US citizen, on a cruise ship in Mexican territorial waters. The federal Court of Appeals analysis was as follows:

International law supports extraterritorial jurisdiction in this case. Two principles of international law permitting extraterritorial jurisdiction are potentially relevant: the territorial principle and the passive personality principle. Under the territorial principle, the United States may assert jurisdiction when acts performed outside of its borders have detrimental effects within the United States. The sexual contact occurred during a cruise that originated and terminated in California. Neil's conduct prompted an investigation by the FBI, and an agent arrested Neil in the United States. The victim was an American citizen who lives and goes to school in the United States, and who sought counseling in this country after the attack. These facts are enough to support jurisdiction under the territorial principle.

. . .

Extraterritorial jurisdiction is also appropriate under the passive personality principle. Under this principle, a state may, under certain circumstances, assert jurisdiction over crimes committed against its nationals. . . . Citing the Restatement [(Third) of Foreign Relations Law of the United States §402, in a similar case] we noted that, in general, the passive personality principle has not been accepted as a sufficient basis for extraterritorial jurisdiction over *ordinary* torts and crimes. . . . By contrast, [US Criminal Code] §2244(a)(3) . . . invokes the passive personality principle by *explicitly* stating its intent to authorize extraterritorial jurisdiction, to the extent permitted by international law, when a foreign vessel departs from or arrives in an American port and an American national is a victim (italics added).[17]

Do you agree that this court properly exercised: (a) territorial jurisdiction; and (b) protective jurisdiction, as articulated by the PCIJ in the already discussed *S.S. Lotus* case? Would one of these two principles of jurisdiction be more appropriate than the others? Why do the courts more narrowly apply the protective principle of extraterritorial criminal jurisdiction?

PROTECTIVE PRINCIPLE

Under this theory, the criminal act must threaten the security (territorial integrity, or political independence) of the State. The protective principle allows a State to prosecute its own citizens, as well as citizens of other States, for their relevant conduct outside of its territory. The perpetrator may choose not to enter the State whose laws have been violated. That State will then have to seek his or her extradition from a State where the offending individual is found. In any event, and as acknowledged by the US Supreme Court, "under the 'protective principle' of international law, a nation is permitted 'to assert jurisdiction over a person whose conduct outside the nation's territory threatens the nation's security.'"[18]

The protective principle differs from the analogous territorial principle because the effect of the criminal's conduct does *not* have to be felt within the territory of the offended State. In a US case distinguishing these two principles, a Canadian citizen made false statements while trying to obtain a visa from the US Consulate in Montreal. The court noted that "the objective principle [requiring that the effects of the crime be directly felt within the territory] is quite distinct from the protective theory. Under the latter, all the elements of the crime occur in the foreign country and jurisdiction exists because these actions have a '*potentially* adverse effect' upon security or governmental functions . . . and there *need not be any actual effect* within the country as would be required under the objective territorial principle."[19]

Because of the potential for abuse, national legislation which relied on this vintage principle to assert jurisdiction normally required that high officials undertake discretionary reviews of its proposed use against conduct abroad which might not be criminal under foreign law, for example, when a Swedish national acted legally abroad in a way that harmed Swedish interests. The basic concern is the subjugation of aliens to Swedish law for acts undertaken far from Sweden, which *might* have some effect (unlike the territorial principle which requires that effect to be felt within the prosecuting nation).

Contemporary applications of the protective principle also require double criminality. The Swedish prosecution of a person (Swedish or otherwise) for a crime against Swedish interests requires that the crime also be a violation of the nation where the act was perpetrated. Furthermore, Sweden will not impose a sanction, which is greater than the place of occurrence would levy.

The primary reason for imposing modern limitations is the 1970 European Convention on the International Validity of Criminal Judgments. The Convention strengthened individual rights, while bringing State exercises of criminal jurisdiction more into line with the realities of the modern world. As noted in the lone book which focuses exclusively on this principle: "With greatly increased international mobility, it was no longer felt to be reasonable to use the criminal law to impose unconditionally Swedish norms of behaviour on nationals and domiciled aliens when they were abroad."[20]

In the aftermath of corporate accounting scandals in the United States, especially those involving Enron and Worldcom, the US Congress responded with legislation with an extraterritorial effect. It effectively asserts jurisdiction over foreign accounting firms. European Union (EU) countries were upset, because their laws already dealt with such matters—thus obviating the need for this "intrusion." In the words of one French journalist: "After the Enron and Worldcom affairs one would have thought that the United States was in a poor position to give the world lessons about corporate governance."[21] One provision in this legislation singles out foreign accounting firms. It asserts jurisdiction over them, if they play "a substantial role in the preparation and furnishing" of accounting statements filed with the Security and Exchange Commission.[22] This legislation is similar to the 1996 Helms-Burton Act (textbook §13.1). Its provisions penalize non-American firms for "trafficking" in property expropriated by Cuba in 1959. Both statutory regimes are examples of laws designed to secure US economic interests.

Most states do not use this theory for exercising jurisdiction. In the leading treatise on International Law as applied by Canada, the authors explain that the focus on "security" underscores the potential for abuse:

A state may exercise jurisdiction over acts committed abroad that are prejudicial to its security, territorial integrity and political independence. For example, the types of crime covered could include treason, espionage, and counterfeiting of currency, postage stamps, seals, passports, and other public documents.

Canada and other countries such as the United Kingdom have not favored this principle when unaccompanied by other [jurisdictional] factors such as nationality or other forms of allegiance tying the accused to the forum.[23]

UNIVERSALITY PRINCIPLE

Certain crimes spawn a "universal interest" because they are sufficiently heinous to be considered crimes against the entire community of nations. The perpetrators of these crimes are deemed to be enemies of all mankind. Any nation where the perpetrator is found is expected to arrest and try the perpetrator, or to extradite the criminal to a State that will prosecute. Genocide (§11.1) is the classic example. The universality principle is not applied to "common crimes" such as murder, because it is not sufficiently outrageous. This section will help you in the quest for determining whether an event like "9-11" is a *universal* crime, or the *national* crime of (mass) murder.

One distinguishing feature of universal jurisdiction is that it is "criminal jurisdiction based solely on the nature of the crime, without regard to where the crime was committed, the nationality of the alleged or convicted perpetrator, the nationality of the victim, or any other connection to the state exercising such jurisdiction."[24] Unlike all of the other bases for a State to exercise its jurisdiction over matters arising beyond its boundaries, the jurisdictional linchpin is the nature of the crime— rather than any connection to a particular country.

There are several other well-recognized universal crimes beyond piracy and genocide. Some commentators include the harming of diplomats and the hijacking of aircraft. A contemporary short list, the work product of the 2001 *Princeton Project*, lists the following as universal crimes: "(1) piracy; (2) slavery; (3) war crimes; (4) crimes against peace; (5) crimes against humanity"[25]—the latter three being the fundamental Nuernberg allegations you will study in §9.5. While some commentators may disagree with the length or completeness of this list, its moral accuracy cannot be contested.

One of the most prominent examples of a prosecution for a universal crime involved acts perpetrated during the Nazi Holocaust in World War II. In *Israel v. Eichmann,* Israel prosecuted Adolf Eichmann, Hitler's chief exterminator, under its Nazi Collaborators Punishment Law. That legislation and the ensuing prosecution were based on the application of universal jurisdiction. None of the other jurisdictional principles were available to Israel. The territorial principle could not apply, because Israel did not become a State until 1948. The nationality principle was inapplicable, because *Germany* would have to be the prosecuting State for that principle to apply. The passive personality principle did not apply, because no victim could possibly be a citizen of the State of Israel before it came into existence. In the absence of an Israeli State during the period in which Eichmann engaged in his atrocities, the protective principle could not be invoked to protect the interests of a nation which did not yet exist.

Eichmann committed the crime of genocide against the citizens of various European States before Israel existed. Eichmann was abducted from Argentina by Israeli commandos to stand trial in Israel. The resulting prosecution was undertaken in Israel's capacity as a member of the community of nations. It asserted its universal jurisdiction to prosecute Eichmann. In the opinion of Israel's Supreme Court:

> The crimes defined in this [Israeli] law must be deemed to have always been international crimes, entailing individual criminal responsibility: customary international law is analogous to the Common Law and develops by analogy and by reference to general principles of law recognized by civilized nations; these crimes share the characteristics of crimes . . . which damage vital international interests, impair the foundations and security of the international community, violate universal moral values and humanitarian principles . . . and the principle of universal jurisdiction over "crimes against humanity" . . . similarly derives from a common vital interest in their suppression. The State prosecuting them acts as agent of the international community, administering international law.[26]

The universality principle might be invoked if none of the other principles apply. Piracy, for example, was (and is) usually committed on the high seas rather than within the territorial waters of any nation. Pirates often flee to distant lands or waters. In November 2005, for example, pirates attacked a luxury cruise liner, with a rocket-propelled grenade and machine guns, off the coast of east Africa. Several ships per month are so attacked, valuables are stolen, and crews are held hostage for ransom. Under the universal principle, all nations have the jurisdiction and the duty to apprehend pirates, when they are present and thus subject to capture or extradition. Aerial piracy is the modern analogy, serving as a basis for applying this vintage jurisdictional concept. In the 1970s, it became quite evident that: aircraft could be seized by individuals of unknown nationality; they answered to no State authority; and that their interferences with navigation was taking place over the high

seas, Antarctica, and elsewhere on the planet that were outside the territorial jurisdiction of any nation.[27]

The most prominent future application could be the trial of Usama bin Laden, if some country other than the United States or the United Kingdom were to capture him (Problem 5.B and text §10.7), and it was not one of the eighty-one countries whose citizens were lost in 9-11. If that country decided not to turn bin Laden over for trial to any other national or international tribunal, then it would be exercising universal jurisdiction.

The most intriguing universal jurisdiction application involved the extent to which customary practice recognized a Belgian prosecution—where there was *no* other jurisdictional link between the perpetrator and the prosecuting State, as illustrated in the following case:

Case Concerning the Arrest Warrant of 11 April 2000

(DEMOCRATIC REPUBLIC OF THE CONGO V. BELGIUM)

International Court of Justice
General List No. 121 (Feb. 14, 2002)
<http://www.icj-cij.org/icjwww/idecisions.htm>
Go to course Web page at
<http://home.att.net/~slomansonb/txtcsesite.html>.
Under Chapter Five, click <u>Belgian Arrest Warrant</u>.

The US House of Representatives had its own reaction to Belgium's exercise of universal jurisdiction, May 2003, H.R. 2050, the "Universal Jurisdiction Rejection Act of 2003." This bill was presented on the House floor, "[t]o prohibit cooperation with or assistance to any investigation or prosecution under a universal jurisdiction statute." It specifically referred to a suit brought by Palestinians against Israeli Prime Minister Ariel Sharon for acts occurring in Lebanon in 1982; that the relevant massacres had been investigated under Israel's Commissions of Inquiry Law that year; and that this suit was thus politically motivated. It was subsequently dismissed and Belgium limited its unique universal jurisdiction law.

Internet Application   Now that you have studied the five jurisdictional principles, we can focus on their application in a fresh context: the Internet. As of November 2005, 15 percent of the planet's 6 billion inhabitants already have access to the Internet. Almost 52 percent of these cybernauts are located in Canada, Europe, and the United States. These percentages will increase dramatically by the next edition of this book. Sovereign nations fully understand the implications, and have reacted in predictable ways.

One attribute of the contemporary *Information Revolution* is that States are finding it increasingly unmanageable. Individuals and corporations are using the Internet to challenge the State's traditional ability to control activities occurring within—and in many cases beyond—its borders. They have numerous reasons for attempting to control the Internet, especially in the current global War on Terror. One example is the use of the Internet by al-Qaida. In a prominent scenario, an Egyptian member registered a domain name and rented a server in China in February 2000. It served as a hub for this group's activities in various countries. The US president, for example, has unreservedly acknowledged his authorization of electronic surveillance of various communications media. This has been done, without judicial approval, in the name of national security, to wage the War on Terror.[28]

Previously addressed jurisdictional theory, such as the "effects doctrine" and other internationally recognized bases for governmental control, are ineffective solutions to the jurisdictional issues posed by the Internet. The intersection of law and the Internet presents problems, which have not been adequately addressed in the emerging shift from a traditional, territorial domain to a virtual, electronic environment. States are therefore attempting to apply traditional legal principles to retain what power they can summon to control either Internet commerce or Internet content, which may be offensive to public policy.[29]

In Spring of 2004, the People's Republic of China (PRC) closed down 8,600 Internet cafes, mostly for illegally admitting juveniles. China bans them from operating within 220 yards of schools, to avoid students being exposed to pornography or addicted to online video games. The General Administration for Industry and Commerce provided a statement, regarding the above closures, that "cafes admitting children have brought great harm to the mental health of teenagers and interfered with school teaching, which has aroused strong reaction from the public."[30]

Many other nations, espousing admirable objectives, exhibit like concerns. The 2001 Council of Europe Cybercrime Convention, for example, facilitates cooperation in the investigation and prosecution of Internet based offenses.[31] This Convention applies to any Internet service provider (ISP) having a fixed location within the EU. It created the new criminal offense "illegally accessing an information system." The European Network and Information Security Agency, operational as of 2004, is designed to help governments, businesses, and consumers protect their computers and privacy interests. Further, at the invitation of the Swiss Federal Data Protection Commissioner, the 27th International Conference of Data Protection and Privacy Commissioners met and produced the September 2005 Montreux Convention. It "encourages international and supra-national organizations to commit . . . to complying with principles . . . compatible with . . . data protection and privacy . . . [and] software manufacturers to develop products and systems integrating privacy enhancing technologies." The goal is to control the risks associated with biometrics in government-issued passports, identity cards, travel documents.

The United Nations deserves the "spotlight" as well. During Saddam Hussein's rule, it prevented Iraq from importing most computer equipment. At the same time, Iraq severely limited citizen access to cyberspace. After the regime changed, the November 2005, UN-sponsored World Summit on the Information Society convened in Tunis. One objective was to promote UN participation in controlling the Internet. This program has been labeled, however, as a digital Trojan Horse. Under the guise of making the Internet more accessible to the world's population, its working group (including China, Cuba, Iran, and Saudi Arabia) hopes to concentrate control within the United Nations. Some of the most repressive regimes therefore seek to wrestle Internet control from the private organization now controlling domain names and the other trappings of Internet governance.[32]

Governmental control is, however, difficult to maximize. You probably have access to a computer terminal and the Internet, both at home and at school. Yet your digital machinations have only the most tenuous connection to your physical location. Nations wishing to participate in modern commerce will have to strike a balance between what their governments wish to regulate, and grasping the immense value that the information age now offers. Two leading analysts thus pose the following dose of cyberspace reality:

Law and Borders—The Rise of Law in Cyberspace

BY DAVID JOHNSON AND DAVID POST

48 *Stanford Law Review* 1367 (1996)

Cyberspace radically undermines the relationship between legally significant (online) phenomena and physical location. The rise of the global computer network is destroying the link between geographical location and: (1) the power of local governments to assert control over online behavior; (2) the effects of online behavior on individuals or things; (3) the legitimacy of a local sovereign's efforts to regulate global phenomena; and (4) the ability of physical location to give notice of which sets of rules apply. . . .

Cyberspace has no territorially based boundaries, because the cost and speed of message transmission on the Net is almost entirely independent of physical location. Messages can be transmitted from one physical location to any other location without degradation, decay, or substantial delay, and without any physical cues or barriers that might otherwise keep certain geographically remote places and people separate from one another. The Net enables transactions between people who do not know, and in many cases cannot know, each other's physical location. . . . The system is indifferent to the physical location of those machines, and there is no necessary connection between an Internet address and a physical jurisdiction. Although the domain name initially assigned to a given machine may be associated with an Internet Protocol address that corresponds to that machine's physical location (for example, a ".uk" domain name extension), the machine may be physically moved without affecting its domain name.

Alternatively, the owner of the domain name might request that the name become associated with an entirely different machine, in a different physical location. Thus, a server with a ".uk" domain name need not be located in the United Kingdom, a server with a ".com" domain name may be anywhere, and users, generally speaking, are not even aware of the location of the server that stores the content that they read.

. . .

They [governmental authorities] assert jurisdiction only over the physical goods that cross the geographic borders they guard and claim no right to force declarations of the value of materials transmitted by modem. Banking and securities regulators seem likely to lose their battle to impose local regulations on a global financial marketplace. And state attorneys general face serious challenges in seeking to intercept the electrons that transmit the kinds of consumer fraud that, if conducted physically within the local jurisdiction, would be easier to shut down.

. . .

The foregoing excerpt illustrates the inherent difficulty with placing new wine (Internet transactions) into old bottles (territorial jurisdiction). As national authorities struggle to control this communications medium, they are relying on jurisdictional principles dating from the 1648 Treaty of Westphalia. Such efforts are bound to result in national apprehension after Nation No.1 attempts to regulate the Internet, followed by Nation No.2 responding in kind.

The foremost case to capture the essence of this dilemma is the *French Yahoo* case:

Union des Etudiants Juifs de France
Ligue contre le Racisme et l'Antisémitisme

v.

Yahoo! Inc. and Yahoo France

COURT OF GREAT INSTANCE OF PARIS (2000)

Go to course Web page at <http://home.att.net/~slomansonb/txtcsesite.html>.

Click <u>French Yahoo! Judgment</u>

◆ 5.3 EXTRADITION

INTRODUCTION

Section 5.2 presented the five jurisdictional bases for prosecuting individuals engaged in international criminal activity. The theoretical availability of jurisdiction is pointless, however, if the alleged criminal is not present. Some States try criminals *in absentia* under their internal laws. This is not very satisfying, however, if the State cannot enforce its judgment because the convicted criminal is absent. There is no global extradition treaty. Instead, there are hundreds of bilateral treaties listing mutually agreeable conditions for the surrender of accused or convicted criminals to stand trial in the requesting State. An extradition request by State X asks State Y to turn over an individual located in State Y who has committed a crime which violated the laws of State X. State X normally seeks extradition of the individual via diplomatic channels. If State Y agrees to X's request, then Y surrenders the accused to X authorities.

This process has ancient origins. The first recorded extradition treaty dates back to 1280 BC, when an Egyptian Pharaoh foiled an attempted invasion by the bordering Hittite nation. The ensuing peace treaty provided for the exchange of the activists who had returned to their respective nations, where they sought shelter after the unsuccessful invasion attempt.[33]

UTILITY

Extradition treaties are necessary because extradition is not automatic. There is no *duty* to surrender an individual to another nation. As articulated by the US Supreme Court: "in the absence of a conventional or legislative provision, there is no authority vested in any department of the government to seize a fugitive criminal and surrender him to a foreign power. . . . There is no executive discretion to surrender him to a foreign government, unless that discretion is granted by law. It necessarily follows that as the legal authority does not exist save as it is given by act of Congress or by the terms of a treaty, it is not enough that statute or treaty does not deny the power to surrender. It must be found that [some] statute or treaty confers the power."[34]

When granted, extradition overcomes a major jurisdictional limitation closely linked to State sovereignty. Extradition allows States to accomplish indirectly what they cannot do directly. Austria's police agents cannot enter Germany to apprehend a criminal. Austria's desire to prosecute that criminal is met, however, should Germany grant Austria's extradition request. Extradition circumvents the limitation that Austria's territorial jurisdiction cannot extend beyond its borders into Germany. Extradition also accomplishes the broader objective of facilitating international assistance in the apprehension of criminals. The British jurist Lord Russell stated in a classic case that "the law of extradition is . . . founded upon the broad principle that it is in the interest of civilised communities that crimes . . . should not go unpunished, and it is a part of the comity of nations that one State should afford to another every assistance towards bringing persons guilty of such crimes to justice."[35] The nation that honors a request for extradition today may want the requesting nation to return that favor tomorrow.

Extradition treaties typically list a mutually acceptable schedule of offenses which are subject to extradition. The crimes are usually major offenses against the law of both parties to the treaty. For example, Article II of the 1978 Treaty on Extradition Between the United States of America and Japan provides as follows: "Extradition shall be granted in accordance with the provisions of this Treaty for any offense listed in the Schedule annexed to this Treaty . . . when such an offense is punishable by the laws of both Contracting Parties by death, by life imprisonment, or by deprivation of liberty for a period of more than one year; or for any other offense when such offense is punishable by the federal laws of the United States and by the laws of Japan by death, by life imprisonment, or by deprivation of liberty for a period of more than one year."[36] The extraditable offenses in this treaty include murder, kidnaping, rape, bigamy, robbery, inciting riots, piracy, drug law violations, bribery, evasion of taxes, unfair business transactions, and violations of export/import laws.

Some countries prohibit or greatly limit extradition. The Honduran Constitution, for example, has historically prohibited the extradition of Honduran citizens to the United States. The constitutions of both Colombia (from 1991 to 1997) and Slovenia have barred extradition of their citizens to *any* foreign country. In 1993, a Pennsylvania judge claiming to be a Slovenian national fled from the United States to Slovenia after being convicted of corruption—where he remains a fugitive, and is beyond the reach of US authorities. A related limitation is that, even when States X and Y have entered into an extradition treaty, the criminal may find a safe haven in State Z, if it is not a party to the X–Y treaty.

On the other hand, there may be an *internationally* derived duty to surrender a fugitive for trial, which does not depend on a treaty as a legal basis for seeking extradition. The classic instance involves two Libyan intelligence officers who were indicted by the United Kingdom and the United States for their alleged role in the 1988 terrorist bombing of Pan Am Flight 103. The plane blew up over Lockerbie, Scotland, which claimed the lives of 270 people.[37] Libya refused to surrender them for trial. Several UN Security Council resolutions demanded their release for trial. Ultimately, negotiations with Libya resulted in their being extradited to The Netherlands to stand trial before three Scottish judges. In the interim, Libya countered with a lawsuit in the International Court of Justice, claiming that the United Kingdom and United States violated an air treaty to which all three (and most nations of the world) are parties. Libya claimed that it complied with this treaty. The United Kingdom and United States allegedly violated that treaty because a State in whose territory an offender is found has the obligation to try or extradite such individuals. Having submitted them to prosecution in Libya, there was supposedly no further Libyan obligation to extradite. Because of massive international pressure, Libya nevertheless surrendered them for trial abroad.[38]

Case Study In the United States, extradition not based on a bilateral treaty is exceedingly rare. In the following case, however, the President committed the United States to supporting the UN's International Criminal Tribunals for both the former Yugoslavia and Rwanda, without Senate involvement (a scenario further addressed in §8.3 of this book.)

In 1996, the United States was about to surrender a Rwandan national—residing in Texas, since leaving Rwanda two years earlier—to the International Criminal Tribunal for Rwanda (ICTR). This is the only case where transfer to one of the UN's ad hoc international criminal tribunals was litigated in a US court. A federal magistrate denied the ICTR's extradition request. He ruled that the federal statute authorizing such transfers was unconstitutional. Historical practice requires a bilateral treaty, even for the extradition of a foreign national from the United States. Another trial judge later decided that Mr. Ntakirutimana *could* be surrendered to the ICTR.

The appellate court delayed his extradition, but ultimately approved his surrender to the ICTR. A two-judge majority opinion recalled prior US Supreme Court case law, whereby "no statutory basis conferred the power on the Executive to surrender a citizen to the foreign government." However, even if Congress has rarely exercised the power to extradite by statute, rather than by executive treaty, "a historical understanding exists nonetheless that it may do so. . . . [I]n some instances in which a fugitive would not have been extraditable under a treaty, a fugitive has been extradited pursuant to a statute that 'filled the gap' in the treaty."

One of the two judges approving this extradition to the ICTR filed a concurring opinion in *Ntakirutimana*. He presented the following plea to the participating US Department of State:

I . . . invite the Secretary to closely scrutinize the underlying evidence as she makes her decision regarding whether Ntakirutimana should be surrendered to the International Criminal Tribunal for Rwanda. The evidence supporting the request is highly suspect. Affidavits of unnamed Tutsi witnesses acquired during interviews utilizing questionable interpreters in a political environment that has all the earmarks of a campaign of tribal retribution raises serious questions regarding the truth of their content.

It defies logic, and thereby places in question the credibility of the underlying evidence, that a man who has served his church faithfully for many years, who has never been accused of any law infraction, who has for his long life been a man of peace, and who is married to a Tutsi would somehow suddenly become a man of violence and commit the atrocities for which he stands accused.

The third judge on this panel dissented, as follows:

Our Constitution is the result of a deliberate plan for the separation of powers, designed to prevent both the arrogation of authority and the potential for tyranny. Notwithstanding our nation's moral duty to assist the cause of international justice, our nation's actions taken in that regard must comport with the Constitution's procedures and with respect for its allocation of powers. That is why we claim to be a nation ruled by law rather than men. . . .

The Attorney General's litigation position in this case has apparently been chosen for the purpose of validating a constitutional shortcut which would bypass the Treaty Clause. She stakes her case on the validity and enforceability of a warrant issued by the United Nations International Criminal Tribunal for Rwanda, which is a nonsovereign entity created by the United Nations Security Council, purporting to "DIRECT" the officials of our sovereign nation to surrender the accused. . . .

A structural reading of the Constitution compels the conclusion that most international agreements must be ratified according to the Treaty Clause of Article II. The history of national and international practice indicate that extradition agreements fall into this category. Our Founding Fathers intended that the President have authority to negotiate such agreements, but also that they be ratified pursuant to a special process intended to set a higher standard of legislative agreement than that required for ordinary legislation.[39]

◆ *Notes & Questions*

1. There were three distinct opinions issued by the three judges on this appellate panel. Given the expectation that the President will exercise the constitutional treaty power to extradite individuals from the United States in conjunction with the Senate, should the court have approved Ntakirutimana's extradition to the ICTR?
2. The second judge stated that the ICTR indictment in this case "defies logic." The defendant was a minister, had no prior criminal record, and was married to a member of the Rwanda Tutsis, who were slaughtered by the majority Hutus. Would it be better for the US court to resolve this issue, as part of the extradition process, or leave it to the foreign tribunal to resolve the logic of the charges? The ICTR ultimately found this defendant guilty of the charges of aiding and abetting genocide, but *not* conspiracy to commit genocide, nor crimes against humanity, nor murder or cruel treatment of persons not taking an active part in hostilities. At his sentencing, he was found to be "a person of good moral character until . . . 1994 during which he was swept along with many Rwandans into criminal conduct." Prosecutor v. Elizaphan & Gerad Ntakirutimana, Case Nos. ICTR-96-10, ICTR-96-17-T.
3. More detailed analyses of the US extradition proceedings are available in L. Klarevas, The Surrender of

Alleged War Criminals to International Tribunals: Examining The Constitutionality of Extradition Via Congressional-Executive Agreement, 8 UCLA J. INT'L L. & FOREIGN AFF. 77 (2003) & Casenote, Validating a Constitutional Shortcut–The "Congressional-Executive Agreement": Ntakirutimana v. Reno, 184 F.3d 419 (5th Cir. 1999), 69 UNIV. CINCINNATI L. REV. 1055 (2001).

"IRREGULAR" ALTERNATIVES

States do not always depend on extradition treaties when seeking to prosecute certain individuals. They may expel or deport "wanted" individuals without going through a formal extradition process, regardless of whether there is an applicable extradition treaty. States have also resorted to kidnaping.[40] The State whose sovereignty has thus been violated may protest. The individual defendant does not always have the legal capacity to rely on this violation of International Law as a defense to his or her criminal prosecution. In the *Eichmann* case (§5.2), for example, Israel violated the territorial sovereignty of Argentina when its commandos secretly entered Buenos Aires to capture him for trial in Tel Aviv. He was not able to successfully invoke this violation as a defense to his prosecution in the Israeli court. In the South African case, which follows (the US Supreme Court case in this section), the individual defendant was able to secure a dismissal of the case against him on this procedural ground.

The most notorious defendants typically claim that they cannot be prosecuted because of an "irregular" extradition, regardless of the merits of the accusations. Slobodan Milosevic, the Federal Republic of Yugoslavia's former president, claims that he was improperly "deported" from Yugoslavia to the UN's criminal tribunal in The Netherlands—rather than being properly "extradited" under Yugoslavian law. President Vojislav Rostunica, Milosevic's successor, publicly commented that the Yugoslavian constitution "does not allow extradition of Yugoslav citizens to a foreign court, so any talk about possible extradition is not legally founded."[41] Yugoslavia's Constitutional Court subsequently voted unanimously to suspend his extradition to the UN war crimes tribunal. Prior to his departure, Milosevic's defense lawyer characterized any attempt to extradite him as an "outright kidnaping, an act of legal terrorism."[42] Ultimately, an official other than the new Yugoslavian president authorized Milosevic's departure, allegedly because of the threatened withdrawal of a $1.3 billion US aid package related to the North Atlantic Treaty Organization (NATO) bombing campaign in Yugoslavia.

In cases like that of Adolf Eichmann (chief architect of the Holocaust's "Final Solution"), however, few nations are likely to protest an irregular extradition (abduction). In 1994, Carlos "The Jackal" was finally brought to justice in France. He is the world-famous terrorist who allegedly trained many European and Middle East terrorist organizations during the 1970s and 1980s. As he was undergoing a medical operation in the Sudan, he was drugged and smuggled from the Sudan to Paris. While the Sudanese themselves may have arranged this kidnaping, his technical complaint about the method of capture and informal extradition were rejected by the French court wherein he was prosecuted.

In one of the most internationally criticized cases ever decided by a national tribunal, the US Supreme Court reasoned that the *absence* of an express provision in a US-Mexico extradition treaty, which would have expressly barred international kidnaping, did not deprive the US courts of the jurisdiction to try a kidnaped defendant. In 1985, a US Drug Enforcement Administration (DEA) agent, Enrique Camerena, was brutally tortured for many hours in Mexico. A Mexican doctor reportedly kept him alive so that Mexican drug lords could torture him. This was one of the most sadistic murders in recorded history, and the first death of a US drug agent on Mexican soil.

Although there were earlier denials, the US president conceded that a "system of rewards," specifically, a $50,000 bounty, was established to ensure the capture of the doctor who allegedly kept Camerena alive. A Mexican policeman was supposed to deliver this doctor to US authorities, but this arrangement fell through. Doctor Alvarez-Machain was then released from a Mexican jail. A private team of current and former US police officers assisted some Mexican nationals with the kidnaping of this doctor from his office in Guadalajara, Mexico. He then "appeared" in a Los Angeles federal court to face criminal charges related to the Camerena murder. The Mexican government protested, demanding that Doctor Alvarez-Machain be released, because of what it characterized as a violation of the general principle of International Law prohibiting violations of territorial sovereignty.

◆

United States v. Humberto Alvarez-Machain

SUPREME COURT OF THE UNITED STATES
504 US 655, 112 S.Ct. 2188, 119 L. Ed. 2d 441 (1992)

AUTHOR'S NOTE: The defendant's lawyers defended him on several grounds, including the procedural argument that the way by which he appeared before the court was so outrageous that the US courts did not have jurisdiction to hold him for trial. Since the nineteenth century, the US courts had ruled that an individual criminal defendant may not obtain a dismissal, based on how he or she was brought before the court—with the modern exception of conduct "shocking the conscience" of the court. In this instance, it was argued that the case against the doctor should be dismissed, because the manner of obtaining his presence for trial in the United States violated the basic tenets of "due process of law."

The US government did not dispute the facts of this kidnaping. The trial judge in Los Angeles dismissed this case against the doctor, because of the "shocking" conduct of the US agents in violation of the laws of Mexico and the 1980 extradition treaty between the US and Mexico. In the words of the trial judge: "This court lacks jurisdiction to try this defendant." The intermediate Court of Appeals affirmed this dismissal—holding that the proper remedy was to release this Mexican national from US custody so that he could return to Mexico. The majority of the US Supreme Court judges reversed, as follows:

COURT'S OPINION: The Chief Justice delivered the opinion of the Court.

The issue in this case is whether a criminal defendant, abducted to the United States from a nation with which it has an extradition treaty, thereby acquires a defense to the jurisdiction of this country's courts. We hold that he does not, and that he may be tried in federal district court for violations of the criminal law of the United States. . . .

Respondent moved to dismiss the indictment, claiming that his abduction constituted outrageous governmental conduct, and that the District Court lacked jurisdiction to try him because he was abducted in violation of the extradition treaty between the United States and Mexico. . . .

In the instant case, the Court of Appeals affirmed the district [trial] court's finding that the United States had authorized the abduction of respondent, and that letters from the Mexican government to the United States government served as an official protest of the Treaty violation. Therefore, the Court of Appeals ordered that the indictment against respondent be dismissed and that respondent be repatriated to Mexico. We granted certiorari, and now reverse [for purposes of authorizing further proceedings in the US]. . . .

In *Ker v. Illinois*, . . . [this court held] in line with "the highest authorities" that "such forcible abduction is no sufficient reason why the party should not answer when brought within the jurisdiction of the court which has the right to try him for such an offence, and presents no valid objection to his trial in such court." . . .

The only differences between *Ker* and the present case are that *Ker* was decided on the premise that there was no governmental involvement in the abduction; and Peru, from which Ker was abducted, did not object to his prosecution. . . . Therefore, our first inquiry must be whether the abduction of respondent from Mexico violated the extradition treaty between the United States and Mexico. If we conclude that the Treaty does not prohibit respondent's abduction, the rule in *Ker* applies, and the court need not inquire as to how respondent came before it.

In construing a treaty, as in construing a statute, we first look to its terms to determine its meaning. The Treaty says nothing about the obligations of the United States and Mexico to refrain from forcible abductions of people from the territory of the other nation, or the consequences under the Treaty if such an abduction occurs.

More critical to respondent's argument is Article 9 of the Treaty which provides: "1. Neither Contracting Party shall be bound to deliver up its own nationals, but the executive authority of the requested Party shall, if not prevented by the laws of that Party, have the power to deliver them up if, in its discretion, it be deemed proper to do so." "2. If extradition is not granted pursuant to paragraph 1 of this Article, the requested Party shall submit the case to its competent authorities for the purpose of prosecution, provided that Party has jurisdiction over the offense." . . .

[But] Article 9 does not purport to specify the only way in which one country may gain custody of a national of the other country for the purposes of prosecution. . . .

The history of negotiation and practice under the Treaty also fails to show that abductions outside of the Treaty constitute a violation of the Treaty. As the [US] Solicitor General notes, the Mexican government was made aware, as early as 1906, of the *Ker* doctrine, and the United States' position that it applied to forcible abductions made outside of the terms of the United States-Mexico extradition treaty. Nonetheless, the current version of the Treaty, signed in 1978, does not attempt to establish a rule that would in any way curtail the effect of *Ker*. Moreover, although language which would grant individuals exactly the right sought by respondent [Doctor Alvarez] had been considered and drafted as early as 1935 by a prominent group of legal scholars sponsored by the faculty of Harvard Law School [*see* note 7 to this chapter], no such clause appears in the current Treaty.

The language of the Treaty, in the context of its history, does not support the proposition that the Treaty prohibits abductions outside of its terms. The remaining question, therefore, is whether the Treaty should be interpreted so as to include an implied term prohibiting prosecution where the defendant's presence is obtained by means other than those established by the Treaty.

Respondent contends that the Treaty must be interpreted against the backdrop of customary international law, and that international abductions are "so clearly prohibited in international law" that there was no reason to include such a clause in the Treaty itself. The international censure of international abductions is further evidenced, according to respondent [doctor], by the United Nations Charter and the Charter of the Organization of American States. Respondent does not argue that these sources of international law provide an independent basis for the right respondent asserts not to be tried in the United States, but rather that they should inform the interpretation of the Treaty terms. . . .

In sum, to infer from this Treaty and its terms that it prohibits all means of gaining the presence of an individual outside of its terms goes beyond established precedent and practice . . . [and] to imply from the terms of this Treaty that it prohibits obtaining the presence of an individual by means outside of the procedures the Treaty establishes requires a much larger inferential leap, with only the most general of international law principles to support it. The general principles cited by respondent simply fail to persuade us that we should imply in the United States-Mexico Extradition Treaty a term prohibiting international abductions.

Respondent [Alvarez] . . . may be correct that respondent's abduction was "shocking," and that it may be in violation of general international law principles.

Mexico has protested the abduction of respondent through diplomatic notes, and the decision of whether respondent should be returned to Mexico, as a matter outside of the Treaty, is a matter for the Executive Branch. We conclude, however, that respondent's abduction was not in violation of the Extradition Treaty between the United States and Mexico, and therefore the rule of *Ker v. Illinois* is fully applicable to this case. The fact of respondent's forcible abduction does not therefore prohibit his trial in a court in the United States for violations of the criminal laws of the United States.

The judgment of the Court of Appeals is therefore reversed, and the case is remanded for further proceedings consistent with this opinion.

◆ *Notes*

1. In the following year: (a) Costa Rica's Supreme Court discarded the US-Costa Rican extradition treaty on grounds that the *Alvarez-Machain* decision made a mockery of extradition treaties to which the United States is a party; (b) Mexico and the United States also began to renegotiate the 1978 extradition treaty interpreted in this case, a process that remains unresolved. *See* Mexico-US Protocol to the Extradition Treaty, done at Washington, DC, Nov. 13, 1997, reprinted in 37 INT'L LEGAL MAT'LS 154 (1998); and Doctor Alvarez-Machain, who was released for lack of evidence, filed a $20 million lawsuit against the United States. It included allegations of torture by US agents related to the abduction.

2. The doctor's civil case successfully asserted that State-sponsored abduction in another country violated the international laws regarding the preservation of sovereignty, as well as the international human rights norms protecting the plaintiff. His claim was permitted to proceed against the named individual Mexican defendant involved in the abduction, including five unnamed Mexican nationals currently in the US federal witness protection program. But the other co-defendant, the United States, was *initially* dismissed from this case (by the trial court) on the grounds that the Federal Torts Claims Act did not apply to the Drug Enforcement Administration's conduct in Mexico. The federal appellate court reversed, thus reinserting the United States back into this case. The DEA was thus required to defend its conduct, which allegedly infringed upon various fundamental rights.

The reviewing court, citing the United States' obligations under the 1988 United Nations Convention Against Illicit Traffic in Narcotic Drugs and Psychotropic Substances (analyzed in the §5.2 Judge Guillaume opinion in the *Belgian Warrant Case*) noted that "[a] Party shall not undertake in the territory of another Party the exercise of jurisdiction and performance of functions which are exclusively reserved for the authorities of that other Party by its domestic law." Alvarez-Machain v. U.S., 266 F.3rd 1045, (9th Cir. 2001).

In June 2004, the US Supreme Court—after the United States had been dismissed—determined the remaining portion of this case involving the Mexican policeman who allegedly arranged the Doctor's kidnaping. That case, Alvarez-Machain v. Sosa, held that the Mexican defendant's actions did not violate International. (It is the principal case in §11.5 of this book.)

3. In a major 1975 federal case from New York, the defendant—an Italian citizen living in Uruguay—moved to dismiss the indictment against him on facts similar to *Alvarez-Machain*. He was abducted from his home by Uruguay's police, turned over to Brazilian police, tortured, sedated, and flown to the US—where he was immediately placed in the custody of the US Drug Enforcement Administration. He claimed

that US officials participated in the abduction and torture. While the alleged conduct was not ultimately proven, the appellate court did rule on this potential defense as follows: "[W]e view due process as now requiring a court to divest itself of jurisdiction . . . where it has been acquired as the result of the government's *deliberate, unnecessary and unreasonable* invasion of the accused's constitutional rights. This conclusion represents but an extension of the well recognized power of federal courts in the civil [case] context . . . to decline to exercise jurisdiction over a defendant whose presence has been secured by force or fraud." US v. Toscanino, 500 F.2d 267, 275 (2d Cir. 1974) (italics added). This approach has not been adopted in other federal circuits. It has been raised by many defense attorneys, however, as a desirable exception to the general rule that defendants cannot rely on the circumstances of their arrest in another country, to avoid a US prosecution.

Toscanino is cited in the following case from South Africa, dealing with precisely the same issue. The South African court, unlike Alvarez-Machain where Mexico protested the kidnaping of a defendant, received no protest from Swaziland. Nevertheless, its reasoning and result are quite different from the foregoing US Supreme Court decision:

State v. Ebrahim

APPELLATE DIVISION FOR EAST/SOUTH-EAST CIRCUIT, 1991
31 INT'L LEGAL MAT'LS 888 (1992)

AUTHOR'S NOTE: Ebrahim, a citizen of South Africa, previously completed a fifteen-year jail term in South Africa. In 1980, he left South Africa for Swaziland, because he was a leading member of the African National Congress (Nelson Mandela's political party). He was forcibly abducted from Swaziland in 1986 by unidentified persons. He was taken to the Republic of South Africa where he was formally arrested, tried, convicted of treason, and sentenced to twenty more years of imprisonment. Unlike the situation in Alvarez-Machain, in which Mexico protested the US assertion of jurisdiction, Swaziland did not object to the kidnaping in this case. This appeal (decided fifteen months before Alvarez-Machain) raises the same question: Whether a person abducted by State agents is amenable to the criminal jurisdiction of the courts of the State to which he is abducted. Ebrahim lost his jurisdictional plea in the lower court.

This appellate court decision first examines the historical antecedents, including the Roman and Dutch laws that are still applied in South Africa. Previous judicial decisions, in which criminal jurisdiction had been "properly" exercised over abducted persons, were rejected as a result of this case.

COURT'S OPINION: Appellant argues that the abduction was a violation of the applicable rules of international law, that these rules are part of our law, and that the violation of these rules deprived the trial court of competence to hear the matter. . . .

In Nduli and Others v. Minister of Justice [1978] this court decided that where the accused were abducted from Swaziland by members of the South African Police in breach of orders from their commanding officer, the South African state was not responsible and accordingly there was no violation of international law. Consequently the trial court was not deprived of its competence to try the accused. In that case, as in the present case, the accused were formally arrested in South Africa. In the present case, . . . the appellant was abducted from Swaziland to South Africa by persons who were not police but who acted under the authority of some state agency. . . .

According to [Roman Law] Digest 2.1.20:

"Paul Edict book 1: One who administers justice beyond the limits of his territory may be disobeyed with impunity." . . .

This limitation on the legal powers of Roman provincial governors and lawgivers is understandable and was unavoidable in the light of the great number of provinces comprising the Roman Empire in classical times, with their ethnic and cultural diversity, and their different legal systems which the politically pragmatic Romans allowed to remain largely in force in their conquered territories. Until late in the history of the Roman Empire certain provinces were controlled by the Senate and others by the Emperor. Intervention by one province in the domestic affairs of another was a source of potential conflict. . . .

It is inconceivable that the Roman authorities would recognize a conviction and sentence, and allow them to stand, when they were the result of an abduction of a criminal from one province on the order or with the cooperation of the authority of another province. This would not only have been an approval of illegal conduct, and therefore a subversion of authority, but would also have threatened the internal interprovincial peace of the Empire. . . .

One of the foremost Roman-Dutch jurists was Johannes Voet (1647–1713), a Professor of Law in the University of Leiden. According to Voet in his Commentarius and Pandectas 48.3.2:

So far however must the limits of jurisdiction be observed in seizing a person accused of crime that, if the judge or his representative pursues him when he has been caught in the judge's own area and has taken flight, he nevertheless cannot seize or pursue further than the point at which the accused has first crossed the boundaries of the pursuer. A judge is regarded as a private person in the area of another, and thus he would in making an arrest in that area be exercising an act of jurisdiction on another's ground, a thing which the laws do not allow. . . .

From the repeated exposition and acceptance of the above rule in its different forms it is clear that the unlawful removal of a person from one jurisdiction to another was regarded as an abduction and as a serious breach of the law in Roman-Dutch law. . . .

It is therefore clear that in Roman-Dutch law a court of one state had no jurisdiction to try a person abducted from another state by agents of the former state. The question must now be considered whether this principle is also part of our present law.

Our [English-based] common law is still substantially Roman-Dutch law as adjusted to local circumstances [in South Africa]. No South African statute grants or denies jurisdiction to our courts to try a person abducted from another state and brought into the Republic of South Africa. . . .

Several fundamental legal principles are contained in these rules, namely the protection and promotion of human rights, good inter-state relations and a healthy administration of justice. The individual must be protected against illegal detention and abduction, the bounds of jurisdiction must not be exceeded, sovereignty must be respected, the legal process must be fair to those affected and abuse of law must be avoided in order to protect and promote the integrity of the administration of justice. This applies equally to the state. When the state is a party to a dispute, as for example in criminal cases, it must come to court with "clean hands." When the state itself is involved in an abduction across international borders, as in the present case, its hands are not clean.

Principles of this kind testify to a healthy legal system of high standard. Signs of this development appear increasingly in the municipal law of other countries. A telling example is that of United States v. Toscanino 500 F. 2d 267, to which [defendant's counsel] Mr. Mahomed referred us. The key question for decision in that [1974 US] case was formulated as follows:

In an era marked by a sharp increase in kidnaping activities, both here and abroad . . . we face the question as we must in the state of the pleadings, of whether a Federal Court must assume jurisdiction over the person of a defendant who is illegally apprehended abroad and forcibly abducted by Government agents to the United States for the purpose of facing criminal charges here.

The [South African] Court refused to follow the decisions of Ker v. Illinois, 119 US 342 (1886), and Frisbie v. Collins, 342 US 519 (1952), for the following reasons:

Faced with a conflict between the two concepts of due process, the one being the restricted version found in *Ker-Frisbie* and the other the expanded and enlightened interpretation expressed in more recent decisions of the Supreme Court, we are persuaded that to the extent that the two are in conflict, the *Ker-Frisbie* version [whereby the offended State but not the abducted individual] must yield. Accordingly we view due process as now requiring a court to divest itself of jurisdiction over the person of a defendant where it has been acquired as the result of the Government's deliberate, unnecessary and unreasonable invasion of the accused's constitutional rights. This conclusion represents but an extension of the well-recognized power of federal courts in the civil context to decline to exercise

jurisdiction over a defendant whose presence has been secured by force or fraud (at 275). . . .

It follows that, according to our common law, the trial court had no jurisdiction to hear the case against the appellant. Consequently his conviction and sentence cannot stand.

AVOIDING EXTRADITION

Extradition Limitations   States do not always honor valid extradition requests. The laws of the requesting State may be perceived as violating fundamental human rights. For example:

◆ Canada does not apply the death penalty in criminal cases. The United States does. Canada initially refused extradition of a US citizen accused of the sex-torture slaying of thirteen people in 1985 in California. In 1991, a Canadian jet flew this individual to the United States after the Canadian Supreme Court restricted Canada's death-penalty extradition exception by interpreting the Canadian rule as being inapplicable to non-Canadian citizens. In 1989, however, the European Court of Human Rights barred Great Britain from extraditing a West German citizen to the United States—where he would face the death penalty.

◆ In April 2005, the European Court of Human Rights similarly noted the violation of the European Convention on Human Rights for extraditing a prisoner under circumstances likely to result in persecution or death. Certain Georgians and Russians, who were ethnic Chechens, thus avoided extradition from Georgia to Russia. The Court noted the increasing volume of applications to the Court from other applicants—also concerned about the persecution and killings of persons of Chechen origin in Russia.[43]

◆ In March 2004, Norway did not extradite two airplane hijackers to Iran, who hijacked a Russian plane in 1993, served prison sentences in Russia, and then returned to Oslo. They risked torture if they were returned home. The Iranian government labeled this decision as a "reward for terrorist."

Extradition treaties typically require that extraditable offenses be those, which violate the laws of both parties

to the treaty. The conduct charged may violate the laws of one country but not the other. State practice varies on whether a treaty party can refuse extradition—opting, instead, to try the accused. Roorkee University (India) Professor Prakash Chandra comments on this contrast as follows: "Some jurists—Grotius, Vattel and Kent among them—hold that a state is bound to give up such fugitives but the majority . . . appear to deny such obligation. But mutual interests of states for the maintenance of law and order and the common desire to ensure that serious crimes do not go unpunished require that nations should cooperate with one another in surrendering fugitive criminals to the state in which the crime was committed."[44]

There is a tendency to strictly interpret extradition treaties and their implementing statutes. For example, extradition may be granted only when a crime has been committed within the territorial jurisdiction of the offended State seeking extradition from the State where the fugitive is located. In 1997, the Nova Scotia Supreme Court denied extradition in a case in which Taiwanese crewmembers threw several Romanian stowaways overboard to their deaths. This was done in circumstances in which the stowaways could not reasonably survive. While both Romania and Taiwan desired the crewmembers be extradited for murder, the Canadian court determined that extradition was not warranted because the crime was not committed within Romanian or Taiwanese territory.[45]

Political Offense Exception   Another reason for refusing extradition is the "political offense" exception. Treaties typically include some form of escape clause. The requested State thus has an opportunity to deny extradition on political grounds, although the extradition would otherwise be legally required. An all-too-familiar reason for such refusals is that the requested State clandestinely supports the acts of the individual charged with a crime in the requesting State. Extradition can be denied when the requested State characterizes the crime as a "*political offense*." In an amendment to the 1986 US-UK extradition treaty, for example, "extradition shall not occur if . . . the request for extradition has in fact been made with a view to try to punish him on account of . . . political opinions."

The application of the political defense exception to extradition produced a useful breakthrough in the stormy political relationship between Taiwan and China. In 1994, China conceded that Taiwan could exclude certain hijackers from repatriation to China if a Taiwanese court found that the hijackers acted out of political motives. Between April 1993 and August 1994, there had been twelve such aircraft hijackings from China by dissidents seeking asylum in Taiwan. China ultimately decided to recognize this defense, avoiding the closing of this avenue of escape. As a result, China now recognizes the right of Taiwanese vessels to patrol the waters of the Taiwan Straits as well as the jurisdiction of Taiwanese courts over such matters.

What *is* a political offense? This question is subject to much debate. The 1935 Draft Extradition Treaty produced by the Harvard Research in International Law project used this perennial definition: "[T]he term 'political offense' includes treason, sedition and espionage, whether committed by one or more persons; it includes any offense connected with the activities of an organized group directed against the security or governmental system of the requesting State; and it does not exclude other offenses having a political objective." The commentary to this proposed article adds that no "satisfactory and generally acceptable definition of a political offense has been found yet, and such as have been given are of little practical value."[46] Nearly seven decades later, there is still little consensus on what constitutes a political crime for the purpose of avoiding extradition.[47]

State practice thus vests the decision about the "political" nature of the defendant's crime with the requested State which has the offender in custody. Interpretations often depend on the circumstances of the particular case. Under Article IV of the above US-Japan extradition treaty, for example, extradition "shall not be granted . . . [w]hen the offense for which extradition is requested is a political offense or when it appears that the request for extradition is made with a view to prosecuting, trying or punishing the person sought for a political offense.

If any question arises as to the application of this provision, the decision of the requested Party shall prevail." The common "political offense" treaty exception is left purposefully vague. The requested party thus enjoys a wide latitude of discretion when handling future cases.

Article 1F of the 1951 Refugee Convention (textbook §4.2) bears upon this issue:

The provisions of this Convention shall not apply to any person with respect to whom there are serious reasons for considering that:

(a) he has committed a crime against peace, a war crime, or a crime against humanity, as defined in the international instruments drawn up to make provision in respect of such crimes;

(b) he has committed a serious non-political crime outside the country of refuge prior to his admission to that country as a refugee;

(c) he has been guilty of acts contrary to the purposes and principles of the United Nations.

This provision has been the subject of great debate for a half-century. Serious crimes such as murder have been treated differently, often because of overt or clandestine support for the motive of the offender who seeks asylum rather than extradition to the place where the crime was committed. A revealing analysis was provided in 2002, by the Refugee and Humanitarian Division of the Department of Immigration and Multicultural and Indigenous Affairs in Canberra, Australia:

[T]he UNHCR [UN Human Rights Committee] Handbook expressly suggests a need to strike a balance between the nature of the offence presumed to have been committed and the degree of persecution feared. . . .

The United States, United Kingdom, New Zealand, and Canada do not recognise any requirement under Article 1F to balance the nature of the crime with the degree of persecution feared. . . .

Similarly, in Australian case law, there is no such requirement to balance the degree of harm feared against the seriousness of the crime committed. The judgements in [cases omitted] . . . confirm that once the crime committed outside the country of refuge is properly characterised as an Article 1F crime, the provisions of the Convention do not apply and that there is no obligation to go further and weigh up the degree of seriousness of the crime against the possible harm to the applicant if returned to his or her state of origin.[48]

One who thus commits a crime, which falls within the earlier discussed Refugee Convention subsection (a) category, will not be eligible for asylum under the political offense exception. He or she is therefore someone who should be extradited under the applicable treaty, for lack of eligibility for such international protection.

Most problems arise under subsection (b) of the Convention. Is a murderer eligible for asylum, and thus able to avoid extradition by the arresting nation, because his conduct may be characterized as falling within the "political offense" exception to extradition? This question is of immense practical concern in the aftermath of "9-11." In the following 2002 case, the applicant for asylum in Australia murdered a policeman in India. The applicant was the chief communications officer for a leading antigovernmental organization. Judge Calligan of the High Court of Australia provides as precise a response that one might expect—given the characteristic penchant for flexibility:

> The underlying, inescapable, moral question which the Convention does not answer is, however, do the ends of a political cause justify any means, including murder and assassination?
>
> In a sense, violence, especially in its final and worst manifestation, killing, is the antithesis of political activity. Politics is the art or science of government. Murder can hardly be fairly characterisable as an activity in furtherance of, or part of the practice of, an art or science.
>
> . . .
>
> A crime, in my opinion, murder, especially premeditated murder, or its planning or furtherance, will practically never be a political crime. I say "practically never" because, as I have already intimated, it is impossible to predict precisely what circumstances and cases of desperation, and justification, may come before the courts.
>
> A crime, in my opinion, will be a political crime if, first, it is done genuinely and honestly for political purposes, that is in order to change or influence an oppressive government or its policies, and, secondly, the means employed, although of a criminal nature according to the law of the country in which they are employed, are reasonably, in all of the circumstances, adapted to that purpose.[49]

The 1977 European Convention on the Suppression of Terrorism contains a regional response. Its first article contains a list of offenses for which extradition may not be denied under the political offense doctrine. These include crimes under the multilateral treaties governing aircraft, crimes against diplomats, the taking of hostages, and bombing of civilians. In the aftermath of 9-11, a pending protocol has expanded this list of crimes, which may not be characterized as political offenses. The 1998 UN Convention for the Suppression of Terrorist Bombings was the first global treaty to specifically prohibit a party from allowing this defense to extradition.[50]

Rendition   A rendition is the act of surrendering an individual to a foreign government, in the absence of any treaty. The contrast between extradition and rendition is vivid. Extradition is an open procedure under which a fugitive is lawfully sent to a requesting State where he has committed a serious crime. Rendition is a covert operation under which even an innocent person may be forcibly transferred to a State where he has committed no crime. The rendered individual is deprived of the benefits of access to counsel and a hearing.

Since 9-11, US intelligence agencies have "rendered" terrorists to friendly governments, mostly in the Islamic world, for detention and interrogation. Rendered individuals cannot be lawfully extradited because they have committed no crime in the State to which they are rendered. Sometimes, the friendly government does not know the identity or activities of the person prior to rendition—especially when the individual is not a national of the receiving State.

Human rights groups claim that these renditions facilitate a US policy whereby ghost detainees can be dispatched from Afghanistan, Iraq, and Cuba to the third countries. This practice has created a remarkable rift between the United States and its allies. Dozens of suspected terrorists have thus been secretly sent for questioning to locations outside of the United States. Upon arrival, these individuals are subject to being tortured. In May 2005, for example, the Canadian Defense Minister testified in Ottowa that his office was upset because of the US transfer of a dual national Syrian-Canadian from New York to Syria (while en route to Canada, upon his return from Tunisia). Alex Neve, the head Amnesty International officer in Canada also commented that "[t]he concern is, do we have a Canadian version of the notorious American practice of extraordinary rendition?"

A 2005 US Department of State report noted that Egypt and Syria (countries to which some individuals have been rendered) practice torture in their prisons.[51]

◆ 5.4 INTERNATIONAL JUDICIAL ASSISTANCE

Service of a State X subpoena in State Y, requiring an individual to do something—such as returning to State X to testify in a criminal matter—is an act of executive/judicial administration which many countries consider a violation of their territorial sovereignty. State Y's consent should be obtained, either on an *ad hoc* basis (e.g., via a State X consular official in State Y), or on a treaty basis where State Y gives its advance consent to specified forms of process as set forth in the treaty. Service of process in a civil matter may likewise offend a foreign nation's sensibilities, especially if it requires a State Y citizen to take action—like hiring a defense lawyer in one or both countries—to respond to the State X civil proceedings.

In the *Blackmer* decision (§5.2 Nationality Principle), the US Supreme Court validated the US consular official's service of the subpoena in France, referring only to the US statute authorizing service abroad. There was no mention of *France's* position on a US subpoena being served within French territory. The court did say, merely in passing, that "The mere giving of such a notice to the citizen in the foreign country of the requirement of his government that he shall return is in no sence [*sic*] an invasion of any right of the foreign government and the citizen has no standing to invoke any such supposed right."[52] Thus, the court was not at all concerned about the related feature of this case which was not addressed: whether Nation X or its citizens can effect service of criminal subpoenas or civil summons in Nation Y without Y's consent.

Modern cases distinguish between the mere giving of notice of a proceeding, as opposed to service of a document requiring action, which avoids some sanction in the nation issuing such process. One of the classic articulations surfaced when the US Federal Trade Commission sought to enforce an investigatory subpoena, served upon a French corporation by registered mail:

> When the individual being served is not an American on U.S. soil but a foreign subject on foreign soil, the distinction between the service of *notice* and the service

of *compulsory* process takes on added significance. When process in the form of summons and complaint is served overseas, the informational nature of that process renders the act of service relatively benign. When compulsory process is served, however, the act of service itself constitutes an exercise of one nation's sovereignty within the territory of another sovereign. Such an exercise constitutes a violation of international law. [FN67] . . . Given the compulsory nature of a subpoena, . . . service by direct mail upon a foreign citizen on foreign soil, without warning to the officials of the local state and without initial request for or prior resort to established channels of international judicial assistance, is perhaps maximally intrusive.

> [FN67] "(T)he first and foremost restriction imposed by international law upon a State is that failing the existence of a permissive rule to the contrary it may not exercise its powers in any form in the territory of another State." Case of The S.S. "Lotus," (1927) [§5.2]. *See also* 1 L. Oppenheim, International Law §144b (8th ed. Lauterpacht 1955) ("States must not perform acts of sovereignty within the territory of other States").

The court added that "not only does it represent a deliberate bypassing of the official authorities of the local state, it allows the full range of judicial sanctions for noncompliance with an agency subpoena to be triggered merely by a foreign citizen's unwillingness to comply with directives contained in an ordinary registered letter."[53] There are now several *multilateral* treaties, whereby State parties agree to permit such acts of foreign administration within their territories under specified conditions. Examples include the Hague Service Convention (HSC) for serving civil process, the Hague Evidence Convention (HEC) for obtaining evidence in pending civil and criminal matters, and the Inter–American Convention on Letters Rogatory (IAC) governing most details in this class of litigation.[54]

The basic service provision requires an attorney in State X to forward process to a Central Authority in State Y, rather than directly to the target defendant. Then, the local Authority delivers the document to the witness or defendant—rather than a plaintiff or prosecutor in State X attempting to do so directly. This added layer of service delays litigation. However, it ameliorates concerns with abuses of process, which violate State Y's territorial sovereignty. The EU has a draft regional treaty, for example, which would designate transmitting agencies. Community Regulation 1348/2000, effective in May 2001, exempts all submitted documents from various formalities which accompany the discussed global treaties.[55]

These model treaties are often ratified by nations that tender reservations, which vary the terms of the general treaty provision as applied to that nation. (Chapter 8 deals with the treaty process, including the importance of reservations.) Thus, citizens in Nation X must be aware of an applicable treaty, whether it has been ratified, and whether the nation—wherein someone is targeted for service—has any local limitations expressed in a treaty reservation.[56]

Some nations, regardless of treaty commitments, issue guidelines for service of process abroad. Rule 4(f) of the US Federal Rules of Civil Procedure, for example, provides that "if there is no internationally agreed means of service or the applicable international agreement allows other means of service [which are not treaty-based]," then such other means are appropriate "provided that service is reasonably calculated to give notice . . . in the manner prescribed by the law of the foreign country . . . [or] as directed by the foreign authority in response to a letter rogatory" [request for the appropriate authority to effect service, or] . . . by other means not prohibited by international agreement as may be directed by the court.

A US federal statute classically illustrates the flexibility needed for good international relations, without regard to any specific treaty agreement. In 2004, the US Supreme Court demonstrated its commitment to the judiciary in different parts of the world, to work with them to accommodate the needs of private litigants in their respective proceedings:

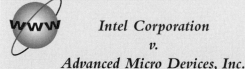

Intel Corporation
v.
Advanced Micro Devices, Inc.

UNITED STATES SUPREME COURT
542 U.S. 241, 124 S.Ct. 2466,
159 *L. Ed.* 2d 355 (2004)

Go to course Web page at
<http://home.att.net/~slomansonb/
txtcsesite.html>.
Under Chapter Five, click <u>Intel v. Micro Devices</u>.

◆ PROBLEMS

Problem 5.A (end of §5.1)   Review the definition of statehood in §2.1. The United States attacked Iraq on March 18, 2003. In June 2003, the United States announced that it wished to abandon its plan to have Iraqis from a provisional government because of internal rivalries. The United States instead appointed an interim government in July 2003. UN Security Council Resolution 1511 recognized the legitimacy of the appointed interim government, while calling for a timetable for Iraqi self-governance. The coalition announced that such governance would be achieved by June 2004, though the coalition forces would remain in Iraq.

The United States could not establish a stable government. It therefore asked for the help of the United Nations. On January 1, 2004, Lakhdar Brahimi was appointed as a special UN envoy. By March 2004, the various factions agreed on an interim constitution. During the spring of 2004, terrorist attacks escalated, as the date for handing over sovereignty—from the US-appointed governor to the interim government—approached. In June 2004, the Security Council unanimously passed resolution 1546. It legitimized the authority of the interim government about to assume power in Iraq—the Iraqi Governing Council (IGC). The resolution also authorized the multinational force to provide security in partnership with the new government; established a leading role for the United Nations in helping the political process over the next year; and called upon the international community to aid Iraq in its transition. The IGC chose Iyad Allawi as Iraqi Prime Minister. Allawi is a Shi'ite and was a member of Saddam Hussein's Ba'ath party. The terrorist attacks continued, with reports that the insurgents wanted the United States and United Kingdom out of Iraq. The illusive Iraqi Constitution was finally presented to the people in Fall 2005. During this period, between 150,000 and 180,000 coalition troops—mostly from the United States—remained in Iraq, and likely to remain for several more years, while an Iraqi police and military forces are being trained.

In September 2005, an eighteen-member National Sovereignty Committee of elected Iraqi legislators in the governing Iraqi National Assembly released a report. It claimed that the presence of the US military prevented Iraq from becoming a full sovereign nation. The Committee's report called for the multinational forces to leave. It said that to end the "occupation," the

United States would have to set a timetable for departure. As of that point, the United States steadfastly refused to do so. Iraq's government officials, who depend on the United States for security and financial backing, later opposed either withdrawal or a timetable. This Committee also asked the United Nations to pass a resolution ending the immunity of foreign nationals from prosecution in Iraqi courts.[57]

During this period, was Iraq: (1) a State, operating under the §2.1 classic definition of statehood in the Montevideo Convention? (2) a sovereign nation? (3) a territory in transition, working its way toward achieving its own sovereignty? (4) an occupied territory? (§6.2); (5) operating under the shadow of another more powerful government—like Afghanistan under Soviet occupation (1979–1989)?

Four students or groups will debate this matter. One will be Iraqi Prime Minister Iyad Allawi. The second will be the National Sovereignty Committee. The third will be the United States and/or the Coalition forces in Iraq. The fourth will be a representative of one of the §3.5 international organizations in which Iraq participated before the 2003 Iraq War.

Problem 5.B (end of §5.2) In 1988, two Libyan citizens planned and executed the bombing of Pan Am Flight 103 over Lockerbie, Scotland. All 259 passengers aboard the flight plunged to violent deaths. More people were killed on the ground, when the plane fell to earth. Pan Am was a US corporation. There were both UK and US citizens aboard this ill-fated flight.

The United Kingdom and the United States indicted these individuals, demanding that Libya surrender them for trial. This demand was backed by a UN Security Council resolution. Libya initially said that it would cooperate, but only if former US President Ronald Reagan and former UK Prime Minister Margaret Thatcher were to be tried simultaneously for bombing Tripoli in 1986. That bombing was a US reprisal for Libya's earlier bombing of a Berlin discotheque wherein a number of US soldiers died. The perpetrators were ultimately extradited to The Hague for trial before a special international tribunal agreed to by the United States, United Kingdom, and Libya.

Assume, *instead,* that Libya has not yet agreed to release its two intelligence officers accused of that crime. On what bases could the United Kingdom and the United States apply their criminal jurisdiction consistently

with the basic principles of "international criminal jurisdiction"?

Problem 5.C (end of §5.2) The context is the September 11, 2001, terrorist attack on the United States. (1) Which jurisdictional principles would apply, were the United States to capture Usama bin Laden and wish to prosecute him in the United States? (2) Which principles would apply to those individuals, previously residing in the United States, who hijacked the commercial aircraft on that day?

Problem 5.D (after §5.4 French Yahoo! Judgment) Four students (or groups) will participate in this exercise. The first two are French lawyers who previously represented the respective parties in the French court Yahoo! case. The other two are American lawyers who have represented the parties in this second round of the case in the US court. They will be prepared to analyze the following questions:

1. Paragraph [8] of the French case states that "looking at such objects [Nazi memorabilia on the web] obviously causes a wrong in France." Was the wrong caused "in" France?
2. Paragraph [10] resolves that "A tying link of the present case with France . . . gives this Court full jurisdiction to hear the claims. . . ." Does this so-called link really exist?
3. Paragraph [14] refers to the Court's previous May 22nd announcement which "Order[ed] Company Yahoo! France to give to any internaut, before he opens the link . . . a notice informing him that, if the result of his search . . . leads him to point to sites, pages or forums, the title and/or contents of which constitute a violation of the French law, . . . then he must stop the consultation of the site concerned . . . ." Would compliance with this order present Yahoo! with an insurmountable technical problem? Does paragraph [30] provide any insight?
4. Paragraph [53.6] states that "it would be appropriate to ask the internauts, when their IP address is ambiguous, that they subscribe a declaration of nationality. Would French subscribers—knowing that accessing the Nazi memorabilia web page is illegal in France— be likely to declare their French nationality? Is this a viable alternative?
5. Paragraph [71] concludes that "most certainly it would cost Yahoo! Inc. very little to extend the above

prohibitions to symbols of nazism. . . ." Yahoo! could have settled the French case, thus avoiding the costs including those of the expert consultants—not to mention the costs associated with the related US litigation. Was Yahoo! thus taking a principled approach to its dilemma, because it was an advocate of First Amendment freedom of speech? Was Yahoo! actually fighting for some other purpose? Was the French judge wrong in his assessment that developing more software programs to fix the nationality of the user would cost Yahoo! "very little?"

6. Paragraph [i] of the US federal court's subsequent opinion notes that while the procedural question regarding jurisdiction might present a "higher threshold" for foreign defendants, constitutional concerns sometimes trump such limitations. What was the gist of Yahoo's! constitutional argument?

7. If the Holocaust had occurred in the United States, would the US court be as likely to liberally interpret First Amendment freedom of expression?

Problem 5.E (after §5.4 French Yahoo! Judgment)
In January 1998, a German prosecutor charged the former German Chief of Staff for CompuServe, a US-based ISP, with transmitting child pornography over the Internet. In May 1998, a German trial court in Munich imposed a two-year term of probation and a DM 100,000 fine (US $57,000).

An expert for the defense testified that the defendant could not have known about the child pornography being transmitted over the Internet by some CompuServe customers. The prosecutor dropped the charge, although the judge still found Felix Somm guilty. He was thus legally accountable for pornographic content transferred from private individuals to German citizens over the Internet via CompuServe, even when the Internet traffic may be as high as 100 gigabytes per day. Further details are available at <www.freudenstadt.net/somm/english.html>.

Assume that "Joe," one of those child pornography providers, posted offensive materials on the Internet. Joe is a private CompuServe customer, living in New Jersey. He uses CompuServe as his ISP to send such information to other interested individuals. His materials are viewed in Germany. The German prosecutor issues an arrest warrant and thereafter seeks Joe's extradition to Germany for prosecution. This will be an important test case for the German government in its efforts to keep Internet pornography from coming into Germany. Joe is about to be extradited to Germany for sending an e-mail attachment to German citizens (and the rest of the cyberworld). It contained samples of the pornographic materials that are on his personal Web site. This site is provided by CompuServe, a US corporation. Joe's personal Web site (and its e-mail capacity) is one of the thousands of "pages" that CompuServe customers have established, thereafter inserting their desired content.

Extradition in this case could spawn future foreign prosecutions, and like extradition requests, by other countries of the world. These governments would be interested in controlling the information made available to their citizens—because of e-mails sent by, and personal Web sites maintained by, millions of US citizens. The German government's interests include blocking the transmission of illegal materials via the Internet. The US interests include not wanting other governments to impose their views of what is illegal on US citizens.

Two students will represent the respective German and US Departments of State. They will debate whether extradition is a good idea in this case.

Problem 5.F (after §5.3 State v. Ebrahim case) The US Supreme Court and the South African Supreme Court arrived at very different conclusions about whether a court had jurisdiction to proceed with the prosecution, when the custodial State's agents arranged the abduction of the defendant from foreign soil.

Assume that a South African citizen is abducted through arrangements made by US agents to secure his presence for trial in the United States. South Africa protests, based on an extradition treaty between the two countries. That treaty does not prohibit such abductions, nor does it condone them. South Africa and the United States decide to resolve this matter in the International Court of Justice (ICJ). The issue for the ICJ is whether the United States has the jurisdiction, under International Law, to proceed with the criminal case against the South African defendant.

Two students (or groups) will argue this matter before three class members, who will serve as the ICJ judges. They will announce their decision in this case, based upon the presentations and the relevant legal principles. The resulting decision will not necessarily be unanimous. But it should be quite useful for generating the ensuing class discussion.

◆ BIBLIOGRAPHY

§5.1 Definitional Setting

A. Chayes & A. Chayes, The New Sovereignty: Compliance with International Regulatory Agreements (Cambridge, MA: Harvard University Press, 1995)

L. Henkin, The Mythology of Sovereignty, ch. 24, in R. MacDonald (ed.), Essays in Honour of Wang Tieya 351 (Dordrecht, Neth.: Martinus Nijhoff, 1994)

H. Hensel (ed.), Sovereignty and the Global Community: The Quest for Order in the International System (Dobbs Ferry, NY: Oceana, 2004)

The Jurisdiction of States, ch. XII, in O. Schachter, International Law in Theory and Practice 250 (Dordrecht, Neth.: Martinus Nijhoff, 1991)

R. Lapidoth, Sovereignty in Transition, 45 J. Int'l Affairs 2 (1992)

W. Reisman, The Library of Essays in International Law: Jurisdiction in International Law (Aldershot, Eng.: Ashgate, 2000)

§5.2 Jurisdictional Principles

P. Berman, The Globalization of Jurisdiction, 151 Univ. Penn. L. Rev. 311 (2002)

M. Franda, Launching into Cyberspace: Internet Development and Politics in Five World Regions (Boulder, CO: Rienner, 2002)

International Conflict of Laws, ch. 10, in M. Janis, An Introduction to International Law 317 (4th ed. Boston: Aspen Law & Business, 2003)

Jurisdiction over Persons, ch. 9, in G. von Glahn, Law Among Nations: An Introduction to Public International Law 146 (7th ed. Boston: Allyn and Bacon, 1996)

J. Rogers, Treaties and Statutes Against the Background of Customary International Law, ch. 9, in International Law and United States Law 170 (Aldershot, Eng.: Ashgate, 1999)

UNESCO, The International Dimensions of Cyberspace Law (Aldershot, Eng.: Ashgate, 2000)

UN, World Public Sector Report 2003: E-Government at the Crossroads (New York: UN, 2003)

§5.3 Extradition

M. Bassiouni, International Extradition: United States Law and Practice (3d ed. Dobbs Ferry, NY: Oceana, 1996)

J. Gurule, Terrorism, Territorial Sovereignty, and the Forcible Apprehension of International Criminals Abroad, 17 Hastings Int'l & Comp. L. Rev. 457 (1994)

E. Nadelmann, Cops Across Borders: The Internationalization of US Criminal Law Enforcement (University Park, PA: Penn. State Univ. Press, 1993)

A. Sambei, Extradition Law Handbook (Oxford, Eng.: Oxford Univ. Press, 2004)

§5.4 International Judicial Assistance

B. Ristau, International Judicial Assistance (Wash., DC: Int'l Law Inst., 1984–) (six volume looseleaf treatise with frequent updates)

US Department of State treaties, reservations, and explanatory reports Web page: <http://www.travel.state.gov/judicial_assistance. html#evidence>

Additional Internet Resources

Chicago-Kent College of Law, Internet Jurisdiction (research resources): <http://www.kentlaw.edu/cyberlaw>

Internet Archive (digital library of Internet sites): <http://www.archive.org>

Ogilvy Renault, Jurisdiction and the Internet: Are Traditional Rules Enough? Uniform Law Conference of Canada (1998): <http://www.law.ualberta.ca/alri/ulc/current/ejurisd.htm>

UN Model Agreement on the Transfer of Foreign Prisoners and Recommendations on the Treatment of Foreign Prisoners: <http://www.icpa.ca/un/docs/un_5.html>

◆ ENDNOTES

1. B. Jankovic, Public International Law 115-117 (Dobbs Ferry, NY: Transnational, 1983) (Pravo translation).

2. The individual states within the United States must yield to the federal powers created by the US Constitution. This is the exception, not the rule in state-federal relations. The constitutional delegates established a federated system consisting of thirteen States and a federal district. But they also feared the reestablishment of *another* excessively powerful central federal government. Under the Tenth Amendment: "The powers not delegated to the United States by the Constitution, nor prohibited by it to the States, are reserved to the States respectively, or to the people."

3. Pennoyer v. Neff, 95 U.S. (5 Otto) 714, 722, 24 L. Ed. 565 (1877) (partially overruled on other grounds).

4. J. Jackson, Sovereignty-Modern: A New Approach to an Outdated Concept, 97 Amer. J. Int'l L. 782 (2003).

5. U.S. v. Palmer, 16 U.S. (3 Wheat.) 610, 630, 4 L.Ed. 471 (1818) (involving US jurisdiction over foreign pirates on a Spanish vessel on the high seas).

6. The piracy connection with 9–11 may be discerned from the piracy-terrorism discussion in the leading treatise on piracy: A. Rubin, "Piracy Today," ch. 6, in The Law of Piracy 373, at 378 (2d ed. Irvington-on-Hudson, NY: 1998) [hereinafter *Law of Piracy*].

7. Murray v. The Charming Betsy, 6 U.S. (2 Cranch) 64, 118, 2 L.Ed. 208 (1804).

8. *See generally Spying:* Territory and Espionage, ch. 3, in J. Kish, International Law and Espionage (The Hague. Neth.: Martinus Nijhoff, 1995). *Counter-terrorism:* G. Rivers, The Specialist: Revelations of a Counterterrorist (New York: Stein & Day, 1985).

9. The United States has received the most attention on this point. See, e.g., *Hostage law:* 18 United States Code §1203. *Drug law:* 46 USC §1901 et. seq. *Environmental case:* Environmental Defense Fund, Inc. v. Massey, 986 Fed.2d 528 (D.C. Cir. 1993). *Abduction case: see* text of US v. Alvarez-Machain case in §5.3. *Antitrust case:* Hartford Fire Insur. Co. v. Merrett Underwriting Agency Management. Ltd., 509 US 764 (1993).

Refugee case: see text of Sale v. Haitian Council case in §4.2. *Milan kidnaping:* news story at E. Povoledo, Italy Demands 'Full Respect' From U.S. Over Terror Suspect's Seizure, International Herald Tribune (NYT on the Web) (July 1 & 2, 2005) & legal analysis at F. Kirgis, ASIL Insight: Alleged CIA Kidnapping of Muslim Cleric in Italy (July 2005), available at: <http://www.asil.org/insights/2005/07/insights050707.html>.

10. Further readings are available in J. Paust et al., INTERNATIONAL CRIMINAL LAW: CASES AND MATERIALS (2d ed. Durham, NC: Carolina Academic Press, 2000); and L. Sunga, THE EMERGING SYSTEM OF INTERNATIONAL CRIMINAL LAW (The Hague, Neth.: Kluwer, 1997).

11. I. Cameron, THE PROTECTIVE PRINCIPLE OF INTERNATIONAL CRIMINAL JURISDICTION 11-12 (Aldershot, Eng.: Dartmouth, 1994) [hereinafter *Protective Principle*].

12. The Research in International Law of the Harvard Law School, Jurisdiction with Respect to Crime, 29 AMER. J. INT'L L. SUPP. 443 (1935) [hereinafter *Harvard Research*].

13. H. Maier, Jurisdictional Rules in Customary International Law, ch. IV, in K. Meessen (ed.), EXTRATERRITORIAL JURISDICTION IN THEORY AND PRACTICE 64, at 65 (London: Kluwer, 1996).

14. Regarding Penati, Case No. 30, reported in 46 ANNUAL DIGEST AND REPORTS OF PUBLIC INT'L L. CASES 74.

15. Human rights violations concern all States. Chapter 11 will explore the contemporary applicability of International Law to a State's treatment of its own citizens within its own borders.

16. The S.S. Lotus (France v. Turkey), PCIJ, SER. A, NO. 10 (1927) (Judge Moore, dissenting).

17. U.S. v. Neil, 312 F.3d 419, 422-423 (9th Cir. 2002).

18. U.S. v. Cardales, 168 F.3d 548, 553 (1st Cir. Puerto Rico, 1999).

19. US v. Pizzarusso, 388 Fed.2d 8 (2d Cir. 1968), cert. den'd, 392 US 936 (1968) (italics added).

20. For a historical overview of the protective principle jurisdiction in the Swedish Criminal Code. See *Protective Principle* 97, at 101 (cited in note 11 above).

21. Laurent Cohen-Tanugi, La Chronique de Gouvernement d'entreprise Sous Pavillon Americain, Les Echos (Aug. 20, 2002), at 35. The translation was provided by D. Vagts, Extraterritoriality and the Corporate Governance Law, 97 AMER. J. INT'L L. 289n.2 (2003).

22. Sarbanes-Oxley Act, Pub. L. No. 107-204, 116 Stat. 745 (2002) (principally codified in titles 15 and 18 of the United States Code) §106.

23. H. Kindred et al., INTERNATIONAL LAW: CHIEFLY AS INTERPRETED AND APPLIED IN CANADA 518 (6th ed. Toronto: Edmond Montgomery, 2000).

24. Principle 2.1—Serious Crimes Under International Law, in The Princeton Principles of Universal Jurisdiction 28 (Princeton, NJ: Princeton Univ., 2001).

25. *Id.,* at 29. Further detail on this project is available in S. Macedo, UNIVERSAL JURISDICTION: NATIONAL COURTS AND THE PROSECUTION OF SERIOUS CRIMES UNDER INTERNATIONAL LAW (Philadelphia: Univ. Penn. Press, 2003).

26. Attorney-General of Israel v. Adolf Eichmann, Dist. Ct. of Jerusalem; reported in 36 INT'L LAW REP. 5, 15 (1968) (decided in 1961).

27. See *Law of Piracy* (cited in note 6 above), Aircraft Hijacking, in Piracy in the Twentieth Century, ch. 5, at 321.

28. *Al-Qaida: See* A. Higgins, K. Leggett, and A. Cullison, How al Qaeda Put Internet to Use: From Britain, Webmaster Kept 'The Brothers' Abreast on Terror, Wall Street J. (Nov. 12, 2002). US reaction: See Eric Lightblau, Judges and Justice Dept. Meet Over Eavesdropping Program, New York Times on the Web, Jan. 10, 2006.

29. A host of policy implications are assessed in K. Boele & C. Kessedjian (ed.), INTERNET: WHICH COURT DECIDES? WHICH LAW APPLIES? (The Hague: Kluwer, 1998) & its Selected Bibliography at 177. Additional commercial applications are analyzed in Symposium on Borderless Electronic Commerce, 35 INT'L LAWYER 1–106 (2001).

30. China Shuts Down 8,600 Internet Cafes, People's Daily Online (May 6, 2004), available at: <http://english1.people.com.cn/200405/06/eng20040506_142470.html>.

31. Reprinted in 41 INT'L LEGAL MAT'LS 282 (March 2002).

32. *Montreux Declaration*: <http://www.privacyconference2005.org/index.php?id=6>. *UN World Summit*: at <http://www.un.org>, click—Main Bodies, General Assembly, Search, UN Search. See J. Gurwitz, U.N. Oversight of Internet Threatens Freedom of Information, Los Angles Daily Journal, Nov. 23, 2005).

33. B. Yarnold, INTERNATIONAL FUGITIVES: A NEW ROLE FOR THE INTERNATIONAL COURT OF JUSTICE 11 (New York: Praeger, 1991).

34. Valentine v. United States ex rel. Neidecker, 299 US Rep. 5, 9 (1936).

35. Re Arton, 1 Queen's Bench 108, 111 (1896).

36. 31 US Treaties 892 (1979); US TREATIES AND OTHER INTERNATIONAL AGREEMENTS SERIES, No. 9625 (1980).

37. *See generally* R. Wallis, LOCKERBIE: THE STORY AND THE LESSONS (Westport, CT: Preager, 2001).

38. *See* Questions of Interpretation and Application of the 1971 Montreal Convention Arising from the Aerial Incident at Lockerbie (Libyan Arab Jamahiriya v. United Kingdom), on the ICJ's Web site at <www.icj-cij.org/idocket/iluk/iluk2frame.htm>.

39. Ntakirutimana v. Reno, 184 F.3d 419 (5th Cir. 1999). *Majority quote:* at 426. *Concurring quote:* at 430-431. *Dissenting quote:* at 431.

40. *Exclusion and deportation:* Evans, Acquisition of Custody over the International Fugitive Offender-Alternatives to Extradition: A Survey of United States Practice, 40 BRIT. YEARBOOK. INT'L L. 77 (1964). *Force:* M. Glennon, State-Sponsored Abduction: A Comment on United States v. Alvarez-Machain, 86 AMER. J. INT'L L. 746 (1992).

41. Quote from State run Tanjug News Agency, as reported by Associated Press on January 15, 2001.

42. Associated Press, Milosevic Extradition Decree Suspended, June 28, 2001, at <http://www.globalpolicy.org/intljustice/tribunals/2001/0628milo.htm>.

43. *Candadian case:* In February, 2001, the Canadian Supreme Court unanimously ruled that *no one* facing the death penalty

would be extradited, unless there were an assurance that there would be no execution. This decision thus barred the extradition to the United States of two men charged with murder in the State of Washington. *European Court case:* Shamayev and 12 Others v. Georgia and Russia (April 12, 2005), available on the Court's Web site (in French). *See* <http://www.echr.coe.int>.

44. P. Chandra, International Law 80 (New Delhi: Vikas Pub.). *See also* The Eisler Extradition Case, 43 Amer. J. Int'l L. 487 (1949), a British case in which the relevant substantive law of Great Britain differed from that of the United States.

45. Romania v. Cheng, 114 C.C.C.3rd 289 (Nova Scotia S.Ct, 1997).

46. Draft Convention on Extradition, Harvard Research, at 112–113 (cited in note 12 above).

47. G. Gilbert, The Political Offence Exemption, ch. 6, in Transnational Fugitive Offenders in International Law: Extradition and Other Mechanisms 203 (The Hague, Neth.: Martinus Nijhoff, 1998).

48. DIMIA, A Paper Prepared as a Contribution to the UNHCR's Expert Roundtable Series 25-26 (2002), available at: <www.immi.gov.au/refugee/publications/convention2002/05_exclusion.pdf>.

49. Minister for Immigration and Multicultural Affairs v. Singh [2002] Hca 7 (7 March 2002), para. 160-168, available at: <http://www.austlii.edu.au/au/cases/cth/high_ct/2002/7.html>.

50. Art. 5, reprinted in 37 Int'l Legal Mat'ls 249 (1998).

51. *See* C. Krauss, Canada May Have Reaped Information via Torture, New York Times News Service, reprinted in San Diego Union-Tribune, p. A3 (Sept. 17, 2005).

52. Blackmer v. US, 284 U.S. 421, 439 (1932).

53. F.T. C.v. Compagnie De Saint-Gobain-Pont-a-Mousson, 636 F.2d 1300, 1313 n.67, 1314 (D.C. Cir., 1980) (italics added and footnotes omitted).

54. *HSC:* 4 Int'l Legal Mat'ls 341 (1965). *HEC:* 8 Int'l Legal Mat'ls 37 (1969). *IAC:* Inter-American Convention on Letters Rogatory, 14 Int'l Legal Mat'ls 339 (1975) & Protocol: 18 Int'l Legal Mat'ls 1238 (1979).

55. Official Journal of the European Communities (L 160) 37, June 30, 2000.

56. *See, e.g.* Dr. Ing. H.C.F. Porsche A.G. v. Superior Ct., 123 Cal.App.3d 755, 762, 177 Cal.Rptr. 155, 159 (3d Dist.1981) (HSC preempts state mail service alternative) & Securities and Exchange Comm'n v. International Swiss Investments Corp., 895 F.2d 1272 (9th Cir.1990) (IAC inapplicable at time of service because treaty signed but not yet ratified).

57. See N. Youssef, U.S. Presence Blocking Sovereignty, Iraqi Panel Says, Knight Ridder News Service (Sept. 14, 2005).

CHAPTER SIX

Range of Sovereignty

INTRODUCTION

Chapter 2 introduced the fundamentals of statehood. Chapter 5 added the related limitation that one State cannot unilaterally act within the territorial boundaries of another State. This chapter augments these themes by illustrating the scope of sovereign power exercisable in, over, and outside of a State. The essential question is this: To what extent may a State exercise its sovereign powers abroad, without violating the sovereign rights of another State?

States routinely exercise their sovereign powers in zones that are the common heritage of all nations. These areas include the sea, airspace, and outerspace—which many States and their citizens simultaneously occupy. Furthermore, commercial interests dictate that Nation X's ships and aircraft be able to enter and traverse State Y's land, water, and airspace for the mutual benefit of all. This chapter deals with the twilight zone between

DISCUSSION AMONG THE OFFICERS OF THE USS Enterprise, upon learning that persistent travel at certain warp speeds (faster than light) is damaging the fabric of outer space:

Captain Picard: Ah, we've received new directives from the Federation Council on this matter. Until we can find a way to counteract the warp field effect, the Council feels the best course is . . . [that travel in] areas of space found susceptible to warp fields will be restricted to essential travel only and effective immediately, all Federation vehicles will be restricted to a speed of warp 5, except in cases of extreme emergency.

Worf: The Klingons will observe these restrictions, but the Romulans will not.

Troi: And what about the Ferrengi, and the Cardassians for that matter?

Picard: The Federation is sharing all our data with warp capable species. We can only hope that they realize it's in their best interest to take similar action.

— *Star Trek: The Next Generation,* Force of Nature, Episode No. 158 (1994), reprinted in M. Sharf & L. Roberts, The Interstellar Relations of the Federation: International Law and "Star Trek: The Next Generation," 25 UNIV. TOLEDO LAW REV. 577, 594 (1994).

absolute sovereign power to exclude another nation's entry, and the practical need to encourage commercial and other forms of international interaction.

◆ 6.1 CATEGORIES OF TERRITORY

Four species of territory emerged with the modern system of States:

◆ Territory owned by a sovereign State (sovereign territory)
◆ Territory not owned by any State due to its special status (trust territory)
◆ Territory capable of ownership, although not yet under sovereign control (*terra nullius*)
◆ Territory that cannot be owned by any nation (*res communis*)

SOVEREIGN TERRITORY

States possess the right to control the land located within their territorial boundaries. The extent of that sovereignty is ordinarily defined by oceans, mountains, and other natural frontiers. One attribute of the State-centric system inherited from the seventeenth century is that all land is subject to sovereign control. As recounted by the London research consultant Peter Hocknell: "Some 127 new states have emerged since 1945, and the number of recognised international land boundaries has increased from approximately 280 in the late 1980s to about 315 today. New land is not being created; instead, states have fragmented into smaller states and other political structures. Ever since 1648, international law, the basis of the Westphalian state system, has abhorred undefined territory and portrayed international boundaries as inviolable."[1]

TRUST TERRITORY

A second land category is that land which is not subject to the sovereignty of *any* State because of some special status. Certain territories were League of Nations "mandates" or post-World War II UN "Trust Territories" (§3.3). The League and the United Nations placed such areas under the protection of established States to promote the self-determination of the inhabitants. No State, including the protecting State in whose care such a territory had been placed by the organization, could claim title to that land. This category of territory was under a temporary disability to engage in self-governance, usually because it lacked political infrastructure.

At present, there are no such trust territories. Kosovo, while under UN administration after the 1999 North Atlantic Treaty Organization (NATO) bombing campaign (§3.5), would be a contemporary equivalent—although administered by the international organization, rather than a State member.

TERRA NULLIUS

Certain territories were once capable of being legally acquired. At one time, no State controlled them. These locations were referred to, in earlier colonial eras, as territories that were thus *terra nullius*. They were conveniently characterized as belonging to no nation, but capable of being legally acquired by the colonial European powers. International Law, after all, was shaped by the more powerful European States who determined that an existing State was competent to designate certain territories as *terra nullius*. In 1885, for example, the States attending the Conference of Berlin declared that most of the African continent was *terra nullius,* on the basis that the inhabitants of the continent were supposedly incapable of governing themselves.

In a 1971 International Court of Justice (ICJ) case, South Africa argued that it continued to be seized with the sovereign right to control South West Africa (now Namibia). The people of that protectorate were supposedly incapable of governing themselves. The Court seized this opportunity to unreservedly declare a "blunder" by those States that had characterized African territory as *terra nullius*. As stated by the Court:

African law illustrated . . . the monstrous blunder committed by the authors of the Act of Berlin, the results of which have not yet disappeared from the African political scene. It was a monstrous blunder and a flagrant injustice to consider Africa south of the Sahara as *terrae nullius,* to be shared out among the Powers for occupation and colonization, even when in the sixteenth century Victoria had written that Europeans could not obtain sovereignty over the Indies by occupation, for they were not *terrae nullius*.

By one of fate's ironies, the declaration of the 1885 Berlin Congress which held the dark continent to be *terrae nullius* related to regions which had seen the rise and development of flourishing States and empires. One should be mindful of what Africa was before there fell upon it the two greatest plagues in the recorded history of mankind: the slave-trade, which ravaged Africa for centuries on an unprecedented scale, and colonialism, which exploited humanity and natural wealth to a relentless extreme. Before these terrible plagues overran their continent, the African peoples had founded states and even empires of a high level of civilization. . . .[2]

More than one State may attempt to control the activities of the people who inhabit areas that are *terra nullius.* This conflict has generated the occasional question regarding which State may legitimately claim territorial sovereignty—when the area is not controlled exclusively by either? In the famous 1928 Island of Palmas arbitration, the United States and the Netherlands both claimed the exclusive right to an island located in the Philippine archipelago. The resulting arbitral opinion could be characterized as a restatement of the imperialistic nature of the regime of *terra nullius,* carried forward into twentieth-century legal thought:

Territorial sovereignty belongs always to one [State] . . . to the exclusion of all others. The fact [is] that the functions of a State can be performed by any State within a given zone . . . in those parts of the globe which, like the high seas or lands without a master, cannot or do not yet form the territory of a State. . . .

In the exercise of territorial sovereignty there are necessarily gaps, intermittence in time and discontinuity in space. This phenomenon will be particularly noticeable in the case of colonial territories, partly uninhabited or as yet partly unsubdued.[3]

As a condition for establishing its right to claim sovereignty, a State must normally establish that the particular zone was, in fact, *terra nullius* and thereby available for occupation and the ensuing claim to title. The ICJ's 1974 Western Sahara case analyzed this prerequisite in a dispute between Spain and Morocco over control of a portion of the Western Sahara desert. The Court confirmed the international expectation that mere occupation is not enough to justify a claim of sovereignty over an occupied area. It also must have been a *terra nullius* if the claimant State seeks exclusive

sovereign control. The Court therein traced the history of the term:

[The] expression "terra nullius" was a legal term of art employed in connection with "occupation" as one of the accepted legal methods of acquiring sovereignty over a territory . . . [and it] was a cardinal contention of a valid "occupation" that the territory should be *terra nullius* "a territory belonging to no-one" at the time of the act alleged to constitute the "occupation.". . . A determination that the Western Sahara was a *terra nullius* at the time of colonization by Spain would be possible only if it were established that at that time the territory belonged to no-one in the sense that it was then open to acquisition through the legal process of "occupation."[4]

RES COMMUNIS

A fourth category of territory is incapable of ever being legally owned or controlled; it is typically referred to as *res communis.* It belongs to no one and must remain available for all to use. Under International Law, the entire community of nations must have unfettered access to such areas. These territories cannot be lawfully controlled by any State or group of States without the approval of the community of nations. The clearest examples of *res communis* are the high seas and outer space, which are discussed later in this chapter.

It has been argued that Antarctica is a "land" area that is res communis. Article 4 of the 1959 Antarctic Treaty provides that States shall not recognize, dispute, or establish territorial claims there, and no new claims may be asserted by parties to this treaty. Some commentators have characterized Antarctica as res communis because of the harsh weather conditions making it difficult to occupy. Some scholars analogize Antarctica to the high seas, the deep seabed, outer space, and the Arctic (which has no land mass).[5] Chilean Professor Emilio Sahurie disputes the "occupation" analog, however. He notes that even the high seas have been appropriated (illustrated by §6.3 sea zones). "Occupation" is becoming obsolete with advances in modern technology. Traditionalist scholars should acknowledge that only the moon and other celestial bodies are actually *res communis.* There is no territory on earth that is totally incapable of exploitation, "which would be a more accurate measure of sovereignty than "occupation." [6]

◆ 6.2 DOMINION OVER LAND

A State ordinarily possesses the exclusive right to the use of its territory and to exclude other nations from being present without its consent. However, disputes over ownership and control have existed for centuries—and directly responsible for untold loss of life, countless human rights violations, devastation of economic resources, diplomatic conundrums, and numerous broken commitments.[7] Israel's occupation of the Palestinian territory stems from land taken by conquest during the 1967 Middle East War. Argentina's 1982 invasion of the Falkland Islands was the contemporary phase of a dispute with England, dating from 1833. England's possession of Ireland's northern six counties, and continuing territorial conflict in the Balkans, are just a few examples.

The peaceful resolution of such disputes is often complicated because judges, arbitrators, or diplomats have to rely on documents, which are centuries old. In a 1953 ICJ case, England and France both claimed the exclusive right to two islets within the English Channel. The ICJ analyzed a number of medieval treaties in its effort to establish which State was entitled to this territory: the Treaty of Lambeth of 1217, the Treaty of Paris of 1259, the Treaty of Calais of 1360, and the Treaty of Troy of 1420. The ICJ even considered a papal declaration in 1500, which transferred the Channel Islands from the French Diocese of Coutances to the English Diocese of Winchester. None of these documents specifically mentioned the disputed islets. The Court ultimately granted title to Great Britain based on its acts of possession.

Uti possidetis juris is a more blunt instrument that originated in Roman law. It later facilitated border resolutions in Latin America, Africa, Asia, the former Soviet Union, and Yugoslavia. It conveniently defined the borders of newly sovereign States, on the basis of prior externally imposed administrative frontiers. Europe, for example, divided Africa according to "spheres of influence." The collapse of colonial rule resulted in the drawing of abstract lines, based on latitudes and longitudes. These were roughly equivalent to the previous administrative zones. The resulting cross-border ethnic division effectively encouraged groups to attempt secession from their parent States. Such reunification efforts met with severe resistance from the international community, which was intent on establishing concrete borders.[8]

The materials in this section analyze the general modes for establishing sovereign title. The historical approach is presented first, followed by contemporary criticisms of these modes.

HISTORICAL APPROACH

The traditional methods for acquiring sovereignty over territory are as follows: occupation, conquest, cession, prescription, and accretion.

Occupation

Historical Perspective Exclusive occupation for an extended period of time is the most common basis for claiming sovereignty over a particular geographical area. This mode of acquisition is referred to as an "original" claim to territory, as opposed to a "derived" basis for claiming sovereign title. In the latter instance, title may be expressly derived from a document, such as a treaty in which two or more States formally agree on exclusive or shared sovereignty over a particular territory.

During the previous colonization era, effective occupation required that the State occupy an area that was originally *terra nullius*—owned by no other country, but capable of ownership. The World Court has repeatedly stated that occupation is "legally an original means of peaceably acquiring sovereignty over territory . . . [however] it was a cardinal condition of a valid 'occupation' that the territory should be terra nullius—territory belonging to no-one—the time of the act alleged to constitute the 'occupation.'"[9]

This method for authenticating sovereign title was typically proven by "discovery." The medieval perspective was that mere discovery, without actual possession, was sufficient to establish valid title. State practice in the later centuries of Europe's colonial expansion retreated from that view. After territory was discovered, there had to be at least some symbolic act signifying possession. State representatives planted flags or created more substantial ties, such as establishing a settlement within the discovered territory. Discovery, coupled with such acts, established a colorable title, which was thus initiated but not necessarily perfected.

The nineteenth-century European powers relied on discovery as a basis for initiating claims of exclusive land title. They carefully protected their respective colonial claims to the territories of the African Continent. The 1885 Berlin Conference, whereby well-established African tribes were deemed incapable of self-governance, echoed the then prevailing State practice that *any* form of occupation should be immediately communicated to the other colonial powers. Formal notification to all signatories was designed to prevent or ameliorate problems of successive discoveries of the same territory.

There is no general agreement about the effect of "discovery" on modern claims to State territory. Though some countries assert that discovery alone generates legal rights, others disagree. The US government, for example, claims that mere discovery yields no rights. When the United States entered into an 1824 treaty with Russia, establishing the boundaries of Alaska, the United States declared that "dominion cannot be acquired but by a real occupation and possession, and an intention to establish it [by mere discovery] is by no means sufficient."[10] Under this view, some form of occupation was necessary to claim legitimate sovereignty over territory. The US astronaut, who planted a flag on the moon in 1969, did not establish any US sovereign rights or title to that territory.

Discovery was supposed to be followed by *effective* occupation. States generally agreed that they did not have to physically occupy the territory in question. They did have to conduct some activity, however, to confirm the existence of some form of actual governmental administration. The Permanent Court of International Justice [PCIJ (located in The Netherlands)] validated this requirement in the 1933 Danish-Norwegian dispute over eastern Greenland. The Court declared that sovereign claims to territory often depend "upon continued display of authority, involv[ing] two elements each of which must be shown to exist: the intention and will to act as sovereign, and some actual exercise or display of such authority."[11] Denmark did not physically occupy the contested portion of eastern Greenland. It did not establish settlements or send governmental officials to administer the area. Yet Denmark's title was successfully predicated upon "the peaceful and continuous display of authority over the island." This was an *effective* occupation during the several centuries that Denmark engaged in diplomatic exchanges with other governments concerning eastern Greenland. These acts demonstrated the requisite degree of dominion to support Denmark's claim to sovereignty.

In November 2002, Italian divers planted a flag, 26 feet beneath the sea, on a normally submerged volcanic island between Italy and Sicily. Italy thus claimed title to this island via discovery. It has emerged four times in recorded history. The last occasion was in 1831, when it reached a height of 213 feet and a 3-mile circumference. It is also claimed by the United Kingdom ("Graham Island"),

Sicily ("Ferdinandea"), and Spain. Under International Law, however, the inability of any sovereign to establish control moots its susceptibility to ownership.[12]

Belligerent Occupation Contemporary occupations, resulting from a hostile takeover of territory, are often described by the occupying government as being temporary in nature. Some last far longer than initially predicted. As noted by Oxford University's Professor of International Relations, Adam Roberts: an implicit assumption is that "military occupation is a provisional state of affairs, which . . . will be transformed into some other status through negotiations conducted at or soon after the end of the war. However, many episodes during this [twentieth] century have called into question the assumption that occupations are of short duration."

The key international instruments are the 1907 Hague Regulations and the 1949 Fourth Geneva Convention. Article 43 of the Hague Regulations provided that the occupying power "shall take all the measures . . . to restore and ensure, as far as possible, public order and [civil life], while respecting . . . the laws in force in the [occupied] country." This article was incorporated into the analysis of the post–World War II Nuremberg Trials. Articles 47 and 64 of the Geneva Convention—the contemporary governing rule according to the Red Cross—provide a similar but more detailed articulation of the law of occupation. Their key provisions state that (47) "persons who are in the occupied territory shall not be deprived . . . of the benefits of the present Convention by any change introduced . . . into the institutions or government of the said territory . . . nor by any annexation. . . ." Furthermore (64), the occupying power may "subject the population . . . to [penal] provisions which are essential to enable the Occupying Power . . . to maintain the orderly government of the territory. . . ."

Occupiers are thereby supposed to remain, after the cessation of hostilities, only until a final peace treaty establishes the fate of the occupied territory. As aptly articulated by Wayne State University's Professor Gregory Fox, rather than *regime change,* a focal point for the US War in Iraq, "an occupier enjoys no general legislative authority to make permanent changes to legal and political structures in the territory. These are instead choices reserved to an indigenous government upon its return to power at the end of the occupation."[13]

In 2003, after the US invasion of Afghanistan and Iraq, the 70th biennial reunion of Belgium's Institut de Droit International produced its Brugge Declaration on the Contemporary International Law on the Use of Force. Since 1873, this widely respected non-governmental organization has considered it a duty to comment upon, and reaffirm, which State applications of force lie within and beyond International Law. Its Brugge Declaration contains a contemporary restatement of the law of belligerent occupation, based upon the rules codified in the Hague Regulations of 1907 on humane treatment of civilians and Prisoners of War (POW); the Fourth Geneva Convention of 1949 regarding civilian protection in time of war; and the First Additional Protocol, including colonial domination and alien occupation, as follows:

—Belligerent occupation does not transfer sovereignty over territory to the occupying power.

—The occupying power can only dispose of the resources of the occupied territory to the extent necessary for the current administration of the territory and to meet the essential needs of the population.

—The occupying power assumes the responsibility and the obligation to maintain order and to guarantee the security of the inhabitants of the territory and to protect its historical heritage, cultural property, and basic infrastructure essential to the needs of the population.

—The occupying power has the obligation to meet the basic needs of the population.

—The occupying power has the obligation to respect the rights of the inhabitants of the occupied territory which are guaranteed by international humanitarian law and international human rights law. . . .[14]

Contemporary examples of what are, or are destined to become, prolonged occupations include:

◆ *Cyprus.* The northern part of Cypress has been occupied by Turkish military forces since 1974 (see §2.4 *Cyprus v. Turkey*). Turkey supports the supposedly distinct State-like entity known as the Turkish Republic of Northern Cyprus (TRNC). No other country in the world recognizes the TRNC as the *de jure* government of this occupied area of Cyprus.

◆ *Lebanon.* Israel established a special "zone of peace" in the southernmost portion of Lebanon in 1978. Because of many attacks from this area, Israel claimed a critical need for this zone—about 10 percent of Lebanon's landmass—under the guise of self-defense.[15] It was designed to provide a buffer between rival forces, because Syria also began its own occupation of Lebanon in 1978. Syria also claimed the critical need for a military foothold in a land that bordered Israel. Given Israel's earlier withdrawal, and the pendency of the Iraq conflict, the September 2004 UN Security Council Resolution 1559 called upon Syria to respect the "sovereignty, territorial integrity, unity, and political independence from Lebanon. . . ." Given Syria's weak economy, not well suited to withstand UN economic sanctions, Syria withdrew in May 2005. The Syrian presence was not necessarily over. In November 2005, Syria's exiled former vice-president accused President Assad of personally ordering the assassination of Lebanon's prime minister. Assad rejected any related discussion with UN investigators.

◆ *Afghanistan and Iraq.* US preemptive strikes, launched in the name of the War on Terror, resulted in what was clearly an initial period of belligerent occupation. Interim "official" transfers of sovereignty, and ensuing elections in both nations, brought these formal occupations to an end, from the US viewpoint. (The United States proclaimed the end of its occupation of Iraq, for example, in June 2004.) As of September 2005, Afghanistan had successfully conducted nationwide elections, choosing from 6,000 candidates for 249 parliamentary seats—plus legislative councils in each of its thirty-four provinces. Many Middle East nations, however, characterize the continued presence—in both nations—of (a) US military forces; (b) civilians working for entities such as the US Central Intelligence Agency, and (c) "US-installed" governments, as clear evidence of a contemporary form of continuing occupation. That the United States has not renounced the possibility of having permanent military bases in each country only adds to this perception. In November 2005, the UN Supreme Court extended the then 180,000-strong multinational force in Iraq for another year. At the close of 2005, shortly after parliamentary elections, it also closed the political process, as defined by the UN SC.

◆ *Palestinian territories.* The legal distinction between occupation and conquest has blurred in this long-term conflict between Israel and displaced Palestinians. Having successfully concluded several military campaigns, Israel occupied the West Bank of Jordan and the Gaza Strip formerly belonging to Egypt; Syria's Golan Heights (which Israel annexed in 1981); and Egypt's Sinai Desert (for a comparatively brief period). In 1967, the United Nations responded with Resolution 242, whereby Israel was advised to (a) withdraw its armed forces from those territories; (b) terminate all claims or any belligerent occupation; and (c) respect "the sovereignty, territorial integrity and political independence of every state in the area and their right to live in peace within secure and recognized boundaries free from threats or acts of force." The Security Council has since issued further resolutions referring to its this Resolution, but to no avail.

This "occupation" ("conquest" from the Palestinian perspective) once again received worldwide attention in 1997. Israel had built approximately 200 settlements in the West Bank, Gaza Strip, and the Golan Heights. On three occasions in four months, the UN General Assembly adopted resolutions condemning Israel for housing its citizens in these territories. During the first "emergency session" of the General Assembly in fifteen years, the vote was virtually unanimous: 131-3, with Israel, Micronesia, and the United States voting against the last resolution. Article 49 of the 1949 Geneva Conventions provides that an occupying nation may not "transfer parts of its own civilian population into territory it occupies." A series of agreements have failed to resolve various territorial disputes.[16] Israel left Gaza in August 2005. Its national security interests nevertheless render Gaza subject to renewed, but presumably temporary, occupation by Israeli military forces until a functioning Palestinian State is established. In December 2005, for example, Israel established a security zone in northern Gaza, to prevent Palestinian rocket attacks upon Israel.

With the launch of the second Intifada, and its suicide bombings, Israel constructed a security wall. It fenced in 8 to 16 percent of the West Bank (depending on whose estimate one uses) that is undoubtedly part of the Palestinian Territory. The General Assembly then exercised its Charter-based authority to refer this matter to the ICJ for an advisory opinion on the legality of Israel's construction of this wall. In July 2004, the ICJ rendered its opinion about the legality of this device for dealing with the suicide bombings.[17]

◆

Legal Consequences of the Construction of a Wall in the Occupied Palestinian Territory

INTERNATIONAL COURT OF JUSTICE
9 July General List No. 131 (2004)
Go to course Web page at
<http://home.att.net/~slomansonb/txtcsesite.html>.
Under Chapter Six, click Palestinian Wall Case.

The US House and Senate responded to the court's illegality decision in their respective July 2004 resolutions deploring this "perversion of justice." Fourteen months later, the Israeli Supreme Court concluded that one area of the Wall was illegal because its presence violated the international law of belligerent occupation. The rest, however, may protect Israel in a manner that the Israeli court will ultimately characterize as properly assuring the security that all persons are entitled to expect of an occupying nation. At the opening of the 2005 UN annual session, Israeli Prime Minister Ariel Sharon added that this barrier has blocked many potential bombers; specifically, stating: "This fence is vitally important [to Israel's national security]. This fence saves lives."[18]

Conquest Another historical method for establishing title to territory is conquest. Nations historically acquired territory by forcefully taking it. Twentieth century examples include the following: Israel conquered the West Bank of Jordan during its 1967 war with neighboring Arab nations. Germany annexed Austria in 1939. Japan annexed Korea in 1910. Belgium annexed the Congo in 1908.

In much of the Middle East, Great Britain's colonial boundaries devolved upon its former protégés in a way, which spawned much dissension because of lines drawn literally in the sand. This early twentieth-century geopolitical boundary making is ably depicted by Oxford Professor John Wilkinson as a regime that defies adherence to any evolved notion of International Law:

Not one of the states of the Arabian Peninsula recognized by the international community, Kuwait,

Saudi Arabia, Behrain, Qatar, the United Arab Emirates, Oman, and Yemen could put up a watertight case to the International Court at The Hague to retain the territory it actually occupies. Each one of their boundaries could be challenged, in whole or in part, by its neighbour or a third party. . . .

There are two reasons for this state of affairs. Firstly, the boundaries have not fully met the precepts of international law. Secondly, local concepts of territorial organization have been largely ignored in imposing or otherwise deciding boundaries. . . .

Because the legal rulings that an international body would apply in arbitrating the disputes would generally have been unfavourable to Britain's attempts to maintain a permanent sphere of territorial control, Britain decided in 1955 to resolve the situation by unilaterally declaring a frontier [in] which it stated defined territory that incontestably belonged to its protégés. . . .[19]

The twentieth-century development of rules prohibiting the use of force outlawed conquest as a legitimate basis for ceding or claiming title to State territory. In 1945, the UN Charter expressly prohibited the use of force in international relations. After two world wars initiated by the expansionist territorial policies of numerous States, the Charter's drafters effectively vitiated conquest as a basis for claiming title to property. Although there have been scofflaws, most States have observed this norm most of the time.

While the "right" of conquest is no longer legally viable, there remains the practical problem of certain ethnic subdivisions—claiming the right of self-determination—never amassing the requisite political basis for national recognition, absent some degree of territorial conquest. One could argue that a permanent state of civil war is too great a price to pay for blind adherence to the norm prohibiting conquest as a legal basis for achieving self-determination. As asserted by Sharon Korman, formerly of St. Anthony's College (Oxford):

Given that a right of conquest is no longer recognized, what is to be done about a state—the recent history of Bosnia-Herzegovina provides a possible illustration of the problem—which has no real existence or central authority capable of maintaining orderly government in its territory, and whose violent intercommunal hatreds are likely to lead to a permanent state of war, with all the dangers to international order which that entails? . . . While old-fashioned partition . . . must, in the late twentieth century, be regarded as an unacceptable and barbaric solution, has contemporary international society devised any alternative procedures for preserving the interest of order in a case of this kind? Does an insistence on the legitimacy of impractical boundaries, in the name of preserving the territorial integrity of a state whose ethnic composition makes it inherently ungovernable, not tend to exacerbate rather than alleviate the problem?[20]

Cession An international agreement that deeds territory from one nation to another is called a *cession*. The grantee nation's right to claim title to the granted land is derived from that agreement. In the 1928 Island of Palmas Arbitration, the Permanent Court of Arbitration (Netherlands) addressed the viability of transferring title by cession. The United States unsuccessfully claimed sovereignty over an island in the Philippine archipelago, founded on the 1898 Treaty of Paris between Spain and the United States. Spain did not have proper title to the Island of Palmas at the time it ceded its treaty rights to the United States. Spain could not, therefore, cede more rights to the United States than Spain itself possessed. The opinion generally addressed the way in which title by cession is established:

[Titles] of acquisition of territorial sovereignty in present-day international law are either based on . . . occupation or conquest, or, like cession, presuppose that the ceding [grantor] and the cessionary [grantee] Power, or at least one of them, have the faculty of effectively disposing of the ceded territory. . . . The title alleged by the United States of America . . . is that of cession, brought about by the Treaty of Paris, which cession transferred all rights of sovereignty which Spain may have possessed in the region indicated in Article III of the said Treaty and therefore also those concerning the Island of Palmas or Miangas.[21]

Cession spawns smoldering hostility when it is forced on the granting State because it has lost a war. Germany was required to cede land to Poland after World War I. The ceded territory contained more than 1 million ethnic Germans. For them, this change meant a drastic role reversal. The Polish government was suddenly confronted with a significant German minority in a region where power relationships had been quite different for more than a century. There may have been a legally sufficient transfer of title to this territory, but the German minority refused to consider itself subject to Polish rule. Germany, in turn, refused to formally renounce the region, although it had been forced to do so by the Treaty of Versailles. Poland was determined to create a homogeneous society in this region, and there were lingering socio-economic differences between the new "Polish" Germans and the other citizens of this new ceded territory, formerly in Germany and now in Poland.[22]

The former Yugoslavia splintered into multiple countries during the 1990s. There were, and are, continuing border and personal property ownership disputes. The 2001 Agreement on Succession Issues Between the Five Successor States of the Former State of Yugoslavia addressed some of these disputes. Property of the former Yugoslavia was thereby legally transferred to the successor State in whose territory it is now located.[23]

Prescription State A may derive title to territory within State B, by occupying some part of it without objection. After some period of time (not uniformly defined), A may thus validate its title to the land, which was in B, if B does not effectively protest a prolonged presence.

Prescription is not universally accepted as a method for acquiring sovereign title. Some nineteenth-century jurists rejected the view that prescription is recognized under International Law. They asserted that one State could *not* legally claim title by merely taking over another's territory. Abandonment was an unacceptable legal fiction. The purported acquiescence in the prescriptive rights of the new occupant was characterized as merely a face-saving device. Most States, however, now recognize prescription as a valid basis for claiming sovereignty over territory.

One practical reason is that ineffective or excessively delayed opposition to hostile occupation conveniently removes defects in sovereign claims to disputed territory. Prescription is thus a common means for resolving long-term border disputes. The ICJ addressed the underlying practicalities when it resolved a sixty-year-old boundary dispute between France (on behalf of Cambodia) and Thailand (formerly Siam). Each claimed sovereign rights to the area surrounding a sacred temple on the Siamese-Cambodian border. In the 1962 *Case Concerning the Temple of Preah Vihear,* Thailand claimed title under a 1904 treaty. It did not, however, rebuff Cambodia's occupation of the disputed area until it

seized the temple in 1954. The Court affirmed the utility of prescription, as a device for acquiring title to property, on the basis that this scenario

appears to have amounted to a tacit recognition by Siam of the sovereignty of Cambodia . . . over [the Temple] Preah Vihear, through a failure to react in any way, on an occasion that called for a reaction in order to affirm or preserve title in the face of an obvious rival claim. . . . In general, when two countries establish a frontier between them, one of the primary objects is to establish stability and finality. This is impossible if the line so established can, at any moment . . . be called in question . . . indefinitely [because] finality would never be reached. . . .[24]

Accretion The other historical method for establishing sovereign title is accretion. A State's territory may be augmented by new formations of land gradually deposited from bodies of water. Examples include additions to territory by the formation of islands within a State's territorial waters, or a natural change in the flow of an international river.

In November 1998, China, Russia, and North Korea extended a World War II-era border agreement regarding the Tumen River. It flows from one of China's northern provinces into the Sea of Japan, separating the northern tip of North Korea from Russia. Its course has changed in the decades since the war. The three nations finally resolved resulting border issues, which had been on hold since a 1991 agreement between Russia and China. North Korea effectively delayed implementation for political reasons. However, such border disputes are sometimes even more complex, because of the passage of time coupled with *both* gradual and sudden changes in a river on an international border.

Sudden changes do not affect the boundary between two nations. The change must be gradual and imperceptible. The *Chamizal Arbitration* between the United States and Mexico dealt with both types of change. One of the major boundaries between these two nations is the Rio Grande River. Treaties in 1848 and 1852 fixed this international boundary at a point farther north than that existing at arbitration in 1911. In the interim period, the gradual southward movement of the Rio Grande exposed a tract of land that was formerly *within* the river. This movement was exacerbated by a sudden flood in 1864. Both the gradual accretion and the instantaneous flooding altered the course of the Rio Grande, producing a 600-acre tract that became the subject of a territorial land dispute. The Mexican and US arbitrators thus described the legal impact of accretion in this instance as follows:

> [Because of] the progressive movement of the river to the south, the American city of El Paso has been extending on the accretions formed by the action of the river on its north bank, while the Mexican city of Juarez to the south has suffered a corresponding loss of territory. . . . The contention on behalf of the United States of Mexico is that this dividing line was fixed, under those treaties, in a permanent and invariable manner, and consequently that the changes which have taken place in the river have not affected the boundary line which was established and marked in 1852.
>
> On behalf of the United States of America it is contended that . . . if the channel of the river changes by gradual accretion, the boundary follows the channel, and that it is only in a case of a sudden change of bed that the river ceases to be the boundary, which then remains in the abandoned bed of the river.[25]

The arbitrators resolved this US-Mexican dispute by dividing the tract in accordance with the usual international rules applicable to accretion. They decided that the United States was entitled to sovereignty over that portion of the Chamizal Tract resulting from the gradual southward accretion of land prior to the 1864 flood. Mexico was entitled to the remaining acres exposed by the flood. In 1967, the United States put an end to the matter by formally transferring this portion of the Chamizal Tract to Mexico.

CRITICISMS OF THE HISTORICAL APPROACH

Contemporary scholars have criticized the historical modes for acquiring sovereignty over State territory. According to Oxford University Professor Ian Brownlie, "[m]any of the standard textbooks, and particularly those in English, classify the modes of acquisition in a stereotyped way which reflects the preoccupation of writers in the period before the First World War."[26] Some significant claims also arose (or resurfaced) after World War II. Professor Brownlie depicts some of the reasons why such claims will continue to adversely affect international relations in the following way:

> The pressures of national sentiment, new forms of exploitation of barren and inaccessible areas, the strategic significance of barren and inaccessible areas previously neglected, and the pressure of population on resources, give good cause for a belief that territorial disputes will increase in significance. This is especially so in Africa and Asia, where the removal of foreign political domination has left the successor states with a long agenda of unsettled [sovereignty] problems, legal and political.[27]

The following excerpt provides a representative Chinese perspective on Western development of the modes for acquiring State territory. It addresses why those historical modes are unacceptable.

A Criticism of Bourgeois International Law on the Question of State Territory

HSIN WU

KCWTYC (newspaper) No. 7:44–51 (1960)

Reprinted and translated in J. Cohen & H. Chiu, Vol. 1

People's China and International Law, 323 Princeton University Press (1974)

Bourgeois international law sums up the various methods by which imperialist countries have historically seized territory by classifying them. Methods of acquiring territory are divided into "*original* acquisition" and "*derivative* acquisition" according to the different owners of the annexed territory.

Methods of acquiring territory are divided into "acquisition by means of treaty" or "acquisition not by means of treaty" according to the different methods adopted at the time of annexation. All these methods of acquiring territories are given legal status, and beautiful legal terms are used to conceal the reactionary essence of these actions. Let us now strip off the legal covers to see what is meant by . . . [these Western terms].

"Original Acquisition": According to the explanation of bourgeois international law, acquisition of land "without an owner" [*terra nullius*] is "original acquisition." What is land "without an owner"? Colonialists do not conceal the fact that this is not land which is entirely uninhabited, but merely land inhabited by what they do not regard as a "civilized people." They regard the vast lands in Asia, Africa, and Latin America as lands "without an owner," despite the fact that millions of owners live there and various nations exist there. They regard those people and nations as "barbarous" and "backward" and believe that they cannot be the owners of those lands. The lands should be occupied by "civilized" people and the acquisition of this territory by "civilized" countries is proper; it is a legitimate method of "original acquisition." In the words of the American scholar Hyde: "If the inhabitants of the territory concerned are an uncivilized or extremely backward people, deemed to be incapable of possessing a right of sovereignty, the conqueror may, in fact, choose to ignore their title, and proceed to occupy the land as though it were vacant." This statement shows how this authoritative American bourgeois scholar unabashedly defends aggressors. His reactionary theory is extremely absurd.

The inhabitants of lands "without an owner" are by no means the kind of people whom colonialists and bourgeois scholars have described as barbarous, ignorant, willing to be slaves, and unable to exercise sovereignty. These descriptions are a great insult and defamation to these inhabitants. The true situation is that, whether it was in Asia, Africa, or Latin America, the indigenous inhabitants all had their own excellent cultures. Bourgeois scholars may consider Africa, for example, as the most barbarous land. But, everyone knows that the African people once had excellent civilizations in the Nile River region, the Congo River region and in Carthage. Long before their contact with Europeans, the Africans were experts in various handicraft skills and technology and were able to refine iron and other mineral ores. They could make various instruments of production, weapons, and furniture. In certain areas of Africa,

national art already had reached a comparatively high standard. African folk literature was rich, colorful, and full of attraction. The allegation that they were willing to become slaves and were unable to exercise sovereignty is a lie inconsistent with history. . . . It was not that they were unable to exercise sovereignty but rather that they were prevented from exercising their sovereignty by colonialists' use of massacre and suppression.

It should be pointed out that there has been a change in the view of bourgeois international law concerning the methods of "original acquisition." At first, bourgeois scholars argued that "occupation" was one method of "original acquisition," that is, a state which "first discovered a land" without an owner should be the owner of that piece of land. It was through this method of acquisition that Portugal and Spain, two of the earliest colonial powers, occupied a large number of colonies. Later, bourgeois scholars proposed the view of "effective occupation." . . . The theory of "occupation" did not meet the desire of the powerful imperialist countries that subsequently emerged, while "effective occupation" provides them with a legal basis for redistribution of the spoils.

"*Derivative Acquisition*": Bourgeois international law holds that the difference between "derivative acquisition" and "original acquisition" is that the former does not refer to the method of acquiring territory without an owner but refers to the method of acquiring territory originally belonging to another state. The imperialist powers "plundering of foreign territory naturally would not be limited to [only] lands without an owner." After lands "without an owner" were carved up, they naturally would plunder lands "with an owner." Lenin said: "When the whole world had been divided up, there was inevitably ushered in an era of monopoly ownership of colonies, and, consequently, of particularly intense struggle for the division and redivision of the world." There is no limitation on imperialism's ambition with respect to plundering territory. . . .

Sometimes, imperialism nakedly uses the method of aggressive war forcibly to seize another state's territory; sometimes it uses camouflaged measures or various pretexts to force another state in fact to place its territory under imperialism's occupation. In order to prove the legality of the above-stated methods of seizing territory, bourgeois international law further classifies "derivative acquisition" into acquisition by means of treaty and acquisition not by means of treaty.

What are the methods of "derivative acquisition" by means of *treaty?* Bourgeois international law considers cession one of these methods. Every country has the right to cede its territory, and it has the right to acquire ceded territory. . . . In a discussion on the form of cession [by treaty], "Oppenheim's International Law" described the annexation of Korea in 1910 by Japanese imperialism and the annexation of the Congo in 1908 by Belgian colonialists as a method of acquiring ceded territory through *peaceable* negotiation. But everyone knows that Korea was forcibly occupied by Japanese bandits and the Congo was a victim of the colonial system. From these instances, we may clearly discern that countries which ceded their territories were all under compulsion and that they were either weak, small, or defeated countries. Countries which acquired ceded territories were all imperialist countries engaging in territorial expansion. Bourgeois international law writings have never been able to cite a single case in which an imperialist power ceded its territory to a weak or small country. Therefore, it can be said that cession of territory is a method of plundering the territories of weak and small or defeated countries used by imperialist countries through the use of war and threat of force.

. . . Most outspoken on this point is the American scholar Hyde, who writes in his book "International Law, Chiefly as Interpreted and Applied by the United States": "The validity of a transfer of rights of sovereignty as set forth in a treaty of cession does not appear to be affected by the motives which have impelled the grantor to surrender them." Obviously, according to such an interpretation, it was legitimate for Japan to force the Manchu government of China to cede Taiwan and Penghu through the unequal Treaty of Shimonoseki of 1895, after the Sino-Japanese War. This is tantamount to saying that if a robber steals property by brandishing a dagger before an owner and by threatening his life forces him to put his fingerprint on a document indicating his consent, then the act of robbery becomes legal. Is that not absurd? No wonder bourgeois international law has sometimes been described as the law of bandits. There is no exaggeration in such a description.

Besides cession, bourgeois international law also considers lease as a method of "derivative acquisition" of territory by means of treaty. . . . In 1898 Germany leased Kiaochow Bay, Britain *leased* Wei-hai-wei, and France leased Kuang-chou Wan from China. These leases were acquired by concluding unequal treaties.

These unequal treaties absolutely were not concluded through "peaceable negotiations" as described by bourgeois international law. As a matter of fact, lease of the above-mentioned Kiaochow Bay and other places was executed under threat of force. In November 1897 Germany sent four men-of-war to Kiaochow Bay to occupy Tsingtao on the ground that its missionaries had been killed. It was under these circumstances of armed occupation that the "Treaty of the Lease of Kiaochow" was concluded. The leases of Wei haiwei and Kowloon were also obtained under similar conditions. . . .

Bourgeois international law considers "conquest" a method of *acquiring territory where no treaty exists.* So-called conquest means that a state uses its armed forces for long-term occupation of the territory or a part of the territory of another state. Undoubtedly, this is a savage and aggressive act. Bourgeois international law, however, considers such a method of acquiring territory lawful, even though it does not go through the process of concluding a treaty. In analyzing the causes of war, "Oppenheim's International Law" states: "If . . . territory cannot be acquired by peaceable means, acquisition by conquest alone remains if International Law fails to provide means of peaceful change in accordance with justice." Charles Rousseau, Professor of International Law at the University of Paris, in his book "Principles Generaux du Droit International Public," held that conquest is a means of acquiring sovereignty over a certain territory. The British jurist Schwarzenberger held: "In the international society law is subordinate to the rule of force. If the whole State machinery [of the defeated State] has collapsed, conquest would permit acquisition of title to the territory of this State." According to these theories, colonial wars or other aggressive wars started by imperialist countries in order to annex territories of other countries are lawful. The Japanese seizure of China's three northeastern provinces, Italy's annexation of Ethiopia, and Fascist Germany's occupation of Poland, Czechoslovakia, and so forth were all lawful.

"Prescription" is also considered a method of "derivative acquisition" of territory not by means of treaty. According to the explanation of bourgeois international law, "prescription" means the acquisition by a state of title to a territory through prolonged occupation. Obviously, this recognizes imperialism's acquisition of legal title to a territory through prolonged occupation by force. "Oppenheim's International Law" held that "a State is considered to be the lawful owner even of those parts of its territory of which originally it took possession wrongfully and unlawfully, provided that the possessor has been in undisturbed possession for such a length of time as is necessary to create the general conviction that the present condition of things is in conformity with international order." This means that any country, regardless of its motive or the means it used—whether by way of annexation or aggression—as long as it has the power to be in prolonged occupation by force of the territory of another state, may consider its aggressive act as "lawful." History shows that colonialists in fact frequently used the concept of "prescription" to plunder the territory of other countries. Even recently, in certain countries, certain persons in power and bourgeois scholars have attempted to resort to the concept of "prescription" as a legal basis for putting certain territory of China's Tibet under the jurisdiction of another country.

In view of the foregoing, the "derivative acquisition" either by means of treaty or not by means of treaty mentioned by bourgeois international law is a general term which describes the various methods used by imperialist countries to plunder the territory of colonized countries and weak and small countries.

NEW MODES OF TERRITORIAL ACQUISITION

Title may now be acquired in ways other than those developed over the centuries since the 1648 Treaty of Westphalia, which yielded the modern system of States (§2.1). These newer methods include renunciation, joint decision, and adjudication.

Renunciation   A nation may relinquish title to its territory by renunciation. There is no transfer of title, unlike the "treaty cession" that *formally* cedes sovereignty to the grantee nation. In 1947, Italy renounced title (previously obtained by conquest) to its territories in northern Africa. These were involuntary renunciations orchestrated by the victorious Allied powers after Italy lost the war. A State may voluntarily relinquish its territorial sovereignty as well. This method of transferring sovereignty is sometimes referred to as acquiescence, estoppel, and even prescription.

The distinction between these results is sometimes rather blurred. They do share a common denominator. A State may not assert a territorial claim in a manner that is inconsistent with its conduct. In the 1968 Rann of Kutch arbitration, for example, Pakistan implicitly relinquished its title to an area on its common border with India. For more than 100 years, Pakistan's predecessor did not react to obvious assertions of sovereignty (by England and then India) in this disputed border area. The arbitrators determined that Pakistan had acquiesced in India's exercise of sovereignty over the suddenly disputed area. Pakistan could not reclaim this land after another State had peacefully occupied it for so long a period of time.[28]

Joint Decision   A joint decision by the victors of war is a twentieth-century device for transferring sovereignty over State territory. After each world war, victorious States claimed and exercised a right to dispose of certain property that the defeated States had obtained by forceful conquest. After World War I, certain victors decided to jointly dispose of the territory of the losers. The PCIJ acknowledged this method for transferring sovereign territory in 1923. After World War II, the victorious nations felt compelled to impose security measures on the losing nations. One such measure was the joint decision of the Allies to reduce certain German frontiers. As a result, Germany was forced to yield its sovereignty over that territory.[29]

Adjudication   This is another method for legitimizing the transfer of sovereignty. Title disputes to State territory are often examined by judges or arbitrators. Although many have classified adjudication as an independent mode for "acquiring" title to State territory, this is a misnomer. International tribunals have no more power than that granted to them by the sovereign States that create them. Adjudication is the result of an international agreement that authorizes a mutually acceptable tribunal to resolve a dispute between the participating States. The tribunal is merely interpreting the agreement.

Title by adjudication is similar to a treaty cession from a grantor to a grantee State. In both instances, the participating States enter into an agreement about how they will fix a boundary line. By adjudication, the parties agree to establish sovereign rights after the tribunal examines the facts and renders its decision. The ICJ has resolved more territorial disputes than any other issue before the court.

◆ 6.3 LAW OF THE SEA

INTRODUCTION

The widely heralded "freedom of the seas" norm is also a limitation. It was crafted to restrict national attempts to unreasonably extend coastal sovereignty into international waters. In its heyday, free seas conflicted with the rights of all States to fish in, and navigate through commercial trade routes on the high seas. The approximately three-mile "cannon-shot rule" is often attributed to an influential Dutch jurist who refused to recognize greater sovereignty than that recognized under late medieval practice.[30] As characterized in a study by Yale Law School scholars:

> The concept of "freedom of the seas" entered the law of nations as a reaction against broad claims to territorial sovereignty over vast sea areas put forward by Spain, Portugal, England, and other states in the sixteenth and seventeenth centuries. The object of these claims was to monopolize fisheries, and trade with areas thought particularly rich in resources. . . . No interference whatever with navigation was justified because effective occupation was impossible by the nature of the sea itself. The same principle was applicable to fisheries . . . for the additional reason that the resources of the sea were [then considered] inexhaustible. . . . The claim of the Dutch to free navigation . . . [evinces the] common interest in navigation and fishing [which] triumphed over monopoly, and that the great principle of "freedom of the seas" became in this sense universally accepted.[31]

Freedom of the seas then served the interests of the more powerful European nations. It authorized their vessels to navigate, fish, and mine without limitation. A coastal State was precluded from interfering with a foreign vessel's activities, just beyond the accepted marine-league territorial sea. As customary State practice evolved, the sovereignty of the nation whose flag a ship sailed under often claimed rights, which trumped those of port authorities. By the dawn of the contemporary system of State sovereignty, introduced by the 1648 Peace of Westphalia, European powers assumed that the ocean's resources were unlimited. Thus the area beyond 3 nautical miles was an area, which was conveniently characterized as *res communis*—meaning open to all comers. As succinctly described by University of Ottawa Professor Donat Pharand:

> Beginning in the seventeenth century, the Law of the Sea was developed and maintained to accommodate the interests of the major maritime powers. They developed a legal regime which protected their colonial, commercial and military interests. That legal regime was characterized by two basic principles: the freedom of the seas and the sovereignty of the flag State. The expression "freedom of the seas" designated mainly two types of freedom, fishing and navigation. It was thought that biological resources of the sea were inexhaustible and that any State, having the necessary fishing capability, could simply go out and help itself without any restriction whatever. As for the sovereignty of the flag State, it meant that the country under whose flag the ship was sailing had exclusive jurisdiction over all activities aboard the ship. Certainly this was the case when the ship was on the high seas, that is beyond the traditional three-mile territorial sea. Aside from two exceptions covering slave trade and piracy, this principle of sovereignty of the flag State remained untouched. In a nutshell this represented the state of the law of the sea until after World War II.[32]

The end of World War II signaled many beginnings. One was the coastal State tendency to extend sovereignty into marine areas well beyond the traditional 3-mile limit of the "territorial" sea. Twentieth-century technology caused the free seas pendulum to swing in the opposite direction. Free accessibility to the *high seas* resulted in a depletion of global marine resources, as well as a reevaluation of the international penchant for a *laissez faire* ocean policy. As suggested by All Soul's College (Oxford) Professor David Attard, however, replacement of a free access regime, by a treaty-based extension of sovereignty, comes with a price. Thus, "the division of the oceans today on the basis of sovereignty . . . is a solution as dangerous and as obsolete as the maintenance of an unrestricted concept of the freedom of the seas. Clearly, therefore, neither sovereignty nor freedom today provide an acceptable basis for a viable regime to regulate uses of the sea beyond the territorial sea."[33]

Various coastal zones surfaced. Some States claimed full sovereignty over large areas, while other claims were comparatively limited. Indeed, all States had an important interest in guarding against illegal drug trafficking, immigration, and pollution. The less-developed States watched in dismay, while the more-developed States entered their general maritime regions to fish and exploit the nearby oceans with technology unavailable to the coastal State. As more seagoing nations began to extract resources from the sea, pressure mounted to compress the notion of freedom of the seas. The colonial period was in decline (§2.2). The new resource-rich, but technology-poor, coastal States began to espouse the view that freedom of the seas continued to serve the ever-present colonial purposes of many large and economically powerful nations. The historical regime of freedom of the seas did not incorporate the interests of the newer members of the international community, especially those coastal nations seeking to facilitate a more equitable distribution of the ocean's resources. Former colonies, not sovereign States until the 1960s, were excluded from any role in the evolution of the Law of the Sea segment of International Law.

The United Nations thus sponsored various treaties with two objectives in mind: first, acknowledging the need to limit freedom of the seas; second, incorporating new coastal State perspectives about evolving sea zones which were unheard of before World War II. The most important and comprehensive of these treaties effectively codified a new constitution of the oceans, finally entering into force in 1994.

In November 1994, the most ambitious and comprehensive treaty of all time entered into force: the 1982 UN Convention on the Law of the Sea (UNCLOS).[34] It was the work product of the third multilateral treaty negotiation on the law of the sea, consisting of numerous meetings of the national delegates from 1974 to 1982. One-hundred and seventeen nations originally signed this treaty in 1982. As of 2001, more than double this number of States had ratified the treaty (157).[35]

US President Clinton submitted this treaty to the US Senate for its approval in 1994. The Senate Foreign Relations Committee recommended that the full Senate approve the treaty in March 2004. The Committee then noted that the Convention "advances national security interests by preserving the rights of navigation and overflight across the world's oceans on which our military relies to protect U.S. interests around the world,

and it enhances the protection of these rights by providing binding mechanisms to enforce them." The United States, however, has yet to ratify UNCLOS. The Bush Administration's general avoidance of international mechanisms suggests that ratification will not occur until some president is willing to embrace the bipartisan recommendation of the US Senate Foreign Relations Committee.

The UNCLOS is the global maritime constitution. Much of the UNCLOS codifies prior State practice. A number of provisions resulted from a progressive evolution during the eight years of negotiations. Some of its provisions were quite novel. This portion of the textbook thus addresses this revised maritime legal regime—proceeding outward from the coastline, through the various sea zones:

(1) Internal waters
(2) Territorial sea
(3) High seas
(4) Contiguous Zone (CZ)
(5) Exclusive Economic Zone (EEZ)
(6) The Continental Shelf (CS)
(7) The deep seabed

Exhibit 6.1 depicts these zones, at the outset, to illustrate the first major theme of this section: The coastal State may control certain activities in ocean waters, including portions of the high seas, in a way which limits the activities of other States. Its control of these various zones is itself limited, however. The farther away from the coast that the coastal State desires to act, the less a State may impede the conduct of other States.

INTERNAL WATERS

UNCLOS Article 8.1 defines internal waters as the "waters on the landward side of the baseline of the territorial sea." As with its land, a State has the sovereign right to control its bays, rivers, and other internal waters. Like repelling foreign invaders from its soil, a State has a strong interest in monitoring the military and commercial activities of foreign vessels within its internal waters. As depicted in Exhibit 6.1, the coastal baseline is the point where the sea intersects with the edge of the land at the seacoast. The baseline is a geographical yardstick for distinguishing internal waters from the sea and the starting point for measuring the various ocean water zones.

EXHIBIT 6.1 SEA ZONES

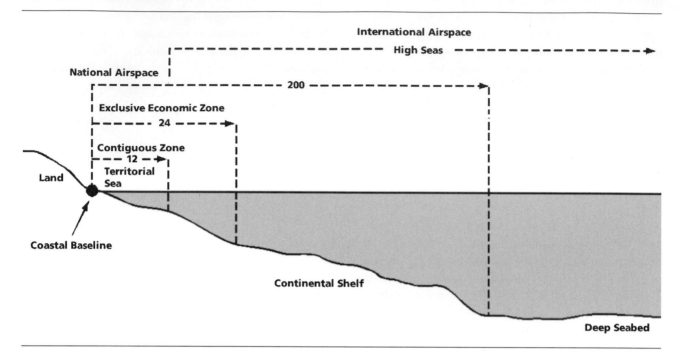

Two settings complicate the application of the exclusive jurisdiction of the coastal State over its internal waters. One is the problem of jurisdiction over events occurring on a foreign vessel while it is in port. The other scenario involves conflicting rights in certain large coastal bays because they contain more open seas than the typical bay.

Ports For the purpose of separating a State's internal waters from the territorial waters off its coast, a port extends to the outermost permanent harbor facility forming an integral part of that harbor's system. A long entryway consisting of natural twists and turns is a part of the port. An artificial buoy area constructed outside of the mouth of that entryway, however, is usually not part of the port.

Each State has the absolute right to control the internal waters contained within its ports. Customary practice has incorporated some limitations, however. When a foreign warship enters internal waters with permission, the port authorities do not board it, for mutual security reasons. Neither State wants to subject its military secrets to unnecessary scrutiny when its naval vessels enter a foreign port. A different limitation applies to merchant and other private vessels. They have the implied right to enter the internal waters of another State without express permission. They are routinely boarded, however, for customs or immigration purposes.

The UNCLOS does not cover the important jurisdictional problem associated with a member of a foreign crew who commits a crime while in port (as opposed to one committed on a ship passing through the TS). When the vessel's sailors go ashore, they subject themselves to the laws or jurisdiction of the coastal State. When a crime is committed on board a foreign vessel in a port, however, either the laws of the coastal State or the laws of the State to which the vessel is registered (the flag State) might be applied.

The ancient rule was that any ship entering another nation's port became subject to the latter's complete control. Modern customary and treaty practice has altered that rule. In the case of crimes that do not affect the port's tranquility, the State—rather than the port State—usually has the primary jurisdiction to prosecute the criminal. That concession facilitates the smooth progress of international commerce. It also avoids undue interference in a ship's movements by the port State. But when the onboard crime causes a significant intrusion on the port's tranquility, the perpetrator becomes subject to prosecution by the port State.

Not all States automatically cede jurisdiction over on-board crimes to the flag State. In some regions, all crimes occurring within the internal or territorial waters trigger the coastal nation's competence to prosecute foreign sailors (absent the usual treaty exception for military personnel). Under customary practice, the flag State is competent to act if the port State chooses not to prosecute. For example, a court in Argentina had to determine the question of Argentina's jurisdiction over a theft that occurred aboard an Argentine merchant vessel at anchor in the port of Rio de Janeiro, Brazil. The ship left the Brazilian port and returned to Argentina with the thief still aboard. The thief was prosecuted in the Argentine court system. Although his lawyer argued that Argentina had no jurisdiction because the crime occurred in Brazil, the court disagreed in the following terms:

According to the rules of public international law . . . offences committed on board a private ship fall within the jurisdiction of the courts of the flag State if the ship is on the high seas, and fall within the jurisdiction of a foreign State only in the event that such offences have been committed while the ship is in the [internal or] territorial waters of that other State. . . . [The court then decided that Argentina nevertheless had jurisdiction because this] principle is not an absolute rule . . . for if the foreign State does not choose to exercise its right to institute proceedings because it considers that the act has not affected the community at large or the peace of the port (as maintained in French and Italian doctrine), the flag [State] may then assert full authority over the ship for the purpose of restoring order and discipline on board or protecting the rights of the passengers. . . .[36]

The rights of the port and flag States are not always left to judicial interpretation under *customary* International Law. The respective jurisdictional rights are often agreed to by treaty. Such treaties typically cede primary jurisdiction to the flag State. They frequently contain a "port tranquility" exception, permitting the port State to prosecute foreign sailors in specified situations.

What type of criminal conduct activates the "port tranquility" exception to the primary jurisdiction of the flag State? The US Supreme Court addressed this question in the following case, relied on by US courts on subsequent occasions:

Mali v. Keeper of the Common Jail of Hudson County (Wildenhus Case)

SUPREME COURT OF THE UNITED STATES
120 US 1, 7 S.Ct. 385, 30 *L. Ed.* 565 (1887)
Go to course Web page at
<http://home.att.net/~slomansonb/txtcsesite.html>.
Under Chapter Six, click Port Tranquility Case.

Bays   Most bays consist of only internal waters. Large bays with wide mouths present the issue of whether they contain only internal waters, or whether they *also* contain territorial and international waters (high seas). This type of bay illustrates the natural tension between freedom of the seas in international waters and the coastal State need to control activities in a strategic bay that penetrates deep into its coastline.

A classic illustration of this tension drew worldwide attention in 1986 when US warplanes were attacked over the Gulf of Sidra in the large southern indentation of the Mediterranean Sea on Libya's coastline. Libya's leader, Mu'ammar Gadhafi, had proclaimed a "Line of Death" across the mouth of this gulf, approximately 300 miles across. At its deepest indentation on Libya's coastline, this gulf extends well over 100 miles into Libya's coastline on the Mediterranean Sea. Libya considers the entire gulf to be internal waters subject to its exclusive control. The US warplanes were operating over the gulf on the premise that it contains international waters because of its immense width.

Article 10 of the UNCLOS defines a bay as "a well-marked indentation whose penetration . . . constitute[s] more than a mere curvature of the coast. An indentation . . . [must be] as large as, or larger than, that of a semicircle whose diameter is a line drawn across the mouth of that indentation." The mouth of a bay consists of its natural entrance points.

A coastal State may normally exercise complete sovereignty up to 12 nautical miles from its coast (see "Territorial Sea" later). In the case of a bay, if the Article 10 semicircle diameter of the bay is *less* than 24 miles—between each side of the mouth of the bay—its waters consist solely of internal waters. If the diameter is *greater* than 24 miles, the bay also contains high seas (international waters) in the center of the mouth; and, territorial waters up to twelve miles from the entire coastline that forms the land boundary of the bay.

Bays are quite important to the national interests of coastal States.[37] The 1910 North Atlantic Coast Fisheries arbitration between England and the United States addressed this significance in the following terms: "[A]dmittedly the geographical character of a bay contains conditions [that] concern the interests of the territorial sovereign to a more intimate and important extent than do those [interests] connected with an open coast. Thus conditions of national security and integrity, of defense, of commerce and of industry are all vitally concerned with the control of the bays penetrating the national coastline. This interest varies, speaking generally, in proportion to the penetration inland of the bay. . . ."[38]

An *historic* bay may contain only internal waters (as opposed to the "territorial" waters discussed below), although its mouth may be wider than the above 24-miles limitation of the UNCLOS. Over a long period of time, a State may claim exclusive sovereignty over a large bay that would normally contain one or more of the other categories of ocean waters (Exhibit 6.1)—because the distance between its natural entrance points is more than 24 miles across. If other States do not dispute such a claim, they effectively acquiesce in the coastal State's treatment of the large historic bay as consisting of only internal waters.

One of the classic disputes is the aging US objection to Canada's claim that Hudson Bay is a "historic" bay, allegedly consisting solely of internal waters. It is 50 miles wide at its mouth. As stated by the Canadian Minister of Northern Affairs and Natural Resources in 1957, "the waters of Hudson Bay are Canadian by historic title. . . . Canada regards as inland waters all the waters west of a line drawn across the entrance to Hudson Strait. . . ."[39] The United States characterizes most of the Hudson Bay as international waters, however, on the basis that the United States has consistently disputed Canada's claim that it is exclusively internal waters. The international status of this bay has not been resolved, since neither nation has a strong enough interest to actually resolve this dispute.

TERRITORIAL SEA

States have historically disagreed about the dividing line between the high seas and the territorial sea. Bold, unilateral expansions of exclusive sovereignty crested during the fifteenth and sixteenth centuries. The range of these national claims extended deep into what is now considered the high seas. Denmark and Sweden claimed large portions of the globe's northern seas. Each claimed complete sovereignty over the entire Baltic Sea. England claimed the entire English Channel and much of the North Sea. A land demarcation by the Pope, as Head of the Holy See (Vatican State), effectively ceded most of the Atlantic and Pacific Oceans to Spain and Portugal in 1492.

Under the United Nations' 1982 treaty, the territorial sea extends outward 12 nautical miles from the national coastline. A coastal State exercises sovereignty over this portion of its territory, essentially to the same extent that it does so over its landmass. Its range of sovereignty includes the air over the territorial sea belt adjacent to the coast, the seabed below, and the subsoil within this zone.

Unlike the other zones addressed later, a State *must* exercise its sovereign power in this adjacent strip of water. The minimum expectation is that the coastal State will chart the waters, this close to its coast, to provide warning of navigational hazards. As stated in a 1951 decision by the ICJ: "To every State whose land territory is at any place washed by the sea, international law attaches a corresponding portion of maritime territory consisting of what the law calls territorial waters. . . . No maritime States can refuse them. International law imposes upon a maritime State certain obligations and confers upon it certain rights arising out of the sovereignty which it exercises over its maritime territory. The possession of this territory is not optional, not dependent upon the will of the State, but compulsory."[40]

Treacherous definitional undercurrents muddied the territorial sea before the UNCLOS was negotiated. These included the location of the "baseline," the "breadth" of the territorial sea, what constitutes "innocent" passage, and the extent to which there exists a right to pass through straits, which formerly contained international waters.

Baseline   The territorial sea begins at the baseline (depicted in Exhibit 6.1). Each begins where the ocean's edge meets the coastline. Under Article 5 of the UNCLOS, the "normal baseline for measuring the breadth of the territorial sea is the low-water line along the coast as marked on large-scale charts officially recognized by the coastal State." The baseline is the yardstick for marking the inner boundary of the various coastal sea zones described in this chapter (see Exhibit 6.1).

The demarcations on the coastal State's official baseline charts do not mandate international recognition of its placement of the baseline. Coastal baselines must follow the general direction of the coast. However, unnatural land contours make it difficult to establish indisputable baselines. Article 7.3 of the UNCLOS espouses the general principle that "the sea areas lying within the [base]lines must be sufficiently closely linked to the land domain to be subject to the regime of internal waters." This language, of course, begs the question of proper baseline placement for the inner edge of the TS on erratic coastlines.

The ICJ furnished guidelines, not bright lines, in its 1951 Anglo-Norwegian Fisheries case. When Norway announced the location of its baselines after World War II, it included a substantial portion of what were previously international fishing areas within its internal and territorial waters. Norway has many ramparts of rocks and small islets that interrupt the natural course of its coastline. Norway drew straight baselines, conveniently encompassing the rocks and islets off its coast, rather than using the traditional method of tracking the contour of its irregular coastline. By placing its baselines at the outer edge of these rock and islet configurations, Norway thus claimed a greater share of the common fishing area than Great Britain was willing to recognize. British fishermen had operated off Norway's coast (within the straight baseline area set by Norway) since the early 1900s. The parties to this dispute had exchanged diplomatic correspondence about their respective rights to these fishing grounds for many years.

The ICJ delineated the general rules applicable to baseline placement for cases involving such unusual coastlines in the following passage:

> The delimitation of sea areas has always an international aspect; it cannot be dependent merely upon the will of the coastal State as expressed in its municipal [internal] law. . . .
>
> It is the land which confers upon the coastal State a right to the waters off its coasts. It follows that while such a State must be allowed the latitude necessary in order to be able to adapt its delimitation to practical needs and local requirements, the drawing of baselines must not depart to any appreciable extent from the general direction of the coast.
>
> Another fundamental consideration . . . is the more or less close relationship existing between certain sea areas and the land formations which divide or surround them. The real question raised in the choice of baselines is in effect whether certain sea areas lying within these lines are sufficiently closely linked to the land domain to be subject to the regime of internal waters. This idea, which is at the basis for the determination of the rules relating to bays, should be liberally applied in the case of a coast, the geographical configuration of which is as irregular as that of Norway.
>
> Finally, there is one consideration not to be overlooked, the scope of which extends beyond purely geographical factors: that of certain economic interest peculiar to a region, the reality and importance of which are clearly evidenced by a long usage.[41]

The majority of the ICJ's judges thereby approved Norway's straight baseline method in these unusual circumstances, because the resulting straight lines were sufficiently aligned with the general direction of the Norwegian coast. Although this method did not produce the usual replica of the coastal nation's coastline, it was acceptable in international practice. Exhibit 6.2 illustrates the Court's description of the method that Norway used to establish its baselines.

Territorial Sea Breadth   The breadth of the territorial sea has long been controversial. In 1492, for example, Spain claimed exclusive territorial sovereignty over the entire Pacific Ocean. Portugal similarly claimed the Indian Ocean and most of the Atlantic Ocean.[42] Claims to entire oceans, however, were never recognized under International Law. States recognized the existence of a much narrower belt of water subject to the coastal State's exclusive control. In 1702, the writings of an often-quoted Dutch judge articulated the vintage State perception of the breadth of this particular coastal zone: "Wherefore on the whole it seems a better rule that the control of the land [of its adjacent Territorial Sea] extends as far as a cannon will carry; for that is as far as we seem to have both command and possession. I am speaking, however, of our own times, in which we have those engines of war; otherwise, I should have to say in general terms that the control of the land ends where the power of men's weapons ends; for it is this, as we have said, that guarantees possession."[43]

This often-cited passage reveals that the 3 mile shooting range of the eighteenth-century cannon established the width of the territorial sea. The coastal State could claim no more than it could control. Under this view, the maximum range of existing weapons was the yardstick for measuring the breadth of the territorial sea. Had this view persisted until the 1960s, the range of

EXHIBIT 6.2 STRAIGHT BASELINE METHOD

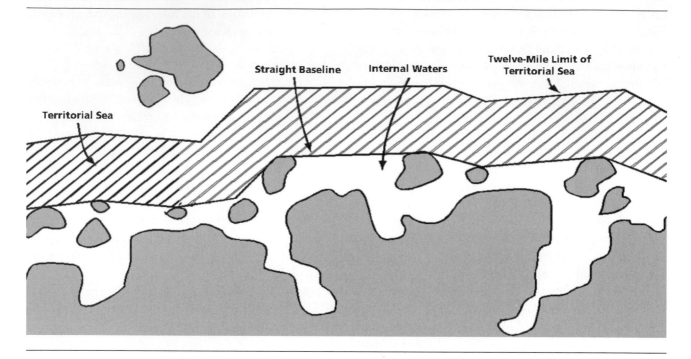

intercontinental missiles would make entire oceans the territorial waters of the launching nation.

After the American War for Independence, the United States claimed a territorial sea extending from the outer tips of various capes on its eastern coast. It used a straight baseline method, which did *not* conform to its coastline. The resulting baselines were not a natural extension of the coastline—unlike Norway's straight baselines that connected the nearby rocks and islets immediately adjacent to its coasts. The US territorial sea thus purported to extend its exclusive jurisdiction far beyond 3 miles from its shores. Various nations objected to this departure from international practice. In 1793, Secretary of State Thomas Jefferson responded by suspending this cape-to-cape baseline method. He formally advised England and France, noting the customary "cannonball" measure of the breadth of the territorial sea:

[The] President of the United States, thinking that, before it shall be finally decided to what distance from our seashores the territorial protection of the United States shall be exercised . . . finds it necessary in the meantime to fix provisionally on some distance for the present government of these questions. You are

sensible that very different opinions and claims have been heretofore advanced on this subject. The greatest distance to which any respectable assent among nations has been at any time given, has been the extent of human sight, estimated at upwards of twenty miles, and the smallest distance . . . is the utmost range of a cannonball, usually stated at one sea league [three nautical miles]. Some intermediate distances have also been insisted on, and that of three sea leagues has some authority in its favor. The . . . President gives instructions to the officers acting under his authority to consider those heretofore given are restrained for the present to the distance of one sea league or three geographical miles from the seashores.[44]

Certain coastal States claimed territorial sea boundaries much wider than the customary limit. Most of these claims were made by lesser-developed nations with significant fishing or seabed resources adjacent to their coasts—while lacking the superior technology possessed by developed nations to take advantage of these resources. In 1952, Chile, Ecuador, and Peru claimed a territorial sea of 200 nautical miles from their coasts. In 1956, a number of other nations in the same region of the world attended the Meeting of the Inter-American Council of Jurists in Mexico City. They adopted the following principle, which differed from the prevailing yardstick for a uniform approach to measuring the territorial sea: "The distance of three miles as the limit of territorial waters is insufficient, and does not constitute a general rule of international law. Therefore, the enlargement of the zone of the sea traditionally called "territorial waters" is justified. *Each State is competent to establish its territorial waters* within reasonable limits, taking into account geographical, geological, and biological factors, as well as the economic needs of its population, and its security and defense."[45]

Such statements generated worldwide pressure to expand the historical 3-mile limit.

In 1958, under sponsorship of the United Nations, representatives of eighty-six nations gathered in Geneva, Switzerland, to pursue a global agreement about the breadth of the various sea zones. The Geneva Convention on the Territorial Sea and Contiguous Zone (1958 LOS Convention) expressly adopted the customary 3-mile limit. However, many nations subsequently extended their territorial sea zones to 12 nautical miles. The 1982 Conference on the Law of the Sea (attended by 148 States) adopted this development in State practice. Under Article 3 of the UNCLOS, every "State has the right to establish the breadth of its territorial sea up to a limit not exceeding 12 nautical miles. . . ."

Although some 140 nations adopted a 1-mile limit at the United Nations' 1982 Conference, the United States rejected the entire convention (as discussed later under deep seabed mining analysis). Shortly after independence from Great Britain, the United States announced its adherence to the customary 3-mile limit and retained that limit for two centuries. In 1988, however, President Reagan unilaterally extended the US territorial sea from 3 to 12 miles in "accordance with international law, as reflected in the applicable provisions of the 1982 United Nations Convention on the Law of the Sea."[46]

This quadrupling of the territorial waters zone had two major effects upon the Law of the Sea. First, it limited freedom of the seas because coastal States could regulate more activities because of the 9-miles expansion from 3 to 12 nautical miles. That development simultaneously extended the existing rules of "innocent passage." Second, many straits, through which ships pass from one part of the high seas to another, no longer contained international waters (high seas). Ships passing through such waters suddenly became subject to regulation by the coastal State on either side of the strait. Both of these developments were addressed in the UNCLOS as follows in Exhibit 6.3.

Innocent Passage   One of the most tangible impacts of the change to a 12-mile territorial sea was the extension of coastal State rules of "innocent passage." Article 18.1 of the UNCLOS Convention defines passage as "navigation through the territorial sea for the purpose of: (a) traversing that sea without entering internal waters . . . or (b) proceeding to or from internal waters. . . ."

But when is the passage "innocent"? In 1986, two US naval vessels entered the Black Sea via the Turkish Straits. They were equipped with electronic sensors and sophisticated listening devices. Their disclosed purpose was to exercise what the US naval authorities characterized as their "right of innocent passage" through the territorial waters of the Soviet Union. The Soviet Union placed all of its Black Fleet military vessels on combat alert. The Soviet Union protested this entry as unnecessarily provocative because it was a clear violation of its territorial sovereignty. But innocent passage violations are usually not so confrontational. As illustrated in a 2005 US Supreme Court case, Russian forces apprehended and boarded an American commercial vessel—traversing territorial waters, before Alaska was ceded to the United States in 1867. The Court described its voyage as not being innocent, due to its "purpose of procuring . . . Indians to hunt for sea otter on the said coast."[47]

Under Article 19 of the UNCLOS, "innocent" passage means passage that is "not prejudicial to the peace, good order, or security of the coastal State." The passing vessel may not stop or anchor, unless incidental to ordinary navigation or undertaken for the purpose of the authorized entry into a foreign port. A vessel may thus proceed to or from port, and render assistance to persons, ships, or aircraft needing emergency assistance.

Article 19 further requires foreign vessels to ascertain and comply with the innocent passage regulations promulgated by coastal States. Regulations relating to customs, immigration, and sanitation protect the coastal nation's interests in its territorial waters. An ocean liner carrying passengers into another country's territorial waters must comply with local tax laws affecting its cargo, passport regulations affecting its passengers, and waste-offloading requirements. Military vessels, when expressly authorized to enter a foreign port, normally

EXHIBIT 6.3 BAY, BASELINE, HARBOR, ISLAND, AND TERRITORIAL SEA

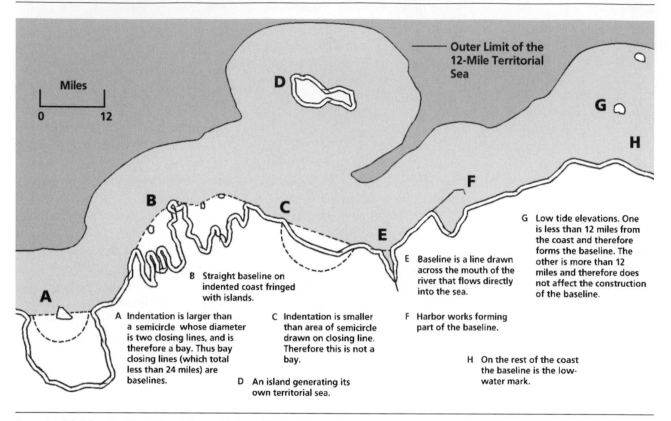

E Baseline is a line drawn across the mouth of the river that flows directly into the sea.

F Harbor works forming part of the baseline.

G Low tide elevations. One is less than 12 miles from the coast and therefore forms the baseline. The other is more than 12 miles and therefore does not affect the construction of the baseline.

H On the rest of the coast the baseline is the low-water mark.

A Indentation is larger than a semicircle whose diameter is two closing lines, and is therefore a bay. Thus bay closing lines (which total less than 24 miles) are baselines.

B Straight baseline on indented coast fringed with islands.

C Indentation is smaller than area of semicircle drawn on closing line. Therefore this is not a bay.

D An island generating its own territorial sea.

Source: Modified from R. Churchill & A. Lowe, *The Law of the Sea* 39 (Manchester, Eng.: Manchester University Press, 1988).

give notice of their intended arrival at least several days in advance.

The application of the "innocent passage" regime is nevertheless elastic and ill-defined. Nations sometimes disagree about whether certain conduct poses a threat. A "threat" can take many forms, often being in the eyes of the coastal State beholder. There are, of course, clear breaches. A foreign military ship authorized to enter the territorial waters of another State could undertake military exercises upon arrival. Submarines might navigate below the surface in territorial waters, undetected by the coastal authorities. In September 1996, for example, a North Korean submarine went aground when passing through South Korean territorial waters, clearly violating the principles that prohibit military entry without permission and entering such waters submerged. In November 2004, Japan filed a protest when a Chinese nuclear submarine entered its territorial waters without notice or identification.

Less threatening activities can be labeled as threats by a coastal State. Foreign vessels can also collect hydrographic information, conduct research, fish, or disseminate propaganda via electronic means. During the Cold War, Soviet "fishing" trawlers with elaborate electronic devices aboard hovered just outside the US 3-mile territorial water limits to gather information. Suppose that a private vessel called the *Greenpeace* distributes leaflets or displays signs against nuclear weapons to ships passing through the territorial waters of a major nuclear power. That State's coast guard vessel may stop the dissemination of such information because the activities of the *Greenpeace* would not be considered innocent. The UNCLOS provisions are ambiguous, but a better option than no definition at all.

The coastal State's discretion to arbitrarily apply locally defined rules of innocent passage are limited by the UNCLOS. Article 24 imposes a duty not to "impair" the innocent passage of foreign ships. The coastal State cannot impose navigational requirements that effectively deny the right of innocent passage. Failure to publicize dangers to navigation in the State's official navigational charts, for example, would make territorial sea passage impractical and dangerous. Article 24 also prohibits coastal States from promulgating regulations that discriminate against the ships or cargo of a particular nation, or ships carrying cargo to or from certain nations. The Arab embargo of Israeli shipping and goods would breach this provision of the treaty (§10.1).

Strait Passage   The second major effect of expanding the territorial sea, from 3 to 12 nautical miles, surfaced in a number of strategic straits. These are the natural sea passages connecting two large maritime areas. The Strait of Hormuz connects the Persian Gulf and the Indian Ocean. The Strait of Gibraltar connects the Mediterranean Sea and the Atlantic Ocean.

The relatively narrow width of the these straits presents a problem. When the navigable channel of such a strait is more than 12 miles from each of the national coasts bordering on the strait, it still contains some international waters or "high seas." Ships are entitled to unrestricted passage through the high seas portion of such straits, assuming that their activities are not repugnant to the coastal State's interests in other zones, such as the CZ or EEZ described below. When such a strait is less than 24-miles wide at its narrowest point, however, it contains only territorial waters.

As a result of this UNCLOS augmentation of coastal jurisdiction by nine additional miles, approximately 116 of these comparatively narrow "international straits— formerly containing High Seas—suddenly embodied Territorial Seas only." Under customary State practice, coastal States would appropriately apply their "innocent passage" rules to such waters. Under the UNCLOS "strait passage" articles, however, the coastal State's innocent passage rules do *not* apply to these special straits. Military and commercial vessels are entitled to free transit in them, just as if those special straits still contained slices of high seas within them.

The Bering Strait between Russia (Siberia) and the United States (Alaska) provides a useful illustration. That strait is 19 miles wide at its narrowest point. Ships pass through it when going between the Arctic and the northern Pacific Oceans. The former Soviet Union claimed a 12-mile territorial sea. Prior to 1988, the US 3-mile territorial sea claim left a 4-mile slice of high

seas at the narrowest point of this strait. Military and commercial vessels could freely navigate in that strip of international waters in the middle of the Bering Strait. When the United States adopted a 12-mile territorial sea in 1988, there were no high seas left in that strait. All States would otherwise be subject to the arguably subjective "innocent passage" rules promulgated by Russia (the eastern border of the strait) and the United States (the western border). At its narrowest point, the Bering Strait now contains only the territorial sea of both the United States and Russia. Such a strait is normally delimited by an equidistance principle directing ships to pass in the middle of the navigable channel.

Under the regime of "transit passage" proposed by the United States, which would govern straits traditionally used for such international navigation, all States could navigate the Bering Strait as if it still contained a slice of high seas in the middle of the navigable channel. A number of States rejected this UNCLOS provision by tendering reservations to its application when they ratified the treaty.

The UNCLOS's "transit passage" provisions are designed to balance two competing national interests: the *pre*-1982 right to transit through straits containing some international waters—through the high seas, when the norm was a 3-mile territorial sea limit—and the *post*-1982 UNCLOS extension of the coastal State jurisdiction from 3 to 12 miles. Under Article 38.2, ships and aircraft may undertake "transit passage" through such straits now containing only territorial waters that formerly contained international waters "solely for the purpose of continuous and expeditious transit of the strait between one part of the high seas. . . and another part of the high seas. . . ." The coastal State or States may not impede such transit on the arguable basis that the otherwise amorphous rules of innocent passage apply to these waters that otherwise contain only territorial waters because of the narrowness of such a key navigational strait.

Assume that the United States and Russia were to agree upon applying this Article 38 transit passage provision. A Chinese ship, passing through the Bering Strait between the Arctic and northern Pacific oceans, would not be subject to either US or Russian innocent passage rules—although that strait would otherwise be territorial waters at its narrowest point (19 miles). Neither coastal State could prohibit the foreign commercial vessel from traversing their overlapping territorial waters, although the Chinese vessel would pass less than

12 miles from the coasts of both the United States and Russia. As long as the Chinese vessel was merely passing through this strait, the potential US-Russian adoption of the transit passage provisions under Article 38 of the UNCLOS would entitle that ship to pass freely through the strait, just as if it still contained high seas.

HIGH SEAS

The high seas, also referred to as "international waters," covers 71 percent of the earth's surface, hosts 80 percent of the planet's life forms, and absorbs more carbon dioxide than the forests. They consist of that part of the ocean not subject to the complete territorial sovereignty of any State. States have "exclusive" jurisdiction *only* over their 12-mile territorial seas. They have *some* powers in the zones seaward of their territorial waters. The degree of jurisdictional power is inversely correlated to the distance of the particular zone from the coastal baseline.

The most fundamental division among the various zones discussed in this section of the textbook is the distinction between the territorial sea and the high seas. (Two additional ocean water zones, the CZ and the EEZ, also begin at the coastal State's baseline.) As depicted in Exhibit 6.1, the outer edge of the territorial sea zone marks the inner edge of the high seas.

Freedom of the high seas has long been a universal tenet of International Law. In 1927, the PCIJ reaffirmed the principle that this freedom was virtually absolute. The Court's comment, noting that this liberty was subject to only those special limitations expressly recognized by State practice, was as follows: it "is certainly true that . . . vessels on the high seas are subject to no authority except that of the State whose flag they fly. In virtue of the principle of the freedom of the seas, that is to say, the absence of any territorial sovereignty upon the high seas, no State may exercise any kind of jurisdiction over foreign vessels upon them. If a war vessel, happening to be at the spot where a collision occurs between a vessel [from its own country] . . . and a foreign vessel, were to send on board the latter an officer to make investigations or to take evidence, such an act would undoubtedly be contrary to international law."[48] The 1958 UN Law of the Sea Conference delegates restated the rule of complete freedom of the high seas in Article 1 of the 1958 Convention on the High Seas. It defined the high seas as "all parts of the sea that are not included in the Territorial Sea or in the internal waters of a State." Article 2 added that

the "high seas being open to all nations, no State may validly purport to subject any part of them to its sovereignty."[49]

Freedom of the seas is no longer absolute. The 1958 treaty was drafted just before the decolonization period of the 1960s. The maritime pendulum thus began to swing in the other direction. During the 1974–1982 UNCLOS process: the territorial sea was quadrupled, the size of the CZ was doubled, and a 200-mile EEZ was created. The impact has been a "territorialization" of the oceans, once thought to belong to all. One result of these expansions, and creation of the new economic zone, was the extension of coastal sovereignty into the high seas. The remainder is scheduled for control by an International Seabed Authority, which regulates all resource-extraction activities in the far reaches of the oceans under the UNCLOS regime described below. The high seas could hardly continue to be characterized as *res communis* (belonging to all). As aptly stated by Professor Francis Ngantcha, in his book published by the Geneva Institute of International Studies:

> The Law of the Sea has traditionally been aimed at protecting the international community's interests over the inexhaustible uses of ocean space. To this end, the main pillar of the law has been freedom of the sea—with the implication that seagoing vehicles may freely roam the oceans. When much of the ocean space was considered *res communis,* this tenet was considered unquestionable.
>
> The "territorialization" of the ocean space, *i.e.,* its division into zones of coastal State sovereignty and/or jurisdiction, has put a stop to the "old" system of "free" global maritime communication and transportation. Consequently, the international networks of trade and commerce, naval mobility, overflight, etc., have come to depend upon the national maritime spaces of third States for purposes of passage.[50]

There remains a major issue regarding coastal State jurisdiction in the high seas: the degree to which it can protect itself against criminal activities which threatens its national interests. Drug trafficking threatens coastal State interests, long before the drugs reach any of the UNCLOS treaty zones. Consider the following scenario, wherein US customs inspectors seized drugs and arrested the leader of an international drug-smuggling ring near Singapore's coastline:

United States of America v. Larsen

UNITED STATES COURT OF APPEALS, NINTH CIRCUIT

952 Fed. Rptr. 2d 1099 (1991)

AUTHOR'S NOTE: The defendant was convicted of "aiding and abetting the knowing and intentional possession with intent to distribute marijuana" under national controlled substances laws. The appellate court held that Congress intended that the applicable statute should be applied outside the US where "necessary." US customs agents were thus authorized to seize a private vessel and arrest its crew in the High Seas near Singapore—thousands of miles from the California forum where the defendant was brought to trial for his violation of this statute.

COURT'S OPINION: Before Browning, Alarcon, and T.G. Nelson, Circuit Judges.

Charles Edward Larsen was convicted for his involvement in an international marijuana smuggling operation. . . . Larsen challenges the legality of his conviction on numerous grounds, including the court's extraterritorial application of 21 USC §841(a)(1) [the controlled substances law serving as the basis for his arrest near Singapore]. We affirm.

Larsen's conviction was based on evidence which established that he, along with codefendants and numerous other individuals, conspired to import shipments of Southeast Asian marijuana into the United States from 1985 to 1987, and to distribute the marijuana in the United States. The profits from these ventures were concealed by a fictitious partnership created by the defendant and others. This partnership was used to purchase the shipping vessel intended to transport the marijuana. During some of the smuggling operations, Larsen served as captain of the vessel.

Under Count Eight, Larsen was convicted of aiding and abetting codefendant Walter Ulrich in the crime of knowing and intentional possession with intent to distribute marijuana in violation of 21 USC §841(a)(1). The marijuana was seized by [US] customs inspectors from a ship on the high seas outside of Singapore. Larsen claims that the district court erred when it denied his motion to dismiss Count Eight because 21 USC §841(a)(1) does not have extraterritorial jurisdiction. . . .

Congress is empowered to attach extraterritorial effect to its penal statutes so long as the statute does not violate the due process clause of the Fifth Amendment. There is a presumption against extraterritorial application when a statute is silent on the matter. However, this court has given extraterritorial effect to penal statutes when congressional intent to do so is clear. Since 21 USC §841(a)(1) is silent about its extraterritorial application, we are "faced with finding the construction that Congress intended."

The [US] Supreme Court has explained that to limit the locus of some offenses "to the strictly territorial jurisdiction would greatly curtail the scope and usefulness of the statute and leave open a large immunity for frauds as easily committed by citizens on the high seas and in foreign countries as at home." "Congressional intent to attach extraterritorial application" may be inferred from the nature of the offenses and Congress "other legislative efforts to eliminate the type of crime involved."

Until now, the Ninth Circuit [where appeals from California federal trial courts are heard] has not applied this "intent of congress/nature of the offense test" to 21 USC §841(a)(1); however, four other circuits have. They all held that Congress did intend the statute to have extraterritorial effect.

The Fifth Circuit held that Congress intended that 841(a)(1) have extraterritorial effect because it was a part of the Comprehensive Drug Abuse Prevention and Control Act of 1970, and the power to control illegal drug trafficking on the high seas was an essential incident to Congress' intent to halt drug abuse in the United States.

The Third Circuit held that Congressional intent to apply 841(a)(1) extraterritorially could be implied because "Congress undoubtedly intended to prohibit conspiracies to [distribute] controlled substances into the United States . . . as part of its continuing effort to contain the evils caused on American soil by foreign as well as domestic suppliers of illegal narcotics. . . . To deny such use of the criminal provisions 'would be greatly to curtail the scope and usefulness of the statute."

The First Circuit concluded that the district court had jurisdiction over a crime committed on the high seas in violation of 841(a)(1) because "[a] sovereign may exercise jurisdiction over acts done outside its geographical jurisdiction which are intended to produce detrimental effects within it." The Second Circuit similarly held that "because section 841(a)(1) properly applies to schemes to distribute controlled substances within the United States," its extraterritorial application was proper.

Extraterritorial application of a drug possession/distribution statute comports with the reasoning behind the Supreme Court's Bowman decision, since such a statute is "not logically dependent on locality for the Government's jurisdiction, but [is] enacted because of the right of the government to defend itself against obstruction, or fraud wherever perpetrated" and "[i]t would be going too far to say that because Congress does not fix any locus it intended to exclude the high seas in respect of this crime" [citation omitted]. . . .

Larsen cites to a passing reference in Hayes which stated that Congress accepted the views of representatives from the Department of Justice and the DEA who testified that the Comprehensive Drug Abuse Prevention and Control Act of 1970 did not apply to American ships on the high seas. While the Hayes court acknowledged that some might conclude that §841(a)(1) does not apply extraterritorially because of this Congressional testimony, the court nevertheless held that §841(a)(1) did have extraterritorial application.

In affirming Larsen's conviction, we now join the First, Second, Third, and Fifth Circuit Courts in finding that 21 USC "841(a)(1) has extraterritorial jurisdiction. We hold that Congress" intent [to apply this drug law to the High Seas] can be implied because illegal drug trafficking, which the statute is designed to prevent, regularly involves importation of drugs from international sources.

[Conviction] AFFIRMED.

◆ Notes & Questions

1. Larsen deals with something different than extracting resources from the high seas. The United States was prosecuting a US citizen for criminal conduct occurring on the high seas. Should the United States have such jurisdiction to apply its laws anywhere on the high seas under International Law?

2. A 2002 Canadian Supreme Court decision articulated a representative perspective regarding the extraterritorial application of domestic law:

> A judgment of this Court, *Daniels v. White,* (1968) S.C.R. 517, sets out when international law is appropriately used to interpret domestic legislation. In that case, Pigeon J. held at p. 541 that:
>
> > . . . this is a case for the application of the rule of construction that Parliament is not presumed to legislate in breach of a treaty or in any manner inconsistent with the comity of nations and the established rules of international law. *It is a rule that is not often applied, because if a statute is unambiguous, its provisions must be followed even if they are contrary to international law.* . . . (Emphasis added [by the court].)

The questions at stake fall within the purview of the domestic legislation. Indeed, it can be argued that the domestic legislation is more specific than the rules set out by the international legal principles and as such, there would be little utility in examining international legal principles in detail. In other cases, international law principles might have a more direct impact and the disposition of the matter might turn on their interpretation and application.

Schreiber v. Canada (Attorney General), (2002) 3 S.C.R. 269, 2002 SCC 62 (CanLII), para. 50–51, available at: <http://www.canlii.org/ca/cas/scc/2002/2002scc62.html>.

3. Assume that the drug seizure and Larsen's arrest occurred in one of the following sea zones:

   (a) Singapore's EEZ
   (b) Singapore's CZ
   (c) Singapore's territorial sea.

Would Singapore be more concerned about the location of the arrest and seizure in any particular zone, as opposed to another? Might the United States be violating any rights of the coastal State if the events in Larsen occurred in *any* of these zones (Exhibit 6.1)?

4. In December 2002, Spain stopped and boarded the So San, about 600 miles off the coast of Yemen. The So San was a Yemen vessel carrying fifteen Scud missiles and 85 tons of chemicals buried under 40,000 bags of cement. Yemen disavowed knowledge of its destination. This vessel was not flying any flag. The then new US Bush Administration policy was to interdict shipments of arms capable of carrying weapons of mass destruction. Thus, any government could board the vessel to determine its cargo and destination. It was placed under control of a US admiral, then escorted by the Spanish Navy to a US military base in the Indian Ocean. Did this exercise of Spanish and US jurisdiction violate the rules applicable to the high seas (including freedom of the seas)?

The term "high seas" may have a distinct meaning under the national law of certain countries. In 1996, TWA Flight 800 crashed 8 miles off the Long Island shore. The Death on the High Seas Act (DOSHA) provides for limited liability when a death occurs on the "high seas." The version of this act, effective at the time of the 1996 disaster, provided that high seas meant "beyond a [three-mile] marine league from the shore of any State. . . ." A two-judge majority held that this event did *not* occur on the high seas. The dissenting judge, displeased with the majority's application of the federal act, countered:

> [President Reagan's] Proclamation changed the meaning of the U.S. territorial sea—and thus its complement the "high seas"—for international, but not domestic, law purposes. . . . The majority ignores that [in] the DOHSA Congress, by using the phrase "high seas beyond one marine league from the shore of any State," intended both to define and to indicate the geographical boundary line at which the high seas began—three nautical miles from the U.S. coast—because that boundary line coincided with the outer border of the states' territorial seas. Congress wished to preserve state [legal] remedies in state waters, and to provide a separate remedy, *i.e.* DOHSA, to waters subject only to federal jurisdiction, *i.e.,* "the high seas" beyond a [three-mile] marine league. Simply stated, it is irrelevant whether Congress shared the international legal understanding of 'high seas' as 'non-sovereign waters,' because its only concern at the time of DOHSA's passage was state, and not federal, boundaries. Nothing in

DOHSA's language or legislative history supports the majority's conclusion that Congress intended 'high seas' to be a variable term 'subject to change' because of evolving international concepts.[51]

Four years later, Congress amended the DOHSA to change the statutory boundary between US territorial seas and the high seas from "one marine league" to "twelve nautical miles."[52]

CONTIGUOUS ZONE

Coastal State sovereignty is *exclusive* in the territorial sea belt immediately adjacent to its landmass. A coastal State may also exercise *limited* jurisdiction in the CZ. It extends from the baseline to 24 nautical miles from the coast. As depicted in Exhibit 6.1, the outer edge of the territorial sea is the midpoint of the CZ.

Why *is* there a CZ? Sovereign rights in the CZ allow a coastal State to effectively preserve various national policies. Under Article 33.1 of the UNCLOS, the activities of foreign States or their vessels in the CZ are subject to the coastal State's jurisdiction for the express purposes of enforcing "customs, fiscal, immigration, or sanitary laws."

The CZ's proximity to the coastline requires a balance of international and coastal State rights to respectively use and control these waters. Enforcement of special maritime laws in this zone is not an unreasonable infringement of the international right to freely navigate through them. During the eighteenth and nineteenth centuries, State practice acknowledged the right to seize foreign and domestic vessels and arrest their occupants in international waters at some distance beyond the 3-mile territorial sea. Coastal States were unwilling to ignore harmful or illegal activities occurring in this fringe area just beyond their territorial seas. The classic illustration was rumrunners during the US alcohol Prohibition era of the 1920s. They would hover there, without dropping anchor. They sought opportunities to enter the territorial sea; or, to turn over their contraband to smaller boats, which could then offload it at undisclosed locations ashore. This gave rise to the "hovering laws" extending coastal jurisdiction for the limited purpose of fending off anticipated violations of US liquor laws. The same concern exists today, given the "invasion" by international drug traffickers.

A number of early twentieth-century developments impacted the creation and subsequent extensions of the CZ. The 1928 meeting of Stockholm's Institut de Droit International (Institute of International Law) was the first international attempt to react by assessing the proper scope of such hovering laws. The 1929 Harvard Law School study of the Law of Territorial Waters stated that "navigation of the high seas is free to all States. On the high seas adjacent to the marginal [territorial] sea, however, a State may take such measures as may be necessary for the enforcement within its territory or territorial waters of its customs, navigation, sanitary or police laws or regulations, or for its immediate protection."[53] The League of Nations 1930 Conference on the Law of the Sea did not reach any express agreement about the precise scope or breadth of the CZ. The participants did agree on one important matter. Unlike territorial waters, where a coastal nation must exercise its sovereign control, a State had to expressly declare its claim to jurisdiction over a CZ. Under International Law, the CZ is not a necessary adjunct of the inherent scope of the territorial sovereignty of coastal States.

This consensus placed the burden on coastal States to justify any extension of sovereignty beyond their territorial seas. Other States did not have to recognize unusual jurisdictional claims in this area beyond the historic 3-mile territorial sea. A major difference between the two zones was that a coastal State could not claim exclusive sovereignty over its CZ for all purposes. It could monitor and exclude hovering activities there. It could not limit passage that was otherwise unharmful to coastal State interests.

One problem with the 1958 UN Convention on the Law of the Sea was the specific 12-mile breadth of the CZ. Its establishment may have been a step backward. The drafters' intent was to place a single limit on the diverse national interests claimed by coastal States in this zone. States that wanted jurisdiction over a larger sea zone, however, did not ratify this provision of the 1958 Convention. They did not acquiesce in the prospect of their coast guard cutters idly standing by while contraband was being unloaded just outside the proposed 12-mile CZ. In a related extension, the 1958 UN Law of the Sea Convention provided for coastal jurisdiction over the CS "to where the depth of the superjacent waters admits of the exploitation of the natural resources. . . ." This provision effectively permitted coastal States to monopolize the marine resources in and over their CSs—normally including and extending beyond the CZ.[54]

The third UN Law of the Sea Conference produced some answers to these problems through seaward extensions of sovereign control. The UNCLOS delegates expanded the territorial sea from the coastal baseline to 12 miles and the CZ to 24 miles. This treaty-based expansion, which codified existing State practice, formally resolved the simmering disputes over the acceptable breadth of the CZ.

EXCLUSIVE ECONOMIC ZONE

During the 1974–1982 UNCLOS negotiations, State representatives proposed a novel plan to accommodate the competing interests of freedom of the high seas versus natural resource depletion. Customary State practice had condoned the offshore regulation of fishing, mining, security, and certain other activities of interest to coastal States. These national interests were effectively codified by the 1982 treaty provisions, expressly adopting a 200-mile EEZ. This "economic" zone starts at the coastal baseline and overlaps the 24 miles CZ, as well as the 12-mile territorial sea.

Although the EEZ is now firmly established in International Law, the vagueness of the 1982 Convention—typical of any multilateral treaty where a wide degree of consensus is sought—masks continued disagreement about the respective rights of different States in *overlapping* EEZs. The difficulty in reaching any agreement over the eight-year negotiating period was partially overcome by employing vague language, thereby enabling all participants to claim that their varied objectives had been achieved.

Under Article 56 of the UNCLOS, the coastal State enjoys sovereign rights in the EEZ for the purposes of "exploring and exploiting, conserving and managing the natural resources . . . of the waters superjacent to the seabed and its subsoil, and with regard to other activities for the economic exploitation and exploration of the zone, such as the production of energy from the water. . . ." This language provides no objective yardstick for measuring the discretion of the coastal State to exclude the activities of other States in its EEZ. For example, the coastal State may determine the "allowable catch" of fish to be taken by other States from its EEZ. This treaty language contains no concrete standard to define just what constitutes an allowable catch. Under Article 62, when a State fails to determine its allowable catch, or does not have the "capacity to harvest the entire allowable catch, it shall, through agreements . . . give other states access to the surplus of the allowable catch. . . ." This article requires the coastal State to provide for access to the surplus by other nations. Unfortunately, this provision means no more than an agreement to agree at a later time—without the benefit of guidelines to define specifically another State's right of access to the surplus resources of the EEZ.

Article 73 presents another example of the confusion spawned by treaty language, which is forever in need of judicial interpretation. The following case illustrates this predicament. The UNCLOS International Tribunal for the Law of the Sea, seated in Hamburg, Germany, is the treaty-based entity for resolving maritime disputes.[55] In its first judgment in 1997, the Tribunal was acutely divided over several issues, including what type of activity would result in a violation of coastal State fishing regulations in its EEZ:

Application for Prompt Release
The Camouco Case

(Panama v. France)

INTERNATIONAL TRIBUNAL FOR THE LAW
OF THE SEA

Judgment of 7 February 2000 (Tribunal Case No. 5)
<http://www.un.org/Depts/los/itlos_new/
Case5_Camouco/Jud-Camouco.htm>
Provided by the Division for Ocean Affairs and the Law of the Sea, Office of Legal Affairs, United Nations, New York.

Go to course Web page at
<http://home.att.net/~slomansonb/txtcsesite.html>.
Under Chapter Six, click Camouco Case

This newest sea zone is a product of the tension between historical expectations associated with freedom of the seas and modern pressures to decentralize the exploitation of ocean resources. After World War II, the more developed nations used their superior technology to extract the rich fishing and mineral resources contained in the sea and under the ocean's floor. Many of these natural resources were located just beyond the territorial seas of the lesser-developed nations. They witnessed the resulting depletion of these natural resources, virtually within sight but beyond their grasp. Even some developed nations were concerned about protecting the resources off their own coasts from unlimited exploitation by other economic powerhouses. The sovereignty equation struck in the EEZ does not preclude all activity in this portion of the high seas, which could be characterized as being "economic."

Although the coastal State effectively enjoys the economic fruits of this area, UNCLOS Article 58 provides that other States retain the right therein to navigate, overfly, and lay submarine cables and pipelines "compatible with . . . this Convention." As a result of the treaty-based creation of this zone, the less powerful coastal States can now share in the wealth of natural resources adjacent to their shorelines. They established a licensing regime for recapturing a percentage of the revenues derived by the extraction of natural resources from the sea, or the subsoil under the sea, up to 200 nautical miles from their coasts.

Unfortunately, States do not uniformly apply the terminology properly associated with this zone. As recently lamented by a judge on the Law of the Sea Tribunal:

The "Juno Trader" Case

(Saint Vincent and the Grenadines v. Guinea-Bissau)

THE INTERNATIONAL TRIBUNAL FOR THE LAW OF THE SEA
44 INT'L LEGAL MAT'LS 498 (2005)
Application for Prompt Release
December 18, 2004

Declaration of Judge Kolodkin

1. Every year, the United Nations General Assembly in its annual resolutions on the oceans and the law of the sea appeals to all States to harmonize their legislation to bring it into in compliance with the United Nations Convention on the Law of the Sea.

2. Unfortunately, not all States Members of the United Nations that are parties to the United Nations Convention on the Law of the Sea have heeded those appeals. In the "Juno Trader" Case it has been found that a coastal State, the Respondent, has used the expression "the

maritime waters of Guinea-Bissau" to mean not only territorial sea of Guinea-Bissau, but also its exclusive economic zone.

3. On 19 October 2004, the Interministerial Maritime Inspection Commission adopted the Minute in which was stated that the Juno Trader ". . . was arrested . . . in the maritime waters of Guinea-Bissau . . .". However, it is known that the Juno Trader was arrested in the exclusive economic zone of Guinea-Bissau and, under the United Nations Convention on the Law of the Sea, exclusive economic zones do not form part of the territorial sea or "maritime waters" of any State.

4. There is another trend in the application of the United Nations Convention on the Law of the Sea: some coastal States are demanding, in their domestic legislation, prior notification by vessels intending to enter their exclusive economic zones even if only for the purpose of transiting them in application of the freedom of navigation which is guaranteed by article 58, paragraph 1, of the United Nations Convention on the Law of the Sea.

Anatoly Kolodkin

The international adoption of the EEZ regime has had the following impact upon the International Law of the sea. Over one-third of all ocean space, containing 90 percent of global fishing resources, is now subject to the sovereignty of the coastal nations of the world. Now that the 1982 UNCLOS has been ratified by enough countries for it to enter into force, the lesser-developed nations have achieved one objective in their proposed redistribution of world wealth: an increase in the national sovereignty of such nations over global economic resources in the ocean waters near their shores, but beyond both the older territorial sea and the CZs.

On the other hand, there is no evidence that international approval of the 1982 Convention's EEZ articles have helped or will actually help the poorer or underdeveloped States as envisioned by its proponents. As stated by Professor Arvid Pardo, Malta's former ambassador to the United Nations and an UNCLOS participant:

[T]he Convention is grossly inequitable not only as between coastal States and landlocked and geographically disadvantaged States, but also as between coastal States themselves: only ten of these in fact obtain more than half of the area which the Convention places under national control [since so many nations separated by international waters are less than four hundred miles apart]. . . . It should be noted that adequate scientific capability, appropriate technology and substantial financial resources are required to effectively develop offshore resources, particularly mineral resources; thus, only wealthy countries and a few large developing countries such as China, Brazil, India and a few others have the means themselves to engage in significant offshore development. This could mean that marine areas under the jurisdiction of many small developing countries . . . could be exploited in practice predominantly for the benefit of technologically advanced countries with far-reaching political consequences.[56]

This perspective illustrates that comparatively wealthy and developed States can still extract the usual benefits from their international ventures in the EEZs of other nations.

Some of the most powerful States have also *extended* this zone, by augmenting it to accommodate what they characterize as special circumstances. In 1994, Canada enacted "emergency" legislation authorizing the arrest of violators of its new ban on catching the endangered "turbot" fish in the Grand Banks area, 220 miles off Newfoundland. In March 1995, Spanish and Portuguese fishing trawlers were either seized or threatened with capture. The European Union then engaged in unsuccessful diplomatic attempts to convince Canada to cease this interference with the recognized right to fish in international waters *beyond* the 200-mile EEZ. Spain's resulting case against Canada was dismissed by the ICJ on the basis of Canada's not having consented to the Court's jurisdiction.[57] This jurisdictional defect was tendered to avoid a resolution of this issue on its merits. The sovereignty scenario is analogous to the previously discussed "historic bay." Such bodies, normally containing *both* internal waters and high seas because of their size, may be characterized as exclusively "internal" waters. Canada, similarly, was hereby attempting to expand its sovereignty because of its historic claim to an area, which spilled over the outer limits of the 200-mile EEZ.

After the UNCLOS has entered into force (1994), coastal States began to enjoy greater profits from their EEZs. They may, as illustrated in the above *Camouco Case,* charge licensing fees for taking fish or minerals from those zones. They may erect artificial islands or structures to harvest fish in the waters and minerals in the seabed of the EEZs. They may also conduct marine research and legitimately exclude other States from engaging in such activity.

One recurring problem with creation of the EEZ, and its attendant expansion of the range of coastal sovereignty, is that many States cannot possibly claim an exclusive 200-mile EEZ. Their shorelines may be less than 400 nautical miles from another nation. Or, adjacent nations may share an irregular geographical land configuration, which necessarily limits their respective abilities to claim a full 200-nautical mile swath of ocean waters without crossing over into one another's EEZs. Under Article 74 of the UNCLOS, States with opposing or adjacent coastlines are thus expected to resolve any inconsistent claims to their respective EEZs "by agreement on the basis of international law . . . in order to achieve an equitable solution." A similar problem arises with delimitation in facing or adjacent CSs (later). Between 1969 and 1993, for example, the ICJ heard six cases wherein it was called upon to establish respective rights in such EEZs or CSs in various regions of the world. The Court has not been able to produce a uniform principle other than its routine articulation of the rather vague notion of "equidistance," so that geographical limitations require them to claim only their share of a limited resource. However, "equidistance" is a term meaning different things to different nations.

In practice, some nations have established their respective rights to overlapping coastal zones by using an equidistance principle. Italy and what was the former Yugoslavia, for example, faced one another across the Adriatic Sea. It is only 100 miles across at many points. UNCLOS Article 74 mandates an agreement to "achieve an equitable solution" to the geographic inability of both nations to claim an entire 200-mile width across the Adriatic as their EEZ. Under customary State practice, the Italian and (former) Yugoslavian

EEZs would extend to a median line that is equidistant from both coasts. Italy and Yugoslavia would be entitled to comparable EEZs of some 50 nautical miles at certain points from their respective shores.

Article 59 of the 1982 LOS Convention provides that conflicts over the control and the breadth of the EEZ are supposed to be resolved "on the basis of equity and in light of all the relevant circumstances, taking into account the respective importance of the interests involved to the parties as well as to the international community as a whole." This article is obviously vague. It does not define *equity, relevant,* or *interests.* There is, however, a degree of accuracy that is self-defeating. This treaty, in other words, illustrates that consensus was once again achieved through the use of broad terminology, thus yielding the flexibility that sovereigns love to retain.

CONTINENTAL SHELF

Historical Development   The United States devised a novel approach for protecting its natural resources: It claimed a right to control the resources over its CS. In 1946, President Truman unilaterally announced a "fishing conservation zone" beyond what was then a 3-mile territorial sea. The United States claimed limited jurisdiction over the CS adjacent to its coasts, a distance extending approximately 200 nautical miles from both coasts.

President Truman did not thereby claim exclusive sovereignty in this area of the high seas. He expanded coastal sovereignty for the limited purpose of controlling economic activity in the waters over the CS. Other nations retained the right to pass freely through the high seas over these shelves. They could not fish there, however, without observing new US coastal fishing regulations. This Continental Shelf Doctrine was later adopted by some other nations and was the central theme of the 1958 United Nations Convention on the Continental Shelf (CS).[58]

Many States have a CS that differs drastically from that of the United States. Chile, Ecuador, and Peru, for example, have shelves extending out to only a few miles from their coastlines. Their shelves then drop off to great depths. They took a more direct approach to preserving adjacent economic resources in the high seas. In 1952, these States claimed a 200-mile-wide territorial sea. Unlike the United States, they claimed *exclusive* territorial sovereignty in this extended area adjacent to their coasts—which unlike the United States, had no large CS.

They perceived little difference between their claim of exclusivity, and the US claim of more limited sovereignty over its respective CSs.

UNCLOS Treatment   Article 76 of the 1982 Law of the Sea treaty defines the CS as the coastal State's "seabed and subsoil of the submarine areas that extend beyond its territorial sea throughout the natural extension of its land territory. . . ." The range of the CS may vary from [a minimum of] 200 nautical miles from the coastal baseline to 350 nautical miles, depending on the natural extension of the coastal State's underwater landmass—which often drops off to great depths relatively close to many coastlines. The CS depicted in Exhibit 6.1 naturally slopes off, as is the case with countries like the United States, where there is no sudden drop. There is no CS to speak of off coastal States such as Chile, Ecuador, and Peru.

What happens when two or more coastal States share the same CS? What are their respective rights regarding the use of their shared CS? The ICJ addressed this matter in its 1969 North Sea Continental Shelf case decision. Germany, Denmark, and the Netherlands disputed the respective CS delimitations in the North Sea on each of their coasts. The Court stated that there was no obligatory method of delimitation. However, the delimitation was to be arranged "by agreement in accordance with equitable principles . . . in such a way as to leave as much as possible to each party all those parts of the continental shelf that constitute a natural prolongation of its land territory into and under the sea, without encroachment on the natural prolongation of the land territory of the other[s]. . . ."[59]

The 1982 UNCLOS essentially codified the North Sea Continental Shelf Cases decision in Article 83.1. States with opposite or adjacent coasts must thereunder enter into an "agreement on the basis of international law." Unfortunately, this is merely an agreement to agree, although typical of multilateral conventions, and interpretive judicial decisions, where consensus is achieved by the use of question-begging language with which no State could disagree.

DEEP SEABED

Historical Regime   Exploitation of marine life was only the first of two major reasons for international interest in extending national sovereignty into the high seas. The second reason was control of mineral exploitation in the seabed, just beyond the territorial sea and CZ. After World War II, the technology for deep seabed mining advanced quickly. Valuable ore deposits beyond the territorial sea became increasingly accessible and were extracted on a first-come, first-served basis. The coastal State could exercise exclusive sovereignty in the territorial sea, limited sovereignty in the CZ, but no further control in the high seas. Under International Law, the high seas beyond these zones were *res communis*—belonging to no one, and thus accessible by all. Many coastal States could not obtain, nor could they prevent other States from extracting, the mineral resources under these waters just beyond their sovereign control.

In 1970, the UN General Assembly proposed another ocean regime designated the "Common Heritage of Mankind" (CHM). In Resolution 2749, the Assembly attempted to institutionalize the CHM in areas beyond national jurisdiction. Management, exploitation, and distribution of the resources of the ocean area beyond the national control of the coastal States should be governed by the international community rather than by the predilections of the more technologically advanced States and their multinational corporations. To this end, the UN General Assembly called for the convening of a new law of the sea conference that would reflect this change in attitude; and, to draft articles for consideration by the international community.[60]

UNCLOS Provisions   The work of the ensuing conference produced the most drastic revision of the historical conception of "freedom of the seas." The 1982 Law of the Sea Treaty provisions on resources in the deep seabed, Part XI (Articles 136–153), address what is called the "Area." These provisions delayed the treaty's entry into force for more a decade. Developed nations had been profitably mining the oceans under the high seas for decades before promulgation of the 1982 UNCLOS.

Article 1 of the UNCLOS defines the "Area" as the ocean floor and its subsoil "beyond the limits of national jurisdiction." Article 136 provides that the "Area and its resources are the common heritage of all mankind." This is the area under the oceans that does not otherwise fall within any of the zones described earlier in this section of the book. There are valuable minerals located in the high seas, or the area beyond the territorial seas and the CZ and EEZ.

While no State may exercise its exclusive or limited jurisdiction within "the Area," a treaty-based organization called the International Seabed Authority (ISA, or "the Authority") would materialize. It was designed to control virtually all aspects of deep seabed mining in the Area. Article 137.2 of the UNCLOS contained a feature which drew harsh objections from the major maritime powers: "All rights in the resources of the Area are vested in mankind as a whole, on whose behalf the [International Seabed] Authority shall act. These rights are not subject to alienation [sale or licensing by a national authority]. The minerals recovered from the Area, however, may only be alienated in accordance with this Part [XI] and the rules, regulations and procedures of the Authority."

Under the 1982 Convention, the ISA consists of all national participants in the UNCLOS. It is based in Jamaica and funded by assessed contributions from UN members. The ISA is expected to organize and control all economic activities in the Area. Mineral resources within it are *beyond* national jurisdiction (outside of the EEZ of 200 miles), and thus *within* the Authority's control.

The ISA commenced operations in 1996. It is one of the three new international institutions, including the previously discussed LOS Tribunal in Germany, created upon the entry into force of the UN Convention on the Law of the Sea. As an autonomous but UN-related organization, the ISA is responsible for organizing, monitoring, and controlling specific issues covered in Part XI of the Convention. Part XI of the treaty focuses on activities such as mining on the international seabed beyond the limits of national jurisdiction of coastal States.

ISA activities include the following:

reviewing work plans for seabed exploration and exploitation—particularly in the area of solid, liquid or gaseous mineral resources

monitoring compliance with the rules, regulations and procedures for seabed exploration and exploitation

promoting and monitoring scientific research, data collection and the development of sustainable marine technology

and developing recommendations on mining standards for the protection and preservation of the marine environment[61]

These tasks are assigned to the "Authority." It thus operates the "Enterprise," the mineral exploration, and the exploitation organ of the ISA. Under the LOS treaty, the Enterprise monitors the commercial production of all mineral resources in the Area. The revenues derived from the Enterprise will be the royalty payments or profit shares of national or individual miners who extract minerals from seabeds in the area. The collection of these revenues and potential transfer of mining technology to the Authority's Enterprise are designed to circumvent what some 1982 Law of the Sea Conference delegates characterized as the monopolistic behavior of the larger developed nations. A small group within the community of nations possesses the requisite technology for mining these deep seabed resources.

Under UNCLOS Article 150g, however, the Enterprise is tasked with the responsibility to ensure the "enhancement of opportunities for all . . . irrespective of their social and economic systems or geographical location, to participate in the development of the resources of the Area and the prevention of monopolization of activities in the Area."

Agreement on Implementation of Part XI In 1994, the then US Secretary of State, Warren Christopher announced the US intent to sign the 1982 UNCLOS. The United States realized that the UNCLOS would soon enter into force in November 1994, because the minimum number of ratifications (sixty) had already been deposited with the United Nations. This realization was a motivating factor for the July 1994 United States "signing" (but not ratifying) this treaty (see §8.2 for distinction). The US Senate has not voted on whether to ratify the UNCLOS, because the former Chair of the Senate Foreign Relations Committee would not conduct hearings on this issue.

While treaty ratification stalled in the US Senate, executive-branch support is rooted in the successful negotiation of a separate agreement entitled the "Agreement Relating to Implementation of Part XI of the United Nations Convention on the Law of the Sea." Former Secretary of State Christopher lamented that the original UNCLOS Part XI provisions are "seriously flawed." Yet "it is imperative from the standpoint of our security and economic interests that the United States become a [ratifying] party to this Convention. . . . Its strategic importance cannot be overstated. . . . The result is a regime that is consistent with our free market principles and provides the United States with influence over decisions on deep seabed mining commensurate with our interests." He thus expressed the US intent to become a party to the UNCLOS if it can simultaneously ratify the two agreements (i.e., the 1982 Treaty and the special 1994 Agreement adopted by the UN General Assembly in 1994) as if they were a single instrument.[62]

The July 1994 Special Agreement, approved by the General Assembly, restructured Part XI of the 1982 Treaty as a compromise designed to achieve more universal participation in a global law of the sea. The major maritime powers were reluctant to ratify Part XI as approved in the original treaty text of 1982. The 1994 Report of the Section of International Law and Practice of the American Bar Association recommended that the US sign (and ratify) the 1982 UNCLOS, because of "new threats to United States security posed by the end of the Cold War and by the rise of new nations and regional powers [make] . . . it important to seek long-term stability of rules related to the oceans."

The original treaty text suggests the creation of a new form of cartel—the Enterprise. This entity would be responsible for the mandated sharing of technology, the degree of production control and pricing, and an infrastructure not unlike that of the Organization of Petroleum Exporting Countries, which is responsible for worldwide price increases and production quotas—hardly a free market enterprise. As stated in the Congressional Record, the objections of industrialized States to Part XI of the 1982 treaty included that "it established a structure for administering the seabed mining regime that did not accord industrialized States influence in the regime commensurate with their interests; [and] it incorporated economic principles inconsistent with free market philosophy. . . ."[63]

The special 1994 Agreement removes a number of such objections to the deep seabed mining provisions, articulated by the major industrialized powers. It removes objections to deep seabed mining resource allocation, which had excluded the input of the major powers within the ISA. It negates mandatory technology transfer; production limitations; more onerous financial obligations for the private enterprises of the economically powerful mining nations; and a subsidized international entity (the enterprise), which could otherwise compete unfairly with existing commercial enterprises. The essential objective of the fresh agreement was to retain a free market-oriented regime, whereby the major powers have flourished since World War II.

The 1994 Agreement specifically permits an industrialized nation to veto the financial or budgetary decisions of the ISA. This agency could otherwise decide to

use revenues derived from the Enterprise to fund some national liberation movement, which is not in harmony with that nation's political interests. Under the 1994 Special Agreement, the mandatory technology transfer provisions are supplanted by more cooperative arrangements, such as joint ventures involving procurement on the open market. The Enterprise will not have to be financed by the developed States only. There is also a "grandfathering" provision which allows mining contracts, which were already licensed under national law, to continue on the same favorable terms as those previously granted by the Authority to French, Japanese, Indian, and Chinese companies whose mine site claims were already registered. To meet yet another objection to the wording of the Part XI provisions of the UNCLOS, certain financial obligations imposed on mining nations, at the exploration stage, were eliminated under the special 1994 Agreement.

For those nations that are already parties to the 1982 LOS Convention, there is no specific time frame for either the Enterprise's commencement of mineral production; nor for the Authority's equitable distribution of Enterprise-generated revenues. Upon ratification by a sufficient number of nations, however, the Authority began its every-five-year review of progress made toward these production and distribution goals. There will be another international review conference 15 years after the Authority begins its commercial production of minerals in the Area. That conference will monitor the Authority's progress toward exploration, exploitation, conservation, and distribution of the resources from the ocean areas beyond national control.

PROGNOSIS

Individual conference participants in the drafting of the 1982 Treaty have provided mixed reviews about its achievements. Tommy Koh, Singapore's ambassador to the United Nations and President of the Conference, described the Area and Authority provisions as a success. In his view, the delegates reconciled the competing interests of many diverse groups of nations. Per his positive assessment:

[T]he international community as a whole wished to promote the development of the seabed's resources as did those members of the international community which consume the metals extracted from the . . . nodules [in the ocean's floor]. The developing countries, as co-owners of the resource, wanted to share in the benefits of the exploitation of the resources and to participate in the exploitation. . . . A seabed miner will have to pay to the International Seabed Authority either a royalty payment or a combination of a royalty payment and a share of his profits. . . . Under the Convention, a seabed miner may be required . . . to sell his technology to the Authority. This obligation has caused great concern to the industrialised countries. It should be borne in mind, however, that the obligation [to transfer technology] cannot be invoked by the Authority unless the same or equivalent technology is unavailable in the open market. A contract study by the US Department of the Interior indicates that there is a relatively large number of suppliers of ocean mining system components and design construction services. If this is true, then the precondition [requiring technology transfer to the Authority] cannot be met and the obligation can never be invoked.[64]

The perspective of Arvid Pardo, Malta's Ambassador to the UN Conference on the Law of the Sea, was not as rosy as that of Ambassador Koh's. Per Ambassador Pardo's contrasting perspective:

[T]he Convention reflects primarily the highly acquisitive aspirations of many coastal States, particularly of those developed and developing States with long coastlines fronting on the open ocean and of mid-ocean archipelagic States. Perhaps as much as forty percent of ocean space, by far the most valuable in terms of economic uses and accessible resources, is placed under some form of national control [by adoption of the exclusive economic zone]. . . . Additionally, elaborate provision is made for [the Authority's] international management of the mineral resources of the seabed beyond national jurisdiction. Nevertheless, the approach of the Convention to problems of marine resource management appears seriously deficient in several respects. . . . [T]he common heritage regime established for the international seabed is a little short of disaster. The . . . competence of the Authority is limited strictly to the exploration and exploitation of mineral resources; the decision-making procedures . . . ranging, according to the nature of the question, from a two-thirds majority to a consensus, are such as to render unlikely appropriate

and timely decisions on important questions. . . . Thus, there arises the unpleasant prospect of the establishment of new and expensive international organizations incapable of effectively performing the functions for which they were created. . . . It is a pity that this side of the Convention has not been developed in a practical way. Instead a truly historic opportunity to mold the legal framework governing human activities in the marine environment in such a way as to contribute effectively to the realization of a just and equitable international order in the seas . . . has been lost.[65]

The ambitious provisions of the UNCLOS have not all been implemented. But the following events are all very positive developments, ranking it among the most successful multilateral treaties in history: ratification by 149 nations (and signature by some dozen others); UN General Assembly's acceptance of a renegotiated Part XI on deep seabed mining; establishment and functioning of a Law of the Sea Tribunal; and the convention's regime for compulsory dispute resolution.

◆ 6.4 AIRSPACE ZONES

This section of the chapter identifies the various air zones, and the degree to which State authority may be exercised in those zones. It analyzes State's rights and obligations:

(1) In national airspace
(2) In that of other States
(3) Over international waters belonging to no one
(4) In outer space

DOMESTIC AIRSPACE

Few branches of International Law developed as rapidly as International Air Law. Prior to World War I, there were no norms to govern international flight. The military use of aircraft quickly filled this vacuum. Hostile aircraft could approach more swiftly than approaching armies or warships. Rapid advancements in the technology of air travel profoundly accelerated the need to establish norms to control national airspace. Almost immediately, States claimed the right to include airspace within the definition of their "territory."

State practice quickly reflected the impact of air travel on international trade. A 1942 commentary in the

American Journal of International Law addressed the significance of commercial air travel for internal security and foreign competition:

> The unprecedentedly accelerated speed of change in the last thirty years has been such that, politically, air navigation has already passed through many of the phases which it took sea navigation centuries to span.
>
> As to air navigation, it may be observed that in 1910, the states were preoccupied only with guaranteeing the safety of their territory; the necessity of permitting other states to navigate freely to and over their territory was recognized to the fullest extent where this freedom did not affect the security of the state. The period 1910–1919 can thus be compared with that period in the history of shipping in which the adjacent seas were appropriated primarily to secure the land from invasion.
>
> In 1919, the first consideration was still the security of the states, but . . . some small clouds were already appearing on the horizon of the free sky. In the minds of some . . . the idea took shape to use the power of the state over the air to protect its own air navigation against foreign competition. As in shipping, the pretensions to the appropriation of the sea and the power to restrict foreign sea commerce grew in proportion to the increase in the direct profits to be expected from them, so in aviation the pretensions to unrestricted sovereignty—not in doctrine but in practice—grew in proportion to the development of aviation during the period from 1919 to 1929.[66]

National legislation imposed various limitations on international air travel. It prohibited the unauthorized entry of aircraft. These laws restricted freedom of navigation, types of importable cargo, and conditions of passenger travel. States soon recognized the need to enter into international treaties for the purposes of establishing mutual expectations and facilitating international trade.

Paris Convention The vertical extension of State sovereignty first appeared in the 1919 Paris Convention Relating to the Regulation of Aerial Navigation. Article 1 provided "that every Power has complete and exclusive sovereignty over the airspace above its territory." Under Article 15, each State party to this treaty could "make conditional on its prior authorisation the establishment

of international airways and the creation and operation of regular international air navigation lines, with or without landing, on its territory."[67] As international commerce grew, the international community needed to solidify its expectations so that there could be a comprehensive air-treaty regime.

1944 Chicago Convention The next multilateral air treaty became the cornerstone of International Air Law: the 1944 Chicago Convention on International Civil Aviation. Most nations of the world are parties to this treaty. Its fundamental provisions are:

Article 1 The contracting States recognize that every State has complete and exclusive sovereignty over the airspace above its territory.

Article 2 For the purposes of this Convention the territory of a State shall be deemed to be the land areas and territorial waters adjacent thereto under the sovereignty . . . of such State.

. . .

Article 5 Each contracting State agrees that all aircraft of the other contracting States, being aircraft not engaged in scheduled international air services, shall have the right . . . to make flights into or in transit non-stop across its territory and to make stops for non-traffic purposes without the necessity of obtaining prior permission, and subject to the right of the State flown over to require landing.

Article 6 No scheduled [commercial] international air service may be operated over or into the territory of a contracting State, except with the special permission or other authorization of that State. . . .

These provisions codify the sovereign right to completely exclude air travel through the airspace above the State's landmass and above the territorial waters adjacent to its coastlines. France, for example, legally denied US President Ronald Reagan's request that US military aircraft fly over France during a 1986 retaliatory bombing mission in Libya. US warplanes were required to fly a circuitous route *around* France's territorial airspace. They proceeded on a much longer route, through the Straits of Gibraltar, in order to gain access to Libya via the western entrance to the Mediterranean Sea.

In most instances, States encourage *commercial* flights through their airspace in order to maintain economic ties with other States. The Chicago Convention governs both the nonscheduled flights of private aircraft and the scheduled flights of commercial passenger and cargo air services. The key articles, their intended applications, and the essential provisions on military and other state aircraft are abstracted later.

Private Aircraft Noncommercial private aircraft enjoy the general right to fly into or over state territory (Article 5 above). They may land for refueling and other purposes without prior permission. An English citizen may land to refuel his plane at a French airport while en route to Germany. That pilot must, however, file a flight plan at the flight's point of origin. France may require an alteration of that flight plan, if the intended flight path interferes with any French regulation or security concerns. State practice is more restrictive in the case of commercial aircraft (Article 6 above). They may not fly over or land in the territory of another country without advance routing or landing arrangements. Otherwise, the impacted State may undertake necessary measures to divert an intruding aircraft or require it to land.

Commercial Aircraft The International Civil Aviation Organization (ICAO) regulates international commercial aviation. Established by the State parties to the Chicago Convention, this international organization schedules air routes, cargo delivery, and passenger service. Under Article 44 of the Chicago Treaty, the ICAO promotes "the safe and orderly growth of international civil aviation throughout the world . . . [by] development of airways, airports, and air navigation facilities . . . [and avoidance of] economic waste caused by unreasonable competition."

The organization's member States are encouraged to use a neutral tribunal to resolve disputes involving the ICAO's administrative decisions. Article 84 provides that States may appeal such decisions "to an *ad hoc* arbitral tribunal agreed upon with the other parties to the dispute or to the Permanent Court of International Justice."[68] In 1989, the ICJ reviewed an ICAO decision whereby the United States was not legally responsible when one of its naval vessels shot down an Iranian commercial aircraft over the Persian Gulf. Iran filed a suit, asking the court to declare the ICAO's decision erroneous. The parties ultimately dismissed this suit in 1994 after a number of delays in its pleading phase.

The 1944 Chicago Convention did not resolve many of the problems associated with the scheduling of air services. The commercial airlines of the world formed a private organization called the International Air Transport Association (IATA), which has focused its work on achieving the Chicago Convention goal of avoiding "unreasonable competition." The IATA is essentially a cartel of private airlines attempting to avoid destructive or excessive competition among international airlines—an unusually competitive business. The IATA, for example, ensures that flights by competing airlines do not leave the same airport at the same time. Such competition would ultimately destroy one or more of the competitors.

In a related development, "Open Skies Agreements" create a free market for aviation services and provide substantial benefits for travelers, shippers, and communities as well as for the economy of each country. These agreements give the airlines of two or more countries the right to operate air services from any point in one country to any point in the other, as well as to and from third countries. These rights enable airlines to network by using strategic points across the globe. In November 2000, for example, Brunei, Chile, New Zealand, Singapore, and the United States concluded the Multilateral Agreement on the Liberalization of International Air Transportation to replace the bilateral agreements between them.

Some airlines have claimed that there is, in fact, a great deal of anticompetitive activity in international aviation. In 1983, Laker Airways of England filed lawsuits in Great Britain and the United States, claiming that various Belgian, British, and Dutch airlines (IATA members) conspired to bankrupt Laker Airways because it offered very competitive airfares to the public. Members of the IATA allegedly perceived Laker's operations as a threat to the price structure established by their association. Plaintiff Laker claimed that the IATA airlines "agreed to set rates at a predatory level to drive Laker out of business." Laker also alleged that these international air carriers conspired to stop Laker from expanding its international air routes.[69]

Restrictive business practices in the international airlines industry are not limited to just private airline carriers. Many governments subsidize their government-owned or certain private international airlines, a practice facilitating continuing operation and increasing their share of the international market. These subsidies permit the favored airlines to charge lower fares or operate at a better profit margin, even when they charge the same or lower fares than their competitors. Subsidizing countries thereby create artificial economic barriers to normal market competition. They impose limitations on certain categories of importable cargo and on frequency of passenger aircraft entry into their airspaces. (Similar barriers to international competition are addressed in Chapter 13.) In 1998, a European Union court thus annulled France's 1994 plan to provide 20 billion francs—about US $3.3 billion—to Air France.

The nations of the world recognized the need for an orderly disposition of claims against international air carriers, not long after the advent of commercial aviation. The 1929 Warsaw Convention thus applies "to all international transportation of persons, baggage or goods performed by aircraft for hire."[70] The purpose of this constitution of the airways is to unify International Air Law, whereby any conflicting national laws of the State parties are supplanted by a treaty agreement. As noted in an annotated handbook on this convention, it "seeks to limit international air carriers' potential liability in case of accidents, facilitate speedy recoveries by passengers, [and] unify laws in treaty countries. . . ."[71]

State Aircraft Public (as opposed to private) aircraft are operated by the military, customs, and police authorities. These flights are not generally governed by the 1944 Chicago Convention, although it does make certain limited provisions for such aircraft. Under Article 3:

(a) This convention shall be applicable only to civil aircraft, and shall not be applicable to state aircraft.

(b) Aircraft used in military, customs and police services shall be deemed to be State aircraft. [However,]

(c) No state aircraft . . . shall fly over the territory of another State or land thereon without authorization by special agreement.

Unlike nonscheduled private aircraft, government aircraft cannot enter another State's national airspace without its express prior consent. These agreements are often made on a case-by-case basis and otherwise by treaty arrangements between friendly countries. Before making an emergency landing in another State, a military pilot must seek permission to enter that State's airspace (and to land). This requirement prevents one State from sending its planes on a hostile mission under the pretext of a feigned emergency. Military flight agreements, such as those governing a State aircraft's entry into foreign airspace during joint military exercises, are normally made by formal agreements between affected States.

There are many gaps in treaty coverage, however. China claims a right to prohibit aerial surveillance over the South China Sea, in an area well beyond its 12-mile territorial sea. The United States has occasionally claimed special "defensive sea areas," extending beyond its territorial sea—in time of war or declared national emergency. Article 3(c) of the Chicago Convention came into play when a US reconnaissance aircraft flew over international waters, about 50 miles southeast of China's Hainan Island in April 2000. It collided with a Chinese jet fighter, which had been tracking its movements. Chinese authorities proclaimed that the US aircraft swerved and hit the Chinese jet. American authorities claimed that the Chinese jets that track the movements of US surveillance planes fly too close to them for safe aerial operations. The Chinese pilot was allegedly at fault.

The pilot of the US aircraft did not obtain verbal permission for the emergency landing in China. The Chicago Convention is not designed for noncommercial State aircraft. However, Article 3(c) provides that state aircraft may not overfly the territory of another State, and may not land without authorization by special agreement. Although the US plane landed on Chinese territory without verbal clearance, it did so under distress. There is no express exception to Article 3(c) for State aircraft in distress. Customary International Law recognizes that ships at sea have a right to enter another nation's ports when in distress. A similar right arguably applies to aircraft in distress, including state aircraft. Article 25, which does not apply to noncommercial state aircraft like the ones in this instance, provides that "Each contracting State undertakes to provide such measures of assistance to aircraft in distress as it may find practicable. . . ."[72]

The following case is a classic illustration of the tension associated with the presence of foreign State aircraft flying directly over another State's territory, even for a plane with no weapons systems. It further illustrates that more than one State can violate International Law, when a single plane makes an unauthorized entry into another nation's airspace:

Powers Case

UNION OF SOVIET SOCIALIST REPUBLICS
MILITARY COLLEGIUM OF THE SOVIET SUPREME COURT (1960)
30 INTERNATIONAL LAW REPORTS 69 (1966)

AUTHOR'S NOTE: In 1960, the US authorized the flight of a U-2 military aircraft over the former Soviet Union. The U-2 is a reconnaissance plane with no weapons capability. After the U-2 was shot down, the Soviet Union prosecuted the US pilot for espionage. The following excerpts are from the military panel of the Soviet Supreme Court.

COURT'S OPINION: On May 1, 1960, at 5 hours 36 minutes, Moscow time, a military unit of the Soviet anti-aircraft defence in the area of the city of Kirovabad, the Tajik S.S.R., at an altitude of 20,000 metres, unattainable for planes of the civil air fleet, spotted an unknown aircraft violating the State frontier of the USSR.

The military units of the Soviet anti-aircraft defence vigilantly followed the behaviour of the plane as it flew over major industrial centres and important objectives, and only when the intruder plane had penetrated 2,000 kilometres into Soviet territory and the evil purpose of the flight, fraught with disastrous consequences for world peace in an age of thermonuclear weapons, became absolutely obvious, a battery of ground-to-air missiles brought the aggressor plane down in the area of Sverdlovsk at 8 hours 53 minutes as ordered by the Soviet Government.

The pilot of the plane bailed out and was apprehended upon landing. On interrogation, he gave his name as Francis Gary Powers, citizen of the United States of America. Examination of the wreckage of the plane which had been brought down showed that it was of American make, specially designed for high-altitude flights and fitted with various equipment for espionage reconnaissance tasks.

In April 1956, Powers was recruited by the Central Intelligence Agency of the United States for special intelligence missions in high-altitude aircraft.

After he had concluded a secret contract with the United States Central Intelligence Agency for a term of two years, Powers was allotted a high salary of 2,500 dollars a month for espionage activity. He underwent special training and was assigned to the intelligence air detachment under the code name of "Ten-Ten," stationed at the American-Turkish war base of Incirlik, near the town of Adana, in Turkey.

The Court has established that the detachment "Ten-Ten" is a special combination of the United States military and civilian intelligence designed for espionage against the Soviet Union with the help of reconnaissance planes sent into Soviet airspace. . . .

Having taken off from Peshawar airport in Pakistan, Powers flew over the territory of Afghanistan and for more than 2,000 kilometers over the Soviet Union in accordance with the established course. Besides Powers' testimony, this is confirmed by the American flight map discovered in the debris of the U-2 plane and submitted to the Court, bearing the route plotted out by Major Dulak, navigator of the detachment "Ten-Ten," and also notes and signs made by Powers, who marked down on this map several important defence objectives of the Soviet Union he had spotted from the plane.

Throughout the flight, to the very moment the plane was shot down, Powers switched on his special intelligence equipment, photographed important defence objectives and recorded signals of the country's anti-aircraft radar installations. The development of the rescued aerial photography films established that defendant Powers photographed from the U-2 plane industrial and military objectives of the Soviet Union—plants, depots, oil storage facilities, communication routes, railway bridges and stations, electric transmission lines, aerodromes, the location of troops and military equipment.

The numerous photos of the Soviet Union's territory, taken by defendant Powers from an altitude of 20,000 metres, in possession of the Military Collegium of the USSR Supreme Court, make it possible to determine the nature of industrial establishments, the design of railway bridges, the number and type of aircraft on the airfields, the nature and purpose of military material.

Powers tape-recorded impulses of certain radar stations of the Soviet Union with a view of detecting the country's anti-aircraft defence system.

Powers himself admitted that he realized when intruding into the airspace of the Soviet Union that he was violating the national sovereignty of the USSR and flying over its territory on an espionage mission, whose main purpose consisted of detecting and marking down missile launching sites. . . .

In considering the Powers case, the Military Collegium of the USSR Supreme Court takes into account that the intrusion of the American military intelligence plane constitutes a criminal breach of a generally recognized principle of international law, which establishes the exclusive sovereignty of every State over the airspace above its territory. This principle, laid down by the Paris Convention of October 13, 1919, for the regulation of aerial navigation, and several other subsequent international agreements, is proclaimed in the national legislations of different States, including the Soviet Union and the United States of America.

Violation of this sacred and immutable principle of international relations creates in the present conditions a direct menace to universal peace and international security.

At the present level of military technology, when certain States possess atomic and hydrogen weapons, as well as the means of delivering them quickly to targets, the flight of a military intelligence plane over Soviet territory could have directly preceded a military attack. This danger is the more possible in conditions when the United States of America, as stated by American generals, constantly keeps bomber patrols in the air, always ready to drop bombs on earlier marked-out targets of the Soviet Union.

Under these conditions the aggressive act of the United States of America, carried out on May 1 of this year by defendant Powers, created a threat to universal peace. . . .

After that the American leaders—President Eisenhower, Vice-President Nixon and State Secretary Herter—admitted that spying flights over Soviet territory by American planes constitute part of the "calculated policy of the United States of America."

Thus, the leaders of the United States of America proclaimed the violation of the sovereignty of other States and espionage against them as the official State policy of America. . . .

The Military Collegium of the Supreme Court of the Soviet Union has established that Powers could not have carried out the spy missions assigned to him without the use of the United States of America, for aggressive purposes, of the war bases and aerodromes on the territories of the States neighboring on the Soviet Union, including the territories of Turkey, Iran, Pakistan and Norway.

Powers' flight has proved that the Government of the United States of America, having bound Turkey, Iran, Pakistan, Norway and other States by bilateral military agreements, has established war bases and aerodromes on their territories for dangerous provocative actions, making these States accomplices in the aggression against the Soviet Union.

◆ *Notes & Questions*

1. Did the United States violate Soviet airspace? If so, did any other nation incur State responsibility for breaching International Air Law?
2. Was the Soviet Union being overly technical about the threat posed by this unarmed plane with no military capability?

There are a number of unresolved problems in International Air Law. Two of them are particularly sensitive. States have not agreed on the permissible degree of response to violations of national airspace, or the altitude that constitutes the upper limits of their territorial airspace. The upper limit is important, because it separates national airspace from outer space—the latter being *res communis,* and thus available to all nations.

Excessive Force How much force may a State use to repel intruders? A number of military planes have purposefully or accidentally entered foreign airspace. A number of commercial aircraft have also encroached on territorial airspace. In some parts of the world, these unexpected intrusions are routinely ignored. In some cases, however, the intruder has been ordered to change course, escorted out of the offended State's territorial airspace, fired on as a warning, forced to land, or actually shot down.

In the decade after World War II, deadly force was employed in many incidents involving nonmilitary aerial intrusions into national airspace. In the major international incident of 1955, an Israeli commercial plane flew into Bulgarian airspace while en route from Austria to Israel. A Bulgarian military aircraft shot it down over Bulgaria, killing all fifty-eight passengers. Israel instituted proceedings in the ICJ. The court decided, however, that it could not hear the case because Bulgaria had not consented to the court's jurisdiction to hear such cases.[73] Israel and Bulgaria ultimately negotiated a compensation agreement in 1963.

In 1983, a Korean Air Lines passenger jet, KAL Flight 007, was shot down over the Sea of Japan after it strayed into Soviet airspace. All 269 passengers and crew were killed. The Soviet pilot knew that it was a passenger aircraft. This incident generated a number of diplomatic protests, ICAO deliberations, and several meetings of the United Nations Security Council. It also demonstrated the importance that the former Soviet Union attributed to the presence of any nonscheduled aircraft in its national airspace.

The United States did not institute litigation against the Soviet Union (the ICJ being a likely forum). KAL settled with families of the deceased victims in some 100 civil suits against the airline in the United States. KAL was found liable for the willful misconduct of the crew, which had flown off-course for a number of hours. Suits involving such incidents have reached the US Supreme Court on more than one occasion.[74]

Unfortunately, some States still use deadly force to react to nonmilitary intrusions of their airspace. In September 1999, Ethiopia shot down a private jet flying over Ethiopia while it was en route from Egypt to South Africa, killing the British and Swedish copilots. It was registered to a US company. Ethiopia had declared a "no-fly zone" in the vicinity of the disputed border between Ethiopia and Eritrea. The flight and plan had been approved by both countries.

Upper Limit   The upper limit of territorial airspace has not been precisely established. While the 1944 Chicago Convention is the centerpiece of International Air Law, it does not define the extent or height of national airspace. Different States, with varying political agendas, therefore claim different limits for distinguishing national airspace from outer space. As noted by Robert Goedhart, in his work at the University of Utrecht in the Netherlands: "In spite of extensive discussions, anything but agreement on the said boundary has been arrived at . . . neither at a political level nor at a legal level, for which the tensions and enmity between the main spacefaring nations, the former Soviet Union and the United States, as a consequence of the Cold War are partly to blame."[75]

As a practical matter, territorial airspace is limited to the navigable airspace over State territory and its adjacent territorial seas—12 nautical miles from the coastline under the Law of the Sea Treaty. This is the limit used by most States when they characterize the extent of their territorial airspace. Navigable airspace is the highest altitude attainable by military aircraft not in orbit.

AIRSPACE ABROAD

Although the 1944 Chicago Convention on International Civil Aviation is the fundamental air treaty, other treaties were needed to address issues, which evolved during air travel after World War II. For example, could a State exercise jurisdiction over criminal offenses aboard its own aircraft when it was flying over international waters or in the airspace of another State? The need to expand jurisdiction over crimes aboard civil (nonmilitary) aircraft became apparent as States began to experience prosecutorial limitations because of treaty voids.

A classic instance of this vacuum emerged in 1950 when a US passenger assaulted several US citizens aboard a plane registered under a US airline company while it was flying over international waters. The Chicago Convention vests jurisdiction in the State where an incident occurs. But this event took place beyond national airspace. The American prosecutor resorted to US internal law. Under US law, there had to be a statute that specifically made the passenger's conduct a criminal act. The only relevant statute made it a crime to assault passengers on "vessels" that were "on the high seas." The plane was neither a vessel within the meaning of the only applicable statute nor was it "on" the high seas.[76] The United States was unable to prosecute this individual, however, because of the absence of an applicable national law. The case was dismissed. The defendant was thus released from custody. The US Congress reacted by expanding this statute to include aerial offenses. This incident suggested the need for an international approach. State representatives ultimately negotiated and ratified a series of international treaties to fill such legal gaps.

Tokyo Convention After World War II, the wartime concern about hostile flights appeared to be eclipsed by another problem. Airlines with large fleets of commercial aircraft were understandably concerned about their aircraft being subjected to the exclusive control of foreign nations while operating within foreign airspace. Within two decades after the war ended, members of the airline industry convinced their respective governments to negotiate the first multilateral air treaty containing several jurisdictional alternatives—the 1963 Tokyo Convention on Offences and Certain Other Acts Committed on Board Aircraft. It became effective in 1969 and has been ratified by most nations of the world.[77]

The Tokyo Convention established a framework for punishing individuals who commit violent crimes during international flights. This treaty emphasizes the jurisdiction of the aircraft's State of registration (often called the *flag State*) rather than that of the airspace of the State where the offense is committed. This treaty facilitated prosecution under jurisdictional principles not contemplated by the 1944 Chicago Convention while effectively expanding the range of sovereignty now exercisable in the airspace above distant lands. Because States had the exclusive sovereign power over the airspace above them (Chicago Convention), they had the correlative right to yield this total control of their airspace for mutually acceptable purposes. Under Article 3 of the Tokyo Convention, the "State of registration of the aircraft is competent to exercise jurisdiction over offences and acts committed on board [and each participating State] shall take such measures as may be necessary to establish its jurisdiction as the State of registration over offences committed on board aircraft registered in such State."

Under Article 4 of the Tokyo Convention, a State that is not the State of registration cannot interfere on the basis that its territorial criminal jurisdiction also applies in its own airspace—except in the following specific cases (see §5.2 on extraterritorial jurisdiction):

(a) The offense has an effect on the territory of such State (territorial principle).

(b) The offense has been committed by or against a national or permanent resident of such State (nationality and passive personality principles).

(c) The offense is against the security of such State (protective principle).

Assume that a Japanese airliner is flying in an easterly direction 25,000 feet over Hawaii en route to Canada. A German passenger assaults and kills a French citizen during the flight. All of these countries are parties to both the Chicago and the Tokyo conventions. Under the territorial principle of international criminal jurisdiction, the incident occurred "in" the United States because the Japanese aircraft was flying within the navigable airspace of a state of the United States. Under the 1944 Chicago Convention, the United States has "complete and exclusive sovereignty over the airspace above its territory." Japan is the State of registration (*i.e.,* the flag State). Under Article 3 of the 1963 Tokyo Convention, Japan would be "competent to exercise jurisdiction over offences and acts committed on board [its airliner and should] take such measures as may be necessary to establish its jurisdiction." Since the United States is a party to the Tokyo Convention, it will yield its territorial right to Japan to prosecute the German passenger. Japan will be obliged to prosecute this German citizen for the offense aboard the Japanese aircraft (unless it accedes to a United States request to have the perpetrator tried in the United States).

Under Article 4 of the Tokyo Convention, States other than the State of registration should not interfere by exercising their criminal jurisdiction over the offender. While the United States has territorial jurisdiction over the German passenger, it should assist Japan in the latter's efforts to prosecute him. If the plane lands in Hawaii, the United States should grant Japan's extradition request.

There are significant exceptions to the treaty norm of ceding jurisdiction to the State of registration. Other States may prosecute the German citizen in four situations. First, another State may prosecute him if his crime has an effect on its territory. This exception draws from the "effects doctrine" established by the PCIJ in the *SS Lotus Case* in 1927 (§5.2). The Tokyo Convention thus provides for applications of the territorial principle of international criminal jurisdiction. If the captain of the Japanese airliner has to alter course or altitude to respond to the incident, that action might violate navigational rules established for the safety of aircraft. The United States could then request the plane to land and prosecute the German for various crimes against the United States—over Japan's objection. This is an example of the territorial principle of jurisdiction, which remains available under the terms of the Tokyo Convention.

The second and third bases for States other than Japan (the State of the aircraft's registration) to exercise jurisdiction over the German citizen employ the nationality and passive personality principles of criminal jurisdiction. Germany and France may prosecute the German passenger under Article 4b of the above Convention: The "offense has been committed by or against a national or permanent resident of such State [that is a treaty party]." Germany may prosecute its national under the nationality principle; and France may prosecute the German passenger for killing a French citizen, under the passive personality principle.

The fourth exception to Japan's primary jurisdiction as the flag State involves the protective principle of jurisdiction. The German passenger may be prosecuted outside of Japan if this "offense is against the security" of some other State. It is unlikely that the United States would actually claim that its security was threatened by the killing of the French citizen or, alternatively, by the unusual maneuvers of the Japanese aircraft over Hawaii. Suppose, however, that the French citizen was working for the US Central Intelligence Agency and was carrying sensitive documents, which the German stole and was the reason for the murder aboard the aircraft. US security interests might support the exercise of US jurisdiction, under the "security exception" to Japan's primary jurisdiction over its aircraft.

These additional jurisdictional bases for extending the range of State sovereignty have invoked all the typical rationales for international criminal jurisdiction except for one—the universality principle. The Hague Convention (discussed below) was required because the Tokyo Convention was not intended to cover such interferences with civil aviation. The Tokyo Convention paid lip service to primary jurisdiction of the State of registration, while at the same time retaining all of the criminal jurisdictional principles. These were employed as express exceptions to the rule that the flag State would have the initial option to prosecute criminal conduct occurring aboard its aircraft operating over another State and international waters.[78]

Hague Convention The 1970 Hague Convention for the Suppression of Unlawful Seizure of Aircraft added another jurisdictional alternative for prosecuting crimes on international flights. The universality principle provides that certain crimes are sufficiently heinous to be considered crimes against all States. Every State would thus have the jurisdiction to capture and punish or to extradite the perpetrator of such crimes (§5.2). The Hague Convention extends the universality principle of jurisdiction to aircraft hijacks.

The treaty's fundamental theme is that all States must take the necessary steps to prosecute or extradite those who unlawfully seize commercial aircraft. This treaty is a direct response to the rash of international hijacks that began in the late 1960s. Too many nations clandestinely supported the political goals underlying those hijacks, seeking to publicize the political problems of the Middle East. These nations characterized brutal crimes aboard hijacked aircraft as "political conduct" rather than extraditable common crimes (§5.3). They granted asylum to, or did not otherwise prosecute, the responsible hijackers. Consequently, there was a growing international desire to deny such asylum to those involved in what was otherwise a "universal" crime. The 1970 Hague Convention neither addresses nor precludes this practice. Under the 1976 European Convention on the Suppression of Terrorism, however, offenses governed by the 1970 Hague Convention cannot be characterized as "political" offenses. This European treaty applies to only a handful of nations, however, that are parties to the Hague Convention.[79]

The Hague Convention was nevertheless the first *multilateral* step toward establishing air hijacking as a universal crime. More than 140 nations are parties to this treaty. It permits the exercise of jurisdiction over international flights by States other than the State of registration. Under Article 4 of the Hague Convention, each "[c]ontracting State shall take such measures as may be necessary to establish its jurisdiction over the offense . . . [and] shall likewise take such measures as may be necessary to establish . . . jurisdiction over the offense in the case where the alleged offender is present in its territory and it does not extradite him. . . ." Article 8 provides that the "offense shall be treated, for the purposes of extradition between Contracting States, as if it had been committed *not only* in the place in which it occurred *but also* in the territories of the States required to establish their jurisdiction in accordance with Article 4" (italics added).

Assume that the hypothetical German terrorist mentioned in this section forcefully takes control of the Japanese airliner over Hawaii. The hijacker causes it to land in Canada to refuel. The plane is then diverted to Libya. That nation does not comply with its treaty obligation to capture and prosecute the hijacker, who has committed a universal crime under the Hague Convention. The terrorist then escapes to Lebanon. All of these nations are parties to the Hague Convention. What States may thereby exercise jurisdiction over the German terrorist under the 1970 Hague Convention? Under Article 4, each State party must take measures to ensure that jurisdiction is somehow established. In this case, Japan could exercise its jurisdiction over the terrorist, but only if Lebanon were convinced to surrender the terrorist to Japan. The latter is the State of registration of the aircraft with "territorial" jurisdiction over events occurring aboard it anywhere in the world.

Under Article 6, any State "in the territory of which the offender or the alleged offender is present shall take him into custody or take other measures to ensure his presence." Canada or Lebanon would have the obligation to exercise jurisdiction in the case of such a "universal" crime. The Hague treaty requires them to take the necessary steps to prosecute or extradite the terrorist—either when the plane landed for refueling in Canada, or when it arrived at the final destination of Libya.

Because neither Canada nor Libya actually captured the hijacker, Lebanon would incur the ultimate obligation of prosecution or extradition under the Hague Convention. Lebanon would be justified in treating the terrorist's act "as if it had been committed not only in the place in which it occurred but also in the territories of the States required to establish their jurisdiction" over this hijacking incident. Lebanon is thereby obligated to capture this terrorist upon arrival in its territory. Mere custody of the terrorist would give Lebanon the right (or obligation) to either try or extradite him to Japan, Canada, or the United States. Parts of the crime occurred in their respective territories.

Unfortunately, certain States have clandestinely supported hijacking incidents while appearing to satisfy their Hague Convention prosecution obligations. Under Article 7, a State that does not extradite a hijacker is "obliged, without exception whatsoever . . . to submit the case to its competent authorities for the purpose of prosecution." States that are sympathetic to the political cause of a particular hijacker, however, have sometimes allowed the terrorist to "escape." Alternatively, they have conducted mock trials for the purpose of concluding that the terrorists were not guilty of

hijacking charges in violation of the Hague Convention. In 1973, for example, an Italian court released the hijackers of an Israeli passenger plane and tried them in absentia. Cyprus released Arab terrorists who attacked an Israeli plane in Cyprus after they were sentenced to imprisonment. These States technically met their treaty obligation to "prosecute" terrorists who seize commercial aircraft.[80]

Montreal Sabotage Convention   The related 1971 Montreal Sabotage Convention similarly establishes universal jurisdiction over those who bomb or sabotage (rather than merely seize) commercial aircraft.[81]

The terrorist bombing of Pan Am Flight 103 over Lockerbie, Scotland in 1988 triggered the criminal liability of the Libyan individuals allegedly responsible for the deaths of 270 passengers. Libya had the responsibility to prosecute these perpetrators, or to turn them over for trial in the United Kingdom or the United States, where they were indicted. UN Security Council Resolution 731 of 1992 determined that Libya must release them for trial. Libya responded with a suit in the ICJ, claiming that the United States and the United Kingdom had themselves breached the Montreal Convention. Libya presented the theory that the United States and the United Kingdom had rejected Libyan efforts to resolve this matter in good faith. Libya claimed that the United States and the United Kingdom allegedly threatened the use of force. It requested that the ICJ issue an order prohibiting those countries from acting in any way that would further threaten peaceful relations. Libya was presumably concerned that, like the 1986 US bombing of Tripoli in response to another terrorist incident, these nations might undertake a military mission to extract the Libyan agents allegedly responsible for the bombing of Pan Am Flight 103.[82]

The Court decided not to grant Libya's request for these measures pending the resolution of this matter between Libya, the United States, and the United Kingdom. The essential stumbling block was that another UN organ, the Security Council (Resolution 731), had already demanded that Libya turn over the terrorists for trial elsewhere. The ICJ did not want to be in the awkward position of rendering an injunction against US-UK action under the existing norm of International Law that prohibits the use of force to resolve disputes. The Court avoided this dilemma by noting that Libya chose instead to base its request for relief on the

Montreal Convention, which does not address reprisals. As described by ICJ Judge Shahabuddeen (Guyana),

> the decision [that] the Court is asked to give [in favor of Libya] is one [that] would directly conflict with a decision of the Security Council. . . . Yet, it is not the jurisdictional ground for today's Order [denying Libya's request that the US and UK not take any action involving the use of force until this case is resolved on its merits]. This [denial] results not from any collision between the competence of the Security Council and that of the Court, but from a collision between the obligations of Libya under the decision of the Security Council and any obligation it may have under the Montreal Convention. The [UN] Charter says that the former [must] prevail.

In 1998, almost six years after Libya instituted this suit, the ICJ finally ruled that it had jurisdiction to hear this case.[83] In so doing, the ICJ acknowledged the potential for conflict between the UN Charter and other international agreements. Libya's claim under the Montreal Convention was that it was competent to investigate its own agents who were in Libya. But the Security Council had ordered Libya to release them for trial elsewhere, given Libya's apparent responsibility for this act of State terrorism. Under Article 25 of the UN Charter, UN members agree to comply with decisions of the Security Council. Under Article 103 of the Charter, the Charter prevails "[i]n the event of a conflict between the obligations of the Members of the United Nations under the present Charter and their obligations under any other international agreement. . . ." Thus, Libya's treaty-based right to investigate and try these individuals was superseded by the Security Council action and the conflict resolution mechanism expressed in Charter Article 103.

Libya finally turned these two men over for trial at The Hague, in part attributable to negotiations involving the potential lifting of sanctions against Libya. The judges are Scottish, Scottish law applies, and sentences will be served in The Netherlands (§9.5).

OUTER SPACE

Introduction   The exploration of outer space began in 1957, when the Soviets launched their Sputnik satellite. This was the first man-made object to orbit the Earth. In 1961, the UN General Assembly resolved that

international "law, including the Charter of the United Nations, applies to outer space and celestial bodies."[84] See Exhibit 6.4.

The following Charter-based principles for peaceably governing activities in the rest of the universe exist, but have yet to be fully defined.

Moon Treaty   The current status of outer space is analogous to the historical maritime concept of *res communis*. The high seas are *res communis*. They cannot be owned. They, therefore, remain open to the peaceful use of all States. Under International Law, space and the planets within it are governed by the same regime. The 1967 UN Treaty on Principles Governing the Activities of States in the Exploration and Use of Outer Space, Including the Moon and Other Celestial Bodies Outer Space Treaty is the *Magna Carta* of outer space. It established mutual State expectations about international relations in outer space. Its essential provisions are as follows:

◆ *Article I:* [the] "exploration and use of outer space . . . shall be carried out for the benefit and in the interests of all countries, irrespective of their degree of economic or scientific development, and shall be the province of all mankind."
◆ *Article II:* "Outer space, including the moon and other celestial bodies, is not subject to national appropriation by claim of sovereignty, by means of use or occupation, or by any other means."
◆ *Article III:* [the] "activities in the exploration and use of outer space . . . [are governed by] international law, including the Charter of the United Nations, in the interest of maintaining international peace and security and promoting international cooperation and understanding."
◆ *Article VIII:* "A State Party to the Treaty on whose registry an object launched into outer space is carried shall retain jurisdiction and control over such object, and over any personnel thereof, while in outer space or on a celestial body. . . ."[85]

International Law thus mandates free access to outer space, the moon, and other celestial bodies. For example, the United States landed on the moon in 1969. Under the 1967 Moon Treaty, it did not thereby acquire any sovereign rights. The Soviet Union was the first to land unmanned spacecraft on the moon,

EXHIBIT 6.4 OUTER SPACE "CHARTER"

1958 UNGA RESOLUTION	UN General Assembly Res. 1348(XIII): Peaceful use of outer space and avoidance of national rivalries in outer space.
1959 UNGA RESOLUTION	Res. 1472(XIV): Freedom of space exploration *and* UN establishes the Committee on the Peaceful Uses of Outer Space
1961 UNGA RESOLUTION	Res. 1721(XIV): Space to be used for benefit of all humankind
1962 UNGA DECLARATION	General Assembly Declaration of Legal Principles Governing the Activities of States in the Exploration and Use of Outer Space: Resolved to conclude a nuclear test ban treaty; did not specifically recognize military use of outer space (3 ILM 157)
1963 TREATY	Treaty Banning Nuclear Weapon Tests in Atmosphere, Outer Space and Under Water: No nuclear explosions are permitted in outer space (2 ILM 883)
1963 UNGA RESOLUTION	Res. 1884(XVIII) Regarding Weapons of Mass Destruction: US and USSR are not to station nuclear or other weapons of mass destruction in outer space (2 ILM 1192)
1967 UNGA TREATY REGIME	Principles Governing the Activities of States in the Exploration and Use of Outer Space, Including the Moon and Other Celestial Bodies Outer Space Treaty: The Magna Carta of outer space regime; no weapons of mass destruction allowed; no military bases or maneuvers in space, although use of military for science; implicit acceptance of conventional weapons (6 ILM 386)
1971 CONVENTION	International Liability for Damage Caused by Space Objects: Launching State liable for damage caused by falling space debris (Liability Convention) (10 ILM 965)
1979 UNGA RESOLUTION	Moon Treaty: Clarifies ambiguities in 1967 Outer Space Treaty; moon subject to same demilitarization regime as other bodies. "Peaceful purposes" remains undefined (18 ILM 1434)
VARIOUS BILATERAL TREATIES	Most prominent are the SALT I and II Agreements between the US and former USSR providing for strategic arms limitations (20 ILM 477; 26 ILM 232)

Note: ILM—International Legal Materials.

Venus, and Mars. But neither nation can thus claim any of these celestial bodies, nor preclude other nations from gaining access to it. The universe may be thus explored for scientific purposes, but not to expand national sovereignty.

The Moon Treaty text purports to demilitarize outer space. Its national signatories "undertake not to place in orbit around the Earth any objects carrying nuclear weapons or any other kinds of weapons of mass destruction, install such weapons on celestial bodies, or station such weapons in outer space in any other manner . . . [because the] moon and other celestial bodies shall be used by all State Parties to the Treaty exclusively for peaceful purposes." The treaty does permit a limited military presence in space. Article IV concurrently provides that the "use of *military* personnel for scientific research or for any other peaceful purposes shall not be prohibited" (emphasis added).

Nuclear Test Ban Treaty The ostensible demilitarization language in the 1967 Outer Space Treaty was drawn in part from the 1963 Nuclear Test Ban Treaty, whose original members were the United Kingdom, the former Soviet Union, and the United States. Most nations of the world are parties to the Nuclear Test Ban Treaty (§10.4). Article I of the Moon Treaty contains a promise that each member "undertakes to prohibit, to prevent, and not to carry out any nuclear weapon test explosion, or any other nuclear explosion, at any place under its jurisdiction or control. . . ."

This language, contained in both the Test Ban Treaty and the Outer Space Treaty, is ambiguous. It was the product of a compromise, to ensure the participation of the then-existing space powers in the Outer Space Treaty. They would not approve a *total* ban on a military presence in space. But in 1998, India and Pakistan's respective nuclear testing programs generated a fresh resolve to broaden participation in this particular treaty. Suddenly, the world seemed poised to deal with another crisis, this time between regional rivals. That year, the US Departments of State and Defense thereby objected to President Clinton's approval of the sale of satellite technology to the Peoples Republic of China. This was a "dual technology" transfer. It focuses on commercial communications equipment, but readily convertible to weapons guidance systems. It arguably violated various treaties, including the 1972 Anti-Ballistic Missile Treaty, which outlaws missiles in outer space.

The treaty concern about the potential militarization of space was also the basis for the Soviet claim that the United States would have violated the Moon Treaty, if it had implemented the so-called Star Wars Strategic Defense Initiative announced by the Reagan administration in 1983. Under that proposal, the United States considered placing "defensive" nuclear military installations in outer space to neutralize Soviet weapons—and those of other countries—before they could reach the United States. Then, in 1997, the US military announced its plans to aim a laser at a US satellite in space. The purpose was to test methods for protecting satellites from jamming and being otherwise disabled. This spawned concern in the US Congress that Russia might respond by resurrecting its own testing involving ballistic missile shots at its satellites. The US executive branch would later rachet up the tension by several notches.

In May 2001, US President Bush took steps to negate the US treaty commitment not to place missiles in space (and resurrecting the Reagan proposal of 1983), to the disappointment of many US allies.[86] US Defense Secretary Rumsfeld ordered the Pentagon to review missile defense options and to consider outer space as the battlefield of the future, but not to answer questions regarding whether the United States plans to develop space weapons. This capability would, under the aegis of avoiding a space-based Pearl Harbor, possibly deploy space weapons to defend US satellites and to destroy those of its foes.[87]

Liability Convention The Moon Treaty incorporates some nonmilitary concerns of the international community. It requires participants to assume full civil liability for their activities in outer space that cause harm to any of Earth's inhabitants. Under Article VI, launching nations "bear international responsibility for national activities in outer space. . . ." This requirement inspired the creation of the 1971 Liability Convention, under which ratifying States have accepted automatic responsibility for damage caused by their spacecraft upon reentering Earth's atmosphere.

Under Article II of the 1971 Liability Convention, a "launching State shall be absolutely liable [even if its conduct is not negligent] to pay compensation for damage caused by its space object on the surface of the earth or to aircraft in flight." Over 17,000 man-made objects have fallen back to earth. There are still 8,300 such objects orbiting in outer space. The launching State must provide advance notification of an anticipated breach of airspace caused by a falling object. This convention was applied in 1979 when Canada lodged a claim against the former Soviet Union, alleging that the latter nation did not comply with its treaty obligation to notify Canada of a nuclear-powered satellite's potential reentry into Canadian airspace. Canada claimed that when "Cosmos 954" fell, it deposited harmful radioactive debris in various parts of Canada's Northwest Territories. Canada's claim was later resolved diplomatically.[88]

The research and exploration of outer space is essentially "on hold," in the sense that there is no longer a space race between the two superpowers of the Cold War. Further, economic considerations make it difficult for the United States and Russia to continue the massive planning that occurred immediately after the Soviet Sputnik went into orbit in 1957. Yet all States are interested in pursuing the age-old dream of space travel. With world financial markets on a virtual roller coaster, international cooperation may be the only way to tap the many resources available in outer space. In the interim, private investment is taking the lead by evolving telecommunications projects in outer space.[89]

The Future "Where do we go from here?" This familiar question has special meaning in the context of outer space. The population continues to outgrow food supply. The environment is unable to meet demands being currently placed on it. So it is not surprising that there are over 500 satellites operating in space. Hundreds more are expected to be in orbit in the coming decade, especially as the information age evolves via space technology. As described in the following *Outlook on Space Law* excerpt, there is no guarantee that existing charters and organizations will be able to meet the evolving demands of life in the twenty-first century.

The Achilles heel in the United Nations' Moon Treaty system is the lack of specificity regarding the most sensitive issues. As already described, space is not supposed to be militarized. Yet treaty articles permit a military presence in space, as long as it is "for scientific research or for any other peaceful purposes." As lamented by the Director of the UN Office for Outer Space Affairs, and President of the International Institute of Space Law:

> The five [mulilateral] outer space treaties lay out general legal rules without providing specific standards or procedures by which the treaties are to be implemented and by which space activities are to be controlled. In doing so, they create technical and legal weaknesses in the treaties. To give just two examples: in the Outer Space Treaty, Article XI requires States to "adopt appropriate measures" so as to avoid the harmful contamination of the Earth and outer space environments while conducting space activities. However, the treaty does not recommend the measures that are to be taken. . . . In the Liability Convention, procedures for rendering assistance as provided for in Article XXI (which deals with large scale danger to human life by damage caused by a space object [falling] on Earth) are not established.[90]

The UN Committee on the Peaceful Uses of Outer Space has been the standing committee for dealing with space issues for the last half of the twentieth century. The time may be ripe for a World Space Organization—known in contemporary pop culture as the "Federation Council" (see *Star Trek* episode appearing at the beginning of this chapter). Such a new international organization would receive and provide the specialized expertise for achieving objectives like those enshrined in the UN Charter at the dawn of what was then a new era in international relations. The international political environment appears to be more amenable to augmenting the United Nations' outer space programs, in the new

millennium of interplanetary relations—now that Cold War confrontation is no longer an irrefutable fact of life. Yet the cost and complexity of space exploration is astronomical. This organization could be the catalyst, however, for managing resources, technology, and manpower for the benefit of all nations—not unlike the work of the United Nations' ISA for the oceans of the globe.[91]

In the twenty-first century, people will likely inhabit space stations and other planets for extended periods of time, if not permanently. Commencing in 1984, the United States forged a cooperative effort with fourteen other countries and the European Space Agency—Canada, Japan, Brazil, United Kingdom, France, Germany, Belgium, Italy, The Netherlands, Denmark, Norway, Spain, Switzerland, Sweden—to develop an International Space Station. In November 1998, Russia launched the initial module of the International Space Station. Fifteen nations now participate in this project, consisting of 100 elements, which was scheduled for completion by 2006. The living space will be about the size of the cabins of two 747 jets. It will be an orbital home for at least 15 years, and a stepping-stone for the potential habitation of other planets.[92]

Will those societies govern themselves in accordance with the peaceable norms of International Law developed on the Planet Earth? The critical questions that will have to be answered include the following:

1. Will interplanetary colonization result in "States" as we now know them?
2. Will the UN Charter's prohibition against the use of force actually be extended into space? Or be abandoned? Supplanted by some other regime?
3. Will the national entities on Earth, referred to as States, apply Earth-bound legal principles to the vast reaches of outer space?
4. Will various social groupings in space apply different paradigms, which each planet or solar system considers appropriate for their independent galaxies separated by light years of travel?
5. Will the existence and discovery of another species of life make these questions irrelevant?

The following essay projects the likely integration of law and technology, which will be required by the demands of space travel, and the potential for either introducing or joining colonies on other planets:

Outlook on Space Law Over the Next 30 Years

Gabriel Lafferranderie (Editor), *Introduction,* at 6

Kluwer Law International (1997)

The global nature of this field of law can be seen from the [following] range of commercial activities. It is called upon to regulate (international trade and launch services, insurance and liability, copyright, intellectual property rights) by the new legal concerns which it is quite naturally called upon to accommodate, as new legal instruments are negotiated. . . . A paradigm case is the international space station, a cooperative venture involving a number of states and designed to support a very wide range of activities covering scientific research and applications, with people of various nationalities called upon to handle experiments proposed by various investigators and users. The station, linked directly to laboratories on the ground and resupplied by a fleet of space vehicles coming under the jurisdictions of a number of countries, gives rise to something akin to "global law," a "melting-pot" of various national legal provisions fashioned for the purposes of the utilisation of space, . . . in pursuance of international cooperative activities undertaken for the benefit of all mankind but with due regard for the specific interests, rights and obligations of the promoters.

. . .

Most activities undertaken on Earth can also be carried out in space—in Earth orbit, on the Moon, en route to other celestial bodies. Securing understanding of the Earth's environment and hence a better standard of living for the whole planet . . . improving our knowledge of the Universe and hence our origins and our future: space as the new cradle of mankind to adapt Tsiolkowski's well-known expression. Activities in these various areas—research, exploration, and now the utilisaton of space—imply the need for legal provisions and these must encompass the securing of the necessary financial and technological resources. . . . In many fields

of law a major question today is whether it is possible to stand aside from the construction of this global law [as well as] . . . the contribution which space exploitation can make to the maintenance of international peace and security.

. . .

The players: space law is no longer the sole prerogative of States. Space activities will in the future be conducted on three fronts—by States, international organization and the private sector. International organizations have come to the fore as structures for cooperation and as generators of legal texts; they should aim for similar prominence in the development of [space law] norms.

. . .

Defining space activity and the use of space for peaceful purposes, delimiting airspace and outerspace; from the outset opinions were divided on the case for legal definitions of these concepts. . . . Astronauts in space or on the Moon thus be able to rely on a special regime and would have their rights and obligations more clearly defined. Well-established themes such as liability, registration and settlement of disputes will themselves be affected by new forms of space activity and will have to be further developed and perhaps adapted to new circumstances.

. . .

[A]rticle IV of the [1967 Moon] Treaty fails to address the question of the militarisation off space. This is an astonishing omission if one looks back to the emergence of projects such as the [Reagan, and now Bush "Star Wars"] Strategic Defense Initiative and considers that space is today an integral part of military planning . . . , with the development of anti-satellite weapons etc.

◆ PROBLEMS

Problem 6.A (after §6.2 Bruges Declaration)   Note the following time line—January 2003: US President Bush announced his readiness to attack Iraq, regardless of whether the United States could secure an authorizing

UN Security Council resolution. March 2003: The United States attacks Iraq. April 2003: Baghdad falls to US forces. May 2003: President Bush declares an end to major combat operations, and a US diplomat replaces a US general as Iraq's governor. July 2003: Iraq's Interim

Governing Council—composed of 25 Iraqis appointed by American and British officials—is inaugurated, although US diplomat Paul Bremer retains ultimate authority. October 2003: Coordinated suicide attacks in Baghdad launch a campaign where hundreds die and thousands are wounded over the next two years. Insurgents increasingly victimize civilians, Iraqi security forces, and foreign aid agencies—not just US troops. December 2003: A directive issued by the US Deputy Secretary of Defense bars France, Germany, and Russia from bidding on lucrative contracts for rebuilding Iraq.

March 2004: The Iraqi Governing Council signs an "interim" constitution. April 2004: The United States agrees to a UN proposal to replace this Council with a caretaker government. June 2004: The US announces the end of its occupation of Iraq.

September 2004: Estimated Iraqi civilian deaths, since the start of the Iraq War, range from 12,000 to 14,000. September 15, 2004: UN Secretary-General Kofi Annan says the war against Iraq was illegal and a violation of the UN Charter. The Bush Administration requests that the Senate divert $3.4 billion of the $18.4 billion Iraq reconstruction budget to improve its security. The worsening security situation—with pockets of Iraq essentially under the control of insurgents—threatens to disrupt national elections (then scheduled for January 2005). November 2004: US forces initiate a major assault on Falluja, which has been under the control of insurgents since May. Falluja had been severely damaged by artillery, air and tank bombardments, while most of the city's 300,000 residents had not returned.

January 2005: Iraq's elections select a National Assembly. A total of 8.5-million people voted, representing about 58 percent of those Iraqis eligible to vote. Violence accompanies the voting, with 260 attacks taking place on election day, the largest number since the war began. June 2005: The US commander of US forces in the Middle East states that the Iraq insurgency remains as strong as it had been at the start of 2005 and the number of Iraqi civilian deaths was then estimated to be 25,000. A private estimate claims that these deaths exceed 100,000.

Assume that the Bruges Declaration is an accurate restatement of the contemporary law of belligerent occupation. Did the United States comply with it? Four students or groups will debate this matter. They will represent (1) Iraq's new government; (2) the United States; (3) Iraqi insurgents, seeking the departure of US military personnel and bases closures; and (4) the United Nations.

Problem 6.B (end of §6.2)   Assume the following facts: Iran (or its predecessor Persia) has exercised sovereignty over the island of Kais in the Persian Gulf near Iran's coastline, as a result of a military conquest 500 years ago. Iran and Iraq are now at war (during their 1980–1988 war). Iraq's military forces seize Kais and refuse to return it to Iranian control. Iraq does not physically occupy Kais, but its military vessels prohibit Iran from gaining any access to Kuis. Iran takes no action until 15 years later when it lodges a formal diplomatic protest with Iraq, disputing Iraq's current control of Kais, and its surrounding waters. Iran insists that Kais remains under Iraq's historical territorial sovereignty.

Two students will act as representatives for Iran and Iraq. They will deliberate whether Kais is now legally owned by Iran or Iraq.

Problem 6.C (§6.3 at end of (2) Territorial Sea) The United States and the hypothetical nation of Estado are on the verge of a military confrontation. A sizable US fleet is steaming toward Estado to engage in what some cantankerous senators have branded *gunboat diplomacy*—a show of force designed to illustrate the US decision to back up its political position with a show of military strength.

The US fleet crosses into what Estado has claimed to be its 200-nautical mile "territorial sea" (announced in 1952). Estado has never announced a sovereign claim to any other sea zone. Estado claims exclusive sovereignty over all of Bahia Grande, the large bay adjacent to its northern coastal border. This would be the first time that foreign vessels have ever entered Bahia Grande without Estado's permission.

The fleet continues to head directly for Estado's Port El Centro on the southern edge of Bahia Grande. The bay's east-west mouth is 40 nautical miles wide. The Port's outer harbor facilities are on the coastal baseline. That point is 20-miles south of the mouth (or entrance points of the bay). These facilities are on a point of the bay's coastline that is equidistant from the entrance points forming the mouth of the Bahia Grande. No branch of the Estado government has defined the term "bay." A 2005 US Supreme Court decision, drawing upon a common treaty definition, defines it as "a well-marked indentation whose penetration . . . constitute[s] more than a mere curvature of the coast. An indentation shall not, however, be regarded as a bay unless its area is as large as, or larger than, that of the semi-circle whose diameter is a line drawn across the mouth of that indentation."[93]

The US military forces pass through the center of the bay's navigable channel in the middle of the mouth of the bay. The armada pauses at a point 15 miles from the outer edge of Port El Centro (from the baseline) and equidistant from the sides of the semicircular coastline forming the edges of Bahia Grande. This resting point is also 5 miles south of a line that could be drawn across the bay between its entrance points.

When the US forces come to rest, are they located in the internal waters of Estado or in some other zone defined by the UN Law of the Sea Treaty?

Problem 6.D (end of §6.3)   Refer to Problem 6.C, wherein the US fleet steams into Estado's Bahia Grande. Assume that Bahia Grande is not a historic bay that contains only internal waters. Refer to the Exhibit 6.1 Sea Zones chart at the beginning of §6.3. Assume that Port El Centra's outer harbor facilities are located on that chart at the point marked "Coastal Baseline." Apply the 1982 UNCLOS principles, and any applicable Customary International Law principles, to answer the following questions:

1. Did the United States violate Estado's territorial waters when it crossed into Estado's 200-mile "territorial sea?"
2. What sea zone did the US fleet first enter when it was en route to Estado?
3. Did the US fleet ever enter Estado's contiguous zone? If so, where?
4. Did the US fleet ever enter Estado's territorial waters?
5. Where do Estado's internal waters meet its territorial sea?

Problem 6.E (§6.3 at end of (2) Territorial Sea)   A US Navy vessel and a US passenger ship are about to pass through an international strait between two coastal nations. The strait's natural width varies from 15 to 25 nautical miles between the bordering coastal States. Each State has ratified the 1982 Convention on the Law of the Sea. The navigational officer (NO) does not know whether the two coastal States have ratified Articles 37–44 of the UN Convention on the Law of the Sea authorizing "strait passage." The NO's petty officer is researching this matter, and will subsequently report to the captain.

NO 1 is the navigational officer aboard the Navy vessel. NO 2 is the navigational officer aboard the passenger ship. The NOs will advise their respective captains (the class) of the rights of each ship and the coastal States. The NOs will review the various rules of passage outlined in the materials in the "territorial sea" section of the book.

Problem 6.F (end of §6.3)   Assume that the United States and the hypothetical nation of Estado enter into a treaty giving US corporations the right to establish business operations in Estado. Assume that a large multinational enterprise called Mineco is the US-based corporate parent for many worldwide subsidiary corporations. Mineco has established a foreign corporate subsidiary in Estado. None of Mineco's key management personnel are citizens of Estado, although all of Mineco's bluecollar workers are Estado nationals.

Under the Estado-US licensing agreement, Mineco is solely responsible for all mining of Wondore, a valuable ore found mainly in and near Estado. Wondore is used to create cheap energy. US scientists are now exploring whether it can also serve as an alternative to oil. Under the licensing agreement with Estado, Mineco has the exclusive right to do all of the drilling in and near this resource-rich nation. There are vast reserves of Wondore in the seabed adjacent to Estado's shores—up to 300 nautical miles from its coastline. Mineco is now examining the viability of drilling under the ocean floor, in a corridor stretching from Estado to 300 nautical miles seaward from its coast.

Assume that Estado is a party to and has ratified the 1982 Law of the Sea Treaty, which entered into force in 1994. The US position is not relevant, because any rights involving mining in or near Estado waters will depend on Estado's position regarding the UNCLOS. You should assume the following alternatives: (a) Estado *is* and (b) Estado *is not* a party to the special 1994 Agreement (prompted by the United States to avoid the impact of the UNCLOS's Part XI provisions regarding the mining of deep seabed resources). How does the new UNCLOS affect Estado's and Mineco's right to extract these minerals from the 300-mile corridor?

Problem 6.G (§6.4 after Powers Case)   The United States and a Caribbean neighbor are engaged in what may turn out to be a hostile conflict. A US fleet containing US marine and naval forces is now steaming toward the hypothetical State of Estado. A US multinational corporation owns a satellite that is in geostationary orbit over Estado, at an altitude of 22,500 miles. That corporation allows the US forces to use its satellite to monitor events occurring in Estado. This sophisticated satellite permits a monitor aboard the fleet command ship to count individual troops in Estado. US fighter-bomber aircraft are launched in international waters and fly over Estado, after the satellite confirms that all Estado military aircraft are on the ground.

Does the *presence* of the privately owned satellite "over" Estado violate its airspace under any of the treaties in §6.4?

Problem 6.H (end of Air Space portion of §6.4) A group of Estado extremists seizes a US commercial airliner as it flies over Jamaica. There are eighty US citizens on board the aircraft. The hijackers divert the plane to Estado. En route, they broadcast that their reason for seizing the aircraft is to bring world attention to the plight of Estado. They proclaim that their only way of dealing with US imperialism is to capture one of its aircraft and bring the US hostages to Estado. The plane arrives, and the hostages are hidden from public view. It is not clear whether Estado's government played a role in planning this hijacking.

The Estado hijackers are tried in an Estado "People's Tribunal" and found not guilty. The tribunal decides that the defendants have committed a "political" crime rather than an ordinary crime under Estado law. Estado is a party to all of the multilateral treaties dealing with commercial air flights described in the air zones section of this chapter. Estado is not a party to any regional air treaty, such as the referenced European Convention on the Suppression of Terrorism. Has Estado breached the air treaties to which it is a party? How?

Problem 6.I (end of §6.4) Section 10.7 of this text addresses various issues spawned by the September 11, 2001, terrorist attack on the United States. Which, if any, treaties in §6.4 of the textbook on International Air Law were thereby violated? By whom?

Problem 6.J (end of space law portion of §6.4) In July 2000, a French prosecutor commenced an investigation of whether the US global surveillance system ("Echelon") is a threat to France. France's counter intelligence agency appraised whether this system, that listens in on millions of telephone calls and sends faxes/e-mails

each day, "is harmful to the vital interests of the nation." The French concern is that this Cold War development is now being used to further US economic interests. The European Parliament commissioned an earlier report (written by a British journalist). It determined that Echelon had twice helped US companies gain an advantage over Europeans, although the specific details were never made public. Europeans are generally concerned because the United Kingdom is a US partner in the use/development of Echelon—although France supposedly operates a similar system on a smaller scale. *Source:* NYT News Service, July 5, 2000.

In February 2005, unmanned US surveillance drones overflew Iran, seeking evidence of a nuclear weapons program. Both sides to the above Echelon affair might have used this detail in any debate about the Echelon system. In December 2005, the European Union launched its first satellite, in a bid to break the US monopoly on space-based networks. Given its greater accuracy, it is likely that coexisting military uses will materialize. Assume that France and the United States are parties to all the treaties contained in §6.4 on outer space. Could the US/UK use of Echelon violate any of those treaties? How?

◆ BIBLIOGRAPHY

§6.1 Categories of Territory

M. Dixon & R. McCorquodale, Sovereignty over Territory, ch. 7, in CASES AND MATERIALS ON INTERNATIONAL LAW 248 (4th ed. London: Oxford Univ. Press, 2003)

W. Resiman et al., Land, Part III, in INTERNATIONAL LAW IN CONTEMPORARY PERSPECTIVE 746 (New York: Foundation Press, 2004)

§6.2 Dominion Over Land

J. Allain, INTERNATIONAL LAW IN THE MIDDLE EAST: CLOSER TO POWER THAN JUSTICE (Aldershot, Eng.: Ashgate, 2004)

M. Bassiouni (ed.), DOCUMENTS ON THE ARAB-ISRAELI CONFLICT (Irvington, NY: Transnational, 2004)

B. Brown, Intervention, Self-Determination, Democracy and the Residual Responsibilities of the Occupying Power in Iraq, 11 DAVIS J. INT'L L. & POL. 23 (2004)

P. Huth, STANDING YOUR GROUND: TERRITORIAL DISPUTES AND INTERNATIONAL CONFLICT (Ann Arbor, MI: Mich. Univ. Press, 1996)

A. Kacowicz, PEACEFUL TERRITORIAL CHANGE (Columbia: Univ. So. Caro. Press, 1994)

C. Rubenberg, THE PALESTINIANS: IN SEARCH OF A JUST PEACE (Boulder, CO: Rienner, 2003)

S. Sharma, TERRITORIAL ACQUISITION, DISPUTES AND INTERNATIONAL LAW (The Hague, Neth.: Martinus Nijhoff, 1997)

E. Rogan & A. Shlaim (ed.), THE WAR FOR PALESTINE: REWRITING THE HISTORY OF 1948 (Cambridge, Eng.: Cambridge Univ. Press, 2001)

§6.3 Law of the Sea

R. Churchill & A. Love, THE LAW OF THE SEA (3d ed. Manchester, Eng.: Juris, 1999)

G. Galdorisi & K. Vienna, BEYOND THE LAW OF THE SEA: NEW DIRECTIONS FOR US OCEANS POLICY (Westport, CT: Praeger, 1997)

Law of the Sea Forum: The 1994 Agreement on Implementation of the Seabed Provisions of the Convention on the Law of the Sea, 88 AMER. J. INT'L LAW 687 (1994)

R. Lee & M. Hayashi, NEW DIRECTIONS IN THE LAW OF THE SEA: REGIONAL & NATIONAL DEVELOPMENT (Dobbs Ferry, NY: Oceana, 1995) (three looseleaf volumes)

T. McDorman et al., INTERNATIONAL OCEAN LAW: MATERIALS AND COMMENTARIES (Durham, NC: Carolina Acad. Press, 2005)

V. Prescott & C. Schofield, THE MARITIME POLITICAL BOUNDARIES OF THE WORLD (2d ed. 2005)

L. Sohn & J. Noyes, CASES AND MATERIALS ON THE LAW OF THE SEA (Irvington, NY: Transnational, 2004)

G. Walker & J. Noyes, Definitions for the 1982 Law of the Sea Convention: Part I, 32 CAL. WEST. INT'L L.J. 343 (2002) & Part II, 33 CAL. WEST. INT'L L.J. 191 (2003)

F. Vicuna, EXCLUSIVE ECONOMIC ZONE: A LATIN AMERICAN PERSPECTIVE (Boulder, CO: Westview Press, 1984)

P. Yuan, The United Nations Convention on the Law of the Sea from a Chinese Perspective, 19 TEXAS INT'L L.J. 415 (1984)

§6.4 Airspace Zones

AIR SPACE

I. Diederiks-Verschoor, AN INTRODUCTION TO AIR LAW (The Hague, Neth.: Kluwer, 1997)

C. Johnsson, INTERNATIONAL AVIATION AND THE POLITICS OF REGIME CHANGES (New York: St. Martin's Press, 1987)

OUTER SPACE

P. Dempsey (ed.), SPACE LAW (Dobbs Ferry, NY: Oceana, 2004) (five loose leaf volumes)

N. Jasentuliyana (ed.), SPACE LAW: DEVELOPMENT AND SCOPE (Westport, CT: Praeger, 1992)

K. Li (ed.), WORLD WIDE SPACE LAW BIBLIOGRAPHY (Montreal: McGill Univ. De Daro Pub., 1978) (two volumes with annual supplements)

N. Matte (ed.), SPACE ACTIVITIES AND EMERGING INTERNATIONAL LAW (Montreal: McGill Univ., 1994)

Additional Internet Resources

Atmosphere and Space Treaties: <http://fletcher.tufts.edu/multi/atmos.html>

Marine and Coastal Treaties: <http://fletcher.tufts.edu/multi/marine.html>

UN Division for Ocean Affairs and the Law of the Sea all Treaty Web ite: <http://www.un.org/Depts/los/index.htm>

◆ ENDNOTES

1. Peter Hocknell, BOUNDARIES OF COOPERATION: CYPRUS, DE FACTO PARTITION, AND THE DEMOLITION OF TRANSBOUNDARY RESOURCE MANAGEMENT 2 (London: Kluwer, 2001).
2. Namibia (South-West Africa) Case, 1971 ICJ REP. 55.
3. US v. Netherlands, Permanent Court of Arbitration, No. XIX, 2 REP. INT'L ARB. AWARDS 829 (1949).
4. 1975 ICJ REP. 4 (a principal case in §2.4 of this text).
5. Regarding both regions, see The Legal Regimes of the Polar Regions, Part II, in D. Rothwell, THE POLAR REGIONS AND THE DEVELOPMENT OF INTERNATIONAL LAW 49 (Cambridge, Eng.: Cambridge Univ. Press, 1996).
6. Antarctica res communis: Balch, The Arctic and Antarctic Regions and the Law of Nations, 4 AMER. J. INT'L L. 265 (1910); not res communis: E. Sahurie, THE INTERNATIONAL LAW OF ANTARCTICA 420 (Dordrecht, Neth.: Martinus Nijhoff, 1992). Treaty text: see 54 AMER. J. INT'L L. 476 (Supp. 1960) or 19 INT'L LEGAL MAT'LS 860 (1980).
7. See generally S. Sharma, TERRITORIAL ACQUISITION DISPUTES AND INTERNATIONAL LAW (The Hague, Neth.: Martinus Nijhoff, 1997); and G. Goetz & P. Diehl, TERRITORIAL CHANGES AND INTERNATIONAL CONFLICT (London: Routledge, 1992). Contemporary examples also include the delay of the 1999 Sharm el-Sheikh Memorandum on Implementation Timeline of Outstanding Commitments of Agreements Signed and the Resumption of Permanent Status Negotiation, available at: <http://www.israel-mfa.gov.il/mfa/go.asp?MFAH0fnq0>; the year 2000 Vatican agreement with the PLO, warning Israel that any unilateral decision on Jerusalem would be "morally and legally unacceptable," source: Reuters News Service, Feb. 15, 2000; and the British Parliament's Northern Ireland Act 2000 Act, designed to suspend the Northern Ireland Assembly. The Act comes into force on any date that the British Secretary of State decides to so order, without the need of Parliamentary approval. No Irish Assembly would be entitled to meet or conduct any business. This legislation was enacted in February, 2000, although its first suspension occurred shortly thereafter. See <http://www.hmso.gov.uk/acts/acts2000/20000001.htm>.
8. Judicial approach: The Miniquiers and Ecrehos Case (France v. United Kingdom), 1953 ICJ REP. 47 (1953). Administrative approach: E. Hasani, Uti Possidetis Juris: From Rome to Kosovo, 27 FLETCHER FORUM WORLD AFFAIRS 85 (2003).
9. Western Sahara Case (Spain v. Morocco), 1975 ICJ REP. 3, citing the Permanent Court of International Justice Legal Status of Greenland Case, PCIJ SER. A/B, NO. 53 (1933) (hereinafter Greenland Case.)
10. See G. von Glahn, Title to Territory, Air, and Space, ch. 14, in LAW AMONG NATIONS 297 (7th ed. Boston: Allyn & Bacon, 1996).
11. Greenland Case (cited in note 9 above).

12. Reuters, Volcanic Island Could Rise After 170 Years Under Sea, NYT on the Web (Nov. 26, 2002).

13. *Short duration:* Adam Roberts, Prolonged Military Occupation: The Israeli-Occupied Territories 1967–1988, ch. 1 in E. Playfair, INTERNATIONAL LAW AND THE ADMINISTRATION OF OCCUPIED TERRITORIES: TWO DECADES OF ISRAELI OCCUPATION OF THE WEST BANK AND THE GAZA STRIP 25, at 28 (Oxford, Eng.: Clarendon Press, 1992). *Treaty provisions:* E. Benvenisti, THE INTERNATIONAL LAW OF OCCUPATION at 7 & 98 (Princeton, NJ: Princeton Univ. Press, 1993). *Occupier's role:* G Fox, The Occupation of Iraq, 36 GEORGETOWN J. INT'L L. 195, at 199 (2005).

14. *Institute:* see <http://www.idi-iil.org/idiE/navig_history.html>. *Declaration:* Institut de Droit International, Bruges Declaration on The Use of Force (Sept. 2, 2003), available at: <www.idi-iil.org/idiE/declarationsE/2003_bru_en.pdf> .*Commentary:* E. McWhinney, The Institute de Droit International Adopts Bruges Declaration on Contemporary International Law on the Non-Use-of-Force and on Belligerent Occupation, 2 CHINESE J. INT'L L. 567 (2003).

15. *See* S. Subedi, LAND AND MARITIME ZONES OF PEACE IN INTERNATIONAL LAW (Oxford, Eng.: Clarendon Press, 1996).

16. *1995 Interim Agreement:* 36 INT'L LEGAL MAT'LS 551 (1997). *1997 Note for the Record:* 36 INT'L LEGAL MAT'LS 650 (1997). *1998 Wye River Agreement:* <http://www.mfa.gov.il/mfa>, search "Wye." Numerous settlement maps, photos, diagrams, and tables are available in the work product of the Israeli Information Center for Human Rights in the Occupied Territories in Y. Lein, LAND GRAB: ISRAEL'S SETTLEMENT POLICY IN THE WEST BANK (Jerusalem: B'Tselem, 2002).

17. A symposium on this case is available at Agora: ICJ Advisory Opinion on Construction of a Wall in the Occupied Palestinian Territory, 99 AMER. J. INT'L L. 1–141 (2005). The Palestinian Initiative for the Promotion of Global Dialogue & Democracy also provided detailed reactions. *See, e.g.,* S. Zunes, Implications of the U.S. Reaction to the World Court Ruling against Israel's "Separation Barrier," available at: <http://www.miftah.org/Display.cfm?DocId=6322&CategoryId=5> (Jan. 18, 2005).

18. *House:* commending President Bush for "his leadership in marshaling opposition to the misuse of the ICJ . . . ." H. Res. 713. 108th Congress, 2nd session (July 15, 2004). *Senate:* "supporting the construction by Israel of a security fence to prevent Palestinian terrorist attacks, [and] condemning the decision of the International Court of Justice on the legality of the security fence. . . . ." S. Res. 408, 108th Congress, 2nd session (July 20, 2004). *Israeli Supreme Court:* Judgment on the Fence Surrounding Alfei Menashe–HCJ 7957/04 (Sept. 15, 2005). *Israeli Prime Minister:* M. Lavie, Israeli Court Rejects Opinion on Fence (Sept. 17, 2005), available at: <http://politics.yahoo.com/s/cpress/20050915/ca_pr_on_wo/israel_barrier_world_court>.

19. J. Wilkinson, ARABIA'S FRONTIERS: THE STORY OF BRITAIN'S BOUNDARY DRAWING IN THE DESERT ix (London: I.B. Tauris, 1991).

20. S. Korman, THE RIGHT OF CONQUEST: THE ACQUISITION OF TERRITORY BY FORCE IN INTERNATIONAL LAW AND PRACTICE 306 (1996).

21. 1928 Permanent Court of Arbitration No. XIX, 2 REP. INT'L ARB. AWARDS 829 (1949).

22. *See* R. Blanke, ORPHANS OF VERSAILLES: THE WEST GERMAN MINORITY IN WESTERN POLAND, 1918–1939 (Lexington: Univ. Press of Kentucky, 1993).

23. Agreement on Succession Issues Between the Five Successor States of the Former State of Yugoslavia, 41 INTL LEGAL MAT'LS 3 (2002).

24. 1962 ICJ REP. 6.

25. Award by the United States-Mexico International Boundary Commission Constituted by Treaty of June 24, 1911, 11 REP. INT'L ARB. AWARDS 309 (1962).

26. I. Brownlie, PRINCIPLES OF PUBLIC INTERNATIONAL LAW 126 (6th ed. Oxford, Eng.: Oxford Univ. Press, 2003) (footnote omitted).

27. *Id.,* at 123 (footnote omitted).

28. *See* Summary of the Indo-Pakistan Western Boundary (Rann of Kutch) Case (India v. Pakistan), 1968 INT'L L. REP. 2 (1976); excerpts reprinted in 7 INT'L LEGAL MAT'LS 635 (1968).

29. *PCIJ application:* Jaworzina Boundary Case, PCIJ, ser. B, No. 8 (1923). *Post-World War II application:* I. Brownlie, INTERNATIONAL LAW AND THE USE OF FORCE BY STATES 408 (Oxford, Eng.: Oxford Univ. Press, 1963).

30. C. van Bynkershoek, DE DOMINIO DISSERTATIO (Possession of the Sea Dissertation), reprinted in ch. 2, CLASSICS OF INTERNATIONAL LAW 44 (Wash., DC: Carnegie Endowment for Int'l Peace, Magoffin translation, 1923) [hereinafter *Bynkershoek*].

31. M. McDougal & N. Schlei, The Hydrogen Bomb Tests in Perspective: Lawful Measures for Security, 64 YALE L. J. 648, 661–662 (1964).

32. The Law of the Sea: An Overview, ch. 1, in D. Pharand & U. Leanza, THE CONTINENTAL SHELF AND THE EXCLUSIVE ECONOMIC ZONE: DELIMITATION AND LEGAL REGIME 5 (Dordrecht, Neth.: Martinus Nijhoff, 1993).

33. D. Attard, THE EXCLUSIVE ECONOMIC ZONE IN INTERNATIONAL LAW 308–309 (Oxford, Eng.: Clarendon Press, 1987).

34. UN Doc. A/CONF. 62/122 (1982), reprinted in 21 INT'L LEGAL MAT'LS 1261 (1983), available at: <http://www.un.org/Depts/los/convention_agreements/convention_overview_convention.htm>.

35. Signature and ratification information for: (1) the *basic treaty* (entered into force 1994), (2) the revised *Part XI* treaty (in force 1996/discussed below), and (3) the associated *Fish Stocks* treaty (entered into force 2001) is available on the UN's Web site at the above note 34 Web site.

36. Re Bianchi, Camara Nacional Especial [special chamber of the national court of] Argentina, 24 INT'L L. REP. 173 (1961) (decided in 1957).

37. *See* G. Westerman, THE JURIDICAL BAY (Oxford, Eng.: Clarendon Press, 1987).

38. Tribunal of the Permanent Court of Arbitration, reprinted in Sen. Doc. No. 870, Vol. I, 61st Congress, 3rd Sess., at 64 (1912).

39. Excerpt from Canadian Parliamentary debate, reprinted in H. Kindred et al., INTERNATIONAL LAW CHIEFLY AS INTERPRETED AND APPLIED IN CANADA 869 (6th ed. Toronto: Edmond Montgomery Pub., 2000).

40. Anglo-Norwegian Fisheries Case (England v. Norway), 1951 ICJ REP. 116, 160 (Judgment of Dec. 18, 1951).

41. *Id.,* 18 INT'L LAW REPORTS 86, at 95.

42. *See* 2 YEARBOOK. INT'L L. COMM. 36, UN Doc. A/CN.4/17 (1950) on the Vatican's proclamations, which preceded these claims.

43. *Bynkershoek* (cited in note 30 above), at 44.

44. J. Moore, DIGEST OF INTERNATIONAL LAW 702–703 (Wash., DC: US Gov't Print. Off., 1906).

45. *1952 declaration:* see US Naval War College, 51 INT'L LAW SITUATION AND DOC. *1956,* at 265 (1957). *1956 declaration:* see US Naval War College, 50 INT'L LAW SITUATION AND DOC. *1955,* at 244 (1957) (italics added).

46. Presidential Proclamation on the Territorial Sea of the United States, 24 Weekly Compilation of Presidential Documents 1661 (1989), reprinted in 28 INT'L LEGAL MAT'LS 284 (1989).

47. *Black Sea incident:* The US and the USSR subsequently decided that their respective commercial vessels could enter their ports and pass through territorial waters. A minimum of two days notice was required. This 1990 agreement expressly excluded "war vessels." Agreement Regarding Certain Maritime Matters between the Government of the United States of America and the Government of the Union of Soviet Socialist Republics, US TREATIES AND OTHER INTERNATIONAL AGREEMENTS SERIES, No. 11453 (1990). *Alaskan incident:* Alaska v. United States, 125 S.Ct. 2137, 2147 (2005) [hereinafter *Alaska*].

48. The SS Lotus (France v. Turkey), PCIJ, SER. No. 10 (1927) (case set forth in §5.2).

49. 450 UN TREATY SERIES 82 (1963).

50. F. Ngantcha, THE RIGHT OF INNOCENT PASSAGE AND THE EVOLUTION OF THE INTERNATIONAL LAW OF THE SEA: THE CURRENT REGIME OF "FREE" NAVIGATION IN COASTAL WATERS OF THIRD STATES 1 (London: Pinter, 1990).

51. In re Air Crash Off Long Island, New York, on July 17, 1996, 209 F.3d 200, 216 (2nd Cir., 2000) (J. Sotomayor, dissenting).

52. 46 UNITED STATES CODE App. §761.

53. Harvard Research Draft, Art. 20, reprinted in 23 AMER. J. INT'L L. 250 (1929).

54. *Expanded CZ:* Convention on the Territorial Sea and Contiguous Zone, Art. 24.2, 516 UN TREATY SERIES 205 (1964). *Shelf agreement:* Convention on the Continental Shelf, Art. 1, 499 UN TREATY SERIES 311 (1964).

55. Details about this tribunal are available in P. Rao & R. Khan (ed.), THE INTERNATIONAL TRIBUNAL FOR THE LAW OF THE SEA: LAW AND PRACTICE (The Hague: Kluwer, 2001) or H. Caminos, The Creation of Specialized Courts: The Case of the International Tribunal for the Law of the Sea, in N. Ando, E. McWhinney & R. Wolfrum, 1 LIBER AMICORUM: JUDGE SHIGERU ODA 569 (Hague: Kluwer, 2002) & P. Rao, The International Tribunal for the Law of the Sea: An Evaluation, id., at 667.

56. A. Pardo, The Convention on the Law of the Sea: A Preliminary Appraisal, in F. Snyder & S. Sathirathai, THIRD WORLD ATTITUDES TOWARD INTERNATIONAL LAW 737, 741, and 747 n. 32 (Dordrecht, Neth.: Martinus Nijhoff, 1987) [hereinafter *Third World Attitudes*].

57. Case Concerning Fisheries Jurisdiction (Spain v. Canada). The final decision (1998) is available at: <http://www.icj-cij.org/icjwww>, click Decisions.

58. *Truman's CS declaration:* 10 Fed. Register 12304, 59 STATUTES AT LARGE 884 (1945), Presidential Proclamations 2667 and 2668. *CS Convention:* 400 UN TREATY SERIES 311 (1961). The evolution of Continental Shelf principles is presented in D. Pharand & U. Leanza (eds.), THE CONTINENTAL SHELF AND THE EXCLUSIVE ECONOMIC ZONE: DELIMITATION AND LEGAL REGIME (Dordrecht, Neth.: Martinus Nijhoff, 1993).

59. 1969 ICJ REP. 3, 53.

60. *CHM Resolution:* Gen. Ass. Reso. 2749 (XXV), UN Gen. Ass. Off. Rec. (GAOR), 25th Sess., Supp. No. 28, at 24, reprinted in 10 INT'L LEGAL MAT'LS 220 (1971). *Analysis:* Joyner, Legal Implications of the Concept of the Common Heritage of Mankind, 35 INTL & COMP. L.Q. 190 (1986).

61. Introduction to International Seabed Authority Web site at: <http://www.unac.org/players/isa.html>.

62. *1994 Agreement:* Annex I to Consultations of the Secretary-General on Outstanding Issues Relating to the Deep Seabed Mining Provisions of the United Nations Convention on the Law of the Sea, UN Doc. A/48/950 (1994) (revising UN DOC. SG/ LOS/CRP.1/Rev.1), reprinted in 33 INT'L LEGAL MAT'LS 1309 (1994). *Christopher quote:* United States to Move Ahead with the Law of the Sea Convention, 140 CONGRESSIONAL RECORD-SENATE, 103 Cong., 2nd Sess. (June 30, 1994). An extensive review of Law of the Sea developments is available in J. Noyes, International Legal Developments in Review: 1996 Public International Law of the Sea, 31 INT'L LAWYER 703 (1997).

63. *See* transmittal document to the Senate Foreign Relations Committee, Treaty Doc. 103–39, 103rd Cong., 2nd Sess., Oct. 7, 1994, regarding Part XI and Agreement on Implementation of Part XI, at 59.

64. T. Koh, Negotiating a New World Order for the Sea, in *Third World Attitudes* 715, 725–726 (cited in note 56 above).

65. *Third World Attitudes* 737, 741–744 (cited in note 56 above).

66. D. Goedhuis, Civil Aviation After the War, 36 AMER. J. INT'L L. 596, 605 (1942) (referring to World War I).

67. 11 LEAGUE OF NATIONS TREATY SERIES 173 (1922). The United States was never a party to this first international air treaty.

68. In 1972, the ICJ decided that it could review ICAO decisions in Jurisdiction of the ICAO Council (India v. Pakistan), 1972 ICJ REP. 46.

69. Laker Airways v. Sabena, 731 Fed.2d 909 (D.C. Cir. 1984). A history of the various English and American cases regarding Laker is available in 1 RESTATEMENT OF THE FOREIGN RELATIONS LAW OF THE UNITED STATES 252–253 (3d ed. Wash., DC: Amer. Law Inst., 1987).

70. Convention for the Unification of Certain Rules Relating to International Carriage by Air, Signed at Warsaw on

12 October 1929 (Warsaw Convention), Art. 1, available at <http://www.jus.uio.no/lm/air.carriage.warsaw.convention .1929/doc.html>.

71. L. Goldhirsch, THE WARSAW CONVENTION ANNOTATED: A LEGAL HANDBOOK 5 (2d ed., Kluwer Law Int'l, 2000). *See generally* The Warsaw System: Past, Present and Future, Part Two, in Chia-Jui Cheng & Doo Hwan Kim (ed.), THE UTI-LIZATION OF THE WORLD'S AIR SPACE AND FREE OUTER SPACE IN THE 21ST CENTURY at 63 (The Hague: Kluwer, 2000) [hereinafter *Air Space and Outerspace*].

72. For a valuable description of the legal issues, see F. Kirgis, United States Reconnaissance Aircraft Collision with Chinese Jet, ASIL Flash Insight No. 66 (Apr., 2001), available at <http://www.asil.org/insights/insigh66.htm>.

73. Case Concerning the Aerial Incident of July 27, 1955 (Israel v. Bulgaria), 1957 ICJ REP. 182.

74. *Analysis:* G. Fitzgerald, The Use of Force Against Civil Aircraft: The Aftermath of the KAL Flight 007 Incident, 22 CANADIAN YEARBOOK INT'L L. 291 (1984). *US case example:* Dooley v. Korean Air Lines, 524 U.S. 116, 118 S.Ct. 1890, 141 L.Ed.2d 102 (1998), superceded by legislative amendment.

75. R. Goedhart, THE NEVER-ENDING DISPUTE: DELIMITATION OF AIR SPACE AND OUTER SPACE 4 (Gif-sur-Yvette, France: Editions Frontieres, 1996).

76. US v. Cordova, 89 Fed.Supp. 298 (E.D. N.Y. 1950).

77. 704 UN TREATY SERIES 219 (1969).

78. *See* M. Milde, Law and Aviation Security, in T. Masson-Zwaan & P. Mendes de Leon, AIR AND SPACE LAW; DE LEGE FERENDA, ESSAYS IN HONOR OF HENRI A. WASSENBERGH 93 (Dordrecht, Neth.: Martinus Nijhoff, 1992).

79. Reprinted in 15 INT'L LEGAL MAT'LS 1272 (1976).

80. These and similar examples of the era are collected in W. Slomanson, ICJ Damages: Tort Remedy for Failure to Punish or Extradite International Terrorists, 5 CALIF. WEST. INT'L L.J. 121 (1974).

81. 610 UN TREATY SERIES 205 (1967).

82. *See generally,* R. Wallis, LOCKERBIE: THE STORY AND THE LESSONS (Westport, CT: Praeger, 2001.

83. *Preliminary jurisdictional ruling:* Questions of Interpretation and Application of the 1971 Montreal Convention Arising from the Aerial Incident at Lockerbie (Libyan Arab Jamahiriya v. United Kingdom), Request for the Indication of Provisional Measures, reprinted in Official Documents, 86 AMER. J. INT'L L. 638 (1992). *Case quote:* id., at 651 (Shahabuddeen, J., Separate Opinion). *Final jurisdictional decision:* see ICJ Web site at <www.icj-cij.org>, click Decisions.

84. Gen. Ass. Reso. 1721(XVI) of Dec. 20, 1961.

85. 610 U.N. TREATY SERIES 205 (1967).

86. The legal debate about the legality of the US posture is conveniently chronicled on the American Society of International Law *Insights* Web site: F. Kirgis, Proposed Missile Defenses and the ABM Treaty, at: <http://www.asil.org/ insights/insigh70.htm> (May, 2001) & Addendum, at: <http:// www.asil.org/insights/insigh70.htm#addendum> (Aug., 2001). A. de Hoogh, Response to Addendum, at: <http://www.asil.org/insights/insigh70.htm#response> (Aug., 2001) & D. Sloss, Reply to Response, at: <http:// www.asil.org/insights/insigh70.htm#reply> (Aug., 2001).

87. O. Kreisher, Rumsfeld is Coy on Weapons in Space, San Diego Union Tribune (May 9, 2001), available at: <http://copleydc .com/Archives-2001/kreisher_5-9-01.htm>.

88. The diplomatic exchanges between Canada and the former USSR are reproduced in 18 INT'L LEGAL MAT'LS 899 (1979).

89. *See* N. Jasentuliana, The Future of International Telecommunications Law, in A. Anghie & G. Sturgess (ed.), LEGAL VISIONS OF THE 21ST CENTURY: ESSAYS IN HONOUR OF JUDGE CHRISTOPHER WEERAMANTRY 391 (The Hague: Kluwer, 1998).

90. N. Jasentuliyana, Space Activities and Plans Within the United Nations: Preparing for the 21st Century, in *Air Space and Outerspace* 231, at 237 (cited in note 71 above).

91. *See* S. Cortex, Towards a World Space Organization?, in G. Lafferranderie & D. Crofter (ed.), OUTLOOK ON SPACE LAW OVER THE NEXT 30 YEARS 423 (The Hague: Kluwer, 1997).

92. Useful details and illustrative charts are available on the National Aeronautic and Space Administration Web site at: <http://spaceflight.nasa.gov/station>.

93. *Alaska* (cited in note 47 above), ___ U.S., at ___, 125 S.Ct., at 2151 (2005).

Diplomatic Relations

INTRODUCTION

Diplomacy plays a significant role in shaping international legal developments. Kings, queens, and presidents rely on their diplomats to address the day-to-day crises that are often resolved through quiet diplomacy. UN Secretary-Generals have not merely presided over various UN operations. Under Article 99 of the UN Charter, they "may bring to the attention of the Security Council any matter which in his opinion may threaten the maintenance of international peace and security."

This chapter depicts the working environment and legal status of diplomats, foreign travelers, and others who are protected by International Law. You will explore how diplomatic relations are initiated and broken. The fundamental questions include: What is the nature of diplomatic and consular functions? What is the legal effect of acts within an embassy, which do not conform to the laws of the host country? What are the relevant legal principles governing the famous cases involving diplomatic asylum? Do newspaper stories and books—like the foregoing

A WOMAN IS BRUTALLY RAPED, YET HER ATTACKER goes free. A man is fatally hit by a car, and the driver is not charged with a crime. Drug smugglers are seized, kidnappers identified, thieves caught in the act—and all go free.

. . .

Most of these given this enormous exemption from civilized behavior are not diplomats. They are the wives, children, drivers, and valets of ambassadors and ministers sent to this country to represent their nations. . . .

This immunity is particularly bizarre since it is not limited to incidents occurring in the course of "official duties" but rather serves as an absolute security blanket.

—C. Ashman & P. Trescott, DIPLOMATIC CRIME at back cover & 14–15 (New York, NY: Knightsbridge Publishing, 1988).

excerpt—fairly depict supposedly deplorable situations when some diplomat has "once again" avoided civil or criminal prosecution?

◆ 7.1 FOREWORD TO DIPLOMACY

HISTORICAL DEVELOPMENT

For centuries, special envoys have represented the interests of their rulers in other regions of the world. A treatise apparently written in 300 BC described Greek practice in 800 BC. There were already three categories of what we now call diplomats, consuls, and couriers: those with ministerial rank, those with slightly lesser rank, and the conveyors of messages. The Greek city-states developed lasting rules of diplomatic exchanges, inaugurating the practice that protected messengers who brought bad news from distant lands.[1]

Around AD 1500, permanent representatives called "ambassadors" were first established in Italy. This institution then flourished elsewhere in Western Europe, although other nations resisted it for several more centuries. As chronicled by London School of Economics Professor M. S. Anderson:

> [B]y the middle of the fifteenth century there were clearly taking root in Italy new diplomatic techniques and institutions. These formed the basis of a system of interstate relations recognizable as the direct ancestor of the one which exists today. . . . [M]ost of the Italian peninsula was divided between a fairly small number of relatively well-organized states. . . . These competed with one another intensely for power, for territory, [and] in the last analysis for survival. It was therefore essential for their rulers to watch closely each other's doings and to be as well informed as possible about each other's policies and ambitions. . . . In Italy it was therefore possible to raise day-to-day government to a high pitch of efficiency, to control the territory of these states effectively from a single centre, in a way which was still impracticable in France, Spain, or the growing Habsburg [dynasty in Hungary]. . . .
>
> Fifteenth-century Italy, then, was in miniature what in the following hundred years most of western Europe and later the rest of the continent [and modern diplomacy] was to become.[2]

The 1814–1815 Vienna Congress focused on the norms for engaging in international diplomacy. Most European States thereby established the mutually acceptable institutions that governed their international relations. Previously considered a somewhat discredited activity, diplomacy was finally perceived as a very positive institution. Preventative diplomacy was viewed as a vehicle that would not necessarily prevent war, but would serve the long-term interests of the international community.

The drafters of the 1945 UN Charter included a provision implicitly recognizing the importance of maintaining diplomatic ties. Should a State fail to carry out its peaceful membership obligations, Article 41 authorizes the Security Council to call on its members to sever or limit diplomatic relations with the offending State. This sanction was conceived as a technique for disrupting conduct that threatened international peace. The target State would lose the benefit of trade and other ties with the remaining UN member States. In 1992, for example, the United Nations imposed sanctions against Libya for its failure to surrender the two Libyan terrorists allegedly responsible for the bombing of Pan Am Flight 103 over Lockerbie, Scotland, in 1988. Those sanctions prohibited arms sales to Libya and commercial flights into that country, thus forcing the scaling back of Libya's diplomatic missions throughout the world. When Libya finally turned them over for trial (§9.5), as well as admitting responsibility for the death of a British policewoman, England restored diplomatic ties in 2001. The European Union likewise imposed sanctions on Libya, as a result of a bombing in West Berlin, killing approximately 160 victims and injuring 200. In August 2004, Libya agreed to pay $35 million to compensate the victims of this nightclub disaster (Problem 7.D).

States are expected to employ diplomatic alternatives before resorting to international courts or the use of force. In 1957, the International Court of Justice (ICJ) aptly articulated this practical norm when India objected to Portugal's premature filing of a case against India in the ICJ. The Court's formulation of this principle was that "Portugal, before filing her application in the present case, did not comply with the rule of customary international law requiring her to undertake diplomatic negotiations and continue them to the point where it was no longer profitable to pursue them. . . ."[3] The diplomatic function is not only to prevent the premature resort to third party resolution. It is primarily to prevent disputes from escalating into violent conflicts.[4]

PERCEPTIONS OF THE DIPLOMATIC ROLE

Fighter or Negotiator?   The role of the diplomat has not been characterized uniformly. Host governments have often considered them to be "spies."

In Czarist Russia, leaders feared that the presence of foreign ambassadors would be an invitation to spy on Russia. Allegations of espionage continued to plague international diplomacy during the Cold War.[5] In 1985, the former Soviet Union charged some US diplomatic personnel stationed in Moscow with spying. They were required to leave Russia. The United States responded by ejecting a number of Soviet diplomats from the United Nations in New York City. In 1987, the United States refused to occupy a newly constructed diplomatic complex in Moscow because the walls contained hidden listening devices. In 1994, the United States expelled a diplomat identified as Russia's senior intelligence agent. Then in March 2001, the FBI learned that one of its senior agents had been spying for Russia for 15 years. The Bush Administration then immediately ordered a half-dozen Russian diplomats to leave the United States, with more to follow.

Russia fielded *more* spies after the Cold War, during the first 5 years of (former KGB) President Putin's term. As of 2005, according to the Moscow Times, Russia has more than 100 spies working under diplomatic cover in just Washington and New York. The United Kingdom likewise reported an increase in the number of post-Cold War Russian spies. One reason is that, in the aftermath of 9-11, both the United States and United Kingdom have shifted their resources away from counterespionage toward counterterrorism.[6]

Claims of espionage continue to resonate anywhere there is a foreign diplomatic presence. France expelled four American diplomats in 1995 for their alleged industrial and political espionage. The US Central Intelligence Agency's station in Paris supposedly obtained secrets about France's nuclear arsenal and its planned trade posture toward US industry. In June 2004, the United States expelled two Iranian guards from Iran's UN mission in New York. Taking pictures of city infrastructure was deemed "incompatible with their stated duties."

The nineteenth-century European conception was that diplomacy was the art of negotiation or communication. Harold Nicolson, a twentieth-century British diplomat and prolific writer, thus defined international diplomacy as "the application of intelligence and tact to the conduct of official relations between the governments of independent states."[7] Most contemporary commentators perceive diplomats in the more familiar context of being foreign-based emissaries who promote friendly relations. Their role includes maintaining the vigilance necessary to ensure that State interaction is harmonious and that all the relevant legal relationships conform to expectations.

The Chinese have characterized the diplomat as a "fighter." During the 1966–1976 Cultural Revolution, the Chinese press often referred to diplomats in this context, as illustrated in the following excerpt:

> The diplomatic personnel of great socialist China are proletarian diplomatic fighters. At any time and in any place, they . . . show a dauntless revolutionary spirit, a firm and correct political orientation, an unconquerable fighting will. They are capable of accomplishing all the missions of proletarian revolutionary diplomacy however complicated or perilous the situation. The proletarian fighters on the diplomatic front . . . can distinguish friends from enemies. They are most modest in their attitude toward [other] revolutionary people and countries; they respect them; they resolutely support their revolutionary struggles, displaying the proletarian internationalist spirit. They repudiate all manifestations of great-power chauvinism. They wage a firm, blow-for-blow struggle against the imperialists, modern revisionists and all reactionaries, and relentlessly rebuff their provocations.[8]

Idealist or Realist? During the emergence of the "realist" period of international relations during the 1960s, renowned US commentator, Hans Morgenthau, criticized the legalistic perception of modern diplomacy as myopic idealism. Diplomats, in reality, were thus characterized as practical manipulators of power relationships—and *not* facilitators of International Law. Under this view, diplomats merely negotiate on the basis of the respective strength of the States they represent. This role parallels the Chinese view that the diplomat is a fighter. Morgenthau thus contended that international "politics, like all politics, is the struggle for power [and that the] means at the disposal of diplomacy are three: persuasion, compromise and threat of force." US President Nixon and Secretary of State Kissinger restated this theme as their justification for unpopular tactics utilized during the Vietnam War, specifically echoing Morgenthau's sentiment that we "must negotiate from a position of strength."

A closely related realist perspective is that the State is not imbued with ethical expectations in the conduct of its diplomatic functions. Under this view, there is no external authority to which the State must answer. Wales University College of Swansea's Professor David Boucher thus comments: "The state itself is [often] implicitly and explicitly personified. It, like individuals, has interests, and is motivated by the same psychological factors.

The state as the creator and sustainer of morals internal to itself is not itself constrained by a moral code in its relations with other states. The international sphere is *devoid* of the notions of justice and injustice because no ultimate authority exists to subordinate the individual states to it and create the conditions necessary for the emergence of morality."[9]

Former Canadian Prime Minister Lester Pearson advocated the realist theory—that the character of diplomacy depends on the particular issue at hand. In his assessment of nuclear diplomacy, he stressed that force must be recognized as the essential backdrop for successful control of the arms race. In his words: "Protection from these grim consequences of our own [nuclear] genius requires possession of overwhelming, destructive power" to avoid mutual destruction. Those States with nuclear power options must negotiate from a position of strength. This power theory is echoed by the leading Soviet publicist, Moscow State University's Professor Grigori Tunkin. He characterizes diplomacy as the most important means of accomplishing a State's foreign policy. He defines diplomacy as the activity of "heads of states, of governments, of departments of foreign affairs, of special delegations and missions, and of diplomatic representations appertaining to the effectuation by peaceful means of the purposes and tasks of the foreign policy of a state."[10]

In an informative exchange at the 1983 annual meeting of the American Society of International Law in Washington, DC, two diplomats espoused their respective idealist and realist perspectives on the degree to which diplomats rely on International Law. The summary of that exchange includes Canada's ambassador to the United States, Ambassador Gottlieb, aptly describing the idealist perspective on the conduct of diplomacy. He states that there is a "need to anchor the conduct of diplomacy in international law, as well as the need to develop this body of law. . . . [One] hope[s] that international law would keep pace with the demands imposed by these trends and that, in some cases, international law might even exceed the requirements placed on it." In contrast, the Venezuelan ambassador to the United States expressed his view that international law was not important in the conduct of diplomacy, which is controlled primarily by the will of governments rather than rules of law. Ambassador Perez-Chiriboga's "realist" perspective was that "international law did play a[n effective] role in the practice of international diplomacy,

but that not all steps taken in the conduct of diplomacy fell within the parameters of international law. . . . [D]iplomacy was conditioned by the will of governments and the role of international law in this field would increase [only] if governments respected international law."[11]

Any attempt to synthesize these varied definitions and perspectives on diplomacy produces at least two related conclusions: (1) Diplomats often deal with each other from diverse political perspectives about the fundamental nature of their respective roles; and (2) diplomatic practice has necessarily adapted to changing international environments. These starting points in a discourse on diplomacy provide some insight into why diplomatic negotiations often deteriorate: The participants often pursue varying purposes from different moral, political, and sociological perspectives.[12]

Diplomats must decide what particular methods are best suited to achieve their respective foreign policy objectives. To do this, they must first determine what those objectives are and what alternatives are available to accomplish them. Diplomats must be prepared, for example, to deal with different constitutional and social systems in the host State. A new ambassador cannot expect to achieve diplomatic goals without knowing what results can be realistically achieved. The ambassador must continue to assess the objectives of the host State and the degree to which he or she can reasonably negotiate in favor of the home State. Next, the diplomat must gauge the extent to which the objectives of the sending and receiving States are compatible. Finally, the diplomat must employ suitable means to pursue desired objectives—often in a different cultural context.[13]

Cultural Component Overlooking cultural differences sows seeds of mistrust in both private and international relations. First, there is the comparatively minor irritant associated with failing to appreciate a cultural contrast in a way that tends to undermine relationships. This recurring problem often surfaces when two nations possess unequal bargaining power. The conduct of the stronger nation's representative may indicate unawareness or ignorance. Protocol missteps are thus spawned by communication gaps.

During President Clinton's first official dinner function in a foreign nation (July 1993), he unexpectedly invited a translator to stand between himself and South

Korea's President Kim, who was seated near the lectern. This event would have no cultural significance in the United States. In Korea, however, it is an insult for anyone to stand between two heads of state. Strictly observed rules of etiquette apply in Korea, even between family members in private dinner settings. To add insult to injury, there had been an agreement that each president would deliver postdinner remarks in their native tongues, without the aid of an interpreter. The invitation to the translator to stand between them spawned yet another cultural *faux pas,* although there were no *perceptible* consequences.

The more significant form of cultural difference arises when an agreement is reached, but applied differently by the parties to the same agreement in good faith. What often appears perfectly clear to both sides, when formulated in abstract principles, may be interpreted quite differently. Intelligent diplomacy requires the representatives to take account of cultural differences because they should be seeking a lasting result that will be satisfying to all participants. It is no secret that one should attempt to negotiate from a position of strength. Yet raw power politics, although a fact of international life, does not ultimately succeed as well as attempting to accommodate the cultural values of the "other side" in international relations. As articulated by St. John's University (New York) Professor Frank Ninkovich:

> Although diplomacy functions within cultural and intercultural contexts, historians of diplomacy have traditionally slighted cultural explanations of foreign policy in favor of tried and true concepts of power and interest . . . [but] insightful statesmen have always recognized that diplomacy also requires reckoning with cultural values which, because of their crucial role in shaping perceptions, are more significant than either ideological beliefs or abstract ideals. In one way or another, nearly all the major US statesmen of the twentieth century took cultural factors into account as part of their approach to diplomacy; indeed, culture played a prominent and often decisive role in their decision–making.[14]

ALTERED DIPLOMATIC STATUS

The technological innovations of the twentieth century changed diplomacy in two dramatic ways. First, they altered the status of the diplomat. Nineteenth-century diplomats, serving far from the seat of their governments, had much wider discretion when reacting to problems at their outposts. Travel and communications were difficult and slow. An ambassador had to react to local crises without the benefit (or detriment) of immediate directions from his government. Instantaneous Internet communications and supersonic travel now limit the need to rely on such undirected judgment.

The role of the diplomat in international relations—once the sole province of ambassadors and consular officers—has been minimized, in comparison to that of his or her nineteenth-century counterpart. In the United States, for example, there has been an increasing tendency toward the centralization of foreign policy decisions at the White House.[15] Modern "shuttle diplomacy," typified by President Nixon's dispatching of Secretary of State Henry Kissinger, in Middle East and Vietnamese negotiations, further limited the degree of autonomy once enjoyed by US ambassadors.

The scope of diplomacy itself was also changed. Summit diplomacy by heads of State has also impacted the role of ambassadors. Presidents, prime ministers, emperors, and sheikhs attend well-publicized conferences on major issues. In 1972, Richard Nixon, the first US president to visit the PRC, personally directed the establishment of more friendly international relations between these two powers. In 1992, the fifteen heads of State in the nations then serving on the UN Security Council met for the first time. They directly discussed their respective interests in the operations of the Council. Most of the world's heads of State met in New York for the year 2000 Millennium Summit, and again for the five-year review Summit.[16]

Another twentieth-century development significantly influenced the role of the diplomat. International terrorism is now more effective, because of improvements in electronic communication, travel speed, and weapons technology. Diplomats must sometimes conduct their affairs in the hostile shadow of intimidation from terrorist groups. The Brazilian senior UN diplomat, as well members of his staff, were killed in an August 2003 Baghdad truck bombing at UN headquarters. A number of obscure groups have been clandestinely supported by certain governments as a crude instrument for furthering their foreign policy objections. Diplomats at all levels of government have encountered the threat of assassination by those States or individual groups whose political philosophies differ from their own.

Rescuers carry a woman from the US embassy over the rubble of a collapsed building next to the embassy in Nairobi, Kenya. Terrorist bombs exploded minutes apart outside the US embassies in the Kenyan and Tanzanian capitals on August 7, 1998. Twelve Americans were among the dead, and the US ambassador to Kenya was injured, according to the US State Department. The bombings killed 224 people and wounded 5,000. AP photo by Khalil Senosi (reprinted with permission of AP/World Wide Photos).

The student of diplomacy must also recognize that modern diplomacy has been used as both a sword and a plowshare. The 1994 US-North Korea (NK) energy aid agreement is a positive example of economic diplomacy. In 1993, NK announced its intent to withdraw from the Nuclear Nonproliferation Treaty (§10.4), which had been signed by 153 nations. NK denied access to its nuclear facilities to inspectors from the UN's International Atomic Energy Agency. The United States, after a round of preliminary negotiations, threatened sanctions. The international community was concerned that NK's aging leader was unwilling to move beyond the Cold War era—in order to cooperate in international controls on nuclear proliferation. Under the 1994 agreement, the United States is providing $4 billion of energy aid to ameliorate NK's desperate economic situation and to dissuade the further nuclear weapons development. This program is designed to provide economic assistance, vitiate NK's isolationism, and promote diplomatic ties. NK nevertheless conducted a missile test in 1998, with a trajectory that overflew Japan. This event has significant political and military implications for regional stability. NK would not likely risk confrontation with the United States and the loss of financial gains from the prior economic aid deal. NK made like threats during Summer 2005, and was rewarded with further concessions.

The Arab boycott of Israeli goods could be described as one of the worst examples of economic diplomacy. The Arab League's official policy was to influence other

States not to buy from or sell to Israel—a scenario that was not expected to survive the diplomatic breakthrough associated with the 1993 Israeli-Palestine Liberation Organization (PLO) Peace Accords signed in Washington (§10.1).

SECRET DIPLOMACY

What diplomats do is sometimes less important than *how* they do it. For example, should diplomacy be conducted openly or in secret? President Woodrow Wilson's famous "Fourteen Points" speech to the US Congress in 1918 advocated "[o]pen covenants of peace, openly arrived at, after which there shall be no private international understandings of any kind but diplomacy shall proceed always frankly and in public view." Wilson was thereby admonishing certain governments who had engaged in secret arrangements, which led to World War I. The skillful British diplomat and commentator, Sir Harold Nicolson, articulated the position that international policy making should never be undertaken in secret. Consider his remarks, regarding World War II, which have unarguably retained their appeal to this day: "No system should ever again be tolerated [that] can commit men and women, without their knowledge or consent, to obligations which will entail upon them, either a breach of national good faith, or the sacrifice of their property and lives."[17]

The pendulum may now be swinging in the other direction. In March 1986, US Secretary of State George Shultz complained that diplomats and heads of State cannot effectively conduct their affairs in public. Shultz felt that US Cold War relations with the Soviet Union were becoming far less productive. Diplomatic exchanges about nuclear arms control were being conducted in public forums. He perceived the presence of the media as unduly influencing the effectiveness of these critical diplomatic efforts. He called on the leaders of both Cold War powers to engage in a more "quiet" diplomacy conducted via private discussions rather than open conversations effectively directed at the public and the media—as opposed to only the respective negotiators. In 1994, US Secretary of State Warren Christopher received a rather blunt lecture about secret diplomacy from the Chinese Communist Party's leader. Christopher met secretly with China's leading dissident, while on a trade mission to Beijing. The Chinese leader claimed that this meeting unnecesssarily inflamed public opinion, and

that US officials had thus made accusations against China which would not survive public scrutiny in other countries. The Chinese reaction made it far more difficult for the United States to exact human rights concessions in exchange for the United States continuing to grant China favorable trade status.

◆ 7.2 DIPLOMATIC AND CONSULAR FUNCTIONS

SYSTEMIC OVERVIEW

Establishing Relations When two States agree to establish diplomatic relations, they first exchange representatives who usually work in the respective capitals of each State. The representative is often referred to as "ambassador," "minister," or "head of mission." A *chargé d'affaires* is normally the second-ranking official in the delegation. He or she takes charge of the mission and the premises in the absence of the primary diplomat.

No State has established diplomatic offices in every other State of the world. Many consulates and embassies have even closed for financial reasons. The United States maintains approximately 140 embassies abroad. It hosts about 130 foreign embassies in Washington, DC. The United States also maintains more than 100 "consular posts" to deal with commercial matters throughout the world. Certain States, however, can afford embassies in only a few places. In 1993, the Philippines announced that it would close its consulates in a number of US cities. It also closed its embassies in Cuba, Jordan, Micronesia, Morocco, Peru, Poland, Romania, Senegal, and Sri Lanka.

The host State may close, or withhold occupancy of, an embassy—without necessarily breaking diplomatic relations. The United States closed Rwanda's Washington embassy in July 1994. The Rwandan diplomats were ordered to leave the United States with only five days' notice. (The United States then sought to remove the Rwandan representative from the UN Security Council.) President Clinton explained that the United States was not breaking formal ties with Rwanda, but attenuating relations to a lower level of interaction. President Clinton noted that "The US cannot allow representatives of a regime that supports genocidal massacres to remain on our soil." In 1990, the military government of Lebanon was no longer recognized by the United States. Despite claims emanating from "leaders" in Lebanon, the United States refused to allow Lebanon's former representative to occupy the Lebanese embassy in Washington. In 1981 and 1992, China downgraded the Beijing missions of France and the Netherlands, respectively, because of their sales of fighter planes and submarines to Taiwan.

Accreditation often becomes a problem during the postwar occupation by another country. Shortly after the first phase of the 2003 Iraq War, there were a number of foreign diplomats in Baghdad. These diplomats had been accredited to, and by, the regime of Saddam Hussein. Many still resided in former mission residences in Iraq. The US State Department's position was as follows: "They're accredited to a regime that is no longer existent, and, therefore, their accreditation would have lapsed."[18]

The process of exchanging diplomats begins with an "accreditation." The State A host government must consent to the particular diplomat dispatched from State B. State B's agent typically presents his or her "credentials" to a representative of the head of State A. The credential is a document that identifies the State B agent as State B's official representative. State A's consent is confirmed by an *agrément* which indicates its approval of State B's diplomat.[19] During the failed 1991 coup by certain Russian military leaders against Mikhail Gorbachev, the ranking US diplomat refused to present his credentials to the coup's leaders. He was forced to leave Russia but was hastily replaced by a new US ambassador who immediately presented his credentials to Gorbachev as a show of US support for maintaining the democratic reforms sought by Gorbachev.

Foreign diplomats must navigate the host State's accreditation process in order to be actually "accredited." In one of few cases on point, a Gambian citizen in Florida pled guilty to the charge of paying a gratuity in violation of US law. The defendant was designated by Gambia as a Special Advisor to the Special Mission in the United States. Gambia therefore claimed diplomatic immunity under the Vienna Convention on Diplomatic Relations (VCDR). A federal judge denied that request, however. Gambia did not submit Mr. Sissoko, or his credentials, for certification by the US Department of State. Thus, there had been no performance of the accreditation process set forth in the Convention and the governing host-State Diplomatic Relations Act. There is a UN Convention on Special Missions. As it had not been signed by Gambia, the United States, or the UN Security Council, it could not be proffered by the defendant as evidence of Customary International Law (§1.2).[20]

Certain States have arranged for multiple accreditations, whereby the same diplomatic premises contain the embassies of more than one foreign government. Conversely, some States do not have any diplomatic presence, and often rely on their United Nations mission in New York or Geneva to promote their diplomatic interests with other countries.

The location of the diplomatic premises occasionally signals a political aperture. Foreign missions are normally located in the capital city of the host State. Massachusetts Avenue in Washington, DC, is commonly referred to as "Embassy Row," because of the large number of foreign missions on that street. In Israel, most States have located their diplomatic premises in Tel Aviv. They do not recognize Jerusalem as the capital of Israel, which Israel has claimed since 1950. In 1993, the essentially Muslim State of Kyrgyzstan established its embassy in Jerusalem—a religious center for Muslims. Only El Salvador and Costa Rica had previously maintained embassies in Jerusalem. In 1998, US Speaker of the House, Newt Gingrich acquiesced in a White House request that he did not visit the proposed site of the new US embassy in Jerusalem. Both Israel and Palestine claim Jerusalem as their capital city. His visit would have triggered more bloodshed in Middle East peace negotiations.

Breaking Relations   Diplomatic relations, once established, do not always proceed smoothly. An adverse development in the international relations between two States may occur. A diplomat may act in a manner considered unacceptable to the host State and may then be asked to leave—with or without specified reasons. The host State would thus declare the sending State's diplomat *persona non grata* (unwelcome), necessitating his or her departure. On the eve of the 1991 UN-imposed Iraqi departure date from Kuwait (and the ensuing Persian Gulf War), Iraq's ambassador was summoned to the US State Department in Washington and advised that he must reduce the size of his diplomatic staff to four people who could travel no farther than twenty-five miles from their embassy. The rest of the staff was ordered to leave the United States, including the Iraqi ambassador himself. While the United States did not then "break" diplomatic relations with Iraq, it did close its US embassy in Baghdad.

Not all States follow this customary practice of merely withdrawing a particular diplomat's acceptability.

Contrary to International Law, diplomats are sometimes held captive and have even been prohibited from exiting the host State. During its Cultural Revolution, the People's Republic of China (PRC) withdrew the diplomatic status of a representative in the Indian embassy and forbade his departure until he was punished for the "crimes" with which he had been charged. In a similar episode during the same period, a Dutch *chargé d'affaires* in China was declared *persona non grata*. Rather than facilitating his return to the Netherlands, China did not grant this officer an exit visa until after five months of confinement. In response to this episode, Chinese diplomats in the Netherlands remained secluded in their offices—to avoid having to testify about this affair to Dutch officials. China's actions violated both the customary practice of States and the fundamental diplomatic treaty discussed later. This incident illustrates how host States can readily interrupt and interfere with the normal conduct of diplomatic relations.[21]

Suspension or termination of diplomatic relations is completely discretionary under State practice. International Law does not require a legal basis for such disruptions. States may abruptly refuse to deal with each other. The sending and host States may opt to recall their respective diplomatic agents. During the student demonstrations in Beijing in 1989, the United States did not break diplomatic relations with China. The United States did prepare its diplomats to leave Beijing for their safety—an action designed to demonstrate the US protest of the massacre of students seeking democratic reform in China.

In 1979, the United States recognized the government of the PRC as the political entity responsible for "China." The United States continued to maintain diplomatic relations with Taiwan. It is treated as a State and is permitted access to US courts—unlike the PRC, and the former Soviet Union, when they were not recognized by the United States. Prior to 1993, when mainland China and Taiwan took some preliminary steps to resolve 40 years of political hostility, their proximity required unofficial communications on a regular basis—notwithstanding lack of diplomatic ties and their mutual nonrecognition.[22] As succinctly described by the University of Leicester's G. R. Berridge: "Intermediaries are valued by hostile states seeking some kind of accommodation when at least one of the parties regards the political price of direct talks as unacceptably high, or believes that the participation of a third party in any negotiation with its enemy will bring it material gain and additional security from any settlement."[23]

Broken Relations   Severing diplomatic ties does not necessarily cut off the continuing need to deal with each other—even when there are no "official" links. This unconventional diplomacy—when States and other entities without diplomatic relations must nevertheless talk to the enemy—is a worldwide phenomenon. This form of diplomatic exchange is the product of the need for communication between States or other entities publicly at war but privately seeking a reconciliation or some other mutually recognized objective.

One of the more common devices for this shadowy form of diplomacy is to employ the diplomatic corps of third parties who enjoy good relations with both hostile States. Cuba and the United States have had indirect dealings with each other ever since Fidel Castro assumed political power in 1959. The United States broke diplomatic relations with Cuba, but the Swiss and former Czechoslovakian embassies in Havana exchanged information on behalf of the US and Cuban government for many years. The Cuban Interest Section of the former Czechoslovakian embassy in Washington, DC, also acted as a go-between in such matters. In March 1995, an Iraqi court sentenced two Americans to an eight-year prison term because they strayed into Iraqi territory during a visit with friends in the demilitarized zone between Kuwait and Iraq. The United States and Iraq had no official diplomatic ties. Poland had such ties with both countries. Its diplomats served as go-betweens to negotiate the release of the US citizens. The Swiss also assisted Iran, when unmanned US surveillance drones overflew Iran during the winter of 2005, seeking evidence of a nuclear weapons program. Iran lodged its formal protest with the United States via the good offices of the Swiss government.

States also undertake other forms of unconventional diplomacy when they do not recognize one another. Israel and the PLO secretly communicated for many years before their 1993 Washington peace accord. The United Kingdom and Sinn Fein (the nongovernmental organization seeking independence for Northern Ireland) engaged in private negotiations before the 1994 announcement of their new working relationship. The clandestine methods for international communication include disguised embassies and ceremonial occasions such as the "working funeral" when a prominent dignitary has died.

No Relations   Some countries have no official relations. Before the United States attacked Afghanistan in response to "9-11," there were no diplomatic ties (nor during the prior Soviet occupation). Pakistan was one of only several nations that recognized Afghanistan's fundamentalist Taliban government. After the war's commencement, the Taliban ambassador to Pakistan remained in Pakistan, gave press conferences, and ultimately requested asylum. Pakistan refused. A brief but notable period passed, during which he did not return to Afghanistan. Pakistan thus handed him over to the United States. He was then transferred to a US warship, and then the Guantanamo Bay detention facility in Cuba, where he remained until released in September 2005. Although his prior status as an ambassador requesting asylum was murky, one could argue that Pakistan or the United States should have returned him to Afghanistan as a diplomat entitled to protection under the VCDR. On the other hand, his asylum request, Pakistan's denial, and his choosing to remain in Pakistan all suggest that he had effectively relinquished his protected status.

The respective 1961 and 1963 VCDR are the current encyclopedias of diplomatic practice. They are the core materials for this chapter.

1961 VIENNA CONVENTION ON DIPLOMATIC RELATIONS

Diplomatic functions are globally defined in the VCDR.[24] The diplomat thus:

(a) Represents the sending State in the receiving State;

(b) Protects the interests of the sending State and of its nationals, within the limits permitted by the receiving State's internal laws and International Law;

(c) Negotiates with the Government of the receiving State;

(d) Ascertains, by lawful means, conditions and developments in the receiving State, and reports them to the Government of the sending State; and

(e) Promotes friendly relations between the sending State and the receiving State by prodding the development of their economic, cultural, and scientific relations.[25]

Protecting the interests of State A includes providing diplomatic (or consular) assistance to a State A citizen who is present in and has allegedly been harmed by host State B or its agents (§4.2). The State A representative in State B may have to deal with a variety of problems confronting his or her fellow citizens who are visiting or residing in State B. Normally, a diplomat deals with the host government on intergovernmental issues. While a diplomat's tasks could include making arrangements for a criminal defense, or transferring of deceased individuals or their property between the host State and the home State, such details generally fall within the province of consular officials.

1963 VIENNA CONVENTION ON CONSULAR RELATIONS

Consular officials are not usually "diplomatic" representatives. They are not generally accredited to the host State, although they are official agents of the sending State. Consular officers often conduct "diplomatic" negotiations in international trade matters, however. Such matters are sometimes handled through the institution of the honorary consul. This is an individual who assists in the promotion of trade policies. He or she is typically a national of the *host* State, possessing expertise in host State business matters.

One of the most sensitive consular functions is providing access to nationals of the home State who are arrested in the host State. Denial of access, or delays, often generate friction in international relations. In 1993, for example, the United States protested to Israel about its treatment of three jailed Palestinian-Americans from Chicago. They were visiting relatives in the occupied West Bank, where they were arrested and confined, without prompt access to either lawyers or US consular officials. The resulting US protest occurred during the period when the United States was attempting to bring Israel and the PLO together for the long-awaited peace accords (ultimately achieved in Washington several months later).

Historical Evolution   Consular institutions have had a longer, and more varied, history than the diplomatic mission described earlier.

Consular officials once possessed broad powers in both the trade and judicial matters. However, the judicial function is now limited to any express treaty provision which may confer some judicial powers on a consular officer—such as serving notice of judicial proceedings (§5.5). As noted by the US Supreme Court in 1875:

Historically, . . . as shown by numerous authorities quoted by Mr. Warden in his treatise on "*The Origin and Nature of Consular Establishments,*" that the consul was originally an officer of large judicial as well as commercial powers, exercising entire municipal authority over his countrymen in the country to which he was accredited. But the changed circumstances of Europe, and the prevalence of civil order in the several Christian States, have had the effect of greatly modifying the powers of the consular office; and it may now be considered as generally true, that, for any judicial powers which may be vested in the consuls accredited to any nation, we must look to the express provisions of the treaties entered into with that nation, and to the laws of the States which the consuls represent.[26]

The forerunner of the modern consul appeared almost as early as people began to trade. The Preamble to the 1963 Vienna Convention acknowledges that "consular relations have been established between peoples since ancient times." As succinctly described by Professor Luke Lee of American University in Washington, DC:

Among the many political contributions of the Greek city-states . . . [include] the early development of the consular system; the *prostates* and the *proxenos* are considered forerunners of the modern consuls. The *prostates* were chosen by Greek colonists to live abroad to act as intermediaries in legal and political relations between the foreign (Greek) colony and the local government [of a distant land]. About the sixth century BC the Egyptians allowed Greek settlers . . . to select *prostates,* who administered Greek law to the Greeks. In the same period, similar institutions could be found in certain parts of India.

During the first millennium BC, *proxenoi* were appointed in the Greek city-states to look after the interests of the appointing [city-]State. The *proxenos,* though more a political than commercial agent, has been likened to the modern honorary consul, and was [thus] chosen from the nationals of the receiving State.[27]

Modern Treaty The 1963 Vienna Convention on Consular Relations contains the globally defined consular functions. Consular officials thus:

(a) Protect the interests of the sending State and its nationals, within the limits permitted by International Law

(b) Further the development of commercial, economic, cultural, and scientific relations—and otherwise promote friendly relations

(c) Ascertain conditions and developments in the commercial, economic, cultural, and scientific life of the receiving State—and report thereon to the government of the sending State and other interested persons

(d) Issue passports and travel documents to nationals of the sending State, and visas or appropriate documents to persons wishing to travel to the sending State

(e) Safeguard the interests of nationals, including minors and other persons lacking full capacity of the sending State

(f) Represent or arrange appropriate representation for nationals of the sending State before the tribunals and other authorities of the receiving State—where such nationals are unable to assume the defense of their own rights and interests—including the transmission of judicial documents or the taking of evidence for the courts of the sending State

(g) Exercise rights of supervision and inspection provided for in the laws and regulations of the sending State for vessels having the nationality of the foreign State, as well as aircraft registered in that State

(h) Assist vessels and aircraft and their crews, or take statements regarding the voyage of a vessel, examining and stamping the ship's papers, or conduct investigations into any incidents that occurred during the voyage (§6.3 "Port Tranquility" case).[28]

Consular officers thus prepare trade reports, gather information relevant to international trade, and investigate alleged infractions of commercial treaties. Consuls also aid in the supervision of international shipping. Seagoing vessels must be registered to a particular country and fly that country's flag. Consuls authenticate the registration papers of their home State's ships in the host State. Consuls help their home State's nationals resolve host State customs and immigration problems. Consuls also provide needed services to fellow citizens who become ill or indigent while in the host State. They take charge of the estates of deceased home State nationals and arrange for property distribution under the host State's laws. Unlike diplomats, consuls often directly assist their fellow nationals with *personal* problems—such as obtaining legal representation in host State courts.

As of July 2001, only four of 123 foreigners on America's death row (in the previous quarter-century) were promptly told that they could seek help from their consulates. Amnesty International stated that since 1976, at least fifteen foreign citizens had been executed; three were freed after appeals or retrials; and eight had their death sentences overturned on appeal.[29] A number of these communication gaps violated a treaty that also protects the roughly 2,500 Americans detained abroad each year. The following case illustrates how this treaty should operate:

◆

www *Torres v. Oklahoma* (Mullin)

OKLAHOMA COURT OF CRIMINAL APPEALS

42 INT'L LEGAL MAT'LS 1227 (2004)

Go to course Web page at
<http://home.att.net/~slomansonb/txtcsesite.html>.
Under Chapter Seven, click <u>Torres v. Mullin.</u>

As noted in *Torres,* Texas initially advised the federal government that it did not intend to comply with President Bush's demand that it conduct further reviews, in response to the International Court of Justice *Avena* case. Texas does not, however, seek to keep such prisoners in its jails. On the contrary, it has a model plan for implementing the repatriation of foreign nationals, where federal treaties so provide. They may thereby serve the remainder of their terms in their home country. This model plan mandates that a correctional official notify the foreign national of this right. Other states have adopted this model plan. In California, for example, the Governor signed into law a 2005 revision, which expands state participation in the international prisoner transfer process. Under California law:

> Upon the entry of any person who is currently or was previously a foreign national [naturalized citizen] into a facility operated by the Department of Corrections, the Director . . . shall inform the person that he or she may apply to be transferred to serve the remainder of his or her prison term in his or her current or

former nation of citizenship. The director shall inform the person that he or she may contact his or her consulate and shall ensure that if notification is requested by the inmate, that the inmate's nearest consulate or embassy is notified without delay of his or her incarceration.[30]

◆ 7.3 EXTRATERRITORIALITY AND DIPLOMATIC ASYLUM

Prior sections discussed diplomatic and consular functions. There are two important corollaries. First: What is the effect of an act undertaken in a foreign embassy or consulate, when the legal consequences would be different under the laws of the host State where the building is located? Second: May a foreign State give diplomatic asylum within its embassy or consular premises, when to do so offends the host State?

EXTRATERRITORIALITY FICTION

The special international status of embassies and consular premises long ago generated the question of whether they are legally a part of the host State or the sending State. Historically, they were considered an extraterritorial extension of the sending State. This legal fiction meant that acts done within an embassy or consulate would be governed by the law of the sending State, even when contrary to host State law.

The historical basis for this view is derived from the practice of medieval "Christian" States. Their consuls exercised full civil and criminal jurisdiction over their fellow nationals located in non-Christian States. This exclusion from the jurisdiction of local tribunals was rooted in the convenient legal fiction of "extraterritoriality." Foreign nationals could invoke the protection of the more favorable laws of their own home States—a subtle form of extraterritorial jurisdiction (§5.1). The Sino-Russian Treaty of Nerchinsk of 1689 provided that criminals would be delivered to the consular officers of their own countries for prosecution. The Franco-US Consular Convention of 1788 similarly provided for consular jurisdiction of the respective nations over civil disputes between Frenchmen when both were in the United States, and between Americans when both were in France. The Japanese-American Treaty of 1858 was a model for a number of similar pacts that provided for this extraterritorial regime, conferring jurisdiction to resolve such disputes on foreign consular officers located in the host State.[31]

Contemporary courts apply a pragmatic analysis of such immunity, thereby rejecting this historical fiction. Under the historical view, Egypt's consulate in London would have been characterized as being located on "Egyptian" soil. The contemporary approach is that the Egyptian consulate in London is located in England for all purposes. But the Consular Convention protects the premises. The putative conflict is illustrated in the following case:

Radwan v. Radwan

FAMILY DIVISION OF LONDON, ENGLAND

3 *All England Reports* 967 (1972)

AUTHOR'S NOTE: Mr. Radwan was an Egyptian national who entered into a polygamous marriage with an English woman in the Egyptian consulate in Paris.

Mr. Radwan subsequently moved to London. He entered the Egyptian consulate there, for the purpose of divorcing his English (second) wife. He thus employed the "talaq" procedure. In her absence, he orally decreed, three times, that they were divorced. This talaq procedure constituted a valid divorce under the laws of Egypt—but not under English law.

Several years later, his English wife filed her own divorce suit in the English courts, anticipating a more favorable divorce decree under English law than under Egyptian law. Her English lawyer argued that the talaq "divorce," while performed within the Egyptian consulate in London, was not entitled to recognition under English law. It should not be recognized as a divorce performed "outside of" England. Mr. Radwan, hoping to avoid a comparatively unfavorable English divorce decree, responded to this "wife's" suit on the basis that he had already obtained a valid divorce. Thus, he argued, his prior talaq divorce was effective, because it was legally performed on "Egyptian territory" (i.e., in Egypt's consulate in London).

The court's footnotes are omitted.

COURT'S OPINION: I have read the relevant subparagraph of the petition whereby the talaq divorce is pleaded. The husband put in evidence the affidavit of Mustapha Kamil Abdul Fata, Deputy Consul General of the Consulate General of the United Arab Republic of Egypt in Kensington Palace Gardens in London. In it he swore [in his capacity as an expert on Egyptian law] as follows:

(1) The Egyptian Consulate in London is regarded as being Egyptian territory on Egyptian soil.

(2) The divorce . . . registered in Cairo . . . is valid and recognised by Egyptian law. . . .

I also received the affidavit of Jamil Nasir, a person qualified in Egyptian law. In that affidavit he says that

. . . under Egyptian law the Consulate General of the United Arab Republic in London is regarded as Egyptian territory. He does not give any reasons for that opinion, but I note that it corresponds with the [above-quoted] statement of the deputy consul of the Consulate General in London. . . .

The facts are as follows. The husband was born in Cairo. He is and at all material times was a Mohammedan. He was and remains a subject of the United Arab Republic. . . . On 1st [of] April 1970 he entered the Egyptian Consulate in London; the procedure stated in the affidavit of the deputy consul of the Consulate General was followed. The husband three times declared the prescribed [talaq] form of divorce in the presence of two witnesses. All the steps were carried out in accordance with Egyptian law. After the prescribed 90 days the divorce was finalised in accordance with Egyptian law, and in accordance with that law it was no impediment to the efficacy of the proceedings that the wife knew nothing about it at all. . . .

The question for my decision is whether by English law the Consulate General of the United Arab Republic is part of a country outside the British Isles within the meaning of the Recognition of Divorces and Legal Separations Act of 1971. By that Act the relevant sections providing for recognition will have effect in respect of overseas divorces if they have been obtained by means of judicial or other proceedings in any country outside the British Isles, and it is necessary for the efficacy of the talaq divorce that it should have been obtained outside the British Isles by reason of the fact that at the material time the husband had acquired English domicile [emphasis supplied by author].

Curiously, the question has not arisen for decision in England before, that is, the question whether the premises of an embassy or consulate are part of the territory of the sending state as compared to the territory of the receiving state.

I quote and adopt the observations of [legal commentator] Mr J E S Fawcett:

There are two popular myths about diplomats and their immunities which we must clear away: one is that an embassy is foreign territory, and the other is that a diplomat can incur no legal liabilities in the country in which he is serving. The first is a confusion between territory or property and jurisdiction over it, and it is important to clarify it for it has sometimes arisen over ships and aircraft. The building occupied by a foreign embassy and the land on which it stands are part of the territory of what we call the receiving state: it is therefore under the jurisdiction of that state. But the members of the mission and their activities in the embassy are primarily under the control and jurisdiction of the sending state. International law avoids conflict between these jurisdictions by laying down rules to cover the whole field of diplomatic relations. These rules have been embodied in the Vienna Convention [on Diplomatic Relations of] 1961, which may be taken as reflecting existing law and practice. This Convention, and that on Consular Relations drawn up in 1963, are among the first steps . . . in the successful codification of international law. The premises of a mission are inviolable, and the local authorities may enter them only with the consent of the head of the mission. But this does not make the premises foreign territory or take them out of the reach of the local law for many purposes: for example, a commercial transaction in an embassy may be governed by the local law, particularly tax law; marriages may be celebrated there only if conditions laid down by the local law are met; and a child born in it [the diplomatic premises] will, unless his father has diplomatic status, acquire the local nationality.

Judge Cummins then considered similar cases involving this issue arising in other countries. This is a useful illustration of how a decision maker resorts to customary State practice as a basis for ascertaining the content of International Law.

FRANCE: *Nikitschenkoff* case: The court was dealing with murderous assaults on the first secretary of the Russian embassy in the Russian embassy in Paris, and an argument was submitted that the place of the crime being the premises of the Russian embassy was a place situated outside the territory of France and not governed by French law. The decision was a decision under art. 3 of the Code of Napoleon. The court said:

[that] all those who live in the territory [France] are subject to [French] police and security laws; Whereas, admitting as exceptions to this rule of public law the immunity which, in certain cases, international law accords to the person of foreign diplomatic agents and the legal fiction in virtue of which the premises they occupy are deemed to be situated outside the territory of the sovereign to whom they are accredited; Whereas, nevertheless, this legal fiction cannot be extended but constitutes an exception to the rule of territorial jurisdiction . . . and is strictly limited to the ambassador or minister whose independence it is designed to protect and to those of his subordinates who are clothed with the same public character; Whereas the accused is not attached in any sense to the Russian Embassy but, as a foreigner residing for the time in France, was subject to French law; and Whereas the place where the crime which he is charged with committing cannot, in so far as he is concerned, be regarded as outside the limits of [French] territory . . . the jurisdiction of the French judiciary [is] clearly established.

GERMANY: *Afghan Embassy* case.

ITALY: [citing several cases].

In all these cases the court rejected the argument that diplomatic premises were not part of the territory of the receiving state. . . .

Although international conventions [treaties] do not have the force of law unless embodied in municipal legislation [of an individual state], they may in the field of international law be valuable as a guide to the rules of international law which this country as a signatory respects. . . .

If it was the view of the high contracting parties [to the Vienna Convention] that the premises of missions were part of the territory of the sending state, that would undoubtedly be formulated [within the language of those treaties].

◆ *Notes & Questions*

1. In this *initial* phase of a stormy divorce, Judge Cummins ruled that Mr. Radwan did not legally divorce his English wife in a place "outside of" England, although he performed the talaq procedure in the Egyptian consulate. Thus, all the relevant activity was performed in England and Mr. Radwan's prior talaq "divorce" was not entitled to recognition as a foreign judgment. Mr. Radwan remained married to his English wife. Mrs. Radwan was thus able to prosecute her subsequent divorce action in the English courts.

2. The same Judge Cummins subsequently decided a related question: whether the original Radwan "marriage" was governed by Egyptian or French law. Their marriage was performed in the Egyptian consulate in Paris. Judge Cummins ruled, in "Radwan 2," that their marriage occurred in France rather than in Egypt. He noted that the extraterritoriality fiction regarding foreign consulates was not recognized under French law (nor under English law, as he had decided in "Radwan 1"). The marriage ceremony performed in the Egyptian consulate in Paris was *also* void under host State (French) law. *Radwan v. Radwan* (No. 2), 3 ALL ENGLAND LAW REPORTS 1026 (1972).

3. The popular misconception—even today—is that embassies and consulates are on "foreign" soil. The Vienna Conventions, mentioned in the *Radwan* opinion, effectively replaced the extraterritoriality fiction—with an *express* protection for diplomatic premises. Judge Cummins based the above London "talaq" opinion on what is *not* said in those treaties. Why does their silence support the proposition that "extraterritoriality" is a fiction no longer necessary under International Law?

4. In June 2000, a court in Alexandria, Egypt ruled that while a husband may divorce his wife by saying "I divorce you" three times (talaq procedure), he cannot do this by e-mail. The court decided that Islam, the basis of family law in Egypt, does not recognize electronic documents as evidence. The wife of the man who attempted this divorce was not free to marry, when he changed his mind and she the so-called e-mail divorce. *Source*: NYT News Service.

DIPLOMATIC ASYLUM

A host-State political refugee may request that a foreign-State diplomat provide asylum (protection) from local arrest or extradition to another nation.

There have been a number of prominent instances where this protection has been requested and then granted, to the dismay of the host State. During the 1989 Tiananmen Square demonstrations in the PRC, the United States granted asylum to China's top dissident. He and his wife stayed in the US embassy in Beijing. Chinese authorities had ordered his arrest for treason, demanding that the US government surrender him to the local authorities waiting outside the US embassy in Beijing. At the same time, the Chinese sealed their international borders to prevent any clandestine escape attempts.

The Vatican has been a prominent participant in asylum and other diplomatic contexts.[32] United States invaded Panama in 1989. Its dictator, General Manuel Noriega, remained in hiding for five days. He then entered the Vatican embassy in Panama City, after evading US military personnel seeking to take him to the United States for trial on drug-trafficking charges. The Vatican diplomat initially refused to turn Noriega over to the invading US forces—which had surrounded the embassy with US troops, tanks, and helicopters to prevent any possible escape. After an agreement with US authorities, the Vatican decided to surrender Noriega to the US forces. He was brought to the United States for trial. Whether the Vatican actually granted him asylum became a moot issue. Noriega was able to obtain temporary refuge in the embassy until he could arrange a satisfactory bargain with the US authorities. This was not the first time that the Vatican effectively granted asylum to someone wanted by US authorities. In 1866, Pope Pius XI granted diplomatic asylum to John Surratt, Jr., who had conspired with John Wilkes Booth to assassinate US President Lincoln. Ultimately, the Pope surrendered Surratt to the United States for prosecution.

Other sensational asylum cases have generated the popular belief that individuals are routinely granted such refuge in foreign embassies. Political relations may be harmed, however, when asylum is granted. A classic case was that of Hungary's Cardinal Jozsef Mindszenty, who remained within the premises of the US embassy in Budapest, Hungary, for *fifteen years*. He had been arrested for antigovernment activities in 1948, jailed in 1949, and freed for several days during a popular revolt in 1956. He then sought refuge in the US embassy. Although the United States did not normally grant asylum, it considered this particular request a special case. Mindszenty remained in the embassy under a grant of diplomatic asylum from 1956 to 1971, when Hungary finally agreed to his safe passage out of Hungary and to the Vatican.

In the leading international judicial opinion on diplomatic asylum, the ICJ articulated the general principle that State practice does not recognize a *right* of asylum. Diplomatic asylum had been granted with some frequency, however, in Latin America. The following case presents a unique scenario. The Court failed to acknowledge the regional custom of granting asylum, a decision for which it would be criticized for years to come.

Asylum Case: *Colombia v. Peru*

INTERNATIONAL COURT OF JUSTICE
1950 *ICJ Rep.* 266 (1950)

AUTHOR'S NOTE: Haya de la Torre was a Peruvian national. He led an unsuccessful rebellion against Peru in 1948. The Peruvian government issued a warrant for his arrest on criminal charges related to this political uprising. He fled to the Colombian embassy in Lima. He therein requested, and was granted, diplomatic asylum by the Colombian ambassador on behalf of the government of Colombia. Colombia then requested permission from Peru for de la Torre's safe passage from the Colombian embassy, through Peru, and into Colombia. Peru refused.

Colombia then brought this suit against Peru in the ICJ, asking the Court to declare that Colombia had properly granted asylum, pursuant to a recognized regional practice of granting asylum in such political cases. Peru's lawyers responded that Colombia could not unilaterally grant asylum over Peru's objection. De la Torre had committed a common crime, subjecting him to prosecution by Peru, just like any other criminal. Colombia had no right to employ asylum as a means of avoiding Peru's criminal laws.

COURT'S OPINION: In the case of diplomatic asylum, the refugee is within the territory of the State where the offence was committed. A decision to grant diplomatic asylum involves a derogation from the sovereignty of that State. It withdraws the offender from the jurisdiction of the territorial State and constitutes an intervention in matters which are exclusively within the competence of that State [Peru]. Such a derogation from territorial sovereignty cannot be recognised unless its legal basis is established in each particular case. . . .

The Havana Convention on Asylum of 1928 . . . lays down certain rules relating to diplomatic asylum, but does not contain any provision conferring on the State granting asylum a unilateral competence to qualify the offence with definitive and binding force for the territorial State. . . .

A competence of this kind is of an exceptional character. It involves a derogation from the equal rights of qualification which, in the absence of any contrary rule, must be attributed to each of the States concerned; it aggravates the derogation from territorial sovereignty constituted by the exercise of asylum. Such a competence is not inherent in the institution of diplomatic asylum. This institution would perhaps be more effective if a rule of unilateral and definitive qualification were applied. But such a rule is not essential to the exercise of asylum. . . .

The Colombian Government has finally invoked "American international law in general" [to justify its grant of asylum]. In addition to the rules arising from agreements, . . . it has relied on an alleged regional or local custom peculiar to Latin-American States. The Party which relies on a custom of this kind must prove that this custom is established in such a manner that it has become binding on the other Party, . . . that it is in accordance with a constant and uniform usage practised by the States in question, and that this usage is the expression of a right appertaining to the State granting asylum and a duty incumbent on the territorial State. This follows from Article 38 of the Statute of the Court, which refers to international custom "as evidence of a general practice accepted as law." . . .

[T]he Colombian Government has referred to a large number of particular cases in which diplomatic asylum was in fact granted and respected. But it has not shown that the alleged rule of unilateral and definitive qualification was invoked or . . . that it was, apart from conventional stipulations, exercised by the States granting asylum as a right appertaining to them and respected by the territorial States as a duty incumbent on them and not merely for reasons of political expediency. The facts brought to the knowledge of the Court disclose so much uncertainty and contradiction, so much fluctuation and discrepancy in the exercise of diplomatic asylum and in the official views expressed on various occasions, there has been so much inconsistency in the rapid succession of conventions on asylum, ratified by some States and rejected by others, and the practice has been so much influenced by considerations of political expediency in the various cases, that it is not possible to discern in all this any constant and uniform usage, mutually accepted as law, with regard to the alleged rule of unilateral and definitive qualification of the offence.

The Court cannot therefore find that the Colombian Government has proved the existence of such a custom. But even if it could be supposed that such a custom existed between certain Latin-American States only, it could not be invoked against Peru which, far from having by its attitude adhered to it, has, on the contrary, repudiated it by refraining from ratifying the Montevideo Conventions of 1933 and 1939, which

were the first to include a rule concerning the qualification of the offence [as "political" in nature] in matters of diplomatic asylum. . . .

Article 2 lays down in precise terms the conditions under which asylum shall be granted to [political] offenders by the territorial State . . . the essential justification for asylum being in the imminence or persistence of a danger for the person of the refugee. It was incumbent upon the Government of Colombia to submit proof of facts to show that [this] condition was fulfilled. . . .

Asylum may be granted on humanitarian grounds . . . to protect political offenders against the violent and disorderly action of irresponsible sections of the population. It has not been contended that Haya de la Torre was in such a situation at the time when he sought refuge in the Colombian Embassy at Lima. . . .

In principle, it is inconceivable that the Havana Convention could have intended the term "urgent cases" to include the danger of regular prosecution to which the citizens of any country lay themselves open by attacking the institutions of that country, nor can it be admitted that in referring to "the period of time strictly indispensable for the person who has sought asylum to ensure in some other way his safety," the Convention envisaged protection from the operation of regular legal proceedings. . . .

In principle, asylum cannot be opposed to the operation of justice. An exception to this rule can occur only if, in the guise of justice, arbitrary action is substituted for the rule of law. Such would be the case if the administration of justice were corrupted by measures clearly prompted by political aims. Asylum protects the political offender against any measures of a manifestly extralegal character which a Government might take or attempt to take against its political opponents. The word "safety," which . . . determines the specific effect of asylum granted to political offenders, means that the refugee is protected against arbitrary action by the Government, and that he enjoys the benefits of the law. On the other hand, the safety which arises out of asylum cannot be construed as a protection against the regular application of the laws and against the jurisdiction of legally constituted tribunals. Protection thus understood would authorise the diplomatic agent to obstruct the application of the laws of the country whereas it is his duty to respect them; it would in fact become the equivalent of an immunity, which was evidently not within the intentions of the draftsmen of the Havana Convention.

It has not been shown that the existence of a state of siege [in Peru] implied the subordination of justice to the executive authority, or that the suspension of certain constitutional guarantees entailed the abolition of judicial guarantees. . . .

The Court cannot admit that the States signatory to the Havana Convention intended to substitute for the practice of the Latin-American republics, in which considerations of courtesy, good-neighbourliness and political expediency have always held a prominent place, a legal system which would guarantee to their own nationals accused of political offences the privilege of evading national jurisdiction. Such a conception, moreover, would come into conflict with one of the most firmly established traditions of Latin-America, namely, nonintervention [for example, by Colombia into the internal affairs of another State like Peru]. . . .

[The court must] reject the argument that the Havana Convention was intended to afford a quite general protection of asylum to any person prosecuted for political offences, either in the course of revolutionary events or in the more or less troubled times that follow, for the sole reason that it must be assumed that such events interfere with the administration of justice. It is clear that the adoption of such a criterion would lead to foreign interference of a particularly offensive nature in the domestic affairs of States; besides which no confirmation of this criterion can be found in Latin-American practice, as this practice has been explained to the Court.

In thus expressing itself, the Court does not lose sight of the numerous cases of asylum which have been cited. . . .

If these remarks tend to reduce considerably the value as precedents of the cases of asylum cited . . . they show none the less, that asylum as practised in Latin-America is an institution which, to a very great extent, owes its development to extra-legal factors. The good-neighbour relations between the republics, the different political interests of the Governments, have favoured the mutual recognition of asylum apart from any clearly defined juridical system. Even if the Havana Convention, in particular, represents an indisputable reaction against certain abuses in practice, it in no way tends to limit the practice of asylum as it may arise from agreements between interested Governments inspired by mutual feelings of toleration and goodwill. . . .

The Court considers that there did not exist a danger constituting a case of urgency within the meaning of Article 2, paragraph 2, of the Havana Convention.

◆ *Notes*

1. The ICJ decided that Haya de la Torre's asylum should be terminated because Colombia could not properly grant it. Colombia's unilateral decision that de la Torre was engaged in "political activity," rather than a "common crime" against Peru, was not entitled to recognition by other countries.

2. Although the ICJ ruled that Colombia's granting asylum was not legally valid, Peru's citizen was effectively sheltered anyway. Peru could not enter the Colombian embassy to force his surrender. Colombia, on the other hand, could not force Peru to grant de la Torre safe passage out of Peru. After this decision, Colombia and Peru ultimately negotiated an end to the stalemate by permitting de la Torre to leave Peru for Colombia.

3. Four years after this judgment, Peru ratified the Caracas Convention on Diplomatic Asylum. Article 2 therein provides that "every State has the right to grant asylum. . . ." Article 4 adds that it "shall rest with the State granting asylum to determine the nature of the offense [common crime versus political act] or the motives for the persecution." These provisions require treaty signatories to recognize unilateral grants of asylum rather than depend on a distant court's interpretation or application of the general International Law that may differ from a regional State practice. See Comment, Diplomatic Asylum in the United States and Latin America: A Comparative Analysis, 13 BROOKLYN J. INT'L L. 111 (1987).

4. The ICJ's judgment in the Asylum case was criticized by many States—especially in Latin America. There, diplomatic asylum was a common regional practice. Commentators characterized the Court as suffering from the continuing influence of irrelevant European

judicial perspectives. A representative criticism by a Brazilian author is as follows:

[The various judicial pronouncements in the Asylum case] received wide publicity and were the object of various learned papers; those written in Spain and Latin America were, with rare exception, highly critical of the stand taken by the [ICJ]. . . .

From a Latin American point of view, [the judgment] contains certain affirmations which simply went to prove that the Court was not qualified to pass judgment since it had examined a typical Latin American juridical institution [diplomatic asylum] exclusively from a European and biased point of view. . . . Just as the [reasoning] . . . of the International Court of Justice on the question of the international status of South-West Africa made most Afro-Asian States distrust the court, the Haya de la Torre case alienated most Latin American States, contributing to the atmosphere of ill-will which characterizes the relations of most States with the principal judicial organ of the United Nations [the ICJ].[33]

In the referenced *South-West Africa* case, decided by the ICJ in the same year as the *Asylum* case, the Court ruled that South Africa had no obligation to place South-West Africa (a former League "mandate") under the UN Trusteeship system. As a result, this territory remained subject to domination by the white minority government until independence forty years later (as the new State of Namibia). *See* International Status of South-West Africa, 1950 ICJ REP. 128.

5. In May 1999, João Vieira, the president of Guinea-Bissau, was driven from power by a segment of his nation's army. He successfully sought political asylum in the Portuguese embassy in the capital city of Bissau. Vieira's nineteen-year rule had been criticized on the basis of entrenched corruption. Portugal's prime minister provided Vieira asylum. As is typical in such cases, however, there was no guarantee that Vieira would be able to leave the Portuguese embassy to travel out of Guinea-Bissau to go to Portugal.

6. In April 2005, Brazil granted asylum to Ecuador's former President Lucio Gutierrez. He had just been removed from office by the Congress, for his alleged attempts to overhaul the Supreme Court. He was the

third president in eight years. The first in this grouping was declared mentally unfit to govern, and fled into exile. The interim president was ousted by a coup, led by Gutierrez (then an army colonel). Demonstrators closed down the airport, when an arrest warrant was issued for his arrest. Brazil then entered into negotiations with Ecuador for his safe passage out of Brazil.

◆ 7.4 IMMUNITIES AND ABUSE OF IMMUNITY

This section addresses two integral themes in the International Law of Diplomacy: (1) the extent to which the sending State, and its representatives may invoke immunity from prosecution in the host State; and (2) the pressure to seek a waiver of immunity, when a diplomat engages in conduct unbecoming his or her position.

DIPLOMATIC AND CONSULAR IMMUNITIES

Evolution   Many centuries ago, it was customary to protect the representatives of other governments. Otherwise, they could not perform their economic and political functions without fear of injury or death. Protective measures—now referred to as immunities—were created to limit the absolute power or jurisdiction of the host States to which they had traveled to convey their message. The mutual interests of the sending and receiving States required the creation of special privileges and immunities from local prosecution. Diplomats were thus protected from both host State authorities, and private citizens, in civil and criminal matters. The foreign envoy could then focus on diplomatic endeavors, without fear of arrest or time-consuming involvement in litigation unrelated to the official's diplomatic functions.

Oxford University Professor Ian Brownlie explains the rationale for diplomatic immunity as follows: "The essence of diplomatic relations is the exercise by the sending government of state functions on the territory of the receiving state by license of the latter. Having agreed to the establishment of diplomatic relations, the receiving [host] state must take steps to enable the sending state to benefit from the content of the license. The process of giving 'full faith and credit' to the license results in a body of 'privileges and immunities.'"[34]

This vintage practice, now known as *diplomatic immunity,* has additional roots in the medieval State practice that recognized the need for safe passage through third States. In the fifteenth and sixteenth centuries, a ruler who hoped to defeat an alliance between two other rulers would literally select their respective emissaries as targets. He needed only to kill or imprison any intermediary who was passing through his kingdom. For example, the French envoys Rinco and Fregoso were murdered by Emperor Charles V. Spain's Ambassador Mendoza was imprisoned in France for four months while on a mission to England. Incidents such as these ultimately led to State recognition of diplomatic immunities and privileges.[35] Unfortunately, many States failed to appreciate the practicality of "not shooting the messenger." Ultimately, certain States began to codify their expectations about diplomatic immunity in their internal laws. England's Diplomatic Privileges Act of 1708, for example, was a direct result of the arrest and detention of the Russian ambassador and his coach by English authorities. The Act was designed "to prevent like insolences for the future."[36]

Reciprocity, as a basis for this immunity, may echo through the ages. However, the various reasons for diplomatic immunity changed over the centuries—depending on whether the prevailing custom favored hospitality, status, some legal regime, or a functional approach. As Montana and Kansas state history professors Linda and Marsha Frey note, in their seminal work on the history of diplomatic immunity: "The weight of this study falls within the Western tradition, because the establishment of resident envoys is exclusively a Western development and because the expansion of European powers across the globe brought in its wake European international law. Admittedly, in other civilizations some envoys stayed in their host country for long periods. For example, in China in the sixteenth century, envoys from Russia and Central Asia remained in the capital for three or four years; in the eighteenth century, they remained even longer. This practice remained anomalous, however, and was never institutionalized [*i.e.,* in a multilateral treaty]."[37]

Consular immunity is more limited than diplomatic immunity. The diplomat and his or her immediate staff are normally granted full immunity from the jurisdiction of the host State. Consular officers enjoy less insulation from host State arrest or civil litigation. One reason for this distinction is that they usually represent less sensitive interests than ambassadors. As restated by Stefan Sawicki in the Polish Yearbook of International Law, "members of the consulate enjoy the immunity *only* in relation to official acts considered as [an] expression of a sovereign State. . . ."[38]

Modern Treaty Paradigm   The contemporary rules of diplomatic immunity are contained in the Vienna Convention on Diplomatic Relations of 1961, ratified by almost 180 State parties. Its key provisions are as follows:

Vienna Convention on Diplomatic Relations

500 United Nations Treaty Series 95–239 (1961)
<http://fletcher.tufts.edu/multi/texts/BH408.txt>

Article 22.1

The premises of the mission shall be inviolable. The agents of the receiving State may not enter them, except with the consent of the head of the mission. 2. The receiving State is under a special duty to take all appropriate steps to protect the premises of the mission against any intrusion or damage and to prevent any disturbance of the peace of the mission or impairment of its dignity. 3. The premises of the mission, their furnishings and other property thereon and the means of transport of the mission shall be immune from search, requisition, attachment [seizure resulting in custody and control by a court] or execution [sale of property to satisfy court judgment].

. . .

Article 24

The archives and documents of the mission shall be inviolable at any time and wherever they may be.

. . .

Article 27.1

The receiving State shall permit and protect free communication on the part of the mission for all official purposes. In communicating with the Government and the other missions and consulates of the sending State, wherever situated, the mission may employ all appropriate means, including diplomatic couriers and messages in code or cipher. However, the mission may install and use a wireless transmitter only with the consent of the receiving State. 2. The official correspondence of the mission shall be inviolable. Official correspondence means all correspondence relating to the mission and its functions. 3. The diplomatic bag shall not be opened or detained. . . . 5. The diplomatic courier, who shall be provided with an official document indicating his status and the number of packages constituting the diplomatic bag, shall be protected by the receiving State in the performance of his functions. He shall enjoy personal inviolability and shall not be liable to any form of arrest or detention.

. . .

Article 29

The person of a diplomatic agent shall be inviolable. He shall not be liable to any form of arrest or detention. The receiving State shall treat him with due respect and shall take all appropriate steps to prevent any attack on his person, freedom or dignity.

Article 30.1

The private residence of a diplomatic agent shall enjoy the same inviolability and protection as the premises of the mission. 2. His papers, correspondence and . . . his property shall likewise enjoy inviolability. . . .

Article 31.1

A diplomatic agent shall enjoy immunity from the criminal jurisdiction of the receiving State. He shall also enjoy immunity from its civil and administrative jurisdiction [regarding torts, contracts, and other legal matters].

. . .

A number of these provisions—found also in the 1963 Vienna Convention on Consular Relations[39]—were the subject of worldwide attention during the Iranian Hostage Crisis of 1979–1980. Their continuing vitality, notwithstanding a 444-day diplomatic stalemate between Iran and the United States, was illustrated by the fact that *no* country supported Iran's actions. The UN Security Council unanimously resolved that Iran should immediately release the diplomatic and consular personnel who were seized at the US embassy and various consular offices in Iran. The crisis, together with its international legal implications, is analyzed in the following case:

Case Concerning United States Diplomatic and Consular Staff in Tehran

INTERNATIONAL COURT OF JUSTICE

Judgment on the Merits (1980)

Gen. List No. 64

19 Int'l Legal Mat'ls 553 (1980)

AUTHOR'S NOTE: On November 4, 1979, the US embassy in Tehran, Iran, was overrun by several hundred of the 3,000 Iranians who had been demonstrating at the embassy gates. They seized diplomats, consuls, and Marines, as they began their occupation of the embassy premises. Two US consulates in other cities in Iran were also occupied and closed on the following day. The embassy personnel in Tehran were physically threatened and denied any communication with either US officials or relatives. Several hundred thousand demonstrators converged on the US embassy premises on November 22, 1979. The Iranian government made no effort to intervene or to assist the hostages inside the building. While a few hostages were released, most were removed to unknown locations beyond the embassy's premises.

The US instituted this suit against the International Court of Justice, alleging that Iran breached the Vienna Conventions on Diplomatic and Consular Relations, the Vienna Convention on the Prevention of Crimes against Internationally Protected Persons, and the 1955 US-Iran Treaty of Amity.

The position of the Iranian government is contained in correspondence it submitted to the court. Iran refused to send lawyers to represent Iran, to file any official papers, or to directly participate in these proceedings. The ICJ nevertheless considered Iran's correspondence and made preliminary reference to it as follows.

IRANIAN CORRESPONDENCE: The Government of the Islamic Republic of Iran . . . draws the attention of the Court to the deeprootedness and the essential character of the Islamic Revolution of Iran, a revolution of a whole oppressed nation against its oppressors and their masters, the examination of whose numerous repercussions is essentially and directly a matter within the national sovereignty of Iran. . . .

For this question [regarding detention of the diplomatic hostages] only represents a marginal and secondary aspect of an overall problem, one such that it cannot be studied separately, and which involves . . . more than 25 years of continual interference by the United States in the internal affairs of Iran, the shameless exploitation of our country, and numerous crimes perpetrated against the Iranian people, contrary to and in conflict with all international and humanitarian norms.

The problem involved in the conflict between Iran and the United States is not [merely] one of the interpretation and the application of the treaties upon which the American Application is based, but results from an overall situation containing much more fundamental and more complex elements. Consequently, the Court cannot examine the American Application divorced from its proper context, namely the whole political dossier of the relations between Iran and the United States over the last 25 years. This dossier includes . . . all the crimes perpetrated in Iran by the American Government, in particular the coup d'etat of 1953 stirred up and carried out by the CIA, the overthrow of the lawful national government of Dr. Mossadegh, the restoration [then] of the Shah and of his regime which was under the control of American interests, and all the social, economic, cultural and political consequences of the direct interventions in our internal affairs, as well as grave, flagrant and continuous violations of all international norms, committed by the United States in Iran.

COURT'S OPINION:

. . .

22. The persons still held hostage in Iran include, according to the information furnished to the Court by the United States, at least 28 persons having the status, duly recognized by the Government of Iran, of "member of the diplomatic staff" within the meaning of the Vienna Convention of Diplomatic Relations of 1961; at least 20 persons having the status, similarly recognized, of "member of the administrative and technical staff" within the meaning of that Convention; and two other persons of United States nationality not possessing either diplomatic or consular status. Of the persons with the status of member of the diplomatic staff, four are members of the Consular Section of the Mission.

23. Allegations have been made by the Government of the United States of inhumane treatment of hostages; the militants and Iranian authorities have asserted that the hostages have been well treated, and have allowed special visits to the hostages by religious personalities and by representatives of the International Committee of the Red Cross. The specific allegations of ill-treatment have not however been refuted. Examples of such allegations, which are mentioned in some of the sworn declarations of hostages released in November 1979, are as follows: At the outset of the occupation of the Embassy some were paraded bound and blindfolded before hostile and chanting crowds; at least during the initial period of their captivity, hostages were kept bound, and frequently blindfolded, denied mail or any communication with their government or with each other, subjected to interrogation, threatened with weapons.

24. Those archives and documents of the United States Embassy which were not destroyed by the staff during the attack on 4 November have been ransacked by the militants. Documents purporting to come from this source have been disseminated by the militants and by the Government-controlled media.

. . .

36. . . . [T]he seizure of the United States Embassy and Consulates and the detention of internationally protected persons as hostages cannot [despite Iran's written communication to the ICJ] be considered as something "secondary" or "marginal," having regard to

the importance of the legal principles involved. It also referred to a statement of the Secretary-General of the United Nations, and to Security Council resolution 457 (1979), as evidencing the importance attached by the international community as a whole to the observance of those principles in the present case as well as its concern at the dangerous level of tension between Iran and the United States.

. . .

46. [The court is able to hear this case because the] United States' claims here in question concern alleged violations by Iran of its obligations under several articles of the Vienna Conventions of 1961 and 1963 with respect to the privileges and immunities of the personnel, the inviolability of the premises and archives, and the provision of facilities for the performance of the functions of the United States Embassy and Consulates in Iran. . . . By their very nature all these claims concern the interpretation or application of one or other of the two Vienna Conventions.

47. The occupation of the United States Embassy by militants on 4 November 1979 and the detention of its personnel as hostages was an event of a kind to provoke an immediate protest from any government, as it did from the United States Government, which despatched a special emissary to Iran to deliver a formal protest. . . .

It is clear that on that date there existed a dispute arising out of the interpretation or application of the Vienna Conventions and thus one falling within the scope of the Protocols [which are a part of the Vienna Conventions on Diplomatic and Consular Relations requiring States to submit such disputes to the ICJ for resolution].

. . .

61. The conclusion just reached by the Court, that the initiation of the attack on the United States Embassy on 4 November 1979, and of the attacks on the Consulates at Tabriz and Shiraz the following day, cannot be considered as in itself imputable to the Iranian State does not mean that Iran is, in consequence, free of any responsibility in regard to those attacks; for its own conduct was in conflict with its international obligations. By a number of provisions of the Vienna Conventions of 1961 and 1963, Iran was placed under the most categorical obligations, as a receiving State, to take appropriate steps to ensure the protection of the United States Embassy and Consulates, their staffs, their archives, their means of communication and the freedom of movement of the members of their staffs.

62. Thus, after solemnly proclaiming the inviolability of the premises of a diplomatic mission, Article 22 of the 1961 Convention continues in paragraph 2:

The receiving State is under a special duty to take all appropriate steps to protect the premises of the mission against any intrusion or damage and to prevent any disturbance of the peace of the mission or impairment of its dignity. [Italics added by the Court.]

So, too, after proclaiming that the person of a diplomatic agent shall be inviolable, and that he shall not be liable to any form of arrest or detention, Article 29 provides:

The receiving State shall treat him with due respect and *shall take all appropriate steps to prevent any attack on his person, freedom or dignity.* [Italics added by the Court.]

The obligation of a receiving State to protect the inviolability of the archives and documents of a diplomatic mission is laid down in Article 24, which specifically provides that they are to be "inviolable at any time and wherever they may be." Under Article 25 it is required to "accord full facilities for the performance of the functions of the mission," under Article 26 to "ensure to all members of the mission freedom of movement and travel in its territory," and under Article 27 to "permit and protect free communication on the part of the mission for all official purposes." Analogous provisions are to be found in the 1963 [Consular] Convention regarding the privileges and immunities of consular missions and their staffs (Art. 31, para. 3, Arts. 40, 33, 28, 34 and 35). In the view of the Court, the obligations of the Iranian Government here in question are not merely contractual obligations established by the Vienna Conventions of 1961 and 1963, but also obligations under general international law.

63. The facts set out in paragraphs 14 to 27 above establish to the satisfaction of the Court that on 4 November 1979 the Iranian Government failed altogether to take any "appropriate steps" to protect the premises, staff and archives of the United States mission against attack by the militants, and to take any steps either to prevent this attack or to stop it before it reached its completion. They also show that on 5 November 1979 the Iranian Government similarly failed to take

appropriate steps for the protection of the United States Consulates at Tabriz and Shiraz. In addition they show, in the opinion of the Court, that the failure of the Iranian Government to take such steps was due to more than mere negligence or lack of appropriate means. . . .

77. . . . Paragraphs 1 and 3 of that Article [22] have also been infringed, and continue to be infringed, since they forbid agents of a receiving State to enter the premises of a mission without consent or to undertake any search, requisition, attachment or like measure on the premises. Secondly, they constitute continuing breaches of Article 29 of the same Convention which forbids any arrest or detention of a diplomatic agent and any attack on his person, freedom or dignity. Thirdly, the Iranian authorities are without doubt in continuing breach of the provisions of Articles 25, 26 and 27 of the 1961 Vienna Convention and of pertinent provisions of the 1963 Vienna Convention concerning facilities for the performance of functions, freedom of movement and communications for diplomatic and consular staff, as well as of Article 24 of the former Convention and Article 33 of the latter, which provide for the absolute inviolability of the archives and documents of diplomatic missions and consulates. This particular violation has been made manifest to the world by repeated statements by the militants occupying the Embassy, who claim to be in possession of documents from the archives, and by various government authorities, purporting to specify the contents thereof. Finally, the continued detention as hostages of the two private individuals of United States nationality entails a renewed breach of the obligations of Iran under Article 11, paragraph 4, of the 1955 Treaty of Amity, Economic Relations, and Consular Rights.

. . .

79. . . . [J]udicial authorities of the Islamic Republic of Iran and the Minister for Foreign Affairs have frequently voiced or associated themselves with a threat first announced by the militants of having some of the hostages submitted to trial before a court or some other body. These threats may at present merely be acts in contemplation. But the Court considers it necessary here and now to stress that, if the intention to submit the hostages to any form of criminal trial or investigation were to be put into effect, that would constitute a grave breach by Iran of its obligations under Article 31, paragraph 1, of the 1961 Vienna Convention. This paragraph states in the most express terms: "A diplomatic agent shall enjoy

immunity from the criminal jurisdiction of the receiving State." Again, if there were an attempt to compel the hostages to bear witness, a suggestion renewed at the time of the visit to Iran of the Secretary-General's Commission, Iran would without question be violating paragraph 2 of that same Article of the 1961 Vienna Convention which provides that: "A diplomatic agent is not obliged to give evidence as a witness."]

. . .

83. In any case, *even if the alleged criminal activities of the United States in Iran could be considered as having been established,* the question would remain whether they could be regarded by the Court as constituting a justification of Iran's conduct and thus a defence to the United States' claims in the present case. The Court, however, is unable to accept that they can be so regarded. This is because diplomatic law itself provides the necessary means of defence against, and sanction for, illicit activities by members of diplomatic or consular missions. [Italics added by author.]

. . .

85. Thus, it is for the very purpose of providing a remedy for such possible abuses of diplomatic functions that Article 9 of the 1961 Convention on Diplomatic Relations stipulates:

1. The receiving State may at any time and without having to explain its decision, notify the sending State that the head of the mission or any member of the diplomatic staff of the mission is persona non grata or that any other member of the staff of the mission is not acceptable. In any such case, the sending State shall, as appropriate, either recall the person concerned or terminate his functions with the mission. A person may be declared non grata or not acceptable before arriving in the territory of the receiving State.

2. If the sending State refuses or fails within a reasonable period to carry out its obligations under paragraph 1 of this Article, the receiving State may refuse to recognize the person concerned as a member of the mission.

86. Even in the case of armed conflict or in the case of a breach in diplomatic relations those provisions require that both the inviolability of the members of a diplomatic mission and of the premises, property and

archives of the mission must be respected by the receiving State. Naturally, the observance of this principle does not mean—and this the Applicant Government expressly acknowledges—that a diplomatic agent caught in the act of committing an assault or other offence may not, on occasion, be briefly arrested by the police of the receiving State in order to prevent the commission of the particular crime.

87. . . . The Iranian Government did not, therefore, employ the remedies placed at its disposal by diplomatic law specifically for dealing with activities of the kind of which it now complains. Instead, it allowed a group of militants to attack and occupy the United States Embassy by force, and to seize the diplomatic and consular staff as hostages; instead, it has endorsed that action of those militants and has deliberately maintained their occupation of the Embassy and detention of its staff as a means of coercing the sending State. It has, at the same time, refused altogether to discuss this situation with representatives of the United States. The Court, therefore, can only conclude that Iran did not have recourse to the normal and efficacious means at its disposal, but [instead] resorted to coercive action against the United States Embassy and its staff. . . .

◆ *Notes & Questions*

1. What rules of International Law did Iran breach?
2. Assume that the United States was in fact responsible for the violations of International Law—as asserted by Iran in the preliminary passage of this case, where the ICJ mentions Iran's correspondence with the court. Do such violations justify Iran's taking over the embassy/consulates and kidnaping the diplomatic and consular personnel?
3. Would the ICJ rule differently if Iran were *not* a party to the respective Vienna Conventions on Diplomatic and Consular Relations? On what basis?
4. The ICJ ruled that Iran was responsible to make reparations to the United States. The Court also left this matter to subsequent negotiation between the parties. Failing an agreement, the United States was free to return for a judicial resolution of the form and amount of Iranian reparations. One year later, however, Iran had not made reparations but the United States did not request the Court to reconsider the judgment for the purpose of a final resolution. The United States thus requested a dismissal, based on the Algiers Accord providing for the release of all US hostages. See International Court of Justice: Order on Discontinuance and Removal of Case Concerning United States Diplomatic and Consular Staff in Tehran (United States v. Iran), 20 INT'L LEGAL MAT'LS 889 (1981).
5. In April 2005, 20,000 anti-Japanese demonstrators roamed through the streets of Shanghai. Upon arrival at the Japanese Consulate, they stoned it, smashed cars and shops in the area. China is upset with Japan's bid for a permanent seat on the UN Security Council. There has been a long history of animosity in China, because of Japan's pre–World War II and war-related atrocities in China. One of the prominent examples is depicted in J. Yin & S. Young, THE RAPE OF NANKING: AN UNDENIABLE HISTORY IN PHOTOGRAPHS (Chicago: Innovative Publishing Group, 1997).

   Numerous Chinese police were present, but did very little to restrain the crowd. Japan lodged a formal protest, given like events in various cities in the PRC for a three-week period. The PRC government responded that Japan had sparked these protests because of its "wrong attitudes and actions on a series of issues such as its history of aggression." (Numerous newspaper articles depicted the government's efforts to likewise orchestrate public protest against the United States, when its accidentally bombed the Chinese embassy in Belgrade during the 1999 NATO bombing campaign.) The PRC's failure to do all that possible to avoid persistent riots at the steps of the Japanese Consulate was a clear violation of the Vienna Convention's "inviolability of the premises" requirement.
6. In October 2004, the Islamic militant group al-Qaida in Mesopotamia kidnapped a Moroccan diplomat. He was travelling in Iraq from Jordan. This group posted a Web site death threat, intending it "to be an example for others who are still thinking to challenge the mujahadeen." Assume that this diplomat was killed. The United States had announced the official end of its occupation of Iraq several months earlier. Approximately 150,00 of its troops remained, however, to assist the new Iraqi government to maintain security. If Morocco seeks retribution, to whom should it direct its protest?

General (Mis)perception There are many criticisms of diplomatic immunity. Journalists have sensationalized abuses of diplomatic immunity with a view toward revisiting the protection afforded by the VCDR.[40] This perspective is not unique. Not all States observe the general international rule of diplomatic immunity from criminal prosecution. During the Cultural Revolution (1966–1976), representatives of the PRC "declared that diplomatic immunities were of bourgeois origin and . . . had no place in a socialist society."[41]

The 1961 VCDR nevertheless codified State expectations, most of which were rooted in reciprocity. The British University of Reading's Craig Barker illustrates that "[e]ven if it were considered desirable to amend the law to deal with the problem of abuse, the question must be asked as to whether such amendment is possible, given the reciprocal nature of diplomatic relations and the manifest desire of each State to ensure the fullest protection for its diplomatic personnel working abroad. On the other hand, does that mean that abuse of diplomatic privileges is simply a necessary evil which must be endured in order to ensure the greater good that is the maintenance of proper international relations?"[42]

Contemporary Alternatives The foregoing examples of moral indignation with diplomatic immunity do not always acknowledge that there are alternatives available to coping with such abuses, as suggested in paragraph 86 in the Hostage case dicussed earlier. The participation of nearly 180 nations in the Vienna Convention on Diplomatic Relations (VCDR) suggests that the overall benefit has not been vitiated by the occasional burdens. Assume that a State A diplomat commits a crime in host State B. The interests of both States are better served if State B declares State A's offending ambassador *persona non grata* (§7.2). If State B were to arrest the State A diplomat, State B would risk reciprocal treatment. The authorities in State A might one day respond by arresting a State B diplomat or consular officer, who commits a crime or civil wrong while present in State A.

Insuring against the diplomat's conduct is an alternative to VCDR remedies. State B citizens can be protected against certain consequences of diplomatic conduct through this risk-shifting device. A portion of the risk of having A's diplomats in State B can thus be borne by State A. This insurance may thus benefit State B nationals. While the State A diplomat is not thereby subject to suit in State B's courts, a State B insurer can thereby assume a portion of the risks associated with the diplomat's negligence (assuming that State A has paid the insurance premium). State B nationals would thus have a monetary remedy like that available to them when they insure themselves against the conduct of private, nondiplomatic individuals in State B. This convenient compromise permits the A diplomat to continue his or her duties without the inconvenient disruption of having to defend lawsuits in B's courts. The insurer will do this instead. The culpable diplomat does not fully "escape" liability. The US Department of State has promulgated standards regarding compulsory diplomatic insurance.[43]

"Waiver" of diplomatic immunity presents an alternative, which depends on the discretion of the sending State. Assume that an individual is entitled to immunity under the Vienna Diplomatic or Consular Convention. She has committed a serious criminal offense. The host State might request that the sending State waive the consular immunity of this agent. States are not precluded from requesting such waivers on an *ad hoc* basis, when circumstances so warrant. The sending State could ensure the continuance of mutually beneficial relations if one of its diplomats committed a serious crime (which violates the laws of both nations).

There is a blossoming culture of acquiescence in host-State requests for waivers of diplomatic immunity. In 1996, Zaire's president waived diplomatic immunity for the country's ambassador to France. This ambassador's speeding caused a car accident in Menton, France, that killed two 13-year-old French children and protests by 5,000 marchers. In 1997, the Republic of Georgia's second-ranking diplomat was drinking and speeding in Washington, DC. He thereby caused four other cars to crash, resulting in the death of a 16-year old girl. The US Department of State immediately sought and obtained a waiver of his diplomatic immunity from Georgia. This request was premised on the then-recent statement by Georgia's President Shevardnadze, that the moral principle of just punishment outweighed what he considered to be the antiquated, Cold War-era practice of diplomatic immunity. The former Georgian diplomat is now serving a twenty-one year sentence.

Four years after the Vienna Conventions entered into force, the UN General Assembly reacted to an alarming increase in crimes against diplomats and other persons in need of special protection under International Law. The Assembly's International Law Commission (§3.3) thus produced draft articles. These were adopted by the Assembly, which thereby requested States to become parties to this special regime: the 1973 Convention on the Prevention and Punishment of Crimes Against Internationally Protected Persons, including Diplomatic Agents.[44] Heads of State, diplomats, and various governmental agents are the subject of special legislation under the local law of treaty parties. Such laws are designed to ensure special attention to their safety, as well as members of their immediate households. Aircraft hijackers, assassins, and perpetrators of violent crimes against these protected persons must be prosecuted or extradited, without regard to political motive.

Diplomatic Bag Complaints about diplomatic immunity include the occasional problem with the "diplomatic bag." Article 27.3 of the Vienna Convention on Diplomatic Relations provides that a "diplomatic bag shall not be opened or detained." The following excerpt from the French *Review of Public International Law* demonstrates the competing considerations that often arise when there has been an abuse:

Seizure of Arms in Baggage of Diplomat in Transit

78 *Revue Generale de Droit International Public* 247 (1974)

Five hand grenades, five revolvers, eight kilos of explosive devices, and 21 letter bombs not yet addressed, rifles and ammunition were discovered on the evening of October 23, 1972, by Dutch customs officers at the airport of Schiphol in the baggage of an Algerian diplomatic agent accredited to a South American nation which the Dutch Minister of Justice refused to identify. Aged 32, born in Jordan, but carrying an Algerian diplomatic passport, the diplomat, who was identified only by the initials II.R., came from Damascus via Frankfurt and was en route to Rio de Janeiro. He declared himself to be entirely ignorant of the contents of his baggage, explaining only he thought he was carrying documents delivered to him in Damascus and destined for an Algerian embassy in a South American republic, which he declined to identify further. He added nevertheless he had bought the rifles, which were found separately, for diplomatic colleagues. The Queen's prosecutor [of the Netherlands] did not institute judicial proceedings against the diplomat because in his judgment it had not at all been established that the diplomat was actually aware of the contents of his baggage. As a result the diplomat was authorized to continue his trip to South America, but his bags were retained for an investigation.

Following the discovery, the Israeli government—which was convinced the arms seized were to be used in organizing an attack upon its embassy in Brazil—requested an explanation from the Dutch government, because in its opinion the Algerian diplomat should have been held by the authorities at the airport "because diplomatic immunity applies only in the countries where diplomatic agents are accredited and not in the countries through which they are only in transit." One should have some reservations about this assertion which is contrary to established practice and is contradicted by Article 40 of the Vienna Convention of April 18, 1961, on Diplomatic Relations by whose terms a diplomatic agent in transit through the territory of a third state is given "inviolability and every other immunity necessary for his passage or return." But, inasmuch as the acts here were outside official functions, the immunity of agents in transit, already subject to strict limitations, obviously ceases in a case of flagrant offense.

What constitutes a diplomatic bag is arguably open to question. In March 2000, Zimbabwean authorities impounded a *seven-ton* shipment of supposedly routine equipment for building communications facilities, as well as the tools for its installation. England recalled its ambassador from Zimbabwe, to protest the opening of this British diplomatic "bag" by customs authorities. They asserted a right to open such unusually large diplomatic packages. British officials countered that the Vienna Convention generally exempts "diplomatic bags" from inspection.

The UN's International Law Commission has been working on draft provisions that would amend the status of the diplomatic courier and the diplomatic bag—through optional protocols to the Vienna Convention. The objective is to provide the State parties to the VCDR an opportunity to place further restrictions on such immunity, in a way that would better control potential abuse. The UN's Sixth Committee (Legal) is conducting informal consultations on the question whether the General Assembly should convene an international conference for the purpose of creating draft articles on this sensitive topic.[45]

◆ PROBLEMS

Problem 7.A (end of §7.1)   US President Bush has engaged in varied forms of diplomacy in his speeches. He responded to "9-11" with the prodigious comment that "You are either with us, or against us," referring to the then fresh War on Terrorism; defined an Axis of Evil (prewar Iraq, Iran, and NK); commented that he would "not rule out a military strike" against Iran's nuclear program; and personally chastised the United Nations for not authorizing force, prior to the US preemptive strike in Iraq.

To develop a practical sense of what diplomats do, to best advise a president or prime minister, assume that you are a Department of State representative in your powerful country. Your country has decided to go to war with Iraq. You have *credible* intelligence that Iraq possesses weapons of mass destruction. If so, possessing such weapons could dramatically impact the balance of power in the Middle East, and maybe globally. You also know that in 1981, Israel bombed Iraq's nuclear weapon plant, which delayed Iraq's pending acquisition of nuclear power. Saddam Hussein is a brutal dictator, having gassed 5,000 Iraqi Kurds in northwestern Iraq in 1988. He annexed Kuwait three years later. This occupation led to the first Persian Gulf War, conducted by a large coalition of international military forces. Since then, he has ignored UN resolutions demanding accountability for the presumed presence of weapons of mass destruction in the post-9-11 era. Would you recommend that your government:

◆ Try to *negotiate* or to *impose* a settlement?
◆ Consider the wishes of the public on whether to go to war?
◆ Compromise with Iraq, which might make things worse in the long run?[46]

(The UK's Lord Chamberlain appeased Hitler prior to World War II.)

Four students or groups will now debate these options. Given the 20-20 nature of hindsight, there should be no reference to any development *after* the US-UK launch of the March 2003 Iraq War. These students will represent the following entities: the United States, people of Iraq, United Nations, and the regional international organizations of which Iraq is a member (§3.5).

Problem 7.B (end of §7.3)   In 1992, Peru's ex-President Alan Garcia sought refuge in the Colombian embassy in Peru. This Peruvian president (from 1985 to 1990) was an outspoken opponent of his successor. Garcia went into hiding when the new Peruvian president dissolved the Peruvian Congress and temporarily closed the Peruvian courts. Colombia decided to grant Garcia diplomatic asylum. Colombia began to process Garcia's orderly departure from Peru. Did Colombia violate International Law by granting diplomatic asylum to former President Garcia in 1992? Would Peru be required to let Garcia leave the Columbian Embassy and leave Peru?

Problem 7.C (end of §7.4)   In 1994, a Berlin appellate court reinstated a German arrest warrant issued for Syria's former Ambassador "S." It determined that neither the Vienna Convention on Diplomatic Relations (VCDR) nor customary International Law, prohibited his arrest and prosecution for assisting in the 1983 bombing of a French arts center in (the former) West Berlin. Explosives used in this attack had been temporarily stored in the Syrian embassy in (the former) East Berlin. Syria's Ambassador S. was instructed by his government to aid the terrorist organization led by the infamous terrorist "Carlos the Jackal" to carry out this attack. It claimed one life and severely injured twenty-three people. Although the Syrian embassy officer declined to transfer the explosives to West Berlin, storage there did help to conceal their whereabouts. The German court determined that the diplomatic immunity accorded to a Syrian head of mission by the German Democratic Republic (East Germany) was not binding on third States—including the Federal Republic of Germany ("West Germany" before reunification in 1990). In the court's words: "Diplomatic immunity is only effective in the receiving state. Third states have not consented to the diplomat's activity. . . ." The court also reasoned that the incorporation of former East Germany into the new Germany did not require (reunified) Germany to respect the immunity accorded by a "third state" to this diplomat.

S. v. Berlin Court of Appeal and District Court of Berlin-Tiergarten, 24 EUROPAISCHE GRUNDECHTE-ZEITSCHRIFT 436 (1994). *See* B. Fassbender, International Decisions, 92 AMER. J. INT'L LAW 74 (1998).

Three students or groups will debate the soundness of West Germany's decision. One will act as the German prosecutor who argued this case on appeal. The other will represent Syria. A third will represent the UN International Law Commission (§3.5)—having been summoned as a "friend to the court" to advise all parties about the proper application of the VCDR to this case.

Problem 7.D (end of §7.4) The following hypothetical is adapted from actual events. Many of the applicable rules of International Law are set forth in the 1961 Vienna Convention on Diplomatic Relations and the ICJ's 1980 Hostage case. Students will engage in diplomatic negotiations to achieve what they believe to be the best resolution. This exercise is designed to illustrate the rules of immunity—and, some of their practical limitations:

The Problem. Rieferbaans is a discotheque in Germany near a US military base. US soldiers often socialize at Rieferbaans. Magenta is a State that has an embassy in Germany but no diplomatic relations with the United States. Magenta's embassy is ten minutes from Rieferbaans by car.

The first secretary of Magenta's diplomatic mission in Germany is *Chargé d'Affaires* Mann. The leader of Mann's home State (Magenta) has directed Mann to openly criticize the United States and take all steps necessary to publicize Magenta's belief that the United States should withdraw its troops from Western Europe. Magenta's leader directs *Chargé d'Affaires* Mann to set off a bomb at the discotheque when it is crowded with US soldiers. Mann and the Magenta head of State communicate secretly via coded radio signals.

Unknown to Mann, the Army Intelligence Office at the US military base, in conjunction with a government radio station in Germany, has broken Magenta's code for diplomatic transmissions. The US and German governments are fully aware of the terrorist plot. They want it to develop, however, to a point where Magenta cannot deny responsibility.

Chargé d'Affaires Mann has assembled a group of armed anti-US "freedom fighters" at Magenta's embassy premises and at various points between the embassy and Rieferbaans. The Army Intelligence Office learns that

there will be a very extraordinary (but apparently innocuous) message transported directly from Magenta's leader to Mann. It will enter Magenta's embassy via diplomatic pouch. It contains the signal to carry out the terrorist bombing at the Rieferbaans Disco. Magenta's diplomatic courier arrives at a German airport, is detained by US soldiers, and is then arrested by German police. The State of Magenta's official diplomatic pouch is seized and opened. The US soldiers and the German police intercept the message that would have resulted in the bombing of the discotheque and a massive loss of life.

German police later surround Magenta's embassy where Magenta's "freedom fighters" are located. They advise *Chargé d'Affaires* Mann by telephone that the plot has been discovered and that the courier and pouch have been seized due to Magenta's "abuse of transit" via the diplomatic pouch brought into Germany. Everyone in the embassy is ordered to immediately come outside and cross the street onto "German soil."

Three students will act as diplomatic representatives. Student 1 will be Hans Smit, a German career diplomat assigned to negotiate a successful conclusion to this crisis. Student 2 will be Joanna Shultz, the US Ambassador to Germany. Student 3 will assume the role of *Chargé d'Affaires* Mann, Magenta's ambassador to Germany.

Part One. Hans Smit (student 1) and Joanna Shultz (student 2) confer at a government building in Germany near the Magenta embassy. They are trying to decide whether *Chargé d'Affaires* Mann should be invited to join them. Germany, the United States, and Magenta are parties to the Vienna Convention on Diplomatic Relations. Smit and Shultz should assess whether Mann can be characterized as having waived the treaty's immunity provisions. If Mann decides to confer with them outside the Magenta embassy, they should further assess the possibility of revoking his diplomatic immunity to arrest him.

Part Two. Assume that Smit and Shultz decide to invite Mann to negotiate, but *not* to arrest him. Can Mann reasonably claim that Germany and the United States have violated the Vienna Convention? What specific claims will Mann likely assert?

Part Three. The three ambassadors are discussing whether the "freedom fighters" in the Magenta embassy should be permitted to go free—from Germany to

France, as they have requested. If Germany decides against this resolution, what can it do to the "freedom fighters?"

Note: The incident on which this problem is based occurred in 1986 in what was then West Berlin. Two US soldiers and a Turkish citizen were killed by a bomb blast in the Berlin discotheque "La Bella" (229 others were wounded). It finally reached closure after a four year trial of various defendants including: a German who carried the bomb into the disco; a Palestinian working in the Libyan embassy who organized the bombing; and a Libyan diplomat—all of whom were given prison sentences at the conclusion of their trial in November 2001. One of the victims' estates later sued Libya in the United States.[47]

Libya was supposedly retaliating for the US sinking of two Libyan boats near Libya in 1986. Ten days after the disco bombing, President Reagan ordered retaliatory strikes in Libya, one of which supposedly killed Libyan President Gadhafi's daughter. Two years later, Libyan intelligence officers bombed Pan Am 103 over Lockerbie, Scotland (killing 270 people). They were finally tried in The Netherlands in 2000 (§9.5). Relations thawed after Libya compensated victims' families for the tragic 1988 Pan Am 103 bombing incident. Libya participated in the US coalition in Afghanistan reacting to September 11, 2001 (§10.7).

◆ BIBLIOGRAPHY

§7.1 Foreword to Diplomacy

J. Chay (ed.), Diplomatic History and International Relations, ch. 3, in CULTURE AND INTERNATIONAL RELATIONS 34 (New York: Praeger, 1990)

R. Cohen, NEGOTIATING ACROSS CULTURES: COMMUNICATION OBSTACLES IN INTERNATIONAL DIPLOMACY (Wash., DC: US Inst. Peace, 1991)

Y. Dinstein, Diplomatic Protection of Companies Under International Law, in K. Wellens (ed.), INTERNATIONAL LAW: THEORY AND PRACTICE–ESSAYS IN HONOUR OF ERIC SUY 505 (Hague: Martinus Nijhoff, 1998)

J. Findling, DICTIONARY OF AMERICAN DIPLOMATIC HISTORY (2d ed. New York: Greenwood Press, 1989)

D. Mak & C. Kennedy, AMERICAN AMBASSADORS IN A TROUBLED WORLD: INTERVIEWS WITH SENIOR DIPLOMATS (Westport, CT: Greenwood Press, 1992)

§7.2 Diplomatic and Consular Functions

H. Heath, Non-compliance with the Vienna Convention on Consular Relations and its Effect on Reciprocity for United States Citizens Abroad, 17 N.Y. INT'L L. REV. 1 (2004)

A. Kapur (ed.), DIPLOMATIC IDEAS AND PRACTICES OF ASIAN STATES (Leiden, Neth.: E.J. Brill, 1990)

A. Kremenyuk (ed.), INTERNATIONAL NEGOTIATION, ANALYSIS, APPROACHES, ISSUES (San Francisco: Jossey-Bass Pub., 1991)

H. Langholtz & C. Stout (ed.), THE PSYCHOLOGY OF DIPLOMACY (Westport, CT: Praeger, 2004)

B. Sen, A DIPLOMAT'S HANDBOOK OF INTERNATIONAL LAW AND PRACTICE (3d ed. Dordrecht, Neth.: Martinus Nijhoff, 1988)

§7.3 Extraterritoriality and Diplomatic Asylum

R. Jennings & A. Watts, So-Called Diplomatic Asylum, §495, in 2 OPPENHEIM'S INTERNATIONAL LAW 1082 (9th ed. Essex, Eng.: Longman, 1993)

C. Ronning, DIPLOMATIC ASYLUM: LEGAL NORMS AND POLITICAL REALITY IN LATIN AMERICAN RELATIONS (Hague, Neth.: Martinus Nijhoff, 1965)

L. Schuster, THE USE AND ABUSE OF POLITICAL ASYLUM IN BRITAIN AND GERMANY (London: Schuster, 2003)

§7.4 Immunities and Abuse of Immunity

Comment, Limiting Diplomatic Immunity: Lessons Learned from the 1946 Convention on the Privileges and Immunities of the United Nations, 28 BROOK. J. INT'L L. 989 (2004)

J. Ure, DIPLOMATIC BAG: AN ANTHOLOGY OF DIPLOMATIC INCIDENTS AND ANECDOTES FROM THE RENAISSANCE TO THE GULF WAR (London: John Murray Pub., 1994)

M. Zaid, Diplomatic Immunity: To Have or Not to Have, That Is The Question, 4 ILSA J. INT'L & COMP. LAW 623 (1998)

A. Zeidman, Abuse of the Diplomatic Bag: A Proposed Solution, 11 CARDOZO LAW REVIEW 427 (1989)

Additional Internet Resources

Electronic Embassy Web site: <http://www.embassy.org> Governments on the WWW: <http://www.gksoft.com/govt/en/>

Internet Diplomacy: <http://www.diplomacymonitor.com/stu/dm.nsf/opener?OpenForm>

Visa Information: <http://travel.state.gov> and <http://www.projectvisa.com>

Wikipedia, The Free Encyclopedia, Diplomatic Immunity: <http://en.wikipedia.org/wiki/Diplomatic_immunity>

◆ ENDNOTES

1. See B. Murty, Diplomacy in Historical Perspective, §1.2, in THE INTERNATIONAL LAW OF DIPLOMACY: THE DIPLOMATIC INSTRUMENT AND THE WORLD PUBLIC ORDER 3 (New Haven, CT: New Haven Press, 1989) [hereinafter *Law of Diplomacy*].

2. M. Anderson, THE RISE OF MODERN DIPLOMACY 1450–1919, at 2-3 (London: Longman, 1993).

3. Right of Passage Case (Preliminary Objections), 1957 ICJ REP. 125, 130.

4. See M. Lund, PREVENTING VIOLENT CONFLICTS: A STRATEGY FOR PREVENTATIVE DIPLOMACY (Wash., DC: US Inst. Peace Press, 1996).

5. J. Kish, INTERNATIONAL LAW AND ESPIONAGE (The Hague, Neth.: Martinus Nijhoff, 1995).

6. A. Medetsky, Russia Still Fields Cold War Army of Spies, Moscow Times on the Web (Feb. 9, 2005).

7. *European perspective:* Garden, 1 TRAITE COMPLET DE DIPLOMATIE OU THEORIE GENERALE DES RELATIONS EXTERIEURES DES PUISSANCES DE L'EUROPE 1 (Paris 1833) (diplomacy is the science or "art of negotiation"); C. Calvo, 1 DICTIONNAIRE DE DROIT INTERNATIONAL PUBLIC ET PRIVIE 25 (Berlin, 1885) (science of state relations, or simply the "art of communication"). *Nicolson perspective:* H. Nicolson, The "Old" and the "New" Diplomacy, in R. Pfaltzgraff (ed.), POLITICS AND THE INTERNATIONAL SYSTEM 425 (2d ed., Philadelphia: Lippincott, 1972).

8. Translation provided by P. Ardant, Chinese Diplomatic Practice during the Cultural Revolution, ch. 3, in CHINA'S PRACTICE OF INTERNATIONAL LAW: SOME CASE STUDIES 92–93 (Cambridge, MA: Harv. Univ. Press, 1974) [hereinafter *Chinese Practice*].

9. *Morgenthau view:* H. Morgenthau, POLITICS AMONG NATIONS 541 (3d ed. New York: Knopf, 1960) [hereinafter *Morgenthau*]. *Boucher view:* D. Boucher, Reconciling Ethics and Interests in the Person of the State: The International Dimension, ch. 3, in P. Keal (ed.), ETHICS AND FOREIGN POLICY 44, 46 (St. Leonards, Aust.: Allen & Unwin, 1992) (italics added).

10. L. Pearson, DIPLOMACY IN THE NUCLEAR AGE 64 (Cambridge, MA: Harv. Univ. Press, 1959); G. Tunkin, THEORY OF INTERNATIONAL LAW 273 (Cambridge, MA: Harv. Univ. Press, 1974).

11. *Idealist* (Canadian): Panel, International Law in International Diplomacy, in PROCEEDINGS OF THE 77TH ANNUAL MEETING OF THE AMERICAN SOCIETY OF INTERNATIONAL LAW 99 (Wash., DC: Amer. Soc. Int'l Law, 1985). *Realist* (Venezuelan): *id.*, at 103.

12. *See generally* K. Hamilton & R. Langhorne, THE PRACTICE OF DIPLOMACY: ITS EVOLUTION, THEORY AND ADMINISTRATION (London: Routledge, 1995).

13. *Morgenthau,* at 539–540 (cited in note 9 above).

14. F. Ninkovich, Culture in US Foreign Policy Since 1900, ch. 8, in J. Chay (ed.), CULTURE AND INTERNATIONAL RELATIONS 103 (New York: Praeger, 1990).

15. *See* Bacuss, Diplomacy for the 70's: An Afterview and Appraisal, 68 AMER. POL. SCIENCE REV. 736 (1974) (post-World War II tendency encouraged by all US presidents).

16. *See* United Nations Millennium Declaration, at <http://www.un.org/millennium/declaration/ares552e.htm>.

17. *Wilson quote:* 2 SELECTED LITERARY AND POLITICAL PAPERS AND ADDRESSES OF WOODROW WILSON (New York: Grosset & Dunlap, 1927). *Nicolson quote:* reprinted in T. Couloumbis & J. Wolfe, INTRODUCTION TO INTERNATIONAL RELATIONS 161 (3d ed. Englewood Cliffs, NJ: Prentice-Hall, 1986).

18. Details are available in F. Kirgis, ASIL Insight: Diplomatic Immunities in Iraq (June 2003) available at: <http://www.asil.org/insights/insigh109.htm>.

19. *See* Vienna Convention on Diplomatic Relations of 1961, Articles 1–5, 500 UN TREATY SERIES 95 (1964), reprinted in 18 INT'L LEGAL MAT'LS 149 (1979), available at: <http://fletcher.tufts.edu/multi/texts/BH408.txt> [hereinafter *Diplomatic Convention*].

20. U.S. v. Sissoko, 995 F. Supp. 1469 (S.D. Fla., 1997).

21. Accounts of these incidents are available in *Chinese Practice* (cited in note 8 above), at 100 (Raghunath Affair) and 103 (Jongejans Affair).

22. *See* Taiwan Relations Act of 1979, 22 UNITED STATES CODE §3303 (1986) (change of recognition status of Taiwan does not affect legal rights vested prior to recognition of the PRC) & §2.3 of this book on the specific legal effects of nonrecognition.

23. G. Berridge, TALKING TO THE ENEMY: HOW STATES WITHOUT "DIPLOMATIC RELATIONS" COMMUNICATE 129 (New York: St. Martin's Press, 1994).

24. *See generally* E. Denza, DIPLOMATIC LAW: COMMENTARY ON THE VIENNA CONVENTION ON DIPLOMATIC RELATIONS (2d ed. Oxford, Eng.: Clarendon Press, 1998) (article by article analysis of this treaty).

25. *Diplomatic Convention,* Art. 3 (cited in note 19 above].

26. Dainese v. Hale, 91 U.S. 13, 15–16 (1 Otto) (1875) regarding American consular powers in Turkey and Egypt.

27. L. Lee, Historical Evolution, ch. 1, in CONSULAR LAW AND PRACTICE 4 (2d ed. Oxford, Eng.: Clarendon Press, 1991) [hereinafter *Consular Law*].

28. 596 UN TREATY SERIES 261 (1967), Art. 5, reprinted in E. Osmanczyk, ENCYCLOPEDIA OF THE UNITED NATIONS AND INTERNATIONAL AGREEMENTS 987 (2d ed. New York: Taylor & Francis, 1990) [hereinafter *Consular Convention*].

29. Eun-Kyung Kim, Convicts' Treaty Rights Withheld, Associated Press (July 10, 2001).

30. *Texas model:* see Calif. Senate Bill No. 1608 §1(b)(2). *California version:* Cal. Penal Code §5028.

31. *See* Extraterritoriality, in *Consular Law,* at 7 (cited in note 27 above).

32. Accounts of papal diplomacy in contemporary conflicts are available in P. Kent & J. Pollard (ed.), PAPAL DIPLOMACY IN THE MODERN AGE (Westport, CT: Praeger, 1994).

33. G. Do Nascimento e Silva, DIPLOMACY IN INTERNATIONAL LAW 104–106 (Leiden, Neth.: Sijthoff, 1972). In the South-West Africa Cases (Ethiopia and Liberia v. South Africa), 1966 ICJ REP. 6, the ICJ held that the plaintiff States did not have a sufficient interest to represent the rights of persecuted natives in South Africa. The suit was dismissed, leaving those natives without an effective remedy.

34. I. Brownlie, PRINCIPLES OF PUBLIC INTERNATIONAL LAW 343 (6th ed. Oxford, Eng.: Oxford Univ. Press, 2003).

35. Claims to Formal Bases of Capability, ch. 7, in *Law of Diplomacy* 333, 424–425 (cited in note 1 above).

36. *See* Empson v. Smith, 2 ALL ENGLAND REP. 881, 883 (1965) (discussing the Russian ambassador's detention).

37. L. Frey & M. Frey, THE HISTORY OF DIPLOMATIC IMMUNITY, at 5 (Columbus, OH: Ohio State Univ. Press, 1998) (footnote omitted).

38. XV POLISH YEARBOOK. INT'L L. 119, 120 (1986) (italics added).

39. *Consular Convention* (cited in note 28 above).

40. The *classic* illustration appears in the text box on the first page of this chapter.

41. *See Chinese Practice,* at 94 (cited in note 8 above).

42. J. Barker, THE ABUSE OF DIPLOMATIC PRIVILEGES AND IMMU-NITIES: A NECESSARY EVIL? 12 (Aldershot, Eng.: Dartmouth, 1996).

43. *Insurance analysis:* Note, Insuring Against Abuse of Diplomatic Immunity, 38 STANFORD L. REV. 1517 (1986). *US Government standards:* Regulations on Compulsory Liability Insurance for Diplomatic Missions and Personnel, 22 CODE OF FED. REGS. 151 (1980), reprinted in 18 INT'L LEGAL MAT'LS 871 (1979). *Federal statute:* 22 US CODE §254e.

44. UN Gen. Ass. Reso. 3166(XXVII) of 14 Dec. 1973, 13 INT'L LEGAL MATERIALS 43 (1974), and available at: <http://fletcher.tufts.edu/faculty/rubin/courses/l201/L201_XII4_ProtectedPersons.doc>.

45. Report of the Secretary-General on United Nations Decade of International Law, UN DOC. A/47/384, para.153, at 49 (Aug. 26, 1992). *See also* ILC's Web page on inviolability of the unaccompanied diplomatic bag at <http://www.un.org/law/ilc/guide/gfra.htm>, scroll to 9. Law of International Relations.

46. *Israeli bombing:* See T. McCormack, SELF-DEFENSE IN INTERNATIONAL LAW: THE ISRAELI RAID ON THE IRAQI NUCLEAR REACTOR (New York: St. Martin's Press, 1996). *Diplomat's advice:* see S. Murphy, Peacemaking: The Interaction of Law, Politics, and Diplomacy—Comments on Senator Mitchell's Lecture, in 97 AMER. SOC. INT'L L. PROCEEDINGS 177 (2003).

47. Beecham v. Socialist People's Libyan Arab Jamahiriya, 424 F.3d 1109 (D.C.Cir. 2005). This case was filed in 2004. Libya's appeal on sovereign immunity grounds was dismissed in September 2005. As of January 2006, the case was still in progress.

CHAPTER EIGHT

Treaty System

INTRODUCTION

States have used treaties to establish their mutual expectations for many centuries—both orally and in writing.[1] Today's primary method of determining mutual expectations is the written treaty, governed by the 1969 Vienna Convention on the Law of Treaties.[2] From the end of World War II through 2003, the United Nations, which receives copies of most treaties, has registered over 50,000 bilateral and multilateral treaties. The contributors include: China—more than 6,000; France—almost 7,000; the United States and Japan—approximately 10,000 each.[3]

◆ 8.1 DEFINITION AND CLASSIFICATION

DEFINITIONAL CONTOURS

The word "treaty" means different things to different people. Some three dozen terms are used interchangeably with that word. Thus, there have been several prominent studies. A major Harvard Law School analysis

◆

Moscow—Russia and China signed a treaty of friendship and cooperation yesterday, binding the two nations closer together over the next 20 years.

The treaty also commits them to jointly oppose much of the framework for international security that the United States is seeking to erect in the post-Cold War era.

. . . [T]he treaty formally joins Russia and China in opposing the U.S. plans for missile defense and places Russia more firmly behind China's claim of sovereignty over Taiwan.

It also strengthens military cooperation between Beijing and Moscow and rejects the kind of humanitarian intervention that NATO undertook in the Balkans in 1999.

. . .

One Russian commentator here described the treaty as "an act of friendship against America."

—Patrick Tyler, Russia, China sign strategic accord to meet all threats, NYT News Service, July 17, 2001.

described treaty law as "confusing, often inconsistent, unscientific and in a perpetual state of flux." The UN International Law Commission (ILC) undertook an exhaustive study of this term. The ILC characterized the word treaty as a "generic term covering all forms of international agreement in writing concluded between states."[4] This analysis nevertheless concluded that "judicial differences, in so far as they exist at all . . . lie almost exclusively in the method of conclusion and entry into force." The legal distinctions among these various terms are minimal, however, in the sense that each synonym depicts obligations, which are binding under International Law.[5]

Article 2.1 of the 1969 Vienna Convention on the Law of Treaties (VCLT) defines a treaty as "an international agreement concluded between states in written form and governed by international law, whether embodied in a single instrument or in two or more related instruments and whatever its particular designation." This "constitution" on treaty law does not address *oral* agreements, because of the comparative prominence of written instruments as a basis for contemporary international obligations.

Treaties may be made by States and international organizations.[6] In 1991, for example, the International Monetary Fund (IMF) signed an accord with the Soviet Union (on the eve of its demise). That agreement established a special association, whereby the IMF could advise the Soviets on economic and fiscal policy during its transition to a market economy. The 1969 VCLT deals only with *State* treaties. The drafters wanted to mold the State treaty regime first—saving the international organizational regime for another day. The 1986 Vienna Convention on the Law of Treaties Between States and International Organizations or Between International Organizations is the organizational counterpart of International Treaty Law.[7]

Treaty disputes have adversely affected international relations on many occasions, and in a variety of contexts. There have been many issues of interpretation with the formation, observation, and termination of treaties. The United Nations thus developed the VCLT, as a code to govern international agreements—a treaty on treaties. It governs written treaties made after 1980, when the convention was ratified by the required minimum number of nations to become effective. It provides the best insight into the treaty practice of States, and is the core of this chapter on the treaty system.

Analogy to Contract Law? There is a daunting question about whether public treaties between nations are analogous to private contracts between individuals (including corporate "persons"). By producing a global yardstick, the VCLT drafters arguably oversimplified treaty

law. As described by Professor Andreas Gasis of the Hellenic Institute of International and Foreign Law (Greece):

As is well known, man, when faced with a problem not previously encountered, frequently resorts to a familiar solution, derived from an analogous situation. . . . This practice is widespread in the realm of European Continental Law, where the more elaborated Civil Law of Roman origin has systematically been used as the root onto which new branches of law have been grafted. . . .

The . . . phenomenon has also appeared in the realm of international law, where there has been an attempt to codify a Law of Treaties in recent years. Thus, the relevant Vienna Convention on the Law of Treaties, 1969, takes a notoriously narrow "contract" view of Treaties. . . . Hence, when reading the text . . . , one cannot escape the impression of being at the forefront of . . . a Continental Civil Code governing [the] private law [of] contract. . . .[8]

When drafting or applying a treaty between sovereigns, however, there is often a need for more flexibility than expected of a business relationship between individuals. As aptly articulated by the University of New South Wales senior lecturer Shirley Scott: "A *legal* interpretation of a multilateral treaty takes the treaty at face value. The preamble is read as indicative of the goals of the treaty. From the perspective of the *political* interpretation of a treaty, the treaty per se is not considered to have goals. The preamble points to, but does not define, a principle whose acceptance as a basis of negotiation was essential to the conclusion of the treaty. Whereas from a legal perspective all preambular paragraphs are of equal importance, from a political perspective those making reference to the foundation[al] ideology . . . are of greater political importance than the others.[9]

The VCLT is thereby characterized as failing to incorporate the fact that an international treaty is something different than a contract governing private relationships between individuals, who often speak the same native language. The above scholars argue that a treaty should not be thought of as a "concluded" agreement expressing the complete intent of the parties to the treaty. Instead, it is merely evidence of an underlying legislative purpose to be ascertained by international consensus. Even an agreed-upon meaning associated with a particular treaty word can undergo subsequent alteration, when there has been a lapse of time or a change in State practice regarding the application of that term. The nineteenth-century legal writer, Robert Phillimore, thus cautioned that "due construction of the instrument may require a [k]nowledge of the antiquated as well as the present use of the words. . . ."[10]

States generally prefer less specific agreements than do private international traders, in order to retain maximum flexibility in their respective dealings. University of Helsinki Professor Jan Klabbers comments that many "formal and visible agreements make it politically difficult for states to change their policies. The necessity of sending proposed agreements through cumbersome procedures of approval in their national legislatures reduces states' freedom of action. Further, agreements allowing for quick renegotiation or modification are by definition not as inflexible as agreements which do not make [such an] allowance. Finally, agreement can be reached more swiftly . . . the more informal the proposed instrument is considered to be."[11] One should acknowledge that the twentieth-century "public treaty as private contract" analogy is not without its critics. A lawyer in a treaty-drafting process may prefer to "cross all the t's." A political scientist might focus on the relationship between the four corners of the document. A diplomat must view the process through both lenses.

"Unequal" Treaties International agreements are supposedly the product of a mutually beneficial decision to create rights and honor obligations. Unfortunately, a number of treaties have been imposed by one State on another because of their inherently unequal bargaining positions.

During the seventeenth and eighteenth centuries, writers first raised the question of whether treaties were valid in the absence of any real bargaining or negotiations. In 1646, the famous Dutch author Hugo Grotius distinguished between equal and unequal treaties. He described an unequal treaty as one that is forced on one nation by another, rather than being the product of a negotiated process. In 1758, Swiss author E. de Vattel examined the problem of unequal treaties—concluding that States, like individuals, should deal fairly with one another. De Vattel hypothesized that because States "are no less bound than individuals to respect justice, they should make their treaties equal, as far as possible." Neither of these influential writers, however, questioned the legal *validity* of such treaties. A bargained-for exchange was not considered a

necessary prerequisite for a valid treaty between sovereign States. But as later stated by American author H. Halleck in 1861, "the inequality in the . . . engagements of a treaty does not, in general, render such engagements any the less binding upon the contracting parties."[12]

Examples of unequal treaties include Napoleon's 1807 threat to place the king of Spain on trial for treason, unless the king surrendered his throne. Having no choice, King Ferdinand entered into an agreement with France that was devoid of any bargained-for advantages for Spain. In the 1856 Treaty of Paris, Russia was prohibited from maintaining a naval fleet on the Black Sea at its geographically sensitive southwestern border. In 1903, a US condition for recognizing Cuba's independence from Spain was the Guantanamo Naval Base Treaty. The United States thereby "acquired" a permanent lease for a military base that proved critical to US interests. The 1903 Panama Canal Treaty with Colombia validated US control over the Canal (until relinquished in 1977). The Treaty of Versailles, which ended World War I, was signed by German delegates who had unsuccessfully objected to draconian terms requiring that Germany pay the victors for damages incurred during World War I. Just prior to World War II, Hitler threatened to bomb Czechoslovakia to force the adoption of a treaty placing the Czechs under German "protection."[13]

In the twentieth century, legal commentators began to question the historical presumption that unequal treaties are valid. National Chengchi University (Taipei) Professor Hungdah Chiu summarized them as follows:

After the 1917 Bolshevik revolution in Russia, the Bolshevik government offered to abolish and later did abolish some former Tzarist treaties imposed upon China, Persia, and Turkey; and Soviet writers then began to discuss the question of the validity of those "coercive, predatory, and enslaving" treaties, although the term "unequal treaties" was not widely used after World War II. This early development in the Soviet Union, however, was generally ignored by Western scholars.

In the 1920s, however, the problem of unequal treaties received world-wide attention when China demanded the abolition of some treaties that it termed unequal. Only then did some Western writers renew interest in the problem. In 1927, at the annual meeting of the American Society of International Law, a session was devoted to the discussion of China's unequal treaties. With the abolition of what were presumed to be the last of China's unequal treaties in the early 1940s, Western scholars again lost interest in the subject.

With the emergence of many new states in Asia and Africa in the 1960s, the question of unequal treaties again began to attract worldwide attention. When the Draft Articles on the Law of Treaties prepared by the United Nations International Law Commission was sent to UN member states for comment, many states expressed concern about the question of unequal treaties.[14]

CONTEMPORARY CLASSIFICATION

The convenience of any treaty classification system is rivaled by the danger of oversimplification. Four common distinctions illustrate the general nature of most treaties: oral versus written; bilateral versus multilateral; lawmaking versus contractual; and self-executing versus declaration of intent.

Oral versus Written   The VCLT was drafted in terms of "written" treaties. While most treaties are written, States routinely incur international obligations based on oral agreements. State representatives may orally incur a binding international obligation.

In a prominent example, Denmark and Norway established Denmark's sovereignty over Eastern Greenland in a manner, which was far less formal than a written treaty. The right to this vast area had been disputed since the 1819 termination of the union between what is now Denmark and Norway. In a recorded conversation in 1919, the Norwegian Minister of Foreign Affairs and a Danish diplomat agreed that Norway would not object to Danish control over all of Greenland, including the disputed portion of its eastern coast. The Permanent Court of International Justice (PCIJ) held that this oral understanding resulted "in the settlement of this [sovereignty] question."[15] The Court accorded great weight to the context in which this particular conversation occurred. Although certainly not as formal as a written treaty, this agreement was nevertheless binding on Norway, because of the subject matter of this diplomatic discussion. Two diplomats had orally resolved a question falling within the negotiating authority conferred upon them by their respective nations.

A writing does not have to be a formal treaty to create international obligations. In 1994, the International Court of Justice (ICJ) reviewed some documents related to a maritime boundary dispute. These were the 1987 exchanges of letters between the King of Saudi Arabia and the Emir of Qatar, and between the King of Saudi Arabia and the Emir of Bahrain; and, a 1990 document entitled "Minutes," signed at Doha by the Ministers for Foreign Affairs of Bahrain, Qatar, and Saudi Arabia. These exchanges constituted international agreements, which obligated the State Parties to abide by the terms of those agreements, including the undertaking to submit their long-term maritime boundary dispute to the Court.[16]

Bilateral versus Multilateral   A bilateral treaty establishes mutual rights and obligations between two States. It normally affects only them, but not others. Other States typically derive no benefits or duties from such a treaty. The States entering into this type of treaty do not intend to establish rules, which contribute to the progressive development of International Law. For example, there are hundreds of bilateral extradition treaties. Each one lists the circumstances under which the two treaty parties agree to return criminals to the State requesting extradition. The respective States do not intend to make a change to international practice, merely by agreeing on which crimes are thereby subject to mutual extradition.

Bilateral treaties do not confer benefits on or create obligations for nonparties, unless that is the *express* intent of the contracting parties. Nor does a multilateral treaty necessarily do that. However, its contents may be evidence of accepted State practice which lies within the parallel universe of Customary International Law (§1.2).[17] A multilateral treaty, on the other hand, is an international agreement among three or more States. Most of the military, political, and economic organizations discussed in this book were created by multilateral treaties. They expressed the rights and duties of the member States, and the competence of the particular organization created by their treaty.

There was a significant proliferation of multilateral treaties in the twentieth century. Writing on the impact of the 1982 UN Convention on the Law of the Sea, for example, George Washington University Professor Louis Sohn traces the comparative deluge after World War II:

International lawyers have by now accepted the fact that rules for drafting and putting into force such [multilateral] agreements are flexible. . . .

This flexibility is due primarily to the tremendous increase in the last fifty years in the role being played by international institutions and multipartite diplomacy. Originally, evidence of the existence of a rule of international law could be found only in books written by eminent professors or in briefs prepared by practitioners in disputes involving international law. . . . The Hague Peace Conferences of 1899 and 1907 inaugurated a new approach: the contracting parties, acting on behalf of "the society of civilized nations," agreed on a number of lawmaking conventions . . . [regarding] "the principles of equity and right on which are based the security of States and the welfare of peoples . . . and the dictates of public conscience."

During the period of the League of Nations, while the 1930 Codification Conference [on treaty practice] did not prove successful, the number of multipartite treaties increased considerably. Professor Manley O. Hudson collected in the first eight volumes of International Legislation, covering the period 1918 to 1941, 610 international multipartite treaties of that period. Since the Second World War, the United Nations, acting not only through the International Law Commission, but also through its specialized agencies and special conferences . . . together with the increasing number of regional organizations and various groups of states dealing with specific topics of international law, has given birth to several thousands of multipartite agreements covering practically every conceivable subject [more than 33,000 when this article was written].[18]

Lawmaking versus Contractual   Treaties may also be classified as either "lawmaking" or "contractual." A lawmaking treaty creates a new rule of International Law designed to modify existing State practice. The 1982 United Nations Law of the Sea Treaty contains a number of new rules governing jurisdiction over the oceans. Although it codifies (restates) some previously existing rules that States applied in their mutual relations, this multilateral treaty also contains some novel lawmaking provisions. For example, the new International Seabed Authority was created to control the ways in which the ocean's resources are globally (re)distributed. Free "transit passage" would replace the otherwise applicable regime of restricted "innocent passage" through the territorial waters of coastal States (§6.3).

Ratification of some of the associated provisions would *change* State practice, which had not previously required either an equitable redistribution of global resources or transit passage.

On the other hand, some treaties are merely "contractual." An import-export treaty sets forth the terms of a contract, which the State parties agree to for a specified period of time. For example, under the GATT/WTO regime (§13.2), State X agrees to charge an 8 percent tariff on incoming State Y wine. State Y may export up to 100,000 bottles of wine per year to State X. This arrangement is a simple contract. It does not purport to create, alter, or abrogate any of the norms, which govern international trade.

French Professor Paul Reuter, in his distinguished treatise on treaty law, succinctly recounted that "[t]he development of treaties during the second half of the nineteenth century prompted several new doctrinal distinctions. . . . [T]he expressions 'law-making treaties' and 'contractual treaties' came into use, the former referring to the treaties [that] first laid down general conventional rules governing [all of] international society. . . . It is important to make clear, when speaking of treaties as either [normative] 'legislation' or [mere] 'contracts,' whether they are being viewed from [either] a legal or sociological standpoint."[19]

An entire treaty, or parts of it, may break new legal ground. The North American Free Trade Agreement (NAFTA) associated Canada, Mexico, and the United States into a large free-trade area. That development was "lawmaking" because it created a new international organization. Yet there was nothing novel or lawmaking about their reduction of trade barriers to form a common economic market. Many other countries, as in the European Union, had already done so. In this sense, NAFTA merely created an international contract governing the respective goods and services exchange among the State parties, just like a private contract would do, between three merchants engaged in a similar cross-border transaction. One could distinguish the 1995 World Trade Organization (WTO), however. It replaced the established 1947 General Agreement on Tariffs and Trade (GATT) process. The physical bulk of the WTO process merely continued the GATT process of publishing national tariff schedules. But establishing an authoritative WTO process involved fresh lawmaking, because of the way in which nations therein decided to resolve their international trade disputes.

Self-Executing versus Declaration of Intent A treaty may be further classified as "self-executing" when it expressly imposes immediate obligations. A self-executing treaty requires no further action to impose binding obligations on its signatories. It is instantly incorporated into both International Law and the internal law of each treaty member by the express terms of the treaty. There is no need for additional executive or legislative action by the State parties to immediately create binding legal obligations. Alternatively, a treaty may be a declaration of intent. It would thereby contain general statements of principle, which set forth a hortatory standard of achievement for all parties. Such treaties require follow up, individual State action before any of the parties incur actual legal—as opposed to moral—obligations under the treaty.

Bilateral treaties concluded by two States are normally self-executing. The contracting States would have no treaty, if they were unable to agree to all of its terms. Not so with a multilateral treaty. Most multilateral treaties are not self-executing. The State drafters who sign them intend them to be statements of principle, which do not impose immediate *legal* obligations to act in a particular way. Such treaties are intended to articulate mutually agreeable goals or standards of achievement. Each participant must undertake some subsequent act under its internal law, for the stated standard to then ripen into a binding legal obligation.

If all treaties were self-executing, few States would participate. There is a vast difference in economic, cultural, political, or military capabilities to immediately institute all features of certain multilateral treaties. An initial agreement on the aspirational goal accommodates these differences via the expression of commonly understood objectives. As acknowledged by UN Secretary General Kofi Annan, in his Millennium Summit invitation for nations of the world to ratify the twenty-five core multilateral treaties:

> Since the founding of the United Nations in 1945, over 500 multilateral treaties have been deposited with the Secretary General. . . . Without exception, all of these treaties have been the result of meticulous negotiations and reflect a careful balance of national, regional, economic and other interests. . . . The aspirations of nations and of individuals for a better world governed by clear and predictable rules agreed upon at the international level are reflected in these instruments. They constitute a comprehensive international legal framework covering the whole spectrum of human activity, including human rights, humanitarian affairs, the environment, disarmament, international criminal matters, narcotics, outer space, trade, commodities and transportation. . . .

> Some of these multilateral treaties, though negotiated many years ago, are still to receive the minimum number of ratifications and accessions required for their entry into force. Others are still far from achieving universal participation. It is my hope that Heads of State and Government will . . . rededicate themselves to the multilateral treaty framework and thereby contribute to advancing the international rule of law and the cause of peace. . . .[20]

The following case arose in the now familiar context of the Vienna Convention on Consular Relations. In the §7.2 *Torres* case, you observed the sensitive fallout from failure to provide consular access to an arrested foreign national. In a related case, the US Supreme Court analyzed whether that treaty is self-executing:

Medellin v. Dretke

SUPREME COURT OF THE
UNITED STATES
__ U.S. __ , 125 S.Ct. 2088, 161 *L. Ed.* 2d
982(2005)
Go to course Web page at
<http://home.att.net/~slomansonb/txtcsesite.html>.
Under Chapter Eight, click <u>Medellin v. Dretke.</u>

◆ 8.2 FORMATION, PERFORMANCE, CESSATION

This section of the book deals with the treaty process: how a treaty is formed, expectations regarding its performance, and when performance may be interrupted. Although this section focuses on the main international treaty on treaties, local procedures for adopting it vary from country to country. As noted by the Council of Europe: "Treaty-making constitutes the very basis of the international legal order and influences international relations.

It channels the expression by States of consent to be bound and defines the commitments they enter into. However, the national procedures by which States express their consent to be bound vary considerably, depending on constitutional, legal and political conditions which reflect the history of each country."[21]

TREATY FORMATION

The chronological phases in the formation and implementation of a multilateral treaty are negotiation, signature, ratification, reservations (if any), entry into force, and registration.

Negotiations The emergence of a multilateral treaty often begins when an international organ such as the UN General Assembly decides to study some problem of global concern. The Assembly might resolve that the problem should be the subject of an international conference. State representatives commence the treaty process with preliminary negotiations during an international conference. Most nations of the world first met in 1974, for example, to draft an International Law of the Sea treaty. These initial discussions expanded, over the course of the next eight years, during which many nations thus negotiated their respective positions on proper use of the oceans and its natural resources. These representatives drafted, and redrafted, a "constitution" of the oceans. They produced a final treaty text, which was satisfactory, at least in principle, to the participants (§6.3).

Conference representatives must possess the authority to negotiate on behalf of their respective States. Not unlike diplomats who present their credentials to host State authorities, conference participants are normally vested with "full powers" by the State they represent. A document from each State's government is presented to a chair or conference committee at the inception of the conference. That document normally vests the representative with various powers: to negotiate, provisionally accept, or perform any act necessary for completing this initial phase of the treaty process. The "full power" instrument facilitates assurances that conference developments will be acceptable to the governments that will one day have to decide whether to ratify the final draft of the treaty text negotiated by their respective conference representatives.

The lack of such authority adversely affected international relations when a former US minister to Romania signed two bilateral treaties, but without the president's authority to do so. Regarding one of those treaties, the US minister improperly advised the president that he was signing a different treaty than the one he actually signed with Romania. As to the other agreement, he had no authority whatsoever to actually bind the United States. The US attempt to avoid its obligations under those treaties was resisted by Romania because the United States had already officially entered into these two agreements.[22]

To help clarify treaty expectations in such instances, Article 8 of the VCLT provides that any "act relating to the conclusion of a treaty performed by a person who cannot be considered . . . as authorized to represent a State for that purpose is without legal effect unless afterwards confirmed by the competent authority of the State." This language theoretically creates the potential for abuse, whereby a State representative can enter into a treaty, and the home State can subsequently disavow the authority of its representative. In practice, however, the representative's presentation of documentary powers at the inception of a conference contains clear notification to all participants about the extent of a particular delegate's powers (which may be limited by the dispatching government).

In the 1960s, many of the new nations and former colonies in Africa and Asia advocated the proposition that (the previously discussed) "unequal treaties" were no longer acceptable under International Law. One prominent forum for advocating this perspective was the drafting negotiations for the 1969 VCLT. Article 2.4 of the UN Charter requires all members to "refrain in their international relations from the threat or use of force . . . [which is] inconsistent with the purposes of the United Nations." If force was illegal in international relations, then coercion in the treaty process should invalidate the legality of any treaty forced upon these former colonies whose bargaining power was no match for their former occupiers.

The result of the VCLT negotiations was the incorporation of two articles applicable to treaties concluded after the effective date of the VCLT (January 27, 1980). Article 51 provides that the "expression of a State's consent to be bound by a treaty which has been *procured by the coercion of its representative* through acts or threats directed against him shall be without any legal effect" (italics added). Article 52 provides that a "treaty is void if its conclusion has been *procured by the threat or use of force* in violation of the principles of international law embodied in the Charter of the United Nations" (italics added). Although coerced treaties that concluded prior to the VCLT were presumed valid by some writers, Articles 51 and 52 expressly negated that presumption for subsequent treaties. As stated by the ICJ, there "can be little doubt, as is implied in the Charter of the United Nations and recognized in Article 52 of the

Vienna Convention on the Law of Treaties, that under contemporary international law an agreement concluded under the threat or use of force is void."[23]

During the VCLT negotiations, a number of Eastern communist bloc and African states advocated the view that Article 52's prohibition against force should expressly include "economic, military, and political" coercion. Their attempts to ban treaties procured through these categories of force were rebuffed by Western representatives. The Western position was that, given the difficulty of defining "force" in the treaty process, it would be too difficult to determine whether a treaty was invalid because it was allegedly signed as a result of such duress.

Article 52 of the VCLT therefore does not contain a specific definition of force. Instead, it generally prohibits the threat or use of force in violation of the principles of International Law embodied in the UN Charter. That language thus meant that "the precise scope of the acts covered by this definition should be left to be determined in practice by interpretation of the relevant provisions of the [UN] Charter." Yet Article 2.4 of the Charter also begs the question of what is the intended meaning of the term "force." It vaguely prohibits the use of force "against the territorial integrity or political independence of any state. . . ." The Vienna Convention Article 52 definition of force in the treaty process was likewise left purposefully vague, because it incorporated the Charter's inherently vague definition of force.[24]

Some ambiguity about the scope of the term "force" was offset at the conclusion of the VCLT. The delegates adopted the separate Declaration on the Prohibition of Military, Political, or Economic Coercion in the Conclusion of Treaties. They therein stated that the United Nations Conference on the Law of Treaties "solemnly condemns the threat or use of pressure in any form, whether military, political, or economic, by any State in order to coerce another State to perform any act relating to the conclusion of a treaty in violation of the principles of the sovereign equality of States and freedom of consent. . . ."[25] This Declaration was actually made independently of the VCLT rather than directly expressed within the text of the Article 52 prohibition of force in the conclusion of treaties. This exclusion—which more precisely defined force, but in the supplemental text not officially a part of the VCLT itself—was a compromise. It ameliorated Western opposition to nonmilitary duress as a basis for invalidating a treaty. Because the VCLT itself defines coercion only by the reference to the "principles of international law embodied in the Charter of the United Nations," it is difficult to determine when a treaty would be void on the basis of duress in its creation.

Signature   The next significant step in the treaty process is "opening for signature." States, and any participating international organizations, are invited to sign (which is distinct from subsequent ratification). A State that *signs* a treaty has agreed, in principle, to the general wording of the articles appearing in the text of its final draft. Drawing upon the example of the Vienna Convention on Diplomatic Relations (§7.2), negotiations were concluded in 1969. The representatives had thereby finished drafting this new "constitution" governing diplomatic issues.

In one sense, this was only the beginning. Under Article 81 of the VCLT, "[t]he present Convention shall be open for signature by all States Members of the United Nations . . . and by any other State invited by the General Assembly to become a party to the Convention . . ." States that did not participate in the drafting conference may subsequently "accede" to a treaty. That State thereby consents to be bound, albeit in principle, like any States that signed the treaty at or near the conclusion of the drafting conference. Alternatively, accession *may* express a State's willingness to accept the treaty's obligations as being immediately binding, without the necessity of ratification (discussed below).

Unanimous and immediate consent of all States is possible, but quite atypical—for reasons addressed in the "reservations" portion of this section. Fully embracing the treaty's commitments normally evolves through two related stages. The first stage is *provisional* acceptance of the treaty by the conference delegates. This stage expresses consent to the general wording of the final conference draft. Unless otherwise specified, the signature of a representative on a multilateral treaty merely indicates that his or her State agrees in principle with the essence of the treaty. *Final* acceptance would follow, when a State expresses its willingness to be legally bound by the treaty's terms, expressed in that State's ratification of the treaty.

Ratification   Postconference ratification is the typical mode for each State's full acceptance of a treaty. The conference delegate has already submitted the provisionally accepted treaty text to the proper authority in his or her State for final approval. This ratification is then determined in accordance with each State's internal laws on treaty acceptance. Oxford University's Sir Humphrey Waldock provides a useful explanation for the necessity of *postconference* ratification by each potential

State party: "[T]he interests with which a treaty deals are often so complicated and important that it is reasonable that an opportunity for considering the treaty as a whole should be reserved. A democratic state must consult public opinion, and this can hardly take shape while the negotiations, which must be largely confidential, are going on."

As classically articulated in a 2005 US Court of Appeals decision, drawing from two leading treatises on International Law:

> The ratification process, in whatever form it may take serves several functions. First and foremost, "it affords a state the chance to scrutinize closely the provisions of a complicated agreement" after signing it. "The need for an institution such as ratification is principally that, for various reasons, states need time after agreement has been reached upon a definitive text of a treaty before they feel able to commit themselves to it." In addition, in the time between signing and ratification, States are able . . . (1) to effect changes in domestic law that may be necessary for the implementation of a treaty, (2) to seek and obtain the consent of legislative bodies as may be required, and (3) to re-examine the relevant provisions before committing to them.[26]

Reservations   Acceptance of a multilateral treaty is usually not an "all-or-nothing" proposition. A reservation is a State's unilateral variation from the language of some general term contained in the negotiated text. Notwithstanding ratification of the overall treaty, a State may exclude, or modify, the legal effect of *its* obligations, which would otherwise arise under the general language of the "model" article in the final draft of the treaty. The reserving State is expressing its agreement with the text generally; but it does not wish to become obligated on all terms. A State's provisional acceptance at the drafting conference does not preclude it from tendering a reservation, although it may have signed the treaty.

A reservation to a specific provision in a treaty is a conditional consent. If the reservation is acceptable to the other parties, it limits the scope of the reserving State's general consent to the rest of the treaty. The reserving State is not bound by what it thus identifies as an "objectionable" treaty provision. It is bound by all other terms of the ratified treaty to which it has not submitted a reservation.

In the case of a bilateral treaty between just two nations, reservations are generally nonexistent. One of the two parties may still have a "reservation" to a tentative agreement. But any reservation is effectively a fresh proposal, which is a counteroffer to change their treaty. Both States must agree on all terms of a bilateral agreement. Otherwise, it cannot become uniformly applicable for each treaty party.

Hypothetical reservation illustration: Assume that the representatives of States A, B, C, and D provisionally accept the final text of a treaty at the conclusion of their four-nation drafting conference. They express their agreement to be bound by the broadly worded principles stated in the treaty. They open this treaty for signature (and subsequent ratification). The terms of the treaty are not self-executing because the conference delegates did not have the power to ratify the treaty immediately upon conclusion of the drafting stage. No State is yet entitled to the rights, nor bound to perform the obligations, specified in the treaty. Each State must subsequently accept the treaty through the respective national ratification processes. State A's leaders review this treaty for possible ratification. They decide to object to the application of one treaty clause. State A will thus tender a reservation to that particular provision of the treaty. Assuming that A's reservation is acceptable to B, C, and D. State A is excused from performing that particular provision of the treaty. Assume that B, C, and D do not tender the same reservation when they ratify this treaty. Unlike State A, they are bound to perform whatever is required by this treaty clause among themselves. However, the three countries do not have to perform that obligation in their respective dealings with State A.

Why are reservations permitted? They encourage wider participation in multilateral treaties via the practical compromise, that is, permitting reservations. Broad participation is better than limited participation by only those few States that might be willing to accept *every* term in a draft treaty. For example, few States would agree to be sued in the International Court of Justice (ICJ) if they were unable to make reservations to the final draft treaty provision regarding the ICJ's competence to hear and decide its own cases. Article 36.6 of the UN's Statute of the ICJ provides that any disputes over the Court's jurisdiction, or power to hear the particular case, are to be determined by the Court itself. Every UN member is automatically a party to this Statute, which is itself a treaty.

States often object to the Court's jurisdiction to hear a case, which has just been filed against them. Those States may do so, if they had previously decided not to give their full consent to Article 36.6 of the ICJ Statute. Many States tendered reservations to this treaty-based competence of the ICJ to decide its own jurisdiction. They reserved the question of the Court's power to hear a case unto themselves, when they would be summoned as a defendant in a future case before the Court. This common reservation precludes the ICJ from deciding its own jurisdiction under the ICJ's Statute. This complex feature of the Court's jurisprudence is analyzed in §9.4. Suffice it to say that at this juncture, there was a practical need for compromise. Without the possibility of such a treaty reservation, a number of major powers would not have recognized a distant Court—sitting in Europe—as having the absolute power to hear all international controversies. Reservations like this one accommodate the special interests of States, which would not otherwise participate in the overall process of international adjudication by the ICJ. Half a loaf is better than none.

Such conditional assent cannot be used in *all* treaties. The drafting conference negotiators may decide to insert a prohibition against reservations within the express language of the final treaty text. The 1995 Agreement for Implementation of the Provisions of the United Nations Convention on the Law of the Sea of 10 December 1982 relating to the Conservation and Management of Straddling Fish Stocks and Highly Migratory Fish Stocks prohibits reservations. Predictably, such a provision can limit effective participation. While the US Senate gave its approval to this treaty in 1996, members of that body warned other nations that this should not be construed as US acquiescence in future treaties containing a like provision.[27]

Many treaties say nothing about the possibility of the parties being able to tender reservations to the final text. Silence normally cannot be construed as supporting or defeating the right to become a party, while attempting to do so via a reservation to a key text provision. This can yield a very sensitive debate. The classic example is the United Nations Genocide Convention.[28] The principles enshrined in this 1948 instrument were unanimously adopted by all UN members in the aftermath of Nazi Germany's Holocaust. Many States, however, did not ratify the Genocide Convention. The term "genocide" has meant different things to different people. States were thus reluctant to accept it without knowing what specific obligations might one day materialize. They feared that the absence of a reservation provision in the Genocide Treaty might one day subject them to scrutiny on grounds that they had never contemplated. The United States, for example, did not become a party until nearly forty years later (1986) because of prior senatorial concern about the meaning and application of its various terms.

The International Court of Justice *Reservations Case* addresses this issue. In 1948, the UN General Assembly unanimously adopted the Convention on Genocide. It began as a General Assembly resolution, and thus not directly binding upon UN members, without further action via individual State ratifications (§1.2 Sources). In 1950, the UN General Assembly requested an advisory opinion from the ICJ. The 1948 Convention had just entered into force, because of the deposit of the minimum number of ratifications by 1950. There was no provision on the extremely sensitive question of whether reservations would be permitted. If reservations *were* to be allowed, then States could theoretically exclude certain forms of genocide from their consent to be bound by this treaty. The General Assembly asked the Court to interpret the Genocide Convention, to determine whether a State might ratify the Convention and simultaneously tender a limiting reservation to its egalitarian terms.

Reservations to the Convention on Genocide

INTERNATIONAL COURT OF JUSTICE

1951 ICJ REPORTS 15 (1951)

AUTHOR'S NOTE: The Court chose to articulate a somewhat abstract analysis of this sensitive question. Noting the apparent divergence of State views on the possibility of reservations to this particular treaty, the ICJ decided that it implicitly contained the right to become a party and to simultaneously present a reservation—as long as it was "compatible" with the language and purpose of the treaty. The relevant portion of the opinion follows—unsigned by any member of the Court.

COURT'S OPINION: [T]he precise determination of the conditions for participation in the [Genocide]

Convention constitutes a permanent interest of direct concern to the United Nations which has not disappeared with the entry into force of the Convention. . . .

It is well established that in its treaty relations a State cannot be bound without its consent, and that consequently no reservation [by one state] can be effective against any [other] State without its agreement thereto. It is also a generally recognized principle that a multilateral convention is the result of an agreement freely concluded upon its clauses and that consequently none of the contracting parties is entitled to frustrate or impair, by means of unilateral decisions or particular agreements, the purpose and raison d'etre of the convention. To this principle was linked the notion of the integrity of the convention as adopted, a notion which in its traditional concept involved the proposition that no reservation was valid unless it was accepted by all the contracting parties without exception, as would have been the case if it had been stated during the negotiations.

This concept, which is directly inspired by the notion of contract, is of undisputed value as a principle. However, as regards the Genocide Convention, it is proper to refer to a variety of circumstances which would lead to a more flexible application of this principle. Among these circumstances may be noted the clearly universal character of the United Nations under whose auspices the Convention was concluded, and the very wide degree of participation envisaged by Article XI of the [Genocide] Convention. Extensive participation in conventions of this type has already given rise to greater flexibility in the international practice concerning multilateral conventions. More general resort to reservations, very great allowance made for tacit assent to reservations, the existence of practices which go so far as to admit that the author of reservations which have been rejected by certain contracting parties is nevertheless to be regarded as a party to the convention in relation to those contracting parties that have accepted the reservations—all these factors are manifestations of a new need for flexibility in the operation of multilateral conventions.

It must also be pointed out that although the Genocide Convention was finally approved unanimously, it is nevertheless the result of a series of majority votes. The majority principle, while facilitating the conclusion of multilateral conventions, may also make it necessary for certain States to make reservations. This observation is confirmed by the great number of reservations which have been made in recent years to multilateral conventions.

In this state of international practice, it could certainly not be inferred from the absence of an article providing for reservations in a multilateral convention that the contracting States are prohibited from making . . . reservations. Account should also be taken of the fact that the absence of such an article or even the decision not to insert such an article can be explained by the desire not to invite a multiplicity of reservations. The character of a multilateral convention, its purpose, provisions, mode of preparation and adoption, are factors which must be considered in determining, in the absence of any express provision on the subject, the possibility of making reservations, as well as their validity and effect. . . .

The Court recognizes that an understanding was reached within the General Assembly on the faculty [ability] to make reservations to the Genocide Convention and that it is permitted to conclude therefrom that States becoming parties to the Convention gave their assent thereto. It must now determine what kind of reservations may be made and what kind of objections may be taken to them.

The solution of these problems must be found in the special characteristics of the Genocide Convention. The origins and character of that Convention, the objects pursued by the General Assembly and the contracting parties . . . furnish elements of interpretation of the will of the General Assembly and the parties. The origins of the Convention show that it was the intention of the United Nations to condemn and punish genocide as "a crime under international law" involving a denial of the right of existence of entire human groups, a denial which shocks the conscience of mankind and results in great losses to humanity, and which is contrary to moral law and to the spirit and aims of the United Nations (Resolution 96(I) of the General Assembly, December 11th, 1946). The first consequence arising from this conception is that the principles underlying the Convention are principles which are recognized by civilized nations as binding on States, even without conventional obligation. A second consequence is the universal character both of the condemnation of genocide and of the cooperation required "in order to liberate mankind from such an odious scourge" (Preamble to the Convention). The Genocide Convention was therefore intended by the General Assembly and by the contracting parties to be definitely universal in scope. It was in fact approved on December 9th, 1948, by a resolution which was unanimously adopted by fifty-six States.

The objects of such a convention must also be considered. The Convention was manifestly adopted for a purely humanitarian and civilizing purpose. It is indeed difficult to imagine a convention that might have this dual character to a greater degree, since its object on the one hand is to safeguard the very existence of certain human groups and on the other to confirm and endorse the most elementary principles of morality. In such a convention the contracting States do not have any interests of their own; they merely have, one and all, a common interest, namely, the accomplishment of those high purposes which are the raison d'etre of the convention. Consequently, in a convention of this type one cannot speak of individual advantages or disadvantages to States, or of the maintenance of a perfect contractual balance between rights and duties. The high ideals which inspired the Convention provide, by virtue of the common will of the parties, the foundation and measure of all its provisions.

The foregoing considerations, when applied to the question of reservations, and more particularly to the effects of objections to reservations, lead to the following conclusions.

The object and purpose of the Genocide Convention imply that it was the intention of the General Assembly and of the States which adopted it that as many States as possible should participate. The complete exclusion from the Convention of one or more States would not only restrict the scope of its application, but would detract from the authority of the moral and humanitarian principles which are its basis. It is inconceivable that the contracting parties readily contemplated that an objection to a minor reservation should produce such a result. But even less could the contracting parties have intended to sacrifice the very object of the Convention in favour of a vain desire to secure as many participants as possible. The object and purpose of the Convention thus limit both the freedom of making reservations and that of objecting to them. It follows that it is the compatibility of a reservation with the object and purpose of the Convention that must furnish the criterion for the attitude of a State in making the reservation on accession as well as for the appraisal by a State in objecting to the reservation. Such is the rule of conduct which must guide every State in the appraisal which it must make, individually and from its own standpoint, of the admissibility of any reservation.

Any other view would lead either to the acceptance of reservations which frustrate the purposes which the General Assembly and the contracting parties had in mind, or to recognition that the parties to the Convention have the power of excluding from it the author of a reservation, even a minor one, which may be quite compatible with those purposes.

It has nevertheless been argued [independently of these proceedings] that any State entitled to become a party to the Genocide Convention may do so while making any reservation it chooses by virtue of its sovereignty. The Court cannot share this view. It is obvious that so extreme an application of the idea of State sovereignty could lead to a complete disregard of the object and purpose of the Convention.

◆ *Notes & Questions*

1. What test did the International Court of Justice use to determine whether a reservation to a multilateral treaty is permissible?

2. There would be a devastating impact on human rights programs if there were a flood of reservations to the various instruments—in the absence of provisions regarding whether reservations are permissible. For fascinating analyses, *see* L. Lijnzaad, RESERVATIONS TO UN—HUMAN RIGHTS TREATIES: RATIFY AND RUIN? (Dordrecht, Neth.: Martinus Nijhoff, 1995) &

J. Gardner (ed.), HUMAN RIGHTS AS GENERAL NORMS AND A STATE'S RIGHT TO OPT OUT: RESERVATIONS AND OBJECTIONS TO HUMAN RIGHTS CONVENTIONS (London: Brit. Inst. Comp. Law, 1997).

3. The United States ratified the International Covenant on Civil and Political Rights (§11.2). This treaty is often referred to as the international guarantor of Due Process of Law—especially its first two dozen articles. Upon ratification, the United States included two pages of "Reservations," "Understandings," and "Declarations." One of latter states as follows: "(1) That the

United States declares that the provisions of articles 1 through 27 of the Covenant are not self-executing." Could it be argued that the United States did not realistically ratify this treaty? Is this declaration "compatible with the object and purpose of the treaty?"

4. The text and commentaries in the Draft Guidelines on Reservations to Treaties was provisionally adopted by the International Law Commission in 2001. This project is designed to clarify mostly procedural issues related to reservations, especially when a nation ratifies a treaty and then wishes to later augment its earlier position with a limiting interpretation of its existing reservation. In reference to the European Convention on Human Rights: "Any State may, when signing this Convention or when depositing an instrument of ratification, make a reservation in respect of any particular provision of the Convention to the extent that any law then in force in its territory is not in conformity with the provision. Reservations of a general character shall not be permitted under this Article." ILC, Conventions and Other Texts, available at: <http://www.un.org/law/ilc/convents.htm>, scroll to "Topics currently under consideration," last entry under "Reservations to treaties," at 497 (pdf at 61), n. 1200.

5. In 1999, Trinidad and Tobago reacceded to the Optional Protocol to the International Covenant on Civil and Political Rights. This Protocol included the provision that ratifying nations were to allow prison inmates to file claims with the UN Human Rights Committee regarding alleged human rights violations. Trinidad and Tobago therein tendered a reservation, which purported to vitiate the ability of its death row inmates to submit such communications for external review. The UN Committee decided that this reservation was incompatible with the purpose of the protocol. It thus decided that it *could* hear such a petition from an inmate, notwithstanding the acceding country's reservation to its obligations under the treaty protocol. *See* Decision of the Human Rights Committee Under the Optional Protocol to the International Covenant on Civil and Political Rights, U.N. GAOR, Hum. Rts. Comm., 67th Sess., Annex, ¶ 7, U.N. DOC. NO. CCPR/C/67/D/845/1999 (1999).

6. Certain treaties do not permit *any* reservations. Examples include the Statute of the International Criminal Court (§9.5), and the proposed World Health Organization Framework Convention for Tobacco Control. The latter requires governmental control of the tobacco industry. Article 30 provides as follows: "No reservations may be made to this Convention." In May 2003, the United States forcefully objected to this nonreservation clause. It was willing to become a party, but only if it could attach reservations to the treaty provisions setting minimum sizes for tobacco package warnings, restricting free distribution, and limiting advertising promotions. See D. Fidler, World Health Organization's Framework Convention for Tobacco Control, ASIL Insight (Mar. 2003), available at: <http://www.asil.org/insights/insigh100.htm>. This convention entered into force in February 2005, without US ratification.

Entry into Force   The next phase of the treaty process is "entry into force." The participants may have provisionally accepted the treaty's final draft language at the drafting conference, followed by final acceptance of the treaty by their individual ratifications. Unlike bilateral treaties, where only two States have to agree on all terms for a treaty to come into force, multilateral treaties usually require greater indicia of international consensus before they are binding. An "entry into force" provision ensures that an agreed-upon minimum number of States ratify the treaty before it becomes binding on those which have signed.

The manner and date of entry into force is determined from the particular treaty's express provisions. Multilateral treaties normally enter into force when a minimum number of ratifications are deposited at some central location, such as the United Nations. The 1948 Genocide Convention, for example, did not enter into force until twenty States had deposited their ratifications with the UN Secretary-General. The 1982 UN Law of the Sea Convention did not enter into force until 1994, one year after the sixtieth State (Bosnia) ratified it, pursuant to an express provision so stating in that treaty.

States that have not ratified a treaty are not bound by its terms just because it has entered into force. They may be bound by its underlying norms if the treaty codifies the existing practice of most States. Those States may consent to be bound by submitting a subsequent ratification/accession.

Registration   Treaties must be registered, meaning that they are normally sent to the UN Secretariat, or another appropriate international institution most directly involved with the object of the particular treaty. Both of the Vienna Conventions, which govern the treaties of *States* and of international *organizations,* mention this obligation.[29] UN Charter Article 102 provides that "Every treaty and every international agreement entered into by any Member of the United Nations after the present Charter comes into force shall as soon as possible be registered with the Secretariat and published by it." The United Nations thus maintains both print and electronic versions of its *United Nations Treaty Series*.[30] Registration approximates the filing of an important document with a court such as a pleading, which can be accessed by all interested parties at a known location where it is archived. Registration also ensures that international agreements are public, as opposed to the secret treaties that led to World Wars I and II. Treaties are usually registered at the UN, or at the headquarters of the international organization

The publication of treaties is typical, but not always accomplished. Certain countries, especially those with the economic capacity to do so, publish all of their treaties. While some government representatives might prefer to engage in "quiet" diplomacy and treaty negotiations, the product of their efforts must be subject to public scrutiny. The US Congress therefore requires publication in the comprehensive source United States Statutes at Large. Once published therein, US laws and treaties "shall be legal evidence of laws . . . treaties, and international agreements other than treaties [that is, executive agreements]."[31]

There is a peculiar difference between the League of Nations Covenant and the UN Charter regarding the registration requirement embraced by both documents. Article 18 of the Covenant contained an outright bar, which vitiated the legality of unregistered treaties. Secret treaties were thus characterized as being void from the outset. UN Charter Article 102, on the other hand, provides that a party to an unregistered treaty may not "invoke that treaty or agreement before any organ of the United Nations." This does not "void" the treaty. It declares that the particular instrument cannot be used in any proceedings involving the United Nations, such as judicial proceedings in the International Court of Justice. In 1992, a London newspaper reported that presidential candidate Bill Clinton had struck a secret deal with the head of the European Community. A new world trade agreement (§13.2 WTO, effective 1995) would be delayed until after his election, which he denied. Such an agreement would be completely void

under League practice, but effective under UN practice as long as it was not relied upon in any UN proceeding.

As a practical matter, many treaties are not registered (published). Because of the time and money inherent in the registration/publication process, certain international organizations have narrowly construed the meaning of the word "treaty" to limit which treaties are subject to the UN Charter registration requirement. The United Nations, although subject to budgetary constraints, has resolved to improve the availability of its documents on the Internet. General Assembly Resolution 211(C) of 1997 "[r]equests the Secretary-General to ensure that the texts of all new public documents . . . are made available through the United Nations Web site . . . and are accessible to Member States without delay. . . ."

TREATY OBSERVANCE

There are several yardsticks for determining whether a State has performed or properly rebuked "its end of the deal": good faith performance of national treaty obligations; changed circumstances justifying nonperformance; express and implied consent to suspension or termination of a treaty; material breach by one party justifying another's nonperformance; impossibility of performance; and conflict with a peremptory norm of International Law.

Good Faith Performance   Under Article 2.2 of the United Nations Charter, "Members . . . shall fulfill in good faith the obligations assumed by them in accordance with the present Charter." The universal character of this norm was aptly articulated by the former Dutch ambassador to the United Nations in 1967: "The principle of good faith itself . . . extends beyond the scope of this article and is generally recognized as expressing a fundamental concept underlying the entire structure of the international public order. It applies to the observance and interpretation of treaties and even to the obligation not to frustrate the object of a treaty prior to its entry into force, as well as to the fulfillment of obligations arising from other sources of international law. Particularly in the context of the law of treaties the principle of good faith . . . clearly emerges as having a fundamental and universal nature."[32]

State must not act in a way which would frustrate the purpose of a treaty, which it has signed or ratified. It may not pass subsequent internal legislation that is inconsistent with those obligations. In a US-UK treaty delineating the fishing rights of US citizens in Canadian waters, the UK's posttreaty regulations limited those rights in a way that was not contemplated by the wording of the treaty. The arbitrators in this famous proceeding noted that such regulations had to be "drawn according to the principle of international law that treaty obligations are to be executed in perfect good faith, therefore excluding the right to legislate at will concerning the subject-matter of the treaty, and limiting the exercise of sovereignty of the States . . . to such acts as are consistent with the treaty. . . ."[33]

Various cases decided by the International Court of Justice illustrate the problems with *applying* the unassailable good faith performance standard. In two significant cases, the ICJ dealt with what it perceived to be tardy claims, not made in good faith. In the 1960 *Case Concerning the Arbitral Award Made by the King of Spain,* a bilateral treaty required Honduras and Nicaragua to arbitrate their boundary dispute. Spain's king was the agreed-upon arbitrator after the treaty-designated arbitrator failed to act. When the king decided this boundary dispute in 1960, neither country objected to his decision. Years later, Nicaragua challenged the validity of his award because the king "was not designated arbitrator in conformity with the provisions of the . . . Treaty [which] had elapsed before he agreed to act as arbitrator." Honduras responded that Nicaragua was thereby acting in bad faith, waiting too long to assert this potential bar to enforcement of the king's award. The ICJ held that Nicaragua could not in good faith raise such procedural problems, so many years after the arbitration was complete and the treaty purpose fulfilled. In the words of the ICJ: "It would be contrary to the principle of good faith governing the relations between States were it [Nicaragua] permitted now to rely upon any irregularity in the appointment to invalidate the Award. Its conduct up to the moment of the Award operated in my opinion so as to preclude it thereafter from doing so. . . ."[34]

In another illustration, Cambodia and Siam (now Thailand) agreed to a boundary delimitation made by a "Mixed Commission" of individuals from Thailand and Cambodia. The commission's work was completed in 1907. A subsequent dispute arose over an important religious site situated at the border, but not mentioned in surveys conducted by the commission's officers. The surveys apparently placed the temple area within the territory comprising French Indochina (included in what is now Cambodia). The commission members from Siam received copies of the surveys and did not object at the time of that body's findings. Years later, Thailand refused to cede authority over the area to Cambodia. In the 1960 proceedings before the ICJ, Thailand had two objections to the treaty-based boundary of 1907: First, the surveys were not actually the work of the treaty-designated commission; second, they contained material errors in the placement of the Thai-Cambodian boundary. The ICJ rejected Thailand's claim for two reasons: It was not made in good faith because of the tardiness in asserting it; also, Thailand had apparently acquiesced in the boundary line fixed by the commission decades before it presented an objection. Both forms of conduct led to the Court's useful articulation regarding the importance of good faith performance:

> The primary foundation of this principle is the good faith that must prevail in international relations, inasmuch as inconsistency of conduct or opinion on the part of a State to the prejudice of another is incompatible with good faith. Again, I submit that such inconsistency is especially inadmissible when the dispute arises from bilateral treaty relations. A secondary basis of the principle is the necessity for security in contractual relationships. A State bound by a certain treaty to another State must rest in the security that a harmonious and undisturbed exercise of the rights of each party and a faithful discharge of reciprocal obligations denote a mutually satisfactory state of things which is permanent in character and is bound to last as long as the treaty is in force. A State cannot enjoy such a situation and at the same time live in fear that some day the other State may change its mind or its conduct and jeopardize or deny rights that for a long time it has never challenged. A continuous and uncontroverted fulfillment of a treaty is tantamount to a pledge, a security renewed day by day that the treaty rights, passiveness or any form of express or tacit acquiescence, and other disputes have been decided against litigant States on the general basis of inconsistency between the claims of States and their previous acts."[35]

The lack of a precise definition of "good faith treaty performance" has spawned the occasional question of whether it is in fact a general principle of International Law. Professor Charles Fenwick, former director of the Department of Legal Affairs of the Pan American Union, asserted the doubtful existence of this norm. He used treaties of peace, imposed by the victor on the vanquished, as his prime example that good faith was not seriously expected in treaty matters. When a vanquished State wanted to repudiate a treaty imposed on it by a victorious nation, the simple solution was another war. Given this fact of international life, he argued that "[a]ppearances could be saved, if [even] necessary, by finding other grounds of war, and then, if the outcome were successful, taking back what had been previously granted under duress. . . . Thus the faithful execution of treaties of peace was adjusted to shifts in the balance of power, and the principle of good faith was maintained while being indirectly undermined."[36]

Various organizations have thus attempted to articulate a standard for resolving questions about the precise content of the rather elastic "good faith performance" yardstick—often referred to as *pacta sunt servanda*. The UN International Law Commission (ILC) commenced its study of this "norm" shortly after the United Nations was created. The ILC's first work product on this subject was the Draft Declaration on the Rights and Duties of States. Article 13 provided that every "State has the duty to carry out in good faith its obligations arising from treaties . . . and it may not invoke provisions in its constitution or its [internal] laws as an excuse for failure to perform this duty."[37] This limitation was almost too acceptable, because it was not a functional description of the norm's supposed content.

Two decades later, some of the Vienna Convention on the Law of Treaties delegates thus argued in favor of *eliminating* the term from international treaty law, because of its perennial ability to mean different things to different people.[38] The wording chosen for Article 26 of the VCLT was general enough to achieve a consensus. It provides that every treaty "is binding upon the parties to it and must be performed by them in good faith." That language is no more specific than any earlier attempt to define good faith. Thus, good faith performance of treaty obligations does not mean literal compliance, and should be assessed by reference to the circumstances of each particular case.

Change in Circumstances A treaty is no longer binding if there has been a "fundamental change in circumstances," also referred to as the doctrine of *rebus sic stantibus*. While a treaty is a solemn contract between States, a party may invoke changed circumstances as an excuse for suspending or terminating that contract.

The Vienna Convention's essential provision is Article 62.1. It provides as follows:

A fundamental change in circumstances which has occurred with regard to those existing at the time of the conclusion of a treaty, and which was not foreseen by the parties, may not be invoked as a ground for terminating or withdrawing from the treaty unless: (a) the existence of those circumstances constituted an essential basis of the consent of the parties to be bound by the treaty; and (b) the effect of the change is radically to transform the extent of obligations still to be performed under the treaty.

This theme often surfaces as a defense to the good faith performance requirement. Defining "changed circumstances" is as amorphous an venture as defining "good faith." Commentators, diplomats, and jurists are unable to agree on the precise circumstances for properly invoking this basis for avoiding treaty obligations. This obstacle has not impeded the evolution of a spectrum of divergent views. For example, *rebus sic stantibus* has been characterized as (1) a "clearly a reasonable doctrine [that] . . . international law should recognize;" (2) an "alleged principle of international law;" and (3) an "unsuitable method for altering treaty obligations to accommodate changed conditions."

The prolific Chinese scholar Wang Yao-t'ien dubbed changed circumstances as a contrivance fashioned by capitalist States to abrogate treaties at will. In his 1958 treatise on trade treaties, he wrote that two States should renegotiate their treaty, rather than one of them unilaterally suspending or terminating its treaty obligations. In his words: "There is a doctrine of '*rebus sic stantibus*' in the works of bourgeois international law. . . . In international relations, sometimes it is necessary to revise or abrogate a treaty in the light of fundamental change of circumstances. However, capitalist states frequently use this principle as a pretext to justify their unilateral [abrogation] of treaties. Generally, the process should be: When a fundamental change of circumstances occurs, the contracting states should seek revision or reconclusion of the original treaty through diplomatic negotiation."[39]

Columbia University Professor Oliver Lissitzyn aptly referred to the changed circumstances doctrine as a right with unsettled contours. In his words: "After centuries of doctrinal discussion, the existence, scope and modalities of such a right remain controversial and perplexing. Its practical importance may at times be exaggerated; but nations dissatisfied with the *status quo* continue to regard it as a welcome device for escaping from burdensome treaties, while others fear it as a threat to stability and to their interests. Terminology has complicated the problem. . . . Governments, in asserting the right, have variously employed or refrained from employing such terms as *rebus sic stantibus*."[40]

Changed circumstances does not permit an outright unilateral abrogation of treaty commitments. When circumstances beyond the control of the parties necessitate the alteration of a treaty commitment, the remedy is usually suspension or termination of the treaty—depending on the nature and extent of the conditions which have changed. The reality may be that the State claiming changed circumstances may no longer want to fulfill commitments that have become inconvenient or not as beneficial as anticipated. During the 1960s, the drafters of the Vienna Convention on the Law of Treaties attempted to clarify the legal contours of the changed circumstances doctrine. The drafting committee articulated its concern as follows: "Almost all modern jurists, however reluctantly, admit the existence in international law of the principle . . . commonly spoken of as the doctrine of *rebus sic stantibus*. . . . Most jurists, however, at the same time enter a strong caveat as to the need to confine the scope of the doctrine within narrow limits and to regulate strictly the conditions under which it may be invoked; for the risks to the security of treaties which this doctrine presents . . . [are] obvious. The circumstances of international life are always changing and it is easy to allege that the changes render the treaty inapplicable."[41]

The existence of the changed circumstances doctrine has been reluctantly conceded in international litigation. The Permanent Court of International Justice grudgingly recognized its vitality. The Court refused to assess its contours, however, ultimately choosing not to apply it.[42] In the early 1970s, the International Court of Justice effectively characterized Iceland's changed circumstances defense as an unacceptable attempt to unilaterally terminate its treaty obligations. The segment of this case dealing with changed circumstances is presented below. It echoes the sentiment of the VCLT (which came into force seven years after this case was decided) that renegotiation, or judicial settlement, is the preferred alternative to unilateral termination supposedly based on "changed circumstances." The dissenting opinion, on the other hand, vividly portrays the perennial problem associated with larger nations historically taking advantage of smaller ones:

Fisheries Jurisdiction Cases
(*Germany v. Iceland*)

INTERNATIONAL COURT OF JUSTICE
Gen. List No. 56, 1973 *ICJ Reports* 49 (1973)
Go to course Web page at
<http://home.att.net/~slomansonb/txtcsesite.html>.
Under Chapter Eight, click <u>Fisheries Jurisdiction Cases.</u>

TREATY TERMINATION AND SUSPENSION

The stability of the treaty system is nourished by the fulfillment of treaty commitments. Yet a State may legitimately terminate or suspend its treaty obligations, by employing recognized methods for suspending or terminating a treaty.

Express Consent   States typically enter into treaties of indefinite duration. Some treaties, however, terminate by its their own terms—in conformity with the expressed desire of the treaty parties. For example, the expiration of a specified time of duration is a routine basis for termination. The People's Republic of China commonly makes treaties that remain in force only for a designated period. For example, the 1950 Sino-Soviet Treaty of Friendship, Alliance, and Mutual Assistance provided that the "present treaty will be valid for thirty years. If neither of the contracting parties . . . desire[s] to renounce the treaty, it shall remain in force for another five years and will be extended in compliance with this rule."[43]

Treaties that do not expire under their own terms typically contain provisions for advance notification of termination. The 1955 Sino-Indonesian Treaty on Dual Nationality provided that if "after the expiration of twenty years, one party requests its termination, it must so notify the other party one year in advance and in written form; and the present treaty shall be terminated one year after the tendering of such notification." The 1954 Mutual Defense Treaty between the United States and the Republic of China (Taiwan) provided that it would remain in force "indefinitely [although] either Party may terminate it one year after notice has been given to the other Party." In 1978, President Carter gave notice that he intended to terminate the treaty with Taiwan. That treaty was terminated by the United States one year later when he officially recognized the People's Republic of China (mainland China) as the *de jure* government of China.

A treaty may be terminated or suspended even when it does not contain revocation or notice provisions. The participants may simply repeal it in another treaty. Under Article 58 of the Vienna Convention on the Law of Treaties, two (or more) nations may suspend a treaty as it relates to their mutual obligations to one another.

States sometimes withdraw from treaties on political grounds, unrelated to any breach. In September 2002, Mexico announced its intent to withdraw from the key Organization of American States 1947 hemispheric defense treaty. Mexico was frustrated over the United States' more restrictive US immigration policy imposed in the aftermath of 9-11.

Implied Consent   Treaty parties can effectively disapprove it by implication. If a subsequent treaty is silent about the continued validity of a prior treaty on the same subject, termination or suspension can be implied from the circumstances. The State parties may enter into a later agreement on the same subject matter as an earlier treaty. If provisions in the second treaty conflict with the first, then the first is canceled via the implied consent of the parties. The supposedly conflicting provisions must be incompatible in order to impliedly terminate the earlier treaty.

Examples include the 1939 Permanent Court of International Justice (PCIJ) case, wherein a majority of the Court had decided that two related agreements were compatible. Justice Anzilotti's dissent succinctly stated the general requirements for implicit treaty abrogation: There "was no express abrogation [of the 1931 treaty]. But it is generally agreed that, beside express abrogation, there is also tacit abrogation resulting from the fact that the new provisions are incompatible with the previous provisions, or that the whole matter which formed the subject of these latter [understandings] is henceforth governed by the new provisions."[44] Under Article 59(b) of the 1969 VCLT, the parties may consent by implication to treaty termination when a subsequent treaty is "so far incompatible with the earlier one that the two treaties are not capable of being applied at the same time."

Failure of compliance is another basis for implied consent to a treaty's termination. A treaty can be negated by implication when all of the parties unabashedly ignore it. The absence of objections constitutes an implied understanding that the treaty is no longer in force.

Finally, Customary International Law may evolve in a way, which effectively supercedes an existing treaty. There may be some disagreement among the treaty parties about whether a specific custom in fact conflicts with the treaty. Even assuming that a conflict does exist, State reaction varies as to whether the particular custom trumps the treaty. The common resolution is to revise the treaty. A posttreaty rule may evolve, which possesses the attributes of *jus cogens*—a peremptory norm from which no State may deviate. The VCLT provides that such a rule trumps the treaty. It is otherwise silent, however, about the interplay of a new customary State practice conflicting with a prior treaty when that fresh norm is *not jus cogens*. In this instance, the Brussels writer Nancy Kontou has analyzed the jurisprudence of international tribunals assessing the impact of supervening custom on prior incompatible treaties. That research yielded the "proposition that one party has the right to call for the termination or revision of a treaty on account of the development of new custom."[45]

Material Breach   One party's treaty breach may allow the other(s) to consider the treaty as either suspended or terminated.[46] The breach must be material, not minor. Under Article 60 of the VCLT, the material breach of a *bilateral* treaty by one party permits the other party "to invoke the breach as a ground for terminating the treaty or suspending its operation in whole or in part." Material breach of a *multilateral* treaty similarly entitles "the other parties . . . to suspend the operation of the treaty . . . in the relations between themselves and the defaulting State [but not between one another]. . . ." The clearest example of a material breach under Article 60 would be an outright repudiation of a treaty. The other party would then be authorized to suspend or terminate its own obligations under that treaty.

In practice, it is often difficult to establish what constitutes a material breach and which party is actually responsible for the breach. In 1966, North Vietnam claimed that South Vietnam had materially breached the Geneva Accords. That international agreement, agreed to by representatives of both governments, called for a cessation of hostilities in Vietnam, the reduction of military forces, and reunification through free elections. The North Vietnamese claimed that South Vietnam had materially breached the Accords, premised on the introduction of US military forces into the Southern portion of the country. The United States justified South Vietnam's departure from the Geneva agreement on the basis of a material breach by North Vietnam. The United States claimed that the "substantial breach of an international agreement by one side [North Vietnamese aggression in South Vietnam] permits the other side to suspend performance of corresponding obligations under the agreement. South Vietnam was allegedly justified in refusing to implement the provisions of the Geneva Accords," which otherwise would have required it to limit expanded military involvements and to arrange unification elections. South Viet Nam thus claimed that the introduction of military personnel into the southern portion of the country "was justified by the international law principle that a material breach of an agreement by one party [North Vietnam] entitles the other [South Vietnam] at least to withhold compliance . . . until the defaulting party is prepared to honor its obligation."[47] North Vietnam and South Vietnam thus accused each other of materially breaching their respective commitments under the Geneva Accords.

In a 1972 case in the International Court of Justice, Pakistan complained that India materially breached several aviation treaties. An Indian aircraft had been hijacked and diverted to Pakistan. India then revoked Pakistan's right to fly over Indian territory. For reasons unrelated to the merits of this case, the ICJ did not resolve whether India breached the aviation treaties when it refused to allow Pakistani aircraft in Indian airspace. It did find, however, that the Indian suspension of Pakistan's treaty rights to pass over Indian territory, and to land in India, constituted material breaches of this aviation treaty.[48]

Impossibility of Performance   A treaty party may invoke impossibility of performance as a basis for suspending or terminating its obligations. Article 61 of the VCLT provides that impossibility "results from the permanent disappearance or destruction of an object indispensable for the execution of the treaty." The drafters of the VCLT used the following examples: submergence of an island that is the object of a treaty relationship, the drying up of a river, and the destruction of a dam or hydroelectric installation indispensable for the execution of a treaty. The permanent or temporary impact of such circumstances would terminate (or suspend) rights and obligations arising under a treaty governing their use.[49]

A fundamental change that radically alters the nature of treaty obligations has been characterized by some jurists as impossibility of performance—presenting a fine-line distinction from the above "changed circumstances"

analysis. Although there are similarities, the criteria employed for applying "impossibility" differ. Every impossibility of performance involves a changed circumstance, but not every changed circumstance constitutes impossibility of performance. The changed circumstances doctrine may excuse difficulty of performance, while impossibility excuses only that performance that would be totally impossible. This excuse exonerates one or both parties from treaty performance when the relevant circumstance renders the treaty meaningless.[50]

Assume that Spain and Portugal establish their respective rights to fish in an area on either side of a boundary in the international waters off their adjacent coasts. They agree to regulate their respective fishing fleets on either side of the line separating Spain's area from Portugal's area. The purpose of this treaty is to maintain the equal distribution of the resources near their respective coasts. If the fish unexpectedly migrate into Portugal's area, then the treaty would be suspended. The changed circumstance is that fish are temporarily unavailable in equal numbers to both Spain and Portugal. Spain's fishermen might be permitted to fish in Portugal's area of the high seas, because of the treaty's mutually agreed purpose of equitable distribution. The same fishing treaty would be terminated under the impossibility doctrine, if all of the fish were permanently driven away by contamination of the treaty area. The treaty would be meaningless because the object of that agreement would no longer exist.[51]

Conflict with Peremptory Norm   A treaty is void if it conflicts with a peremptory norm of International Law. The common descriptive term for such a norm is *jus cogens,* referring to a supposed universally acknowledged law from which no State could deviate. Article 53 of the Vienna Convention on the Law of Treaties defines that term as a norm which is "accepted and recognized by the international community of States as a whole as a norm from which no derogation is permitted and which can be modified only by a subsequent norm of general international law having the same character." However, the VCLT does not provide examples of what constitutes such a norm.

The International Law Commission's July, 2001 Articles on State Responsibility provide no substantive clues regarding *which* norms fall within this category. Article 26 states only that "Nothing in this Chapter precludes the wrongfulness of any act of a State which is not in conformity with an obligation arising under a peremptory norm of general international law." Article 40 follows with "the international responsibility which is entailed by a serious breach by a State of an obligation arising under a peremptory norm of general international law . . . [which] is serious if it involves a gross or systematic failure by the responsible State to fulfil the obligation."

Some jurists and commentators deny the functional existence of *jus cogens,* because even the most generally accepted rules have not achieved universality. Moscow State University's Professor Grigori Tunkin explains that the "arguments of opponents of *jus cogens* can be reduced to the fact that such principles are possible only in a well-organized and effective legal system, and since international law is not such a system, the existence of principles of general international law having the character of *jus cogens* is impossible."[52]

One can make a reasonable theoretical argument that applying *jus cogens* (assuming that it actually exists) would render certain treaties void. When two States have entered into a treaty in which they agree to invade another country, that agreement violates the most fundamental UN Charter article: Article 2.4's prohibition on the use of force in international relations. Such a treaty would violate an undisputable Charter norm. Today, Stalin and Hitler's then secret 1939 agreement to divide Europe could not legitimately circumvent the Article 2.4 prohibition of force.

VCLT Applied In 1997, the ICJ adjudicated the following dispute between Hungary and Slovakia. Hungary relied on the VCLT's provisions discussed in this section of the book—as its rationale for terminating its 1977 Budapest Treaty with (what was then) Czechoslovakia.

◆

Case Concerning the Gabcíkovo-Nagymaros Project
(Hungary v. Slovakia)

INTERNATIONAL COURT OF JUSTICE (1997)
Gen. List No. 92
Go to course Web page at
<http://home.att.net/~slomansonb/txtcsesite.html>.
Under Chapter Eight, click <u>Hungary/Slovakia Treaty Breach Case.</u>

Limitations Suspension or termination is subject to other restrains. The severance of diplomatic or consular relations does not necessarily affect treaty rights and obligations. Article 2.3 of the Vienna Convention on Consular Relations (VCCR) provides that the "severance of *diplomatic* relations shall not ipso facto [automatically in and of itself] involve the severance of *consular* relations" (italics added). Article 45 of the VCCR expressly provides that a break in diplomatic relations does *not* alter the continuing obligation to honor treaty obligations having nothing to do with diplomatic or consular matters. Therefore, war and other hostile relationships do not terminate all treaty obligations of parties to the conflict. States are expected to continue to perform their obligations under treaties like the Geneva Conventions of 1949 dealing with Red Cross assistance, the laws of war, and treatment of prisoners of war (§10.6).

Theory and practice, however, often diverge when nations are at war. The outbreak of war does not automatically terminate treaty obligations. The US war with Germany did not automatically terminate the 1923 US treaty obligation to transmit property of deceased individuals to German citizens.[53] A prolonged state of war often presents problems with the performance of treaty requirements, and continuing these obligations may make no sense.

◆ 8.3 UNITED STATES TREATY PRACTICE

Under International Law, there are two general principles for resolving conflicting laws. One is that the UN Charter prevails when it conflicts with another international instrument.[54] The other is that a nation's internal law cannot be used as a defense to its breach of an international obligation.

How various nations make treaties is beyond the introductory scope of this book. Suffice it to say that the range of practice includes "legislative" and "executive" treaties.[55]

TREATY VERSUS EXECUTIVE AGREEMENT

One must begin with three essential components of US treaty practice. The first is the constitutional articulation of the president's treaty power. Under Art. II, Section 2, clause 2: "He shall have Power, by and *with the Advice and Consent of the Senate*, to make Treaties, provided that two thirds of the Senators present concur . . . [italics added]."

Second, there is an oceanic distinction between the constitutionally articulated "treaty" power and the nearly simultaneous appearance of the president's "executive agreement" power. All presidential agreements with other nations or international organizations are treaties. But under US practice, executive agreements are undertaken by the president alone—without the advice and consent of the Senate.

The third major theme is the relative ranking of treaties (either type), the US Constitution, and federal statutes when any of them conflict. The debate sometimes splits legal hairs regarding whether the president—who makes all treaties, with or without the Senate's consent—can use the executive's treaty-making power to trump some constitutionally required legislative involvement in certain foreign affairs. In 1977, for example, sixty members of the US House of Representatives unsuccessfully sued President Carter when he relinquished US control of the Panama Canal. Article IV, Section 3, clause 2 of the Constitution provides that the "Congress [both houses] shall have Power to dispose of . . . Property belonging to the United States. . . . In the view of these members of the House, President Carter had improperly relied on the Constitution's Treaty Power when he successfully sought the "Advice and Consent of the Senate"—rather than seeking the Canal's transfer to Panama via *both* houses of Congress.

The "treaty" versus "executive agreement" distinction was spawned by early US practice. During the Constitutional Convention of 1787, the House of Representatives was ultimately excluded from an express treaty-making role, which would have been exercised in conjunction with the Senate, as originally proposed. After debating the matter, the delegates acknowledged the widespread feeling that diplomatic negotiations required a degree of secrecy possible only in the smaller senatorial body (then twenty-six senators from the thirteen former colonies). The fervor of this debate effectively overshadowed the importance of what remained in the final draft of the Constitution—excluding the House completely, and including the president as the constitutional maker of US treaties.[56]

Almost immediately, US presidents, without seeking the consent of the Senate, began to enter into "executive agreements." This contrast evolved, in part, because the US Constitution does not actually *define* the term "treaties." When it was adopted in 1787, its drafters apparently saw no need to define a concept that was then well known in international practice.[57] The Treaty Clause has

never been judicially interpreted by the judicial branch of the US government—to mean that the president must have the Senate's advice and consent for all international agreements.

Two types of "executive agreements" evolved. One is the *congressional-executive* agreement. The president also requests approval of certain executive agreements by joint resolution of both houses of Congress. Columbia University Professor, Louis Henkin presents the following vindication for this implied presidential power: "Neither Congresses, nor Presidents, nor courts, have been seriously troubled by these conceptual difficulties and differences. Whatever their theoretical merits, it is now widely accepted that the Congressional-Executive agreement is available for wide use . . . and is a complete alternative to a treaty: The President can seek approval of any agreement by joint resolution of both houses of Congress rather than by two-thirds of the Senate. Like a treaty, such an agreement is the law of the land, superseding inconsistent state laws, as well as inconsistent provisions in earlier treaties, in other international agreements, or in acts of Congress."[58]

The other category of executive agreement is the "*sole executive* agreement." While congressional approval for executive agreements is often sought, it has been completely avoided in some instances. The president has exercised the inherent power to incur an international obligation independently of the Senate (Article II treaty) or both houses of Congress (congressional-executive agreement). Columbia University Professor Oliver Lissitzyn succinctly describes the historical but troubled development of the president's executive agreement power:

The making of executive agreements is a constitutional usage of long standing [that] apparently rests upon the President's vast but ill-defined powers in the fields of foreign relations and national defense. Neither the usage nor the decisions of courts, however, provide clear-cut guidance as to the scope of the treaty-making power and the scope of the executive agreement-making power [which] are not mutually exclusive. What may be properly accomplished by executive agreement may also be accomplished by treaty. . . .

It is not believed that any attempt to delimit rigidly the scope of the executive agreement-making power is likely to be successful or to result in a correct portrayal or prediction of actual practice. Some writers, while refusing to regard the executive agreement-making power as co-extensive with the treaty-making power, wisely refrain from attempting to define the scope of the former. . . .

It may be proper, therefore, to regard the executive agreement-making power as extending to all the occasions on which an international agreement is believed by the Chief Executive to be necessary in the national interest, but on which resort to the treaty-making procedure is impracticable or likely to render ineffective an established national policy. The test here suggested is the only one that adequately accounts for the variety of situations in which the President, with or without the approval of Congress, has resorted to the executive-agreement procedure. It also accounts for the increasing frequency of resort to the executive-agreement method in recent years, with the growth of complexity in international affairs and of pressure of work in the Senate.[59]

Not all Commonwealth countries allow executive agreements to have automatic effect as domestic law. Such a treaty is binding under International Law standards. Under Australia's Constitution, however, an executive agreement cannot have any internal effect until it is enabled into law via legislation.

Exhibit 8.1 illustrates the historical comparison between "treaties," in the constitutional sense of requiring the Senate's advice and consent, and "executive agree-

ments," undertaken as either the congressional or sole variations of that term. It is readily evident that the executive agreement has far surpassed the treaty in terms of how the president exercises the treaty-making power.

The Senate has occasionally expressed concern about this spiraling use of executive agreements, which has arguably emasculated its constitutional role in the treaty-making process. The most heated debate occurred between 1952 and 1957. Senator John Bricker generated an intense challenge by his proposed amendment to the Constitution's Treaty Clause. He advocated that all international agreements by the United States should become effective only when legislation passes in both the House of Representatives and the Senate. If he had been successful, the proposed constitutional amendment would have eliminated the president's ability to enter into any international agreement without express congressional approval. He or she would thus have been more of a negotiator than a *maker* of treaties.

Although the Bricker Amendment failed, Congress did pass the Case Act in 1972. It requires the president to advise Congress (in writing) of all international agreements made without the consent of the Senate or without a joint resolution of Congress. The president may believe that public disclosure would prejudice national security, however. In this instance, he or she may secretly enter into and later transmit a completed executive agreement to the Senate Committee

EXHIBIT 8.1 ARTICLE II—TREATY EXECUTIVE AGREEMENT COMPARISON

Treaties and Executive Agreements Concluded by the United States from 1789–2004

Period	Treaties	Executive Agreements	Treaty/Exec Agreements (%)
1789–1839	60	27	69/31
1839–1889	215	238	47/53
1889–1939	524	917	36/64
1939–1989	702	11,698	6/94
1990–1999	249	2,847	8/92
2000–2004	84	977	8/92
Total	1,834	16,704	10/90

The author's percentage calculations are expressed in rounded numbers. Data on the period since 1945 has been furnished by the US Department of State, Office of the Assistant Legal Adviser for Treaty Affairs. Data prior to 1945 is from the Congressional Record, May 2, 1945, at 4118 & E. Borchard, Treaties and Executive Agreements, 40 AMER. POL. SCIENCE REV. 735 (Aug. 1947). This table was adapted from, and further detail is available at: <http://frwebgate.access.gpo.gov/cgi-bin/getdoc.cgi?dbname=106_cong_senate_print&docid=f:66922.wais>. The more recent numerical comparisons were forwarded to the author by Jennifer Elsea, Legislative Attorney, Congressional Research Service.

on Foreign Relations and the House Committee on Foreign Affairs.[60]

The US Supreme Court has occasionally described, but not clearly defined, the scope of the president's executive agreement power. In a case growing out of President Carter's 1979 executive agreement with Iran—which ended the hostage crisis (§7.4), and provided a basis for resolving business claims against Iran—the Court characterized that general power as follows: "In

addition to congressional acquiescence in the President's power to settle [such] claims, prior cases of this Court have also recognized that the President does have *some* measure of power to enter into executive agreements without obtaining the advice and consent of the Senate."[61] The following case illustrates the difficulty in drawing a precise legal demarcation between the president's executive agreement power and the Senate consent required under the US Constitution:

Weinberger v. Rossi

SUPREME COURT OF THE UNITED STATES
456 U.S. 25, 102 S.Ct. 1510, 71 *L. Ed.* 2d 715 (1982)

AUTHOR'S NOTE: In 1968, President Johnson made an executive agreement with the Republic of the Philippines. It provided for the preferential employment of Filipino citizens at US military bases in the Philippines. Its purpose was to ensure the availability of suitable employees on those bases, including individuals who could speak the local language. The underlying rationale was that giving these jobs to local Filipino nationals would result in lower wage costs and less turnover in these positions, than if the same jobs were available to US military dependents. The President thus decided to favor foreign nationals in the hiring process on these bases.

Three years later, Congress enacted a law prohibiting any employment discrimination against US citizens on US overseas military bases—unless a "treaty" expressly permitted such discrimination as being necessary to US national interests. Four more executive agreements followed, providing for preferential treatment of foreign citizens at overseas military bases—after passage of the 1971 nondiscrimination legislation. However, none of these postlegislation agreements were submitted to the Senate for its advice and consent, as arguably required by the 1971 law.

In 1978, several US citizens working at one of the US naval bases in the Philippines were notified that their jobs had been converted into "local" positions (pursuant to the intentional discrimination authorized by executive agreement with the Philippines). This meant that they would be discharged from their employment with the US Navy—so that "local" citizens could obtain those jobs at the US military bases. The Rossis, and others who

had lost their jobs, sought reinstatement in their employment. They sued the US government (naming Secretary of Defense Weinberger) for violating the 1971 antidiscrimination statute.

The Supreme Court had to interpret the "treaty" exception in Section 106 of the 1971 anti-discrimination statute. It prohibited such discrimination, unless a "treaty" authorized this discrimination against US citizens, in favor of local nationals. But did this exception mean that discrimination against US citizens would be permitted only under a constitutional "treaty"—which requires Senate consent to discriminate against US citizens abroad? Alternatively, did Congress intend to leave the President's power to enter into an executive agreement permitting job discrimination intact, when it passed the 1971 Act?

The Supreme Court's task was to construe the federal statute, which provides as follows: "Unless prohibited by treaty, no person shall be discriminated against . . . in the employment of civilian personnel . . . in any foreign country because such person is a citizen of the United States or is a dependent of a member of the Armed Forces of the United States." Justice Rehnquist's opinion illustrates the difficulties with distinguishing between "Article II treaties" and "executive agreements." The Court's analysis arose in a very sensitive context, with significant foreign policy ramifications.

COURT'S OPINION: Our task is to determine the meaning of the word "treaty" as Congress used it in this statute. Congress did not separately define the word, as it has done in other enactments. We must therefore ascertain as best we can whether Congress intended the word "treaty" to refer solely to [the Constitution's] Art. II, §2, cl. 2, "Treaties" those international agreements concluded by the President with the advice and consent of the Senate—or whether Congress intended "treaty" to also include executive agreements such as the BLA [Base Labor Agreement, which permitted discrimination].

The word "treaty" has more than one meaning. Under principles of international law, the word ordinarily refers to an international agreement concluded between sovereigns, regardless of the manner in which the agreement is brought into force. Under the United States Constitution, of course, the word "treaty" has a far more restrictive meaning. Article II, cl. 2, of that instrument provides that the President "shall have Power, by and with the Advice and Consent of the Senate, to make Treaties, provided two thirds of the Senators present concur."

Congress has not been consistent in distinguishing between Art. II treaties and other forms of international agreements. For example, in the Case Act, 1 U. S. C. §112b(a), Congress required the Secretary of State to "transmit to the Congress the text of any international agreement, other than a treaty, to which the United States is a party" no later than 60 days after "such agreement has entered into force." Similarly, Congress has explicitly referred to Art. II treaties in the Fishery Conservation and Management Act of 1976, 16 U.S.C. §1801, and the Arms Control and Disarmament Act, 22 U.S.C. §2551.

On the other hand, Congress has used "treaty" to refer only to international agreements other than Art. II treaties. In 39 U.S.C. §407(a), for example, Congress authorized the Postal Service, with the consent of the President, to "negotiate and conclude postal treaties or conventions." A "treaty" which requires only the consent of the President is not an Art. II treaty. It is not dispositive that Congress in §106 used the term "treaty" without specifically including international agreements that are not Art. II treaties [emphasis supplied]. . . .

Thus, if Congress intended to limit the "treaty exception" in "106 to Art. II treaties, it must have intended to repudiate these executive agreements that affect the hiring practices of the United States only at its military bases overseas. One would expect that Congress would be aware that executive agreements may represent a quid pro quo [bargained for exchange whereby] the host country grants the United States base rights in exchange for the preferential hiring of local nationals [of the host State]. . . .

At the time §106 was enacted, there were in force 12 agreements in addition to the BLA providing for preferential hiring of local nationals on United States military bases overseas. Since the time of the enactment of §106, four more such agreements have been concluded, and none of these were submitted to the Senate for its advice and consent. We think that some affirmative expression of congressional intent to abrogate the United States" international obligations is required in order to construe the word "treaty" in §106 as meaning only Art. II treaties. We therefore turn to what legislative history is available in order to ascertain whether such an intent may fairly be attributed to Congress.

The legislative history seems to us to indicate that Congress was principally concerned with the financial hardship to American servicemen which resulted from discrimination against American citizens at overseas bases. As the Conference Committee Report explains:

> The purpose of [§106] is to correct a situation which exists at some foreign bases, primarily in Europe, where discrimination in favor of local nationals and against American dependents in employment has contributed to conditions of hardship for families of American enlisted men whose dependents are effectively prevented from obtaining employment.

The Conference Report, however, is entirely silent as to the scope of the "treaty" exception. Similarly, there is no mention of the 13 agreements that provided for preferential hiring of local nationals. Thus, the Conference Report provides no support whatsoever for the conclusion that Congress intended in some way to limit the President's use of international agreements that may discriminate against American citizens who seek employment at United States military bases overseas.

On the contrary, . . . Congress was not concerned with limiting the authority of the President to enter into executive agreements with the host country, but with the ad hoc decisionmaking of military commanders overseas. In early 1971 [just before Congress passed §106], Brig. Gen. Charles H. Phipps, Commanding General of the European Exchange System, issued a memorandum encouraging the recruitment and hiring of local nationals instead of United States citizens at the system's stores [on US military bases]. The hiring of local nationals, General Phipps reasoned, would result in lower wage costs and turnover rates. Senator Schweiker, a sponsor of §106, complained of General Phipps' policy [of discriminating against US nationals on US military bases in Europe]....

While the question is not free from doubt, we conclude that the "treaty" exception contained in §106 extends to executive agreements as well as to Art. II treaties [characterizing these executive agreements as "treaties" for the purpose of authorizing discrimination against US nationals on foreign US military bases]....

◆ *Notes & Questions*

1. The Supreme Court effectively "lent its hand" to the president's intentional discrimination against US citizens who hoped to work on US military bases abroad. This meant that military dependents, typically spouses of enlisted personnel, with a generally lower wage structure than that of military officers, would be unable to work, and in many cases thus unable to accompany their military spouses during overseas assignments. What was the rationale for promoting US interests via intentional discrimination in favor of foreign nationals?

2. The materials in this section suggest a two-part process for deciding whether the president's exercise of the executive agreement power transgresses any limits contained in the constitutional Treaty Clause or limiting congressional legislation. First, the president (through the appropriate federal agency) must determine whether his or her proposed executive agreement instead falls within the parameters of the Treaty Clause, which would require Senate consent. Second, the president must examine existing congressional legislation and attitudes to determine whether congressional approval should be obtained. As stated in the principal treatise on US constitutional law in the US, L. Tribe, Treaties and Executive Agreements, §4-4, in 1 AMERICAN CONSTITUTIONAL LAW 648–649 (3d ed. New York: Foundation Press, 2000):

> The precise scope of the President's power to conclude international agreements without the consent of the Senate is unresolved. At one extreme, the proposition that the treaty is the exclusive medium for affecting foreign policy goals and, consequently, that executive agreements are *ultra vires* [unconstitutional] seems adequately refuted....
>
> At the other extreme the notion that executive agreements know no constitutional bounds proves equally bankrupt. Executive agreements, no less than treaties, must probably be limited to appropriate subject matter. The more difficult question is whether there exist species of international accord that may take the form of a treaty, but not that of an executive agreement.

3. In September 2004, a federal appellate court resolved a conflict akin to *Rossi*—in this instance between a president's military Status of Forces Agreement (SOFA) with the United Kingdom and the US Foreign Sovereign Immunities Act (FSIA) (§2.6). During a bar fight in Tacoma, Washington, several members of the British military started a fight with and severely injured a US civilian. The 1976 FSIA is ordinarily the "exclusive" source of jurisdiction over suits involving foreign States and their instrumentalities. While foreign States are generally presumed to be immune from suit, this conduct fell within the FSIA's "noncommercial tort" exception. The civilian plaintiff could thus sue the United Kingdom.

The 1951 SOFA executive agreement between the United States and the United Kingdom was created to avoid just such disruptions in military service obligations. Local plaintiffs in either country may proceed with their suits, but against the host country—just as if its own soldiers had committed the wrongful act. The United Kingdom was thus immune from suit under the SOFA, but liable under the FSIA. The US court applied the familiar rule that US legislation should not be applied in a way that violates international obligations, unless Congress expressly says otherwise. Thus, the United Kingdom was dismissed, and the local citizen's claim was instead deemed to be against the United States, under the Federal Tort Claims Act. *Moore v. United Kingdom,* 384 F.3d 1079 (9th Cir. 2004).

4. Some US labor unions brought an action challenging constitutionality of North American Free Trade Agreement (NAFTA). President Clinton entered into that treaty, on behalf of the United States, with Canada and Mexico without Senate consent. The issue was whether NAFTA required an "Article II Treaty" requiring Senate ratification. The federal appeals court "decided" that this was a nonjusticiable, political question (§1.4). Thus:

> The appellants [unions] concede, as they must, that the Constitution affords the political branches substantial authority over foreign affairs and commerce. The appellants also concede that the Supreme Court has recognized the constitutional validity of the longstanding practice of enacting international agreements which do not amount to full-fledged treaties. . . .
>
> Indeed, just as the [Art. II] Treaty Clause fails to outline the Senate's role in the abrogation of treaties, we find that the Treaty Clause also fails to outline the circumstances, if any, under which its procedures must be adhered to when approving international commercial agreements. . . .
>
> Significantly, the appellants themselves fail to offer, either in their briefs or at argument, a workable definition of what constitutes a "treaty." Indeed, the appellants decline to supply any analytical framework whatsoever by which courts can distinguish international agreements which require Senate ratification from those that do not.
> —*Made in the USA Foundation v. U.S.,* 242 F.3d 1300, 1314–1315 (11th Cir., 2001).

CONFLICT RESOLUTION

The other major problem in US treaty practice arises when there is a conflict among the US Constitution, a federal statute, and/or an international treaty commitment.

In parts of Europe, Mexico, and certain other regions, treaties must take precedence over internal law in the event of a conflict.[62] The constitutions of Burkina Faso, Congo, Mauritania, and Senegal expressly provide that a treaty is superior to internal law—although there is apparently no reported judicial decision that affirms this elevated status.

The US Constitution does not provide a direct answer to the resolution of such conflicts. Article VI provides only that the "Constitution, and the Laws [federal statutes] of the United States which shall be made in Pursuance thereof and all Treaties made . . . shall be the supreme Law of the Land. . . ." This wording does not establish any relative hierarchy in the event of a conflict. An internal law of the United States may occasionally clash with, and supersede, a prior international agreement. This portion of the treaty chapter addresses the resolution of such conflicts under US law, as opposed to International Law, where a State may not rely on its internal law to avoid international obligations.

Treaty versus Constitution   The US Supreme Court has consistently held that the Constitution prevails when it conflicts with statutes or treaties. Both a federal statute and a treaty (executive agreement) were in conflict with the Constitution in the 1957 case of *Reid v. Covert.*[63] The Court held that civilian wives who had killed their military husbands on US bases, in England and Japan, could not be tried by a military court-martial. The Supreme Court examined several distinct sources of US law to arrive at this conclusion. The Uniform Code of Military Justice (UCMJ) is federal legislation, which then provided for a court-martial in this situation. Presidential executive agreements governing crimes occurring on US bases abroad, incorporated these provisions of the UCMJ, which was thus expressly applicable to these civilian wives. The court found that neither the Military Justice Code nor the executive agreements could deny the spouses' constitutional rights to indictment by a civilian grand jury, and to a jury trial by their peers. These rights enshrined in the US Constitution could not be vacated by either the federal statute (UCMJ), or by an executive agreement, which purported to apply the UCMJ to military dependents abroad.

Treaty versus Statute   Treaties and federal statutes are on equal footing under Article VI of the Constitution. Each is therein referred to as the "supreme law of the land." Neither is superior to the other, under the express terms of the Constitution.

The US Supreme Court applies the following rule: "The last in time prevails." As stated in the above *Reid* decision, the Court has "repeatedly taken the position that an Act of Congress . . . is on full parity with a treaty, and that when a statute which is subsequent in time is inconsistent with a treaty, the statute to the extent of conflict renders the treaty null."[64] The Court affirmed this position in 1998, when construing the 1996 Antiterrorism and Effective Death Penalty Act. A Paraguayan defendant was thus foreclosed from appealing the failure of the Virginia state court system to notify Paraguay of his arrest and detention. Such notification is required by the 1963 Vienna Convention on Consular Relations (§7.2).[65] Congress may thus denounce it prior treaties under US law. In its comprehensive Anti-Apartheid Act of 1986, Congress expressly repudiated a presidential executive agreement providing for air service with South Africa (prior to the improvement in international relations, when the white minority relinquished power in 1993).[66]

The US Supreme Court illustrated this progression in a case involving civilian wives who murdered their military husband's abroad. The case involved all three: the US Constitution's Bill of Rights, a federal statute (UCMJ), and a prior treaty regarding which country would have jurisdiction to try civilian spouses. When conflicts arise, the "Court has . . . repeatedly taken the position that an Act of Congress, which must comply with the Constitution, is on a full parity with a treaty, and that when a statute which is subsequent in time is inconsistent with a treaty, the statute to the extent of conflict renders the treaty null."[67] So in the event of a conflict:

(1) The Constitution prevails over International Law.
(2) A statute (UCMJ) and a bilateral Status of Forces treaty—regarding which country would try these civilians—were on the same legal footing.
(3) The later in time—either treaty or federal statute—trumps the prior of the two.

◆ PROBLEMS

Problem 8.A (after §8.1 Medellin case)   Reconsider the ICJ 1980 *Hostage Case,* and the 1961 Diplomatic Relations Convention provisions, both set forth in §7.4 of this book. Answer the following questions based on the materials in §8.1:

1. Did the Vienna Convention on Diplomatic Relations have to be "self-executing" for the United States to claim that Iran breached it?
2. Are those provisions (text, p. 342) self-executing? Can this be answered by reading the given articles?
3. Based on the *Medellin* case analysis, how would you resolve the question of whether the Diplomatic Relations treaty is self-executing?

Problem 8.B (after §8.2 Reservations case)   The treaties you will study in Chapter 11 illustrate the UN promotional role in human rights. One of them is the UN Convention on the Elimination of All Forms of Discrimination Against Women (CEDAW), available at: <http://www.un.org/womenwatch/daw/cedaw/cedaw.htm>. Read and compare the following information regarding the reservations submitted to this convention by Bangladesh, Saudi Arabia, and the United States:

◆ Bangladesh: "On reading the Bangladeshi reservation to the Women's Convention, indicating that it will implement this convention in accordance with Islamic Sharia Law, the advocates of women's rights cannot but be extremely skeptical about the possible contribution of the Convention (as amended by the [Sharia Law] reservation) to the improvement of the situation of women in Bangladesh." (Insight about that law is available in §1.3 of this textbook.) L. Lijnzaad, RESERVATIONS TO UN-HUMAN RIGHTS TREATIES: RATIFY AND RUIN? 3 (Dordrecht, Neth.: Martinus Nijhoff, 1995).

◆ Saudi Arabia: "In case of contradiction between any term of the Convention and the norms of islamic law, the Kingdom is not under obligation to observe the contradictory terms of the Convention."

◆ United States: The United States has signed (1980) but not ratified CEDAW. The United States is therefore committed in principle, but has yet to merge word and deed via Senate confirmation. Per materials in §8.2 of the textbook, a signatory cannot take any action that is inconsistent with the object and purpose of a signed treaty.

Determine the following:

(1) Do the Bangladesh and Saudi Sharia Law reservations comply with the ICJ *Reservations Case* "compatibility" test?

(2) Does the United States have a higher duty to avoid discrimination against women—than *either* of the above two ratifying nations—based on the United States signing the CEDAW? Does the post-*Reparations Case* note, on the Draft Guidelines on Reservations to Treaties, help to resolve these questions?

Problem 8.C (after §8.2 Reservations case)   Article 17(2) of the 1969 VCLT states that when "it appears from the . . . object and purpose of the treaty that the application of the treaty *in its entirety* between all the parties is an *essential condition* of the consent of each one to be bound by the treaty, a reservation requires acceptance by all the parties" (italics added). VCLT Article 19(1)(a) provides that the legal effect of a reservation is that it "[m]odifies for the reserving state the provisions of the treaty to which the reservation relates to the extent of the reservation."

Assume the following facts: La Luce del Pueblo—meaning "Light of the People," or LLP—is an ultra-radical group of citizens within a hypothetical Caribbean State called Haven. Last September, Haven's military leader placed the LLP in charge of guarding some kidnaped US citizens. They were being held incommunicado during political hostilities with the United States. Without authority from the country's leader, some members of LLP decided to mistreat the US citizens. Several were beaten. One was brutally murdered. His body was then dumped on the steps of the US embassy in Haven, where journalists had gathered to learn about the latest developments in the escalating hostilities.

A number of foreign newspapers printed a picture of the body of the dead US citizen on the US embassy steps. Their news story about the beatings and execution assigned responsibility to "LLP, the zealous group of Haven idealists who say that they resent the decades of the US dominance in hemispheric affairs." This newspaper account included LLP's statement to these journalists: "We plan, for the benefit of the People's Revolutionary Party (led by Haven's military leader), to eliminate all US citizens in Haven who hinder our progress." Subsequently, US citizens were randomly attacked and beaten in Haven's restaurants and bars. Nationals from other countries were not harmed in these incidents. Haven's leader denied any involvement with what he characterized as "an idealistic, but irresponsible splinter group of radicals to be dealt with if found." Worldwide media attention now focused on Haven and its growing confrontation with the United States.

Some US senators thus stated for the Congressional Record that "Haven had added genocide to the long list of international obligations breached by Haven in the last decade. Haven has failed to adhere to the bilateral treaties between the two nations, to the wishes of the Organization of American States, and to the unmistakable minimum standards of international behavior." Under the Genocide Convention, *genocide* is the killing of members of a particular ethnic group with the intent to destroy it (as analyzed in §9.5 *Radio Machete* case).

Under the applicable US-Haven treaty, murder is an extraditable offense. Last October, the US Department of State demanded that Haven extradite those responsible for killing the US citizen so that they could be tried either in the United States or in some international tribunal for the crime of genocide. Haven refused this extradition request because "those who have killed the US citizen may have committed murder, but they could not possibly be thereby responsible for the bizarre claim of genocide."

Assume that Haven, attempting to show its solidarity with the world community, chooses this point in time to become a party to the Genocide Convention. Haven tenders its consent to the appropriate international authority. It also submits the following reservation: "Haven hereby adopts the Genocide Convention as binding. Haven reserves the sovereign right, however, to use any means at its disposal to eliminate external threats to Haven's territorial integrity."

Can Haven legitimately tender this reservation to the Genocide Convention, under the ICJ's *Reservations Case*? The Vienna Convention on the Law of Treaties?

Problem 8.D (§8.2, after "Invalidity" Materials)   In 1980, the VCLT became effective when the minimum number of national ratifications were deposited with the United Nations. During the negotiating process, US hostages initially remained captive in the American embassy and, for most of the time, at other locations in Iran. The United States and Iran had no direct diplomatic relations. Algeria assisted US President Jimmy Carter in negotiating a treaty with Iran to secure the liberation of these hostages. They were released in exchange for the simultaneous expungement of Iranian assets in the United States, which had been frozen by Carter near the outset of the crisis. The United States also agreed to return assets subject to its control that belonged to the family of the former Shah of Iran. Various documents about that treaty and related matters are reprinted in 20 Int'l Legal Mat'ls 223–240 (1981). A criticism of the US Department of State's decision not to raise the question of force in this particular treaty process is presented in *Iranian Hostage Agreements,* in Malawer book, at 27 (cited in note 14 below).

A very sensitive provision of this treaty required arbitration of any subsequent disputes related to the "Hostage Crisis." This provision precluded the hostages, their families, or any governmental entity from suing Iran in the United States, the International Court of Justice, or anywhere else. President Carter's economic sanctions were not working, and he did not want to undertake further military action to retrieve the hostages from Iran, after a failed rescue attempt in 1979. Instead, he entered into an *executive agreement* to resolve this crisis and obtain the guaranteed safety of the hostages. Subsequent suits by several hostages were dismissed by US courts, on the basis of the president's agreement not to permit suits against Iran that were spawned by the Hostage Crisis.

The US Senate attempted to abrogate this agreement (the Algiers Accords) on several occasions, as recently as 2003. This is a recurring legislative response to cases like the July 2003 District of Columbia federal case, where Iran was potentially subject to a judgment in a hostage families' class action lawsuit. Iran had been designated a terrorist State, under an amendment to the Foreign Sovereign Immunities Act (textbook §2.6). The executive branch nevertheless intervened to obtain a dismissal of this action. Its lawyers successfully argued that the Algiers Accords were not affected by Iran's subsequent "terrorist" status under US law.[68]

Assume that the US Senate is debating the propriety of President Carter's negotiations leading to the above executive agreement between the United States and Iran. The topic of this hypothetical Senate debate is not whether the Senate's advice and consent were necessary for the hostage-release agreement with Iran. The Senate has instead chosen to debate whether it can avoid the US obligations under the treaty, on the basis that the president had to enter into the hostage-release treaty under duress.

Senator Dove represents a number of colleagues who do not wish to alter or negate the effect of the president's arrangement with Iran. They do not want to risk renewed hostilities or create the impression that America goes back on its obligations. Dove contends that "there was no physical, military, or economic coercion that forced this powerful nation into President Carter's treaty. It was the

United States that employed forceful tactics, rather than Iran, when Carter's military rescue mission failed."

Senator Hawk represents an opposing group of senators. She and her colleagues hope to refreeze Iranian money accounts and gold bullion still within the United States or controlled by private US businesses in foreign countries. She wants to renew the 1980 *Hostage Case* litigation in a separate phase in the ICJ. (*See* §7.4 for ICJ case excerpts on the Court's order that Iran free the US hostages.) Relying on Article 52 of the VCLT, Hawk believes that the ICJ should render an authoritative decision characterizing the hostage treaty as being invalid on the basis of VCLT duress.

Senator Hawk thus contends that "the Iranian treaty would never have seen the light of day if we were not forced into it by the hostage situation." Senator Dove's litmus test for validating the treaty is an imaginary bright line that separates military and nonmilitary coercion in all circumstances. "The proper approach, in my not so humble opinion, is to invalidate the sham, and shameful, Iranian deal by distinguishing between lawful and unlawful coercion—rather than Senator Dove's approach, which isolates military duress to invalidate the treaty from nonmilitary duress, whereby the treaty would be unaffected."

Make the following assumptions:

(a) Iran is a party to the VCLT.
(b) It did not make any reservations.
(c) The hostages have been released, but the Iranian assets are still frozen/available for seizure.
(d) The Carter hostage release agreement was made *after* the January 27, 1980 "start" date for the prospective applicability of the VCLT.

Two students will present the arguments that Senators Dove and Hawk might use in their Senate debate on the applicability of the VCLT. Can the United States void its treaty obligations to Iran under President Carter's executive agreement?

Problem 8.E (after §8.2 Fisheries Jurisdiction cases) The United States and the hypothetical Latin American State of Estado entered into a 1953 Treaty of Friendship, Commerce, and Navigation (FCN). This treaty initiated their international relationship and covered a number of details. In the relevant treaty clause, the United States agreed that Estado could nationalize American business interests. In return, Estado was required to provide reasonable compensation, which was defined in the treaty as "the fair market value of all nationalized assets."

The US-Estado relationship has turned sour. The Estado government nationalizes a major US corporation's property in Estado, but does not tender *any* compensation. Estado resisted the US claim of entitlement to compensation under the 1953 friendship treaty. Estado's Minister of State issued the following statement:

A fundamental change in circumstances has precluded the continued viability of the 1953 FCN Treaty. The 1974 United Nations Declaration on the Establishment of a New International Economic Order obviously necessitates termination of the decades earlier compensation requirements of the outmoded US-Estado FCN Treaty [see §4.4 of this text on the NIEO]. The changed circumstance is that our nation, which the Creator has endowed with natural resources, need no longer fall prey to another nation's multinational enterprises. The United States corporation has plundered untold billions of dollars in excessive profits from the very core of Estado. All of the profits have been repatriated back into the United States, rather than remaining here to benefit Estado's economy. The content of International Law was developed by powerful nations over the many centuries before Estado even existed. It is a self-perpetuating vehicle used by countries like the United States to justify its asserted right to compensation in the amount of the "fair market value" of nationalized property. Due to these changed circumstances, Estado may reasonably justify its refusal to pay any compensation to a corporation that has already acquired much more than it could ever repay to Estado. As a showing of good faith on the part of my Government, Estado will not seek reimbursement in an international forum, settling instead for the fair market value of the nationalized assets, which is only a small fraction of what the United States enterprise has itself expropriated natural resources from the people of Estado.

Can Estado properly invoke the doctrine of *rebus sic stantibus* to terminate its treaty obligation to repay fair market value for nationalizing the US corporation?

Problem 8.F (end of §8.2) Refer to Problem 8.E above Assume that Estado later repealed all treaty com-

mitments with the United States after the US senators widely condemned its nationalization of the US corporate property. Questions:

(1) Is the United States now required to perform its obligations under any treaty with Estado?
(2) Does the United States have any remedies under the Vienna Convention on the Law of Treaties?

◆ BIBLIOGRAPHY

§8.1 Definition and Classification

J. Grenville & B. Wasserstein (ed.), THE MAJOR INTERNATIONAL TREATIES OF THE TWENTIETH CENTURY (3d ed. New York: Routledge, 2001)

D. Johnson, CONSENT AND COMMITMENT IN THE WORLD COMMUNITY: THE CLASSIFICATION AND ANALYSIS OF INTERNATIONAL INSTRUMENTS (Irvington-on-Hudson, NY: Transnational, 1998)

Li Zhaojie, Cultural Relativity and the Role of Domestic Courts in the Enforcement of International Human Rights: A Survey of the Practice and Problems in China, in E. Mendez & A. Traehold (de.), HUMAN RIGHTS: CHINESE AND CANADIAN PERSPECTIVES 185 (Ottawa: Univ. Ottawa, 1997)

§8.2 Formation, Performance, Cessation

V. Gowlland-Debbas (ed.), MULTILATERAL TREATY-MAKING: THE CURRENT STATUS OF CHALLENGES TO AND REFORMS NEEDED IN THE INTERNATIONAL LEGISLATIVE PROCESS (Hague: Martinus Nijhoff, 2000)

F. Horn, RESERVATIONS AND INTERPRETIVE DECLARATIONS TO MULTILATERAL TREATIES (The Hague, Neth.: T.M.C. Asser Inst. 1988)

S. Rosenne, BREACH OF TREATY (Cambridge, Eng.: Grotius, 1985)

S. Rosenne, THE LAW OF TREATIES: A GUIDE TO THE LEGISLATIVE HISTORY OF THE VIENNA CONVENTION (Dobbs Ferry, NY: Oceana, 1970)

A. Vamvoukos, TERMINATION OF TREATIES IN INTERNATIONAL LAW: THE DOCTRINES OF REBUS SIC STANTIBUS AND DESUETUDE [acquiescence] (Oxford, Eng.: Clarendon Press, 1985)

P. Wesley-Smith, UNEQUAL TREATY: 1898–1997 (rev. ed. Hong Kong: Oxford Univ. Press, 1984)

§8.3 United States Treaty Practice

R. Dalton, United States, Ch. 20, in D. Hollis, M. Blakeslee & L. Ederington (ed.), NATIONAL TREATY LAW AND PRACTICE 765 (Leiden, Neth.: Martinus Nijhoff, 2005)

M. Glennon, The Senate Role in Treaty Ratification, 77 AMER. J. INT'L L. 257 (1983)

E. Surrency, How the United States Perfects an International Agreement, 85 LAW LIB. JOURNAL 343 (1993)

D. Vagts, The United States and its Treaties: Observance and Breach, 95 AMER. J. INT'L L. 313 (2001)

Electronic Resources

ASIL Guide to Electronic Resources for International Law (Treaties): <http://www.asil.org/resource/treaty1.htm>

Frequently Cited Treaties: <http://www.law.umn.edu/library/tools/pathfinders/most-cited.html>

◆ ENDNOTES

1. *See generally* D. Bederman, INTERNATIONAL LAW IN ANTIQUITY [Cambridge. Eng.: Cambridge University Press (2001)].

2. The text of this convention is reprinted in 63 AMER. J. INT'L L. 875 (1969), 8 INT'L LEGAL MAT'LS 679 (1969), and <http://fletcher.tufts.edu/multi/texts/BH538.txt> [hereinafter *VCLT*].

3. D. Hollis, A Comparative Approach to Treaty Law and Practice, ch. 1, in D. Hollis, M. Blakeslee & L. Ederington (ed.), NATIONAL TREATY LAW AND PRACTICE (Leiden, Neth.: Martinus Nijhoff, 2005), containing chaptered analyses on the treaty practice of nineteen nations.

4. Comment (2) to Art. 2, Int'l L. Comm'n, Commentary on the Vienna Convention on the Law of Treaties, in Official Documents-United Nations Reports of the International Law Commission, 61 AMER. J. INT'L L. 248, 287 (1967) [hereinafter *Commentaries*]. The ILC study did not address "oral" agreements, because of the comparative prominence of written instruments as a basis for international obligations.

5. *Harvard study:* Draft Convention on the Law of Treaties, 29 AMER. J. INT'L L. 652, 712 (Supp., 1935). *Multiple terms:* A comprehensive table depicting these terms, with accompanying details, is available in D. Myers, The Names and Scope of Treaties, 51 AMER. J. INT'L L. 574, 576 (1957). ILC study: *Commentaries,* Comment (3) to Art. 2, at 288 (cited note 4 above).

6. *See* M. Kaniel, THE EXCLUSIVE TREATY-MAKING POWER OF THE EUROPEAN COMMUNITY UP TO THE PERIOD OF THE SINGLE EUROPEAN ACT (The Hague: Kluwer, 1996).

7. UN Gen. Ass. Doc. A/CONF.129/15 of March 20, 1986, reprinted in P. Menon, THE LAW OF TREATIES BETWEEN STATES AND INTERNATIONAL ORGANIZATIONS 159 (Lewiston, NY: Edwin Mellon Press, 1992).

8. A. Gasis, Preface to E. Raftopoulos, THE INADEQUACY OF THE CONTRACTUAL ANALOGY IN THE LAW OF TREATIES XIII (Athens: Hellenic Inst. Int'l & Foreign Law, 1990) [hereinafter *Contractual Analogy*].

9. S. Scott, Proposing a Political Theory of Treaty Interpretation, ch. 5, in THE POLITICAL INTERPRETATION OF MULTILATERAL TREATIES 97, at 111 (Leiden, Neth.: Martinus Nijhoff, 2004) (italics added).

10. R. Phillimore, 2 COMMENTARIES UPON INTERNATIONAL LAW 99 (3d ed. London: Butterworths, 1892).

11. *Scientific approach:* The Public Law View of Treaties in the 19th and the Early 20th Century, ch. 5, in *Contractual Analogy* text, at 151 (cited note 8 above). *Informal approach:* Treaty-Like Instruments: An Overview, ch. 1, in J. Klabbers, THE CONCEPT OF TREATY IN INTERNATIONAL LAW 27 (The Hague: Kluwer, 1996).

12. *Grotius:* 2 DE JURE BELLI AC PACIS [The Law of War and Peace] 394 (Kelsey translation, Wash., DC: Carnegie Endowment for Int'l Peace, 1925). *E. de Vattel:* 3 LE DROIT DE GENS OU PRINCIPES DE LA LOI NATURELLE [The Law of Nations or Principles of Natural Law] 165 (Wash., DC: Carnegie Endowment for Int'l Peace, 1916 reprint of 1758 treatise). *American author:* H. Halleck, INTERNATIONAL LAW 196 (San Francisco: Bancroft, 1861).

13. *Treaty of Paris:* An account of this event and its related treaty validity problems is provided in J. L. Brierly, THE LAW OF NATIONS 332–333 (Waldock 6th ed. London: Oxford Univ. Press, 1963) [hereinafter *Brierly*]. *Treaty of Versailles:* This treaty and its consequences are described in C. Fenwick, INTERNATIONAL LAW 531–532 (4th ed. New York: Appleton, 1965) (Fenwick translation from the French) [hereinafter *Fenwick*]. *Hitler treaty:* A detailed account of the events is provided in G. Von Glahn, LAW AMONG NATIONS 479–480 (7th ed. Boston: Allyn and Bacon, 1996).

14. H. Chiu, Comparison of the Nationalist and Communist Chinese Views of Unequal Treaties, in J. Cohen (ed.), CHINA'S PRACTICE OF INTERNATIONAL LAW: SOME CASE STUDIES 241–242 (Cambridge, MA: Harv. Univ. Press, 1972) (footnotes omitted). A brief assessment and criticism of the Soviet writers on this subject is available in S. Malawer, Soviets and Unequal Treaties, in ESSAYS ON INTERNATIONAL LAW, at 101 (Buffalo, NY: Hein, 1986).

15. Status of Eastern Greenland (Denmark v. Norway), 1933 PCIJ, SER. A/B, No. 53.

16. Maritime Delimitation and Territorial Questions between Qatar and Bahrain (Qatar v. Bahrain), Judgment of 16 March 2001, available at <http://www.icj-cij.org/icjwww/idocket/iqb/iqbframe.htm>.

17. The general rule against creation of third-party obligations is exhaustively examined in C. Chinkin, States as Third Parties to Treaties: Formal Prescriptions, ch. 2, in THIRD PARTIES IN INTERNATIONAL LAW 25 (Oxford, Eng.: Clarendon Press, 1993). Potential exceptions are also addressed in A. Verdross, VOLKERRECHT 143–144 (5th ed. Vienna: Springer Verlag, 1964). An English-language restatement of the Verdross Position is provided in G. I. Tunkin, THEORY OF INTERNATIONAL LAW 93 (Cambridge, MA: Harv. Univ. Press, 1974) (Butler translation from Russian language) [hereinafter *Tunkin*].

18. L. Sohn, International Law Implications of the 1994 Agreement, 88 AMER. J. INT'L L. 696, 701–702 (1994).

19. P. Reuter, INTRODUCTION TO THE LAW OF TREATIES 20 (2d ed. London: Pinter Pub., 1989) (Mico & Haggenmacher translation).

20. K. Annan, *Foreword,* MILLENNIUM SUMMIT MULTILATERAL TREATY FRAMEWORK: AN INVITATION TO UNIVERSAL PARTICIPATION ix (New York: UN, 2000).

21. Council of Europe (ed.), Foreword, TREATY MAKING-EXPRESSION OF CONSENT TO BE BOUND BY A TREATY (Hague: Kluwer, 2001).

22. An account of this event is provided in 4 G. Hackworth, DIGEST OF INTERNATIONAL LAW 467 (Wash., DC: US Gov't Print. Off., 1942).

23. Fisheries Jurisdiction (U.K. v. Iceland), 1973 ICJ REP. 1, 14 (decided after 1969 VCLT conference, but before the VCLT's 1980 effective date).

24. *Communist-African position:* An account of the varied perspectives of the participants is available in R. Kearney & R. Dalton, The Treaty on Treaties, 64 AMER. J. INT'L L. 495, 532–535 (1970) [hereinafter *Treaty on Treaties* article]. *Force left undefined: Commentaries,* Art. 49 [now Art. 52], Comment (3), at 407 (*VCLT* cited in note 2 above).

25. UN Doc. A/CONF. 39/26, contained in Documents of the Conference, at 285, May 22, 1969. The text is reprinted in 8 INT'L LEGAL MAT'LS 733 (1969).

26. *Waldock quote: Brierly,* 319–320 (cited in note 13 above). *Court quote:* Avero Belgium Ins. v. American Airlines, Inc., 423 F.3d 73, 80 (2d Cir. 2005) (citing Oppenheim & Brownlie treatises).

27. *Treaty:* UN Doc. A/Conf. 164/37 (1995), reprinted in 34 INT'L LEGAL MAT'LS 1542 (1995). *Senate caveat:* [T]he Senate's approval of this treaty should not be construed as a precedent for acquiescence to future treaties containing such a provision. Dep't State Files L/T, discussed in 90 AMER. J. INT'L L. 270 (1996).

28. Convention on the Prevention and Punishment of the Crime of Genocide of December 9, 1948, 78 UN TREATY SERIES 277 (1951), available at <http://fletcher.tufts.edu/multi/texts/BH225.txt>.

29. *States:* VCLT, Art. 80.1 (cited in note 2 above). *Organizations: Organizational* Treaty, Art. 81.1 (cited in note 2 above).

30. This UN publication, approaching nearly 1,500 print volumes, is available in electronic form at <http://untreaty.un.org/> (subscription required). The United Nations charges a fee for using this site. Researchers can obtain no-cost electronic versions of many major multilateral treaties from online university collections and the Web pages of individual professors.

31. 1 US CODE §112.

32. P.-H. Houben, Principles of International Law Concerning Friendly Relations and Cooperation among States, 61 AMER. J. INT'L L. 703, 725 (1967).

33. North Atlantic Coast Fisheries Arbitration, Permanent Court of Arbitration No. VII (1910), 11 ROYAL INST. FOREIGN AFFAIRS 167 (1932).

34. Honduras v. Nicaragua, 1960 ICJ REP. 192 (Judgment of Nov. 18, 1960).

35. Case Concerning the Temple of Preah Vihear (Cambodia v. Thailand), 1962 ICJ REP. 6 (Judgment of June 15, 1962).

36. *Fenwick,* at 531 (footnote omitted) (cited in note 13 above).

37. *See* Proposed Article 13, Report of the International Law Commission Covering Its First Session, contained in UN GAOR, 4TH SESSION, SUPP. NO. 10, DOC. A/925, at 8 (1949).

38. *See Treaty on Treaties* article, at 516–517 (cited in note 24 above). The proposed exclusion is therein reported by members of US Department of State participants in the VCLT.

39. *Spectrum of views:* The quoted characterizations are contained in the *Brierly* treatise, at 338 (cited in note 13 above) (clearly reasonable); Briggs, The Attorney General Invokes Rebus Sic Stantibus, 36 AMER. J. INT'L L. 89, 93 (1942) (alleged principle); M. Akehurst, A Modern Introduction to International Law 145 (7th ed. London: Routledge, 1997) (unsuitable). *Chinese view:* This excerpt is from International Trade Treaties and Agreements (Peking: 1958) and is reprinted in 2 J. Cohen & H. Chiu

40. O. Lissitzyn, Treaties and Changed Circumstances (Rebus Sic Stantibus), 61 AMER. J. INT'L L. 895 (1967) [hereinafter *Changed Circumstances*].

41. *Commentaries,* Art. 59 (now Art. 62), at 428-429 (cited in note 4 above).

42. *See* The Free Zones of Upper Savoy and the District of Gex (Switzerland v. France), 1929 PCIJ, SER. A, NO. 22, and ser. A/B No. 46, 2 WORLD COURT REP. 448 (1971).

43. Translation provided in 2 J. Cohen & H. Chiu, *People's China* 1166, 1167 (cited in note 39 above).

44. Electricity Company of Sofia and Bulgaria (Belgium v. Bulgaria), 1939 PCIJ, SER. A/B, NO. 77, at 64 (dissenting opinion of Judge Anzilotti).

45. N. Kontou, THE TERMINATION AND REVISION OF TREATIES IN THE LIGHT OF NEW CUSTOMARY INTERNATIONAL LAW 2 (Oxford, Eng.: Clarendon Press, 1994).

46. *See generally* M. Gommaa, SUSPENSION OR TERMINATION OF TREATIES ON GROUNDS OF BREACH (The Hague: Martinus Nijhoff, 1996).

47. The US government's brief is reprinted in US Department of State, The Legality of United States Participation in the Defense of Viet-Nam, 60 AMER. J. INT'L L. 565, 585 (first quote) and 577 (second quote) (1966). For additional detail, see American Society of International Law, THE VIET-NAM WAR AND INTERNATIONAL LAW (Princeton: Princeton Univ. Press, 1968) (three volumes).

48. Appeal Relating to the Jurisdiction of the ICAO Council (India v. Pakistan), 1972 ICJ REP. 46 (Judgment of Aug. 18, 1972).

49. *Commentaries,* Art. 58 (now Art. 61), Comment (2), at 427 (cited in note 4 above).

50. *Changed Circumstances* article (cited in note 40 above).

51. *See* American Law Institute, RESTATEMENT SECOND OF THE FOREIGN RELATIONS LAW OF THE UNITED STATES, §153, Illustration 1 (St. Paul: West, 1965). (Unlike the prior *Restatement,* the new *Restatement Third* does not use illustrations in the replacement §336.)

52. *Judicial denial:* see *Commentaries,* Comment (1) to Art. 50 (now Art. 53), at 409 (cited in note 4 above). *Academic denial: Tunkin,* at 149 (cited in note 17 above).

53. Clark v. Allen, 331 U.S. 503, 67 S.Ct. 1431, 91 L. Ed. 1633 (1947).

54. *See* ICJ's analysis regarding the Pan Am Flight 103 Libyan terrorist bombing case in §6.4 of this book under Montreal Sabotage Convention. UN Charter Article 103 was thus characterized as controlling, notwithstanding the conflicting treaty that would otherwise accord Libya the exclusive right to resolve this matter within its judicial system.

55. *See* S. Reisenfeld & F. Abbott (eds.), PARLIAMENTARY PARTICIPATION IN THE MAKING AND OPERATION OF TREATIES: A COMPARATIVE STUDY (Dordrecht, Neth.: Martinus Nijhoff, 1994).

56. The process is recounted in A. Bestor, Advice from the Very Beginning, Consent When the End is Achieved, in L. Henkin, M. Glennon & W. Rogers, FOREIGN AFFAIRS AND

(eds.), PEOPLE'S CHINA AND INTERNATIONAL LAW, at 1257 (Princeton: Princeton Univ. Press, 1974) [hereinafter *People's China*].

THE U.S. CONSTITUTION 6 (Ardsley-on-Hudson, NY: Transnat'l Pub.: 1990).

57. An analysis of the drafters' intent is available in L. Henkin, International Concern and the Treaty Power of the United States, 63 AMER. J. INT'L L. 272 (1969).

58. L. Henkin, FOREIGN AFFAIRS AND THE US CONSTITUTION 217 (2d ed. Oxford, Eng.: Clarendon Press, 1996) (footnotes omitted).

59. O. Lissitzyn, The Legal Status of Executive Agreement on Air Transportation, 17 J. AIR L. & COMM. 436, 439–442 (1950) (footnotes omitted).

60. The relevant section of the *Case Act* is contained in 1 US Code §112b(a).

61. Dames & Moore v. Regan, 453 U.S. 654, 682, 101 S.Ct. 2972, 2988, 69 L. Ed. 2d 918 (1981) (noting that the President's power to settle claims regarding international relations had been exercised for 200 years with congressional acquiescence) (italics added).

62. *Switzerland:* Librairie Hachette, S.A. v. Societe Cooperative, XXV Annuaire Suisse de Droit International 239 (1968).

Belgium: Minister for Economic Affairs v. S.A. Fromagerie Franco-Suisse, 1972 Common Market Law Rep. 330. *Mexico:* Constitution, Art. 133.

63. Reid v. Covert, 354 U.S. 1, 77 S.Ct. 1222, 1 L. Ed.2d 1148 (1957).

64. *Reid,* 354 U.S. at 18, 77 S.Ct. at 1231.

65. Breard v. Greene, 523 U.S. 371, 118 S.Ct. 1352, 140 L.Ed.2d 529 (1998).

66. *See* South African Airways v. Dole, 817 Fed. Rptr. 2d 119 (D.C. Cir. 1987).

67. Reid v. Covert, 354 U.S. 1, 18, 77 S.Ct. 1222, 1231, 1 L. Ed. 2d 1148 (1957). Subsequent legislation includes the 2000 Military Extraterritorial Jurisdiction Act, first applied to a woman who stabbed her husband to death on an Air Force base in Turkey in May 2003. The US Justice Department may thereby prosecute civilians who accompany military personnel on international assignments. See 18 U.S.C.A. § 3261.

68. *See* Roeder v. Islamic Republic of Iran, 333 F.3d 228 (D.C. Cir. 2003), *cert den'd,* 542 U.S. 915 (2004).

Arbitration and Adjudication

INTRODUCTION

This chapter examines the primary third-party dispute resolution mechanisms: arbitration and adjudication. Its essential objective is to unveil the circumstances whereby States are willing to rely on some third party, not directly involved in their disputes, as an alternative to more hostile alternatives.

After an overview of the international arbitration and litigation models, the materials in this chapter will proceed through the maze of global, regional, and national court alternatives for resolving contemporary international controversies.

IRRELEVANCE OF OFFICIAL CAPACITY

This Statute shall apply equally to all persons without any distinction based on official capacity. In particular, official capacity as a Head of State or Government, a member of a Government or parliament, an elected representative or a government official *shall in no case exempt a person from criminal responsibility* under this Statute, nor shall it, in and of itself, constitute a ground for reduction of sentence.

—Statute of the International Criminal Court, Article 27.1(italics added), adopted July 1998, at <www.un.org/icc/romestat.htm>

◆ 9.1 ARBITRATION AND ADJUDICATION BLUEPRINT

The common inquiries are as follows:

- ◆ Who can pursue a remedy for a violation of International Law?
- ◆ Where can a violation of International Law be adjudicated?
- ◆ Should it be resolved by arbitrator or by judges?

◆ How feasible is third-party dispute resolution in cases involving international relations between States? Between a State and an international organization? Between individuals or corporate entities? In cases involving the most sensitive matters, as opposed to those of lesser concern to national interests?

ARBITRATION: HISTORICAL DEVELOPMENT

The city-States of ancient Greece used arbitration as a peaceful alternative for resolving their disputes. A treaty in 445 BC grew out of the Peloponnesian War between Athens and Sparta. They agreed not to resort to war, as long as the other was willing to resolve a dispute via arbitration. A violation of this treaty subsequently resulted in a ten-year war, where after the parties once again agreed not to engage in war—with a renewed commitment to resolving any future disputes via arbitration.[1]

Modern commercial law is based on European medieval practices developed by international merchants. Their standard expectations were called the "Law Merchant." This body of law was created and developed by specialized tribunals in various Mediterranean ports—where private merchants resolved both internal and international business disputes in an arbitral setting. The Law Merchant thus flourished in the twelfth-century Italian city-States, later spreading to other commercial centers. The customary practices developed by these tribunals were ultimately incorporated into the commercial laws of many nations.

International arbitration had its own "Dark Ages," lasting until just before the nineteenth century. The famous 1794 Jay Treaty between Great Britain and the United States established a regime whereby an equal number of British and American nationals were selected to serve on an arbitral commission. It settled disputes arising out of the Revolutionary War, which could not be resolved by British-American diplomacy.[2] The former enemies further encouraged the use of international arbitration in their 1871 Treaty of Washington Arbitration. The United States claimed that Great Britain had violated the neutrality rules arising under customary State practice (§2.3). Great Britain had aided the South during the American Civil War by building ships for the Confederate Navy. This arbitral tribunal ordered Great Britain to compensate the United States for its resulting losses. When Great Britain complied, there was a renewed interest in international arbitration. The national practice of inserting arbitration clauses into treaties increased dramatically.

Russia's Czar Nicholas invited the international community to meet at the Netherlands city of The Hague. Numerous national delegates attended the Hague Peace Conferences of 1899 and 1907. The resulting 1899 Hague Convention for the Pacific Settlement of International Disputes recognized arbitration as "the most effective and at the same time the most equitable means of settling disputes which diplomacy has failed to settle." The 1907 Convention for the Pacific Settlement of Disputes was the first multilateral treaty to provide that "International Arbitration has for its object the settlement of disputes between States by judges of their own choice and on the basis of respect for law." Before these Conventions materialized, arbitrations were usually *ad hoc*. Arbitrators were typically limited to available heads of State, academics, national agencies, and politicians.[3] The Hague Conference process thus produced the Permanent Court of Arbitration (PCOA) in 1907, which still functions a century later.

Articles 12 and 13 of the Covenant of the League of Nations "mandated" that League members could not go to war, if the subject of their dispute had been submitted previously to arbitration. Three months were to elapse after an award before a State party could resort to war. This Covenant also created the first "World Court." It was named the Permanent Court of International Justice (PCIJ), and was also located at The Hague. But resort to international arbitration declined—from the PCIJ's inception in 1920, until after World War II.

Those corners of the globe not served by such judicial organs sometimes establish *ad hoc* tribunals, especially for resolving postwar claims. The December 2005 Eritrea-Ethiopia Claims Commission, for example, addressed claims arising from Eritrea's 1998 invasion of Ethiopia. This Commission determined that Eritrea's aggressive actions did not constitute lawful self-defense, merely because of a border dispute.

With establishment of the second World Court—the International Court of Justice (ICJ) at The Hague in 1945—the State members of the international community once again envisioned the submission of international legal disputes to a permanently constituted judicial body, as opposed to *ad hoc* arbitrations. The foremost collection of data regarding international arbitrations has been compiled by Nijmegen University (Netherlands) Professor A. M. Stuyt. His Survey of International Arbitrations lists nearly 180 inter-State arbitrations between 1900 and 1945. In the last half of the twentieth century, roughly the same period of years (1945–present) produced only forty-three inter-State arbitrations.[4]

A number of prominent disputes have nevertheless been submitted to various permanent arbitral tribunals. One reason is the delay factor often associated with the litigation alternative. The States involved must first consent to being sued in international tribunals (as with arbitration). States must be willing to await their turn on the particular court's docket, should they decide to submit their dispute to a third-party institution, such as the ICJ. Since the 1980s, the average length of a judicial proceeding, from filing to disposition, has grown from 2.5 to 4 years.[5] While States generally moved away from inter-State arbitration, other forms of international arbitration involving private parties began to flourish, as described in §9.3 later.

Arbitration is usually the preferable option—for those disputes susceptible to resolution by arbitration. Less sensitive matters, such as commercial disputes, are often more amenable to resolution by arbitration. More sensitive problems, such as an offensive use of force, spawn more publicity in a litigation context. Global venues, such as the ICJ or the International Criminal Court (ICC), may generate more public attention than an attempt to resolve differences via some bilateral, ad hoc claims commission process.[6]

An increasing number of courts encourage: (1) both domestic and foreign arbitration of matters previously resolved only by local tribunals; (2) the application of foreign law to local arbitral proceedings; and (3) the local enforcement of foreign arbitral awards. As articulated by the United Arab Emirates Supreme Court of Cassation: "in the absence of an agreement, an arbitration award must be issued by the UAE. However there is nothing to prohibit the parties from agreeing on the issuance of the arbitration award outside the UAE. In such a case the procedure applicable in the foreign country will be applicable to the arbitration award. . . . Thus it is not contrary to UAE law for the parties to agree on foreign arbitration or foreign arbitrators. Such an agreement is not contrary to UAE public policy."[7]

ADJUDICATION: HISTORICAL DEVELOPMENT

Diplomatic Initiatives Litigation has not been a viable option in situations involving sensitive disputes or open hostilities. States are understandably reluctant to admit that they have breached International Law. The pursuit of litigious remedies in an open forum may thus be more complicated than quiet diplomacy. The allegedly offending State will not readily admit its liability, even in the clearest of circumstances. For example, the United States never admitted its liability when an American U-2 reconnaissance aircraft violated Russian airspace in 1960. The plane was shot down 2,000 kilometers inside the Soviet border. The pilot claimed that he had merely strayed off course (§6.4 *Powers* case). In 1983, the Soviet Union did not admit liability when a Russian pilot shot down a Korean commercial aircraft that strayed off course over Russian territory. Nearly three hundred civilian passengers and crew were killed. The aircraft posed no security threat to Russian sovereignty. The Soviets claimed that warnings were given, and that this response to an intrusion of its airspace did not involve the use of "excessive force."

In November 2003, Ukraine agreed to pay approximately $1,000,000 for each of the seventy-eight Israeli and Russian passengers on a jet that Ukrainian forces accidentally shot down over the Black Sea, while it was en route to Tel Aviv from Russia in October 2001. Ukraine never admitted legal responsibility, which was abundantly clear. Under the terms of the accompanying agreement, Ukraine instead stated as follows:

> Ukraine recognizes the Aerial Catastrophe as a terrible human tragedy and expressed deep regret over the loss of lives. . . . Ukraine has not acknowledged any legal liability or responsibility.
>
> . . .
>
> [T]he Ukranian Side shall pay, on an *ex gratia* basis, to the Israeli Side [dollar amount] . . . without any responsibility arising therefrom for Ukraine.
>
> . . .
>
> The Israeli Side acknowledges that Ukraine . . . shall be immune from any and all Claims before the courts of the State of Israel. . . .[8]

The difficulty with obtaining an apology does not mean that it is never pursued at the international level. An apology, or a promise that the offending act will not reoccur, is often unattainable for a host of reasons. But in almost every case, the concerned States will undertake a diplomatic exchange, with a view toward amicably resolving their differences. As succinctly articulated by the United Kingdom's former Legal Advisor to the Foreign Office: "In international relations apology lies at the crossroads of the diplomatically commendable and the legally dangerous. In international life as in private life, saying 'sorry' does much to neutralize the diplomatic fall-out from an unfortunate incident; but saying 'sorry' may also imply an admission of legal liability. The art lies (from one point of view) in achieving the diplomatic benefits while avoiding the legal risks: but (from the other point of view) . . . in maximizing the legal gain while not wholly negating the diplomatic achievement."[9]

States may have something to learn from the private sector. In March 2004, a major US law firm with offices in Tokyo placed notices in two leading Japanese newspapers. This was a condition for settling a suit against the firm by a former client that allegedly became bankrupt, partially due to the law firm's role in the client's development of luxury hotels around the world.[10]

Early Conferences   Some national leaders wanted more durable dispute-resolution alternatives. The Latin American participants in the Hague Conferences proposed, and then implemented, a judicial response to the perennial problems with inter-State dispute resolution. They established the Central American Court of Justice in 1908, the first international court designed to address regional disputes. It closed in 1918. One reason was the forecast that the French-conceived League of Nations and the Permanent Court of International Justice (PCIJ) would supplant any need for a regional court. A global court would, it was hoped, shift the resolution of inter-State disputes from the battlefield to the courtroom. The States creating the PCIJ wanted it to play a role in the achievement of world peace through law. Some believed that this court would function as a judicial buffer between adversaries, who would otherwise resolve their disputes in a military arena. Others anticipated that a world court would, at the very least, be a neutral forum for settling certain disputes. A number of national leaders, including US President Woodrow Wilson, believed that an international court could positively influence national adherence to International Law.

The concept of a world (as opposed to regional) international court evolved through two phases, each commonly associated with a particular international organization: the former PCIJ and the current ICJ. The PCIJ was not a part of the League, however. A State desiring to use it would enter into a treaty with another State. Several hundred bilateral treaties among the various nations of the world conferred jurisdiction on the PCIJ. On the other hand, States joining the United Nations are automatically parties to the Charter's companion treaty—the Statute of the ICJ. While they are not required to use the ICJ, this symbiotic nexus with the Court's Statute attested to the judicial role, which the Charter drafters envisioned for the fledgling UN organization.

The PCIJ was the first permanently constituted dispute-resolution mechanism available to all nations of the world. In the case of States unwilling to actually litigate their differences, organs within the League of Nations could (and did) request "advisory" opinions from the PCIJ, which had the power to theoretically apply International Law to situations where a potentially liable State was unwilling to appear in judicial proceedings as a defendant. From 1922 to 1940, the PCIJ heard twenty-nine cases between adversaries who litigated their cases in the court. It also rendered twenty-seven "advisory opinions," a special form of decision making available in international (but usually not national) courts (§9.4).[11]

Two paradoxes contributed to the demise of the PCIJ. First, while this court was sponsored by the League of Nations, it was not an official organ of the League. Second, while US President Wilson played a fundamental role in developing international support for the League, the US did not join the League and never appeared as a litigant before the PCIJ. The Senate blocked US participation in the League. Because of rampant post-World War I isolationist sentiment, US senators feared any international alliances because any one of them might one day draw the United States into a second world war.

The 1939 outbreak of World War II destroyed the potential effectiveness of the PCIJ. The court conducted its last public sitting in that year—when most of the judges fled to Geneva to take advantage of Switzerland's wartime neutrality.

The dream of a global judicial body was not totally shattered by the abrupt reality of war. In 1943, the "Four Powers" (China, the Soviet Union, Great Britain, and the United States) determined that another global international organization should replace the League of Nations. The possibility of another world court was also rekindled by Great Britain's invitation to a group of International Law experts who met in London. These experts agreed that another global court was needed. It would have to be a fresh and innovational court in order to diffuse the criticism of the earlier PCIJ—perceived by many States as a European institution designed by European jurists to dominate the legal affairs of other regions of the world.

◆ 9.2 ALTERNATIVE DISPUTE RESOLUTION

Modern International Law emerged from the seventeenth century Peace of Westphalia (§1.1). The notion of State entities was not accompanied by a world government to control their predictable use of force. As the international community grew in size, there was less to share—and more pressures on peaceful cohabitation of the planet, given limited landmasses, oceans, natural resources (and ultimately air space). Disputes became a not so surprising feature of international relations.

The United Nations has a variety of devices for alternative dispute resolution (ADR) between nations. Relevant examples appear in both the UN Charter and ensuing resolutions. For example: (1) "The parties to any dispute . . . shall, first of all, seek a solution by negotiation, enquiry, mediation, conciliation, arbitration, judicial settlement . . . or other peaceful means of their own choice;" and (2) States "shall accordingly seek early and just settlement of their international disputes by negotiation, enquiry, mediation, conciliation. . . ."[12]

Post–World War II State practice matured to the point where leaders and merchants alike acknowledged the advantages of bloodless alternatives. As succinctly portrayed by London School of Economics Professor Christine Chinkin:

> Among their most frequently cited advantages are cheapness, flexibility and privacy compared to litigation. The parties' freedom of choice with respect to third party facilitators allows them to draw upon appropriate technical, legal, cultural or other expertise, and even to bring together a balanced team of experts. The consensual nature of the [various ADR] processes is said to be empowering for the disputants who can craft for themselves a mutually acceptable outcome, unfettered by the restrictions of legal procedures and remedies. The parties' retention of control over the outcome is thought likely to produce a potentially more durable, forward-looking settlement to the dispute than one imposed by a court, which will almost inevitably be framed in a "win/lose" formulation. Further, since the dispute need not be presented in the bilateral model required by litigation, third party and collective interests can be more readily accommodated, at least in theory."[13]

Today's devices can be more effective, and less formal, than arbitration and court proceedings. They include the following primary means of ADR: negotiation, inquiry, mediation, conciliation, and minitrial.

NEGOTIATION

Negotiation differs from the other informal modes of ADR because its conduct is completely controlled by the immediate parties to the dispute. Negotiations between States are normally conducted through diplomatic channels. They may be performed by heads of State, ambassadors, draft treaty conference participants, or other designated representatives.

The parties may thus consult with one another in their attempt to resolve a dispute. Consultation facilitates problem solving before any adverse action has been taken by either party. After the 1982 Falkland Islands War, Argentina and Great Britain hoped to avoid unnecessary confrontations because of the presence of their respective military forces in the same area. In 1990, they entered into an Interim Reciprocal Information and Consultation System. It applies to "movements of units of their Armed Forces in Areas of the South West Atlantic. The aims of this system are to increase confidence between Argentina and the United Kingdom and to contribute to achieving a more normal situation in the region [including a direct communication link]."[14]

INQUIRY

Unlike direct negotiations, the other ADR modes invoke the assistance of a third party. An inquiry is conducted by someone, not a party to the dispute, who attempts to provide adversaries with an objective assessment of the respective positions. A stalemate may otherwise lead to a more confrontational mode of dispute settlement. The presence of a third party facilitates the injection of a more balanced and informed approach to resolving the dispute—before it erupts into hostilities.

The term "inquiry" is commonly used in two senses. The broader connotation refers to the process itself. A court, arbitral body, international organization, or individual tries to resolve a dispute between other States or entities. The narrower connotation of this term, as used in this section of the book, refers to an arrangement, which requires that the third party conduct an independent investigation of the underlying facts.[15]

In the famous *Dogger Bank Inquiry,* a group of Russian war vessels were en route from the Baltic Sea to the Far

East in 1904 to engage hostile forces in the war with Japan. The Russian ships steamed directly into a fleet of private British fishing vessels at the Dogger Bank in the North Sea. The Russian fleet assumed that it was under attack by British war vessels, which were reportedly in the area. The Russians fired on the fishing vessels, sinking one, damaging others, and killing and wounding a number of civilian fishermen. Great Britain then made plans to intercept the Russian fleet. France intervened, convincing Russia and Great Britain to establish a commission of inquiry under the 1899 Hague Convention on the Pacific Settlement of International Disputes. Five admirals from Austria-Hungary, Great Britain, France, Russia, and the United States spent two months hearing evidence from witnesses. This commission found that the Russian admiral had no justification for opening fire—although the report was worded so as to not discredit the Russian admiral. Russia received the commission's findings and decided to pay damages as a result of the conduct of this Russian squadron.[16]

MEDIATION

Mediation also invokes the assistance of an "outsider" who is not a party to the dispute. Unlike the commission of inquiry, which is basically a fact-finding tool, the mediator is typically authorized to advance his or her own proposal for resolving the dispute. Nothing is binding about the mediator's role. Otherwise, he or she would really be an arbitrator or judicial officer, who is seized with the power to require a particular result. There is no prior commitment by the parties to accept the mediator's proposal.

The mediator can make his or her proposals informally, based on information supplied by the parties. The mediator does not undertake an independent investigation, as would a commission of inquiry. Where negotiations are deadlocked, the mediator can attempt to move the parties in the direction of at least considering his or her proposal (or that of the other party). Such proceedings are normally informal and private, unlike an arbitration or judicial proceeding, with its formal procedures for taking evidence from witnesses in an open-hearing context. The Red Cross often acts as a mediator in those conflicts where the parties are unlikely to negotiate face-to-face. Algeria served in this capacity, mediating the Iran-US Hostage Crisis in 1979–1980.

On the other hand, a proliferation of well-intentioned mediators can add a degree of complexity, which includes some less well-intentioned competition marked by turf battles, such as the many mediations leading to the Dayton Peace Accords (which was to bring peace to Bosnia.)[17] As acknowledged by the editors of a major analysis of international mediation: "The multiplication of mediators is less a matter of choice than a fact of life in today's world. This complexity has been brought on by the end of the Cold War and by the increasing involvement of a wide array of both state and nonstate actors in the more fluid and less structured relationships of the current era.[18]

"Good offices" is a variant of the mediation technique. A third party communicates the statements of the disputing parties to one another. This is a useful technique when the dispute involves States that do not maintain diplomatic communications. Good offices may involve the "outsider" inviting the disputing parties to a settlement conference or undertaking other steps to facilitate their communications. This theme was the focal point of the 1936 Inter-American Good Services and Mediation Treaty, as well as the 1948 American Treaty on Peaceful Settlement of Disputes (the Bogotá Treaty). The UN Secretary-General has often used his position to facilitate inter-State settlement of disputes through the "good offices" of the UN.

In October 1998, four nations used various features of the mediation technique to resolve a border dispute between two other nations. From 1941 to 1995, Ecuador and Peru had fought three wars over a 48-mile strip of jungle on their 1,050-mile common border. Argentina, Brazil, Chile, and the United States mediated during three years of deadlocked negotiations. The disputing parties felt that they had not obtained all that they were entitled to receive under this mediation. However, their joint agreement ended this dispute on terms that were an acceptable alternative to another war.

The December 2004 Report of the UN High-level Panel on Threats, Challenges and Change strongly recommended additional mediation training and applications:

> 100. United Nations efforts . . . are often inhibited by the reluctance of Member States to see their domestic affairs internationalized. But more effort . . . should be made in this area, particularly through the appointment of . . . regionally experienced envoys, mediators and special representatives, who can make as important a contribution to conflict prevention as they do to conflict resolution.

101. . . . This would be made easier by the establishment of a facility for training and briefing . . . United Nations mediators, and we so recommend.

102. . . . The [UN] Department of Political Affairs should be given additional resources and should be restructured to provide more consistent and professional mediation support.

103. . . . [T]he details of such a restructuring . . . should take into account the need for the United Nations to have . . . (c) Greater interaction with national mediators, regional organizations and non-governmental organizations involved in conflict resolution.[19]

CONCILIATION

Conciliation is third-party dispute resolution in a more formalized setting than negotiation or mediation. Like the commission of inquiry, a conciliation commission may engage in a fact-finding role. Yet, a conciliation commission normally attempts to promote a resolution. This is a step beyond mere fact-finding inquiries, yet it is less formal than an arbitration or judicial proceeding.

The textbook definition of conciliation was provided by late Professor Clive Parry of Cambridge, England. It is the "process of settling a dispute by referring it to a commission of persons whose task it is to elucidate the facts and (usually after hearing the parties and endeavoring to bring them to an agreement) to make a report containing proposals for a settlement, but not having the binding character of an [arbitral] award or [court] judgment."[20] The conciliator thus attempts to reconcile differences by portraying the negative aspects of the respective positions.

In 1922, the League of Nations General Assembly resolved that States should conclude treaties requiring the submission of disputes to conciliation commissions—unless the parties preferred to resolve the dispute via arbitration or litigation in the PCIJ. Some twenty treaties contained a conciliation requirement. These included the famous post-World War I Locarno agreements between Germany on the one hand, and Belgium, France, Czechoslovakia, and Poland on the other. The Locarno Treaty was then incorporated into the League's 1928 General Act for the Pacific Settlement of Disputes. League members established both *ad hoc* and permanent conciliation commissions to act. Nearly 200 such treaties were concluded before the outbreak of World War II.

MINITRIAL

While quite similar to conciliation, the minitrial is a fresh approach to international dispute resolution. It is not a real trial. The parties confront one another in a similar context, however, and must verify their positions before a neutral third party. The "judge" is typically an expert in the particular field, and not necessarily a sworn judicial officer (or lawyer). These "trials" often take place before negotiators who are senior employees of the respective parties. Each negotiator, in turn, then proceeds to illustrate the weaknesses to his or her employer's position long before a costly arbitration or judicial proceeding at some point in the future.

Italy's Mauro Rubino-Sammartano, who practices in French and Italian courts, illustrates the successes with this comparatively new device in his book on international arbitration:

◆

Illustration[s]

Xerox Corporation entered into a distribution agreement with a Latin American company. . . . [T]he distributor construed the contract as applying (i) not to one line of computers only, but to all the computers sold by Rank Xerox (ii) throughout Latin America rather than in a more limited territory.

One year after proceedings had been started before the California Courts, an extremely quick mini-trial took place (Rank Xerox presenting its case in 1 hour and 40 minutes), which produced a positive result ending in a promptly reached settlement.

Another positive mini-trial is the *Telecredit-TRW* dispute concerning trademarks, conducted before the parties' negotiators and a neutral advisor; the dispute was settled by the parties' CEOs in 30 minutes after 14 hours of mini-trial.

A third positive mini-trial is reported as having taken place between a German manufacturer and an American distributor. Settlement was reached after a presentation of [just] one hour by each party.[21]

There are inherent limitations with this ADR device. Goodwill is an essential element in such a process. Large corporate enterprises, however, have little to lose by such devices—as opposed to the time and expense associated with the more formal resolution mechanisms addressed in the remaining sections of this chapter.

◆ 9.3 ARBITRAL CLASSIFICATIONS AND TRIBUNALS

Arbitration is a comparatively formal mode of dispute resolution. Adversaries rely on a third party to hear the evidence and resolve the dispute by issuing a binding arbitral award. This section of the book covers the types of arbitration and some prominent arbitral tribunals.

CLASSIFICATION

Arbitration may be classified as follows: *ad hoc* versus permanent; by the nature of the parties; composition of the tribunal; and category of dispute.

Ad Hoc versus Permanent Historically, arbitrations have been *ad hoc*. After a dispute arises, the parties determine what will be decided and who will do the deciding. They agree on the general terms and limitations that they will impose on the arbitrators. *Ad hoc* arbitration presents the recurring problem of not having procedures already in place, with the resulting lack of predetermined procedures and loss of time for resolving the dispute. On a more positive note, the overwhelming number of parties to these arbitrations have fulfilled their international obligations established by binding arbitration.[22]

Assembling an *ad hoc* international arbitration may leave much to the discretion of the arbitrator and the participants. In 1988, for example, an international arbitration panel ruled in Egypt's favor in a border dispute with Israel, leaving the parties to work out the details of actually determining the precise boundary line. The parties tend to encounter less flexibility, however, when they submit their case to a standing arbitral tribunal—with its own preestablished set of rules and procedures. Permanently established arbitration tribunals have the advantage of predictability and stability in resolving business disputes. As aptly depicted by Canada's McGill University Professor Stephen Troope:

Since the 1960s, the international business community has manifested an increasing interest in arbitration as a dispute resolution mechanism. Concurrent with this increased attraction to arbitration has been the emergence and growth of more and more arbitral institutions . . . providing facilities and organisational mechanisms for the arbitral resolution of commercial disputes . . . [and] with the increasing scale of international trade, arbitration has very much come into its own. . . .

Because of the potential application of contemporary commercial arbitration in many economic contexts . . . one can understand the superficial attraction of institutional arbitration which provides a stable organisational base for an arbitration, a staff trained to administer arbitration and more importantly, a set of pre-established procedural rules which should prevent renegotiation during a heated dispute, thereby helping to ensure that the arbitration goes forward even in the face of a recalcitrant party. It is asserted, therefore, that institutional arbitration enhances the values of certainty and predictability.[23]

Nature of Parties Arbitration historically involved inter-State disputes, achieving its heyday in the first half of the twentieth century. The prime example is the Permanent Court of Arbitration (PCOA), a product of the 1899 Hague Peace Conference. Various nations met in Holland to explore ways to achieve peace and disarmament. They adopted the Convention on the Pacific Settlement of International Disputes. Treaty participants viewed the PCOA as an egalitarian device, which would implement their goal of peacefully resolving international disputes. It commenced operations in 1913 and still functions today at its seat in The Hague.

The PCOA is not a court. Its "judges" are mostly lawyers who have expertise in international business matters and are willing to travel. They serve on small arbitration panels. Each of the seventy-five participating countries appoints four individuals to provide arbitration services for a fixed number of years. The national parties to a dispute choose several of these experts to serve on a panel, which will deliberate their particular problem.

The number of inter-State arbitrations has declined significantly since World War II. The post-World War I creation of the Permanent Court of International Justice in The Hague, diverted national attention from the PCOA. Prior to 1931, the PCOA heard twenty-four cases. Since then, it has heard only several, including the Iran-US Claims Tribunal. The sixty-five-year-old PCOA was the convenient forum for carrying out the details of the US-Iran 1980 Hostage Treaty. The PCOA could immediately begin to consider the difficult compensation issues arising out of that dispute.

Another "States-only" arbitral tribunal was established by the Charter of the Organization of African Unity (OAU): the OAU's Commission of Mediation, Conciliation, and Arbitration, is seated in Addis Ababa, Ethiopia. Its twenty-one members have "jurisdiction" (noncompulsory) to resolve any inter-State dispute referred to it by the parties or by certain governmental entities of the OAU or its State members. The essential role of the OAU Commission is to facilitate alternative dispute-resolution mechanisms among the various African States.

The lion's share of contemporary "international" arbitrations involve either private individuals/corporations and a State; or, settle disputes between private persons/corporations, and international organizations. Contracts between private corporations normally contain a forum selection clause. The parties thus agree in advance to dispute resolution in a designated institution with the appropriate expertise.[24]

Inter-State treaties are not always locked into a particular arbitral body. The 1987 France-United Kingdom Channel Tunnel Treaty expressly authorizes the reference of disputes to arbitral tribunals for disputes between: (a) the State parties, (b) States and concessionaires, or (c) just concessionaires. All public and private entities (concessionaires) have access to a convenient dispute-resolution mechanism—without regard to the status of any particular tunnel-service provider. There are no sovereign immunity problems for concessionaires. A claimant does not have to surmount potential sovereignty objections between the States involved in the tunnel's operation. There is no need for a business entity to first enlist the assistance of its home State in order to present a claim against an international person (i.e., France or the United Kingdom). A private nongovernmental corporation may then arbitrate a dispute with its own home State. It does not have to first resort to the traditional International Law requirement that it seek sovereign representation at the international level. The major multilateral treaties that provide for this form of mixed State-private party arbitration are the New York Convention, the Inter-American Convention on International Commercial Arbitration, and the Washington Convention.[25]

Composition and Category A functional classification of arbitration would be: (a) mixed international arbitration, (b) private disputes involving a public interest, and (c) administrative arbitration.

In a "mixed" arbitration, one party is a State and the other is either a private party or a business entity. A classic instance is the Algiers Accords—the agreement creating the Iran-United States Claims Tribunal in 1981.[26] The US hostages being held in Iran were released. Iran was able to regain control over some of its assets, which had been frozen at the inception of this major international dispute. US individuals and corporations were provided with a means of redress against Iran. The Tribunal then began its task of resolving claims against the Iranian funds, which would be disbursed as a result of its decisions. Due to the animosity between the parties and the high claims at stake, the Tribunal's lasting value was rather evident. It was unlikely that a negotiated settlement between the United States and Iran could have been reached without this independent mechanism for "posthostility" claims adjudication typical of postwar tribunals formed to resolve private claims against State parties.[27]

In 1991, the UN Security Council established the UN Compensation Commission (UNCC), headquartered in Geneva. Its mandate is to process, determine, and pay any claims against Iraq arising from the 1991 Persian Gulf War. This tribunal was created under the Council's Chapter VII powers whereby it takes various measures to control threats to peace. The UNCC's function is to decide the amount and validity of claims arising on or after August 2, 1990—the date of Iraq's invasion of Kuwait. Its decisions have announced settlements in claims involving serious personal injury or death that resulted from Iraq's annexation of Kuwait. In 1996, the UNCC began to issue checks based on money obtained from Iraqi oil sales—30 percent of which is retained for the payment of UNCC claims.[28]

Another form of international arbitration is "commercial" arbitration between business enterprises.[29] While there are a number of such tribunals, several bear special mention. The International Court of Arbitration of the International Chamber of Commerce (ICC Court) is a prominent arbitral organization based in Paris. It has resolved commercial disputes since 1923. It currently receives approximately 350 cases per year. Under Article 1.1 of the ICC's Rules of Conciliation and Arbitration, the "function of the Court is to provide for the arbitration of business disputes of an international character. . . ."[30] The parties submit their requests for dispute resolution assistance to the Secretariat of the ICC Court of Arbitration. The "court" then delegates the power to arbitrate matters referred to it. The Secretariat appoints an odd number of individuals (either one or three) to consider the dispute, depending on its complexity. These individuals sit on the ICC National Committee located in each participating country.[31]

The International Centre for Settlement of Investment Disputes (ICSID) is another prominent commercial arbitral body. The 1966 Convention on the Settlement of Investment Disputes Between States and Nationals of Other States established the ICSID.[32] The host organization is the UN's International Bank for Reconstruction and Development located in Washington, DC. The ICSID was designed to develop confidence in private foreign investment through arbitration. It differs from other international arbitral bodies, such as the Hague PCOA, because use of ICSID facilities is not limited to governmental parties. An individual or corporation may arbitrate directly with a foreign State ("mixed" arbitration). An individual does not need to seek and obtain governmental or diplomatic assistance from one's own country to arbitrate an international claim. Like the ICC's International Court of Arbitration, the ICSID does not directly arbitrate disputes at its headquarters. It maintains panels of legal and business experts who are willing to arbitrate claims submitted to it. They arbitrate many contract disputes between private corporations and the foreign States with which they deal.[33] In 1993, the ICSID rendered the first award ever given under a bilateral investment treaty to which the United States was a party.[34] The 2003 *Loewen* case, featured in §4.4 of this textbook, is an ICSID case.

There are also "special purpose" commercial arbitral bodies that specialize in specific areas of law or trade. The World Intellectual Property Organization (WIPO) is a specialized agency of the United Nations with headquarters in Geneva. It maintains panels for resolving international problems involving alleged copyright, patent, and trademark-infringement claims. This body published its revised ADR rules, which became effective in 1994. It has become a particularly expeditious and suitable means for accommodating the special problems associated with intellectual-property disputes. A patent or trademark holder may have instant access to a body of intellectual-property experts. A claim that a foreign company is illegally making or marketing the owner's product—without entering into a licensing arrangement

with that patent or trademark owner—may be lodged with the WIPO. The owner does not have to pursue either diplomatic or judicial remedies, which would depend on the willingness of the owner's home State to one day pursue such claims (should such a case become a priority for the State).

In a classic illustration of this entities utility, the WIPO process yielded a swift result, at a minimum of cost, with an instantly available worldwide result. In 1999, US citizen Michael Bosman registered the Internet domain name <worldwrestlingfederation.com> with an Australian company. Bosman then contacted the World Wrestling Federation (WWF), a US company, offering to sell that domain name to the WWF for US $1,000. The WWF then electronically submitted a complaint to WIPO's Arbitration and Mediation Center in Geneva. The Panel concluded that Bosman's offer to sell that the domain name had been registered in bad faith. His failure to establish a Web site under the referenced domain name indicated that Bosman had not in fact "used" the domain name. The use requirement is intended to discourage such registrations, by cybersquatters who do so only for the purpose of resale.[35]

Certain commercial treaties expressly provide for judicial conformation of international arbitral awards. The North American Free Trade Agreement (NAFTA) protects private investors in Canada, Mexico, and the United States. They may obtain awards from a NAFTA tribunal, and then enforce them in the courts of each NAFTA country. In one case, a US citizen obtained a $50,000,000 NAFTA panel award against Mexico, which was confirmed by a Canadian court.[36]

"Administrative" arbitration typically involves the inner workings of international organizations. In a representative case, a UN staff member from the Russian delegation at the United Nations in New York applied for asylum in the United States. He also requested a career appointment at the United Nations, based on his excellent service record. When his request was denied, he filed an administrative action in the UN Administrative Tribunal. The UN Tribunal decided that the Secretary-General's decision was "flawed," although it would not reverse the UN's nonemployment decision In a 2004 decision, a former UN employee living in France was charged with Rwandan war crimes for killing his colleagues in 1994. He was initially awarded six months' back pay. His appeal resulted in his winning thirteen months pay, instead, on the basis that he was unfairly dismissed.[37]

◆ 9.4 INTERNATIONAL COURT OF JUSTICE

INTRODUCTION

The dream of world peace, entwined with a judicial body for resolving international disputes, is not new. The medieval Florentine poet Dante's *De Monarchia,* proposed a world State which would be incomplete without a central court of justice. The twentieth century was the first to yield world organizations dedicated to peace. In 1943, the Four Powers (China, Soviet Union, United Kingdom, and United States) agreed that another global international organization should replace the defunct League of Nations. These were debated during the 1945 UN development conference in San Francisco. Fifty nations met there, to forge the principles now contained in the UN Charter and its annexed Statute of the International Court of Justice (ICJ). The UN Charter drafters decided that the powers of the new Court must be directly incorporated into the UN Charter. The status of this *second* World Court would, in principle, be on a par with the other major organs of the United Nations. The ICJ was designated as the judicial arm of the United Nations. It would share responsibility with the other major UN organs for monitoring national observance of the principles set forth in the UN Charter.

This section of the textbook describes the contemporary operations of the Court—what it is, and is *not,* designed to do.

CHARTER PROVISIONS

The UN's founding members decided to place the constitutive ICJ provisions directly in the UN Charter. This integrated the international organization and its new World Court, unlike the loose "association" existing between the League of Nations and the *distinct* PCIJ.[38]

The UN Charter sets forth the general functions of the Court in Articles 92 through 96. The Statute of the ICJ contains the procedures for submitting and resolving national disputes. The following materials survey the UN Charter provisions on the Court, summarize the Court's functions under its statute, and analyze how State practice has affected its roles *after* the Charter materialized in 1945.

The UN Charter provides that: (1) all member States are automatically parties to the Statute of the ICJ; (2) members promise to comply with the decisions of the Court; and (3) the Security Council may undertake enforcement

measures if this promise is breached. To encourage national use of the ICJ, Article 93.1 of the Charter requires all State members to become "parties to the Statute of the International Court of Justice." This statute is often referred to as being "annexed" to the Charter. The drafters wanted the Charter and the Court's Statute to be jointly adopted by every State that joined the United Nations. This Statute, discussed below, became operative in 1951. Several States, which were not UN members (for several decades after it came into existence), initially became parties to the ICJ Statute, but not to the UN Charter (Liechtenstein, San Marino, and Switzerland).

Under Article 94.1 of the Charter, each UN member "undertakes to comply with the decision of the International Court of Justice in any case to which it is a party." This is a fundamental requirement of any organized judicial system. While the judgments of the ICJ have been honored by most State parties, some States have ignored its judgments. And, as usual, certain commentators have focused on this feature of the judicial process, construing the conduct of several scofflaws as a fatal blow to the continuing willingness of most States to abide by ICJ judgments. As will be seen, getting a State to consent to the jurisdiction of the Court is not always given. Once consent has been obtained, however, State practice has routinely complied with the Court's judgments.

The conspicuous examples of State defiance of ICJ decisions include the following. For over a decade, Libya disobeyed the Court's order to turn over the two Libyan terrorists allegedly responsible for blowing up Pan Am Flight 103 over Lockerbie, Scotland, in 1988. South Africa refused to honor the Court's "advisory" order in the 1971 *Namibia Presence* case to terminate control of the area of South-West Africa (now the independent State of Namibia). In the 1973 *Fisheries Jurisdiction* cases, the ICJ ordered Iceland and the United Kingdom to negotiate an equitable solution to foreign fishing rights in the international waters near Iceland's coast (§8.2). This matter was not seriously negotiated and has not been resolved. In the 1980 *Hostage Case,* Iran refused to release the US diplomats held hostage in Tehran. And from 1984 to 1988, the United States refused to participate in, or honor, the ICJ's judgments in the *Nicaragua* case (discussed below).

Defiance of the Court's orders and judgments is not without a remedy under the UN Charter. Article 94.2 provides that if "any party to a case fails to perform the obligations incumbent upon it under a judgment rendered by the Court, the other party may have recourse to the Security Council, which may, if it deems necessary, make recommendations or decide upon measures to be taken to give effect to the judgment." A State may notify the Security Council when another State has failed to comply with any Charter obligations.

By the early 1950s, a handful of States had failed to perform their obligations as determined by the Court. Although the Charter does not specify what measures may be taken in this instance, the Security Council could have devised and announced postjudgment compliance measures, pursuant to its Chapter VII powers to maintain world peace.

The Security Council formulated what was probably its most significant (although unsuccessful) ICJ enforcement measure, after the Court rendered its opinion in the 1971 *Namibia Presence* case (§2.4). The Court ordered South Africa to terminate its control of South-West Africa (Namibia). The Council then ordered South Africa to comply with the ICJ's judgment. It also ordered other States to abstain from dealing with South Africa in any way that was inconsistent with the ICJ's investment divestment opinion. South Africa ultimately agreed to cooperate with the United Nations. Two decades later, South-West Africa finally achieved its independence from South Africa.

The Security Council has had very limited experience with enforcing judgments, and little incentive to develop enforcement measures. Under UN Charter Article 36.3, "legal disputes should as a general rule be referred by the parties to the International Court of Justice in accordance with the provisions of the Statute of the Court." States do not, as a general rule, refer their more sensitive legal disputes to the ICJ. This is one reason why States litigating disputes in the ICJ have generally complied with its judgments. A potentially adverse result is usually not particularly detrimental to the critical political or economic interests of the litigants.

UN TRUST FUND

One reason for limited use of the ICJ is the financial condition of the UN's smaller States. As noted in §7.2, many of them do not have the resources to maintain a diplomatic presence in other countries. Many cannot operate any embassy, anywhere, because of quite limited financial resources. The same problem has historically limited their access to the ICJ as a dispute-resolution center. It is costly to maintain a local presence at The Hague (Netherlands), where the ICJ is located, even for the limited purpose of filing pleadings, conducting the research necessary to adequately participate in judicial proceedings on a distant continent, and paying the cost of scientific studies and expert testimony in the Court's proceedings. A partial remedy has been proposed at the United Nations.

In UN Secretary-General Boutros Boutros-Ghali's 1992 report on preventive diplomacy, he recognized that while the Court's docket has grown, it is an underutilized resource. He urged UN members to "support the Trust Fund established to assist countries unable to afford the cost involved in bringing a dispute to the Court. . . ."[39] This is an inducement to States to submit their disputes to the ICJ. This fund constitutes a form of international legal aid, as envisioned by Secretary-General Javier Perez de Cuellar in 1989. It is financed by voluntary contributions from the comparatively prosperous States, international organizations, and nongovernmental organizations. Thirty-four States had contributed over a half-million dollars to the fund as of the Secretary-General's 1992 annual report. Chad is one State that disclosed its ability to participate in ICJ proceedings, only because of the availability of this fund (during a public hearing at the ICJ on July 14, 1993, in the ICJ Territorial Dispute case between Libya and Chad). While some commentators view this fund as a make-work device for the Court, the ICJ itself is not an intended beneficiary. A permanent fund is preferable to the common scenario whereby needy States must seek financial assistance from other States. The latter may, of course, exact a future concession for such grants or loans.

As reported by a staff member of the ICJ, the fund's resources were essentially depleted (after only two successful applications). Thus, "new incentives are needed to raise the level of contribution by wealthier states and enable a larger number of less fortunate states to settle their disputes peacefully in the World Court."[40] It is unfortunately evident that smaller States' access to the ICJ is not a priority of the larger States. The United Nations still has a long way to go in currying support for funding the UN Secretary-General's Trust Fund.

ICJ STATUTE

Earlier materials in this section identified the basic UN Charter provisions on the ICJ. The various provisions of the companion "Statute of the International Court of

Justice" provide additional details regarding the judges, court functions, the pivotal "optional" clause, and the Court's "advisory" jurisdiction (as opposed to its "contentious" jurisdiction).[41]

Judges The ICJ is composed of fifteen judges, each from a different UN member State. Recurring suggestions that there be more judges are not very practical. The United Nations does not have the resources to pay the salaries of a large number of jurists. There has been a rather limited caseload to date.

The UN Secretary-General invites State members who are parties to the Permanent Court of Arbitration to submit names of judicial candidates. They are then elected by the UN General Assembly and Security Council. There are triennial elections of five judges to the Court, each serving a nine-year term.

Article 2 of the Statute of the International Court of Justice establishes the eligibility requirements for its judges. They must be independent, "elected . . . from among persons of high moral character, who possess the qualifications required in their respective countries for appointment to the highest judicial offices, or are jurisconsults [learned in International Law] of recognized competence. . . ." About one-third of the judges actually have been judicial officers in their countries. Most have been law professors and practicing lawyers. Some judges have been senior government administrators, and two were heads of State.[42]

Unlike other branches of the UN or certain regional tribunals, ICJ judges do not represent their governments. They must act independently. Under Articles 16 and 17 of the Statute, judges cannot "exercise any political or administrative function, or engage in any other occupation of a professional nature." Nor can they "act as agent, counsel, or advocate in any case." Since the judges are not national delegates, their respective governments cannot dismiss them from the ICJ for their judicial opinions. Only the Court itself can vote to dismiss a judge. It has never done so.

Functions and Limitations The Court's basic function is to hear and determine cases involving interpretations and applications of the principles set forth in the UN Charter. Under ICJ Statute Article 36.1, the Court's jurisdiction consists of "all cases [that] the parties refer to it and all matters specially provided for in the Charter of the United Nations or in treaties. . . ." Under Article 38,

the Court relies on the following sources of International Law to disputes submitted for its consideration: treaties; customary State practice; general principles of law applied by civilized nations; national or other international court decisions; and scholarly writings of the experts in International Law (§1.2).

The Court's first contentious case was the 1948 *Corfu Channel* litigation. The United Kingdom sued Albania when UK warships hit mines laid in Albania's territorial waters. The Court decided that the United Kingdom had a right to navigate through these waters, holding Albania responsible for the damage to the UK war vessels. In the 1950 *Protection of French Nationals and Protected Persons in Egypt Case,* France sued Egypt for harming French citizens residing in Egypt. After the suit was filed, Egypt rescinded its objectionable measures. The ICJ discontinued the proceedings because Egypt's remedy satisfied France. The Court was apparently headed for a bright future.

Some built-in jurisprudential problems impacted the Court's ultimate performance, however. Nigeria's former Judge and President of the ICJ, T.O. Elias, observed that "[t]he ICJ or World Court is unique in a number of ways and, as such, generates no international legal system of its own." Unlike national tribunals, the ICJ has no bailiffs or prison system to ensure compliance with its interim orders and judgments.[43] There were no special forces dispatched, for example, when the Court ordered Libya to turn over its two citizens allegedly responsible for the 1988 bombing of Pan Am Flight 103 over Lockerbie, Scotland. When Libya finally turned over those individuals for trial, there was no UN jail at the disposal of the ICJ. This void necessitated reliance, instead, on the aid of a national UN member to facilitate the execution of such orders. Thus, when those individuals were tried in The Hague in 2000, it was not in the ICJ (where only States may appear). The defendants were turned over for trial to a special tribunal agreed upon by England, Libya, the United States, and the Netherlands. They were thus tried before a panel of Scottish judges, applying Scottish law, at a former US military base known as Camp Zeist.[44] After one of them was found guilty and sentenced to a lengthy jail term, he was committed to a special jail facility in The Netherlands not associated with the ICJ.

There is another significant jurisprudential problem with the Court: It is a trial court, not an appellate court. Reviewing tribunals in national legal systems routinely rely on an extensive judicial record generated by a lower court, whose lawyers refine and advocate the respective view of the precise nature of the issue to be resolved. New York University Professor Thomas Franck notes the inherent limitation of not having a record from which to draw:

> [T]he Court, as both trial court and court of ultimate jurisprudential recourse, is in a far more difficult position than domestic [national] courts, where it is customary to make fact-determination the principal concern of the lower court while leaving it to a higher tribunal to devote itself almost exclusively to the jurisprudential issues applicable to predetermined facts. Moreover, to this burden of duality should be added the disadvantage of distance. That The Hague is very far . . . [from] the forests of El Salvador or the jungles of Thailand and the desert of Western Sahara, is self-evident. Less immediately apparent is the . . . Court's cultural diversity, [because] few members can draw upon personal experience to imagine the substantive realities as to which the pleadings establish contradictory assertions. . . . In the [ICJ's] Peace Palace, the judges . . . cannot . . . reach into their life experiences to weigh the comparative probabilities. Even where contradictory witnesses are concerned, how can they rely on socio-culturally conditioned instinct to feel who is likely to be lying . . . when the witnesses are from a culture that is wholly unfamiliar to most members of the Court."[45]

While the ICJ has always functioned as a trial court, it could arguably undertake a form of judicial review of UN agency actions. In several instances, certain UN members have claimed that the ICJ must review and overrule Security Council sanction decisions that were allegedly beyond the Council's powers under the UN Charter. In its *Namibia Case,* however, the Court stated: "Undoubtedly, the Court does not possess powers of judicial review or appeal in respect of the decisions taken by the United Nations organs concerned [which included the Security Council]."[46] The express power to judicially review the Council's action is not suggested in the UN Charter, nor in the companion Statute of the ICJ or its Rules of Court. However, as reasoned by Cambridge University Professor Dapo Akande, "lack of an express power of review is not . . . determinative. What is more important is lack of an express prohibition from engaging in judicial review."[47]

By analogy, the US Supreme Court decided, early in the new Republic's existence, that it necessarily possessed the power of judicial review. As of 1803, that Court may trump the acts of the other, political branches of government. In the Court's words: "It is emphatically the province and duty of the judicial department to say what the law is. Those who apply the rule to particular cases, must of necessity expound and interpret that rule. If two laws conflict with each other, the courts must decide on the operation of each."[48] In a democratically constituted national court system, then, such a balance-of-power principle unquestionably authorizes judicial review of the constitutionality of executive action.[49] The ICJ has never reviewed a Security Council sanction decision to determine whether it complied with the UN Charter. However, further study of this question reveals that there is a full spectrum of opinions as to whether the ICJ *could* find—as have many national courts in democratic countries—that the judicial branch must have that power for a democratic regime to survive.[50]

OPTIONAL CLAUSE

"Compulsory" Jurisdiction   All State members of the United Nations are automatically parties to the ICJ Statute per Article 93.1 of the UN Charter. Its terms "dictate" as follows: "All Members of the United Nations are *ipso facto* parties to the Statute of the International Court of Justice." That rather commanding language does not actually mandate ICJ dispute resolution, however. This "requirement" is one of form, not substance. Those who created the ICJ anticipated that sovereign States would not be willing to vest the ICJ with the full judicial power necessary to require them to appear in a lawsuit filed by another State. The prospect of a distant tribunal, rendering judgments against the more powerful nations of the world, was too myopic to compel compulsory jurisdiction in all cases. If such a mandate had been placed in the Charter or ICJ Statute, the United Nations would be a far smaller organization than it is today.

Instead, the drafters of the ICJ Statute provided that a nation could join the United Nations and decide later whether or not to accept the Court's compulsory (mandatory) jurisdiction. Article 36 of the Statute thus provides that the ICJ will have jurisdiction to hear and decide cases against a consenting State:

◆ in "cases the parties refer to it" [for example, by inserting a treaty clause specifically referring disputes to the ICJ; or]

◆ "States parties to the present Statute may . . . [unilaterally by an appropriate filing with the UN Secretary-General that the filing State] recognizes as compulsory . . . the jurisdiction of the Court in all legal disputes concerning:

(a) the interpretation of a treaty;
(b) any question of international law;
(c) the existence of any fact which, if established, would constitute a breach of an international obligation;
(d) the nature or extent of the reparation [such as damages] to be made for the breach of an international obligation."

The Court's "compulsory jurisdiction" depends completely on the will of States to accept the Court's power over them—in the specific circumstances expressed in each Declaration of Acceptance. The specific methods for exercising these alternatives are succinctly summarized by Polish Academy of Sciences Professor Renata Szafarz in his book on the ICJ's so-called compulsory jurisdiction:

The consent may be expressed *ad hoc* once a dispute has arisen. It may also be expressed *post hoc* by a party to the dispute when the case has been brought before the court by another party. Finally, consent may be expressed *ante hoc,* in advance, with reference to all legal disputes to be submitted in the future or to certain categories of dispute. The latter form of jurisdiction is usually, though not very precisely, termed compulsory or obligatory jurisdiction. Since the compulsory jurisdiction of the ICJ results either from the acceptance by states of the so-called optional clause . . . or from the acceptance of judicial clauses contained in treaties a considerable majority of states have accepted the compulsory jurisdiction of the ICJ, at least to some extent . . . even though . . . there should be more than the present 54 declarations accepting the optional clause and that there should be fewer reservations to [such] judicial clauses.[51]

Optional Clause Applied The UN blueprint for judicial dispute resolution was a practical compromise. The organization's judicial process could not reasonably mandate compulsory jurisdiction for all members, all of the time. State sovereignty necessitated avoidance of a pollyannaish framework, which would otherwise have locked each State into submitting each dispute to this fledgling, untested tribunal. The Optional Clause compromise represented a unique variation from the "compulsory" jurisdiction commonly exercised by national courts. States joining the United Nations would automatically "accept" the ICJ Statute, which contained a "compulsory jurisdiction" clause. That clause would be triggered, however, *only* by the member State's subsequent decision to expressly subject itself to the jurisdiction and judgments of the UN's judicial arm. Requiring truly compulsory jurisdiction as a condition of joining the United Nations would have been a disaster. Thus, the optional acceptance of its power to adjudicate was not an all-or-nothing proposition.

This unique limitation is found in Article 36.2 of the ICJ Statute: States party "to the present Statute *may at any time* declare that they recognize as compulsory . . . the jurisdiction of the Court in all legal disputes. . ." [italics added]. Lacking this option, the world's more powerful nations would otherwise be unlikely to swell the membership ranks of the new world organization. This is one reason why the UN Charter also incorporated other dispute-resolution mechanisms (§9.2).

The "compulsory" jurisdiction to hear cases is the most controversial and misunderstood feature of the ICJ's jurisdiction. States have unilaterally tendered a variety of acceptances: (a) very narrow acceptances of the ICJ's compulsory jurisdiction; (b) very broad ones; and (c) others lying somewhere in-between. Egypt's 1957 declaration of acceptance was probably the narrowest. The ICJ would have the power to resolve cases *only* in the event of an international dispute directly involving its operation of the Suez Canal. The broadest acceptance comes from countries like Nicaragua, which have submitted unconditional unilateral acceptances of the ICJ's jurisdiction—authorizing the ICJ to hear *any* case involving Nicaragua. That country has little to lose in a forum where it can theoretically "square off" with the major powers of the world. Somewhere in between lies the declaration accepting ICJ jurisdiction on specified terms, such as an acceptance that functions for a limited period of years (subject to renewal). Under Article 36.3, national declarations opting to accept the compulsory jurisdiction of the ICJ may thus be made as follows: (1) unconditionally, (2) for a limited time, or (3) on the condition of reciprocity (explained in the *Norwegian Loans* case below).

Jurisdiction to Determine Jurisdiction   State practice spawned a nonstatutory limitation on ICJ jurisdiction. It clashes with the express terms of the ICJ Statute. Article 36.6 provides that in "the event of a dispute as to whether the Court has jurisdiction, the matter shall be settled by the decision of the Court." This provision was interpreted by the ICJ in the Court's 1955 Nottebohm case (§4.2). The relevant passage addresses the virtually global practice that courts have the jurisdiction to determine their own jurisdiction, when one of the parties questions whether a court has the power to hear the case:

> Paragraph 6 of Article 36 merely adopted . . . a rule consistently accepted by general international law . . . [whereby] an international tribunal has the right to decide to [resolve questions about] its own jurisdiction and has the power to interpret for this purpose the instruments which govern jurisdiction. This principle, which is accepted by general international law in the matter of arbitration, assumes particular force when the international tribunal . . . is an institution which has been pre-established by an international instrument defining its jurisdiction and regulating its operation, and is in the present case the principal judicial organ of the United Nations. . . . The judicial character of the Court and the rule of general international law referred to above are sufficient to establish that the Court is competent to adjudicate on its own jurisdiction in the present case.[52]

The ICJ does not possess the exclusive power to decide its own jurisdiction. The more powerful UN members began to limit their declarations when they filed *so-called* acceptances of the Court's "compulsory jurisdiction." Their reservations to this statutory language, when tendered in advance of any dispute, specified that the defendant State—not the ICJ—would decide whether the Court could actually require them to appear as a defendant. Try to imagine a national judge's reaction, if a defendant were to tell the judge that the court did not have the power to act; that the *defendant* had decided this question; and, that the judge could do nothing about it. This is exactly what many States did by cautiously limiting the scope of their "acceptances" of the Court's compulsory power to hear cases. The ICJ Statute was not worded, so as to *require* UN members to accept the Court's jurisdiction. The Court has therefore been powerless to act in some widely publicized instances.

France's acceptance (withdrawn in 1974) is a good example. Its acceptance was quite narrow, because it "does not apply to differences relating to matters that are essentially within the national jurisdiction *as understood by the Government of France* [italics added]." In this instance, France warmly embraced Article 2.7 of the UN Charter. It provides that "Nothing contained in the present Charter shall authorize the United Nations to intervene in matters [that] are essentially within the domestic jurisdiction of any state. . . ." France (and a number of other nations) thereby invoked the UN Charter's own limitation on its general power to act as the basis for the following State practice: (a) *appearing* to submit to the jurisdiction of the Court, while (b) actually retaining the ability to avoid certain ICJ disputes—by classifying them as falling within their "domestic" jurisdiction, and supposedly not "international" in scope.

Canada's acceptance of the ICJ's compulsory jurisdiction was limited as follows: In a 1994 reservation to the UN Law of the Sea Treaty, its Declaration of Acceptance consented only to jurisdiction "over all disputes . . . other than . . . disputes arising out of or concerning conservation and management measures taken by Canada with respect to vessels fishing in the NAFO Regulatory Area . . . and the enforcement of such measures." This area is the subject of conflicting fishing rights and an ICJ case wherein Spain sued Canada because of its assertion of fisheries jurisdiction beyond the economic zone established in the UN treaty.

Reciprocity   This basis for accepting—yet limiting the scope of national acceptances of the ICJ's compulsory jurisdiction—acknowledged that not all States would recognize the Court's jurisdiction on the identical grounds. A potential defendant State might consider it unfair for a plaintiff State, which had previously tendered a narrower acceptance of the Court's jurisdiction before any dispute arose, to sue in circumstances whereby the plaintiff State would not be similarly amenable to the Court's jurisdiction.

The following ICJ case illustrates the problems spawned by such national declarations, some of which were not included in the ICJ Statute. This case simultaneously demonstrates how the domestic jurisdiction limitation, and the reciprocity limitation, combined to deprive the ICJ of its otherwise available power to decide a case arising under International Law.

Case of Certain Norwegian Loans (*France v. Norway*)

INTERNATIONAL COURT OF JUSTICE

1957 *ICJ Reports* 9 (1957)

AUTHOR'S NOTE: From 1885 to 1909, the Norwegian Government borrowed money from French sources. Norway's loans were secured by banknotes, whereby the Norwegian government promised to repay the loans in gold. In 1914 (when World War I began in Europe), Norway wanted to retain its gold reserves. It therefore suspended the convertibility of its banknotes into gold for an indefinite period. Norwegian law provided that when creditors refused to accept payment in Bank of Norway notes (rather than the promised gold), Norwegian debtors could postpone payment of their loans in gold. French citizens were unable to obtain their repayment in gold, as they had been promised under the express terms of their loans to Norwegian borrowers.

The French government suggested that this dispute be submitted to either an international commission of financial experts, or any mutually acceptable arbitral body—or, to the International Court of Justice. Norway consistently refused all of these alternatives on the basis that this matter should be heard only in Norway's judicial system. Norway considered this problem to be a local matter, involving no more than an alleged breach of contract governed by the domestic laws of Norway. France finally filed this case in the ICJ. In its application for relief, the French government sought a judgment that Norway could discharged these loans only by payment in gold—as originally promised.

The ICJ did not reach the merits of France's case. The Court could not hear and decide it, because its inherent judicial power to proceed was vitiated by the combined effect of France's "domestic jurisdiction" reservation, and Norway's "reciprocity" reservation.

The opinion of the majority of the judges discusses why the ICJ did not have the power to act. Judge Lauterpacht's separate opinion concurred with the result (that the court lacked the power to proceed). He based his conclusion, however, on different footing: France's purported submission to the compulsory jurisdiction of the court was illusory—a rather daunting theme that continues to plague the Court to this day.

COURT'S OPINION: The Application [by France for a judgment against Norway] expressly refers to Article 36, paragraph 2, of the Statute of the Court and to the acceptance of the compulsory jurisdiction of the Court by Norway on November 16th, 1946, and by France on March 1st, 1949. The Norwegian Declaration reads:

> I declare on behalf of the Norwegian Government that Norway recognizes as compulsory ipso facto and without special agreement . . . on condition of reciprocity, the jurisdiction of the International Court of Justice in conformity with Article 36, paragraph 2, of the Statute of the Court, for a period of ten years as from 3rd October 1946.

The French Declaration reads:

> On behalf of the Government of the French Republic, and subject to ratification [which was later given], I declare that I recognize as compulsory ipso facto and without special agreement . . . on condition of reciprocity, the jurisdiction of the International Court of Justice . . . for all disputes which may arise [unless] the parties may have agreed or may agree to have recourse to another method of peaceful settlement. This declaration does not apply to differences relating to matters which are essentially within the national jurisdiction [of France] as understood by the Government of the French Republic. . . .

The Norwegian Government maintained that the subject of the dispute was within the exclusive domain of the municipal [internal] law of Norway, and that the Norwegian Government relied upon the reservation in the French Declaration [excluding] matters which are essentially within the national jurisdiction [of France] as understood by the French Government. . . .

[Norway explained that] There can be no possible doubt on this point. If, however, there should still be some doubt, the Norwegian Government would rely upon the reservations made by the French Government in its Declaration of March 1st, 1949. By virtue of the principle of reciprocity, which is embodied in Article 36, paragraph 2, of the Statute of the Court and which has been clearly expressed in the Norwegian Declaration of November 16th, 1946, the Norwegian Government cannot be bound, vis-à-vis the French Government, by undertakings which are either broader or stricter than those given by the latter Government [of France]....[In a subsequent portion of the opinion, the Court responded as follows.] In the Preliminary Objections filed by the Norwegian Government it is stated:

> The Norwegian Government did not insert any such reservation in its own Declaration. But it has the right to rely upon the [narrower] restrictions placed by France upon her own undertakings.
>
> Convinced that the dispute, which has been brought before the Court by the Application of July 6th, 1955, is within the domestic jurisdiction, the Norwegian Government considers itself fully entitled to rely on this right [as France would do if a defendant in this Court]. Accordingly, it requests the Court to decline, on grounds that it lacks jurisdiction, the function which the French Government would have it assume.

In considering this ground of the Objection, the Court notes in the first place that the present case has been brought before it on the basis of Article 36, paragraph 2, of the Statute and of the corresponding Declarations of acceptance of compulsory jurisdiction; that in the present case the jurisdiction of the Court depends upon the Declarations made by the Parties in accordance with Article 36, paragraph 2, of the Statute on condition of reciprocity; and that, since two unilateral declarations are involved, such jurisdiction is conferred upon the Court only to the extent to which the Declarations coincide in conferring it. A comparison between the two Declarations shows that the French Declaration accepts the Court's jurisdiction within narrower limits than the Norwegian Declaration; consequently, the common will of the Parties, which is the basis of the Court's jurisdiction, exists within these narrower limits indicated by the French reservation....

France has limited her acceptance of the compulsory jurisdiction of the Court by excluding beforehand dis-putes relating to matters which are essentially within the national jurisdiction as understood by the Government of the French Republic. In accordance with the condition of reciprocity to which acceptance of the compulsory jurisdiction is made subject in both Declarations and which is provided for in Article 36, paragraph 3, of the Statute, Norway, equally with France, is entitled to except from the compulsory jurisdiction of the Court disputes understood by Norway to be essentially within its national jurisdiction....

The Court does not consider that it should examine whether the French reservation is consistent with the undertaking of a legal obligation and is compatible with Article 36, paragraph 6, of the Statute [the core of Justice Lauterpacht's concurring opinion] which provides:

> In the event of a dispute as to whether the Court has jurisdiction, the matter shall be settled by the decision of the Court.

The validity of the [French] reservation has not been questioned by the Parties....

The Court considers that the Norwegian Government is entitled, by virtue of the condition of reciprocity, to invoke the reservation contained in the French Declaration of March 1st, 1949; that this reservation excludes from the jurisdiction of the Court the dispute which has been referred to it by the Application of the French Government; that consequently the Court is without jurisdiction to entertain the [French] Application....

The ICJ then voted twelve to three that it lacked the necessary jurisdiction to hear and determine France's claim.

Separate Opinion of Judge Sir Hersch Lauterpacht

While I concur in the operative part of the Judgment inasmuch as the Court has declared itself incompetent to decide on the merits of the case submitted to it, I much regret that I do not find myself in agreement with the grounds of the Judgment....

I consider it legally impossible for the Court to act in disregard of its Statute which imposes upon it the duty and confers upon it the right to determine its jurisdiction. That right cannot be exercised by a party to the dispute. The Court cannot, in any circumstances, treat as admissible the claim that the parties have accepted its jurisdiction subject to the condition that they, and not the Court, will decide on its jurisdiction. To do so is in my view contrary to Article 36 (6) of the Statute which, without any qualification, confers upon the Court the right and imposes upon it the duty to determine its jurisdiction. Moreover, it is also contrary to Article 1 of the Statute of the Court and Article 92 of the Charter of the United Nations which lay down that the Court shall function in accordance with the provisions of its Statute. It is that question which I now propose to consider in connection with the examination of the validity of the French Acceptance [whereunder it decides jurisdiction rather than the ICJ]. . . .

Moreover, the particular [French] reservation now at issue is not one that is contrary to some merely procedural aspect of the Statute. It is contrary to one of its basic features. It is at variance with the principal safeguard of the system of the compulsory jurisdiction of the Court. Without it, the compulsory jurisdiction of

the Court being dependent upon the will of the defendant party, expressed subsequent to the dispute having been brought before the Court, has no meaning. Article 36(6) is thus an essential condition of the system of obligatory judicial settlement as established in the Statute. That provision was inserted in the Statute with the deliberate intention of providing an indispensable safeguard of the operation of the system. Article 36 (2) speaks of the recognition by the parties to the Statute of the "compulsory" jurisdiction of the Court. But there is no question of compulsory jurisdiction if, after the dispute has arisen and after it has been brought before the Court, the defendant State is entitled to decide whether the Court has jurisdiction. . . .

Accordingly, in my view the entire French Declaration of Acceptance must be treated as devoid of legal effect and as incapable of providing a basis for the jurisdiction of the Court. It is for that reason that, in my view, the Court has no jurisdiction over the dispute.

◆ *Notes & Questions*

1. Both litigants had expressly agreed, long before this dispute arose, to use the World Court to decide international disputes. Yet the terms of their conditional consents, i.e., reservations to the treaty (§8.2), reserved their respective rights to avoid the Court's "compulsory" jurisdiction over them as specified in their reservations to its jurisdiction. France's comparatively narrow acceptance reserved its ability to characterize any claim as one arising under France's internal law—regardless of whether the claim arose under International Law. Norway merely piggybacked onto France's narrower Declaration of Acceptance. Norway had accepted the ICJ's compulsory jurisdiction, subject to its own Declaration of Acceptance based on "reciprocity," thus allowing it to borrow the same terms contained in the plaintiff nation's own reservation to the jurisdiction of the Court.

2. Consider the following questions:
   (a) Under the Statute of the ICJ, who decides whether the Court has jurisdiction?
   (b) What is the "optional clause," and which State or States invoked it in *Norwegian Loans*?
   (c) When a State accepts the optional clause, what obligation does it thereby incur?

   (d) The text of the optional clause includes the word "compulsory." What does this term mean? What limitations does the ICJ Statute contain?
   (e) States do not have to unconditionally accept the jurisdiction of the ICJ in all matters. How did Norway limit the declaration, in which it previously submitted itself to the compulsory jurisdiction of the ICJ?
   (f) Why was Norway able to avoid litigating the *Norwegian Loans* case?
   (g) Why did Judge Lauterpacht characterize France's submission to the compulsory jurisdiction of the ICJ as being invalid?

3. Spain [representing the interests of the European Union (EU)] sued Canada in the ICJ, claiming that Canada's special fisheries jurisdiction some 220 nautical mile off Canada's coast, and well beyond the 200-mile Exclusive Economic Zone violates International Law. In December 1998, the ICJ dismissed this suit on the basis that it lacked jurisdiction to hear Spain's case. One year before enacting this special legislative fishing-conservation zone, Canada tendered a fresh acceptance to the compulsory jurisdiction of the ICJ. Canada thus limited its consent to suit in the ICJ by accepting any case against Canada regarding Canada's amended

Coastal Fisheries Protection Act. The Court rejected Spain's assertion that the Canadian reservation could not be invoked. Further details are available on the ICJ Web site at: <http://www.icj-cij.org/idocket/iec/iecframe.htm>.

4. In June 2000, the ICJ determined that it did not have jurisdiction to hear Pakistan's case against India, which had allegedly shot down a Pakistani military aircraft in Pakistan. They argued the issues whether: (a) British India's 1931 accession to the PCIJ's 1928 jurisdictional Act had survived the demise of the League of Nations; and (b) if so, whether India and Pakistan had become parties, upon their accession to independence. In a 1974 communication to the United Nations, India "never regarded [itself] as bound . . . since Independence in 1947 by succession or otherwise. . . ." The ICJ concluded that India could not be regarded as having been a proper party to the 1928 Act.

Also, India's declaration accepting the compulsory jurisdiction of the ICJ contains a reservation whereby "disputes with the government of any State which is or has been a Member of the [British] Commonwealth of Nations" are excluded from the Court's jurisdiction. Regardless of why India limited the scope of its acceptance, the Court could not accept Pakistan's argument that India's reservation was "extra-statutory" (à la Lauchterpacht) or obsolete. Aerial Incident of 10 August 1999 (Pakistan v. India), ICJ summary, at: <http://www.icj-cij.org/icjwww/ipresscom/IPress-2000/ipresscom2000-19_ipi_20000621.htm>.

ADVISORY JURISDICTION

The ICJ also renders "advisory" opinions, wherein no State is a party to the proceedings. The Court's Statute invites States and international organizations to provide information to assist in its advisory deliberations. Unlike the ICJ's contentious litigation, there is no named plaintiff or defendant. A particular State, however, may be the conspicuously absent target of the Court's opinion.

The ICJ succinctly summarized the fundamental difference between its contentious and advisory jurisdiction as follows:

The participation of interested States had conferred on the present proceedings a wholly unusual character tending to obscure the difference in principle between contentious and advisory proceedings. Whereas in contentious proceedings the Court has before it parties who plead their cause and must, where necessary, produce evidence in support of their contentions, in advisory proceedings it is assumed that the Court will itself obtain the information it needs, should the States not have supplied it. In contentious proceedings, if a party does not succeed in producing good grounds for a claim, the Court has only to dismiss it, whereas in advisory proceedings the Court's task is not confined to assessing the probative force of the information supplied by States, but consists in trying to arrive at an opinion with the help of all the elements of information available to it.[53]

The ICJ's advisory jurisdiction resolves sweeping questions of International Law in a comparatively nonadversarial context. An advisory resolution fills the gap created by the general lack of State commitment to resolving sensitive international disputes in contentious (adversarial) litigation. Many States are normally unwilling to submit their major disputes to the Court. Some States have even registered objections, when a UN agency has sought an advisory opinion. An early ICJ opinion on point (1950) determined that State consent is *not* required for an advisory opinion: "It follows that no State, whether a Member of the United Nations or not, can prevent the giving of an Advisory Opinion which the United Nations considers to be desirable in order to obtain enlightenment as to the course of action it should take. The Court's [advisory] Opinion is given not to the States, but to the organ which is entitled to request it; the reply of the Court, itself an 'organ of the United Nations,' represents its participation in the activities of the Organization, and, in principle, should not be refused."[54]

Who initiates advisory proceedings and why? Under Article 65 of the Statute of the ICJ, the "Court may give an advisory opinion on any [international] legal question at the request of whatever body may be authorized by or in accordance with the Charter of the United Nations to make such a request." An individual State may bring a problem to the attention of one of these bodies. Under UN Charter Article 96, however, only the General Assembly, the Security Council, and specialized agencies authorized by the General Assembly may "request advisory opinions of the Court on legal questions arising within the scope of their activities." The Court then interprets and applies International Law in the absence of State litigants. In 1993, for example, the General Assembly's World

Health Organization sought an advisory opinion from the ICJ requesting guidance on the question of whether the threat or use of nuclear weapons is permitted in any circumstances.

This UN judicial organ may also resolve conflicting interpretations of the Charter by different UN organs. In the 1945 Statement on Charter Interpretation contained in UN Conference Document No. 933, the drafting committee provided as follows: "Difficulties may conceivably arise in the event that there should be a difference of opinion among organs of the Organization concerning the correct interpretation of the Charter. Thus, two organs may conceivably hold and may express or even act upon different views. . . . [I]t would always be open to the General Assembly or to the Security Council . . . to ask the International Court of Justice for an advisory opinion concerning the meaning of a provision of the Charter."

Another reason for the ICJ's advisory jurisdiction is that only *States* may be parties in the Court's contentious cases. Unlike certain regional international courts (§9.6), other international organizations, their agencies, and individuals cannot be parties in ICJ litigation.

Among the Court's more prominent advisory opinions are the 1950 *Competence of the Assembly* case, the 1951 *Genocide Reservations* case, and the 1988 *PLO UN Mission* case. In the first of these opinions, the ICJ resolved a dispute involving the respective powers of the UN's General Assembly and Security Council. The Court decided that the UN Charter could not be interpreted to permit the General Assembly to unilaterally admit members to the United Nations. It was unwilling to condone the suggestion—contrary to the Charter's language—that a recommendation of the Security Council was not required. In the second of the above advisory opinions, the General Assembly sought guidance about the permissibility of potential reservations to the Genocide Treaty. While the court did not clearly answer this question (§8.2), it did decide that State treaty reservations must be generally compatible with the underlying purpose of a treaty. In the 1988 Palestine Liberation Organization (PLO) UN Mission case, the Court decided that the US could not close the mission of the PLO in New York. The US obligations to the United Nations precluded closure of the PLO's UN Mission, although it had been accused of engaging in terrorism.[55]

Given the political interest that States sometimes exhibit in proceedings related to an advisory opinion, the difference between advisory and contentious litigation can be obscured. Normally, the Court obtains what information it desires when exercising its advisory jurisdiction—particularly when one or more interested States are not forthcoming in providing factual details for the Court's legal analysis. But in some advisory cases, State interest generates a degree of participation virtually on a par with that manifested by the ICJ's contentious cases.

In the 1975 *Western Sahara* advisory opinion (§2.4), for example, the UN General Assembly requested an ICJ advisory opinion regarding the status of the referenced territory. The Court called upon Spain, Morocco, and Mauritania to submit information regarding their respective claims to this region. The proceedings resembled contentious litigation, because of the presentation of conflicting adversarial views to the Court—although the case technically involved only the advisory jurisdiction of the Court. As aptly articulated by professor Peter Kovacs of Hungary's Miskolc University, regarding the 2004 *Palestinian Wall* case: "Does this very special advisory opinion—which was, in fact, a *quasi* judgment (even if, of course, without a direct, binding nature)—falling upon a State in a lawsuit launched on a very peculiar basis remain an isolated phenomenon or does it mean the opening of a new jurisprudence . . . .?"[56]

The Court's 2004 *Palestinian Wall* opinion ranks among the most notable and sensitive exercises of advisory jurisdiction in ICJ history. The substantive issues addressed by the ICJ were presented in the edited version of this case, which appears in textbook §6.2. The following portion of the same opinion provides an excellent assessment of the rationale for this form of dispute resolution found in few national court systems:

Legal Consequences of the Construction of a Wall in the Occupied Palestinian Territory

INTERNATIONAL COURT OF JUSTICE
9 July General List No. 131 (2004)
Go to course Web page at
<http://home.att.net/~slomansonb/txtcsesite.html>.
Under Chapter Nine, click Palestinian Wall Advisory Jurisdiction case.

Chambers Option Under Article 26 of the ICJ Statute, the "Court may form from time to time one or more chambers, composed of three or more judges . . . for dealing with particular categories of cases." Upon the request of a party to a dispute, the president of the ICJ determines whether the other party is agreeable to the formation of a chamber to hear the dispute. The original intent to provide chambers to hear labor, transit, and communications cases expanded in 1982. Various ICJ chambers began to consider border disputes between the United States and Canada, Mali and Upper Volta, and El Salvador and Honduras, Benin and Niger.[57]

The chamber mode of dispute resolution offers two advantages. One is that the judges may decide matters on a summary basis. Article 29 of the ICJ Statute provides that with "a view to the speedy dispatch of business, the Court shall form annually a chamber composed of five judges which, at the request of the parties, may hear and determine cases by summary procedure." The judges can dispense with certain court rules and procedures when deemed appropriate. The other advantage is that States do not have to submit their cases for consideration by the full Court. The entire tribunal of fifteen jurists may include judges from States having poor relations with a party to a particular dispute.

In 1993, the United States and Russia tendered a joint proposal at the United Nations which encouraged greater use of the ICJ via a "chambers" process. The objective is to encourage resort to a convenient dispute-resolution mechanism, at least in cases involving the terrorism and narcotics treaties signed by both States in the aftermath of the Cold War. The other UN Security Council members—France, Great Britain, and China—were asked to support and ultimately join the US-Russia chambers proposal. Disputes would be resolved by "panels" of fewer than all fifteen judges. But Great Britain and a number of commentators characterized this proposal as a step backward. It supposedly discouraged use of full-court powers. France and China remain so suspicious of the ICJ that their endorsement of this plan never surfaced.[58]

Stare Decisis In many countries, a judicial decision is characterized as having a *stare decisis* effect—that the legal point it decides is applicable to future cases involving the same issue. Article 59 of the ICJ Statute is an arguable manifestation of a general sovereign mistrust of "outside" judicial resolutions of local disputes. The Courts' decisions "have no binding force except as between the parties and in respect [only] of that particular case." Although the Court is expected to aid in the progressive development of International Law, its Statute expressly limits the binding effect of the ICJ's judgments for use in subsequent cases. Decisions legally bind only the immediate parties in the immediate suit. The parties are not necessarily bound in the event of a similar issue arising between them in the future. *Stare decisis* is generally rejected in countries employing Civil Law jurisprudential principles (e.g., France)—as opposed to Common Law countries (e.g., England), where case precedent is a central feature of the nation's jurisprudence. The Court has nevertheless relied on its prior decisions as evidence of the content of International Law. It would be a waste of judicial resources, however, to completely disregard earlier decisions when the same point of law is later presented in another case.[59]

ICJ ASSESSMENT

Hope and Reality Jeremy Bentham, the British philosopher and oft-described "Father" of modern International Law, wrote a global peace plan in 1789, reflecting upon both the long and arduous war which led to creation of the seventeenth-century nation-State, and the many conflicts since its appearance:

> The maintenance of . . . pacification might be considerably facilitated, by the establishment of a common court of judicature, for the decision of differences between the several nations, although such court were not to be armed with any coercive powers.
>
> . . .
>
> While there is no common tribunal, something might be said for this. Concession to notorious injustice invites fresh injustice. Establish a common tribunal, the necessity for war no longer follows from difference of opinion. Just or unjust, the decision of the arbiters will save the credit, the honour of the contending party.
>
> . . .
>
> There might, perhaps, be no harm in regulating, as a last resource, the contingent to be furnished by the several states for enforcing the decrees of the court. But the necessity for the employment of this resource would, in all human probability, be superseded for ever by having recourse to the much more simple and less burdensome expedient, of introducing into the instrument by which such court was instituted, a clause guaranteeing . . . that the diet [parliament]

might find no obstacle to its giving, in every state, to its decrees, and to every paper whatever which it might think proper to sanction with its signature, the most extensive and unlimited circulation.[60]

Bentham would likely observe little change, were he alive to assess the "realization" of his dream. Of the "Permanent Five" members of the UN Security Council—who wield the most power—only the United Kingdom remains committed to ICJ membership. China, France, and the United States have withdrawn. The Soviet Union/Russia were never parties. Given that none of these powers have committed to the now functioning International Criminal Court, one might reason that the concept of global adjudication as an alternative to war too idealistic to be workable.

It is unlikely that States will rekindle the resilient interest in international adjudication, like that which blossomed between 1944 and 1946. In 1944, even before World War II ended, some of the world's most powerful nations planned a global organization of States, which would avert further wars. In 1945, they drafted unassailable principles calling for the peaceful settlement of disputes. These norms were then incorporated into both the UN Charter and the ICJ Statute. The language in these constituting documents expressed the hope that the Court would play a prominent role in managing subsequent hostilities. UN Charter Article 36.3 states "that legal disputes should as a general rule be referred by the parties to the International Court of Justice in accordance with the provisions of the Statute of the Court." The Court was designed to serve as a buffer for adversaries who would otherwise resort to the familiar forms of hostility to settle disputes. If an offending State failed to comply with the Court's interim orders, or final judgments, the Security Council would surely devise measures to ensure compliance. After all: "Most professors of international law say that compliance with international law is no worse than that of any other law. Indeed, national court decisions are not always complied with."[61]

In the UN Secretary-General's 1992 special report to the UN Security Council, Boutros Boutros-Ghali recommended the following steps to reinforce the role of the ICJ: "(a) All member States should accept the general jurisdiction [rather than the usual reliance on special treaty clauses] of the International Court . . . without any reservation, before the end of the United Nations Decade of International Law in the year 2000. (b) When submission of a dispute to the full Court is not practical, the Chambers jurisdiction should be used. (c) States should support the Trust Fund established to assist countries unable to afford the cost involved in bringing a dispute to the Court. . . ."[62]

The 1999 comment of the Court's past president, on the eve of the new millennium was that "today, 53 years after its creation, the International Court of Justice has more than justified [the] perception . . . [that] a world court can fundamentally foster peace through the adjudicated settlement of international disputes and the development of the body of international law."[63]

This statement is in marked contrast to that of Jawaharlal Nehru University's R. Anand—one of the premiere spokespersons for Third World views on International Law. Referring to the positive sentiments expressed when a world court was reestablished after World War II:

These hopes were however woefully belied after 1945 in the tension-ridden bipolar world . . . that ensued between the Communist and the non-Communist States. Although 23 countries which had accepted the jurisdiction of the Permanent Court were deemed to have accepted the jurisdiction of the ICJ . . . in 1945, not many more countries came forward to accept the jurisdiction of the new court. In fact 17 countries . . . let their declarations lapse or terminated them. In 1990, out of the 164 members . . . only 51 States (about 30%) had accepted the jurisdiction of the International Court. . . . These included 16 States from Africa, 9 from Latin America, 3 from Asia and 23 from Western European and other States. . . . Not only have very few countries accepted the jurisdiction of the Court but even these declarations under the Optional Clause have been made with far-reaching reservations which are found in almost 40 out of 51 declarations."[64]

There are, of course a variety of methods for participation in ICJ proceedings. A State may decide to do so on an ad hoc basis, without the necessity of a prior submission to the court's jurisdiction. It has thus been argued that "neither the number nor the quality of acceptances . . . provide a reliable pointer to States' readiness to use judicial settlement."[65]

The existing geopolitical terrain has not closed the gap between hope and reality. Many of the original UN members refused to yield sovereign control over their own disputes to an international organization headquartered in a distant land (New York City) or its judicial organ (in The Hague). Many UN delegates at the 1945 UN drafting conference mistrusted the first World Court (PCIJ), which had been conceived by the French and staffed with mostly European judges. The UN delegates were likely to give only lip service to a model, which appeared to entrust sensitive disputes to a judicial body hundreds or thousands of miles away in Europe. Socialist States would routinely avoid the submission of their disputes to this tribunal, which was seen as a bourgeois threat to their sovereign decision-making prerogatives. Many lesser developed States lacked familiarity with formal adjudication and were thus rather cautious about formal mechanisms like "compulsory jurisdiction."[66]

Finally, one of the plausible answers for the failure to embrace a Bentham-like "common court of judicature" is the perceived lack of impartiality. Can it be said that the judges vote impartially, when they vote for their own nations, ninety percent of the time? When their home State is not a party, the judges still vote in favor of the litigant whose position most closely resembles their home State. As statistically demonstrated by the University of Chicago's Eric Posner, wealthy judges vote for wealthy nations, and poor judges for poor nations.[67]

ICJ Utility   Although numerous criticisms persist, the ICJ has been useful. It has decided a number of significant disputes. Most of its decisions have been implemented by the participating States. In 1992, for example, El Salvador and Honduras accepted an ICJ border-dispute judgment that ended *two-centuries* of friction in their international relations. As stated by the Honduras President Rafael Callejas, two Central American States thus illustrated "that any dispute, however complex, can be resolved in a civilized and conciliatory way." The Court has also been able to proceed to an important judgment even in the absence of the defendant State. Such cases have aided in the progressive development of International Law; for example, the *Nicaragua* judgment against the United States, after its unsuccessful withdrawal from the proceedings (§10.2), and a long overdue international judicial pronouncement regarding at least some notable issue in the Palestinian territories.

The utility of the ICJ includes the plaintiff State's ability to file a case with a view toward encouraging settlement when diplomatic negotiations are deadlocked. Nicaragua filed a transborder armed-conflict claim

against Honduras in 1988. Honduras responded by attacking the jurisdiction of the Court. The Court determined that it did have jurisdiction over this dispute. The parties then reached an out-of-court agreement, likely facilitated by the Honduran recognition that it could obtain more via settlement, than by a possibly all-or-nothing court judgment. Nicaragua then requested that this case be discontinued, after the two nations fully resolved their dispute diplomatically.

One must acknowledge that in many cases, the applicant State is seeking something more than the mere resolution of a dispute. Litigation in the ICJ provides the opportunity to alert the international community to the illegal conduct of another State.[68]

Success must be tempered by the realization that States tend not to submit their most sensitive disputes to the Court. The Court has played a tangible role in facilitating the continuous development of International Law as it ebbs and flows with the complex developments of State practice. Through no fault of its own, however, it has not contributed significantly to the preservation of world peace. It cannot realistically control disputes when the participants, who would be benefitted by its jurisprudence, fail to employ its resources.

Can the ICJ be fairly accused of failing? It was never vested with the independent power to require the participation of potential defendant States or render enforceable legal solutions. In the last analysis, the "compulsory" jurisdiction of the Court is solely dependent on State consent for its very existence. Some States have even deprived the Court of the otherwise universally exercised judicial power to determine its own jurisdiction to proceed. England's Sir Hersch Lauterpacht, one of the most prominent members of the Court, explained that "it would be an exaggeration to assert that the Court has proved to be a significant instrument for maintaining peace. The degree of achievement of this end by an international court, as indeed by any other court, is dependent upon the state of political integration of the society whose law it administers. But international society has in this respect, in the years following the two World Wars, fallen short of the expectation of those who in the Covenant of the League of Nations and in the Charter of the United Nations intended to create, through them, the basis of the future orderly development of the international community."[69]

Some commentators claim that the ICJ is the classic ivory tower, occupied by a group of theoreticians.

Its jurists supposedly generate pointless discourses that are unrelated to how States actually behave in the real world. These criticisms are misdirected. The United Nations was not intended to be the judge of any world governance system. It was not empowered to replace the primacy of national sovereignty. The ICJ was not intended to be a true world court, in the sense that it would be a primary tool for dispute resolution. The optional nature of the ICJ's so-called "compulsory" power to hear and determine cases arising under International Law is the Court's legal Achilles heel.

The United Nations has not replaced States as the core element in the superstructure of the international legal system. Its members never transferred the necessary jurisdictional powers to it, or its judicial organ, the ICJ or the necessary enforcement powers to the United Nations. States did not want to vest such organizational entities with the power to resolve international disputes, absent the full consent of the participating States on an almost case-by-case basis. The original fifty-one members of the United Nations had various reasons for limiting the power of this judicial body. The older and more developed powers perceived the potential change in the postwar composition of the community of nations as an unwelcome shift in the balance of power.

Nearly three-fourths of current UN members did not exist in 1945, when the other quarter created the organization. The newer States do not share the same political and economic perspectives of certain of the older, powerful, and more economically established members. Beginning in the 1960s, these "third world" States expressed the common view that they should become members of the international community on equal terms with the original UN members. From the perspective of new States, many aspects of modern International Law developed by Europeans incident to the 1648 Peace of Westphalia discouraged the third world's from achieving a comparable military and economic statute. One might argue that the ICJ, and the ability of the more powerful UN members to manipulate it, is just another facade for perpetuating the dominance of the older members of the international community. This perspective suggests that until international tribunals command a wider constituency, national courts provide a more realistic medium for judicial development of International Law. The ICJ cannot be a talismanic cure for international disputes, given the contemporary degree of political integration (or lack thereof) within the community of nations.

Many observers of the International Court of Justice exude a religious reverence for the Court, and a demonic disdain for States that have not used it. This perspective is also misleading. The ICJ is not like a national supreme court, typically exercising the powers to command the presence of adversaries and to enforce its court judgments. The States that sired the ICJ brought it into a community where there is no world government. They did not want the ICJ to function like their own national courts. If "weakness" is an appropriate characterization, why blame the child for the infirmity of its parents?

US Position   The United States has been rather reserved about the ICJ from the outset. In 1946, the US Senate debated whether the United States should accept the jurisdiction of the UN's new court. Senator Connally, Chairman of the Senate Foreign Relations Committee, expressed his concern that the United States would be effectively surrendering the fate of important national interests to the United Nations by generally accepting the Court's compulsory jurisdiction. In his words: "I am in favor of the United Nations, but I am also for the United States of America. I do not want to surrender the sovereignty or the prestige of the United States with respect to any question which may be merely domestic in character . . . [when the] best hope of the world lies in the survival of the United States with its concepts of democracy, liberty, freedom, and advancement under its [own] institutions."[70]

The United States nevertheless "accepted" the ICJ's jurisdiction in 1946, but not without reservations. The key US limitations, precluding the Court from hearing international cases, were those instances where those cases were: (a) entrusted to *other* tribunals by a distinct treaty provision; (b) essentially within the domestic jurisdiction of the United States, *as determined by the United States;* and (c) cases arising under a multilateral treaty—unless all parties to the dispute were also parties to the particular treaty *and* all agreed to the submission of the dispute to the ICJ.

After accepting the Court's jurisdiction, subject to the above limitations, the United States publicly supported an increased use of the ICJ. In 1974, the US Senate asked the US president to consider the feasibility of increasing the nation's participation in the ICJ. In 1977, the resulting US Department of State study concluded that the "underlying presumption of this Senate Resolution is that it is desirable to widen access to the International Court of Justice in order to increase its activity, use and contributions to the development of international law. As a general proposition, the Department of State strongly endorses that presumption."[71]

In the 1980s, the pendulum reversed course. The United States began to withdraw from various organs of the United Nations, as well as refusing to pay its assessed share of UN dues (§3.3). In 1984, the United States refused to participate in Nicaragua's suit against the United States, which claimed that the US Central Intelligence Agency had arranged the mining of key Nicaraguan harbors. The United States withdrew its acceptance of the Court's jurisdiction—virtually on the eve of the filing of the case by Nicaragua. In its 1946 declaration accepting the jurisdiction of the ICJ, the United States had promised a minimum of six months' notice for any withdrawal. US Secretary of State George Schultz nevertheless stated that the immediate withdrawal from any case involving any Central American State was necessary "to foster the continuing regional dispute settlement process which seeks a negotiated solution to the interrelated political, economic, and security problems of Central America." Although the United States could not *legally* withdraw without giving six month's notice, the Court proceeded with the case and entered a judgment against the United States.[72]

A sharp debate arose regarding both the legality and political propriety of the US withdrawal. George Mason University (Virginia) Professor Stuart Malawer made the following observation in opposition to the US withdrawal from this case:

> The World Court [judges] in absolutely astonishing majorities rejected the American arguments concerning the lack of jurisdiction and inadmissibility of Nicaragua's claim against it. Reading the recent court decision, one must wonder how anyone ever believed the [Court's] decision could have been otherwise. Why is it that the United States, the country which has championed international law in foreign affairs and the development of the World Court, has gotten itself into such an embarrassing position, and is now on the verge of being branded an outlaw state, when the transgressions of so many others are so great? My answer is simple. The legal advice given by the lawyers in the State Department must have been terrible.[73]

Although scholars may debate the legality of the US withdrawal, one conclusion is inescapable. The United States did not comply with its reservation promising to give six month's notice of its intent to withdraw its acceptance of the Court's compulsory jurisdiction. Then in 1985, the United States terminated its *general* acceptance (1946) of ICJ compulsory jurisdiction. The US position was that, of the five permanent members of the UN Security Council, only the United States and the United Kingdom had previously accepted the Court's compulsory jurisdiction (albeit in rather limited circumstances). The United States had never been able to bring a case against another State, while being sued there three times. Therefore, the US presidential administration publicly "blamed" Nicaragua, Cuba, and the former Soviet Union for using the Court's processes as a political weapon in the Cold War.

The last indication of the US posture on the Court can be gleaned from the 1993 Final Report of the United States Commission on Improving the Effectiveness of the United Nations. This special government commission was established by the US Congress under the Foreign Relations Authorization Act of 1988. It studied the role of the United Nations and its place in US foreign policy. In the Findings and Recommendations, this Commission (consisting of House members and other special appointees) determined that the United States should take the lead in advocating wider acceptance of the compulsory jurisdiction of the Court. The Commission recommended as follows: "that, to set a standard of leadership, the US consider reaccepting the compulsory jurisdiction of the Court. . . ."[74] As to the Court's *advisory* jurisdiction, the Commission also recommended a gradual expansion of this facet of the ICJ's competence. Specifically, *other* States were thus encouraged to refer questions of International Law from their national courts to the ICJ.

◆ 9.5 INTERNATIONAL CRIMINAL COURTS

INTRODUCTION

Victors often punish the vanquished. In earlier eras, the motivation was revenge. If the twenty-first century experience with an International Criminal Court (ICC) is an accurate barometer, the contemporary motivation is to punish those guilty of outrageous human rights violations. The most famous criminal tribunal to date has been the post–World War II "Nuremberg Trial" of Nazi Germany's notorious war criminals. The 1990s dabbling with a new version yielded two temporary alternatives: the currently functioning *ad hoc* tribunals for crimes occurring in the former Yugoslavia and Rwanda. This section of the textbook presents a critical question: whether the "permanent" ICC will effectively transform dream to reality.

In a 1997 Red Cross plea for establishing a permanent ICC: "The topic under discussion today is particularly important for the ICRC [International Committee of the Red Cross]. Through its activities, the ICRC witnesses the commission of atrocities on a wide scale, including war crimes, which are all too often left unpunished. This situation simply cannot continue, and we firmly believe that the international community must ensure that those responsible are made accountable for their acts. Although States already have a duty to prosecute, and also to undertake all the necessary steps to adapt their national legislation and to provide effective penal sanctions, today's reality shows that this duty is not fulfilled. It is in this context that the establishment of an international criminal court is so important to change this pattern of impunity."[75]

On the other hand, some commentators urged that altering the existing Statute of the existing ICJ would have been preferable. Rather than create a *new* criminal tribunal, to deal with the criminal prosecution of individuals, States could have changed the ICJ limitation which authorizes only States to be parties to its proceedings. As succinctly articulated by Florida International University's Professor Barbara Yarnold: "[T]he International Court of Justice is the best forum for the adjudication of state and international crimes, for several reasons. . . . Certainly, this recommendation that the International Court of Justice be given jurisdiction over international crimes [rather than leaving it to State jurisdiction] . . . will be opposed by those superpowers in the world community that historically have favored the use of force over the rule of law."[76] After studying these materials, you will be able to judge for yourself.

Background   The concept of a war crimes trial is not unique to the revered Nuremberg Trial. There are accounts of a war crimes trial in 405 BC near what is now Turkey; the trial of a European governor for his actions in 1427, when his troops raped and killed innocent

individuals; and the post–World War I trial of a submarine commander who torpedoed a British hospital ship and then sank its lifeboats. The League of Nations produced an international penal code and a Convention on the Establishment of the ICC (within the PCIJ). It was signed by Belgium, Bulgaria, Cuba, Czechoslovakia, France, Greece, Spain, Monaco, the Netherlands, Romania, Turkey, the USSR, and Yugoslavia. This treaty never entered into force, however, because of the lack of sufficient ratifications.[77]

In theory, the trial of "international" criminals is best accomplished by an international court—as opposed to a national court. The 1921 Leipzig trials of German nationals in Germany for war crimes against the Allies, plus the 1961 Israeli trial of Hitler's chief exterminator, Adolf Eichmann, are classic examples of the judicial dilemma associated with such national tribunals. In 1994, Ethiopia commenced war crimes trials against the leaders of its former Marxist dictatorship. After these leaders seized power in 1974, some 250,000 people were killed or died in forced relocation programs. In one 6-hour period during 1988, 2,500 civilians were killed by helicopter gunships and fighter planes. It was arguably difficult for those respective judicial bodies to exercise impartiality, which is the hallmark of an international tribunal. As stated in a prominent study of the future of international courts:

The existence of international crimes and the recognition of individual responsibility for such crimes logically suggests that there should be an international tribunal with power to try individuals for the commission of international crimes. It is just as important to have an international criminal court to administer international criminal law as it is to have national criminal courts to administer national criminal law. For however objective and impartial national courts in fact may be, because they are courts of particular states there will inevitably be a suspicion of bias when a national court tries an international criminal. . . .

[T]rying international criminals before municipal courts is haphazard, unjust and militates against the development of a universal criminal law. The administration of international criminal law will only become systematic, just and universal when the organ of its administration is a permanent international criminal court.[78]

Between 1946 and 1993 (the dates of establishment of the Nuremberg and Bosnia-oriented tribunal for crimes in the former Yugoslavia), there were many calls for the creation of the second exclusively *criminal* international tribunal to try various types of "international" crimes. These crimes would serve as a basis for universal jurisdiction (§5.2) over war crimes, terrorism, and hijacking. Building on the 1934 League of Nations draft Convention for the Creation of an ICC, an unofficial nongovernmental organization attempted to assert pressure on the community of nations to bring such a tribunal into existence. The organization, the Foundation for the Establishment of an ICC, conducted two drafting conferences in 1972. These gatherings were attended by experts from all over the world.[79] In 1986, the US Congress asked President Reagan to explore the possibility of international pressure being exerted to establish an ICC to deal with international terrorists.

In the aftermath of September 11, 2001, however, when the World Trade Centers and the Pentagon were struck by hijacked aircraft, the United States opted for a military response—rather than a judicial one.[80] That response should come as no surprise. Before 9-11, the US threatened the capture and prosecution of those responsible for: the first World Trade Center attack (1993); the subsequent bombing of the USS Cole in Yemen; and the bombing of various US installations in other countries.

Securing the extradition of criminals who commit *universal* crimes has been a major obstacle to bringing them to justice. One would think that an asylum-granting State would be in an awkward position, if it refused to yield such an offender to an international criminal tribunal. But that is no more awkward than traditional reliance on the "political offense" exception contained in numerous extradition treaties (§5.3). This form of political end-run became the object of ridicule, after the rash 1970s aircraft hijackings in the Middle East. Branding terrorist acts as "political" crimes, rather than as common (or universal) crimes has often been an extradition stumbling block because it is a convenient basis for refusing to extradite individuals and conduct that the holding State clandestinely supports.[81] Libya ignored international pressure for more than a decade after the 1988 *Pan Am 103* bombing. In 1992, the UN Secretary-General thus appointed a Commission of Experts to document violations of humanitarian law (§10.6 Laws of War) in the former Yugoslavia, preceding the UN's establishment of the Yugoslavian tribunal in 1993.

Given the debate about whether national or international tribunals should be trying international criminals, there has always been the underlying question about whether there is actually an "international criminal law,"[82] or just international crimes that fall within the jurisdiction of either national courts or the *ad hoc,* limited-purpose tribunals established by the UN Security Council in the mid-1990s (Yugoslavia and Rwanda). They will be closed in the not-too-distant future, after they have tried the few aging individuals turned over for some very expensive prosecutions. The trial of Slobodan Milosevic began in 2002. It was predicted that his trial would take six years to complete. The permanent ICC commenced its prosecutorial functions in 2005. If it remains permanently open and effective, it might then become the international "point person" in the progressive development of International Criminal Law.[83]

NUREMBERG AND TOKYO TRIBUNALS

The eleven-nation International Military Tribunal of the Far East, tried twenty-five Japanese defendants for war crimes. All were found guilty. Seven were sentenced to death. The most famous tribunal, however, was the four-nation body established by the Nuremberg Charter. The United States, Great Britain, France, and the former Soviet Union created the Nuremberg Tribunal by international agreement. The fundamental objective was to try Nazi "war criminals whose offenses have no particular geographical location whether they be accused individually or in their capacity as members of [military] organizations" of the German government.[84] It was hoped that those limited-purpose tribunals would deter future war crimes by heads of State and military leaders.

The constituting treaty, known as the Nuremberg Charter, contained what the Allied powers perceived as a novel method for deterring the national misuse of force. Germany's key planners were thus tried, and imprisoned or executed, for the various crimes defined in the case below. The following excerpt from the resulting Nuremberg Judgment analyzes the role that International Law played in assessing the tactics planned and executed by German leaders during World War II:

Nuremberg Trial Proceedings (1946)

CHARTER OF THE INTERNATIONAL
MILITARY TRIBUNAL
INDICTMENT OF THE DEFENDANTS
WITNESS EXAMINATION (OTTO OHLENDORF)
JUDGMENT OF THE INTERNATIONAL
MILITARY TRIBUNAL
22 INTERNATIONAL MILITARY TRIBUNAL:
TRIAL OF THE MAJOR WAR CRIMINALS 411 (1948)
Go to course Web page at
<http://home.att.net/~slomansonb/txtcsesite.html>
Under Chapter Ten, click Nuremberg Trial.

The principles enshrined in the Nuremberg Judgment were later approved by the UN General Assembly. In 1946, shortly after the Judgment was published, the Assembly adopted Resolution 95(1) to express its sentiment that the "Nuremberg principle" had been incorporated into International Law. The UN General Assembly's International Law Commission completed its restatement of the Principles of International Law Recognized in the Charter of the Nürnberg Tribunal in 1950.[85]

Under this principle, a State and its agents who wage an aggressive war commit the supreme international crime. It is punishable by any nation able to bring the perpetrators to justice. The responsible leaders thereby incur criminal responsibility arising directly under International Law for their conduct, which makes them liable for this crime. The validity under the internal laws of Germany did *not* provide them with a defense, although it was considered as a mitigating factor in their sentencing. They were tried and punished for their participation as agents of the State in its unlawful use of force against other States. As articulated by the judges at Nuremberg, "[C]rimes against international law are committed by men, not by abstract entities, and only by punishing individuals who commit such crimes can the provisions of international law be enforced."

Neither the Nuremberg principles, nor the ensuing UN resolution, had a significant impact on subsequent decisions to use or refrain from using force. This was the last time that victorious nations ever established a tribunal to try agents of a defeated nation for waging war.

(The 1993 UN Yugoslavian and subsequent Rwandan tribunals, discussed below, do not involve victors imposing such jurisprudence on the vanquished. They were the product of UN Security Council resolutions.) In 1974, the University of Michigan's renowned Professor William Bishop expressed his frustration with this predicament. He thus posed the following question:

> What then, has . . . international law done for the welfare of humanity since its promulgation? The answer is clear and simple: nothing. Since Nuremberg, there have been at least eighty or ninety wars (some calculators exclude armed invasions of neighbors too weak to attempt resistance), some of them on a very large scale. The list includes the Korean War, the Suez invasion [by France and Great Britain] of 1956, . . . the four Arab-Israeli wars, the Vietnam wars (including the accompanying fighting in Laos and Cambodia), and the invasion of Czechoslovakia by the Soviet Union and its myrmidons. In none of these cases, nor in any other, was an aggressor arrested and brought to the bar of international justice, and none is likely to be. For all the good it has done, the doctrine that aggressive war is a crime might as well be relegated to the divinity schools.[86]

For many years, DePaul University (Chicago) Professor M.C. Bassiouni and Benjamin Ferencz of New York, kept the vision of a permanent ICC from fading into obscurity. Their exhaustive studies served as models for the UN's creation of the current *ad hoc* tribunals for atrocities committed in the former Yugoslavia and Rwanda.[87] Ultimately, the UN Security Council employed its Chapter VII powers for this contribution to the continuing UN role in the preservation of human rights. However jubilant international lawyers might be about this development, one should not lose sight of the questionable financial commitment of the international community to these tribunals. Specifically, "from this perspective, financing is the most delicate and revealing issue. . . . It has been reported that the Fifth Committee of the General Assembly has been extremely reluctant in appropriating the necessary funds for investigative purposes."[88]

AD HOC INTERNATIONAL CRIMINAL TRIBUNALS [89]

Yugoslavia   Unlike the Allied Powers treaty arrangement establishing the Nuremberg and Tokyo tribunals, the current Yugoslavian and Rwandan ICCs were established by UN Security Council Resolutions. In 1993, the first of the two specialized tribunals was the International Criminal Tribunal for the Prosecution of Persons Responsible for Serious Violations of International Humanitarian Law Committed in the Former Yugoslavia since 1991 (ICTY). As explained in the resolution creating this court, the Security Council "[e]xpressing once again, its grave alarm at continuing reports of widespread and flagrant violations of international humanitarian law occurring within the territory of the former Yugoslavia . . . including reports of mass killings, massive, organized and systematic detention and rape of women, and the continuance of the practice of ethnic cleansing . . . Decides hereby to establish an international tribunal for the sole purpose of prosecuting [the] persons [who are] responsible. . . ."[90]

This court has brought individuals to justice who committed major atrocities in Bosnia from 1991 to 1995 (from the breakup of the former Yugoslavia through the restoration of peace). Its seat is in The Hague. Its most prominent case has been the trial of the former president of the former Yugoslavia, Slobodan Milosevic.[91] It is notable because this was the first trial of a head of State by an international tribunal.

The ICTY consists of trial chambers and an appellate chamber. The executive organs include a registry for the court and a prosecutor's office. In September 1993, the UN General Assembly elected eleven judges to serve four-year terms from a slate of candidates nominated by the UN Security Council. The judges are professors and lawyers from various nations. The first president of the International Tribunal (and its appellate chamber) was from Italy. The vice-president was from Costa Rica. A female judge from the United States was the first president of one of the two trial chambers. This choice was particularly significant because of the alleged mass rapes of Muslim women by Serbian soldiers as part of an ethnic-cleansing plan.[92] A Nigerian was the first president of the other trial chamber.

The ICTY applies the rules of international humanitarian law applicable to armed conflict. These are the 1949 Geneva Convention for the Protection of War Victims, the 1948 Genocide Convention, the crimes against humanity formulation contained in the above 1946 Nuremberg Judgment, and the 1907 Hague Convention on the Laws and Customs of War on Land (§10.6). Prosecution focuses on crimes including murder, rape, torture, ethnic cleansing, and other human rights violations.[93] Four countries—Finland, Italy,

Norway, and Sweden—agreed with the ICTY to provide cells for those serving prison terms.[94]

Since its inauguration, the ICTY has rendered a number of spectacular decisions in the sense of a contemporary implementation of the Nuremberg principles. One comparative advantage is that the ICTY is an impartial tribunal not composed of victors' judges. Prominent examples of its work product include:

◆ *Rape*—sexual violence and enslavement as a war crime, and a crime against humanity;
◆ *Genocide*—mass extinction of 7,800 Muslims by Serbian forces in seven days and first ever judicial condemnation of an "ethnic cleansing" policy; and
◆ *International humanitarian law*—killings, beatings, and sexual mutilation (see *Tadic* later).[95]

The tribunal's first verdict in 1997 was possibly its most significant because of the legal precedents it established for subsequent prosecutions:

Prosecutor v. Dusko Tadic aka "Dule"

INTERNATIONAL TRIBUNAL FOR THE PROSECUTION OF PERSONS RESPONSIBLE FOR SERIOUS VIOLATIONS OF INTERNATIONAL HUMANITARIAN LAW COMMITTED IN THE TERRITORY OF FORMER YUGOSLAVIA SINCE 1991 (ICTY)

Case No. IT-94-1-T, 7 (May 1997)

Go to course Web page at
<http://home.att.net/~slomansonb/txtcsesite.html>.
Under Chapter Nine, click Tadic Case.

In 2004, its Appeals Chamber delivered its judgment in the Srebrenica case. In 1995, 7,800 Muslim men and boys were slaughtered by Bosnian Serb forces commanded by Radislav Krstic. This event took only three days, and was the worst mass murder in Europe since World War II. The appellate panel found that the evidence was not conclusive that Krstic personally harbored genocidal intent, although he was aware of that specific intent on the part of his Drina Corps personnel such as Tadic. His sentence for genocide as reduced to aiding and abetting genocide. In mitigation, he had just assumed command, was not present, and had promulgated written orders to treat Muslims humanely.[96]

Rwanda   In the year after the UN Security Council's establishment of the ICTY (1993), the Council established the International Criminal Tribunal for the Persons Responsible for Genocide and Other Serious Violations of International Humanitarian Law Committed in the Territory of Rwanda and Rwandan Citizens Responsible for Genocide and Other Such Violations Committed in the Territory of Neighbouring States between 1 January 1994 and 31 December 1994 (ICTR) in Arusha, Tanzania. This tribunal has tried and convicted various individuals, including a mayor and the former premier of Rwanda (life terms) for their roles in the genocidal massacre (including rape and other crimes) of some one-half million Tutsis by the ruling Hutu majority government in 1994.[97]

This court was also established by the UN Security Council: "having received the request of the Government of Rwanda, to establish an international tribunal for the sole purpose of prosecuting persons responsible for genocide and other serious violations of international humanitarian law committed in the territory of Rwanda and Rwandan citizens responsible for genocide and other such violations committed in the territory of neighbouring States, . . . and to this end to adopt the Statute of the International Criminal Tribunal for Rwanda annexed hereto. . . ."[98]

The Security Council opted against a Rwandan location on a variety of grounds including security risks, lack of appropriate infrastructure, and perceptions of judicial partiality normally associated with conducting trials in the very nation where the atrocities occurred. Rwanda did not support establishment of this tribunal, partially because it was outside Rwanda. In 1998, one of six judges at the Tribunal stepped down, claiming mismanagement and a lack of leadership. The UN Secretary-General had previously fired the administrative head of the tribunal. Rwanda suspended cooperation with the ICTR because: (1) a former Foreign Ministry official was released because he was held too long, in violation of the Court's speedy trial guarantee, in Arusha, Tanzania—the seat of the Tribunal; and (2) Rwanda has criticized the Court's slow pace and lack of a death penalty. This development restricted the tribunal's genocide and human rights investigations.[99]

In the Rwandan premier's case, the ICTR drew upon the Appellate Tribunal's analysis contained in the ICTY's above *Tadic* case. The ICTR judges were ruling on a decisive defense motion, which unsuccessfully challenged the court's jurisdiction to hear and determine such cases. This phase, of this particular proceeding, effectively illustrated that the Security Council had properly invested the *ad hoc* Rwandan court with the express power to prosecute.[100] Its analysis also paved the way for drafting a permanent ICC treaty, pursuant to the 1998 Rome Conference (below).

There were five principle objections, all rejected by the ICTR, which provide insight about future issues which may arise, now that the permanent ICC treaty has entered into force. First, Rwanda's State sovereignty had been allegedly violated because the ICTR was not created by a treaty ratified by Rwanda. One defect with this allegation was that Rwanda had requested establishment of an *ad hoc* ICC to adjudicate cases involving the 1994 genocide occurring within its borders. And, its rationale for not approving the final ICTR draft statute did *not* raise sovereign objections. Also, Article 25 of the UN Charter requires States to comply with Security Council decisions. Should the permanent ICC not materialize, or not function as anticipated, it is arguable like defenses in any future *ad hoc* tribunal would likewise be denied. Should the State where the atrocities occur not request formation of such an *ad hoc* tribunal (as for Rwanda), one might expect a UN Charter Article 2.7 defense—that the UN cannot interfere in matters which that State considers as falling exclusively within its domestic adjudicatory power.

Second, the defense asserted that the UN Security Council exceeded its authority when it relied on its "Chapter VII" powers to create this tribunal. The Rwandan genocide was allegedly *not* a threat to international peace. This argument presented the view that the UN Charter never contemplated formation of such a judicial tribunal to preserve peace. However, the Rwandan genocide (and other violations of international human rights) inherently supported the Council's authority to prevent such threats to peace—then (ICTR), and in the future (permanent ICC).

Third, the former Rwandan premier's defense team challenged the primacy of the international tribunal vis-à-vis the national courts of Rwanda. "Primacy" in ICTY proceedings is expressed in Article 9(2) of the ICTY Statute, whereby it "shall have primacy over national courts. . . . [ICTY] may formally request national courts to defer to the competence of the International Tribunal. . . ." The Trial Chamber of the ICTR acknowledged the applicability of the general principle that persons accused of crimes should retain their right to be tried by the customary domestic court, as opposed to a politically founded *ad hoc* tribunal which might fail to provide impartial justice. The Appellate Chamber decision in the ICTY's *Tadic* case led to the ICTR's assessment, however, that its establishment under the Security Council's Chapter VII powers enabled the ICTR to prosecute a Rwandan citizen—even in the absence of Rwandan consent.[101]

Fourth, the defense argued that the UN Charter did not encompass the possibility that a UN-based tribunal could confer jurisdiction over individuals, as opposed to States (see §9.4, regarding only States being parties to contentious ICJ cases). Also, the Council had never done so in the past, when clear violations of human rights laws had occurred. The Court responded that by establishing the ICTR (and ICTY), the Security Council had effectively extended international criminal responsibility directly to individuals for their violations of international humanitarian law. This was another instance where the Nuremberg Principles provided a precedent for such actions, although that case was tried by the four Allied Powers (independently of the United Nations).

Finally, the defense raised the other potentially recurring issue: that the ICTR is not an impartial entity, because of its establishment by a political entity (Security Council). However, the Tribunal's judges are not accountable to the Council. Also, the ICTR's Statute explicitly requires a fair trial. Ironically, the defense did not mention the *advantage* of being tried by the ICTR, rather than in the national courts of Rwanda—where the death penalty not only applies, but has been applied to a number of defendants convicted of like crimes. In April 1998, despite pleas for clemency by Pope John Paul II, twenty-two men were tied to stakes and shot. Large crowds witnessed this mass execution. In some instances, the convicts had no lawyers, and no witnesses were called in their defense in the national proceedings.[102]

The ICTR's *Radio Machete* case provides excellent insight into the actual operations of the ICTR. The activities giving rise to this case are vividly depicted in the 2005 movie *Hotel Rwanda*:

The Prosecutor
v.
Ferdinand Nahimana,
Jean-Bosco Barayagwiza
& Hassan Ngeze
INTERNATIONAL CRIMINAL
TRIBUNAL FOR RWANDA
TRIAL CHAMBER I
Case No. ICTR-99-52-T (2003)
<http://www.ictr.org/default.htm>
Go to course Web page at
<http://home.att.net/~slomansonb/txtcsesite.html>.
Under Chapter Nine, click Radio Machete.

The ICTR experience has received mixed reviews. As stated by two of the leading commentators on the proceedings of the ICTR (and ICTY):

The establishment of the Rwanda Tribunal constitutes one of the most important milestones in the history of international criminal law. The significance of this event becomes clear only when it is viewed in its historical context, taking into account the difficulties encountered in previous efforts to create ad hoc international criminal tribunals and in the continuing efforts to create a permanent international criminal court.

. . .

While some of the causes of the delay were perhaps unavoidable, the major cause of the delay resulted from the need to build an entire international institution from the ground up. . . . Yet the delay could have been avoided if there had existed a permanent international criminal court. . . . Since the establishment of the Rwanda Tribunal, the members of the Security Council have experienced . . . "tribunal fatigue." . . . Notwithstanding a host of other atrocities . . . at least one permanent member of the Security Council [possessing the right of veto] "China" has openly expressed concern about using the Yugoslavia and Rwanda Tribunals as precedent for the creation of other *ad hoc* [by country or by incident] criminal tribunals. Moreover, the expense of establishing ad hoc tribunals, each with its own staff and facilities, is simply seen as too much for an organization [UN] whose budget is already stretched too thin. Thus, the requests by Burundi and Cambodia to establish similar tribunals to address the atrocities committed in those countries have not received a favorable response by the Security Council to date.[103]

Similar expense and time delays were not avoided in the Netherlands-based Lockerbie *Pan Am 103,* Tokyo's *Women's International War Crimes Tribunal* judgments, or the Sierra Leone tribunal.[104]

Hybrid Sierra Leone Tribunal   In August 2000, UN Security Council Resolution 1315 requested the Secretary-General to negotiate with the government of Sierra Leone to create a "Special Court" for atrocities in Sierra Leone. Since 2002, eleven judges have been sworn in. Two are from Sierra Leone. Most were chosen by the UN Secretary-General. The others were chosen by Sierra Leone's government. This is the first time that a court was established, based on a treaty between the UN and a national government—unlike the mentioned *ad hoc* tribunals established by the UN Security Council. Like the ICTY and ICTR, the UN-Special Court for Sierra Leone may request that a national court in Sierra Leone transfer a particular case to the Special Court. In contrast, the permanent International Criminal Court (ICC) is generally expected to yield to national court prosecutions.

Unlike the other internationally created criminal courts, the Sierra Leone court is located in the country where the alleged crimes occurred. This process thus facilitates more timely access to evidence and less costly proceedings. It should also promote local media coverage, whereby the victims can more clearly see the results—unlike the other criminal courts located well beyond the borders of where atrocities occurred. The permanent court is authorized to convene in locations other than in The Hague. This global court could occasionally convene in Sierra Leone, a nation that has ratified the ICC Statute, and thus a potential venue for African ICC prosecutions. (Tanzania's *ad hoc* ICTR has a limited mandate, and is expected to conclude its work within the next decade).

The Special Court is designed to prosecute for crimes committed in Sierra Leone *after* November 30, 1996 (as opposed to the conflict's 1991 commencement). Its work is supposed to be completed by 2007. This limitation takes into account the period during which the most heinous crimes were committed and the potential judicial workload. Its special emphasis is gender-related crimes. As related by its Chief Investigator: "let me mention . . . [something] that makes this special tribunal unique. Gender crimes will be emphasized as a war crime and will be pursued from the outset. . . . We are making gender crimes a top priority . . . because rape, and sexual assault used as a tool of war needs to be prosecuted."[105]

This court's key task is the potential prosecution of former Liberian President Charles Taylor. In May 2004, the Appeals Chamber determined that his serious "international crimes" in Sierra Leone included responsibility for terrorizing the civilian population of Sierra Leone, sexual and physical violence, use of child soldiers, forced labor, and attacks on peacekeepers and humanitarian assistance workers.[106] This prosecution is especially important because of its unwavering pursuit of this former head of State. It is thus lending its support to the practice of the UN ad hoc tribunals and the ICC. There, heads of State are no longer insulated from international prosecution for conduct unbecoming a national leader.

There have been criticisms of the companion, but distinct, Truth and Reconciliation Commission (TRC) process. The Sierra Leone Statute does not mention the TRC. Nor do Special Court prosecutors use information obtained from TRC hearings in this court's prosecutions. Objectors have expressed like concerns about perpetrators escaping justice in similar proceedings in South Africa, Afghanistan, and Latin America.[107] The tradeoff is obtaining public disclosure by perpetrators, and thus more detail about who did what to whom. But one must acknowledge the extraordinary number of child combatants employed in Sierra Leone since 1991.

Lack of funding is another problem. As noted in the UN Secretary-General's Report on the Special Court, it will be realistically financed only via assessed contributions from UN member nations. That will effectively transform the Sierra Leone Special Court from a treaty-based to UN-based court. One may expect donor fatigue in a system based on voluntary donations, especially in view of the UN's problem with threats to cut payments of its already limited resources; e.g., the threatened US 50 percent cut in dues payments presented in text §3.3.[108]

PERMANENT ICC[109]

Evolution In July 1998, representatives of approximately 150 UN members gathered in Rome to draft the first global ICC Statute.[110] One hundred twenty voted in favor of establishing this permanent ICC; twenty countries abstained; and seven opposed. At the UN's 2000 Millennium Summit, national leaders supported the evolution of this tribunal in their following resolution: "We resolve, therefore . . . [t]o ensure the implementation, by States Parties, of treaties in areas such as arms control and disarmament, and of international humanitarian law and human rights law, and call upon all States to consider signing and ratifying the Rome Statute of the International Criminal Court."[111]

The treaty creating the ICC entered into force in July 2002. There are now 100 State Parties. In March 2005, the Iraqi Interim Government nullified a previous decree, whereby Iraq would have acceded to the ICC treaty. On February 15, 2005 the Council of Ministers of Iraq's Interim government issued Order Number 20, announcing Iraq's decision to accede to the Rome Statute. The Council decided to join the Court because the provisions of the Rome Statute embody the highest values shared by all of humanity and also because most of its provisions can be found in existing international treaties. But unlike Afghanistan, which ratified the ICC treaty, Iraq has yet to sign it.[112]

This global criminal court, located in The Hague, is the contemporary Nuremberg Tribunal. Its task is to prosecute individuals charged with genocide, crimes against humanity, and war crimes.[113] If nations negotiate to produce a treaty definition of "aggression," the ICC prosecutor will be empowered to also charge individuals with crimes of aggression.

Unlike the Nuremberg and Tokyo tribunals, there is no death penalty. Rather than dealing with such crimes on an *ad hoc* basis—as have the Yugoslavian and Rwandan Tribunals established by UN Security Council vote—this State treaty-based ICC will be a permanent fixture on the international landscape. Ironically, the use of poison gas and exploding bullets are punishable, but not the use of nuclear weapons, land mines, or chemical weapons. As discussed in §8.2 of this book, however, many compromises are often necessary to achieve broad participation in a multilateral treaty.

The ICC will not act unless the nation where the alleged crimes occurred either waives local prosecution, or refuses to extradite in cases where the duty to prosecute

is crystal clear. The latter option is triggered by a UN Security Council resolution, which requires the blessing of the five permanent members of the Security Council, but not necessarily the blessing of the country involved. In March 2005, the Security Council made its first reference to the ICC. It referred a list of fifty-one government officials and other Sudanese citizens for potential prosecution in the ICC—for their alleged complicity in various atrocities in Sudan's remote Darfur region.[114]

Sudan is not a party to the ICC. Two days after the UNSC referred Sudan to the ICC, Sudanese President Omar Bashir vowed to defy the UN vote. He stated that "We will never give up any Sudanese national for trial outside Sudan." The potential defendants include senior government and army officials, and some rebel and commanders. The Sudan then created its own criminal court to try those accused of war crimes. The ICC had already opened its criminal investigation. Under Article 17 of the Court's Statue, the ICC may declare a case inadmissible for prosecution when the same matter "is being investigated or prosecuted by a State which has jurisdiction . . . unless the State . . . is unwilling or unable genuinely to carry out the investigation or prosecution." Article 18 of the Court's Statute, in turn, allows the ICC Prosecutor to challenge the genuineness of the State proceedings.

In December 2005, the Chief ICC prosecutor briefed the UN Security Council on the respective local and international Darfur investigations. He focused on the ICC's statute in his assessment of whether the ICC should defer to the related proceeding in The Sudan. In his telling comment, he characterized the United Nations investigation as being "specific to the cases selected for prosecution, not the state of the Sudanese justice system as a whole." One may thus anticipate that the ICC will retain its jurisdiction to pursue this particular case—notwithstanding the Sudanese government's attempt to trump the ICC's process with its own proceeding.

The large nation objections include Articles 17 and 20, which authorize the ICC to ignore national rules providing for amnesty and other limitations on its jurisdiction. In January 1999, the French Constitutional Council ruled—in a case brought by France's president and prime minister—that the French Constitution would have to be amended before France could ratify the ICC Statute. Article 27 waives immunity from any criminal responsibility of a head of State or government or members of a ratifying government and parliament. The Council held that this treaty provision would contradict the constitutional provisions regarding the special responsibility of State officials. In terms of the UN Security Council's "Permanent 5," France's ratification was followed by the United Kingdom.[115] While Russia signed this treaty, China and the United States publicly dissented (including President Bush's unsigning the ICC treaty).

US Position on ICC   The US delegation participated extensively in the preparatory negotiations which began in 1995. President Clinton frequently spoke in favor of the ICC and appointed a first-ever Ambassador at Large for War Crimes Issues to focus the administration's efforts. Clinton commented, upon the US signing (but not ratifying) the ICC treaty: "The United States has a long history of commitment to the principle of accountability, from our involvement in the Nuremberg Tribunals that brought Nazi war criminals to justice to our leadership in the effort to establish the international criminal tribunal for the former Yugoslavia and Rwanda. Our action today sustains that tradition of moral leadership."

The US position drastically changed during the ensuing Bush Administration. The United States is now a fierce dissenter—although it nurtured the creation of the previously mentioned Nuremberg, Tokyo, Rwanda, and Yugoslavian international tribunals. Although President Clinton signed the ICC treaty on behalf of the United States, President Bush "unsigned" it, early in his first term. He is dead set against the ICC prosecution of any US citizen. The president's stated fear is that the ICC will be used for political prosecutions against US soldiers, US government officials, and any other American who might be charged with the above international crimes. The secretary of state has thus negotiated bilateral Article 98 treaties with as many nations as possible. That provision of the ICC treaty authorizes exemption from extradition to the ICC, between any nations that so agree.

The United States successfully lobbied the UN Security Council, on two ICC anniversary occasions, to exempt its citizens/soldiers from ICC prosecutions. This band-aid approach provided wiggle room to continue negotiating numerous bilateral Article 98 treaties. These are designed to achieve essentially the same result as the two earlier SC moratoria, but on a country-by-country basis. Some commentators question whether either tactic

remains justified, in the aftermath of the Iraq Abu Grahib Prison scandal (§10.6).[116]

The US Congress supports this approach. One month after the ICC treaty entered into force, Congress passed the so-called Hague Invasion Act to protect the US military. The president is thereby authorized to use all means necessary to facilitate the release of any person who is being detained by, or on behalf of, the ICC. The key provisions of this federal law, known as the American Servicemembers' Protection Act of 2000, are as follows:

. . . no United States Court, and no agency or entity of any State or local government, including any court, may cooperate with the International Criminal Court in response to a request for cooperation submitted by the International Criminal Court pursuant to the Rome Statute.

. . . no agency . . . may extradite any person from the United States to the International Criminal Court. . . .

Members of the Armed Forces of the United States may not participate in any [UN] peacekeeping operation . . . unless the President has submitted to the appropriate congressional committees a certification . . . with respect to such operation.

. . . no United States military assistance may be provided to the government of a country that is a party to the International Criminal Court.

The President may . . . waive the [above] prohibition . . . with respect to a particular country if he determines . . . that it is important to the national interest of the United States to waive such prohibition.

The President may [also] . . . waive the [above] prohibition . . . if he determines and reports to the appropriate congressional committees that such country has entered into an agreement with the United States pursuant to Article 98 of the Rome Statute preventing the International Criminal court from proceeding against United States personnel present in such country.

The President is authorized to use all means necessary and appropriate to bring about the release of any person [US citizen] . . . who is being detained or imprisoned by, on behalf of, or at the request of the International Criminal Court.

Nothing in this subchapter shall prohibit the United States from rendering assistance to international efforts to bring to justice Saddam Hussein, Slobodan Milosovic, Osama bin Laden, other members of Al Queda, leaders of Islamic Jihad, and other foreign nationals accused of genocide, war crimes or crimes against humanity.

The prominent *New York Times* liberal commentator, Nicholas Kristof, characterized this legislative policy as one which "undermines our friends and confirms every prejudice that people abroad have about Americans."[117]

Exempting US citizens from prosecution in the ICC does not mean absolution from conduct governed by international treaties such as the Geneva Conventions. This only means no prosecution by the ICC, as opposed to other forums. US Army Sgt. Lyndie England, who worked at Iraq's Abu Ghraib prison, is one US citizen who deservedly knows this all too well.

The United States has negotiated with most countries of the world, seeking Article 98 exemptions for the United States from ICC proceedings. As of Fall 2005, ninety-nine countries had agreed to such exemption treaties. Forty-five countries had publicly refused to sign an exemption agreement with the United States. China refused, on the basis of US abuses related to the Abu Ghraib prison scandal in Iraq (§10.6). The United States has also withdrawn its soldiers from some UN peace-keeping operations as well. If a head of State can be prosecuted, UN peacekeepers likewise lack immunity from prosecution.

The United States is using economic pressure to secure these agreements. Many commentators have criticized the United States for this. But the balance sheet must take account of similar circumstances whereby US financial backing has prompted prosecutions in other international tribunals, as evinced by the last statutory provision above regarding specific individuals and groups. Belgrade received sizeable economic incentives, for example, to entice Serbia to turn over former President Slobodan Milosevic for trial in the International Criminal Tribunal for the Former Yugoslavia. The United States also offered a $5,000,000 reward each, for information leading to the extradition of the two individuals (Karadzic and Mladic) who were indicted by the ICTY regarding the Srebrenica, Bosnia, massacre of 1995. The United States has made major financial and political contributions to this, and to the UN's Rwanda tribunal.

Responses & Limitations   The Rome Treaty contains a number of procedural safeguards designed to allow such prosecutions only in the most egregious of circumstances. A case is inadmissible, if it is "not of sufficient gravity to justify further action by the Court."

Under the Article 124 "transitional clause," a State—upon becoming a party to the Statute—may declare that, for a period of seven years, it does not accept the jurisdiction of the Court over war crimes committed by its nationals or in its territory.

While the Rome Treaty entered into force, its "crime of aggression" provision did not. In the early negotiations, various nations raised the issue that the time had come to define this crime. But there were other priorities.[118] Until the Rome Treaty's "crime of aggression" is addressed and then defined by treaty, this potential basis for prosecutorial charging is completely out of the question. While aggression was ever so briefly defined by a 1974 UN General Assembly Resolution regarding State conduct,[119] the Rome Statute is a State-based treaty geared toward individual prosecutions. A sufficiently specific and prosecutable definition of aggression was left open to a future protocol.

As you will recall from Chapter 8 on multilateral treaty formation, one must acknowledge that there is a price to be paid for obtaining the support of many diverse nations. The Rome Treaty is fraught with further compromises which allow States or the Security Council to delay investigations or delay prosecutions. An ICC investigation, for example, may be commenced only by one of three triggering mechanisms: a Security Council resolution, the request of a State party to the Rome Statute, or by the ICC Prosecutor.[120]

For investigations launched by a State or the ICC Prosecutor, the Court will need the consent of either the State on whose territory the crime occurred or the State of the nationality of the accused. This is referred to as "complementarity." A case cannot be heard when a State with jurisdiction is already investigating a crime, unless: (a) that state "is unable or unwilling genuinely to carry out the investigation;" (b) a State has made a good faith decision not to investigate; or (c) the accused has already been tried for the conduct alleged. As succinctly explained by Professor Mauro Politi of the University of Trento, Italy:

I now come to the principle of "complementarity" . . . that, instead of replacing national jurisdictions, the Court will intervene only in those situations where national justice systems are unavailable or ineffective. Unlike the

Yugoslav or Rwanda Tribunals, the ICC does not have "primacy" over national jurisdictions. . . .

The main question is what criteria should determine the application of complementarity. In other words, when should the Court be authorized to act instead of a national jurisdiction? In which cases should a national justice system be deemed "unable or unwilling genuinely to carry out" an investigation or prosecution, to use the formula of Article 17?

Here, I do not share the pessimism of some commentators. Under Article 17, the Court will be able to affirm its competence in many significant situations: for example, after the total or partial collapse of a national judicial system, or in the presence of "sham" proceedings undertaken to shield the accused from criminal responsibility. . . .

Furthermore, it is always up to the Court to decide on issues of complementarity. This helps to reinforce the independence and the effectiveness of the Court. . . .[121]

The ICC may otherwise act, only if there is a UN Security Council referral, which can be blocked by the veto of any of the five permanent members. The ICC's first such case was so referred in March 2005. (The ICC's very first case—based upon an agreement signed by the United Nations and Uganda government—began with the ICC Prosecutor's June 2004 announcement launching an investigation into the Lord's Resistance Rebel Group for war crimes and crimes against humanity.) The Security Council's March 2005 reference of the Darfur case to the ICC was an historic occasion. It provided the much-needed spark for illuminating the dark sixty-year gap between the Nuremberg/Tokyo tribunals and today's functional ICC:

United Nations Security Council Resolution 1593

REPORTS OF THE SECRETARY-GENERAL ON THE SUDAN

Adopted by the Security Council at its 5158th Meeting
31 March 2005

The Security Council,

Taking note of the report of the International Commission of Inquiry on violations of international humanitarian law and human rights law in Darfur (S/2005/60),

Recalling article 16 of the Rome Statute under which no investigation or prosecution may be commenced or proceeded with by the International Criminal Court for a period of 12 months after a Security Council request to that effect,

Also recalling articles 75 and 79 of the Rome Statute and encouraging States to contribute to the ICC Trust Fund for Victims,

Taking note of the existence of agreements referred to in Article 98.2 of the Rome Statute [an unnecessary reference to the Article 98 treaties the US has pursued with many signatories, but a likely "requirement" for the US abstention from the Security Council vote],

Determining that the situation in Sudan continues to constitute a threat to international peace and security,

Acting under Chapter VII of the Charter of the United Nations,

1 *Decides* to refer the situation in Darfur since 1 July 2002 [because the Statute operates only prospectively from the date of its entry into force] to the Prosecutor of the International Criminal Court;

2. *Decides* that the Government of Sudan and all other parties to the conflict in Darfur, shall cooperate fully with and provide any necessary assistance to the Court and the Prosecutor pursuant to this resolution and, while recognizing that States not party to the Rome Statute have no obligation under the Statute, urges all States and concerned regional and other international organizations to cooperate fully;

3. *Invites* the Court and the African Union to discuss practical arrangements that will facilitate the work of the Prosecutor and of the Court, including the possibility of conducting proceedings in the region, which would contribute to regional efforts in the fight against impunity;

4. *Also encourages* the Court, as appropriate and in accordance with the Rome Statute, to support international cooperation with domestic efforts to promote the rule of law, protect human rights and combat impunity in Darfur;

5. *Also emphasizes* the need to promote healing and reconciliation and encourages in this respect the creation of institutions, involving all sectors of Sudanese society, such as truth and/or reconciliation commissions, in order to complement judicial processes and thereby reinforce the efforts to restore longlasting peace, with African Union and international support as necessary;

6. *Decides* that nationals, current or former officials or personnel from a contributing State outside Sudan which is not a party to the Rome Statute of the International Criminal Court shall be subject to the exclusive jurisdiction of that contributing State for all alleged acts or omissions arising out of or related to operations in Sudan established or authorized by the Council or the African Union, unless such exclusive jurisdiction has been expressly waived by that contributing State;

7. *Recognizes* that none of the expenses incurred in connection with the referral including expenses related to investigations or prosecutions in connection with that referral, shall be borne by the United Nations and that such costs shall be borne by the parties to the Rome Statute and those States that wish to contribute voluntarily;

8. *Invites* the Prosecutor to address the Council within three months of the date of adoption of this resolution and every six months thereafter on actions taken pursuant to this resolution [also referring the names of fifty-one Sudanese officials and other citizens to the ICC Prosecutor based on reports provided by the UN Secretary-General];

9. *Decides* to remain seized of the matter.

The UN Security Council will not always act, however, as it did in the case of Darfur. In this particular instance, the United States abstained, rather than veto Security Council action regarding Sudan. The genocide in Darfur did not involve any US defendant. This particular prosecution was in keeping with the US president's (and Prime Minister Blair's) 2005 Donor Nations for Africa Initiative. Whether the new ICC will effectively control despotic governments will depend on the will of the international community, which has the historically under-utilized power to turn promise into reality. As concluded by a former legal advisor to the US Department of State and the past president of the American Society of International Law—on the price of opting out:

> After World War II, the United States was the chief architect of the United Nations . . . and associated international institutions. All of them bear many of the marks of the American political and legal experience. More recently, U.S. trade negotiators pushed steadily for the increasing legalization of the GATT and ultimately the creation of the World Trade Organization. Over the past fifty years, the United States has been a major participant in these institutions, exercising a predominant influence in their implementation and evolution.
>
> . . .
>
> Consistent with its own conception of its global position, the United States should be taking the lead in shaping these new institutions. It is not too late. By signing the treaty, . . . the United States would strengthen its ability to participate as an observer in the early phases of implementation. If the United States stands aside from the process, it will miss an opportunity of serious dimensions. And the loss will have an impact on national interests far beyond the work of prosecuting war crimes.[122]

◆ 9.6 REGIONAL COURT ADJUDICATION

INTERNATIONAL LAW IN REGIONAL COURTS

Article 33 of the UN Charter provides that the "parties to any dispute . . . shall, first of all, seek a solution by negotiation, . . . arbitration, . . . resort to regional agencies or arrangements, or other peaceful means of their own choice." This section of the book thus surveys *regional* litigation, the apparent advantages over dispute resolution by a global entity, and some practical problems with this form of international dispute settlement.

For many centuries, international disputes were not resolved by international courts. Diplomatic negotiations and occasional *ad hoc* arbitrations served this purpose. Successful postwar diplomacy, beginning in the nineteenth century, began to establish international "Claims Commissions." These temporary bodies heard evidence from representatives of the States involved in a particular dispute. The resolution of claims dissolved the commission.

The modern trend has been away from the use of *temporary* regional tribunals toward more permanent institutions. During the twentieth century, a number of regional courts (and two global courts) have been created by international agreement. Full-time judges and permanent staffs are available to the parties who may thus submit disputes to these tribunals. Unlike the Yugoslavian and Rwandan criminal tribunals, one does not have to await a several-year organizing process before filing an action and proceeding with a comparatively prompt resolution. There is no need for creating a new *ad hoc* tribunal, negotiating its rules of engagement, and selecting the judges.

In theory, regional courts should be more viable dispute-resolution mechanisms than global courts. Like the ICJ, they are generally underutilized. Mistrust of international institutions with distant seats, as opposed to a national court, should be less of a problem in a regional court. Local judges from the affected region are arguably in a better position to resolve international problems originating within their own region. They are likely to be familiar with regional norms of conduct, which may not be universal. The two "World Courts," both seated in the heart of Europe, have been criticized for not fully comprehending the impact of regional practices (e.g., §7.3 *Asylum Case*).

The comparative ability to enforce judgments is a related benefit of regional dispute resolution. Unlike judgments from the UN's ICJ, which have sometimes been ignored, judgments from the regional tribunals, especially in Western Europe, are unquestionably incorporated into the fabric of the member States. With the exception of this particular region, however, it is not clear that regional courts have been more effective than global courts. A number of regional courts have not survived. Those that have, do not hear and resolve many cases. A Central American Court, the first regional international court, was established by treaty in 1907. The State participants soon decided that any need for regional courts would be supplanted by the Permanent Court of International Justice. The Central American Court was therefore disbanded in 1918.

The success of regional adjudication depends on the solidarity of the member States. In many instances, the political and economic unity of the region has been minimal. This discourages national resort to such courts for resolving disputes. In the EU, on the other hand, members have demonstrated the necessary cohesiveness to support a regional court system now spanning more than four decades. The participating States possess similar economic and political interests—a political and economic reality which has contributed significantly to the success of the EU and its judicial dispute-resolution. In most regions, the lack of political solidarity among nations has limited the potential for a more effective regional court process.

Not all citizens relish the concept of an international tribunal, on foreign soil, having authority over their affairs. One example is the comparatively successful European Court of Human Rights (ECHR), as illustrated in the following complaint:

> Many Britons—not only lawyers like myself—find it an insult to national pride that . . . the two 15-year-old Liverpool boys convicted five years ago by an English court of murdering 2-year-old James Bulger in a crime that shocked the world, will be allowed by the European Court of Human Rights in Strasbourg, France, to argue that the English legal system breached their human rights. . . .
>
> For many, myself included, the court is unpopular, despite the good work it has done. It is generally perceived as arrogant, unwieldy and the source of much chaos and delay. It is absolutely typical that when I telephoned recently to check the name of the chief judge, they were all at lunch. A recorded voice told me in French and English that someone would get back to me but, of course, no one did.[123]

In a perfect world, the resolution of international disputes would not be affected by political considerations. The decision about whether to go to court, however, is itself a major political consideration. Many States avoid regional (and global) courts for reasons unrelated to the legal issues or merits of their disputes. National leaders may decide that the filing of a lawsuit in a public forum will only exacerbate national differences, which might otherwise be managed more effectively through quiet diplomacy. A State may oppose judicial resolutions of international disputes, because a public airing of the problem may escalate (or create) a rift in international relations. In a different political environment, the same State may seek a judicial resolution. Amicable relations may be preserved by submission of the case to an impartial international tribunal.

Another problem, strikingly reminiscent of the global court paradigm, is that States have not given most of the regional courts the compulsory jurisdiction to litigate. When States have created regional courts, they theoretically agree that the availability of a standing tribunal is a good idea. In practice, however, they do not require themselves to submit to the judicial processes of the regional courts they create. They fear the loss of the sovereignty they typically associate with submitting sensitive cases to a public forum, which they do not control.

The lack of a defined relationship between the global and regional court systems further limits the potential for the judicial resolution of international disputes. Issues arising under International Law have been adjudicated both in the various regional courts and in the ICJ. UN Charter Article 95 grants the ICJ the power to hear cases arising under International Law. No Charter provision, however, creates or even suggests a relationship between the ICJ and the various regional courts. Charter Article 33 merely provides for prior resort to "regional agencies or arrangements" for the resolution of international disputes. The same case could be lodged in a regional court, the ICJ, and a national court. Certain State violations of an individual's human rights, for example, could be heard in the ECHR (against an individual defendant), the ICJ (only State defendants), or the UN's ICC for the trial of war crimes in the former Yugoslavia (although it possesses "primacy" over parallel national litigation).

The lack of a hierarchy among national, regional, and global courts is a related limitation on the viability of regional adjudication. While the litigants are expected to exhaust local remedies in national courts before coming to the ICJ (§2.5 State Responsibility), the ICJ has never required its litigants to resort first to available regional courts. Neither the UN Charter nor the Statute of the ICJ give the ICJ power to suspend regional court proceedings so the ICJ might provide a global response to the problem at hand.

There is yet another significant problem. Regional courts operate independent of national courts, the ICJ, and each other. Regional international courts function as trial courts from which there is no right of appeal. States normally do not cede appellate powers to regional (or global) courts, so that they could judicially review decisions by the national judiciary. States generally avoid the common model existing within their own court systems. In many national court systems, cases normally proceed through a hierarchy of judicial levels. This progression creates a trial-court record resolving factual issues so that an appellate tribunal may then concentrate on the legal issues involved in the dispute. This review process thus promotes uniformity of decision within national legal systems. A higher appellate court may then provide guidance to the various national trial/lower appellate courts to promote uniformity of the applicable law within that national system.[124]

The general lack of a legal relationship among regional courts, and between regional courts and the ICJ, has generated other problems. The predicament of having entirely independent regional court systems was forecast by prominent British commentator Professor Jenks. In 1943, prior to creation of the regional courts that exist today, he cautioned against such a system because "[t]he coexistence of the Permanent Court of International Justice and of entirely independent regional international courts would involve at least two dangers. There would be a danger of conflicts regarding jurisdiction, and a danger that regional courts might be inspired by regional legal conceptions to such an extent that their decisions might prejudice the future unity of the law of nations in respect of matters regarding which uniform rules of worldwide validity are desirable."[125]

Jenks' concern about parochial definitions of International Law was well founded. The interpretation of what constitutes a local custom has jeopardized prospects for a smooth relationship among national, regional, and global courts. What one international court perceives as falling within the general parameters of International Law may present a rather parochial perspective. The ICJ's 1950 *Asylum Case* (§7.3) illustrates this problem. Colombia relied on a regional practice to establish its claim that Peru had failed to honor the right of asylum existing in the Latin American region of the world. There was, in fact, support for Colombia's position. The ICJ did not affirm the right of asylum, however, because it was not practiced on either a regional level in Europe or on a global level. The ICJ ruled that Colombia "failed to meet its burden" of proving the existence of such a right under International Law. The ICJ was harshly criticized for its failure to recognize and apply this regional practice.

The following subsection surveys the operations and aspirations of the prominent regional courts. See Exhibit 9.1.

REGIONAL COURTS

EXHIBIT 9.1 SELECTED REGIONAL INTERNATIONAL COURTS

Court	Location (Date)[a]	Bench	Primary Affiliation	Cases Heard
Court of Justice of the European Communities[b]	Luxembourg (1973)	15 judges: 1 from each European Union member State; and president	European Union	◆ Commission v. State ◆ Private v. EU institution ◆ Cases referred from national courts
European Court of First Instance[b]	Luxembourg (1989)	15 judges: 1 from each European Union member State	European Union	◆ Actions brought by individuals ◆ Appeals to Court of Justice
European Court of Human Rights[b]	Strasbourg, France (1958)	3-judge Committees 7-judge Chambers 17-judge Grand Chamber (40 total from Council of Europe members)	Council of Europe	Determines State violations of European Convention on Human Rights
Inter-American Court of Human Rights	San Jose, Costa Rica (1979)	6 part-time judges 1 full-time president (all from OAS member States)	Organization of American States	Determines State violations of American Convention on Human Rights
Central American Court of Justice	(1907 & 1965)[c]	Presidents of member State judiciaries	Organization of American Central States	Disputes between States and between individual and State[d]
Arab Court of Justice	Cairo, Egypt (1965)	[d]	League of Arab States	[d]
O.P.E.C. Judicial Tribunal	Kuwait (1980)	7 part-time Arab judges	Oil Producing Exporting Countries	◆ interpretation of OPEC Agreement ◆ disputes between member country and petroleum company operating in its territory
African Economic Community Court of Justice[e]	(1991)	[d]	Organization of African Unity	[d]
African Court on Human and Peoples' Rights	To be determind by OAU Assembly (2003)	11 judges from OAU States	Organization of African Unity	Interprets African Charter on Human and Peoples' Rights

---

EXHIBIT 9.1 SELECTED REGIONAL INTERNATIONAL COURTS (CONTINUED)

Court	Location (Date)[a]	Bench	Primary Affiliation	Cases Heard
Caribbean Court of Justice	Seat not yet selected (1999)	President and not more than nine other Judges	Caribbean Community and Common Market	[f]
Islamic Court of International Justice	[d, g]		Organization of Islamic Conference	

---

[a]Date established, reestablished

[b]Compulsory jurisdiction over member States

[c]Hiatus from 1918 until reconstituted in 1965; *see* D. Bowett, THE LAW OF INTERNATIONAL INSTITUTIONS 287 (4th ed. London: Stevens & Sons, 1982). not mentioned in 5th ed.

[d]Proposed but not yet operational

[e]*See* A. Yusuf (Ed.), 1 AFRICAN YEARBOOK OF INTERNATIONAL LAW 237 (Art. 7) & 241 (Art. 18) (Dordrecht, Neth.: Martinus Nijhoff, 1994), and <http://www.oau-oua.org/document/Treaties/Treaties.htm>, 1991 treaty Sections 18–20.

[f]Disputes between Contracting State Parties; State Parties & Community; referrals from national courts or tribunals; applications by nationals re any treaty right. See <http://www.sice.oas.org/trade/ccme/ccj1.asp>

[g]See c above, Sands & Klein 5th ed. of Bowett, at 391.

There have been other dormant or defunct regional courts. The former Central American Court of Justice ceased to function in 1918. While it was supposedly reestablished in 1965, it has not yet issued a case. The Court of Justice of the European Coal and Steel Community was replaced by the current European Court of Justice (ECJ) in 1973. The League of Arab States has contemplated establishing an Arab Court of Justice since 1950. The proposed court is described in a draft statute. However, insufficient political solidarity in the region has prevented its activation.[126]

Several regional courts currently hear issues arising under International Law. They include the following courts, which are discussed below: (1) the ECJ, (2) the ECHR, (3) the Inter-American Court of Human Rights (IACHR), and (4) the Andean Court of Justice. These courts essentially interpret the treaties that created the political or economic organizations they serve.

European Court of Justice The 1957 Treaty of Rome established the first European regional court: the Court of Justice of the European Coal and Steel Community. Article 3 of the 1973 Convention on Certain Institutions Common to the European Communities transferred the powers of this court to the current ECJ, which is located in Luxembourg. The ECJ's judges from EU member countries decide about 200 cases per year.

The ECJ, sometimes called the "Supreme Court of Europe," resolves disputes between the national laws of member States and European Community law. For example, EU nations are not supposed to create import duties or nontariff barriers on most products imported from other EU members. This Court decided that Italy violated community transportation rules by prohibiting an Irish airline from picking up passengers in London and flying them to Milan.

The judicial power of this remarkably successful tribunal is succinctly described by the UK's University of Exeter Professor John Bridge, as follows:

The ECJ is an "international court" in more than one sense of that term. It is international in the fundamental sense that it is a creation of international law through the joint exercise of the treaty-making powers of the Member States. In organizational terms it is international in that it is composed of judges of the different nationalities of the [EU] Member States. In jurisdictional terms it is international in the classic sense that it is competent to hear and determine cases alleging the failure of Member States to fulfill treaty obligations. Another aspect of its international character lies in its authority to review, with reference to the Treaties, the legality of acts and omissions by the institutions set up by the Treaties to serve the purposes of

---

the Communities. The ECJ also has jurisdiction to rule on the compatibility with the EEC Treaty of proposed agreements between a Community and either third states or an international organization. It also serves as an international administrative tribunal through its jurisdiction in disputes between the Communities and its servants.[127]

The ECJ differs from the traditional international tribunals. Unlike the practice of the global ICJ, where only States may be parties, individuals and corporations may participate in certain proceedings before the ECJ (especially through its Court of First Instance). The first two cases heard by the European Court were filed by private (nongovernmental) corporations. Individuals who have been fined by an administrative body of the EU may appeal to the ECJ. Individuals and corporations may also ask the ECJ to annul administrative decisions and regulations of EU agencies, which allegedly violate EU norms. In one case, a British citizen filed suit in the ECJ to recover damages incurred during an assault in Paris. The administrator of a French fund for French citizens had denied the British citizen's claim on the basis of his foreign nationality. In another case of great constitutional significance, a French political group was able to successfully attack the European Parliament's allocation of funds from its budget to certain political parties. This clarified the Court's position that the decisions of all EU institutions, including the European Parliament, were open to judicial review via suits brought by private individuals or nongovernmental entities.[128]

National tribunals may also invoke the expertise of the ECJ. Under Article 177 of the EEC Treaty and Article 150 of the Euratom Treaty, courts and other tribunals from within the EU's member States have requested the ECJ to rule on a treaty matter arising within their particular national systems.

This Court's practice further differs from international litigation in the UN's ICJ. Unlike the twenty-five nations EU, the United Nations is composed of 191 member States. The objectives of the UN members are quite diverse in comparison with those of the much smaller EU, whose member States are comparatively homogeneous. Also, the respective constitutional charters are quite different. The UN Charter is not a legally enforceable document. It did not create immediately enforceable obligations applicable to all member States. These were, instead, standards of achievement, or a form of global political aspiration (§8.1). On the other hand,

the various treaties applicable to the comparatively integrated EU were intended to create legal obligations from the outset. EU member States are thus subject to the economic directives contained in its various self-executing treaties. The EU may enforce those provisions in the same manner that a national court may require compliance with its internal law.

This difference accounts for the comparative volume of cases heard by the ECJ. The range of the ECJ's jurisdiction has had an impact on States outside of the EU—including the United States. There is an understandable global obsession with the "extraterritorial application" of the laws of the United States (§5.2). The ECJ exercises similar power, however, under its own case law, which allows it to enforce Community legislation against even nonmembers. The ECJ has thus relied on US antitrust case law in support of its judicial authority over corporate anticompetitive conduct beyond the EU.

European Court of Human Rights   This court (ECHR) is the other major international court in Europe. It was established by the Council of Europe—now forty nations via the 1950 European Convention for the Protection of Human Rights and Fundamental Freedoms. The ECHR was operational in 1958. In 1959, it began to hear cases arising under the European Convention in Strasbourg, France.

Article 45 of the Convention provides that the ECHR may hear "all cases concerning the interpretation and application of the present Convention." The Court's basic role is to provide judicial protection for the fundamental rights of the individual. Thus, it may hear cases that might not be heard under the laws of the aggrieved individual's home State. In Great Britain, for example, there is no written constitution that enumerates a list of individual rights. Great Britain's commitment to the preservation of human rights under the European treaty, however, does provide certain guarantees. Its citizens may file claims against their government in the ECHR at its seat in Strasbourg France (see also §11.3).[129]

ECHR judgments are directly *enforced* in the national courts of the parties to the European Convention on Human Rights. This eliminates the major enforcement problem plaguing the ICJ (§9.4). Even when States appear and litigate in the ICJ's proceedings, there is no supranational executive body to oversee national compliance with the ICJ judgments. Nor is there a comparable treaty provision making ICJ judgments directly enforceable by treating them as if they were made by a national court of the State parties to the dispute. The following case offers a dramatic illustration how States yielded the requisite degree of sovereignty to an international court, so as to effectuate its judgments—and thus, achieve the common objectives of those member States.

The year 1992 was a stormy one in Ireland in terms of the very sensitive issue of abortion. Ireland's Constitution prohibits abortion, as the result of a referendum of its voters in 1983. It is also a crime punishable by life imprisonment. A 1979 law had previously been enacted, making it unlawful to advocate or assist in the obtaining of an abortion in any manner. Here, a lower Irish court prohibited a raped fourteen-year-old girl from going abroad for the purpose of obtaining an abortion. After it became clear that she would commit suicide, the Irish Supreme Court overruled that opinion in a rather succinct one-sentence opinion, which did not squarely resolve the issue, at least for future cases where a potential defendant wished to obtain abortion information.

The EU's ECJ, seated in Luxembourg, determined that it had no jurisdiction with regard to Ireland's national abortion law. Any issues related to that national law were characterized as "lying outside the scope of [European] Community Law." This case was then lodged with the European Court of Human Rights. The following decision did not address whether family planning counselors in Ireland could advise women about the option of traveling to England, where abortion is legal. The defendants' lawyers claimed that Ireland's judicial action, prohibiting abortion counseling, violated the European Human Rights Convention. In a companion case, some student newspapers were charged with publishing information about pregnancy alternatives, in violation of Irish law. The ensuing opinion of the ECHR, seated in France, effectively reversed the Irish Supreme Court injunction against the various defendants in these companion cases. It is also a classic illustration of how an international organization can require a State to act in a way that is contrary to its national law:

◆

Case of Open Door and Dublin Well Woman v. Ireland

EUROPEAN COURT OF HUMAN RIGHTS, 1992

No. 64/1991/316/387–388

<http://www.echr.coe.int/echr>

AUTHOR'S NOTE: The Irish Supreme Court affirmed a lower Irish court order requiring the defendants— Open Door Counselling, Ltd., Dublin Well Woman, Ltd., and certain individuals—to cease counseling on the availability of abortions outside of Ireland. The court order had already resulted in the closure of defendant Open Door. The defendants applied to the ECHR for relief under the European Convention on Human Rights (European Convention) provisions—which protect freedom of expression, and prevent disclosure of information received in confidence.

The ECHR did not rule directly on Ireland's constitutional ban on abortions. The majority of the Court's judges did rule, however, that preventing women from getting information on how to get abortions outside of Ireland violated the European Convention. Ireland could no longer use its own anti-abortion laws to deprive its citizens of human rights guaranteed by the European Convention. This was nevertheless an excep-

tionally divided court, the majority opinion resolving this matter by a vote of fifteen to eight of the judges. Seven of twenty-three judges wrote their own separate opinions. The Court's paragraphs numbering is omitted.

COURT'S OPINION: The case was referred to the Court by the European Commission on Human Rights [and] . . . by the Government of Ireland. . . . It originated in two applications against Ireland lodged with the Commission . . . by Open Door Counselling Ltd, a company incorporated in Ireland; the second by another Irish company, Dublin Well Woman Centre Ltd., and one citizen of the United States of America, . . . and three Irish citizens, Ms Ann Downes, Mrs X and Ms Maeve Geraghty [two employed as trained counsellors for one of these companies and two in their capacity as women of child-bearing age residing in Ireland]. . . .

The applicants complained of an injunction imposed by the Irish courts on Open Door and Dublin Well

Woman to restrain them from providing certain information to pregnant women concerning abortion facilities outside the jurisdiction of Ireland. . . .

On 19 December 1986 Mr Justice Hamilton, President of the High Court [lower Irish court], found that the activities of Open Door and Dublin Well Woman in counselling pregnant women . . . to travel abroad to obtain an abortion or to obtain further advice on abortion within a foreign jurisdiction were unlawful [under] . . . the Constitution of Ireland.

He confirmed that the Irish criminal law [thus] made it an offence to procure or attempt to procure an abortion. . . . Furthermore, Irish constitutional law also protected the right to life of the unborn from the moment of conception onwards.

An injunction was accordingly granted " . . . that the Defendants [Open Door and Dublin Well Woman] and each of them, their servants or agents, be perpetually restrained from counselling or assisting pregnant women within the jurisdiction of this court [Ireland] to obtain further advice on abortion or to obtain an abortion."

Open Door and Dublin Well Woman appealed against this decision to the [Irish] Supreme Court which in a unanimous judgment . . . rejected the appeal [affirming the lower court's injunction requiring the defendants to cease giving information about the availability of abortions in Great Britain].

On the question of whether the above activity should be restrained as being contrary to the [Irish] Constitution, Mr Justice Finlay C. J. stated:

. . . the issue and the question of fact to be determined is: were they thus assisting in the destruction of life of the unborn?

I am satisfied beyond doubt that . . . the Defendants were assisting in the ultimate destruction of the life of the unborn by abortion.

[In a companion case, an Irish anti-abortion society applied to the lower Irish court to restrain the publication of information in student newspapers regarding abortion information. That court referred this, and the Open Door and Well Woman matter, to the European Court of Justice in Luxembourg for a determination of whether this issue fell within the ambit of Community Law. But on appeal of that case referral, the Irish Supreme Court instead restrained the student publication from

further publishing abortion counseling information. The dispositive statement from the Irish Supreme Court in the related newspaper case is provided by the ECHR in its Open Door and Dublin Well Woman decision at this point in the opinion.]

. . . I reject as unsound the contention that the activity involved in this case of publishing in the students' manuals the [Great Britain abortion clinic information] . . . can be distinguished from the activity condemned by this Court in [the Open Door Counselling case]. . . . It is clearly the fact that such information is conveyed to pregnant women, and not the method of communication, which creates the unconstitutional illegality. . . .

[The ECHR next returned to its analysis of the Open Door and Dublin Well Woman defendants.]

Section 16 of the Censorship of Publications Act 1929 . . . provides that: It shall not be lawful for any person, otherwise than under and in accordance with a permit in writing granted to him under this section . . . to print or publish . . . any book or periodical publication (whether appearing on the register of prohibited publications or not) which advocates . . . the procurement of an abortion. . . .

. . . In their applications lodged with the Commission . . . the applicants complained that the injunction[s] in question constituted an unjustified interference with their right to impart or receive information contrary to Article 10 of the [European Human Rights] Convention. . . .

[The Commission had then ruled that the Irish Supreme Court injunctions did violate the European Convention, triggering the ECHR's jurisdiction to hear this case. Its analysis continues with the Open Door and Dublin Well Woman defendants.]

The applicants . . . invoked [Convention] Article 10 which provides:

1. Everyone has the right to freedom of expression. This right shall include freedom to hold opinions and to receive and impart information and ideas without interference by public authority and regardless of frontiers [within the Community].

2. The exercise of these freedoms . . . may be subject to such formalities, conditions, [and] restrictions . . . necessary in a democratic society . . . for preventing the disclosure of information received in confidence. . . .

In their submissions to the Court the [Irish] Government contested these claims and also contended that Article 10 should be interpreted against the background of Articles 2 . . . and 60 of the Convention the relevant parts of which state:

1. Everyone's right to life shall be protected by law. . . .

60. Nothing in [the] Convention shall be construed as limiting or derogating from any of the human rights and fundamental freedoms which may be ensured under the laws of any High Contracting Party. . . .

The Court cannot accept that the restrictions at issue pursued the aim of the prevention of crime since . . . neither the provision of the information in question nor the obtaining of an abortion outside the jurisdiction [*i.e.,* in Great Britain] involved any criminal offence. However, it is evident that the protection afforded under Irish law to the right to life of the unborn is based on profound moral values concerning the nature of life . . . [which was] reflected in the stance of the majority of the Irish people against abortion as expressed in the 1983 referendum. . . .

The Court [however] is not called upon to examine whether a right to abortion is guaranteed under the Convention or whether the foetus is encompassed by the right to life as contained in Article 2. . . .

The only issue to be addressed is whether the [Irish] restrictions on the freedom to impart and receive information contained in the relevant part of the [Irish court's] injunction are necessary in a democratic society for the legislative aim of protection of morals. . . .

[T]he national authorities enjoy a wide margin of appreciation in matters of morals, particularly [when they] . . . touch on matters of belief concerning the nature of human life. . . .

However this power of appreciation is not unlimited. It is for the Court . . . to supervise whether a restriction [like this one] is compatible with the Convention. . . .

In this context, it is appropriate to recall that freedom of expression is also applicable to "information" or "ideas" that offend, shock or disturb the State or any sector of the population. Such are the demands of that pluralism, tolerance and broadmindedness without which there is no "democratic society." . . .

The [Irish] Government . . . [has] submitted that Article 10 should not be interpreted in such a manner as to limit, destroy or derogate from the right to life of the unborn which enjoys special protection under Irish law. . . . [T]he Court recalls [however] that the injunction . . . [and] the information that it sought to restrain was available from other sources. Accordingly, it is not the interpretation of Article 10 but the position of Ireland as regards the implementation of the [anti-abortion] law that makes possible the continuance of the current level of abortions obtained by Irish women abroad.

In light of the above, the Court concludes that the restraint imposed on the applicants from receiving or imparting information was disproportionate to the [governmental] aims pursued. Accordingly there has been a breach of Article 10.

◆ *Notes*

1. The Court held that Ireland violated Article 10 of the Convention and that it must pay damages to the defendant entities Open Door and Dublin Well Woman. These private corporations, and the individuals who were parties to this suit, were capable of personally enforcing their treaty rights provoked by Ireland's violations of the European Human Rights Convention. In the UN's ICJ, however, only States may be parties to such enforcement proceedings (§9.4). *Open Door* illustrates how an international organization may vary the rule of International Law that otherwise requires a State to bring an action on behalf of its injured citizens at the international level. Ireland would not, of course, exercise its discretion in such matters to advocate such treaty rights on behalf of its natural or corporate citizens. Further contextual perspectives are available in J. Kingston & A. Whelan,

ABORTION AND THE LAW: AN IRISH PERSPECTIVE (Dublin: Street & Maxwell, 1997).

2. In March 2002, Irish voters rejected a referendum, which would have overruled a 1992 Irish court decision holding that the potential suicide of the mother was grounds for an abortion. This vote handed a stunning defeat to the government and the Roman Catholic Church.

3. In July 2004, the ECHR held that France did not violate the right to life of a six-month old fetus, when a doctor mistakenly pierced the mother's amniotic sac—thinking that she was another woman. A criminal court in Lyon, France, acquitted the doctor of any criminal wrongdoing. An appellate court reversed, imposing a fine and six-month jail term. The French Court of Cassation reversed the intermediate appellate court's ruling. The high court commented that this was a matter of national law, as there was no majority consensus on this point in member States. The ECHR ultimately determined that France did not violate the rights of the fetus, by failing to punish the doctor by making his conduct a criminal offense. Vo v. France, [GC] No. 53924/00, CEDH/ECHR 2004-VIII, summary available at: <http://www.echr.coe.int/echr>.

4. Two years after the US Supreme Court's *Roe v. Wade* decision, the comparable German Constitutional Court decided contrary to the United States and the ECHR:

    1. . . . The State's duty to protect forbids not only direct state attacks against life developing itself, but also requires the state to protect and foster this life.
    2. The obligation of the state to protect the life developing itself exists, even against the mother.

See German Constitutional Court Abortion Decision, BVerfGE 39, 1, English translation available at: <http://www.swiss.ai.mit.edu/~rauch/germandecision/german_abortion_decision2.html>.

5. In 2002, the Mexican government allegedly violated the right of a thirteen-year old girl to have an abortion—after being raped in her home by an intruding heroin addict. Baja California state officials, priests, and the Attorney General discouraged her from aborting, although Mexican law permits abortions in this situation. She then filed a petition in the Inter-American Court of Human Rights, seeking an unspecified amount of monetary restitution on behalf of her family. Details are available at: <http://www.crlp.org/pr_03_0904Paulina.html>.

Inter-American Court of Human Rights   Organization of American States (OAS) member State representatives drafted the American Convention on Human Rights, which became effective in 1978.[130] Approximately two-thirds of the more than thirty-member States have adopted this treaty (not including the United States).

In 1979, the OAS established the IACHR in San Jose, Costa Rica. It has since heard several contentious cases and has rendered about a dozen advisory opinions. The court's primary function is to interpret the American Convention. The IACHR hear claims alleging that an individual's civil and political rights have been infringed by State action. Unlike the practice developed in Europe's regional courts, individuals can never appear either directly or indirectly in the IACHR. Under Article 61(1) of the Convention, "only States Parties and the [Human Rights] Commission shall have the right to submit a case to the Court."

The IACHR hears disputes between States when one accuses another of violating individual freedoms guaranteed under the American Convention. The participating States must consent, however, to the jurisdiction of this Court to resolve such disputes. Unlike the practice of the two European international courts (discussed earlier), only a few OAS member States have accepted the compulsory jurisdiction of the IACHR.

Like the International Court of Justice, the IACHR may also issue "advisory" opinions. These do not depend on the presence/consent of an offending nation. The purpose of this power, similar to that of the ICJ's advisory jurisdiction, is to provide judicial guidance to member States about certain practices that violate the Human Rights Convention.[131] The Court is thereby able to develop the regional Latin American norms regarding State compliance with the American Convention.

One of the Convention's key provisions prohibits States from harming their citizens for political purposes. In a landmark trial in 1988, the IACHR heard the first contentious trial against a Latin American State for the politically motivated murders of its own citizens. Honduras was tried for the disappearance and murders of 90,000 people since the 1950s.[132] The IACHR is only the second regional court (after the ECHR) to judge States for violations of internationally recognized human rights.

In what may be the Court's most significant case, it rejected Peru's July 2000 decision, purporting to withdraw from the Court's contentious jurisdiction. The IACHR had recently determined that Peru would have to retry four people convicted of treason. They had been tried and convicted by a military, rather than a civilian, tribunal. Peru's antiterrorism legislation had authorized civilians to be tried in military courts for the terrorism-related offence of "treason." The IACHR determined that Peru should amend this law, because the independence and impartiality of its national court system was seriously in doubt. The Court said that Peru's failure to carry out the Court's decisions, before and after Peru's attempt to withdraw from the Court's jurisdiction, went "to the very essence of international law, *i.e.* good-faith performance of treaty obligations." Peru ultimately acknowledged the Court's jurisdiction, rather than face possible expulsion form the OAS.[133]

The IACHR is something more than a temporary arbitral body, but something less than a permanent judicial institution. Its seven jurists, from different OAS nations, do not conduct proceedings on a full-time basis. Funding has been withheld, pending development of the Court's jurisprudence to a point where full-time judges are necessary. This part-time status is, unfortunately, unique among the regional courts of the world. The Court's former Chief Justice, and now member of the ICJ, lamented that ". . . a part-time tribunal might give that body an ad hoc image, likely to diminish the prestige and legitimacy it might need to obtain compliance with and respect for its decisions in the Americas. But the [OAS] General Assembly opted instead for a tribunal composed of part-time judges . . . [who are] free to practice law, to teach, and to engage in whatever other occupations they may have in their native countries."[134]

This tribunal oversees the rather ambitious set of goals set forth in the various regional human rights documents. Its theoretical utility, however, has not been matched by State usage. This region does not enjoy the comparatively lengthy period of development, and degree of solidarity that exists in Europe's regional tribunals. In the absence of the long-term evolution of liberal democracy, as enjoyed in some other regions of the world, the tangible progress of this Court may remain comparatively limited. As aptly described by University of Canterbury (New Zealand) Professor Scott Davidson:

"The malaise [that] the nonuse of the contentious procedure signifies lies deeper than the pure mechanics of making an instrument and its institutions work more efficiently: it lies more likely in the political and economic structures of the states of the region and in the perceptions which these structures engender. If certain states continue to see the inter-American human rights system as a threat to entrenched positions rather than an aid to furthering support for the forms of liberal democracy which the Court and the instruments upon which it relies clearly support, then such states are unlikely to encourage its [expanded] use."[135]

Andean Court of Justice The 1969 Treaty of Bogotá, often referred to as the "Andean Pact," was adopted by five South American nations. They hope to develop an economic union similar to that of the EU. The national members are Bolivia, Colombia, Ecuador, Peru, and Venezuela. (Chile previously withdrew.)

In 1983, the Andean Pact countries created the Andean Court of Justice (ACJ), which sits in Quito, Ecuador. It has five judges—one from each member State. Contrary to the more flexible practice in the Inter-American Court of Justice, the judges of the ACJ must live near Quito. They may not undertake any other professional activities.[136]

Under Article 32 of the ACJ agreement, judgments are directly enforceable in the national courts of member States. There is no need for any national incorporation of the regional court's judgments into internal law. Similar to the practice in the ECJ, Article 33 provides that States cannot submit any controversy arising under the Andean Pact "to any [other] court, arbitration system or any other procedure not contemplated by this Treaty." This limitation is designed to promote uniformity of decision and application of the same judicial standards to economic disputes arising throughout the region. Judges of national courts within Andean Pact states may also request that the regional court interpret the Andean Pact's economic provisions when such issues are litigated in their national courts. This power encourages regional solidarity in matters of Latin American economic integration.

The court is able to overrule decisions by the Andean Pact's other major organs. A member State's alleged noncompliance with the Pact's economic integration plan is first considered by either the Commission, the Pact's major administrative organ or the Junta, its chief executive organ. These bodies may submit a dispute with a member nation to the Court. The Court can nullify decisions of the Commission or the Junta and require the offending State to comply. In the ACJ's first case, decided in 1987, Colombia questioned a resolution of the Junta. The Court ruled that the Junta improperly limited Colombia's introduction of protective measures against imports from Venezuela.[137]

Under Article 25 of the treaty creating the ACJ, the offending nation's noncompliance permits the court to "restrict or suspend, totally or partially, the advantages deriving from the Cartagena [Andean Pact] Agreement which benefit the noncomplying member country." Suppose that a member State does not reduce its tariffs on exports of another member State as required by the terms of the Andean Pact regulations. The ACJ Court has the power to render a judgment requiring the offending State to comply with the treaty or its related regulatory rules. The Court has never issued such an opinion, however. Like other international courts, the ACJ may also render advisory opinions.

The ACJ has not been utilized extensively for a variety of economic and political reasons. The underlying Cartagena Agreement (Andean Pact) was modified in 1989 by the Quito Protocol with a view toward bringing the Andean regional process in line with that of the EU. In that year, the member States also issued a manifesto whereby they committed themselves to fully implementing the Andean Common Market. Should that degree of integration materialize, then the Andean Pact has the theoretical ability to mature into a viable international judicial process—but not before.[138]

◆ PROBLEMS

Problem 9.A (§9.4 after Norwegian Loans) The ICJ *Reservations to the Convention on Genocide* opinion is set forth in §8.2. The Court therein held that a reservation must be "compatible" with the underlying purposes of the treaty. In *Norwegian Loans*, France's reservation provided that France would decide if the ICJ has jurisdiction—over cases which *France* could characterize as falling within its domestic jurisdiction. Under the ICJ Statute, the *ICJ* decides whether it has the power to act. Is France's reservation compatible with the underlying purpose of the ICJ Statute (which is a treaty)?

Problem 9.B (after §9.4 ICJ Statute materials) Two groups of students will meet separately to draft their versions of a new "World Court Statute." Each group must draft clauses defining the court's power to act. These clauses will address whether the UN membership should do any of the following:

1. Automatically be parties to this new World Court Statute.
2. Have the option to accept the court's "compulsory" jurisdiction:
   a. without any possible reservation, or
   b. with reservations.
3. If 2(b) is permitted, should the new draft Statute authorize *conditional* acceptances, to ensure wider participation in the new "World Court Statute?"

Problem 9.C (after §9.4 Palestinian Wall advisory opinion) The ICJ possesses advisory jurisdiction to hear a case referred to it by a UN organ such as the General Assembly. The US dissenter, Judge Buergenthal, claimed that the ICJ should not have considered and decided its *Palestinian Wall* case (§9.6). Three questions: (1) what was the gist of his §9.6 dissenting opinion; (2) do you agree; and (3) did he appear to dissent, based on his belief that Israel should be permitted to protect itself against suicide bombings originating from the West Bank?

Four students will assume the roles of: (a) Judge Buergenthal; (b) pro and con debaters, on whether he was correct; and (c) a potential critic, who will assess whether this judge's US citizenship should have affected his vote as the lone dissenter.

Problem 9.D (§9.5, after ICTY Tadic Case) Defendant Tadic was sentenced to twenty years in prison, after his killings, sexual assaults, torture, and so forth. The possible sentences for his various crimes added up to a total of ninety-seven years. The court opted to minimize his sentence by having the respective sentences served concurrently. He was not given the ultimate sentence of life in prison.

Neither the ICTY nor the Rwandan tribunal has the power to sentence a convicted war criminal to death. One reason is the growing sentiment that the death penalty violates International Law. A Protocol to the International Covenant on Civil and Political Rights prohibits the death penalty in member nations (§11.2). The tribunal remarked that Tadic was a lower level functionary, operating out of a deep hatred spawned by a party and governmental campaign of terror which many individuals carried out—while only a few were captured and prosecuted.

Should the tribunal have sentenced Tadic to life in prison? Would a "life" sentence be more than the minimum necessary to send a message that war criminals can no longer undertake such acts, with the impunity that so many of them have savored since Nuremberg? Would "life" have suggested that the judges were unnecessarily flexing their judicial muscles, in an effort to make an example of this lower level criminal? Alternatively, was the tribunal too lenient, because it sentenced Tadic to only twenty years of the possible ninety-seven-year sentence?

Two students will represent, respectively, the ICTY prosecutor's office and Tadic's defense counsel. They are conducting a "rehearing" in the mock penalty phase of this trial. They will debate these (and any related) factors which should impact the length of Tadic's sentence. . . .

◆ BIBLIOGRAPHY

§9.1 Arbitration and Adjudication Blueprint

M. Butlerman & M. Kuijer (eds.), COMPLIANCE WITH JUDGMENTS OF INTERNATIONAL COURTS (The Hague, Neth.: Martinus Nijhoff, 1996)

A. Lowenfeld, INTERNATIONAL LITIGATION AND ARBITRATION (St. Paul, MN: West, 1993)

S. Muller & W. Mijs (eds.), THE FLAME REKINDLED: NEW HOPES FOR INTERNATIONAL ARBITRATION (Dordrecht, Neth.: Martinus Nijhoff, 1994)

S. Rosenne (ed.), THE HAGUE PEACE CONFERENCES OF 1899 AND 1907 AND INTERNATIONAL ARBITRATION: REPORTS AND DOCUMENTS (The Hague: Kluwer, 2001)

V. Shany, THE COMPETING JURISDICTIONS OF INTERNATIONAL COURTS AND TRIBUNALS (Oxford, Eng.: Oxford Univ. Press, 2003)

§9.2 Alternative Dispute Resolution

A. O'Shea, AMNESTY FOR CRIME IN INTERNATIONAL LAW AND PRACTICE (The Hague: Kluwer, 2002)

R. Ostrihansky, The Future of Dispute Settlement within GATT: Conciliation v. Adjudication, in M. Brus, S. Muller, & S. Weimers (eds.), THE UNITED NATIONS DECADE OF INTERNATIONAL LAW: REFLECTIONS ON INTERNATIONAL DISPUTE RESOLUTION 125 (Dordrecht, Neth.: Martinus Nijhoff, 1991)

Panel, New Trends in International Dispute Settlement, in PROCEEDINGS OF THE 87TH ANNUAL MEETING OF THE AMERICAN SOCIETY OF INTERNATIONAL LAW 2 (1993)

§9.3 Arbitral Classifications and Tribunals

A. Lowenfeld, INTERNATIONAL LITIGATION AND ARBITRATION (St. Paul: West, 1993)

T. Varady, J. Baccelo & A. von Mehren, Introduction, ch.1, in INTERNATIONAL COMMERCIAL ARBITRATION: A TRANSNATIONAL PERSPECTIVE 1–61 (St. Paul, MN: WestGroup, 1999)

§9.4 International Court of Justice

W. Coplin & J. Rochester, The Permanent Court of International Justice, the International Court of Justice, the League of Nations and the United Nations: A Comparative Empirical Survey, 66 AMER. POL. SCI. REV. 529 (1972)

T. Gill, THE WORLD COURT: WHAT IT IS AND HOW IT WORKS (6th Leiden, Neth.: Martinus Nijhoff, 2003)

S. Gorove, Formation of Internal Subdivisions of International Tribunals: Some Comparative Highlights and Assessment, 38 AMER. J. INT'L LAW 353 (1990)

M. Hudson (ed.), WORLD COURT REPORTS: A COLLECTION OF JUDGMENTS, ORDERS AND OPINIONS OF THE PERMANENT COURT OF INTERNATIONAL JUSTICE (Buffalo, NY: Hein, 2000) (four volumes, originally published 1934–1943)

H. Thirlway, The Law and Procedure of the International Court of Justice 1960–1989, 63 BRITISH YEARBOOK INT'L LAW 1 (1992)

A. Zimmerman (ed.), THE STATUTE OF THE INTERNATIONAL COURT OF JUSTICE: A COMMENTARY (Oxford, Eng.: Oxford Univ. Press, 2006)

§9.5 International Criminal Courts

K. Askin, WAR CRIMES AGAINST WOMEN: PROSECUTION IN INTERNATIONAL WAR CRIMES TRIBUNALS (The Hague: Martinus Nijhoff, 1997)

B. Brown, U.S. Objections to the Statute of the International Criminal Court: A Brief Response, 31 NYU J. INT'L LAW & POLITICS 855 (1999)

A. Cassese, THE ROME STATUTE OF THE INTERNATIONAL CRIMINAL COURT: A COMMENTARY (Oxford, Eng.: Oxford Univ. Press, 2002)

O. Elagab, The Hague as the Seat of the Lockerbie Trial: Some Constraints, 34 INT'L LAWYER 289 (2000)

J. Jones, THE PRACTICE OF THE INTERNATIONAL CRIMINAL TRIBUNALS FOR THE FORMER YUGOSLAVIA AND RWANDA (Ardsley, NY: Transnational, 1998)

G. Knoops, AN INTRODUCTION TO THE LAW OF THE INTERNATIONAL CRIMINAL TRIBUNALS (Irvington-on-Hudson, NY: Transnational, 2003)

B. Roling, THE TOKYO TRIAL AND BEYOND: REFLECTIONS OF A PEACEMONGER (Cambridge, Eng.: Blackwell, 1995)

C. Romano, INTERNATIONALIZED CRIMINAL COURTS: SIERRA LEONE, EAST TIMOR, KOSOVO, AND CAMBODIA (Oxford, Eng.: Oxford Univ. Press, 2004)

Ling Yan, The Beijing Symposium on the Comparative Study of International Criminal Law and the Rome Statute, 3 CHINESE J. INT'L L. 305 (2004)

V. Morris & M. Scharf, AN INSIDER'S GUIDE TO THE INTERNATIONAL CRIMINAL TRIBUNAL FOR THE FORMER YUGOSLAVIA: A DOCUMENTARY HISTORY AND ANALYSIS (Irvington-on-Hudson, NY: Transnat'l Pub., 1994) (two volumes)

§9.6 Regional Court Adjudication

J. Bengoextea, THE LEGAL REASONING OF THE EUROPEAN COURT OF JUSTICE: TOWARD A EUROPEAN JURISPRUDENCE (Oxford, Eng.: Clarendon Press, 1993)

V. Berger, CASE LAW OF THE EUROPEAN COURT OF HUMAN RIGHTS (Dublin: Round Hall Press, 1991) (two volumes)

J. Pasqualucci, THE PRACTICE AND PROCEDURE OF THE INTER-AMERICAN COURT OF HUMAN RIGHTS (Cambridge, Eng.: Cambridge Univ. Press, 2003) VT, USA: Dartmouth Press, 1992)

J. Delgado, The Inter-American Court of Human Rights, 5 ILSA JOURNAL OF INT'L & COMP. L. 541 (1999)

M. Janis, INTERNATIONAL COURTS FOR THE TWENTY-FIRST CENTURY (Dordrecht, Neth.: Martinus Nijhoff, 1992)

P. Kempees, A SYSTEMATIC GUIDE TO THE CASE-LAW OF THE EUROPEAN COURT OF HUMAN RIGHTS 1960–1994 (The Hague, Neth.: Martinus Nijhoff, 1996) (currently four volumes)

Electronic Resources

International Courts, Commissions & Tribunals: <http://www.worldcourts.com>

Max Planck Institute—National Prosecution of International Crimes: <http://www.iuscrim.mpg.de/forsch/straf/projekte/natstraf2_mat_e.html

Nuremberg Trials Project: Digital Document Collection: <http://nuremberg.law.harvard.edu/php/docs_swi.php?DI=1&text=overview>

United Nations, War Crimes Commission's Law Reports of Trials of War Criminals: <http://www.ess.uwe.ac.uk/genocide/war_criminals.htm>

World Court Digest (ICJ case summaries): <http://www.virtual-institute.de/en/wcd/wcd.cfm>

◆ ENDNOTES

1. *See* L. Sohn, International Arbitration in Historical Perspective: Past and Present, in A. Soons (ed.), INTERNATIONAL ARBITRATION: PAST AND PROSPECTS 9 (Dordrecht, Neth.: Martinus Nijhoff, 1990).

2. 8 US STATUTES AT LARGE 196 (1802), US TREATY SERIES NO. 108.

3. *See* Introduction, in A. Stuyt, SURVEY OF INTERNATIONAL ARBITRATIONS: 1794–1989, at 3 (3d ed. Dordrecht, Neth.: Martinus Nijhoff, 1990) [hereinafter *Arbitration Survey*].

4. *See generally*, *Arbitration Survey* (cited in note 3 above).

5. ICJ COMMUNIQUÉ NO. 98/14, 6 Apr. 1998, at 1, para. 4.

6. Section 4.4 of this book contains several useful examples: the *Roberts v. Mexico* imprisonment case; and the *Loewen v. US* arbitration regarding the Mississippi state court trial proceedings against the non-resident Canadian defendant.

7. Abu Dhabi Court of Cassation Judgment No. 514/19 (1 June 1999), as summarized in R. Price & E. Tamimi (ed.), UNITED ARAB EMIRATES COURT OF CASSATION JUDGMENTS 1998–2003, at 287 (Leiden, Neth.: Brill, 2005).

8. Agreement between the Government of Ukraine and the Government of the State of Israel on the Settlement of Claims Arising form the Aerial Catastrophe of 4 October 2001 (Nov. 20, 2003), available at: <http://www.asil.org/ilm/Ukraine_Israel.pdf>.

9. A. Watts, The Art of Apology, ch. 10, in M Ragazzi (ed.), INTERNATIONAL RESPONSIBILITY TODAY: ESSAYS IN MEMORY OF OSCAR SCHACHTER 107 (LEIDEN, NETH.: MARTINUS NIJHOFF: 2005).

10. *See* J. Ryan, Story Behind U.S. Law Firm's Japanese Apology Continues, Los Angeles Daily Journal (legal newspaper), at 1 (Mar. 15, 2004), available at: <http://www.dailyjournal.com/law>, subscription required.

11. Details about the PCIJ are available in S. Rosenne, THE LAW AND PRACTICE OF THE INTERNATIONAL COURT, 1920–1996 (The Hague, Neth.: Martinus Nijhoff, 1997) (four volumes) [hereinafter *Rosenne*]. *See also* A. Zimmern, THE LEAGUE OF NATIONS AND THE RULE OF LAW 1918–1935 (Gaunt [Holmes Beach, FL] reprint of London: MacMillan & Co., 1936).

12. *Quote (1):* UN Charter Art. 33.1 (1945). *Quote (2):* UN Gen. Ass. Res. 2625(XXV) of 1970.

13. C. Chinkin, Alternative Dispute Resolution under International Law, ch. 7, in M. Evans (ed.), REMEDIES IN INTERNATIONAL LAW: THE INSTITUTIONAL DILEMMA 123–124 (1998).

14. Reprinted in *Appendix A* to J. Merrills, INTERNATIONAL DISPUTE SETTLEMENT 312 (3d ed. Cambridge, Eng.: Grotius, 1998) [hereinafter *International Dispute Settlement*].

15. An excellent discussion of this distinction, and ADR modes in general, is available in Office of Legal Affairs, HANDBOOK ON THE PEACEFUL SETTLEMENT OF DISPUTES BETWEEN STATES (New York, UN: 1992) (Inquiry, at 24).

16. The facts are available in *International Dispute Settlement,* at 44–46 (cited in note 14 above).

17. General Framework Agreement, available at: <http://www.nato int/ifor/gfa/gfa-home.htm>.

18. C. Crocker, F. Osler & P. Aall, Rising to the Challenge of Multiparty Mediation, ch. 25, in HERDING CATS: MULTIPARTY MEDIATION IN A COMPLEX WORLD 666 (Wash., DC: US Inst. Peace, 1999).

19. Report of the UN High-level Panel on Threats, Challenges and Change, at 37 (Dec. 2, 2004), at <http://www.un.org/secureworld>, click Document [bolding removed].

20. C. Parry et al., PARRY AND GRANT ENCYCLOPAEDIC DICTIONARY OF INTERNATIONAL LAW 71 (2d ed., New York: Oceana, 2004).

21. M. Rubino-Sammartano, Arbitration and Alternative Disputes Resolution, ch. 1, in INTERNATIONAL ARBITRATION LAW AND PRACTICE 15–16 (Deventer, Neth.: Kluwer, 2001) (footnotes omitted).

22. *See generally, Arbitration Survey* (cited in note 3 above). In the prior edition of that work, the author reported that a party failed to comply with only 3 of 443 reported decisions.

23. S. Troope, MIXED INTERNATIONAL ARBITRATION 200–201 (Cambridge, Eng.: Grotius, 1990).

24. J. Goldsmith (ed.), INTERNATIONAL DISPUTE RESOLUTION: THE REGULATION OF FORUM SELECTION (Irvington-on-Hudson, NY: Transnational, 1997).

25. *New York Convention:* United Nations Convention on Recognition and Enforcement of Arbitral Awards, 330 UN

TREATY SERIES, No. 4739 (1958) (more than 90 State parties). *Inter-American Convention: See* US implementing statutes in 9 US CODE §§301–307 (1990) (approximately thirteen State parties and likely to increase with US ratification). *Washington Convention:* Convention on the Settlement of Investment Disputes Between States and Nationals of Other States, 575 UN TREATY SERIES 159 (1965) (more than 100 State parties) [hereinafter *Washington Convention*].

26. *See* G. Aldrich, THE JURISPRUDENCE OF THE IRAN-UNITED STATES CLAIMS TRIBUNAL: AN ANALYSIS OF THE DECISIONS OF THE TRIBUNAL (Oxford, Eng.: Clarendon Press, 1996).

27. *See* T. von Mehren, The Iran-US Arbitral Tribunal, 31 AMER. J. COMP. L. 713 (1983); A. Mouri, THE INTERNATIONAL LAW OF EXPROPRIATION AS REFLECTED IN THE WORK OF THE IRAN-U.S. CLAIMS TRIBUNAL (Dordrecht, Neth.: Martinus Nijhoff, 1994); and R. Lillich & D. Magraw (ed.), THE IRAN-UNITED STATES CLAIMS TRIBUNAL: ITS CONTRIBUTION TO THE LAW OF STATE RESPONSIBILITY (Irvington-on-Hudson, NY: Transnational, 1998).

28. *See* R. Lillich (ed.), THE UNITED NATIONS COMPENSATION COMMISSION (Ardsley, NY: Transnational, 1995).

29. *See generally,* W. Reisman et. al., INTERNATIONAL COMMERCIAL ARBITRATION: CASES, MATERIALS AND NOTES ON THE RESOLUTION OF INTERNATIONAL BUSINESS DISPUTES (Westbury, NY: Foundation Press, 1997).

30. The ICC's arbitration rules are reprinted in 15 INT'L LEGAL MAT'LS 395 (1976).

31. Further detail about the work of the ICC is available in S. Jarvin, Y. Derains, & J. Arnaldez, COLLECTION OF ICC ARBITRAL AWARDS: 1986–1990 (Deventer, Neth.: Kluwer, 1994).

32. *See Washington Convention* (cited in note 25 above).

33. Further detail about the work of the ICSID is available in R. Rayfuse (ed.), ICSID REPORTS (Cambridge, Eng.: Grotius, 1993).

34. Amer. Manufacturing & Trading, Inc. v. Republic of Zaire, ICSID Case Arb/93/1, reprinted in 36 INT'L LEGAL MAT'LS 1531 (1997).

35. World Wrestling Federation Entertainment, Inc. v. Michael Bosman, Case No. D99-0001 (Jan. 14, 2000), available at: <http://arbiter.wipo.int/domains/decisions/html/1999/d1999-0001.html>.

36. Feldman v. Mexico, ARB(AF)/99/1 (2002), available at: <http://www.dfait-maeci.gc.ca/tna-nac/documents/FeldmanAward.pdf>. For a useful legal analysis, see R. Sharma & A. Goldman, ASIL Insight: Intoario Court of Appeals Upholds NAFTA Chapter 11 Award, available at: <http://www.asil.org/insights/2005/02/insight040214.html>.

37. *Russian UN employee:* Yakimetz v. Secretary-General of the United Nations, Judgment No. 333, Doc. No. AT/DEC/333, (1984), reviewed in the International Court of Justice advisory opinion, Application for Review of Judgment No. 333 of the United Nations Administrative Tribunal (1987), available at: <http://www.icj-cij.org/icjwww/idecisions/isummaries/irjysummary870527.htm>. Rwandan UN employee: see J. Perlez, Accused of Killings, He Still Gets Back Pay, New York Times on the Web (Oct. 17, 2004).

38. Further detail is available in M. Hudson, INTERNATIONAL TRIBUNALS 145 (Wash., DC: Carnegie Endowment for Int'l Peace, 1944).

39. B. Boutros-Ghali, AN AGENDA FOR PEACE 23 (New York: UN, 1992), first printed in 31 INT'L LEGAL MAT'LS 953 (1992) [hereinafter *Agenda for Peace*]. This proposal was repeated in his 1995 SUPPLEMENT TO AGENDA FOR PEACE 54 (New York: UN, 1995)

40. *Commentators: See* O'Connell, International Legal Aid: The Secretary General's Trust Fund to Assist States in the Settlement of Disputes through the International Court of Justice, ch. 12, in M. Janis, INTERNATIONAL COURTS FOR THE TWENTY-FIRST CENTURY 235 (Dordrecht, Neth.: Martinus Nijhoff, 1992) [hereinafter *International Courts*]. *Resources quote:* P. Bekker, International Legal Aid in Practice: The ICJ Trust Fund, 87 AMER. J. INT'L L. 659, 668 (1993).

41. The full ICJ Statute is reprinted in E. Osmanczyk, ENCYCLOPEDIA OF THE UNITED NATIONS AND INTERNATIONAL AGREEMENTS 454 (2d ed. New York: Taylor & Francis, 1990) [hereinafter *UN Encyclopedia*] and on the Court's Web site at <http://www.icj-cij.org/icjwww/ibasicdocuments/ibasictext/ibasicstatute.htm>.

42. A more detailed description is available in *Rosenne*, at 23 (cited in note 11 above).

43. The World Court and the International Legal System, ch. 8, in T. O. Elias, THE UNITED NATIONS CHARTER AND THE WORLD COURT 111 (Lagos, Nigeria: Nigerian Inst. Advanced Legal Studies, 1989).

44. Background details are available in M. Scharf, A Preview of the Lockerbie Case, ASIL Insight 44 (May, 2000), available at: <http://www.asil.org/insights/insigh44.htm>. For his review of the results, see M. Scharf, The Lockerbie Trial Verdict, ASIL Insight 61 (Feb., 2001), available at: <http://www.asil.org/insights/insigh61.htm>.

45. T. Franck, Fact-Finding in the ICJ, in R. Lillich, FACT-FINDING BEFORE INTERNATIONAL TRIBUNALS 21–22 (Ardsley-on-Hudson, NY: Transnat'l Pub., 1992) [hereinafter *Fact Finding*].

46. Legal Consequences for States of the Continued Presence of South Africa in Namibia (South-West Africa) 276 (1970), 1971 ICJ REP., para. 89, at 45.

47. D. Akande, The International Court of Justice and the Security Council: Is there Room for Judicial Control of Decisions of the Political Organs of the United Nations?, 49 INT'L & COMP. L. QUARTERLY 326 (1997).

48. Marbury v. Madison, 5 U.S. (1 Cranch) 137, 177 (1803).

49. *See generally* M. Andenas (ed.), JUDICIAL REVIEW IN INTERNATIONAL PERSPECTIVE (The Hague: Kluwer, 2000).

50. *See generally,* §5.3.6 Judicial Review by the Court of Security Council Decisions, in D. Schweigman, THE AUTHORITY OF THE SECURITY COUNCIL UNDER CHAPTER VII OF THE UN CHARTER: LEGAL LIMITS ON THE ROLE OF THE INTERNATIONAL COURT OF JUSTICE 267–272 (The Hague: Kluwer, 2001).

51. R. Szafarz, THE COMPULSORY JURISDICTION OF THE INTERNATIONAL COURT OF JUSTICE X (Dordrecht, Neth.; Martinus Nijhoff, 1993) (explanatory clauses deleted).

52. Nottebohm Case, 1953 ICJ REP. 119–120 (preliminary order) [a principal case in §4.2].

53. Western Sahara Case (Advisory Opinion), 1975 ICJ REP. 3, 104 (Judge Petren's separate opinion).

54. Interpretation of Peace Treaties with Bulgaria, Hungary and Romania (Advisory Opinion), 1950 ICJ REP. 71, para.71.

55. *Competence case:* Competence of the General Assembly for the Admission of a State to the United Nations, 1950 ICJ REP. 4. *Reservations case:* Reservations to the Convention on Genocide, 1951 ICJ Rep. 15. *PLO case:* Applicability of the Obligation to Arbitrate Under Section 21 of the United Nations Headquarters Agreement of 26 June 1947, 1988 ICJ REP. 12.

56. Peter Kovacs, Rather Judgment than Opinion? Or Can We Speak About a Third Type of Judicial Procedure before the International Court of Justice?, XX ANUARIO DE DERECHO INTERNACIONAL 447, at 465 (Universidad de Navarra 2004).

57. S. Schwebel, Ad Hoc Chambers of the International Court of Justice, 81 AMER. J. INT'L L. 831, at 843 (1987). A July 2005 chambers decision resolved a major boundary dispute between Niger and Benin, regarding islands in the River Niger. A summary is available at: <http://www.icj-cij.org/icjwww/ipresscom/ipress2005/ipresscom2005-02_bn_summary_20050712.htm>.

58. A comprehensive analysis is available in & M. Leigh & S. Ramsey, Confidence in the Court: It Need Not Be a "Hollow Chamber," in L. Damrosch, THE INTERNATIONAL COURT OF JUSTICE AT A CROSSROADS 106, 112–117 (Dobbs Ferry, NY: Transnat'l Pub., 1987) [hereinafter *ICJ at a Crossroads*].

59. *See generally,* M. Shahabuddeen, PRECEDENT IN THE WORLD COURT (Cambridge, Eng.: Grotius, 1996).

60. J. Bentham, A Plan for an Universal and Perpetual Peace, Essay 4, Vol.2 THE PRINCIPLES OF INTERNATIONAL LAW 535–560 (1789) (1843 Bowring Edition of the first publication of Bentham's works, available at: <http://www.la.utexas.edu/research/polthcory/bentham/pil/pil.e04.html>.

61. H. Schermers, Evaluation, in M. Bulterman & M. Kuijer (ed.), COMPLIANCE WITH JUDGMENTS OF INTERNATIONAL COURTS 129 (The Hague: Martinus Nijhoff, 1996).

62. *Agenda for Peace* (cited in note 39 above), at 22–23].

63. S. Schwebel, Perspectives for the First Century of the Third Millennium, ICJ Press Communiqué 99/46 of 26 October 1999.

64. R. Anand, The World Court on Trial, ch. 5, in STUDIES IN INTERNATIONAL LAW AND HISTORY: AN ASIAN PERSPECTIVE 159, at 160–161 (Leiden, Neth: Martinus Nijhoff, 2004).

65. J. Merrills, The Optional Clause at Eighty, in N. Ando, E. McWhinney & R. Woldrum (ed.), 1 LIBER AMICORUM: JUDGE SHIGERU ODA 829 (The Hague: Kluwer, 2002) [hereinafter *Liber Amicorum*].

66. Insightful analyses of this mistrust are available in R. Anand, Attitude of the "New" Asian-African Countries Toward the International Court of Justice, in F. Snyder & S. Sathirathai, THIRD WORLD ATTITUDES TOWARDS INTERNATIONAL LAW 163 (Dordrecht, Neth.: Martinus Nijhoff, 1987) & E. Whinney, THE WORLD COURT AND THE CONTEMPORARY INTERNATIONAL LAW-MAKING PROCESS (Alphen aan den Rijn, Neth.: Sijthoff & Noordhoff, 1979).

67. E Posner, All Justice, Too, is Local, New York Times on the Web (Dec. 30, 2004). See also, J. Goldsmith, THE LIMITS OF INTERNATIONAL LAW (Oxford, Eng.: Oxford, 2005).

68. See generally, I. Brownlie, Why Do States Take Disputes to the International Court?, in *Liber Amicorum* (cited in note 63 above), 435, at 449–450.

69. H. Lauterpacht, THE DEVELOPMENT OF INTERNATIONAL LAW BY THE INTERNATIONAL Court 4 (Cambridge, Eng.: Grotius Publications, 1982).

70. 92 CONGRESSIONAL RECORD 10,696 (1946).

71. *See* Department of State Study on Widening Access to the International Court of Justice, 16 INT'L LEGAL MAT'LS 187 (1977).

72. Case Concerning the Military and Paramilitary Activities in and Against Nicaragua (Nicaragua v. USA), 1986 ICJ REP. 98.

73. S. Malawer, WORLD COURT AND THE US, IN ESSAYS ON INTERNATIONAL LAW 95 (Buffalo, NY: Hein, 1986). The Department of State's position is summarized in Stevenson, Conclusion, in *ICJ at a Crossroads* 459–461 (cited in note 58 above).

74. Copies are obtainable from the UN Sales Office in New York City. Quotation drawn from Final Report, at 28.

75. Statement of the International Committee of the Red Cross before the United Nations Preparatory Committee for the Establishment of an International Criminal Court, New York, February 14, 1997.

76. B. Yarnold, The International Court of Justice as an Adjudicator of State Transnational and International Crimes, ch. 7, in INTERNATIONAL FUGITIVES: A NEW ROLE FOR THE INTERNATIONAL COURT OF JUSTICE 104–105 (New York: Praeger, 1991).

77. *Early trials: See* R. Hingorini, MODERN INTERNATIONAL LAW 353 (2d ed. New York: Oceana, 1984). *League of Nations ICC:* This account is available in *UN Encyclopedia,* at 202 (cited in note 41 above).

78. J. Bridge, The Case for an International Court of Criminal Justice and the Formulation of International Criminal Law, ch. 11, in *International Courts* 213, 223 (cited in note 40 above).

79. *See* R. Gross, International Terrorism and International Criminal Jurisdiction, 67 AMER. J. INT'L L. 508 (1973).

80. Section 10.7 of this book provides a detailed discussion of the US response.

81. J. Stone & R. Woetzel (ed.), TOWARD A FEASIBLE INTERNATIONAL CRIMINAL COURT (GENEVA: WORLD PEACE THROUGH LAW CENTER [now World Jurist Ass'n], 1970). *See* also, The Political Offense Exemption, ch. 6, in G. Gilbert, ASPECTS OF EXTRADITION LAW 113, 156–162 (Dordrecht, Neth.: Martinus Nijhoff, 1991).

82. *See generally,* C. Van den Wyngaert (ed.), INTERNATIONAL CRIMINAL LAW: A COLLECTION OF INTERNATIONAL AND EUROPEAN INSTRUMENTS (2d rev. ed. The Hague: Kluwer, 2000).

83. *See generally,* J. Paust et al., INTERNATIONAL CRIMINAL LAW: CASES AND MATERIALS (2d ed. Durham, NC: No. Carolina

Acad. Press, 2000); L. Sunga, THE EMERGING SYSTEM OF INTERNATIONAL CRIMINAL LAW: DEVELOPMENTS IN CODIFICATION AND IMPLEMENTATION (The Hague: Kluwer, 1997); and Symposium: Developments in International Criminal Law, 93 AMER. J. INT'L LAW, 1–123 (1999).

84. *Tokyo Trial: See* T. Maga, JUDGMENT AT TOKYO: THE JAPANESE WAR CRIMES TRIALS (Lexington, KY: Univ. Press of Kentucky, 2001); J. Ginn, SUGAMO PRISON, TOKYO: AN ACCOUNT OF THE TRIAL AND SENTENCING OF JAPANESE WAR CRIMINALS IN 1948 (Jefferson, NC: McFarland & Co., 1992); and J. Keenan & B. Brown, CRIMES AGAINST INTERNATIONAL LAW (Wash., DC: Public Affairs Press, 1950). *Nuremberg Trial:* G. Ginsburgs & V. Kudriavtsev, THE NUREMBERG TRIAL AND INTERNATIONAL LAW (Dordrecht, Neth.: Martinus Nijhoff, 1990); J. Fried, The Great Nuremberg Trial, 70 AMER. POL. SCI. REV. 192 (1976).

85. Text available on ILC Web site at: <http://www.un.org/law/ilc/texts/nurnfra.htm>.

86. W. Bishop, JUSTICE UNDER FIRE 284 (New York: Prentice-Hall, 1974).

87. *See, e.g.,* M. Bassiouni, The Time Has Come for an International Criminal Court, 1 INDIANA INT'L & COMP. L. REV. 1 (1991) (one of this author's *many* publications in this field) & B. Ferencz, AN INTERNATIONAL CRIMINAL COURT: A STEP TOWARD WORLD PEACE–A DOCUMENTARY HISTORY AND ANALYSIS (New York: Oceana, 1980) (two volumes).

88. C. Tomuschat, International Criminal Prosecution: The Precedent of Nuremberg Confirmed, ch. 1, in R. Clark & M. Sann (ed.), THE PROSECUTION OF INTERNATIONAL CRIMES 21 (New Brunswick, NJ: Transaction Publishers, 1996) (see comprehensive authority contained in its herein omitted footnote 8).

89. A combined digest of ICTY and ICTR cases is available at: <http://hrw.org/reports/2004/ij/digest.pdf>.

90. UN Security Council Reso. 827, 25 May 1993, available at: <http://daccess-ods.un.org/TMP/8079314.html>(underlining deleted).

91. For details, see L. Sadat, ASIL Insight, The Trial of Slobodan Milosevic, available at: <http://www.asil.org/insights/insigh90.htm>.

92. R. May et al. (ed.), ESSAYS ON ICTY PROCEDURE AND EVIDENCE: IN HONOUR OF GABRIELLE KIRK MCDONALD (The Hague: Kluwer, 2001).

93. *See generally,* V. Morris & M. Scharf, AN INSIDER'S GUIDE TO THE INTERNATIONAL CRIMINAL TRIBUNAL FOR THE FORMER YUGOSLAVIA (Irvington-on-Hudson, NY: Transnational, 1995) (two volumes).

94. *See* ICTY Press Communiqué at <http://www.un.org/icty/pressreal/p382-e.htm>.

95. Summaries are available (press releases) on the ICTY Web site. *Rape:* Judgment of Trial Chamber II in the Kunarac, Kovac and Vukovic Case (Feb. 22, 2001), at <http://www.un.org/icty/pressreal/p566-e.htm>. *Genocide:* Judgment of Trial Chamber I in the Krstic Case (Aug. 2, 2001), at <http://www.un.org/icty/pressreal/p609-e.htm>. *Humanitarian Law:* Judgment of Trial Chamber II in the Tadic Case (May 7, 1997), at <http://www.un.org/icty/pressreal/p190-e.htm> (see *Tadic* case on course Web page).

96. See <http://www.un.org/icty>, click SREBRENICA for details & ICTY Cases & Judgments for this decision.

97. *Mayor case:* Prosecutor v. Jean-Paul Akayesu, Case No. ICTR-96-4-T (Judgment), <www.un.org/ictr/english/judgements/akayesu.html>. *Premier case:* Prosecutor v. Jean Kambanda, Case No. ICTR 97-23-S (Judgment and Sentence), www.un.org/ictr/english/judgements/kambanda.html>.

98. UN Security Council Reso. 955, 8 November 1994, available at: <http://daccess-ods.un.org/TMP/9548435.html>.

99. *See* K. Vick, Rwandan Genocide Case puts U.N. Court in Trial, Wash. Post on the Web, at A15 (Mar. 10, 2000).

100. Prosecutor v. Kanyabashi, Case No. ICTR-96-15-T (Jurisdiction, 18 June 1997). The ICTY case relied on by the ICTR in ruling on jurisdictional objections is Prosecutor v. Tadic, Decision on Jurisdiction, No. IT-94-1-T (Aug. 10, 1995), *aff'd*, Appeal on Jurisdiction, No. IT-94-1-AR72 (Oct. 2, 1995).

101. *See* B. Brown, Primacy or Complementarity: Reconciling the Jurisdiction of National Courts and International Criminal Tribunals?, 23 YALE J. INT'L L. 383 (1998).

102. An excellent summary of the various objections is available in B. Oxman, International Decisions, 92 AMER. J. INT'L L. 66 (1998). A Cambodian tribunal later emerged.

103. V. Morris & M. Scharf, The Rwanda Court as a Prelude to a Permanent International Criminal Court, Vol.1 THE INTERNATIONAL CRIMINAL TRIBUNAL FOR RWANDA, 707–709 (Irvington-on-Hudson, NY: Transnational, 1998).

104. *Lockerbie trial:* a comprehensive collection of web-based original trial materials and analyses are available at: <http://www.thelockerbietrial.com>. *See also,* R. Wallis, LOCKERBIE: THE STORY AND THE LESSONS (Westport, CT: Praeger, 2001). *Japanese trial:* the 1998 Tokyo judgment—the only successful compensation claim for sexual slavery against Japan, for its 1930s and 1940s conduct in the Asia Pacific region—was overruled in 2001. *See also,* Problem 11.C & Editorial Comments, Women's International Tribunal on Japanese Military Sexual Slavery, 95 AMER. J. INT'L LAW 335 (2001). *Sierra Leone tribunal:* see M. Scharf, The Special Court for Sierra Leone, ASIL Insight 53 (Oct. 2000), available at: <http://www.asil.org/insights/insigh53.htm>.

105. This account and useful background insight are provided in N. Stafford, A Model War Crimes Court: Sierra Leone, 10 ILSA J. INT'L & COMP. L. 117, at 131 (2003). See also, A. Kanu & G. Tortora, The Legal Basis of the Special Court for Sierra Leone, 3 CHINESE J. INT'L L. 515 (2005).

106. For a succinct but comprehensive analysis, see C. Jalloh, ASIL Insight, Immunity from Prosecution for International Crimes: The Case of Charles Taylor at the Special Court for Sierra Leone, is available at: <http://www.asil.org/insights/insigh145.htm>.

107. *Generally:* Truth Commissions: A Comparative Assessment, An Interdisciplinary Discussion Held at Harvard Law School in May 1996, available at: <http://www.law.harvard.edu/ programs/hrp/Publications/truth1.html>; *Afghanistan* (proposed): Human Rights Watch, Afghanistan: Bring War Criminals to Justice Special Court Needed For Past Atrocities, available at: <http://hrw.org/reports/

2005/afghanistan0605>; and *South Africa:* South African Truth and Reconciliation Commission Web site, available at: <http://www.doj.gov.za/trc>

108. Report of the Secretary-General on the Establishment of a Special Court for Sierra Leone, UN Doc. S/2000/915, UN SCOR, 55th Sess., para. 71 (2000), available at: <http://www.hri.ca/fortherecord2000/documentation/security/s-2000-915.htm>.

109. *ICC Journal:* See Official Journal of the International Criminal Court, available at: <http://www.icc-cpi.int/officialjournal.html>. *Academic Symposium:* A. von Bogdandy & R. Wolfrum (ed.), ICC and International Criminal Law, Part II, 7 MAX PLANCK YEARBOOK OF UNITED NATIONS LAW 329–735 (Leiden, Neth.: Martinus Nijhoff, 2004). *Drafting Commentary:* A. Cassese (ed.), THE ROME STATUTE FOR AN INTERNATIONAL CRIMINAL COURT: A COMMENTARY (Oxford, Eng.: Oxford Univ. Press, 2002) (two volumes).

110. The ICC "Rome Statute" is available on the UN's Web page at: <www.un.org/icc/romestat.htm>. Participating nations are listed at: <http://untreaty.un.org/ENGLISH/bible/englishinternetbible/PartI/chapterXVIII/treaty10.asp>.

111. UN Millennium Declaration, Part II. Peace, Security and Disarmament, point 9, available at: <http://www.unitednations.org.uk/info/millenniumdec.html>. For Conference details, see M. Scharf, Results of the Rome Conference for an International Criminal Court, ASIL Insight 23 (Aug., 1998), available at: <http://www.asil.org/insights/insigh23.htm>.

112. A press release is available at: <http://www.picosearch.com/cgi-bin/ts.pl>, search "Iraq."

113. Crimes within the Court's Jurisdiction are available on the UN's Web page at: <http://www.un.org/icc/crimes.htm>.

114. For details, see W. Hoge, International War-Crimes Prosecutor Gets List of 51 Sudan Suspects, New York Times on the Web, Apr. 6, 2005.

115. *French ratification: see* story (in French) at: <www.conseil-constitutionnel.fr/decision/98/98408/index.htm>. *England's ratification: see* House of Lords International Criminal Court bill at: <http://www.parliament.the-stationery-office.co.uk/pa/ld200001/ldbills/008/2001008.htm>.

116. *Treaty listing:* see Coalition for the ICC, Documents on Impunity Agreements, available at: <http://iccnow.org/documents/otherissuesimpunityagreem.html>. *Post-Abu Grahib reaction: See, e.g.,* A. Abass, The Competence of the Security Council to Terminate the Jurisdiction of the International Criminal Court, 40 TX INT'L L.J. 263, 265 (2005).

117. *Statutes:* The referenced federal statutes, in order of appearance are: 22 U.S.C. § 7423(c); (d); § 7424(b); § 7426(a); (b); (c); § 7427(a); § 7433. *Critiques:* N. Kristof, Schoolyard Bully Diplomacy, New York Times on the Web (Oct. 16, 2005). An analysis by the President of the American Society of International Law is available in A. Rovine, Notes from the President, ASIL Newsletter (Jan.–Feb., 2001).

118. M. Shukri, Will Aggressors Ever be Tried Before the ICC?, ch. 3, in M. Politi & G. Nesi (ed.), THE INTERNATIONAL CRIMINAL COURT AND THE CRIME OF AGGRESSION 33 (Aldershot, England: Ashgate Publishing, 2004).

119. UN Gen. Ass. Reso. 3414 (XXIX), available at: <http://www.un.org/documents/ga/res/29/ares29.htm>, scroll to 3414.

120. The triggering mechanisms are exhibited on the UN's Web page at <http://www.un.org/icc/trigger.htm>.

121. M. Politi, The Rome Statute of the ICC: Rays of Light and Some Shadows, in M. Politi & G. Nesi (ed.), THE ROME STATUTE OF THE INTERNATIONAL CRIMINAL COURT: A CHALLENGE TO IMPUNITY 14–15 (Aldershot, England: Ashgate Publishing, 2001).

122. A. Chayes & A. Slaughter, The ICC and the Future of the Global Legal System, ch. 14, in S. Sewall & C. Kaysen, THE UNITED STATES AND THE INTERNATIONAL CRIMINAL COURT: NATIONAL SECURITY AND INTERNATIONAL LAW 244–246 (Lanham, MD: Rowman & Littlefield, 2000).

123. Fenton Bresler, Can Foreign Court Pronounce on British Justice?, National Law Journal, June 8, 1998 (US legal newspaper).

124. *See* authorities in *Fact Finding* (cited in note 45 above).

125. C. Jenks, Regionalism in International Judicial Organization, 37 AMER. J. INT'L L. 314 (1943).

126. *Central American Court:* P. Sands & P. Klein, Regional Courts, in BOWETT'S LAW OF INTERNATIONAL INSTITUTIONS 391 (5th ed. London: Street & Maxwell, 2001). *Arab Court: See* E. Foda, THE PROJECTED ARAB COURT OF JUSTICE: A STUDY IN REGIONAL ADJUDICATION WITH SPECIFIC REFERENCE TO THE MUSLIM LAW OF NATIONS (Westport, CT: Hyperion Press, 1981).

127. *International Courts* 87–88 (cited in note 40 above).

128. Case 294/83, Partie Ecologiste "Les Verts" v. European Parliament, 1986 EURO. CT. REP. 1339, analyzed in Judicial Review of Community Acts, ch. 7, in L. Brown & T. Kennedy, THE COURT OF JUSTICE OF THE EUROPEAN COMMUNITIES 123, 128 et seq. (4th ed. London: Street & Maxwell, 1994).

129. *See* F. Newman, Legal Anomaly: Lacking Bill of Rights, Britons Seek Redress at a Court in France, Wall Street Journal, Oct. 21, 1985, at 1.

130. Reprinted in 9 INT'L LEGAL MAT'LS 673 (1970).

131. *See* T. Burgenthal, The Advisory Practice of the Inter-American Human Rights Court, 79 AMER. J. INT'L L. 1 (1985).

132. A detailed account of this and two related cases is available in C. Cerna, The Inter-American Court of Human Rights, in *International Courts,* 117, 131 (cited in note 40 above).

133. *See* Peru to recognize human rights court, USA Today (on the web) (Jan. 12, 2001), available at: <http://www.usatoday.com/news/world/nwsfri01.htm>.

134. T. Burgenthal, The Inter-American Court of Human Rights, 76 AMER. J. INT'L L. 231, 233 (1982).

135. S. Davidson, THE INTER-AMERICAN COURT OF HUMAN RIGHTS 207 (Aldershot, Eng.: Dartmouth Press, 1992).

136. *Andean Pact:* reprinted in 8 INT'L LEGAL MAT'LS 910 (1969). *Andean Court agreement:* reprinted in 18 INT'L LEGAL MAT'LS 1203 (1979).

137. Pierola, The Andean Court of Justice, 2 J. INT'L DISPUTE RESO. 11, 35–36 (1987).

138. *Alignment with European process:* Quito Protocol, 28 INT'L LEGAL MAT'LS 1165 (1989). *Implementation goal:* Manifest of Cartagena de Indias, 28 INT'L LEGAL MAT'LS 1282 (1989).

CHAPTER TEN

Use of Force

INTRODUCTION

The introductory chapters on States, international organizations, and the individual occasionally depicted the hostile environment associated with issues arising under International Law. This chapter focuses first on the many faces of "force," when force may be legitimately invoked, and its capacity to disrupt international relations. The remaining sections will depict some rather sensitive issues involving force—including humanitarian intervention, rescue missions, the Laws of War, and post-911 applications by the United States.

◆ 10.1 DEFINING "FORCE"

WHAT IS FORCE?

The word "force" is mentioned, but not defined, in the UN Charter. States have embraced or vilified its use in

[W]E LIVE . . . IN AN AGE OF LAW AND AN AGE OF reason, and age in which we can get along with our neighbors.

. . . It will be just as easy for nations to get along in a republic of the world as it is for us to get along in the republic of the United States.

. . . [I]f Kansas and Colorado have a quarrel . . . they don't call out the National Guard of each State and go to war over it. They bring suit in the Supreme Court and abide by its decisions. There isn't a reason in the world why we can't do that internationally.

—Speech on June 28, 1945, reprinted in PUBLIC PAPERS OF THE RESIDENTS: HARRY S. TRUMAN, at 151 (1961).

YOU ARE EITHER WITH US OR AGAINST US IN THE fight against terror. . . . That means different things for different nations. Some nations don't want to contribute troops. . . . Other nations can contribute intelligence-sharing. . . . But all nations . . . must do something.

—US President George Bush, Joint news conference with French President Jacques Chirac (Nov. 6, 2001).

a variety of circumstances.[1] Under Article 13.1(a) of the UN Charter, the General Assembly is responsible for "promoting international co-operation in the political field and encouraging the progressive development of

445

international law and its codification." The Assembly thus resolved to fill the Charter's definitional gap with several major resolutions regarding the use of force.

Friendly Relations Declarations   In the first of two related resolutions, the UN General Assembly broadly defined the term "force" in its Declaration on Principles of International Law concerning Friendly Relations and Cooperation among States in Accordance with the Charter of the United Nations (1970).[2] This comparatively lengthy Declaration contains provisions drawn from a variety of interim UN documents regarding the use of force. The purpose of the 1970 Declaration was to collate them, and to affirm what States should be willing to accept as a post-Charter norm.

The 1970 Declaration "recalls" the duty of States to refrain from military, political, economic, or any other form of coercion directed at the political independence or territorial integrity of another State. It specifies that such "a threat or use of force constitutes a violation of international law and the Charter of the United Nations and shall never be employed as a means of settling international issues." This Declaration provides that a State may not use "propaganda," "terror," or "finance" to coerce another State into acting in a particular way.

The 1970 Declaration was not the product of a negotiated process. The UN membership did not exchange concessions to produce a binding agreement. It was a statement in principle, containing common sense provisions that arguably belabored the obvious. The final paragraph, for example, provides that the "principles of the Charter [that] are embodied in this Declaration constitute basic principles of international law, and consequently [it] appeals to all States to be guided by these principles in their international conduct and to develop their mutual relations on the basis of the strict observance of these principles."

In 1987, the General Assembly approved a similar declaration. It augmented the earlier declaration. This was the Declaration on the Enhancement of the Effectiveness of the Principle of Refraining from the Threat or Use of Force in International Relations. This ensuing attempt to more clearly define aggression was the product of ten years of committee work. Like the UN's 1970 Declaration on Friendly Relations, the General Assembly ultimately adopted the 1987 UN Declaration without a vote.[3]

The 1987 Declaration contains some general clarifications. States must:

- refrain from "organizing, instigating, or assisting or participating in paramilitary, terrorist or subversive acts, including acts of mercenaries, in other States;"
- abstain from threats against the economic elements of another State; and
- avoid "economic, political or any other type of measures to coerce another State" for the purpose of securing advantages of any kind.

There are two significant similarities in these UN Declarations. First, they broadened the Charter rule prohibiting force, by expressly prohibiting particular uses of force, which were not mentioned in the 1945 Charter. Second, they share the same infirmity. The national members of the General Assembly did not include concrete measures to enforce the principles they purported to add to the UN's trilogy of basic articles on force (§10.2). These declarations are arguably just that: declarations—as opposed to multilateral treaties with specific obligations. On the other hand, they do serve as indicators of what conduct States deem to be, in principle, included within the Charter's prohibition on the use of force.

"Aggression"   The General Assembly's interim 1974 definition of the term "aggression" came as no surprise. It stated the obvious and meant different things to different people. UN General Assembly Resolution 3314, like the Assembly's 1970 and 1987 declarations, was also adopted without a vote. There was no debate as to specific applications:

Definition of Aggression
UNITED NATIONS GENERAL ASSEMBLY RESOLUTION 3314 (XXIX) (1974)
<http://www.un.org/documents/ga/res/29/ares29.htm>

Article 1
Aggression is the use of armed force by a State against the sovereignty, territorial integrity or political independence of another State, or in any other manner inconsistent with the Charter of the United Nations, as set out in this Definition.

Article 2

The first use of armed force by a State in contravention of the Charter shall constitute prima facie evidence of an act of aggression although the Security Council may, in conformity with the Charter, conclude that a determination that an act of aggression has been committed would not be justified in the light of other relevant circumstances, including the fact that the acts concerned or their consequences are not of sufficient gravity.

Article 3

Any of the following acts, regardless of a declaration of war, shall, subject to and in accordance with the provisions of article 2, qualify as an act of aggression:

(a) The invasion or attack by the armed forces of a State of the territory of another State, or any military occupation, however temporary, resulting from such invasion or attack, or any annexation by the use of force of the territory of another State or part thereof;

(b) Bombardment by the armed forces of a State against the territory of another State or the use of any weapons by a State against the territory of another State;

(c) The blockade of the ports or coasts of a State by the armed forces of another State;

(d) An attack by the armed forces of a State on the land, sea or air forces, or marine and air fleets of another State;

(e) The use of armed forces of one State which are within the territory of another State with the agreement of the receiving State, in contravention of the conditions provided for in the agreement or any extension of their presence in such territory beyond the termination of the agreement;

(f) The action of a State in allowing its territory, which it has placed at the disposal of another State, to be used by that other State for perpe-

trating an act of aggression against a third State;

(g) The sending by or on behalf of a State of armed bands, groups, irregulars or mercenaries, which carry out acts of armed force against another State of such gravity as to amount to the acts listed above, or its substantial involvement therein.

Article 4

The acts enumerated above are not exhaustive and the Security Council may determine that other acts constitute aggression under the provisions of the Charter.

. . .

Article 6

Nothing in this Definition shall be construed as in any way enlarging or diminishing the scope of the Charter, including its provisions concerning cases in which the use of force is lawful.

Article 7

Nothing in this Definition, and in particular article 3, could in any way prejudice the right to self-determination, freedom and independence, as derived from the Charter, of peoples forcibly deprived of that right and referred to in the Declaration on Principles of International Law concerning Friendly Relations and Cooperation among States in accordance with the Charter of the United Nations, particularly peoples under colonial and racist regimes or other forms of alien domination: nor the right of these peoples to struggle to that end and to seek and receive support, in accordance with the principles of the Charter and in conformity with the above-mentioned Declaration.

Article 8

In their interpretation and application the above provisions are interrelated and each provision should be construed in the context of the other provisions.

◆ *Notes & Questions*

1. There are of course many questions about how to apply this definition to specific cases. Article 1 prohibits "the use of armed force by a State," for example, against the sovereignty of another State. Should that include a nation clandestinely funding the al-Qaida terrorist organization?

2. Does Article 3(a) mean that the US pursuit of Taliban and al-Qaida members in Afghanistan, in response to 9-11, was an act of aggression? The discussion below regarding UN Charter Article 51 may help you resolve this question. Should it matter that, unlike the Iraq War, few States objected to the US invasion of Afghanistan—in its pursuit of those responsible for 9-11?

3. Would Article 3(b) mean that the 1999 North Atlantic Treaty Organization (NATO) nation bombing of Serbia and its Kosovo province—to prevent ethnic cleansing—constitutes an "act of aggression?"

4. Does Article 3(g) mean that paramilitary groups sent into South Africa—by surrounding African nations during the Apartheid era—rendered the sending nations guilty of "acts of aggression" within the meaning of this General Assembly resolution?

5. Does the Article 7 preservation of the rights to "self-determination, freedom and independence" mean that Palestinian suicide bombers are subjecting the Palestinian Authority to prosecution for the "crime of aggression?"

These UN resolutions—adopted without a vote, and thus no debate—may be likened to the US Supreme Court's attempted definitions of "obscenity." One has difficulty defining the term, yet all claim to know it when they see it.[4] You will recall, from your study of Chapter 2 on States, that express State consent is necessary to create binding obligations. A multilateral treaty would be the best evidence of such obligations. An international organization's resolution is *not* the equivalent. Pursuant to your study of Chapter 3 on organizations, a resolution is at least a non binding statement of general principles that States *should* observe in their mutual relations. The Friendly Principles and Aggression declarations provide guidance about the direction in which International Law points. Beware of those who characterize such resolutions as actually defining the specific content of International Law—as well as those who deny their suitability for any purpose.

The treaty on the International Criminal Court (ICC) (§9.5) did nothing to aid the progressive development of the law on this point. It does provide definitions for three of the four chargeable crimes: genocide, crimes against humanity, and war crimes. The fourth category of chargeable crimes is in ICC Statute, set forth in its Article 5.1(d) as "The crime of aggression." However, the ICC treaty did not define "aggression." As you learned in Chapter 8, one can expect many compromises in a multilateral treaty whose participants hope to include as many participants as possible. Instead, the 1998 conference delegates added Article 5.2: "The Court shall exercise jurisdiction over the crime of aggression once a provision is adopted . . . defining the crime and setting out the conditions under which the Court shall exercise jurisdiction with respect to this crime."[5]

This compromise had the advantage of retaining the prospect of future definitional negotiations, presumably at the Article 123 seven-year review of this treaty (2009). The disadvantage was the continuing lack of a negotiated agreement within the international community on the elements of this arguably theoretical crime. As articulately concluded by the Legal Advisor to the Egyptian Delegation to the United Nations, this compromise "was not without a price; it resulted in a main defect in the Statute . . . [which] does not contain a readily applicable provision on aggression which, according to the whole international community, represented by the General Assembly, is 'the gravest of all crimes against peace and security throughout the world', without the punishment of which the ICC would not really become the ultimate long awaited [vessel for applying] international criminal jurisdiction."[6]

SPECIFIC APPLICATIONS

Force has been applied when States are at war, on the brink of war, exchanging political or economic potshots, and when one adversary is unaware of the clandestine acts of the other. States have also invoked measures, short of war, which have had devastating effects on the target nation.

"Brinksmanship"   Nonviolent force has been used in a variety of contexts which might be characterized as brinkmanship: lighting the fuse, without actually firing—often referred to as "saber rattling." One of the classic examples appears on the border between North and South Korea. Since the Korean War ended in 1953, both the United States and North Korea have stationed tens of thousands of military troops and munitions at this potential flashpoint.[7] Other brinksmanship examples include reprisals and gunboat diplomacy.

A *reprisal* is a coercive measure typically involving a government-authorized seizure of property or persons in another country. It retaliates for a prior wrong to the initiating State or its citizens. While not uncommon during war, it is not authorized during times of peace. Unlike the 1789 US Constitution, the 1970 UN Declaration on Principles of International Law Concerning Friendly Relations and Cooperation Among States in

Accordance with the Charter of the United Nations explicitly prohibits acts of reprisal.[8]

Reprisal was more commonly invoked before the twentieth century. It took the forms of public and private reprisals. Public reprisals were once confined to injuries sustained by the State itself. In the eighteenth century, however, governments began to authorize reprisals for injuries to their citizens caused by foreign governments. When the ship of an English Quaker was seized in French waters, for example, England's Lord Cromwell demanded redress from the French government. When he was ignored, he sent orders to English warships to seize the French vessels and goods. Private reprisals were executed by individuals, as opposed to State military forces. Individuals would petition their home States for the issuance of "letters of marque and reprisal." In times of peace, the carrier of such a letter would be authorized—within his or her home State—to seize property or citizens of the offending State under authority of the issuing State's letter.[9]

Gunboat Diplomacy is one State's somewhat threatening conduct designed to intimidate another State. In the International Court of Justice's 1949 *Corfu Channel* judgment, for example, Albania had contested the presence of foreign military vessels in the channel between Albania and the Greek Island of Corfu. A British warship hit a mine while navigating within those waters. The presence of British warships was a hostile act, which apparently provoked Albania to take mining countermeasures. Before the Viet Nam War, US warships were continuously present off the coast of North Vietnam, as more US military advisors were being introduced into South Vietnam. The message to North Vietnam, sent by the mere presence of these vessels, was that the United States was literally always on the horizon.

More recent examples of this form of force involve the post-Persian Gulf War (PGW) tension between Iraq and the United States. Iraq engaged in cat-and-mouse diplomacy with its 1994 military buildup in southern Iraq, near Kuwait's northern border. The United States responded to this show of force by conducting military exercises in the immediate area. US warplanes then dropped bombs on Iraqi tanks abandoned in the Kuwait desert during the PGW. In March 1995, Iraq deployed some 6,000 troops and chemical weapons near the edge of the Persian Gulf. This buildup was apparently well beyond Iraq's reasonable defense requirements. It was apparently intended as a regional show of force. In 1998,

two US military buildups, in and around the Persian Gulf, sent the message that the United States was willing to launch a major military attack against Iraq. The message, occasioned by the presence of the US forces, was that Iraq must rescind its decision to thwart UN weapons inspectors from doing their job of monitoring Iraq's potential for producing weapons of mass destruction. Then in the months before the Iraq War began, President Bush threatened Saddam Hussein with a hostile reaction if Hussein did not permit access to inspect for weapons of mass destruction.

Countermeasures A *sanction* usually responds to internationally wrongful conduct. Sanctions include the confiscation of goods, or the freezing of assets—when US President Carter froze Iranian bank accounts during the hostage crisis of 1979–1980 (§7.4). A *countermeasure* might be imposed for purely political reasons. A State might decide to withdraw or expel a diplomat because of some political rift in international relations with another country. While a reprisal is a countermeasure, the peacetime use of this individualized remedy is rare. That is because countermeasures are typically launched by States on the basis of self-defense. While legitimate self-defense is a justification for the use of force, countermeasures undertaken for other purposes are not justifiable.[10]

A State that clandestinely finances a terrorist or terrorist group is effectively launching a countermeasure against the State where the terrorist strikes. Individuals like India's Prime Minister Gandhi, Egypt's President Sadat, and the prime ministers of Argentina and Italy were killed by terrorist acts allegedly financed from external sources. These leaders were punished for legitimate political conduct while in office, through the clandestine support of other States. In a more contemporary context, fifteen of the nineteen 9-11 aircraft hijackers were Saudi Arabian nationals. If their activities were financed by their homeland, or some other nation, this would be an extreme form of State-sponsored countermeasure against the US—and quite a stretch, if done in the name of self-defense.

Economic Coercion This application of force has many faces. One example is the nearing five-decade US economic embargo of Cuba.[11] Many nations including staunch US allies nevertheless trade with Cuba. In fact, a number of them joined in the October 2005 demand that the United States abide by the thirteen successive

UN General Assembly resolutions calling on the United States to end its Cuban embargo.

The most turbulent illustration of economic coercion is the Arab nation boycott of Israeli products, which began in 1954. For the next half-century, it would be a vivid reminder of how nonmilitary force can be used for the most sensitive of political purposes: to drive a nation out of existence. Members of the Council of the Arab League of Nations drafted and unanimously approved the 1954 Unified Law on the Boycott of Israel. The Council was composed of State representatives from each State in the League. The Council was established to promote cooperation through periodic meetings of the foreign ministers of each Arab State. The Arab States agreed to prohibit the purchase of Israeli exports when they approved the Unified Law as follows:

1. All persons within the enacting country [in the Arab League] are forbidden to conclude any agreement or transaction, directly or indirectly with any person or organization (i) situated in Israel; (ii) affiliated with Israel through nationality; or (iii) working for or on behalf of Israel, regardless of the place of business or residence; and
2. Importation into the enacting country [adopting this boycott] is forbidden of all Israeli goods, including goods manufactured elsewhere [outside of Israel] containing ingredients or components of Israeli origin or manufacture.

The 1968 Palestinian Charter affirmed the principle reason for the Arab boycott as follows:

The partition of Palestine in 1947 and the establishment of the state of Israel are entirely illegal, regardless of the passage of time, because they were contrary to the will of the Palestinian people and to their natural right in their homeland, and inconsistent with the principles embodied in the Charter of the United Nations, particularly the right to self-determination.

. . . Judaism, being a religion, is not an independent nationality. Nor do Jews constitute a single nation with an identity of its own; they are citizens of the states to which they belong. [12]

In 1972, the Arab League announced a revision of the boycott law called the General Principles for the Boycott of Israel. This version retained the broad language of the original agreement and supplemented it by imposing three specific categories of prohibitions. A *primary* boycott barred Arab nations from exporting goods to and importing goods from Israel. A *secondary* boycott generally banned trade between League members and countries that trade with Israel. Israel's trading partners are thus placed on a blacklist that limits their ability to trade with nations in the Arab League.

A *tertiary* boycott further discouraged trade with Israel. League members could not deal with companies that did any business with blacklisted countries, such as a company which had contracted to supply buses to Saudi Arabia. When the Saudis learned that the seats were made by a firm located in a blacklisted country, they threatened to cancel the bus order. The bus manufacturer then substituted seats with those made by a different firm that was *not* located in a blacklisted country. The Saudis only then considered the contract to be acceptable. The buses could thus be delivered to Saudi Arabia. [13]

The Arab League's Unified Law further prohibited trade with persons "affiliated with Israel through nationality." Some commentators asserted that this language was a euphemism for persons of the Jewish faith. If so, the Arab boycott applies to *all* Jewish-owned businesses, wherever they are located throughout the world. Some States, including the United States, passed legislation to punish compliance with this boycott. League members rejected this characterization of the boycott as being overly inclusive. [14]

The Arab boycott of Israel exhibited a comparatively hostile form of non military pressure. Travelers in the Middle East were not surprised to see lists at airport customs booths, listing Israeli-made goods or those from "offending" countries that dealt with Israel, thereby precluding travelers from bringing such goods to Arab nation's port of entry.

Several events impacted the solidarity once enjoyed by the twenty-one member States of the Arab League (§3.5). Egypt broke ranks with the League by its decision to even negotiate with Israel—incident to the 1979 "Camp David" agreements facilitated by US President Carter. A dozen years later, Kuwait no longer supported the Arab boycott of Israeli goods, when the US rescued Kuwait from an Iraqi conquest. That particular war pitted various Arab League members against its own League member Iraq. The 1993 Washington Peace Accords between PLO Chairman Yasir Arafat and Israeli

Prime Minister Yitzhak Rabin presented an important breakthrough for ending the Arab boycott of Israel, which had threatened international relations in the Middle East for more than four decades.

There was still work to be done to end this boycott. In 1997, US Defense Secretary William Cohen learned that the air force was excluding Jews from working for a private contractor on a US military base in Saudi Arabia. That predicament was spawned by lingering vestiges of the decades-old boycott. Given the US law that prohibits compliance with that discriminatory boycott, the secretary ordered all US military installations to ensure strict compliance with the US anti-discrimination law designed to counter the effects of the Boycott. In the 1998 Washington-brokered peace effort, Israel and the PLO finally agreed on the removal of the language from the Palestinian National Charter that called for the dismantling of Israel.

Boycotts are, of course, not unique to the Middle East. Economic boycotts and embargoes have been used by other countries as an alternative to military coercion. The United States, for example, has participated in boycotts against Cuba, Iran, Nicaragua, North Korea, and Vietnam.[15] The United Nations has established its own boycotts. The international boycott of South Africa was based in part on UN resolutions that condemned apartheid.

In 1998, the United Nations passed General Assembly Resolution 53/10 on the Elimination of Coercive Economic Measures as a Means of Political and Economic Compulsion. It thus urged States not to unilaterally impose coercive economic measures. The underlying concern was the severe impact that such measures have on the economy and free trade of the State against whom they are directed. The Assembly therein called for the repeal of unilateral, extraterritorial laws which impose such "sanctions on corporations and nationals of other States." It also called on States to cease applying or recognizing such unilateral measures.

Many nations have used economic sanctions to achieve political ends. There are reports about a grassroots effort in a number of Arab countries to boycott American goods as well. The primary impetus is the US support of Israel, during its Spring 2002 offensive in the occupied Palestinian territories. The Al Montazah supermarket chain in Bahrain, for example, is enforcing this boycott. It has replaced some 1,000 US-made products otherwise available to its estimated 10,000 daily

customers. Syria had already barred US products for some time.[16]

Low-intensity Conflict This point on the use of force spectrum lies between the categories of all-out war and small-scale hostilities. Low-intensity conflicts continued to surface, with increasing frequency, in the aftermath of the Cold War. The post-1945 Soviet objective of worldwide communism, and the alleged US exaggeration of the Soviet threat (so as to manipulate US allies), are no longer factors in the suppression of low-intensity conflict.[17]

The word "war" conjures visions of the two world wars of the twentieth century, and the more contemporary PGW (1991), in which two-dozen States joined in the fight to liberate the oil-rich sheikhdom of Kuwait from Iraq. But there have been hundreds, if not thousands, of conflicts of a lesser magnitude, wherein death and destruction have been just as exacting for the affected individuals. Residents of Somalia, for example, would hardly consider that 1993 conflict as being anything less intense than a large geopolitical conflict like World War II. An event like 9-11 can ignite, then fuel, external military and political sparks to fan the flames of war beyond the flashpoint.

The US military definition of low-intensity conflict provides useful insight into the conduct of contemporary foreign affairs: "Low-intensity conflict is a politico-military confrontation between competing states or groups below conventional war and above the routine, peaceful competition among states. It frequently involves protracted struggles of competing principles and ideologies. Low-intensity conflict ranges from subversion, such as training and paying paramilitary rebels, to the use of armed force. It is waged by a combination of means, employing political, economic, informational, and military instruments. Low-intensity conflicts are often localized, generally in the Third World, but contain regional and global security implications."[18] Examples include: interventions like the 1994 US military operation in Haiti to restore democracy; border wars between Third World countries; and wars involving national liberation fronts, such as the mid-1980s US support of the Contras—who sought to topple Nicaragua's Sandinista government (§10.2 *Nicaragua Case*).

An analysis in a 1988 US Government Printing Office publication reported the findings of the Commission on Integrated Long-Term Strategy. While it was prepared (just) before the collapse of the Soviet Union, this analysis still suggests the continuing stake in low-intensity conflict and its implications for US national security:

To help protect US interests and allies in the Third World we still need more of a national consensus on both means and ends. Our means should include:

◆ Security assistance at a higher level and with fewer legislative restrictions. . . .
◆ Versatile mobile forces, minimally dependent on overseas bases, that can deliver precisely controlled strikes against military targets.
◆ In special cases, US assistance to . . . insurgents who are resisting a hostile regime that threatens its neighbors. The free world will not remain free if its options are only to stand still and retreat.[19]

War   War was not condemned in ancient Greece or Rome. On the other hand, Aristotle wrote that it was regarded as the antithesis of happiness and leisure: "We make war in order that we may live at peace. . . . Nobody chooses to make war or provokes it for the sake of making war; a man would be regarded as a bloodthirsty monster if he made . . . [friendly nations] into enemies in order to bring about battles and slaughter."[20]

War appeared to be a necessary evil in the nation-State system spawned by the 1648 Peace of Westphalia. The cornerstone, State sovereignty, demanded territorial protection. Breaches meant war, which had to be waged to protect even barren hinterlands from foreign occupation or trespass. Yale University Professor Michael Reisman penned a valuable insight in his provocative essay on a global system that continues to promote war:

The rhetoric of peace is more than neutralized by the symmetrical prominence of the military in competing governments. The manifest drive is for security, in a system which is structured for insecurity. . . . The allocation of power is, of course, an inescapable concern, but one of the functions of a system of nation-states . . . is to perpetuate insecurity through artifacts such as the "balance" or imbalance of power. . . . While a war system requires a culture of parochialism, self-sacrifice, and the paraphernalia of wars, it does not require wars. Rather it requires a pervasive expectation of impending violence in order to sustain and magnify personal insecurity. Small wars can be nourished as a neat means of keeping this expectation alive. . . .

The viciousness of a war system is circular as well, for even those who concede its horror and absurdity [can readily] perceive . . . a situation in which the sense of insecurity can be quite accurate and rational . . . In international politics there is, indeed, a very real enemy with very real operations-plans [prepared in anticipation of war].[21]

During the evolution of modern International Law in the eighteenth and nineteenth centuries, the use of force was often characterized as a "necessity." The more powerful European States developed convenient justifications for their aggressive uses of force, including the so-called "just war." They commonly claimed that force was the only effective method for enforcing International Law. An aggrieved State could not allow the violation of International Law to go unpunished, for fear of anarchy. Force was characterized as an inherent right—beyond question—when a State, in its unbridled discretion, deemed it necessary to use force in the name of God and country.

Great Britain's Sir Hersch Lauterpaucht was one of the most prolific legal historians, teachers, writers, and judges [International Court of Justice (ICJ)] of all time. His ubiquitous writings on war aptly described it as the ultimate instrument for enforcing national policy. It was also the self-acclaimed enforcement mechanism of International Law, given the absence of an international organization to control uses of force (prior to the twentieth century). Lauterpaucht traced the development of the legal justification for unilateral uses of force as follows:

[T]he institution of war fulfilled in International Law two contradictory functions. In the absence of an international organ for enforcing the law, war was a means of self-help for giving effect to claims based or alleged to be based on International Law. Such was the legal and moral authority of this notion of war as an arm of the law that in most cases in which war was in fact resorted to in order to increase the power and the possessions of a State at the expense of others, it was described . . . as undertaken for the defence of a legal right. This conception of war was intimately connected with the distinction, which was established in the formative period of International Law and which never became entirely extinct, between just and unjust wars. . . .

In the absence of an international legislature it was a crude substitute for a deficiency in international organization. As [the English legal analyst] Hyde, writing in 1922, said "It always lies within the power of a State to gain political or other advantages over another . . . by direct recourse to war." International Law did not consider as illegal a war admittedly waged for such purposes. . . .

War was in law a natural function of the State and a prerogative of its uncontrolled sovereignty.[22]

In the nineteenth century, the limitless use of force became the centerpiece of national policy for certain leaders. They employed it to preserve the "national security."[23] However, the self-righteous implications of that term provided only a thin veneer for the aggressive nature of their realpolitik. Napoleon used force to dominate Europe in the late eighteenth and early nineteenth centuries. Hitler's twentieth-century use of force expanded Germany's national frontiers and influence throughout Europe. His aggressive policies sparked World War II.

Many military conflicts have erupted since the end of World War II—mostly in the third world. These have been declared or undeclared wars; large-scale military combat or low-intensity conflict; and civil or international wars. In all such instances, the conduct of the belligerents and the treatment of the victims are governed by International Humanitarian Law including the 1949 Geneva Conventions (GCs). These will be addressed in §10.6 and §10.7 later.

Force as Politics The use of force has become a natural feature of many political struggles for achieving national objectives. The use of force is necessary to achieve political power, both internally and in international relations. China's revolutionary leader from a recent generation in Chinese political thought, Mao Tse-Tung, thus viewed "politics as war without bloodshed and war as politics with bloodshed."[24] During and after his rise to power in 1949, Mao asserted that war would no longer be necessary, after international communism eliminated the world's social and economic classes. In the interim, aggressive military means were justified by the end.

The former Soviet Union championed a distinct communist articulation, purportedly designed to *avoid* the use of force. Prior to the Soviet demise, the use of force was characterized as becoming obsolete as other nations embraced the principle of "peaceful coexistence," which was enshrined in the Soviet Constitution. The basic premise was that two nations with opposed

political and economic ideologies could nevertheless coexist in peace—if each was able to pursue distinct social, political, and economic goals during the global transition from capitalism to communism. Commentators often referred to this Soviet foreign policy with the West as "détente." It necessitated tolerance of the Western capitalist system, until it could be overcome by the fall of capitalism. Moscow State University Professor Grigori Tunkin explains it as follows:

The principle of peaceful coexistence of states with different social systems presupposes the existence of other major principles of international law, such as non-use of force or threat of force, respect for sovereignty and non-intervention in internal affairs. It reflects their substance in a general form even though it goes beyond these principles. The principle of peaceful coexistence prohibits policies that are directed at confrontation between states belonging to different social systems and requires that policies be directed at developing cooperation between them, in short, be policies of détente. . . .

It follows that the principle of peaceful coexistence is directed against anti-communism in interstate relations. That is why it is so strongly disliked by reactionary circles of capitalist countries who assert that this principle does not exist in international law.[25]

Contemporary political science "realists" discount the accuracy of claims that history has ever produced binding limitations on the use of force. Their perspective is that international rules about force are meaningless in a crisis. There is no practical utility in the legal formulations that purport to justify, or limit, the national employment of force. Analyzing the legitimacy of aggressive conduct is, in reality, theoretical and unproductive. The role of law in international relations, in their view, is overstated. One supporting example is that States retained the inherent right to use force, notwithstanding the contemporary prohibition on the threat or use of force in Article 2.4 of the UN Charter. It is thus unrealistic to expect States to justify their conduct to anyone. Australian National University Professor D. W. Greig describes this view as follows:

The extent to which a state is entitled to use force in the conduct of its international relations raises a profusion and a confusion of politico-legal problems [that] are scarcely capable of analysis, let alone solution. . . .

In no area is international law more vulnerable to the taunt that *"it really doesn't work"* than in the context of the rules which are claimed to exist [about] prohibiting or restricting the use of force. The reason why this type of assertion is made is partly due to the fact that widespread publicity is given to instances of the use of force by states, while peaceful inaction or cooperation, that is, the normal situation in the relations of states, merits scarcely a mention in the news media. However, the making of such an assertion discloses a fundamental misunderstanding of the role of international law. It has already been demonstrated that legal principles are only allowed to be the sole determinants within a limited area (i.e. mainly within the jurisdictional competence of the International Court). The more important the issue, the less traceable it is to anything other than political compromise in which the part played by the legal rules is correspondingly limited. And if one assumes that states will only have recourse to force as a last resort when they consider their vital interests most gravely threatened or affected, the role of legal principle may well vanish altogether, even though the states concerned will often advance reasons which purport to establish the legality of their actions within the existing or supposed legal order.[26]

In practice, a number of States do not characterize force, or certain of its applications, as being inherently mischievous. For some, it is a natural instrument of foreign policy.[27] Many nations have thus employed combinations of military action, threats, and economic coercion to achieve political objectives such as the multi faceted US reaction to the terrorist attacks in the United States on September 11, 2001 (§10.7). Most nations ostensibly characterize force as being "bad" in the abstract. It often becomes a "necessary evil," if not inherently "just," when such a critical national interest is at stake. One of the most difficult decisions a leader can make is whether to use force, and the degree to which it is in the national interest. The US Congress, for example, has declared war only five times in the nation's history. A major Brookings Institution (think tank) study revealed that the US President was "called upon" to employ US forces 215 times between 1946 and 1975—and hundreds more, before and after the Viet Nam War.[28]

The preceding summary yields only a small slice of the spectrum. Many shades of gray emerge when viewing this subject in depth—more so than with any other

surface on the International Law canvas. The underlying concern is this: Will the international community effectively control national uses of aggressive force, now that sophisticated weaponry can consummate Armageddon?

VARIABLES AFFECTING LEGITIMACY

Economic and Political Force   States compete with one another, employing various forms of economic and political force. There is often a fine line between economic competition and aggression. The Arab boycott of Israel classically illustrates economic intimidation designed to drive a State out of existence. Just after the establishment of the State of Israel, members of the Arab League unanimously planned the economic collapse of Israel as follows: a primary boycott of Israeli goods sold in the international marketplace; a secondary boycott, whereby Arab States discouraged other States from trading with Israel; and a tertiary boycott, whereby other States which traded with Israel were blacklisted from obtaining international contracts of any kind with the boycott's overseers (§8.4).

In 1979, US President Carter ordered a freeze on the transferability of billions of dollars worth of Iranian assets, found in the United States or controlled by US entities, in response to Iran's seizure of US diplomats. Freezing Iran's vast financial assets in the United States ultimately played a significant role in the resolution of this diplomatic conflict (§7.4).

Collectively imposed sanctions often bring more "force" to bear than State-sponsored sanctions. The breakdown of South African apartheid, for example, was to a significant degree facilitated by UN-imposed sanctions. These were leveled against South Africa because of its official policy of separating the races at all levels of society. The United Nations directed its member States to boycott South African goods and investments. The long-term effects of this economic deprivation were partially responsible for that government's decision to abandon apartheid in order to avoid the adverse long-term effects of this external economic pressure. Unlike the Arab boycott of Israel, these economic sanctions were not designed to drive South Africa out of existence, but rather its official policy of racial discrimination.

One must acknowledge, however, that multinationally imposed economic sanctions are another form of force. Such sanctions are presumably far less forceful than military alternatives. That is not always the case. In his revealing study, former Iraqi Ambassador to the United

States and the United Kingdom, Amir Al-Anbari, points out that:

> Economic sanctions are generally conceived as peaceful measures preferable to the use of force. In reality, however, economic sanctions are by no means peaceful and quite often are deadlier and more destructive than military action.
>
> . . .
>
> Consequently, economic sanctions imposed [by the UN] on states or governments degenerate into a collective punishment of the people. It is almost a cliché to hear that the suffering of the civilians particularly children and women is a collateral or unintended side effect. Be that as it may, when the main victim of the sanction is the civilian population then the sanctions have to be terminated or modified . . . to ensure the safety and human rights of the civilian population. Under the present Charter there is no such requirement.[29]

Aggressive versus Defensive Force   The actor's posture—aggressor or a victim with no choice—is a significant factor in determining whether the use of force is acceptable or not. As acknowledged in this section's materials on self-defense, this distinction is often rather ambiguous. The underlying question is whether the particular use of force resembles a sword more or a shield.

State versus Organizational Actor   One distinction focuses on whether the State actor is undertaking *unilateral* action, or acting at the directive of an international organization attempting to restore peace.

A classic illustration of a unilateral use/threat of force arose in 1998, when the United States engaged in two, proximate military buildups in the Persian Gulf. Iraq had consistently thwarted UN efforts to conduct inspections in search of weapons of mass destruction. In 1991, UN Security Council Resolution 678 authorized the use of "all necessary force" to eject Iraq from Kuwait. Seven years later, however, it was not clear that the United States could continue to rely on an aging Council resolution to use additional force against Iraq. In the absence of a fresh resolution, the UN Secretary-General advised the United States that a new one would be necessary for the US employment of forceful measures in the latter scenario. Three Council members [France, People's Republic of China (PRC), and Russia] objected to the

US assertion of virtually *carte blanche* authority to invade Iraq. The United States was not defending Kuwait's sovereignty in 1998. There was no longer a widely accepted Arab coalition, which favored multilateral action against Iraq. The United States nevertheless responded that it retained the authority to use force. That was because Iraq had failed to comply with UN weapons-inspection mandates after the PGW. The United States thus asserted that it did not need *fresh* Council authority to attack Iraq. However, other nations countered that a US attack would have constituted an *aggressive* use of force in violation of UN Charter principles.

For PGW II (2003), the United States was unable to secure a UN resolution backing its intended use of force. In September 2004, the Secretary-General announced that the Iraq War was illegal, after eighteen months of expressing reservations. It was the other post-attack events, however, that trimmed back international support for the United States and Coalition presence in Iraq. These events included the:

◆ Withdrawal of certain Coalition nations such as Spain, when the 2004 Madrid metro bombings effectively unelected the previously pro-war government;
◆ Leaking of the previously secret, March 2003 Downing Street memo wherein: (a) Great Britain's Attorney General advised the Prime Minister, before the war started, regarding the illegality of launching an Iraq War; (b) that the White House viewed military action against Saddam Hussein as inevitable since 9-11; and (c) that "the intelligence and facts were being fixed around the policy;[30]
◆ Failure to find any weapons of mass destruction;[31] and
◆ Swelling of foreign insurgents able to aid the insurrection—an estimated total strength of 200,000, as opposed to the US military's 150,000 troops.

◆ 10.2 UN PRINCIPLES ON FORCE

The UN Charter contains deceptively simple directives on the use of force:

(1) States may not use or threaten the use of force.
(2) States may use force defensively, when responding to an "armed attack."
(3) The UN Security Council possesses the legal monopoly on the use of force.

The UN Charter's drafters hoped to control the aggressive outbursts of behavior, which led to the demise of the post–World War I League of Nations, as well as World War II. The key Charter provisions on the use of force were cast in the following terms:

United Nations Charter
United Nations Conference on International Organization
signed 26 June 1945, San Francisco, California
<http://www.un.org/aboutun/charter>

Chapter I.
Purposes and Principles

Article 2.4
All Members shall refrain in their international relations from the threat or use of force against the territorial integrity or political independence of any state, or [behave] in any other manner inconsistent with the Purposes of the United Nations.

Article 2.7
Nothing contained in the present Charter shall authorize the United Nations to intervene in matters which are essentially within the domestic jurisdiction of any state . . .; but this principle shall not prejudice the application of [UN Security Council] enforcement measures under Chapter VII.

Chapter VII.
Actions with Respect to
Threats to the Peace, Breaches of the Peace,
and Acts of Aggression

Article 39
The Security Council shall determine the existence of any threat to the peace, breach of the peace, or act of aggression and shall . . . decide what measures shall be taken in accordance with Articles 41 and 42, to maintain or restore international peace and security.

Article 41
The Security Council may decides what measures not involving the use of armed force are to be employed to give effect to its decisions, and may call upon Members of the United Nations to employ such measures. These may include complete or partial interruption of economic relations and of rail, sea, air, postal, telegraphic, radio, and other means of communication, and the severance of diplomatic relations.

Article 42
Should the Security Council consider that measures provided for in Article 41 would be inadequate . . ., it may take such action by air, sea, or land forces as may be necessary to restore international peace and security. Such action may include demonstrations, blockade, and other operations by air, sea, or land forces of Members of the United Nations.

Article 51
Nothing in the present Charter shall impair the inherent right of individual or collective self-defence if an armed attack occurs against a Member of the United Nations, until the Security Council has taken measures necessary to maintain international peace and security. Measures taken by Members in the exercise of this right of self-defence shall be immediately reported to the Security Council and shall not in any way affect the authority and responsibility of the Security Council to maintain or restore international peace and security.

The International Law Commission (§3.3) is an organ of the General Assembly. In July 2001, it promulgated the text of its years-in-the-making *Draft Articles on State Responsibility*. Its treatment of countermeasures addresses State activity undertaken for purposes ranging from the imposition of economic sanctions to military self-defense:

International Law Commission
Titles and Texts of the Draft Articles on
Responsibility of States for Internationally Wrongful Acts

(adopted by the Drafting Committee on second reading)

UNGA Doc. A/CN.4/L.602/Rev.1 (26 July 2001)
<http://www.un.org/law/ilc/sessions/53/english/602rev1e.pdf>

Chapter II
Countermeasures

Article 49
Object and Limits of Countermeasures

1. An injured State may only take countermeasures against a State which is responsible for an internationally wrongful act in order to induce that State to comply with its obligations under Part Two [Content of the International Responsibility of a State].
2. Countermeasures are limited to the non-performance for the time being of international obligations of the State taking the measures towards the responsible State.
3. Countermeasures shall, as far as possible, be taken in such a way as to permit the resumption of performance of the obligations in question.

Article 50
Obligations Not Affected by Countermeasures

1. Countermeasures shall not affect:
   (a) The obligation to refrain from the threat or use of force as embodied in the Charter of the United Nations;
   (b) Obligations for the protection of fundamental human rights;
   (c) Obligations of a humanitarian character prohibiting reprisals;
   (d) Other obligations under peremptory norms of general international law.
2. A State taking countermeasures is not relieved from fulfilling its obligations:
   (a) Under any dispute settlement procedure applicable between it and the responsible State;
   (b) To respect the inviolability of diplomatic or consular agents, premises, archives and documents.

Article 51
Proportionality

Countermeasures must be commensurate with the injury suffered, taking into account the gravity of the internationally wrongful act and the rights in question.

Article 52
Conditions Relating to Resort to Countermeasures

1. Before taking countermeasures, an injured State shall:
   (a) Call on the responsible State, in accordance with article 43, to fulfil its obligations under Part Two;
   (b) Notify the responsible State of any decision to take countermeasures and offer to negotiate with that State.
2. Notwithstanding paragraph 1(b), the injured State may take such urgent countermeasures as are necessary to preserve its rights.
3. Countermeasures may not be taken, and if already taken must be suspended without undue delay if:
   (a) The internationally wrongful act has ceased, and
   (b) The dispute is pending before a court or tribunal which has the authority to make decisions binding on the parties.
4. Paragraph 3 does not apply if the responsible State fails to implement the dispute settlement procedures in good faith.

Article 53
Termination of Countermeasures

Countermeasures shall be terminated as soon as the responsible State has complied with its obligations under Part Two in relation to the internationally wrongful act.

◆ *Notes & Questions*

1. Do the General Assembly's above International Law Commission Articles provide the specific circumstances under which a State may react, when an adversary's conduct is not unmistakable military aggression? Do they adequately define the behavior that appropriately triggers resort to force in the name of self-defense?[32]

2. For an analysis of the ILC's draft Articles, see J. Crawford, J. Peel & S. Olleson, The ILC's Articles on Responsibility of States for Internationally Wrongful Acts: Completion of the Second Reading, 12 EUROPEAN J. INT'L L. 963 (2001), available at: <http://www.ejil.org/journal/new/new0109.html>.

CAROLINE AND PGW 1 APPLICATIONS

Note that the above UN International Law Commission's Article 52.2 authorizes only such countermeasures as are "*necessary*." Article 51 limits countermeasures to those commensurate with the injury suffered, pursuant to its title "*Proportionality*." These integrated requirements are key ingredients for the many applications you will encounter in this chapter.

Most courses in International Law mention a widely accepted, and debated, test of "necessity" which dates back to 1842. US Secretary of State Daniel Webster rejected a British claim of self-defense, as follows: Great Britain claimed a necessity when it raided the steamship Caroline, which some Canadian forces were using in support of a Canadian insurrection (prior to independence in 1867). A British raiding party boarded the ship when it was moored on the New York side of the Niagara River. They attacked those on board, and set the ship afloat so that it plunged over Niagara Falls. Webster said that although Great Britain possessed a right of self-defense, the exercise of that right should be confined to cases in which the "necessity of that self-defence is instant, overwhelming, and leaving no choice of means and no moment for deliberation."[33]

Which of these key variables—necessity and proportionality—is more easily decided and applied: necessity or proportionality? Are they applied universally? A useful response is offered by University of Adelaide Professor Judith Gardam:

Although it is true to say that there will be a theoretical divide between States involved in an armed

conflict in terms of their respective legal position under the [UN] Charter ban on the use of force, its practical impact is *negligible*. With some notable exceptions [however], States *invariably* conduct themselves on the basis that, whatever the legal status . . . proportionality and necessity govern their actions. Even States that claim expansive rights to resort to force do not regard themselves as having the right to use unlimited force.

. . .

On reflection, proportionality . . . can be seen as somewhat of a success story. Despite the limitations in that regime and the controversy it always seems to generate, it has been possible to incorporate the restraints of proportionality into concrete norms that have proved capable of broad application to particular situations. . . .

The application of the requirement of necessity is more straightforward than proportionality. There are not so many variables that can contribute to the decision-making process in determining the necessity to resort to forceful measures in any given situation. . . . [N]ecessity plays a significant role as a restraint in the use of force under current international law . . . [and] the mere fact of the intense debates . . . where forceful action is [being] considered indicates the constraining role of necessity.

The need for further refinement of these norms has been highlighted by the revival of the global terrorist threat and the 2001 National Security Strategy of the United States in relation to the use of preemptive force. With the constraints of the Charter norms on the use of force subjected to considerable strain, necessity and proportionality arguably are all that is left uncontested in the legal regime.[34]

To what extent are these vintage principles of real significance to States on the brink of war? This may be the most sensitive subject of all. The late Ocsar Schachter, former Legal Advisor to the United Nations, responded that:

In virtually all wars, questions of necessity and proportionality have given rise to controversy that is troubling and divisive.

. . .

However, centuries of discussion by philosophers and jurists about the meanings of necessity and proportionality in human affairs do not seem to have produced general definitions capable of answering concrete issues. As with many abstract concepts, the answers to specific questions depend on the circumstances, appraised in the light of the humanitarian ends that justify the[se two] restraints. Determining the proper relation between means and ends in situations of great complexity and uncertainty is never easy. Decision makers . . . cannot forget the risks and costs of restraint, yet they must also be mindful of the legal imperative to avoid unnecessary and disproportionate force.[35]

You have now had an opportunity to grapple with some applications of the easily stated, but difficult to apply, dual requirements of necessity and proportionality. Having initially considered this preliminary building block, it should be easier to digest the following materials. They delve into the three specific Charter provisions often applied in use of force analyses.

UN CHARTER PROHIBITION ON FORCE

Article 2.4 enshrines *the* most fundamental principle in International Law. States may not use, or threaten to use, force in their international relations. This undefined but fundamental ban almost immediately spawned debates about whether it is, in fact, a meaningful norm. Unlike earlier multilateral treaties on the use of force—such as the 1928 Paris Peace Pact that expressly condemned war—the UN Charter mentions, but does not define, the terms "war" or "aggression." Some commentators have therefore argued that Article 2.4 is deficient as a legal norm. It is too broad to have any specific meaning. Others have argued that the drafters' use of such broad terms was intended to avoid any narrow interpretation of this centerpiece of the UN Charter. Columbia University Professor Oscar Schachter, former Director of the UN Legal Division, asserts that Article 2.4 was intended to broadly outlaw *all* forms of aggressive force:

Admittedly, the article does not provide clear and precise answers to all the questions raised. Concepts such as "force," "threat of force" or "political independence" embrace a wide range of possible meanings. Their application to diverse circumstances involves choices as to these meanings and assessments of the behavior and intentions of various actors. Differences of opinion are often likely even among "disinterested" observers; they are even more likely

among those involved or interested. But such divergences are not significantly different from those that arise with respect to almost all general legal principles. . . . [A]rticle 2.4 has a reasonably clear core meaning. That core meaning has been spelled out in [subsequent] interpretive documents . . . adopted unanimously by the General Assembly. . . . The International Court and the writings of scholars reflect the wide area of agreement on its [intended] meaning. It is therefore unwarranted to suggest that article 2.4 lacks the determinate consent necessary to enable it to function as a legal rule of restraint.[36]

Some States and commentators interpret Article 2.4 far more narrowly. They do not view economic coercion, for example, as falling within the meaning of the Charter's prohibition against force. Under this delimiting view, a State-imposed trade embargo against a particular State's products is not "force" within the meaning of the Charter.[37]

This legal debate began to take shape in 1952. The General Assembly established the Special Committee on the Definition of Aggression. Many States, particularly those in the Western hemisphere, urged that since International Law had already banned the use of force, further definitions of "aggression" were unnecessary. The Committee and the General Assembly ought to concentrate, it was argued, on defining the Charter terms "armed attack" and "self-defence." A more detailed definition of aggression would only serve to hamper the UN's organs in ways that might preclude the Security Council (SC) from exercising its "Chapter VII" powers to control breaches of the peace. This blocking move was countered with the argument that the major powers, in reality, thus sought to retain their own discretion to act in ways not expressly prohibited by the UN Charter.

In its 1956 Report to the United Nations Special Committee on the Definition of Aggression, the US representative asserted the futility of attempting to achieve globally acceptable refinements. The United States had signed a number of more specific regional definitions, including the Organization of American States (OAS) 1947 Inter-American Treaty of Reciprocal Assistance. Such "instruments belonged to the same geographical area and were united by many bonds, including a feeling of solidarity, which were not present to the same degree among the Members of the United Nations."[38] Further articulations would be best deduced by a *regional* refinement process (which the United States could better control).

ICJ Position on "Force" The ICJ 1986 *Nicaragua* case took the position that the Article 2.4 "armed attack" provision of the UN Charter is not the exclusive blueprint for employing force in International Law. While Nicaragua and the United States agreed that Article 2.4 is the fundamental norm, the Charter's language is but one module of the legal foundation for the use of force:

Military and Paramilitary Activities in and Against Nicaragua
(*Nicaragua v. United States*)

INTERNATIONAL COURT OF JUSTICE, 1986
1986 *ICJ Reports* 14

AUTHOR'S NOTE: Nicaragua alleged that the US had mined its harbors, trained counterinsurgents, and promoted civil dissent against the Sandinista government, which was unpopular with the US. The excerpted paragraphs address the interplay of Article 2.4 and customary State practice.

COURT'S OPINION.

. . .

183. . . . [T]he Court has next to consider what are the rules of customary international law applicable to the present dispute. For . . . the Court recently observed,

> It is of course axiomatic that the material of customary international law is to be looked for primarily in the actual practice and *opinio juris* [commonly accepted practice] of States, even though multilateral conventions [such as the UN Charter] may have an important role to play in recording and defining rules deriving from custom, or indeed in developing them.

. . .

188. The Court thus finds that the Parties thus both take the view that the fundamental principle in this area is expressed in the terms employed in Article 2, paragraph 4, of the United Nations Charter. . . . The Court has however to be satisfied that there exists in customary international law . . . [State acceptance of] the binding character of such abstention. This may . . . be deduced from . . . the attitude of the Parties and the attitude of States towards certain General Assembly resolutions, and particularly . . . [the 1970 Declaration concerning Friendly Relations]. The effect of [unanimous] consent to the text . . . may be understood as an acceptance of the validity of the rule or set of rules declared by the resolution themselves. The principle of non-use of force, for example, may thus be regarded as a principle of customary international law. . . .

191. As regards . . . the principle in question, it will be necessary to distinguish the most grave forms of the use of force (those constituting armed attack) from other less grave forms. In determining the legal rule which applies to these latter forms, the Court can again draw on the formulations contained in the Declaration [concerning Friendly Relations]. . . . Alongside certain descriptions which may refer to aggression, this text includes other . . . less grave forms of the use of force. In particular, according to this resolution:

> . . . Every State has the duty to refrain from organizing or encouraging the organization of irregular forces or ar.med bands . . . for incursion into the territory of another State.
>
> Every State [also] has the duty to refrain from . . . assisting or participating in acts of civil strife or terrorist acts in another State or acquiescing in organized activities within its territory directed towards the commission of such acts, when the acts . . . involve a threat or use of force.

192. Moreover, in the part of this same resolution devoted to the principle of non-intervention in matters within the national jurisdiction of States, a very similar rule is found:

> Also, no State shall organize, assist, foment, finance, incite or tolerate subversive, terrorist or armed activities directed towards the violent overthrow of the regime of another State, or interfere in civil strife in another State.

In the context of the inter-American system, this approach can be traced back at least to 1928 (Convention on the Rights and Duties of States in the Event of

---

Civil Strife, Art. 1 (1)); it was confirmed by resolution 78 adopted by the General Assembly of the Organization of American States on 21 April 1972. The operative part of this resolution reads as follows:

The [OAS] General Assembly Resolves:

1. To reiterate solemnly the need for the member states of the Organization to observe strictly the principles of nonintervention and self-determination of peoples as a means of ensuring peaceful coexistence among them and to refrain from committing any direct or indirect act that might constitute a violation of those principles.

2. To reaffirm the obligation of those states to refrain from applying economic, political, or any other type of measures to coerce another state and obtain from it advantages of any kind.

3. Similarly, to reaffirm the obligation of these states to refrain from organizing, supporting, promoting, financing, instigating, or tolerating subversive, terrorist, or armed activities against another state and from intervening in a civil war in another state or in its internal struggles. . . .

◆ *Notes & Questions*

1. The ICJ ruled against the United States in the preceding case in 1986. Nicaragua's claim for reparations was pending before the ICJ during the ensuing five years. In 1991, the Nicaraguan government notified the Court that it had decided to "renounce all further right of action based on the case and did not wish to go on with the proceedings. . . ." As is typical in such cases, where a party has requested a discontinuance of the case, the United States was given an opportunity to object to the "discontinuance." Two weeks later, the Legal Adviser to the US Department of State responded with a letter to the Court, "welcoming the discontinuance." The case was removed from the ICJ's list of active cases.

2. In February 2001, the US Bush Administration approved $4 million in aid to dissidents who opposed Iraq's President Saddam Hussein. Sharif Ali, spokesperson for the London-based Iraqi National Congress, responded that "We will use that [money] to enhance our own network there [in Iraq], to penetrate the Iraqi regime and to expose the crimes of the regime." The expressed objective of this grant was to develop a legal case, which establishes Hussein's crimes against humanity. The "Congress" is an umbrella organization opposed to the Hussein government. *Question:* Did the unilateral decision by the United States, to aid those who are contra (as in Nicaragua's "Contras") to the Iraqi regime, violate the spirit of the ICJ's 1986 Nicaragua judgment against the United States?

UN CHARTER ARTICLE 51

Article 51 authorizes force for the limited purpose of self-defense. The never-ending international debate about what circumstances properly trigger its application has evolved through three phases—each arguably associated with a particular event and approximate date:

(1) Armed attack (1945)
(2) Anticipatory self-defense (1962)
(3) Preemptive self-defense (2002)

Armed Attack In 1945, the UN Charter expressed that self-defense could be justified only in the case of "armed attack." That year was also the dawn of the nuclear age when the United States dropped atomic bombs on Hiroshima and Nagasaki, effectively ending World War II. The development of weapons technology mushroomed in the ensuing decades. The claimed scope of self-defense would be expanded by national concerns with limiting self-defense to only the moment when an attack was underway.

Is Article 51 the *exclusive* source for defining the parameters of the permissible "self-defense?" Prior to World War II, an armed attack was not synonymous with annihilation of an entire country or region of the world. In 1945, however, only one nation had the monopoly on nuclear weapons. As new alliances formed, and technical information was thus shared, the sophistication of intercontinental weapon systems began to heavily influence international relations during the Cold War. The Charter-based definition of self-defense quickly became obsolete.

Rather than States being limited to "armed attack," nations and commentators—arguably using revisionist history—asserted that the Charter's drafters could *not* have intended to prohibit self-defense until missiles were actually launched. The *inherent* right of self-defense of course antedated the expression of that right in the UN Charter. But some analysts clung to the view that this UN Charter provision had only one clear meaning. Self-defense was thereby perceived as being properly invoked, only in cases where an "armed attack" was underway. Australian National University Professor D. W. Greig criticizes the circuitry of this narrow "plain meaning" argument as an unrealistic interpretation of the UN Charter. By using this term, the Charter did not become the *sole* source for defining the contours of self-defense. Customary State practice was thus a viable alternative for defining the contours of the justifications for self-defense. In Greig's aptly worded account:

> Because Article 51 refers solely to situations where *armed* attack has actually occurred, it has been argued that the Charter only reserves the right of self-defense to this limited extent. Supporters of this view have inevitably been led into tortuous distinctions between different situations to decide whether each situation qualifies as an "armed attack." Once a missile is launched, it may be said that the attack has commenced; but does it also apply to the sailing of an offensive naval force? Does the training of guerrillas and other irregular forces for use against another state constitute an armed attack? . . .
>
> However, there would appear to be no need to adopt such an unrealistic approach to Article 51, because it is possible to reconcile its wording with the reasonable interests of states. It has already been pointed out that [under] Article 51 [a State] retains the "inherent right of self-defence" independently of other provisions of the Charter in cases of an armed attack. In cases where there is no armed attack but where, under traditional [customary] rules of international law, there existed a wider right of action in self-defence . . . [it] still continues to exist, though made subject to the restrictions contained in the Charter [prohibiting the aggressive use of force].[39]

Anticipatory Self-Defense Under Article 51, the right of self-defense may be invoked only until the Security Council (SC) has undertaken measures against the aggressor. This is a reason why the victim is supposed to immediately report any defensive activity to the Council. Article 51 intended that the attacked nation would immediately discontinue its defensive actions, once the SC implemented countermeasures on its behalf, under the Council's various Chapter VII powers.

A variety of post-Charter developments, including Cold War veto practice (§3.3), precluded the Council from performing this ostensible function. As noted by one of the foremost authorities on Charter interpretation, Professor Brunno Simma of the University of Munich, one must conclude that "[t]here is no consensus in international legal doctrine over the point in time from which measures of self-defense against an armed attack may be taken."[40] One can nevertheless resort to State practice, for the purpose of drawing conclusions about its acceptable contours.

The Cuban Missile Crisis of 1962 presented the next round in the debate on the outer limits of self-defense applications:

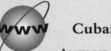

Cuban Missile Crisis

ANTICIPATORY SELF-DEFENSE DEBATE
(Article 51 Force in Self-Defense)
Go to course Web page at
<http://home.att.net/~slomansonb/txtcsesite.html>.
Under Chapter 10, click Cuban Missile Crisis.

The United States premised its Article 51 self-defense posture on the progressive development of International Law, which then arguably acknowledged "anticipatory" self-defense. A State could not stand by, without taking decisive action, when an arch-rival's missiles appeared on platforms only 90 miles away. But the UN Security Council was not given an opportunity to take control of this crisis, as envisioned by Article 51. It provides that a State may take unilateral action "until Security Council has taken measures necessary to maintain international peace and security." Under the US view, the Charter may have rendered the SC l the primary entity for monitoring the defensive use of force. It was not the *exclusive* one, however.

President Kennedy was fully aware that the Soviet Union would undoubtedly block any SC action by exercising its veto power. Kennedy's legal advisor, Leonard Meeker, later wrote, "The quarantine was based on a collective judgment and recommendation of the

American Republics made under the [OAS] Rio Treaty. It was considered not to contravene Article 2, paragraph 4, because it was a measure adopted by a regional organization in conformity with the provisions of the [UN] Charter. Finally, in relation to the Charter limitation on threat or use of force, it should be noted that the quarantine itself was a carefully limited measure proportionate to the threat and designed solely to prevent any further build-up of strategic missile bases in Cuba."[41]

The former Soviet Union and the PRC opposed the legality of the US-imposed "quarantine" of Cuba. They did not perceive it as a measure, which reasonably reacted to any imminent danger. The Soviet Union introduced a resolution in the SC condemning the US "blockade" of Cuba. It characterized this US action as a hostile act of aggression, and *not* defensive in nature, because the United States did not first seek the SC's approval. While the Council did not act on the Soviet resolution to condemn the US action in Cuba, there was a general consensus that the UN Secretary-General should have been given the opportunity to negotiate a settlement. And in November 1962, an article in the Chinese Government's Chinese People's Daily newspaper summarized the Sino–Soviet perspective on why this was an illegal blockade under International Law:

Disregarding the severe condemnation and strong protest of the world's people, United States President Kennedy ruthlessly declared that a military blockade of Cuba was being put into effect. . . .

It is extremely clear that American imperialism frivolously hopes to use the military blockade to exterminate the revolutionary regime of Cuba, to wipe out the Cuban people's right of self-determination. It is a serious act of criminal intervention in the internal affairs of Cuba and infringement of the sovereignty and independence of Cuba. This naked aggression is also a

thorough undermining of the Charter of the United Nations [Article 2.4] . . . and even [Article 15] of the "Charter of the Organization of American States". . . .

This further proves that any rules or any rights confirmed by the Charter . . . can be torn to pieces by the United States in accordance with its own needs of aggression and war.[42]

Pre-emptive First Strike   In 1992, UN Secretary-General Butros Butros-Ghali issued a warning that the traditional Laws of War would not suffice for future conflicts. His warning was virtually ignored, when promulgated in 1992:

The new breed of intra-State conflicts have certain characteristics that present [the] United Nations . . . with challenges. . . .

They are usually fought not only by regular armies but also by militias and armed civilians with little discipline and with ill-defined chains of commend. They are often guerilla wars without clear front lines. Civilians are the main victims and often the main targets. Humanitarian emergencies are commonplace and the combatant authorities . . . lack the capacity to cope with them. . . .

Another feature of such conflicts is the collapse of State institutions, especially the police and judiciary, with resulting paralysis of governance, a breakdown of law and order, and general banditry and chaos.[43]

This theme unfortunately deserved center stage, in the midst of calls for change as of the horrific events of September 11, 2001 (chronicled in §10.7). As to the matter of national self-defense, the US Permanent Representative to the United Nations informed the SC (less than one month later) of the following change in US defense policy:

Letter dated 7 October 2001 from the Permanent Representative of the United States of America to the United Nations addressed to the President of the Security Council
UN Doc. S/2001/946 (7 October 2001)
<http://www.un.int/usa/s-2001-946.htm>

In accordance with Article 51 of the Charter of the United Nations, I wish, on behalf of my Government, to report that the United States of America,

together with other States, has initiated actions in the exercise of its inherent right of individual and collective self-defence following the armed attacks that were carried out against the United States on 11 September 2001.

. . . Since 11 September, my Government has obtained clear and compelling information that the Al-Qaeda organization, which is supported by the Taliban regime in Afghanistan, had a central role in the attacks. There is still much we do not know. Our inquiry is in its early stages. We may find that our self-defence requires further actions with respect to other organizations and other States.

The attacks on 11 September 2001 and the ongoing threat to the United States and its nationals posed by the Al-Qaeda organization have been made possible by the decision of the Taliban regime to allow the parts of Afghanistan that it controls to be used by this organization as a base of operation. Despite every effort by the United States and the international community, the Taliban regime has refused to change its policy. From the territory of Afghanistan, the Al-Qaeda organization continues to train and support agents of terror who attack innocent people throughout the world and target United States nationals and interests in the United States and abroad.

In response to these attacks, and in accordance with the inherent right of individual and collective self-defence, United States armed forces have initiated actions designed to prevent and deter further attacks on the United States. These actions include measures against Al-Qaeda terrorist training camps and military installations of the Taliban regime in Afghanistan. . . .

I ask that you circulate the text of the present letter as a document of the Security Council.

John D. Negroponte

Unlike the Cuban Missile Crisis, the United States was *actually* attacked in New York, Washington, DC, and Pennsylvania. The perpetrators employed flying "bombs" (the hijacked commercial aircraft). When the United States first responded with military and ground forces in Afghanistan, there was no claim that "Afghanistan" had incurred State responsibility for these attacks. While the United States was displeased with the Taliban's refusal to turn over the prime suspect, Usama Bin Laden, the United States did not purport to be protecting itself from either the country it was bombing or its Taliban government. Although the US Congress did not actually declare war, the President repeatedly stated that America was "at war."

Also unlike the 1962 Cuban Missile Crisis and the 2003 Iraq War, the US military response in Afghanistan *did* have some advance blessing by the United Nations, in two resolutions passed the day after the September 11th attacks. The first was the General Assembly's September 12th global call for "international cooperation to prevent and eradicate acts of terrorism, . . . [so] that those responsible for aiding, supporting, or harbouring the perpetrators, organizers and sponsors of such acts will be held accountable." Second, the SC's like resolution recognized "the inherent right of individual or collective self-defence *in accordance with the Charter*" (italics added). However, the Council carefully expressed "its readiness to take all necessary steps to respond to the terrorist attacks of 11 September 2001, and to combat all forms of terrorism, in accordance with its responsibilities under the Charter of the United Nations—as proclaimed by the Council's resolution wording 'to remain seized of the matter'."

Article 51 of the UN Charter envisions UN oversight so that the SC can orchestrate the resulting scenario spawned by State claims of self-defense, once the initial threat is contained. But SC control was never achieved because of the supreme national interests at stake for the United States. Turning the war over to the SC did not conform to the US desire to retain maximum flexibility. This would be a "war" against individuals and nongovernmental organizations, which could, and has, lasted for years. The United States would soon follow the above UN Ambassador's letter to the President of the SC by making its unilateral claim to the right of preemptive self-defense. Unlike the Cuban Missile Crisis claim of anticipatory self-defense, where the water was boiling, the United States claimed the right to attack when it was merely simmering—as determined by the United States.

On September 17, 2002, President Bush announced the new US approach to self-defense. He therein stated the rationale in support of pre-emptive first-strikes as part of the war on terror. When formulating your reaction to the questions in this exercise, consider the following:

◆ The unparalleled threats with which the United States must now contend.

- That the four other permanent members of the UN Security Council have not openly embraced this National Defense Strategy.[44]
- The position of other world leaders, who must also assess the new US National Security Strategy (NSS) in a remarkably charged context.

A regional alliance, led by Russia and China, ultimately reacted by calling upon the United States to withdraw from Afghanistan. The Shanghai Cooperation Organization urged the United States to set a deadline for withdrawal, because of the decline of

The National Security Strategy of the United States of America

PRESIDENT GEORGE W. BUSH

The White House (Sept. 17, 2002)
<www.whitehouse.gov/nsc/nss.pdf>
Go to course Web page at
<http://home.att.net/~slomansonb/
txtcsesite.html>. Under Chapter Ten,
click National Security Defense Exercise.

International Law and The War in Iraq

John Yoo

97 AMERICAN JOURNAL OF INTERNATIONAL LAW 563 (2003)

. . .

Despite the long-standing recognition of a nation's right to self-defense, some argue that Article 51 has limited the right to permit only a response to an actual "armed attack." Some even argue that an armed attack must occur across national borders to trigger Article 51. Under this interpretation, the UN Charter superseded the existing right under customary international law to take reasonable anticipatory action in self-defense. There is no indication that the drafters of the UN Charter intended to limit the customary law in this way, nor that the United States so understood the Charter when it ratified. Instead, Article 51 merely partially expressed a right that exists independent of the UN Charter.

. . .

The use of force in anticipatory self-defense must be necessary and proportional to the threat. At least in the realm of WMD, rogue nations, and international terrorism, however, the test for determining whether a threat is sufficiently "imminent" to render the use of force necessary at a particular point has become more nuanced than Secretary Webster's nineteenth-century formulation [in the above 1837 Caroline incident]. Factors to be considered should now include the probability of an attack; the likelihood that this probability will increase, and therefore the need to take advantage of a limited

window of opportunity; whether diplomatic alternatives are practical; and the magnitude of the harm that could result from the threat. If a state instead were obligated to wait until the threat were truly imminent in the temporal sense envisioned by Secretary Webster, there is a substantial danger of missing a limited window of opportunity to prevent widespread harm to civilians. Finally, in an age of technologically advanced delivery systems and WMD, international law cannot require that we ignore the potential harm represented by the threat.

Applying the reformulated test for using force in anticipatory self-defense to the potential use of force against Iraq reveals that the threat of a WMD attack by Iraq, either directly or through Iraq's support for terrorism, was sufficiently "imminent" to render the use of force necessary to protect the United States, its citizens, and its allies. The force used was proportionate to the threat posed by Iraq; in other words, it was limited to that which is needed to eliminate the threat, including the destruction of Iraq's WMD capability and removing the source of Iraq's hostile intentions and actions, Saddam Hussein.

. . .

International law permitted the use of force against Iraq on two independent grounds. First, the Security Council authorized military action against Iraq to implement the terms of the cease-fire that suspended the hostilities of the 1991 Gulf war. Due to Iraq's material breaches of the cease-fire, established principles of international law—both treaty and armistice law—permitted the United States to suspend its terms and to use force to compel Iraqi compliance. Such a use of force was consistent with U.S. practice both with regard to Iraq and with regard to treaties and cease-fires. Second, international law permitted the use of force against Iraq in anticipatory self-defense because of the threat posed by an Iraq armed with WMD and in potential cooperation with international terrorist organizations.

. . .

The use of force in anticipatory self-defense against terrorist groups armed with WMD, or against the rogue nations that support them, will depend on three factors that go beyond mere temporal imminence. First, does a nation have WMD and the inclination to use them? . . .

Second, nations will have to use force while taking into account the available window of opportunity. If a state waits until a terrorist attack is on the verge of being launched, it likely will be unable to protect the civilians who are being targeted, especially against suicide bombers who seem immune to traditional methods of deterrence. . . .

Third, nations will have to take into account that the degree of harm from a WMD attack would be catastrophic. The combination of the vast potential destructive capacity of WMD and the modest means required for their delivery make them more of a threat than the military forces of many countries. . . .

The Concept of the US National Security and International Law: A View from Moscow

Igor I. Lukashuk and Darya S. Boklan
2 CHINESE JOURNAL OF INTERNATIONAL LAW 587 (2003)

. . .

The [US National Security] Strategy is characterized by the absolute primacy of national interests to the detriment of national interests. . . .

Having come to power in 2000, the new American Administration proclaimed that in its future endeavors, it would proceed from the national interests and not from those of some illusory international community.

. . .

The . . . Strategy . . . lies in the assumption that the USA enjoys unprecedented power, and thus, is bound to form an international order and oversee its enforcement. History testifies to the fact that mighty empires have existed in the past, but . . . their attempts aimed at establishing dominance over other nations ended in failures. It is worthwhile to consider that in the past such claims were much more modest that the global claims of the USA today.

. . . As some experts note, "the most controversial elements in the *Security Strategy* are those which seem to treat [first strike] pre-emption as normal rather than an exceptional response. It is not clear that states will accept pre-emption as a general doctrine of international law in context[s] going beyond the war against terrorism.

The efficiency of international law . . . may be compared to traffic rules that are honored due to the understanding of their necessity. If someone should drive a tank in the opposite lane, it would inevitably cause a disaster.

. . .

There are "Bushmen" also amongst Russian political scientists. . . . The [referenced] author believes that Americans, without any reservations, are establishing and strengthening the new unilateral world order: "American order is better and safer for us than terrorist disorder. It's better to have a World sheriff than the World killers."

. . .

The [April 2003] meeting of the Russian President V. Putin, the French President J. Chirac, and the German Chancellor G. Schroeder with international lawyers from various countries . . . is quite remarkable in this context. . . . Speaking about the interrelation of power and law, participants of the conference proceeded from [the] J. Chirac formulation that "respect of law is not recognition of weakness, but [a] moral and political imperative, and the foundation of efficiency. . . .

The US *National Security Strategy* and the New "Bush Doctrine" on Preemptive Self-defense

Christine Gray

1 Chinese Journal of International Law 587 (2002)

The *US National Security Strategy* ... is a dramatic document, a mixture of triumphalism at the victory of the West in the Cold War and alarmism about the threat of terrorism.

. . .

The series of terrorist attacks after September 11, on a nightclub in Bali, a Moscow theater, and a French supertanker in Yemen, confirmed the continuing danger, but also made clear the difficulties with any strategy based on fighting terrorism by the use of force.

. . .

The threatened extension of the war against terrorism beyond Afghanistan to the states of the Axis of Evil [*e.g.*, Iraq in 2003] and the claims to a wide right of preemptive action against states in possession of, or in the process of developing, weapons of mass destruction have proved divisive.

. . .

The US, with the UK and Israel, have supported a wider right of self-defense than most states. This has long been controversial and is certainly not as generally accepted as the *Security Strategy* suggests.

. . .

In the famous case of the 1981 attack by Israel on the Iraqi nuclear reactor,[a] the UN Security Council unanimously condemned the Israeli action in Resolution 487. ...The US—very unusually—voted in favour of the resolution on the ground that Israel had not exhausted peaceful means for the resolution of the dispute.

. . .

The new doctrine goes far beyond the previous rare claims to preemptive action. There is a central uncertainty in that it is not at all clear what will trigger an attack; there is also uncertainty as to what form the preemptive action will take, and as to the role, if an, envisaged for the UN. In 2002, President Bush is reported to have authorized the CIA to return to the controversial policy of assassination[b] of foreign heads of states, such as Saddam Hussein, and of terrorists, a policy abandoned

in 1976. ...There is an inherent problem with proportionality in any preemptive use of force; in the absence of clear evidence as to the nature and scope of a particular threat the requirement that any response be proportionate is necessarily difficult to apply.

. . .

The new *Security Strategy* seemed to be designed with Iraq [rather than Afghanistan] in mind, on the basis that preemptive military action will be needed to prevent its development of nuclear weapons and supply of those weapons to terrorists.

. . .

The question also arises how far, if at all, the US would be willing to accept the application of these new doctrines on the use of force by other states. Does the *Security Strategy* offer a green light for states wishing to suppress independence movements, to invite outside help for that purpose and to take cross-border action?

. . .

A new Bush doctrine is emerging. ....The uncertainties at its heart increase the doubts as to the legality of the radical new doctrine; its impact will depend on the reaction of the rest of the world and to date the other states have proved distinctly cautious.[c] The Security Strategy may yet prove more a rhetorical device [that was] designed to put pressure on Iraq than a serious attempt to rewrite [the] international law on self-defense.

---

[a] (Textbook author's footnote) See T. McCormack, Self-Defense in International Law: The Israeli Raid on The Iraqi Reactor (Jerusalem: Magnes Press, Hebrew University, 1996).

[b] Regarding assassination as a government policy, see M. Scharf, In the Cross Hairs of a Scary Idea, Washington Post (Apr. 25, 2004), at B-1.

[c] The referenced caution intimates that the Bush doctrine, regarding pre-emptive first strikes, could one day be more widely accepted by the international community (although possibly limited to just the terrorist context).

active fighting in Afghanistan. The United States rejected that request in July 2005. The reaction of several prominent academics to the 2002 US National Security Strategy include the preceeding three excerpts.

The apparent UN response to the US 2002 NSS may be drawn from its December 2004 report, providing a modified version of the comparatively uncontentious Customary International Law requirements of necessity and proportionality:

Report of the UN High-level Panel on Threats, Challenges and Change
A More Secure World: Our Shared Responsibility
<http://www.un.org/secureworld> click <u>Document</u> (Dec. 2, 2004)

. . .

In all cases, we believe that the Charter of the United Nations, properly understood and applied, is equal to the task: Article 51 needs neither extension nor restriction of its long understood scope, and Chapter VII [*e.g.*, Art. 39 threat assessment and Art. 42 collective use of military force] fully empowers the Security Council to deal with every kind of threat that States may confront. The task is not to find alternatives to the Security Council as a source of authority but to make it work better than it has.

That force *can* legally be used does not always mean that . . . it *should* be used. We identify a set of five guidelines—five criteria of legitimacy—which we believe that the Security Council (and anyone else involved in these decisions) should always address in considering whether to authorize or apply military force. The adoption of these guidelines (seriousness of threat, proper purpose, last resort, proportional means and balance of consequences) will not produce agreed conclusions with push-button predictability, but should significantly improve the chances of reaching international consensus on what have been in recent years deeply divisive issues [p.53].

. . .

188. . . . The problem arises where the threat in question is not imminent but still claimed to be real: for example the acquisition, with allegedly hostile intent, of nuclear weapons-making capability.

189. Can a State, without going to the Security Council, claim in these circumstances the right to act, in anticipatory self-defence, not just pre-emptively (against an imminent or proximate threat) but preventively (against a non-imminent or non-proximate one)? Those who say "yes" argue that the potential harm from some threats (e.g., terrorists armed with a nuclear weapon) is so great that one simply cannot risk waiting until they become imminent, and that less harm may be done (e.g., avoiding a nuclear exchange or radioactive fallout from a reactor destruction) by acting earlier.

190. The short answer is that if there are good arguments for preventive military action, with good evidence to support them, they should be put to the Security Council, which can authorize such action if it chooses to. If it does not so choose, there will be, by definition, time to pursue other strategies, including persuasion, negotiation, deterrence and containment–and to visit again the military option.

191. For those impatient with such a response, the answer must be that, in a world full of perceived potential threats, the risk to the global order and the norm of non-intervention on which it continues to be based is simply too great for the legality of unilateral preventive action, as distinct from collectively endorsed action, to be accepted. Allowing one to so act is to allow all [to do so].

Nuclear Weapons: A Special Problem In 1996, the ICJ addressed the unthinkable situation whereby a nation State might one day use this particular weapon in the name of Article 51 self-defense:

◆ *Notes*

1. *See* general notes at the end of the "Nuclear Weapons Case" on the course Web page.

Legality of the Threat or Use of Nuclear Weapons

INTERNATIONAL COURT OF JUSTICE
General List No. 95
Advisory Opinion of 8 July 1996
Go to course Web page
<http://home.att.net/~slomansonb/txtcsesite.html>.
Under Chapter Ten, click Nuclear Weapons Case.

2. The ICJ's decision was not very satisfying. It is susceptible to varied interpretations. As aptly characterized by St. John's University (New York) Professor Charles Moxley, author of a book-length analysis of this book-length case:

> From a litigator's point of view, one—from either side of the issue—can find much language and expressed sentiment to quote and manipulate in arguing the issue in the next case [assuming there is one], or in justification of policy decisions and contingency planning and military training . . . in the meantime.
>
> For *proponents* of nuclear weapons, there is the wide-open barndoor of self-defense, and the basis to argue that . . . nuclear weapons, like any other weapon, may be used, and, indeed, that arguably they may be used in extreme circumstances of self-defense regardless of the dictates of other provisions of international law.
>
> For the *opponents* of nuclear weapons, there is the recognition of the "general" unlawfulness of nuclear weapons and the suggestion that all uses of nuclear weapons would be unlawful if the contention of the nuclear powers is disproved that they can deliver modern precision low-yield nuclear weapons at a target, discriminating between military and non-military targets and controlling collateral effects, particularly radiation.[45]

3. Professor Moxley's comprehensive analysis does note, however, that the case is not without contemporary utility: "Most fundamentally, the decision contains a grand and historic invitation: Show us the facts. . . . When viewed in light of the extraordinary fact . . . that the United States defended the lawfulness only of the modern precision low-yield nuclear weapons, the Court's invitation becomes focused and real: Give us the facts as to the type of weapons whose legality is being defended and the putative circumstances of such lawful use, and the issue can be decided." Characterization of the Court's Decision, in Chapter 3 of C. Moxley, Jr., NUCLEAR WEAPONS AND INTERNATIONAL LAW IN THE POST COLD WAR WORLD 249, at 250 (Lanham, MD: Austin & Winfield, 2000). See "Bunker Buster" Problem 10.G.

One of the most serious problems with implementing multilateral agreements on the control of force surfaced in 1991. The Cold War had ended. North Korea had been admitted to the United Nations in 1991 as a "peace-loving state" under Article 4.1 of the UN Charter. It signed a Treaty of Reconciliation with South Korea. The United States had announced a major withdrawal of its troops, stationed in South Korea since the Korean War. North Korea had announced its agreement, in principle, with a US plan to purge the Korean peninsula of nuclear weapons. The United States had already removed its nuclear weapons from South Korea.

Suddenly, it appeared that one remnant of the Cold War was about to resurface, another major threat to regional and global stability centered on the possession of nuclear weapons of mass destruction. North Korea announced that it would no longer permit inspections by the UN International Atomic Energy Agency as conducted under the 1968 Nuclear Non-Proliferation Treaty. All foreigners, except accredited diplomats, were asked to leave North Korea in 1993 as this disruptive scenario continued to unfold. North Korea then announced its withdrawal from the 1968 nuclear control treaty, which was later scaled back to a "suspension" after extensive UN-sponsored negotiations. Japan and South Korea pleaded with the United States not to impose sanctions on North Korea. The world was once again perceived by many commentators as being near the brink of nuclear confrontation. In 1994, the United States sent in scores of Patriot surface-to-air anti-missile batteries to block North Korean Scud missiles in the event of the North's attack of the South. Later in 1994, North Korea finally agreed to permit inspectors to re-enter the country to determine its nuclear weapons capability.

While the tension was ultimately diminished, the related compromise has arguably set a risky precedent. The United States agreed to North Korea's demand that inspections of its suspected nuclear sites be postponed for several years. The US provision of $4 billion in aid would help North Korea pursue alternative energy resources. North Korea would freeze all nuclear programs for several years. This incident may have sent an unintended message to rogue States: Violating the 1968 treaty has its rewards. North Korea is effectively free to proceed as it wishes. The international community was "put off" for several years, and North Korea remained again free to disregard the nuclear control treaty when that time frame elapses.

During Summer 2005, six nations revived discussions on North Korea's evolving nuclear weapons capability—China, Japan, North Korea, Russia, South Korea, and the United States. The PRC supplies North Korea with 70 percent of its oil, and one-third of its food. But China does not want to risk reducing or eliminating such exports, fearing that to do so would render North Korea more belligerent. The US secretary of state has repeatedly advised this member of the president's "Axis of Evil" that the United States does not intend to invade. North Korea nevertheless fears that the new US National Security Strategy, that guided the Iraq War, would logically place North Korea in America's weapons of mass destruction cross hairs. In a September 2005 accord, North Korea agreed to: scrap all of its existing nuclear weapons and production facilities; rejoin the Nuclear Non-proliferation Treaty; and to readmit international nuclear inspectors. The other nations assured North Korea's security, and to provide economic and energy benefits—reminiscent of the earlier US agreement with North Korea. On this round, however, five additional nations are parties to this security arrangement.

The potential for nuclear weapons in space is another source of friction. In 2001, US President Bush expressed the desire to amend the 1972 US-Russian Anti-Ballistic Missile Treaty. Doing so would remove this restriction on building a space-based missile defense system—aka the "Star Wars" defense shield during the Reagan presidency. The United States based this intention on its concern with what it called "rogue nations," such as North Korea. They might use whatever nuclear weapons capability they have to politically blackmail the United States. Russia's President Putin stated that if "the United States

abandons the 1972 agreement, we will have the right to pull out not only of Start II but also from the entire arms reductions and control system." Putin previously announced Russia's stance on the potential use of nuclear arms in January 2000, when he appeared to lower the nuclear threshold: "The Russian Federation considers it possible to use military force to guarantee its national security according to the following principle: the use of all forces and equipment at its disposal, *including nuclear weapons,* if it has to repel armed aggression if all their means of resolving the crisis have been exhausted or proved ineffective." In December 2002, the United States provided notice of its withdrawal.[46]

There has been another prominent US disengagement from the Cold War-era nuclear arms control regime (Exhibit 10.2). The 185 signatories of the 1968 Nuclear Proliferation Treaty pledged never to acquire, nor help another nation acquire, nuclear weapons. By the turn of the century, however, seven nations including rivals India and Pakistan are now declared nuclear powers. A total of forty-four nations are believed to have varying capacities to produce nuclear weapons.

In October 1999, the US Senate voted to reject the 1996 Comprehensive Test Ban Treaty (CTBT), which had been signed by Russia, China, and the United States. They strongly urged the United States to ratify this treaty, which had languished in Senate controversy for the three years since President Clinton signed it. Archrivals India and Pakistan did not sign the CTBT, which was a priority for the Clinton Administration because of their vernal nuclear capability. It requires nuclear-capable nations to halt their weapons testing. Nations ratifying the CTBT agreed to accept increased international monitoring for detecting unauthorized testing. The US Senate opponents, however, complained that other nations could cheat. Their taking advantage of an arguably unenforceable treaty would ultimately erode the US nuclear advantage.

One downside of the US decision not to ratify the CTBT is the example that it set for others. When the United States rejected this major arms control treaty, 151 nations had signed and fifty-one of those had ratified it. These numbers then included twenty-six of the forty-four nuclear-capable nations. This treaty was supposed to enter into force when all nations believed to have nuclear capacity had ratified it.

One might thus conclude with the following question: How well can existing arms control agreements effectively suppress mutually assured destruction, while the nuclear community continues to grow, mature, and test nuclear weapons in the name of preserving national security?

COLLECTIVE SELF-DEFENSE

Nicaragua Application   The United States relied on "collective" self-defense to vindicate its actions in a major ICJ case filed by Nicaragua. The United States had supported anti-government forces, for the purpose of undermining the mid-1980s Sandinista government. This case presented an opportunity for the ICJ to address the applicability of collective self-defense arguments, which had not been determined during the Cuban Missile Crisis but were now ripe for decision. The issue was whether the United States could assert collective self-defense as a legal justification for its political actions, which included the work of US CIA operatives who arranged the mining of strategic harbors in Nicaragua. The United States asserted that its interference was justified as a form of self-defense against some future armed attack by Nicaragua on other OAS members. Nicaragua was allegedly helping anti-government forces in countries such as El Salvador overthrow democratically elected governments in the region.

The ICJ was not receptive to the US claim of justifiable intervention in the name of collective self-defense. For such a general right to legally materialize, the United States would have to prove a fundamental modification of the Customary International Law principle of non-intervention. The ICJ disapproved the US basis for intervention in Nicaraguan affairs, reasoning that it could not be justified on a collective self-defense rationale. In the Court's words:

the United States has not claimed that its intervention, which it justified in this way on the *political* level, was also justified on the *legal* level, alleging the exercise of a new right of intervention regarded by the United States as existing in such circumstances. As mentioned above, the United States has, on the legal plane, justified its intervention expressly and solely by reference to the "classic" rules involved, namely, collective self-defence against an armed attack. Nicaragua, for its part, has often expressed its solidarity and sympathy with the opposition [anti-government forces] in various States, especially in El Salvador. . . .

The Court therefore finds that no such general right of intervention, in support of an opposition

within another State, exists in contemporary international law. The Court concludes that acts constituting a breach of the customary principle of non-intervention will also, if they directly or indirectly involve the use of force, constitute a breach of the principle of non-use of force in international relations.[47]

Kuwait Application   The next major opportunity to analyze Article 51 occurred during the PGW. Four days after Iraq invaded Kuwait, the UN Security Council issued Resolution 661. That statement identified the application of self-defense by ". . . [a]ffirming the inherent right of individual and collective self-defence, in accordance with Article 51 of the Charter. . . ."[48] The dozen SC resolutions during that war reflected a *clear* consensus about the existence of the inherent right of collective self-defense.

The question was whether either individual or collective self-defense could be undertaken, at any time, without the direct participation of the Council. Article 51 authorizes self-defense "until the SC has taken measures necessary to maintain international peace and security." Although time was allegedly of the essence, the text of Article 51 does not condone a wholly unilateral exercise by a group of States, without some UN involvement. The Council was motivated to quickly, and incessantly, issue resolutions so as to remain openly involved with the US-directed process of forcing Iraq to withdraw from Kuwait.

Embassy Bombing Application   The pre-Charter elements of *necessity* and *proportionality* were arguably stretched to the limits, when the United States launched cruise missile attacks into Afghanistan and Sudan in 1998, in retaliation for the August bombings of US embassies in Kenya and Tanzania. Some 250 people had been killed on these embassy bombings, including twelve American citizens. More than 5,000 people were wounded. Neither Afghanistan nor Sudan took any action to find the perpetrators, who demonstrated their continued interest in directing more terrorist attacks toward US embassies.

The United States considered these embassy bombings as armed attacks on the United States. Both attacks occurred half a world away from US shores. Only a small fraction of those harmed were US citizens. Those found to be responsible for the bombings were not State agents of either Afghanistan or Sudan. At that point in time, there was no overwhelming concern about such an attack ever reoccurring. And there was no resort to the UN Security Council. Doing so would likely compromise the secrecy and timeliness of any forceful US reaction to these embassy bombings in Africa. To label the US response "acceptable" under International Law, would require characterization of the missile attack as constituting a limited right of reprisal launched in the name of self-defense.

September 11, 2001 Application   For the first time in NATO's history, the North Atlantic Council implemented the collective self-defense provision, which is Article 5 of the Washington Treaty (NATO's constitutive document):

> The Parties agree that an armed attack against one or more of them in Europe or North America shall be considered an attack against them all and consequently they agree that, if such an armed attack occurs, each of them, in exercise of the right of individual or collective self-defence recognised by Article 51 of the Charter of the United Nations, will assist the Party or Parties so attacked by taking forthwith, individually and in concert with the other Parties, such action as it deems necessary, including the use of armed force, to restore and maintain the security of the North Atlantic area.
>
> Any such armed attack and all measures taken as a result thereof shall immediately be reported to the Security Council. Such measures shall be terminated when the Security Council has taken the measures necessary to restore and maintain international peace and security.

The European and North American treaty members thus agreed that in the event of an attack within the meaning of Article 5, each would assist the attacked party and take such action as necessary. The commitment to collective self-defense embodied in this 1949 treaty was entered into in a different era. There are now a host of security risks quite unlike those, which effectively called NATO into existence. International terrorism rendered that long-term collective self-defense commitment no less valid, especially now that Russia and the United States are working hand-in-hand to respond.

One day after the 9/11 attack, NATO allies unequivocally activated their treaty-based commitment to work with the United States to respond to international terrorism. British commandoes entered the ground war and other NATO members made various economic, legislative, and diplomatic contributions to the organization's joint response to the attack of September 11th. This uniform resolve thus solidified one of the most clearly supported instances of collective self-defense in history.

The second paragraph of Article 5 includes a NATO commitment to the United Nations. NATO members therein agreed that they would defer on self-defense measures, when the UN Security Council has taken its own measures to maintain the peace. This scenario presents a fresh example of the persistent tug-of war between NATO and the United Nations regarding the ultimate scope of collective self-defense. NATO conducted the Kosovo bombing without the imprimatur of the UN Security Council (§10.5). On the other hand, the Council is unlikely to pull rank by stepping in when a common objective is being successfully pursued by NATO. The United Nations may once again effectively look the other way; delegate its Chapter VII peacekeeping powers to this regional organization—rather than risk a turf war which would impede a successful anti-terrorism campaign; or effectively give its stamp of approval by undertaking a peacekeeping operation in a post-Taliban Afghanistan.

UNSC CHAPTER VII POWERS

Organizational Force   Charter Article 39 provides that the "Security Council shall . . . decide what measures shall be taken in accordance with Articles 41 and 42, to maintain or restore the peace." The latter articles provide that the Council may initiate appropriate countermeasures. Those *not* involving force include the interruption of economic relations with the offending States. Countermeasures that *do* authorize the organization's use of force include "action by air, sea, or land forces . . . includ[ing] demonstrations, blockade, and other operations by air, sea, or land forces of Members of the United Nations."

"Sanctions" is a word used by journalists and other commentators, although typically avoided in international documents. It suggests the imposition of punishment rather than mere deterrence. The UN Charter is most discreet in its Article 39 reference to "measures . . . to maintain or restore international peace and security."

The UN Charter envisions regional organizational measures, undertaken to promote regional dispute resolution. Like SC oversight, such action is not supposed to be unilaterally inflicted in the absence of organizational endorsement. For example, the European Community's anti-investment measures against South Africa were imposed as a means of participating in the broader UN policy of encouraging member States to dismantle apartheid. The Organization of American States imposed economic sanctions on Haiti in 1991, after military leaders deposed that country's first democratically elected leader. The 1992 OAS sanctions barred oil deliveries to Haiti, as a measure for securing Haiti's observation of the democratic principles contained in the OAS Charter. The OAS also considered sanctions against Peru in 1992, when its leader closed Congress and suspended the Peruvian Constitution.

The application of sanctions on this international level, as opposed to being unilaterally imposed, increases the likelihood of consensus. Organizational sanctions may thus help to eliminate threats to peace. Unilaterally imposed sanctions, on the other hand, tend to encourage the escalation of threats to peace. When implementing countermeasures are imposed by a multilateral body, the sanctioning State (or States) is not as readily perceived to be an aggressor. A single State may thus be perceived as taking advantage of the situation, to achieve some less-than-altruistic objective. The same country, which has the backing of an international organization, is more likely to be characterized as furthering multinational objectives. US President Carter, for example, applied a series of sanctions against Iran during the 1979–1980 Hostage Crisis (§7.4). Virtually every nation of the world condemned Iran's actions when it seized diplomatic hostages. With the backing of the UN Security Council and the ICJ, the US sanctions directed at Iran were far more acceptable than any action which the United States might have taken without that level of international support.

Persian Gulf War I Application Iraq invaded Kuwait in 1991. The UN's expressed objective was to defeat Iraq, and then contain it, with sufficient force to eliminate its potential for further threats to international peace. The Council thus resolved as follows: "Acting under Articles 39 and 40 . . . *Demands* that Iraq withdraw immediately and unconditionally all its forces" and "Acting under Chapter VII of the Charter [commencing with Art. 39] . . . *Decides* as a consequence, to take the following measures to secure compliance of Iraq . . . and to restore the authority of the legitimate Government of Kuwait . . . Decides that all States shall prevent: (a) The import into their territories of all commodities and products originating in Iraq or Kuwait exported therefrom after the date of the present resolution; . . . [and other measures designed to boycott Iraq]."[49]

The ensuing SC Resolution 687 was a milestone in UN history. This cease-fire resolution, among the many issued by the Council during and after the cessation of hostilities,[50] was a major break from the Council's past assertions of power. One reason was 687's breadth; another was its purported control over future State behavior. The SC ordered unprecedented and unparalleled controls, in terms of observing international border delimitations, non-use of chemical and nuclear weapons, sanctions, and required war reparations. The relevant paragraphs of this particular resolution are reprinted here:

United Nations Security Council Resolution 687

2981st Meeting (3 April 1991)
<http://www.un.org/Docs/scres/1991/687e.pdf>

The Security Council . . .
   Welcoming the restoration to Kuwait of its national sovereignty, independence, and territorial integrity and the return of its legitimate government, . . .
   2. *Demands* that Iraq and Kuwait respect the inviolability of the international boundary.

. . .

   4. Decides to guarantee the inviolability of the above-mentioned international boundary and to take as appropriate all necessary measures to that end in accordance with the Charter;

. . .

8. *Decides* that Iraq shall unconditionally accept the destruction, removal, or rendering harmless, under international supervision, of:

(a) all chemical and biological weapons and all stocks of agents . . . ;

(b) all ballistic missiles with a range of greater than 150 kilometers and related major parts, and repair and production facilities;

. . .

14. *Takes note* that the actions to be taken by Iraq . . . represent steps towards the goal of establishing in the Middle East a zone free from weapons of mass destruction and all missiles for their delivery and the objective of a global ban on chemical weapons;

. . .

24. *Decides* that, in accordance with Resolution 661 (1990) and subsequent related resolutions and until a further decision is taken by the Council, all States shall continue to prevent the sale or supply . . . to Iraq by their nationals . . . of:

(a) arms and related materiel of all types. . . .

25. *Calls upon* all States and international organizations to act strictly in accordance with paragraph 24 above, notwithstanding the existence of any [prior] contracts, agreements, licenses, or any other arrangements;

. . .

30. *Decides* that, in furtherance of its commitment to facilitate the repatriation of all Kuwaiti and third party nationals, Iraq shall extend all necessary cooperation to the International Committee of the Red Cross

. . .

32. *Requires* Iraq to inform the Council that it will not commit or support any act of international terrorism.

. . .

34. *Decides* to remain seized of the matter and to take such further steps as may be required for the implementation of this resolution and to secure peace and security in the area.

The quoted portions of Resolution 687 provide the foremost statement of conditions ever made by the SC, because of their comprehensive nature and their purported control of future action by Iraq and all members of the international community. The Cold War veto power, held by the five permanent members of the SC (§3.3), precluded a similar resolution in prior conflicts. This resolution signaled a zenith in the willingness of the Council to implement its Charter task of maintaining global peace and security.

Adherence to this resolution was not as forthcoming as expected. Iraq chose to limit UN agents from conducting inspections of its war potential. Iraq even seized certain agents during their UN-sanctioned visits. In spite of such problems with implementation, this resolution heralded what would appear to be the effective return of the SC from its Cold War hiatus.

Prior exercises of the Council's Chapter VII powers politically necessitated a more restrained approach, when flexing its muscles by applying force to maintain peace. But Resolution 678 authorized "all necessary means" to force Iraq's withdrawal from Kuwait, as well as imposing a post-cessation of hostility regime. Such organizational force had previously authorized less

forceful measures, before resorting to such forceful measures. The Council had previously authorized forcible sanctions only after less severe ones failed to work. However, its activism in this instance indicated that the Charter should also be a flexible document in terms of the Council's scope of authority to carry out its mandate to control threats to international peace.

David Scheffer of the Carnegie Endowment for International Peace therefore commented that "[t]he Iraq-Kuwait crisis served to remind us that the Charter is a flexible document that can be interpreted as such. Narrow, rigid interpretation of the Charter by U.N. enthusiasts may have the unintended result of creating unnecessary obstacles to the effective implementation of critical Charter provisions. For example, there was some discussion during the early months of the Iraq-Kuwait crisis that trade sanctions must be proven to have failed before the Security Council could authorize use of force under Article 42 of the Charter. However, the text of Article 42 offers more latitude. . . . The Security Council could make a determination at any time that trade sanctions 'would be inadequate' [under Article 41] and move on to Article 42 and the use of force."[51] Professor Scheffer's argument thus favored a liberal Charter interpretation. It was ultimately corroborated by the fact that Iraq was militarily defeated in the PGW, yet it restationed a large military force near the Kuwait border in late 1994 to avoid full inspections of its capacity for producing weapons of mass destruction.

Security Council Activism Resolution 687 was part of a larger development. The SC's Gulf War activism triggered divergent perceptions: that the United Nations was casting off the fetters of the Cold War; and, suspicion by nations that could be the next object of powerful member hegemony. Many "third world" countries (a label reminiscent of the Cold War) perceived the PGW, and the Council's related activism, as providing the cannon fodder for a new form of control by the post-Cold War dominant States. This concern is aptly articulated by Kyoto University's Professor Yoshiro Matsui:

The Gulf War symbolizes the United Nations activism after the end of the Cold War. The Security Council adopted many resolutions under Chapter VII of the Charter during and after the Gulf War, without being disturbed by the veto of its permanent Members, and this fact is highly appreciated . . . as illustrating a "rebirth" of the United Nations' collective security. . . .

But . . . there spreads a wide suspicion, especially among the nonaligned and developing countries, that this United Nations activism may be a Great Power hegemony in disguise, since they are the only possible targets of this activism. This suspicion seems to be reinforced by the fact that almost all the resolutions . . . have not specified the concrete article of the Charter as their basis [for Council actions against Iraq]. This ambiguous constitutionality . . . is not a happy one for the United Nations activism, and Member States have legitimate interests to see that the Security Council acts within the framework of the Charter which they have accepted.[52]

Professor Matsui attributes this suspicion to the inherently limited scope of available UN controls. The Charter, the SC, and precedent do not give the Secretary-General authority to act in a military operation. The superpowers ensured their control of their own destiny in 1945, when the Charter emerged just short of providing such authority to the head of the United Nations. No State later chose to provide the standing

military forces called for in Article 43 of the Charter—as opposed to the resulting *ad hoc,* case-by-case approach, whereby each nation must consent to provide supporting military forces on an incident-by-incident basis.

Article 2.7 of the UN Charter presents another facet regarding the constitutionality of the SC's post-Cold War/PGW activism. It provides that "[n]othing contained in the present Charter shall authorize the United Nations to intervene in matters which are essentially within the domestic jurisdiction of any state or shall require the Members to submit such matters to settlement under the present Charter; but this principle shall not prejudice the application of enforcement measures under Chapter VII."

Prior to the Gulf War, the Cold War period bred a restrictive application of Chapter VII. It was historically difficult for the SC to take an activist role in maintaining international peace. With world opposition to Iraq's invasion of Kuwait, however, the Council was willing to employ more ambitious applications of its Charter VII powers—with less concern about encroaching upon the Article 2.7 qualifier. This atmosphere set the stage for potential SC intervention in Yugoslavia (humanitarian aid), Somalia (where force was used first by UN troops), Rwanda (humanitarian relief), and the UN administration of troubled areas such as East Timor and Kosovo (peacekeeping).

Subsequent "Unilateral" Action? For a number of years after the PGW, Iraq played the cat and mouse game of frequently testing the UN resolve to ensure that any weapons of mass destruction would be found and dismantled. The United States finally mounted a massive military presence in the Persian Gulf in 1998. The United States relied on the language of the UN's PGW resolutions from 1991, including one that called on States to take all necessary measures to ensure the preservation of peace and Iraq's restoration of sovereignty to Kuwait. The counter to the US perspective that it could still act, under authority of the then seven-year-old SC resolutions, was that Charter Article 2.4 prohibits the use of force—the exceptions being Article 51 self-defense and/or SC authorization under Article 42.

This stalemate was broken, but not legally resolved, by a Memorandum of Understanding between the United Nations and the Republic of Iraq, brokered by UN Secretary-General Kofi Annan.[53] This agreement thus put off the question of whether the United States could legally attack Iraq without the benefit of a *fresh* UN Security Council resolution authorizing this particular use of force—*seven years* after the PGW resolutions had accomplished the objective of Iraq departing from Kuwait.

Bosnia-Herzegovina Application   The SC's activism was temporarily shelved, as events were unfolding in the former Yugoslavia. Several regional entities voted for independence and were recognized by the international community. Throughout the 1991–2000 period, when the United Nations reacted to various events in the former Yugoslavia, the basis for SC action was by no means conspicuous. One reason was that the UN's role in the deployment of its peacekeeping force (UNPRO-FOR), gradually assumed enforcement characteristics. As characterized by David Schweigman, of the T.M.C. Asser Institute in The Hague: "The Council generally refrained from specifying the exact legal basis for its actions. In most cases the Council merely stated that it 'was acting under Chapter VII of the Charter,' after a prior determination that a threat to peace and security existed. . . . The deployment of UNPROFOR against the will of the states concerned, however, raises the interpretive issues as to the legal basis for UNPRO-FOR's continued presence in Yugoslavia."[54]

At the beginning of the PGW period, the first SC Resolution demanding Iraqi retraction from its invasion of strategically located and oil-rich Kuwait came 10 hours after the invasion. The Council never "took charge," however, in the less strategically located and resource-poor arena of Bosnia-Herzegovina. The Bosnian Serbs perpetrated a full-scale war, marked by the brutal infliction of extreme violations of humanitarian norms on Bosnia's Muslim and Croatian civilian population. Bosnian Serbs mistreated those in detention, ignored the basic international safeguards intended to protect civilians and medical facilities, and perpetrated a policy of "ethnic cleansing," resulting in the disappearance or uprooting of hundreds of thousands of refugees on the basis of their ethnicity and religion.

Unlike the Council's activism during the PGW, there was a waning optimism about the SC's continued role in actively maintaining peace in the Bosnian theater. It engaged in a form of political "hot potato," regarding who should take charge of the international response to the Bosnia crisis. The Council authorized the use of force in three resolutions:

(1) Resolution 770—"all necessary measures" could be "taken nationally or through regional agencies or arrangements" to deliver humanitarian assistance when needed in Bosnia-Herzegovina.

(2) Resolution 816—States and regional groups may use necessary means that they may determine for enforcing no-fly zones established by the Council to contain this conflict.

(3) Resolution 836—UN member States "acting nationally or through regional organizations or arrangements" could employ air power to protect UN peacekeepers on the ground in Bosnia. It appeared that the United Nations was thus in search of a significant role to play in bringing the Bosnian conflict under control.

The NATO-based ultimatum, that Serb guns withdraw from UN-designated safe havens, was the most effective tool for shifting political and military responsibility. NATO was simultaneously courting Russian membership, while the United Nations was hoping for a face-saving device in the aftermath of Serb defiance of various UN directives. The United Nations would thereby exercise some degree of control, via its plan to give NATO authority to order air strikes as needed to control Serbian nationalism.

The United Nations' most effective Bosnian-related development was the SC's establishment of the ICC. It made a number of prominent contributions to the evolution of individual responsibility for war-related conduct (§9.5). But the Council had nothing to do with the cessation of the Bosnian conflict.

Kosovo Administration   In 1999, the UN Security Council employed an unheralded degree of activism, and the most striking to date. When NATO's Kosovo airstrikes stopped in June 1999, the SC immediately adopted Resolution 1244. It created a transitional civil administration in Kosovo, known as the United Nations Interim Administration Mission in Kosovo (UNMIK). This would be the UN's second such administration, whereby it would be the only international organization to ever administer sovereign territory.[55]

Relying on several prior resolutions, promulgated pursuant to its Chapter VII powers, the Council thus established a framework for nation building.[56] Under this co-operative venture: the United Nations heads the civil administration of Kosovo; NATO provides military security; the European Union (EU) is responsible for

Kosovo's physical reconstruction; the Organization for Security and Cooperation in Europe is in charge of institution-building and democratization (and the UN High Commission for Refugees humanitarian mission has since dissolved).[57]

While this blueprint is extraordinary, in terms of nation-building in the aftermath of-long-term ethnic hostilities, the UN's efforts to rebuild the judicial system has experienced local challenges to its credibility and legitimacy. It did not incorporate resources from the local population. As recommended by those with direct personal experience: "A number of the problems experienced by the international community could be avoided in future situations by using a more developed, phased approach, which ultimately allows for full participation by the local population, but in the short-term relies on international standards and expertise."[58]

FUTURE ORGANIZATIONAL FORCE

Rapid Deployment Force?   Former UN Secretary-General Butros Butros-Ghali advocated a more forceful method for applying Charter principles to future hostilities. In 1992, he proposed that UN forces be made available for the rapid deployment of force under the Charter's Chapter VII powers. There had never been a standing army as envisioned by UN Charter Article 43. Yet the time was ripe in the aftermath of the Cold War to establish some force capable of quickly responding to threats to peace.

In his *Agenda for Peace,* which was prepared in response to a request from the heads of State of the Council members (*see Summit,* later), Butros-Ghali proposed that the PGW had taught the community of nations an important lesson. A permanent body should be on call, to serve as a deterrent to future threats to peace. He thus proposed "peace-enforcement units." Under this proposal, the "ready availability of armed forces could serve, in itself, as a means of deterring breaches of the peace since a potential aggressor would know that the Council had at its disposal a[n immediate] means of response."

This never-implemented proposal sought the introduction of a UN rapid deployment force into any conflict deemed appropriate by the SC. Butros-Ghali's perspective was that the Council should consider "the utilization of peace-enforcement units in clearly defined circumstances."[59] In his view, adoption by the Council would have bolstered the UN's diplomatic role, while simultaneously providing the manpower to be an effective-*peacemaker*—rather than continuing to serve in its perennial role as mere *peacekeeper.*

First Security Council Summit   In the same year (1992), world leaders conducted a summit-level meeting of the UN Security Council members in New York. This was the 3,046th meeting of the Council, but the first meeting of its heads of State. As proclaimed by Britain's SC President, on behalf of the UNSC to the participating heads of State, at their final gathering:

> This meeting takes place at a time of momentous change. The ending of the Cold War has raised hopes for a safer, more equitable and more humane world. . . .
>
> Last year, under authority of the United Nations, the international community succeeded in enabling Kuwait to regain its sovereignty and territorial integrity, which it had lost as a result of Iraqi aggression.

> The members of the Council also recognize that change, however welcome, has brought new risks for stability and security. Some of the most acute problems result from changes to State structures [§2.4]. . . .

> The international community therefore faces new challenges in the search for peace. All Member States expect the United Nations to play a central role at this crucial stage. The members of the Council stress the importance of strengthening and improving the United Nations to increase its effectiveness.

Rather than taking the initiative, by resolving *how* this "strengthening and improvement" would occur, the SC's heads of State instead requested the UN Secretary-General to assume this task. In his responsive work product (*Agenda for Peace,* earlier) Butros Butros-Ghali therein made specific recommendations in three areas:

(1) *Preventative diplomacy*—formal fact-finding mandated by the SC; meeting "away" from the Council's New York headquarters, notwithstanding this Charter requirement, so as to directly diffuse any underlying disputes based on the Council's presence in a major city of the major superpower.

(2) *Peacemaking*—mediation or negotiation by an individual to be designated by the SC; that the Council devise means for using financial institutions and other components of the UN system to insulate certain

States from the economic consequences of economic sanctions under Article 41; that States undertake to make armed forces available to the Council, on a permanent basis, when it decides to initiate military action under Article 42; that the Council utilize peace-enforcement measures only in "clearly defined circumstances and with their terms of reference specified in advance.

(3) *Peacekeeping*—that regional arrangements be undertaken in a manner that would effectively contribute to a deeper sense of participation, consensus, and democratization in international affairs.

US "Monkey Wrench"   In 1994, President Clinton responded to the 1992 Summit meeting with new guidelines for US participation. His directive would do two things. First, it would greatly limit future US involvement in UN operations involving the use of force. The essential feature is that "the President will never relinquish command over US forces. However, the President will, on a case-by-case basis, consider placing appropriate US forces under the operational control of a competent UN commander for specific UN operations authorized by the Security Council."

There may be room, within this US executive policy, for supporting the rapid deployment force, proposed two years earlier by the Secretary-General. It is unlikely, however, that it would survive either executive or congressional scrutiny. The Clinton Directive modified the prior Bush Administration's expansive UN policy, during a post-Cold War period, which experienced an unparalleled increase in UN peacekeeping operations associated with the SC's renaissance during the PGW.

The following analysis could not be directly based on the President's classified Directive, although the US Department of State provided a separate analysis summarizing the key elements. The first paragraph addresses the general US voting posture in future SC matters. The second provides specifics about the conditions for committing US troops to such actions:

We have determined that the United States should support international action when a threat exists to international or regional peace and security, such as international aggression, an urgent humanitarian disaster or interruption of established democracy or gross violation of human rights that is coupled with violence. In determining whether to support international action, the US will consider whether operations have clear objectives, a defined scope, and an integrated politico-military strategy to achieve our objectives. An international "community of interests" should exist to support multilateral operations. For Chapter VI [presumably meaning Chapter VII] operations, a ceasefire should be in place. The availability of financial and human resources to carry out the strategy will be a critical factor in US deliberations, as will the linkage of expected duration to clear objectives and realistic exit criteria for the operation.

The standards will be even more stringent when the United States considers deploying American forces to participate in UN peacekeeping operations. The United States will only participate in a peace operation when:

◆ It advances US interests and the level of risk is acceptable;
◆ US participation is necessary for the success of the operation;
◆ An integrated politico-military strategy exists to achieve our objectives;
◆ The personnel, funds, and resources are available to support the strategy;
◆ Command and control arrangements are satisfactory;
◆ Likely duration and exit conditions have been identified; and
◆ Domestic and Congressional support exists or can be marshaled.

We believe these factors are critical to the successful conduct of peace operations and to building public and Congressional support for US involvement in those operations. As for command and control arrangements, the President will never relinquish command over US forces. However, the President will, on a case-by-case basis, consider placing appropriate US forces under the operational control of a competent UN commander for specific UN operations authorized by the Security Council.[60]

◆ *Notes & Questions*

Assume you represent another member of the UN Security Council. How will you advise your country about the potential for US involvement in a UNSC action that your country is about to advocate to the rest of the Council?

GENDER PERSPECTIVES

Rape has been used as an instrument for achieving military objectives, since long before the seventeenth-century appearance of the modern nation-State. It would thus appear unexplainable that gender-specific crime was historically beyond the scope of International Law.[61] As vividly encapsulated by one of the foremost authorities, US Professor Kelley Askin:

Gender based issues have been viewed as private matters, "not suitable for aggressive governmental intervention."... The international community holds violence against women as private, falling under the exclusive authority of the State.... Thus, when gender-specific abuses are relegated to the state, and the state then banishes them to the private sphere, they continue to be marginalized. Domestic attitudes transcend international law; the sexist stereotypes and patriarchal practices which prevail at the state level are projected onto the international stage. Consequently, women's issues are ... unworthy of international concern.[62]

There has been an unusual increase, not in gender-related war crimes, but in their prosecution in international courts in the last decade. The primary impetus was the establishment of the International Criminal Tribunal for the Former Yugoslavia (ICTY). Rape was, for the first time, therein prosecuted as a crime against humanity. The systematic rape and sexual slavery by the Japanese, of some 200,000 "comfort women" was ignored by the post-World War II prosecutors at the Tokyo Tribunal (Problem 11.C). The UN's Rwanda Tribunal, however, has prosecuted such cases as both crimes against humanity and as a crime of war. The latter's *Akayesu* judgment (discussed at length within the §9.5 *Radio Machete* case), was the first to treat rape as an instrumentality of genocide (as well as a crime against humanity). Several ICTY cases have involved convictions for like crimes on like grounds.[63]

Unlike the post-World War II Nuremberg and Tokyo treaties, the Rome Statute of the ICC was the first to explicitly authorize prosecution of the following as war crimes and crimes against humanity: rape, sexual slavery, forced prostitution, forced sterilization, forced pregnancy, and "any other kind form of sexual violence of comparable gravity."[64]

Providing a snapshot of International Law in one volume necessitates some difficult choices. One of them is whether to divide this book's primary gender analyses between this chapter on the use of force, and the next one on human rights. The scant coverage of gender-related crimes at this point means only that a monolithic topic, suitable for an entire course of its own, is best addressed in the Human Rights chapter.

◆ 10.3 PEACEKEEPING OPERATIONS

Regional powers have established several significant *non*-UN peacekeeping operations. This section concentrates on UN peacekeeping and how it evolved—without any express provision for it in the UN Charter.

NON-UN PEACEKEEPING OPERATIONS

The United Nations is not the only international organization for dispatching international peacekeeping forces. NATO, OAS, EU, and other peacekeeping forces have attempted to control State uses of force.

NATO has authorized the use of air strikes since 1993, for example, under extensive international pressure to react to the Bosnian Serb attacks on civilian targets. NATO awaited UN authorization before it carried out its "threat" by bombing some Serbian positions when the Serbs failed to retreat and then attacked UN-designated safe havens in Bosnia. NATO's 1994 air strikes were the first attacks on ground troops in NATO's existence. In 2001, NATO assembled a European Defense Force to deal with future problems—first, in Macedonia to disarm Albanian rebels. The United States apparently objects to this presence, because President Bush came into office in 2001, criticizing NATO-based peacekeeping. The United States was involved with that force in Kosovo, because of the US stand against the Yugoslavia's prior Belgrade government.

Other less-publicized operations and proposals have been conducted by several international organizations, including the following (listed chronologically in Exhibit 10.1):

EXHIBIT 10.1 NON–UN PEACEKEEPING FORCES

African Union (2004)	80 military observers and 300 soldiers in the Darfur region of The Sudan (a September 2004 UN Security Council resolution endorsed troop expansion)
Coalition (2003)	UN Security Council resolution authorizes US-led force in Iraq, mandating establishment of democracy
African Union (2003)	AU's first PKO of 2,700 troops in Burundi (until takeover by UN peacekeepers in May 2004)
West African PKO (2003)	3,250 troops headed by Nigeria
Int'l Stabilization Force (2001)	Initial 15-nation peacekeeping 5,000 member force in post-Taliban Afghanistan; replaced by NATO and US-led Coalition (2003)
NATO (2001)	European Defense Force of 3,500 British, French, and Italian troops in Macedonia and Kosovo
OAU (1998)	African foreign ministers met in Ethiopia, rejecting Western nations' proposal to help train potential OAU peacekeeping force on the African continent
ECOMOG (1997)	Economic Community of Western African States "Military Observer Group" was authorized by the UN Security Council to intervene to maintain order in Sierra Leone's civil war (between 7,000 and 20,000 peacekeepers by January 1999)
High Readiness Brigade (1996)	Seven nations signed an agreement in December 1996 to deploy a 4,000-person force to crisis spots under the direction of the Security Council: Austria, Canada, Denmark, Poland, Netherlands, Norway, and Sweden
Georgia-Russia (1994)	Primarily Russian peacekeeping force assisting Georgia with its separatist Abkhazia province, which has claimed independence/2001: Georgia Parliament asks Russia to withdraw its troops from this force
OAS (1993)	A sixteen-nation OAS civilian observer force was present in Haiti to assess the effect of the coup of its first democratically elected leader in 1991
WEU (1992)	The Western European Union assisted NATO with enforcing a UN-imposed blockade. The warships of certain European States kept all vessels from passing in or out of the Adriatic Sea near the former Yugoslavia
WAC (1990)	The sixteen-member West African Community sent a five-nation peacekeeping force into Liberia during its civil war to locate the leader of the rebel forces in Liberia
British Commonwealth (1979)	One thousand troops from five nations of the British Commonwealth were sent into Southern Rhodesia. Their goal was to keep the peace achieved as a result of a ceasefire agreement between anti-government guerrillas and the government of Southern Rhodesia. The presence of this force enabled Southern Rhodesia to transfer political power to the new Zimbabwe government in 1980
Arab League (1976)	The six-nation Inter-Arab Deterrent Force was sent into Lebanon by the Arab League. On Lebanon's request, the League sent more than 30,000 troops there to monitor the peace "established" by an agreement between Muslim and Christian factions during Lebanon's civil war
OAS (1965)	The Dominican Republic was on the verge of a civil war. The US sent more than 20,000 troops in a unilateral action that violated standing OAS regional security agreements. The OAS later replaced those troops with its own much smaller Inter-American Peace Force

The Organization on Security and Cooperation in Europe is assuming a prominent organizational role in maintaining peace in Europe. It has monitored election results, for example, and is a potential NATO "competitor" for broadening regional peacekeeping activity. However, it may be difficult to cultivate a smooth functioning relationship with the UN Security Council, a problem experienced throughout much of the "UN" peacekeeping process. As University of Pisa Professor Natalino Ronzitti writes:

> The usual pattern has been established by relations between the UN and regional organizations: regional organizations are entitled to take enforcement measures if so authorized by the UN Security Council [which] . . . can "utilize" regional organizations for enforcement action "under its authority." This concept is based on the supremacy of the Security Council, under the authority of which regional organizations can act.
>
> The way in which this concept has been implemented in practice is a moot point. During the Cold War, regional organizations often acted without any authorization from the Security Council (the best example is the Organization of American States). Even in the post-Cold War period, relations between regional organizations and the Security Council are still not easy (UNPROFOR and NATO in Bosnia and Herzegovina is a case in point) and regional organizations sometimes act without real directions from the Security Council, as proven in the case of NATO in former Yugoslavia (Bosnia and Herzegovina), where the UN adopted an "enabling resolution" putting NATO under the nominal authority only of the UN.[65]

UN PEACEKEEPING

Introduction UN peacekeeping has been a focus of worldwide attention since its inception. The United Nations' first such mission was the 1948 UN Truce Supervision Organization. It is still carrying out its mission with observers who remain in the Middle East to monitor ceasefires, supervise armistice agreements, and attempt to prevent escalation of the conflict.

The United Nations has actually conducted a number of "peacekeeping" operations, although the term was not employed officially until the 1956 Suez Canal Crisis. Since then, approximately one-half million UN troops have been deployed in many regions of the globe. As of the end of 2000, 1,650 UN international civil servants thereby lost their lives. A listing of the numerous UN peacekeeping missions is available on the UN Web site.[66]

The scope of these operations has dramatically increased over time, particularly during the period after the Cold War and just prior to the UN's end-of-millennium financial crisis. In 1992, the number of UN forces quadrupled from 11,000 to 44,000. By the end of 1993, there were 80,000 UN peacekeepers. As of December 2004, this number was down to 60,000. And for the first time in UN history, US combat troops were assigned as UN peacekeepers, sent to Macedonia to aid in containing the Bosnian conflict so that it would not spill over into bordering States.

At the turn of the century, world leaders made a commitment to act upon a contemporary report which called for more peacekeeping resources to facilitate conflict management—in the following terms: "We resolve, therefore . . . [t]o make the United Nations, more effective in maintaining peace and security, by giving it the resources and tools it needs for conflict prevention, peaceful resolution of disputes, peacekeeping, post-conflict peace building and reconstruction. In this context, we take note of the Report of the Panel on United Nations Peace Operations and request the General Assembly to consider its recommendations expeditiously."[67]

The UN's December 2004 High-level Panel Report reconfirmed this commitment. It further noted that the "developed States have particular responsibilities here, and should do more to transform their existing force capacities into suitable contingents for peace operations."[68]

Limitations From the outset, there were problems with the laudatory objective of the UN as keeper of the peace. No standing army ever materialized, as arguably contemplated by some participants in the drafting of Article 43 of the Charter. The Cold War blocked effective peace*making*. Contemporary UN peacekeeping problems include inadequate funding, insufficient national resolve to continue participation, and the severely limiting US guidelines promulgated by President Clinton in 1994 (§10.2).

Member State unwillingness to cede the requisite degree of State sovereignty to the United Nations is the basic limiting factor. The Charter was drafted with a view toward ensuring that the UN would not become a form of world government possessing the preeminence to override national sovereignty (§3.3). Therefore, Article 2.7 of the Charter retained the primacy of State sovereign power, in the following terms: "Nothing contained in the present Charter shall authorize the United Nations to intervene in matters [that] are essentially within the domestic jurisdiction of any state. . . ." This constitutional limitation historically precluded the organization from operating in any theater, absent consent of the State, giving rise to the perennial UN role as "peacekeeper" rather than "peacemaker."[69]

The United Nations learned this lesson the hard way in the unique expansion of its "Operation Restore Hope" in Somalia. In practice, a peacekeeping invitation had always been understood to mean that the UN troops would take on a somewhat passive role. UN "Blue Helmets" would not actively participate in local military conflicts. These neutral "troops" would serve only as a buffer between hostile forces, only *after* a hostility-ending agreement with all sides. UN troops in Somalia seized arms and conducted raids, however, in search of a particular Somalian warlord. This organizational activity violated the practice that this organization would not use its presence to act in ways not authorized under its non-Chartered peacekeeping role.

Another preliminary handicap limited the UN's peacekeeping potential. France had unsuccessfully attempted to gather support for an international police force during the League of Nations drafting conference. At the Dumbarton Oaks UN preparatory conference, however, Article 43 was worded as follows:

1. All Members of the United Nations, in order to contribute to the maintenance of international peace and security, undertake to make available to the Security Council, on its call and in accordance with a special agreement or agreements, armed forces . . . necessary for the purpose of maintaining international peace and security.

. . .

3. The agreement or agreements shall be negotiated as soon as possible on the initiative of the Security Council. They shall . . . be subject to ratification by the signatory states in accordance with their respective constitutional processes.

Article 43 was inserted into the UN Charter as an open-ended provision that was, in effect, only an agreement to agree. The Charter did not specify the intended *composition* of the UN force. The members opted not to stock the putative "armed forces." There would never be a standing military force. The Council was not destined to have an immediately available, and thus rapidly deployable, military subdivision at its disposal when hostilities arose.

So that the SC would not be totally out of the loop, national staffing agreements were to be approved by the SC. Article 47 even provided for a Military Staff Committee, which would supposedly facilitate the Council's role in developing "military requirements for the maintenance of international peace and security, the employment and command of forces placed at its disposal, the regulation of armaments, and possible disarmament."

Thus, the general lack of specificity allowed the national representatives to quickly conclude the drafting of the UN Charter. Unfortunately, it also vitiated the SC's power to effectively maintain peace, since it had no standing army available for potential police actions to deal with threats to international peace.[70]

The Soviet-US Cold War was an insurmountable problem. For four decades, the UN peacekeeping operations would not be established within any US or Soviet sphere of direct influence. William Durch, a prominent policy analyst at the Henry Stimson Center in Virginia, notes that "the UN offered a nominally impartial alternative that could meet this objective. . . . Peacekeeping missions more often served the West's interests in regional stability. Since Moscow's interest . . . was to foster regional *instability* . . . lead[ing] to radical political change and greater Soviet regional influence, Soviet support for UN peacekeeping was intermittent at best throughout this period."[71]

Uniting for Peace Resolution Frustration with the SC's potential for inaction led the GA to adopt the 1950 Uniting for Peace (UFP) Resolution. With the SC effectively precluded from controlling hostilities—because of the veto power of any one of the five permanent members—the UN General Assembly decided to fashion its *own* method for taking action independently of the Council, and, mentioned nowhere in the Charter.

The Assembly's UFP Resolution was designed to remedy the potential failure of the SC to discharge its responsibilities on behalf of the General Assembly's numerous member States. The resolution's supporters devised a strategy, not contemplated by the terms of the Charter, purporting to authorize the *General Assembly* to initiate measures to restore peace—including the use of armed force. This novel resolution is set forth below:

Uniting for Peace, Resolution 377 (V)

UN GENERAL ASSEMBLY OFFICIAL RECORD
5th Session (1950), Supp. No. 20 (A/1775), p.10

. . . *Conscious* that failure of the Security Council to discharge its responsibilities on behalf of all the Member States . . . does not relieve Member States of their obligations or the United Nations of its responsibility under the Charter to maintain international peace and security,

Recognizing in particular that such failure does not deprive the General Assembly of its rights or relieve it of its responsibilities under the Charter in regard to the maintenance of international peace and security,

Recognizing that discharge by the General Assembly of its responsibilities in these respects calls for possibilities of observation which would ascertain the facts and expose aggressors; for the existence of armed forces which could be used collectively; and for the possibility of timely recommendation by the General Assembly to Members of the United Nations for collective action which, to be effective, should be prompt . . .

Resolves that if the Security Council, because of lack of unanimity of the permanent members, fails to exercise its primary responsibility for the maintenance of international peace and security in any case where there appears to be a threat to the peace, breach of the peace, or act of aggression, the General Assembly shall consider the matter immediately with a view to making appropriate recommendations to Members for collective measures, including in the case of a breach of the peace or act of aggression the use of armed force when necessary, to maintain or restore international peace and security. If not in session at the time, the General Assembly may meet in emergency special session within twenty-four hours of the request therefor. Such emergency special session shall be called if requested by the Security Council on the vote of any seven Members, or by a majority of the Members of the United Nations [General Assembly]. . . .

This resolution was not used excessively, but was nevertheless important to the future of UN peacekeeping operations. The League of Nations had failed to prevent the outbreak of World War II. The promoters of this resolution did not want history to repeat itself. If the SC were unsuccessful in exercising its "primary" responsibility to maintain peace, because of permanent member vetoes, then the General Assembly must assist in the achievement of the fundamental objectives of the organization. This resolution effectively amended the UN Charter's SC provisions by augmenting the organizational source for dispatching peacekeeping forces. The Uniting for Peace Resolution was the basis for the next UN peacekeeping operation: the 1956 Suez Canal Crisis.

The Middle East has been the site of a number of UN peacekeeping operations, including the very first one, which (as noted earlier) is still in existence. In 1956, the president of Egypt nationalized the Suez Canal, one of the major trans-shipping points of the world. Its closure would require time and great cost to circumnavigate continents to deliver goods and troops. Control of the canal could also affect the price of transporting Middle Eastern oil to the rest of the world.

The significant economic and military threats posed by Egypt's control of the Suez Canal concerned the entire international community. Great Britain, France, and Israel secretly decided that Israel would attack Egypt. Great Britain and France would rely on that attack as the basis for their own police action. After the Israeli attack, Great Britain and France then vetoed a SC resolution, calling on Israel and Egypt to cease their hostilities. These vetoes by permanent members of the Council temporarily precluded the establishment of a UN peacekeeping force. Great Britain, France, and Israel thus presumed that they could protect their own interests in the canal without any UN interference.[72]

The United Nations Emergency Force (UNEF) was established in 1956. The General Assembly invoked the Uniting for Peace Resolution to enable it to act, after the SC was stalemated by the British and French vetoes. A 5000-troop force was drawn from States, which were not members of the SC. They were deployed to Egypt to serve as a buffer between Egypt and its British, French, and Israeli adversaries. In 1967, at the request of Egypt, the UN Secretary-General took the controversial step of withdrawing this force at the time of the Six Day War between Israel and its Arab neighbors. This suspended the UNEF operation until 1973, when it was revived to keep peace and order in the Sinai Desert and Gaza Strip. This time, the SC exercised its Charter powers to establish the next of many Council operations in that theater.

Contemporary Blemishes   Two events have especially tarnished the reputation of the UN's otherwise popular "Blue Helmets." In July 1995, 7,800 Muslim men and boys of military age were gathered at a UN safe haven in Srebrenica, Bosnia. They were drawn there, on the basis of promised UN protection to them from the region's violent ethnic conflict. The UN's 750 peacekeepers were suddenly vastly outnumbered by Serb forces. The Serbs thus slaughtered these refugees in three days. This became Europe's worst such genocidal act since the Holocaust. The Dutch government fell, when this event was made public, because the Dutch troops took no action to stop the killing. The families of those killed filed a lawsuit against the United Nations and the Dutch government in November 2003.

In December 2004, there were some 150 *reported* rapes of young girls in The Congo. UN peacekeepers were accused and are being investigated. UN Secretary-General Kofi Annan responded that there was "clear evidence that acts of gross misconduct have taken place. This is a shameful thing for the United Nations to have to say, and I am absolutely outraged by it." There have been some dismissals, but no prosecutions—apparently on grounds of organizational immunity (§3.6).

◆ 10.4 MULTILATERAL AGREEMENTS

This section summarizes the many treaty-based attempts to control the use of force by States. The quest to limit the use of military force is not just a twentieth-century phenomenon. In 1789, English writer Jeremy Bentham published arms-control proposals emphasizing disarmament as the prerequisite to achieving peace. He hoped to pacify Europe via treaties to limit the number of troops that States could maintain. As an alternative, he envisioned an international court which would resolve any disputes regarding implementation of his proposed regime. He did caution, however, with a relevance that has not faded with the passage of time that "such a court was not to be armed with any coercive powers."[73]

In the nineteenth century, a number of European States considered the efficacy of drafting rules on the laws of war. They produced the Paris Declaration of 1856, a collection of principles on the methods for employing and conserving the use of force in armed conflicts. The ensuing treaty regime would not materialize, however, until the turn of the century.

HAGUE CONFERENCES

In 1899, Russia's Czar Nicholas invited a number of national representatives to The Hague, in the Netherlands, for the first of two turn-of-the-century international peace conferences. The second occurred in 1907. The objective was to limit the national use of armaments. Once the conference participants realized that there would be no international agreement eliminating war, the central theme became how to conduct war. For example, the representatives agreed to provide advance warning when any nation intended to use force to settle a dispute. The conference delegates also prepared numerous declarations in the form of draft treaties. A representative list is provided below:

1899 Hague Conference
- Convention for the Adaption to Maritime Warfare of the Principles of the Geneva Convention of 1864 on the Laws of War
- Declaration on Prohibiting Launching of Projectiles and Explosives from Balloons
- Declaration on Prohibiting the Use of Projectiles Diffusing Suffocating Gas
- Declaration on Prohibiting the Use of Expanding Bullets
- Hague Convention with Respect to the Laws and Customs of War on Land

1907 Hague Conference

◆ Convention for the Pacific Settlement of International Disputes

◆ Convention Respecting the Limitation of the Employment of Force for the Recovery of Contract Debts

◆ Convention Relative to the Opening of Hostilities

◆ Convention Respecting the Rights and Duties of Neutral Powers and Persons in War on Land

◆ Convention Respecting Bombardment by Naval Forces in Time of War

The Hague Conference representatives did not establish a system to *remedy* violations of the principles contained in the above agreements. There would be no international military force to act as a peacekeeper/peacemaker at the scene of hostilities. Instead, they announced an arbitration system to settle international disputes (§9.1 Permanent Court of Arbitration). But no nation was *required* to resort to arbitration before using force. This round of draft treaties contained rights without effective remedies. Obligations were thus unenforceable.

Many of the Hague Conference principles nevertheless served as bases for later treaties, conferences, and the Nuremberg Trials. The Hague draft agreement on suffocating gas was reconsidered during the 1925 Geneva Protocols on the manufacturing of chemical weapons for future use. These post–World War I agreements prohibited the use of poisonous gases in warfare, although nations could continue to stockpile such weapons. In 1971, UN delegates considered both of these earlier documents, when they resolved to prohibit the development, production, and stockpiling of biological and toxic weapons. The Hague Conference chemical weapons principles resurfaced in 1989. Discovery of a chemical weapons plant in Libya focused new attention on the need for international control of chemical weapons to avoid their use by terrorists. There was a renewed fear about the effects described in the preparatory work for the early twentieth-century chemical weapons conferences. The former Soviet Union and the United States then pledged that they would reduce their arsenals of chemical weapons. Iraq was "required" to end its production of any such weapons as a consequence of the 1991 PGW. The UN weapons inspectors would be frustrated (and even taken hostage), however, in their efforts to assure that Iraq was not producing weapons of mass destruction—a theme which would rekindle international interest after September 11, 2001.

LEAGUE OF NATIONS

The 1919 Treaty of Versailles established peace expectations after World War I, then referred to as "the war to end all wars." That treaty prohibited war until three months after an arbitral or judicial decision considering the particular dispute (League of Nations Covenant, Article 12).[74]

Article 16 of the League's Covenant contained a significant innovation. It established the first collective security measure adopted by an international organization: War against one member of the League was tantamount to war against all. The League's representatives believed that they could deter hostile actions by agreeing to an interrelated mutual defense system. They opted for economic rather than military enforcement measures. Article 16 provided that "[s]hould any of the . . . Parties break or disregard its covenants under Article XII, it shall thereby ipso facto [by that act automatically] be deemed to have committed an act of war against all the other members of the League, which hereby undertake immediately to subject it [the offending nation] to the severance of all trade or financial relations, the prohibition of all intercourse between their nationals and the nationals of the covenant breaking State, and the prevention of all financial, commercial, or personal intercourse between nationals of the covenant breaking State and the nationals of any other State, whether a member of the League or not."

This Article was first tested in the mid–1930s during Italy's war against Abyssinia (now Ethiopia). The League did not intervene, even when Abyssinia sought its assistance to control Italy's aggression. The League instead responded by directing several nations to draft a report on Italy's hostile acts. Great Britain and France, with League approval, established an embargo against certain Italian exports. The products that were the object of this embargo, however, were insignificant. Great Britain and France did not want to risk war with their Italian trading partners. Japan then attacked Manchuria in 1939. The League's inability to respond decisively destroyed its credibility and exposed its inability to control the State use of force.[75]

KELLOGG-BRIAND PACT

The 1928 Treaty for the Renunciation of War, or Kellogg-Briand Pact, was advocated by France and the United States. It was not designed to be merely a regional peace process. The participants focused on Europe, however. It was the region most affected by World War I, not to mention the region most engaged in wars since creation of the modern State in 1648 (§2.1 Peace of Westphalia). Napoleon unwittingly spawned the first international attempt to declare war illegal. In 1814, after his defeat, Austria, Prussia, Russia, and Napoleon himself, all agreed that any attempt to declare war, or to wage it, was illegal.[76]

This pact was an outright *condemnation* of war. It contained the agreement that States "shall" use only peaceful means to settle their differences. Under Articles 1 and 2, the "Parties solemnly declare in the names of their respective peoples that they condemn recourse to war for the solution of international controversies, and renounce it as an instrument of national policy in their relations with one another. The . . . Parties agree that the settlement or solution of all disputes or conflicts of whatever nature or of whatever origin they may be . . . shall never be sought except by pacific means." It contained unassailable principles, but it also lacked any effective enforcement provisions to stop the outbreak of another world war.

LATIN AMERICAN INITIATIVES

Other significant peace initiatives also condemn war, on a regional level. The 1933 Montevideo Treaty provided that "settlement of disputes or controversies shall be effected only by the pacific means [that] shall have the sanction of international law." The 1948 Charter of the OAS also prohibits the aggressive use of force. Its Article 21 provides that the "American States bind themselves in their international relations not to have recourse to the use of force." This treaty does not contain a specific arms control regime, however.

MULTILATERAL AGREEMENTS

There are numerous treaty-based regimes for controlling the use of force—on both regional and multilateral levels. Exhibit 10.2 provides a snapshot of selected instruments, designed to control modern applications of military force.

◆ 10.5 HUMANITARIAN INTERVENTION

Humanitarian intervention is not mentioned in the UN Charter, the NATO Charter, or any like document. Thus, any rules that have emerged are the by-product of Customary International Law. A commonly cited UN General Assembly contribution is the 1965 Inadmissibility of Intervention in Domestic Affairs Resolution

2131—often associated with the decolonization movement of the 1960s, which focused on self-determination on the African Continent. It then reaffirmed the principle of nonintervention proclaimed in numerous global and regional charters. It recognized "that full observance of the principle of non intervention of States in the internal affairs of other States is essential to the fulfillment of the purposes and principles of the United Nations."

What this resolution did not do was to foresee the many failed States and governments that would wreak havoc on their own people, in Africa and other regions, after the end of the Cold War. In October 2003, for example, Russia announced the reservation of its right to intervene militarily in former Soviet States where the human rights of ethnic Russians were being violated.[77]

Such interventions may be military or non-military, unilateral or collective. The United Nations has authorized collective interventions with military forces that were designed to endorse the Charter's humanitarian objectives. Charter Article 2.7 eschews UN intervention, however, "in matters essentially within the domestic jurisdiction of any State." But this sovereignty-driven principle does "not prejudice the application of enforcement measures under Chapter VII"?

The UN Security Council has thus relied on its Chapter VII powers to establish the *ad hoc* International Criminal Tribunals for Rwanda and Yugoslavia (§9.5). Because Article 39 authorizes the Council to "decide what measures shall be taken . . . to maintain or restore international peace and security," it authorized this form of nonmilitary intervention to address the atrocities perpetrated within those arenas by forces within those countries.

Unilateral humanitarian intervention may conflict with the norms associated with territorial sovereignty and the use of force. The extent to which a *State* may unilaterally intervene for various purposes, including the rescue of political figures and hostages is fraught with complex issues of legitimacy. This section focuses on situations which some States have conveniently characterized as "humanitarian" interventions, especially when they have a dual purpose in mind.

DEFINITIONAL CONTOURS

As classically articulated by the nineteenth-century British philosopher, John Stuart Mill: "To go to war for an idea, if the war is aggressive, not defensive, is as criminal as to go to war for territory or revenue; for it is as little justifiable to force our ideas on other people, as to compel them to submit to our will in any other respect. But there assuredly are cases in which it is allowable to go to war, without having been ourselves attacked, or threatened with attack; and it is very important that nations should make up their minds in time, as to what these cases are."[78]

The latter portion of Mill's articulation finds contemporary expression in the widely heralded 2001 report International Commission on Intervention and State Sovereignty—endorsed by the UN Secretary-General and recommended to all States for consideration. While noting the primacy of State sovereignty, the Commission cautioned that primary responsibility for the protection of its people lies with the State itself. The second of its two main principles thus acknowledges that: "Where a population is suffering serious harm, as a result of internal war, insurgency, repression or state failure, and the state in question is unwilling or unable to halt or avert it, the principle of non-intervention yields to the international responsibility to protect."

In its Principles for Military Intervention, the Commission defines its "Just Cause Threshold" as follows (bolding in the original):

Military intervention for human protection purposes is an exceptional and extraordinary measure. To be warranted, there must be serious and irreparable harm occurring to human beings, or imminently likely to occur, of the following kind:

A. **large scale loss of life,** actual or apprehended, with genocidal intent or not, which is the product either of deliberate state action, or state neglect or inability to act, or a failed state situation; or

B. **large scale 'ethnic cleansing',** actual or apprehended, whether carried out by killing,—forced expulsion, acts of terror or rape.

This formulation arguably builds upon the rhetoric of the ICJ in its 1986 *Nicaragua* case (§10.2), wherein the Court commented as follows:

There can be no doubt that the provision of *strictly humanitarian aid* to persons or forces in another country, whatever their political affiliations or objectives, *cannot be regarded as unlawful intervention, or as in any other way contrary to international law.* The characteristics of such aid were indicated in the first and second of the fundamental principles declared by the Twentieth International Conference of the Red Cross, that

"The Red Cross, born of a desire to bring assistance without discrimination to the wounded on the battlefield, endeavours—in its international and national capacity—to prevent and alleviate human suffering wherever it may be found. Its purpose is to protect life and health and to ensure respect for the human being. It promotes mutual understanding, friendship, cooperation and lasting peace amongst all peoples."[79]

There may thus be a *duty* to intervene, in appropriate circumstances. Gross violations of fundamental human rights that would violate the Genocide Convention enable the United Nations to act under Article VIII of the Convention "to take such action under the Charter of the United Nations as they consider appropriate for the prevention and suppression of acts of genocide." But as University of Zagreb Professor Budislav Vukas notes: "Unfortunately, the United Nations often are not acting in accordance with this provision. . . . Notwithstanding the ongoing genocide of the population of the Darfur region in Sudan, the United Nations are not even considering an efficient action which would what the Security Council called [2005] 'the world's worst current humanitarian disaster.'"[80] One can only hope that the March 2005 SC reference of fifty-one perpetrators to the International Criminal Court prosecutor will have a deterring effect there and elsewhere. And as stated in the UN's December 2004 High-level Report on Threats, Challenges, and Change:

201. The successive humanitarian disasters in Somalia, Bosnia and Herzegovina, Rwanda, Kosovo and now Darfur, Sudan, have concentrated attention not on the immunities of sovereign Governments but their responsibilities, both to their own people and to the wider international community. There is a growing recognition that the issue is not the "right to intervene" of any State, but the "responsibility to protect" of *every* State when it comes to people suffering from avoidable catastrophe—mass murder and rape, ethnic cleansing by forcible expulsion and terror, and deliberate starvation and exposure to disease.

. . .

203. We endorse the emerging norm that there is a collective international responsibility to protect, exercisable by the Security Council authorizing military intervention as a last resort, in the event of genocide and other largescale killing, ethnic cleansing or serious violations of international humanitarian law which sovereign Governments have proved powerless or unwilling to prevent.[81]

EXHIBIT 10.2 SELECTED MULTILATERAL ARMS CONTROL REGIMES

Date*	Title	Scope
1957	International Atomic Energy Agency	Intergovernmental organization to promotes peaceful uses of nuclear energy
1959/ 1961	Antarctic Treaty	Prohibits establishment of military bases, maneuvers, and testing
1963 1963	Treaty Banning Nuclear Weapon Tests in the Atmosphere, in Outer Space and under Water	Signed by the Original Parties: USSR, the UK, and the US
1967	Outer Space Treaty	Prohibits orbit of weapons of mass destruction and military presence in space or on a celestial body
1967/ 1968	Treaty of Tlatelolco (Latin America)	Regional nuclear-free zone and prohibits acquisition, manufacture, or any use of nuclear weapons
1968/ 1970	Nuclear Non-Proliferation Treaty	Nuclear States may not transfer and others may not receive, manufacture, or develop nuclear weapons; effect limited because it lacks ratification by key parties
1971/ 1972	Seabed Treaty	Prohibits nuclear weapons and other weapons of mass destruction on the seabed and ocean floor and in subsoil
1972/ 1975	Biological Weapons Convention	Prohibits the production and stockpiling of bacteriological and toxic weapons. Seeks destruction or diversion of weapons to peaceful purposes. National sovereignty withdrawal clause has rendered it ineffective
1972	Anti-Ballistic Missile Treaty (US-Russia)	Forbids deployment of a missile defense system/North Korea withdraws in Jan. 2003/US announces plans to withdraw by end of 2004
1977/ 1978	Enmod Convention	Prohibits military or other hostile use of environmental modification in, over, and above the Earth
1977	Mercenarism Convention (Africa)	Organization of African Unity prohibits placing or training mercenaries in Africa. Created crime of mercenarism whereby guilty person is denied POW status.
1979	SALT II Treaty (US-Russia)	FIrst ceiling on strategic nuclear weapons
1980/ 1983	Inhumane Weapons Convention	Prohibits or restricts certain conventional weapons deemed too injurious: mines, booby traps, incendiary devices
1985/ 1986	Treaty of Rarotonga (South Pacific)	Declares nuclear-free zone/Prohibits acquisition, testing of nuclear weapons, waste dumping
1986	Confidence and Security Building	Facilitates abstention from threat or use of force, including advance Measures and Disarmaments (CSCE; notification of certain military activities such as major troop and now OSCE) (Europe) battle tank movements

*Second date: year of entry into force, by minimum number of ratifications or by other special agreement.

EXHIBIT 10.2 SELECTED MULTILATERAL ARMS CONTROL REGIMES (CONTINUED)

Date*	Title	Scope
1991	START I Treaty (US-Russia)	Slashed nuclear arsenals by one-third
1992	Conventional Armed Forces in Europe Treaty	Former Warsaw Pact nations to destroy 50,000 major weapons/ NATO nations to destroy few weapons/All to reduce ground- and air weapons/Ceilings set on certain combat equipment.
1993/ 2000	START II Treaty (US, Russia, and three other former Soviet republics)	Cut nuclear stockpiles by another thirds
1991	Missile Technology Control Regime	UN Security Council permanent members sponsored arms-export limitations and shared information regarding sales of all military weapons and control of missiles capable of delivering biological, chemical, nuclear weapons
1992/ 1997	Chemical Weapons Convention	UN General Assembly Resolution 47/39 prohibits use, development, and stockpiling of chemical weapons/Seeks destruction 10 years after entry into force
1992	Nuclear Power in Outer Space	UN General Assembly Resolution 47/68 would control use of nuclear power in outer space
1992	General and Complete Disarmament	UN General Assembly Resolution 46/36: 12 resolutions calling for complete disarmament rather than mere controls/Annex establishes UN Register of Conventional Arms to track importing or exporting of specified types of military systems.
1996	UN Comprehensive Test Ban Treaty	Designed as universal and verifiable nuclear test ban, including duty not to explode nuclear weapons within their jurisdiction or control
1997/ 1999	Land Mine Treaty	Prohibits use, stockpiling, production, and transfer of antipersonnel mines and requires their being found and destroyed within 10 years/Not signed by Russia, China, or the US
1999	Protocol II to 1980 Inhumane Weapons Convention (mines, booby-traps, and related devices)	Ratified by US
2002	US-Russia Nuclear Missile Reduction Treaty	Cuts respective nuclear arsenals—from about 6,000 each, to about 2,000—or two-thirds, by 2012
2003	UN Convention on Conventional Weapons	Clearing unexploded weapons/designing to explode on impact
2005	International Convention for the Suppression of Acts of Nuclear Terrorism	Measures each State is to adopt, including criminalizing relevant conduct under national law/Does not address legality of use/threat of nuclear weapons

The case of Rwanda would of course be the last decade's worst case scenario (ICTR *Radio Machete* case §9.5). The international community was hesitant to label Darfur—aka slow motion Rwanda—as "genocide." The Genocide Convention Article VIII—international responsibility to intervene would be triggered by the application of that term. However, the costs, UN limitations, donor fatigue, the priority for saving strangers, and a host of other priorities explain why the international community is so slow to act in such cases.[82] The facts are often crystal clear, but not the motives.

Multilateral intervention is often undertaken by a regional or global organization, for the purpose of aiding people who are enduring intolerable conditions. The underlying cause may be a civil war or degradation at the hands of a despotic political regime. The intervention may take the form of military or economic action, designed to bring about a policy change by the targeted State. Too often, intervention has been a euphemism for political domination. States have long recognized the practical utility of characterizing their actions as a moral and legal benevolence, which has been undertaken for "humanitarian" purposes.[83]

This strain of force is often justified by a State or an international organization on the basis that the inhabitants of some nation are not receiving the protection they deserve under the International Law of Human Rights. In other words, the government is accused of arbitrarily and persistently abusing its inhabitants, or a particular ethnic group. The United States unilaterally intervened in Cuba in 1898, for example, to "put an end to barbarities, bloodshed, starvation, and horrible miseries."[84]

The permissible contours of "humanitarian intervention" have not been defined in a way that represents a meaningful State consensus. One reason is that this term became part of the customary post-Cold War lexicon; however, neither word in this phrase has been precisely defined. The US Department of State's Sean Murphy comments on this vacuum:

> The adjective "humanitarian" is very broad and in common parlance is used to describe a wide range of activities of governmental and nongovernmental actors that seek to improve the status and well-being of individuals. . . . The international community is not fully in agreement on the normative content of many human rights. . . .
>
> Assuming certain core human rights upon which there is more or less universal agreement, there is nevertheless an inherent subjectivity in assessing whether, for any given situation, those rights are threatened and must be protected. This subjectivity in turn raises important questions about who is competent to make the assessment. Is it important that the international community regard an intervention as "humanitarian," or is it sufficient that the state or group conducting the intervention consider it humanitarian? . . .
>
> The noun "intervention" is, likewise, quite broad and has been the subject of extensive debate in the United Nations and of scholarly treatises on international law. When a state, group of states, or international organization takes action against a state . . . [it] "intervenes" in the affairs of that state in the lay sense of the term, even if no military coercion is brought to bear. Indeed, all of international law and international relations consists of varying levels of states interacting and thereby "intervening" in each other's affairs. [85]

The following analytical essay surveys some muddy footing in the humanitarian intervention terrain. It vividly presents the choices, which sometimes spawn an intervention, in ways not imaginable during the Cold War:

Realpolitik and the CNN Factor of Humanitarian Intervention

Edward Newman, Researcher in Law, University of Kent

IN THE UNITED NATIONS IN THE NEW WORLD ORDER:
THE WORLD ORGANIZATION AT FIFTY 191–194 (HAMPSHIRE, UK: MACMILLAN, 1995)

Humanitarian Intervention is action across recognizable territorial boundaries ostensibly aimed at alleviating grave human need, be it the result of starvation, disease, atrocity or gross persecution, widespread dispossession,

---

Reprinted with permission of Macmillan Ltd. Footnotes omitted.

or the imminent danger of these or other threats. It has been used to describe short term action in response to immediate need, either with or without the consent of the recipient territory, longer term reconstruction involving the distribution of food, medical equipment, shelter, and also military protection and rescue. This type of action has been conducted on a unilateral or multilateral basis. Humanitarian intervention has been associated with situations, of government persecution of the citizens of another state within its territory, civil war, conditions of failed statehood and anarchy, and in cases of natural disaster.

It is essential to emphasize that failing statehood has prompted much of the debate concerning humanitarian intervention. Although this is not a new phenomenon, if one were seeking a point of departure from the Cold War to the post-Cold War humanitarian agenda, this would undoubtedly form part of the equation. As Falk has stated, "the challenge of the weak state is moving to the center of concern," and the attitude of the international community in response forms a major part of the subject of humanitarian intervention. Vulnerable state are those chiefly of the Third World, typically struggling under the legacy of spurious colonial boundaries in the case of Africa, the collapse of dictatorial rule and the semblance of authority and order, premature decolonization, and abject poverty. Although many tribal and ethnic animosities are indigenous in origin, there is a strong argument to suggest that the colonial overlords, where they existed, and in turn the interference of Cold War politics, severely weakened or destroyed traditional structures of authority. During the Cold War the sovereignty of many such states was partially propped-up by aid and the support of vying superpowers. Now that the support is gone, the corrupt leaders are being toppled, leaving anarchy and a glut of weapons. Fragmentation and ethnic hostility are the only identities which exist, and the lawlessness which often accompanies this can result in the most harrowing of human suffering. It is, therefore, correct to suggest that the "[i]nstabilities and insecurities that abound in the Third World are largely a function of the historical juncture at which most Third World states find themselves."

In addition to the moral responsibility to intervene where possible to alleviate the suffering which usual follows state collapse, there is a real need to consider the international repercussions of state failure. The spill-over from such circumstances can create innumerable problems; as [former UN Secretary-General] Boutros-Ghali has suggested "[y]ou will pay the price sooner or later if you don't intervene. And later it will cot you 10 times more." However, humanitarian intervention in such circumstances almost inevitably leads to further tasks of reconstruction. There is no hope of the "surgical operation" so beloved in the West, and a host of problems arise requiring great commitments by the international community. Yet if the failing of states becomes "a familiar facet of international life", the international community must respond with more understanding and farsightedness than has been demonstrated so far.

An important distinction must be made between intervention which is under the auspices of the United Nations—either directly coordinated, or authorized, by the Security Council—and that which is not. The most important distinction, however, is between action which has the consent of the recipient state—either expressly or tacitly—and that which does not, through the opposition of the government or in circumstances where a government can no longer be said to exercise legal jurisdiction. From these factors—the *what*, *when*, and *who* of humanitarian intervention—one can draw a loose legal and political framework which has a bearing upon the usual questions raised with this subject: is intervention necessary and legal in a particular case? Is humanitarian intervention the prerogative of the strong against the weak, or the North against the South? Can it involve structural change in the recipient state? Is humanitarian intervention a mask for ethnocentrism or neo-colonialism? Or can humanitarian intervention in the post-Cold War world, free from the geopolitics of bipolarity and spheres of influence, finally live up to its altruistic rhetoric? What is the relationship between the United Nations and non-governmental organizations (NGOs) in the provision of humanitarian assistance? Can the international community devise an acceptable blueprint and multilateral mechanisms for intervention which would overcome the present disagreements on when to assist, and how to coordinate and pay for these operations?

Before addressing such questions it is essential to distinguish between the different agendas underpinning humanitarian intervention. In particular, one can identify the separate, but by no means mutually exclusive, political, strategic, legal, moral, practical, and financial dimensions which sometimes converge but often compete be hind the stances of governments and by extension the activities of the UN. This is an important exercise: it is the alignment of these factors which largely determines whether a humanitarian operation will be initiated under the UN and if it will have the support necessary for success. These factors should be the focus of attention, for they form the basis of unilateral and collective action under the UN.

. . .

The legal basis for humanitarian intervention . . . is surrounded in a vague legality. The fundamental factor is the question of consent and sovereign territorial integrity. . . . Further to this, the existence and nature of Security Council support for humanitarian intervention is of great importance.

Historically, humanitarian intervention in breach of the sovereignty of a state has been condemned by treaty and customary international law. The statist Westphalian conception of international society, reflected in countless legal instruments, has culminated in the legal, if not sanctity of state sovereignty. The UN Charter, most notably Article 2(4) and 2(7), and a number of landmark resolutions support this. Generally, state practice also reflects this [sanctity], including the questionable legality of forceful humanitarian intervention. . . . Cases such as the successive Belgian interventions in the Congo, the US intervention in the Dominican Republic in 1965, the 1976 Israeli raid at Entebbe in Uganda, and the 1980 attempt by the US

to release members of its embassy from Iran, were widely questioned from a legal standpoint and often defended more in terms of an extended form of self-defence. . . . [F]orce can sometimes be used and not necessarily be directed at the territorial integrity or political independence of a state if it is limited to legitimate and temporary humanitarian objectives and not directed against the structure or domestic institutions of the county. It is an issue of territorial inviolability.

Clearly, Article 2(7) of the Charter does not preclude action authorized by the Security Council without the consent of the target state if a threat to the maintenance of peace and security in the context of Chapter VII exists. . . .

However, since the end of the Cold War there arguable has been progress in state practice through the United Nations, and in attitudes, towards an adjustment of the balance between human needs and state sovereignty. . . . In this respect a most important legal trend would be a wider acceptance of the idea that humanitarian suffering on a large scale represents a threat to international peace and security and that there is an obligation to respond to this new dimension of collective security. . . . Finally, one might expect a greater recognition from the legal perspective that the concepts of sovereignty and consent, in the context of failed statehood, are no longer inviolable in absolute terms.

Collective intervention is readily more justifiable than a unilateral intervention by one State. Chapter VII of the Charter gives the SC broad powers to intervene, when there are threats to peace, although the Charter contains potentially conflicting norms. Members are expected to avoid the use of force because it threatens peace, while at the same time not acquiesce in ongoing human rights atrocities. The Charter's expressed expectation is that UN members pledge "to take joint and separate action" in cooperation with the United Nations for the achievement of its humanitarian purposes. They must therefore promote "universal respect for, and observance of, human rights and fundamental freedoms for all without distinction as to race, sex, language, or religion."[86] As acknowledged in the *Restatement of Foreign Relations Law of the United States:* "Whether a state may intervene with military force in the territory of another state without its consent . . . is

not agreed or authoritatively determined. Such intervention might be acceptable [however] if taken pursuant to [a] resolution of a United Nations body or of a regional organization such as the Organization of the American States."[87]

The UN Charter further authorizes regional arrangements in Chapter VIII. It does not specify the interplay between that chapter of the Charter and the SC's Chapter VII enforcement powers. A collective regional action, undertaken in the name of humanitarian intervention, would not be necessarily authorized by SC inaction or silence. Under Article 53, regional *enforcement* actions require authorization from the SC.[88] On the other hand, there is room for the argument that customary State practice may augment or clarify the meaning of the term "humanitarian intervention," given the inherently imprecise nature of that term. As articulated by the ICJ in its 1986 *Nicaragua* case:

"There can be no doubt that the provision of *strictly* humanitarian aid to persons or forces in another country, whatever their political affiliation or objectives, cannot be regarded as unlawful intervention, or as in any other way contrary to international law."[89] This "right" might support one State's providing humanitarian supplies in specified emergencies. It would not include the right of armed penetration, or intervening in a way which violates the intervener's duty of neutrality in a civil war.

Post-Cold War international humanitarian interventions "rescued" Bosnia and Kosovo.[90] Claims of ethnic cleansing by Serbian military forces, mass rapes of Muslim women as a military tactic to achieve "ethnic cleansing," and other atrocities gave rise to the first ICC since Nuremberg. NATO air strikes on Serb positions provided some small relief for the suffering of the civilian populace.

In a January 1993 speech, the Pope claimed that the international community had a "duty to disarm the aggressor" if other means failed. This sentiment was premised, in part, on the appeal of non-Serbian leaders for any form of intervention which would balance the playing field in the Bosnian war. The Serbs stood accused of genocidal acts and defying UN mandates in violation of human rights.

The resulting 1999 NATO bombing in Yugoslavia was a classic illustration of a collective use of force, applied in the name of humanitarian intervention, being subjected to intense scrutiny. After the bombing began, the Federal Republic of Yugoslavia (FRY) filed a lawsuit in the ICJ. The FRY sought "interim measures" from the Court, requesting an interim order that the United States and its NATO allies cease their bombing campaign until the merits could be litigated at a later date:

The Application of The Federal Republic of Yugoslavia Against The United States of America For Violation of the Obligation Not to Use Force

(Yugoslavia v. United States of America)
29 April 1999 General List No. 114
<http://www.icj-cij.org/icjwww/idocket/iyus/iyusframe.htm>

Application Instituting Proceedings
The subject-matter of the dispute are acts of the United States of America [and nine other NATO countries] by which it has violated its international obligation banning the use of force against another State, the obligation not to intervene in the internal affairs of another State, the obligation not to violate the sovereignty of another State, the obligation to protect the civilian population and civilian objects in wartime, the obligation to protect the environment, the obligation relating to free navigation on international rivers, the obligation regarding fundamental human rights and freedoms, the obligation not to use prohibited weapons, the obligation not to deliberately inflict conditions of life calculated to cause the physical destruction of a national group.

Request for the Indication of Provisional Measures
. . .

There are many casualties, including a large number of civilian deaths. Even residential areas have been attacked.

Countless dwellings have been destroyed. Enormous damage has been caused to schools, hospitals, radio and television stations, institutions and cultural monuments as well as to places of worship. Many bridges, roads and railway lines have also been destroyed. Industrial facilities have not been spared either. Attacks on oil refineries and chemical plants have had serious environmental effects on some cities, towns and villages in the Federal Republic of Yugoslavia. The bombing of oil refineries and oil storage tanks as well as chemical plants is bound to produce massive pollution of the environment, posing a threat to human life, plants and animals. The use of weapons containing depleted uranium warheads is having far-reaching consequences for human health.

From the onset of the bombing of the Federal Republic of Yugoslavia, over 10 000 attacks were made against the territory of the Federal Republic of Yugoslavia. In air strikes were used: 806 warplanes (of which over 530 combat planes) and 206 helicopters stationed in 30 air-bases (situated in 5 states) and aboard 6 warships in the Adriatic Sea. More than 2,500 cruise missiles were launched and over 7,000 tons of explosives were dropped.

About 1000 civilians, including 19 children, were killed and more than 4,500 sustained serious injuries . . . .

After these military attacks hundreds of thousands of citizens have been exposed to poisonous gases which can have lasting consequences for the health of the entire population and the environment.

. . .

The aviation of the United States of America also targeted many hospitals and health-care institutions, which have been partially damaged or totally destroyed . . . .

Over 2000 schools, faculties and facilities for students and children were damaged or destroyed (over 25 faculties, 10 colleges, 45 secondary and 90 elementary schools, 8 student dormitories, as well as a number of kindergartens). . . .

PUBLIC AND HOUSING FACILITIES (TENS OF THOUSANDS) [plus infrastructure, telecommunications, and cultural-historical monuments and museums]: . . . .

Photo-evidence is supplemented as annex to the Request.

. . .

Possible Consequences in Case Requested Measures are not Adopted

If the proposed measure were not to be adopted, there will be new losses of human life, further physical and mental harm inflicted on the population of the FR of Yugoslavia, further destruction of civilian targets, heavy environmental pollution and further physical destruction of the people of Yugoslavia.

Requested Measures

The Government of the Federal Republic of Yugoslavia request the Court to order the next measure:

The United States of America shall cease immediately its acts of use of force and shall refrain from any act of threat or use of force against the Federal Republic of Yugoslavia.

Belgrade, 28 April 1999
Rodoljub Etinski, Agent for the
Federal Republic of Yugoslavia

◆ *Notes & Questions*

1. In the §3.3 *Bosnia v. FRY* Genocide Convention case, the ICJ determined that it had jurisdiction over the defendant FRY—notwithstanding that entity's unique (non)status at the United Nations from 1992–2000. It was during this unusual period of the former Yugoslavia's "existence" that the FRY brought this suit (1999). The FRY sought an emergency order from the Court, hoping to bar NATO members from continuing with their 1999 bombing campaign in the FRY and Kosovo. The Court denied the requested relief and dismissed this case. The Court found that it clearly lacked jurisdiction. Both the United States and Yugoslavia were parties to the Genocide Convention. However, the US reservation to the Genocide treaty required US consent to be sued in the ICJ (which the United States refused). Thus, the Court found that the "FRY" existed in the earlier case, when it was a defendant nation, but not in this case, when it was a plaintiff nation. Both cases involved claims arising under the Genocide Convention. What was the reason for this difference in the treatment of the FRY at the ICJ? (§9.4)

2. The ICJ denied Yugoslavia's requested measures. The majority of the court had little to say about humanitarian intervention. Vice President Weeremantry filed a standard dissenting opinion in a number of these cases. He therein expressed what to expect, when such cases are heard on the merits:

Human rights violations on [the scale reported in Kosovo] are such as to throw upon the world community a grave responsibility to intervene for their prevention and it is well-established legal doctrine that such gross denials of legal rights anywhere are everyone's concern everywhere. The concept of sovereignty is no protection against action by the world community to prevent such violations if they be of the scale and nature alleged.

. . .

On the other hand, however well intentioned the air strikes that have been launched by NATO powers . . . there are assertions by the Applicant [Yugoslavia] that *this* use of force lacks United Nations sanction and authority and overlooks express Charter provisions [italics added].

The global concern about the morality and legality of NATO's first war is encapsulated in the following analysis:

NATO, the UN, and the Use of Force: Legal Aspects—Kosovo, The Thin Red Line

Professor Bruno Simma,
University of Munich

9 EUROPEAN JOURNAL OF INTERNATIONAL LAW (1999)

Go to course Web page at
<http://home.att.net/~slomansonb/txtcsesite.html>.
Under Chapter Ten, click Thin Red Line.

Various groups have assessed the legal validity of NATO's Kosovo's bombing campaign. In December 1999, the UN International Criminal Tribunal's chief war crimes prosecutor commenced an investigation into the conduct of NATO pilots. In June 2000, the prosecutor resolved that there was no basis for a formal investigation about whether NATO committed war crimes during its Yugoslavia bombing campaign. Carla del Ponte (Switzerland) thus advised the SC that there was no evidence that NATO deliberately bombed civilians, nor did it conduct any unlawful bombing.

In May 2000, England's House of Commons Foreign Affairs Select Committee prepared a report which found that the bombing campaign to be of "dubious legality." It rejected humanitarian intervention grounds for the bombing campaign as being without legal foundation. London-based Amnesty International went a step further, characterizing NATO as having conducted various attacks in which numbers of civilians were certain to be killed. One example was the bombing of Radio Television Serbia, where civilian technicians were killed in a predawn attack. NATO characterized the response to this particular incident as part of the "propaganda machine" of the Yugoslav President Slobodan Milosevic.[91]

One can readily observe the problems associated with a *regional* organization's use of force under the banner of "humanitarian intervention." Without the imprimatur of a UN Security Council prior/subsequent resolution, bombing another nation's territory—to save its populace from its government—is the category of humanitarian intervention which has drawn the most criticism from the international community of nations.

PRIVATE INTERVENTION

Given the difficulties of establishing criteria for legitimate humanitarian intervention, certain *nongovernmental* actors have sought the right to privately intervene into appropriate conflicts. At France's insistence, the General Assembly supported this development in its three resolutions, between 1988 and 1991, on "Humanitarian assistance to victims of natural disasters and similar emergency situations."[92] France sought to establish the right of private French groups to cross international borders, unhindered by sovereign limitations which otherwise prevented them from treating the victims of armed hostilities and other disasters.

These General Assembly resolutions paved the way for the 1991 SC Resolution 688. It demanded that Iraq provide immediate access to those in need of humanitarian assistance—especially its Kurdish population, which had been the subject of government poison gas attacks several years before. Resolution 688 did not, however, authorize *armed* intervention. Council members were then reluctant to set any precedent, regardless of Iraq's extremely provocative conduct, reminiscent of the Nazi Holocaust. International humanitarian organizations, such as the International Red Cross, were thus endowed with a new justification for their ongoing humanitarian relief missions—often blocked by the competing notion of national sovereignty.

It is arguable that States have a duty under International Law to either provide humanitarian assistance to their *own* populations, or, to accept external humanitarian assistance. In appropriate circumstances, other States could provide such help, presumably without the consent of the State whose populace is in need of such "intervention." Because the oft-stated basis for humanitarian intervention is to limit or eliminate human suffering, then accessibility to any afflicted group by nongovernmental organizations would be a reasonable compromise. It would balance sovereign concerns with the evolving human rights regime discussed in the next chapter of this book. As stated by University of Zurich Professor Dietrich Schindler:

> Access by private humanitarian organisations to victims without the consent of the government of the State concerned must be considered lawful in the following two cases. First, in a non-international armed conflict [civil war], an impartial humanitarian body, such as the International Committee of the Red Cross, may bring humane assistance to victims of the insurgent party without the consent of the legal government.... Second, if a State refuses a humanitarian organization [to have such] access to its territory in contradiction to its duties, such organizations can assert the same rights as a State. They may bring assistance to the victims in spite of the refusal of the government. [93]

RESCUE

Certain States employ clandestine forms of coercion in their international relations. One of these is the taking of hostages as a means of placing political pressure on another nation. The aggressor nation takes hostages, or financially supports a group of individuals, to force another nation to act pursuant to the captors demands.

Hostage taking occurred with alarming frequency in the 1970s, when it became a useful tool for accomplishing national political objectives. The United Nations responded to this phenomenon with the 1979 International Convention against the Taking of Hostages. The primary impetus for this convention was Iran's 1979 seizure of American diplomats and military personnel at the US embassy in Tehran. Article 1 of the Hostage Convention provides that any person who detains and threatens to kill another person in order to compel a State "to do or abstain from doing any act as an explicit or implicit condition for the release of the hostage commits the offense of taking hostages." Under International Law, a person acting on behalf of a State may not take a hostage to coerce another State to act in a certain way. When this occurs, the responsible State breaches this prohibition.

Some States have disregarded this principle, giving rise to a related issue in International Law. Danger invites rescue. When one nation's citizens are held hostage in another country, there is intense national pressure to free

them. It is difficult to yield to that pressure because giving in to the captors' demands encourages further hostage taking. This dilemma has triggered the occasional, but widely publicized, use of an innovative form of countermeasure. Rescue missions have been carried out in other States to save hostages facing certain death.

Military rescue missions present both practical and legal problems. The nation launching the rescue mission clearly breaches the territorial sovereignty of the nation where the hostages are held. The rescuing nation claims, however, that necessity dictates this response. One reason for the necessity is that International Law cannot enforce the Hostage Convention's principles when a nation either takes or effectively condones hostage taking. Where no action appears to be on the horizon, other than the usual diplomatic efforts to free the hostages, they have often been harmed or killed. It is therefore argued that the rescuing nation's right of self-defense supports the existence of a limited right to breach the sovereignty of the captor nation for this humanitarian purpose. States and international organizations have undertaken occasional rescue missions to extract their citizens or agents who are likely to die at the hands of some terrorist or government. While not a completely altruistic form of humanitarian intervention, there are similar concerns regarding the violations of sovereignty that may accompany such forms of self-help.

There is a viable legal basis for an *organization's* activities that extract its agents involved in SC enforcement actions. In 1992, a UN antimine team rescued a convoy that had braved two days of crossfire to deliver food to the besieged Bosnian town of Gorazde. While returning to the Bosnian capital of Sarajevo, this convoy was trapped by land mines. Neither warring faction would come to the aid of these UN workers to ensure their safe return. In this instance, no nation would obstreperously object to organizational action to retrieve such international civil servants from their dilemma.

The dominant problem with hostage rescue is the unilateral use of force by a single nation. The United States has been involved in a number of such rescue attempts. In 1980, a failed US military operation in Iran attempted the retrieval of US diplomats held captive for more than one year (§7.4). In 1992, a US Navy SEAL team conducted a secret rescue mission in Haiti. It extracted a handful of former Haitian officials aligned with the then-ousted but democratically elected President Aristide. The lives of these officials were in danger, according to Pentagon officials. US Congressman Charles Rangel condemned this rescue, promising that Congress would conduct an inquiry into this matter. US President Bush did not comment on the raid, although a White House spokesman denied presidential knowledge of the rescue (a highly suspect representation).

The classic hostage rescue mission occurred in 1976. A French passenger plane, containing mostly Israeli citizens, was hijacked in Athens by a Middle East terrorist organization and flown to Entebbe, Uganda. Some newspaper accounts of this event reported that a Middle Eastern nation clandestinely promoted this hijacking. The hijackers threatened to systematically kill the hostages unless other Middle Eastern citizens were freed from Israeli prisons. Uganda's President, Idi Amin, refused to help the hostages. He apparently wished to avoid diluting his political capital with any Arab nation, which may have sponsored the hijacking. A group of Israeli commandos then flew into Uganda in a clandestine hostage rescue mission. They killed a number of Ugandan soldiers at the airport where the hostages were being held. The SC's ensuing debate follows:

Excerpts from United Nations Security Council Debate on the Entebbe Incident

13 UN MONTHLY CHRONICLE
(August–September 1976)

Go to course Web page at
<http://home.att.net/~slomansonb/txtcsesite.html>.
Under Chapter Ten, click Raid on Entebbe.

◆ 10.6 LAWS OF WAR—TRADITIONAL APPLICATIONS

INTRODUCTION

The "Laws of War," also referred to as International Humanitarian Law, consists of customary State practices and treaties. They govern the way in which belligerents conduct war. National laws prohibit war-related crimes, such as espionage or treason. It is International Law, however, which protects the innocent and defenseless

against the excesses of State actors who believe that the end justifies the means. Democratic States tend to include certain of these expectations in their military field manuals.

Expediency during hostilities must sometimes yield to legal and moral concerns about humane treatment. The areas of concern include the following: summary executions of civilians and military personnel; ethnic cleansing and forcible displacement; mistreatment of detained prisoners of war (POW); indiscriminate use of force against nonmilitary targets; attacks on medical and related relief personnel; looting and other destruction of civilian property with no military purpose; terrorizing and starving a civilian population; use of military or civilian human shields against a pending attack; and the use of particular types of warfare condemned under the international agreements mentioned in this section of the book.

HISTORICAL SETTING

History is fraught with accounts of "man's inhumanity to man" in time of war. The Bible's Old Testament contains admonitions prohibiting the following: the slaughter of captured men; the transplanting of innocent women and children; the plunder of animals and other property; and the pillaging and wanton destruction of cities. In the Battle of Teutoburg Forest of AD 9, a Germanic tribal chieftain defeated several Roman legions. He declared at the point of victory that "those prisoners who were not hewn to pieces on the spot were only preserved to perish by a more cruel death in cold blood." During the medieval Crusades, combatant forces routinely slaughtered enemy prisoners. Women were raped, and the inhabitant's goods were forfeited. These prizes of war were available as an incentive for soldiers facing periods of protracted siege.[94]

This is not to say that all societies of the era believed in such cruelty. The religious overtones of the evolving Muslim world were by no means oblivious to the importance of limitations on how war was to be conducted. The Qur'an, for example, provided as follows: "War is permissible in self-defence, and under well defined limits. . . . In any case, . . . women, children, old and infirm men should not be molested, nor trees and crops cut down, nor peace withheld when the enemy comes to terms."[95]

Sporadic efforts have limited the cruelty of warfare. A few military leaders and heads of State required their soldiers to observe certain minimum standards of humane conduct in warfare. In 559 BC and 333 BC, respectively, the King of Persia and Alexander the Great ordered their troops to spare the civilian population of conquered areas. They were also admonished not to intentionally desecrate religious sites. In 70 BC, the Roman commander Titus arranged for the safe departure of women and children from Jerusalem when it was under his siege. In AD 410, the Visigoth leader Alaric known for his cruelty to foreign soldiers forbade his soldiers to violate the women of Rome when he captured the city. In the Middle Ages, certain Christian and Muslim leaders humanized the conduct of war, partially because of a more long-range strategy to avoid an overly desperate enemy otherwise facing some cruel form of extinction.

The notion of the "Just War," of which Aristotle wrote,[96] was sewn into the fabric of the new international legal system established by the seventeenth-century Peace of Westphalia. The European perspective was that if the war was "just," then the enemy was by definition "unjust." Adversaries therefore were not entitled to humane treatment other than that within the discretion of the on-scene military commander.

By the mid-nineteenth century, the various modes for conducting, declaring, and waging war were no more than pretenses for justifying aggressive tendencies. States and private organizations, such as the Red Cross, understood that increasingly sophisticated weapon systems were capable of inflicting alarming consequences. Military theorists, theologians, and moralists believed that certain State practices were too inhumane to be condoned by a civilized society. The desire for controlling such excesses began to materialize in national and treaty-based Laws of War. Although there were several predecessors, the 1864 GC for the Amelioration of the Condition of the Wounded in Armies in the Field was the first such treaty to be drafted and widely ratified. The Laws of War would soon find their way into the national laws of many countries, as well as appear in major international treaties. As stated in a post-Civil War US Supreme Court decision, regarding the treatment of enemy aliens during an internal civil war:

When a rebellion becomes organized, and attains such proportions as to be able to put a formidable military force in the field, it is usual for the established government to concede to it some belligerent rights. This concession is made in the interests of humanity, to prevent the cruelties which would inevitably follow mutual reprisals and retaliations.

. . .

The concession made to the Confederate government in its military character was shown in the treatment of captives as prisoners of war, the exchange of prisoners, the recognition of flags of truce, the release of officers on parole, and other arrangements having a tendency to mitigate the evils of the contest. The concession placed its soldiers and military officers in its service on the footing of those engaged in lawful war, and exempted them from liability for acts of legitimate warfare.[97]

The year 1847 was an important turning point. Swiss General Dufour ordered his officers to protect wounded enemy soldiers who were prisoners of war. He was one of the original members of the "Committee of Five," which became the International Committee of the Red Cross in 1876. The International Red Cross worked with the Swiss government on a project that would one day yield four treaties that are often referred to as the 1949 "Geneva Convention." Thus, it was actually a nongovernmental actor that ignited the international movement for regulating the treatment of civilians and prisoners in times of war.

No multilateral agreement has fully embraced the varied perspectives about the content of the Laws of War. In 1899, Russian Minister and Professor of International Law at Petersburg University Fredrick de Martens drafted the well-known "de Martens" clause. He therein provided that "Until a more comprehensive code of rules of war is prepared, . . . the people and belligerent parties are under the protection of principles of the law of nations stemming from the customs adopted by the civilized peoples, from the rights of humanity and public conscience." Although designed for a turn-of-the-century Hague Convention covering military combatants, it was later incorporated into the 1949 GCs (common article 3). This was designed to be a description of Customary International Law, which would serve as the default provision in the absence of applicable treaty protection.

The Laws of War are not applicable to only adult military combatants. In a 1998 UN report issued by the UN Secretary-General's special representative for children and armed conflict, Olara Otunnu reported that the twentieth-century impact of war on civilians had grown exponentially. In the First World War, civilians constituted 5 percent of all casualties. In the Second World War, this figure rose to 48 percent. By the last decade of the century, 90 percent of such casualties were civilians. He also provided the estimate that 300,000 military combatants are under age of eighteen, many children being used for mine clearance, spying, and suicide bombings. Thus, the need for international control continues to be needed by all sectors of society.

ESSENCE OF LAWS OF WAR

The Laws of War govern how nations may legally wage war. Exhibit 10.3 provides a summary of the major treaties containing the Laws of War.

EXHIBIT 10.3 SELECTED TREATIES ILLUSTRATING THE LAWS OF WAR

Date	Treaty	Scope
1907	Hague Second Conference on Laws and Customs of War (12 treaties, some updating 1899 Hague Conference draft)	Prohibits acts including uncontrolled unanchored contact mines, naval bombardment of undefended towns and capturing hospital ships/Requires humane treatment of POWs who cannot be summarily killed or wounded
1925	Geneva Convention	Prohibits use of asphyxiating, poisonous, and bacteriological warfare
1945	London Charter (the Nuremberg Tribunal)	Prohibits conduct including: murder, ill treatment, deportation to slave labor, plunder of public or private property, destruction of cities in absence of military necessity
1946	UN General Assembly Resolution 95(1)	Prohibits the Crime of Genocide: includes annihilation of particular ethnic or national group
1949	Geneva Convention "I" on the wounded and sick in the field	Updated original 1864 Convention to adapt to modern warfare/Requires respect and care for defenseless combatants
1949	Geneva Convention "II" on the wounded, sick, and shipwrecked at sea	Updated 1868 principles and 1907 Hague Convention laws in conduct of maritime warfare
1949	Geneva Convention "III" on prisoners of war	Most extensive of four 1949 Conventions. Updates 1929 Geneva Convention. Regulates conditions of captivity to safeguard human dignity
1949	Geneva Convention "IV" (Civilian protection in time of war)	Second most extensive Geneva Convention/Prohibits torture, mutilation, violence, outrages on personal dignity/Designed to protect innocent civilians not involved in hostilities from being terrorized by enemy military forces
1972	Bacteriological Warfare Convention	Prohibits the production and stockpiling of bacteriological and toxic weapons/Seeks destruction or diversion to peaceful purposes/National sovereignty withdrawal clause has limited effectiveness
1976	Environmental Modification Convention	Prohibits military or other hostile use of environmental modifications in, over, and above the Earth
1977	Geneva Protocols to 1949 Conventions	Refinements: most significant one protects POWs in conflict described as noninternational or undeclared
1981	Inhumane Weapons Convention	Prohibits and restricts certain conventional weapons deemed too injurious; e.g., land mines, booby traps, incendiary devices, weapons escaping even X-ray detection in human body
1992	Chemical Weapons Convention	Priority is post-Cold War destruction of chemical and bacteriological weapons stock
1997	Land Mine Treaty	Prohibits the use, stockpiling, production, and transfer of antipersonnel mines and requires their destruction

A number of countries have enacted related legislation. The US Congress passed the War Crimes Act of 1996, for example. It amends US law by expressly incorporating the 1949 GCs into US law. It also provides criminal penalties for certain war crimes. US courts may now fine and imprison anyone who, inside or outside the United States, violates the GCs under specified circumstances. This broadens US jurisdiction over war crimes, although the legislation is limited to members of the US armed forces and US citizens:

WAR CRIMES

CRIMES AND CRIMINAL PROCEDURE
United States Code 18 USC §2441
(as amended in 2002)

(a) Whoever, whether inside or outside the United States, commits a war crime, in any of the circumstances described in subsection (b), shall be fined under this title or imprisoned for life or any term of years, or both, and if death results to the victim, shall also be subject to the penalty of death.

(b) The circumstances referred to in subsection (a) are that the person committing such war crime or the victim of such war crime is a member of the Armed Forces of the United States or a national of the United States (as defined in section 101 of the Immigration and Nationality Act).

(c) Definition—As used in this section the term "war crime" means any conduct—

(1) defined as a grave breach in any of the international conventions signed at Geneva 12 August 1949, or any protocol to such convention to which the United States is a party;

(2) prohibited by Article 23, 25, 27, or 28[a] of the Annex to the Hague Convention IV, Respecting the Laws and Customs of War on Land, signed 18 October 1907;

(3) which constitutes a violation of common Article 3 of the international conventions signed at Geneva, 12 August 1949, or any protocol to such convention to which the United States is a party and which deals with non-international armed conflict; or

(4) of a person who, in relation to an armed conflict and contrary to the provisions of the Protocol on Prohibitions or Restrictions on the Use of Mines, Booby-Traps and Other Devices as amended at Geneva on 3 May 1996 (Protocol II as amended on 3 May 1996), when the United States is a party to such Protocol, willfully kills or causes serious injury to civilians.

---

[a]*Author's footnote: see <http://www.yale.edu/lawweb/avalon/lawofwar/hague04.htm>.*

Had the above US legislation been in force before 1996, the most notorious breach would have taken place in the Vietnam village of My Lai in 1968. This military court-martial provides a realistic "in the field" perspective about the soldier who must choose between punishment for disobeying the order of a superior—and, alternatively, like punishment for violating the Laws of War. The dissent raises the troubling question of whether the same yardstick should measure the wartime conduct of all soldiers:

United States v. Calley

US COURT OF
MILITARY APPEALS
22 USCMA 534, 48 CMR 19 (1973)
Go to course Web page at:
<http://home.att.net/~slomansonb/txtcsesite.html>.
Under Chapter Ten, click <u>Calley Court-Martial.</u>

There have been few reported incidents of violations of the naval Laws of War. This does not mean that they have not occurred, or are less heinous in potential effect. During the Nazi war crimes trials at Nuremberg, two U-boat captains were accused of ordering totally unrestricted submarine warfare. One was found guilty of sinking all vessels within a neutral shipping zone. The other was charged (although there was insufficient evidence for conviction) with the crime of killing survivors of sunken ships. Naval captors may not deny quarters to or kill a defenseless enemy. He was not found guilty of this particular charge, partially because the tribunal found that this was also the US practice in the Pacific.[98]

The 1980–1988 Iran-Iraq war provided a fresh opportunity to reexamine the relevant principles, which States consider under the modern naval Laws of War. First, belligerents have a right to visit and search neutral-flagged merchant vessels. While this was done routinely during the Vietnamese conflict, it was basically just one State (the United States) that exercised this "right." Visit and search occurred with much greater frequency during the 1991 PGW, thus giving rise to the rather clear expectation that States at war may undertake this form of intrusion. It is a necessary incident to maintain security from various forms of infiltration by belligerents and violations of neutrality by third parties (§2.3).

Minelaying is permitted, but not without limitations. The 1907 Hague Convention Relative to the Laying of Automatic Submarine Contact Mines precludes indiscriminate minelaying without proper monitoring by the responsible State. States may not lay mines in the high seas, if doing so endangers the shipping of nonbelligerent States. UN Security Council Resolution 540 of 1983 provides that States may not thereby threaten "the right of free navigation and commerce in international waters." Notification is an essential requirement. The ICJ commented on this expectation in both its 1949 *Corfu Channel* case and its 1986 *Nicaragua* decision. In the earlier case, Albania was at fault for not removing surface mines hit by British ships passing through an international strait adjacent to its coast. In the later case, the United States was responsible for assisting indigenous forces to lay mines in key harbors to interrupt Nicaraguan shipping.[99]

This norm was tested during the PGW, when Iran threatened to close the Straits of Hormuz—the only entry to the oil-exporting Persian Gulf. University of Pisa (Italy) Professors Andrea de Guttry and Natalino Ronzitti comment on the scope of this right of passage as follows:

[N]eutral warships are granted the right of passage through international straits even if the littoral [coastal] State is at war. If such right is accorded to warships, so much the more will it be binding for merchant vessels flying a neutral flag. Not all scholars agree on this, but it seems to us that practice in the Gulf is perfectly in tune with what appears to be the dominant trend, a trend which probably now corresponds to precise customary rules.

Faced with Iran's repeated threat to close the Strait, the USA, the United Kingdom, France and Italy . . . firmly emphasized that the right of passage through international straits can never be suspended, even when the littoral State is one of the belligerents.[100]

The comparatively recent appearance of the airplane in military warfare may account for the fact that there were no such charges made at either the Nuremberg or Tokyo trials. The only reference therein was a statement addressing the bombing of a city that kills innocent civilians (without mention of the 1945 US atomic bombings of Hiroshima and Nagasaki). In the words of the Nuremberg Tribunal: "This is . . . an unavoidable corollary of battle action. The civilians are not individualized. The bomb falls, it is aimed at railroad yards, houses along the tracks are hit and many of their occupants killed. But that is entirely different, both in facts and in law, from an armed force marching up to these same railroad tracks, entering those houses abutting thereon, dragging out the men, women, and children and shooting them."[101]

Air warfare tactics are regulated by the 1977 Geneva Protocol and the 1980 Convention on Prohibition or Restrictions on the Use of Certain Conventional Weapons. Article 42 of the Geneva Protocol prohibits ground or air attacks on persons parachuting from aircraft in distress. Such individuals must also be given an opportunity to surrender before engaging them as enemy soldiers. Airborne troops are excepted from this protection. One reason for the protocol was the North Vietnamese position that the 1949 GCs did not apply to undeclared conflicts such as the Vietnam War.

Persian Gulf War I Application The 1992 Report by the US Department of Defense classically presents the dilemmas faced by nations and their field commanders in war zones:

Conduct of The Persian Gulf War: Final Report to Congress

PURSUANT TO TITLE V OF THE PERSIAN GULF CONFLICT
SUPPLEMENTAL AUTHORIZATION AND PERSONNEL BENEFITS ACT OF 1991
(April 1992)

The Conduct of the Persian Gulf War

Saddam Hussein's invasion of Kuwait on August 2, 1990, unleashed an extraordinary series of events that culminated seven months later in the victory of American and Coalition forces over the Iraqi army and the liberation of Kuwait. Pursuant to Title V, Public Law 102-25, this report discusses the conduct of hostilities in the Persian Gulf theater of operations. It builds on the Department's Interim Report of July 1991. A proper understanding of the conduct of these military operations the extraordinary achievements and the needed improvements is an important and continuing task of the Department of Defense as we look to the future.

The Persian Gulf War was the first major conflict following the end of the Cold War. The victory was a triumph of Coalition strategy, of international cooperation, of technology, and of people. It reflected leadership, patience, and courage at the highest levels and in the field. Under adverse and hazardous conditions far from home, our airmen, soldiers, sailors, and marines once again played the leading role in reversing a dangerous threat to a critical region of the world and to our national interests. Their skill and sacrifice lie at the heart of this important triumph over aggression in the early post-Cold War era.

. . .

Role of Legal Advisers

The Office of General Counsel of the Department of Defense (DOD) . . . provided advice to the Secretary of Defense, the Deputy Secretary of Defense, the Under Secretary of Defense for Policy, other senior advisers to the Secretary and to the various components of the Defense legal community on all matters relating to Operations Desert Shield and Desert Storm, including the law of war. For example, the Secretary of Defense tasked the General Counsel to review and opine on such diverse issues as . . . DOD targeting policies; the rules of engagement; the rules pertinent to maritime interception operations; issues relating to the treatment

of prisoners of war; sensitive intelligence and special access matters; and similar matters of the highest priority to the Secretary and DOD. In addition, military judge advocates and civilian attorneys with international law expertise provided advice on the law of war and other legal issues at every level of command in all phases of Operations Desert Shield and Desert Storm. Particular attention was given to the review of target lists to ensure the consistency of targets selected for attack with United States law of war obligations.

. . .

Targeting, Collateral Damage and Civilian Casualties

The law of war with respect to targeting, collateral damage and collateral civilian casualties is derived from the principle of discrimination; that is, the necessity for distinguishing between combatants, who may be attacked, and noncombatants, against whom an intentional attack may not be directed, and between legitimate military targets and civilian objects. Although this is a major part of the foundation on which the law of war is built, it is one of the least codified portions of that law.

As a general principle, the law of war prohibits the intentional destruction of civilian objects not imperatively required by military necessity and the direct, intentional attack of civilians not taking part in hostilities. The United States takes these proscriptions into account in developing and acquiring weapons systems, and in using them in combat. Central Command (CENTCOM) forces adhered to these fundamental law of war proscriptions in conducting military operations during Operation Desert Storm through discriminating target selection and careful matching of available forces and weapons systems to selected targets and Iraqi defenses, without regard to Iraqi violations of its law of war obligations toward the civilian population and civilian objects.

Several treaty provisions specifically address the responsibility to minimize collateral damage to civilian objects and injury to civilians. Article 23(g) of the Annex to Hague IV prohibits destruction not "imperatively demanded by the necessities of war," while Article 27 of that same annex offers protection from intentional attack to "buildings dedicated to religion, art, science, or charitable purposes, historic monuments, hospitals, and places where the sick and wounded are collected, provided they are not being used at the time for military purposes." Similar language is contained in Article 5 of Hague IX, while the conditions for protection of cultural property in the 1954 Hague Cultural Property Convention were set forth in the preceding discussion on the treatment of civilians in occupied territory. In summary, cultural and civilian objects are protected from direct, intentional attack unless they are used for military purposes, such as shielding military objects from attack.

While the prohibition contained in Article 23(g) generally refers to intentional destruction or injury, it also precludes collateral damage of civilian objects or injury to noncombatant civilians that is clearly disproportionate to the military advantage gained in the attack of military objectives, as discussed below. As previously indicated, Hague IV was found to be part of customary international law in the course of war crimes trials following World War II, and continues to be so regarded.

An uncodified but similar provision is the principle of proportionality. It prohibits military action in which the negative effects (such as collateral civilian casualties) clearly outweigh the military gain. This balancing may be done on a target-by-target basis, as frequently was the case during Operation Desert Storm, but also may be weighed in overall terms against campaign objectives. CENTCOM conducted its campaign with a focus on minimizing collateral civilian casualties and damage to civilian objects. Some targets were specifically avoided because the value of destruction of each target was outweighed by the potential risk to nearby civilians or, as in the case of certain archaeological and religious sites, to civilian objects.

Coalition forces took several steps to minimize the risk of injury to noncombatants. To the degree possible and consistent with allowable risk to aircraft and aircrews, aircraft and munitions were selected so that attacks on targets within populated areas would provide the greatest possible accuracy and the least risk to civilian objects and the civilian population. Where required, attacking aircraft were accompanied by support mission aircraft to minimize attacking aircraft aircrew distraction from their assigned mission. Aircrews attacking targets in populated areas were directed not to expend their munitions if they lacked positive identification of their targets. When this occurred, aircrews dropped their bombs on alternate targets or returned to base with their weapons.

One reason for the maneuver plan adopted for the ground campaign was that it avoided populated areas, where Coalition and Iraqi civilian casualties and damage to civilian objects necessarily would have been high. This was a factor in deciding against an amphibious assault into Kuwait City.

The principle of proportionality acknowledges the unfortunate inevitability of collateral civilian casualties and collateral damage to civilian objects when noncombatants and civilian objects are mingled with combatants and targets, even with reasonable efforts by the parties to a conflict to minimize collateral injury and damage. This proved to be the case in the air campaign. Despite conducting the most discriminate air campaign in history, including extraordinary measures by Coalition aircrews to minimize collateral civilian casualties, the Coalition could not avoid causing some collateral damage and injury.

There are several reasons for this. One is the fact that in any modern society, many objects intended for civilian use also may be used for military purposes. A bridge or highway vital to daily commuter and business traffic can be equally crucial to military traffic, or support for a nation's war effort. Railroads, airports, seaports, and the interstate highway system in the United States have been funded by the Congress in part because of US national security concerns, for example; each proved invaluable to the movement of US military units to various ports for deployment to Southwest Asia (SWA) for Operations Desert Shield and Desert Storm. Destruction of a bridge, airport, or port facility, or interdiction of a highway can be equally important in impeding an enemy's war effort.

The same is true with regard to major utilities; for example, microwave towers for everyday, peacetime civilian communications can constitute a vital part of a military command and control (C2) system, while electric power grids can be used simultaneously for military and civilian purposes. Some Iraqi military installations had separate electrical generators; others did not. Industries essential to the manufacturing of

CW, BW and conventional weapons depended on the national electric power grid.

Experience in its 1980–1988 war with Iran caused the Government of Iraq to develop a substantial and comprehensive degree of redundancy in its normal, civilian utilities as back-up for its national defense. Much of this redundancy, by necessity, was in urban areas. Attack of these targets necessarily placed the civilian population at risk, unless civilians were evacuated from the surrounding area. Iraqi authorities elected not to move civilians away from objects they knew were legitimate military targets, thereby placing those civilians at risk of injury incidental to Coalition attacks against these targets, notwithstanding efforts by the Coalition to minimize risk to innocent civilians.

When objects are used concurrently for civilian and military purposes, they are liable to attack if there is a military advantage to be gained in their attack. ("Military advantage" is not restricted to tactical gains, but is linked to the full context of a war strategy, in this instance, the execution of the Coalition war plan for liberation of Kuwait.)

. . .

The Coalition targeted specific military objects in populated areas, which the law of war permits; at no time were civilian areas as such attacked. Coalition forces also chose not to attack many military targets in populated areas or in or adjacent to cultural (archaeological) sites, even though attack of those military targets is authorized by the law of war. The attack of legitimate Iraqi military targets, notwithstanding the fact it resulted in collateral injury to civilians and damage to civilian objects, was consistent with minimizing collateral damage and injury is a responsibility shared by attacker and defender.

. . .

The presence of civilians will not render a target immune from attack; legitimate targets may be attacked wherever located (outside neutral territory and waters). An attacker must exercise reasonable precautions to minimize incidental or collateral injury to the civilian population or damage to civilian objects, consistent with mission accomplishment and allowable risk to the attacking forces. The defending party must exercise reasonable precautions to separate the civilian population and civilian objects from military objectives, and avoid placing military objectives in the midst of the civilian population. As previously indicated, a defender is expressly prohibited from using the civilian population or civilian objects (including cultural property) to shield legitimate targets from attack.

An attacker operating in the fog of war may make decisions that will lead to innocent civilians' deaths. The death of civilians always is regrettable, but inevitable when a defender fails to honor his own law of war obligations or callously disregards them, as was the case with Saddam Hussein. . . . Leaders and commanders necessarily have to make decisions on the basis of their assessment of the information reasonably available to them at the time, rather than what is determined in hindsight.

◆ *Notes & Questions*

1. This US Defense Department Report on the first Persian Gulf War notes that "cultural and civilian objects are protected from direct, intentional attack unless they are used for military purposes, such as shielding military objects from attack." You are the field commander in battle. Assume that you learn that your enemy has moved his troops to the center of an area where there are known cultural objects present. Are you thus entitled to destroy them in the next skirmish with enemy troops? Would the same be true of human shields being used for the same purpose? What international legal guidelines would you apply?

2. The Department of Defense Report also states that the Coalition forces "avoided populated areas, where Coalition and Iraqi civilian casualties and damage to civilian objects necessarily would have been high." Is it easier to disregard necessity and proportionality limitations, when you absolutely cannot loose a particular battle? Should there be a correlation between a commander's ability to minimize or ignore these requirements versus the risk of losing that battle? The entire war?

3. The DOD Report further states that "Iraqi authorities elected not to move civilians away from objects they knew were legitimate military targets, thereby placing

those civilians at risk of injury incidental to Coalition attacks against these targets." If you therefore decided to attack under these conditions, would your decision be a case of "two wrongs making a right?"

4. This segment of the above DOD Report concludes with the following comment: "The death of civilians always is regrettable, but inevitable when a defender fails to honor his own law of war obligations or callously disregards them, as was the case with Saddam Hussein." If you therefore achieved your military objective, but at the cost of killing all Iraqi civilians in the area, does the enemy's failure to abide by the Laws of War absolve you from the necessity and proportionality requirements? Would you need more information to answer this question? What information would be helpful?

Persian Gulf War II Application

◆

 Iternational Legal Issues Surrounding The Mistreatment of Iraqi Detainees by American Forces

By Leila Nadya Sadat, Washington University School of Law American Society of International Law Insight
<http://www.asil.org/insights/insigh134.htm>
(May 2004)

Go to course Web page at
<http://home.att.net/~slomansonb/txtcsesite.html>.
Under Chapter Ten, click Abu Ghraib Prison Scandal.

"Reprinted with permission of the author and American Society of International Law."

In December 2002, the UN General Assembly adopted Resolution A/RES/57/199—thereby promulgating a protocol to the torture treaty, now open for signature by willing States entitled: The Optional Protocol to the Convention Against Torture and Other Cruel, Inhuman or Degrading Treatment or Punishment. Under Article 1: "The objective of this Protocol is to establish a system of regular visits undertaken by independent international and national bodies to places where people are deprived of their liberty, in order to prevent torture and other cruel, inhuman or degrading treatment or punishment." Under Article 3: "Each State party shall set up . . . visiting bodies for the prevention of torture and other cruel, inhuman or degrading treatment or punishment (hereinafter referred to as the national preventive mechanism)." Under Article 30: "No reservations shall be made to the present Protocol."

The United States has neither signed nor ratified this Protocol. The United States subsequently admitted that torture had occurred at the US military base in Guantanamo Bay, Cuba. It relied, however, on the "few bad apples" defense and claimed that its investigation tactics did not violate generally accepted international practice.

The United Kingdom ratified this Optional Protocol in November 2003. The British courts have already dealt with deaths in Iraqi prisons under UK control. Iraq's new government has good reason to consider ratification of the Convention Against Torture, and its new optional Protocol, in the aftermath of both the US Abu Ghraib Prison scandal, and the one which surfaced in late 2005 regarding *Iraq's* treatment of its own detainees.

Three provocative incidents echo the long-term consequences of not observing the Laws of War. *First,* Afghanistan President Hamid Karzai condemned the October 2005 body burning of two Taliban fighters, punctuated by a propaganda campaign against insurgents near Kandahar. The GC provides that disposal of war dead "should be honorable if possible, according to the rites of the religion to which the deceased belonged." This event was particularly offensive to Muslims, who do not permit bodies to face west, and bury them within 24 hours. The US military sentenced the responsible US soldiers, for displaying these bodies in a way that taunted Islamic traditions. Afghanistan reacted by preparing for major riots over the next several weeks. *Second,* in November 2004, the US military used white phosphorus (WP) munitions in Fallujah, Iraq. While it was used "very sparingly for illumination purposes," allegations emerged that the United States had used illegal chemical weapons during this military campaign. Italian public television aired a documentary entitled "Fallujah: The Hidden Massacre." It accused US military forces of using WP, as *ammunition* against insurgents and collaborating civilians. The US military ultimately acknowledged this use of WP as a "potent psychological weapon." *Third,* Israel's Supreme Court banned the use of Palestinian human shields in October 2005. They were being used in arrest raids, to minimize military casualties. The Chief Justice decried this military tactic, however, with his admonition: "You cannot exploit the civilian population for the army's military needs, and you cannot force them to collaborate with the army."[102]

Environmental Warfare   Given modern technology, and geometric advances in weapon system capabilities, one must acknowledge environmental warfare as a fourth dimension of this survey—hovering over warfare on land, at sea, and in the air. The common applications involve bacteriological and gaseous substances. Adolf Hitler considered the use of such weapons in World War II. His field marshals convinced him, however, that Germans would likely suffer more than the enemy. Germany did use Soviet prisoners, and its own citizens, to conduct experiments in anticipation of the war potential for possessing and using biological warfare.[103]

The 1976 Environmental Modification Convention prohibits hostile uses of the environment to destroy the enemy. Ensuing protocols exhibited the international concerns regarding acts that affected lives far beyond the immediate military theater. The 1977 protocol precludes any use that would cause "widespread, severe damage to the environment." Reprisals that use the environment are also prohibited.

These conventions proved ineffective when the most disastrous environmental act of war occurred in 1991. During its retreat from Kuwait at the end of the PGW, Iraq's military forces set fire to over 600 oil wells. This wartime tactic sent flames and smoke into the upper atmosphere for a period of nine months until all wells could be capped. This event also generated the call for a new "Fifth" GC dedicated solely to the protection of the environment in time of armed conflict.[104]

LAWS APPLICABLE TO INTERNATIONAL ORGANIZATIONS

No treaties specifically address the responsibility of an international organization to observe the Laws of War. The United Nations is not a party to the GCs governing the Laws of War. Those Conventions form the heart of the norms that address State practice. By analogy, however, national contingents operating in the service of the United Nations, NATO, or other organizations

should be bound by the same requirements, as if they were operating on behalf of their own States.

The International Committee of the Red Cross has requested that the United Nations promote the practice of having its State members provide renewed instructions to their national contingents prior to departure for UN service. In 1961, there were reports that UN emergency forces were violating the Laws of War during the UN operation in the Congo. Now that the UN peacekeeping operations have exercised the option of firing first, in situations carefully prescribed in the Somalian conflict, this concern has taken on a new significance. GC Articles 47, 48, 127, and 144 incorporate the State responsibility of instructing State military forces about the Laws of War. The Red Cross document, which is addressed to the UN member States within the organization, requests "that such contingents receive, before leaving their own countries, appropriate instruction so that they may acquire a sufficient knowledge of these Conventions."[105]

Members of the Canadian components of the UN peacekeeping mission in Somalia and the NATO action in Bosnia would be the modern test cases. In 1997, the Canadian Army's commanding officer said that forty-seven soldiers in Bosnia were accused of misconduct, including physically abusing mental hospital patients in 1993–1994. Ten other Canadians allegedly killed a Somalian during the UN operation there in an incident that was exposed after a cover-up. Because of a shift from the traditional national defense posture to international peacekeeping, Canada took steps to better train its soldiers in fulfilling these new duties.

In 1999, Kofi Annan thus promulgated a Secretary-General's Bulletin requiring UN forces to observe International Humanitarian Laws:

Section 3 Status-of-forces agreement
In the status-of-forces agreement concluded between the United Nations and a State in whose territory a United Nations force is deployed, the United Nations undertakes to ensure that the force shall conduct its operations with full respect for the principles and rules of the general conventions applicable to the conduct of military personnel.

. . .

Section 5 Protection of the civilian population
5.1 The United Nations force shall make a clear

distinction at all times between civilians and combatants and between civilian objects and military objectives. Military operations shall be directed only against combatants and military objectives. Attacks on civilians or civilian objects are prohibited.[106]

◆ 10.7 LAWS OF WAR—POST "9-11" US APPLICATION

September 11, 2001, is a convenient starting point for examining new US applications of the Laws of War. As a result of the fateful events of that day, the United States undertook some responsive measures that are the subject of this section:

September 11, 2001

Go to course Web page at <http://home.att.net/~slomansonb/txtcsesite.html>. Under Chapter Ten, click September 11, 2001.

Geneva Convention Provisions The following 1960 *Commentary* is the official summary of the critical GC provisions. The quotation marks within this *Commentary* identify the actual language of the listed articles:

The Geneva Conventions of 12 August 1949 Commentary: III Geneva Convention Relative to the Treatment of Prisoners of War

J. Pictet (ed.), INTERNATIONAL COMMITTEE OF THE RED CROSS, (GENEVA: ICRC, 1960).

Article 3

There must be no "outrages upon personal dignity, in particular, humiliating and degrading treatment. It also prohibits the passing of sentences and the carrying out of executions without previous judgment pronounced by a regularly constituted court affording all the judicial guarantees which are recognized as indispensable by civilized peoples."

Article 4

Detainees who are POWs are protected from being punished for refusing to cooperate with interrogators beyond providing name, rank, and serial number. They must also be repatriated upon the conclusion of the hostilities. Protected persons are "those who at a given moment and in any manner whatsoever find themselves, in case of a conflict of occupation, in the hands of a Party to the conflict or Occupying Power of which they are not nationals."

Article 5

"Should any doubt arise as to whether persons, having committed a belligerent act and having fallen into the hands of the enemy, belong to any of the categories enumerated in Article 4, such persons shall enjoy the protection of the present Convention until such time as their status has been determined by a competent tribunal." [The GC does not define the term *competent tribunal*.]

. . .

Article 17

"No physical or mental torture, nor any other form of coercion, may be inflicted on prisoners of war to secure from them information of any kind whatever. Prisoners of war who refuse to answer may not be threatened, insulted, or exposed to unpleasant or disadvantageous treatment of any kind."

. . .

Article 100

"Prisoners of war and the Protecting Powers shall be informed as soon as possible of the offences which are punishable by the death sentence under the laws of the Detaining Power."

. . .

Article 102

"A prisoner of war can be validly sentenced only if the sentence has been pronounced by the same courts according to the same procedure as in the case of members of the armed forces of the Detaining Power, and if, furthermore, the provisions of the present Chapter have been observed."

. . .

Article 104

"In any case in which the Detaining Power has decided to institute judicial proceedings against a prisoner of war, it shall notify the Protecting Power as soon as possible and at least three weeks before the opening of the trial."

Article 105

The prisoner of war shall be entitled to assistance by one of his prisoner comrades, to defence by a qualified advocate or counsel of his own choice, to the calling of witnesses and, if he deems necessary, to the services of a competent interpreter. He shall be advised of these rights by the Detaining Power in due time before the trial.

Failing a choice by the prisoner of war, the Protecting Power shall find him an advocate or counsel, and shall have at least one week at its disposal for the purpose. The Detaining Power shall deliver to the said Power, on request, a list of persons qualified to present the defence. Failing a choice of an advocate or counsel by the prisoner of war or the Protecting Power, the Detaining Power shall appoint a competent advocate or counsel to conduct the defence.

. . .

The representatives of the Protecting Power shall be entitled to attend the trial of the case, unless, exceptionally, this is held in camera in the interest of State security. In such a case the Detaining Power shall advise the Protecting Power accordingly.

Article 106

"Every prisoner of war shall have, in the same manner as the members of the armed forces of the Detaining Power, the right of appeal or petition from any sentence pronounced upon him, with a view to the quashing or revising of the sentence or the reopening of the trial. He shall be fully informed of his right to appeal or petition and of the time limit within which he may do so."

. . .

Article 108

"Prisoners of war shall be released and repatriated without delay after the cessation of active hostilities."

◆

Protocol I
Article 45

1. A person who takes part in hostilities and falls into the power of an adverse Party shall be presumed to be a prisoner of war, and therefore shall be protected by the Third Convention, if he claims the status of prisoner of war, or if he appears to be entitled to such status, or if the Party on which he depends claims such status on his behalf by notification to the detaining Power or to the Protecting Power. Should any doubt arise as to whether any such person is entitled to the status of prisoner of war, he shall continue to have such status and, therefore, to be protected by the Third Convention and this Protocol until such time as his status has been determined by a competent tribunal.

2. If a person who has fallen into the power of an adverse Party is not held as a prisoner of war and is to be tried by that Party for an offence arising out of the hostilities, he shall have the right to assert his entitlement to prisoner-of-war status before a judicial tribunal and to have that question adjudicated. Whenever possible under the applicable procedure, this adjudication shall occur before the trial for the offence. The representatives of the Protecting Power shall be entitled to attend the proceedings in which that question is adjudicated, unless, exceptionally, the proceedings are held in camera in the interest of State security. In such a case the detaining Power shall advise the Protecting Power accordingly.

There are two 1977 protocols to the 1949 GCs.[107] The first protocol includes a reference to the status of those captured during military hostilities. (The second protocol requires humane treatment for individuals who are detained during a conflict that is *not* international in character.)[108]

"Unlawful Combatant" Status The Third GC contains two cardinal principles which are of utmost importance to prisoners. First, POWs cannot be prosecuted and punished, merely for taking part in the hostilities. Second, POWs must be given humane treatment from the time they fall into the power of the enemy until their final release and repatriation. If a person is not given combatant status, he may be tried for having committed an unlawful belligerent act. As such, he would not have had the "licence to kill" as a military combatant, and may thus be subject to the death penalty.

The terms "combatant" and "unlawful combatant" do not appear in the GCs. But the classic illustration would be a civilian spy or mercenary. Neither may properly claim "POW" status. When in doubt, a detainee's status must therefore be determined by an Article 5 "competent tribunal" (see earlier). The GC, however, does not: (1) describe the composition of the tribunal; (2) specify the due process rights of the person undergoing this status determination; nor (3) explain the judicial guarantees to which the detainee is entitled under International Humanitarian Law.[109]

Congress gave the president its support for the US riposte in Afghanistan (and Iraq). This would be—in keeping with the practice since 9-11—labeled a "War on Terror." Congress chose not to declare war. One reason would be that the US military offensive was not mounted against "Afghanistan" as a nation. The United States was, instead, in Afghanistan to defend itself by pursuing individuals such as Usama bin Laden—and nongovernmental international organizations, typified by al-Qaida.[110] September 11th signaled the claimed need to revamp the Laws of War to reflect these contemporary realities.[111] The GC flourished in an era dominated by wars between countries, and between soldiers in uniform.

As high profile detainees were captured—initially in Afghanistan (and later in Iraq), the initial US position was that *no* detainee would be entitled to the mentioned GC protections. One given reason was that these individuals did not wear recognizable uniforms, did not openly display their arms, and never wore traditional military insignia. In February 2002, the Bush Administration partially modified its hard-line stance: *Taliban* detainees would be protected pursuant to GC principles, although they would not be reclassified as "POWs." *Al-Qaida* captives would remain classified as "unlawful combatants" who would not, under any circumstances, be entitled to GC protection.

The International Red Cross, not satisfied with this distinction, responded as follows: "International Humanitarian Law foresees that the members of armed forces as well as militias associated to them which are captured by the adversary in an international armed conflict are protected by the Third Geneva Convention. There are divergent views between the United States and the ICRC on the procedures which apply on how to determine that the persons detained are not entitled to prisoner of war status. The United States and the ICRC will pursue their dialogue on this issue."[112] The US position softened somewhat, when in March 2002, Secretary Rumsfeld announced that he anticipated trying very few of the detainees. The rest were expected to be returned for a suitable disposition in their home countries.

Article 4.1 of the Fourth Geneva Convention specifies as follows: "Persons [also] protected by the Convention are those who, at a given moment and in any manner whatsoever, find themselves, in case of a conflict or occupation, in the hands of a Party to the conflict or Occupying Power of which they are not nationals." This apparently all embracing definition suggests that *any* person would be protected, once within the grasp of a Party to a conflict or occupying power. However, its scope has been reduced by specific exceptions. Also, the Fourth Convention (protecting civilians) has not been applied to individuals protected by the first three (land, sea, and POWs).[113] (Article 49 of this Convention also prohibits "individual or mass forcible transfers . . . from occupied territory to the territory of the Occupying Power or to that of any other country.")

The US ratified all four 1949 Geneva Conventions. It signed the 1977 Protocol I, but has not ratified it. So the Article 5 "competent tribunal" determination would not be binding on the United States as an express treaty obligation.

Question:

How does the above US interpretation, regarding the status of captured Taliban and al-Qaida detainees, differ from the above Geneva Convention language? Which of those Articles are involved in this debate? Are Taliban or al-Qaida members entitled to POW status?

Detainee Cases As these individuals were captured, they were removed from various conflict zones in Afghanistan, and elsewhere. The president used his constitutional power as Commander-in-Chief to detain them at the US military base in Cuba. As word of their presence there began to be reported, the conditions of their confinement spawned a national debate on whether they should be detained—some for years—without being charged with crimes, assisted by lawyers, and all without their status being determined by anyone other than the president. He exercised his power to denominate these approximately 640 suspected terrorists as being "unlawful combatants" who were beyond US borders, and therefore also not entitled to any US constitutional rights. They would not be processed via military courts-martial, as POWs are expected to be, under the Geneva Convention. Nor were they entitled to any of the US constitutional guarantees normally accorded to civilians in US criminal prosecutions.

One of the many problems with such secret incarcerations is the "ghost detainee." US Army jailers in Iraq, acting at the request of the US Central Intelligence Agency (CIA), kept dozens of such prisoners at the Abu Ghraib prison. Under the Geneva Convention, a temporary failure to disclose the identity of prisoners is permitted. However, this exemption is triggered only by military necessity.[114] In December 2004, the House of Lords thus overruled a like British detainee policy that had impacted foreign Muslims. This was a violation of civilian detention requirements under the European Convention on Human Rights (§11.3).

The United States was in the midst of a popular debate, which pitted this application of the 2002 National Security Strategy against the core values which routinely apply to anyone in US custody. Foreign citizens (and two) US civilians were thus denied the right of habeas corpus: to petition a judge, requiring the warden to produce the body, for the purpose of judicially assessing the validity of the incarceration.

US presidents and legislators have occasionally found it necessary to limit such judicial review. Examples include President Adams' approval of the 1798 Alien Sedition Act, and President Lincoln's suspension of the writ of habeas corpus during the US Civil War.

RASUL v. BUSH

SUPREME COURT OF THE UNITED STATES

542 U.S. 466, 124 S.Ct. 2686, 159 *L. Ed.* 2d 548 (2004)

AUTHOR'S NOTE: Alien detainees at the US Naval Base in Guantanamo Bay, Cuba, brought several suits to contest the legality and conditions of their confinement. The federal trial court dismissed this case for lack of jurisdiction. The Court of Appeals for the District of Columbia Circuit affirmed the dismissal. The Supreme Court granted certiorari in these consolidated cases, which were closely watched by supporters and critics of the US War on Terror.

COURT'S OPINION:

JUSTICE STEVENS delivered the opinion of the Court.

These two cases present the narrow but important question whether United States courts lack jurisdiction to consider challenges to the legality of the detention of foreign nationals captured abroad in connection with hostilities and incarcerated at the Guantanamo Bay Naval Base, Cuba.

I

On September 11, 2001, agents of the al Qaeda terrorist network hijacked four commercial airliners and used them as missiles to attack American targets. . . . [T]he President sent U.S. Armed Forces into Afghanistan to wage a military campaign against al Qaeda and the Taliban regime that had supported it.

Petitioners in these cases are 2 Australian citizens and 12 Kuwaiti citizens who were captured abroad during hostilities between the United States and the Taliban.[1] Since early 2002, the U.S. military has held them—along with, according to the Government's estimate,

---

[1]When we granted certiorari, the petitioners also included two British citizens, Shafiq Rasul and Asif Iqbal [who] . . . have since been released from custody.

approximately 640 other non-Americans captured abroad—at the Naval Base at Guantanamo Bay. The United States occupies the Base, which comprises 45 square miles of land and water along the southeast coast of Cuba. . . . Under the [lease] Agreement, "the United States recognizes the continuance of the ultimate sovereignty of the Republic of Cuba over the [leased areas]," while "the Republic of Cuba consents that during the period of the occupation by the United States . . . the United States shall exercise complete jurisdiction and control over and within said areas." . . .

In 2002, petitioners, through relatives acting as their next friends, filed various actions in the U.S. District Court for the District of Columbia challenging the legality of their detention at the Base. All alleged that none of the petitioners has ever been a combatant against the United States or has ever engaged in any terrorist acts.[4] custody. The Australian David Hicks was allegedly captured in Afghanistan by the Northern Alliance, a coalition of Afghan groups opposed to the Taliban, before he was turned over to the United States. The Australian Mamdouh Habib was allegedly arrested in Pakistan by Pakistani authorities and turned over to Egyptian authorities, who in turn transferred him to U.S. custody.

They also alleged that none has been charged with any wrongdoing, permitted to consult with counsel, or provided access to the courts or any other tribunal.

The two Australians, Mamdouh Habib and David Hicks, each filed a petition for writ of habeas corpus, seeking release from custody, access to counsel, freedom from interrogations, and other relief. Fawzi Khalid Abdullah Fahad Al Odah and the 11 other Kuwaiti detainees filed a complaint seeking to be informed of the charges against them, to be allowed to meet with their families and with counsel, and to have access to the courts or some other impartial tribunal. They claimed that denial of these rights violates the Constitution, international law, and treaties of the United States. . . .

Construing all three actions as petitions for writs of habeas corpus, the District Court dismissed them for want of jurisdiction. The court held . . . that "aliens detained outside the sovereign territory of the United States [may not] invok[e] a petition for a writ of habeas corpus." The Court of Appeals affirmed. Reading [Johnson v.] *Eisentrager* [339 U.S. 763, 70 S.Ct. 936, 94 L.Ed. 1255 (1950)], to hold that " 'the privilege of litigation' does not extend to aliens in military custody who have no presence in 'any territory over which the United States is sovereign,'" it [too] held that the District Court lacked jurisdiction over petitioners' habeas actions. . . . We granted certiorari, and now reverse.

II

Congress has granted federal district courts, "within their respective jurisdictions," the authority to hear applications for habeas corpus by any person who claims to be held "in custody in violation of the Constitution or laws or treaties of the United States." 28 U.S.C. §§2241(a), (c)(3). . . . In 1867, Congress extended the protections of the writ to "all cases where any person may be restrained of his or her liberty in violation of the constitution, or of any treaty or law of the United States."

Habeas corpus . . . received explicit recognition in the Constitution, which forbids suspension of "[t]he Privilege of the Writ of Habeas Corpus . . . unless when in Cases of Rebellion or Invasion the public Safety may require it," Art. I, §9, cl. 2.

As it has evolved over the past two centuries, the habeas statute clearly has expanded habeas corpus "beyond the limits that obtained during the 17th and 18th centuries." . . . ("The historic purpose of the writ has been to relieve detention by executive authorities without judicial trial"). . . .

Consistent with the historic purpose of the writ, this Court has recognized the federal courts' power to review applications for habeas relief in a wide variety of cases involving Executive detention, in wartime as well as in times of peace. . . .

The question now before us is whether the habeas statute confers a right to judicial review of the legality of Executive detention of aliens in a territory over which the United States exercises plenary and exclusive jurisdiction, but not "ultimate sovereignty."

III

Respondents' primary submission is that the . . . jurisdictional question is controlled by our decision in

---

[4]Relatives of the Kuwaiti detainees allege that the detainees were taken captive "by local villagers seeking promised bounties or other financial rewards" while they were providing humanitarian aid in Afghanistan and Pakistan, and were subsequently turned over to U.S.

Eisentrager. In that case, we held that a Federal District Court lacked authority to issue a writ of habeas corpus to 21 German citizens who had been captured by U.S. forces in China, tried and convicted of war crimes by an American military commission headquartered in Nanking, and incarcerated in the Landsberg Prison in occupied Germany. . . . [T]his Court summarized the six critical facts in the case:

> We are here confronted with a decision whose basic premise is that these prisoners are entitled, as a constitutional right, to sue in some court of the United States for a writ of *habeas corpus.* To support that assumption we . . . [would have to] hold that a prisoner of our military authorities is constitutionally entitled to the writ, even though he (a) is an enemy alien; (b) has never been or resided in the United States; (c) was captured outside of our territory and there held in military custody as a prisoner of war; (d) was tried and convicted by a Military Commission sitting outside the United States; (e) for offenses against laws of war committed outside the United States; (f) and is at all times imprisoned outside the United States.

On this set of facts, the Court concluded, "no right to the writ of *habeas corpus* appears." Petitioners in these [Cuban detainee] cases differ from the *Eisentrager* detainees in important respects: They are not nationals of countries at war with the United States, and they deny that they have engaged in or plotted acts of aggression against the United States; they have never been afforded access to any tribunal, much less charged with and convicted of wrongdoing; and for more than two years they have been imprisoned in territory over which the United States exercises exclusive jurisdiction and control.

. . .

IV

. . . [R]espondents contend that we can discern a limit on §2241 [habeas corpus] through application of the "longstanding principle of American law" that congressional legislation is presumed not to have extraterritorial application unless such intent is clearly manifested. Whatever traction the presumption against extraterritoriality might have in other contexts, it certainly has no application to the operation of the habeas statute with respect to persons detained within "the territorial jurisdiction" of the United States. . . . Considering that the statute draws no distinction between Americans and aliens held in federal custody, there is little reason to think that Congress intended the geographical coverage of the statute to vary depending on the detainee's citizenship. Aliens held at the base, no less than American citizens, are entitled to invoke the federal courts' authority under §2241.

Application of the habeas statute to persons detained at the base is consistent with the historical reach of the writ of habeas corpus. . . . Later cases confirmed that the reach of the writ depended not on formal notions of territorial sovereignty, but rather on the practical question of "the exact extent and nature of the jurisdiction or dominion exercised in fact by the Crown."

In the end, the answer to the question presented is clear. Petitioners contend that they are being held in federal custody in violation of the laws of the United States.[15] We therefore hold that §2241 confers on the District Court jurisdiction to hear petitioners' habeas corpus challenges to the legality of their detention at the Guantanamo Bay Naval Base.

. . .

VI

Whether and what further proceedings may become necessary after respondents make their response to the merits of petitioners' claims are matters that we need not address now [i.e., mode of trial, access to counsel, etc.] What is presently at stake is only whether the federal courts have jurisdiction to determine the legality of the Executive's potentially indefinite detention of individuals who claim to be wholly innocent of wrongdoing. Answering that question in the affirmative, we reverse the judgment of the Court of Appeals and remand for the District Court to consider in the first instance the merits of petitioners' claims.

---

[15]Petitioners' allegations—that, although they have engaged neither in combat nor in acts of terrorism against the United States, they have been held in Executive detention for more than two years in territory subject to the long-term, exclusive jurisdiction and control of the United States, without access to counsel and without being charged with any wrongdoing— unquestionably describe "custody in violation of the Constitution or laws or treaties of the United States."

It is so ordered.

JUSTICE KENNEDY, concurring in the judgment.

The Court is correct, in my view, to conclude that federal courts have jurisdiction to consider challenges to the legality of the detention of foreign nationals held at the Guantanamo Bay Naval Base in Cuba. . . .

Eisentrager . . . began by noting the "ascending scale of rights" that courts have recognized for individuals depending on their connection to the United States. Citizenship provides a longstanding basis for jurisdiction, the Court noted, and among aliens physical presence within the United States also "gave the Judiciary power to act." . . . The place of the detention was also important to the jurisdictional question, the Court noted. Physical presence in the United States "implied protection," whereas [in *Eisentrager*] . . . "th[e] prisoners at no relevant time were within any territory over which the United States is sovereign." The Court next noted that the prisoners in *Eisentrager* "were actual enemies" of the United States, proven to be so at trial, and thus could not justify "a limited opening of our courts" to distinguish the "many [aliens] of friendly personal disposition to whom the status of enemy" was unproven. Finally, the Court considered the extent to which jurisdiction would "hamper the war effort and bring aid and comfort to the enemy." Because the prisoners in *Eisentrager* were proven enemy aliens found and detained outside the United States, and because the existence of jurisdiction would have had a clear harmful effect on the Nation's military affairs, the matter was appropriately left to the Executive Branch and there was no jurisdiction for the courts to hear the prisoner's claims.

The decision in *Eisentrager* indicates that there is a realm of political authority over military affairs where the judicial power may not enter. . . . A necessary corollary of *Eisentrager* is that there are circumstances in which the courts maintain the power and the responsibility to protect persons from unlawful detention even where military affairs are implicated.

The facts here are distinguishable from those in *Eisentrager* in two critical ways, leading to the conclusion that a federal court may entertain the petitions. First, Guantanamo Bay is in every practical respect a United States territory, and it is one far removed from any hostilities. . . .

The second critical set of facts is that the detainees at Guantanamo Bay are being held indefinitely, and without benefit of any legal proceeding to determine their status. . . . Indefinite detention without trial or other proceeding presents altogether different considerations. It allows friends and foes alike to remain in detention. It suggests a weaker case of military necessity and much greater alignment with the traditional function of habeas corpus. Perhaps, where detainees are taken from a zone of hostilities, detention without proceedings or trial would be justified by military necessity for a matter of weeks; but as the period of detention stretches from months to years, the case for continued detention to meet military exigencies becomes weaker.

In light of the status of Guantanamo Bay and the indefinite pretrial detention of the detainees, I would hold that federal-court jurisdiction is permitted in these cases.

. . .

JUSTICE SCALIA, with whom THE CHIEF JUSTICE and JUSTICE THOMAS join, dissenting.

The Court today holds that the habeas statute extends to aliens detained by the United States military overseas, outside the sovereign borders of the United States and beyond the territorial jurisdictions of all its courts. This is not only a novel holding; it contradicts a half-century-old precedent on which the military undoubtedly relied, *Johnson v. Eisentrager.* . . . This is an irresponsible overturning of settled law in a matter of extreme importance to our forces currently in the field. I would leave it to Congress to change §2241, and dissent from the Court's unprecedented holding.

I

. . .

The reality is this: Today's opinion, and today's opinion alone, overrules *Eisentrager;* today's opinion, and today's opinion alone, extends the habeas statute, for the first time, to aliens held beyond the sovereign territory of the United States and beyond the territorial jurisdiction of its courts. No reasons are given for this result; no acknowledgment of its consequences made. . . . Normally, we consider the interests of those who have relied on our decisions. Today, the Court springs a trap on the Executive, subjecting Guantanamo Bay to the oversight of the federal courts even though it has never before been thought to be within their jurisdiction—and thus making it a foolish place to have housed alien wartime detainees.

II

In abandoning the venerable statutory line drawn in *Eisentrager,* the Court boldly extends the scope of the habeas statute to the four corners of the earth. . . .

The consequence of this holding, as applied to aliens outside the country, is breathtaking. It permits an alien captured in a foreign theater of active combat to bring a §2241 petition against the Secretary of Defense. Over the course of the last century, the United States has held millions of alien prisoners abroad. . . . A great many of these prisoners would no doubt have complained about the circumstances of their capture and the terms of their confinement. The military is currently detaining over 600 prisoners at Guantanamo Bay alone; each detainee undoubtedly has complaints—real or contrived—about those terms and circumstances. The Court's unheralded expansion of federal-court jurisdiction is not even mitigated by a comforting assurance that the legion of ensuing claims will be easily resolved on the merits. To the contrary, the Court says that the "[p]etitioners' allegations . . . unquestionably describe 'custody in violation of the Constitution or laws or treaties of the United States.'" From this point forward, federal courts will entertain petitions from these prisoners, and others like them around the world, challenging actions and events far away, and forcing the courts to oversee one aspect of the Executive's conduct of a foreign war.

. . .

To grant the writ to these prisoners might mean that our army must transport them across the seas for hearing. This would require allocation for shipping space, guarding personnel, billeting and rations. It might also require transportation for whatever witnesses the prisoners desired to call as well as transportation for those necessary to defend legality of the sentence. The writ, since it is held to be a matter of right, would be equally available to enemies during active hostilities as in the present twilight between war and peace. Such trials would hamper the war effort and bring aid and comfort to the enemy. They would diminish the prestige

of our commanders, not only with enemies but with wavering neutrals. It would be difficult to devise more effective fettering of a field commander than to allow the very enemies he is ordered to reduce to submission to call him to account in his own civil courts and divert his efforts and attention from the military offensive abroad to the legal defensive at home. Nor is it unlikely that the result of such enemy litigiousness would be conflict between judicial and military opinion highly comforting to enemies of the United States.

. . .

III

Part IV of the Court's opinion, dealing with the status of Guantanamo Bay, is a puzzlement.

. . .

The Court does not explain how "complete jurisdiction and control" without sovereignty causes an enclave to be part of the United States for purposes of its domestic laws. Since "jurisdiction and control" obtained through a lease is no different in effect from "jurisdiction and control" acquired by lawful force of arms, parts of Afghanistan and Iraq should logically be regarded as subject to our domestic laws. Indeed, if "jurisdiction and control" rather than sovereignty were the test, so should the Landsberg Prison in Germany, where the United States held the *Eisentrager* detainees.

. . .

In sum, the Court's treatment of Guantanamo Bay, like its treatment of §2241, is a wrenching departure from [sixty years of] precedent.

. . .

The Commander in Chief and his subordinates had every reason to expect that the internment of combatants at Guantanamo Bay would not have the consequence of bringing the cumbersome machinery of our domestic courts into military affairs. . . . If [Congress] . . . wished to change federal judges' habeas jurisdiction from what this Court had previously held that to be, it could have done so. And it could have done so by intelligent revision of the statute,[7] instead of by today's clumsy, countertextual reinterpretation that confers upon wartime prisoners greater habeas rights than domestic detainees. The latter must challenge their present physical confinement in the district of their confinement, whereas under today's

---

[7]It could, for example, provide for jurisdiction by placing Guantanamo Bay within the territory of an existing district court; or by creating a district court for Guantanamo Bay, as it did for the Panama Canal Zone, see 22 U.S.C. §3841(a) (repealed 1979).

strange holding Guantanamo Bay detainees can petition in any of the 94 federal judicial districts. . . . For this Court to create such a monstrous scheme in time of war, and in frustration of our military commanders' reliance upon clearly stated prior law, is judicial adventurism of the worst sort. I dissent.

During the War on Terror, various cases worked their way through the courts, presenting the core question: What rights, if any, should suspected terrorists have, after being placed beyond the modern battle fields in the War on Terror?

The US Supreme Court answered some key questions in the preceeding case.

◆ *Notes & Questions*

1. The majority opinion says that "the presumption against extraterritoriality [§5.2] . . . has no application . . . within 'the territorial jurisdiction' of the United States." Scalia's dissent laments that "the Court boldly extends the scope of the habeas statute to the four corners of the earth." Is the majority saying that part of Cuba is now within US territory?

2. Footnote 15 states that the detainees' allegations "unquestionably describe 'custody in violation of the Constitution or laws or treaties of the United States.'" While the majority paints these petitions as "unquestionable," note that: (a) the president chose Guantanamo Bay, Cuba for the port 9-11 detention facility, (b) the two lower courts dismissed these petitions on the basis of the Supreme Court precedent in *Eisentrager;* (c) this issue simmered in the media and on the public conscience for two years before being decided by the highest court in the United States; and (d) the facts spawned three separate opinions—including Justice Kennedy's concurring opinion.

3. Per Justice Scalia's dissent: "No reasons are given for this result. . . ." How would you counter that statement, if you were in the majority of the six judges in this case? Justice Scalia also says: "Today, the Court springs a trap on the Executive, subjecting Guantanamo Bay to the oversight of the federal courts . . . thus making it a foolish place to have housed alien wartime detainees." The Bush Administration's strategy of holding the detainees in Cuba was the best one that could have been made. These suspected terrorists were thus taken out of the military theaters where they were supposedly fighting along with the Taliban or al-Qaida. The 1950 *Eisentrager* case held that alien detainees (Germans), captured outside of the United States (China), and held outside of the United States (on a US base in Germany) could not challenge the legal validity of their detentions in a US civilian court via habeas corpus. Of course, Justice Scalia likely meant that the location of incarceration decision was made "foolish" by the "puzzlement" of the majority's "monstrous" decision in *Rasul.*

4. Six months later, a special panel of the House of Lords ruled 8-1 in favor of nine foreign Muslim men in what human rights organizations refer to as "Britain's Guantanamo." This institutional equivalent of the US Supreme Court determined that Britain's unlimited detention policy for London's Belmarsh prison was Draconian, discriminated against foreigners, and was an unjustifiable violation of the European Convention on Human Rights. In Lord Hoffman's words: "It calls into question the very existence of an ancient liberty of which this country has until now been very proud: freedom from arbitrary arrest and detention . . . posing a greater threat to the nation than terrorism."
A (FC) and others (FC) v. Secretary of State for the Home Department, [2004] UKHL 56, *and* [2005] UKHL 71, available at: <http://www.parliament. the-stationery-office.co.uk/pa/ld200506/ldjudgmt/ jd051208/aand-1.htm>.

5. The Court does not address "[w]hether and what further proceedings may become necessary after respondents [government officials] make their response to the merits of petitioners' claims." This ensuing phase of the Cuban detainee cases is addressed in the next subsection of this section on post-9-11 US applications of the Laws of War regarding trial by a US military commission.

6. Justice Kennedy's concurring opinion refers to the "ascending scale of rights" that "courts have recognized for individuals depending on their connection to the United States." Two related cases were decided by the US Supreme Court on the same day as *Rasul.* Both involved *US* citizens held as enemy combatants on the US mainland. Both cases triggered the potential application of 18 US Code §4001(a): "No citizen shall

be imprisoned or otherwise detained by the United States except pursuant to an Act of Congress."

(a) In Hamdi v. Rumsfeld, 542 U.S. 507, 124 S.Ct. 2633, 159 L.Ed.2d 578 (2004), the detainee was captured on the battlefield in Afghanistan and brought to a naval brig in Charleston, S.C. In his case, the Court held that constitutional due process required that a US citizen, being held as enemy combatant, must be given a meaningful opportunity to contest the factual basis for his detention in the United States. After this decision, the government released Hamdi, and then sent him to Saudi Arabia, where he was raised as a child. Justice O'Conner therein penned the constitutional limitation that "a state of war is not a blank check for the president."

(b) In Rumsfeld v. Padilla, 542 U.S. 426, 124 S.Ct. 2711, 159 L.Ed. 2d 513 (2004), the Court held only that the federal trial court did not have jurisdiction to proceed. Padilla is a US citizen and former Chicago gang member, who was captured in the Chicago airport upon his return from abroad. He was dubbed the "Dirty Bomber," because he allegedly planned to detonate a nuclear-contaminated bomb somewhere in the United States. A federal appeals court (when overruling the trial judge) unanimously ruled that the president *does* have the authority to detain him indefinitely, and without charges, as an "enemy combatant." Padilla v. Hanft, 423F.3d 386 (2005). The US Attorney General then sought authorization to first, transfer Padilla for prosecution in the US criminal justice system; and second, to vacate the favorable Court of Appeals decision. This was an apparent attempt to avoid the case being reviewed by the US Supreme Court. The Attorney General did not want to risk the high court's reversal of the foregoing intermediate appellate decision. That could adversely impact the government's desire to hold even a US citizen, captured on US soil, for an indefinite period (already three-and-a-half years in Padilla's case). The government's motion was denied. The Attorney General then charged Padilla with criminal conduct, to effectuate the plan to transfer Padilla into the civilian criminal justice system. That would hopefully moot any further Supreme Court involvement in the *Padilla* case.

Military Commissions: This method of trial is not unique to the US "9-11" response. Nor was the above *Padilla* detention of a US citizen, for over three years without charges or trial, which would have resulted in a trial by military commission. President Lincoln, and others since, have authorized military commissions to try civilians outside of the civilian criminal justice system. After the US Civil War, for example, a military commission tried a Mississippi newspaper editor. Congress passed a law withdrawing his right to have the Supreme Court decide the validity of his detention via habeas corpus. In PGW of 1991, the United States conducted 1,196 such trials. American military officers therein tried and released three-quarters of the detainees.

In March 2003 (and again in 2005), the Inter-American Commission on Human Rights of the OAS, formally requested—upon receipt of an earlier US response—that the United States "take the urgent measures necessary to have the legal status of the detainees at Guantanamo Bay determined by a competent tribunal." In April 2005, the Council of Europe passed Resolution 1433, therein stating "the Assembly concludes that the circumstances surrounding detentions by the United States at Guantánamo Bay show unlawfulness and inconsistency with the rule of law. . . ." [115]

After the Supreme Court's preceding June 2004 trio of "unlawful combatant" cases, Deputy Secretary of Defense Paul Wolowitz assumed the task of revamping the traditional US approach to the status determinations for captured prisoners. (US Army Regulation 190-8 codified the "Article 5" Geneva Convention process.) The new tribunals were called Combat Status Review Tribunals (CSRT). Under the CSRT process, an enemy combatant was "an individual who was part of or supporting Taliban or al-Qaeda forces, or associated forces that are engaged in hostilities against the United States or its coalition partners. The United States then claimed that the pre-9-11 military regulations no longer applied to the Guantanamo military base—on the basis of the presumption of correctness of the president's determination that they were "enemy combatants." In March 2005, the CSRT process was completed for all detainees. Of the 558 cases, all but thirty-eight were not "enemy combatants."

In a second process, the government devised its Annual Review Boards (ARB). The task of these boards is to determine whether those still detained at Guantanamo present a continuing threat, or any factor which is the basis for continued detention. The three-member ARB panels are military officers. There is no access to counsel, and only closed hearings. In October 2004, a US federal court determined that the right to counsel applied to these detainees. In November 2004, another federal trial judge issued a broad protective order, requiring that the detainee's lawyers meet a series of national security restrictions, such as no disclosure of classified information to the detainees' counsel.[116]

The broadened definition of "enemy combatant" resulted in more litigation in the aftermath of *Rasul* and the new regulations. The US government claimed that *Rasul* resolved only the narrow issue of whether the federal courts had habeas corpus jurisdiction in the case of the Cuban detainees. *Rasul,* it was argued, did not govern the scope of legal rights, if any, possessed by these detainees. In January 2005, two federal judges reached opposite results on this point. In one case, the US Constitution and Geneva Conventions were applied to the Taliban detainees, but not to members of al-Qaida. In the other, no detainees had any such rights.[117]

Congress previously passed the Antiterrorism and Effective Death Penalty Act. It placed all federal court habeas corpus proceedings on a fast track. Prisoners were thus limited to a single habeas petition. The 2006 Defense Reauthorization Act further limited review by habeas corpus. It removed the judicial power to hear such proceedings, in the case of the remaining alien detainees at the US military installation at Guantanamo Bay, Cuba. One appeal is permitted, however, from a detainee's Combat Status Review Tribunal.

The first federal appellate decision to analyze a Guantanamo detainee's objection to trial by a military commission appears later. The detainee admitted that he was Usama bin Laden's driver, bodyguard, and general assistant:

Hamdan v. Rumsfeld

UNITED STATES COURT
OF APPEALS DISTRICT
OF COLUMBIA
Circuit 415 F.3d 33 (2005),
certiorari granted, 126 S.Ct. 622 (2005).
Go to course Web page at
<http://home.att.net/~slomansonb/txtcsesite.html>.
Under Chapter Ten, click Hamdan v. Rumsfeld.

Torture Redefined?   The United States is a party to the UN's 1984 Convention Against Torture and Other Cruel Inhuman, or Degrading Treatment (CAT). Article 2 provides as follows: "No exceptional circumstances whatsoever, whether a state of war or a threat of war, internal or political instability or any other public emergency, may be invoked as a justification against torture."

The United States codified its commitment to the CAT, by defining "torture" in 18 United States Code §2340(1): "'torture' means an act committed by a person acting under the color of law specifically intended to inflict severe physical or mental pain or suffering (other than pain or suffering incidental to lawful sanctions) upon another person within his custody or physical control. . . ." Under §2340(2)A: "'severe mental pain or suffering' means the prolonged mental harm caused by or resulting from . . . the intentional infliction or threatened infliction of severe physical pain or suffering. . . ."

Unlike the Geneva Conventions, those who violate the Torture Convention can be criminally prosecuted. Injured individuals may also allege a claim seeking money damages or other relief against the perpetrator. This level of commitment has not deterred the vast majority of nations from ratifying the Torture Convention.

After 9-11, a revised US interpretation emerged. For two years before its partial repudiation by the White House in June 2004, the administration appears to have relied on various memo written by the Justice Department's Office of Legal Counsel, narrowing the definition of torture stated earlier, to only life-threatening interrogation procedures. Attorney General Alberto Gonzales released these documents in June 2004—noting that such memos were designed only to explore the limits of the legal landscape.

The most criticized document was written on August 1, 2002. It stated that torture covered only that degree of pain that is so intense that it will result in "organ failure, impairment of bodily function, or even death." Torture could then be justified under a theory of national self-defense or as a necessity. Other key provisions of this new presidential interpretation included the following:

In the absence of any textual provision to the contrary, we assume self-defense can be an appropriate defense to an allegation of torture [under the above US Criminal Code].

. . .

In light of the President's complete authority over the conduct of the war, without a clear statement otherwise, we will not read a criminal statute as infringing on the President's ultimate authority in these areas.

. . .

[A] detainee may possess information that could enable the United States to prevent attacks that potentially could equal or surpass the September 11 attacks in their magnitude. Clearly, any harm that might occur during an interrogation would pale to insignificance compared to the harm avoided by preventing such an attack, which could take hundreds of thousands of lives.

. . .

As we have made clear in other opinions involving the war against al Qaeda, the nation's right to self-defense has been triggered by the events of September 11. If a government defendant were to harm an enemy combatant during an interrogation in a manner that might violate [the above US Code] section 2340A, he would be doing so in order to prevent further attacks on the United States by the al Qaeda terrorist network.

. . .

As commander-in-chief, the President has the constitutional authority to order interrogations of enemy combatants to gain intelligence information concerning the military plans of the enemy. Any effort to apply Section 2304A in a manner that interferes with the President's authority of such core war matters as the detention and interrogation of enemy combatants thus would be unconstitutional.[118]

The president therefore believes that his authority is derived from two sources, First, the September 14, 2001 congressional authorization authorized the president to "use all appropriate and necessary force" against those involved in that week's 9-11 "attacks" on US soil. Second, the US Constitution gives the Commander in Chief the responsibility to, above all, protect the national security. There are raging debates about the scope of this power. The real question is whether it's use will be limited to the *crisis du jour*.

The quoted memo subordinates the US Criminal Code (and effectively, the Geneva Conventions) to the president's constitutional powers as Commander-in-Chief—whose first responsibility is national defense. As

a result, the interrogation tactics used at Guantanamo were harsher than those used in Iraq. Unlike Guantanamo's suspected al-Qaida and Taliban Guantanamo detainees, all detainees in Iraq (including those at Abu Ghraib) are to be accorded the traditional Geneva Convention protections—such as the Article 17 prohibition against torture and degrading treatment. All US military defendants, accused of violating either the Geneva Convention or the above US code prohibitions on torture and degrading treatment will no doubt rely on these Justice Department memos in their defense.[119]

New guidelines were approved, but not publicized at first. This list of six Enhanced Interrogation Techniques include "waterboarding." This is a mock execution (by drowning), which is prohibited by the Geneva Convention. Only a handful of CIA officers have applied this technique to high-value detainees. Nevertheless, contemporary critics might draw upon the articulation of the prominent seventeenth-century scholar, Hugo Grotius: "Avenging himself to excess, [a]nd slaughtering the guilty, guily himself became."

The McCain Amendment to the 2006 US Defense Appropriations Law attempts to strike a balance between national security and the prohibition on torture. US Senator John McCain, who was himself tortured for years in North Vietnam, describes it as follows: "It's not about who they are. It's about who we are." His amendment essentially provides: "No person . . . under detention in a Department of Defense facility shall be subject to any technique of interrogation not authorized by the United States Army Field Manual on Intelligence Interrogation. . . . [Further no], individual . . . shall be subject to cruel, inhumane, or degrading treatment of punishment." This law should be welcome news for military leaders in the field. It is designed to remove the ambiguity of any order regarding the treatment of prisoners.

However, upon signing this act into law, the president simultaneously executed a Signing Statement which limits this new torture provision: "The executive branch shall construe . . . the Act, [when] relating to detainees, in a manner consistent with the constitutional authority of the President . . . as Commander in Chief and consistent with the limitations on the judicial power, which will assist in achieving the shared objective of the Congress and the President . . . of protecting the American people from further terrorist attacks."[120] This caveat reserves the president's stated power to bypass the McCain Amendment, based upon a balance of power-free executive determination that torture is required in present (Guantanamo detainee) or future contexts.

TICKING BOMB PROBLEM

The "ticking bomb" hypothetical is often used to focus attention on this debate. Your region of the nation is about to experience a second 9-11. Your detainee admits that he has the information to avoid this tragedy.

(1) If necessary, will you torture him to death to get the bomb location information?
(2) Would your answer be the same if you "suspected"—but did not know for sure—that your detainee had the critical information you need to find the explosive device (or some environmental pollutant that could take hundreds of thousands of lives)? Would a legal or moral dividing line between "knowing" and "suspecting" make a difference? Could such a distinction lead to a slippery slope, where mere suspicion is all that is needed for the government to torture anyone to death? Should there be a distinction between "torture" and "cruel, inhumane, and degrading treatment?"[121]
(3) For those who would not answer "yes" to (1) or (2) above, would it be better to open this question to public debate, and have your country abide by the democratic result?
(4) Could that vote be skewed by geographical proximity to the first 9-11? For example, would a New York City, Madrid, or London resident be entitled to a weighted vote? No vote? The same vote as everyone else?
(5) Should such decisions remain within the government, rather than being subjected to a democratic vote?
(6) You are in your government's legislature. Would you vote to pass legislation that exempts governmental officers from the reach of the above statutes (18 USC §§2304 and 2304A)? Alternatively, would you remind your executive branch that no one is above the law? That is, there is *already* a clear public statement in these statutes—which were passed to implement the US Torture Convention commitment? Do those statutes necessarily preclude permanent implementation of the above August 1, 2002 torture memo?

While answering this "hypothetical," one might ponder the words of a Vanderbilt University Professor, former Member of Congress of the United States, and former Chairman of the Appellate Body of the World Trade Organization:

The Garden

JAMES BACCHUS

28 Fordham Int'l L. J. 308 (2005)

. . .

Separate and apart from the question of whether all of this is legal, is the question of whether it is right or wrong. Still another reason to oppose torture is because torture, whether it is legal or not, is simply immoral. Beyond law is morality. Beyond the quibbling questions of lawyers is the simple question of right and wrong. . . . [Some] may quarrel with the contention of Jefferson and other Enlightenment thinkers that there can be such a thing as a "universal intelligibility" in the world. Others may contend that a "new paradigm" in our post-"9/11" world has somehow altered the previous dictates of both law and morality in ways that must alter also our traditional notions of right and wrong. But I remain with Jefferson. I continue to cling to the belief that there are such absolutes as right and wrong—whatever the circumstances. And the torture of another human being is just plain wrong.

. . .

Does this moral imperative have exceptions? Should it matter who the "others" are? Should it matter if they are "prisoners of war" or not? Should it matter if they are "terrorists" or not? . . . The "war on terror" raises these questions in [its] challenge to this moral imperative. Regardless of what the law may say in answer to these questions, what does morality say? Is there one morality where some of us are concerned, and another morality for some "others?" Jefferson did not think so. "I know but one code of morality for man," he said, "whether acting singly or collectively." We Americans have always agreed with him. For . . . our poor choices from time to time along the paths of our garden, we Americans have always professed an allegiance to one code of morality for all.

. . .

Do we Americans no longer agree with Jefferson that there is only one morality for everyone? Do we believe today in "good torture" and "bad torture?" Have we concluded since September 11, 2001, that there is

more than one code of morality, and that it is permissible to apply a different standard of right and wrong to our actions against "evildoers" because of the extent of the evil of their deeds?

. . .

But there is not one code of morality that is owed to evildoers and another that is owed to the rest of us. There is, as Jefferson said, only one code of morality, and . . . [thus] no such thing as "good torture" and "bad torture." There is only torture. . . . If we choose to believe otherwise, then what has long been special about America, about Americans, and about the American garden, will disappear.

◆ PROBLEMS

Problem 10.A (§10.2 after UN General Assembly resolutions) Refer to the *Alvarez-Machain* case, contained in §5.3 of this book. A similar incident occurred in Panama, two years earlier. Its President, General Manuel Noriega, was extracted by US military forces during the US "invasion" of Panama in 1990 (see §1.4 on Standing), complete with live CNN coverage of the beachhead where US forces landed. Noriega stood trial and was convicted in the United States on international drug-trafficking charges. Panama did not protest. Panama was supposedly glad to be rid of this despot, in part because of his being on the US CIA payroll.

Assume, instead, that Panama's acting President, MiniNorg, decides that he must take decisive action, because of the US abduction—especially because it involves an official of Panama. In a speech to the people of Panama, MiniNorg declares as follows:

The unforgivable atrocity, perpetrated this week by US authorities, demonstrates the unquenchable imperialistic attitude of the US toward Panama's political independence, territorial sovereignty, and indisputable right to self-determination. I am thus forced to take measures to counter this unlawful operation of US forces in our beloved nation. Because humanitarian concerns do not guide the actions of the US, I must focus US attention upon our sovereign rights by using economic countermeasures. This morning, I ordered Panama's Minister of Banking and Commerce to seize all bank accounts and assets belonging to US citizens.

The US president responds to this expropriation by imposing an embargo on all goods from Panama. The US Customs Service refuses to allow any products from Panama to enter the United States.

Given this hypothetical scenario, would Panama's bank account seizures and the US embargo violate the principle of International Law prohibiting the State use of force? What principles in §10.1 and §10.2 would apply?

Problem 10.B (§10.2 after Cuban Missile Crisis Materials) Did the United States properly invoke UN Charter Article 51's provision, which authorizes self-defense?

Problem 10.C (§10.2 after Article 51 Materials) In April 1993, after US President Bush left office, he traveled to Kuwait. After returning, the United States discovered that Saddam Hussein had planned to assassinate ex-President Bush during this visit. The United States responded in June 1993 by launching several missiles into Baghdad. The United States claimed that an unsuccessful armed attack on a former head of State justified this responsive use of force as Article 51 self-defense.

Two students—one representing Iraq, and one representing the United States—will debate whether a State's use of force in these circumstances is justifiable self-defense, as opposed to a mere reprisal. For a useful analysis regarding the Israeli assassination of a Hamas leader, and his predecessor, see M. Patel, Israel's Targeted Killings of Hamas Leaders, ASIL Insight (May 2004), available at: <http://www.asil.org/insights/insigh133.htm>.

Problem 10.D (within §10.2, after *Subsequent Unilateral Action* materials) A major legal question arose, as of the US 1998 military buildup in the Persian Gulf: Could the United States unilaterally attack Iraq, premised on aging 1991 UN resolutions, as opposed to soliciting a *fresh* UN Security Council resolution to authorize an attack on Iraq?

Resolution 678, passed before the PGW began, provided that member States could use "all necessary force" to oust Iraq from Kuwait. However, seven years had passed by the time of this US saber rattling; Iraq had left Kuwait; there had been a cease-fire; the United States did not have the benefit of the same worldwide resolve to go to war in 1998 (i.e., the United States lacked the same support which it previously enjoyed from the permanent SC members China, France, and Russia and the Arab nations which had so staunchly supported the PGW in 1991); there was no provision in any SC resolution authorizing a UN member State to use force on its own initiative; and Article 2.4 of the UN Charter generally prohibits the use of force. This provision could be interpreted to require the *express* authorization of force by a fresh SC resolution, rather than leaving a doubtful situation to the discretion of one member State.

The US position relied on several arguments, including the following: Resolution 678 could still be invoked, because peace and security had not been restored to the area; in 1994, Iraqi forces moved toward Kuwait, then pulled back, when the United States dispatched a naval carrier group to the Gulf; in 1996, Iraq sent forces into Northern Iraq to help a Kurdish group capture a key city inside a safe haven protected by US-led forces; and Article 51 of the UN Charter accorded the right of collective self-defense because of the potential use of the biological and chemical weapons thought to be hidden in Saddam Hussein's large presidential palaces. Thus, the continuing threat of biological warfare could mean that the war had never really ended. Iraqi compliance with the cease-fire agreements could be construed as a condition precedent to an actual cease-fire.

Two students (or groups) will debate whether the United States possessed the authority to attack Iraq—as planned, prior to the Secretary-General's successful intervention—without a *fresh* UN Security Council resolution. The basic arguments have been provided. Others are available in J. Lobel & M. Ratner, Bypassing the Security Council: Ambiguous Authorizations to Use Force, Ceasefires, and the Iraqi Inspection Regime, 93 AMER. J. INT'L LAW 124 (1999). This exercise portrays some problems with potential UN solutions to threats to peace.

Problem 10.E (after §10.2 nuclear weapons materials) The US "bunker buster" nuclear bomb is a low-yield bomb designed for penetrating underground complexes such as those potentially used by armed forces, paramilitary, and al-Qaida in Afghanistan's mountainous terrain. It is quite difficult to search and penetrate all such complexes. This type of landscape may account for the inability to find Usama bin Laden. Using such a tactical weapon would: (a) greatly diminish the potential impact on the above-ground environment; (b) virtually eliminate the possibility of civilian collateral damage; (c) not be prohibited under the 2002 US National Security Strategy (§10.2); and (d) arguably fall within the necessity and proportionality limitations imposed by Customary International Law.

The Bush administration's proposed budget for FY 2006 contains appropriation lines for resuming research on the nuclear bunker-buster. This plan presents the issue of whether such research is illegal under the disarmament obligations established by the Treaty on the Non-Proliferation of Nuclear Weapons (NPT). Article VI of the NPT states: "Each of the Parties to the Treaty undertakes to pursue negotiations in good faith on effective measures relating to cessation of the nuclear arms race at an early date and to nuclear disarmament, and on a Treaty on general and complete disarmament under strict and effective international control." The treaty is available at: <http://www.fas.org/nuke/control/npt/text/npt2.htm>.

The United States is expected to press for tougher global rules on the spread of nuclear weapons and the fuel-cycle technology needed to produce weapons-usable fissile materials. Its main concerns include North Korea's threatened withdrawal from the NPT, its assertion that it has nuclear weapons, nuclear activities being undertaken by Iran, and the threat of terrorist acquisition of nuclear weapons. But the 2002 NSS does not mention its potential use of bunker busters. For a very useful analysis, see A Grotto, ASIL Insight: Nuclear Bunker-Busters and Article VI of the Non-Proliferation Treaty, available at: <http://www.asil.org/insights/2005/02/insight050217.html>.

Two students or groups will debate whether or not the US use of bunker busters would violate International Law.

Problem 10.F (after §10.5) The border separating the hypothetical nations of North Alpha and South Bravo is lined with military installations on both sides.

Both nations are members of the United Nations. Alpha and Bravo recently signed a bilateral treaty in which they agreed that neither State may use coercive measures of an economic or political character. They further agreed that neither could force its sovereign will of the other State, nor attempt to use force to obtain advantages of any kind.

Their international relations are now very poor. A small band of Alpha's military troops covertly crossed the border into Bravo and disappeared into Bravo's heartland. Bravo's leader learns about this clandestine military operation and decides that he must respond to this threat. He takes some prominent visiting Alpha citizens as hostages. He then announces that they will remain under house arrest in an unknown location in Bravo. The Alpha troops in Bravo are given an ultimatum by Bravo's leader in a widely broadcasted radio and television message: The Alpha soldiers must surrender to Bravo authorities, or the Alpha civilian hostages will be executed, one each day, until Alpha's troops surrender.

Alpha's military forces in Bravo decide *not* to surrender. Instead, they plan a hostage-rescue mission. An Alpha military plane, loaded with specially trained Alpha soldiers, flies into Bravo to assist them. All of the Alpha soldiers in Bravo then join forces at a predetermined rendezvous point, near the city where the Alpha citizens are being held. Bravo is not surprised. Bravo's military troops ambush and kill all of the Alpha soldiers. Bravo's leader then orders the mass execution of all Alpha hostages.

Did Alpha's rescue mission violate any international norms? Was there any justification?

Problem 10.G (after §10.7 at end of chapter) Assume that there is going to be another terrorist strike in Baghdad—one of many on United States and Iraqi soldiers and police in Iraq—but this time on the magnitude of 9-11. The US military captures Abu Musab al-Zarqawi, the leader of al-Qaida in Iraq, and the world's second most-wanted person. He is sent to the US military base in Cuba. President Bush immediately determines that al-Zarqawi is an "unlawful combatant." Mr. al-Zarqawi is the most valuable asset ever captured by the United States.

You are the most skilled military interrogator in the US military forces. You learn from other sources about al-Zarkawi's planned nuclear attack of Baghdad. What are your options or limitations for interrogating al-Zarkawi? Assigned students will serve as military liaisons, who will provide you with a brief synopsis of this chapter's mate-

rials on each of the following matters: military necessity and proportionality; the Geneva Conventions; the UN Torture Convention; the 2002 US National Security Strategy; the US president's first obligation as Commander-in-Chief to ensure national security; and Professor Bacchus' perspectives in *The Garden*. You are now ready to interrogate al-Zarqawi, who is known for his ability to withstand extraordinary physical torture. Failure to obtain the information you need will likely result in major coalition casualties, for great distances from the epicenter in Baghdad. What will you do?

◆ BIBLIOGRAPHY

§10.1 Defining "Force" and Its Role

W. Butler, THE NON-USE OF FORCE IN INTERNATIONAL LAW (Dordrecht, Neth.: Martinus Nijhoff, 1989)

J. Ciment (ed.), ENCYCLOPEDIA OF CONFLICTS SINCE WORLD WAR II (Sharpe Reference, 1999) (four volumes)

E. Corr & S. Sloan (eds.), LOW-INTENSITY CONFLICT: OLD THREATS IN A NEW WORLD (Boulder, CO: Westview Press, 1992)

W. Dixon, Democracy and the Peaceful Settlement of International Conflict, 88 AMER. POL. SCI. REV. 14 (1994)

D. Gambetta, MAKING SENSE OF SUICIDE MISSIONS (Oxford, Eng.: Oxford Univ. Press, 2005)

B. Jankovic, International Conflicts, ch. 4, in PUBLIC INTERNATIONAL LAW 347 (Dobbs Ferry, NY: Transnat'l Pub., 1984) (Balkan perspective)

Robert Jervis, Theories of War in An Era of Leading Power Peace: Presidential Address, Amer. Political Science Association, 2001, 96 AMER. POL. SCI. Rev. 1 (2002)

A. Rifat, INTERNATIONAL AGGRESSION: A STUDY OF THE LEGAL CONCEPT: ITS DEVELOPMENT AND DEFINITION IN INTERNATIONAL LAW (Stockholm: Almqvist & Wiksell Int'l, 1979)

§10.2 UN Principles on Force

Y. Arai-Takahashi, Shifting Boundaries of the Right of Self-Defence–Appraising the Impact of the September 11—Attacks, 36 INT'L LAWYER 1081 (2002)

L. Damrosch & B. Oxman, Editors' Introduction: Agora: Future Implications of the Iraq Conflict, 97 AMER. J INT'L L 553 (2003)

C. Gray, INTERNATIONAL LAW AND THE USE OF FORCE (2d ed. Oxford, Eng.: Oxford Univ. Press, 2004)

I. Johnstone, AFTERMATH OF THE GULF WAR: AN ASSESSMENT OF UN ACTION (Boulder, CO: Lynne Reinner, (1994)

A. Lowenfeld, Unilateral Sanctions Versus Collective Sanctions: An American's Perception, ch. 5, in V. Gowlland-Debbas (ed.), UNITED NATIONS SANCTIONS AND INTERNATIONAL LAW 95 (Hague: Kluwer, 2004)

J. Moore, Panel: The Bush Administration Preemption Doctrine and the Future of World Order, in American Society of

International Law, PROCEEDINGS OF THE 98TH ANNUAL MEETING 325 (Wash., DC ASIL, 2004)

S. Scott & R. Withana, The Relevance of International Law for Foreign Policy Decision-making When National Security is at Stake: Lessons Learned from the Cuban Missile Crisis, 3 CHINESE J. INT'L L. 163 (2004)

R. Wolfrum, The Attack of September 11, 2001, the Wars Against the Taliban and Iraq: Is There a Need to Reconsider International Law on the Recourse to Force and the Rules in Armed Conflict?, in A. Bogdandy & R. Wolfrum (ed.), MAX PLANCK YEARBOOK OF UNITED NATIONS LAW 1–78 (2004)

J. Yoo, Using Force, 71 UNIV. CHI. L. REV. 729 (2004)

§10.3 Peacekeeping Operations

D. Daniel & B. Hayes (eds.), BEYOND TRADITIONAL PEACEKEEPING (New York: St. Martin's Press, 1995)

L. Davis, PEACEKEEPING AND PEACEMAKING AFTER THE COLD WAR (Santa Monica, CA: Rand Inst., 1993)

P. Diehl, INTERNATIONAL PEACEKEEPING (Baltimore: Johns Hopkins Press, 1993)

W. Durch (ed.), THE EVOLUTION OF UN PEACEKEEPING: CASE STUDIES AND COMPARATIVE ANALYSIS (New York: St. Martin's Press, 1993)

G. Knoops, THE PROSECUTION AND DEFENSE OF PEACEKEEPERS UNDER INTERNATIONAL CRIMINAL LAW (Ardsley, NY: Transnat'l, 2004)

§10.4 Multilateral Agreements

D. Bourantonis, THE UNITED NATIONS AND THE QUEST FOR NUCLEAR DISARMAMENT (Brookfield, VT: Dartmouth, 1993)

S. Croft (ed.), THE CONVENTIONAL ARMED FORCES IN EUROPE TREATY: THE COLD WAR ENDGAME (Brookfield, VT: Dartmouth, 1994)

D. Dahlitz & D. Dicke (eds.), THE INTERNATIONAL LAW OF ARMS CONTROL AND DISARMAMENT (New York: UN, 1991) (symposium)

D. Paul (ed.), DISARMAMENTS MISSION DIMENSION: A UN AGENCY TO ADMINISTER MULTILATERAL TREATIES (Toronto: S. Stevens, 1990)

R. Powell, Crisis Bargaining, Escalation and MAD, 81 AMER. POL. SCI. REV. 717 (1987)

D. Schindler & J. Toman (ed.), THE LAW OF ARMED CONFLICT: A COLLECTION OF CONVENTIONS, RESOLUTIONS AND OTHER DOCUMENTS (4th ed. Leiden, Neth.: Martinus Nijhoff, 2004)

S. Teifenbrun, A Semiotic Approach to a Legal Definition of Terrorism, Symposium–The Challenge of September 11: International Law and the Control of Violence, 9 ILSA J. INT'L & COMP. L 357 (2003)

§10.5 Humanitarian Intervention

J. Holzgrefe & R. Keohane (ed.), HUMANITARIAN INTERVENTION: ETHICAL, LEGAL, AND POLITICAL DILEMMAS (Cambridge, Eng.: Cambridge Univ. Press, 2003)

A. Kuperman, THE LIMITS OF HUMANITARIAN INTERVENTION: GENOCIDE IN RWANDA (Wash., DC: Brookings Inst., 2001)

J. Moore (ed.), HARD CHOICES: MORAL DILEMMAS IN HUMANITARIAN INTERVENTION (Lanham, MD: Rowman & Littlefield, 1998)

P. Schraeder, INTERVENTION IN THE 1990S: US FOREIGN POLICY IN THE THIRD WORLD (Boulder, CO: Lynne Reinner Pub., 1992)

F. Teson, HUMANITARIAN INTERVENTION: AN INQUIRY INTO LAW AND MORALITY (3d ed. Irvington, NY: Transnat'l, 2005)

§10.6 Laws of War: Traditional Applications

M. Danner, TORTURE AND THE TRUTH: AMERICA, ABU GRAHIB, AND THE WAR ON TERROR (New York: New York Review Books, 2004)

L. Green, ESSAYS ON THE MODERN LAW OF WAR (2d ed. Ardsley, NY: Transnat'l, 1999)

J. Henckaerts & L. Doswald-Beck (ed.), CUSTOMARY INTERNATIONAL HUMANITARIAN LAW (Cambridge, Eng.: Cambridge Univ. Press, 2005)

L. Henkin et al., The Law of War and the Control of Weapons in International Law, in INTERNATIONAL LAW: CASES AND MATERIALS 1054 (4th ed. St. Paul: West, 2001)

W. Krutzsch & R. Trapp, A COMMENTARY ON THE CHEMICAL WEAPONS CONVENTION (Dordrecht, Neth.: Martinus Nijhoff, 1994)

T. McCormack & G. Simpson, THE LAW OF WAR CRIMES: NATIONAL AND INTERNATIONAL APPROACHES (The Hague, Neth.: Kluwer Law Int'l, 1997)

M. McDougal & F. Feliciano, THE INTERNATIONAL LAW OF WAR: TRANSNATIONAL COERCION AND WORLD PUBLIC ORDER (Dordrecht, Neth.; Boston: Martinus Nijhoff, 1994)

J. Moore & R. Turner, NATIONAL SECURITY LAW (2d ed. Durham, NC: Carolina, 2004)

M. Osiel, OBEYING ORDERS: ATROCITY, MILITARY DISCIPLINE & THE LAW OF WAR (New Brunswick, NJ: Transaction Publishers, 1998)

N. Quenivet, SEXUAL OFFENSES IN ARMED CONFLICT AND INTERNATIONAL LAW (Ardsley, NY: Transnat'l, 2005)

§10.7 Laws of War: Post-9-11 US Applications

G. Aldrich, The Taliban, Al Qaeda, and the Determination of Illegal Combatants, 96 AMER. J. INT'L L. 891 (2002)

G. Fox, The Occupation of Iraq, 36 GEORGETOWN J. INTL L. 195-297 (2005)

E. McWhinney, THE SEPTEMBER 11 TERRORIST ATTACKS AND THE INVASION OF IRAQ IN CONTEMPORARY INTERNATIONAL LAW: OPINIONS ON THE EMERGING NEW WORLD ORDER SYSTEM (Leiden, Neth.: Martinus Nijhoff, 2004)

J. Paust, Executive Plans and Authorizations to Violate International Law, 43 COLUM. J. TRANSNAT'L L. 811 (2005)

R. Wolfrum, The Attack of September 11, 2001, the Wars Against the Taliban and Iraq: Is There a Need to Reconsider International Law on the Recourse to Force and the Rules in Armed Conflict?, in A. Bogdandy & R. Wolfrum (ed.), 3 MAX PLANCK YEARBOOK OF UNITED NATIONS LAW 1 (Leiden, Neth.: Martinus Nijhoff, 2004)

J. Yoo, The Status of Soldiers and Terrorists under the Geneva Conventions, 3 CHINESE J. INT'L L. 135 (2004) & J. Aggelen, A Response to John C. Yoo, 4 CHINESE J. INT'L L. 167 (2005)

Electronic Resources

Bibliography of U.S. government documents related to Iraq (City College of New York): <http://www.ccny.cuny.edu/library/Divisions/Government/Iraqbib.html>

Multilateral Arms Regulation and Disarmament Agreements: <http://disarmament2.un.org/TreatyStatus.nsf>

New York Times Guide to Memos on Torture: <http://www.nytimes.com/ref/international/24MEMO-GUIDE.html>

J. Pejic, Three Misconceptions About the Laws of War, CRIMES OF WAR PROJECT MAGAZINE (Oct. 29, 2004): <http://www.crimesofwar.org/onnews/news-miscon.html>

G. Ratteray, STRATEGIC WARFARE IN CYBERSPACE (Cambridge, MA: MIT Press, 2001) US Government Documents on Iraq: <http://www.ccny.cuny.edu/library/Divisions/Government/Iraqbib.html>

◆ ENDNOTES

1. See The Historic Development of International Law on the Use of Force, ch. 3–4, in M. O'Connell, INTERNATIONAL LAW AND THE USE OF FORCE: CASES AND MATERIALS 105 (New York: Foundation Press, 2005).

2. Gen. Ass. Reso. 2625(XXXV 1970), reprinted in 9 INT'L LEGAL MAT'LS 1292 (1970).

3. Gen. Ass. Reso. 42/22 (1987), reprinted in 27 INT'L LEGAL MAT'LS 1672 (1988).

4. The Court's famous passage regarding "hard-core pornography" is: "I shall not today attempt further to define the kinds of material I understand to be embraced within that shorthand description; and perhaps I could never succeed in intelligibly doing so. But I know it when I see it. . . ." Jacobellis v. Ohio, 378 U.S. 184, 197, 84 S.Ct. 1676, 1683, 12 L.Ed.2d 793 (1964) (Justice Stewart, concurring).

5. See M. Bassiouni, Articles 6–8, THE STATUTE OF THE INTERNATIONAL CRIMINAL COURT: A DOCUMENTARY HISTORY 40–45 (Ardsley, NY: Transnational, 1998) & The Rome Statute of the International Criminal Court, available on the Court's Web site at: <http://www.icc-cpi.int/about.html>, click Rome Statute.

6. M. Gomaa, The Definition of the Crime of Aggression and the ICC Jurisdiction over that Crime, ch. 5 in M. Polti & G. Nesi (ed.), THE INTERNATIONAL CRIMINAL COURT AND THE CRIME OF AGGRESSION 56 (Aldershot, Eng.: Ashgate, 2004).

7. For some background, and the Bush plan to scale back US troops, see J. Broke & T. Shanker, U.S. May Cut Third of Troops in South Korea, New York Times on the Web, June 8, 2004.

8. *Constitution:* "The Congress shall have Power To . . . grant Letters of Marque and Reprisal. . . ." US CONST., Art. I, Sec. 8, cl. 11. *UN:* Gen. Ass. Reso. 2625(XXXV), Part 1 Principles (1970).

9. *See* The Development of the Doctrine of Reprisals in the Seventeenth and Eighteenth Centuries, ch. 1, in O. Elagab, THE LEGALITY OF NON-FORCIBLE COUNTER-MEASURES IN INTERNATIONAL LAW (Oxford, Eng.: Clarendon Press, 1988).

10. *See generally* J. Crawford, The Relationship Between Sanctions and Countermeasures, ch. 2., in V. Gowlland-Debbas (ed.), UNITED NATIONS SANCTIONS AND INTERNATIONAL LAW 57 (The Hague: Kluwer, 2004) [hereinafter *UN Sanctions*].

11. M. Krinsky & D. Golove (ed.), United States Economic Measures Against Cuba: Proceedings in the United Nations and International Law Issues (Northampton, MA: Altheia Press, 1993).

12. The Palestinian National Charter: Resolutions of the Palestine National Council July 1-17, 1968, Articles 19 & 20, available at: <http://www.isracl.org/mfa/go.asp?MFAH00pv0>.

13. *See* S. Doyle, International Boycotts, in V. Nanda, THE LAW OF TRANSNATIONAL BUSINESS TRANSACTIONS 13–14 (New York: Clark Boardman, 1984).

14. *Arguable applicability* to all *persons of Jewish faith*: 3 A. Lowenfeld, International Economic Law: Trade for Political Ends 314 (New York: Clark Boardman, 1983). *Laws punishing compliance*: See H. Fenton, United States Antiboycott Laws: An Assessment of Their Impact Ten Years after Adoption, 10 HASTINGS INT'L & COMP. L. REV. 211 (1987) & P. Areeda, Remarks on the Arab Boycott, 54 TEXAS L. R. 1432 (1976).

15. See M. Malloy, UNITED STATES ECONOMIC SANCTIONS: THEORY AND PRACTICE (The Hague: Kluwer, 2001).

16. See, e.g., N. MacFarquhar, An Anti-American Boycott is Growing in the Arab World, New York Times on the Web (May 10, 2002).

17. *See, e.g.,* a representative comment of one critic that "American administrations have exaggerated the Soviet threat so as to keep in line their allies in the North and their clients in the South." Introduction, G. Arnold, WARS IN THE THIRD WORLD SINCE 1945 xii (London: Casell, 1991).

18. Dept. of the Army and the Air Force, Military Operations in Low Intensity Conflict, ARMY FIELD MANUAL 100–20 and AIR FORCE PAMPHLET 3–20, p. 1 (Dec. 1990). *See generally* C. Lynch, Survey: Warfare has become far less deadly in the 21st century, Wash. Post (Oct. 19, 2005).

19. Commission on Integrated Long-Term Strategy, DISCRIMINATE DETERRENCE 2–3 (Wash., DC: US Gov't Print. Off., 1988).

20. Aristotle, NICHOMACHAEAN ETHICS 329 (New York: Penguin, 1976) (H. Tredennick revision, J. Thompson translation).

21. W. Reisman, Private Armies in a Global War System: Prologue to Decision, in M. McDougal & W. Reisman, INTERNATIONAL LAW ESSAYS 142, 154–155 (Mineola, NY: Foundation Press, 1981).

22. War as a *Lawful* Instrument of National Policy, 2 OPPENHEIM'S INTERNATIONAL LAW 177–178 (Essex, Eng.: Longman, 7th ed. 1952) (H. Lauterpaucht edition).

23. *See* M. Mandelbaum, THE FATE OF NATIONS: THE SEARCH FOR NATIONAL SECURITY IN THE NINETEENTH AND TWENTIETH CENTURIES (New York: Cambridge Univ. Press, 1988).

24. On Protracted War (May 1938), ch. 5 On War and Peace, reprinted in QUOTATIONS FROM CHAIRMAN MAO TSE-TUNG, in 59 (2d ed. Peking: Foreign Language Press, 1966).

25. *See* G. Tunkin, Law Functioning in the International System, ch. 2, in LAW AND FORCE IN THE INTERNATIONAL SYSTEM 43, 80 (Moscow: Progress Publ., 1983) (1985 English translation). *See also* E. McWhinney, The Renewed Vitality of the International Law Principles of Peaceful Co-existence in the Post-Iraq Invasion Era: The 50th anniversary of the China/India Pancha Shila Agreement, 3 CHINESE J. INT'L L. 379 (2005).

26. D. Greig, The Use of Force by States, ch. 16, in INTERNATIONAL LAW 867 (2d ed. London: Butterworths, 1976).

27. D. Nowlin & R. Stupak, WAR AS AN INSTRUMENT OF FOREIGN POLICY: PAST, PRESENT, AND FUTURE (Lanham, MD: Univ. Press of Amer., 1998).

28. B. Blechman & S. Kaplan, FORCE WITHOUT WAR 16 (Wash., DC: Brookings Inst., 1978). For both older and more recent data, see R. Grimmett, Instances of Use of United States Armed Forces Abroad, 1798–2004 (Wash, DC: Congressional Research Service, 2004), available at: <http://www.au.af.mil/au/awc/awcgate/crs/rl30172.pdf>. For the text of all related US declarations, see D. Ackerman & R. Grimmett, Declarations of War and Authorizations for the Use of Military Force: Historical Background and Legal Implications, (Wash, DC: Congressional Research Service, 2003 revision), available at: <http://www.ndu.edu/library/docs/crs/crs_rl31133_14jan03.pdf>.

29. A. Al-Anbari, The Impact of United Nations Sanctions on Economic Development, Human Rights and Civil Society, ch. 27, in *UN Sanctions* (cited in note 10 above), at 371–372.

30. M. Smith, Blair Hit by New Leak of Secret War Plan, London Times Online, May 1, 2005, available at: <http://www.timesonline.co.uk/article/0,2087-1592904,00.html>.

31. Iraq destroyed its illicit weapons stockpiles several months after the first Persian Gulf War. For details, see D. Jehl, U.S. Reports Finds that Iraqis Eliminated Illicit Arms in 90's, New York Times on the Web (Oct. 7, 2004).

32. Contemporary resources for analyzing this, and related issues in this self-defense section, include: S. Alexandrov, SELF-DEFENSE AGAINST THE USE OF FORCE IN INTERNATIONAL LAW (The Hague, Neth.: Kluwer, 1996); R. Amer, THE UNITED NATIONS AND FOREIGN MILITARY INTERVENTIONS: A COMPARATIVE STUDY OF THE APPLICATION OF THE CHARTER (Uppsala, Sweden: Uppsala Univ., 1992); D. Daniel & B. Hayes, COERCIVE INDUCEMENT AND THE CONTAINMENT OF INTERNATIONAL CRISES (Wash., DC: US Inst. Peace, 1999); and D. Sarooshi, THE UNITED NATIONS AND THE DEVELOPMENT OF COLLECTIVE SECURITY: THE DELEGATION OF THE UN SECURITY COUNCIL OF ITS CHAPTER VII POWERS (Oxford, Eng.: Oxford Univ. Press, 2000).

33. Further details on pre-Charter applications are available in M. Occelli, 'Sinking' the Caroline: Why the Caroline Doctrine's Restrictions on Self-Defense Should Not Be Regarded as Customary International Law, 4 SAN DIEGO INT'L. L.J. 467 (2003); T. Kearley, Raising the Caroline, 17 WISC. INT'L L.J. 325 (1999); and The Caroline Exchange of Diplomatic Notes between Great Britain and the United States (1842), 2 J. Moore, DIGEST OF INTERNATIONAL LAW 409, 412 (1906).

34. *Quote:* The Place of Necessity and Proportionality in Restraints on the Forceful Actions of States, Ch. 1, in J. Gardam, NECESSITY, PROPORTIONALITY AND THE USE OF FORCE BY STATES 25–27 (Cambridge, Eng.: Cambridge Univ. Press, 2004). *2001 US National Security Strategy*: <http://www.whitehouse.gov/nsc/print/nssall.html>, Sept. 17, 2002.

35. C. Allan, Panel Reporter, on Remarks of Oscar Schachter, Implementing Limitations on the Use of Force: the Doctrine of Proportionality and Necessity, 86 AMER. SOC. INT'L L. PROCEEDINGS 39 (1982).

36. O. Schachter, The Right of States to Use Armed Force, 82 MICH. L. REV. 1620, 1633 (1984).

37. Further details are available in Exceptions to the Prohibition of the Use of Force, ch. 7–10, in Y. Dinstein, WAR, AGGRESSION AND SELF-DEFENCE (3d ed. Cambridge, Eng.: Cambridge Univ. Press, 2001).

38. Report of the Special Committee on the Definition of Aggression, 12 UN GEN. ASS. OFF. REC. (SUPP. NO. 16) 13 (1956). Details are available in H. McCoubrey & N. White, Aggression and Armed Attack, ch. 3, in INTERNATIONAL LAW AND ARMED CONFLICT 39 (Brookfield, VT: Dartmouth Pub., 1992).

39. D. Greig, INTERNATIONAL LAW 892–893 (2d ed. London: Butterworths, 1976) (italics added).

40. B. Simma (ed.), Anticipatory Self-Defense, under Article 51, in THE CHARTER OF THE UNITED NATIONS: A COMMENTARY 675 (New York: Oxford Univ. Press, 1995) [hereinafter *Simma*].

41. L. Meeker, Defensive Quarantine and the Law, 57 AMER. J. INT'L L. 515, 523 (1963).

42. C. Li-hai, American Imperialism Tramples on International Law, Chinese People's Daily, Nov. 14, 1962, at 4; reprinted in Vol. 2 J. Cohen & H. Chiu, PEOPLE'S CHINA AND INTERNATIONAL LAW: A DOCUMENTARY STUDY 1461–1464 (Princeton: Princeton Univ. Press, 1974).

43. UN Secretary-General, AGENDA FOR PEACE 8–9 (New York: UN, 1995).

44. The following textual excerpts indicate that Russia is not in favor of the US National Defense Strategy. However, its Defense Minister stated in September 2004 that Russia reserved the right to carry out pre-emptive strikes, in the aftermath of the Chechen rebel-initiated child-hostage situation in Southern Russia—where 330 civilian hostages died ten days earlier. For story, see V. Isachenkov, Pre-emptive Strikes Threatened by Russia, Associated Press (Sept. 13, 2004).

45. C. Moxley, Jr., NUCLEAR WEAPONS AND INTERNATIONAL LAW IN THE POST COLD WAR WORLD 250 (Lanham, MD: Austin & Winfield, 2000).

46. *2000 announcement:* see M. Evans, Russia alters rules on using nuclear arms, The London Times (Jan 15, 2000), available on Lexis Nexis news database. *2002 announcement:* M. Wines, Moscow Miffed Over Missile Shield but Others Merely Shrug, New York Times on the Web (Dec. 19, 2002) & Associated Press, China Concerned by Missile Defense Plan, New York Times on the Web (Dec. 19, 2002).

47. Military and Paramilitary Activities in and Against Nicaragua, (Nicaragua v. United States), 1986 *ICJ Rep.* 14, para. 208–209 (italics added) [hereinafter *Nicaragua Case*].

48. The various Gulf War resolutions and numerous related documents are collected in W. Weller (ed.), IRAQ AND KUWAIT: THE HOSTILITIES AND THEIR AFTERMATH (Cambridge, Eng.: Grotius Pub., 1993) [hereinafter *Hostilities*].

49. S.C. Reso. 660 (2 August 1990) and 661 (6 August 1990), both available at: <http://www.un.org/Docs/scres/1990/661e.pdf>.

50. A detailed account of the relevant UN "Kuwait" resolutions, and supporting national materials, is available in *Hostilities* (cited in note 48 above).

51. D. Sheffer, Commentary on Collective Security, ch. 8, in L. Damrosch & D. Scheffer (ed.), LAW AND FORCE IN THE NEW INTERNATIONAL ORDER 101, 103–104 (Boulder, CO: Westview Press, 1991) [hereinafter *Law and Force*].

52. Y. Matsui, The Gulf War and the United Nations Security Council, ch. 36, in R. MacDonald (ed.), ESSAYS IN HONOUR OF WANG TIEYA 511 (Dordrecht, Neth.: Martinus Nijhoff, 1994).

53. *See* <http://cnn.com/WORLD/9802/23/un.iraq.agreement/index.html>.

54. D. Schweigman, Former Yugoslavia 1991–2000, §3.6, in THE AUTHORITY OF THE SECURITY COUNCIL UNDER CHAPTER VII OF THE UN CHARTER: LEGAL LIMITS AND THE ROLE OF THE INTERNATIONAL COURT OF JUSTICE 111 (The Hague: Kluwer, 2001).

55. See N. Azimi & Chang Li Lin, THE UNITED NATIONS TRANSITIONAL ADMINISTRATION IN EAST TIMOR (Leiden, Neth.: Martinus Nijhoff, 2003).

56. *See* Symposium: State Reconstruction After Civil Conflict: M. Matheson, United Nations Governance of Postconflict Societies, 95 AMER J. INT'L L. 76 (2001) & H. Strohmeyer, Collapse and Reconstruction of a Judicial System: The United Nations Missions in Kosovo and East Timor, 95 AMER. J. INT'L L. 46 (2001).

57. S.C. Reso. 1244, U.N. SCOR, 54th Sess., 4011th mtg., U.N. DOC. S/RES/1244 (1999), available at: <http://www.un.org/Docs/scres/1999/99sc1244.htm>.

58. W. Betts, S. Carlson, and G. Gisvold, THE POST-CONFLICT TRANSITIONAL ADMINISTRATION OF KOSOVO AND THE LESSONS-LEARNED IN EFFORTS TO ESTABLISH A JUDICIARY AND RULE OF LAW 371, 372–373 (2001). *See generally* H. Krieger, THE KOSOVO CONFLICT AND INTERNATIONAL LAW: AN ANALYTICAL DOCUMENTATION 1974–1999 (Cambridge, Eng.: Cambridge Univ. Press, 2001).

59. B. Boutros-Ghali, Agenda for Peace 25–26 (New York: UN, 1992). and *1995 Supplement* at 55–56.

60. Opening Statement of Dr. Edward Warner before the Senate Armed Services Subcommittee on Coalition Defense and Reinforcing Forces, in US Department of Defense Statement on Peacekeeping, 33 INT'L LEGAL MAT'LS 814 (1994). *See also* D. Scheffer, US Administration Policy on Reforming Multilateral Peace Operations, 33 INT'L LEGAL MAT'LS 795 (1994); and US Department of State Statement on the Legal Authority for UN Peace Operations, 33 INT'L LEGAL MAT'LS 821 (1994).

61. See, e.g., C. Chinkin, Women and Peace: Militarism and Oppression, in K. Mahoney & P. Mahoney (ed.), HUMAN RIGHTS IN THE TWENTY-FIRST CENTURY: A GLOBAL CHALLENGE 408 (Leiden, Neth: Martinus Nijhoff, 1993); E. Kohn, Rape as a Weapon of War: Women's Human Rights During the Dissolution of Yugoslavia, 12 AUSTRALIAN YEARBOOK INT'L L. 205 (1992); and A. Hoiberg, The Other Victims of the Iraq War, San Diego Union Tribune (Aug. 26, 2004), available at: <http://www.signonsandiego.com/uniontrib/20040826/news_lz1e26holberg.html>.

62. K. Askin, The Evolution of the Status of Women in Domestic and International Law and Practice, in WAR CRIMES AGAINST WOMEN: PROSECUTION IN INTERNATIONAL WAR CRIMES TRIBUNALS 204, at 216–217 (The Hague: Kluwer, 1997).

63. K. Askin, A Decade of Development of Gender Crimes in International Courts and Tribunals: 1993–2003, 11 HUMAN RIGHTS BRIEF 16 (Wash., DC: Amer. Univ., 2004).

64. Statute of the ICC, Appendix I, Article 7.1(g) (humanity); Article 8.2(b)(xxii) (war crimes); and (e)(vi) (other serious violations).

65. N. Ronzitti, OSCE Peace-Keeping, ch. 8, in M. Bothe et al. (eds.), THE OSCE IN THE MAINTENANCE OF PEACE AND SECURITY: CONFLICT PREVENTION, CRISIS MANAGEMENT AND PEACEFUL SETTLEMENT OF DISPUTES 250–251 (The Hague, Neth.: Kluwer, 1997).

66. <http://www.un.org/Depts/dpko/dpko/ops.htm>, click <u>Completed Operations & Current Operations.</u>

67. United Nations Millennium Declaration, A/55/L.2 (Sept. 6, 2000) (Heads of State Summit at UN HQ in New York).

68. Report of the UN High-level Panel on Threats, Challenges and Change A More Secure World: Our Shared Responsibility (Dec. 2, 2004), available at : <http://www.un.org/secureworld> click <u>Document</u> [hereinafter *High-level Report*].

69. *See* G. Garvey, United Nations Peacekeeping and Host State Consent, 64 AMER. J. INT'L LAW 642 (1984).

70. A succinct, authoritative account of the UN Charter drafting process, including Article 43, is available in *Simma,* at 636 (cited in note 40 above).

71. W. Durch (ed.), THE EVOLUTION OF UN PEACEKEEPING 7 (New York: St. Martin's Press, 1993) (italics added).

72. A detailed account is provided in D. Neff, WARRIORS AT SUEZ (New York: Simon & Schuster, 1981).

73. This account is provided in J. McNeill, Commentary on Dispute Resolution Mechanisms in Arms Control Agreements, ch. 26, in *Law and Force* (cited in note 51 above), at 258–259.

74. League of Nations Covenant, available at: <http://www.yale.edu/lawweb/avalon/league/league.htm>.

75. An account of this incident is provided in Spencer, The Italian-Ethiopian Dispute and the League of Nations, 31 AMER. J. INT'L L. 614 (1937).

76. The legality of war and the law of armed conflict, ch. 1, in L. Green, THE CONTEMPORARY LAW OF ARMED CONFLICT 3 (2d ed. Manchester, Eng.: Juris Pub., 2000) (see subsections on *Criminalizing war*).

77. *See, e.g.*, T. Shanker, Russian Official Cautions U.S. on Use of Central Asian Bases, New York Times on the Web (Oct. 10, 2003).

78. John Stuart Mill, A Few Words on Non-Intervention (1859), reprinted in ESSAYS ON POLITICS AND CULTURE 382 (New York: Doubleday, 1962).

79. *Commission:* This private Canadian-based entity reported to the UN Secretary-General, and has completed its mission. The Government of Canada continues to lead follow up efforts on the findings of the commission. *Principle:* Synopsis: The Responsibility to Protect: Report of the International Commission on Intervention and State Sovereignty XI (Ottowa: Int'l Devel. Res. Centre, 2001), available at: <http://www.iciss.ca/report-en.asp>. *Just cause: Id.*, at XII (bolding in original text). *Case quote: Nicaragua Case* (cited in note 47 above), at p.14, para. 124.

80. B. Vukas, Humanitarian Intervention and International Responsibility, ch. 21, in M. Ragazzi (ed.), INTERNATIONAL RESPONSIBILITY TODAY: ESAYS IN MEMORY OF OSCAR SCHACHTER 235, at 237 (Leiden, Neth.: Martinus Nijhoff, 2005).

81. *UN High-level Report* (cited in note 68 above).

82. N. Wheeler, SAVING STRANGERS: HUMANITARIAN INTERVENTION IN INTERNATIONAL SOCIETY (Oxford, Eng.: Oxford Univ. Press, 2002).

83. *Historical background:* J. Fonteyne, The Customary International Law Doctrine of Humanitarian Intervention, 4 CALIF. WEST. INT'L L.J. 203 (1974). *Varied definitions*: Bazyler, Reexamining the Doctrine of Humanitarian Intervention in Light of the Atrocities in Kampuchea and Ethiopia, 23 STANFORD J. INT'L L. 547 (1987).

84. *See* T. Franck & N. Rodley, After Bangladesh: The Law of Humanitarian Intervention by Military Force, 67 AMER. J. INT'L L. 275, 285 (1973).

85. S. Murphy, HUMANITARIAN INTERVENTION: THE UNITED NATIONS IN AN EVOLVING WORLD ORDER 8–10 (Phila., PA: Univ. Pennsylvania Press, 1996). This book was written while the author was on leave at the University of Virginia School of Law.

86. *Humanitarian purposes:* Article 55(c). *Action pledge:* Article 56.

87. 2 THIRD RESTATEMENT OF THE LAW OF THE FOREIGN RELATIONS LAW OF THE UNITED STATES §703, Comment *e*. Humanitarian intervention to rescue victims or suppress human rights violations, at 177 (St. Paul, MN: Amer. Law Inst., 1987).

88. *See* R. Lillich (ed.), HUMANITARIAN INTERVENTION AND THE UNITED NATIONS (Charlottesville, Va.: Univ. Press of Va., 1973).

89. *Nicaragua Case,* para. 242 (cited in note 47 above) (italics added).

90. A. Schnabel & R. Thakur (ed.), KOSOVO AND THE CHALLENGE OF HUMANITARIAN INTERVENTION (Tokyo: UN Univ. Press, 2000).

91. *UN Prosecutor Report:* Final Report to the Prosecutor by the Committee Established to Review the NATO Bombing Campaign Against the Federal Republic of Yugoslavia, printed in 39 INT'L LEGAL MAT'LS 1257 (Sept., 2000 issue) and <http://www.un.org/icty/pressreal/nato061300.htm>. *House of Commons Report:* Foreign Affairs Fourth Report, Session 1999–2000, at: <http://www.publications.parliament.uk/pa/cm199900/cmselect/cmfaff/28/2802.htm>. Amnesty International Report: <http://web.amnesty.org>, search "NATO Bombings."

92. UN Gen. Ass. Reso. 43/131, Dec. 8, 1988; 45/100, July 29, 1991; 46/182, Dec. 19, 1991.

93. D. Schindler, Humanitarian Assistance, Humanitarian Interference and International Law, ch. 46, in R. Macdonald (ed.), ESSAYS IN HONOUR OF WANGTIEYA 689, 700 (Dordrecht, Neth.; Boston: Martinus Nijhoff, 1994).

94. These accounts are provided in *Historical Background,* ch. 1, in H. Levie, TERRORISM IN WAR: THE LAW OF WAR CRIMES 9–10 (Dobbs Ferry, NY: Oceana, 1992).

95. Abdullah Yusef Ali, THE HOLY QUR'AN: TEXT, TRANSLATION AND COMMENTARY (rev. 1989 ed.), Al Baqarah, Surah 2, n.204.

96. See Development of the International Law of Conflict Management, ch. 3, in J. Moore & R. Turner, NATIONAL SECURITY LAW, at 34 (Durham, NC: Carolina Acad. Press, 2005).

97. Williams v. Bruffy, 96 U.S. 176, 186–187, 24 L.Ed. 716 (1877).

98. 1 NUREMBERG TRIAL PROCEEDINGS 313, available at: <http://www.yale.edu/lawweb/avalon/imt/proc/v1menu.htm> [hereinafter *Nuremberg Proceedings*]. The print copy of this multivolume set contains an exhaustively complete record of the lengthy proceedings. The same volumes also contain the record of the similar proceedings of the Tokyo defendants also tried by the Allies.

99. *Corfu:* 1949 ICJ Rep. 4, p. 22. *Nicaragua:* 1986 ICJ REP. 14, p.112.

100. A. Guttry & N. Ronzitti (eds.), THE IRAN-IRAQ WAR (1980–1988) and the LAW OF NAVAL WARFARE 7 (Cambridge, Eng.: Grotius, 1993).

101. 4 *Nuremberg Proceedings,* (cited in note 98 above), at 466–467, available at: <http://www.yale.edu/lawweb/avalon/imt/proc/ 01-07-46.htm>.

102. *Burning incident:* Al Skeini v. Secretary of State For Defence, High Court of Justice Queen's Bench Division, Case No: CO/2242/2004, [2004] EWHC 2911 (Admin) (2004) (claims by relatives regarding six Iraqi citizens, who died in provinces of Iraq when the UK was recognized as an occupying power). *UK Case:* E. Schmitt, Army Examining an Account of Abuse of 2 Dead Taliban, New York Times on the Web (Oct. 20, 2005). *Chemical incident:* D. Fidler, The Use of White Phosphorus Munitions by U.S. Military Forces in Iraq, ASIL Insight (Dec. 6, 2005), available at: <http://www.asil.org/insights/2005/12/insights051206.html>. *Human shield incident:* K. Bennhold, Israel Bans Use of Palestinian Civilians as Human Shields, New York Times on the Web (Oct. 6, 2005).

103. 1 *Nuremberg Proceedings* (cited in note 98 above), at 234–235 (German defendants).

104. The London Conference of 1991 is discussed in G. Plant, ENVIRONMENTAL PROTECTION AND THE LAW OF WAR: A "FIFTH GENEVA" CONVENTION ON THE PROTECTION OF THE ENVIRONMENT IN TIME OF ARMED CONFLICT (London: Belhaven Press, 1992).

105. Memorandum of the ICRC to the Governments of States Party to the Geneva Conventions and Members of the United Nations on the Application of the Geneva Conventions by the Armed Forces Placed at the Disposal of United Nations, 10 November 1961, reprinted in INTERNATIONAL REVIEW OF THE RED CROSS (Geneva: 1961).

106. UN DOC. T/SGB/1999/13, available at: <http://www.un.org/peace/st_sgb_1999_13.pdf>.

107. Protocol I: Additional to the Geneva Conventions of 12 August 1949, and Relating to the Protection of Victims of International Armed Conflicts, at: <http://www.unog.ch/frames/disarm/distreat/prt_gen.htm>.

108. This Protocol was spawned by the North Vietnamese position, in relation to its treatment of US POWs during the Viet Nam War—that the Geneva Conventions do not apply to an *internal* civil conflict—as opposed to an *international* conflict [text §11.2]. For Protocol II, see Additional to the Geneva Conventions of 12 August 1949, and Relating to the Protection of Victims of International Armed Conflicts, available at: <http://www.unog.ch/frames/disarm/distreat/prt_gen2.htm>.

109. For a thoughtful analysis, see Y. Asmin Naqvi, Doubtful Prisoner-of-War Status, 84 INT'L REV. RED CROSS (2002) (No. 847).

110. M. Swetnam, USAMA BIN LADEN'S AL-QAIDA: PROFILE OF A TERRORIST NETWORK (Ardsley, NY: Transnat'l, 2001).

111. See J. Paust, Use of Armed Force Against Terrorists in Afghanistan, Iraq, and Beyond, 35 CORNELL INT'L L.J. 533 (2002).

112. ICRC Communication No. 02/11, 8 February 2002. See Agency Differs With U.S. Over P.O.W.'s, NYT (Feb. 9, 2002).

113. Knut Dörmann, The Legal Situation of "Unlawful/Unprivileged Combatants," 85 INT'L REV. RED CROSS 45 (2003), available at: <http://www.icrc.org/Web/Eng/siteeng0.nsf/htmlall/review?OpenDocument>, click No. 849.

114. See See B. Graham & J. White, General Cites Hidden Detainees: Senators Told CIA May Have Avoided Registering Up to 100, Wash. Post (Sept. 10, 2004), at A24 & CBS News, Iraq After Saddam: CIA Detained Dozens Secretly (Aug. 10, 2004), available at: <http://www.cbsnews.com/stories/2004/09/02/iraq/main640611.shtml>.

115. *Inter-American Commission:* Precautionary Measures and Request for Information, Inter-American Commission on Human Rights (Mar, 18, 2003), available at: <http://www.derechos.org/nizkor/excep/cidhresp.html>. *Council of Europe Assembly Resolution:* Lawfulness of Detentions by the United States in Guantánamo Bay, available at: <http://assembly.coe.int/Documents/AdoptedText/TA05/ERES1433.htm>. *US case:* Ex parte McCardle, 74 U.S. 506, 19 L.Ed. 264 (1868).

116. For a succinct but comprehensive overview, see R. Wilson, Defending the Detainees at Guantanamo Bay, 12 HUMAN RIGHTS BRIEF 1 (Wash., DC: Amer. Univ., 2005).

117. In re Guantanamo Detainee Cases, 355 F.Supp.2d 443 (2005) (Taliban, but not al-Qaida have such rights) & Khalid v. Bush, 355 F.Supp.2d 311 (2005) (no detainees have such rights).

118. J. Bybee & W. Haynes, Justice Department's Office of Legal Counsel Memo, Re: Standards of Conduct for Interrogation under 18 U.S.C. 2340–2340A, available at: <http://www.washingtonpost.com/wp-dyn/articles/A38894-2004Jun13.html>, click Aug. 1, 2002, memorandum (PDF). The new 2004 memorandum is analyzed at J. Crook, Contemporary Practice of the United States Relating to International Law: Justice Department Issues New Memo on Torture, 99 AMER. J. INT'L L. 479 (2005).

119. A. Roth, Marine Can Use Justice Memos: Officer is accused in Death of Iraqi, San Diego Union Tribune (Aug. 18, 2004), available at: <http://www.signonsandiego.com>.

120. *Techniques:* J. Yoo (Deputy Assistant Attorney General), Memo to Special Counsel on Application of Treaties and Laws to al Qaida and Taliban Detainees (Jan. 9, 2002) available at: <http://www.nytimes.com/ref/international/24MEMO-GUIDE.html>, click Yoo's Memo on Avoiding Geneva Conventions. *Grotius quote* (quoting King Ovid): reprinted in M. O'Connell, CASES AND MATERIALS ON INTERNATIONAL AND THE USE OF FORCE 155 (New York: Foundaton Press, 2005). *McCain Amendment:* see various features at: <http://jurist.law.pitt.edu/currentawareness/torture.php>. *President's signing reservation:* President's Statement on Signing of H.R. 2863, the "Department of Defense, Emergency Supplemental Appropriations to Address Hurricanes in the Gulf of Mexico, and Pandemic Influenza Act," 2006, available at: <http://www.whitehouse.gov/news/releases/2005/12/20051230-8.html>.

121. *See, e.g.,* J. Waldron, Torture and Positive Law: Jurisprudence fore the White House, 105 Columbia L. Rev. 1681, 1703 (2005) *and* E. Wallach, The Logical Nexus Between the Decision to Deny Application of the Third Geneva Convention to the Taliban and Al Qaeda and the Mistreatment of Prisoners in Abu Grahib36 Case Western Reserve J. Int'l L. 537 (2005).

CHAPTER ELEVEN

Human Rights

CHAPTER OUTLINE

INTRODUCTION

The first ten chapters of this book address the diverse mechanics of International Law. The remaining chapters contain cross-cutting themes, some of which previously played a supporting role: human rights, the environment, and economic relations. Each is typically offered as a separate course in both undergraduate and law schools. This survey course in Public International Law would be incomplete without chapters that touch upon the essentials.

IN 2001, . . . THE UNITED STATES WAS VOTED OUT OF the United Nations Human Rights Commission and the International Narcotics Committee. This shows . . . that it is extremely unpopular for the United States to push double standards and unilateralism on such issues as human rights. . . . We urge the United States to change its ways, give up its hegemonic practice of creating confrontation and interfering with the internal affairs of others by exploiting the human rights issue. . . .

—Chinese Government's White Paper: Human Rights Record of the United States in 2001, Mar. 11, 2002, available at: <www.fmprc.gov.cn/eng/32296.html>.

THE [CHINESE] GOVERNMENT'S HUMAN RIGHTS record . . . remained poor and the Government continued to commit numerous and serious abuses. Authorities still were quick to suppress any person or group . . . that they perceived to be a threat to government power, or to national stability, and citizens who sought to express openly dissenting political and religious views continued to live in an environment filled with repression.

—US Department of State Bureau of Democracy, Human Rights, and Labor, Country Reports on Human Rights Practices 2001, Mar. 4, 2002, available at: <http://www.state.gov/g/drl/rls/hrrpt/2001/eap/8289.htm>.

—*Note*: both announcements were made in the same week.

After a contextual overview, this chapter traverses the terrain which scholars have designated the "International Bill of Human Rights." To stimulate an appreciation of both successes and obstacles, the remaining sections highlight prominent global and regional approaches to human rights. This chapter thus explores the culpability of various entities for human rights violations. Individuals and corporations are now receiving more attention for their inhuman wrongs. This dilating spotlight cannot be used by the State, however, to avoid its obligation as the primary guardian of International Human Rights Law.[1]

◆ **11.1 HUMAN RIGHTS IN CONTEXT**

What does the term "human rights" mean? Internationally defined, human rights cannot be withheld by any State. Judges and scholars typically describe this cornerstone of International Law as "the protection of individuals and groups against violations by governments of their internationally guaranteed rights . . . referred to as . . . international human rights law."[2]

The English Magna Carta (1215), the French Declaration of the Rights of Man (1789), and the US Constitution's Bill of Rights (1791) included inherent, inalienable rights of the individual. The French Declaration and the US Constitution incorporated one of the most fundamental of all contemporary human rights: No person shall be deprived of life, liberty, or property without due process of law. The US Constitution's Bill of Rights was a series of Constitutional amendments which guarantee freedom of religion, speech, press, and assembly—among other rights of the individual.

One must acknowledge, however, that the scope of human rights depends on the nature of the society that lays claim to them. A State's level of economic development cannot be ignored in the application of basic rights. In democratic societies, individual rights routinely focus on political rights. In lesser-developed societies, social and economic rights are the individual's primary concern. Food, shelter, health care, and a minimal education are the "human rights" of primary importance. Many individuals must therein struggle for their daily existence, just to obtain essential food and shelter. Unlike a comparatively developed nation, the government of such a society is not in as good a position to achieve the standards set forth in the fundamental human rights documents addressed in this chapter. There may be budgetary constraints on a particular government's ability to provide the full panoply of rights enjoyed in a more developed nation.

One could view World War II as "the" war that was fought to promote human rights. Certain States had deprived their inhabitants of life, liberty, and property by instituting sweeping social reforms to eliminate particular scapegoats. Germany's Nazi government deported a large portion of the German population to concentration camps in Poland and other occupied areas of Europe. Nazis totally disregarded the inherent dignity of the individual.

If anything positive can be drawn from that experience, it is that the Nazi form of fascism spawned the international consensus that the dignity of the individual is not solely a matter of State consent. After the war, States opposed to that form of government formed an international organization of States—the United Nations. A centerpiece of its *raison d'etre* would be the development of the various human rights initiatives, which are the focus of this chapter. Postwar treaties, declarations, and commentaries stand as evidence of an international moral order that now limits State discretion in the treatment of its citizens. Regimes like the white minority South African government (apartheid), Bosnian Serbs (ethnic cleansing), and Afghanistan's Taliban (religious extremism exemplified by its mistreatment of women) learned that the community of nations would initially watch from afar but ultimately take direct action to topple governments.

A brief history of human rights is provided below by a Canadian scholar. It provides a useful perspective for understanding how the contemporary international human rights regime developed; why certain States began to appreciate the importance of protecting individuals, while clinging to the Westphalian notion of State sovereignty; and in what way this renewed fervor would form the basis of contemporary UN human rights model:

The International Law of Human Rights in the Middle Twentieth Century

John Humphrey
UN DIRECTOR OF DIVISION OF HUMAN RIGHTS FROM 1946 TO 1966
IN THE PRESENT STATE OF INTERNATIONAL LAW AND OTHER ESSAYS WRITTEN IN HONOUR
OF THE CENTENARY CELEBRATION OF THE INTERNATIONAL LAW ASSOCIATION 75
(London: Int'l Law Ass'n, 1973)

I. Traditional Doctrine and Practice

[L]egal historians will surely be saying that one of the chief characteristics of mid-twentieth century international law was its sudden interest in and concern with human rights. The human rights were—and indeed still are—essentially a relationship between the State and individuals—usually its own citizens—residing in its territory . . . considered to fall within domestic jurisdiction and hence beyond the reach of international law, the norms of which governed the relations of States only. . . .

[I]n the nineteenth and early twentieth centuries an increasing number of treaties were entered into the purpose of which was to protect, if only indirectly, the rights of certain classes of people. The most important of these [treaties] were the treaties aimed at slavery and the slave trade. By 1885, it was possible to affirm, in the General Act of the Berlin Conference on Central Africa, that "trading in slaves is forbidden in conformity with the principles of international law." [This European "revelation" appeared after the success of the North in the American Civil War.] And in 1889, the Brussels Conference not only condemned slavery and the slave trade but agreed on measures for their suppression, including the granting of reciprocal rights of search, and the capture and trial of slave ships [on the high seas]. This work was continued by both the League of Nations and the United Nations. Steps were also taken in the nineteenth century for the relief of sick and wounded soldiers and prisoners of war. By the Geneva Convention of 22 August, 1864, twelve States undertook to respect the immunity of military hospitals and their staffs, to care for wounded and sick soldiers and to respect the emblem of the Red Cross. The Convention was revised in 1929 and has been widely ratified.

In 1906, the second Berne Conference opened two conventions for signature which were forerunners of the many labor conventions which, after the First World War, would be adopted by the International Labor Organization: the International Convention respecting the Prohibition of Night Work for Women in Industrial Employment and the International Convention respecting the Prohibition of the Use of White (Yellow) Phosphorus in the Manufacture of Matches.

II. The League of Nations

The peace settlement at the end of the First World War brought still more important developments. Attempts were made to enshrine human rights in the Covenant of the League of Nations. President Wilson sponsored an article on religious freedom, but when the Japanese suggested that mention also be made of the equality of nations and the just treatment of their nationals (which frightened some countries the laws of which restricted Asiatic immigration) both suggestions were withdrawn. Wilson put into his second draft an article under which the League would have required all new States to bind themselves, as a condition precedent to their recognition, to accord all racial and national minorities "exactly the same treatment and security, both in law and in fact, that is accorded the racial and national majority of their [own] people." But the Peace Conference decided that the protection of [certain] minorities . . .would be dealt with not in the Covenant but by other treaty provisions and by declarations which certain States were required to make on their [subsequent] admission to the League. . . .

Human rights were expressly dealt with in Article 23 of the Covenant. Members of the League, it said, would "endeavour to secure and maintain" fair and humane labor conditions, undertake to secure just treatment for the native inhabitants of territories under their control, and entrust the League with the supervision of agreements relating to the [slave] traffic in women and children.

Although President Wilson's suggestion that the Covenant contain a provision protecting minorities was not pursued, the Allied and Associated Powers did require certain newly created States and [other] States, the territory of which had been increased by reason of the war, to grant the enjoyment of certain human rights to all inhabitants of their territories and to protect the rights of their racial, religious and linguistic minorities. These obligations were imposed by treaty and by the declarations which certain States were required to make on their admission to the League—the provisions relating to minorities being put under the guarantee of the League Council. . . .

The League of Nations also did important work on slavery. It created a special committee to study the question, was responsible for the drafting of the Slavery Convention of 1926, and, when Ethiopia applied for readmission to the League, it required from her an undertaking to make special efforts to abolish slavery and the slave trade, Ethiopia recognizing that this was not a purely internal matter but one on which the League had a right to intervene. . . .

To sum up, international law recognized, by the beginning of the Second World War, a whole series of rules and institutions . . . the effect of which was to protect the rights of individuals and groups, even though, in the dominant theory, the individual was neither a subject of international law nor directly protected by it. International law protected the rights of aliens through their States. . . .

III. The Impact of the Second World War and the United Nations

The Second World War and the events leading up to it was the catalyst that produced the revolutionary developments in the international law of human rights that characterize the middle twentieth century. So potent was this catalyst that it produced not only an unprecedented growth in human rights law, but the very theory of international law had to be adapted to the new circumstances. The individual now becomes a subject of international law. . . . He is directly protected by this law

and can even in some cases seek his own remedy. And States can no longer rely on the plea of domestic jurisdiction [over its own citizens to avoid human rights obligations under International Law]. It was not only a matter of new norms being added within the confines of an existing order, but the very nature of that order had changed. What had happened was revolutionary.

The Second World War was, as no other war has ever been, a war to vindicate human rights. This was recognized by the leaders of the Grand Alliance and perhaps best expressed by President Roosevelt when, in January 1941, before the United States entered the war, he defined four freedoms: freedom of speech, freedom of worship, freedom from want, freedom from fear—"everywhere in the world." He said that these were "the necessary conditions of peace. . . ." Yet, when the Dumbarton Oaks Proposals [creating the blueprint for the UN] were published in the fall of 1944 they contained only the [most] general reference to human rights. The United Nations would . . . "promote respect for human rights and fundamental freedoms"—something which considering its context and the generality of the language used hardly met the expectations of a public opinion shocked by the atrocities of the war.

The relatively strong human rights provisions in the Charter . . . were largely, and appropriately, the result of determined lobbying by non-governmental organizations at the San Francisco Conference. Some of the countries represented at San Francisco would have accepted even stronger human rights provisions than found their way into the Charter. There was even an attempt, which failed, to incorporate in the Charter an International Bill of Rights. But the Charter did provide for the creation of a Commission on Human Rights which, as [US] President Truman said in the speech by which he closed the Conference, would, it was generally understood, draft the bill [of rights. The UN Economic and Social Council later established the Commission that drafted the ensuing UN human rights instruments]. . . .

Implementation systems created by treaty have the inherent weakness that they are unlikely to reach those countries where human rights are the least respected and where, therefore, they are the most needed. There is no way by which the governments of such countries can be forced to ratify the treaties. Even those governments which are the most committed to respecting human rights are cautious about committing themselves in advance to limitations on their discretionary powers; and, in the experience of the United Nations in any event, treaty provisions for implementation have been extremely limited in their scope and operation. . . . The principal characteristic of the twentieth century approach to human rights has been its unambiguous recognition of the fact that all human beings are entitled to the enjoyment not only of the traditional civil and political rights but also the economic, social and cultural rights without which, for most people, the traditional rights have little meaning. . . .

The United Nations, however, has always recognized that there is a difference between what can be expected from States in the implementation of economic and social rights and in the enforcement of civil and political rights. The former are looked upon as programme rights, [that is, mutually agreeable principles] the implementation of which is to be progressive. This is particularly true of economically underdeveloped countries with large populations to feed, which can hardly be expected to guarantee the immediate implementation of all economic and social rights. Even highly industrialized States will hesitate before guaranteeing the right, for example, to work—on any literal interpretation of the meaning of that right. . . .

[There is] the question of the increasing politicalization of human rights in the United Nations. Human Rights cannot, nor is it desirable that they should, be divorced from politics. To do so would be to divorce them from reality. And as a matter of fact there has always been a good deal of political controversy in the debates on human rights. . . . In recent years, however, the debates have become political to the exclusion of almost all constructive work, and one has the impression that governments are chiefly motivated by their [unrelated] conflicts with other countries. This, and the absence of any effective public opinion capable of putting pressure on governments, has resulted in a slowing down, in the United Nations at least, of effective work for the international promotion of respect for human rights.

This perspective of the UN's first Human Rights Director depicts the political reasons for disparate applications of the Charter and the ensuing Charter-based human rights declarations. The contemporary International Law of Human Rights had not been adopted by all social and political systems. Thus, some States continued to assert that the scope of human rights remained a matter of internal law.[3] They put forward the conflict between two UN Charter objectives: first, State sovereignty, which precludes UN meddling in "matters [that] are essentially within the domestic jurisdiction of any state" (Art. 2.7); and second, "universal respect for . . . human rights and fundamental freedoms for all" (Art. 55c). Under this view, what constituted such rights was reserved exclusively for national implementation on a discretionary basis, reflecting local rather than internationally defined conditions.

Even today, western scholars acknowledge that a globally defined human rights regime does not flourish in certain national systems. The human rights of the individual does not readily prevail in a society where the rights of the State necessarily take priority over the rights of the individual. Internationally defined human rights are not common to all cultures and cannot be readily incorporated into all of the world's social and political systems. Canadian and US professors Rhoda Howard and Jack Donnelly illustrate this point as follows:

We argue, however, that international human rights standards are based upon a distinctive substantive conception of human dignity. They therefore require a particular type of "liberal" regime, which may be institutionalized in various forms, but only within a narrow range of variation. . . .

Human rights are viewed as (morally) prior to and above society and the state, and under the control of individuals, who hold them and may exercise them against the state in extreme cases.

In the areas and endeavors protected by human rights, the individual is the "king. . . ."

Communitarian societies are antithetical to the implementation and maintenance of human rights, because they deny the autonomy of the individual, the irreducible moral equality of individuals, and the possibility of conflict between the community's interests and the legitimate interests of any individual. . . .

Communist societies obviously must violate a wide range of civil and political rights during the revolutionary transition, and necessarily, not merely as a matter of unfortunate excesses in practice. Even after communism is achieved, the denial of civil and political rights remains necessary to preserve the achievements of the revolution. The permanent denial of civil and political rights is required by the commitment to build society according to a particular substantive vision, for the exercise of personal autonomy and civil and political rights is almost certain to undermine that vision.[4]

One must also acknowledge certain limitations on the UN's ability to consummate its human rights objectives. The UN's annual human rights budget is approximately $11 million, or less than 1 percent of its regular (non-peacekeeping) budget. Yet the work of the UN Commission on Human Rights tripled during the ten years between the early 1980s and the early 1990s. Facing the budget limitations discussed in §3.3, the United Nations has been more active in the oversight of areas torn by *gross* human rights violations—as when the UN embraced the administration of East Timor and Kosovo (§3.3).

GENOCIDE "DEBATE"

You may have previously focused on the specifics of genocide in the §9.5 *Radio Machete* in the International Criminal Court (ICC) for Rwanda. Article 8 of the 1948 Genocide Convention on the Prevention and Punishment of the Crime of Genocide provides as follows: "Any Contracting Party may call upon the competent organs of the United Nations to take such action under the Charter of the United Nations as they consider appropriate for the prevention and suppression of acts of genocide. . . ."

States have been long on rhetoric, but short on embracing the Article 8 call for international action when genocide has no doubt occurred. In 1994, the US Clinton Administration resisted using the word "genocide" when referring to Rwanda. The post-2000 Bush Administration initially avoided that word, when describing the horrors occurring in The Sudan. The US House of Representatives initially considered the conduct of the Sudanese government in Darfur to be "close" to genocide. Then in September 2004, US Secretary of State Colin Powell proclaimed the US view that the systematic and government-sponsored elimination or departure of millions of members of the non-Arab population was in fact "genocide." In his testimony to the US Senate's Foreign Relations Committee, Powell sternly admonished Sudan's government-backed militia. He "concluded that genocide has been committed in Darfur and that the government of Sudan and the Janjaweed [militia] bear responsibility. . . ." Subsequently:

◆ President Bush added: "We urge the international community to work with us to prevent and suppress acts of genocide."

◆ The UN Secretary General's office responded that this was the *first* time—since the Genocide Convention's 1948 inception—that a nation had made such a declaration.

◆ The US Congress passed the December 2004 Comprehensive Peace in Sudan Act of 2004, stating that "through a military coup in 1989, the Government of Sudan repeatedly has attacked and dislocated civilian populations in southern Sudan in a coordinated policy of ethnic cleansing and genocide that has cost the lives of more than 2,000,000 people and displaced more than 4,000,000 people."[5]

In March 2005, the UN Security Council issued its first reference of allegedly responsible individuals to the ICC (§9.5). Although the United States is staunchly opposed to this court, the United States abstained during the Security Council vote. The silent acquiesce of the United States thus supported the first UN reference of a case to the ICC Prosecutor.

Delay has been rampant for a variety of reasons. One is that the use of the very sensitive term "genocide" would antagonize the allegedly responsible government. Even threats of sanctions could backfire. Sudan's Arab-dominated government, for example, backed the Darfur conflict against non-Arabs. The Arab might characterize sanction threats as further evidence of US hegemony in Africa as evidence of some broader anti-Arab sentiment.

Even the United Nations has been reluctant to use the term genocide to describe the activities of a member government. The UN Commission of Inquiry Report on The Sudan concluded that there was mass murder and other atrocities. These would constitute crimes against humanity, according to the UN Commission, but not "genocide."[6] The October 2004 Security Council terrorism resolution tracks the wording of the Genocide Convention, without actually using the word "genocide." Resolution 1566 affirms that "criminal acts, including [those] against civilians, committed with the intent to cause death or serious bodily injury . . . with the purpose to provoke a state of terror in the general public or in a group of persons or particular persons, intimidate a population or compel a government or an international organization to do or to abstain from doing any act, . . . are under no circumstances justifiable . . . and *calls upon* all States to prevent such acts and . . . to ensure that such acts are punished by penalties consistent with their grave nature. . . ."

One must distinguish between mass murder and genocide. The 9-11 perpetrators killed 3,000 people on 9-11.

Without evidence of their intent, this could be "only" mass murder. Article 2 of the Genocide Convention states that "genocide means any of the following acts committed with [the specific] intent to destroy, in whole or in part, a national, ethnical, racial or religious group, as such. . . ." International courts interpreting the Genocide Convention, and International Humanitarian Law (§§10.6 and 10.7), have routinely required a finding that the actor *specifically intended* to destroy, or at least partially destroy, a specified group.[7] There is also the question of whether genocide can be attributed to an association of terrorists, as opposed to a particular State. The *raison d'être* of the 1948 Genocide Convention was to place future States on notice that the individual would no longer be subjected to the whims of a rogue government like the Third Reich.

There is also some debate about whether genocide can be committed only by the State, or some entity closely associated with it—such as the above Janjaweed paramilitary in The Sudan. As noted by William Schabas, Director of the Irish Centre for Human Rights: "Because of the scope of genocide, it can hardly be committed by an individual, acting alone. Indeed, while exceptions cannot be ruled out, it is virtually impossible to imagine genocide that is not planned and organized either by the State itself or by some clique associated with it." On the other hand, neither the Preparatory Commission for the Statute of the ICC, nor the original UN General Assembly Genocide Convention resolution, included such a requirement. Also, certain prominent national court decisions have not required governmental planning as an element of genocide.[8]

"ETHNIC CLEANSING" EUPHEMISM?

Tracing the lineage of "ethnic cleansing" is arguably less daunting, when one considers the State and UN reluctance to apply the term "genocide" to sensitive international relations. The term "ethnic cleansing" was first associated with the 1990s breakup of the former Yugoslavia. As noted in one of the very few reported national court decisions to define it: "The term 'ethnic cleansing' emerged from the tragedy in the former Yugoslavia and is a translation of the Serbo-Croatian term, *etnicko cis cenje*. It is commonly understood to be a euphemism for genocide. Unlike genocide, however, 'ethnic cleansing' is not a legal term of art; therefore, the Court uses quotation marks when citing the term."[9] A 1993 UN report noted that ethnic cleansing is supposedly a relatively new concept, defining it as "rendering an area ethnically homogenous by using force or intimidation to remove from a given area the persons from another ethnic or religious group."[10]

Its potential application actually has an older and contemporary genealogy. In 1972, for example, a British plan would have evacuated 200,000 Catholics from Northern Ireland to "homogenous enclaves within Northern Ireland." This plan was rejected, however, because unless "the [British] government were prepared to be completely ruthless in the use of force, the chances of imposing a settlement consisting of a new partition together with some compulsory transfer of population would be negligible."[11] Israel would arguably be an ethnic cleanser, to the extent that its Jewish settlements in the West Bank and Gaza drove away previous Palestinian residents. During World War II, the United States forced hundreds of thousands of Japanese-Americans into relocation camps. In the nineteenth century, tens of thousands of US native-American Indians were moved from their lands by the federal government.

As to the substantive difference, Genocide Convention Article 8 calls for States to prevent genocide. It does not mention "ethnic cleansing." The latter may easily become the former. Many commentators have not made this important distinction. Professor Schabas (mentioned earlier), perhaps the foremost expert on the study of genocide, offers that the "Special Rapporteur of the Commission on Human Rights on Extrajudicial, Summary and Arbitrary Executions has characterized ethnic cleansing as a euphemism for genocide. The view that the two terms are equivalent or that they overlap is widely held within the diplomatic and academic communities. After many years of sharing such a view [however], I have come to the conclusion that the two concepts are quite distinct and that they do not coexist."[12]

The Genocide Convention requires the specific intent to destroy part or all of a particular group. Ethnic cleansing is not yet a "legal term," in the sense of being the subject of a treaty or having been authoritatively defined in the case law from international tribunals. One could thus argue that any "intent" element for a domestic court's ethnic cleansing prosecution should not be as demanding as that which is necessary for genocide. Merely banishing people from their homes, or from a particular region, may be economically driven. But without more, that does not constitute "genocide." As discussed in the previously referenced *Unocal* case, villagers were driven from their homes to ensure the security of the oil pipeline. Some were killed. But there was no apparent racial or ethnic hatred associated with the government's egregious conduct in that case.[13]

◆ 11.2 UNITED NATIONS PROMOTIONAL ROLE

UN CHARTER PROVISIONS

Because of the atrocities that occurred before and during World War II, the "United Nations" proclaimed a preliminary 1942 Declaration. It was the initial landmark in the evolution of the UN system. Forty-seven Allied Powers therein declared their conviction that "complete victory over their enemies is essential to defend life, liberty, independence and religious freedom . . . to preserve human rights and justice in their own lands as well as in other lands . . . ."[14] In 1945, the UN's charter members thus wove a number of human rights provisions into the fabric of this institution dedicated to worldwide peace:

Charter of the United Nations

San Francisco Conference: April 25–June 26, 1945. Entered into force: October 24, 1945

<http://www.icj-cij.org/icjwww/ibasicdocuments/Basetext/iunchart.htm>

WE THE PEOPLES OF THE UNITED NATIONS DETERMINED

. . .

to reaffirm faith in fundamental human rights, in the dignity and worth of the human person, in the equal rights of men and women and of nations large and small,

. . .

AND FOR THESE ENDS

to practice tolerance and live together in peace with one another as good neighbours, and

. . .

to employ international machinery for the promotion of the economic and social advancement of all peoples,

HAVE RESOLED TO COMBINE OUR EFFORTS TO ACCOMPLISH THESE AIMS

Chapter I
Purposes and Principles

Article 1

. . .

3. To achieve international co-operation in solving international problems of an economic, social, cultural, or humanitarian character, and in promoting and encouraging respect for human rights and for fundamental freedoms for all without distinction as to race, sex, language, or religion; and

. . .

Chapter IX
International Economic and Social Co-operation

Article 55

With a view to the creation of conditions of stability and well-being which are necessary for peaceful and friendly relations among nations based on respect for the principle of equal rights and self-determination of peoples, the United Nations shall promote:

a. higher standards of living, full employment, and conditions of economic and social progress and development;
b. solutions of international economic, social, health, and related problems; and international cultural and educational co-operation; and
c. universal respect for, and observance of, human rights and fundamental freedoms for all without distinction as to race, sex, language, or religion.

Article 56

All Members pledge themselves to take joint and separate action in co-operation with the Organization for the achievement of the purposes set forth in Article 55.

A preliminary question in any human rights dialogue involves the legal nature of the UN Charter: Do the human rights provisions of the UN Charter impose legally binding obligations or are they merely a statement of goals? (This treaty distinction is analyzed in §8.1 of this text.) The Charter contains a statement of aspirational standards for all member States. Article 56 contains the oath that members "pledge themselves to take joint and separate action in cooperation with the Organization" to achieve the human rights goals specified in the Charter. If this language were designed to require immediate steps to implement the Article 56 pledge, however, joining the United Nations would have required instant compliance with the Charter's human rights provisions. States intended the Charter to be a broad statement of principle, requiring a moral commitment to provide the specified rights to all inhabitants.

When the Charter was being drafted, many States were in shambles. It was readily foreseeable that an immediate universal obligation, to provide all the specific human rights which were the subject of many *later* treaties, would be prohibitively expensive—not to mention the cultural relativity which a universal norm might entail. Ultimate compliance was expected to vary with: (1) the respective UN members' economic, social, and political ability to fully implement Charter expectations, and (2) just how the post-World War II interest in human rights would be defined by subsequent human rights instruments. Columbia University Professor Louis Henkin offers this explanation:

> [B]ecause, in general, the condition of human rights seemed to have little relation to the foreign policy interests of states, traditional policy-makers and diplomats tended to have little concern for the human rights movement, but neither did they see any need to court the public embarrassment of opposing it. In the United Nations General Assembly . . . governments could take part in the . . . [human rights] process without any commitment to adhere to the final product, trying nevertheless to shape emerging international norms so that their country's behaviour would not be found wanting . . . and [that] it might even be possible to adhere to them without undue burden if that later appeared desirable.[15]

The transformation from moral imperative to legal duty would be accomplished by: (a) ratifying global treaties such as those in Exhibit 11.1 that follows; (b) ratifying regional treaties containing human rights provisions acceptable to certain UN members in a localized context; and (c) enacting legislation at the national level to finally implement the various UN Charter moral commitments.

One might be tempted to characterize the UN Charter's human rights provisions as saying one thing, but meaning another. No State would dare to openly object to the Charter's human rights provisions. However, no State was obliged to immediately act on the Charter's "Article 56 pledge." Each State was implicitly authorized to defer the decisions regarding "how," "what," and "when" until that point in time and development when implementation would be economically and politically feasible. The statement of South Africa's representative at the Charter drafting conference portrays the underlying concern. In the context of Charter Article 2.7, which prevented UN interference in matters essentially within the jurisdiction of the sovereign State:

> if the United Nations were to be permitted to intervene under Article 55c, which, incidentally, concerns the promotion of human rights . . . then the Assembly would be equally permitted to intervene in regard to matters set out in Article 55a and b, that is economic and social matters, higher standards of living, full employment, health legislation, etc. And I submit that no State on earth would tolerate this.
>
> . . . In conclusion, on this point, I should draw attention to the fact that neither the Charter nor any other internationally binding instrument contains any definition of fundamental human rights. If they had, there would have been no need to set up the [Human Rights] Commission to frame the proposed covenant on human rights.[16]

But as noted by the University of Munich Professor Bruno Simma—regarding the half century of practice since the above articulation: "Today, sweeping statements can often be found, according to which human rights no longer belong to the domestic jurisdiction of States. . . . Such statements are unquestionably true in the sense that States have vastly reduced their sphere of unfettered decision-making by agreeing to a large number of human rights declarations and treaties and by participating in the formulation of a considerable body of customary international human rights law. . . . United Nations organs have identified specific and individual

EXHIBIT 11.1 PRINCIPLE UN HUMAN RIGHTS INSTRUMENTS*

Year	Treaty
1948	Universal Declaration of Human Rights (the lone *declaration* in this list of post-WWII treaties)
1948 **1951**	Convention on the Prevention and Punishment of the Crime of Genocide, affirming Nuremberg Principles
1949 **1951**	Convention for the Suppression of the Traffic in Persons and of the Exploitation of the Prostitution of Others
1951 **1954**	Convention Relating to the Status of Refugees (as a result of WWII)
1966 **1967**	Protocol (regarding *post*-WWII refugee scenarios)
1952 **1954**	Convention on the Political Rights of Women
1954 **1960**	Convention Relating to the Status of Stateless Persons
1957 **1958**	Convention on the Nationality of Married Women
1960 **1962**	Convention Against Discrimination in Education (covers all distinctions not expressed in Charter Articles 1.3 and 55c prohibition on discrimination based on race, gender, language, or religion)
1962 **1964**	Convention on Consent to Marriage, Minimum Age for Marriage and Registration of Marriages
1965 **1969**	International Convention on the Elimination of All Forms of Racial Discrimination
1966 **1976** **—**	International Covenant on Civil and Political Rights
1966 **1976** **—**	Optional Protocol to the International Covenant on Civil and Political Rights (individual victims may submit violations by home State to UN HR Committee)
1989 **1991**	Second Optional Protocol to the International Covenant on Civil and Political Rights (abolition of the death penalty)
1966 **1976**	International Covenant on Economic, Social and Cultural Rights
1968 **1970**	Convention on the Non-Applicability of Statutory Limitations to War Crimes and Crimes Agains Humanity
1973 **1976**	International Convention on the Suppression and the Punishment of the Crime of Apartheid
1979 **1981** **—**	Convention on the Elimination of All Forms of Discrimination Against Women
2000 **2000**	Optional Protocol to the Convention on the Elimination of All Forms of Discrimination against Women (UN Committee to receive and consider communications from individuals)

Second date: year of treaty's entry into force. The bolded entries are the root treaties in contemporary human rights law. Further details: *see* comprehensive University of Minnesota *Human Rights Library*—by topic and searchable by key word at: <http://www1.umn.edu/humanrts/instree/ainstls2.htm>.

EXHIBIT 11.1   PRINCIPLE UN HUMAN RIGHTS INSTRUMENTS (CONTINUED)

Year	Treaty
1981 **1983**	Convention concerning Occupational Safety and Health Convention and the Working Environment
1984 **1987** —	Convention Against Torture and Other Cruel, Inhuman or Degrading Treatment
2002	Optional Protocol (system for monitoring places of detention by independent bodies)
1989 **1990** —	Convention on the Rights of the Child
2000 **2002** —	Optional Protocol One to the Convention on the Rights of the Child (children in armed conflict)
2000 **2002**	Optional Protocol Two to the Convention on the Rights of the Child (sale of children, child prostitution and child pornography)
1989 **1991**	Convention Concerning Indigenous and Tribal Peoples in Independent Countries (maintain distinctions)
1990 **2003**	International Convention on the Protection of the Rights of All Migrant Workers and Members of Their Families
1980 **1981** —	Convention for the Elimination of All Forms of Discrimination Against Women
1999 **2000**	Optional Protocol (Committee investigation of individual complaints)
1994	Draft Declaration on the Rights of Indigenous Peoples
1998 **2002**	Rome Statute of the International Criminal Court (to prosecute war crimes and crimes against humanity)
1999	Convention Concerning the Prohibition and Immediate Elimination of the Worst Forms of Child Labour
2000 **2003** —	UN Convention against Transnational Organized Crime
2000 **2003** —	Protocol to Prevent, Suppress and Punish Trafficking in Persons, Especially Women and Children
2000 **2004**	Protocol against the Smuggling of Migrants by Land, Sea and Air
2001	Universal Declaration on Cultural Diversity (cultural diversity as necessary for humankind as Biodiversity for nature & cannot be invoked to deny internationally recognized human rights)
2002	United Nations High Commissioner For Human Rights Principles and Guidelines on Human Rights and Trafficking
2005	Office of the High Commissioner for Human Rights Human Rights Resolution 2005/35 Basic Principles and Guidelines on the Right to a Remedy and Reparation for Victims of Gross Violations of International Human Rights Law and Serious Violations of International Humanitarian Law

human rights violations and have demanded that governments remedy those violations."[17]

One prominent example is the March 2005 UN Security Council reference of Sudanese State officials to the Prosecutor of the ICC (§9.5). The United Nations had attempted to halt the continuing human rights violations in The Sudan. Its president then vowed to block this international effort on behalf of the residents of Darfur, who were being terrorized by the government-backed militia.

The 1945 UN Charter nevertheless avoided self-executing language, which would have made the UN Charter a legally binding document. In an often-cited judicial pronouncement on this point, the 1952 California Supreme Court candidly analyzed the nonobligatory nature of UN Charter's human rights provisions in the following terms:

It is clear that the provisions . . . are not self-executing. They state general purposes and objectives of the United Nations Organization and do not purport to impose legal obligations on the individual member nations or to create rights in private persons. . . . Although the member nations have obligated themselves to cooperate with the international organization in promoting respect for, and observance of, human rights, it is plain that it was contemplated that future legislative action by the several nations would be required to accomplish the declared objectives, and there is nothing to indicate that these provisions were intended to become rules of law for the courts of this country upon the [US] ratification of the charter.[18]

On the other hand, the Charter's broadly worded provisions did present a malleable standard by which national conduct would be measured. The founding UN members had very practical reasons for creating such a hybrid document. They did not want to accept obligations for themselves, and purport to require such obligations for future applicants for admission, which had not been precisely defined in this new era of attention to "human rights." Given the pre-World War II inattention to this theme, this indefinite term would mean different things to different people. Charter members might otherwise risk the embarrassment of a UN inquiry into unforeseen matters, which they as State sovereigns, might wish to characterize as *national* rather than *international* in scope.

The initial UN members had too many "skeletons in the closet" to intend that the Charter be a legally binding

instrument, without further treaty-based clarifications of what "human rights" meant. South Africa would officially proclaim its apartheid in 1948. Various governmental entities in the United States had officially sanctioned racial segregation and prohibited interracial marriages. The former Soviet Union had its gulags—the forced-labor camps where individuals who resisted State policy in peaceful ways were incarcerated. Nor were the other powerful nations without their own human rights problems.[19]

The UN Charter provided only a skeletal backbone for fleshing out the global and regional human rights regime, which would evolve during the latter half of the twentieth century. Midway, the General Assembly announced the 1970 Declaration on the Occasion of the Twenty-Fifth Anniversary of the United Nations. State representatives therein lauded the UN's work, while recognizing that there remained much to be done. In the words of the Assembly, "serious violations of human rights are still being [routinely] committed against individuals and groups in several regions of the world."[20]

INTERNATIONAL BILL OF HUMAN RIGHTS

While numerous human rights instruments materialized, the four cornerstones of the modern International Bill of Human Rights are:

(1) The 1948 Universal Declaration of Human Rights
(2) The 1966 International Covenant on Civil and Political Rights
(3) Its two optional protocols
(4) The 1966 International Covenant on Economic, Social, and Cultural Rights.

One might expand this list to include a number of significant additions to the cache of contemporary human rights instruments. Exhibit 11.1 provides a snapshot of this formidable array of post-UN Charter human rights treaties.

The United Nations' rather comprehensive human rights program has received remarkable publicity. Commentators argue, however, that many State participants merely "pay lip service" to these programs while their inhabitants suffer. New York University Professor Theodore Meron espouses the representative view that—rather than editing or beefing up existing treaties—a completely new instrument is needed. His perspective is that:

In recent years there has been a proliferation of human rights instruments, not all of them necessary and carefully thought out. It would nevertheless appear that the international community needs a short, simple, and modest instrument to state an irreducible and nonderogable core of human rights. . . .

Some might argue that a solution could be found in better implementation of the existing law, rather than in the adoption of new instruments. But attainment of an effective system to implement the existing law, rather than in the adoption of new instruments. But attainment of an effective system to implement the existing law is not probable in the near future. Neither would it help to remedy the weakness inherent in the quantity and quality of the applicable norms.[21]

On the other hand, some commentators believe that the existing regime should be *supplemented*. Professor Lyal Sunga of the Graduate Institute of International Studies at Geneva proposed an increased emphasis on individual responsibility for human rights violations. His starting point would be the establishment of legal liability of individuals for serious violations in the context of the Laws of War. The Nuremberg Judgment, followed by the 1949 Geneva Conventions, did this on an *ad hoc* basis. Dr. Sunga argues that there should be a general rule of individual responsibility under International Law for serious human rights violations to supplement existing rules of State responsibility for such violations.[22]

Since the presentation of these diverse commentaries, there have been a number of UN developments, which have positively expanded the degree of protection afforded to the human rights of the individual. These include creation of two functioning tribunals for prosecuting human rights violations in the former Yugoslavia and Rwanda, promoting the widely signed (but not yet ratified) ICC Statute (§9.5), and the creation of the UN post for the High Commissioner on Human Rights (addressed below).

THE INTERNATIONAL BILL OF HUMAN RIGHTS AT WORK

Universal Declaration The historical cornerstone in the UN program for spawning a global human rights culture is the Universal Declaration of Human Rights (UDHR). This 1948 UN General Assembly resolution was adopted without dissent—although five members of the Soviet bloc, plus Saudi Arabia and South Africa abstained from voting. This Declaration was the first comprehensive human rights document to be formally declared on a global scale. Its specificity, while not

elaborate, readily eclipsed the UN Charter's minimal references to human rights.

The UDHR promotes two general categories of rights. The first of two, *civil and political rights,* includes the following: the right to life, liberty, and security of the person; the right to leave and enter one's own country; the prohibition of slavery and torture; freedom from discrimination, arbitrary arrest, and interferences with privacy; the right to vote; freedom of thought, peaceable assembly, religion, and marriage. The second category of UDHR rights consists of *economic, social, and cultural rights* including: the right to own property, to work, to maintain an adequate standard of living and health, and the right to education.

Like the UN Charter, this Declaration was also a statement of principles. It did not *require* UN members to immediately provide the listed rights to their citizens. The diversity of economic bases, per capita income, regional cultures, and the like was one reason for this limitation. A lesser-developed country would not be able to give its citizens what a more developed country would consider to be a minimum standard of living or education. But each UN member State *was* expected to pursue the laudatory purposes of the Universal Declaration at its own pace, according to its respective financial ability to comply with the spirit of that trend-setting document.[23]

Eleanor Roosevelt, Chair of the United States Commission on Human Rights and US Representative to the UN General Assembly, gingerly expressed the national sentiment regarding this post-war statement of "universal" principles. She carefully noted that "[i]n giving our approval to the declaration today, it is of primary importance that we keep clearly in mind the basic character of the document. It is not and does not purport to be a statement of law or of legal obligation. It is a declaration of basic principles of human rights and freedoms, to be stamped with the approval of the General Assembly by formal vote of its members, and to serve as a common standard of achievement for all peoples of all nations."[24]

The UDHR was thus initially intended to be a statement of aspirations. Since its adoption in 1948, however, a number of commentators have characterized it as evolving into something more. In 1971, the Vice President of the International Court of Justice (ICJ) perceived the Declaration's human rights provisions as having ripened into general practices that had become "accepted as law." In his separate opinion in the *Namibia* case, Judge Ammoun (Lebanon) expressed the view that:

[The] Universal Declaration of Human Rights . . . stresses in its preamble that "it is essential, if man is not to be compelled to have recourse, as a last resort, to rebellion against tyranny and oppression, that human rights should be protected by the rule of law. . . ." The Court could not remain an unmoved witness in face of the evolution of modern international law which is taking place in the United Nations through the implementation and the extension to the whole world of the principles of equality, liberty and peace in justice which are embodied in the Charter and the Universal Declaration of Human Rights. By referring . . . to the Charter of the United Nations and the Universal Declaration of Human Rights, the Court has asserted the imperative character of the right of peoples to self-determination and also of the human rights whose violation by the South African authorities [the Court] has denounced. . . .

The violation of human rights has not yet come to an end in any part of the world. . . . Violations of personal freedom and human dignity, the racial, social or religious discrimination which constitutes the most serious of violations of human rights . . . all still resist the currents of liberation on the five continents. That is certainly no reason why we should close our eyes to the conduct of the South African authorities. . . . Although the affirmations of the Declaration are not binding *qua* international convention [that is, not possessing legal capacity as an immediately binding treaty obligation] . . . they can bind states on the basis of custom . . . because they have acquired the force of custom through a general practice accepted as law. . . .

The equality demanded by the Namibians and by other peoples of every colour . . . is something of vital interest here . . . because it naturally rules out racial discrimination and apartheid, which are the gravest of the facts with which South Africa, as also other States, stands charged. . . .

It is not by mere chance that in Article 1 of the Universal Declaration of the Rights of Man there stands, so worded, this primordial principle or axiom: All human beings are born free and equal in dignity and rights. . . . The condemnation of apartheid has passed the stage of declarations and entered the phase of binding conventions.[25]

Some US commentators share Judge Ammoun's belief that certain human rights provisions of the UN

Declaration are now binding under customary State practice. In 1987, a nationwide group of US judges, academicians, and government lawyers confirmed that:

Almost all States are parties to the United Nations Charter, which contains human rights obligations. There has been no authoritative determination of the full content of those obligations, but it is increasingly accepted that states parties to the Charter are legally obligated to respect some of the rights recognized in the Universal Declaration. . . . It has been argued that the general pledge of the members in the Charter [to promote human rights] . . . has been made definite by the Universal Declaration, and that failure by any member to respect the rights recognized in the declaration is a violation of the Charter. Alternatively, it has been urged, the Charter, the Universal Declaration . . . and other practice of states have combined to create a customary international law of human rights requiring every state to respect the rights set forth in the Declaration.[26]

Critics have consistently objected to the 1948 UDHR's "Western" (sometimes referred to as "northern") derivation. It lacked input from lesser-developed nations and those with more diverse political and social viewpoints. Norwegian author Ashborn Eide, and Iceland's Gudmundur Alfredsson (of the UN Secretariat) characterize this common criticism as being somewhat overstated. In their leading study of the UDHR, they depict its evolution as follows: "[P]articipants came from all over the world. Admittedly, there was only one participant from the African continent (Egypt). Indigenous peoples and minorities had no representation during the drafting and adoption stages. While this may be true, today the broad wording of the Declaration and its general principles together with subsequent standard-setting and implementation activities [*see* Exhibit 11.1] reduce the value of this statement to history."[27]

Ironically, the June 1993 Vienna World Conference on Human Rights appeared to take a step backward in terms of globally defining human rights entitlements. (China and Indonesia were the front-runners in the final conference statement.) It contends that Western-derived human rights standards should be tempered by "regional peculiarities and various historical, cultural and religious backgrounds." This perspective, promulgated in the Vienna Declaration and Programme of Action,[28] arguably diminishes the efforts to eliminate barriers to the internationalization of human rights enforcement.

Furthermore, some nations considered the UDHR as somewhat "treacherous." The annual reports of Amnesty International (AI) furnish insight into this reasoning. In its 1988 report, AI observed that many UN member nations consider the 1948 Declaration of Human Rights "subversive." It was the first UN document to assert that individuals have a right to direct protection by the *international community,* as opposed to their own States. The concern is that such a protraction clashes with the national right to freedom from international meddling with matters essentially within the local jurisdiction of a sovereign State. As reported by AI: "In at least half the countries of the world, people are locked away for speaking their minds, often after trials that are no more than a sham. In at least a third of the world's nations, men, women and even children are tortured. In scores of countries, governments pursue their goals by kidnaping and murdering their own citizens. More than 120 states have written into their laws the right to execute people convicted of certain crimes, and more than a third carry out such premeditated killings every year."[29]

International Covenants In 1966, the UN General Assembly added two core documents to the International Bill of Human Rights. These are the:

- International Covenant on Civil and Political Rights (ICCPR)
- International Covenant on Economic, Social, and Cultural Rights (ICESCR)

Unlike the 1948 UDHR, they are not mere declarations of principle. Both covenants were expressly cast as multilateral treaties. Adopting States could thus ratify their legally binding provisions. By 1976, the minimum number of States had ratified both treaties. This development signaled an accord within the post-World War II international community. It solidified the international augmentation of protection for the individual—who before World War II was required to rely exclusively on his or her home State. Such pre-Covenant reliance had a predictable chilling effect on human rights: the victim was beholden to the violator.

These two covenants share a number of common substantive provisions. Both restate the human rights provisions contained in the Universal Declaration. The distinguishing feature of the Covenants, vis-a-vis the 1948 UDHR, is that they *obligate* ratifying States to establish conspicuous and effective machinery for filing charges and then dealing with alleged violations of human rights.

Covenant on Civil and Political Rights (ICCPR) The essential provisions in this treaty,30 ratified by over 150 nations, include the following:

International Covenant on Civil and Political Rights

Article 2

1. Each State Party to the present Covenant undertakes to respect and to ensure to all individuals within its territory and subject to its jurisdiction the rights recognized in the present Covenant, without distinction of any kind, such as race, colour, sex, language, religion, political or other opinion, national or social origin, property, birth or other status.

. . .

3. Each State Party to the present Covenant undertakes:
(a) To ensure that any person whose rights or freedoms as herein recognized are violated shall have an effective remedy, notwithstanding that the violation has been committed by persons acting in an official capacity;

. . .

Article 4

1. In time of public emergency which threatens the life of the nation and the existence of which is officially proclaimed, the States Parties to the present Covenant may take measures derogating from their obligations under the present Covenant to the extent strictly required by the exigencies of the situation.

. . .

Article 6

1. Every human being has the inherent right to life. This right shall be protected by law. No one shall be arbitrarily deprived of his life.
2. In countries which have not abolished the death penalty, sentence of death may be imposed only for the most serious crimes in accordance with the law in force at the time of the commission of the crime. . . . This penalty can only be carried out pursuant to a final judgement rendered by a competent court.

Article 7

No one shall be subjected to torture or to cruel, inhuman or degrading treatment or punishment. In particular, no one shall be subjected without his free consent to medical or scientific experimentation.

Article 8

1. No one shall be held in slavery; slavery and the slave-trade in all their forms shall be prohibited.

. . .

Article 9

1. Everyone has the right to liberty and security of person. No one shall be subjected to arbitrary arrest or detention. No one shall be deprived of his liberty except on such grounds and in accordance with such procedure as are established by law.
3. Anyone arrested or detained on a criminal charge shall be brought promptly before a judge or other officer authorized by law to exercise judicial power and shall be entitled to trial within a reasonable time or to release.
4. Anyone who is deprived of his liberty by arrest or detention shall be entitled to take proceedings before a court, in order that court may decide without delay on the lawfulness of his detention and order his release if the detention is not lawful.

. . .

Article 18

1. Everyone shall have the right to freedom of thought, conscience and religion. . . .

Article 19

1. Everyone shall have the right to hold opinions without interference.
2. Everyone shall have the right to freedom of expression; this right shall include freedom to seek, receive and impart information and ideas of all kinds, regardless of frontiers, either orally, in writing or in print, in the form of art, or through any other media of his choice.

Article 20

. . .

2. Any advocacy of national, racial or religious hatred that constitutes incitement to discrimination, hostility or violence shall be prohibited by law.

. . .

Article 23

3. No marriage shall be entered into without the free and full consent of the intending spouses.

. . .

Article 26

All persons are equal before the law and are entitled without any discrimination to the equal protection of the law. In this respect, the law shall prohibit any discrimination and guarantee to all persons equal and effective protection against discrimination on any ground such as race, colour, sex, language, religion, political or other opinion, national or social origin, property, birth or other status.

Article 27

In those States in which ethnic, religious or linguistic minorities exist, persons belonging to such minorities shall not be denied the right, in community with the other members of their group, to enjoy their own culture, to profess and practise their own religion, or to use their own language.

Article 28

1. There shall be established a Human Rights Committee (hereafter referred to in the present Covenant as the Committee). It shall consist of eighteen members . . . .

◆ *Notes*

1. The ICCPR, by its own terms, is a self-executing treaty (see §8.1): "The States Parties to the present Covenant . . . Agree upon the following articles. . .". Were it otherwise, then the 1966 UN objective to augment the 1948 UN Declaration on Human Rights with a ratifiable treaty regime would make little sense. The United States ratified the ICCPR in 1992. It tendered the following, however, as one of its reservations to the ICCPR: "That the United States declares that the provisions of articles 1 through 27 of the Covenant are not self-executing." This reservation can hardly be acceptable, if one applies the §8.2 ICJ *Reservations to the Convention on Genocide Case* definition: a reservation to a multilateral treaty must be "compatible" with its object and purpose. (*See* for the *Reservations Case* text.)

2. Article 4 of the ICCPR denies a treaty party the opportunity to derogate from certain treaty provisions, including Article 6. It provides that the death penalty "can only be carried out pursuant to a final judgement rendered by a competent court." A post-September 11, 2001, presidential executive order provided for a military tribunal, which does not include the constitutional guarantees otherwise accorded to those who are subject to arrest in the United States—as opposed to being tried abroad in Pakistan/Afghanistan or on a US warship in foreign waters, where they would be tried without being given the various guarantees applicable to civilian criminal trials in the United States. If the US Supreme Court were to determine that such military tribunals are not competent courts, then the above so-called ratification/reservation to the ICCPR would protect the United States from claims that it breached Article 6 of the ICCPR.

3. In a February 2004 opinion by the Uganda Supreme Court, two journalists were charged with the criminal offense of "Publication of False News," in violation of Section 50 of Uganda's Penal Code. They republished a story extracted from a foreign newspaper (Indian Ocean Newsletter) claiming among other things that the president of the Democratic Republic of the Congo "has given a large consignment of gold to the Government of Uganda as payment for 'services rendered' by the latter during the struggle against the former military dictator, the late Mobutu Sese Seko." Their defense was that their being prosecuted infringed upon their rights to the freedoms of thought, conscience, belief, and association, and/or freedom to practice their profession. The Supreme Court noted as follows:

> In the International Covenant on Civil and Political Rights, Article 10 provides [that] . . . "Every one shall have the right to freedom of expression; this right shall include freedom to seek, receive and impart information and ideas of all kinds, regardless of frontiers, either orally, in writing or in print, in the form of art, or through any other media of his choice."
>
> From the foregoing different definitions, it is evident that the right to freedom of expression extends to holding, receiving and imparting all forms of opinions, ideas and information. It is not confined to categories, such as correct opinions, sound ideas or truthful information.
>
> . . .
>
> A democratic society respects and promote the citizens' individual right to freedom of expression, because it derives benefit from the exercise of that freedom by its citizens. In order to maintain that benefit, a democratic society chooses to tolerate the exercise of the freedom even in respect of "demonstrably untrue and alarming statements," rather than to suppress it.
>
> . . .
>
> Democratic societies uphold and protect fundamental human rights and freedoms, essentially on principles that are in line with J.J. Rousseau's version of the *Social Contractor* theory. In brief, the theory is to the effect that the pre-social humans agreed to surrender their respective individual freedom of action, in order to secure mutual protection, and that consequently, the *raison d'etre* of the State is to provide protection to the individual citizens. In that regard, the state has the duty to facilitate and enhance the individual's self-fulfilment and advancement, recognising the individual's rights and freedoms as inherent in humanity.

Onyango-Obbo & Mwenda v. Attorney General, Supreme Court of Uganda No. NFOCAS738, Feb. 11, 2004, first printed in *The Monitor* (Kampala newspaper), February 11, 2004 and reprinted in 43 INT'L LEGAL MAT'LS 686 (2004).

4. In August 2003, the United Nations Human Rights Committee, found that the Government of Australia

discriminated against a homosexual man by denying him pension benefits following the death of his male partner (a war veteran). Under Australian law, only heterosexual married couples, or heterosexual couples, who were *de facto* married, were entitled to receive pension benefits. The Committee found that Australia had not demonstrated how a distinction between same-sex partners, excluded from pension benefits, and unmarried heterosexual partners, who were granted such benefits, was objectively reasonable. Article 26 of the Covenant prohibits sexual-orientation discrimination. The UN Committee thus determined that Australia had provided no arguments as to how the distinction between same-sex partners, and unmarried heterosexual partners, was reasonable. Nor had Australia advanced any evidence as to the factors that would be used to justify such a distinction. *Young v. Australia,* views of the Human Rights Committee under the Optional Protocol to the International Covenant on Civil and Political Rights, Communication No. 941/2000 (August 6, 2003), available at: <http://www.unhchr.ch/tbs/doc.nsf/MasterFrameView/3c839cb2ae3bef6fc1256dac002b3034?Opendocument>.

5. In July 2005, the UN's Human Rights Committee, under attack for lack of effectiveness, opened its 2005 annual session with a call for strengthening the UN human rights system. The opening address contained the following plea: "the whole United Nations human rights system, including our Office as well as human rights bodies and mechanisms must be strengthened in order to ensure better implementation of fundamental freedoms and rights worldwide." See: <http://www.unhchr.ch/huricane/huricane.nsf/view01/A2ADEB5EB6983A84C125703D00317628?opendocument>.

Two Optional Protocols to the ICCPR   The first of two protocols to the ICCPR is designed to monitor compliance with the ICCPR via the Article 28 Human Rights Committee.[31] That committee's eighteen national members consist of prominent individual representatives—based on an equitable geographical distribution of membership among the different forms of civilization and world's principal legal systems. The "Committee" examines the periodic compliance reports that the treaty parties must submit to the United Nations. The first optional protocol thus enables the Committee to receive and consider communications from individuals claiming to be victims of violations of the rights set forth earlier in the Covenant. The interim UN Resolution 1503 procedure of 1970 materialized about half-way between the 1966 promulgation of the ICCPR and its entry into force in 1976. It emphasized the need for an individual's right to petition the United Nations as a basic human right. (This Committee will likely by replaced by a much broader group of nations, based on UN reform efforts addressed in §3.3.)

The following example is an individual petition submitted to this Committee under the first optional protocol to the ICCPR. As you read this passage, note the subjectivity of the government's basis for the arrests in this case:

Report of the Human Rights Committee

24 UN MONTHLY CHRONICLE 66 (June 1979)

. . . The Committee also concluded, for the first time, consideration of a communication submitted to it by a Uruguayan national in accordance with the Optional Protocol to the International Covenant on Civil and Political Rights. Under the terms of the Protocol, individuals who claimed that any of their rights enumerated in the Covenant had been violated and who had exhausted all available remedies, might submit written communications to the Committee for consideration. The Committee, after examining the communication in question, took the view that it revealed a number of violations by Uruguay, the State Party concerned, of the Covenant provisions.

It held that the State Party was under an obligation to take immediate steps to ensure strict observance of the Covenant provisions and to provide effective remedies to the victims.

The communication was written by a Uruguayan national residing in Mexico, who submitted it on her own behalf, as well as on behalf of her husband, Luis

Maria Bazzano Ambrosini, her stepfather, Jose Luis Massera, and her mother, Martha Valentini de Massera.

The author alleged, with regard to herself, that she was detained in Uruguay from 25 April to 3 May 1975 and subjected to psychological torture. She stated that she was released on 3 May 1975 without having been brought before a judge.

The author claimed that her husband, Luis Maria Bazzano Ambrosini, was detained on 3 April 1975 and immediately thereafter subjected to torture.

She also claimed that her stepfather, Jose Luis Massera, professor of mathematics and former Deputy to the National Assembly, had been arrested on 22 October 1975 and held incommunicado until his detention was made known in January 1976, and that her mother, Martha Valentini de Massera, had been arrested on 28 January 1976 without any formal charges and that in September 1976 she was accused of "assistance to subversive association," an offence which carried a penalty of two to eight years imprisonment. . . .

The Committee decided to base its views on the following facts which had not been contradicted by the State Party. Luis Maria Bazzano Ambrosini was arrested on 3 April 1975 on the charge of complicity in "assistance to subversive association." Although his arrest had taken place before the coming into force of the International Covenant on Civil and Political Rights and of the Optional Protocol thereto, on 23 March 1976, his detention without trial continued after that date. After being detained for one year, he was granted conditional release, but that judicial decision was not respected and the prisoner was taken to an unidentified place, where he was confined and held incommunicado until 7 February 1977. On that date he was tried on the charge of "subversive association" and remained imprisoned in conditions seriously detrimental to his health.

Jose Luis Massera, a professor of mathematics and former Deputy to the National Assembly, was arrested in October 1975 and has remained imprisoned since that date. He was denied the remedy of habeas corpus [whereby a neutral judge would assess the basis for his incarceration] and another application for remedy made to the Commission on Respect for Human Rights of the Council of State went unanswered. On 15 August 1976 he was tried on charges of "subversive association" and remained in prison.

Martha Valentini de Massera was arrested on 28 January 1976. In September 1976 she was charged with "assistance to subversive association." She was kept in detention and was initially held incommunicado. In November 1976 for the first time a visit was permitted, but thereafter she was again taken to an unknown place of detention. She was tried by a military court and sentenced to three-and-a-half years imprisonment.

The Committee, acting under article 5(4) of the Optional Protocol to the International Covenant on Civil and Political Rights, took the view that those facts, in so far as they had occurred after 23 March 1976, disclosed violations of the International Covenant on Civil and Political Rights [by Uruguay].

◆ *Notes*

Subsequent developments suggest that Uruguay's shift to civilian control had a positive impact on its observance of international human rights norms. Ten years after the Commission's consideration of this claim of human rights abuses (June 1989), a court in Montevideo, Uruguay, ordered Uruguay's Defense Ministry to pay the equivalent of $47 million to an electrician tortured with his own equipment for eighteen months during 1976 and 1977. This was the first time that such a judgment was rendered in Uruguay—where such incidents were commonplace during the military dictatorship of the 1970s to the mid-1980s.

The "1503" (UN Resolution) right of petition has not been particularly successful. Reasons include the difficulty of individual access, which is effectively controlled by those States that did not become parties to the ICCPR. No communication may be received regarding States which are not parties to the optional protocol. Individuals must exhaust administrative remedies of the home State. They must submit evidence of the claimed violation in writing. Submissions may not be anonymous.[32]

The second optional protocol to the ICCPR is a separate treaty also designed to put teeth into ICCPR provisions. Article 6 of the ICCPR attempts to limit death penalty practice. Article 37(a) of UN Convention on Rights of the Child prohibits the death penalty for minors under the age of eighteen. As of 2000, six nations put juvenile offenders to death: Iran, Nigeria, Pakistan, Saudi Arabia, Yemen, and the United States. States ratifying the second protocol thereby agree not to impose the death penalty under any circumstances.[33]

There is a flourishing movement in the international community to treat this common feature of State practice as a violation of International Law.[34] The International Criminal Tribunals (Yugoslavia and Rwanda) and the Rome Statute for a permanent tribunal all bar the death penalty. Their ultimate sanction in those tribunals is life imprisonment (§9.5). Under the second ICCPR protocol, reservations are permitted only for "the most serious crimes of a military nature" committed during the time of war. During a 1994 debate in the UN General Assembly's Social, Humanitarian and Cultural (Third) Committee, the Chair summarized the respective arguments by various national representatives for and against the death penalty as follows:

[T]he Committee had clearly been divided into two camps: those favoring the abolition of capital punishment and those wishing to retain it. Arguments in favor of abolishing the death penalty had been the following: States could not impose the death penalty as a means of reducing crime because there was no evidence that it had a deterrent effect; the right to life was the most basic human right and, consequently, States did not have the right to take the life of any individual; the death penalty sometimes veiled a desire for vengeance or provided an easy way of eliminating political opponents; the death penalty, once applied, could not be reversed in the event of a judicial error; and capital punishment was excluded from the penalties used by international tribunals . . . and should consequently be less prevalent in national legislation.

Arguments in support of maintaining the death penalty had been the following: certain legislative systems were based on religious laws; it was not possible to impose the ethical standards of a single culture on all countries; there was a need to discourage extremely serious crimes; and, in some countries, capital punishment was a constitutional or even a religious obligation.

At the same time, all members agreed on certain fundamental points: the death penalty should be applied only in exceptional circumstances and subject to strict preconditions; and its scope of application should be extremely limited.[35]

International Covenant on Economic, Social, and Cultural Rights (ICESCR) The other major 1966 UN human rights work product was the ICESCR.[36] It requires State parties to provide adequate or improved living conditions for its inhabitants and to facilitate international cooperation to achieve this objective.

This second basket of rights was the subject of a separate 1966 UN draft treaty for good reason. It would be neither practical nor politically feasible to lump its nonpolitical rights into a comprehensive treaty governing the "universe" of rights set forth in the 1948 UDHR (from which both the CPR Covenant and the ESC Covenant drew their inspiration.) There was too much diversity in the political, economic, social, and cultural fabric of the UN membership. Two respective half-loaves were better than none.

This reality was especially evident to the treaty drafters because of the influx of new UN member States as a result of the decolonization movement of the 1960s. Some developing nations would consider the achievement of *economic* rights a more pressing goal than the *political* rights contained in the other 1966 treaty. They would naturally focus on basic food and shelter requirements,[37] as opposed to societies where such rights are far more prominent. Many lesser-developed nations would have economic limitations precluding them from making any commitment regarding the furnishing of *either* basket of rights to their populace.

The essential treaty provisions are as follows:

International Covenant on Economic, Social and Cultural Rights

Article 3
The States Parties to the present Covenant undertake to ensure the equal right of men and women to the enjoyment of all economic, social and cultural rights set forth in the present Covenant.

. . .

Article 6
1. The States Parties to the present Covenant recognize the right to work, which includes the right of

everyone to the opportunity to gain his living by work which he freely chooses or accepts, and will take appropriate steps to safeguard this right.

2. The steps to be taken by a State Party to the present Covenant to achieve the full realization of this right shall include technical and vocational guidance and training programmes, policies and techniques to achieve steady economic, social and cultural development and full and productive employment under conditions safeguarding fundamental political and economic freedoms to the individual.

Article 7

The States Parties to the present Covenant recognize the right of everyone to the enjoyment of just and favourable conditions of work, which ensure, in particular:

  (a) remuneration which provides all workers, as a minimum, with:

    (i) fair wages and equal remuneration for work of equal value without distinction of any kind, in particular women being guaranteed conditions of work not inferior to those enjoyed by men, with equal pay for equal work;

    (ii) a decent living for themselves and their families in accordance with the provisions of the present Covenant;

  (b) safe and healthy working conditions;

  (c) equal opportunity for everyone to be promoted in his employment to an appropriate higher level, subject to no considerations other than those of seniority and competence;

  (d) rest, leisure and reasonable limitation of working hours and periodic holidays with pay, as well as remuneration for public holidays.

. . .

Article 9

The States Parties to the present Covenant recognize the right of everyone to social security, including social insurance.

Article 10

2. Special protection should be accorded to mothers during a reasonable period before and after childbirth. During such period working mothers should be accorded paid leave or leave with adequate social security benefits.

3. Special measures of protection and assistance should be taken on behalf of all children and young persons without any discrimination for reasons of parentage or other conditions. Children and young persons should be protected from economic and social exploitation. . . .

Article 11

1. The States Parties to the present Covenant recognize the right of everyone to an adequate standard of living for himself and his family, including adequate food, clothing and housing, and to the continuous improvement of living conditions. The States Parties will take appropriate steps to ensure the realization of this right . . . .

2. The States Parties to the present Covenant, recognizing the fundamental right of everyone to be free from hunger, shall take, individually and through international co-operation, the measures, including specific programmes, which are needed.

. . .

Article 13

1. The States Parties to the present Covenant recognize the right of everyone to education.

. . .

Article 15

1. The States Parties to the present Covenant recognize the right of everyone:

  (a) to take part in cultural life. . . .

Article 16

1. The States Parties to the present Covenant undertake to submit in conformity with this part of the Covenant reports on the measures which they have adopted and the progress made in achieving the observance of the rights recognized herein.

2. (a) All reports shall be submitted to the Secretary-General of the United Nations, who shall transmit copies to the Economic and Social Council for consideration in accordance with the provisions of the present Covenant.

Article 17

2. Reports may indicate factors and difficulties affecting the degree of fulfilment of obligations under the present Covenant.

. . .

Economic, social, and cultural rights were thus segregated as a distinct category of rights, based on their historical origins. As noted in a leading commentary about the evolution of the rights governed by the ICESCR treaty:

> Economic, social, and cultural rights are frequently termed "second generation" rights, deriving from the growth of socialist ideals in the late nineteenth and early twentieth centuries and the rise of the labor movement in Europe. They contrast with the "first generation" civil and political rights associated with the eighteenth-century [French] Declaration on the Rights of Man, and the "third generation" rights of "peoples" or "groups," such as the right to self-determination and the right to development. In fact the reason for making a distinction between first and second generation rights . . . [was] the ideological conflict between East and West pursued in the arena of human rights during the drafting of the covenants. The Soviet States, on the one hand, championed the cause of economic, social, and cultural rights, which they associated with the aims of socialist society. Western States, on the other hand, asserted the priority of civil and political rights as being the foundation of liberty and democracy in the "free world." The conflict was such that during the drafting of the International Bill of Rights the intended treaty was divided into two separate instruments which were later to become the ICCPR and the ICESCR.[38]

Like the Committee that monitors political rights under the ICCPR, the ICESCR is also evolving within a UN committee structure: the UN Committee on Economic, Social and Cultural Rights. It is the focal institution for the normative development of such rights. It did not begin that way, however.

Both the West and the Soviets had distinct reasons for *opposing* an economic committee overseer which could act as a substitute for world court dispute resolution. Western nations wanted a committee process for overseeing political rights, but not for monitoring the economic treaty rights quoted above. They did not believe that there could be an effective enforcement mechanism for this category of human rights. The Soviets, as the self-appointed champions of the economic rights treaty regime, had problems with *either* a political or economic UN enforcement regime under the auspices of an international organization. The more that such bodies developed competence and expertise, the more they would be perceived as infringing on matters within the State's domestic competence. This disconnect thus spawned what has turned out to be a comparatively ineffective mechanism for implementing economic human rights vis-a-vis political human rights.[39]

Human Rights "Czar" In 1993, the UN General Assembly added another cog to its wheel of human rights machinery. The Assembly established the post of UN High Commissioner for the Promotion and Protection of All Human Rights—a proposal first made by Uruguay in 1951. The Commissioner is now appointed by the Secretary-General, subject to approval by the General Assembly. The first Commissioner was Jose Ayala Lasso, Ecuador's Education Ambassador to the United Nations (appointed in 1994).[40]

The Commissioner is the focal point for coordinating the UN's fragmented efforts to implement the rights enshrined in its numerous problem-specific treaties (Exhibit 11.1). This UN official manages the UN's Center for Human Rights, which is expected to move more swiftly than the overburdened International Covenant on Civil and Political Rights Human Rights Commission—whose workload tripled between the early 1980s and the early 1990s.

The task of the first UN Commissioner began with a compromise. Western States agreed to modify language that would have given the Commissioner responsibility for "elimination and prevention" of human rights violations. The Commissioner's task is now worded so as to require only "an active role in removing the current obstacles" to the global enjoyment of human rights. This attenuated version of the Commissioner's role may ultimately relegate this office to bureaucratic obscurity.

This office performs a quite valuable function. It questions certain State practices through the medium of the annual report process. The following is a classic instance:

Israeli Interrogation Cases

UNITED NATIONS HIGH COMMISSIONER ON HUMAN RIGHTS CONSIDERATION OF REPORTS SUBMITTED BY STATES PARTIES UNDER ARTICLE 19 OF THE CONVENTION (ISRAEL) BY COMMITTEE AGAINST TORTURE CAT/C/33/Add.2/Rev.1 (18 February 1997)
Go to course Web page at <http://home.att.net/~slomansonb/txtcsesite.html>. Under Chapter Eleven, click Israeli Interrogation Cases.

Nevertheless, the UN Human Rights Commission has been the object of a great deal of criticism. The Secretary-General's August 2005 report—In Larger Freedom: Towards Security, Development, and Human Rights for All—was designed to generate a dialogue for the September 2005 Millennium Summit (fifth year review of the achievement of the §3.3 Millennium Declaration). He therein proposed a new Human Rights Council. It would be a principal organ of the General Assembly. The existing UN Human Rights Commission has been a persistent embarrassment, because of participation and control by countries themselves accused of gross human rights abuses. (Libya chaired this body in 2003). The new Human Rights Council will, instead, operate year-round, thus allowing it to act more frequently because of numerous recesses. Other key goals include establishing criteria for membership, selection by a two-thirds UN GA vote, and the weeding out of violators such as The Sudan (for example, the UN SC 2005 reference of numerous government officials for criminal prosecution to the ICC, discussed in §9.5).

This section's human rights dialogue would be incomplete without scrutinizing the United Nations own performance. As noted in §10.3 of this book, UN peacekeepers in Africa violated the terms of the UN presence there. Some have engaged in conduct unbecoming an international representative who is expected to come to the aid of victims, not create more of them. And in §3.3, you studied the oil-for-food scandal.

It took advantage of the Iraqi people during the international sanctions regime imposed in the aftermath of the first Persian Gulf War.

The United Nations has another major human rights problem, which has received virtually no attention. That is, its detention policies in the locations it has administered (East Timor and Kosovo). None of the relevant East Timor regulations—for the comparatively brief period of direct UN administration there—would hold the UN responsible in situations where a State would be responsible.[41] But during the UN administration of Kosovo, which began in 1999:

The SRSG's [Special Representative for the Secretary-General] use and abuse of executive orders in Kosovo demonstrates the problems that arise from a virtually unchecked centralized authority. The case of Afrim Zeqiri emphasizes the need to rethink the means by which the Security Council applied and enforced human rights standards on interim administrations. U.N. police arrested Zeqiri, an ethnic Albanian, for the murder of three Serbs and the attempted murder of two in the Kosovo village Cernica. He was arrested in May 2000 and held . . . based on judicial detention orders until late July 2000. Following the lapse of the judicial detention order, . . . [the UN] extended Zeqiri's detention . . . because local prosecutors chose to abandon the case. . . . When the series of executive orders and judicial decisions to extend detention expired in November 2000, Zeqiri remained in a detention center at the U.S. Army Base. In response to the [Organization for Security and Co-operation in Europe] Ombudsperson's request for clarification of the legal basis for the prolonged detention, the [UN] Director of the Department of Judicial Affairs wrote that Executive Order detentions were lawful based on the broad mandate of Resolution 1244 which permitted the SRSG to take "any measure necessary to ensure public safety and order and the proper administration of justice." After nearly two years in prison, KFOR released Zeqiri from detention because of the lack of evidence against him.[42]

The United Nations took over Kosovo, two days after North Atlantic Treaty Organization's (NATO) less than democratic bombing campaign ousted Serbian forces and political control of its southern province. The United Nations has to "do it better." Otherwise, how can the United Nations be a role model for State administration, in accordance with its own International Bill of Human Rights?

◆ 11.3 REGIONAL HUMAN RIGHTS APPROACHES

Several regional human rights programs coexist with the UN program. The degree to which they have been successful in comparison to the UN's global program depends on the political solidarity of the particular region. This section highlights some human rights initiatives in Europe, Latin America, Africa, and Asia.

The UN Charter encouraged the development of regional processes. It did not provide for any juridical link between the UN's International Court of Justice and the various human rights courts that evolved (Exhibit 9.1). The ICJ is called upon to adjudicate any type of dispute between States, arising anywhere in the world. Regional human rights courts, on the other hand, entertain a comparatively limited scope of jurisdiction, based on local human rights treaties.

Defendant States may act not only beyond their borders, but also their region. Enforcement entities should not engage in extraterritorial applications of regionally defined human rights norms. The Inter-American Human Rights Commission would not purport to officially question any action taken by the United States in Afghanistan or Iraq. But ordering the United States to take the "urgent measures necessary," to accord the Guantanamo Bay detainees' human rights guaranteed under a local treaty regime, is another matter (§10.7).[43]

EUROPEAN PROGRAMS

Historical Evolution The Council of Europe (1949) is an international organization composed of forty-three European nations. The Council's essential goal is the maintenance of political and economic stability in Europe. Member States have characterized the preservation of individual rights as being an important method for achieving those goals. The constitution of the Council of Europe provides that each member must ensure "the enjoyment by all persons within its jurisdiction of human rights and fundamental freedoms." This provision was implemented by the creation of two human rights treaties: the Convention for the Protection of Human Rights and Fundamental Freedoms (EHR) and the European Social Charter. Upon ratification, the national

participants bind themselves to grant the rights contained in various regional treaties to their inhabitants.[44] One of these is the 1992 Treaty of Maastricht, which deals with economic development. The pervasiveness of human rights as an element of development is evident in Article 130(u). It provides that "Community policy . . . shall contribute to the general objective of developing and consolidating democracy and the rule of law, and to that of respecting human rights and fundamental freedoms."

The EHR treaty contains civil rights that are virtually identical to those set forth in the foregoing United Nations Covenant on Civil and Political Rights. The EHR treaty protects the rights to life, public and fair hearings, peaceful enjoyment of possessions, an education, freedom from torture or other degrading treatment, and the freedoms of thought, conscience, religion, expression, and peaceful assembly.

The European Social Charter provides for economic and social rights that are similar to those set forth in the above United Nations Covenant on Economic, Social, and Cultural Rights. The European Social Charter guarantees the rights to work, safe working conditions, employment protection for women and children, vocational training, and the right to engage in gainful occupations in the territories of other member states.

Enforcement The European Court of Human Rights may be *the* most effective tool in this region's human rights arsenal. This is the judicial arm of the EHR treaty. The Court hears cases arising under the EHR treaty (§9.6). The Court is seated with the Council of Europe in Strasbourg, France. It was this court's predecessor that directed Ireland to permit a pregnant minor to leave the country for the purpose of obtaining an abortion in Great Britain, although the Irish Constitution forbade abortions under the circumstances.[45]

In 1998, a reconstituted court replaced the two prior entities responsible for ensuring that the Contracting Parties comply with their obligations under the Convention: a court with the same name, and the European Commission on Human Rights. The reform was spawned by the growing difficulty experienced by the prior judicial body and the former administrative Commission's efforts to cope with an ever-increasing volume of cases. The reconstitution of the European Court of Human Rights into various chambers, and the elimination of the European Commission on Human Rights, avoided the time-consuming examination of the same cases by two separate bodies. Under Protocol No. 11 to the European Convention on Human Rights (ECHR), the Court's jurisdiction is now compulsory. Under the prior system, acceptance of both the right of individual petition to the Commission and the Court's jurisdiction were optional. Another feature of the revised structure is that the adjudicative role of the Committee of Ministers of the Council of Europe was eliminated. The Committee of Ministers will, however, retain its present responsibility for supervising the execution of the Court's judgments.[46]

The European Court of Human Rights has been a very useful force for preserving human rights in Europe. One reason is that, unlike other international venues, individuals may themselves be parties—rather than States only.[47] In a 1998 decision, for example, the Court rendered a unanimous judgment against Bulgaria that had been brought by several individuals. They successfully claimed that, while a father had hit his plaintiff son on the day that injuries were also allegedly caused by the police, Bulgaria violated the ECHR. It failed to investigate "torture or degrading treatment or punishment" by public authorities, and thus failed to provide an effective remedy for police misconduct. The police also failed to adequately review the lawfulness of the son's two-year detention, during which the case should have come to trial.[48]

It would appear that school dress codes would be one of the more likely subjects for the application of State law. France and Great Britain, for example, are two of the most diverse societies in Europe. Each has had to respond to enormous pressure regarding Muslim practices. In August 2004, French hostages pled for their lives when their captors in Iraq demanded that France rescind its ban on Muslim headscarves in French public schools. This demand echoed amidst beheadings, and other pressures exerted by such groups, seeking the exodus of foreign military troops from Iraq. While the kidnappers would surely disagree, the French law did not target Muslims. It banned all insignia that "conspicuously manifest a religious affiliation," such as Jewish yarmulkas, large Christian crosses, and Muslim head scarves.

A British court likewise ended a two-year legal battle in March 2005. The case in question involved a Muslim teenager sent home from school for wearing a *jilbab*. It is a long, flowing gown that covers the entire body (except for hands and face). Overruling the initial trial court decision, an appellate panel determined that this ban "unlawfully denied her the right to manifest her religion." She was legally represented by Cherie Booth, the wife of Prime Minister Tony Blair.[49]

A September 2004 German Federal Constitutional Court case likewise upheld the right of a female Muslim teacher to wear a headscarf in her classes. Thus, the regional law could no longer ban religious symbols in German classrooms. All of these examples can be analogized to the current leading case from the European Courts of Human Rights. Its facts predate all of the preceding examples:

Leyla Sahin v. Turkey

EUROPEAN COURT OF
HUMAN RIGHTS
STRASBOURG, FRANCE
Application No. 44774/98
Judgment on the Merits (June 29, 2004)

Go to course Web page at
<http://home.att.net/~slomansonb/txtcsesite.html>.
Under Chapter Eleven, click Muslim Headscarf Case.

The European Court of Human Rights is a forum that also advocates limits on State excesses which can threaten regional stability. The following case is a classic illustration:

K.-H. W. v. Germany

EUROPEAN COURT OF
HUMAN RIGHTS
STRASBOURG, FRANCE
Application no. 37201/97
Judgment on the Merits (22 March 2001)

Go to course Web site
<http://home.att.net/~slomansonb/
txtcsesite.html>.
Under Chapter 11, click Berlin Wall Border Guard Case.

The existence of this comprehensive human rights machinery does not mean that the interests of the national participants always yield to the rights of the individual. For example, Great Britain's 1988 Prevention of Terrorism Act extended prearraignment detention for those suspected of terrorism from two to seven days. In the major national case to be prosecuted under that act, four men from Northern Ireland were held for periods of from five to seventeen days. They were never charged with a crime. They were unable to seek redress in the English courts and thus filed a claim in the European Court of Human Rights. The Court in Strasbourg held that England's law permitting police to detain suspected terrorists for even seven days without a hearing, violated the ECHR. The ECHR requires "prompt" access to a judicial officer after an arrest. The ECHR also provides for "an enforceable right to compensation." However, rather than complying with the court's ruling, the British government announced that it would withdraw from the applicable sections of the ECHR treaty. (The 1,100 suspected terrorists detained in the United States under its Patriot Act—between September 11, 2001 and the November 2001—fared no better.[50])

Notwithstanding occasional setbacks, this regional human rights process is the model for all regions of the world. The work of the ECHR and the national willingness to abide by its judgments has greatly contributed to overcoming the historical national sovereignty barriers to effective enforcement of International Human Rights Law. As summed up by University of Connecticut Professors Mark Janis and Richard Kay:

Nowadays, the European Court of Human Rights regularly finds nations in breach of their obligations under the international human rights law. . . . Remarkably, sovereign states have respected the adverse judgments of the Court . . . [and] have reformed or abandoned police procedures, penal institutions, child welfare practices, administrative agencies, court rules, labor relations, moral legislation, and many other important public matters. The willingness with which the decisions of the European Court have been accepted demonstrates the emergence of a crucial new fact in the Western legal tradition: an effective system of international law regulating some of the most sensitive areas of what previously had been thought to be fields within the exclusive domain of national sovereignty.[51]

In February 2005, the court ruled against Russia on six cases involving incidents occurring in Chechnya between October 1999 and February 2000. In each case, Russia violated Article 2 (right to life) and Article 3 (right to an effective remedy) of the European Convention on Human Rights. The applicants complained of various wrongs, including:

(a) Extra-judicial executions of their family members by Russian military forces

(b) Russian criminal investigations failing to identify those responsible, although a civilian court ordered the Russian Ministry of Defense to pay money damages to the families of the deceased

(c) The bombing of civilians attempting to escape the fighting in Chechnya's Grosny region

(d) The intentional and unnecessary destruction of civilian property.[52]

OSCE Process   Another European process has emerged as the regional guardian of human rights. Under the "Helsinki Final Act" of 1975, thirty-five nations (now fifty-five) convened the Conference on Security and Cooperation in Europe (CSCE—now OSCE). The initial driving force for this development was the former Soviet Union and other Warsaw Pact nations. They pursued the concept of a regional political and security arrangement for several decades. Canada and the United States were invited to participate because of their prominent positions in NATO.[53] The organization now has several institutions dedicated to the preservation of human rights,[54] including a High Commissioner on National Minorities and an OSCE Elections Commission whose task is to observe elections as an international observer.[55]

These entities are playing possibly their most prominent human rights role ever, working with the United Nations in its administration of Kosovo. The OSCE is the key agency responsible for human rights monitoring, protection, promotion, and capacity building. Its human rights monitors are deployed throughout Kosovo. They report human rights violations and assist in building a local capacity to self-monitor, report, and advocate human rights. Together with the United Nations High Commissioner for Refugees, the OSCE Mission's human rights teams have conducted surveys on the situation of ethnic minorities in the province.

The Final Act is not a treaty in the traditional sense. Its human rights work product more closely resembles the aspirational nature of the UN Charter and UDHR—which is not surprising given the comparatively large number of members from all over Europe. They are not integrated in the many ways enjoyed by members of the Council of Europe. The Act is a declaration of "Principles Guiding Relations Between Participating States." It is a political statement of principles not intended to be immediately binding. It provides a regional standard of achievement. The State participants decided not to commit themselves to anything other than general principles, due to a lack of consensus on the question of how to achieve regional security.

The fundamental human rights provision of the Helsinki Final Act is Principle VII of its Declaration of Principles. It provides that in "the field of human rights and fundamental freedoms, the participating States will act in conformity with the purposes and principles of the Charter of the United Nations and the Universal Declaration of Human Rights. They will also fulfill their obligations as set forth in the international declarations and agreements in this field, including inter alia the [1966] International Covenants on Human Rights. . . ."

International disagreements, about the individual's right to travel, was one reason for the early inability of conference participants to achieve a concrete agreement on security and human rights. Certain nations, particularly the United States, actively pursued implementation of the right of international travel. The US State Department issued annual reports for ten years after the initial 1975 CSCE conference, focusing on travel restrictions between East and West. The United States therein denounced Eastern European travel restrictions, typified by the former "Berlin Wall," as being contrary to the human rights principles stated in the Helsinki Declaration (*see, e.g.*, above *Berlin Wall Border Guard Case*).

The OSCE played a notable, but ultimately unsuccessful, role in monitoring the Russian assault on Chechnya that began in 1994. In 1995, Russian President Boris Yeltsin agreed to allow a OSCE human rights mission to maintain a permanent presence in the region. Yeltsin assured the foreign ministers of Germany, France, and Spain, while on a mission from the European Union, that Russia was committed to a political settlement of the Chechnya crisis to be undertaken in conformity with OSCE human rights objectives. The OSCE contribution in other fields is addressed in §3.5 (international organizations).

In April 2004, delegates from fifty-five OSCE nations met in Berlin for the OSCE Conference on Anti-Semitism, spawned in part by the notable increase in anti-Semitism in France. Leaders there unveiled their landmark "Berlin Declaration" against anti-Semitism, pledging to "intensify efforts to combat anti-Semitism in all its manifestations and to promote and strengthen tolerance and non-discrimination." Its key provisions are as follows:

> Recalling that Article 18 of the Universal Declaration on Human Rights and Article 18 of the International Covenant on Civil and Political Rights state that everyone has the right to freedom of thought, conscience and religion,
>
> . . .
>
> Recognizing that anti-Semitism, following its most devastating manifestation during the Holocaust, has assumed new forms and expressions, which, along with other forms of intolerance, pose a threat to democracy, the values of civilization and, therefore, to overall security in the OSCE region and beyond,
>
> . . .
>
> 3. Declare unambiguously that international developments or political issues, including those in Israel or elsewhere in the Middle East, never justify anti-Semitism. . . .[56]

LATIN AMERICAN PROGRAMS

Treaties   Human rights norms are expressed in the Charter of the Organization of American States (OAS),[57] the American Declaration of the Rights and Duties of Man, and the American Convention on Human Rights. These norms are monitored by the Inter-American Commission on Human Rights.

The OAS Charter and the American Declaration of the Rights and Duties of Man were both proclaimed in 1948. The latter declaration of principles echo the political and civil rights contained in the UN's 1948 UDHR (§11.2). Its duties include the individual's required obedience of the law and the general duty to conduct oneself in a way that serves the immediate community and the nation.

Like the UN Charter and the UDHR, the rights contained in the American Declaration were not intended to immediately bind the participating Latin American States. It would be better to obtain State participation in a process that at least paid lip service to modern human rights perspectives rather than risk an OAS with very few members. Yet the signatories did agree to a general statement of principles which set the normative stage for embracing the democratic ideals of the modern human rights agenda.

The most recent Latin American human rights document is the American Convention on Human Rights. In the mid-1970s, OAS members decide to expand the minimal human rights provisions contained in the 1948 OAS Charter (as amended in 1970) and the 1948 American Declaration of the Rights and Duties of Man. They were concerned because the latter document emphasized the duties of the individual rather than those of the State. The product of their work was the American Convention on Human Rights. It contains many of the human rights mentioned in the UN Charter and Universal Declaration of Human Rights. The American Declaration was one response to the excesses of the military governments of the 1960s and 1970s.

Prior to its entry into force in 1978, the existing Inter-American Commission on Human Rights did not have a reliable legal foundation, which could be traced to any document drawn by OAS member nations. The American Convention provided an express source for the Commission's power to hear and determine human rights violations. As you read its following provisions, as note the similarity to the UN program (§11.2):

American Convention on Human Rights

1969 Pact of San Jose, Costa Rica
<http://www.oas.org>

The American states signatory to the present Convention . . .

Recognizing that the essential rights of man are not derived from one's being a national of a certain state, but are based upon attributes of the human personality, and that they therefore justify international protection in the form of a convention reinforcing or complementing the protection provided by the domestic law of the American states;

. . .

Have agreed upon the following:

Part I State Obligations and Rights Protected

Article 1. Obligation to Respect Rights

1. The States Parties to this Convention undertake to respect the rights and freedoms recognized herein and to ensure to all persons subject to their jurisdiction the free and full exercise of those rights and freedoms, without any discrimination for reasons of race, color, sex, language, religion, political or other opinion, national or social origin, economic status, birth, or any other social condition.

. . .

Chapter II Civil and Political Rights

Article 4. Right to Life

1. Every person has the right to have his life respected. This right shall be protected by law and, in general, from the moment of conception. No one shall be arbitrarily deprived of his life.
2. In countries that have not abolished the death penalty, it may be imposed only for the most serious crimes and pursuant to a final judgment rendered by a competent court and in accordance with a law establishing such punishment, enacted prior to the commission of the crime. The application of such punishment shall not be extended to crimes to which it does not presently apply.

Article 5. Right to Humane Treatment

2. No one shall be subjected to torture or to cruel, inhuman, or degrading punishment or treatment. All persons deprived of their liberty shall be treated with respect for the inherent dignity of the human person.

. . .

Chapter III Economic, Social, and Cultural Rights

Article 26. Progressive Development

The States Parties undertake to adopt measures, both internally and through international cooperation, especially those of an economic and technical nature, with a view to achieving progressively, by legislation or other appropriate means, the full realization of the rights implicit in the economic, social, educational, scientific, and cultural standards set forth in the Charter of the Organization of American States

. . .

Chapter VII Inter-American Commission on Human Rights

Article 41. [Functions]

The main function of the Commission shall be to promote respect for and defense of human rights.

. . .

Article 44. [Competence]

Any person or group of persons, or any nongovernmental entity legally recognized in one or more member states of the Organization, may lodge petitions with the Commission containing denunciations or complaints of violation of this Convention by a State Party.

There have been mixed reactions to the region's apparent human rights achievements. The OAS Inter-American Commission on Human Rights, for example, conducted an early human rights investigation when Cuba's Castro regime imprisoned anyone suspected of disloyalty to the 1959 revolution. Cuba did not allow the Commission to conduct inspections. Its members thus conducted hearings in Florida where it interviewed Cuban refugees. The Commission found that there was a widespread suspension of the human rights guaranteed by various regional instruments. Cuba was ultimately expelled from the OAS. Yet many commentators, who noted that similar violations occurred in the same period elsewhere in Latin America, espoused the conviction that superpower Cold War politics played a larger role in this expulsion than human rights abuse. Numerous military dictatorships in Latin America had employed similar tactics to control their people, but were not the object of such detailed human rights scrutiny.

One must acknowledge the seeming paradox that Latin America enunciated more than its share of normative human rights values, while at the same time enduring a tradition of repressive regimes. Contrasting the political underpinnings in Western Europe and Latin America during the evolution of their respective human rights regimes in the 1970s provides a rather provocative insight. As portrayed by a past president of the Inter-American Commission on Human Rights:

Western Europe's human rights institutions, the Commission and the Court [of Human Rights], also charged governments with violations of human rights. . . . Moreover, both competitive elections and . . . constitutional restraints enforced by independent courts broadly limited their ends and means to those generally consistent in fact with internationally recognized human rights. . . .

Latin American constitutions also contained long lists of protected rights and corresponding checks on government action. But few, if any, countries had effectively independent judiciaries available and committed to enforcing them. Furthermore, on close inspection constitutional restraints were often riddled with specific exceptions and were for the most part subject to derogation in times of emergency. And the region's constitutional courts had shown little zeal for auditing executive branch claims that the required emergency existed and that the particular suspension of guarantees was reasonably necessary to protect public order. Their determined passivity may not have been entirely unconnected to the fact that judges . . . came from the same middle and upper classes suffused with anxiety about Leftist threats to the established order of things. Serving in the midst of what luminaries of that order . . . declared to be a global Cold War and in ideologically polarized societies, judges would naturally be inclined to concede to governments a very large margin of appreciation about the requirements of domestic security. In actual fact, however, governments . . . committed the most flagrant human rights delinquencies secretly or at least behind the often thin veil of official denial.[58]

There was another disconnect with the apparent regional human rights renaissance in Latin America. There had been a shift from military to democratic governments everywhere except in Cuba. Chile's Pinochet was not unique (case presented in §2.6). In the 1960s and the 1970s, the military dictators in this region were well known for their *desaparecidos*. These were the "disappeared" individuals who were political or personal enemies of government officials. These dictatorships, which had exhibited little concern for human rights, suddenly shifted to democracies in the 1980s. The evidence of improvement, however, was far from conclusive. Commentators were at best reluctantly positive. Many charged that little had actually changed when military rule was replaced with civilian rule. The collapse of military dictatorships did not minimize the degree of human rights violations for years to come. The following 1987 excerpt from the US-based Pacific News Service explains the apparent paradox:

The most telling clue to what sustains terror in democracies lies in Argentina where last April [1987], President Raul Alfonsin reached an accord with military officers. The accord followed protests in which some military [personnel] occupied bases to block the prosecution of fellow officers for human rights abuses committed during the 1970s.

The Argentine military functions almost like an American political party—with its own leaders, hierarchy, and civilian constituents who support it either out of blood ties or . . . the conviction that any drastic action to preserve law and order is justified. But it is a party with a difference—it has a monopoly on modern weapons and a fiercely loyal membership. Government officials have little weight with military officers, who have risen in rank because of their allegiance to generals, not to democracy.

Threatened with a coup, President Alfonsin agreed not to prosecute lower ranking officers—and to preserve democratic rule. He made a "convivencia," or "living together" [arrangement of convenience]. . . .

Nor is the convivencia unique to Argentina. Similar agreements exist in Guatemala, Peru, Columbia, Ecuador, Bolivia, El Salvador, and Uruguay, where civil-

ian governments no longer [bother to] determine the level of human rights abuse.

In democratically ruled Guatemala, infamous secret police still "disappear" government critics—425 political assassinations were recorded by the local press in the first two months of 1987 alone, according to US Embassy sources. . . .

And death squads continue to haunt such democratically run countries as Brazil, El Salvador, and Ecuador.[59]

Cases While the foregoing account does not paint a comforting picture, there is clear evidence that the Inter-American judicial process has had its very positive moments. To its credit, the Inter-American Commission on Human Rights, working in conjunction with the Inter-American Court of Human Rights, has prosecuted violations and has even allowed *amicus curiae* (friends of the court briefs) by some very prominent human rights NGOs from a distant member State. A classic illustration of judicial independence, in a very sensitive context, appears in the following case where legal briefs were submitted by Amnesty International, the Association of the Bar of the City of New York, the Lawyers Committee for Human Rights, and the Minnesota Lawyers International Human Rights Committee:

www **Velasquez Rodríguez Case**

INTER-AMERICAN COURT
OF HUMAN RIGHTS
Inter-Am. Ct. H.R. (Ser. C) No. 4
Judgment of July 29, 1988
Go to course Web page
<http://home.att.net/~slomansonb/txtcsesite.html>.
Under Chapter Eleven, click
Rodríguez v. Honduras.

Certain countries (including the United States) have not ratified the American Convention on Human Rights. Their rationale is that they cannot determine the extent of their commitments under the "full and free exercise of human rights" provision of the Convention. Without specific obligations being set forth in that agreement, they are unwilling to commit themselves to a process that does not fully identify the outer parameters of State responsibility to the individual.

Some OAS nations have been reluctant to ratify the 1978 American Convention for yet another reason. A unique human rights provision was inserted into the 1978 American Convention, stating that judicial remedies for certain rights cannot be suspended. The treaty-based right of *habeas corpus* means that prison officials can be forced to produce a prisoner for a prompt judicial examination of the legality of an incarceration. Under the Convention, that right cannot be suspended, even in time of emergency.[60]

Section 9.4 of this book addressed the extent to which the UN's International Court of Justice could advance International Law via its advisory opinions. This facet of the ICJ judicial power may be initiated only by a UN organ when it is unlikely that the disputing States will agree to an adversarial resolution by the ICJ. In Latin America, by contrast, the ability of the Inter-American Court of Human Rights to enhance the development of human rights is broader. In addition to OAS organs, any member State—not just the State parties to the Inter-American Convention—may request an advisory opinion. Further, the Court's Article 64.1 advisory jurisdiction is not limited to interpreting just the Convention. It extends to all "other treaties concerning the protection of human rights in the American States."

The following case illustrates the Court's advisory jurisdiction at work:

---

www **Interpretation of the American Declaration of Rights and Duties of Man Within the Framework of Article 64 of the American Convention on Human Rights**

ADVISORY OPINION OC-10/89
INTER-AMERICAN COURT OF HUMAN
RIGHTS, 1989
<http://www.corteidh.or.cr/seriea_ing/
index.html>, click Series A No. 10
Go to course Web site at
<http://home.att.net/~slomansonb/txtcsesite.html>.
Under Chapter Eleven, click American
Declaration Case.

In 1994, the OAS promulgated two new human rights instruments: (1) the Inter-American Convention on Forced Disappearance of Persons; and (2) the Inter-American Convention on the Prevention, Punishment and Eradication of Violence Against Women.[61] The impact of the dictatorships of twenty plus years ago is fading. The OAS is increasingly engaging in regional and international business ventures (§13.3). It is taking significant steps to eliminate the historical characterization of Latin America as a region where States are committed only in principle to the rule of law in human rights matters. The Form For Presenting Petitions on Human Rights Violations is prominently posted on the OAS Web site.[62] All such international instruments are geared toward eliminating "'Disappearances' [which] have come to be regarded as a quintessential evil practiced by abusive governments."[63]

AFRICAN PROGRAMS

The Organization of African Unity (OAU) became Africa's political organization of States (§3.5). The 1963 OAU Charter reaffirmed the human rights principles of the UN Charter and the UN's Universal Declaration of Human Rights. It added certain rights not contained in those documents, such as the rights to the "eradication of colonialism" and the well-being of the African people.

Like other regional human rights documents, the OAU Charter provisions are moral rights that exist on paper awaiting implementation. University of Calabar (Nigeria) Professor U. O. Umozurike characterizes this situation as follows:

During the 1970s human rights appeared to enjoy low esteem in Africa. . . . The O.A.U. maintained an indifferent attitude to the suppression of human rights in a number of independent African states by unduly emphasizing the principle of noninterference in the internal affairs of member states at the expense of certain other principles, particularly the customary law principle of respect for human rights. . . . For instance, the massacres of thousands of Hutu [tribal people] in Burundi in 1972 and 1973 were neither discussed nor condemned by the O.A.U., which regarded them as matters of [Burundi's] internal affairs. The notorious regimes of Idi Amin of Uganda (1971-1979) [and other African leaders] escaped the criticism of the O.A.U. and most of its members.[64]

One could of course add a score of other subsequent disasters, including the 1994 Rwanda genocide where

800,000 citizens were hacked to death while the OAU, neighboring African nations, and the United Nations knowingly failed to react.[65]

In his 1993 treatise on International Law, Professor Umozurike characterized the positive potential of the Banjul (African) Charter on Human and Peoples' Rights, which entered into force in 1986. It contains rights like those in the above UN's 1966 Covenants (§11.2). A number of those rights can be derogated by law, however, without any significant limitations on the State parties. While the African Charter internationalizes human rights on the African Continent, "there are practically no effective measures for enforcement."[66]

Why do human rights in Africa not enjoy the degree of recognition found in Europe or the Americas? One reason is that the question just posed contains a degree of cultural relativism. The latter societies tend to perceive the human rights as having a broader basis than just the individual. A Danish scholar who has written extensively on comparative human rights issues commented as follows on the divergent paradigms:

[W]hile the American approach reflects a strong ideological stance favorable to universality of human rights, the Europeans base their conclusions more on the degree to which the universality is reflected empirically in the various instruments.

The African approach can mainly be divided into two schools, the first of which constitutes the most radical opposition to [a] universalist approach. The main argument here is rooted in the different philosophical basis of Western Europe and Africa, with a particular emphasis on the lack of an individualistically perceived personality in traditional African culture, which would render most human rights inapplicable.[67]

The African perspective is generally one involving a distrust of internationally derived human rights measures. Some African scholars perceive these "global" rights as being yet another attempt to impose Western cultural values on the African continent. University of Cape Town Professor T. W. Bennett summarized this position in his study of human rights in southern Africa (in 1991, just prior to South Africa's cessation of minority white political governance):

The talk about human rights that currently permeates discussions about South African law has its origins in the [external] international and constitutional human rights movement. The universality claimed for this movement should not obscure its actual cultural provenance. Although the accession of many developing countries to United Nations declarations and international [human rights] conventions gives a superficial impression of universalism, human rights are the product of bourgeois western values. In many parts of Africa this has given cause for suspicion about a renewed attempt to impose western cultural hegemony.

[The author then refutes the argument that human rights are irrelevant to the situation in Africa, with counter arguments including the following:] . . . Feminist studies, for instance, have revealed that women used to be assured of material protection and support within the framework of the extended family; after the introduction of capitalism, however, the system of labour migration caused the breakdown of this family structure to the detriment of women (amongst others). They have now been rendered vulnerable, and at the same time forced to undertake roles (for which they have no formal legal powers) that were previously prescribed for all men.[68]

Like Latin America's 1948 American Declaration on the Rights and Duties of Man, the 1986 Banjul (African) Charter on Human Rights focuses on duties. The individual has the duty to preserve family, society, the State, and even the OAU. For example, individuals must care for their parents and always conduct themselves in a way that "preserves social and national solidarity."

The fulfillment of such duties may be perverted by a national leader. Idi Amin suppressed individual rights in Uganda, leading to thousands of citizens being killed or jailed without just cause in the 1970s. While no human rights document would mean anything to a leader like Amin, the 1986 African Charter conveniently emphasized duties rather than the minimal rights denied to Ugandans under Amin. As stated by Professor Umozurike, the "concept of duties stressed in the Charter is quite likely to be abused by a few regimes on the continent, if the recent past can be any guide to future developments. Such governments will emphasize the duties of individuals to their states but will play down their rights and legitimate expectations."[69]

Like other global and regional instruments, the 1986 African Charter established an administrative commission for overseeing the observance of human rights. The African

Commission on Human Rights is an eleven-member body composed of representatives from the fifty-two member nations of the OAU. Seated in Bangul, Gambia, the Commission is tasked with managing alleged human rights violations on the African Continent. It may only study, report, and recommend. It has no enforcement powers. It conducts country studies and makes recommendations to member governments. The Commission has the power to publish its reports when it concludes that an OAU State has violated the human rights provisions of the African Charter.[70] This Commission's very existence, however, represents a significant aspirational improvement after centuries of slave trade, colonialism, and despotic regimes. But that regional mechanism was nevertheless unable to regulate the egregious human rights violations exemplified by the Rwandan slaughter of 1994.

If one were to characterize the Commission's power of publication of negative reports as a voice for enforcing human rights in Africa, then that voice may be easily silenced. Individuals and States may report violations of the African Charter to the commission. The Commission then explores the basis for such claims, drafts confirming reports, and may publish them in all OAU countries. The allegedly offending nation's leader may, however, avoid such negative publicity by requesting a vote from the OAU Assembly (Africa's heads of State) to block publication. Since its creation, the Commission has not published one adverse report of mistreatment of individuals by an OAU member State.

There is a fresh perspective, however. The October 2002 Cairo-Arusha principles on Universal Jurisdiction in Respect of Gross Human Rights Offenses are an attempt to use universal jurisdiction (§5.2) in a unique way. Universal jurisdiction would apply to gross violations in both war and "even in peacetime." It would not be limited to just individual defendants, but would be extended to legal entities such as States or corporations. Crimes that the Cairo-Arusha Principles add to the usual list of universal crimes (specifically referring to the Statute of the International Criminal Court) would include acts of plunder, gross misappropriation of public resources, trafficking in human beings, and serious environmental crimes.[71] The use of truth and reconciliation commissions, and other alternative forms of justice, would not relieve States of their "responsibility and their duty" to prosecute, extradite, or transfer persons suspected or accused of gross human rights violations under International Law. The principles also provide that the victims of these offenses should receive reparation, "to the extent possible." The cost of this civil remedy, if implemented, would be extraordinary—a main objective of the Cairo-Arusha Principles.

In December 2003, a protocol to the African Charter presented State members with the opportunity to establish an African Court on Human and Peoples' Rights. The body is supposed to compliment and reinforce the functions of the above Commission on Human and Peoples' Rights. Pursuant to this Protocol, the Court "will address the need to build a just, united and peaceful Continent free from fear, want, and ignorance . . . [and it will] enhance the African Union's Commitment to the realisation of human rights . . . on the Continent." This treaty entered into force in 2004.

ASIAN PERSPECTIVES

A number of Chinese scholars view the existing International Law of Human Rights as a pretext for intervention in the internal affairs of socialist nations. They believe that the field of human rights is primarily a matter governed by the internal law of a State rather than one falling within the competence of International Law. Any pressure on China to apply Western standards to the government's treatment of its own citizens would interfere with Chinese sovereignty. The Chinese were quite offended, for example, when the 1989 government restraints of the student uprisings in Beijing were characterized by the Western press as a return to Maoist-era restrictions on internationally recognized human rights. See Fig.11.1.

A representative Chinese scholar from the earlier Maoist era rationalized such treatment with the perspective that human rights have been intact in China for some time. Thus, there is no need to embrace the approach expressed in the UN's International Bill of Human Rights. The elimination of private ownership of property, for example, is perceived as a guarantee of the genuine realization of human rights of the Chinese people. Chinese Professor Ch'ien Szu stated in 1960 that the "rights of landlords and bourgeoisie arbitrarily to oppress and enslave laboring people are eliminated; the privilege of imperialism and its agents to do mischief . . . is also eliminated. To the vast masses of people, this is a wonderfully good thing; this is genuine protection of the human rights of the people. The bourgeois . . . international law scholars, however, consider this to be a bad thing, since it encroaches upon the 'human rights' of the oppressors and exploiters."[72]

A Chinese man stands alone before a row of Chinese tanks at the time of the 1989 Tianenman Square massacre in Beijing, China. AP photo by Jeff Widener reprinted with permission of AP/World Wide Photos.

Contemporary human rights perspectives are not as State-centric as in previous eras. In the aftermath of the Cultural Revolution of 1966–1976, Professor Szu's perspective would no longer be representative of recent Chinese scholarship on human rights. Contemporary thought is that the way in which one country or group establishes a human rights model is not necessarily the sole criterion for judging the performance of other countries. Chinese citizens enjoy far greater human rights protection now than in the Maoist era.[73] Yet the People's Republic of China (PRC) was rather irritated when Hong Kong incorporated the UN Covenant on Civil and Political Rights into its domestic law just prior to the PRC's takeover by China. The 1991 Bill of Rights Ordinance made the UN Covenant the essential source of human rights law in Hong Kong.[74]

Scholars in Asia's democratic States have a distinct criticism for what they characterize as arrogant Western human rights standards. Indian scholars believe that the Western-derived concepts of human rights, stated in the UN Charter and the various regional programs modeled after the Charter, benefit only developed States. Thus, the UN's international human rights program has little meaning for a State whose people do not all have the basic necessities of life. As articulated by Patna University (India) Dean Hingorini, traditional "human rights have no meaning for these States and their peoples. Their first priority is [obtaining] basic necessities of life. These are bread, clothing and shelter. These necessities of life could be termed as basic human rights for them."[75]

Dean Hingorini's perspective does not mean that Indian scholars *oppose* the human rights principles set forth in the various United Nations and regional charters. Those politically oriented rights are irrelevant for the time being and of little practical value to the people of India today. Attaining such rights, as expressed in what might be considered an advanced UN model, cannot take precedence over India's need to first provide the more basic essentials to its populace. The more developed nations can afford to be the champions of political and economic human rights such as the rights to work and education.

Indian scholars also perceive developed nations as proclaiming the importance of such advanced rights for the convenient purpose of ensuring that their multinational corporations can exploit the Indian masses. As East Indian Professor S.B.O. Gutto recalls:

Historical developments in the Third World countries in the last few decades have firmly fashioned the Third World as theaters for the violation of human rights. . . . Classical international law, under the umbrella of "law of nations" developed as a major super-structural tool for facilitating and justifying the actions of some states and their agents, in ensuring the dominant economic classes and institutions, and in dividing the world into spheres where . . . enslavement, dehumanization, super-exploitation of peoples labour and resources takes place. The unsatisfactory condition of human rights in the Third World today is therefore not solely a reflection of inherent social factors in the Third World but rather products of the historical relations in the world system corresponding to the international division of labor.[76]

The contemporary scope of national economic development may thus be correlated to the degree of affordable human rights enjoyed by a nation's populace. A high percentage of unemployment may be characterized under prevailing human rights norms, such as a State's failure to afford the right to work. An underdeveloped country like India is not economically equipped to create and implement such human rights, however, or to establish commissions to monitor human rights observance. Such countries must first achieve a comparatively minimal degree of economic development. India's Professor T. O. Elias, formerly a judge of the ICJ, articulated the following assessment of this correlation when he described the 1964 Seminars on Human Rights in Developing Countries conducted in Kabul, Afghanistan: "[T]he

existence of adequate material means and a high standard of economic development were essential prerequisites of the full and effective enjoyment of economic, social and cultural rights, and contributed to the promotion of civil and political rights. . . . [T]he right to work was meaningless in countries where employment opportunities were grossly inadequate owing to overpopulation combined with economic underdevelopment."

In the last two decades, some 10 million female fetuses have been aborted, because of the availability of ultrasound equipment to identify gender. The law officially prevents doctors from revealing this information to the parents. But as explained by Bombay's Doctor Shirish Sheth: "Daughters are regarded as a liability. . . . In some communities where the custom of dowry still prevails, the cost of her dowry could be phenomenal."[77]

Given these realities, a comparatively poor and undeveloped economy simply cannot afford the contemporary package of human rights espoused by the more developed nations. Any attempt to implement Western political and economic rights would detract less developed nations from other national priorities—one of which is the right to development.[78] They must necessarily delay realization of these "advanced" rights contained in the prevailing human rights instruments until the far more "basic" human rights to food and adequate living conditions are first realized.

Muslim Perspectives International human rights norms are supposed to exert external limitations on how a State governs its inhabitants. But as benchmarks for modern constitutional democracies, they are not necessarily as fungible as you and I might have expected. The key measurements should include: Does a given State tolerate open discussion by diverse segments of its population? Does it allow the weak a voice in their political and personal affairs? It is at this point that one can compare contemporary Muslim States, in terms of their internal human rights philosophy and practice.

University of Illinois Professor Maimul Ahsan Khan is one of the foremost analysts of human rights in the Muslim world. His work illustrates the clash of ideals between the majority of contemporary Muslim States and today's growing number of constitutional democracies:

Islamic Legal Philosophy and Human Rights

Maimul Ahsan Khan

HUMAN RIGHTS AND THE MUSLIM WORLD:
FUNDAMENTALISM, CONSTITUTIONALISM, AND INTERNATIONAL POLITICS 237–242

(Durham, NC: Carolina Academic Press, 2003)

. . .

[V]ery rarely can we find a Muslim nation-state that can boast of having a functional constitutional system with long-lasting effects on the rule of law and human rights. The Muslim governments have been failing for a long time in developing their own constitutional system based on the legal doctrines presented in the Islamic sources.

. . . The tragedy of the Muslim people is that the ruled Muslim lacks consciousness and awareness regarding the necessity of a strong constitutional system, and the Muslim rulers are indifferent to the basic human rights of their own people.

. . .

The unfortunate reality is that today Muslims predominantly remain illiterate, and in this respect the situation in the oil-rich Arab countries is no better than that of their fellow non-Arab poor Muslim nations.

. . .

The main indicator of the success and failure of the Western and secular concepts of human rights is material achievement, while spiritual salvation is the prime concern of Islamic concepts of human rights. In material terms, a state or society may be rich, but its humane character may be horribly poor because of its weak moral, ethical, and spiritual foundation. . . .

. . .

The real state of affairs concerning basic human rights in the modern Muslim nation-states does not fulfill the demands of the day. The poor performance of Muslim governments in realizing various human rights in their societies remains as a colonial legacy, and no Westernization process has helped Muslim societies achieve good governance on their own. . . . [They] have in fact adversely affected the general welfare and standard of the rule of law sustained by autocratic Muslim leaders and politicians.

. . .

With the help of their Western allies, many Muslim governments have been brutal in exercising state powers over their own people. That very unfortunate phenomenon has been met with popular uprisings in the Muslim world. This is the backdrop of the wide-ranging violations of human rights by the Muslim governments and the resurgence of Muslim militant groups throughout the world.

◆ 11.4 OTHER HUMAN RIGHTS ACTORS

NONGOVERNMENTAL ORGANIZATIONS

Previous sections of this chapter addressed the regional and global efforts of international organizations to secure the human rights of the individual. Other human rights organizations and entities are also effective advocates. The most prominent are the privately constituted nongovernmental organizations (§3.2). They have undertaken the rather daunting task of prodding the national observance of international human rights norms, especially where State actors have paid only lip service to this objective. The State-centric system of International Law brands them as "nongovernmental" institutions a.k.a. NGOs.[79]

There are limitations on the resources that States are actually willing to commit to human rights objectives. This is where NGOs routinely assist, but not without occasional blemishes on the State-NGO relationship. In mid-1993, for example, 167 State representatives convened the Second UN World Human Rights Conference in Vienna. Their work product was the "Vienna Declaration and Programme of Action."[80] Their key objectives were to advocate creation of an ICC and the Office of the UN High Commissioner for Human Rights. Both were achieved. The primary credit for these developments in the International Law of Human Rights was attributed to other public institutions. The UN Security Council established the first *ad hoc* ICC in 1993. The UN General Assembly finally established the Office of the High Commissioner in 1994.

One thousand five hundred NGOs sent representatives. The United Nations ousted them from the drafting of the Conference's Vienna Declaration and Programme for Action. The more powerful NGOs such as Amnesty International bitterly protested. But China's threatened boycott convinced the United Nations to bar NGOs from direct participation. China's perspective was that the United Nations does not need NGOs. The PRC's position reflects that of many Asian States. They perceive western States as attempting to impose their religious and cultural values under color of UN authority, when they denounce human rights abuses in politically targeted regions or countries. The NGOs responded to this ouster by accusing the United Nations of bowing to national pressure and thereby retarding the achievable degree of accountability for human rights violations.

These private organizations have nevertheless played a very critical role in human rights monitoring. The International Red Cross is one of the most prominent. Its efforts included relentless pressure for internationalizing the Laws of War (§10.6). The most significant work product was the 1949 Geneva Conventions and their Protocols, which deal with the treatment of civilians and prisoners during the time of war and related hostilities (Exhibit 10.3). The Red Cross is the NGO that routinely inspects various national detention centers that hold political prisoners so that inmates might receive medical and other basic necessities.

The Red Cross also pressured the US military to cease its torture of prisoners at the US government's Guantanamo Bay prison in Cuba. Upon release, victims can seek the aid of Redress, the London-based human rights organization for assisting released tortured individuals to reintegrate into society.[81]

Doctors Without Borders is another prominent NGO that aids those afflicted by military conflict. In June 2004, this organization lost five more members in Afghanistan, bringing its death toll to thirty-two. As claimed by a Taliban representative: "We killed them because they worked for the Americans against us, using the cover of aid work. We will kill more foreign aid workers."

Amnesty International (AI) is probably the most prominent watchdog group. This NGO has offices and individual members throughout the world. AI produces annual reports on national compliance with the various human rights treaties and declarations on human rights. It is one of the many private monitors that publicize the human rights problems discussed in this chapter. As noted by Iceland's A.I. Director, in describing the power of the individual to change the behavior of governments all over the world: "The two pillars of Amnesty International's effectiveness are reliable research and the ability to mobilise people around the world for action. . . . The research work is backed up by visits to the countries for fact-finding investigations, trial observations and meetings with both governmental and nongovernmental bodies. . . . The government in question will start receiving appeals from the rest of the world."[82]

The major human rights NGOs enjoy consultative status in various international. organizations including the Council of Europe, the OAS, and UNESCO. Their representatives present reports to these organizations as a way of maintaining public scrutiny of offending State practices.

A prominent but admittedly incomplete listing of the major human rights NGOs (and headquarters) includes: AI (London), Canadian Human Rights Foundation (Montreal), Civil Liberties Organization (Nigeria), Committee for the Defense of Democratic Freedoms and Human Rights in Syria (Damascus), Doctors Without Borders (Paris), Human Rights Watch (New York), International Association of Democratic Lawyers (Brussels), International Commission of Jurists (Geneva), International Committee of the Red Cross (Geneva), International Federation for the Rights of Man (Paris), International Helsinki Federation for Human Rights (Vienna), International League for Human Rights (New York), Lawyers Committee for Human Rights (New York), Lawyers Without Borders (Connecticut), and Punjab Human Rights Organization (Chandigarh).[83]

PRIVATE CORPORATIONS

Can a private corporation violate human rights law? Recent US litigation has begun to address the reality of multinational corporate entities that either promote or engage in human rights violations against individuals abroad. The foreign government will of course claim sovereign immunity. But corporate actors have been increasingly scrutinized for their conduct undertaken in concert with a State actor that tramples on the rights of the individual. The following is a classic illustration, in what is probably the most prominent case to go to trial:

John Doe 1 v. Unocal Corporation

UNITED STATES COURT OF APPEALS,
NINTH CIRCUIT
395 F.3d 932 (2002)

Go to course Web page at
<http://home.att.net/~slomansonb/txtcsesite.html>.
Under Chapter Eleven, click Corporate Human
Rights Case.

In August 2003, the UN Sub-Commission for the Promotion and Protection of Human Rights unanimously adopted a resolution entitled Draft Norms on the Responsibility of Transnational Corporations and Other Business Enterprises with Regard to Human Rights. Under two of its key norms:

◆ (c)(3): Transnational corporations and other business enterprises shall not engage in nor benefit from war crimes, crimes against humanity, genocide, torture, forced disappearance, forced or compulsory labour, hostage-taking, extrajudicial, summary or arbitrary executions, other violations of humanitarian law and other international crimes against the human person as defined by international law, in particular human rights and humanitarian law.

. . .

◆ (h)(18): Transnational corporations and other business enterprises shall provide prompt, effective and adequate reparation to those persons, entities and communities that have been adversely affected by failures to comply with these Norms through, inter alia, reparations, restitution, compensation and rehabilitation for any damage done or property taken. In connection with determining damages in regard to criminal sanctions, and in all other respects, these Norms shall be applied by national courts and/or international tribunals, pursuant to national and international law.

Under a quotable but Pollyannaish resolution, this subcommittee decided "to invite the transnational corporations or other business enterprises concerned to

provide any comments they may wish within a reasonable time. . . ."[84]

That these norms are available does not mean that transnational corporations will readily agree to incorporate them into their contractual and corporate culture. The United States, for example, has not agreed to the Kyoto Protocol on greenhouse gas emissions because of the expense to its corporations (§12.2). Nevertheless, the UN's promulgation of *some* human rights norms for corporate behavior is a step forward. Some companies have actually agreed to "road test" these principles.[85]

Until this point, attempts to control human rights abuses have been geared toward State and individual actors. That focus resulted from the State-centric system which essentially shielded business enterprises—throughout the Industrial Revolution—from claims that they too can be liable for human rights abuses.

GENDER PERSPECTIVES

A State actor incurs international liability for gender discrimination in the rare instances where national objectives include official crimes against women as such. Examples of State responsibility for discrimination against women would be the Bosnian Serb *de facto* State tactic of encouraging the rape of Muslim (and other) women as a method for driving them out of a particular area of Bosnia. Afghanistan's Taliban government officially treated women different than men, which has its religious roots in the *Qur'an*. That government would, of course, accuse the West of cultural relativism. Its treatment of any person within its borders would thus be considered a matter of local law, rather than falling within the province of International Law.

The historical "public/private" International Law dichotomy does not favor females who are harmed by non-State actors, such as their husbands or fathers. Perpetrators have historically acted just beyond the grasp of International Law—which governs the conduct of *nations* in their mutual relations. However, certain legal theorists characterize this traditional policy as perpetuating a disengagement of the State from historical, economic, and political reality. While the State is the primary actor in International Law, human rights law is designed to guarantee freedom and equality of the individual on the international level—premised upon the pervasive rights of liberty and equality of the individual.

The University of Sydney's Shelley Wright, in a 1993 study by the American Society of International Law, notes that "international law depends on an ambiguous definition of the state which includes [the elements of] territory, population, and government. The indeterminate nature of this definition means that women's unequal participation in the habitation, ownership, and use of territory and other material sources; women's primary role in the reproduction of population; and their absence from government is left unrecognized in international law. This [indifference] in turn ensures that male control of these processes at a national and global level remains undisturbed by international regulation."[86]

One of the foremost analysts, the University of Minnesota's professor Cheryl Thomas, aptly articulates the pressure on the international community of States to bring women's rights under the umbrella of international human rights law:

Evidence from every region of the world indicates that when women turn to their legal systems for recourse from violence in their homes, the treatment they receive is frequently hostile, with authorities failing to acknowledge the crime of wife assault and doing nothing to prevent further violence.

. . .

In the United States, police have been described as 'largely indifferent' to domestic violence.

. . .

[A]ccording to Bulgarian law, in the case of medium-level injuries, the law distinguishes between an assault by a stranger and one by a relative. Those injured by a relative are not entitled to involvement by the state prosecutor's office. They may prosecute their own cases but must do so alone; they must locate and call their own witnesses and present their own evidence in court. A prosecutor from Sofia, Bulgaria, explained in 1995: "A woman must decide for herself whether she wants to harm the family relationship through prosecution; the state will not damage the family by assisting her."[87]

The 1979 Convention on the Elimination of All Forms of Discrimination Against Women—a product of the UN Decade of the Woman—entered into force in 1981. It specifically observes that, despite the existence of the UN Charter and the Universal Declaration of Human Rights, "extensive discrimination against women continues to exist. Recalling that discrimination against women violates the principles of equality of rights and respect for human dignity, [it] is an obstacle to the participation of women, on equal terms with men, in the political, social, economic and cultural life of their countries [which] hampers the growth and prosperity of society and the family and makes more difficult the full development of the potentialities of women in the service of their countries and humanity." In 1988, the UN General Assembly called upon all States to ratify this treaty. There have been mixed reactions, even in western democracies. For example, Canada and Mexico have ratified this treaty, but not the United States.

An illustration of its application appeared in a 1999 Canadian Supreme Court case, involving a woman who said "no" three times, before an employer engaged in intimate relations without *express* consent. The court held that Canadian law no longer recognizes the defense of *implied* consent to sexual assault. Justice McLachlin stated that "[t]he specious defence of implied consent (consent implied by law), as applied in this case [by the trial judge], rests on the assumption that unless a woman protests or resists, she should be 'deemed' to consent. . . . On appeal, the idea also surfaced that if a woman is not modestly dressed, she is deemed to consent. Such stereotypical assumptions find their roots in many cultures, including our own. They no longer, however, find a place in Canadian law." In a concurring opinion, Justice L'Heureux-Dube noted that the General Assembly's 1988 Declaration on the Elimination of Violence Against Women sets a *common international standard,* whereby nations should adopt measures to eliminate prejudices based on stereotyped roles for men and women. She thus claimed that "[t]his case is not about consent, since none was given . . . [but is about] [m]yths of rape . . . [and] . . . [s]tereotypes of sexuality. . . ."

In 2000, the US Supreme Court determined that the 1994 *federal* Violence Against Women Act (VAWA) was unconstitutional. The majority opinion concluded its analysis as follows: "Petitioner Brzonkala's complaint alleges that she was the victim of a brutal assault. But Congress' effort in § 13981 [VAWA] to provide a federal civil remedy can be sustained neither under the [federal Constitution's] Commerce Clause nor under . . . the Fourteenth Amendment. If the allegations here are true, *no civilized system of justice could fail to provide her a remedy* for the conduct of respondent Morrison. But under our federal system that remedy must be provided by the

Commonwealth of Virginia, and not by the United States [i.e., not the *federal* government]."[88] The court ignored the Discrimination Against Women treaty, and focused exclusively on US law (the federal statute being trumped by constitutional limitations), because the United States is not a party to this treaty. Thus, one could consider this case as an example of a traditional national approach, whereby neither International Law nor nationwide law applies to the protection of women as a distinct group.

The following excerpt offers a paradigm for incorporating feminist perspectives into International Law discourse:

Accountability in International Law for Violations of Women's Rights by Non-State Actors

Rebecca J. Cook

RECEIVING REALITY: WOMEN AND INTERNATIONAL LAW

pp. 93–106 (Washington, D.C.: American Society of International Law, 1993)

Introduction

It can be shown that many states fail to discharge obligations under customary international law to protect women's human rights, and that they fail to protect such rights to which they have expressly committed themselves through voluntary membership of international human rights conventions, including the Convention of the Elimination of All Forms of Discrimination Against Women. Failures can be directly attributed to the executive, judicial and legislative organs of states. It may therefore be asked what is added to states' obligations by attempting to demonstrate and enforce their accountability in international law for violations of women's rights by non-state actors, including private persons. . . .

Women's human rights warrant defense when their violation originates in state action and also in private action. It is not a reason to disregard privately originating violations because violations also occur in the public sector of national life, or because they remain unremedied when they are directly attributable to organs of the state, or because they are more difficult to tackle when they arise through non-state actors. It will advance women's rights to address violations that occur both through direct state action and through state responsibility for the conduct of non-state actors. The pursuit of remedies for violations of rights originating through organs of state and through the conduct of non-state actors can be undertaken in tandem, and if such pursuit is frustrated in one area it nevertheless may be advanced in the other. The identification of violations of women's rights both by organs of state and by conduct of non-state actors for which the state can be shown accountable are complementary goals, and not alternatives to or in competition with each other. . . .

Customary international law and treaty law provide a number of approaches to engaging the responsibility of states. These approaches are addressed to consider how they might be applied to some of the more pervasive causes of violations of women's human rights by non-state actors.

Background Law

The law of state responsibility has evolved over the centuries as a principal area of concern within public international law, and has become subject to official codification under the League of Nations and the United Nations. The modern phase of codification, endorsed by the U.N. General Assembly in 1963, has produced the International Law Commission's Draft Articles on State Responsibility, Part I of which was adopted by the Commission between 1973 and 1980.

Article 11 (1) of the ILC Draft contains the classical proposition that the conduct of a person or a group of persons not acting on behalf of the state shall not be considered as an act of the state under international law. Detailed provisions govern when states may delegate powers to private persons, and when private persons may become empowered to act on behalf of a state, but the Article reflects the general propositions that private persons are not subjects of international law and that "[t]he acts of private persons or of persons acting . . . in a private capacity are in no circumstances attributable to the State."

It does not follow, however, that a state cannot incur international responsibility of its own because of the acts of private persons. When a state owes an obligation, for instance to protect a foreign diplomat or visitor, an act of a private citizen that harms such a protected person engages the responsibility of the state. It must provide adequate protection against repetition, police inquiries to identify and prosecute a criminal suspect, and access to due process in its justice system to compensate the victim.

State responsibility for failure to take proper measures to protect nationals of other countries, and to offer means of redress for their grievances, has been extended by international human rights law to require states to protect and provide justice for their own nationals. Where nationals are injured by acts of private persons, the state will have no greater accountability than under international customary law regarding the protection of nationals of other countries, unless the state has accepted a treaty obligation to assure that injury to its own national will not occur, or to afford a national victim justice through its own institutions and reasonable safeguards against the predictable repetition of private persons' injurious misconduct. . . .

State Responsibility for Non-State Actors Under Treaty Law

The evolution of post-1945 international human rights law has been to amplify and reinforce the legal protection that individuals enjoy against state power exercised by governments of their own nations. Accordingly, human rights treaties bind states in their treatment particularly of their own nationals. States are not obliged in principle to ensure compliance with treaty provisions in private law relations conducted between individuals or among non-state actors. In specific regards, states parties to treaties may commit themselves to a higher level of obligation, but the thrust of international human rights treaties is to hold states accountable only for violations of individual rights committed by state actors.

I. The Scope of State Responsibility

While it is obvious that states parties are responsible for their interference with human rights protected by treaties, a critical question concerns responsibility for failure of state action against private conduct that so denies individual rights protected by treaties as to impoverish a victim's enjoyment of life and citizenship. A state may be responsible for its failure to make its legal protection available to individuals against private action. Criminal law provides for the punishment and deterrence of private persons whose actions against victims endanger the well-being of the community. Civil courts enable individuals to employ the authority of the state to achieve justice for themselves in private relations. If the state refuses or fails to employ the state's protective power of individuals through its police and criminal justice system, or denies individuals reasonable access to self-protection through resort to the civil courts, the state may be considered in breach of its treaty obligation to protect human rights.

State responsibility for failure of its criminal law system was recognized by the European Court of Human Rights in *X and Y v. The Netherlands,* where the state had not enacted adequate criminal legislation to vindicate the rights of a mentally handicapped rape victim, and to deter such future assaults as required by the European Convention on Human Rights. Responsibility for failure to make civil justice accessible to individuals pursuing similarly protected rights was recognized by the Court in *Airey v. Ireland,* where the state offered no legal assistance to an applicant to a civil court whose processes were too complex for a lay person to undertake without legal aid. State responsibility is not for the conduct of private individuals that created the need for resort to the courts, but of the state's denial of justice to victims of crime and potential civil litigants when treaty rights have been violated. . . .

V. The Guarantee of the Elimination of All Forms of Discrimination Against Women

. . . By becoming states parties to the Women's Convention, states agree to "condemn discrimination in all its forms." The Preamble to the Women's Convention notes that the UN Charter, the Universal Declaration of Human Rights, the Women's Declaration, the two international human rights Covenants and UN and specialized agencies' resolutions, declarations and recommendations promote equality of rights of men and women. However, the drafters expressed concern in the Preamble "that despite these various instruments extensive discrimination against women continues to exist." The Preamble concludes with an expression of determination "to adopt the measures required for the elimination of such discrimination in all its forms and manifestation." . . .

The importance of eliminating all forms of discrimination against women is underscored by Recommendation 19 on Violence against Women of the Committee on the Elimination of Discrimination Against Women (CEDAW), established to monitor states parties' compliance with the Women's Convention, the draft UN Declaration on the Elimination of Violence against Women and the draft Inter-American Convention on Violence against Women. . . .

VI. Specific Guarantees

The Women's Convention commences with the agreement of states parties "to pursue by all appropriate means and without delay" a policy of eliminating discrimination against women, and to observe specific undertakings. Included are the significant commitments: "To take all appropriate measures to eliminate discrimination against women by any person, organization or enterprise" and "To take all appropriate measures, including legislation, to modify or abolish existing laws, regulations, customs and practices which constitute discrimination against women." The Convention follows with a number of specific duties by which states accept obligations, a number of which are "to ensure" outcomes such as the full development and advancement of women in such fields as politics, economics and culture, retention of nationality despite marriage, equal rights to education, and employment equity.

◆ Notes & Questions

1. International organizations are bringing attention to the plight of females in a variety of traditional International Law contexts. The UN International Children's Emergency Fund 1997 *Progress of Nations Report* announced that violence against women is the world's most pervasive form of human rights abuse. As stated by its Executive Director, "[i]n today's world, to be born female is to be born high risk." In 1999, the World Bank reported that female suicide in the PRC is the highest in the world. Fifty-six percent of the world's female suicides (500 per day) occur in China. The problem is attributed to the male control of family assets, women not dining with husbands and sons, and the comparatively low status of women in China.

2. In §2.3 of this text, you studied State recognition of other States and governments. Afghanistan's Taliban government conducted what the West would characterize as gender apartheid. Assuming that Afghanistan incurred State responsibility for violating the human rights of its female population, one might question what the international community could have done

to effectuate change—other than going to war. The prewar options included:

(a) *Withholding or withdrawing recognition* (neither of which would affect Afghanistan's de facto status as a State). US President George Bush withheld recognition of six former Soviet republics until it was clear that they would adopt democratic principles of governing their peoples. Russia's President Boris Yeltsin called upon the three States that first recognized the Taliban government to withdraw their recognition.

(b) *Altering the offending government's status in an international organization.* The former Yugoslavia was relegated to a shadowy status at the United Nations. The remaining rump State was not authorized to occupy the seat for "Yugoslavia," although it was not actually expelled from the UN (§2.4). This unusual tactic was a sanction for its aggression in Bosnia, and some other human rights abuses described in earlier chapters.

(c) *Imposing an embargo.* In April 1998, the UN Security Council imposed an arms embargo on

"Yugoslavia," because of its violence against ethnic Albanians in the Kosovo region, near Yugoslavia's border with Albania.

(d) *Pressing for change via treaty commitments.* The UN Declaration on the Elimination of Violence Against Women limits the conduct of ratifying States, by providing treaty-based protections for women. However, it is *non-State* actors who typically batter or harass women. As noted in the earlier account, the responsible individuals normally incur no liability under International Law. Their liability is limited to *national* laws, to the degree they protect women from abuse. A State would be responsible, only if it had an express policy or implicit practice condoning violence against women—such as Afghanistan's Taliban government.

Which, if any, of these options would have been a viable strategy for exerting international pressure on Afghanistan to reverse its gender apartheid policies? Would it be fair to say that the US invasion of Afghanistan was the only plausible way of affecting such change—especially in view of the Muslim human rights excerpt presented earlier in this section?

3. A number of commentators have expressed concern about the role of "Islam," regarding the rights of women who have been subjected to centuries of disparate treatment based on gender. In December 1997, the eighth annual Islamic Summit Conference, conducted in Iran, proclaimed the following objective intended to respond to these negative perspectives:

> "20. Emphasize their full respect for the dignity and rights of Muslim women and enhancement of their role in all aspect[s] of social life in accordance with Islamic principles, and call on the [Islamic] General Secretariat to encourage and coordinate participation of women in the relevant activities of the OIC [Organization of the Islamic Conference]."

Islamic Summit Conference: Tehran Declaration, 37 INT'L LEGAL MAT'LS 938 (1997). The phrases "all aspects of *social* life" and "in accordance with Islamic principles" might provide only rhetorical lip service to women's rights—arguably inserted to counter the western perception that Islam and the disparate treatment of Muslim women are the redundant terms.

One must be cautious about unintentionally injecting cultural relativism into any debate regarding the universal application of human rights norms spawned primarily by western culture. As noted by New York's International Centre for Transitional Justice scholar Vasuki Nesiah: "While both sides of the universalism-cultural relativism dichotomy have haunted third world feminism, [it] . . . has also pushed against both sides of the dichotomy. . . . If we return to the debate about veiling and school girls in France, the principal who enforced the suspension of the girls in scarves in the name of secular-universalism, was enforcing a conception . . . that can itself be grounded in a particular tradition . . . including liberal statecraft (and the attendant project of French nation building), [and] protestant Christianity. . . ." V. Nesiah, The Ground Beneath Her Feet, ch. 7, in A. Anghie et al. (ed.), THE THIRD WORLD AND INTERNATIONAL ORDER: LAW, POLITICS AND GLOBALIZATION 133, at 138–139 (Leiden, Neth.: Martinus Nijhoff, 2003).

The United Nations, in addition to most of its State members, has not enjoyed an historical reputation for its equal treatment of women. The Security Council therefore demonstrated great insight, by finally taking action to incorporate a pervasive gender perspective into an organization whose own constitution requires member States to promote "universal respect for, and observance of, human rights and fundamental freedoms for all without distinction as to race, sex, language, or religion" in Charter Article 55(c).

On October 31, 2000, the Security Council—the organ tasked primarily with monitoring threats to peace—thus articulated a striking principle by: affirming the role of women in preventing and resolving conflicts as well as in peace-building; stressing the importance of women's equal participation and full involvement in all efforts to maintain and promote peace and security; focusing on the need to increase the role of women in decision making for conflict prevention and resolution; and by urging member States to ensure their increased representation at all decision-making levels. Fully embracing this theme will result in a more balanced implementation of every feature of the UN Charter—while directly addressing some anachronistic features of the nation-State system:[89]

United Nations Security Council Resolution 1325

UN DOC. S/RES/1325 (2000)

Adopted by the Security Council at its 4213th meeting,
<http://www.un.org/Docs/scres/2000/res1325e.pdf>

. . .

Reaffirming the important role of women in the prevention and resolution of conflicts and in peace-building, and *stressing* the importance of their equal participation and full involvement in all efforts for the maintenance and promotion of peace and security, and the need to increase their role in decision-making with regard to conflict prevention and resolution,

. . .

1. *Urges* Member States to ensure increased representation of women at all decision-making levels in national, regional and international institutions and mechanisms for the prevention, management, and resolution of conflict;

. . .

5. *Expresses* its willingness to incorporate a gender perspective into peacekeeping operations, and *urges* the Secretary-General to ensure that, where appropriate, field operations include a gender component;

. . .

9. *Calls upon* all parties to armed conflict to respect fully international law applicable to the rights and protection of women and girls, especially as civilians, in particular the obligations applicable to them under the Geneva Conventions of 1949 and the Additional Protocols thereto of 1977, the Refugee Convention of 1951 and the Protocol thereto of 1967, the Convention on the Elimination of All Forms of Discrimination against Women of 1979 and the Optional Protocol thereto of 1999 and the United Nations Convention on the Rights of the Child of 1989 and the two Optional Protocols thereto of 25 May 2000, and to bear in mind the relevant provisions of the Rome Statute of the International Criminal Court;

. . .

13. *Encourages* all those involved in the planning for disarmament, demobilization and reintegration to consider the different needs of female and male ex-combatants and to take into account the needs of their dependants;

. . .

15. *Expresses* its willingness to ensure that Security Council missions take into account gender considerations and the rights of women, including through consultation with local and international women's groups;

. . .

17. *Requests* the Secretary-General, where appropriate, to include in his reporting to the Security Council progress on gender mainstreaming throughout peacekeeping missions and all other aspects relating to women and girls;

18. *Decides* to remain actively seized of the matter.

◆ 11.5 NATIONAL HUMAN RIGHTS PERSPECTIVES

Space limitations preclude anything but selective coverage of national approaches to human rights problems. After two novel examples from Belgium and Iraq, these materials will focus on the world focus on US human rights issues.

BELGIUM

Adequate coverage of what the various nations of Europe are doing, on a State-by-State basis, is beyond the scope of this text. However, one case bears specific mention. In a landmark decision, four Rwandans were tried in Belgium for alleged human rights violations during the 1994 genocide in Rwanda. For the first time, an ordinary jury of individual citizens in Europe—as opposed to an international court such as the UN's Rwandan tribunal—determined the culpability of individual defendants' for violating International Humanitarian Law in *another* country.[90]

Genocide was not among the charges. It was not a crime under Belgian law in 1994, when the events allegedly took place in Rwanda. It became a crime under a 1999 Belgian law. The four defendants were all charged with violations of the Geneva Conventions, in addition to murder—which would not by itself trigger universal jurisdiction (§5.2). Common Article 3 of the four Geneva Conventions covers internal armed conflicts. It requires all parties to a conflict to treat noncombatants humanely, without discrimination, and prohibits violence against persons such as murder, mutilation, and cruel or degrading treatment.

In June 2000, the defendants were convicted of collaborating with the Hutu militia to kill Tutsis seeking refuge at the Sovu convent in Butare, Rwanda. Two of the defendants were Benedictine nuns. Sister Maria was accused of supplying petrol to the militia to burn the Tutsis who refused to leave the building in which they had sought shelter. A number of witnesses were flown to Belgium from Rwanda. The NGO African Rights provided the detail that the leader of the local militia admitted his part in the genocide. He said that the nuns provided vehicles, information, and support for the killing of the Tutsis by the crowd, which had gathered outside of the convent. He said that "[t]hose two nuns collaborated with us in everything we did. They shared our hatred for the Tutsis. I did not do anything without first discussing it with Kisito and Gertrude. They handed over innocent people, without being threatened in any way, and without us having to use force."

As noted by Professor Linda Keller of the Thomas Jefferson School of Law, in her valuable analysis from which the above account was drawn, this trial suggested an extension of the *Pinochet* precedent (§2.6). This Belgian case prosecuted violations of the Geneva Convention, determined by a local jury under a national law incorporating international human rights. Thus, "Belgium is one of the first countries to turn the principle of universal jurisdiction into a legal reality. Although many international human rights treaties provide that states must prosecute or extradite offenders, very few countries have passed implementing legislation."[91]

Belgium subsequently rescinded this broadest of possible applications of universal jurisdiction. US Secretary of Defense Rumsfeld threatened to move NATO headquarters from Brussels, if Belgium insisted on pursuing this unique application of universal jurisdiction.[92] While the above defendants were living in Belgium when arrested, they did not have to have *any* connection with Belgium for it to prosecute (§5.2 *Belgian Arrest Warrant* case). Nevertheless, Belgium's former, and unique, application of universal jurisdiction temporarily exposed an approach to human rights that—if it *were* acceptable to the international community—would instantly destroy a wall of impunity, behind which the world's tyrants have often hidden to avoid justice.

France   During Fall 2005, France declared a twelve-day state of emergency to curb its worst civil disturbances in four decades. The government invoked a 1955 law, enacted during its Algerian War, to curtail civil liberties, particularly in immigrant neighborhoods. It therefore imposed a curfew; authorized raids without warrants; restricted freedom of press and assembly; shut down theaters and bars; and arrested individuals whose activities were deemed dangerous to the maintenance of law and order.

Such emergency measures were necessary, however, to respond to escalating violence; the burning of schools, churches, and over 5,000 cars with gasoline bombs; and dozens of police being wounded. The disparate impact on ethnic neighborhoods was regrettable. But the earlier law's riot control measures were no *ad hoc* exercise of the police power without legislative authority. This application of the 1955 law not only trumped guarantees otherwise available in regional and international human rights measures—it was authorized by universal treaty provisions which recognize the government's right to suspend normal civil rights in such emergencies.

Iraq   In December 2003, the Coalition Provisional Authority established the Iraqi Special Tribunal for Crimes Against Humanity. Its jurisdiction covers genocide, crimes against humanity, war crimes, and violations of certain Iraqi laws. It will prosecute crimes occurring between 1968, when Saddam Hussein took power, and the formal end of the Iraq War in May 2003. The reach of this legislation is to prosecute primarily crimes arising under International Humanitarian Law (§10.6).

It also has the earmarks of human rights law, in that defendants will enjoy various rights enshrined in the International Covenant on Civil and Political Rights (ICCPR), including: the right to legal assistance if the defendant cannot afford a lawyer. There is also a novel right to non-Iraqi legal representation, as long as the principal lawyer is an Iraqi citizen. On the other hand, the Tribunal may impose the death penalty—which is no change from prior Iraqi law.

There are three notable departures from the ICCPR:

(1) The Iraqi Special Tribunal's Statute does not require the accused to be informed of charges in a language he or she understands, nor the related requirement that an interpreter be provided at trial.

(2) The ICCPR prohibits prosecuting a person twice for the same act. Under the Iraqi Statute, a defendant can be retried for an offense, if a new fact surfaces and the Appeals Chamber allows another trial.

(3) This Iraqi Statute does not authorize compensation for a defendant whose conviction is reversed, or pardoned on the basis of a newly discovered fact.[93]

UNITED STATES

Treaty Participation Dilemma The United States is not a party to a number of international human rights instruments (Exhibit 11.1). When ratification *has* occurred, it has typically taken decades. For example, the US Senate did not ratify the 1948 Genocide Convention until 1986.[94] It did not ratify the 1966 International Covenant on Civil and Political Rights (ICCPR) until 1992. When it did so, its reservation was comparable to Swiss cheese. Its various "Declaration" (reservation) clauses include that "the United States declares that the provisions of articles 1 through 27 of the Covenant are not self-executing." (The referenced ICCPR articles are listed under the previously mentioned "International Covenants.) As you learned in §8.2 of this book, a treaty or clause that is not self-executing creates no specific obligation. While a number of bilateral treaties with other countries contain human rights provisions, the United States has not been willing to ratify a number of multilateral human rights agreements. *Why?*

One reason is that—at the time of the 1945 UN Charter—the 1948 Universal Declaration of Human Rights, and the 1948 American Convention on Human Rights, racial discrimination was permitted or, in some instances, mandated in the United States. Black soldiers were buried at Arlington National Cemetery in a segregated plot. Many southern Senators were not willing to embrace the post-World War II wave of UN human rights instruments. They feared that they could thereby subject the United States to embarrassing international inquiries, based on noncompliance with certain human rights instruments.

This form of discrimination was not limited to the south. In 1948, US Supreme Court Justice Black lamented that the majority of the judges (in the particular case before the Court) ignored the UN Charter's human rights provisions. The US Supreme Court's judges thus allowed US states to legally discriminate against Japanese citizens residing in the United States. Aliens were thereby prohibited from owning land under California law—in a state which had hosted wartime Japanese interment camps. In Justice Black's words:

> California should not be permitted to erect obstacles designed to prevent the immigration of people whom Congress has authorized to come into and remain in the country. . . . [I]ts law stands as an obstacle to the free accomplishment of our policy in the international field. One of these reasons is that we have recently pledged ourselves to cooperate with the United Nations to "promote . . . universal respect for, and observance of, human rights and fundamental freedoms for all without distinction as to race, sex, language, or religion." How can this nation be faithful to this international pledge if state laws which bar land ownership and occupancy by aliens on account of race are permitted to be enforced?[95]

It was not until 1954 that the US Supreme Court would decide in *Brown v. Board of Education*: that "separate but equal facilities" were unconstitutional under US law. *De facto* racial discrimination did not end with *Brown,* however. US government agencies continued to struggle with the full implementation of *Brown* and its progeny.[96]

At the same time, Ohio's Senator John Bricker sought an amendment of the US Constitution's treaty power clause, which would have eliminated the president's executive agreement power (textbook §8.3). If successful, that measure would have required the president to obtain the advice and consent of the Senate for *all* treaties—and thereby exclude executive agreements from being included in the term "treaty." Senator Bricker's underlying fear was spawned in part by the California *Sei Fujii* case (§8.1). The trial court had just ruled against discriminatory land laws which barred alien ownership. This decision could be embraced by a presidential executive agreement without any input from Congress (a possibility that never occurred). He was further troubled by the statement of US Supreme Court Justice Holmes that "It is open to question whether the authority of the United States means more than the formal acts prescribed to make the convention."[97] Coupled with the specter of a self-executing treaty (§8.1), more specifically an executive agreement under US practice, Bricker relentlessly expressed his concern that numerous state and federal laws might fall in the wake of presidential agreements that the Senate would not be able to bar or control.

In the 1960s and 1970s, Presidents Kennedy and Carter submitted various human rights treaties to the US Senate for its advice and consent. Few were ratified. The Genocide Convention was ratified during the Reagan years, but not without significant concern about how it might later "haunt" the United States. Like most multilateral instruments, that widely ratified treaty is broadly worded with unassailable statements of general principle which do not contain definitions.

A new constitutional concern supplanted the intergovernmental balance of power concerns earlier expressed by Senator Bricker. Threats to the constitutionally protected right to freedom of speech emerged as the contemporary argument for opposing US ratification of human rights treaties. Under US law, treaties cannot override the Constitution. A variety of international provisions might require the United States to abandon its staunchly ingrained judicial posture that the US Constitution cannot be overcome by a treaty. When the US Senate finally ratified the 1948 Genocide Convention, forty years after the UN General Assembly's unanimous adoption, it appended a reservation providing that "nothing in the [Genocide] Convention requires or authorizes legislation or other action by the United States of America as interpreted by the United States." It is thus open to question whether the United States is actually a party, given the famous Lauchterpacht ICJ opinion that such broadly worded reservations do not agree to accepting any treaty obligation.[98]

Like a number of other human rights instruments, this Convention contains wording that prohibits racial or religious hatred, which constitutes an incitement to discrimination of any kind. In 1978, the American Civil Liberties Union successfully litigated the First Amendment right of Neo-Nazis to parade in Skokie, Illinois—complete with swastikas.[99] Assuming that the United States had ratified the Genocide Convention before the time of that march, absent the preceding treaty reservation, the judicial approval and city-issued permit for this march would likely subject the United States to international responsibility for a government-approved activity that incited religious hatred. Under US law, this march was a constitutionally protected activity under the First Amendment.

The question of whether ratification of human rights treaties would yield unintended consequences (State responsibility for breach of a treaty) is not limited to the free speech concerns discussed. For example, many countries have abolished the death penalty.[100] Many states of the United States, however, impose the death penalty. Also, various US invasions might have violated some segment of the 1977 Geneva Convention Protocol relating to the protection of civilian victims in armed conflict. The US Senate declined ratification on grounds that it was "fundamentally unfair and irreconcilably flawed" because it "would undermine humanitarian law and endanger civilians in war." The US bombing of Kosovo in 1999, and the invasions of Afghanistan and Iraq could conceivably trigger like concerns—at least before 9-11, and the resulting 2002 National Security Strategy's nascent methodology for fighting the War on Terror (textbook §10.7).

Executive Branch Policies In December 1998, President Clinton issued the Executive Order on Implementation of Human Rights Treaties. Section 1 provides that it will be United States "policy and practice . . . to fully respect and implement its obligations under the human rights treaties to which it is a party," specifically referring to the International Covenant on Civil and Political Rights; the Convention Against Torture and Other Cruel, Inhuman or Degrading Treatment or Punishment; and the Convention on the Elimination of All Forms of Racial Discrimination. Each executive department and agency of the US government was thereby directed to appoint a contact person who would be responsible for coordinating the implementation of human rights obligations within that department or agency. An Interagency Working Group on Human Rights was established to coordinate human rights implementation activities. These include the preparation of responses to allegations of US human rights violations submitted to international organizations; the development of mechanisms to review legislation for conformity with human rights obligations; the monitoring of actions by state, municipal, and territorial governments for conformity with international human rights obligations; and the direction of an annual review of US reservations, declarations, and understandings to human rights treaties.[101]

After 9-11, the United States assumed a national defense posture raising questions about the US commitment to human rights. A number of journalists, academicians, and human rights advocates included the following as evidence of this concern:

(1) The US Patriot Act, where certain rights were compromised in the name of national defense.

(2) The Abu Ghraib prison scandal, where it did not take long to discount the military's initial claim that only a few "bad apples" were at fault (§10.6).

(3) The lengthy detention of "unlawful combatants" at the US military base in Cuba, without access to the rights normally accorded to those imprisoned by the United States (§10.7). On the other hand, the novel 2002 National Security Strategy (§10.2) conveyed the intended message that many of the traditional rules are *passe*—arguably ill-suited for the post-9-11 world.

While it may be too soon to resolve this particular debate, there are enough US policy perspectives in place to suggest that even with occasional bumps in the road the path is still relatively clear. The following materials illustrate why.

Legislative Perspectives   The US Congress has enacted some remarkable legislation, to implement the rich human rights tradition which the United States has traditionally claimed as a hallmark of western democracy. The following are three key examples:

Foreign Assistance Act: Certain statutes target conduct abroad that adversely impacts human rights. One of them is Title 22 of the United States Code, containing the Foreign Assistance Act. Sections 2304(a)(1) and (a)(2) provide:

◆ The United States shall, in accordance with its international obligations as set forth in the Charter of the United Nations and in keeping with the constitutional heritage and traditions of the United States, promote and encourage increased respect for human rights and fundamental freedoms throughout the world without distinction as to race, sex, language, or religion. Accordingly, a principal goal of the foreign policy of the United States shall be to promote the increased observance of internationally recognized human rights by all countries.

◆ Except under circumstances specified in this section, no security assistance may be provided to any country the government of which engages in a consistent

pattern of gross violations of internationally recognized human rights.

This legislation prohibits providing police training to any offending foreign government unless the president certifies to Congress that extraordinary circumstances exist to warrant such assistance. The Act defines gross violations as "torture or cruel, inhuman, or degrading treatment or punishment, prolonged detention without charges and trial, causing the disappearance of persons by the abduction and clandestine detention of those persons, and [any] other flagrant denial of the right to life, liberty, or the security of person. . . ."

Section 2151(n) of the Foreign Assistance Act is also designed to protect abused children. No assistance may be provided to any government that fails to take appropriate measures, within its means, to protect children from exploitation, abuse, or forced conscription into military or paramilitary service. The "within its means" provision recognizes that certain governments may not have the economic competence to provide the degree of protection expected under US standards.

Under the Foreign Assistance Act, the US Secretary of State must transmit an annual report to the Speaker of the House of Representatives and the Senate Committee on Foreign Relations on practices of assisted nations involving "coercion in population control, including coerced abortion and involuntary sterilization. . . ." This provision places the relationship between the United States and the PRC at odds because of the PRC's official policy of depriving State benefits to parents who have more than one child (generally enforced in urban areas).[102]

The Foreign Assistance Act *formerly* provided for an Assistant Secretary of State for Human Rights and Humanitarian Affairs. This position was statutorily repealed in 1994 under Vice President Gore's "restructuring" program to reduce the size of US government. The new title for the officer in charge of this monitoring function is the Assistant Secretary of State for the Bureau of Democracy, Human Rights, and Labor. This seemingly inconsequential title change illustrates that the "restructuring" effectively contracted this officer's human rights monitoring duties because of the significantly expanded job description.[103]

US Alien Tort Statute "The district courts shall have original jurisdiction of any civil action by an alien for a tort only, committed in violation of the law of nations or a treaty of the United States."[104] Congress thus gave the federal courts the power to hear appropriate cases not involving breach of contract. The predecessor of this statute was enacted in the original Judiciary Act of 1789. There is some debate about the reasons for this early legislation in the country's first legislative statement of the federal judicial power, as addressed later in the *Sosa* case.

The modern debate focuses on the statute's underlying purpose. The various theories include the following:

◆ To provide a remedy for an international scandal involving a French noble who attacked a French diplomat.

◆ To provide federal control over cases where the rights of foreign citizens had been deprived, thereby spawning international repercussions.

◆ To give the courts of a weak, young nation—anxious to avoid foreign intervention—the ability to react quickly to such transgressions in US courts.[105]

There is at least one basis for agreement: its scope includes suits between non-US citizens for conduct occurring abroad. In October 2005, for example, two Kurds filed a class action in the United States against Saddam Hussein and his former defense minister ("Chemical Ali"). These plaintiffs sought relief for the defendants' gassing and torching their village. This was one of forty genocidal incidents resulting in the 1988 deaths of over 5,000 Iraqi Kurds.

One critical limitation is that notice of suit must be served on the defendant while present in the United States. This provides a territorial element to the exercise of US jurisdiction in such circumstances (§5.2). This distinguishes US law from the prior Belgian law (which did not require *any* jurisdictional nexus with the defendant). The US Supreme Court authoritatively interpreted the Alien Tort Statute (ATS), 215 years after its 1789 enactment:

◆

www **Sosa v. Alvarez-Machain**

UNITED STATES SUPREME COURT
542 U.S. 692, 124 S.Ct 2739, 159 L.Ed.2d 718
(2004)
Go to course Web page at
<http://home.att.net/~slomansonb/txtcsesite.html>.
Under Chapter Eleven, click Alien Tort
Statute Case.

The *Filartega* case mentioned in *Sosa* unleashed the long dormant ATS. The US Supreme Court's *Sosa* decision did not overrule *Filartega,* but it clearly chose not to embrace it. Several scathing academic rebuttals by prominent writers resisted *Filartiga's* sweeping application of the ATS. Chief among them is Tufts University Professor Alfred Rubin. In his view: (1) It is by no means clear that the "law of nations" was meant to apply to individuals, as opposed to States—especially in 1789, when the ATS was enacted; (2) rather than "torture," the *Filartiga* plaintiffs alleged a "wrongful death" claim in their complaint—raising doubts as to whether the "law of nations" could provide a remedy in an action for "wrongful death;" (3) attempts to recover money damages from convicted Nazi war criminals, or their heirs, had been rejected by both East and West German courts; (4) the first Congress did not intend that civil lawsuits would supplant criminal offenses against the law of nations; and (5) *Filartiga* signaled a vast expansion of the rules of national jurisdiction which had been rejected in the early days of the nation.[106]

Between the 1980 *Filartega* case and the 2004 *Sosa* case, there were many §1350 cases, which were better candidates for application of the ATS. A federal appellate court in California, for example, was the first to decide that a political leader could be held liable for *peacetime* human rights violations committed by subordinates. After a fourteen-year rule in the Philippines, Ferdinand Marcos moved to Hawaii in 1986, where he was served with process. The plaintiff Filipino victims and families received a huge money damage award based on the disappearances, summary executions, and torture that occurred under Marcos' command authority while he was dictator.[107]

The textbook §1.4 *Kadic v. Karadzic* case is another example. A Bosnian Serb leader was responsible for the slaughter of 7,800 Muslim men and boys in several days. Victims' relatives hired a New York human rights foundation, whose lawyers served Karadzic with process in a §1350 case (while he was attending peace negotiations at the UN's New York headquarters).

Torture Victim Prevention Act In 1991, Congress added a refinement to the ATS. It effectively adopted the *Filartega* decision, in a limited application of its principles to "torture" and "extrajudicial killings." The congressional purpose was to fulfill the US commitment, after ratification of the UN Torture Convention. Its essential provisions are as follows:

Torture Victim Protection Act

Pub. L. 102–256, Mar. 12, 1992, 106 Stat.73, 28 U.S.C.A. §1350

<http://thomas.loc.gov/cgi-bin/query/z?c102:H.R.2092.ENR:>

[Preamble]

An Act to carry out obligations of the United States under the United Nations Charter and other international agreements pertaining to the protection of human rights by establishing a civil action for recovery of damages from an individual who engages in torture or extrajudicial killing.

. . .

Sec. 2. Establishment of civil action

(a) *Liability*. An individual who, under actual or apparent authority, or color of law, of any foreign nation—

  (1) subjects an individual to torture shall, in a civil action, be liable for damages to that individual; or

  (2) subjects an individual to extrajudicial killing shall, in a civil action, be liable for damages to the individual's legal representative, or to any person who may be a claimant in an action for wrongful death.

. . .

Sec. 3. Definitions

(a) *Extrajudicial killing*. For the purposes of this Act, the term "extrajudicial killing" means a deliberated killing not authorized by a previous judgment pronounced by a regularly constituted court affording all the judicial guarantees which are recognized as indispensable by civilized peoples. Such term, however, does not include any such killing that, under international law, is lawfully carried out under the authority of a foreign nation.

(b) *Torture*. For the purposes of this Act—

  (1) the term "torture" means any act, directed against an individual in the offender's custody or physical control, by which severe pain or suffering . . . whether physical or mental, is intentionally inflicted on that individual for such purposes as obtaining from that individual or a third person information or a confession, punishing that individual for an act that individual or a third person has committed or is suspected of having committed, intimidating or coercing that individual or a third person . . . ; and

  (2) mental pain or suffering refers to prolonged mental harm caused by or resulting from—

    (A) the intentional infliction or threatened infliction of severe physical pain or suffering;

    (B) the administration or application, or threatened administration or application, of mind altering substances or other procedures calculated to disrupt profoundly the senses or the personality;

    (C) the threat of imminent death; or

    (D) the threat that another individual will imminently be subjected to death, severe physical pain or suffering, or the administration or application of mind altering substances or other procedures calculated to disrupt profoundly the senses or personality.

The Torture Victim Prevention Act (TVPA) limits claims to "individuals." That prevents claims from being asserted against foreign nations who are otherwise subject to suit *only* under the terms of the Foreign Sovereign Immunities Act (FSIA). The classic illustration of this limitation is contained in the US Supreme Court *Nelson* decision (§2.6). It precluded a claim under the FSIA when Saudi Arabian officials tortured Mr. Nelson for diligently carrying out his hospital management responsibilities. Because his torture was perpetrated by the Saudi government, Mr. Nelson had no legally viable claim against Saudi Arabia. After the §11.4 *Sosa* decision, the courts will have to address whether the TVPA applies to private corporations as well.

Unlike the above Alien Tort Claims Act regarding suits between aliens, the 1991 Torture Victim Protection

Act authorizes claims made by or against US citizens. This means that US perpetrators and victims are subject to, and have remedies under, this legislation. Various post-9-11 executive branch torture memos, however, purported to trump the applicability of this remedy with national security concerns (§10.7).

The TVPA nevertheless codifies the universally accepted norm prohibiting torture by a governmental official. The TVPA extends the ATS to summary executions, even when not perpetrated in the course of committing genocide or war crimes. This conduct may now be prosecuted under the TVPA, when committed by foreign state officials. In the *Karadzic* case mentioned earlier, the Bosnian Serb leader was characterized as a "state official" because of his self-claimed authority over Serb forces in Bosnia. His alleged conduct was deemed to be a violation of the TVPA. Thus, the plaintiffs could pursue their claim for civil damages on the facts of this case under both federal statutes.[108] If Karadzic had been a *private* citizen, who acted in a way that violated International Law, he would also be subject to liability under the ATS (but not the TVPA).

The September 2000 statement by the same respected federal appeals court that decided *Karadzic* and *Filartega* provides the ideal closure/new beginning for the human rights chapter in an International Law course. It depicts the appropriate level of commitment needed at all levels of government to solidify the rule of law in International Human Rights Law:

The TVPA [Torture Victim Protection] thus recognizes explicitly what was perhaps implicit in the [Alien Tort Claims] Act of 1789—that the law of nations is incorporated into the law of the United States and that a violation of the international law of human rights is (at least with regard to torture) *ipso facto* a violation of U.S. domestic law.

. . .

[P]laintiffs make a strong argument in contending that the present law . . . expresses a policy favoring receptivity by our courts to such suits. . . . This evolution of statutory language seems to represent a more direct recognition that the interests of the United States are involved in the eradication of torture committed under color of law in foreign nations.

. . .

The new formulations of the Torture Victim Protection Act convey the message that torture committed

under color of law of a foreign nation in violation of international law is "our business," as such conduct not only violates the standards of international law but also as a consequence violates our domestic law.[109]

◆ PROBLEMS

Problem 11.A (after §11.1 Genocide Debate) The events of 9-11 suggest an act designed to send a message to moderate Arab governments that they should eschew western ideology. The citizens of eighty-one countries were killed in New York City's World Trade Center that day. The vast majority of the victims were Americans. Some commentators referred to this event as "genocide." The 9-11 al-Qaida hijackers—fifteen of nineteen being Saudi nationals—could have broadcasted their supposed intent that 9-11 was part of a grand design to kill all US citizens—or as many as possible. They could have logically announced: "We are now acting on the 1998 fatwa issued by Usama bin Laden, for Muslims to kill all Americans." They of course did not want to bring early attention to their evolving plot. Had they done so, in this manner, there would be a better argument for characterizing the 3,000 deaths on 9-11 as "genocide."

Five students will present their respective arguments on whether 9-11 was an act of genocide. They will include, but not be limited to, textbook materials that bear upon their respective arguments. Student No.1 is Saudi Arabia's Ambassador to the United States. Student No.2 is the US Ambassador to the United Nations (who knows that members of the bin Laden family were permitted to depart the United States during the brief no-fly period just after 9-11). Student No.3 is the Taliban's former Ambassador to Pakistan (one of three nations which then recognized the Taliban as the *de jure* government of Afghanistan—and the only nation to do so for several months after 9-11). Student No.4 is a senior law student at your university, who will be working for the diplomatic corps next fall. Student No.5 is a journalist who has not taken this course, but was invited by your professor to participate; who knows "genocide when s/he sees it;" and cannot believe that this subject is even debatable.

Problem 11.B (after §11.3) The United Kingdom Human Rights Act of 1998 gives further effect to rights and freedoms guaranteed under Europe's Convention for the Protection of Human Rights and Fundamental Freedoms (ECHR).[110] Sections 2 and 3 of that legislation implement certain human rights provisions of the Convention. All British courts recognize these Convention rights when resolving pending cases. Legislation in the United Kingdom must also be interpreted in a way that is compatible with Convention rights. Any legislation, which is apparently *in*compatible with Convention rights, requires the court to issue a declaration of incompatibility between the statute and the human rights protected by the ECHR. Such a declaration does not affect the validity of the legislative provision that is arguably inconsistent with that treaty. But a judicial declaration of incompatibility may thus serve as the basis for the Minister of the Crown to amend English law to remove or reword the provision that is incompatible with the treaty.

Section 19 of the Act introduced a "Statement of Compatibility" into Great Britain's parliamentary procedure. After rereading a Bill in the Parliament, the Minister of the Crown has to either: (1) make a Statement of Compatibility with the ECHR, saying that, in his or her view, the provisions of the Bill are compatible with rights which are available under the treaty; or (2) announce for the record that he or she is unable to make such a Statement. Parliament may nevertheless wish to proceed with the legislative process—having been duly advised of this executive branch concern.

Assume that legislation is introduced that would codify a woman's right to an abortion, as it exists under British case law—similar to the right as it exists in the United States under the 1974 *Roe v. Wade* decision by the United States Supreme Court (410 U.S. 113). The ECHR, however, contains a provision that specifically recognizes the "right to life" as follows:

Article 2–Right to life
1. Everyone's right to life shall be protected by law. No one shall be deprived of his [or her] life intentionally save in the execution of a sentence of a court following his conviction of a crime for which this penalty is provided by law.
2. Deprivation of life shall not be regarded as inflicted in contravention of this article when it results from the use of force which is no more than absolutely necessary:
   a. in defence of any person from unlawful violence;
   b. in order to effect a lawful arrest or to prevent the escape of a person lawfully detained;
   c. in action lawfully taken for the purpose of quelling a riot or insurrection.

Two students will participate in a House of Commons debate about the compatibility of the pending legislation—which would legislatively authorize abortions in the United Kingdom—versus the right-to-life provision of the European Convention. Student 1 is the Minister of the Crown, who will present a Statement of Compatibility, for the legislative passage in question, with the treaty's right-to-life provision. Student 2 is a member of the House of Commons who demands that the Minister must conclude that a Statement of Compatibility between the proposed British "pro choice" law and the ECHR is not possible.

Both students may rely on the resources in this chapter on human rights, including the various instruments of the International Bill of Human Rights. All of them contain a right-to-life provision. The question is whether the legislation expressly authorizing abortion in England is compatible with the ECHR's Article 2.1 right-to-life provision.

Problem 11.C (after §11.3) Nicaragua's Sandinista government of the mid-1980s learned about a US Central Intelligence Agency plot. Key Nicaraguan harbors were mined and US financial aid was provided clandestinely to a rebel group known as the "Contras." In a widely reported announcement, US President Reagan said, "I, too, am a Contra" (§10.2).

Assume that you are the national leader in Nicaragua. You have just learned about this foreign "presence" in your country. To defend your borders against this form of aggression, you declare martial law. Your military forces now control all of Nicaragua. Civil rights, including access to the courts, are suspended. Martial law has further limited opposition from the Roman Catholic Church and Nicaragua's various human rights groups. Any individual may incur criminal liability for the crime of "civil disobedience," which you imposed under martial law. Nicaragua previously ratified and has publicly embraced the UN's International Bill of Human Rights.

You now decide to dispatch a series of warnings to local groups that you suspect are supporters of the antigovernment Contras. The basic Contra objective is to unseat your government. First, you warn the Catholic Bishop of Nicaragua that "the Church must stay out of political affairs and cannot be used as a vehicle for influencing governmental decision making on behalf of the people of Nicaragua." Amnesty International (AI) is part of a worldwide organization designed to monitor progress toward the accomplishment of UN human rights goals. AI has more offices in the United States than in any other country. AI's local office in Nicaragua opposes martial law. You thus close the AI office in Nicaragua, which has been distributing unapproved literature that must first be approved by your Minister of Defense.

Martial law has thus resulted in the arrest of numerous Nicaraguan citizens charged with "civil disobedience." You believe that their detention is necessary because they are probably aiding the rebel Contra forces. On the basis of this national emergency, you have established "People's Tribunals" to accelerate the prosecution of subversion cases. You are concerned that military tribunals will not appear to be as impartial as tribunals staffed by the people themselves. You are, of course, careful to staff them with conservative people who are sworn to defend Nicaragua against all enemies of the State.

These tribunals have the power to summarily imprison anyone in Nicaragua. They have exercised this power to jail Nicaraguan citizens who are Catholic, members of AI, and suspected of "civil disobedience." This term is not legislatively or judicially defined. Arresting authorities and the prosecuting tribunals may thereby have the necessary discretion to deal with the rebellion and foreign intrusion/attack on a case-by-case basis.

You rely on this national emergency to temporarily suspend "due process of law," which is a fundamental guarantee in all human rights treaties which your country has ratified. The inhabitants of Nicaragua are thus charged with violating the broadly worded crime of "civil disobedience" at the time of their arrests. There is no independent judicial officer available to verify the propriety of incarcerations by the agents of the People's Tribunals. Each local tribunal has the complete discretion to orchestrate what Amnesty characterizes as the "disappearance" of many Nicaraguan citizens. No one jailed under your proclamation can question the legal basis for his or her incarceration. You will, of course, revive this right after this crisis passes and you can abolish martial law.

While in jail, prisoners are routinely tortured. Although this is not an official State policy, it is difficult to control. Your police force is your first line of defense in finding information about the US-supported Contras. Given this emergency, torture is an unpleasant necessity for extracting the vital information necessary to identify all citizens who seek the imminent overthrow of your government. You thus impose curfews on travel at night and travel between the rural and urban areas of Nicaragua— both of which require a government-issued permit. The Contra forces are located mostly in rural areas of your country, although they might now be anywhere because of massive assistance provided by the United States.

You have undertaken all of these steps to maintain public order in Nicaragua. It is clear to you that a major foreign power has effectively launched a military assault on your nation. Your harbors have been bombed. The antigovernment Contras have been well financed. The Catholic Church, and other private organizations in your country, are disseminating information to incite the populace to rise up against your government.

Have you violated the UN's International Bill of Human Rights? If so, how? Were you justified in doing so?

Problem 11.D (after §11.4 Gender Perspectives)
Fifteen women from China, Taiwan, South Korea, and the Philippines sued Japan in a US court for money damages. They were forced into sexual slavery before and during World War II. They, and many others, were called "comfort women" by the Japanese military forces. In June 2005, having already been to the Supreme Court, but remanded back to the Washington, DC federal Court of Appeals, the latter court decided that their case presented a "nonjusticiable political question [text §1.4], namely, whether the governments of the appellants' countries foreclosed the appellants' claims in the peace treaties they signed with Japan." Thus, due to a "series of treaties signed after the war" that "clearly aimed at resolving all war claims against Japan." The "comfort women" cases were then dismissed. The Court reasoned that Japan had signed peace treaties long ago with all of the governments of the appellants' countries. This potential "judicial intrusion into the relations between Japan and these other foreign governments would impinge upon the ability of the President to conduct the foreign relations of the United States." The United States argued in its "Statement of Interest of the United States" that it would be "anomalous" to allow foreign nationals to sue Japan in the courts of the United States, while US nationals would be precluded from doing so under those treaties. Hwang Geum Joo v. Japan, 413 F.3d 45 (D.C. Cir., 2005).

Several individuals have been convicted of the crime of mass rape—in the International Criminal Court for the former Yugoslavia (ICTY)—for this (and much worse) wartime tactics designed to shame Muslim women into leaving Bosnia during the Serb ethnic cleansing campaign (§9.5 ICTY). There were no treaties with Yugoslavia that, unlike Japan, merged these victims' claims into a post-conflict settlement between the parties.

The "comfort women" case was filed after the mass rape convictions in the ICTY. If Japan does not have to answer for its conduct regarding the "comfort women," should China, Taiwan, South Korea, the Philippines, and the United States bear at least the moral responsibility for effectively burying their claims in the post-World War II treaty settlements?

Problem 11.E (after §11.4)   In 2002, a Pakistani woman named Mukhtar Mai was gang raped on orders from a village council. This was a punishment decreed after her thirteen-year-old brother supposedly had an illicit affair with a woman from a family in a higher caste. Mukhtar Mai and her family not only denied her brother's affair, but claimed that her brother was sexually molested by members of the other family. While this was a stunning news account in other countries, it was not a unique "punishment" for someone in Mukhtar Mai's position—whose family member supposedly had sexual relations out of wedlock, especially with a woman not in his "caste."

In 2002, the eight men on the village council were acquitted of all charges. In March 2005, a lower court acquitted five others of the total of thirteen men involved in the rape (and commuted the death sentence of a sixth man to life in prison). They were temporarily held in custody (to protect Mukhtar Mai), until a final resolution of this matter. In June 2005, an intermediate court ordered the release of all thirteen men. In June 2005, the Pakistani Supreme Court ordered that these men be rearrested.

The Asian-American Network Against Abuse of Women invited Mukhtar Mai to speak about her ordeal in the United States. She stated that she "wanted to go (abroad) as [an] ambassador to Pakistan." She could not accept, however, because President Musharraf banned her from travel, to prevent her from casting Pakistan in a bad light. The Pakistani government withheld her passport. In June 2005, he lifted her travel ban, in the aftermath of a strong condemnation of that restriction from Washington.[111]

Students or groups will debate whether Pakistan has: (a) violated International Law; and (2) if so, *which* major

human rights instruments in this chapter were violated. One student will be a Pakistani government lawyer, who will represent Pakistan in its defense that the State has not violated International Law. A second lawyer represents Mukhtar Mai and her family. The third will be the UN High Commissioner for Human Rights.

Problem 11.F (after §11.5)
Background   In a December 1993 report, the World Health Organization (WHO) estimated that "over 80 million [living] female infants, adolescents, and women in over 30 countries . . . have been subject to female genital mutilation." In its 1997 Progress of Nations Report, the UNICEF Executive Director identified this figure as being 130 million living women. Further details are available from the UN Commission on the Status of Women, based on a report from the NGO called Equality Now, UN Doc. E/CN.4/Sub.2/1997/NGO/31, 7 August 1997; E. Hicks, Infibulation: Female Mutilation in Islamic Northeastern Africa (New Brunswick, NJ: Transaction, 1993); and J. Berkey, Circumcision Circumscribed: Female Excision and Cultural Accommodation in the Medieval Near East, 28 INT'L J. MID. EAST STUDIES 19 (1996).

This procedure is commonly referred to as "female circumcision." At an average age of ten, a young girl is held down by several women while a "practitioner" who does not necessarily have medical training uses a razor or paring knife to do this procedure in the home. It is extremely painful and performed without anesthesia. The WHO is concerned about the resulting hemorrhaging, tetanus, infection, infertility, and death that has occurred in an increasingly reported number of cases. Further details are provided on the AI Female Genital Mutilation (FGM) Web site at: <http://www.amnesty.org/ailib/intcam/femgen/fgm1.htm>.

It is a tradition that dates from ancient Egypt. It is estimated that in Somalia, for example, *all* females undergo this process. The estimate for Egypt is 70 to 90 percent. Young women, mostly in Africa and the Middle East, are social outcasts if they do not endure this procedure, which has been associated with the retention of virginity and lack of physical sensation. In countries where this technique is practiced, most men will not marry women who have not undergone this procedure.

In a December 2000 CNN report of a case in Kenya, a father lost his battle to force his daughters to undergo this procedure. His concern was that without it, any potential husband might return the daughter and demand return of the dowries. The court's reported reason for breaking precedent, by deciding against the father, was based on the particular magistrate's discretion rather than the law. This was the first time that a Kenyan court ruled *against* the forced circumcision of girls. There is no legislative provision on this point in Kenya. Some groups, among them the Kenya Family Planning Association, want to preserve the ritual connected with female circumcision. However, they favor a symbolic ceremony that does *not* involve any cutting of the female genitalia, thereby preserving the importance of this local "right of passage" to womanhood.[112]

While it appears that no religion specifically endorses it, some Muslim scholars have endorsed female circumcision as "a noble practice [that] does honor to women" (Washington Post, Apr. 11, 1995, p. A14). While it is not officially endorsed as a State policy in any country, female circumcision is effectively condoned in a number of countries that have never taken any steps to curtail it, regardless of the known health risks. Many Muslims advocate that Islam—contrary to popular belief—does *not* support this practice. The Egyptian Organization for Human Rights specifically disputes this Koran-related claim. Some Egyptian Christians still follow this practice, which *predates* Islam by 1,500 years.

In June 1997, an Egyptian court overruled a one-year-old government decree that had banned this practice. The judge noted that he was not ruling on the health aspects of the case, but rather on the legality of the ban that unduly restricted doctors from practicing medicine as they wish. The court ruling did not disturb that portion of the ministerial decree, however, which unreservedly bars unlicensed and untrained midwives from performing this procedure.

In the West, women's rights groups seek the global abolition of female circumcision (the National Organization for Women, Global Campaign for Women's Human Rights, Population International, and Women's International Network). This procedure is outlawed in France, Great Britain, and the United States as of 1996. In 1993, US House of Representatives Resolution 3247 was the first congressional bill to deal with what Western newspapers have described as "the most widespread existing violation of human rights in the world." In 1994, the State Department first focused on this treatment of women in its annual human rights report, referring to this practice as "ritual mutilation." An analysis of this

phenomenon is available in Eugene Gifford, The Courage to Blaspheme, 4 UCLA WOMEN'S L.J. 329 (1994).

In 1994, a US immigration judge in Boston considered whether two US-born Nigerian girls aged five and six would be returned to their father in Nigeria, or remain in the United States with their mother after their parents divorced. The judge decided to overturn the mother's deportation order on humanitarian grounds. There are an estimated 2 million living women in Nigeria who have undergone this "treatment." The judge permitted the daughters to remain in the United States with their mother. Had the girls returned home with their father, they would have been required to undergo this traditional procedure, just like their mother had when she was a child in Nigeria. In the US judge's words: "This court attempts to respect traditional cultures, but this is cruel and serves no medical purpose." *INS v. Oluloro,* an unreported case reviewed in the *Maui News,* March 29, 1994. In a more recently reported case, the Board of Immigration Appeals (BIA) accepted the argument that a Togolese woman who fled her home country was being persecuted because she was threatened with forced genital mutilation. The BIA concluded that, despite her persecutor's benevolent intent, petitioner Kasinga was a "refugee" because female genital mutilation constitutes "persecution" within the meaning of the Act. In re Fauziya Kasinga, Int. Dec. 3278, at 12 (BIA June 13, 1996) (*en banc*) (designated as precedent by the BIA), reprinted in 35 INT'L LEGAL MAT'LS 1145 (1996).

As a result of the *Kasinga* case, the US Criminal Code now prohibits this procedure from being performed on any person who is *under eighteen* years of age. This law provides that "no account shall be taken . . . that the operation is required as a matter of custom or ritual." (18 US Code §116c). Furthermore, the US Immigration and Nationality Act provides that "[i]n consultation with the Secretary of State, the Commissioner of Immigration and Naturalization shall identify those countries in which female genital mutilation is commonly practiced. . . ." The INS and Department of State thus make available to "all aliens who are issued immigrant or non-immigrant visas, prior to or at the time of entry into the United States . . . [i]nformation on the severe harm to physical and psychological health caused by female genital mutilation . . . compiled and presented in a manner [that] is limited to the practice itself and respectful to the cultural values of the societies in which such practice takes place" (8 US Code §1374). Both statutes were enacted in 1996.

In July 1999, the US Circuit Court of Appeals in New York held that US immigration officials erred in denying a woman from Ghana's application for asylum on the grounds of forced genital mutilation. That decision thereby blocked the imminent deportation of Adelaide Abankwah, who had been held at a detention facility in Queens, New York, for two and half years.

In April 2004, the federal Ninth Circuit Court of Appeals was the first court to rule that women who have already undergone this procedure can claim asylum under the 1988 Torture Convention. In addition to the mother's claim, if she were deported to Nigeria, her eight-year-old daughter—a US citizen—would have to undergo this procedure. Azanor v. Ashcroft, 364 F.3d 1013 (9th Cir. 2004).

Problem   Assume that a wealthy African family vacations in the United States each year when the heat is most intense in their home nation, herein referred to as Country X. Mrs. X is a citizen of Country X. Her husband is a ranking government official in Country X. While he considers it inappropriate for him to ever attend one of his wife's "procedures," he nevertheless agrees with the purpose of her work—as do most of the officials in the State X government, who are fully aware of this common practice in State X and neighboring countries.

Mrs. X is a devout religious woman who has undergone the "procedure" herself and performed it on her own daughters, as well as hundreds of ten- to twelve-year-old girls in Country X. This practice has been passed on from generation to generation in her family for hundreds of years. She believes that it is her "God-given" duty to perpetuate her faith by performing this ritual. She believes that this work is especially important in contemporary times when adolescent behavior in other regions of the world subject young women in Country X to many adverse influences which will certainly debase her family's cultural and religious beliefs.

During her annual vacation in New York City, Mrs. X is served with process in a US lawsuit accusing her of torture in violation of International Law, the Alien Tort Statute, and the Torture Victim Protection Act (§11.5). The plaintiff is the mother of a Middle Eastern girl who underwent this procedure in Country X—only after Mrs. X convinced the mother that this tradition cannot be changed. She advised the mother that "The Divine Order" requires that only faithful women can thus be made suitable for marrying Country X males. "Otherwise,"

Mrs. X explained to the plaintiff mother, "the social, cultural, and religious traditions of Country X will be vitiated by Western influences." Although unusual, this particular child died of complications several very painful weeks after Mrs. X performed the "procedure." This is the *only* death attributable to Mrs. X's procedure, which she has performed hundreds of times in her career as a State X midwife.

Proceedings   The plaintiffs' law firm, the New York Center for Constitutional Rights, files this case in a New York court against Mrs. X. The deceased child's mother therein alleges torture resulting in her daughter's death. The plaintiff's lawyer decides not to sue on the basis of the gender-discrimination provisions in International Human Rights Law. Those instruments address *State* responsibility for discrimination rather than individual responsibility under International Law. The plaintiff's lawyer further decides not to name the father as a defendant in this matter because he would be entitled to diplomatic immunity. Assume, for the purpose of this problem, that Mrs. X is not entitled to diplomatic immunity.

The lawyer for the deceased child's mother also decides to bring this matter to the attention of the United Nations by filing a §1350 petition with the UN Human Rights Commission. In the petition, the plaintiff mother claims that her daughter's rights were violated by Country X because it has failed to provide sufficient information about the dangers of this procedure. It did not mandate any medical licensing or training for Country X midwives who perform this procedure. Thus, State X is responsible for the human rights violations of her deceased daughters and all female children who have undergone this procedure in State X.

Four students or groups will play the following roles in this hypothetical case:

Session No. 1   Two New York trial lawyers are debating this matter in a New York trial court. The plaintiff's lawyer represents a relative of the deceased child. That individual filed this test case to establish some precedents about the applicability of §1350 in such cases. The plaintiff relative's complaint relied on §1350 jurisdiction—arising under the Alien Tort Statute and the Torture Victim Protection Act. The relative's goal is to hold the defendant, Mrs. X, civilly liable for damages in the death of the child, for surgery performed in Country X. The defense lawyer for Mrs. X claims that the New York court should not proceed with this case because no law has been violated. There is a federal law against FGM, but Mrs. X has never performed this procedure in the United States.

The trial judge must decide whether to dismiss this case because the defendant supposedly did nothing wrong. Questions: (1) Is Mrs. X liable for violations of: (a) the Alien Tort Statue; and/or (b) the Torture Victim Protection Act? (2) Would the US Supreme Court's *Sosa* decision play any role in analyzing the legal liability of Mrs. X under US law? (3) Does the location of the surgical procedure matter?

Session No.2: Two career UN diplomats are engaged in proceedings before the UN Human Rights Commission. The diplomat who represents the international community claims that State X is liable under International Law for acquiescing in, and therefore passively approving of the torture of all female children who undergo this procedure in State X. The diplomat who represents State X claims, however, that no UN entity could possibly decide this petition against State X, because it has not violated International Human Right Law. This procedure has been done for centuries in a number of countries, including State X. Also, it is always performed with the consent of the child's parents. Would State X be liable for torture, or any other human rights violation, under International Law?

How should the US judge (Session No.1) and UN High Commissioner for Human Rights (Session No.2) rule in their respective state and international venues?

◆ BIBLIOGRAPHY

§11.1 Human Rights in Context

A. Bell-Fialkoff, ETHNIC CLEANSING (New York: St. Martin's Press, 1996)

W. Benedek & A. Yotopoulos-Marangopoulos (ed.), International Anti-Terrorist Measures and Human Rights, Part One, in INTERNATIONAL ANTI-TERRORIST MEASURES AND HUMAN RIGHTS (Leiden, Neth.: Martinus Nijhoff, 2004)

S. Blanton, Promoting Human Rights and Democracy in the Developing World: U.S. Rhetoric versus U.S. Arms Exports, 44 AMER. J. POL. SCI. 1 (2000)

L. Henkin, et al., HUMAN RIGHTS (New York: Foundation Press, 1999)

G. Hoog & A. Steinmetz (eds.), INTERNATIONAL CONVENTIONS ON PROTECTION OF HUMANITY AND ENVIRONMENT (Berlin: Walter de Gruyter & Co., 1993) (forty-eight treaties full text)

S. Power, A PROBLEM FROM HELL: AMERICA AND THE SAGE OF GENOCIDE (London: Flamingo, 2003)

D. Robertson, A DICTIONARY OF HUMAN RIGHTS (London: Europa, 1997)

H. Steiner & P. Alston, INTERNATIONAL HUMAN RIGHTS IN CONTEXT: LAW, POLITICS, MORALS (Oxford, Eng: Clarendon Press, 1996)

§11.2 United Nations Promotional Role

P. Alston (ed.), THE UNITED NATIONS AND HUMAN RIGHTS: A CRITICAL APPRAISAL (Oxford, Eng.: Clarendon Press, 1992)

A. Eide & G. Alfredsson (eds.), THE UNIVERSAL DECLARATION OF HUMAN RIGHTS: A COMMENTARY (Oslo, Norway: Scandinavian Univ. Press, 1992)

B. Harff, No Lessons Learned from the Holocaust?, Assessing Risks of Genocide and Political Mass Murder Since 1955, 97 AMER. POL. SCI. REV. 1 (2003)

L. Holmstrom (ed.), CONCLUSIONS AND RECOMMENDATIONS OF THE UN COMMITTEE AGAINST TORTURE (Hague: Martinus Nijhoff, 2000)

L. Holmstrom (ed.), CONCLUDING OBSERVATIONS OF THE UN COMMITTEE ON ECONOMIC, SOCIAL AND CULTURAL RIGHTS (2003)

C. Ingelse, THE UN COMMITTEE AGAINST TORTURE: AN ASSESSMENT (Dordrecht, Neth.: Kluwer, 2001)

S. Joseph, J. Schultz & M. Castan, THE INTERNATIONAL COVENANT ON CIVIL AND POLITICAL RIGHTS: CASES, MATERIALS, AND COMMENTARY (Oxford Eng.: Oxford Univ. Press, 2005)

UN, THE UNITED NATIONS AND HUMAN RIGHTS: 1945–1995 (New York: UN, 1995)

§11.3 Regional Human Rights Approaches

AFRICA

F. Ouguergouz, THE AFRICAN CHARTER ON HUMAN AND PEOPLES' RIGHTS: A COMPREHENSIVE AGENDA FOR HUMAN DIGNITY AND SUSTAINABLE DEMOCRACY IN AFRICA (The Hague: Martinus Nijhoff, 2003)

V. Nmehielle, THE AFRICAN HUMAN RIGHTS SYSTEM ITS LAWS, PRACTICE AND INSTITUTIONS (The Hague: Kluwer, 2001)

EUROPE

R. Creech, Language Rights as Human Rights, ch. V, in LAW AND LANGUAGE IN THE EUROPEAN UNION: THE PARADOX OF A BABEL "UNITED IN DIVERSITY" 129 (Groningen, Germ: Europa Law, 2005).

W. Kemp (ed.), QUIET DIPLOMACY IN ACTION: THE OSCE HIGH COMMISSIONER ON NATIONAL MINORITIES (The Hague: Kluwer Law Int'l July 2001)

A. Rosas (ed.), INTERNATIONAL HUMAN RIGHTS NORMS IN DOMESTIC LAW: FINNISH AND POLISH PERSPECTIVES (Helsinki: Finnish Lawyers' Pub., 1990)

INTER-AMERICAN

T. Burgenthal & D. Shelton, PROTECTING HUMAN RIGHTS IN THE AMERICAS: CASES AND MATERIALS (4th rev. ed. Kehl, Germany: N.P. Engel, 1995)

O. Fitzgerald, UNDERSTANDING CHARTER REMEDIES (Scarborough, Ontario: Craswell, 1994) (Canada)

A. Mower, REGIONAL HUMAN RIGHTS: A COMPARATIVE STUDY OF THE WEST EUROPEAN AND INTER-AMERICAN SYSTEMS (New York: Greenwood Press, 1991)

MIDDLE EAST

Human Rights and Peace in the Middle East: A Conference, 13 SYRACUSE J. INT'L L. & COMM. 391 (1987)

GLOBAL

B. Conforti & F. Francioni (eds.), ENFORCING INTERNATIONAL HUMAN RIGHTS IN DOMESTIC COURTS (The Hague: Martinus Nijhoff, 1997)

Symposium: Human Rights: Global Issues and Information Sources, 25 INT'L J. LEGAL INFO. 3–200 (1997)

UN, A COMPILATION OF INTERNATIONAL INSTRUMENTS: REGIONAL INSTRUMENTS (Vol. 1) (New York: Geneva Centre for Human Rights, 1994)

§11.4 Other Human Rights Actors

E. Dungo, MULTINATIONAL CORPORATIONS AND INTERNATIONAL LAW: ACCOUNTABILITY AND COMPLIANCE ISSUES IN THE PETROLEUM INDUSTRY (Ardsley, NY: 2003)

The Frontiers of Gender, Part III, in K. Hastrup & G. Ulrich (ed.), DISCRIMINATION AND TOLERATION: NEW PERSPECTIVES 187 (The Hague: Martinus Nijhoff, 2002)

J. McDowell, The International Committee of the Red Cross as a Witness before International Criminal Tribunals, 1 CHINESE J. INT'L L. 158 (2002)

J. Paust, Human Rights Responsibilities of Private Corporations, 35 VANDERBILT J. INT'L L. 801 (2002)

P. Willetts (ed.), THE CONSCIENCE OF THE WORLD: THE INFLUENCE OF NONGOVERNMENTAL ORGANIZATIONS IN THE U.N. SYSTEM (Wash., DC: Brookings Inst., 1996)

§11.5 National Human Rights Perspectives

DEVELOPING COUNTRIES

S. Chowdhury, E. Denters, & P. Waart, THE RIGHT TO DEVELOPMENT IN INTERNATIONAL LAW (Dordrecht, Neth.: Martinus Nijhoff, 1992)

HUMAN RIGHTS IN DEVELOPING COUNTRIES 1986–1994 (Oslo, Norway: Norwegian Inst. Human Rts, 1994) (seven volumes)

LANGUAGE & RELIGION

F. de Varennes, Language, MINORITIES AND HUMAN RIGHTS (The Hague: Martinus Nijhoff, 1996)

J. van der Vyver & J. Whitte, Jr. (eds.), RELIGIOUS HUMAN RIGHTS IN GLOBAL PERSPECTIVE: LEGAL PERSPECTIVES (The Hague: Martinus Nijhoff, 1996)

MINORITIES

S. Amaya, INDIGENOUS PEOPLES IN INTERNATIONAL LAW (New York: Oxford Univ. Press, 1996)

S. Chandra (ed.), INTERNATIONAL PROTECTION OF MINORITIES (Delhi, India: Mitral, 1986)

WOMEN & CHILDREN

P. Alston et al. (eds.), CHILDREN, RIGHTS AND THE LAW (rev. ed. Oxford, Eng.: Clarendon Press, 1993)

K. Eagle, International Human Rights and Feminism: When Discourses Meet, 13 MICH. J. INT'L L. 517 (1992)

M. Halberstam & E. Defels, WOMEN'S LEGAL RIGHTS: INTERNATIONAL COVENANTS AN ALTERNATIVE TO ERA? (Ardsley-on-Hudson, NY: Transnat'l Pub., 1987)

Frances T. Pilch, The Crime of Rape in International Humanitarian Law, 9 USAFA J. LEGAL STUD. 99 (1998)

D. Rhode & C. Sanger (ed.), GENDER AND RIGHTS (Aldershot, Eng.: Ashgate, 2005)

G. van Bueren, INTERNATIONAL LAW ON THE RIGHTS OF THE CHILD (Dordrecht, Neth.; Boston: Martinus Nijhoff, 1994)

UNITED STATES

H. Hannum & D. Fischer (eds.), UNITED STATES RATIFICATION OF THE INTERNATIONAL COVENANTS ON HUMAN RIGHTS (Irvington-on-Hudson, NY: Transnational, 1993)

M. Gibney (ed.), WORLD JUSTICE? US COURTS AND INTERNATIONAL HUMAN RIGHTS (Boulder, CO: Westview Press, 1991)

K. Randall, FEDERAL COURTS AND THE INTERNATIONAL HUMAN RIGHTS PARADIGM (Durham, NC: Duke Univ. Press, 1991)

OTHER

J. Acker et al. (eds.), AMERICA'S EXPERIMENT WITH CAPITAL PUNISHMENT: REFLECTIONS ON THE PAST, PRESENT, AND FUTURE OF THE ULTIMATE PENAL SANCTION (Durham, NC: Carolina Acad. Press, 1998)

S. Chowdhury, THE RULE OF LAW IN A STATE OF EMERGENCY: THE PARIS MINIMUM STANDARDS OF HUMAN RIGHTS NORMS IN A STATE OF EMERGENCY (New York: St. Martin's Press, 1989)

M. Jakobson, ORIGINS OF THE GULAG: THE SOVIET PRISON-CAMP SYSTEM, *1917–1934* (Lexington, KY: Univ. Press of Kentucky, 1992)

N. Rodley, THE TREATMENT OF PRISONERS UNDER INTERNATIONAL LAW (2d ed. Oxford, Eng.: Oxford Univ. Press, 1999)

Additional Electronic Resources

Country Reports on Human Rights Practices (US Dep't State): <http://www.state.gov/g/drl/rls/hrrpt/>

Muslim World Journal of Human Rights: <http://www.bepress.com/mwjhr>

Protection Project (database of foreign laws on trafficking in women and children): <http://www.protectionproject.org/>

Racism: <http://www.un.org/search/>, search World Conference Against Racism

University of Minnesota Human Rights Library: <http://www1.umn.edu/humanrts>

Yale Law School Avalon Project: <http://yale.edu/lawweb/avalon/avalon.htm>

◆ ENDNOTES

1. M. Evans, International Wrongs and National Jurisdiction, Ch. 11, in M. Evans (ed.), REMEDIES IN INTERNATIONAL LAW: THE INSTITUTIONAL DILEMMA 173 (Oxford, Eng.: Hart, 1998).

2. T. Buergenthal, Historical Antecedents of International Human Rights Law, ch. 1, in INTERNATIONAL HUMAN RIGHTS IN A NUTSHELL 1 (3d ed. St. Paul: West, 2002).

3. See J. Gardner (ed.), HUMAN RIGHTS AS GENERAL NORMS AND A STATE'S RIGHT TO OPT OUT: RESERVATIONS AND OBJECTIONS TO HUMAN RIGHTS CONVENTIONS (London: Brit. Inst. Comp. Law, 1997).

4. R. Howard & J. Donnelly, Human Dignity, Human Rights, and Political Regimes, 80 AMER. POL. SCI. REV. 801 (1986).

5. *Powell testimony:* See S. Weisman, Powell Says Rapes and Killings in Sudan are Genocide, NYT on the Web (Sept. 9, 2004). *Legislative history:* 50 US CODE § 1701 (2004) §3 Findings.

6. *Analysis:* F. Kirgis, ASIL Insight: UN Commission's Report on Violations of International Humanitarian Law in Darfur, available at: <http://www.asil.org/insights/2005/02/insight050204.html>.

7. Further 9-11 details are available in §10.7

8. *Schabas quote:* W. Schabas, The Mental Element or *Mens Rea* of Genocide, ch. 5, in GENOCIDE IN INTERNATIONAL LAW 207 (Cambridge, Eng.: Cambridge Univ. Press, 2000). *ICC:* Article 30 (Mental Element). *Resolution:* UN Gen. Ass. Reso. 96(I), 1 U.N.GAOR, U.N. DOC. A/64/Add.1, at 188–89 (1946). *Case:* see this text's §1.4 Kadic v. Karadzic case, 70 F.3d 232, 241, (2d Cir., 1995), cert. den'd, 518 U.S. 1005 ("genocide is a crime under international law that is condemned by the civilized world, whether the perpetrators are 'private individuals, public officials or statesmen'") [hereinafter *Karadzic*].

9. Presbyterian Church of Sudan v. Talisman Energy, Inc., 244 F.SUPP.2d 289 (S.D.N.Y., 2003) (citing §1.2 *Flores* and §5.3 *Alvarez-Machain* principle cases regarding sources of permissible human rights claims).

10. Final Report of the United Nations Commission of Experts Established Pursuant to Security Council Resolution 780, UN. SCOR, Annex IV, at 16, UN Doc. S/25274 (1993).

11. Associated Press, Northern Irish Ethnic Cleansing Mulled in 70's, NYT on the Web (Jan. 1, 2003) (quoted from secret British documents made public in 2002).

12. See W. Schabas, Problems of International Codification—Were the Atrocities in Cambodia and Kosovo Genocide?, 35 NEW ENG. L. REV. 287, 295 (2001).

13. Further analyses are available in J. Webb, Genocide Treaty—ethnic Cleansing—substantive And Procedural Hurdles in the Application of the Genocide Convention to Alleged Crimes in The Former Yugoslavia, 23 GA. J. INT'L & COMP. L. 377 (1993) & Comment, Genocide and Ethnic Cleansing: Why the Distinction? A Discussion in the Context of Atrocities Occurring in Sudan, 35 CAL. WEST. INT'L L.J. 303 (2005).

14. Reprinted in E. Lawson, ENCYCLOPEDIA OF HUMAN RIGHTS 346 (2d ed. London Taylor & Francis, 1996) [hereinafter *Encyclopedia*].

15. L. Henkin, Idealism and Ideology: The Law of Human Rights, ch. 12, in HOW NATIONS BEHAVE: LAW AND FOREIGN POLICY 231 (2d ed. New York: Columbia Univ. Press, 1979).

16. See B. Simma (ed.), The Position of the Principle of Non-Intervention in the Legal System of the United Nations, in 1 THE CHARTER OF THE UNITED NATIONS: A COMMENTARY 148 (1st ed. Oxford: Oxford Univ. Press, 1994) [hereinafter *Simma*].

17. *Simma,* 2d ed. (2002), at 161 (cited in note 16 above).

18. Sei Fujii v. State of California, 38 Cal. 2d 718, at 722, 242 P.2d 617, at 620 (1952). This case is employed §8.1 to illustrate the distinction between "self-executing" treaties and those instead containing "standards of achievement."

19. *South Africa apartheid: see Encyclopedia* 81–94 (cited in note 14 above). *US segregation:* Plessy v. Ferguson, 163 US 537, 16 S.Ct. 1138, 41 L. Ed. 256 (1898). *Plessy* was not overruled until nearly ten years after the Charter was drafted (1954). *US interracial marriages:* The relevant state prohibitions were not ruled unconstitutional until more than twenty years after the Charter was created. Loving v. Virginia, 388 US 1, 87 S.Ct. 1817, 18 L. Ed. 2d 1010 (1967). *Soviet gulags:* A. Solzhenitsyn, THE GULAG ARCHIPELAGO (New York: Harper & Row, 1974).

20. Gen. Ass. Reso. 2627(XXV) of Oct. 24, 1970, reprinted in *Encyclopedia* 376 (1st ed.: 1991) and referenced in 2d ed., p. 1483 (cited in note 14 above).

21. T. von Meron, On the Inadequate Reach of Humanitarian and Human Rights Law and the Need for a New Instrument, 77 AMER. J. INT'L L. 589, 604–605 (1983).

22. L. Sunga, INDIVIDUAL RESPONSIBILITY IN INTERNATIONAL LAW FOR SERIOUS HUMAN RIGHTS VIOLATIONS (Dordrecht, Neth.: Martinus Nijhoff, 1992).

23. H. Hannum, The Status of the Universal Declaration of Human Rights in National and International Law, 25 GEO. J. INT'L & COMP. LAW 287 (1996).

24. M. Whiteman, 5 DIGEST OF INTERNATIONAL LAW 243 (Wash., DC: US Gov't Print. Off., 1965).

25. Namibia (South-West Africa) Advisory Opinion, 1971 ICJ REP. 16, 55 (Concurring Opinion of Judge Ammoun).

26. American Law Institute, 2 RESTATEMENT OF THE FOREIGN RELATIONS LAW OF THE UNITED STATES §701, at 153 and 155 (3d ed. Wash., DC: Amer. Law Inst., 1987).

27. A. Eide & G. Alfredsson (ed.), "Western Approach?," in THE UNIVERSAL DECLARATION OF HUMAN RIGHTS: A COMMENTARY 11 (Oslo, Norway: Scandinavian Univ. Press, 1992). *See also* UN Permanent Forum for Indigenous Issues, ECOSOC Doc. E/2000/23 (Part I) 28 July 2000 <http://www.unhchr.ch/huridocda/huridoca.nsf/(Symbol)/E.RES.2000.22.En?Opendocument>.

28. Reprinted in 32 INT'L LEGAL MAT'LS 1661 (1993).

29. Rights Report Finds Continuing Abuses around the Globe, Los Angeles Daily Journal, October 5, 1988, p. 1.

30. *ICCPR:* 999 UNITED NATIONS TREATY SERIES 171 (1976), available at: <http://www1.umn.edu/humanrts/instree/b3ccpr.htm>. *Leading treatise:* M. Nowak, U.N. COVENANT ON CIVIL AND POLITICAL RIGHTS: CCPR COMMENTARY (2d ed. Kehl, Germany: N.P. Engel, 2005).

31. Optional Protocol to the International Covenant on Civil and Political Rights, 999 UNITED NATIONS TREATY SERIES 302, entered into force in 1976, available at: <http://www1.umn.edu/humanrts/instree/b4ccprp1.htm>.

32. P. Ghandhi, The Operation of the Individual Communication Procedure, ch. 3, in THE HUMAN RIGHTS COMMITTEE AND THE RIGHT OF INDIVIDUAL COMMUNICATION: LAW AND PRACTICE 48 (Aldershot, Eng.: Ashgate, 1998).

33. Second Optional Protocol to the International Covenant on Civil and Political Rights, aiming at the Abolition of the Death Penalty, U.N. DOC. A/44/49 (1989), entered into force in 1991, available at: <http://www1.umn.edu/humanrts/instree/b5ccprp2.htm>.

34. W. Schabas, THE ABOLITION OF THE DEATH PENALTY IN INTERNATIONAL LAW (3d ed. Cambridge, Eng: Cambridge Univ. Press, 2002) [hereinafter *Death Penalty*].

35. UN DOC. A/C.3/49/SR.43, §§74–76.

36. *ICESCR:* 993 UNITED NATIONS TREATY SERIES 3 (1976), available at: <http://www1.umn.edu/humanrts/instree/b2esc.htm>. *Leading treatise:* M. Craven, THE INTERNATIONAL COVENANT ON ECONOMIC, SOCIAL, AND CULTURAL RIGHTS: A PERSPECTIVE ON ITS DEVELOPMENT (Oxford, Eng.: Clarendon Press, 1995) [hereinafter *Craven*].

37. *See, e.g.,* A. Eide et al. (eds.), FOOD AS A HUMAN RIGHT (Tokyo: UN University, 1984).

38. *See Craven,* at 8–9 (cited in note 36 above).

39. *See generally,* M Craven, The UN Committee on Economic, Social and Cultural Rights, ch.24, in A. Eide et al. (eds.), ECONOMIC, SOCIAL AND CULTURAL RIGHTS: A TEXTBOOK 455 (2d ed. Dordrecht, Neth.: Martinus Nijhoff, 2001).

40. Gen. Ass. Reso. 48/141, of Dec. 20, 1993, reprinted in 33 INT'L LEGAL MAT'LS 303 (1994).

41. See UNATET Regulations, available at: <http://www.un.org/peace/etimor/untaetR/r-1999.htm>.

42. Comment, The Sins of The Savior: Holding The United Nations Accountable to International Human Rights Standards for Executive Order Detentions in Its Mission in Kosovo, 52 AMER. UNIV. L. REV. 1291 (2003).

43. *World Court jurisprudence:* A. Kiss, The Impact of Judgments and Advisory Opinions of the PCIJ-ICJ on Regional Courts of Human Rights, N. Ando, E. McWhinney & R. Wolfrum (ed.), 2 LIBER AMICORUM JUDGE SHIGERU ODA 1469 (The Hague: Kluwer, 2002). *Regional jurisprudence:* J. Cerone, The Application of Regional Human Rights Law Beyond Regional Frontiers: The Inter-American Commission on Human Rights and the US Activities in Iraq, ASIL Insight (Oct. 25, 2005), available at: <http://www.asil.org/insights/2005/10/insights051025.html>.

44. *Convention:* Convention for the Protection of Human Rights and Fundamental Freedoms, 213 UNITED NATIONS TREATY SERIES 221 (1955). *Charter. See* D. Harris, THE EUROPEAN SOCIAL CHARTER (Charlottesville, VA: Univ. Press of Va., 1984).

45. Case of Open Door and Dublin Well Woman v. Ireland, set forth in §9.6 of this book.

46. Further details are available on the Court's Web site at: <http://www.echr.coe.int/Eng/General.htm>, click on Historical Background of the Court.

47. *See* European Convention for the Protection of Human Rights and Fundamental Freedoms: Report Regarding Its Differences from the UN Covenants, 9 INT'L LEGAL MAT'LS 1310 (1970).

48. Assenov and Others v. Bulgaria, 90/1997/874/1086 (Judgment of Oct. 28, 1998).

49. *France:* see E. Ganley, French Students Face New Head Scarf Ban, Associated Press (Sept. 2, 2004). *Britain:* see T. Hundley, Europe Juggles Freedom and Security, Chicago Tribune (July 27, 2005). For an online resource, see L. Louis-Jacques, Researching the Right to Wear Religious Garb in Public Schools in Europe—The Muslim Headscarf Issue: Religion and International Human Rights Law and Policy, available at: <http://www.lib.uchicago.edu/~llou/religion.html>.

50. *See, e.g.,* Title V—Removing Obstacles to Investigating Terrorism, in Uniting and Strengthening America by Providing Appropriate Tools Required to Intercept and Obstruct Terrorism (USA PATRIOT ACT) Act of 2001, available at: <http://jurist.law.pitt.edu/terrorism/hr3162.htm>.

51. M. Janis and R. Kay, EUROPEAN HUMAN RIGHTS LAW, vii (Hartford, CT: Univ. of Conn. Law School Foundation Press, 1990).

52. European Court of Human Rights Press Release, Chamber Judgments in Six Applications Against Russia, available on the court's Web site at: <http://press.coe.int/cp/2005/088a(2005).htm>.

53. *Final Act:* Reprinted in Declaration of Principles Guiding Relations between Participating States, 70 AMER. J. INT'L L. 417 (1976). *Conference documents:* A. Bloed (ed.), THE CONFERENCE ON SECURITY AND CO-OPERATION IN EUROPE: ANALYSIS AND BASIC DOCUMENTS, 1972–1993 (Dordrecht, Neth.: Martinus Nijhoff, 1993); and A. Bloed (ed.), THE CONFERENCE ON SECURITY AND CO-OPERATION IN EUROPE: BASIC DOCUMENTS, 1993–1995 (The Hague: Martinus Nijhoff, 1997).

54. *See generally,* M. Amor & M. Estebanez, The High Commissioner on National Minorities: Development of the Mandate, ch. 5, in M. Bothe, N. Ronzitti & A. Rosas (ed.), THE OSCE IN THE MAINTENANCE OF PEACE AND SECURITY: CONFLICT PREVENTION, CRISIS MANAGEMENT AND PEACEFUL SETTLEMENT OF DISPUTES 123 (The Hague: Kluwer, 1997) [hereinafter *OSCE* collection] and the OSCE Human Rights Web page at: <http://www.osce.org/kosovo/human_rights/>.

55. Further detail is available in M. Pentiken, The Role of the Human Dimension of the OSCE in Conflict Prevention and Crisis Management, ch. 4, p. 83 in *OSCE* collection (cited in note 54 above).

56. Available on the OSCE Web site at: <http://www.osce.org/documents/cio/2004/04/2828_en.pdf>.

57. 119 UNITED NATIONS TREATY SERIES 3 (1952) (as amended), available at: <http://www.oas.org/>, click on Documents & Treaties and Conventions.

58. T. Farer, The Rise of the Inter-American Human Rights Regime: No Longer a Unicorn, But Not Yet an Ox, Ch. 2, in D. Harris & S. Livingstone (ed.), THE INTER-AMERICAN SYSTEM OF HUMAN RIGHTS 33-34 (Clarendon Press: Oxford Univ. Press, 1998).

59. Robin Kirk, Human Rights Challenge: Why Terror Still Persists in Latin American Democracies, Los Angeles Daily Journal, July 14, 1987, at 4.

60. *See generally,* Hartman, Derogation from Human Rights Treaties in Public Emergencies, 22 HARV. INT'L L.J. 1 (1981).

61. Forced Disappearance treaty: <http://www.oas.org/juridico/english/Treaties/a-60.html>. Violence Against Women treaty: <http://www.oas.org/cim/English/Convention%20Violence%20Against%20Women.htm>.

62. *See* <http://www.cidh.oas.org/email9.asp>.

63. *See* Human Rights Watch, "Disappearances" in Law and History, Part IV of The United States' "Disappeared": The CIA's Long-Term "Ghost Detainees" (Oct. 2004), available at: <http://www.hrw.org/backgrounder/usa/us1004/4. htm#_Toc84652972>.

64. U. Umozurike, The African Charter on Human and Peoples' Rights, 77 AMER. J. INT'L L. 902–903 (1983) [hereinafter *African Charter*].

65. International Panel of Eminent Personalities, Report on the 1994 Genocide in Rwanda and Surrounding Events, 40 INT'L LEGAL MAT'LS (2001).

66. U. Umozurike, *Human Rights,* ch. 12, in INTRODUCTION TO INTERNATIONAL LAW 153 (Ibadan, Nigeria: Spectrum Law Pub., 1993).

67. Lone Lindholt, A Universal Concept of Human Rights?, Ch. 3, in QUESTIONING THE UNIVERSALITY OF HUMAN RIGHTS: THE AFRICAN CHARTER ON HUMAN AND PEOPLES' RIGHTS IN BOTSWANA, MALAWI AND MOZAMBIQUE 27 (Aldershot, Eng.: Dartmouth, 1997).

68. T. Bennett, A SOURCEBOOK OF AFRICAN CUSTOMARY LAW FOR SOUTHERN AFRICA viii (Wetton, So. Africa: Juta & Co., 1991).

69. *African Charter,* at 911 (cited in note 64 above).

70. *See* E. Ankumah, THE AFRICAN COMMISSION ON HUMAN AND PEOPLES' RIGHTS: PRACTICE AND PROCEDURES (The Hague: Martinus Nijhoff, 1996).

71. *Summary*: Africa Legal Aid Association, Cairo-Arusha Principles on Universal Jurisdiction in Respect of Gross Human Rights Offences (Oct. 21, 2002), available at: <http://www.afla.unimaas.nl/en/pubs/quarterly/Final%20Summary.doc>. *Analysis*: E. Ankumah, The Cairo-arusha Principles on Universal Jurisdiction in Respect of Gross Human Rights Offenses: an African Perspective, 98 AMER. SOC. INT'L L. PROCEEDINGS 238 (2004).

72. C. Szu, A Criticism of the Views of Bourgeois International Law on the Question of Population, reprinted in 1 J. Cohen and H. Chiu, PEOPLE'S CHINA AND INTERNATIONAL LAW 607 (Princeton: Princeton Univ. Press, 1974).

73. H. Chiu, CHINESE ATTITUDES TOWARD INTERNATIONAL LAW OF HUMAN RIGHTS IN THE POST-MAO ERA, IN CONTEMPORARY ASIAN STUDIES: PAPER NO. 5 (Baltimore: Univ. of Maryland, 1989).

74. R. Lillich, Sources of Human Rights Law and the Hong Kong Bill of Rights, in H. Chiu (ed.), 10 CHINESE YEAR-BOOK INT'L L. & AFFAIRS 27 (Baltimore: Chinese Soc. Int'l Law, 1992).

75. R. Hingorini, MODERN INTERNATIONAL LAW 258 (New York: Oceana, 1984).

76. S. Gutto, Violation of Human Rights in the Third World: Responsibility of States and TNCs, reprinted in F. Snyder and S. Sathirathai (ed.), THIRD WORLD ATTITUDES TOWARD INTERNATIONAL LAW 275 (Dordrecht, Neth.: Martinus Nijhoff, 1987).

77. *African conference:* T. Elias, NEW HORIZONS IN INTERNATIONAL LAW 167 (Alphen an den Rijn, Neth.: Sitjhoff & Noordhoff, 1979). *India abortions*: A. Gentleman, Millions of Abortions Of Female Fetuses Reported in India, New York Times on the Web (Jan. 10, 2006).

78. M. Bulajic, PRINCIPLES OF INTERNATIONAL DEVELOPMENT LAW: PROGRESSIVE DEVELOPMENT OF THE PRINCIPLES OF INTERNATIONAL LAW RELATING TO THE NEW INTERNATIONAL ECONOMIC ORDER (2d rev. ed. Dordrecht, Neth.: Martinus Nijhoff, 1993).

79. C. Welch (ed.), NGOS AND HUMAN RIGHTS: PROMISE AND PERFORMANCE (Philadelphia: Univ. Penn. Press, 2001).

80. Reprinted in 32 INT'L LEGAL MAT'LS 1661 (1993).

81. *Red Cross:* see N. Lewis, Red Cross Finds Detainee Abuse in Guantanamo, New York Times on the Web (Nov. 30, 2004). *Redress:* Redress: Seeking Reparation for Torture Survivors Web page, available at: <http://www.redress.org>.

82. J. Eyjolfsdottir, Amnesty International: The Cradle of Hope, in G. Alfredsson et al., INTERNATIONAL HUMAN RIGHTS MONITORING MECHANISMS: ESSAYS IN HONOUR OF JAKOB TH. MOLLER 855, at 856–857 (2000).

83. *See* M. Posner & C. Whittome, The Status of Human Rights NGOs, 25 COLUM. HUM. RTS. L. REV. 269 (1994). Lawyers Without Borders peace/human rights program: <http://www.Lawyerswithoutborders.org/default.asp?page=1>.

84. *Norms:* U.N. Doc. E/CN.4/Sub.2/2003/12/Rev.2 (2003), available at: <http://www1.umn.edu/humanrts/links/norms-Aug2003.html#approval>. *Resolution:* Sub-Commission resolution 2003/16, U.N. Doc. E/CN.4/Sub.2/2003/L.11 at 52 (2003), available at: <http://www1.umn.edu/humanrts/links/res2003-16.html> (para. 5). *Commentary:* Current Developments: Norms on the Responsibilities of Transnational Corporations and Other Business Enterprises with Regard to Human Rights, 97 AMER. J. INT'L L. 901 (2003).

85. See Amnesty International, UN Human Rights Norms for Business available on it's Web site at: <http://www.amnestyusa.org> (pdf booklet).

86. S. Wright, Economic Rights, Social Justice and the State: A Feminist Reappraisal, in D. Dallmeyer (ed.), RECONCEIVING REALITY: WOMAN AND INTERNATIONAL LAW 117, 135–136 (Wash., DC: Amer. Soc. Int'l L., 1993) [hereinafter *Reconceiving Reality*].

87. C. Thomas, Domestic Violence, in K. Askin & D. Koenig (ed.), 1 WOMEN AND INTERNATIONAL HUMAN RIGHTS LAW 220, 222, and 227 (Ardsley, NY: Transnat'l Publishers, 1999). This is the foremost resource available on this general subject (four volumes).

88. *Convention:* UN Gen. Ass. Res. 34/180, 34 U.N. GAOR Supp. (No. 46) at 193, U.N. Doc. A/34/46, entered into force Sept. 3, 1981. *Resolution:* UN Gen. Ass. Res. 43/100 of Dec. 8, 1988, calls upon all nations that have not yet ratified or acceded to this treaty to do so as soon as possible. *Canadian case:* R. v. Ewanchuk, [1999] 1 S.C.R. 330, 131 C.C.C. (3d) 481 (1999). *US case:* U.S. v. Morrison, 529 U.S. 598, 627 (2000) (italics added).

89. Background reading is available in *Reconceiving Reality* (cited in note 86 above); V. Peterson (ed.), GENDERED STATES: FEMINIST (RE)VISIONS OF INTERNATIONAL RELATIONS THEORY (Lynne Reinner, 1992); M. Meyer & E. Prugl (ed.), GENDER POLITICS IN GLOBAL GOVERNANCE (Lanham, MD: Rowman & Littlefield, 1999); and J. Steans, GENDER AND INTERNATIONAL RELATIONS: AN INTRODUCTION (New Brunswick, NJ: Rutgers Univ. Press, 1998).

90. Regarding the genocide itself, see A. Kuperman, THE LIMITS OF HUMANITARIAN INTERVENTION: GENOCIDE IN RWANDA (Wash., DC: Brookings Institution Press, 2001).

91. L. Keller, Belgian Jury to Decide Case Concerning Rwandan Genocide, ASIL Insight No. 72 (May 2001), available at: <http://www.asil.org/insights/insigh72.htm>.

92. Human Rights Watch, Belgium: Universal Jurisdiction Law Repealed, available at: <http://www.hrw.org/press/2003/08/belgium080103.htm>.

93. These and other features of the Iraqi Statute are addressed at the Commonwealth of Australia Parliamentary Library Department of Parliamentary Services, Research Note No. 34, February 10, 2004, available at: <www.aph.gov.au/library/pubs/rn/2003-04/04rn34.pdf>.

94. Genocide Convention Implementation Act of 1987, codified at 18 USC §1091.

95. Oyama v. California, 332 U.S. 633, 649–50, 68 S.Ct. 269, 277, 92 L. Ed. 249 (1948) (Justice Black, concurring opinion).

96. *Brown case:* 347 US 483, 74 S.Ct. 686, 98 L. Ed. 873 (1954). *Sei Fujii case:* 38 Cal.2d 718, 242 P.2d 617 (1952) (California Supreme Court upheld state's land law barring alien ownership, notwithstanding UN Charter prohibition on racial discrimination). *Racial rationale: see* The US Senate and Human Rights Treaties, §7.3 in *Nutshell* (cited in note 2 above).

97. *Holmes statement:* State of Missouri v. Holland, 252 U.S. 416, 433, 40 S.Ct. 382, 383 (1920). *Bricker proposal:* Note, The Bricker Amendment, T. Franck & M. Glennon, FOREIGN RELATIONS AND NATIONAL SECURITY LAW: CASES, MATERIALS AND SIMULATIONS 297 (2d ed. St. Paul, MN: West, 1993).

98. Separate Opinion of Judge Sir Hersch Lauterpacht, in Case of Certain Norwegian Loans (France v. Norway), 1957 ICJ REPORTS 9 (1957), set forth in §9.4 of this textbook.

99. See *Collin v. Smith,* 578 F.2d 1197 (7th Cir. 1978), *cert. den'd* 439 U.S. 916.

100. *Treaties:* Second Protocol, International Covenant on Civil and Political Rights (§11.2) and Organization of American States Protocol on the American Convention on Human Rights to Abolish the Death Penalty, 29 INT'L LEGAL MAT'LS 1447 (1990). *Scholarship: Death Penalty* (cited in note 34 above).

101. Executive Order 13107 of Dec. 10, 1998: <http://www.fas.org/irp/offdocs/eo13107.htm>.

102. For a discussion of this US statute and related policy analysis, see S. Cohen, Conditioning US Security Assistance on Human Rights Practices, 76 AMER. J. INT'L L. 246 (1982).

103. *Repealed position:* 22 US Code §2384(f). *New job description:* Provided by telephone call to US Department of State from author on January 18, 1995.

104. 28 UNITED STATES CODE §1350.

105. B. Stevens & M. Ratner, §1.3 The History and Intent of the ATCA, in INTERNATIONAL HUMAN RIGHTS LITIGATION IN US COURTS 12 (Irvington-on-Hudson, NY: Transnational, 1996) & R. Steinhardt & A. D'Amato, THE ALIEN TORTS CLAIMS ACT: AN ANALYTICAL ANTHOLOGY (Ardsley, NY: Transnational, 1999).

106. A. Rubin, US Tort Suits by Aliens Based on International Law, 18 FLETCHER FORUM 65 (1994).

107. Hilao v. Estate of Marcos, 103 F.3d 789 (9th Cir., 1996). The estate pa id $150 million to settle this case in February 1999.

108. *Karadzic* (cited in note 8 above). The facts are also set forth in §2.1 of this book, after the excerpt *On Condition of Statehood.*

109. Wiwa v. Royal Dutch Petroleum Co., 226 F.3d 88, 105–106 (2d Cir., 2000), *cert. den'd,* Royal Dutch Petroleum Co. v. Wiwa, 121 S.Ct. 1402 (2001).

110. Government's Internet version: <www.hmso.gov.uk/acts/acts1998/19980042.htm>.

111. Salman Masood, Pakistan Lifts Travel Restrictions on Rape Victim, NYT on the Web (June 16, 2005).

112. Story source: Nairobi, Kenya (AP), Dec. 14, 2000.

CHAPTER TWELVE

Environment

CHAPTER OUTLINE

INTRODUCTION

World wars, the Cold War, and the possibility of nuclear holocaust have all subsided as perceived threats to the earth's inhabitants. Events like September 11, 2001, and the War on Terror now occupy center stage. But environmental degradation may prove to be the apocalyptic threat to humanity.

This chapter presents the essential features of State responsibility for "transboundary environmental interference." The environment knows no boundaries. The UN's dramatic environmental program therefore seeks to shift the current legal regime from the many "soft law" norms to "hard law" via more treaty ratifications.

These materials analyze the somewhat counterintuitive objective of "sustainable development." This touchstone seeks to strike a balance between the interests of the international community's "haves" and "have nots."[1]

ON THE NIGHT OF DECEMBER 2–3, 1984, THE MOST tragic industrial disaster in history occurred in the city of Bhopal . . . India . . . [where] there was a chemical plant owned and operated by Union Carbide. . . . Methyl isocyanate (MIC), a highly toxic gas, . . . leaked from the plant in substantial quantities for reasons not yet determined.

The prevailing winds . . . blew the deadly gas into the overpopulated hutments adjacent to the plant and into the most densely occupied parts of the city. The results were horrendous. Estimates of deaths directly attributable to the leak range as high as 2,100. No one is sure exactly how many perished. Over 200,000 people suffered injuries—some serious and permanent—some mild and temporary. Livestock were killed and crops damaged. Businesses were interrupted. [The official death count rose to 10,000, plus injuries to *another* 380,000 people.]

—In re Union Carbide Corporation Gas Plant Disaster at Bhopal, India, 634 F. Supp. 842, 844 (SDNY, 1986), *aff'd*, 809 F. 2nd 195 (2nd Cir., 1987), *cert. den'd*, 484 US 871 (1987).

◆ 12.1 HISTORICAL DEVOLUTION

Ancient Greek and Roman smelters emitted enough lead to contaminate the entire northern hemisphere, rivaling gasoline as a cause of pollution in the modern era. The silver refining of 2,500 years ago was the oldest large-scale hemispheric pollution ever reported prior to the Industrial Revolution of the nineteenth century.

A few treaty-based limitations surfaced in the jurisprudence of the Permanent Court of International Justice in the 1920s and 1930s. Those cases dealt with State activity in rivers and canals used for international navigation or irrigation.[2]

The radioactive fallout from the US bombing of Nagasaki and Hiroshima initially killed 100,000 people, and ultimately killed or harmed an additional 100,000 people within several years. The following Cold War round of nuclear weapons development would spawn extensive atmospheric and underground testing, which wreaked havoc on more than just the political environment.[3]

Like problems surfaced early in the jurisprudence of the current International Court of Justice (ICJ). The ICJ's first environmental decision (1949) pronounced the obligation of States not to allow the use of their territories to interfere with the rights of other States. Albania was liable for its failure to notify Great Britain about the presence of mines in Albanian waters within the international strait adjacent to its coastline. The exploding mines served a military purpose, while doing a great disservice to the environment. In 1974, the Court ordered France to cease its nuclear atmospheric testing in the South Pacific. Otherwise, radioactive fallout would further prejudice health and agricultural interests of the citizens of Australia, New Zealand, and all downwind islands.

Downriver problems are augmenting downwind disasters with increasing frequency. After a November 2005 chemical plant explosion in northern China, near the Russian border, a 50 mile long benzene slick began its ill-fated downstream journey. The pollutants affected seventy Russian cities and villages—and potentially over a million residents along the Songhua and Amur Rivers. China's extraordinary economic development thus left its mark on a bordering nation. This scenario classically illustrates the tension between economic growth and environmental pollution. A recent study suggests some *political* pollution, if China does not meet its environmental targets before the 2008 Olympic Games. About 70 percent of China's rivers, lakes, and air space are sufficiently polluted to make them unsafe for humans and animals alike. Some 400,000 people die prematurely each year from diseases linked to air pollution.[4]

Trail Smelters Arbitration This 1941 case study classically articulated a fundamental norm which still resonates in contemporary International Environmental Law (IEL), more than sixty years later: "The Tribunal, therefore, finds . . . that, under the principles of international law, as well as of the law of the United States, no State has the right to use or permit the use of its territory in such as manner as to cause injury by fumes in or to the territory of another or the properties or persons therein, when the case is of serious consequence and the injury is established by clear and convincing evidence."[5]

This was the first tribunal to deal authoritatively with cross-border air pollution. A Canadian smelter 7 miles from the US state of Washington emitted extraordinary amounts of sulfur dioxide fumes, harming the atmosphere and the agricultural industry in Washington for more than a decade. The United States and Canada established a three-member arbitral tribunal that consisted of Canadian, United States, and Belgian arbitrators (the third being a neutral arbitrator selected by the other two). The tribunal determined that Canada had incurred State responsibility for environmental damage, although the smelter was privately owned and operated.

In one passage, the arbitrators effectively predicted the direction of the "sustainable development" analysis (§12.2), when referring to the competing interests of industrial development and agricultural degradation in the region surrounding British Columbia and Washington. Drawing from commonly accepted sources, the arbitral decision also determined that "[i]t would not be to the advantage of the two countries concerned that industrial effort should be prevented by exaggerating the [environmental] interests of the agricultural community. Equally, it would not be to the advantage of the two countries that the agricultural community should be oppressed to advance the interest of industry."

While the State parties purported to seek a final resolution of this major environmental decision for the next forty years, *Trail Smelter* authoritatively set the stage for an emerging principle routinely cited in national and international litigation. A State must not knowingly permit the use of its territory to harm other States. It has the obligation to protect other States from the injurious acts of individuals and corporations within its borders. Sovereign rights also meant corresponding responsibility to respect the territory of other sovereigns.

Selected Disasters A number of disasters in the last decade of the twentieth century dramatically illustrated the importance of solidifying a global environmental protection regime. Two years after the Bhopal, India, disaster,[6] an explosion at the Chernobyl nuclear reactor in the Ukraine caused the first *officially* reported radiation deaths from a nuclear power plant accident. The reactor released radioactive material into the atmosphere and was carried as far away as the United States. Also in that year, a fire in Switzerland resulted in 30 tons of hazardous chemicals being washed into the Rhine River, one of Europe's most serious environmental catastrophes. In 1991, near the close of the Persian Gulf War, retreating Iraqi forces set fire to over 600 Kuwaiti oil wells. That single military campaign sent millions of tons of contaminants into the biosphere during the nine months it took to extinguish all of these fires. In 1993, a Norwegian tanker spilled 4,000 tons of sulfuric acid into the sea off the Mexican coast.

These are examples of *sudden* disasters. There have been equally severe *incremental* threats: ozone depletion, climate change, deforestation of entire regions, and many other potentially incalculable dangers to human survival. Many of these hazards have reportedly caused skin cancer, cataracts, suppression of the human immune system, and agricultural degradation. The circulation of industrial contaminants throughout the atmosphere may further lead to catastrophic rises in sea levels.

In 1993, Russia's head environmental adviser revealed that the former Soviet Union had clandestinely dumped vast amounts of highly radioactive waste at sea during the previous thirty years. This was twice the *combined* amount of the other major nuclear nations. This total included 2.5-million curies of radioactive waste and eighteen nuclear reactors dumped into the Arctic Sea and the Sea of Japan. In the northern Arctic, there are vast depots of aging post-Soviet nuclear weapons, submarines, and leaking nuclear fuel assemblies.

The pivotal crisis in the "incremental" category of environmental degradation may ultimately be overpopulation. In 1994, the Worldwide Watch Institute, a Washington, DC, research academy, issued its grimmest annual report ever. According to Worldwide Watch, this planet is nearing its capacity to produce food. If the earth's growing population remains uncontrolled and soil and water resources continue to be degraded, then there will be no positive correlation between food production and human consumption. The Institute projected that the world's population (then 5.4 billion) would increase by 3.6 billion in the next forty years. The world's per capita seafood catch fell 9 percent during that same period. Grain production, which expanded by 3 percent between

1950 and 1984, dropped to a 1 percent annual growth rate between 1984 and 1994. Just as ideological conflict dominated the last four decades of the Cold War, the Earth's physical capacity to satisfy the growing demand for food may dominate the ensuing four decades.[7]

The related problem of shelter is no less in crisis. The 1996 UN Conference on Human Settlements issued its Istanbul Declaration and the Habitat Agenda. It reported that by the year 2001, more than 50 percent of the world's population would be residing in cities. Housing has thus become an even greater problem for local and national governments. An estimated 1 billion people in developing nations do not have adequate shelter.

It was statistics such as these that motivated 180 nations to develop a twenty-year plan for slowing population growth at the 1994 UN Population Conference in Cairo. This conference focused on birth control, economic development, and providing women in certain societies and religious backgrounds with more power over their lives. The Vatican had rejected the final documents of the earlier world population conference debates held in 1974. At the 1994 conference, however, the Pope partially supported the results in principle—although he remained averse to the abortion alternative. The Cairo Program of Action calls on States to provide better education for women in traditionally male-dominated societies, wider access to modern birth control methods, and the right to choose if and when one becomes pregnant. This program purports not to conflict with national laws, religious beliefs, and cultural norms—which does not necessarily match word and deed.[8]

◆ 12.2 UN ENVIRONMENTAL DEVELOPMENT PROGRAM

The 1972 Conference on the Environment spawned an unprecedented political and diplomatic awakening. The United Nations, together with regional environmental organizations and world leaders, repositioned international environmental issues from the periphery to the center of national political and diplomatic agendas. Conferences of States, UN initiatives, and intergovernmental treaties permeated the public consciousness in the last portion of the twentieth century.

This subsection provides a snapshot of the major international environmental instruments. The following overview (Exhibit 12.1) will help you visualize the various campaigns designed to save the environment from unrestrained assaults:

EXHIBIT 12.1 MAJOR ENVIRONMENTAL INSTRUMENTS

Year	Event
1972	Stockholm Declaration of UN Conference on Human Environment: First global statement of environmental principles (11 INT'L LEGAL MAT'LS [ILM] 1416)
1972	UN Gen. Ass. Reso. 2997 on Institutional and Financial Arrangement for International Environment Cooperation: established UN's environmental fund and Governing Council for policy guidance (13 ILM 234)
1973	UN Gen. Ass. Reso. 3129 on Cooperation in the Field of the Environment Concerning Natural Resources Shared by Two or More States: governing Council reports on measures taken (17 ILM 1097)
1974	Convention for the Prevention of Marine Pollution from Land-Based Sources: ecological protection (13 ILM 352)
1977	Environmental Modification Convention: prohibits military and other hostile uses of the environment (16 ILM 88).
1978	Protocol Relating to International Convention for the Prevention of Pollution from Ships: ecological protection (17 ILM 546)
1980	Gen. Ass. Reso. 35/48 on Historical Responsibility of States for Preservation of Nature for Present and Future Generations (UN Doc. A/35/48, GAOR, 35th Session, Supp. No. 48)
1983	World Charter for Nature: nature's essential processes not to be impaired; genetic viability not compromised; all areas of earth subject to conservation; ecosystems managed for optimum sustainable productivity; no degradation by warfare or other hostile activities (22 ILM 455)
1985	Vienna Convention for the Protection of the Ozone Layer: protects layer of atmospheric zone above planetary layer (26 ILM 1529)
1985	◆ Montreal Protocol on Substances that Deplete the Ozone Layer: specific obligations to limit and reduce use of chlorofluorocarbons and possibly other chemicals depleting the ozone (26 ILM 516 (1987))
1989	◆ Helsinki Declaration on the Protection of the Ozone Layer: agrees to phase out CFCs not later than the year 2000; to phase out other ozone-depleting substances; to develop acceptable substitute technologies; to transfer technology and replacement equipment to developing countries at minimum cost (28 ILM 1335)
1986	International Atomic Energy Agency Convention on Early Notification of a Nuclear Accident: designed to minimize consequences and protect life, property, and environment (25 ILM 1369)
1987	Experts Group on Environmental Law of World Commission on Environment and Development: Legal principles for maintaining "sustainable development" of developing countries (UN Doc. WCED/86/23/Add. 1)
1988	Protocol to the 1979 Convention on Long-Range Transboundary Air Pollution Concerning the Control of Emissions of Nitrogen Oxides or Their Transboundary Fluxes: States to control or reduce emissions to 1987 levels (28 ILM 212; 1979 treaty in 18 ILM 1442)
1989	Hague Declaration on the Environment: Cooperation in controlling ozone-layer deterioration caused by emissions from industrialized States adversely affecting the right to live (28 ILM 1308)
1989	Basel Convention on the Control of Transboundary Movements of Hazardous Wastes and Their Disposal (28 ILM 649)
1991	Protocol on Environmental Protection to the Antarctic Treaty: updates 1959 treaty prohibiting nuclear testing and hazardous-waste disposal (19 ILM 860) to enhance protection of all ecosystems, prevent jeopardy of endangered species, and prohibit mineral resource activities except scientific (30 ILM 1461)

EXHIBIT 12.1 MAJOR ENVIRONMENTAL INSTRUMENTS (CONTINUED)

Year	Event
1992	Rio Declaration on Environment and Development: Second major conference of States; establishes current program for global partnership discouraging environmental degradation while encouraging sustainable development (31 ILM 874)
1992	Agenda 21: most extensive statement of priorities including review and assessment of International Law, development of implementation and compliance measures, effective participation by all States in lawmaking process, study of range and effectiveness of dispute resolution procedures (800-page Action Plan)
1992	Framework Convention on Climate Change: measures to combat greenhouse effect of emissions of carbon dioxide and similar gases and to finance controls (31 ILM 849)
1997	◆ Kyoto Protocol to strengthen Climate Change Convention by promise to reduce greenhouse emissions to 1990 levels between 2008 and 2012 (37 ILM 22)
2005	◆ Asia Pacific Partnership for Clean Development and Climate (Australia, China, India, Japan, South Korea, and United States): Supposed complement to Kyoto Protocol, that will develop cleaner energy technologies to combat global warming—but members may to set their goals for reducing emissions individually, with no mandatory enforcement mechanism.
1992	Convention on Biological Diversity: national monitoring and strategies for conserving biological diversity of all ecosystems (31 ILM 818)
1992	Statement of Principles for Global Consensus on the Management, Conservation and Sustainable Development for All Types of Forests: principles encourage sustainable development, reforestation, and reduction of pollutants, especially acid rain (31 ILM 881)
1992	Convention on the Protection and Use of Transboundary Watercourses and International Lakes (31 ILM 1312)
1999	◆ Protocol on Water and Health: requires parties to provide access to drinking water and sanitation; establish targets for standards and levels of performance (achieved/maintained) for increased protection against water-related diseases (38 ILM 1708)
1993	UN Gen. Ass. Reso. on Institutional Arrangement to Follow Up the [1992] UN Conference on Environment and Development: UN General Assembly follow-up resolution welcoming adoption of Agenda 21, stressing integration of environmental protection and sustainable development (32 ILM 238)
1994	UN Convention to Combat Decertification (33 ILM 1328 (1994))
1997	UN Convention on International Watercourses: framework for development, conservation, management, and protection (36 ILM 700)
1997	IAEA Joint Convention on Safety of Spent Fuel Management and on the Safety of Radioactive Waste Management: obligation to establish a legislative and regulatory framework to govern spent fuel from both civilian reactors and military or defense programs (36 ILM 1431)
1998	Convention on Prior Informed Consent Procedure for Certain Hazardous Chemicals and Pesticides in International Trade: requires consent for importation of hazardous materials (38 ILM 1)
1999	Convention on Access to Information, Public Participation in Decision-making and Access to Justice in Environmental Matters (38 ILM 517)
2001	Stockholm Convention On Persistent Organic Pollutants: encourages parties not having regulatory and assessment schemes for pesticides and industrial chemicals to develop such programs (40 ILM 532)
2005	Annex VI to the Protocol on Environmental Protection to the Antarctic Treaty, Liability Arising from Environmental Emergencies (http://www.ats.org.ar/Atcm/atcm28/att/atcm28_att102_rev1_e.doc)

1972 STOCKHOLM CONFERENCE

Emerging Principles This was the first of three major UN Conferences on the environment.[9] The resulting proclamations recognized that preservation of the environment is essential to the continued enjoyment of life itself. The importance of preserving the environment was succinctly stated in the aspirational proclamation providing (in part) as follows:

1. . . . In the long and tortuous evolution of the human race on this planet a stage has been reached when, through the rapid acceleration of science and technology, man has acquired the power to transform his environment in countless ways and on an unprecedented scale. . . . [M]an's environment . . . [is] essential to his well-being and to the enjoyment of basic human rights—even the right to life itself.

2. The protection and improvement of the human environment is a major issue [that] affects the well-being of peoples and economic development throughout the world; it is the urgent desire of peoples of the whole world and the duty of all Governments.

The bulk of the Stockholm Conference work product consists of twenty-six principles that call on States and international organizations to "play a co-ordinated, efficient and dynamic role for the protection and improvement of the environment" (Principle 25). This conference thus established the Governing Council of the United Nations Environment Program. The Council's function include implementation of environmental programs and "[t]o keep under review the world environmental situation in order to ensure that emerging environmental problems of wide international significance receive appropriate and adequate consideration by Governments. . . . "[10] The key provisions are Principles 21 and 22, which set the stage for an evolving regime for establishing both standards and remedies:

Principle 21
States have, in accordance with the Charter of the United Nations and the principles of international law, . . . the responsibility to ensure that activities within their jurisdiction or control do not cause damage to the environment of other States or of areas beyond the limits of national jurisdiction.

Principle 22
States shall cooperate to develop further international law regarding liability and compensation for the victims of pollution and other environmental damage caused by activities within the jurisdiction or control of such States beyond their jurisdiction.

Sustainable Development Proclamation 4 of the 1972 Stockholm Resolution provides that "[i]n the developing countries most of the environmental problems are caused by under-development. . . . Therefore, the developing countries must direct their efforts to development, bearing in mind their priorities and the need to safeguard the environment." One might characterize this aspiration as an attempt to impose the rough equivalent of an environmental impact statement when a government undertakes any project with the potential for causing transboundary pollution on land, in the sea, or in the air. The focus of IEL soon became *sustainable development*.

This phrase represents a somewhat symbiotic relationship between economic development (the benefit) and environmental degradation (the burden). In an ideal world, the improvement of underdeveloped economies would not be accompanied by unacceptable costs to the environment. The more developed countries are generally calling for environmental control. The less-developed countries counter that today's powerful nations had their Industrial Revolution. It is now someone else's turn to reap the same benefits.

This is perhaps the major impasse in IEL today. It effectively pits the industrialized north against the lesser-developed south. Nations of the former group seek comparatively more regulation to control environmental degradation. Lesser-developed nations seek economic prosperity. They are more willing to accept its attendant costs to the environment.

To address this disconnect, a UN group of experts drafted principles which have served as a yardstick for measuring the acceptable scope of "sustainable development" for developing countries. In 1983, the Experts Group on Environmental Law of the World Commission on Environment and Development promulgated its Principles for Environmental Protection and Sustainable Development. Brundtland defined sustainable development as "development which meets the needs of the present generation without compromising the ability of future generations to meet their needs."

The Brundtland Report became the most influential perspective on sustainable development, which was the topical focus of the UN's ensuing 1992 Rio Conference, as well as the contemporary sustainable development dialogue:

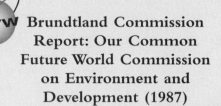

Brundtland Commission Report: Our Common Future World Commission on Environment and Development (1987)

Go to the course Web page <http://home.att.net/~slomansonb.index.html>. Under Chapter Twelve, click <u>Brundtland Commission Report</u>. The full text of this 312-page report is available at:

<http://www.are.admin.ch/are/en/nachhaltig/ international_uno/unterseite02330>

In one of the few environmental cases decided by the ICJ Vice-President Gregory Weermantry succinctly articulated the interplay of the rights to "development," "environmental protection," and "sustainable development:"

A. The Concept of Sustainable Development

. . .

The people of both Hungary and Slovakia are entitled to development for the furtherance of their happiness and welfare. They are likewise entitled to the preservation of their human right to the protection of their environment. . . . The present [1997] case thus focuses attention, as no other case has done in the jurisprudence of this Court, on the question of the harmonization of developmental and environmental concepts. . . .

Article 1 of the [UN] Declaration on the Right to Development, 1986, asserted that "The right to development is an inalienable human right." This Declaration had the overwhelming support of the international community. . . .

The protection of the environment is likewise a vital part of contemporary human rights doctrine, for it is a sine qua non [indispensable prerequisite] for numerous human rights such as the right to health and the right to life itself. It is scarcely necessary to elaborate on this, as damage to the environment can impair and undermine all the human rights spoken of in the Universal Declaration and other human rights instruments. . . .

While, therefore, all peoples have the right to initiate development projects and enjoy their benefits, there is likewise a duty to ensure that those projects do not significantly damage the environment. . . .

After the early formulations of the concept of development, it has been recognized that development cannot be pursued to such a point as to result in substantial damage to the environment within which it is to occur. Therefore development can only be prosecuted in harmony with the reasonable demands of environmental protection. Whether development is sustainable by reason of its impact on the environment will, of course, be a question to be answered in the context of the particular situation involved.

It is thus the correct formulation of the right to development that that right does not exist in the absolute sense, but is relative always to its tolerance by the environment. The right to development as thus refined is clearly part of modern international law. It is compendiously referred to as sustainable development.[11]

The 1982 UN Conference on the Law of the Sea produced a Convention, which entered into force in 1994 (§6.3). Article 235 contains an important statement of the applicable environmental norms which echo the Brundtland principles mentioned earlier:

1. States are responsible for the fulfillment of their international obligations concerning the protection and preservation of the marine environment. They shall be liable in accordance with international law.

2. States shall ensure that recourse is available in accordance with their [national] legal systems for prompt and adequate compensation or other relief in respect of damage caused by pollution of the marine environment by natural or juridical [that is, corporate] persons within their jurisdiction.

"Transborder Environmental Interference" This term of art is commonly used to describe State liability, for both permissible or impermissible activities that cause environmental damage to another State and its inhabitants.

The *Brundtland Report* also determined that State responsibility should attach, even when a transboundary environmental harm results from permissible activities. The rationale for liability for unintentional cases was appropriate when "the overall technical and socio-economic cost . . . far exceeds the long run advantage" of the particular activity. A State should thus be responsible for both intentional and inattentive uses or misuses of its resources which cause an adverse environmental impact in another State.

The prevailing Brundland Report remedies provide that the offending State must then: (1) cease the wrongful act; or (2) reestablish the environmental circumstances, as they were prior to the wrongful act; or (3) provide compensation to the State harmed by the transborder environmental interference; or (4) some combination of all three as the circumstances merit. These remedies are not supposed to be applied cumulatively, so as not to punish a State excessively for its transboundary environmental interference. They are the alternatives to be used in an appropriate combination, depending on the facts of the given case.

There were (and still are) some questions, which have not been satisfactorily resolved. Even assuming that liability is clear, *which* of these remedies should a decision-maker employ? Should the responsible State pay damages for the "environmental interference"? If so, *how much* would appropriately compensate the harmed State? Would it be more fair to require the offending State to restore the *status quo* as it existed prior to the environmental degradation? The "sustainable development" paradigm is supposed to balance the competing interests of protecting the environment, while encouraging underdeveloped nations to improve industrial growth. But striking this balance makes both liability and remedy assessments rather complex, given the ambiguities associated with the ill-defined term "sustainable development."

The current state of liability for such harm is briefly restated by Rene Lefeber, an environmental scholar-practitioner in The Hague:

[C]ontemporary international law and municipal law generally provide for the injurious consequences of harm to lie where they fall, unless the occurrence of harm is imputable, in the sense of the wrongful conduct, to the source of the harm . . . . Thus, if a victim cannot prove that the source of the harm has violated the law . . . the law does not afford protection to the victim with the result that the innocent victim will have to bear the injurious consequences of harm alone . . . . Having considerations of fairness, justice, and equity in mind, there is increasing support for the principle that the innocent victim should not be left to bear the loss, at least not alone . . . [and] should be borne by the source of the harm or should, at least, be shared by means of some kind of burden-sharing arrangement irrespective of whether the source of the harm has violated the law or not. The idea that the injurious consequences of harm should be shifted to the source of the harm also finds support in the polluter-pays principle. The object . . . is to channel the costs of prevention and reparation of environmental interference to the source of that interference.[12]

There are, of course, defenses to an alleged "transboundary environmental interference." The very nature of the environment can obscure the diagnosis of how a degradation occurred. One must sometimes search for a causal link between the result and the responsible actor. An adverse result may occur long after the incident (if *one* is identifiable) that allegedly caused the degradation. *Existing* pollution may also be a factor. Carbon dioxide (in the form of acid rain) was discharged into the atmosphere in the *Trail Smelter Arbitration* across the border from Canada to the US state of Washington. Assuming that the Washington fog became thicker and more dense over a period of time, it would be difficult for the state of Washington to conveniently trace the fog problem directly or exclusively to the Canadian smelter. Other contaminants in the United States may have contributed to that fog, including industrialization in the region near the border. The pollution on the US side may have originated from a variety of sources, including US automobiles, forest depletion machinery operations, and other industrial activities—in addition to smelter operations on either side of the international border.

The 1991 joint research project of the Italian universities of Sienna and Parma succinctly describes the practical problem with international responsibility for environmental harm. The then president of the European Council for Environmental Law therein cautions that environmental damage cases are not comparable to a linear progression from Point A directly to Point B. His analogy is that "[t]he procedure of compensation for environmental damage can be compared to a steeplechase where different obstacles must be overcome before arriving to the final result. Some obstacles—and maybe the hardest ones to overcome—result from [trying to determine what are] the *facts* while others have a *legal* character [lacking a lineage traceable to uncluttered precedent]."[13]

The following case is the most prominent environmental decision by the ICJ, in a contentious case with actual litigants—as opposed to the ICJ *Nuclear Weapons Case* below (an advisory opinion requested by the World Health Organization). The *Gabcíkovo* case involved a joint construction project on the Danube, agreed to by Hungary and Czechoslovakia in 1977. After the breakdown of the former Soviet Union, there was a dispute regarding how to carry out the respective treaty obligations. Public opposition to this project had surfaced in Hungary. The following ICJ opinion did a great deal to solidify the basket of norms that had evolved in IEL, especially during the two decades spanning the litigants' 1977 treaty and the Court's decision:

Case Concerning the Gabcíkovo-Nagymaros Project
(*Hungary v. Slovakia*)
INTERNATIONAL COURT OF JUSTICE
General List No. 92
(Judgment of 25 September 1997)

Go to course Web page at:
<http://home.att.net/~slomansonb/txtcsesite.html>.
Under Chapter Twelve,
click <u>Gabcíkovo-Nagymaros Project</u>.

The ICJ considered its first *contentious* environmental case in 1993. The small, formerly resource-rich State of Nauru alleged that Australia had incurred State responsibility for the environmental degradation of Nauru. It claimed that Australia (and others) mined the phosphate-rich soil of Nauru to satisfy the fertilizer needs of Australia's agricultural industry, but at great expense to Nauru's future. Nauru received a woefully inadequate share of the profits from its natural resources in addition to experiencing a depletion that also degraded its economic, social, and cultural environment as previously announced by an independent Commission of Inquiry.[14]

The parties settled this case shortly after the ICJ announced its Environmental Chambers Constitution in 1993 (§12.3). One might presume that the Court's pending consideration of Nauru's contentious case, coupled with the establishment of a specialized environmental chamber, may have combined to pressure Australia into pursuing a settlement—rather than face the consequences of an adverse ICJ judgment. One possible consequence could have been a court-mandated requirement that Australia restore Nauru to the position it would have enjoyed but for the environmental degradation. Australia would not necessarily honor such a decision because of the immense economic impact of such a mandate. Australia would then have been in the unenviable position of ignoring a world court order.

A book-length account of the work of the Commission of Inquiry (undertaken before Nauru's postindependence ICJ litigation) depicts the resulting environmental degradation of Nauru by the partnership of Australia, New Zealand, and Great Britain. A scientific report used by the Commission of Inquiry illustrates the relevant findings:

Land shortage resulting from mining has given Nauru one of the most important social problems which the country now faces.

In relation to fauna and flora, [scientists who prepared this report] . . . have described how centuries will be needed for the forest to reestablish itself naturally even in modified form, and how numerous plant species are scattered and stunted as compared with their growth in the unmined forest. . . . These scientists have stressed "the disastrous effects and almost total disruption of island ecosystems that resulted from inappropriate development projects and land use." Natural forest microclimates have been transformed into new microclimates with increased sunlight and lower humidity, resulting in greatly altered patterns of vegetation. A number of indigenous plant species are endangered.

With the changes in vegetation, Nauruan diet too has suffered a drastic change.[15]

"Soft" Law V. "Hard" Law Section 1.5 of this text-book presents the question: *Is International Law Really Law?* Section 8.1 presents the treaty subclassification of self-executing versus declaration of intent treaties. In both instances, you were asked to reflect upon whether a nonbinding custom or instrument can ultimately ripen into one that is widely recognized as binding law. In the field of IEL, more so than in any other subset of International Law, critics are fond of using the term "soft law" to describe the numerous instruments produced since the seminal 1972 Stockholm Declaration.

One who does not appreciate the underlying evolution of the law as process can easily fail to see the forest for the trees. The process, from establishing initial norms to treaty ratification, resembles the adage about one having to learn to crawl before one walks and eventually runs. As explained by a group of prominent commentators in their book on IEL:

International Environmental Law and Policy

E. WEISS, S. McCAFFREY, D. MAGRAW, P. SZASZ, AND R. LUTZ

Aspen Law & Business 189, 190–191 (New York: 1998)

Hard international law . . . is, by definition, legally binding, at least on some international entities (states and IGOs), although not necessarily on all. By contrast, what some commentators refer to as "soft international law" is not binding, though perhaps superficially it may appear to be so. Nevertheless, the international entities concerned habitually comply with it, and it is this feature that arguably makes it appropriate to refer to it as "law."

Soft law manifests itself in various ways. One is horatory rather than obligatory language [which would be] set out in otherwise binding instruments, such as when in a treaty in force certain actions to be taken are preceded by "should" rather than by "shall." . . .

According to one view, such nonbinding precepts (rather than obligations) can be considered as soft law only if international entities, particularly states, habitually comply with them—or at least pretend to do so, thus to effect acknowledging their authority. Such behavior, even in the absence of a strict legal obligation, may be due to various factors, such as the existence of a control mechanism that notes and may report on noncompliance; it may also be due to a mere expectation of compliance expressed by other states and by the general public . . .

Soft law is generated as a compromise between those who desire a certain matter to be regulated definitely and those who, while not denying the merits of the substantive issue, do not wish (at least for a time) to be bound by a rigid and obligatory rule—perhaps because they cannot obtain the necessary domestic legislative approval.

In any event, there is an ever-growing amount of soft law, most particularly in respect to the environment, expressed in the form of standards, guidelines, and rules formulated by expert organs and often promulgated by the executive head of a technical IGOs or organ, such as UNEP [the UN Environmental Program]. . . . Similarly, when such norms are to be amended or supplemented, this often can be done much more rapidly and simply than even a simplified treaty-amending procedure.

Inherently even less binding than soft law instruments that at least in form suggest an expectation of compliance, are those that are merely presented as model legislation, regulations, or treaties. . . .

Diplomatic and academic commentators have spent the last two decades attempting to invoke Customary International Law by elaborating rules of State responsibility for transboundary pollution. States have begun to develop principles for the prevention of harmful environmental activity. They also have been experimenting with different modes of regulation for special environmental problems. Numerous intergovernmental organizations now monitor pollution and regulate environmentally harmful behavior.[16] In the last decade of the prior millennium, a number of academic publications suddenly emerged as the core for teaching and research efforts to "catch up" with developments in IEL.[17]

One unifying theme is quite evident: States may no longer rely on territorial sovereignty to invoke the familiar UN Charter Article 2.7 defense that certain matters fall exclusively within national jurisdiction and are not subject to international legal controls.

1992 RIO CONFERENCE

On the twentieth anniversary of the Stockholm Conference, nations assembled once again to reassess the interplay between the potentially conflicting objectives of maintaining the Earth's environment and sustaining development of the southern tier of nations. Nearly 180 States, and 100 heads of government, all gathered in Rio de Janeiro, Brazil, for the second United Nations Conference on Environment and Development (UNCED). The fundamental principle resolved by this conference was that a State is liable for its conduct or omission that is a "transboundary environmental interference."

How to manage the connected but sometimes competing objectives of economic development and environmental protection was a central issue. As provided in the resulting UN declaration, the Rio objectives are "to promote the further development of international environmental law, taking into account the [1992] Declaration of the UN Conference on the Human Environment, as well as the special needs and concerns of developing countries, and to examine . . . the feasibility of elaborating general rights and obligations of states, *as appropriate*, in the field of the environment. . . ."[18]

This widely heralded gathering of diverse States produced the five major documents of the international environmental agenda for the twenty-first century. The primary components of "Rio 1992" are the following:

(1) Agenda 21
(2) Rio Declaration
(3) Biological Diversity Convention
(4) Framework Convention on Climate Change
(5) The Forest Principles

Agenda 21 This is the 800-page blueprint for managing all sectors of the environment in the twenty-first century.[19] Many of the action items are quite specific. Yet they aspire to degrees of protection which are well beyond the existing capacity of many States.

The most controversial of these was protection of the atmosphere. Financing is the critical issue. There was an agreement that fresh funding sources were needed if the objective of sustainable development were to be something more than just lip service to an unattainable ideal.

However, the developed States did not succumb to pressure to commit even a small fraction of their GNP to assisting developing States.

Agenda 21 has other drawbacks. It does not contain any mandatory rules and depends largely on follow-up processes to attain the laudable goals of its 800-page *Program of Action*. Stanley Johnson, author of several environmental books, laments in his description of *Agenda 21* that it

> may suffer from its own sheer bulkiness . . . as well as from the fact that it does not lay down any mandatory rules, nor on the whole does it require truly bankable commitments to be made by any of the [State] parties involved. Agenda 21 is in reality the softest of "soft law," exhortory in nature, a cafeteria where self-service is the order of the day.
>
> Much hope is placed in the "follow-up" process, i.e., how the implementation of Agenda 21 at [the] national and international level will be monitored, but this is an area where much confusion still has to be dissipated.
>
> UNCED [merely] agreed on new institutional arrangements, particularly an inter-governmental Commission on Sustainable Development reporting to the General Assembly through ECOSOC [Economic and Social Council in §3.3 of this text], whose primary responsibility would be to investigate the extent to which states were fulfilling their duties under Agenda 21. . . . With so many uncertainties, it is hard to enthuse . . . over the creation of another new institution in the UN framework [referring to the UN Commission for Sustainable Development].[20]

Rio Declaration The Rio Declaration on Environment and Development consists of twenty-one principles.[21] The several key themes include Principle 2. It repeated verbatim the quoted Stockholm Principle 21 on the general duty not to permit any use that harms another State's interests. The Rio Declaration also expanded the quoted Stockholm Principle 22 statement of environmental expectations. Rio's articulation distinguished between the responsibilities of developed and other countries, specifically referring to the new goal of "sustainable development."

Under Principle 7: "States shall cooperate in a spirit of global partnership to conserve, protect and restore the health and integrity of the Earth's ecosystem. In view of the different contributions of global environmental degradation, States have common but differentiated responsibilities. The developed countries acknowledge the responsibility that they bear in the international pursuit of sustainable development in view of the pressures their societies place on the global environment and of the technologies and financial resources they command."

Principle 15 of the Rio Declaration is referred to as the "Precautionary Principle." Certain types of environmental damage are so severe, that any related State action employing them may be required as follows: "Where there are threats of serious or irreversible damage, [the] lack of full scientific certainty shall not be used as a reason for postponing cost-effective measures to prevent environmental degradation." Global fisheries conservation provided the genesis for this theme. Threats to the world's turbot, bluefin tuna, and swordfish stocks, for example, spawned various capacity limits on these increasingly fragile species. But they have been difficult to achieve. As vividly depicted by Senior Lecturer Rosemary Rayfuse of the University of New South Wales, capacity limits have proved difficult to enforce, because of "proposals from the EU and Japan repeatedly failing due to the concerns of Iran, India and other developing states[,] that proposed limits would prevent growth in their fishing industries while at the same time guaranteeing existing levels of excessive capacity for the developed distant water fishing states."[22]

A half-dozen years later, the Wingspread Statement on the Precautionary Principle added *some* clarity to the defined expectations: "When an activity raises threats of harm to human health or the environment, precautionary measures should be taken even if some cause-and-effect relationships are not fully established scientifically. In this context the proponent of an activity, rather than the public, should bear the burden of proof. The process of applying the precautionary principle must be open, informed and democratic and must include potentially affected parties. It must also involve an examination of the full range of alternatives, including no action."[23] One could add that this addition is so broadly worded that it is likely impossible to effectuate.

A generally cautious application of the precautionary principle does not negate the fact that specific examples can be found. In 2003, for example, Azerbaijan, Iran, Kazakstan, the Russian Federation, and Turkmenistan signed a Framework Convention for Protection of the Marine Environment of the Caspian Sea. Under Article 2,

its objective is to protect "the Caspian environment from all sources of pollution including the protection, preservation, restoration and sustainable and rational use of the Caspian Sea." Article 5 adopted the Rio Principle 15 precautionary principle, adding an agreement that "the polluter pays." Polluters thereby assume the obligations to prevent, control, reduce, and report any pollution of the Caspian Sea.[24] Also, a September 2004 UN annual conference on global warming—carbon dioxide emissions—drew a number of industrial nations, but not the United States. However, nine states of the United States sent delegates. More than two dozen US states have taken action to reduce carbon dioxide emissions by ordering cuts in power-plant emissions, and limiting state government purchases of purchases of sport utility (fuel-inefficient) vehicles.[25]

Principle 24 addresses the relationship between novel environmental concerns and traditional international legal theory. It provides as follows: "Warfare is inherently destructive of sustainable development. States shall therefore respect international law providing protection for the environment in times of armed conflict and cooperate in its further development, as necessary." The drafters likely had in mind the virtually incomprehensible devastation then recently wrought by Iraq's armed forces during their retreat from Kuwait. They set fire to over 600 Kuwaiti oil wells. It took *nine months* to bring these infernos fully under control. In the interim period, millions of tons of hazardous gases belched into the air over Kuwait. UN Security Council Resolution 687 affirmed that Iraq was "liable under International Law for any direct loss, [or] damage, including environmental damage and the depletion of natural resources . . . as a result of Iraq's unlawful invasion and occupation of Kuwait."[26]

The ICJ 1996 *Nuclear Weapons Case* explores the environmental fallout associated with the potential use of this unique weapon. Black marketeers, ethnic or religious zealots, and terrorists may all be playing a clandestine role. One group used poisonous gas in Tokyo's subways in 1995, which attests the potential danger of nuclear environmental pollution. When the US military was first present in Afghanistan after September 11, 2001, the president noted that Usama bin Laden claimed to have nuclear capability. The United States had recently lifted economic sanctions against India and Pakistan, which had been imposed as a consequence of their nuclear testing programs.

Even before these events, the UN's World Health Organization requested an advisory opinion from the ICJ. This UN agency sought guidance from the Court about the legality of a State's potential *use* or *threat* to use nuclear weapons. All States and international organizations with an interest in the resolution of this case submitted their written input to the Court. One of the issues was how to balance environmental degradation with the national prerogative to use *any* means available to preserve the State. The relevant portions of the Court's 1996 decision follow:

Legality of the Threat or Use of Nuclear Weapons

INTERNATIONAL COURT OF JUSTICE

General List No. 95 (Advisory Opinion of 8 July 1996)

<http://www.icj-cij.org/icjwww/idecisions.htm>

AUTHOR'S NOTE: You studied this case in §10.2. The World Health Organization requested an advisory opinion from the ICJ regarding this following issue: "Is the threat or use of nuclear weapons in any circumstance permitted under international law"? The Court did not authoritatively resolve the question presented. Nor did it provide a definitive statement on the legality of using nuclear weapons in self-defense. The Court did, however, enunciate some useful environmental guidelines. That portion of the case, addressing nuclear weapons in an environmental context, is set forth immediately below.

COURT'S OPINION: The Court . . . gives the following Advisory Opinion:

. . .

27. In both their written and oral statements, some States furthermore argued that any use of nuclear weapons would be unlawful by reference to existing norms relating to the safeguarding and protection of the environment, in view of their essential importance.

Specific references were made to various existing international treaties and instruments. These included Additional Protocol I of 1977 to the Geneva Conventions of 1949, Article 35, paragraph 3, of which prohibits the employment of "methods or means of warfare which are intended, or may be expected, to cause widespread, long-term and severe damage to the natural environment"; and the Convention of 18 May 1977 on the Prohibition of Military or Any Other Hostile Use of Environmental Modification Techniques, which prohibits the use of weapons which have "widespread, long-lasting or severe effects" on the environment (Art. 1). Also cited were Principle 21 of the Stockholm Declaration of 1972 and Principle 2 of the Rio Declaration of 1992 which express the common conviction of the States concerned that they have a duty "to ensure that activities within their jurisdiction or control do not cause damage to the environment of other States or of areas beyond the limits of national jurisdiction." These instruments and other provisions relating to the protection and safeguarding of the environment were said to apply at all times, in war as well as in peace, and it was contended that they would be violated by the use of nuclear weapons whose consequences would be widespread and would have transboundary effects.

28. Other States [countered, and thus] questioned the binding legal quality of these precepts of environmental law; or, in the context of the Convention on the Prohibition of Military or Any Other Hostile Use of Environmental Modification Techniques, denied that it was concerned at all with the use of nuclear weapons in hostilities. . . .

It was also argued by some States that the principal purpose of environmental treaties and norms was the protection of the environment in time of peace. It was said that those treaties made no mention of nuclear weapons. It was also pointed out that warfare in general, and nuclear warfare in particular, were not mentioned in their texts and that it would be destabilizing to the rule of law and to confidence in international negotiations if those treaties were now interpreted in such a way as to prohibit the use of nuclear weapons.

29. The Court recognizes that the environment is under daily threat and that the use of nuclear weapons could constitute a *catastrophe* for the environment. The Court also recognizes that the environment is not an abstraction but represents the living space, the quality of life and the very health of human beings, including

generations unborn. The existence of the general obligation of States to ensure that activities within their jurisdiction and control respect the environment of other States or of areas beyond national control is now part of the corpus of international law relating to the environment.

30. . . . The Court does not consider that the treaties in question could have intended to deprive a State of the exercise of its right of self-defence under international law because of its obligations to protect the environment. Nonetheless, States must take environmental considerations into account when assessing what is necessary and proportionate in the pursuit of legitimate military objectives. Respect for the environment is one of the elements that go to assessing whether an action is in conformity with the principles of necessity and proportionality.

This approach is supported, indeed, by the terms of Principle 24 of the Rio Declaration, which provides that:

Warfare is inherently destructive of sustainable development. States shall therefore respect international law providing protection for the environment in times of armed conflict and cooperate in its further development, as necessary.

31. The Court notes furthermore that Articles 35, paragraph 3, and 55 of [Geneva Convention] Additional Protocol I provide additional protection for the environment. Taken together, these provisions embody a general obligation to protect the natural environment against widespread, long-term and severe environmental damage; the prohibition of methods and means of warfare which are intended, or may be expected, to cause such damage; and the prohibition of attacks against the natural environment by way of reprisals.

These are powerful constraints for all the States having subscribed to these provisions.

32. General Assembly resolution 47/37 of 25 November 1992 on the Protection of the Environment in Times of Armed Conflict, is also of interest in this context. It affirms the general view according to which environmental considerations constitute one of the elements to be taken into account in the implementation of the principles of the law applicable in armed conflict: it states that "destruction of the environment, not justified by military necessity and carried out wantonly, is clearly contrary to existing international law." Addressing the reality that certain instruments are

not yet binding on all States, the General Assembly in this resolution "[a]ppeals to all States that have not yet done so to consider becoming parties to the relevant international conventions." . . .

33. The Court thus finds that while the existing international law relating to the protection and safeguarding of the environment does not specifically prohibit the use of nuclear weapons, it indicates important environmental factors that are properly to be taken into account in the context of the implementation of the principles and rules of the law applicable in armed conflict.

. . .

35. . . . The Court has noted the definitions of nuclear weapons contained in various treaties and accords. It also notes that nuclear weapons are explosive devices whose energy results from the fusion or fission of the atom. By its very nature, that process, in nuclear weapons as they exist today, releases not only immense quantities of heat and energy, but also powerful and prolonged radiation. According to the material before the Court, the first two causes of damage are vastly more powerful than the damage caused by other weapons, while the phenomenon of radiation is said to be peculiar to nuclear weapons. These characteristics render the nuclear weapon potentially catastrophic. The destructive power of nuclear weapons cannot be contained in either space or time. They have the potential to destroy all civilization and the entire ecosystem of the planet.

The radiation released by a nuclear explosion would affect health, agriculture, natural resources and demography over a very wide area. Further, the use of nuclear weapons would be a serious danger to future generations. Ionizing radiation has the potential to damage the future environment, food and marine ecosystem, and to cause genetic defects and illness in future generations.

. . .

57. The pattern until now has been for weapons of mass destruction to be declared illegal by specific instruments. The most recent such instruments are the Convention of 10 April 1972 on the Prohibition of the Development, Production and Stockpiling of Bacteriological (Biological) and Toxic Weapons and on their destruction which prohibits the possession of bacteriological and toxic weapons and reinforces the prohibition of their use and the Convention of 13 January 1993 on the Prohibition of the Development, Production, Stockpiling and Use of Chemical Weapons and on Their Destruction which prohibits all use of chemical

weapons and requires the destruction of existing stocks. Each of these instruments has been negotiated and adopted in its own context and for its own reasons. The Court does not find any specific prohibition of recourse to nuclear weapons in treaties expressly prohibiting the use of certain weapons of mass destruction.

58. In the last two decades, a great many negotiations have been conducted regarding nuclear weapons; they have not resulted in a treaty of general prohibition of the same kind as for bacteriological and chemical weapons.

. . .

60. Those States that believe that recourse to nuclear weapons is illegal stress that the conventions that include various rules providing for the limitation or elimination of nuclear weapons in certain areas (such as the Antarctic Treaty of 1959 which prohibits the deployment of nuclear weapons in the Antarctic, or the Treaty of Tlatelolco of 1967 which creates a nuclear-weapon-free zone in Latin America), or the conventions that apply certain measures of control and limitation to the existence of nuclear weapons (such as the 1963 Partial Test-Ban Treaty or the Treaty on the Non-Proliferation of Nuclear Weapons) all set limits to the use of nuclear weapons. In their view, these treaties bear witness, in their own way, to the emergence of a rule of complete legal prohibition of all uses of nuclear weapons.

. . .

76. Since the turn of the century, the appearance of new means of combat has[,] without calling into question the longstanding principles and rules of international law[,] rendered necessary some specific prohibitions of the use of certain weapons, such as explosive projectiles . . . [c]hemical and bacteriological

weapons . . . weapons producing "non-detectable fragments," of other types of "mines, booby traps and other devices," and of "incendiary weapons," was either prohibited or limited.

. . .

78. . . . In conformity with the aforementioned principles, humanitarian law, at a very early stage, prohibited certain types of weapons either because of their indiscriminate effect on combatants and civilians or because of the unnecessary suffering caused to combatants, that is to say, a harm greater than that unavoidable to achieve legitimate military objectives. If an envisaged use of weapons would not meet the requirements of humanitarian law, a threat to engage in such use would also be contrary to that law.

. . .

93. A similar view has been expressed with respect to the effects of the principle of neutrality. Like the principles and rules of humanitarian law, that principle has therefore been considered by some to rule out the use of a weapon the effects of which simply cannot be contained within the territories of the contending States.

94. The Court would observe that none of the States advocating the legality of the use of nuclear weapons under certain circumstances, including the "clean" use of smaller, low yield, tactical nuclear weapons, has indicated what, supposing such limited use were feasible, would be the precise circumstances justifying such use; nor whether such limited use would not tend to escalate into the all-out use of high yield nuclear weapons. This being so, the Court does not consider that it has a sufficient basis for a determination on the validity of this view.

. . .

◆ *Notes & Questions*

1. What is a State's environmental responsibility when it is contemplating the use of nuclear weapons?
2. Must a State choose between preservation of the environment and self-defense?
3. Nuclear weapons are not mentioned in the hundreds of instruments of IEL generated since the 1972 Stockholm Conference. Does this absence suggest that nuclear weapons fall within, or are beyond the scope of these instruments?
4. Would it be fair to characterize the Nuclear Weapons "decision" as one wherein the judges were unwilling

to be specific, in the absence of a specific set of hypothetical facts? Willing to give a more satisfactory answer, only if some future litigant were to present a case where nuclear weapons were actually used (e.g., the Problem 10.G use of US bunker busters)?

Biological Diversity Convention   While humans do not do things which are fundamentally different from other organisms, they do them to the disadvantage of earth's other inhabitants. Thus, contemporary extinction rates (compared to the last 13,000 years of human inhabitation of the earth) are much higher than normal.

Humans thus appropriate 40 percent of global production to their own use. The consequences include burnt forests, overexploited soils, polluted wetlands and oceans, and little harmony between humans and earth's other species.

The 1992 Rio Conference spawned yet another major dispute. The "Biodiversity Treaty" was opened for signature at the Conference. It mandates national development, monitoring, and preservation of all forms of life.[27] It requires the maintenance of "variability" among living organisms from all sources and ecosystems—a form of endangered-species protection. For example, vessels and planes traversing the world's oceans and airways introduce pollutants that disturb the world's biodiversity. The treaty term "biodiversity" is succinctly defined as follows:

> Biological diversity is an imprecise term that may refer to diversity in a gene, species, community of species, or ecosystem; it is often contracted to *biodiversity*, and used broadly with reference to total biological diversity in an area on the Earth as a whole. Pest resistance in different rice varieties, or the number and kinds of species present in an area of forest, or the changing quality of natural grassland, are all aspects of biodiversity, but whatever the context, [maintaining] the diversity of organisms is central.[28]

The related dispute arose when President George Bush (senior) declared that the United States would not endorse this treaty even in principle. He objected to the required transfer of technology and intellectual property rights held by US corporations, the sharing of access to profitable biotechnologies with developing countries, and a required financial commitment to advance the relative economic position of developing countries. The gist of the US objection was that the United States did not want to donate its biotechnology nor provide financing for other countries to develop competitive capabilities.

The United States then stood alone among the world's leading nations against implementation of the Biodiversity Treaty. Some 120 States had signed this treaty at, or shortly after, the Rio Convention. In 1993, however, President Bill Clinton reversed the US position. He announced that the United States would "sign" this treaty—meaning that the United States would agree in principle, but was not ready to ratify it as a binding instrument. President Clinton announced that the

United States would subsequently work with the European Union to develop an interpretive agreement which would not debase the intellectual property rights of US and European companies that used genetic resources in their research and development programs.

Article 3 of the Biodiversity Treaty contains an important principle designed to dovetail environmental protection and sustainable development: "States have, in accordance with the Charter of the United Nations and the principles of international law, the sovereign right to exploit their own resources pursuant to their own environmental policies, and the [concomitant] responsibility to ensure that activities within their jurisdiction or control do not cause damage to the environment of other States or areas beyond the limits of national jurisdiction." This feature of the sustainable development doctrine now permeates the various international environmental debates.

Framework Convention on Climate Change   This treaty voices environmental concerns about the atmosphere. It addresses greenhouse emissions, especially carbon dioxide. The primary problem is the burning of fossil fuels which thrust heat-trapping "greenhouse gases" into the atmosphere. Some six percent of the world's industrialized population now produces thirty percent of the gases responsible for this greenhouse effect. For example, the average greenhouse releases 23,000 pounds of carbon dioxide per year, compared to a car's release of 10,000 pounds.[29] About 80 percent of the world's carbon dioxide emissions originate outside of the transportation sector—mostly from power generation facilities. Extracting and transporting molasses—like crude oil—requires a great deal of electricity and steam. Each of these require burning a fossil fuel, thus producing massive amounts of carbon dioxide—probably the major global-warming gas. The "greenhouse effect" is the unnatural warming of the biosphere, which results in heat waves, melting of the polar icepacks, and depletion of the ozone layer that protects against the sun's infrared rays.

This climate change treaty thus requires the parties to submit periodic reports about their gaseous emissions, which harm the atmosphere by depleting the ozone layer above the earth. An environmental agency reviews national compliance with the treaty goal of limiting these environmentally adverse emissions to earlier levels—as opposed to unregulated increases. Article 9 calls for continual assessment of scientific evidence, as it becomes available, for controlling climate change and incorporating the relevant technologies for achieving better national control. In 2002, the United States submitted its third climate report to the United Nations, detailing the effect that global warming will have on the environment. The US Climate Action Report calls for voluntary measures.[30] This was the Third National Communication Under the United Nations Framework Convention on Climate Change, submitted in compliance with US obligations under the Climate Change Convention.

The 1992 Climate Change Convention generally strived for a return to the emission levels of 1990 by the year 2000. The United States, for example, has the highest rate of greenhouse gas emissions in the world: 25 percent of the total, which was 20 tons per person as of 1995. At the 1997 (Rio) follow-up conference, thirty-eight industrialized nations agreed to reduce greenhouse emissions to 1990 levels at some point between 2008 and 2012 in the Kyoto Protocol. Unlike the Climate Change Convention, its Kyoto Protocol sets comparatively clear targets for the abatement of greenhouse emissions.[31] Poorer countries, who feel entitled to their own industrial development, are reluctant to be parties to this treaty.

The "Kyoto Protocol" debate focuses on whether the projected greenhouse effect is real, or whether the environmentalists are crying wolf. In June 2001, the UN Intergovernmental Panel on Climate Change received input from 2,000 climate scientists who had examined the evidence in 180 countries. Their consensus arguably puts this debate to rest. Unless changes are forthcoming, the earth's average temperature will rise from somewhere between 2.5 and 10.4 degrees Fahrenheit in the twenty-first century. That increase would be two to ten times the 1.1 degree increase in the last century. The panel said that translates into millions of deaths, huge population migrations, frequent droughts, famines, heat waves, and tropical diseases—all of which will *begin* in coastal cities and the tropics.[32]

But preventative measures are costly. The estimated cost would be a combined $120 billion per year to control global warming. Not many States have the economic capacity to provide the requisite funding. The 1992 Climate Convention was thus supposed to provide financial assistance to the lesser-developed countries. Funding would become available through the Global Environmental Facility of the World Bank. This bank was the intergovernmental institution responsible for

rebuilding postwar Europe through the establishment of national economic-development programs. The Global Environmental Facility would be the world's environmental banker. Given existing concerns with the objectivity of the World Bank, however, it is not clear that the more developed nations will ratify this device for financing sustainable development.[33]

The 1997 Kyoto Protocol presents a compromise. For the first time, developed nations adopted an agreement accepting (in principle) that they must meet specific targets/timetables so that the greenhouse gas cause of adverse climate change will be dealt with in a binding "hard law" treaty. Kyoto's primary innovation is its creation of new mechanisms designed to harness market forces for determining how and where to reduce greenhouse gas emissions. The first of these mechanisms, emissions trading, will allow developed countries to achieve their emissions targets by trading emission credits among themselves. Emission reductions would be achieved in the most cost-effective manner because nations could buy and sell credits earned by reducing their CO_2 emissions. Uniform adoption of the Kyoto Protocol program would result in the 5.2 percent reduction of such gases by 2012.

In July 2001, President Bush announced that the United States would not participate further because of the administration's projected financial impact on US corporations and the public. The United States *signed* the Kyoto Protocol during the Clinton presidency, but has not ratified the 1997 Protocol. Ironically, President Bush was, at the same time of rejecting Kyoto, willing to sign the Stockholm Convention On Persistent Organic Pollutants. The Stockholm treaty bans the dirty dozen toxic chemicals and pesticides linked to cancer, birth defects, and other health problems (Exhibit 12.1). Bush felt that there were too many unanswered questions in the Kyoto Protocol including: how the emissions trading would actually function; and, how to address a ratifying party's failure to comply with the stated targets and time lines.[34]

The December 2005 Montreal Conference, was the first annual international meeting associated with the entry into force of the Kyoto Protocol. There, 157 nations of the 190 attendees agreed to begin talks on specific compliance with Kyoto's mandatory post-2012 reduction of greenhouse gases. Australia and the United States rejected this primary conference pillar, because it was not binding upon developing nations as well. But these dissenting nations at least agreed to the secondary conference platform—beginning a fresh global dialogue about future steps to combat adverse climate changes. One might respond that "half a loaf is better than none."

How one measures costs is a relative matter. The September 2005 post-Katrina report of the US National Center for Atmospheric Research provides an insightful example. One cannot categorically conclude that rising sea-surface temperatures caused a specific storm like Katrina. However, this environmental study does demonstrate the potential for more Katrina-like storms. In the 1970s, there was a yearly average of eleven storms in the powerful Categories 4 and 5. Since 1990—the year to which the Kyoto Protocol is tied—the worldwide average has been eighteen per year. This increase in powerful hurricanes is directly attributable to global warming—coinciding with a rise of nearly 1 degree Fahrenheit in the tropical sea surface. The warm water ocean vapor drives tropical storms. As the water gets warmer, the amount of evaporation increases. That in turn fuels such tempests. The estimated cost of the September 2005 Hurricane Katrina was $300,000,000,000. One might thus question whether it is more costly to evade the Kyoto Protocol than to endure this kind of expense—not to mention the "cost" of the hundreds of lives lost because of Hurricane Katrina.

In 2002, the United States submitted its climate report to the United Nations, detailing the effect that global warming will have on the environment. The US Climate Action Report calls for voluntary measures.[35] This was the Third National Communication Under the United Nations Framework Convention on Climate Change, submitted in compliance with the US obligations under the Climate Change Convention.

While the US rejection of the global warming Kyoto Protocol could have doomed its existence, it nevertheless entered into force in February 2005. The 140 ratifying countries (and now a dozen more) included all members of the European Union, Russia, and both of the US NAFTA partners (Canada and Mexico). China, one of the major industrializing countries of the world, has approved Kyoto in principle. The United States is the only member of the economic group "G-8" [§13.3] that has not ratified Kyoto.[36] The environmentalists claim that the earth will get warmer, which is already occurring. If unchecked, the "greenhouse effect" will cause floods and destroy many natural resources.

The depletion of the ozone layer will also contribute to global health hazards, as the sun's ultraviolet rays more readily penetrate the atmosphere.[37]

Ironically, the US Environmental Protection Agency's Web site offers a rather sinister warning:

Rising global temperatures are expected to raise sea level, and change precipitation and other local climate conditions. Changing regional climate could alter forests, crop yields, and water supplies. It could also affect human health, animals, and many types of ecosystems. Deserts may expand into existing rangelands, and features of some of our National Parks may be permanently altered.

Most of the United States is expected to warm, although sulfates may limit warming in some areas. Scientists currently are unable to determine which parts of the United States will become wetter or drier, but there is likely to be an overall trend toward increased precipitation and evaporation, more intense rainstorms, and drier soils.[38]

The polar opposite is claimed by those who believe that the Kyoto Protocol should be avoided. The University of Virginia's Professor Emeritus of Environmental Sciences, Fred Singer, describes the Kyoto Protocol as "outrageously costly," "completely ineffective," and "essentially defunct." Industrialized nations cannot return to 1990 levels, although they can slow emissions. Countries not covered by the treaty would thus become the biggest greenhouse emitters. Kyoto and the international community should be focusing on other pollutants, rather than being obsessed by this one contributor.[39]

As part of the 2000 United Nations Millennium Declaration, 150 heads of State weighed in with the following statement:

We resolve therefore to adopt in all our environmental actions a new ethic of conservation and stewardship and, as first steps, we resolve:
    ◆ To make every effort to ensure the entry into force of the Kyoto Protocol, preferably by the tenth anniversary of the United Nations Conference on Environment and Development in 2002, and to embark on the required reduction in emissions of greenhouse gases.[40]

. . .

Forest Convention The related segment of the 1992 Rio Convention work product is the Non-Legally Binding Authoritative Statement of Principles for Global Consensus on the Management, Conservation and Sustainable Development for All Types of Forests. Rio's *Forest Principles* thus encourage sustainable development, as well as reforestation and the reduction of pollutants (especially acid rain).[41]

In conjunction with the International Monetary Fund, the World Bank is currently working to fund the cleanup and restoration of the Amazon forests in Brazil. These are often referred to as the earth's "lungs" in the sense that 50 to 80 percent of the Western hemisphere's oxygen comes from these rain forests. Each year, however, approximately 25,000,000 acres of forests are cleared from the world's rain forests. In 1994, the US Agency for International Development estimated that Guatemala and Colombia would ultimately lose 33 percent of their remaining forests; Ecuador and Nicaragua 50 percent. This form of environmental depletion affects all other nations throughout the hemisphere.

So what did the Rio Conference accomplish? On the one hand, only two heads of State attended the first UN environmental conference in Stockholm (India and Sweden). Within twenty years, enough attention was brought to environment to attract over 100 heads of State. And as previously noted in this section, there must often be "soft law" on the table from which nations can move forward toward "hard Law" treaty agreements. However, as ironically noted by New Delhi's Jawaharlal Nehru University Professor R.P. Anand:

> If the purpose of the Rio Conference on Environment and Development . . . was to forge a new global partnership between the rich and the poor countries, and to develop a new law of environment and development for the protection of our small planet which is under serious threat of almost certain doom, it achieved neither. The instruments adopted at the Rio Conference were couched in such general and uncertain language that they entailed no legal, political, or even moral obligation [which] . . . merely shows extreme conservativeness, if not insincerity, of the delegates who were concerned about their "sovereignty" and entrenched "sovereign rights." . . . The differing priorities of the rich developed world for environmentalism, and the poor developing world for development were clearly reflected in the

long and bitter debates at Rio. . . . The proposed Earth Charter led to emotional outbursts, became a "graphic symbol of the North-South divide," and "was converted into a mere, pedestrian, rather wordy declaration. . . ."[42]

2002 JOHANNESBURG WORLD SUMMIT ON SUSTAINABLE DEVELOPMENT

This was the third UN environmental conference. It was attended by more than 100 nations. The Johannesburg Declaration on Sustainable Development was a key work product. It identified the contemporary problems as follows:

> 13. The global environment continues to suffer. Loss of biodiversity continues, fish stocks continue to be depleted, desertification claims more and more fertile land, the adverse effects of climate change are already evident, natural disasters are more frequent and more devastating and developing countries more vulnerable, and air, water and marine pollution continue to rob millions of a decent life.
>
> 14. Globalization has added a new dimension to these challenges. The rapid integration of markets, mobility of capital and significant increases in investment flows around the world have opened new challenges and opportunities for the pursuit of sustainable development. But the benefits and costs of globalization are unevenly distributed, with developing countries facing special difficulties in meeting this challenge.
>
> . . .
>
> 18. We welcome the Johannesburg Summit focus on the indivisibility of human dignity and are resolved through decisions on targets, timetables and partnerships to speedily increase access to basic requirements such as clean water, sanitation, adequate shelter, energy, health care, food security and the protection of bio-diversity. At the same time, we will work together to assist one another to have access to financial resources, benefit from the opening of markets, ensure capacity building, use modern technology to bring about development, and make sure that there is technology transfer, human resource development, education and training to banish forever underdevelopment.
>
> . . .

37. From the African continent, the Cradle of Humankind, we solemnly pledge to the peoples of the world, and the generations that will surely inherit this earth, that we are determined to ensure that our collective hope for sustainable development is realized.[43]

The culmination of this conference was its plan of implementation. It set broad timetables for controlling sanitation, chemical pollution, and endangered species between the 2002 conference and 2022. There would be: (a) the reduction of threats to endangered species by 2010; (b) a reduction of the poor who lack sanitation by 2015; (c) the minimization of health and environmental problems by 2020; and (d) many other pledges.[44]

The more powerful nations blocked efforts to set specific and verifiable timetables for reducing oil and gas consumption. Given the abundance or pledges, and comparative dearth of specific and enforceable timetables, one could conclude that this third UN conference merely added to global warming. Of course if one were to advocate change, one might resort to local government, as opposed to acquiescing in a national government's disdain for global environmental treaties and declarations. As noted by University of New Hampshire Professor of Political Science Stacy D. VanDeveer:

If Americans want more effective environmental law, they should demand that their own government actually abide by the promises it so often makes and so rarely keeps. Because U.S. citizens use a disproportionate share of the Earth's resources, they have a disproportionately large opportunity to improve its environment by enacting strong and sensible policy at home and supporting—rather than undermining—international environmental laws and organizations. If U.S. policy makers don't like the Kyoto Protocol, they could do more than complain that it's unfair to the world's wealthiest and most powerful country. They could adopt reasonable polices of their own to efficiently reduce emissions of carbon dioxide and other greenhouse gases ion the United States. . . .

[S]uccess in protecting the environment will require a more explicit acknowledgment that treaties and high-profile conferences are no substitute for leadership at home. . . . That job is left to us.[45]

◆ 12.3 CONTEMPORARY ENVIRONMENTAL APPLICATIONS

ALTERNATIVE ENVIRONMENTAL FORA

Section 9.4 of this book briefly addressed the "Chambers" process, whereby States may access the expertise of certain ICJ judges to resolve their conflicts—rather than having to resort to the more lengthy process associated with the full bench of fifteen judges. Article 26.1 of the Statute of the ICJ thus provides for "chambers, composed of three or more judges . . ."

In 1993, the ICJ formed a "Chamber of the Court for Environmental Matters," to determine environmental cases on an expedited basis. That Chamber's constitution proclaims that the ICJ is willing to deal with environmental matters on an *ad hoc* basis. The special "Constitution of a Chamber of the Court for Environmental Matters" provides as follows: "In view of the developments in the field of environmental law and protection which have taken place in the last few years [see Exhibit 12.1], and considering that it should be prepared to the fullest possible extent to deal with any environmental case falling within its jurisdiction, the Court has now deemed it appropriate to establish a seven-member Chamber for Environmental Matters. . . ."[46]

The Environmental Chamber has yet to decide any case. Given the intense interest in major environmental disasters of the current generation, however, States will hopefully refer such matters to this specialized forum by treaty or other special agreement. The anticipated advantages include the development of a special body of expertise by a group of judges who are readily available for a quicker resolution than possible under the traditional full Court procedure. Judges can also be selected so as to seat those of particular nationalities rather than the full court, which may be a preferred posture for some litigants.

The crosstown option is The Hague's Permanent Court of Arbitration (PCOA), where ninety-four member States promulgated their June 2001 first of a kind rules relating to the resolution of controversies concerning environmental protection and conservation of natural resources.[47]

WAR AND THE ENVIRONMENT

The following is the decision of the UN Security Council's tribunal for war claims against Iraq.

It is a model for the ICJ, or any other international decision-maker who might seek guidance about how to identify and apply IEL to a military conflict:

United Nations Compensation Commission Governing Council Report and Recommendations Made by The Panel of Commissioners Concerning the Fifth Instalment of "F4" Claims

UN Doc. S/AC.26/2005/10 (June 30, 2005)
<http://www2.unog.ch/uncc/reports/r05-10.pdf>

Go to course Web page at
<http://home.att.net/~slomansonb/txtcsesite.html>.
Under Chapter Twelve, click UNCC Iraq Case.

Criminal Law Paradigm? The frustration with finding an effective environmental control mechanism led the Council of Europe to draft the following treaty, which was opened for signature in 1998. While it has not yet been ratified by enough nations to enter into force, its provisions nevertheless encourage States to enact national legislation to address this key priority:

Convention on the Protection of the Environment Through Criminal Law

European Treaty Series No. 172,
Strasbourg, France, November 4, 1998
<http://conventions.coe.int/Treaty/EN/cadreprincipal.htm>,
search Environment

PREAMBLE
. . .
Convinced of the need to pursue a common criminal policy aimed at the protection of the environment;
. . .
Recognising that, whilst the prevention of the impairment of the environment must be achieved primarily through other measures, criminal law has an important part to play in protecting the environment;

Recalling that environmental violations having serious consequences must be established as criminal offences subject to appropriate sanctions;

Wishing to take effective measures to ensure that the perpetrators of such acts do not escape prosecution and punishment and desirous of fostering international co-operation to this end;
. . .

Have agreed as follows:
. . .

ARTICLE 2-INTENTIONAL OFFENCES
1. Each Party shall adopt such appropriate measures as may be necessary to establish as criminal offences under its domestic law:
   a. the discharge, emission or introduction of a quantity of substances or ionising radiation into air, soil or water which:

(i) causes death or serious injury to any
person, or

(ii) creates a significant risk of causing death or
serious injury to any person;

b. the unlawful discharge, emission or introduction of a quantity of substances or ionising
radiation into air, soil or water which causes or
is likely to cause their lasting deterioration or
death or serious injury to any person or substantial damage to protected monuments, other
protected objects, property, animals or plants;

c. the unlawful disposal, treatment, storage, transport, export or import of hazardous waste
which causes or is likely to cause death or serious injury to any person or
substantial damage to the quality of air, soil,
water, animals or plants;

d. the unlawful operation of a plant in which a
dangerous activity is carried out and which
causes or is likely to cause death or serious

injury to any person or substantial damage to
the quality of air, soil, water, animals or plants;

e. the unlawful manufacture, treatment, storage, use,
transport, export or import of nuclear materials
or other hazardous radioactive substances which
causes or is likely to cause death or serious injury
to any person or substantial damage to the quality
of air, soil, water, animals or plants, when committed intentionally.

. . .

ARTICLE 3-NEGLIGENT OFFENCES
1. Each Party shall adopt such appropriate measures as
may be necessary to establish as criminal offences
under its domestic law, when committed with
negligence, the offences enumerated in Article 2,
paragraph 1 a to e.

. . .

This Convention reflects the concern of the more than fifty member States, expressed in the Preamble, that "the uncontrolled use of technology and the excessive exploitation of natural resources entail serious environmental hazards" and that ratifying parties should take "effective measures to ensure that the perpetrators of environmental hazards having serious consequences do not escape prosecution and punishment." The essential objective is to criminalize certain intentional or negligent forms of environmental offenses, which may be limited to acts of gross negligence. The intentional discharge of ionizing radiation into the air, soil, or water that causes death or serious injury, or creates a "significant risk" of death or serious injury, is thereby prohibited. States may not "unlawfully dispose, treat, store, transport, export, or import hazardous waste" that is likely to cause death or serious injury or "substantial damage to the quality of air, soil, water, animals, or plants." Aiding and abetting the intentional commission of an environmental offense is to be criminalized under domestic law. Both natural and corporate offenders may be imprisoned, fined, and required to reinstate the previous condition of the environment. Each ratifying State would also adopt measures for the confiscation of property and proceeds derived from environmental degradations.[48]

This remains a "soft law" instrument, until ratified by enough nations to enter into force. Also, no nation would likely ratify it unless it had already enacted the relevant legislation or committed to doing so on a date certain. Yet it does present a fresh option in the arsenal of treaty-based initiatives for combating transboundary environmental interferences.

ENVIRONMENTAL HUMAN RIGHTS

State environmental decisions are spawning a growing number of related humans rights claims. In December 2004, for example, the Arctic Inuit tribes announced their plan to seek a startling ruling from the Inter-American Commission on Human Rights. They claim that the United States has substantially contributed to global warming—a direct menace to their existence. These 155,000 natives are seal-hunting peoples scattered around the Arctic Ocean. They claim to be threatened by rising temperatures, caused more by the United States than any other nation. They are seeking legal relief from the Inter-American Commission, which tends to treat environmental degradation as a human rights matter.[49]

Governmental decision making about environmental matters, without due consideration of the human rights of various minorities, is vividly illustrated in the following Japanese case:

◆

www **Kayano and Others
v. Hokkaido
Expropriation Committee**

(Nibutani Dam Decision)

Sapporo District Court, Japan
27 March 1997
38 INTERNATIONAL LEGAL MATERIALS
394 (1999)

Go to course Web page at
<http://home.att.net/~slomansonb/txtcsesite.html>.
Under Chapter Twelve, click Nibutani
Dam Decision.

CORPORATE ENVIRONMENTAL RESPONSIBILITY

The §11.4 *Unocal* case addressed corporate reliance on local paramilitary forces to protect an oil pipeline in Myanmar. The following excerpt about another oil company's activities in Nigeria illustrates the pressures, as consistently proclaimed by numerous human rights and environmental organizations, on nation States and private corporations to acknowledge what is often joint responsibility for environmental fiascos:

According to the complaint, Shell Nigeria coercively appropriated land for oil development without adequate compensation, and caused substantial pollution of the air and water in the homeland of the Ogoni people. . . . Allegedly, Shell Nigeria recruited the Nigerian police and military to attack local villages and suppress the organized opposition to its development activity.

. . . [W]hile these abuses were carried out by the Nigerian government and military, they were instigated, orchestrated, planned, and facilitated by Shell Nigeria under the direction of the defendants. The Royal Dutch/Shell Group allegedly provided money, weapons, and logistical support to the Nigerian military, including the vehicles and ammunition used in the raids on the villages, procured at least some of these attacks, participated in the fabrication of

murder charges against Saro-Wiwa . . . and bribed witnesses to give false testimony against them.[50]

In August 2005, Indonesia brought criminal charges against Newmont, a US mining company that is the world's largest gold producer. The indictment charged that the corporation and it's president allowed its toxic waste to enter the sea, in excess of government regulations. This was an unusual case, because of an American company having to defend itself, in a criminal trial in a developing country. Under a method known as submarine tailing disposal, the company piped waste into the waters about a half-mile offshore. This method is banned in many industrialized countries, including the United States. Newmont claimed that it was unaware of a required permit that it failed to obtain from the Ministry of the Environment.[51]

Various nongovernmental entities have embraced the need to fill gaps left by notions of sovereignty and corporate missions. The Paris-based International Chamber of Commerce's Business Charter for Sustainable Development produced a set of voluntary corporate standards in 1991. Over 1,000 companies have pledged their support of these principles.[52] The first Corporate Priority is "[t]o recognize environmental management as among the highest corporate priorities and as a key determinant to sustainable development; to establish policies, programmes and practices for conducting operations in an environmentally sound manner." Its version of the Precautionary Principle is "[t]o modify the manufacture, marketing or use of products or services or the conduct of activities, consistent with scientific and technical understanding, to prevent serious or irreversible environmental degradation.

At about the same time, after the 1989 Exxon-Valdez oil spill in Alaska, a group of investors and environmental nongovernmental organizations created the Coalition for Environmentally Responsible Economies (CERES). They produced the voluntary Valdez Principles, later renamed the CERES Principles, for participating corporations who are committed to environmental responsibility.[53] As of 2005, there are sixty-five CERES companies, including: American Airlines, Bank of America, Coca-Cola, Ford and General Motors, and Nike. These companies thereby pledge to monitor and improve the environmental impact of their corporate activities, although there is no third-party verification of compliance. Maybe "soft law" is preferable to total environmental anarchy.

The European Union launched its Eco-Management and Audit Scheme in 1993.[54] This regulation became effective in 1995. While participation remains voluntary, this program requires third-party compliance assessment.

One must observe as follows: since the UN's seminal Stockholm Conference in 1972, there have been hundreds of global and regional environmental instruments purporting to regulate environmental degradation. But States are not yet willing to merge word and deed. Thus, there is a frightening disconnect between the lip service being paid to environmental concerns, and the willingness to sacrifice for the benefit of future generations. Between now and a date to be determined, the consequences of this failure will far outdistance the terror spawned by September 11, 2001, or the ensuing War on Terror.

◆ PROBLEMS

Problem 12.A (after §12.2) As you are nearing the end of this course, it will be useful to review some of its key concepts in an environmental context. Now that you have studied the various environmental norms, especially the Kyoto protocol, a few questions: Is your country bound by it? If so, how? If not, why not? Should your country ratify this protocol? Three students or groups will debate these questions, which rest in part on your initial exposure to the materials in §1.2 of this book on Sources of International Law.

The assigned students will thereby facilitate this brief review, in the following representative capacities:

(1) The US secretary of state, who represents the United States and other industrialized nations opposed to the Kyoto Protocol.

(2) Russian and European foreign ministers, who represent nations and an international organization that have ratified the Kyoto Protocol.

(3) Two executives from the UN Environmental Development Program, who will present a global perspective on whether "sustainable development" either demands, or forbids, national adoption of the Kyoto Protocol.

(4) An independent environmental science professor, who will predict what will happen if the international community does—or does not—fully embrace the Kyoto Protocol.

Problem 12.B (after §12.2 ICJ *Nuclear Weapons Case*) In September 2002, NATO disclosed that it had fired thousands of rounds of munitions with uranium tips in Bosnia (1995), Kosovo, and Serbia, and Montenegro (both 1999). While most radioactivity had been depleted before this use, these rounds nevertheless emitted some low-level radiation. Shell casings had broken and uranium deposits, potentially toxic, disintegrated into dust.

The University of Montenegro's nuclear physics Professor, Perko Vukotic, headed a twelve-person cleanup team. He lamented: "We don't understand why anyone would want to attack and contaminate the place on the last day of the war [June 1999]." Both NATO and the US Pentagon acknowledged the radiation; but that it was so low, it could not have been harmful to humans or other parts of the Balkan ecosystem.[55]

In May 1999, while the NATO bombing campaign was still underway, the Prosecutor of the International Criminal Tribunal for Yugoslavia (ICTY) undertook an investigation, to determine whether NATO or its participating members had thereby committed any war crimes. This project was initiated by complaints from Yugoslavia and various nongovernmental organizations, based in part on the use of depleted uranium projectiles. Several NATO attacks, most notably the one on a Serbian petrochemical complex (Pancevo), released stored toxic chemicals into the air and water. A report by the UN Environmental Development Programme concluded "that the Kosovo conflict has not caused an environmental catastrophe affecting the Balkans as a whole [but the] pollution detected at some [of the twenty-one] sites is serious and poses a threat to human health."[56] (Some of this air pollution of course predated the 1999 NATO bombing.) The June 2000 ICTY report was submitted just after the cessation of bombing. It determined that none of the NATO actions rose to the level of criminal conduct that could be prosecuted by the ICTY.[57]

The ICTY prosecutor's investigation focused on Protocol to the Geneva Conventions Relating to the Protection of victims of International Armed Conflictsas being the essential governing law (which the United States has not ratified). Article 35(3) prohibits: "methods and means of warfare which are intended, or may be expected, to cause widespread, long-term, and severe damage to the natural environment." Article 55 adds: "This protection includes a prohibition of the use of methods or means of warfare which are intended or may be expected to cause such damage to the natural environment and thereby to prejudice the health or survival of the population."[58]

The ICTY prosecutor Louise Arbour (a Canadian national) was inundated with the numerous other claims, which attracted more global attention. These included Serbian President Milosevic's genocidal tendencies; for example, the Srebrenica massacre where some 7,800 Muslim men and boys were slaughtered in several days at a UN safe haven in Bosnia (§9.5 ICTY and §10.6 Laws of War). The prosecutor's decision not to pursue the radiation munitions claim against the United States and any participating NATO allies could be abstractly characterized as politically expedient, not prosecutable for evidentiary reasons, or premised upon a variety of theoretical motives.

Class members will now assess whether NATO or the United States thereby incurred any liability under IEL. Five persons or groups will debate this matter. They represent: (1) the UN Environmental Development Programme Administrator; (2) Bosnia and Kosovo, who at different times were liberated from a despotic regime because of the respective NATO and US military actions; (3) Serbia (the prime object of the 1999 NATO bombing campaign); (4) participating NATO nations; and (5) the United States—the country most distant from the environmental "fallout."

Problem 12.C (end of Chapter)

Basic Facts Greenpeace International is a nongovernmental organization (NGO) headquartered in Amsterdam. Its objective is to protect the environment, often by monitoring threats to an increasingly fragile environment. It operated a small ocean-going fleet, including the former British-registered flagship *Rainbow Warrior* which began to make international port calls in 1971. French nuclear testing was then a popular target for Greenpeace activity.

In 1973, New Zealand and Australia sued France in the International Court of Justice, seeking a judgment that would require France to cease its nuclear testing in the South Pacific. The plaintiff States feared that radioactive fallout would adversely affect the atmosphere throughout the South Pacific. Rather than participating in this litigation, France withdrew. The ICJ dismissed the case in 1974 on the basis of France's unilateral declaration that it would cease such testing—which it subsequently resumed.

The private multinational crews of Greenpeace vessels had recently begun to follow various oceangoing vessels suspected of excessive whaling and other fishing enterprises in violation of international norms, transporting and dumping of nuclear fuels and waste materials, and dumping other toxic substances into the ocean. Greenpeace had become the world's foremost environmental NGO. Given the mid-1970s case filed by two State opponents of France's nuclear testing, Greenpeace believed that it was in a good position to bring worldwide attention to France's resumption of nuclear testing.

The most famous "collision" between Greenpeace and the French government occurred in 1980 at a harbor's entrance to a port in France. A Japanese merchant vessel was carrying nuclear reactors to France. Greenpeace characterized this shipment as a major hazard because of potential radiation leaks associated with transferring this material by sea. Put another way, this was a nuclear *Exxon Valdez* waiting to happen. As Greenpeace's *Rainbow Warrior* began to shadow the Japanese vessel, the Greenpeace vessel was rammed by a French police ship. After its seizure by French port authorities, the Greenpeace vessel was released and ordered never to return to French waters.

The primary newsworthiness of the *Rainbow Warrior* was its subsequent "shadowing" of French, Russian, and Spanish naval vessels in attempts to disrupt French nuclear testing in French Polynesia (not far from New Zealand). Greenpeace was the target of a plot by the Directeurat-Generale de Sécurité Extérieure (DGSE), a French governmental intelligence agency. A DGSE agent purporting to be a Greenpeace supporter worked undercover in the Auckland, New Zealand, office of Greenpeace International. She photographed Auckland's harbors as part of a plan to sink the Greenpeace ship after a decade of shadowing French military vessels. New Zealand, as part of its Nuclear Free Zone policy, had banned French nuclear vessels from its harbors. This agent's photographs were sent to Paris for intelligence-gathering purposes, which would soon bring worldwide attention to the ongoing Greenpeace-French connection.

While in Auckland Harbor in 1985, the *Rainbow Warrior* was bombed and sunk by a group of at least eight DGSE agents. Two bombs, exploding near midnight, resulted in the death of a Dutch citizen who was the ship's onboard photographer. The explosion injured several crewmembers of various nationalities (other than New Zealand) and sank this British-flagged ship. Most of the French agents escaped. It appears that a nearby French submarine sank the boat in which they escaped from Auckland Harbor, after bringing them aboard for their probable return to France via French Polynesia.

New Zealand captured two of the French DGSE agents, tried them, and sentenced them to ten-year sentences for manslaughter and arson (to name a few of the charges). New Zealand's citizens were outraged.

The *Rainbow Warrior* incident was the first operation by a foreign government involving a bombing, death, and sinking of a vessel in a New Zealand harbor. New Zealand thus lodged a diplomatic protest with France and demanded reparations based on France's alleged State responsibility for various violations of national and International Law.

The UN Secretary-General then arbitrated an agreement between France and New Zealand whereby: (1) France was to pay damages to New Zealand, but not damages on account of the death or damage to the vessel caused by the bomb blast; (2) New Zealand would transfer the two convicted agents to a prison in French Polynesia to serve out the remainder of their prison sentences; and (3) France would not impose trade barriers against New Zealand's butter and meat exports, as France had threatened to do during the *Rainbow Warrior* negotiations. New Zealand thus agreed to release the two captured French army officers to French custody so that they would serve the remainder of their jail terms in a French Polynesian prison.[59]

Within four years, the two transferred prisoners "escaped" from the French island prison. They were repatriated to France but never taken into custody in France (for what would otherwise be their return to the prison in French Polynesia). France claimed that there was no basis for New Zealand to demand their continued incarceration because they were acting on "superior orders." The other French agents were never arrested or tried. The French government conceded its role in the bombing of the *Rainbow Warrior* but inconsistently claimed that its agents had exceeded their authority. France nevertheless threatened to use further force if any other Greenpeace vessel attempted to disrupt future French nuclear testing.

In 1991, another French agent involved in the *Rainbow Warrior* bombing was arrested in Switzerland. Greenpeace immediately pressured the New Zealand government to seek his extradition from Switzerland. New Zealand opted not to pursue the harbor-bombing incident any further. Switzerland allegedly bowed to French pressure to release the agent from custody, even providing a diplomatic escort to the French border.

Additional "Facts"   In addition to the actual facts, assume the following hypothetical facts. The explosion and sinking of the *Rainbow Warrior* in Auckland Harbor contaminates the harbor due to the nature and large volume of chemicals to be used for testing purposes.

New Zealand and French authorities were unaware of the presence of these chemicals aboard the Greenpeace vessel when it entered the harbor. While Greenpeace testing aboard its vessel did nothing to pollute the air, the combination of existing pollutants in Auckland Harbor and the chemicals aboard the sunken *Rainbow Warrior* further contaminates the fish within the harbor. One month after the explosion and sinking, the fish in Auckland Harbor are no longer fit for human consumption.

France continues to conduct nuclear testing in French Polynesia. France actually conducted fifty such reported tests before and after the 1985 *Rainbow Warrior* incident. The people of New Zealand begin to experience a severe form of "cold" that makes the average healthy person sick for several months at a time. The common symptoms are flu, fever, and skin rash. This form of cold did not exist in New Zealand prior to the start of French and US nuclear testing in the South Pacific in the 1950s. Since the 1970s, a small percentage of the population has exhibited these symptoms. In the last five years, however, it has become a fact of life for most New Zealanders.

New Zealand lodges a diplomatic claim with France in 1995, accusing France of "transboundary environmental interference" within the meaning of the various UN instruments—especially the various 1992 Rio declarations, which New Zealand characterizes as the essence of IEL. New Zealand and France agree to arbitrate this matter. Both are parties to the UN Law of the Sea Treaty, the only agreement in force between them which contains relevant environmental provisions. New Zealand seeks remedies for: (1) the flu that its citizens now suffer; and (2) the contamination of Auckland Harbor.

The Forum   Two students (or groups) will represent France and New Zealand as the arbitrators chosen by the respective parties to today's "Flufish Arbitration." A third student will sit as the third and neutral arbitrator selected by the other arbitrators (or professor). This student is the UN's environmental representative who has been asked to be the neutral on this three-person arbitral tribunal for resolving the Flufish dispute between New Zealand and France.

This arbitral body will first debate/discuss how it would best resolve whether France has incurred State responsibility under International Law for harm to New Zealand. In the event of a split decision, the dissenting arbitrator will report his/her decision for further class discussion. All participants will focus on the following:

Issues for Resolution

1. What rule or rules should the arbitrators use to assess whether France is liable under International Environmental Law?

2. What rules of International Law from *prior* chapters were breached by France in the revised *Rainbow Warrior/Flufish* matter?

3. Is France:

   (a) Responsible for a transboundary environmental interference in New Zealand? Elsewhere?

   (b) Subject to suit in a New Zealand court (or any other national court)? (*See* §2.6 and §1.4).

4. If France were liable for the degradation of New Zealand's environment, what remedy should this international arbitral tribunal require?

Additional Resources

The Application of International Law in the Case of the Rainbow Warrior, Chap. 3.A, in L. Guruswamy et al., INTERNATIONAL ENVIRONMENTAL LAW: A PROBLEM-ORIENTED COURSEBOOK 146–170 (St. Paul, MN: West, 1994)

Rainbow Warrior (New Zealand v. France), 82 INT'L LAW REP. 499 (1990)

◆ BIBLIOGRAPHY

Documents & Dictionaries

THE ENVIRONMENT ENCYCLOPEDIA & DIRECTORY (New York: Taylor & Francis, 1993)

H. Hannum (ed.), GUIDE TO INTERNATIONAL HUMAN RIGHTS PRACTICE (4th ed. Ardsley, NY: Transnat'l, 2004)

H. Hohmann (ed.), BASIC DOCUMENTS OF INTERNATIONAL ENVIRONMENTAL LAW (Dordrecht, Neth.: Graham & Trotman/Martinus Nijhoff, 1992)

MULTILATERAL TREATIES IN THE FIELD OF THE ENVIRONMENT (Cambridge, Eng.: Grotius Pub., 1991) (two volumes)

General

D. Freestone (ed.), LEGAL ASPECTS OF IMPLEMENTING THE KYOTO PROTOCOL MECHANISMS: MAKING KYOTO WORK (Oxford, Eng.: Oxford Univ. Press, 2005)

S. Chowdhury et al., THE RIGHT TO DEVELOPMENT IN INTERNATIONAL LAW (Dordrecht, Neth.: Martinus Nijhoff, 1992)

R. Goldstein (ed.), ENVIRONMENTAL ETHICS AND LAW (Aldershot, Eng.: Ashgate, 2004)

P. Muldoon & R. Lindgren, THE ENVIRONMENTAL BILL OF RIGHTS (Toronto: Edmond Montgomery, 1995)

V. Nanda & G. Pring, INTERNATIONAL ENVIRONMENTAL LAW FOR THE 21ST CENTURY (Irvington, NY: Transnat'l, 2003)

C. Romano, THE PEACEFUL SETTLEMENT OF INTERNATIONAL ENVIRONMENTAL DISPUTES (The Hague: Kluwer, 2000)

J. Woods & H. Lewis, HUMAN RIGHTS AND THE GLOBAL MARKET PLACE: ECONOMIC, SOCIAL, AND CULTURAL DIMENSIONS (Ardsley, NY: Transnat'l, 2004)

Special Problems

K. Kummer, INTERNATIONAL MANAGEMENT OF HAZARDOUS WASTES: THE BASEL CONVENTION AND RELATED LEGAL RULES (Oxford, Eng.: Clarendon Press, 1995)

Permanent Court of Arbitration, INTERNATIONAL INVESTMENTS AND PROTECTION OF THE ENVIRONMENT: THE ROLE OF DISPUTE RESOLUTION MECHANISMS (The Hague: Kluwer, 2001)

G. Reijnen & W. de Graaf, POLLUTION OF OUTER SPACE, IN PARTICULAR THE GEOSTATIONARY ORBIT: SCIENTIFIC, POLICY AND LEGAL ASPECTS (Dordrecht, Neth.: Martinus Nijhoff, 1989)

M. Cordonier-Segger & A Khalfan, SUSTAINABLE DEVELOPMENT LAW: PRINCIPLES, PRACTICES, AND PROSPECTS (Oxford, Eng.: Oxford Univ. Press, 2004)

A. Trouwborst, EVOLUTION AND STATUS OF THE PRECAUTIONARY PRINCIPLE IN INTERNATIONAL LAW (The Hague: Kluwer, 2002)

E. Urbani & C. Rubin (eds.), TRANSNATIONAL ENVIRONMENTAL LAW AND ITS IMPACT ON CORPORATE BEHAVIOR (Irvington-on-Hudson, NY: Transnat'l 1994) (Fletcher symposium)

Regional

M. Faure, CRIMINAL ENFORCEMENT OF ENVIRONMENTAL LAW IN THE EU (The Hague: Kluwer, 2005)

H. Munoz, ENVIRONMENTAL DIPLOMACY IN THE AMERICAS (Boulder, CO: Lynne Rienner, 1992)

G. Goldenman, ENVIRONMENTAL LIABILITY AND PRIVATIZATION IN CENTRAL AND EASTERN EUROPE (Dordrecht, Neth.: Graham & Trotman/Martinus Nijhoff, 1994)

Note, The Long Arm of the Law: Extraterritorial Application of US Environmental Legislation to Human Activity in Outer Space, 6 GEORGETOWN INT'L ENVIR. L. REV. 455 (1994)

Third World

A. Elhance, HYDROPOLITICS IN THE 3RD WORLD: CONFLICT AND COOPERATION IN INTERNATIONAL RIVER BASINS (Wash., DC: US Inst. Peace, 1999)

L. Westra, ECOVIOLENCE AND THE LAW: SUPRANATIONAL NORMATIVE FOUNDATIONS OF ECOCRIME (Irvington, NY: Transnat'l, 2004)

S. Johnson, WORLD POPULATION TURNING THE TIDE: THREE DECADES OF PROGRESS (Dordrecht, Neth.: Kluwer, 1994)

M. Miller, THE THIRD WORLD IN GLOBAL ENVIRONMENTAL POLITICS (Boulder, CO: Lynne Reinner, 1995)

R. Mushkat, Public Participation in Environmental Law Making: A Comment on the International Legal Framework and the Asia-Pacific Perspective, 1 CHINESE J. INT'L L.185 (2002)

Additional Electronic Resources

Columbia University Center for International Earth Science Information Network: <http://www.ciesin.org> (most comprehensive collection available)

Environmental Agencies of the World: <http://www.worldbank
.org/nipr/epas.htm>

The World Wide Web Virtual Library: Sustainable Development:
<http://www.ulb.ac.be/ceese/meta/sustvl.html>

◆ ENDNOTES

1. *See* A. Hurrell & B. Kingsbury, The International Politics of the Environment: An Introduction, ch.1, in THE INTERNATIONAL POLITICS OF THE ENVIRONMENT: ACTORS, INTERESTS, AND INSTITUTIONS (Oxford, Eng.: Oxford Univ. Press, 1992) & A. Boyle, Economic Growth and Protection of the Environment: The Impact of International Law and Policy, ch. 8, in A. Boyle (ed.), ENVIRONMENTAL REGULATION AND ECONOMIC GROWTH (Oxford, Eng.: Clarendon Press, 1994).

2. *See, e.g.,* Territorial Jurisdiction of the International Commission of the River Oder, 1929 PCIJ, SER. A, NO. 23 (Versailles Treaty Commission jurisdiction over river running through former nations at war) & Diversion of Water from the Meuse Case (Netherlands v. Belgium), 1937 PCIJ, SER. A/B, NO. 70 (Belgium's control of canal based on treaty).

3. *See* HELSINKI SYMPOSIUM: NUCLEAR ACCIDENTS: LIABILITIES AND GUARANTEES (Paris: Org. Econ. Coop. & Development, 1993).

4. *Mines case:* Corfu Channel Case (Great Britain v. Albania), 1949 ICJ REP. 4. *Nuclear case:* Nuclear Tests Cases (New Zealand v. France), 1974 ICJ REP. 253. *Pollution survey:* J. Yardley, China's Net Big Boom Could be the Foul Air, New York Times on the Web (Oct. 30, 2005).

5. Trail Smelter (US v. Can.) (1941), 3 UN REP. INT'L ARB. 1938 (1949), reprinted in 35 AMER. J. INT'L L. 684 (1941).

6. J. Cassels, THE UNCERTAIN PROMISE OF LAW: LESSONS FROM BHOPAL (Toronto: Univ. Toronto Press, 1993).

7. *Population:* J. Cohen, HOW MANY PEOPLE CAN THE EARTH SUPPORT? (New York: W. W. Norton, 1995). *Food:* L. Brown, Worldwatch Paper 136, THE AGRICULTURAL LINK: HOW ENVIRONMENTAL DETERIORATION COULD DISRUPT ECONOMIC PROGRESS (Danvers, MA: Worldwatch Inst., 1997).

8. *Conference: See* N. Taub, International Conference on Population and Development (Wash., DC: Amer. Soc. Int'l L., 1994). *Statistics:* World Population Statistics 1985–2025 (appendix) in E. Osmanczyk, THE ENCYCLOPEDIA OF THE UNITED NATIONS AND INTERNATIONAL RELATIONS 1085 (New York: Taylor & Francis, 1990).

9. *See* Report on the UN Conference on the Human Environment, UN Doc. A/CONF.48/14/Rev.1, reprinted in 11 INT'L LEGAL MAT'LS 1416 (1972).

10. Section I, 2(d), Resolution on the Institutional and Financial Arrangement for International Environment Cooperation, Gen. Ass. Reso. 2997, UN DOC. A/8370 (1973), reprinted in 13 INT'L LEGAL MAT'LS 234 (1974).

11. Separate Opinion of Vice-President A. Weeramantry, The Concept of Sustainable Development, in Case Concerning the Gabcíkovo-Nagymaros Project (Hungary v. Slovakia), available at: <http://www.icj-cij.org/icjwww/idecisions.htm>,

click on case link, then scroll left frame Index for this judge's separate opinion.

12. R. Lefeber, TRANSBOUNDARY ENVIRONMENTAL INTERFERENCE AND THE ORIGIN OF STATE LIABILITY at 1–2 (The Hague, Neth.: Kluwer, 1996).

13. A. Kiss, Present Limits to the Enforcement of State Responsibility for Environmental Damage, ch. 1, in F. Francioni & T. Scovazzi, INTERNATIONAL RESPONSIBILITY FOR ENVIRONMENTAL HARM 3, 4–5 (Dordrecht, Neth.: Graham & Trotman/Martinus Nijhoff, 1991) (italics supplied).

14. *Case:* Certain Phosphate Lands in Nauru (Nauru v. Australia), 1989 ICJ REP. 12. *Settlement:* 1993 ICJ REP. 322.

15. C. Weeramantry (ICJ Justice), Social Impact of Phosphate Mining, ch. 3, in NAURU: ENVIRONMENTAL DAMAGE UNDER INTERNATIONAL TRUSTEESHIP 28, 30–31 (Oxford, Eng.: Oxford Univ. Press, 1992).

16. *See* Developments in the Law: International Environmental Law, 104 HARV. LAW REV. 1487 (1991).

17. *Coursebooks:* D. Hunter et al., INTERNATIONAL ENVIRONMENTAL LAW AND POLICY 1–38 (New York: Foundation Press, 1998); L. Guruswamy et al., INTERNATIONAL ENVIRONMENTAL LAW: A PROBLEM-ORIENTED COURSEBOOK 323–359 (St. Paul, MN: West, 1994); Weiss text [above §12.1 excerpt on "Soft Law v. Hard Law"]. *Treatises:* P. Birnie & A. Boyle, INTERNATIONAL LAW AND THE ENVIRONMENT (rev. ed. Oxford, Eng.: Clarendon Press, 1994); A. D'Amato & K. Engel, INTERNATIONAL ENVIRONMENTAL LAW ANTHOLOGY (Cincinnati, OH: Anderson, 1996); V. Nanda, INTERNATIONAL ENVIRONMENTAL LAW & POLICY (Irvington-on-Hudson, NY: Transnational, 1995). *Summary:* L. Guruswamy & B. Hendricks, INTERNATIONAL ENVIRONMENTAL LAW IN A NUTSHELL (2d ed, St. Paul, MN: West, 2003).

18. UN Gen. Ass. Reso. 44/228 (1992) (italics supplied).

19. The full text of *Agenda 21* is available at: <http://sedac.ciesin.org/entri/texts/a21/a21-contents.html>.

20. S. Johnson, Did We Really Save the Earth at Rio?, in Introduction to THE EARTH SUMMIT: THE UNITED NATIONS CONFERENCE ON ENVIRONMENT AND DEVELOPMENT (UNCED) 6 (Dordrecht, Neth.: Graham & Trotman/Martinus Nijhoff, 1993) [hereinafter *Earth Summit*].

21. Rio Declaration: <http://sedac.ciesin.org/entri/texts/rio.declaration.1992.html>.

22. R. Rayfuse, The Challenge of Sustainable High Seas Fisheries, ch. 19, in N. Schrijver & F. Weiss (ed.), INTERNATIONAL LAW AND SUSTAINABLE DEVELOPMENT 467, at 486 (Keiden., Neth.: Martinus Nijhoff, 2004).

23. Science and Environmental Health Network, 1998 Wingspread Statement on the Precautionary Principle, available at <http://www.sehn.org/wing.html>. Details are available in N. Myers & C. Raffensperger (ed.), PRECAUTIONARY TOOLS FOR RESHAPING ENVIRONMENTAL POLICY (Cambridge, MA: MIT Press, 2005).

24. Framework Convention for Protection of the Marine Environment of the Caspian Sea, available at: <http://www.unep.ch/regionalseas/legal/conlist.htm>.

25. See C. Hanley, Two Sets of American "States" Debate Emissions Controls, San Diego Union-Tribune (Dec. 17, 2004), at A28.

26. See Well Blowout Control Claim, UN Doc. S/Dec.40, 36 Int'l Legal Mat'ls 1343 (1997). A succinct analysis is available in R. Alford, International Decisions, 92 Amer. J. Int'l L. 287 (1998).

27. Biological Diversity: <http://sedac.ciesin.org/entri/texts/biodiversity.1992.html>.

28. B. Groombridge & M. Jenkins, The Diversity of Organisms, ch. 2, in Global Diversity: Earth's Living Resources in the 21st Century 12 (Cambridge, Eng.: World Conservation Monitoring Centre, 2000).

29. *Treaty:* Framework Convention on Climate Change, reprinted in 31 Int'l Legal Mat'ls 849 (1992). *Background:* D. Goldberg, Negotiating the Framework Convention on Climate Change, 4 Touro J. Transnat'l Law 149 (1993).

30. Climate Action Report, available at: <http://yosemite.epa.gov/oar/globalwarming.nsf/content/ResourceCenterPublicationsUSClimateActionReport.html>.

31. For a detailed presentation of facts and figures, *see* C. Brown, The Kyoto Protocol Enters into Force, ASIL Insight (Feb. 2005), available at: <http://www.asil.org/insights/2005/03/insights050301.html>.

32. 2001 conference documents: <http://www.unfccc.int/cop7/documents/index.html>.

33. *See generally* B. Brown, The United States and the Politicalization of the World Bank: Issues of International Law and Policy (London: Kegan Paul Int'l, 1992).

34. For a succinct but comprehensive analysis, *see* U.S. Rejection of Kyoto Protocol Process, 95 Amer. J. Int'l L. 647 (2001).

35. Climate Action Report, available at: <http://yosemite.epa.gov/oar/globalwarming.nsf/content/ResourceCenterPublicationsUSClimateActionReport.html>.

36. Kyoto's ratification status is available on the UN Framework Convention on Climate Change Web page, available at: <http://unfccc.int/files/essential_background/kyoto_protocol/application/pdf/kpstats.pdf>.

37. For further details, *see* F. Loy, The United States Policy on the Kyoto Protocol And Climate Change, 15 WTR Nat. Resources & Env't 152 (2001) & R. Ottinger & M. Jayne, Global Climate Change Kyoto Protocol Implementation: Legal Frameworks For Implementing Clean Energy Solutions, 18 Pace Envir. Law Rev. 19 (2000).

38. US E.P.A., Global Warming-Impact, available at: <http://yosemite.epa.gov/oar/globalwarming.nsf/content/Impacts.html>.

39. F. Singer, The Kyoto Protocol: A Post-Mortem, available at: <http://www.thenewatlantis.com/archive/4/singer.htm>.

40. UN Millennium Declaration, UN Doc. A/55/L.2, No. 23, available at: <http://www.un.org/millennium/declaration/ares552e.htm> (Sept. 8, 2000).

41. For the principles and an analysis of their application, *see* Authoritative Statement of Forest Principles, ch. 7, in *Earth Summit* 103–116 (cited in note 20 above).

42. R. Ananad, A New International Economic Order for Sustainable Development?, in Studies in International Law and History: An Asian Perspective 244, at 269–270 (Leiden, Neth.: Martinus Nijhoff, 2004).

43. The Johannesburg Declaration on Sustainable Development (Sept. 4, 2002), available at: <http://www.johannesburgsummit.org/html/documents/summit_docs/1009wssd_pol_eclaration.doc>.

44. UNEP, Plan of Implementation, available at: <http://www.un.org/esa/sustdev/documents/WSSD_POI_PD/English/POIToc.htm>.

45. S. VanDeveer, Green Fatigue, in Symposium: What Good is International Law?, 27 Wilson Quarterly 55, at 59 (2003).

46. International Court of Justice Communique No. 93/20 of 19 July 1993.

47. *ICJ:* The advisory, contentious, and chambers jurisdiction of the Court is discussed in §9.4 of this text. *PCOA:* Optional Rules for Arbitration of Disputes Relating to Natural Resources and/or the Environment, available at: <http://www.pca-cpa.org/PDF/ENRrules.PDF>.

48. Text at: <http://conventions.coe.int/Treaty/EN/cadreprincipal.htm>.

49. See A. Revkin, Eskimos Seek to Recast Global Warming as a Rights Issue, NYT on the Web (Dec. 15, 2004).

50. Wiwa v. Royal Dutch Petroleum Co., 226 F.3d 88, 92–93 (2d Cir. 2000), *cert. denied* 532 U.S. 941 (2001).

51. See J. Perlez, U.S. Company on Trial in Indonesia for Pollution, New York Times on the Web (Aug. 5, 2005).

52. Available at: <http://www.iccwbo.org/home/environment_and_energy/sdcharter/charter/principles/principles.asp>.

53. Investors and Environmentalists for Sustainable Prosperity CERES Principles, available at: <http://www.ceres.org/coalitionandcompanies/principles.php>.

54. Promulgated in 1993 Official Journal L 168/1, available at: <http://europa.eu.int/comm/environment/emas/index_en.htm>.

55. I. Bostian, The Environmental Consequences of The Kosovo Conflict And The Nato Bombing of Serbia, 1999 Colo. J. Int'l Envir. L. & Policy 230 (2000). See also M. Simons, On a Balkan War's Last Day, Trouble from the Sky, New York Times on the Web (Sept. 2, 2002).

56. UNEP Balkans Task Force Final Report, The Kosovo Conflict: Consequences for the Environment and Human Settlements 16 (1999), available at: <http://www.grid.unep.ch/btf/final/index.html>.

57. Committee Established to Review the NATO Bombing Campaign Against the Federal Republic of Yugoslavia, Final Report to the Prosecutor, available at: <http://www.un.org/icty/pressreal/nato061300.htm>.

58. The best analysis of this ICTY proceeding, from which many of the facts were drawn, is available in A. Schwabach, Nato's War in Kosovo and the Final Report to the Prosecutor of the International Criminal Tribunal for the Former Yugoslavia, 9 Tulane J. Int'l & Comp. L. 167 (2000).

59. The UN Secretary-General's arbitral decision is available in 26 Int'l Legal Mat'ls 1346 (1987).

CHAPTER THIRTEEN

Economic Relations

CHAPTER OUTLINE

INTRODUCTION

This final chapter overviews international economic relations. It begins by reviewing the pervasive interplay between international commerce and law—often looming just below the surface of earlier materials you encountered in this course.

Subsequent sections will survey contemporary international economic integration: the essential organizations such as the World Trade Organization (WTO), their basic objectives, and the "globalization" controversy—a convenient segue for the so-called New International Economic Order. These features of the "have" versus "have not" nation dialogue were supposedly designed to close this gap, although there is a raging debate about both of them. No analysis of international

THE APPLICANT [DUTCH EXPORTER] contended that its interest in free international trade should in this case carry much weight, because if the delivery of submarines to Taiwan were canceled, the survival of 1000 or possibly all of the 2000 jobs in its enterprise would be greatly endangered.

. . .

. . . [T]HE RESPONDENT [DUTCH MINISTER for Economic Affairs] further contended that granting the permission . . . [to export the submarines to Taiwan] would impair the interest of the international legal order in yet another respect: continued delivery of submarines implied support for Taiwan's rejection of proposals for peaceful reunification [with the PRC] . . . and was therefore likely to thwart a settlement of the existing conflict between the PRC and Taiwan.

—Wilton Feyenoord BV v. Minister for Economic Affairs, Netherlands Trade and Industry Appeals Tribunal (1984), 101 INT'L LAW REP. 419, 424–426 (1987).

business relations would be complete without some coverage of the role played by corruption.

◆ 13.1 ECONOMICS AND INTERNATIONAL LAW

HISTORICAL EVOLUTION

Pre-World War II Trade was pivotal in the evolution of ancient and medieval areas. Civilization developed in part from the concentration of people on or near major trade routes and ports. Trade ultimately led to diplomatic and other exchanges among these congregations of people. The great powers like Persia and Rome could afford to be somewhat apathetic about foreign trade. They maintained well-developed agricultural bases. For many other population centers, however, trade was a key method for raising revenue and exercising some degree of political power. From ancient Athens through the medieval city-States, the role of trade was to create wealth that, in turn, facilitated other advances. Trade ultimately led to diplomatic and other exchanges among these congregations of people. Trade also provided access to broader social and cultural perspectives as merchants traveled in search of marketing opportunities.

A number of early medieval agreements focused on economic matters. The treaty of 860 AD. between Byzantium, the major trading empire of that era, and Russia formalized their diplomatic and commercial relations. Under Article 4 of that agreement, Russia removed its previous ban on Byzantine exports. Trade was the ideal vehicle for developing international relations and for ushering in an era of relative peace. That concession also launched Russia's development of international trade relations with other nations.[1]

Links between commerce and law were forged by exploration. Many territories of the world were "discovered" by explorers seeking new trading opportunities. The ancient Phoenicians traveled the Mediterranean Sea and the north Atlantic Ocean in search of new trading partners. Portuguese and Spanish explorers discovered the new world during their trade-development programs of the fifteenth and sixteenth centuries.

Modern international commercial law is rooted in the trade practices that developed during the resulting interaction of national legal systems. Many standard contractual expectations were expressed in the medieval "Lex Mercatoria" (Law Merchant). This body of law was created and applied by specialized commercial tribunals, typically located in major port cities. Private merchants could conveniently resolve their local and international business disputes by submitting their disagreements for resolution to a neutral third party. The Lex Mercatoria flourished in the twelfth-century Italian city-States and later spread to other commercial centers. The customary practices of these tribunals were ultimately incorporated into the commercial laws of many nations.[2]

An early twentieth-century English case suggests how judges continued to apply the Lex Mercatoria when resolving maritime disputes. A shipment of goods was en route from San Francisco to London. The contract did not include a clause about *when* payment was due. It thus failed to express the intent of the buyer and seller. While the goods were en route, the seller's agent presented the bill of lading (document of title) to the buyer. The buyer refused payment. He wanted to inspect the goods on arrival in London. The seller sued the buyer for breach of contract before the goods arrived. Under the medieval maritime practice, a buyer was required to pay for goods when the seller's agent provided a bill of lading for cargoes still en route by sea—unless the parties expressly contracted for payment at another time. The London court effectively incorporated this vintage commercial practice into the contract and thus supplied the missing term based on this customary practice.[3] Arbitrators and judges thus incorporated certain commercial practices into the decisional law of maritime nations. Those practices then became customary rules of international commercial law. Some practices were then codified into national legislation and treaties.

Post-World War II The global business climate changed dramatically after World War II. The postwar Marshall Plan announced by the United States in 1947 was the largest and most successful foreign assistance program ever devised. The United States was unable to agree with the Soviet Union about the scope of German reparations for the latter's role in causing Europe's economic devastation. The Marshall Plan was the US substitute for the dismal failure of the post-World War I Versailles Treaty process. It unfortunately isolated Germany, rendered its economy stagnant, and unwittingly contributed to the resurgence of Germany's military power in the 1930s.

After World War II, the United States wanted Germany and Japan to rise from the ashes of defeat to become prosperous allies. Helping them to rebuild their economies was an important factor in maintaining an enduring peace, which would later develop markets for US goods and its lifestyle. A prosperous West Germany would ultimately "showcase" the advantages of market capitalism during the Cold War. Improved economic conditions in Germany and Japan created new long-term markets for US exports. The demise of the Soviet Union drove the West's promotion of democracy via economic initiatives in its former republics. Aid was thus linked to reform, arms control, nonproliferation of nuclear weapons, and the development of new consumer markets.

What occurred in the United States is a good example of the development of economic ties which can lead to lasting peace. US economic interaction with Germany and Japan strengthened the political and economic ties between these nations. The stage was set for a comparative frenzy of international business transactions, unlike the isolationist tendencies of earlier eras. The US government's postwar objectives impacted corporate life in the United States, as well as other countries. Corporate managers had previously concerned themselves only with local or nationwide business ventures. The country's vast internal markets did not encourage medium and small entrepreneurs to engage in *foreign* commerce. By the 1970s, however, foreign competitors began to enter into US markets in unprecedented numbers. The rebuilding programs of an earlier generation created economic Frankensteins. As the US demand for foreign products increased, a trade imbalance developed. US export growth lagged behind that of imports. Jobs in the affected US industries were at risk for enterprises unwilling to accommodate the surge of foreign competition.

A price would have to be paid for the unexpected degree of success of the US plans to develop foreign consumer markets. In order to compete, many US companies had to develop an expertise in problems that they had not previously encountered in local or nationwide business contexts. Even companies that did not engage in international business had to respond in their own markets to foreign competitors. There was a growing consumer demand for foreign-made goods, a major contributor to the commonly articulated problem of "the foreign trade deficit."

On the other hand, multinational enterprises in regions like Europe had never been isolated from international commercial transactions like the US continent bordered by two oceans and only two other countries. Europe's natural proximity to foreign borders—coupled with some limitations in the local availability of natural resources—presented a business environment more intuitively driven toward foreign markets. The same aggregate space between the eastern and western borders of the United States could be geographically occupied by virtually all of Europe with its ubiquitous international frontiers. One reason for the success of the European Union's (EU) economic integration is that many national economies were naturally inclined to operate in an international business climate. European States could not afford to be as isolationist as a nation with little international competition just across a number of nearby borders.

Although the United States had its large conglomerates operating worldwide, there were not as many as in other trading nations. In the post-World War II period, US managers contemplating international business opportunities had to become familiar with the intricacies of importing, exporting, and producing in or for foreign markets. They had to incorporate *governmental* perspectives, to appreciate the range of international economic issues that affect our daily lives. As aptly characterized by perhaps the foremost US authority on international economic issues:

> Indeed, almost every conceivable area of economic activity which for one reason or another attracted governmental concern and often regulation, is now impacted by actual or potential international regulation of one kind or another. Thus we need to step back and ask . . . [about the impact of] often *ad hoc* government responses. The fundamental subject appears to be the question of the "regulation of economic behavior which crosses national borders." How should policy makers (and scholars) approach this broad question? Are the same general principles of government regulatory activity which could be applied in most or all situations involving cross-border economic behavior? Can we develop some sort of general framework for policy analysis of this type? . . . These and many more questions can appropriately engage scholarly and policy-maker's attention for years to come.[4]

A useful restatement of the consequences of ill-fated governmental responses to these questions is provided by University of South Carolina Business School Professor Christopher Korth. "The economy will likely suffer if the government of a country accedes to [excessive] protective pressures, regardless of the specific nature of the argument and regardless of whether the interested group represents the private or governmental sector. Protectionism means that a higher price must be paid by the majority in order to benefit the few. The list of arguments on behalf of controls is long. The list of 'reasonable' arguments from the viewpoint of the public good (as opposed to that of special interest groups) is very short. Even in these cases, however, both national and world efficiency, income, and living standards will decline."[5]

Public International Law textbooks historically avoided any detailed discussion of commercial transactions. The rationale was that a course on Public International Law should deal with *State* behavior, and the work of international organizations of States with political and military objectives. Private International Law, by contrast, was sharply distinguished because it deals with the impact of differing national legal systems on *individuals,* such as merchants engaged in cross-border commercial transactions.[6]

In the late 1970s and 1980s, however, the academic environment began to change. Books and courses began to catch up with global economic developments. Business and undergraduate institutions in the United States had been slow to respond to the internationalization of commercial life. A number of international professors were understandably reluctant to "cram" Private International Law themes into a course in Public International Law. At present, international business and economics courses have become distinct offerings and curricula in many universities. Terms like "Euro," "NAFTA," and "WTO" are relatively commonplace. Students studying this chapter will have the benefit of exposure to the essential role of international economics in the evolution of Public International Law.

INTERNATIONAL LAW LINKS

The following materials focus on the underlying connection between international economic relations and the general body of International Law norms covered in earlier chapters.

Private International Law (Chapter 1)   Whether a contract is enforceable often depends on which nation's tribunals are chosen by one of the parties. Also, traders in different countries may operate in quite diverse negotiating postures. Socialist countries, for example, have historically conducted their trade via national trade agencies rather than through private enterprise. Nonsocialist nations depend on a market economy for the conduct of trade, which is done by private enterprises for profit rather than for the direct benefit of all people of the State. The government agencies in socialist States are characteristically

bureaucratic and desperately in search of predictability. Such intersystem cross-overs are often more cumbersome than transactions between traders in private market economies.[7]

To illustrate how differences might affect a common commercial setting, assume that XCorp agrees to sell a load of widgets to YCorp. XCorp does business in its home country State X. YCorp does business in its home country of State Y. XCorp then sends its first shipment of widgets to YCorp. That shipment contains defects. Their written contract does not include a seller's promise that the goods will arrive without defects. Under the national law of State Y, an importer cannot ask a Y court to *imply* a contractual term not expressed by the parties to a contract. The courts of State Y do not want to thereby rewrite business contracts for the parties which would supply terms. Such terms *might* have been reasonably included in the sales contract but were not necessarily *intended* by the parties to the shipping agreement. Under the national law of the exporting State X, the lack of contractual warranties does not preclude YCorp from seeking a judicial remedy in State X. YCorp could sue for breach of the contract in State X, based on an implied warranty (not mentioned in the contract) that the goods will arrive without substantial defects. In the absence of an international treaty which effectively supplies agreed-upon missing terms to such "private" international law conflicts, the result will depend on the country in which the case is filed and/or enforcement is sought.

Given the recurring problems generated by differences in national legal systems, the United Nations opened the Convention for the International Sale of Goods (CISG) for ratification by interested nations in 1980.[8] Under Public International Law, two States that ratify the CISG thereby choose a uniform rule that governs the contractual relationships of their respective private traders. The CISG does not preclude the parties from a private contractual agreement which differs from the otherwise applicable GISG result under the circumstances of the particular case. Both the buyer and the seller may prefer that the law of one of the involved countries will govern their transaction. The CISG authorizes them to agree that the national law of either State X or State Y will apply to their contract. Freedom of contract is thus preserved.

One of the best articulations for a nation to adopt the CISG was provided by US President Ronald Reagan. It appears in the following excerpt from his letter to the US Senate, recommending that the United States adopt this treaty:

International trade law is subject to serious legal uncertainties. Questions often arise as to whether our law or foreign law governs the transaction, and our traders and their counsel find it difficult to evaluate and answer claims based on one or another of the many unfamiliar foreign legal systems [whose law might apply]. The Convention's uniform rules offer effective answers to these problems. Enhancing legal certainty for international sales contracts will serve the interests of all parties engaged in commerce by facilitating international trade.[9]

Until 1998, there was no authoritative judicial interpretation of the 1980 CISG for US merchants.[10] The following decision illustrates how this treaty facilitates international trade, when US law would have otherwise resulted in a dismissal of this case:

◆

www **MCC–Marble Ceramic Center, Inc. v. Ceramica Nuova D'Agostino, S.P.A.**

UNITED STATES COURT OF APPEALS, ELEVENTH CIRCUIT

144 F.3d 1384 (1998), *cert. denied*, 526 U.S. 1087 (1999)

Go to course Web page at <http://home.att.net/~slomansonb/txtcsesite.html>. Under Chapter Thirteen, click MCC Marble Case.

In July 2005, the UN Commission on International Trade Law adopted a draft Convention on the Use of Electronic Communications in International Contracting. Its purpose is to facilitate legal certainty and predictability for international contracts. Its objectives include identifying the time and place of dispatch and receipt of electronic communications.

Letters of Credit The Letter of Credit (LOC) is probably the most useful mechanism for enabling an international commercial transaction between merchants in distant countries. The term "LOC" is commonly used because it was derived from the following historic practice: the buyer's bank would transmit a letter of credit from the buyer's bank on the buyer's soil to the seller's bank on the seller's soil. The LOC's functional equivalent was used by bankers in ancient Egypt and Greece, Imperial Rome, and Renaissance Europe.[11]

The LOC is especially useful for merchants with little or no prior business dealings. A documentary credit is the written promise of a bank, undertaken on behalf of a buyer, to pay a seller the amount specified in the LOC. The seller must comply with the terms set forth in the underlying contract, as manifested by the LOC agreement. The terms and conditions usually require the presentation of documents that bear title to the goods, which will be shipped by the seller, and the terms of payment. Banks thus act somewhat like escrow agents. They are the intermediaries who collect payment from the buyer, in exchange for transfer of the seller's title documents. This short chain of events enables the buyer to take possession of the goods upon arrival in the buyer's country. LOCs provide an immutable level of protection and security to buyers and sellers. The seller is assured that payment will be made by a bank that is independent of the buyer. The buyer is assured that payment will be released, by the bank to the seller, only after the bank has received the documents of title to the shipped goods which are described in the LOC.[12]

The International Chamber of Commerce (ICC), located in Paris, composes standardized commercial documents, contract terms, and rules of interpretation. One of the ICC's most prominent contributions is the Uniform Customs and Practices for Documentary Credits (UCP). The UCP contains a series of articles that standardize the use of the LOC in international banking. A letter of credit is not required, merely because the contract is international in scope. On the other hand, some governments require it for *all* transactions involving foreign trade.

The LOC has an important but little known connection with Public International Law. It has been used to settle conflicts between States at war and to mitigate problems spawned by poor international relations. The classic illustration arose in the aftermath of the ill-fated 1961 Bay of Pigs invasion of Cuba. US President Kennedy supported Cuban rebels, who had previously migrated to the United States, in this clandestine mission to overthrow Fidel Castro. But they were captured shortly after landing. A US naval destroyer was shelled as it monitored these events. One reason this mission failed was that President Kennedy was reluctant to provide air support once the plot was discovered by Cuban authorities.

A New York law firm attempted to negotiate the release of the invading Cuban immigrants who had been assisted by the US Central Intelligence Agency (CIA).

The ensuing 1962 Cuban Missile Crisis did not derail the negotiations for their release. A secret bargain was struck. Cuba was to receive $53 million worth of food and medical supplies in return for their release. But Cuba had no way of knowing whether the United States would renege on its part of the bargain once Cuba released these prisoners. Even if the United States did comply, there was no guarantee about the quality of supplies that the United States might ultimately ship to Cuba. It would be quite difficult to provide assurances via diplomatic representations—which the Cuban government was understandably unlikely to trust. The absence of formal diplomatic ties between Cuba and the United States was but one of the problems with making this exchange.

The US negotiator successfully requested the Red Cross to apply for a LOC from a Canadian bank executed in favor of Cuba. Once the bank issued an irrevocable LOC, Cuba would collect $53 million from the Canadian bank should the United States fail to provide the supplies or if they were inferior. Cuba could be assured that the bank would make the payment. To subsequently dishonor its LOC, even if prodded to do so by the US government, would ruin that bank's credibility in all future banking matters. LOCs are governed by the marketplace and diplomacy is governed by politics. Nevertheless, the United States and Cuban governments were able to employ a LOC to resolve this most sensitive of matters—at a time when these nations least trusted one another because of the Cuban Missile Crisis (§10.2).[13]

International Legal Personality (Chapters 2 and 3)

After World War II, States engaged in international commercial transactions with individuals and corporations in other States, with each other, and with international organizations such as the United Nations on an unprecedented scale. The increasingly routine appearance of States in the international marketplace, where their profit motive resembled that of any other trader, accordingly created the pressure to alter State sovereign immunity practice (§2.6). National and international tribunals began to reconsider the historical practice of *absolute* immunity, resulting in today's *restrictive* approach to sovereign immunity for States and, increasingly, international organizations (§3.6 *Broadbent* case).

The expansion of organizational legal capacity is classically illustrated by the famous "German Beer" case of 1987. The Commission of the European Communities sued the Federal Republic of Germany, claiming that it had breached obligations arising under regional International Law. The relevant treaty ceded the capacity to the Council of Europe to enact directives which limited a member State's ability to use restrictive business practices against other members of the region's international community. The relevant German law, dating from the year 1516, prohibited using additives in making beer. Germany's national beer law barred the importation of beer from any country whose beer contained substitutes for malted barley—the basic and unadulterated substance for making German beer. Other States in the region wanted to export a different kind of beer to the German market that contained such a substitute for malted barley. Germany defended its restrictive beer law on the basis that consumers would be misled—thinking that imported non-German beer was the same as that produced in Germany for four centuries. The Court of Justice of the European Community ruled that Germany's vintage restrictions did not survive the 1985 European Council Directives barring nontariff barriers (NTBs) to imports from other countries within the European Community. Germany's legislative protection unlawfully impeded the free importation of member—State products throughout the Community.[14]

Sovereignty (Chapters 2, 6)

International organizations can also affect commerce in far more sensitive ways. After Yugoslavia splintered into smaller nations, one of the new republics took the same name as the neighboring Greek province of Macedonia. Greece imposed a trade ban on the new State of Macedonia. As discussed in the materials on statehood and recognition, Greece's objection was not limited to the resulting confusion of two Macedonias sharing a common border. Greece questioned whether this fragment of the former Yugoslavia would ultimately seek to expand its territorial boundaries to include the adjacent Macedonian portion of Greece (Problem 2.B).

In April 1994, the EU threatened legal action against Greece, whose trade blockade against the Republic of Macedonia affected the ability of fellow EU members to access the nearby Greek port of Salonika. This is the customary Greek port for the journey of goods to and from the new Republic of Macedonia. Salonika is the exchange point for 80 percent of Macedonian trade and all of its oil imports. EU member States, Great Britain, and Germany pressured the EU to take this action for political reasons. Greece's continued trade blockade of

Macedonia might trigger a new round of Balkan desta-
bilization. The EU advised Greece of its intent to sue in
the European Court of Justice. This was an awkward
decision for several reasons including that the president
of the EU was a Greek citizen. Greece ultimately
backed down based on assurances that the country of
Macedonia would never expand to include the Greek
province of Macedonia.

Jurisdiction (Chapters 5, 6) The range of State
sovereignty has been recently tested in the French Yahoo
litigation's dueling judgments (§5.2 *French Yahoo Judgment*).
A Parisian court required a California-based Internet
service provider to preclude even *non*-French customers
from accessing illegal Nazi memorabilia information on
the Yahoo Web site. A San Francisco court relied on the
US Constitution's First Amendment right to freedom of
speech, to reach the opposite result. The ultimate resolution will have enormous consequences for international
business, as States attempt to keep the wine which so
many are savoring in the geographical bottle.[15]

Multinational corporations must also beware of such
jurisdictional quicksand. A classic example appeared
when an international cartel, including US wood pulp
producers, allegedly conspired to fix paper prices in
member States of the European Community. The organization's executive and judicial bodies fined them pursuant
to European Community Law, because their price-fixing
conspiracy violated the organization's antitrust laws. These
legal actions, although taken against business entities as far
away as the United States, did not constitute an improper
"extraterritorial" regulation of commercial transactions.
The conduct of the foreign enterprises was characterized
as having the requisite effect within the territory of the
European Community.[16]

There is a "price," however, for applying local law to
foreign enterprises. A major example is the US application
of its law to foreign corporate activity. US state and federal
law often subjects foreign companies to conflicting
demands. The US Supreme Court, for example,
trumped Swiss bank secrecy laws by approving the
application of US law to the US branch of a foreign
commercial enterprise. It was required to disclose information that subjected it to criminal sanctions under
Swiss law.[17] In another case, the Supreme Court decided
that procedures in the Hague Convention for the Taking
of Evidence Aboard in Civil or Commercial Matters
were *optional* rather than mandatory. A French company

thus had to submit documents to an adversary under US
procedural rules—although the French Penal Code *prohibited* the sharing of this technology in the absence of
an express treaty exception.[18]

US allies in Europe have thus enacted "locking
statutes." These statutes are countermeasures whereby
State X "blocks" the potential application of US law
to the corporate activities of State X individuals or
corporations who may be subjected to US legal
processes. Blocking statutes typically make it a crime
for non-US corporations to reveal such information.[19] The Chinese State Secrecy Law, for example,
generally forbids the disclosure of financial data by
Chinese corporations. This statute is designed to protect
Chinese State agencies from disclosing information
requested by authorities in other countries. But it
creates a problem for the Chinese entity that is subject
to conflicting demands. When Chinese companies do
business in the United States, for example, they have
consistently been required to disclose financial information when demanded by a US judge. These companies are held to the more liberal informational
disclosure standard in US litigation. In 1992, a federal
judge in San Francisco imposed a fine of $10,000 per
day for each day that a Chinese corporation refused to
comply with an American company's right to obtain
business information.[20]

Banking and other commercial investment entities
will no doubt be dramatically affected by the Bush
Administration's 2001 antiterrorist legislation. It unreservedly subjects foreign entities to US jurisdiction on
two fronts. First, foreign banks will have to alter their
business practices in their nations, and others outside of
the United States, if they wish to continue doing business
with the United States. Second, because the majority of
Internet messaging is routed through information hubs
in Virginia and California, criminal conduct abroad is
now subject to US jurisdiction—as messages facilitating
the criminal enterprise flow through the United States.
The United States is acting on the ones pertaining to
the discovery and prosecution of individuals related to
September 11, 2001.

Diplomacy (Chapter 7) Diplomacy and the economy
are no strangers. In 1991, the European Community
withheld a $1-billion food and aid package destined for
what was then the crumbling Soviet Union. The Community also delayed execution of a one-half-billion

dollar technical assistance agreement with Moscow, announcing its intent to file a human rights complaint with the Conference on the Security and Cooperation (§3.5). Soviet President Mikhail Gorbachev had just imposed a military "crackdown" on proindependence groups in the Baltic republics of the former Soviet Union. The European Community action effectively protested the Soviet response to the political violence in Latvia. France and Germany simultaneously announced that they would seek to temper the Soviet hard-line attitude toward the independence movement in the Baltic States of Lithuania, Latvia, and Estonia.

The United States also pursued trade-related diplomacy at the time. President George Bush (senior) negotiated with Gorbachev on the basis that the US Congress could grant the (former) Soviets special trading status. The objective was to normalize international economic relations between the two superpowers. Bush's announced "global partnership" was designed to prevent the United States and the crumbling Soviet Union from rekindling the tensions that symbolized the Cold War. This was employing economic incentives to reduce the risk of political and military hostilities while exploring the possibility of new Eastern European markets for US exports.

The United Nations suffered a major blow to its prestige in the Iraq oil-for-food scandal (§3.3). One may question the UN's continuing ability to "take the moral high ground"—given the related corruption which swept the United Nations from its diplomatic pedestal.

Treaty Norms (Chapter 8)   The nearly half-century-old Arab economic boycott of Israel was a centerpiece in its plan to bankrupt Israel. The Arab League sought to drive Israel out of existence—through this multilateral treaty response to the UN's 1947 partition of Palestine to create the State of Israel.

The materials in the remaining sections of this final chapter explore global and regional economic treaty relationships, which evolved out of the desire to advance the commercial interests of the participants.

Adjudication (Chapter 9)   The adjudication chapter dealt with the resolution of disputes by some specialized tribunals created for the finite purpose of winding down hostile relations. Dispute resolution typically plays out in a commercial context. The Iran-US Claims Tribunal is a serviceable example. It still functions in a building near the International Court of Justice (ICJ) in the Netherlands.

A third-party resolution model once again served as the means of clipping the loose economic strings spawned by the Iranian Hostage episode. At the conclusion of the 1979–1980 Iranian Hostage Crisis, Iran released the US hostages to Algeria. The United States released a portion of Iran's assets, which were frozen by US President Jimmy Carter at the outset of the crisis. Since then, the Iran-US Claims Tribunal has steadily worked to resolve the private claims of US businesses. This third-party dispute-resolution mechanism peacefully resolved one of the most sensitive disputes ever to arise under Public International Law.[21] The §12.3 UN Compensation Commission case is engaged in a similar process: addressing damage and reparation disputes spawned by Iraq's torching over 600 oil wells as its military forces withdrew from Kuwait in the first Persian Gulf War.

Use of Force (Chapter 10)   The materials on the use of force could be revisited to cultivate the commercial roots in the genealogy of Public International Law. The UN Security Council, for example, invoked its UN Charter powers to impose international economic sanctions with varying degrees of success on South Africa to eliminate its State policy of apartheid; on parts of the former Yugoslavia, to reduce the flow of arms entering the Bosnian conflict; on Iraq, to keep it from perpetrating additional affronts to Kuwait's sovereignty during and after the 1991 Persian Gulf War; and on the Taliban government in Afghanistan because of its posture in relation to Usama bin Laden.

Modern States are increasingly using economics as their weapon of choice, as opposed to using or threatening military force. After the end of the Cold War, for example, the United States became the lone superpower. It continued to rely on unilateral sanctions policy in certain cases, rather than deferring to either the UN Security Council or World Trade Organization (WTO). Despite being the leading voice in favor of the WTO, the United States has threatened or used various legislative and executive policies without the approval of these international organizations. Under the authority of Title 50 of US Code §1701, for example, the president implemented the Iran and Libya Sanctions Act of 1996. This statute authorizes the targeting of certain countries to "deal with any unusual and extraordinary threat, which has its source in whole or substantial part outside the United States, to the national security, foreign policy, or economy of the

United States, if the President declares a national emergency with respect to such threat."

Since then, political relations between the United States and both of these countries have thawed. Libya surrendered its agents responsible for trial in the Pan Am 103 bombing incident in 1988. Libya also paid each of the victims' families millions of dollars in reparations. Libya wished to be a WTO member, and cast itself free of the interim economic sanctions which crippled its economy. The United States has negotiated in favor of Iran's 1996 application to the WTO, in return for Iran's freezing of its nuclear weapons program.

In addition to the Arab economic boycott of Israel, and sanctions imposed or threatened after the September 11, 2001, attacks on the World Trade Center and the Pentagon, the next most prominent example may be the Helms-Burton legislation. Rather than use economic tools to embrace Cuba, the US Congress arguably perpetuated Cold War tactics with this 1996 law. It was the next step in the more than four decades of US economic embargo of Cuba. That sanction does not have the blessing of the UN Security Council, the EU, and many individual nations including US North American Free Trade Agreement (NAFTA) partners Canada and Mexico.

This economic legislation is a forceful example of the interplay between politics, economics, and International Law. It has prompted diplomatic protests from the above-mentioned organizations and many nations. You may now read the edited versions of the US law, the responsive legislation enacted by Cuba, and references to the official objections to Helms-Burton on the course Web page:

United States 1996 Cuban Liberty and Democratic Solidarity Act and the Responsive Republic of Cuba 1996 Reaffirmation of Cuban Dignity and Sovereignty Act

Go to course Web page at:
<http://home.att.net/~slomansonb/txtcsesite.html>.
Under Chapter Thirteen, click Cuban Liberty and Democratic Solidarity Act & Reaffirmation of Cuban Dignity and Sovereignty Act.

The Helms-Burton legislation was initially vetoed by President Bill Clinton. He later signed it after Cuban military jets shot down two private US aircraft in 1996 (§6.4). This was then the latest incident in the unrelenting friction between the United States and Cuba, initially spawned by Fidel Castro's 1959 *coup d'etat*. Its purpose was to tighten the economic embargo of Cuba by making it a crime to "traffic" in property originally belonging to US nationals but confiscated by Cuba in 1959 after the United States first imposed a quota on Cuban sugar products.

This legislation purports to prohibit third-country companies from "trafficking" in such property, a term previously reserved for US drug laws. It creates civil liability and excludes visits to the United States by officers, controlling shareholders, families of trafficking companies, and anyone else who violates its terms. As noted in the foregoing Web page excerpt, Mexico, Canada, and the EU were prominent US trade partners who characterized this Act as an illegal extraterritorial application of US law.

In 1997, the EU brought a claim in the WTO, regarding this US legislation. The EU dropped its claim against the United States in 1998. One can presume that it sensed that pursuing this claim in the WTO presented a "lose-lose" scenario for the then new WTO dispute resolution process. First, if the EU were to continue to prosecute this matter there, and succeed, the case would have effectively politicized the fledgling global trade organization. It was, after all, designed to *avoid* politics in international trade. There was no guarantee that the United States would remain in the WTO. The United States abandoned the ICJ in the mid-1980s when its supreme national interests were at stake in Nicaragua (§10.2). Second, if the United States were to win this case, its "national security" defense to anticompetitive trade measures would have effectively made a mockery of the WTO. The organization was basically conceived to ensure free, nondiscriminatory trade—which was of course expressly contrary to the *raison d'etre* of the Helms-Burton Act. The United States had its reasons for negotiating with the EU to drop its Helms-Burton case. During the eight-year Uruguay Round, which produced the WTO, the United States was generally the first and loudest proponent to claim that a prospective defendant should not frustrate the dispute settlement provisions of the WTO.

President Clinton waived key portions of Helms-Burton a half-dozen times since its passage (each waiver has a six-month life span). He expressed the concern that there would be retaliation against US companies, especially because foreign businesspeople operating in Cuba could be sued under this US law, regarding any transaction involving "trafficked" property. A 1998 bipartisan campaign was launched in the US Congress to ameliorate the potential impact of this Act and the forty-year embargo on the Cuban people (as opposed to the targeted government). President Bush used his first opportunity to continue the presidential waiver of the Act's trafficking provisions which, if implemented, would offend many nations of the world (not to mention the EU and United Nations). President Bush, notwith-standing his strong anti-Castro rhetoric, has also waived his executive prerogative to fire this economic salvo.

In November 2005, the United Nations again weighed in, with its fourteenth consecutive General Assembly resolution, calling on the United States to cease its economic embargo of Cuba. The 182 to 4 vote indicates the degree to which the international com-munity disagrees with this US policy. That Iran began its campaign in 2005, calling for the demise of the State of Israel, hints at one potential downside of the long-term US policy seeking Cuba's economic demise. The United States does not have a clean slate, in terms of being a nation willing to employ economic and political pressure to damage another nation's economy.

In an analysis of the arguments for and against the legality of Helms-Burton in the American Bar Associa-tion's periodical, *International Lawyer,* the Founding Executive Director of the Legal Center for Inter-American Free Trade and Commerce concludes:

> The moment for multilateral diplomacy with respect for Cuba and the Western Hemisphere could not be any more auspicious. [T]he European Union has adopted a new foreign policy strategy vis-à-vis Cuba. The purpose of the European plan is to address human rights abuses and, consistent with Title II of *Helms Burton,* to foster the transition to a democrat-ically elected government in the Caribbean island. Harmonious with this plan, Pope John Paul II made an unprecedented visit to Cuba during the early part of 1998 as a favorable prelude to the Second Summit of the Americas. As the international legal system approaches the crossroads in its continued develop-ment, the door to multilateral diplomacy is open. The only question is whether the US President and the Congress will make the correct policy choice.[22]

Human Rights (Chapter 11)   There are numerous contemporary examples, but space for only several. In mid-1994, the United States opposed Singapore as the initial host of the WTO's premier 1995 ministerial meeting. The US Trade Representative objected to a Singapore site, because of its 1994 "caning" (severe corpo-ral punishment with a whip-like cane) of an eighteen-year-old US citizen. President Clinton was unable to dissuade Singapore from carrying out this punishment after the youth had spray-painted several cars. There were widely reported global concerns with this form of State action on the basis that it constituted torture or cruel and degrading punishment under International Human Rights Law. While US pressure did not prevent the caning, the United States was able to sidetrack Singapore's bid for hosting this major event at the dawn of the new WTO's operations.[23]

Before the normalization of trade relations with China in 2001, there had been a relatively long and tortuous political history associated with the recurrent decisions of US presidents regarding China's trading status with the United States since World War II (§13.2 Most Favored Nation Treatment). In 1951, in the early stages of the Cold War, US President Harry Truman denied Most Favored Nation (MFN) status to *all* communist countries. President Richard Nixon unsuc-cessfully attempted to extend MFN status to China in 1972 when he initiated US relations with the People's Republic of China (PRC). In 1980, President Jimmy Carter finally extended MFN status to that nation. In 1990, President George Bush decided that China would receive MFN status—but not the former Soviet Union because of obstacles it had erected to Jewish emigration to Israel. This appeared to set a double standard for US MFN policy. Candidate Clinton campaigned in 1991 that, if elected, he would revoke China's MFN status because of continuing concerns with China's human rights performance. In 1993, President Clinton scaled this pledge back to denying MFN status only to State entities. Full MFN status was revived that year and con-tinued thereafter.

The threatened revocation of China's MFN status then became a continuing commercial wrinkle in Sino-US diplomatic relations. It resurfaced with a fury after the PRC's massacre of prodemocratic Chinese students in Tiananmen Square in 1989. In 1994, the US Trade Representative announced a new tactic in the pursuit of Chinese human rights improvement—a cutback of 25 to 35 percent on the US importation of Chinese textiles and clothing. The United States experienced a major trade deficit with the PRC. But the expressed rationale for this particular round of human rights diplomacy was that China had continued to display a poor human rights record after a decade of prodding by various human rights organizations. This particular link between human rights and Sino-US economic relations evaporated with the 2001 entry of China into the WTO.

Environmental Niche (Chapter 12)   The 1992 Rio Conference and ensuing UN environmental programs have strived to accomplish sustainable economic development for the underdeveloped countries of the world. But there is continuing concern about the environmental cost of such development. The flourishing industrial-chemical plants of the 1970s and 1980s in Ireland, for example, helped raise the economic standard of living in Ireland, one of the EU's poorest members. But they also produced one of the most polluted atmospheres in the northern hemisphere.[24]

The citizens of Bhopal, India, certainly gained from the presence of a major US corporate operation in their territory, while it was making chemicals for agricultural use. Thousands of jobs were created. India's economy was favorably impacted by the presence of this multinational corporate enterprise. More money was spent locally in the form of the added spending power of corporate employees, steady jobs, and a decline in unemployment. There would be a significant environmental cost in 1984, however, for hosting a foreign corporation's operations in Bhopal—the site of one of the worst (sudden) environmental disasters in history (§12.1).

◆ 13.2 WORLD TRADE ORGANIZATION

The WTO became effective in 1995, emerging in the form of a 26,228-page document. This global agreement embodies a six-part program designed to reduce barriers to international commerce. Its pillars include the following restraints:

◆ *Tariffs.* Import taxes and other tariff barriers would be reduced on 85 percent of the world's trade. The associated taxes are called customs duties, charges, tolls, assessments, or levies. The most common term is "tariff."

◆ *Dumping.* Resisting the practice of temporarily selling imports at a price below cost in the target market. This is a predatory tool for eliminating local competition. After market access is secured, the pricing structure increases significantly so that ultimate profits recoup previous losses after eradication of most or all competitors.

◆ *Agriculture.* Farm subsidies, which artificially reduce the cost of production, are to be reduced by an average of 36 percent.

◆ *Textiles.* Import quotas on textiles from developing countries—which currently help the local market's competitors maintain a greater market share—would be phased out over a ten-year period.

◆ *Service sectors.* Markets in "service" sectors such as banking, shipping, and insurance are subject to international trade controls for the first time. Only "goods" were regulated under the 1947–1994 version of the WTO (GATT).

◆ *Intellectual property.* The WTO regime extends protection against unauthorized copying of "intellectual" property such as books, films, music, computer programs, and pharmaceutical products—thus providing additional copyright and patent protection on a global basis.

EVOLUTION OF GATT AND WTO

GATT   In the consummate economic world, managerial skill and economic efficiency would be the exclusive market forces that drive international economics. Instead, governments have introduced a variety of impediments to the free flow of cross-border commerce. The tariff is the primary international trade barrier. (Nontariff barriers to free trade will be discussed later in this section.) When the government of State X so taxes a foreign-made commodity, the resulting tariff increases the cost of that product for the State Y exporter wishing to sell it and the State X consumer wishing to buy it. The higher the tariff, the higher the cost—and the less likely the importation of foreign goods and international competition for that particular product (and *service* as now addressed by WTO). While the taxing nation's products are protected by tariffs on imported products, that protection has a price. That nation should expect its trading partners to counter with their own tariffs.

The inverse relationship between the level of tariffs and the level of international trade is classically illustrated by the effect of the US tariff law of 1930. It imposed the highest tariffs ever levied on foreign-made products. The US Congress then believed that this trade restriction would stimulate local industry and agriculture, and that the United States would not be harmed by this tariff legislation. Quite the opposite occurred, however. The other major industrial countries retaliated by placing higher tariffs on US exports. The foreign demand for American products fell immediately, resulting in a dramatic loss of jobs in the United States. These events contributed to the Great Depression of the 1930s and the global recession of that era.

In 1934, US President Franklin Roosevelt and the Congress worked together to reverse this disastrous high-tariff protectionist program to stimulate the domestic economy. Congress enacted the Reciprocal Trade Agreements Program to encourage international competition. It generally reduced tariff rates that, in turn, encouraged similar reductions by other countries. The legislative goal was to vitiate the adverse effect of the high tariffs that had strangled the flow of international commerce—both in and out of the United States. Congress then authorized the president to negotiate mutual tariff reductions with individual nations. The US Trade Representative thus began to negotiate an exhaustive series of bilateral agreements to reduce tariffs. This program increased the volume of US exports, while stimulating worldwide trade benefits as other countries responded by reducing their tariffs. The US tariffs gradually declined to the lowest levels in the nation's history.

During World War II, certain nations explored the possibility of a multilateral trade institution. They advocated a single, global trade agreement that would replace the hundreds of independent bilateral agreements. The United States pursued this objective by lobbying for creation of the International Trade Organization (ITO) to develop and maintain a global trade agreement. Representatives from several nations met to draft an ITO Charter. They simultaneously created a comparatively informal document called the General Agreement on Tariffs and Trade (GATT) at Geneva in 1947. The GATT was originally supposed to be a statement of principles related to, but distinct from, the anticipated ITO Charter.[25]

The ITO never materialized. The US Congress resurrected its isolationist trade posture after World War II. It thus decided against US participation in the proposed ITO. The United States had the most prosperous postwar economy. Many of today's major economic powers were in ruins or economically depressed after the war. Without US support, the ITO became impractical. After that, GATT continued to be a *de facto* arrangement, which was useful, even if not legally enforceable when its obligations (discussed later) were breached by a participating State.

GATT became the device for coordinating global policies on international commerce, accomplishing trade objectives, and overcoming the inertia of the US Congress. In 1948, twenty-two nations executed an interim Protocol of Provisional Application—the original GATT agreement referred to as "GATT 1947." A GATT General Secretariat and administrative staff were established by 1955 in Geneva. Their task was to implement the trade objectives of the participating countries—which could not be called "members," because the GATT did not achieve official status as an international organization of States. GATT did not possess its own power to act when a State decided to ignore its GATT "obligations" during the next forty years.

In 1994, the status of the GATT arrangement changed. Most nations of the world either joined or sought accession to the various agreements produced by its eight-year "Uruguay Round" of GATT negotiations. The resulting "GATT 1994" was the last of five periodic rounds conducted since GATT's inception. During that session, the national representatives produced the "Final Act," referring to the WTO.[26] In January 1995, sixty nations became charter members of the WTO. Some have signed but not yet ratified the WTO agreement. Twenty-one others immediately began to negotiate for admission. Some States, however, remained in just the GATT, rather than accept the mandatory dispute-settlement provisions of the 1995 WTO process. China was finally admitted in November 2001, notwithstanding internal protests because of its closure of State-owned factories and reduction of farm subsidies as conditions of WTO membership.

WTO The shift from GATT to WTO has been very dramatic. The GATT was a temporary arrangement, with no institutional framework, no secretariat, and no ties to an existing international organization.[27] WTO is a truly international organization, which has become the treaty-based centerpiece of International Trade Law.[28] The primary reason for this upgraded status is that the WTO radically changed dispute settlement procedures in international commerce. See Exhibit 13.1.

EXHIBIT 13.1

WTO structure
All WTO members may participate in all councils, committees, etc, except Appellate Body, Dispute Settlement panels, and plurilateral committees.

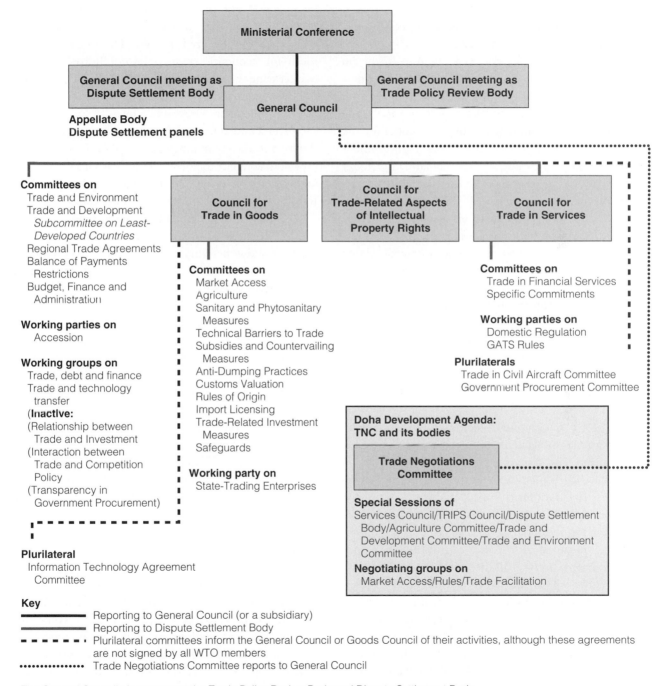

The General Council also meets as the Trade Policy Review Body and Dispute Settlement Body

This chart is available from the WTO Web site at: <http://www.wto.org/english/thewto_e/whatis_e/tif_e/org2_e.htm>.

Overcoming the national distrust associated with submitting sensitive trade disputes to a third-party dispute-resolution body was a primary objective of the switch from GATT to WTO. The following commentary by Ernst-Ulrich Petersmann, the former WTO Legal Adviser, succinctly describes this undercurrent:

> Both the classical international law of coexistence and the post-War international law of economic cooperation, including the General Agreement on Tariffs and Trade (GATT), had focused on the rights of states and governments rather than on the rights of their citizens. . . . While *Alexis de Tocqueville* could describe the US Supreme Court as a model for the judicial control of protectionist abuses of government powers [within a nation], the termination, in October 1985, of the US acceptance of the compulsory jurisdiction of the International Court of Justice . . . revealed a widespread distrust vis-à-vis judicial settlement of disputes with third countries.
>
> How can such distrust of judicial control of foreign policy powers be overcome? How can . . . abuses of foreign policy powers be prevented? How can a liberal international trade order be protected more effectively? . . .
>
> The 1994 WTO Agreement, adopted by 124 countries and the EC . . . [is] arguably the most important worldwide agreement since the UN Charter of 1945. . . .
>
> As a global integration agreement, which regulates international movements of goods, services, persons, capital and related payments in an integrated manner, the WTO agreement reduces the current fragmentation of separate international agreements and organizations. . . . Fifty years after the Bretton Woods Conference, its entry into force on 1 January 1995 completed the legal structure of the Bretton Woods system based on the IMF, the World Bank Group and [now] the WTO. The WTO was designed to serve constitutional functions and rule-making functions . . . , in addition to its executive functions, surveillance functions and dispute settlement functions for the foreign economic policies of member states, more so than the IMF and the World Bank, whose statutes include few substantive rules for the conduct of government policies and for the [much needed] rule-oriented settlement of international disputes.[29]

The new comprehensive title, "WTO" (as opposed to "GATT"), was more than just a name change. First, a *de jure* international economic organization is now endowed with jurisdictional powers ceded by its member States. Second, the WTO has a power that was withheld from the GATT process by its participating States. The WTO can force compliance when one of its nearly 150 member nations breaches organizational obligations (as analyzed below). Third, there is now room for economies that were not historically free-market economies. Both the former Soviet Union and the PRC expressed interest in participating in the earlier GATT agreement. They were initially placed in the Observer Government group. Russia's relatively recent shift to a market economy, assuming that democracy and capitalism continue to flourish, renders it a likely candidate for ultimate inclusion. US President Bush lobbied for Russia's full membership by the end of 2006.

The United States initially opposed China's participation, because of the latter's extensive piracy of patented and copyrighted US materials. These products include computer hardware, software, books, movies, and a host of other items protected by the WTO treaty. US estimates were that China's breach of international copyright and patent treaties has cost US companies more than $1 billion a year in lost revenues. Ninety-four percent of US-made products in China were pirated copies. China and the United States thus entered into a bilateral treaty in November 2001, which enabled China's to enter the WTO.[30]

One major difference between the WTO and GATT is that a GATT member could pick and choose among the various GATT "obligations" based on expediency. This selective incorporation produced a very complex web of varying obligations, doing little to promote GATT's universal appeal. This is one of the reasons why *regional* trade organization (§ 13.3) virtually eclipsed the GATT in importance. The WTO treaty, on the other hand, requires that participating States agree to *all* of the basic provisions (with some temporary exceptions).

The WTO also differs from GATT because GATT was limited only to commodities. WTO membership requires accession to the four fundamental parts of the 1994 Final Act: (1) trade in goods; (2) services; (3) intellectual property rights; and (4) investment rules. The "goods" portion of international commerce continues to be the primary area of concern. It will be summarized below as the focal point in this section. The WTO case selection for this section covers the increasingly important arena of intellectual property.

The primary *legal* difference between GATT and the WTO is the latter's mandatory dispute-resolution mechanism. The former GATT panels of experts often issued their determinations without the ability to force compliance with the basic obligations described below. A far more formal adjudicatory system currently provides enforceable remedies. The significance is conveniently summarized by New York University Professor Andreas Lowenfeld, a prominent international commercial arbitrator:

> Until now dispute settlement in the GATT has generally reflected a certain ambivalence. Some states and many "old GATT hands" within the secretariat and among the delegations in Geneva believed that GATT dispute settlement should aim at lowering tensions, defusing conflicts, and promoting compromise; others, notably American officials and writers, have looked to the dispute mechanism of GATT as an opportunity to build a system of rules and remedies. Over the forty years of GATT dispute settlement, there has been an ebb and flow between the diplomatic and the adjudicatory models. It seems clear that the adjudicatory model prevailed in the Uruguay Round.[31]

Under GATT, the losing party could essentially ignore ("block") a GATT "panel report." States could disregard the findings of the GATT panel when told to cease an offending practice. A powerful trading partner could even block the GATT Secretariat from organizing a panel that was supposed to decide a complaint.[32]

The WTO discourages unilateral fact-finding by an individual member of the organization. The Agreement Establishing the WTO provides that, should a member seek redress for a violation of GATT obligations, it "shall have recourse to, and abide by, the rules and procedures of this Understanding. . . ." Members may not make their own determinations, and must instead seek "recourse to dispute settlement in accordance with the . . . [WTO] Understanding."[33]

Under this Understanding on Rules and Procedures Governing the Settlement of Disputes, there is still an adjudicatory "panel" process. But State members of the WTO can no longer ignore a panel decision for three reasons. First, there is an initial consultation process. The aggrieved party may institute a relatively informal consultation with the allegedly offending party. This informal process has a short fuse so that the aggrieved party may then secure the establishment of a formal panel if the matter remains unresolved for sixty days. Second, one State may not unilaterally block the establishment of a panel when another has lodged a complaint in the WTO's headquarters in Geneva. Third, the unlikely acceptance of an adverse panel decision without any form of review would place the WTO and the entire GATT process at risk.

States have been traditionally reluctant to yield sovereign powers to an external decision maker without any recourse. Panel members can make mistakes. Thus, the losing party may *temporarily* block a panel decision—unlike the former panel "process" which could drag on for months with no resolution. The losing party must now seek immediate appellate review by the WTO's Appellate Body in Geneva. This standing organ consists of seven persons, three of whom review the lower panel decisions. The existence of an appellate process is an innovation that has been criticized, however, on the basis that the availability of appellate review reduces the prestige of the "trial" panel. It also offers a clear advantage: the losing party has the opportunity to rectify a perceived mistake—a common attribute of democratic systems of governance which adds to the integrity of the WTO process.[34]

An international organization may have similar parochial concerns. In the EU, community legislation may be inconsistent with WTO requirements. A "legal person" or business entity may not plead that activities compliant with WTO rules are a defense to contract community rules. In March 2005, the Court of Justice for the European Communities ruled that a Belgian company was unable to import the quantity of bananas it had imported over the prior twenty years. A WTO panel had ruled that the restrictive community regulations were incompatible with the WTO's more liberal rules. As stated by the Court in a March 2005 decision:

> To accept that the Community Courts have the direct responsibility for ensuring that Community law complies with the WTO rules would deprive the Community's legislative or executive bodies of the discretion which the equivalent bodies of the Community's commercial partners enjoy.

It follows from all of the foregoing that an operator [Belgian corporation], in circumstances such as those in the main proceedings, cannot plead before a court of a Member State that Community legislation is incompatible with certain WTO rules, even if the DSB [Dispute Settlement Body] has stated that that legislation is incompatible with those rules.[35]

One reason for such a result is that the WTO above described mandatory dispute-resolution mechanism was a major procedural hurdle to national acceptance. This recent decision echoes the pre-WTO concern of the more powerful nations about a devolution of sovereignty to a distant process in Geneva.[36] This inertia has been partially overcome, now that nearly 150 nations of the world have accepted the WTO and its mandatory settlement provisions. But what are the WTO underlying *substantive* obligations?

WTO OBLIGATIONS

What exactly does participation in the WTO mean? What obligations does a State thereby undertake when it opts to join this international organization of States? The fundamental objective is to combat trade barriers. National representatives thereby attempt to reduce or eliminate the varied forms of trade barriers: tariffs, non-tariff barriers, and discriminatory trade practices.

The essential obligations are set forth in Articles I, II, III, and VI.[37] The relevant portion of each one is provided immediately below, followed by a brief explanation.

Article I *Most-Favored-Nation Treatment*
(1) With respect to customs duties and charges of any kind imposed on or in connection with importation or exportation or imposed on the international transfer of payments for imports or exports, and with respect to the method of levying such duties and charges . . . any advantage, favor, privilege or immunity granted by any contracting country shall be accorded immediately and unconditionally to the like product originating in or destined for the territories of all other contracting parties.

Under International Law, States are generally free to discriminate in their economic dealings. That is an attribute of the sovereign power to engage in international relations with other States. University of London Professor Georg Schwarzenberger explains that in "the absence of bilateral and multilateral treaty obligations to the contrary, international law does not ordain economic equality between States nor between their subjects. Economic sovereignty reigns supreme. It is for each subject of international law to decide for itself whether and, if so, in which form, it desires to grant equal treatment to other States and their subjects or give privileged treatment to some and discriminate against others."[38] A nation's tariffs may thus discriminate against the goods from one country and favor those of another. Groups of States may combine to charge discriminatory tariffs. The States within the EU want to eliminate tariffs on the exported commodities of only its own members. They do not have to extend this favorable tariff treatment to other countries.

The Article I MFN clause has been a centerpiece of GATT, and now the WTO. Even prior to the GATT's appearance in 1947, many bilateral treaties contained such a clause. Each nation thereby promised that the tariff rate on the imports of its trading partner would be the lowest rate imposed on like imports from any other nation. Then under the GATT, member nations agreed to grant MFN status to the imported products from other GATT members. The WTO process is the same. Assume that South Africa imposes a 10 percent tariff on imported Italian shoes. Both of these countries are members of the WTO. The MFN article requires South Africa to charge Italy the lowest shoe tariff that it levies on like shoes from any other country. South Africa may charge a higher, 12 percent tariff on shoes from State X if X is not a WTO member. If South Africa were to reduce its tariff on like shoes from some other nation, South Africa would then have to reduce its tariff to the same rate for State X and other WTO members.

Article II *Schedules of Concessions*
(1.b) The products described in Part I of the Schedule relating to any contracting party, which are the products of territories of other contracting parties, shall, on their importation . . . be exempt from ordinary customs duties in excess of those set forth therein. . . .
(1.c) The products described in *Part II* of the Schedule relating to any contracting party which are the products of territories entitled under Article I to receive preferential treatment upon importation into the territory to which the Schedule relates shall, on their importation . . . be exempt from ordinary customs duties in excess of those set forth and provided for in Part II of that Schedule.

Each State's tariffs on imported products are listed in "concessions," referred to as "schedules." These schedules have been renegotiated during the various periodic GATT rounds since the original 1947 agreement. Members have thereby updated and published their latest tariff schedules, giving their tariff for each item on the list of items governed by the GATT.

There is a dual system of tariffs under the GATT. Article II(1.c) authorizes a GATT member to place the imports of designated nations on its "Part II Schedule" of tariffs. That action results in lower tariffs being imposed on imports from a developing nation. Each GATT member may publish different tariffs for the same category of import on its Parts I and II lists. The lower tariffs on a member's Part II Schedule of tariffs favor the products of certain developing countries. The more they can thus benefit by developing their markets through lower tariff schedules, the larger their markets will be for exports from developed nations.

Since WTO came into existence in 1995, there has been renewed emphasis on assisting developing nations to integrate into the global economy. The post-World War II Marshal Plan for Europe was channeled to specific economic sectors including redevelopment, reconstruction, industry, infrastructure, and the education of skilled labor forces. But the resources allocated to Africa have not been designed to create managerial capabilities, and technical or vocational skills. Under the US African Growth and Opportunity Act of 2005, for example:

Congress finds that—
(1) it is in the mutual interest of the United States and the countries of sub-Saharan Africa to promote stable and sustainable economic growth and development in sub-Saharan Africa;

. . .

(3) sub-Saharan Africa represents a region of enormous economic potential and of enduring political significance to the United States;

. . .

(5) certain countries in sub-Saharan Africa have increased their economic growth rates, taken significant steps towards liberalizing their economies, and made progress toward regional economic integration that can have positive benefits for the region;
(6) despite those gains, the per capita income in sub-Saharan Africa averages approximately $500 annually;

(7) trade and investment, as the American experience has shown, can represent powerful tools both for economic development and for encouraging broader participation in a political process in which political freedom can flourish;

. . .

(9) offering the countries of sub-Saharan Africa enhanced trade preferences will encourage both higher levels of trade and direct investment in support of the positive economic and political developments under way throughout the region.[39]

. . .

This statute encourages enhanced trade and investment incentives. But it does not provide concrete steps for reaching its lofty goal of rebuilding Africa. Such steps may not be economically feasible, because of US taxpayer expense associated with the Iraq War and the financial impact of Hurricane Katrina's.

Direct aid to Africa has always been on a comparatively small scale. So the 2005 US-UK African debt relief initiative and the G-8 debt cancellation program should help.[40] But these programs do not *create* the institutions that can result in the economic power now wielded by the EU members who benefitted from the Post-World War II Marshall Plan. As concisely articulated by Debra Stegar, former Principal Legal Counsel to the Government of Canada for the Uruguay Round of the WTO: "When the world emerged from the ravages of WWII, . . . [it] needed to rebuild the war-ravaged economies of Europe and Asia, in order to ensure economic growth and prosperity. They also realized that with economic growth and prosperity, peace and security would also be maintained."[41]

In November 2000, the *Final Communiqué* from the Meeting of African Trade Ministers in Libreville, Gabon called upon the WTO to assist them as follows. First, they decided to request the following:

7. Call for duty-free and quota-free access to all developed-country markets for products of African origin. . . . We also welcome the efforts by the United States under the African Growth and Opportunity Act and urge that all opportunities be explored to ensure that all African countries and products benefit from the Act;
8. Call for the immediate implementation of G-7 measures to cancel part of the debt of all African

countries and invite other creditors, including the financial institutions, to take similar measures so as to generate surplus resources for technological investments geared towards international trade;

9. Call on the international community to take action for the effective establishment of a World Solidarity Fund aimed at reducing poverty in Africa and world-wide . . . .

12. Call for the streamlining and facilitation of the accession process of African countries, non-Members of the WTO, on terms compatible with their level of development. In this regard, we call for sufficient and adequate technical and financial assistance to these countries . . . . [42]

This is a particularly ambitious Declaration. One reason is suggested by UN Secretary-General Kofi Annan's issuing a like call for aid for developing countries in the form of a Global Health Fund. His primary objective is the spread of HIV/AIDS. At the time of his request, the UN's World Health Organization learned that WTO members were not very favorably disposed to diluting intellectual property rights in favor of creating cheaper generic drugs in the least developed countries.

Article III *National Treatment on Internal Taxation and Regulation*

. . .

(2) The products of the territory of any contracting party imported into the territory of any other contracting party shall not be subject, directly or indirectly, to internal taxes or other internal charges of any kind in excess of those applied, directly or indirectly, to like domestic products.

A tariff increases the cost of selling a particular product in a foreign market. A domestic business in that market obviously does not have to pay any import tariff. It can compete without having to factor in a tariff on its products. If a US company wants to sell steel to Germany, for example, the latter's tariff on that steel is an added cost of doing business in Germany for the American company. German steel producers do not have to pay this same cost in their internal German market. If the international steel market is very competitive, then price differences will normally be minimal. Thus, Germany's tariff may present an insurmountable cost barrier making it unprofitable for a US company to sell steel in the German steel market.

The amount of a *disclosed* tariff can be considered when an international seller is deciding whether the country imposing that tariff would be an efficient market for its products. In addition to direct import tariffs, the importing country might impose an indirect barrier to trade. This would be a NTB to competition for that product. NTBs protect local industries from foreign competition. They create another cost, above that already assessed on the imported product by the published import tax.

Article III(2) prohibits such indirect barriers on imports. If the importing company has already paid an express tax (tariff) on its product, then its cost of doing such business should be transparent—rather than being hidden in the form of some costly restriction imposed after the product has already been taxed via the importing nation's scheduled tariff rate.

Assume that a US steel company determines that, after accounting for the German tariff, it is still profitable to export its American-made steel to the German market. Representatives of the German steel industry then convince the German legislature to enact a law, which requires new inspections for structural defects in steel. This new law applies only to *foreign* steel imported into Germany. The US steel company must now pay the added cost of this new inspection procedure. This law is a prohibited NTB. It discriminates against foreign steel producers without imposing a like cost of doing business on domestic German steel producers.

There are various forms of NTB. The simplest is a quota on the quantity of foreign imports from a particular country. Another example is the "buy national" law. It provides economic incentives to local consumers to buy domestically made products which are in competition with foreign-made products. There is also the dual-purpose protectionist NTB. The US Congress, for example, passed environmental protection legislation in 1986 that discriminated against foreign oil. Congress thereby created a new tax on oil to establish the "Superfund" for cleaning up US waste-disposal sites. The tax was set at 11.7 cents per barrel of *imported* oil, but only 8.2 cents per barrel for *domestic* oil. Many oil-exporting States complained that this was an indirect tariff on their oil sold in the United States. A GATT dispute panel found that this tax violated the GATT, because it was an NTB competition from foreign oil. The United States accepted the findings of the GATT panel and changed the law. [43]

NTBs can discriminate against foreign imports in even more subtle ways. A good example, although arising in a non-GATT context, was a French tax struck down in 1985 by the European Court of Justice. France had imposed a tax on automobiles based on their horsepower. This special French tax applied only to automobiles with a very high horsepower. It was five times the tax imposed on cars with the usual horsepower for cars in France. French automobile makers effectively could not be subject to this tax, because none made vehicles with this high rate of horsepower. Although the French tax law purportedly applied to all automobile makers, its actual impact was limited to foreign makers. France was required to repeal this tax. It was an unlawful NTB to international trade within the European Community, which effectively imposed higher costs on foreign enterprises doing business in the French market.[44]

Article VI *Dumping*

The contracting parties recognize that . . . dumping, by which products of one country are introduced into the commerce of another country at less than the normal value of the products, is to be condemned if it causes or threatens material injury to an established industry in the territory of a contracting party or materially retards the establishment of a domestic industry. . . .

A nation may not "dump" its products onto another nation's market at a price below the *fair market value* at which it is sold in the exporting or third countries. Such conduct normally "causes or threatens material injury to an established industry." Dumping is the type of business conduct that most likely "retards the establishment of a domestic industry" where none is already present in the target market. Cheaper imports are one of the common benefits of participation in the WTO regime.

This antidumping provision controls predatory business plans, such as those designed to initially flood a foreign market with cheap imports. These are first sold at a price below their value (after considering shipping and insurance costs). Upon capturing the foreign market, the importer is then in a position to charge a monopolistic price. Alternatively, there may already be domestic producers of the same product. "Dumping" into the foreign market is designed to manipulate the elasticity of demand, so that consumers will stop buying the domestically made product in favor of the import. When the

local manufacturer goes out of business, or shifts production to a different product, then the foreign company is in a position to raise prices. The increase is more readily accomplished when a dumped product is the only one available—given the absence of competition from former domestic producers.

Should an entity within the exporting nation be suspected of dumping, the importing nation "shall be free . . . suspend the obligation in whole or part or to withdraw or modify the concession." It may thus initiate a Safeguard Measure, when it objectively determines "that such product is being imported into its territory in such increased quantities, absolute or relative to [its] domestic production, and under such conditions as to cause or threaten to cause serious injury to the domestic industry that produced like . . . competitive products."[45]

The United States, for example, instituted a safeguard measure on a wide range of steel imports in 2000, because of the struggling US steel industry. The US measure thereby imposed extra tariffs on foreign steel imports into the United States. The EU responded by threatening to impose counter tariffs on US steel exports. It also filed an action in the WTO. In November 2003, the WTO Appellate Body definitively ruled that the US safeguard measures were, instead, a violation of GATT Article XIX and its related Safeguards Agreement. Both prohibit tariffs designed to subsidize local industry in a way that adversely impacts like products from abroad. President Bush's Trade Representative later claimed that the President had independently reversed course. The President no doubt realized that to ignore the WTO ruling would invite other nations to ignore other rulings in favor of the United States.[46]

Article VI *Countervailing Duties*

In order to offset or prevent dumping, a contracting party may levy on any dumped product an antidumping duty not greater in amount than the margin of dumping in respect to such product.

A State may *augment* its scheduled (published) tariff concession on a product when it determines that imports are being dumped onto its domestic markets. This is an antidumping or countervailing "duty" which is a special tax imposed on imports in addition to the usual tariff for that commodity. The purpose is to offset the anti-competitive effect of the dumped product.[47] The importing State thus elevates the cost of exporting the offending product into the "dumped" market to a level that approximates their normal cost.

A major change from the former GATT to the "New GATT" (*i.e.*, WTO process) is the introduction of the more specific "Agreements on Implementation of the General Agreement on Tariffs and Trade." This new feature embodies the results of the seven-year Uruguay Round of GATT negotiations. Article 3.5 of the Agreement on Implementation of Article VI provides as follows:

> It must be demonstrated that the dumped imports are, through the effects of dumping . . . causing injury within the meaning of this Agreement. The demonstration of a causal relationship between the dumped imports and the injury to the domestic industry shall [include] . . . any known factors other than the dumped imports which . . . are injuring the domestic industry, and the injuries caused by these other factors [such as contraction of demand, developments in technology, or domestic productivity].

Such implementing agreements clarify what factors should (and should not) affect the WTO's determination of whether dumping is actually occurring. They also facilitate the determination of whether dumping is in fact *causing* harm to the importing market's domestic industry.

Dumping accusations are regularly voiced when the importing nation learns that the exporting nation has somehow subsidized a product. With this government assistance, the product becomes marketable at a price that gives the exporting nation's company an improper financial advantage over makers of that product in the importing nation. The advantage makes a product competitive in a foreign market, because it may be sold comparatively cheaply. But subsidies are not known for being transparent. Thus, related litigation often turns on the issue of whether the government involvement constitutes a subsidy. When it is, the importing nation is authorized to levy a countervailing duty on the product. This type of sanction adjusts for the foreign government's interference with unadulterated market forces.[48]

In 1995, for example, an Australian federal court examined Pakistan's price-fixing policy. Pakistan indirectly assisted Pakistani cotton manufacturers, who were thus able to buy raw materials at a price lower than fair-market value in the global market. Although the Australian trial and appellate courts did not find that Pakistani policy sired an unfair "subsidy," the appellate court noted that this particular subsidy did not violate the above antidumping regime. On the facts of this case, the Pakistani government's assistance did not constitute an illegal subsidy because "there was no material injury to an Australian industry producing like goods."[49] Put another way, an exporter can dump at will, as long as in so doing there is no anticompetitive impact in the target market.

The following case demonstrates an actual application of antidumping duties. It arose in the intriguing context of continuing duties, originally imposed on a "Yugoslavian" business entity, after "Yugoslavia" no longer existed:

---

www **Belgian State and Banque Indosuez and Others**

COURT OF JUSTICE OF THE
EUROPEAN COMMUNITIES JUDGMENT
OF THE COURT C-177/96 (1997)
<http://curia.eu.int/en/content/juris/index.htm>
Go to course Web page at
<http://home.att.net/~slomansonb/txtcsesite.html>.
Under Chapter Thirteen, click Banque Indosuez.

INTELLECTUAL PROPERTY

A number of the WTO's cases have dealt with intellectual property issues. This field of the law involves copyright, trademark, and patent issues. There is a growing concern by property owners that their property rights are being diluted as foreign business enterprises do the following: pirate books, films, and videos in the copyright arena; dilute trademarks by opening stores and marketing goods or services which are identified with a particular trademark; and mass produce generic drugs with different names but the identical patented ingredients.

The WTO's August 2001 trademark ruling involving Barcardi rum's confiscated property is an example. It effectively acquiesced in the anti-Cuban US embargo of Cuba (Helms-Burton §13.1), over objections by the EU. The WTO panel found no inconsistency between US law and the WTO's Trade Related Aspects of Intellectual

Property Agreement (TRIPS later) because "TRIPS doesn't regulate the question of the determination of the ownership of intellectual property rights."[50]

In a primer prepared by prominent international intellectual property practitioners, the past chair of the Intellectual Property Committee of both the Section of International Law and Practice and the Antitrust Section of the American Bar Association describes this phenomenon as follows:

> Innovation and product differentiation are essential to competitiveness in a global economy. The costs of constant innovation and product differentiation are exceedingly high and the rewards are uncertain. Participation in such a high-cost risk environment can only be justified by the potential for rewards commensurate with the risks. The protection of intellectual property rights in innovation and product differentiation is essential to reward the entrepreneurs taking these risks.
>
> Innovative industries producing goods and services driven by intellectual property protection compromise a critical sector of, not only the U.S. economy, but also the economies of other developed countries. Indeed, intellectual property protection is arguably a necessary element for the transition of developing nations to advanced industrial economies. In any event, American innovators, particularly those in export-oriented industries such as the computer, entertainment, medical and pharmaceutical industries, are frequently confronted by massive piracy and other infringements of their intellectual property rights which undermine their expenditures on research, development and product differentiation.
>
> The challenge of the Uruguay Round was to sell the vision of intellectual property protection as the engine for innovation and development to countries which see themselves as the victims rather than the beneficiaries of intellectual property protection.[51]

The following intellectual property provisions yield a snapshot of some of the key rights, which are legally protected by WTO members:

Agreement on Trade-related Aspects of Intellectual Property Rights

WORLD TRADE ORGANIZATION TEXT (1995), ANNEX 1C
<http://www.wto.org/english/docs_e/legal_e/27-trips.pdf>

Article 1
Nature and Scope of Obligations
1. Members shall give effect to the provisions of this Agreement. . . . Members shall be free to determine the appropriate method of implementing the provisions of this Agreement within their own legal system and practice.

. . .

Article 8
Principles
1. Members may, in formulating or amending their laws and regulations, adopt measures necessary to protect public health and nutrition, and to promote the public interest in sectors of vital importance to their socio-economic and technological development, provided that such measures are consistent with the provisions of this Agreement.

. . .

Article 14
Protection of Performers, Producers of Phonograms (Sound Recordings) and Broadcasting Organizations
1. In respect of a fixation of their performance on a phonogram, performers shall have the possibility of preventing the following acts when undertaken without their authorization: the fixation of their unfixed performance and the reproduction of such fixation. Performers shall also have the possibility of preventing the following acts when undertaken without their authorization: the broadcasting by wireless means and the communication to the public of their live performance.

. . .

Article 16
Rights Conferred

1. The owner of a registered trademark shall have the exclusive right to prevent all third parties not having the owner's consent from using in the course of trade identical or similar signs for goods or services which are identical or similar to those in respect of which the trademark is registered where such use would result in a likelihood of confusion. In case of the use of an identical sign for identical goods or services, a likelihood of confusion shall be presumed. The rights described above shall not prejudice any existing prior rights, nor shall they affect the possibility of Members making rights available on the basis of use.

. . .

Article 23
Additional Protection for Geographical Indications for Wines and Spirits

1. Each Member shall provide the legal means for interested parties to prevent use of a geographical indication identifying wines for wines not originating in the place indicated by the geographical indication in question or identifying spirits for spirits not originating in the place indicated by the geographical indication in question, even where the true origin of the goods is indicated or the geographical indication is used in translation or accompanied by expressions such as "kind", "type", "style", "imitation" or the like.

. . .

Article 27
Patentable Subject Matter

1. . . . [P]atents shall be available for any inventions, whether products or processes, in all fields of technology, provided that they are new, involve an inventive step and are capable of industrial application. . . .

2. Members may exclude from patentability inventions, the prevention within their territory of the commercial exploitation of which is necessary to protect *ordre public* or morality, including to protect human, animal or plant life or health or to avoid serious prejudice to the environment, provided that

such exclusion is not made merely because the exploitation is prohibited by their law.

3. Members may also exclude from patentability:
   (a) diagnostic, therapeutic and surgical methods for the treatment of humans or animals;
   (b) plants and animals other than micro-organisms, and essentially biological processes for the production of plants or animals other than non-biological and microbiological processes. . . .

Article 28
Rights Conferred

1. A patent shall confer on its owner the following exclusive rights:
   (a) where the subject matter of a patent is a *product,* to prevent third parties not having the owner's consent from the acts of: making, using, offering for sale, selling, or importing for these purposes that product;
   (b) where the subject matter of a patent is a *process,* to prevent third parties not having the owner's consent from the act of using the process, and from the acts of: using, offering for sale, selling, or importing for these purposes at least the product obtained directly by that process.

. . .

Article 31
Other Use Without Authorization of the Right Holder

Where the law of a Member allows for other use of the subject matter of a patent without the authorization of the right holder, including use by the government or third parties authorized by the government, the following provisions shall be respected:

. . .

   (b) such use may only be permitted if, prior to such use, the proposed user has made efforts to obtain authorization from the right holder on reasonable commercial terms and conditions and that such efforts have not been successful within a reasonable period of time. This requirement may be waived by a Member in the case of a national emergency or other circumstances of extreme urgency or in cases of public non-commercial use. In situations of national emergency or other circumstances of extreme urgency, the right holder shall, nevertheless, be notified as soon as reasonably practicable.

. . .

(h) the right holder shall be paid adequate remuneration in the circumstances of each case, taking into account the economic value of the authorization;

(i) the legal validity of any decision relating to the authorization of such use shall be subject to judicial review or other independent review by a distinct higher authority in that Member [nation's judicial or other appropriate authority].

. . .

Article 41
[Enforcement of Intellectual Property Rights]

1. Members shall ensure that enforcement procedures as specified in this Part are available under their law so as to permit effective action against any act of infringement of intellectual property rights covered by this Agreement, including expeditious remedies to prevent infringements and remedies which constitute a deterrent to further infringements. These procedures shall be applied in such a manner as to avoid the creation of barriers to legitimate trade and to provide for safeguards against their abuse.

. . .

4. Parties to a proceeding shall have an opportunity for review by a judicial authority of final administrative decisions and, subject to jurisdictional provisions in a Member's law concerning the importance of a case. . . .

In May 2001, the UN World Health Organization debated whether to adopt an extraordinary proposal to extend access to inexpensive generic HIV/AIDS drugs to affected people. Brazil proposed that locally produced, cheaper generics should be available to save the lives of infected individuals. The European Community's, the United States', and other developed nations' representatives presented the objections on behalf of multinational producers of brand-name products. The World Health Organization's March 2000 study in Geneva provides an informative assessment of the underpinnings of the relationship between health and intellectual property rights.[52]

Six months later, a WTO Ministerial Conference tendered the following response:

Declaration on the TRIPS Agreement and Public Health
WT/MIN(01)/DEC/2 Adopted on 14 November 2001
<http://www.wto.org/english/thewto_e/minist_e/min01_e/mindecl_trips_e.htm>

1. We recognize the gravity of the public health problems afflicting many developing and least-developed countries, especially those resulting from HIV/AIDS, tuberculosis, malaria and other epidemics.

2. We stress the need for the WTO Agreement on Trade-Related Aspects of Intellectual Property Rights (TRIPS Agreement) to be part of the wider national and international action to address these problems.

3. We recognize that intellectual property protection is important for the development of new medicines.

We also recognize the concerns about its effects on prices.

4. We agree that the TRIPS Agreement does not and should not prevent Members from taking measures to protect public health. Accordingly, while reiterating our commitment to the TRIPS Agreement, we affirm that the Agreement can and should be interpreted and implemented in a manner supportive of WTO Members' right to protect public health and, in particular, to promote access to medicines for all.

. . .

5. Accordingly and in the light of paragraph 4 above, while maintaining our commitments in the TRIPS Agreement, we recognize that these flexibilities include:

. . .

c. Each Member has the right to determine what constitutes a national emergency or other circumstances of extreme urgency, it being understood that public health crises, including those relating to HIV/AIDS, tuberculosis, malaria and other epidemics, can represent a national emergency or other circumstances of extreme urgency.

d. The effect of the provisions in the TRIPS Agreement . . . leave[s] each Member free to establish its own regime . . . , subject to the MFN and national treatment provisions of Articles 3 and 4 [set forth above, under general WTO obligations].

6. We recognize that WTO members with insufficient or no manufacturing capacities in the pharmaceutical sector could face difficulties in making effective use of compulsory licensing under the TRIPS Agreement. . . .

7. We reaffirm the commitment of developed-country Members to provide incentives to their enterprises and institutions to promote and encourage technology transfer to least-developed country Members pursuant to Article 66.2. We also agree that the *least-developed country Members* will *not be obliged,* with respect to *pharmaceutical products,* to *implement* or apply . . . the *TRIPS* Agreement or to enforce rights provided for under these Sections *until 1 January 2016,* without prejudice to the right of least-developed country Members to seek other extensions of the transition periods as provided for in Article 66.1 of the TRIPS Agreement [italics added].

. . .

In September 2003, the WTO clarified its position regarding the exceptional circumstances necessary for justifying waivers from obligations set forth in the TRIPS Agreement for pharmaceutical products, mentioned earlier. Eligible importing States must notify the Council for TRIPS of the names and expected quantities of the product needed, and confirm eligibility for the special developing country emergency waivers.[53]

In March 2005, India's lower legislative house approved a more restrictive patent bill that health groups opposed. They claimed that it could increase drug prices for millions of people suffering from diseases including AIDS. Prior law allows Indian pharmaceutical firms to copy patented drugs, as long as they use a different process than the foreign patent holder. If this measure becomes law, patent holders would have more rights, at the expense of local generic drug manufacturers. Life-saving generic drugs would apparently no longer be available at affordable prices. India is one of the world's largest producers of generic drugs.[54]

Having studied the background and institutional framework for the WTO, the following case provides a valuable snapshot of an actual pharmaceutical trade dispute. It pits the United States against India in the very sensitive context of the WTO supposedly protecting the intellectual property rights of its developed State members—while attempting to provide sufficient flexibility to permit the expanded availability of generic pharmaceuticals poor countries need for their inhabitants to survive:

India—Patent Protection for Pharmaceutical and Agricultural Chemical Products

WORLD TRADE ORGANIZATION APPELLATE BODY REPORT
WT/DS50/AB/R 19 DECEMBER 1997
India, *Appellant* United States, *Appellee* European Communities, *Third Participant*
Go to course Web site at:
<http://home.att.net/~slomansonb/txtcsesite.html>.
Under Chapter 13, click <u>WTO TRIPS Intellectual Property Case.</u>

The current DOHA round, however, has not met its initial expectations. The frustration is not limited to the inability to develop a widely acceptable patent-pharmaceutical regime for poor countries, desperately in need of cheap generic drugs for AIDS and other diseases. Participants had also hoped to implement various controls for e-commerce, and international antitrust, no news of which has been negotiated to a common level of satisfaction.[55] In fact, a prominent 2003 report on the WTO predicted many unfortunate developments, including: (a) that the Most-Favored Nation clause had been degraded into an exception amidst the "Spaghetti bowl of Preferential Trade Agreement deals;" (b) that sovereignty was the "matra, red-herring" for protectionism; and (c) problematic retaliation mechanisms due to economic asymmetries between the WTO's rich and poor nations.[56]

One could succinctly sum up the essential problem with the current Doha Round of WTO negotiations, and arguably all others, as offered by the Australian Bond University Professor Ross Buckley: "The challenge does not lie principally in knowing how to improve the multilateral trading system but in summoning the political will to do it. Global prosperity depends on politicians of all nations putting the common good of all their constituents above the interests of selected groups of constituents. The peculiar political challenge is that in all countries[,] vested interest groups will fight far, far harder to not be prejudiced by trade liberalization than the average person will fight to benefit from it."[57]

GLOBALIZATION FISSURE

The majority of WTO member States are developing nations. Between the 1950s and 1980s, many of them had employed trade policies, which included high tariffs and NTBs to protect their emerging industries. As the WTO's roots were blooming in the 1990s, however, it was evident that they would have to liberalize their trade regimes. Failure to join the WTO would marginalize a nation's economy and discourage foreign investment. The developing nations thus made dramatic changes in their economic and development strategies, with a view toward becoming competitive in international trade by developing export-oriented industries. One result was that they would also attract *globally* competitive industries.[58]

The NGO-driven November 1999 "Battle of Seattle" was the site for the 1999 annual meeting of the WTO's trade ministers. This popular protest focused worldwide attention on the "globalization problem"—the liberalized trading processes associated with creation of the WTO (1995). Most protestors did not object to free trade as such. They focused on the severe cutbacks in government spending in health service, education, wages, and farm subsidies, which have negatively impacted living standards in nearly eighty countries. The related objection was the perceived corporate dominance of the methodology for creating worldwide trade rules by the unelected WTO administration. The "undemocratic" corporate influence was viewed as the catalyst for continuing economic colonization of the developing members of the international community. Coupled with IMF and World Bank policies, developing countries were thus perceived as being fully dependent upon their industrialized big brothers. The protest focused on the claim that the real beneficiary of globalization, who had encouraged the developing nation trade liberalization of the 1990s, was multinational corporate enterprise.

The following two excerpts provide fascinating insight into the respective authors' views on how globalization has, and will, evolve:

World on Fire: How Exporting Free Market Democracy Breeds Ethnic Hatred and Global Instability

Professor Amy Chua, Yale Law School
(New York: Anchor Books, 2004)

This book is about a phenomenon-pervasive outside the West yet rarely acknowledged, indeed often viewed as taboo—that turns free market democracy into an engine of ethnic conflagration. The phenomenon I refer to is that of *market-dominant minorities:* ethnic minorities who, for widely varying reasons, tend under market conditions to dominate economically, often to a startling extent, the "indigenous" majorities around them.

Market-dominant minorities can be found in every corner of the world. The Chinese are a market-dominant minority not just in the Philippines but throughout Southeast Asia. In 1998, Chinese Indonesians, only 3 percent of the population, controlled roughly 70 percent of Indonesia's private economy, including all of the country's largest conglomerates. More recently, in Burma, entrepreneurial Chinese have literally taken over the economies of Mandalay and Rangoon. Whites are a market-dominant minority in South Africa—and, in a more complicated sense, in Brazil, Ecuador, Guatemala, and much of Latin America. Lebanese are a market-dominant minority in West Africa. Ibo are a market-dominant minority in Nigeria. Croats were a market-dominant minority in the former Yugoslavia. And Jews are almost certainly a market-dominant minority in post-Communist Russia.

Market-dominant minorities are the Achilles' heel of free market democracy. In societies with a market-dominant ethnic minority, markets and democracy favor not just different people, or different classes, but different ethnic groups. Markets concentrate wealth, often spectacular wealth, in the hands of the market-dominant minority, while democracy increases the political power of the impoverished majority. In these circumstances the pursuit of free market democracy becomes an engine of potentially catastrophic ethnos nationalism, pitting a frustrated "indigenous" majority, easily aroused by opportunistic vote-seeking politicians, against a resented, wealthy ethnic minority. This confrontation is playing out in country after country today, from Indonesia to Sierra Leone, from Zimbabwe to Venezuela, from Russia to the Middle East.

Since September 11, 2001, this confrontation has also been playing out in the United States. Americans are not an ethnic minority (although we are a national-origin minority, a close cousin). Nor is there democracy at the global level. Nevertheless, Americans today are everywhere perceived as the world's market-dominant minority, wielding outrageously disproportionate economic power relative to our size and numbers. As a result, we have become the object; of mass, popular resentment and hatred of the same kind that is directed at so many other market-dominant minorities around the world.

Global anti-Americanism has many causes. One of them, ironically, is the global spread of free markets and democracy. Throughout the world, global markets are bitterly perceived as reinforcing American wealth and dominance. At the same time, global populist and democratic movements give strength, legitimacy, and voice to the impoverished, frustrated, excluded masses of the world-precisely the people, in other words, most susceptible to anti-American demagoguery. In more non-Western countries than Americans would care to admit, free and fair elections would bring to power anti-market, anti-American leaders. For the last twenty years Americans have been grandly promoting both marketization and democratization throughout the world. In the process we have directed at ourselves the anger of the damned.

The relationship between free market democracy and ethnic violence around the world is inextricably bound up with globalization. But the phenomenon of market-dominant minorities introduces complications that have escaped the view of both globalization's enthusiasts and its critics.

To a great extent, globalization consists of, and is fueled by, the unprecedented worldwide spread of markets and democracy. For over two decades now, the American government, along with American consultants, business interests, and foundations, has been vigorously promoting free market democracy throughout the developing and post-socialist worlds. At times our efforts have bordered on the absurd. There is, for example, the sad tale of delegation of American free market advisers in Mongolia. Just before they leave the country, the Americans are thrilled when a Mongolian official asks them to send more copies of the voluminous U.S. securities, laws, photocopied on one side of the page. Alas, it turned out that the Mongolian was interested in the documents not for their content, but for the blank side of each page, which would help alleviate the government's chronic paper shortage.

. . .

In the end, however, stories about American naiveté and incompetence are just a side show. The fact is that in the last two decades, the American-led global spread of markets and democracy has radically transformed the world. Both directly and through powerful international institutions like the World Bank, International Monetary Fund, and World Trade Organization (WTO), the United States government has helped bring capitalism and democratic elections to literally billions of people. At the same time, American multinationals, foundations, and nongovernmental organizations (NGOs) have swept the world, bringing with them ballot boxes and Burger Kings, hip-hop and Hollywood, banking codes and American-drafted constitutions.

The prevailing view among globalization's supporters is that markets and democracy are a kind of universal prescription for the multiple ills of underdevelopment. Market capitalism is the most efficient economic system the world has ever known. Democracy is the fairest political system the world has ever known and the one most respectful of individual liberty. Working hand in hand, markets and democracy will gradually transform the world into a community of prosperous, war-shunning nations, and individuals into liberal, civic-minded citizens and consumers. In the process, ethnic hatred, religious zealotry, and other "backward" aspects of underdevelopment will be swept away.

For globalization's enthusiasts, the cure for group hatred and ethnic violence around the world is straightforward: more markets and more democracy. Thus after the September 11 attacks, Friedman published an op-ed piece pointing to India and Bangladesh as good "role models" for the Middle East and arguing that the solution to terrorism and militant Islam is: "Hello? Hello? There's a message here. It's democracy, stupid!"— "[m]ulti-ethnic, pluralistic, free-market democracy."

By contrast, the sobering thesis of this book is that the global spread of markets and democracy is a principal, aggravating cause of group hatred and ethnic violence throughout the non-Western world. In the numerous societies around the world that have a market-dominant minority, markets and democracy are not mutually reinforcing. Because markets and democracy benefit different ethnic groups in such societies, the pursuit of free market democracy produces highly unstable and combustible conditions. Markets concentrate enormous wealth in the hands of an "outsider" minority, fomenting ethnic envy and hatred among often chronically poor minorities. In absolute terms the majority may or may not be better off—a dispute that much of the globalization debate fixates on—but any sense of improvement is overwhelmed by their continuing poverty and the hated minority's extraordinary economic success. More humiliating still, market-dominant minorities, along with their foreign-investor partners, invariably come to control the crown jewels of the economy, often symbolic of the nation's patrimony and identity—oil in Russia and Venezuela, diamonds in South Africa, silver and tin in Bolivia, jade, teak, and rubies in Burma.

Introducing democracy in these circumstances does not transform voters into open-minded co-citizens in a national community. Rather, the competition for votes fosters the emergence of demagogues who scapegoat the resented minority and foment active ethnonationalist movements demanding that the country's wealth and identity be reclaimed by the "true owners of the nation." As America celebrated the global spread of democracy in the 1990's, ethicized political slogans proliferated: "Georgia for the Georgians," "Eritreans out of Ethiopia," "Kenya for Kenyans," "Whites should leave Bolivia," "Kazakhstan for Kazakhs," "Serbia for Serbs," "Croatia for Croats," "Hutu Power," "Assam for Assamese," "Jews out of Russia." Romania's 2001 presidential candidate Vadim Tudor was not quite so pithy. "I'm Vlad the Impaler," he campaigned; referring to the historically economically dominant Hungarian minority, he promised: "We will hang them directly by their Hungarian tongue!"

When free market democracy is pursued in the presence of a market-dominant minority; the almost invariable result is backlash. This backlash typically takes one of three forms. The fist is a backlash against markets, targeting the market-dominant minority's wealth. The second is a backlash against democracy by forces favorable to the market-dominant minority. The third is violence, sometimes genocidal, directed against the market-dominant minority itself.

. . .

In the contest between an economically powerful ethnic minority and a numerically powerful impoverished majority, the majority does not always prevail. Instead of a backlash against the market, another likely outcome is a backlash against democracy, favoring the market-dominant minority at the expense of majority will. Examples of this dynamic are extremely common. Indeed, . . . the world's most notorious cases of "crony capitalism" all involve a market-dominant ethnic minority-from Ferdinand Marcos's Chinese-protective dictatorship in the Philippines to President Siaka Stevens's shadow alliance with five Lebanese diamond dealers in Sierra Leone to President Daniel Arap Moi's "business arrangements" with a handful of Indian tycoons in Kenya today.

The . . . most ferocious kind of backlash is majority-supported violence aimed at eliminating a market-dominant minority. Two recent examples are the ethnic cleansing of Croats in the former Yugoslavia and the mass slaughter of Tutsi in Rwanda. In both cases a resented and disproportionately prosperous ethnic minority was attacked by members of a relatively impoverished majority, incited by an ethnos nationalist government. In other words, markets and democracy were among the causes of both the Rwandan and Yugoslavian genocides. . . .

To their credit, critics of globalization have called attention to the grotesque imbalances that free markets produce. In the 1990's, writes Thomas Frank in *One Market under God,* global markets made "the corporation the most powerful institution on earth, transformed CEOs as a class into one of the wealthiest elites of all time," and, from America to Indonesia, "forgot about the poor with a decisiveness we hadn't seen since the 1920's." Joining Frank in his criticism of "the almighty market" is a host of strange bedfellows: American farmers and factory workers opposed to NAFTA, environmentalists, the AFL-CIO, human rights activists, Third World advocates, and sundry other groups that made up the protesters at Seattle, Davos, Genoa, and New York Defenders of globalization respond, with some justification, that the world's poor would be even worse off without global marketization. With some important exceptions, including most of Africa, recent World Bank studies shows that globalization's 'trickle down' has produced benefits for the poor as well as the rich in developing countries."

. . .

Essentially, the anti-globalization movement asks for one thing: more democracy. Thus Noam Chomsky, one of the movement's high priests, has clarified that there is no struggle against "globalization" in the general sense, only a struggle against the global "neoliberalism" perpetuated by a few "masters of the universe" at the expense of a truly democratic community. Similarly, at the 2002 World Social Forum in Brazil, Lori Wallach of Public Citizen rejected the label "anti-globalization," explaining that "our movement, really, is globally for democracy, equality, diversity, justice and quality of life." Wallach has also warned that the WTO must "either bend to the will of the people worldwide or it will break." Echoing these voices are literally dozens of NGOS's who call for "democratically empowering the poor majorities of the world."

Given the ethnic dynamics of the developing world, and in particular the phenomenon of market-dominant minorities, merely "empowering the poor majorities of the world" is not enough. Empowering the Hutu majority in Rwanda did not produce desirable consequences. Nor did empowering the Serbian majority in Serbia.

Critics of globalization are right to demand that more attention be paid to the enormous wealth disparities created by global markets. But just as it is dangerous to view markets as the panacea for the world's poverty and strife, so to it is dangerous to see democracy as a, panacea. Markets and democracy may well offer the best long-run economic and political hope for developing and post-Communist societies. In the short run, however, they are part of the problem.

. . .

Will the Nation–State Survive Globalization?

Martin Wolf

Financial Times Associate Editor

80 FOREIGN AFFAIRS 178 (2001)

DEFINING GLOBALIZATION

A specter is haunting the world's governments—the specter of globalization. Some argue that predatory market forces make it impossible for benevolent governments to shield their populations from the beasts of prey that lurk beyond their borders. Others counter that benign market forces actually prevent predatory governments from fleecing their [own] citizens. . . . But is it true that governments have become weaker and less relevant than ever before? And does globalization, by definition, have to be the nemesis of national government?

. . .

CHOOSING GLOBALIZATION

Globalization is not destined, it is chosen. It is a choice made to enhance a nation's economic well-being—indeed, experience suggests that the opening of trade and of most capital flows enriches most citizens in the short run and virtually all citizens in the long run.

. . .

The policy change that has most helped global integration to flourish is the growth of international institutions since World War II. Just as multinational companies now organize private exchange, so global institutions organize and discipline the international face of national policy. Institutions such as the World Trade Organization (WTO), the International Monetary Fund (IMF), the World Bank, the EU, and the North American Free Trade Agreement underpin cooperation among states and consolidate their commitments to liberalize economic policy. The nineteenth century was a world of unilateral and discretionary policy. The late twentieth century, be comparison, was a world of multilateral and institutionalized policy.

. . .

THE CONTINUING IMPORTANCE OF STATES

A country that chooses international economic integration implicitly accepts constraints on its actions. . . .

For example, the assumption that most governments are benevolent welfare-maximizers is naive. International economic integration creates competition among governments—even countries that fiercely resist integration cannot survive with uncompetitive economies, as shown by the fate of the Soviet Union. This competition constrains the ability of governments to act in a predatory manner and increases the incentive to provide services that are valued by those who pay the bulk of the taxes.

. . .

What, then, does globalization mean for states? . . . [I]nternational economic integration magnifies the impact of the difference between good and bad states–between states that provide public goods and those that serve predatory private interests, including those of the rulers.

Finally, as the world economy continues to integrate and cross-border flows become more important, global governance must be improved. Global governance will come not at the expense of the state but rather as an expression of the interests that the state embodies. As the source of order and basis of governance, the state will remain in the future as effective, and will be as essential, as it has ever been.

◆ 13.3 REGIONAL ECONOMIC ASSOCIATIONS

Chapter 3 analyzed various categories of international organizations of States. That material introduced the essential characteristics of such associations, focusing on military and political associations of States. This section of the text concentrates on *economic* associations of States.

REGIONAL ANATOMY

There is a diverse array of economic organizational structures. *Regional* economic organizations virtually eclipsed the importance of global devices like the General Agreement on Tariffs and Trade before the 1995 appearance of the World Trade Organization. The analysis might begin with the basic objectives of the particular economic network. The following are the fundamental categories, in ascending order of degree of integration:

◆ *Preferential trade.* Trade preferences are granted in the form of freer access to the respective members' markets. This is the most basic form of trade association. The United States negotiated this form of agreement with its Caribbean neighbors in the 1983 Caribbean Basin Initiative.

◆ *Free trade area.* Tariffs between the member States are initially reduced and ultimately eliminated. Each member may keep its original tariffs, as against countries outside of the free trade area. There is no organized policy among the members as to other countries. The North American Free Trade Agreement among Canada, Mexico, and the United States is an example.

◆ *Customs union.* The members liberalize trade among themselves, while erecting a common tariff barrier against all nonmember States. The 1969 South African Customs Union is an example.

◆ *Common market.* Usually after a customs union has been established, the members remove restrictions on the internal movement of the means of production and distribution of all commodities. The EU is the most successful of all common markets.

◆ *Economic union.* This is a common market which includes a unified fiscal and monetary policy within the union. The result is similar to the linkage among the fifty states of the United States. The difference is that an economic union consists of international States, rather than states within a federated nation. The EU made a significant step toward becoming a fully integrated economic union through the

implementation of the Single European Act commonly referred to as "1992." In 1999, the eleven members of the EU implemented a common currency for all citizens and agencies within those States. The "Euro" replaced their currency in 2002.[59]

There are numerous regional trading blocs. They function in a variety of ways. Blocs range from those that act like super-States to those that are more like political arrangements merely cast in the form of economic blocs. Many commentators characterize trade blocs as sharing a common bond—each of them, however, being the product of protectionist fears. A Washington, DC, legal practitioner offers the following assessment of the underpinnings of economic integration:

The New World Order of Regional Trade Blocs

Joseph Brand of the District of Columbia Bar

8 AMER. UNIV. J. INT'L LAW & POLICY 155–157 (1992)

. . . Our world today is dividing into trading blocs. Some have the superstructure of nation states. The European Communities (. . . the European Community), with a parliament and courts and the supremacy of Community laws over those of its members, begins to look more and more like a state; others are multinational agreements that may be more political negotiating arrangements than cohesive trading blocs. ASEAN (Association of Southeast Asian Nations) is a relevant candidate. These blocs, however strong or weak, are growing all around the world. Like the empires (from Rome to the Soviet Union) that preceded them, the regional trading blocs of the new economic world order may divide into a handful of protectionist superstates. If by the new political world order we mean increased American hegemony disguised as international cooperation, we may come to know the new economic world order as regional hegemony disguised as free trade. . . .

[A variety of reasons explain the formation of economic associations of States.] First, they are born of political fear. The European Community was proposed . . . just five years after the end of the Second World War. European unity was perceived as the antidote to European war. Fear of war gave birth to the union. Another kind of fear seems relevant to the extension of the US-Canada Free Trade Agreement into a wider hemispheric economic bloc. Critics of the North American Free Trade Agreement (Canada, Mexico, and the United States) believe fear of a successful EC 1992 and the economic eminence of Japan underlies the political imperative that moves these negotiations.

Second, blocs espouse trade liberalization internally, but achieve trade protection externally. For example, the Uruguay Round of trade liberalization is now held hostage to the Europeans' protective treatment of their farmers.

. . .

This rather bleak perspective about the motivation for regional trade groupings is not necessarily the only one. Dalhousie University (Canada) Professor Gilbert Winham espouses a different perspective. It is not as negative, and certainly more buoyant, as noted in his book on

the evolution of trade agreements: "What is the role of international trade agreement[s] in the modern nation-state system? The answer is to reduce protectionist national regulation, but even more important [it is] to reduce the uncertainty and unpredictability of the international trade regime, and to promote stability. The greatest cause of uncertainty in the contemporary trading system comes from the self-serving actions of self-interested nation states. It can be said that one nation's sovereignty is another nation's uncertainty."[60]

This perspective may explain why members of the Association of Southeast Asian Nations (ASEAN)—Brunei, Cambodia, Indonesia, Laos, Malaysia, Myanmar (Burma), Philippines, Singapore, Thailand, and Vietnam—seek regional economic stability in the form of the ASEAN trade agreement. They have thereby engaged in a joint enterprise with similarly situated powers who ultimately seek freedom from external influences over their sovereign affairs. The ASEAN members have traditionally feared Chinese and Japanese territorial aspirations in that region of the world. The ASEAN States have expressed fears that history may repeat itself. Domination by war, or by trade, has been perceived by some as a matter of degree. But the 2003 Protocol to the ASEAN agreement moved a step closer toward integrating China. The adoption of this protocol signals the progressive elimination of tariff and NTBs, liberalization of trade in services, and establishment of an open and competitive investment regime with China by 2012.[61]

Regardless of the motivation for pursuing international trade relations, economic integration is clearly going to be a prominent feature in international relations for the foreseeable future. To appreciate its current contours, Exhibit 13.2 lists the major economic associations of States and summits.

SUMMITS: ECONOMIC DIPLOMACY

The heads of State summit is another organizational structure for facilitating international economic integration. Several examples follow:

"G-8"   National leaders have used economic summits as a basis for developing special-purpose economic associations. Solidarity of approaches to a variety of problems is promoted by emphasizing trade and financial issues. For nearly twenty-five years, the leaders of the world's major industrialized democracies have met at various locations for their annual "G-7" summit.

The Group of Seven consisted of the world's richest countries: Canada, France, Japan, Germany, Great Britain, Italy, and the United States. In mid-1994, the "G-7" became the "G-8" with the admission of Russia. At the Naples meeting of the association, President

Boris Yeltsin described this occasion as a "large step to[ward] full security of peace on Earth." During the Cold War, there could be no such association. The former Soviet Union was politically opposed to democracy and to the capitalist market system. Now these two former rivals have joined in a loose economic association designed to extinguish the mistrust associated with their forty years as political adversaries.

The 1994 summit communiqué of this ostensibly economic grouping of States went much further than just economics. It contained joint positions on Bosnia, Haiti, the Middle East, and North Korea, as well as on nuclear proliferation. At the same time, the two most powerful members, Japan and the United States, are involved in a major economic confrontation over the US trade deficit and US access to Japanese markets. Nevertheless, this annual summit procedure continued to provide the opportunity for the leaders to review their drive toward a coordinated economic policy.

G-8 has endured criticisms. During the decade after the fall of the Soviet Union, G-8 was oriented toward assisting Russia in its transition to a market economy and into the global economy. It has not been very effective in reaching the goal of resisting the advance of economic and political regionalism within the community of nations. Scholars nevertheless perceive G-8 as providing leadership by institutionalizing the summit as one of the positive factors in trade globalization.[62]

Summit of the Americas   In December 1994, the heads of the western hemisphere's thirty-four democracies met in Miami for the first *Summit of the Americas*. Their goal was to convert the hemisphere into a free-trade zone called the Free Trade Area of the Americas (by 2005). The first (and last) summit on this topic was in 1967. Although the GATT has prodded freer trade since 1947, it was the 1993 NAFTA that provided the impetus for this hemispheric economic summit.

The anticipated benefit for the United States is that it will enjoy more trade within Latin America by 2010 than its combined trade with Japan and the EU. This objective also involves much more than what is expressed by its apparent economic emphasis. The Summit's final decree called for joint action to combat crime and poverty. The summit leaders further agreed, in principle, to promote environmental cooperation, democracy, and literacy.

EXHIBIT 13.2 SELECTED REGIONAL ECONOMIC ASSOCIATIONS OF STATES

Name[a]	Members and Objectives[b]
AEC	African Economic Community (1991): Economic organ of Organization of African Unity designed to promote solidarity and collective self-reliance of OAU nations[c]
ANCOM	Andean Common Market: Bolivia, Colombia, Ecuador, Peru, Venezuela: Chile withdrew (1969) as moved toward integration. Conflicting national interests have inhibited achieving common market
APEC	Asia-Pacific Economic Cooperation: Australia, Brunei, Canada, (Chile has applied), China, Hong Kong, Indonesia, Japan, Malaysia, Mexico, New Zealand, Papua New Guinea, Philippines, Singapore, South Korea, Taiwan, Thailand, United States (1990): Pacific Rim trade cooperation [d]
ASEAN	Association of Southeast Asian Nations: Brunei, Indonesia, Malaysia, Philippines, Singapore, Thailand (1976): Vietnam potential member. Promotes regional economic stability and protection from external influences (China, Japan); 1992—program to create common market responding to economic alliances in Europe, North America; 1998—Hanoi Plan of Action to address economic crisis [e] The "ASEAN + 3" pact is the arrangement between ASEAN and China, Japan, and South Korea, all of who seek full membership.
CAFTA	Central American Free Trade Agreement: Central American nations of Costa Rica, Dominican Republic, El Salvador, Guatemala, Honduras, and United States (2005). Designed to pursue enlarged free-trade area.
CARICOM	Caribbean Community and Common Market: Anguilla, Barbados, Belize, Dominica, Grenada, St. Kitts-Nevis, St. Lucia, St. Vincent, Trinidad, Tobago (1974): Elimination of internal trade barriers and common external tariff [f]
ECOWAS	Economic Community of West African States: 16 West African nations (1975): Promotes (Lagos, Nigeria) cooperation and development; seeks creation of a customs union [g]
EFTA	European Free Trade Association: Austria, Denmark, Iceland, Norway, Portugal, Sweden, Switzerland (1959): Great Britain, initially refused membership in EU, led this rival scheme before withdrawing after becoming an EU member [h]
European Union	Only free trade zone with no tariff barriers [i] (see twenty-five State listing in §3.4)
Group of Eight (G-8)	Canada, France, Germany, Great Britain, Italy, Japan, Russia, United States (1974): Annual summits on economic policies of major industrial democracies (was "G-7" before Russia joined) [j]

[a]City: headquarters for those organizations that have a permanent seat

[b](Date): when the association was originally formed

[c]Treaty available in A. Yusef (ed.), 1 AFRICAN YEARBOOK OF INT'L LAW 227 (Dordrecht, Neth.: Martinus Nijhoff, 1993)

[d]K. Okuizumi (ed.), THE US-JAPAN ECONOMIC RELATIONSHIP, IN EAST AND SOUTHEAST ASIA: A POLICY FRAMEWORK FOR ASIA PACIFIC ECONOMIC COOPERATION (Wash., DC: CSI Studies, 1992)

[e]See Framework Agreement on Enhancing ASEAN Economic Cooperation, 31 INT'L LEGAL MAT'LS 506 (1992)

[f]See A. Payne, THE POLITICS OF THE CARIBBEAN COMMUNITY, 1961–1979: REGIONAL INTEGRATION AMONG NEW STATES (New York: St. Martin's Press, 1980)

[g]See ECONOMIC COMMUNITY OF WEST AFRICAN STATES: AN OVERVIEW OF THE ECONOMIES OF WEST AFRICAN STATES (Lagos, Nigeria: ECOWAS Secretariat, n.d.)

[h]See M. Sheridan, J. CAMERON & J. TOULIN, EFTA LEGAL SYSTEMS: AN INTRODUCTORY GUIDE (London: Butterworths, 1993)

[i]See R. Folsom, EUROPEAN COMMUNITY LAW IN A NUTSHELL (St. Paul, MN: West, 1992)

[j]See A. Mep & H. Ulrich, PARTNERS FOR PROSPERITY: THE GROUP OF SEVEN AND THE EUROPEAN COMMUNITY (Upland, PA: Diane Pub., 1994)

EXHIBIT 13.2 SELECTED REGIONAL ECONOMIC ASSOCIATIONS OF STATES (CONTINUED)

Name	Members and Objectives
Gulf Cooperation Council	Bahrain, Kuwait, Oman, Qatar, Saudi Arabia, United Arab Emirates (1981): Standardized subsidies; eliminating trade barriers; negotiating with European Union and other regional organizations to obtain favorable treatment [k]
IECO (Islamabad)	Islamic Economic Cooperation Organization—Iran, Pakistan, Turkey (1964): Seven former Soviet republics joined in 1992 to promote trade among Islamic States
NAFTA	North American Free Trade Agreement: Canada, Mexico, United States (1994): Free trade zone treaty promoting reduction and elimination of tariffs and other trade barriers [l]
OECD (Paris)	Organization for Economic Cooperation and Development (1961): 24 mostly Western European industrialized States. Promotes world trade on nondiscriminatory basis for economic advancement of lesser-developed countries
OPEC (Vienna)	Organization of Petroleum Exporting Countries: Algeria, Ecuador, Gabon, Indonesia, Iran, Iraq, Kuwait, Libya, Nigeria, Qatar, Saudi Arabia, United Arab Emirates, Venezuela (1960): Control production and international pricing of oil [m]
SELA	Acronym for twenty-five nation Latin American Economic System (1975): Goal to establish system for pooling resources, creating agencies to sell resources on world market similar to OPEC
Summit of the Americas	Summit of Western Hemisphere's 34 heads of State (1994): Free Trade Area goal by 2005; 1998 Santiago Declaration and Plan of Action of second summit reaffirming 1994 Miami summit objectives

[k] *See* G. Dietl, THROUGH TWO WARS AND BEYOND: A STUDY OF THE GULF COOPERATION COUNCIL (New York: Advent, 1991)

[l] R. Folsom, M. Gordon & D. Lopez, NAFTA: A PROBLEM-ORIENTED COURSEBOOK (St. Paul, MN: WestGroup, 2000) *and* R. Folsom, NAFTA IN A NUTSHELL (4th ed. St. Paul, MN: WestGroup, 2004)

[m] *See* OPEC OFFICIAL RESOLUTIONS AND PRESS RELEASES 1960–1990 (Vienna: OPEC Secretariat, 1990)

[n] *Miami Summit:* See R. Rosenberg & S. Stein (ed.), ADVANCING THE MIAMI PROCESS: CIVIL SOCIETY AND THE SUMMIT OF THE AMERICAS (Boulder, CO: Miami Univ. North-South Center Press, 1994). *Santiago Summit:* 37 INT'L LEGAL MAT'LS 947 (1998)

The 1998 Santiago Summit of the Americas reconfirmed the Miami Summit programs. The documents signed at both summits are legally binding and signal strong political commitments by the democratic governments of the hemisphere. The Santiago Declaration builds on the first summit's aspirations: more education to improve the living conditions of its inhabitants; the commencement of negotiations for achieving the Free Trade Area of the Americas (by 2005); and renewing the struggle against corruption, money laundering, terrorism, and other impediments to trade and good relations.[63]

The Third Summit of the Americas, held in Quebec City in 2001, focused on the integration of trade and democracy. National leaders assembled to work on a hemispheric free trade agreement. Like the 1999 WTO conference in Seattle, however, thousands of protesters expressed their fear that such an agreement would be another step toward the negative characteristics of "globalization." Continuing to be concerned about lack of a more democratic process, the protesters focused on the free trade pact being negotiated behind closed doors. They set up their own summit called "The People's Summit."

Other impediments may limit the potential for implementation by the target date of 2005. Due to the summit's rather progressive environmental and worker's rights objectives, it will be more difficult for certain States in the hemisphere to adopt or implement every item contained in both final decrees' statements of intent. Further, Latin American States do not support the US policy on Cuba (§10.2), which is the only State not invited to this summit of the hemisphere's democracies.

APEC Summit In 1993, fifteen Pacific rim nations met in Seattle, Washington, for the annual Asia-Pacific Economic Cooperation (APEC) meeting. Members of this "rim" of nations all have borders with the Pacific Ocean. This was the largest of world leaders in the United States since the 1945 UN Conference in San Francisco. It also brought a great deal of attention to APEC in the aftermath of President Clinton's success in negotiating NAFTA. This economic association of States contains just over half of the world's economic production capabilities and approximately 40 percent of the world's population. For the United States, trade across the Pacific surpassed trade across the Atlantic by 1983. By 1992, Pacific trade amounted to $315 billion—one-third more than the US trade across the Atlantic.

APEC has thereby associated the world's three largest economies—China, Japan, and the United States. The 1993 summit was the first opportunity for a US president to meet a Chinese leader since the 1989 Tiananmen Square massacre. That particular event widely impacted subsequent Sino-US trade and human rights discourses. Meeting under the auspices of APEC provided an opportunity to develop a personal dialogue that could ease tensions associated with the Beijing massacre (§11.2) at a time when China was being considered for membership in the WTO.

The APEC nations established an inter-summit Group of Eminent Persons at the 1993 summit. Its task is to follow up on the declarations made at the 1993 summit. In September 1994, this group's report pronounced the objective to "commit the region to achieve trade in all goods, services, capital and investment by the year 2020 with implementation to begin by 2000." The 1994 follow-up summit in Indonesia generated the declaration that the developed members of APEC would remove such barriers by the year 2010.

This group rejected both the EU and the NAFTA trade bloc approach to economic integration. Instead, it encourages "open regionalism." APEC is willing to accept new member States—if they internationalize their economies. Unlike the EU and NAFTA, APEC does not intend to sustain trade discrimination against outsiders. It encourages APEC members to extend trade liberalization to non-APEC members.

APEC solidarity is limited by its being *the* most diverse regional economic organization of States. China has the least codified trade policies. Japan and South Korea have the most intricate NTBs to international trade. China and Taiwan are the two largest economies that were not original members of the GATT. (China immediately sought access to the WTO, while Taiwan did not). The 1993 APEC summit was boycotted by the prime minister of Malaysia, due to a concern that APEC will become a device for forcing western-style democracy and market reforms on its smaller members.

TRADE NGOS

Chapter 3 on "International Organizations," and Chapter 11 on "Human Rights," addressed the role of nongovernmental organizations (NGOs) in these respective arenas. In the current era of economic integration, NGOs are now beginning to play prominent roles in trade-related initiatives. They may start as a regional organization, which emulates global goals of State-based economic organizations.

Jubilee 2000 is a serviceable example. It is a London-based coalition of NGOs, churches, and aid agencies. Its purpose is to seek debt relief for low-income, heavily indebted States. This think-tank is drafting a comprehensive plan for addressing the debt burden of the poor and least developed nations who are seen as victims of globalization. Jubilee is thus committed to:

◆ Developing a new, more accountable, and transparent process for sovereign lending, borrowing, and debt negotiations—with human rights at the center of its focus.
◆ Highlighting and developing policies for financing development in a more self-reliant way, without recourse to dependency on foreign donors and creditors.
◆ Opening up international financial institutions and markets to democratic scrutiny and accountability by civil society.[64]

◆ 13.4 NEW INTERNATIONAL ECONOMIC ORDER

HISTORICAL EVOLUTION

During the nineteenth and twentieth centuries, multinational corporations experienced a commanding expansion that roughly coincided with the decolonization movement of the 1960s (§2.4). Parent companies thus established foreign subsidiaries with the ability to rapidly shift capital in and out of the foreign theater of operations. The foreign subsidiary was incorporated under the national laws of the host State. But the corporate operation was not thereby subject to the effective control of the host State. The corporate parent in a developed State fostered this development, while the host State assisted because it sought the infusion of foreign investment.[65] The people of the host State became more and more dependent on the multinational corporation for economic survival—especially in nations where the cost of labor was cheap due to high unemployment. The multinational corporation's arrival created and supported a job base. This presence conferred economic benefits on the underdeveloped State. It improved the quality of life for its citizens where there was high unemployment.

During the decolonization of the 1960s, many lesser-developed nations of the world sought a forum for the purpose of establishing what they perceived as being a more equitable distribution of global wealth. A deluge of underdeveloped States suddenly appeared on the international level, now armed with access to a world forum where they could express their desire for equality. Lesser-developed States began to articulate their right to economic independence by challenging the international status quo, specifically, the international legal principles on foreign investment, nationalization, and required host State compensation for nationalization. They characterized International Law as a Eurocentric web of control, spun by the more powerful members of the United Nations, to entrap their former colonial "partners."

A series of UN developments surfaced in the 1960s which forged the early statement of this "third world" position. In 1962, the UN General Assembly proclaimed the Resolution on the Permanent Sovereignty over Natural Wealth and Resources. Developing States therein complained about their required abdication of sovereignty—the price tag for encouraging foreign investment. The follow-up Resolution (1973) expressed the essence of the New International Economic Order (NIEO) movement, wherein the General Assembly expressed that it:

2. *Supports resolutely* the efforts of the developing countries and of the peoples of the territories under colonial and racial domination and foreign occupation in their struggle to regain effective control over their natural resources;

3. *Affirms* that the application of the principle of nationalization carried out by States, as an expression of their sovereignty in order to safeguard their natural resources, implies that each State is entitled to determine the amount of possible compensation and the mode of payment, and that any disputes which might rise should be settled in accordance with the national legislation of each State. . . .[66]

G-77 (Group of 77 developing nations) also prompted creation of the United Nations Conference of Trade and Development (UNCTAD) in 1966. This was a form of collective bargaining with the States that G-77 characterized as economic big brothers who were effectively dominating their existence. An UNCTAD resolution purported to demolish the basic tenet that International Law rather than national law provided the yardstick for measuring the scope of compensation for nationalized property. UNCTAD then began to promulgate a series of codes that purported to govern the conduct of multinational corporations. These included a Restrictive Business Practices Code and a Transfer of Technology Code. These were essentially guidelines for an international antitrust law, designed to equitably distribute the proceeds of multinational corporate activity in developing nations. G-77 was also able to enlist the assistance of the industrialized nation Organization for Economic Co-operation and Development (OECD) with similar Guidelines.[67] This influence would later surface in the 1974–1982 negotiations during the UN Conference on the Law of the Sea, producing provisions designed to redistribute the natural wealth found in and under the high seas (§6.3).

The corporate code of conduct theme has lost none of its relevance since it emerged in the 1960s. Today's panorama now includes the possession of comparatively sophisticated technology that divides the have and have not societies. Economic progress and international competitiveness necessitate not only access to knowledge about machines for generating goods and services. The comparatively fresh area of concern is access to expertise about acquiring knowledge itself, including patent, trademark, and patent development. The current and past UNCTAD Secretary-Generals thus describe this critical feature of the evolving code of conduct in the following terms:

International Technology Transfer: The Origins and Aftermath of the United Nations Negotiations on a Draft Code of Conduct

Rubens Ricupero & Gamani Corea

Preface xx (The Hague: Kluwer, 2001)

. . .

In a world of rapid and continuing change, eroding boundaries, multiplying interest groups and an increasingly integrating global economic system, we need to invest more time and energy in the process of constructing shared frameworks . . . that enforce a "level playing field". The objective of the draft International Code of Conduct was exactly that—to establish a shared understanding of where we want to go in matters relating to international technology transfers. The central question provoked by the initiators of the draft Code of Conduct, which is—how can we facilitate a just and mutually beneficial system of technology flows in a world of rapid change and increasing gaps in the technological capability of the developed and the developing countries—is still relevant today. . . . Around the world, the emergence of a global information society is accelerating the pace of change and [also] overwhelming establish methods of organizing production and governing societies that were developed for a world of more limited information flow . . . .

In this respect, the lessons arising from the earlier [UN] efforts to establish a Code of Conduct on the Transfer of Technology through a negotiated agreement will be valuable as we continue to seek an acceptable mechanism for the international transfer of technology. While globalization has opened opportunities, it has also generated new dangers of exclusion and marginalization across and within societies. Exclusion from accessing knowledge is one of the critical factors limiting the capacity of marginalized countries to learn, adjust and integrate effectively into the world economic system. This is not to imply "free-for-all" knowledge transfer, nor to suggest that inventors and innovators should not be adequately rewarded. To the contrary, appropriate reward for innovation is vital for knowledge generation and should be part and parcel of policies to promote the generation and transfer of knowledge. These are in brief some of the issues that will dominate any future discussion on the international transfer of technology.

In 1966, the G-77 established the United Nations Industrial Development Organization (UNIDO). UNIDO's primary objective, contained in Article 1 of its Constitution, was the "promotion and acceleration of industrial development in the developing countries with a view to assist in the establishment of a New International Economic Order."[68]

The third world's NIEO was officially announced at the United Nations in 1974. Its roots may be traced to the early years of the twentieth century. The major political and economic powers engaged in extensive overseas investment and took protective measures to ensure continued profitability. They did not conduct their business operations with a view toward improving conditions in the host countries. The decolonization movement of the 1960s did not extinguish smoldering claims that Western hegemony survived independence. The 1974 NIEO "Charter" was the platform for articulating the perspective about a more rational application of various UN Charter principles, including the following:

◆ "equal rights of . . . nations large and small" (UN Charter Preamble)
◆ "international machinery for the promotion of the economic and social advancement of all peoples" (Preamble)
◆ "international cooperation in solving international problems of an economic . . . character" (Article 1.3)
◆ "the principle of the sovereign equality of all its Members" (Article 2.1)
◆ "promoting international cooperation in the economic . . . field" (Article 13b)

◆ "the United Nations shall promote: higher standards of living . . . and conditions of economic and social progress and development" (Article 55a)

G-77 thus initiated a fresh debate on the question of whether the western foundations of modern International Law could continue, given the inequitable distribution of global wealth. (§6.3).

The UN's establishment of UNIDO and UNCTAD was to be the precursor, whereby developing nations would have a more prominent role on the economic-political horizon. The creation of these institutions reflected the growing thirst of the newly independent States for a greater role in global economic and political affairs. The G-77 nations firmly believed that the GATT operated primarily to preserve the economic hegemony of the relatively powerful and developed States. They were also dissatisfied with the operation of the postwar Breton Woods Agreement establishing the International Monetary Fund. It was not designed to effectively further the economic interests of the developing nations.

The member States of G-77 decided to seek a change in the state of International Law, particularly because of its Eurocentric special protection for aliens. Multinational corporations facing uncompensated nationalizations of their enterprises could resort to the entrenched regime of State responsibility for injury to aliens (§2.5). The "old" international order, established before many decolonized entities became States, precluded reliance on host State law. Developing States perceive this limitation as perpetuating their economic independence. In the following excerpt, University of Kansas Professor Raj Bhala vividly describes the associated, hypocritical trade policies advocated by an unholy alliance between the third world's economic elite:

> There is . . . another dimension to the relationship between the Marxist paradigm and the "anti-Third World claim" leveled at the WTO and international trade law. The critics claim that during the present period of neo-colonialism, as in the colonial era of the past, capitalists advocate free trade policies vis-a-vis developing countries. They push for open markets overseas as an outlet, or vent, for their excess production [not needed for the domestic market]. Simultaneously, they lobby their governments for protection from foreign imports, so as to avoid exacerbating competitive pressures in domestic markets. Here is a

double standard that amounts not to pure free trade, but rather mercantilism in new garments.

> Worse yet, there seems to be nothing in the logic if capitalism is to put an end to the hypocrisy. Marx, and his adherents, . . . observed that the declining rates of return to capital in developed country markets, caused by overproduction and ferocious competition, coupled with the prospect of cheap labour overseas, mandate a push to pry open Third World markets. Yet, independent of this mandate is another: natural resources. Some Third World countries have minerals and other raw materials necessary to fuel the engines of capitalist production.[69]

The G-77 thus promulgated the 1974 UN Charter of Economic Rights and Duties of States.[70] Its essential purpose was to further regulate the multinational corporations and change the legal *status quo*. The NIEO's Economic Charter, supported by a majority of the UN's member States, demanded that International Law be modified to accommodate their economic development in relation to the UN's economically dominant members. G-77's goal was to effectuate a redistribution of global wealth. One of the primary methods would be to recapture some of the wealth derived by multinational corporations, which were otherwise free to operate without constraints in the host State's sovereign territory.

The posture of the ICJ is that there is no clear rule on this perennial debate. The Court explains why in the following passage from a 1970 case, involving a Spanish nationalization of a Canadian corporation, owned by Belgian stockholders: "Considering the important developments of the last half-century, the growth of foreign investments and the expansion of the international activities of corporations, in particular of holding companies, which are often multinational, and considering the way in which the economic interests of States have proliferated, it may at first sight appear surprising that the evolution of law has not gone further and that *no generally accepted rules* in the matter have crystallized on the international plane."[71]

Some western commentators have relied on the Permanent Court of International Justice 1928 *Chorzow Factory* case for its comparatively straightforward compensation requirements. The Court therein stated that established international practice required compensation which would "wipe out all the consequences of the *illegal* act. . . . To this obligation, in virtue of the general principles of international law, must be added that of compensating loss sustained as the result of the seizure."[72] This reliance is misplaced because that case involved an illegal taking of alien property. In that instance, a treaty-based obligation precluded the sovereign State from exercising its inherent power of nationalization.

The promoters of the NIEO hoped to create a legal precedent, which would deem all such compensation decisions as falling *solely* within the discretion of the host State. If, for example, a nationalizing State's court or other tribunal were to find that the multinational enterprise had taken unfair advantage of its position over a period of time, then the host State would not necessarily have to pay any compensation for its taking of property. Compensation would not *have to be the* "prompt, adequate, and effective" the common articulation of the Western-derived principle. Latin American States had already objected to 'international' authority via the Calvo Clause. Now was the time to build on that model via the NIEO perception that host State law should govern such matters.[73]

The 1974 UN Economic Charter was the centerpiece of the NIEO. In its capacity as a sovereign entity, the host State should be able to set the standard of compensation when it nationalizes a foreign enterprise or certain assets. *Whether* and *how much* to compensate a multinational enterprise was now to be characterized as a matter governed by the host State law. The NIEO was designed to trump International Law as formulated by the economically developed States, long before many under-developed nations even existed. Article 2.2 of the NIEO's Economic Charter provides that each State has the following "right":

> To nationalize, expropriate or transfer ownership of foreign property, in which case appropriate compensation should be paid by the State adopting such measures, taking into account its relevant laws and regulations and all circumstances that the State considers pertinent. In any case where the question of compensation gives rise to a controversy, it shall be settled under the domestic law of the nationalizing State and by its tribunals, unless it is freely and mutually agreed by all States concerned that other peaceful means be sought [to resolve compensation issues] on the basis of the sovereign equality of States and in accordance with the principle of free choice of means.[74]

Article 2 presented a variation on the Latin American "Calvo Doctrine" (§4.4). As a condition of doing business, the foreign enterprise must waive the protection of International Law that prohibits the discriminatory treatment of aliens. A Calvo clause, stated either in the contract or mandated by host State law, precludes a nationalized entity from seeking the diplomatic assistance of its home State. The enterprise is thereby treated as if it were a citizen of the nationalizing State—in which case, it must look to *national* law for a remedy. The nationalizing State's decision, whether and *how* to compensate, is thereby based on its national law rather than International Law.

The NIEO's obstacle would be the commonly applied standard, requiring prompt, adequate, and effective compensation for a governmental taking of foreign corporate assets. The source for this principle is ascertainable from customary State practice and international arbitrations. No multilateral treaty exists to express the consensus of States. The decisions of various international tribunals typically reasoned that a nationalizing State must compensate the owner of foreign assets under the "prompt, adequate, and effective" rule (§4.4 Iran-US Claims Tribunal). This meant the fair-market value of the seized property in freely transferable currency, the preferred yardstick of the western capital exporters.

NEW, NEW INTERNATIONAL ECONOMIC ORDER

During the 1980s, the multinational corporations in developed nations—particularly in the United States—reacted to the G-77's UN-based articulation of the NIEO in a way that was not anticipated by its proponents. Corporate management diverted the flow of foreign investment from "third world" nations participating in this attempted paradigm shift to other developed nations. What was thought to be a clear legal standard, permitting nationalization but requiring compensation of foreign investment, had blurred. Corporate management decided to avoid the potential impact of the NIEO, stimulating a capital flight into other nations. The instability wrought by the NIEO backfired on the G-77, although it had grown to 120 nations during the 1970s and 1980s and currently numbers at 133.[75]

As a result, the lesser-developed countries began to negotiate bilateral investment treaties (BITs) with the capital-rich States in order to re-attract foreign investment. These treaties are typified by clauses entitling the multinational corporation to fair-market-value compensation in readily transferrable currency in the event of a nationalization.[76] BITs became the wave of the 1990s. As of 2004, there were more than 1,500 BIT treaties in existence. The Uruguay Round of the GATT process presented a similar device. Trade Related Investment Measures (TRIMs) have been incorporated into the GATT and WTO processes to protect foreign investors and to reverse the capital flight of the 1980s (away from lesser-developed countries, because of the so-called NIEO).

This bilateral treaty approach has not been accepted by all original members of the G-77. The BITs are virtually treasonous competitors with the UN process that pioneered the NIEO. The new NIEO appears to be coming full circle—returning to the *old* order. Foreign investment could not be attracted without sufficient protection from uncompensated nationalizations. Nevertheless, the September 1999 Twenty-third Annual Ministers' Meeting for Foreign Affairs Ministerial Declaration "expressed the urgent need for certain developed countries to immediately eliminate laws with adverse extra-territorial impacts against developing countries . . . [advocating a stronger U.N. system which] would enhance coordination between the UN and multilateral trade institutions . . . [because trade institutions] must take into account the policy framework adopted by the UN and should ensure that their policies are in conformity with the developmental objectives of developing countries . . . [and their] right to development."[77]

An international legal system that *over*emphasizes differences may eclipse values common to all. Central European University (Budapest) Professor Helen Hartnell aptly characterized this problem with the NIEO: "The failed Charter of Economic Rights and Duties of States, like the failed Soviet Union, was built by 'levelers.' Their failure is rooted in [not conceding] the inevitability of diversity. Today's scrambling toward political, economic and legal integration in the eastern and western hemispheres might be seen to stem from fear of the consequences of too much difference, or [alternatively] from a recognition that cooperation can erase destructive differences. In any case, integration always has its limits . . . the point at which differences begin to overshadow common values and interests."[78]

◆ 13.5 CORRUPT INTERNATIONAL TRANSACTIONS

Corrupt business transactions are not limited to a few countries. This is a global phenomenon encompassing every region of the world.[79] The Principle Deputy Assistant US Secretary of Commerce succinctly described its scope as follows:

> By all accounts, however, the corruption problem is most prevalent in the world's transitional economies.
> . . . While the problem is difficult to quantify (i.e., there are no ways of collecting meaningful statistics on corrupt payments), anecdotal evidence indicates that the demand for illicit payments has significantly increased in recent years as these markets have opened their doors to foreign investment and procurement. From Russia to Eastern Europe to China, western businessmen are seeking to participate in these growth markets, thus creating significant opportunities for payments. The size, variety, and prevalence of these foreign payments . . . undoubtedly retards the formation of democratic institutions, economic development, and the rule of law in many societies.
> The problem is perhaps most acute in post-communist societies. After decades of communist dictatorship, with law serving as an instrument of, rather than a check on, arbitrary state power, the rule of law is fragile and largely undeveloped in these countries. . . . While reformist governments are rewriting new anti-corruption laws, business regulations, and ethical guidelines, these regulations contain significant gaps, and the development of institutions to implement and enforce these new laws is a long-term process.[80]

In 1976, the US Securities and Exchange Commission published a report that more than 400 US companies, including 117 of the Fortune 500 companies, made "questionable" payments to foreign officials.[81] In 1977, US President Gerald Ford and the US Congress responded with the Foreign Corrupt Practices Act (FCPA) that: (1) was designed to restore public confidence in US business; (2) would have a significant impact on the ability of US business enterprises to do business abroad; and (3) lead to claims of cultural relativism, because the United States was perceived as trying to legislate morality on an international scale.

While portions of the FCPA appear in various titles of the US Code, the following provisions illustrate its basic content:

◆

1977 Foreign Corrupt Practices Act and International Anti-Bribery and Fair Competition Act of 1998

UNITED STATES CONGRESS

(implementing ratification of the 1997 Bribery Convention)

Go to course Web page <http://home.att.net/~slomansonb/txtcsesite.html>, Under Chapter 13, click Foreign Corrupt Practices Act.

Paying a foreign government official is thus illegal if the payment is intended to induce the recipient to misuse his or her position to direct business to the person who pays the bribe. Foreign officials include any officer or employee of a foreign government, department, agency, member of a royal family, or legislative body who is acting in an official capacity. Payment to an official to induce even a private company to award a contract is also prohibited. The Act excludes payments for routine governmental actions. Although referred to as "grease" payments, fees for obtaining a license or official document, processing governmental papers, or scheduling inspections do not violate the FCPA—as long as such payments are authorized under the written laws of the country where the payment is made.

The FCPA has been prosecuted more heavily than recognized by the general public. In 1995, for example, Lockheed Martin Corporation of Bethesda, Maryland, pled guilty to bribing an Egyptian official to ensure the purchase of three C-130 cargo planes. This resulted in a criminal fine of $21.8 million, a civil settlement of $3 million, and a prison sentence and criminal fine for one of two responsible corporate executives.[82] In February 1999, the CIA received allegations that, between May 1994 and April 1998, bribes were used to influence the outcomes of 239 international contract competitions that totaled $108 billion. Seventy percent were allegedly offered or paid to ministry or executive branch officials.

In March 2005, Titan Corporation, a US defense contractor who provided much of the nonmilitary security in Iraq, paid a $28,500,000 fine. Titan had paid out over $2,000,000 in bribes during the 2001 election campaign in the West African nation of Benin. Titan had 120 agents in 60 foreign countries with no meaningful oversight of their payouts to various government entities. This was the largest fine ever imposed under the FCPA. Halliburton, the major US defense contractor, is under investigation for alleged complicity in paying $180,000,000 in bribes regarding Nigerian gas contracts.[83]

REGIONAL CONTROLS

In the twenty years between the US 1977 FCPA and the 1997 OECD Bribery Convention, some regional organizations drafted interim treaties addressing this market force manipulation. These include the following:

◆ Organization of American States Inter-American Convention Against Corruption (1996) and Quito Declaration on the Impact of Corruption (2004)
◆ European Union Convention on the Fight Against Corruption Involving Officials of Member States of the European Union (1997)
◆ Interim Committee of the Board of Governors of the International Monetary Fund Code of Good Practices on Fiscal Transparency (1998 Declaration on Principles)
◆ Council of Europe's Group of States Against Corruption (2000)
◆ African Union Convention on Preventing and Combating Corruption (2003)[84]

None of these instruments eradicated this commercial nemesis. They did develop an environment conducive to the production of a draft convention for global consideration. A UN General Assembly resolution, and the Secretary-General's report on which it was based,[85] did little to control a problem that all nations acknowledged, but few were willing to act upon.

GLOBAL CONTROLS

UN International Code of Conduct for Public Officials The 1996 UN General Assembly Resolution 51/59, entitled "On Action Against Corruption," provides as follows:

Concerned at the seriousness of problems posed by corruption, which may endanger the stability and security of societies, undermine the values of democracy and morality and jeopardize social, economic and political development, . . .

Convinced that, since corruption is a phenomenon that currently crosses national borders and affects all societies and economies, international cooperation to prevent and control it is essential, . . .

Adopts the International Code of Conduct for Public Officials annexed to the present resolution, and recommends it to member States as a tool to guide their efforts against corruption.[86]

. . .

The UN subsequently promulgated its December 2003 Convention Against Corruption,[87] while proclaiming December 9th as International Anti-Corruption Day. This convention entered into force two years later, after the thirtieth ratification. The intervening UN oil-for-food scandal (§3.3) severely tarnished the UN's image as a competent global corruption fighter. This may explain why, as of Fall 25, only two EU members had ratified it. The United States has not.

The United Nations has also promulgated the UN Convention Against Transnational Organized Crime.

Its two associated protocols are the (1) Protocol to Prevent, Suppress and Punish Trafficking in Persons; and (2) Protocol on Migrant Smuggling. This treaty regime enjoys US support, because of the latter's November 2005 ratification of the basic convention.

OECD Bribery Convention   The twenty-nine members of the Organization for Economic Co-operation and Development (OECD) drafted the most global of corruption treaty alternatives to date. These industrialized nations were joined in the drafting process by five nonmembers: Argentina, Brazil, Bulgaria, Chile, and the Slovak Republic.[88]

The preambular wording states the underlying premise regarding bribery in international business transactions: It undermines good governance and economic development, while distorting competitive conditions in the international marketplace. The twin purpose of this convention is to pressure member nations to criminalize bribery and to facilitate equivalent measures among the ratifying States.

The treaty defines bribery and conspiracy to commit it as follows:

Article 1
The Offence of Bribery of Foreign Public Officials

1. Each Party shall take such measures as may be necessary to establish that it is a criminal offence under its law for any person intentionally to offer, promise or give any undue pecuniary or other advantage, whether directly or through intermediaries, to a foreign public official, for that official or for a third party, in order that the official act or refrain from acting in relation to the performance of official duties, in order to obtain or retain business or other improper advantage in the conduct of international business.

2. Each Party shall take any measures necessary to establish that complicity in, including incitement, aiding and abetting, or authorization of an act of bribery of a foreign public official shall be a criminal offence. Attempt and conspiracy to bribe a foreign public official shall be criminal offences to the same extent as attempt and conspiracy to bribe a public official of that Party.

3. The offences set out in paragraphs 1 and 2 above are hereinafter referred to as "bribery of a foreign public official".

4. For the purpose of this Convention:
   a. "foreign public official" means any person holding a legislative, administrative or judicial office of a foreign country, whether appointed or elected; any person exercising a public function for a foreign country, including for a public agency or public enterprise; and any official or agent of a public international organization;
   b. "foreign country" includes all levels and subdivisions of government, from national to local;
   c. "act or refrain from acting in relation to the performance of official duties" includes any use of the public official's position, whether or not within the official's authorized competence.

. . .

Article 3 of the Bribery Convention requires each ratifying nation to take necessary measures to ensure that a bribe, the proceeds from bribery of a foreign public official, or its corresponding property value are subject to seizure and confiscation—or, alternatively, that monetary sanctions of comparable effect are applicable.

Article 4 provides for both domestic and international jurisdiction, premised on the familiar jurisdictional principles of International Law (text §5.2). Thus, each ratifying State "shall take such measures as may be necessary" to establish its jurisdiction over the bribery of a foreign public official when the offence is committed in whole, or in part, within its territory.

Article 9 requires member States to provide mutual assistance. This means extradition to the most appropriate State under Article 10. To complete this comprehensive guide for ensuring prosecution, each ratifying nation "shall review whether its current basis for jurisdiction is effective" in the fight against the bribery of foreign public officials. If not, then that State must take remedial steps to create or modify its jurisdictional rules to comply with its treaty obligations to prosecute such cases.

What does it all mean? First, under Article 12 of the Bribery Convention, ratifying States will cooperate in carrying out a program of systematic follow-up to monitor and promote full implementation. This will most likely be done within the framework of the OECD working group on Bribery in International Business Transactions. Second, the United States was one of the first nations to have created legislation to ratify and implement the 1997 Bribery Convention (see FCPA Act on course Web page). It thereby took a leadership position, not unlike the lonely vigil it commenced with its 1977 Foreign Corrupt Practices Act. Assuming the requisite degree of acceptance by other ratifications, US enterprises will be freed from the double standard that resulted from the generation of lost bids, when competing with unrestrained bribery in foreign markets. The 1997 Bribery Convention went beyond the US 1977 FCPA by also making it illegal to *receive* a bribe. Third, there is now a uniform standard for defining and combating bribery in international business. Thus, as is the consummate objective of International Law, the same rules will one day apply across the board to State officials—and to officials in international organizations such as the United Nations.

◆ PROBLEMS

Problem 13.A (after §13.2 *MCC Marble* case)   The UN Convention on the International Sale of Goods (CISG) authorizes the legal enforcement of oral contracts—without regard to the amount of money involved. It may also authorize written contract terms that vary from the oral exchange between the parties. In February 2000, a Canadian winery entered into a telephonic agreement with a French subsidiary—located in California—to purchase 1.2 million corks. The parties to the phone conversation agreed upon the amount to be paid, and the shipping terms, but nothing else. There were no prior dealings between the parties.

The French parent company shipped the corks to Canada in eleven shipments. Each shipment included a seller's invoice containing a forum selection clause stating: "Any dispute arising under the present contract is under the sole jurisdiction of the Court of Commerce of the City of Perpigan [France]."

A US court held that this forum selection clause (FSC) was valid and thus enforceable. The trial judge therefore dismissed this case, which had been filed in California. The appellate court reversed that dismissal, thereby reinstating this case for trial in the California forum. The appellate court's rationale was that the eleven identical FSCs were unenforceable. They were not to be considered a part of the agreement between the parties. For additional details, see Chateau des Charmes Wines Ltd. v. Sabate USA Inc., 328 F.3d 528 (9th Cir., 2003), *cert. denied,* 540 U.S. 1049 (2003).

Three students will argue the merits of this case, specifically whether the (post-oral contract) mailing of the written FSC clause(s), along with each of the eleven shipments, should be a valid part of this agreement. Students one and two will represent the respective parties. Student three is a judge who sits on dispute resolution panels of the WTO in Geneva. The judge will comment on whether the enforcement of the FSC will help or hinder international trade.

Problem 13.B (end of §13.2)
Hypothetical Problem   Brazil and the United States are parties to GATT/WTO. In 2003, Brazil announced a major discovery. After years of research in its rain forests, Brazilian chemists developed a generic drug substitute for a popular but expensive drug made by a US company in the United States. The brand name of the

US drug is "A-1." The Brazilian generic substitute is called "B-2." Both drugs are the best nonprescription treatments for the common cold.

Brazen Inc. is a Brazilian State-owned corporation. Brazil uses the profits to raise revenue for the social and economic advancement of its people. Brazen's corporate management realizes the extraordinary potential for B-2 to become a substitute for A-1. The A1 US drug has been used by most US consumers to treat their cold symptoms.

Brazen launches its marketing plan by selling B-2 to associated US companies wishing to compete with the US maker of A-1. A US importer is licensed to market B-2 to US consumers. The price charged is slightly less than what US consumers pay for A-1. The US tariff rate is low enough to make the exportation and sale of B-2 sufficiently profitable to encourage Brazen's entry into the US market.

Brazen exports B-2 to the US, which costs Brazen $2 total per unit shipped. It costs Brazen the equivalent of $1 per unit shipped to produce B-2 in Brazil, and then another $1 to market B-2 in the United States. In 2004, some parts of the US market slowly begin to accept B-2 as the cheaper generic substitute for A-1. Brazen and its US associates then decide to lower the price charged to US consumers to 95 cents per unit. This price reduction yielded immediate benefits for US customers. They paid substantially less for B-2 than for A-1 (95 cents as opposed to just over $2 per bottle of A-1). More consumers can now afford this relatively inexpensive and very effective cold remedy.

B-2's unusually low prices quickly generated a large US demand. A-1's sales plummeted. US consumers could obtain B-2 at a substantially lower cost than A-1. The maker of A-1 reduced its production capacity and began to look for profits in some other line of pharmaceuticals.

In 2005, Brazil's Minister of Commerce authorized an increase in B-2 prices via gradual steps. By the end of the year, the cost to US consumers increased beyond the initial $2 cost of B-2. Brazen began to profit again from the large volume of B-2 sales in the United States. It had lost money during the 2004 marketing campaign. Brazen's below-cost pricing strategy had resulted in US consumers relying almost exclusively on B-2. Brazen's per unit production and shipping costs remained constant, at $2 per bottle of B-2. The retail price of B-2 has now temporarily settled at $2.50 per bottle shipped. That price could increase any day. But charging too

much more for B-2 might encourage other United States or foreign companies to enter or reenter this particular market for cold remedies.

The maker of A-1 reconsiders its decision to completely withdraw from manufacturing A-1. It begins by having its lobbyist in Washington, DC, convince the US Customs Service to issue a new series of special regulations governing the importation of foreign cold remedies. These tests are not conducted on A-1. The expressed purpose of these new requirements is to ensure the quality control and consumability of imported drugs. The new customs procedures reduce the risk of unauthorized or unsafe generic pharmaceuticals entering the United States.

First, the new regulations require special customs inspections for imported cold remedies. Second, the new regulations impose strenuous quality testing of foreign cold remedies arriving at US ports of entry. All of these new procedures the special inspections, and quality testing, are uniformly applied to all foreign pharmaceuticals, regardless of the their national origin. The new regulations result in the rejection of most of the Brazilian B-2, now arriving in the United States.

Brazil lodges a complaint with the US Department of State and the WTO, claiming discriminatory treatment that has targeted foreign-made cold remedies from Brazil. Brazen Inc. is now unable to reap the benefits of the Brazilian discovery of B-2 for Brazil's economy. Brazen may be driven out of this market soon, because so much of its B-2 cold remedy is not permitted to enter the United States by US Customs inspectors.

Questions

1. Did Brazil's state-owned company violate GATT/WTO, because of its marketing activities?
2. Did the United States violate GATT/WTO by instituting its new customs regulations?

Problem 13.C (end of §13.2 or §13.4) Read the WTO TRIPS Intellectual Property Case on the course Web page at: <http://home.att.net/~slomansonb/txtcsesite.html>, scroll to Chap. 13. Four students (or groups) will represent, respectively, India, the United States, the EU, and the WTO. They will present their respective views on the following matter.

Assume these facts: (1) Americorp is a US multinational corporation. It holds the exclusive patent on the drug it has created called "Hivicural." It retards any further development of HIV in HIV positive persons.

(2) Americorp markets its new, patented wonder drug throughout the world. Twenty-one treatments are required. They must be taken consistently, one treatment per week for twenty-one weeks, to arrest the evolution of the HIV virus. The cost to importers in all countries is $100 per treatment. The total wholesale cost is thus US $2,100 per patient. (3) Americorp spent $5 billion in research and development costs which, coupled with the costs of marketing, shipping, and paying tariffs to export Hivicural nevertheless yields a total anticipated profit of about $10 billion during the life of the Hivicural patent. That profit will be distributed to shareholders.

Americorp stock is sold on the New York stock exchange. Numerous investors will be financially rewarded by about $10,000 each. (4) The appearance of any generic substitute would ruin the value of Americorp's drug Hivicural. Any generic derived from Hivicural would almost immediately eliminate demand for this more expensive patented drug. (5) Americorp's claim would be "espoused" by the US Trade Representative in the WTO dispute resolution process.

India is developing a generic pharmaceutical, based on Americorp's patent ingredients in Hivicural. That would make it possible for the Indian government to cheaply dispense a generic copy of Hivicural to save the rapidly increasing percentage of the population infected with HIV. The average annual salary in India, one of the world's most populated—and poorest—countries, is $275.

1. Would the WTO TRIPS agreement, the *US v. India* case, and/or the November 2001 Doha Declaration prohibit the Indian government from making its own generic drug derived from Hivicural?
2. India is a member of G-77. It supports the New International Economic Order. If the answer to (1) would allow India to develop a generic for Hivicural, should India pay compensation for violating Americorp's patent?
3. If India *could* legally use Americorp's patent to produce a generic substitute, are there any WTO-related limits to prevent India from totally ignoring Americorp's rights as the owner of the Hivicural patent?
4. Assume that India ultimately makes and dispenses its own generic substitute for Hivicural only to its own citizens, who are the most affected by HIV. Twenty years later, a completely new disease called "Ebola II" appears. It threatens to kill a large percentage of India's population. Would Americorp be likely to

conduct the research and development to find a cure for Ebola II?

Problem 13.D (end of §13.5)   You are the legal officer for Deftco, a US corporation doing business in Russia. You are transacting business in St. Petersburg, where you meet Misha. He is the personal secretary for the Russian CEO of a state-owned company. This company is accepting bids for refurbishing the Hermitage. That landmark is the Russian government's world-renowned art museum near the center of the city. Misha is also the CEO's brother. Misha maintains copies of all documents involved in the bidding process.

Misha notices that your company has not yet paid the standard "maintenance fee." It is a payment which does not appear in any of the documents regarding this bidding process. Russian law does not prohibit this payment. Nor is there any legal provision authorizing such a fee in either Russia or the United States. You return to your hotel room, open your laptop computer, and research the Foreign Corrupt Practices Act and the OECD Bribery Convention. The United States is a party to the OECD treaty. Russia is not.

You return to Misha's office to explain why you cannot pay this fee. It will subject you to a US prosecution. Your company is the strongest contender for successfully bidding on the Hermitage refurbishing job. Misha, a Russian lawyer, has studied law in the United States—where he obtained a graduate law degree after completing law school in Moscow. He has always been fascinated by what he describes as the "condescending and arrogant attitude of American lawyers, who think that they can impose their parochial values on the world."

Two students will assume your role and that of Misha. They will deliberate about whether the maintenance fee is illegal under either US law or International Law.

◆ BIBLIOGRAPHY

§13.1 Economics and International Law

COURSEBOOKS AND SUMMARIES

R. Folsom et al., INTERNATIONAL BUSINESS TRANSACTIONS: A PROBLEM-ORIENTED COURSEBOOK (7th ed. St. Paul: West, 2004)

R. Folsom et al., INTERNATIONAL TRADE AND ECONOMIC RELATIONS IN A NUTSHELL (3d ed. St. Paul: West, 2004)

J. Jackson et al., LEGAL PROBLEMS OF INTERNATIONAL ECONOMIC RELATIONS: CASES, MATERIALS AND TEXT (4th ed. St. Paul: West, 2002)

A. Swan & J. Murphy, CASES AND MATERIALS ON THE REGULATION OF INTERNATIONAL BUSINESS AND ECONOMIC RELATIONS (2d ed. San Francisco: Matthew Bender, 1999)

DOCUMENTS

P. Kunig, N. Lau, & W. Meng (eds.), INTERNATIONAL ECONOMIC LAW: BASIC DOCUMENTS (2d ed. Berlin: de Gruyter, 1993)

S. Zamora & R. Brand (eds.), BASIC DOCUMENTS OF INTERNATIONAL ECONOMIC LAW (Chicago: CCH, 1990) (two volumes)

TREATISES

A. Cassesse, Legal Attempts at Narrowing the Gap Between North and South, ch. 18, in INTERNATIONAL LAW 394 (Oxford, Eng.: Oxford Univ. Press, 2001)

Y. Lambert, THE UNITED NATIONS INDUSTRIAL DEVELOPMENT ORGANIZATION: UNIDO AND PROBLEMS OF INTERNATIONAL ECONOMIC COOPERATION (Westport, CT: Praeger, 1993)

P. Stephan, D. Wallace, & J. Roin, INTERNATIONAL BUSINESS AND ECONOMICS: LAW AND POLICY (Charlottesville, VA: Michie, 1993)

H. van Houtte, THE LAW OF INTERNATIONAL TRADE (London: Street & Maxwell, 1995–)

§13.2 World Trade Organization and GATT

DOCUMENTS

ABA Int'l Section, Most-Favored-Nation Certification and Human Rights: A Case Study of China and the United States (Chicago: ABA, 1996)

P. Raworth & L. Reif, The Law of the WTO: Final Text of the GATT/Uruguay Round Agreements, Summary & Searchable Diskette (New York: Oceana, 1995–)

TREATISES AND ARTICLES

B. Ahunwan, GLOBALIZATION AND CORPORATE GOVERNANCE IN DEVELOPING COUNTRIES (Ardsley, NY: Transnat'l, 2003)

R. Bjala, MODERN GATT LAW (St. Paul, MN: Thomson, 2005).

P. Chan, The Impact of Globalization on State Sovereignty, 3 CHINESE J. INT'L L. 473 (2005)

B. Chimini, Third World Approaches to International Law: A Manifesto, in A. Anghie, et al. (ed.), THE THIRD WORLD AND INTERNATIONAL ORDER: LAW, POLITICS, AND GLOBALIZATION 47 (Leiden: Brill, 2003)

J. Head, THE FUTURE OF THE GLOBAL ECONOMIC ORGANIZATIONS: AN EVALUATION OF CRITICISMS LEVELED AT THE IMF, THE MULTILATERAL DEVELOPMENT BANKS, AND THE WTO (Ardsley, NY: Transnat'l, 2005)

M. Matsushita, T. Schoenbaum & P. Mavroidis, THE WORLD TRADE ORGANIZATION: LAW, PRACTICE, AND POLICY (2d ed. Stellenbosch, South Africa: Tralac, 2006)

J. Roy, CUBA, THE UNITED STATES, AND THE HELMS-BURTON DOCTRINE: INTERNATIONAL REACTIONS (Gainesville, FL: Univ. Press of Florida, 2000)

Symposium: The Boundaries of the WTO, 96 AMER. J. INTL L. 1–158 (2002)

INTELLECTUAL PROPERTY

G. Dinwoodie, W. Hennesey & S. Perlmutter, INTERNATIONAL INTELLECTUAL PROPERTY LAW AND POLICY (Charlottesville, VA: Lexis/Nexis, 2001)

D. Long & A. D'Amato, A COURSEBOOK IN INTERNATIONAL INTELLECTUAL PROPERTY (St. Paul, MN: 2000)

Symposium: The United States, The Doha Round and the WTO—Where Do We Go from Here?, 37 INT'L LAWYER 651–987 (2003)

§13.3 Regional Economic Associations

J. Adu, OPEC OFFICIAL RESOLUTIONS AND PRESS RELEASES 1960–1990 (Vienna: OPEC Secretariat, 1990)

R. Folsom, M. Gordon & J. Spanogle, HANDBOOK OF NAFTA DISPUTE SETTLEMENT (Ardsley, NY: Transnational, 1998)

V. Nanda, R. Lake, & R. Folsom, EUROPEAN COMMUNITY LAW AFTER 1992: A PRACTICAL GUIDE FOR LAWYERS OUTSIDE THE COMMON MARKET (Boston: Kluwer, 1993)

S. Sullivan, FROM WAR TO WEALTH: 50 YEARS OF INNOVATION (Paris: OECD, 1997) (Organization of Economic Cooperation and Development)

A. Toth, THE OXFORD ENCYCLOPAEDIA OF EUROPEAN COMMUNITY LAW (Oxford, Eng.: Clarendon Press, 1990)

§13.4 New International Economic Order

P. Ghosh (ed.), NEW INTERNATIONAL ECONOMIC ORDER: A THIRD WORLD PERSPECTIVE (Westport, CT: Greenwood Press, 1984)

Panel: The New International Economic Order, in PROCEEDINGS OF THE 87TH ANNUAL MEETING OF THE AMERICAN SOCIETY OF INTERNATIONAL LAW 459 (1993)

D. Saari, GLOBAL CORPORATIONS AND SOVEREIGN NATIONS: COLLISION OR COOPERATION? (Greenwood, 1999)

Thessaloniki Institute of Public International Law and International Relations, NORTH-SOUTH DIALOGUE: THE NEW INTERNATIONAL ECONOMIC ORDER (Thessaloniki, Greece: Inst. Public Int'l Law, 1982)

§13.5 Corrupt International Transactions

C. Anderson Y Y. Tverdova, Corruption, Political Allegiances, and Attitudes Toward Government in Contemporary Democracies, 47 AMER. POL. SCI. REV. 1 (2001)

G. Heine, B. Huber & T. Rose, PRIVATE COMMERCIAL BRIBERY: A COMPARISON OF NATIONAL AND SUPRANATIONAL LEGAL STRUCTURES (Paris: ICC, 2003)

T. Grant, FOREIGN CORRUPT PRACTICES WORLDWIDE: NAVIGATING THE LAWS, REGULATIONS & PRACTICES OF NATIONAL REGIMES (Dobbs Ferry, NY: 2005)

Council of Europe, DIRTY MONEY: THE EVOLUTION OF INTERNATIONAL MEASURES TO COUNTER MONEY LAUNDERING AND THE FINANCING OF TERRORISM (3d ed. Strasborg: COE Pub., 2004)

S. Rose-Ackerman, CORRUPTION AND GOVERNMENT: CAUSES, CONSEQUENCES, AND REFORM (Cambridge, Eng.: Cambridge Univ. Press, 1999)

R. Williams, THE POLITICS OF CORRUPTION SERIES (Cheltenham, Eng.: Elgar, 2000) (four volumes)

Additional Electronic Resources

Abstracts of Decisions of the Appellate Body of the World Trade Organization: <http://www.ejil.org/journal/curdevs/AB.html>

Country Commercial Guides (US Dep't State): <http://www.state.gov/e/eb/rls/rpts/ccg/>

Cultural and business etiquette information: <http://www.kwintessential.co.uk/resources/country-profiles.html>

GATT Archives: <http://gatt.stanford.edu/page/home>

International Trade Library: <http://nt.scbbs.com/trade/>

Tools of Trade Mini-Portal: <http://www.fita.org/tools>

WTO Appellate Body Repertory of Reports and Awards 1995–2004: <http://www.wto.org/english/tratop_e/dispu_e/repertory_e/repertory_e.htm>

◆ ENDNOTES

1. M. Braychevskiy, On the Legal Content of the First Treaty of Russia with the Greeks, 1982 SOVIET YEARBOOK INT'L L. 296 (Moscow: Nauka Pub., 1983) (English translation).
2. See V. Nanda, U. Draetta, & R. Lake, BREACH AND ADAPTATION OF INTERNATIONAL CONTRACTS: AN INTRODUCTION TO LEX MERCATORIA (Salem, NH: Butterworths, 1992).
3. E. Clemens Horst Co. v. Biddell Bros., 1911–1913 ALL ENGLAND LAW REPORTS 93, at 101 (Loreburn, Judge) (London: Butterworths, 1962).
4. J. Jackson, Global Economics and International Economics Law, ch. 22, in THE JURISPRUDENCE OF GATT & THE WTO: INSIGHTS ON TREATY LAW AND ECONOMIC RELATIONS 449, 450 (Cambridge, Eng.: Cambridge Univ. Press, 2000) [hereinafter Jackson]. Professor Jackson is the foremost US authority on International Economics Law.
5. C. Korth, Barriers to International Business, ch. 4, in INTERNATIONAL BUSINESS: ENVIRONMENT AND MANAGEMENT 84 (2d ed. Englewood Cliffs, NJ: Prentice-Hall, 1985).
6. M. Janis, Academic Workshop: Should We Continue to Distinguish between Public and Private International Law?, in PROCEEDINGS OF THE 79TH ANNUAL MEETING OF THE AMERICAN SOCIETY OF INTERNATIONAL LAW 352 (Wash., DC: Amer. Soc. Int'l Law, 1985) (panel discussion).
7. Details on problems and conflict resolution mechanisms in different legal systems are available in P. North & J. Fawcett, PRIVATE INTERNATIONAL LAW (13th ed. London: Butterworths, 1999).
8. Convention: <www.cisg.law.pace.edu>. The text, legislative history, cases, and scholarly analyses are available on this Web site. Analysis: D. Magraw & R. Kathrein (eds.), THE CONVENTION FOR THE INTERNATIONAL SALE OF GOODS: A HANDBOOK OF BASIC MATERIALS (2nd ed. Chicago: Amer. Bar Ass'n, 1990) [hereinafter CISG Handbook].
9. Message from the President of the United States, CISG Handbook, 75 (cited in note 8 above).
10. For the leading contemporary commentary, see P. Schlechtriem & I. Schwenger (ed.), COMMENTARY ON THE UN CONVENTION ON THE INTERNATIONAL SALE OF GOODS (2d ed. Ardsley, NY: Transnat'l, 2005).
11. B. Wunnicke et al., STANDBY AND COMMERCIAL LETTERS OF CREDIT 4 (2d ed. Rexdale, Ont., Canada: John Wiley & Sons, 1996).
12. E. Hinkelman, Letters of Credit, in DICTIONARY OF INTERNATIONAL Trade 305–323 (4th ed. Novato, CA: World Trade Press, 2000).
13. Invasion: An account, including interviews with Fidel Castro, is available in P. Wyden, Bay of Pigs: The Untold Story (New York: Simon & Schuster, 1979). LOC: McLaughlin, How the Marketplace Can Help in International Crises, Los Angeles Daily Journal, Dec. 24, 1992, p. 6.
14. Comm. of European Communities v. Fed. Rep. Germany, Case No. 178/84 (1987).
15. See Course Web Page <http://home.att.net/~slomansonb/txtcsesite.html>, scroll to Chap. 5, click French Yahoo! Judgment.
16. See Ahlstom Oy v. EC Comm., Case No. 89/85, Euro. Ct. Rep. 5193, 4 COMMON MKT L. REP. 901 (1988).
17. Societe Internacionale Pour Participations Industrielles et Commerciales, S.A., 357 U.S. 197, 78 S.Ct. 1087, 2 L.Ed.2d 1255 (1958).
18. Societe Nacionale Industrielle Aerospatial v. United States Dist. Court for the So. Dist. of Iowa, 482 U.S. 522, 107 S.Ct. 2542, 96 L.Ed.2d 461 (1987).
19. See R. Magnuson & K. Whitney, American-Style Discovery in International Locations, ch. 21, in S. Rodriguez & B. Prell (ed.), INTERNATIONAL JUDICIAL ASSISTANCE IN CIVIL MATTERS 193 (Ardsley, NY: Transnat'l Pub., 1999).
20. Chinese case: Richmark Corp. v. Timber Falling Consultants, 959 F.2d 1468 (1992), cert. den'd, 506 U.S. 948 (1992).
21. The economic and political contributions of this tribunal are presented in A. Mouri, THE INTERNATIONAL LAW OF EXPROPRIATION AS REFLECTED IN THE WORK OF THE IRAN-US CLAIMS TRIBUNAL (Dordrecht, Neth.: Martinus Nijhoff, 1994) & J. Westberg, INTERNATIONAL TRANSACTIONS AND CLAIMS INVOLVING GOVERNMENT PARTIES: CASE LAW OF THE IRAN/UNITED STATES CLAIMS TRIBUNAL (Wash., DC: Int'l Law Inst., 1991).
22. G. Giesze, Helms-Burton in Light of the Common Law and Civil Law Legal Traditions: Is Legal Analysis Alone Sufficient to Settle Controversies Arising Under International Law on the Eve of the Summit of the Americas?, 32 INT'L LAWYER 51, 92 (1998).
23. For an insightful analysis of a 1989 Zimbabwe Supreme Court decision involving caning, see H. Hannum, Juvenile v. State, 84 AMER. J. INT'L L. 768 (1990).
24. A fascinating account of this phenomenon is available in R. Allen & T. Jones, GUESTS OF THE NATION: PEOPLE OF IRELAND VERSUS THE MULTINATIONALS (London: Earthscan Pub., 1990).
25. ITO: U.N. ECOSOC Res. 13, UN DOC. E/22 (1946). GATT: 55 UN TREATY SERIES 194 (1950).

26. Final Act, 33 INT'L LEGAL MAT'LS 1143 (1994). Explanatory introductions to the actual agreements are available in A. Porges, General Agreement on Tariffs and Trade: Multilateral Trade Negotiations and Final Act, 33 INT'L LEGAL MAT'LS 1 (1994) (negotiations) and 33 INT'L LEGAL MAT'LS 1125 (1994) (Final Act).

27. The Puzzle of GATT: Legal Aspects of a Surprising Institution, ch. 2, in *Jackson* 17 (cited in note 4 above).

28. The most comprehensive treatise is R. Bhala & K. Kennedy, WORLD TRADE LAW: THE GATT-WTO SYSTEM, REGIONAL ARRANGEMENTS, AND US LAW (Charlottesville, VA: Lexis Law Pub., 1998).

29. *WTO quote:* Ernst-Ulrich Petersmann, INTERNATIONAL TRADE LAW AND THE GATT/WTO DISPUTE SETTLEMENT SYSTEM 7 & 9 (London: Kluwer, 1996). Regarding the referenced international organizations, see *IMF:* E. Reisenhuber, THE INTERNATIONAL MONETARY FUND UNDER CONSTRAINT: LEGITIMACY OF ITS CRISIS MANAGEMENT (The Hague: Kluwer Law Int'l, 2001) & J. Gold, INTERPRETATION: THE IMF AND INTERNATIONAL LAW (London: Kluwer Law Int'l, 1996) & *World Bank:* I. Shihata, The World Bank in a Changing World (The Hague: Martinus Nijhoff, 2000) [three volumes].

30. The Chinese government's "WTO" Web page illustrates what this means to US/Chinese economic relations. *See* <http://www.chinawto.com/wto/>, click on "English."

31. A. Lowenfeld, Remedies Along with Rights: Institutional Reform in the New GATT, 88 AMER. J. INT'L L. 477, 479 (1994) [hereinafter *New GATT*].

32. Blocking examples are available in *New GATT,* 478 notes 7 and 8 (cited in note 31 above).

33. Article 23, Annex 2, Agreement Establishing the World Trade Organization, Final Act Embodying Results of the Uruguay Round of Multilateral Trade Negotiations, GATT Doc. MTN/FA (Dec. 15, 1993), reprinted in 33 INT'L LEGAL MAT'LS 1, 13 (1994). That agreement refers to a "Multilateral" Trade Organization. In a 1994 followup meeting, the State representatives substituted the word "World" in the organization's title.

34. *Rules:* Reprinted in 33 INT'L LEGAL MAT'LS 112 (1994). *Consultations:* Rule 4. *Panels:* Rule 6. *Appeals:* Rule 17. *Criticism of appellate process:* P. Pescatore, The GATT Dispute Settlement Mechanism: Its Present Situation and Its Prospects, 10 J. INT'L ARB. 27 (1993).

35. Léon Van Parys NV v. Belgisch Interventie en Restitutiebureau (Grand Chamber), C-377/02, Para. 53–54, available at: <http://curia.eu.int/en/content/juris/index.htm>.

36. The Great 1994 Sovereignty Debate: United States Acceptance and Implementation of the Uruguay Round Results, ch. 19, in *Jackson* 367 (cited in note 4 above).

37. The various instruments are searchable at: <http://www.jurisint.org/en>.

38. G. Schwarzenberger, Equality and Discrimination in International Economic Law, 25 YEARBOOK WORLD AFFAIRS 163 (London: Sweet & Maxwell, 1971).

39. African Growth and Opportunity Act, 19 U.S. Code §3701 et seq.

40. A. Cowell, Finance Chiefs Cancel Debt of 18 Nations, NYT on the Web (June 12, 2005).

41. D. Stegar, PEACE THROUGH TRADE: BUILDING THE WORLD TRADE ORGANIZATION (London: Cameron May, 2004).

42. Full text of Libreville Declaration available at: <http://www.wto.org/english/news_e/news00_e/libreville_finalcom_e.htm>.

43. *See* 4 BUREAU NAT'L AFFAIRS INT'L TRADE REP. 786 (Wash., DC: BNA, 1987).

44. Humblot v. Directeur (Case No. 112/84), 46 COMMON MKT. L. REP. 338 (London: European Law Centre, 1986).

45. *Suspension authority:* Art. XIX of GATT 1994. *Safeguard measure:* Art. 2. For documents, see <http://www.wto.org/english/docs_e/legal_e/ursum_e.htm#lAgreement>.

46. *Story:* D. Sanger, News Analysis: Backing Down on Steel Tariffs, U.S. Strengthens Trade Group, NYT on the Web (Dec. 5, 2003). *Analysis:* Youngjin Jung & E. Kang, Toward an Ideal WTO Safeguards Regime–Lessons from U.S.-Steel, 38 INT'L LAWYER 919 (2004) & D. Caron, United States—Continued Dumping and Subsidy Offset Act of 2000, 98 AMER. J. INTL L. 150 (2004).

47. G. Marceau, ANTI-DUMPING AND ANTI-TRUST ISSUES IN FREE-TRADE AREAS (Oxford, Eng.: Clarendon Press. 1994).

48. See M. Benitah, THE LAW OF SUBSIDIES UNDER THE GATT/WTO SYSTEM (The Hague: Kluwer, 2001).

49. Rocklea Spinning Mills PTY, Ltd v. Anti-Dumping Authority and Another, 107 INT'L LAW REP. 105 (Australia, Fed. Ct, Gen. Div., 1995).

50. United States Section 211 Omnibus Appropriations Act of 1998, WT/DS176/R (01-3806) panel report of Aug. 6, 2001, available at: <http://www.wto.org/english/tratop_e/dispu_e/distabase_e.htm>.

51. L. Peter Farkas, Trade-Related Aspects of Intellectual Property: What Problems with Transition Rules What Changes to U.S. Law How has Congress Salvaged 337?, ch. 13, in T. Stewart (ed.), THE WORLD TRADE ORGANIZATION: THE MULTILATERAL TRADE FRAMEWORK FOR THE 21ST CENTURY AND U.S. IMPLEMENTING LEGISLATION 463 (Chicago, IL: Amer Bar Ass'n, 1996).

52. Pharmaceuticals and the WTO TRIPS Agreement: Questions and Answers, available on the W.H.O. Web site at: <http://www.who.int/medicines/library/par/hivrelateddocs/Pharmaceuticals_WTO_TRIPS.pdf>.

53. See Implementation of paragraph 6 of the Doha Declaration on the TRIPS Agreement and public health, available at: <http://www.wto.org/english/tratop_e/trips_e/implem_para6_e.htm>.

54. For story, *see* Reuters, Patent Bill in India Could Raise AIDS Drug Prices, NYT on the Web (Mar. 23, 2005).

55. *See* generally Sungjoon Cho, The Troubled Status of WTO Doha Round Negotiations ASIL Insight, available at: <http://www.asil.org/insights/2005/08/insights050825.html> and International Economic Law: Modification of WTO Rules on Protection of Pharmaceuticals, 97 AMER. J. INT'L L. 981 (2003).

56. *See* Sungjoon Cho, The Future of the WTO: Report by the Consultative Board, ASIL Insight, available at: <http://www.asil.org/insights/2005/01/insight050131.htm>.

57. Introduction: The Changing Face of World Trade and the Greatest Challenge Facing the WTO and the World Today, ch. 1, in R. Buckley (ed.), THE WTO AND THE DOHA ROUND: THE CHANGING FACE OF WORLD TRADE 1, at 8 (The Hague: Kluwer, 2003).

58. *See* P. Gallagher, GUIDE TO THE WTO AND DEVELOPING COUNTRIES (London: Kluwer, 2000).

59. *Caribbean initiative:* Caribbean Basin Recovery Act of 1983, as amended, 97 STATUTES AT LARGE 369 (1990). *Free trade area: See* NAFTA textual discussion in this section. *Customs union:* 1969 Agreement Establishing the South African Customs Union, 2 YEARBOOK INT'L ORG. 975 (1990–1991). *Common market: See* R. Keohane & S. Hoffman (ed.), THE NEW EUROPEAN COMMUNITY: DECISIONMAKING AND INSTITUTIONAL CHANGE (Boulder, CO: Westview Press, 1991). *Economic union:* Single European Act, reprinted in 25 INT'L LEGAL MAT'LS 503 (1986). The Treaty of Maastricht anticipated formation of a monetary union—the original objective of the "1992" program. *See* Treaty on the European Union and Final Act, reprinted in 31 INT'L LEGAL MAT'LS 247 (1991).

60. G. Winham, Lessons from History, ch. 1, in THE EVOLUTION OF INTERNATIONAL TRADE AGREEMENTS 3, 21 (Toronto: Univ. Toronto Press, 1992).

61. Protocol to Amend the Framework Agreement on Comprehensive Economic Co-operation between the Association of South East Asian Nations and the People's Republic of China (October 6, 2003), available at: <http://www.aseansec.org/13196.htm>.

62. *See* the collection of diverse and critical opinions in M. Hodges, J. Kirton & J. Daniels (ed.), THE G-8'S ROLE IN THE NEW MILLENNIUM (Aldershot, Eng.: Ashgate, 1999). However, these experts do not recommend any retreat from the G-8's role as a potential institutional leader via its Heads of State summit mechanism, as long as it continues to decentralize.

63. *See* T. Peay, Declaration and Introductory Note, Second Summit of the Americas: Santiago Declaration and Plan of Action, 37 INT'L LEGAL MAT'LS 947 (1998).

64. *About Us,* Jubilee Web page at: <http://www.jubilee2000uk.org/about/about.htm>.

65. *See generally,* M. Sornarajah, THE INTERNATIONAL LAW ON FOREIGN INVESTMENT (Cambridge, Eng.: Cambridge Univ. Press, 1994).

66. *Permanent Sovereignty resolution:* Gen. Ass. Reso. 1803 (XVII), reprinted in 2 INT'L LEGAL MAT'LS 223 (1963). *Followup resolution:* Gen. Ass. Reso. 3171(XXVIII), reprinted in 13 INT'L LEGAL MAT'LS 238 (1974).

67. *Business practices code:* Report of the Intergovernmental Working Group on the Formulation of a Code of Conduct, 16 INT'L LEGAL MAT'LS 719 (1977). *Technology transfer code:* Group of 77 Manila Declaration and Program of Action for Commodities, Trade Negotiations, Transfer of Resources and Technology, and Economic Cooperation, 15 INT'L LEGAL MAT'LS 426 (1976). *OECD: Guidelines for Multinational Enterprises,* 40 INT'L LEGAL MAT'LS 237 (2000).

68. *See* Y. Lambert, THE UNITED NATIONS INDUSTRIAL DEVELOPMENT ORGANIZATION: UNIDO AND PROBLEMS OF INTERNATIONAL ECONOMIC COOPERATION 61 (Westport, CT: Praeger, 1993).

69. R. Bhala, TRADE, DEVELOPMENT, AND SOCIAL JUSTICE 39 (Durham, NC: Carolina Academic Press, 2003).

70. UN Declaration on the Establishment of a New International Economic Order, Gen. Ass. Reso. 3201(S-VI), UN Doc. A/Res/3201(S-VI), reprinted in 13 INT'L LEGAL MAT'LS 715 (1974).

71. Barcelona Light & Traction Company (Belgium v. Spain), 1970 ICJ REP. 3, 46–47, para. 89 (italics supplied). An edited version of this case is set forth in §4.3.

72. 1 WORLD CT. REP. 646 (1928) (italics added).

73. *Classic Western articulation:* 2 RESTATEMENT OF THE LAW OF FOREIGN RELATIONS OF THE UNITED STATES §712 (3d ed. Wash., DC: 1987). *NIEO summary:* G. Sandrino, The NAFTA Investment Chapter and Foreign Direct Investment in Mexico: A Third World Perspective, 27 VAND. J. TRANSNAT'L L. 259 (1994). *Classic Calvo Clause analyses:* A. Freeman, Recent Aspects of the Calvo Doctrine and the Challenge to International Law, 40 AMER. J. INT'L L. 121 (1940) & D. Shea, THE CALVO CLAUSE: A PROBLEM OF INTER-AMERICAN AND INTERNATIONAL LAW AND DIPLOMACY (Minneapolis: Univ. of Minn. Press, 1955).

74. Gen. Ass. Reso. 3281, UN Doc. No. A/9631 (1975), reprinted in 14 INT'L LEGAL MAT'LS 251 (1975).

75. *See e.g.,* M. Rewat, Multilateral Approaches to Improving the Investment Climate of Developing Countries: The Cases of ICSID and MIEA, 33 HARV. INT'L L.J. 102 (1992). G-77's web page claims a current membership of 133 nations. *See* <http://www.g77.org/>.

76. An institutional analysis of BIT development is available in UN Centre on Transnational Corporations, Bilateral Investment Treaties (New York: UN, 1988). *See also* K. Vandevelde, UNITED STATES INVESTMENT TREATIES: POLICY AND PRACTICE (Deventer, Neth.: Kluwer Law and Taxation, 1991).

77. Available at: <http://www.g77.org/Docs/Decl1999.html>.

78. H. Hartnell, The New New International Economic Order: Private International Law, in PROCEEDINGS OF THE 79TH ANNUAL MEETING OF THE AMERICAN SOCIETY OF INTERNATIONAL LAW 352 (Wash., DC: Amer. Soc. Int'l Law, 1985) (panel discussion).

79. Information is available by country in book form and on the Internet. *Book:* J. Bialos & G. Husisian, THE FOREIGN CORRUPT PRACTICES ACT: COPING WITH CORRUPTION IN TRANSNATIONAL ECONOMIES 9–11 (Dobbs Ferry, NY: Oceana, 1996) [hereinafter *Corruption*]. *Internet:* Transparency International (NGOS headquartered in Berlin). See <http://www.transparency.org/>.

80. *Corruption,* 12–13 (cited in note 79 above).

81. S.E.C., Report on Questionable and Illegal Corporate Payments and Practices, 94th Cong., 2d Session 1 (1976).

82. *See* L. Low, Led by the US, the World Wages War on Corruption, National Law Journal B9; and W. Schmidt & J. Frank, FCPA Demands Due Diligence in Global Dealings, National Law Journal B16, (Mar. 3, 1997). *See* update in M.. Morley, Combating Bribery, National Law Journal, B7 (Mar. 27, 2000).

83. SEC probing Halliburton 'bribes,' BBC News (June 11, 2004), available at: <http://news.bbc.co.uk/1/hi/business/3799635 .stm>.

84. *Council of Europe* (2000): <http://www.greco.coe.int/>. *EU:* 37 INT'L LEGAL MAT'LS 12 (1998). *IMF:* 37 INT'L LEGAL MAT'LS 942 (1998); *OAS:* 35 INT'L LEGAL MAT'LS 724 (1996); *African Union:* <http://www.africa-union.org/home/Welcome.htm>.

85. Report of the Secretary-General on Action Against Corruption, submitted to the Commission on Crime Prevention and Criminal Justice, UN DOC. E/CN.15/ 1996/5 (1996).

86. 6 INT'L LEGAL MAT'LS 1039 (1996).

87. Text and analysis available at: <http://www.unodc.org/unodc/ en/crime_convention_corruption.html>.

88. Convention on Combating Bribery of Foreign Public Officials in International Business Transactions (Dec. 18, 1997), 37 INT'L LEGAL MAT'LS 1 (1998).

Index

For page references to legal cases, see "Table of Cases" (vii). For page references to formally titled accords, agreements, conventions, declarations, pacts, protocols, and treaties, see "Table of Treaties" (ix).